An Introduction to Policing

FOURTH EDITION

John S. Dempsey

Captain, New York City Police Department (Retired)
Professor Emeritus of Criminal Justice, Suffolk County
  Community College
Mentor in Criminal Justice and Public Administration,
  SUNY–Empire State College

Linda S. Forst

Captain, Boca Raton Police Department (Retired)
Professor of Criminal Justice, Shoreline Community College

THOMSON

WADSWORTH

Australia • Brazil • Canada • Mexico • Singapore
Spain • United Kingdom • United States

THOMSON

WADSWORTH

An Introduction to Policing, Fourth Edition
John S. Dempsey, Linda S. Forst

Senior Acquisitions Editor, Criminal Justice:
   Carolyn Henderson Meier
Development Editor: *Rebecca Johnson*
Editorial Assistant: *Beth McMurray*
Technology Project Manager: *Amanda Kaufmann*
Marketing Manager: *Terra Schultz*
Marketing Assistant: *Emily Elrod*
Marketing Communications Manager: *Tami Strang*
Project Manager, Editorial Production:
   Jennie Redwitz
Creative Director: *Rob Hugel*
Art Director: *Vernon Boes*
Print Buyer: *Linda Hsu*

Permissions Editor: *Bobbie Broyer*
Production Service: *Sara Dovre Wudali, Buuji, Inc.*
Text Designer: *Carolyn Deacy*
Photo Researcher: *Don Murie, Meyers Photo-Art*
Copy Editor: *Robin Gold, Forbes Mill Press*
Illustrator: *Jill Wolf, Buuji, Inc.*
Cover Designer: *Yvo Riezebos Design*
Cover Images: *Top left: Jeff Greenberg/Alamy;*
   top right: Royalty-Free/Corbis; bottom right:
   Royalty-Free/Corbis; bottom left: Royalty-
   Free/Corbis.
Compositor: *ICC Macmillan Inc.*
Text and Cover Printer: *Edwards Brothers*

© 2008, 2005 Thomson Wadsworth, a part of The Thomson Corporation. Thomson, the Star logo, and Wadsworth are trademarks used herein under license.

ALL RIGHTS RESERVED. No part of this work covered by the copyright hereon may be reproduced or used in any form or by any means— graphic, electronic, or mechanical, including photocopying, recording, taping, Web distribution, information storage and retrieval systems, or in any other manner—without the written permission of the publisher.

Printed in the United States of America
1 2 3 4 5 6 7 11 10 09 08 07

ExamView® and ExamView Pro® are registered trademarks of FSCreations, Inc. Windows is a registered trademark of the Microsoft Corporation used herein under license. Macintosh and Power Macintosh are registered trademarks of Apple Computer, Inc. Used herein under license.

© 2008 Thomson Learning, Inc. All Rights Reserved. Thomson Learning WebTutor™ is a trademark of Thomson Learning, Inc.

Library of Congress Control Number: 2006935543

Student Edition:
ISBN-13: 978-0-495-09545-3
ISBN-10: 0-495-09545-1

Thomson Higher Education
10 Davis Drive
Belmont, CA 94002–3098
USA

For more information about our products,
contact us at:
Thomson Learning Academic Resource
Center
1-800-423-0563
For permission to use material from this text
or product, submit a request online at
http://www.thomsonrights.com.
Any additional questions about permissions
can be submitted by e-mail to
thomsonrights@thomson.com.

Dedication

To my family: Marianne, John, Donna, Cathy, Diane, Daniel, Nikki, Erin Anne Marie, and J.P., and in memory of Anne Marie (1970–2002)—J. S. D.

This book is dedicated to my late husband, Captain James E. Duke, Jr., and our beautiful daughters, Brynn and Juleigh—L. S. F.

About the Authors

John S. Dempsey was a member of the New York City Police Department (NYPD) from 1964 to 1988. He served in the ranks of police officer, detective, sergeant, lieutenant, and captain. His primary assignments were patrol and investigations. He received seven citations from the department for meritorious and excellent police duty. After retiring from the NYPD, Mr. Dempsey served until 2003 as Professor of Criminal Justice at Suffolk County Community College on Eastern Long Island where he won the college's prestigious "Who Made a Difference Award" for his teaching and work with students. In 2005, he was designated Professor Emeritus by the college. Mr. Dempsey also serves as a mentor at the State University of New York–Empire College where he teaches criminal justice and public administration courses and mentors ranking members of law enforcement and criminal justice agencies.

In addition to this book, Mr. Dempsey is the author of *Introduction to Investigations,* Second Edition (Thomson Wadsworth, 2003), and *Introduction to Private Security* (Thomson Wadsworth, 2008).

Mr. Dempsey holds AA and BA degrees in behavioral science from the City University of New York, John Jay College of Criminal Justice; a master's degree in criminal justice from Long Island University; and a master's of public administration degree from Harvard University, the John F. Kennedy School of Government.

He lectures widely around the country on policing and criminal justice issues and is a member of the Academy of Criminal Justice Sciences (ACJS), the International Association of Chiefs of Police, ASIS International, the Northeastern Association of Criminal Justice Sciences (NEACJS), the Criminal Justice Educators Association of New York State, the Pennsylvania Association of Criminal Justice Educators, and the Midwestern Criminal Justice Association. His latest academic distinctions were the Outstanding Contributor Award from the ACJS Community College Section in 2004 and the Fellows Award from the NEACJS in 2005.

Mr. Dempsey is married and has four children and four grandchildren.

Linda S. Forst is a retired police captain from the Boca Raton (Florida) Police Services Department. She joined the department in 1977 and served as a patrol officer, investigator, sergeant, lieutenant, and captain. She spent most of her career in patrol but also worked in investigations, professional standards, training, hiring, and support services. She was the first female field training officer, sergeant, lieutenant, and captain in the department. She has extensive training in accident investigation, domestic violence, sexual violence, community policing, and police management, and served on the board of directors of the local battered women's shelter for many years. She received numerous commendations during her career and brought home many gold medals from the state and International Police Olympics while representing Boca Raton.

Ms. Forst earned her BA in criminal justice, MEd in community college education, and EdD in adult education from Florida Atlantic University. Her dissertation was on acquaintance rape prevention programs. She is a graduate of University of Louisville's Sex Crime Investigation School and Northwestern University's School of Police Staff and Command. She is the author of numerous publications in magazines, journals, and newspapers and presents regularly at conferences and to community groups. She is the author of *The Aging of America: A Handbook for Police Officers.* Ms. Forst has instructed for Northwestern's School of Police Staff and Command as well as Palm Beach Community College and Florida Atlantic University. She is currently a professor of criminal justice at Shoreline Community College in Seattle, Washington, and serves as a member of the Board on Law Enforcement Training Standards and Education for the State of Washington.

Ms. Forst is the mother of two daughters.

Brief Contents

Contents

PART II

The Personal Side of Policing 95

CHAPTER 4

Becoming a Police Officer 96

CHAPTER 5

The Police Role and Police Discretion 122

PART III

Police Operations 227

CHAPTER 9

Patrol Operations 228

CHAPTER 13

Police and the Law 353

PART IV

Critical Issues in Policing 403

CHAPTER 14

Computers, Technology, and Criminalistics in Policing 404

Preface

Introduction to Policing, Fourth Edition, is an introductory text for college students who are interested in learning who the police are, what they do, and how they do it. The policing profession is a noble one and we sincerely hope this text teaches those preparing to enter law enforcement how to continue in this great tradition.

This book provides a general overview of policing in our society so that students can understand why and how policing is performed. It is, above all, a text for students. It will show you the jobs available in policing, how you can go about getting them, what skills you will need, and what you will do when you get those jobs. In addition, we try to give you an idea, a sense, and a flavor of policing. We want you to get a clear look at policing, not only for your academic interest but, more importantly, to help you determine if policing is what you want to do with the rest of your life.

Introduction to Policing explores the subject matter from the perspective of two individuals who have devoted their lives to active police work and education. We wrote this new edition, in part, out of a desire to combine the practical experience gained from a collective 44 years on the job in the field of policing with the equally valuable insights gained from our years of formal education and teaching.

Changes to the Fourth Edition

In response to student and reviewer feedback, this edition provides the latest in academic and practitioner research as well as the latest applications, statistics, court cases, information on careers, and criminalistic and technological advances. As always, coauthor Linda Forst continues to lend additional geographic and gender perspective to the text. And in this edition, even more attention has been given to actual examples of specific police departments—small and large—throughout the nation and world.

We have made a significant change to the Fourth Edition's organization to facilitate more seamless coverage of today's most pressing problems and issues in policing throughout the course. The former Chapter 15, "Specific Police Problems and Issues," has been dissolved and its content absorbed into the remaining chapters, so that these key issues can be treated as they relate to primary policing concepts and traditions rather than being relegated to a catchall chapter or lecture at the end of the book/term.

We have also moved the chapters on police ethics and deviance (which formerly appeared in Part III) and minorities in policing (which formerly appeared in Part IV) forward in the text; they now appear in Part II alongside other foundational aspects of policing to further emphasize the importance of ethics and diversity in today's law enforcement community. Finally, we have divided the two chapters on police operations according to the police functions of patrol (Chapter 9) and investigation (Chapter 10) so they follow the same chronological order as actual police work.

The Fourth Edition continues to reflect the increasing emphasis on policing and homeland security, and we have increased our coverage of such important topics as diversity in policing, rural/local/small-scale police forces, police ethics, and state-of-the-art police technology and criminalistics. We have also provided all-new coverage of the following issues: slave patrols as a possible precursor to the current American policing system; police administration, leadership, and management; Indian Country and Tribal law enforcement; evidence-based policing; multi-agency investigative task forces; the *CSI* effect; and concerns about the USA Patriot Act's effects on civil liberties.

Pedagogical Features

Another significant enhancement we have made to the Fourth Edition is the inclusion of essays from well-respected veterans of law enforcement and higher education. These "Guest Lectures" appear in most chapters and offer practitioner-based insights into crucial law enforcement issues and challenges. In addition, within each chapter, we have included the following pedagogical elements:

- *Chapter Goals* serve as chapter road maps to orient students to the main learning objectives of each chapter.
- *Chapter Introductions* preview the material to be covered in the chapter.
- *Chapter Summaries* reinforce the major topics discussed in the chapter and help students check their learning.
- *Learning Checks* test the student's knowledge of the material presented in the chapter.
- *Definitions of Key Terms* appear at the end of each chapter and in the full glossary at the end of the book.

Boxed Features

To further heighten the book's relevancy for students, we have included the following boxed features in each chapter:

- *You Are There!* These boxes take students back to the past to review the fact pattern in a particular court case or to learn the details about a significant event or series of events in history. They are intended to give the students a sense of actually being at the scene of a police event.
- *On the Job* These features recount personal experiences from our own police careers. They are intended to provide a reality-based perspective on policing, including the human side of policing.

Ancillaries

An extensive package of supplemental aids accompanies this edition of *Introduction to Policing* and is available for instructor and student use. Supplements are available to qualified adopters. Please consult your local sales representative for details.

For the Instructor

- **Instructor's Resource Manual with Test Bank** The thoroughly expanded and revised *Instructor's Resource Manual* provides learning objectives, detailed chapter outlines and summaries, lecture suggestions, key terms with definitions, discussion topics, and testing suggestions that will help you more effectively communicate with your students while allowing you to strengthen coverage of course material. The *Resource Manual*'s integrated Test Bank includes 25 multiple-choice questions, 20 true/false questions, 20 fill-in-the-blank questions, and 5 essay questions for each chapter, saving you hours of test preparation. Each question in the Test Bank has been carefully reviewed by experienced criminal justice instructors for quality, accuracy, and content coverage. Our "Instructor Approved" seal, which appears on the front cover, is our assurance that you are working with an assessment and grading resource of the highest caliber.

- **ExamView® Computerized Testing** The comprehensive *Instructor's Resource Manual* is backed up by ExamView, a computerized test bank available for PC and Macintosh computers. With ExamView, you can create, deliver, and customize tests and study guides (both print and online) in minutes. You can easily edit and import your own questions and graphics, change test layouts, and reorganize questions. And using ExamView's complete word processing capabilities, you can enter an unlimited number of new questions or edit existing questions.

- **WebTutor™ Toolbox on Blackboard® and WebCT®** A powerful combination: easy-to-use course management tools for whichever program you use—WebCT or Blackboard—and content from this text's rich companion website, all in one place. You can use ToolBox as is, from the moment you log on—or, if you prefer, customize the program with web links, images, and other resources.

- **eBank Microsoft® PowerPoint® Slides** These handy, ready-to-use PowerPoint slides, created for each chapter of *An Introduction to Policing*, Fourth Edition, will save you time in preparing engaging lectures and presentations for your course.

- **The Wadsworth Criminal Justice Video Library** So many exciting new videos—so many great ways to enrich your lectures and spark discussion of the material in this text! A list of our unique and expansive video program follows. Or, visit www.thomsonedu.com/criminaljustice/ media_center/index.html for a complete, up-to-the-minute list of all of Wadsworth's video offerings (many of which are also available in DVD format) as well as clip lists and running times. The library includes these selections and many others:

- *ABC® Videos:* Featuring short, high-interest clips from current news events specially developed for courses including Introduction to Criminal Justice, Criminology, Corrections, Terrorism, and White-Collar Crime, these videos are perfect for use as discussion starters or lecture launchers. The brief video clips provide students with a new lens through which to view the past and present, one that will greatly enhance their knowledge and understanding of significant events and open up to them new dimensions in learning. Clips are drawn from such programs as *World News Tonight, Good Morning America, This Week, PrimeTime Live, 20/20,* and *Nightline,* as well as numerous ABC News specials and material from the Associated Press Television News and British Movietone News collections.

- *The Wadsworth Custom Videos for Criminal Justice:* Produced by Wadsworth and Films for the Humanities, these videos include short (5- to 10-minute) segments that encourage classroom discussion. Topics include white-collar crime, domestic violence, forensics, suicide and the police officer, the court process, the history of corrections, prison society, and juvenile justice.

- *Court TV Videos:* One-hour videos presenting seminal and high-profile cases such as the interrogations of Michael Crowe and serial killer Ted Bundy, as well as crucial and current issues such as cyber crime, double jeopardy, and the management of the prison on Riker's Island.

- *A&E American Justice:* Forty videos to choose from, on topics such as deadly force, women on death row, juvenile justice, strange defenses, and Alcatraz.

- *Films for the Humanities:* Nearly 200 videos to choose from on a variety of topics such as elder abuse, supermax prisons, suicide and the police officer, the making of an FBI agent, domestic violence, and more.

- *Oral History Project:* Developed in association with the American Society of Criminology, the Academy of Criminal Justice Sciences, and the National Institute of Justice, these videos will help you introduce your students to the scholars who have developed the criminal justice discipline. Compiled over the last several years, each video features a set of Guest Lecturers—scholars whose thinking has helped to build the foundation of present ideas in the discipline.

- **Classroom Activities for Criminal Justice** This valuable booklet, available to adopters of any Wadsworth criminal justice text, offers instructors the best of the best in criminal justice classroom activities. Containing both tried-and-true favorites and exciting new projects, its activities are drawn from across the spectrum of criminal justice subjects, including introduction to criminal justice, criminology, corrections, criminal law, policing, and juvenile justice, and can be customized to fit any course. Novice and seasoned instructors alike will find it a powerful tool to stimulate classroom engagement.

- **Internet Activities for Criminal Justice, Third Edition** This is the resource that no introductory criminal justice instructor should be without! The user-friendly booklet allows instructors to send their students far beyond the classroom, guiding them online to conduct research and retrieve information. Its URLs and virtual projects, drawn from all foundational criminal justice areas, have been completely revised and expanded for 2008.

- **The Wadsworth Criminal Justice Resource Center** www.thomsonedu.com/criminaljustice Designed with the instructor in mind, this website features information about Wadsworth's technology and teaching solutions, as well as several features created specifically for today's criminal justice student. Supreme Court updates, timelines, and hot-topic polling can all be used to supplement in-class assignments and discussions. You'll also find a wealth of links to careers and news in criminal justice, book-specific sites, and much more.

For the Student

- **Companion Website www.thomsonedu.com/criminaljustice/dempsey** The new companion website provides many chapter-specific resources, including chapter outlines, learning objectives, glossary, flash cards, crossword puzzles, and tutorial quizzing.

- **Careers in Criminal Justice Website www.thomsonedu.com/login** This unique website helps students investigate the criminal justice career choices that are right for them with the help of several important tools:

  - *Career Profiles:* Video testimonials from a variety of practicing professionals in the field as well as information on many criminal justice careers, including job descriptions, requirements, training, salary and benefits, and the application process.

  - *Interest Assessment:* Self-assessment tool to help students decide which careers suit their personalities and interests.

  - *Career Planner:* Résumé-writing tips and worksheets, interviewing techniques, and successful job search strategies.

  - *Links for Reference:* Direct links to federal, state, and local agencies where students can get contact information and learn more about current job opportunities.

- **Wadsworth's Guide to Careers in Criminal Justice, Third Edition** This handy guide, compiled by Caridad Sanchez-Leguelinel, of John Jay College of Criminal Justice, gives students information on a wide variety of career paths, including requirements, salaries, training, contact information for key agencies, and employment outlooks.

- **Writing and Communicating for Criminal Justice** This book contains articles on writing skills, along with basic grammar review and a survey of verbal communication on the job, that will give students an introduction to academic, professional, and research writing in criminal justice. The voices of professionals who have used these techniques on the job will help students see the relevance of these skills to their future careers.

Acknowledgments

So many people have helped us make the successful transition from the world of being street cops to the world of academia and so many more helped in the publication of this book. It is impossible to mention them all but there would be no *Introduction to Policing,* Fourth Edition, without them.

Both authors would like to sincerely thank senior acquisitions editor Carolyn Henderson Meier for her faith, patience, and constant assistance in this project and development editor Rebecca Johnson for her intelligent and insightful assistance in all stages of the development of this book. This edition is a testament to Rebecca's outstanding efforts and advice. Also, we applaud the intelligent and excellent copyediting of Robin Gold and the super production efforts of Jennie Redwitz and Sara Dovre Wudali, as well as photo editor Donald Murie.

To the many students who came to our offices or classes wanting to know about the material we have put into this text, you were the inspiration for this work. This book is for you. To the great men and women we worked with in our police departments, the heart of this book comes from you.

The authors would also like to thank all the professors across the country, particularly those former women and men in blue who have made that transition from the streets to the classrooms, for their adoptions of the first three editions and their kind words and sage advice. They inspired us to prepare this Fourth Edition. We would especially like to thank the reviewers of this edition, who provided outstanding and detailed feedback: George R. Franks, Jr., Stephen F. Austin State University; Kent R. Kerley, University of Alabama at Birmingham; Michael Myer, University of North Dakota; Mahendra Singh, Grambling State University; and R. Alan Thompson, Old Dominion University. Their names appear along with those of the reviewers of previous editions on the list that follows this preface, as a special tribute to all of those who have helped us refine the book over the years.

John Dempsey would like to offer special tribute to his former partners in the NYPD, the late Jimmy Fyfe, Pat Ryan, Bill Walsh, and Vinny Henry, who continually served as my academic and intellectual stimulation. Jim Fyfe, who through his career and academic achievements served as an inspiration to generations of New York City cops, will surely be missed in academia and policing. Anything I have achieved in scholarship I owe to Jim. Also, I would like to mention Dave Owens and thank him for his friendship and leadership in our professional associations, as well as the members of the Great Uncaught, my speaking partners across the country: Lorenzo Boyd, Jim Burnett, Pat Faiella, Jim Ruiz, Donna Stuccio, Tom Lenahan, and Ed Thibault. It is always an honor and privilege to be in your gracious company. Also, to my partner Linda Forst for adding so much to this book.

Again, as always to my family: Marianne, my love and best friend; my children, John, Donna, and Cathy; my daughter-in-law Diane; and in memory of Anne Marie, my special hero—your love and patience has sustained me over the years. Finally, to Danny and Nikki Dempsey and Erin and J. P. Gleeson, my grandchildren: Who loves you more than the Grand Dude?

Linda Forst would like to thank many people who led her down the path to a challenging and fulfilling career in law enforcement. My late father Calvin taught me to have a great respect for the police and regularly "backed up" officers in our small town of Ardsley, New York, where he owned a chicken business, and my mother, Betty, gave me her unwavering support despite her concerns for my safety in my chosen career. I'd like to thank Dr. Bill Bopp, my first criminal justice professor, who welcomed me in his class at Florida Atlantic University when I showed up on a whim. He opened up a whole new world to me and served as a role model and mentor for many years. I hope that I may have the impact on students that he had on me. I am eternally grateful to my late husband, Jim Duke, who supported and encouraged females in law enforcement long before it was politically correct and who was always there for me as I confronted various challenges while rising through the ranks. I also thank attorney Michael Salnick, the best criminal defense attorney in Palm Beach County, for his part in making me a better investigator, as well as for his friendship and support over the years. I continue to be indebted to former Washington State Patrol Captains Steve Seibert and Tom Robbins (Chief of Wenatchee P.D.) for their support and assistance since we first met at Northwestern University's School of Police Staff and Command in 1989.

I thank Jack Dempsey for his confidence in me and his unending support as well as his big heart. I am also blessed with loving and supportive daughters, Brynn and Juleigh, who were understanding of the demands placed on my time. They are an endless source of pride.

I also want to thank the generous practitioners who agreed to share their "stories" throughout the book in an effort to assist students' understanding of the police field: Lorenzo Boyd, Michelle Bennett, David Swim, Jeff Magers, Claudia Leyva, Adolfo Gonzales, Andrew Scott, Michelle Dunkerley, and Jim Nielsen. A special thanks also to Sergeant Cesar Fazz and Officer Eric Cazares of the Yuma, Arizona, Police Department for their time and insights into law enforcement in the southwest.

We both would like to offer a special tribute to all the heroes of September 11, 2001, who rushed in so that others could get out. You are truly symbols of the great public servants who work in emergency services in our nation.

Jack Dempsey
Linda Forst

Reviewers of *An Introduction to Policing*

Frank Alberico, Joliet Junior College

Douglas Armstrong, McNeese State University

Dan Baker, University of South Carolina

Elaine Bartgis, Fairmont State College

Michael Blankenship, Memphis State University

Joseph Bunce, Rockville Community College

Paul Clark, Community College of Philadelphia

Frank Cornacchione, Pensacola Junior College

George Franks, Jr., Stephen F. Austin State University

Alvin Fuchsman, Northern Virginia Community College

Edmund Grosskopf, Indiana State University

Joseph Hanrahan, Westfield State University

John Harlan, Stephen F. Austin State University

Pamela Hart, Iowa Western Community College

Patrick Hopkins, Harrisburg Area Community College

Charles Kelly, Jr., Southeastern Louisiana University

Kent R. Kerley, University of Alabama at Birmingham

Gary Keveles, University of Wisconsin-Superior

Julius Koefoed, Jr., Kirkwood Community College

Tom Lenahan, Herkimer County Community College

Walter Lewis, St. Louis Community College at Merrimac

David Mackey, St. Anselm College

Anthony Markert, Western Connecticut State University

Michael Meyer, University of North Dakota

Kenneth Mullen, Appalachian State University

Hugh O'Rourke, Westchester Community College

David Owens, Onondaga Community College

Gregory Petrakis, University of Missouri–Kansas City

Charles Purgavie, Ocean County Community College

Chester Quarles, University of Mississippi

Jayne Rich, Atlantic Community College

John Sargent, Jr., Kent State University

Mahendra Singh, Grambling State University

William Sposa, Bergen Community College

David Streater, Catawba Valley Community College

Sam Swaim, Indian Hills Community College

R. Alan Thompson, Old Dominion University

Gary Tucker, Sinclair Community College

Roger Turner, Shelby State University

Arvind Verma, Indiana University

William Vizzard, California State University–Sacramento

Police History
and Organization

Jeff Greenberg/Alamy

CHAPTER 1
  Police History

CHAPTER 2
  Organizing Public and
  Private Security in the
  United States

CHAPTER 3
  Organizing the Police
  Department

Police History

© Bettmann/Corbis

GOALS

- To acquaint you with the rich, colorful history of policing
- To show you how the U.S. police and, indeed, the entire U.S. criminal justice system evolved from the English law enforcement experience
- To acquaint you with early American policing—both the colonial experience and the eighteenth and nineteenth centuries
- To introduce you to the history of policing in the first half of the twentieth century
- To acquaint you with the history and development of recent policing, from the 1960s through the present time

Introduction

The word *police* comes from the Latin word *politia,* which means "civil administration." The word *politia* goes back to the Greek word *polis,* or "city." Etymologically, therefore, the police can be seen as those involved in the administration of a city. *Politia* became the French word *police.* The English took it over and at first continued to use it to mean "civil administration." The specific application of *police* to the administration of public order emerged in France in the early eighteenth century. The first body of public-order officers to be named police in England was the Marine Police, a force established in 1909 to protect merchandise in the port of London.[1]

The reference to the police as a "civil authority" is very important. The police represent the civil power of government, rather than the military power of government. We use the military in times of war. The members of the military, of necessity, are trained to kill and destroy. That is appropriate in war. However, do we want to use military forces to govern or patrol our cities and towns? We, the authors of this textbook, do not think so. Imagine that you and some of your classmates are having a party. The party gets a bit loud, and your neighbors call 911. Instead of a police car, an armored personnel carrier and tanks arrive at the party, and 20 soldiers come out pointing AK-47 assault rifles at you. This is a silly example, but think about it. Surely we need a civil police, not the military, in our neighborhoods.[2]

This chapter will discuss early forms of policing and what some believe was the direct predecessor of the American police, the English police. Then the discussion will turn to the United States, beginning with the colonial experience with policing, including the watch and ward in the North and slave patrols in the South—some scholars believe that slave patrols could have been the first modern American police patrol organizations. A summary of the eighteenth- and nineteenth-century experience will focus on the urban, southern, and frontier experiences. The chapter will then turn to modern times—twentieth-century policing—and discuss the American police from 1900 to 1960, the turbulent decades of the 1960s and 1970s, and our generation, the 1980s and 1990s. It will end with a discussion of policing since the onset of the new millennium, emphasizing the dramatic, unprecedented changes in police organization and operations brought about by the terrorist attacks of September 11, 2001, as well as other current events that affected policing, such as Hurricane Katrina in 2005.

Early Police

We do not know much about the very early history of the police. Policing—maintaining order and dealing with lawbreakers—had always been a private matter. Citizens were responsible for protecting themselves and maintaining an orderly society. Uniformed, organized police departments as we think of them today were rare. Actually, as we'll see in this chapter, modern style police departments didn't appear until the fourteenth century in France and the nineteenth century in England.

Around the fifth century B.C.E., Rome created the first specialized investigative unit, called questors, or "trackers of murder."[3] Around the sixth century B.C.E. in Athens and the third century B.C.E. in Rome, unpaid magistrates (judges), appointed by the citizens, were the only people we would consider law enforcement professionals. The magistrates adjudicated cases, but private citizens arrested offenders and punished them. In most societies, people in towns would group together and form a watch, particularly at night, at the town borders or gates to ensure that outsiders did not attack the town.[4]

At about the time of Christ, the Roman emperor Augustus picked special, highly qualified members of the military to form the **Praetorian Guard,** which could be considered the first police officers. Their job was to protect the palace and the emperor. At about the same time, Augustus also established the Praefectus Urbi (Urban Cohort) to protect the city. The Urban Cohort had both executive and judicial power. Augustus also established the Vigiles of Rome. The **Vigiles** began as fire fighters. They were eventually also given law enforcement responsibilities, and they patrolled Rome's streets day and night. The Vigiles could be considered the first civil police force designed to protect citizens. They were considered quite brutal, and our words *vigilance* and *vigilante* come from them.[5]

Also in Rome in the first century C.E., public officials called lictors were appointed to serve as bodyguards for the magistrates. The lictors would

You Are There!

What a Police Officer's Uniform Means

The police badge—known in some departments as the shield, chest piece, or tin—is the outward symbol of a police officer's legal status and entitlement. It is symbolic of the authority vested in that individual by the public. The badge and other parts of the police officer's uniform are vestiges of the armor worn by government warriors centuries ago.

The badge's history can be traced back to two pieces of armor: the hand-held shield used to deflect blows and the chest plating intended to protect the warrior's chest from penetration. The shield often displayed the heraldry and symbols of the warrior's lord or head of state, just as today's badges reflect symbols of the officer's municipality, county, or state.

Shoulder epaulets or shoulder patches represent the shoulder plating worn to protect the warrior from the heavy, flat swords of the time. The officer's hat is reminiscent of helmets worn by warriors in battle. The hat badge or shield is a vestige of the plumage or insignia on the helmets.

SOURCE: *Police Chief*, September 1988, p. 66.

---

bring criminals before the magistrates upon their orders and carry out the magistrates' determined punishments, including the death penalty. The lictors' symbol of authority was the fasces, a bundle of rods tied by a red thong around an ax, which represented their absolute authority over life and limb.

During the twelfth and thirteenth centuries, kings on the European continent began to assume responsibility for the administration of the law. They began to appoint officials for that purpose to replace the watch and other private forms of self-defense. In the thirteenth century in Paris, Louis IX created a provost, who was assigned to enforce the law and supervise the night watch. The provost was assisted by investigating commissioners and sergeants. In 1356, France created a mounted military patrol, the Maréchausée, to maintain peace on the highways. The Maréchausée evolved into the Gendarmerie Nationale, which today polices the areas outside France's major cities.

The city of Paris had an armed, professional police in the eighteenth century that was credited with keeping Paris a safe and orderly city. The city of Munich also had an effective police department.

English Policing: Our English Heritage

The American system of law and criminal justice was borrowed from the English. Therefore, we will now concentrate on the English police experience, which is colorful and related to the development of English society.

Early History

Sir Robert Peel is generally credited with establishing the first English police department, the London Metropolitan Police, in 1829.[6] However, the first references to an English criminal justice or law enforcement system appeared some 1,000 years earlier, in the latter part of the ninth century, when England's king, Alfred the Great, was preparing his kingdom for an impending Danish invasion. Part of King Alfred's strategy against the Danes was maintaining stability in his own country and providing a method for people living in villages to protect one another. To achieve this stability, King Alfred established a system of **mutual pledge** (a form of "society control" where citizens grouped together to protect each other), which organized the responsibility for the security of the country into several levels. At the lowest level were tithings, ten families who grouped together to protect one another and to assume responsibility for the acts of the group's members. At the next level, 10 tithings, or 100 families, were grouped together into a hundred; the hundred was under the charge of a constable. People were supposed to police their own communities. If trouble occurred, a citizen was expected to raise the **hue and cry** (yell for assistance), and other citizens were expected to come to that citizen's assistance. The **constable,** who might be considered the first form of English police officer, was responsible for dealing with more serious breaches of the law.

Groups of hundreds within a specific geographic area were combined to form shires (the equivalent of today's county). The shires were put under the control of the king and were governed by a **shire-reeve,** or sheriff.

Over the centuries, as formal governments were established, early, primitive forms of a formal criminal justice system evolved in England. In 1285 C.E., the *Statute of Winchester* was enacted in England and established a rudimentary criminal justice system in which most of the responsibility for law enforcement remained with the people themselves. The statute formally established (1) the watch and ward, (2) the hue and cry, (3) the parish constable, and (4) the requirement that all males keep weapons in their homes for use in maintaining the public peace.

The **watch and ward** required all men in a given town to serve on the night watch. The watch, therefore, can be seen as the most rudimentary form of metropolitan policing. The watch was designed to protect against crime, disturbances, and fire. The watchmen had three major duties:

1. Patrolling the streets from dusk until dawn to ensure that all local people were indoors and quiet and that no strangers were roaming about.

2. Performing duties such as lighting street lamps, clearing garbage from streets, and putting out fires.

3. Enforcing the criminal law.

Persons serving on the watch, if necessary, would pronounce the hue and cry, and all citizens would then be required to leave their homes and assist the watchmen. The *Statute of Winchester* made it a crime not to assist the watch. The statute also established the office of parish constable, who was responsible for organizing and supervising the watch. The parish constable was, in effect, the primary urban law enforcement agent in England.

In the early fourteenth century, with the rise of powerful centralized governments and the decline of regional ones, we see the beginnings of a more formal system of criminal justice, with a separation of powers and a hierarchical system of authority.

Seventeenth Century and Thief-Takers

In seventeenth-century England, as before, law enforcement was seen as the duty of all the people, even though more and more officials were being charged with enforcing the law and keeping the peace. Already we see the beginnings of a tremendously fragmented and inept criminal justice system. The next criminal justice positions to be created were magistrates and beadles. Magistrates assisted the justices of the peace by presiding in courts, ordering arrests, calling witnesses, and examining prisoners. Beadles were assistants to the constables and walked the streets removing vagrants. The impact of the magistrates, constables, and beadles was minimal, and they were mostly corrupt.

The seventeenth-century English policing system also used a form of individual, private police. Called **thief-takers,** these private citizens, with no official status, were paid by the king for every criminal they arrested—similar to the bounty hunter of the American West. The major role of the thief-takers was to combat highway robbery committed by highwaymen, whose heroes were the likes of such legendary outlaws as Robin Hood and Little John. By the seventeenth century, highwaymen made traveling through the English countryside so dangerous that no coach or traveler was safe. In 1693, an act of Parliament established a monetary reward for the capture of any road agent, or armed robber. A thief-taker was paid upon the conviction of the highwayman and also received the highwayman's horse, arms, money, and property.

The thief-taker system was later extended to cover offenses other than highway robbery, and soon a sliding scale of rewards was established. Arresting a burglar or footpad (street robber), for example, was worth the same as catching a highwayman, but catching a sheep stealer or a deserter from the army brought a much smaller reward. In some areas, homeowners joined forces and offered supplementary rewards for the apprehension of a highwayman or footpad in their area. In addition, whenever there was a serious crime wave, Parliament awarded special rewards for thief-takers to arrest particular felons.

Often criminals would agree to become thief-takers and catch other criminals to receive a pardon from the king for their own crimes. Thus, many thief-takers were themselves criminals. Thief-taking was not always rewarding because the thief-taker was not paid if the highwayman was not convicted. The job also could be dangerous because the thief-taker had to fear the revenge of the highwayman and his relatives and associates. Many thief-takers would seduce young people into committing crimes and then have other thief-takers arrest the youths during the offenses. The two thief-takers would then split the fee. Others framed innocent parties by planting stolen goods on their persons or in their homes. Although some real criminals were apprehended by the professional thief-takers, the system generally created more crime than it suppressed.

Henry Fielding

Henry Fielding, the eighteenth-century novelist best known for writing *Tom Jones,* may also be credited with laying the foundation for the first modern police force. In 1748, during the heyday of English highwaymen, Fielding was appointed magistrate in Westminster, a city near central London. He moved into a house on Bow Street, which also became his office. In an attempt to decrease the high number of burglaries, street and highway robberies, and other thefts, Fielding established relationships with local pawnbrokers. He provided them with lists and descriptions of recently stolen property and asked them to notify him should such property be brought into their pawnshops. He then placed the following ad in the London and Westminster newspapers: "All persons who shall for the future suffer by robber, burglars, etc., are desired immediately to bring or send the best description they can of such robbers, etc., with the time and place and circumstances of the fact, to Henry Fielding Esq., at his house in Bow Street."[7]

Fielding's actions brought about what we can call the first official crime reports. Fielding was able to gain the cooperation of the high constable of Holborn and several other public-spirited constables. Together they formed a small investigative unit, which they called the Bow Street Runners. These were private citizens who were not paid by public funds but who were permitted to accept thief-taker rewards.

Eventually, the government rewarded Fielding's efforts, and his Bow Street Runners were publicly financed. In 1763, Fielding was asked to establish with public funds a civilian horse patrol of eight men to combat robbers and footpads on the London streets. The patrol proved successful but was disbanded after only nine months because of a lack of government support.

Londoners debated whether to have a professional police department. Although certainly enough crime, vice, theft, and disorder occurred to

You Are There!

England's Early Experience with a Civil Police Department

1763	Fielding creates civilian horse patrol in London.
1770	Foot patrol is established in London.
1798	River or marine police to patrol the Thames is established by Patrick Colquhoun. (Some consider this to be England's first civil police department.)
1804	Horse patrol is established in London (England's first uniformed patrol).
1829	Peel's police force, the Metropolitan Police, is established in London (England's first large-scale, organized, uniformed, paid, civil police department).

justify forming a civil police force, most people did not want a formal, professional police department for two major reasons. Many felt that a police force would threaten their tradition of freedom. Additionally, the English had considerable faith in the merits of private enterprise, and they disliked spending public money.

Despite the widespread public fear of establishing a civil police force, a small, permanent foot patrol financed by public funds was established in London in 1770. In 1789, a London magistrate, Patrick Colquhoun, lobbied for the creation of a large, organized police force for greater London, but his ideas were rejected after much government and public debate.

In 1798, Colquhoun was able to establish a small, publicly financed special river or marine police, patterned after Fielding's Bow Street Runners, to patrol the Thames. Some consider Colquhoun's force the first civil police department in England.

In 1804, a new horse patrol was established for central London. It included 2 inspectors and 52 men who wore uniforms consisting of red vests and blue jackets and trousers, making them England's first uniformed civil police department. As the problems of London in the late eighteenth and early nineteenth centuries increased (because of the Industrial Revolution, massive migration to London, poverty, public disorder, vice and crime), the people and Parliament finally surrendered to the idea that London needed a large, organized, civil police department.

© Fox Photos/Getty Images

■ *May 1927: A British "bobby" on his beat.*

Peel's Police—The Metropolitan Police for London

In 1828, Sir Robert Peel, England's home secretary, basing his ideas on those of Colquhoun, drafted the first police bill, the *Act for Improving the Police in and near the Metropolis* (the *Metropolitan Police Act*). Parliament passed it in 1829. This act established the first large-scale, uniformed, organized, paid, civil police force in London. More than 1,000 men were hired. Although a civil, rather than a military, force, it was structured along military lines, with officers wearing distinctive uniforms. The first London Metropolitan Police wore three-quarter-length royal blue coats, white trousers, and top hats. They were armed with truncheons, yesterday's equivalent of today's police baton. The police were commanded by two magistrates, later called commissioners.

London's first two police commissioners were Colonel Charles Rowan, a career military officer, and Richard Mayne, a lawyer. Peel, Rowan, and Mayne believed that mutual respect between the police and citizens would be crucial to the success of the new force. As a result, the early Bobbies (called that in honor of their founder) were chosen for their ability to reflect and inspire the highest personal ideals among young men in early nineteenth-century England.

The control of the new police was delegated to the home secretary, a member of the democratically elected government. Thus, the police as we know them today were, from their very beginning, ultimately responsible to the public.

Peel has become known as the founder of modern policing; however, it must be noted that he was never a member of a police department. His link to policing comes from his influence in getting the new police bill passed. The early London police were guided by **Peel's Nine Principles,** as described by the New Westminster Police Service:

1. The basic mission for which the police exist is to prevent crime and disorder.

2. The ability of the police to perform their duties depends on public approval of police actions.

3. Police must secure the willing co-operation of the public in voluntary observance of the law to be able to secure and maintain the respect of the public.

You Are There!

Sir Robert Peel—The Founder of Modern Policing

Sir Robert Peel was one of the most important persons in nineteenth-century British history. He dominated parliament throughout the period 1830 to 1850. He became a Member of Parliament (MP) in 1809 at the age of 21, after his father bought him a seat in parliament, and he became under-secretary of war and the colonies in 1810.

In 1812, Peel was appointed as Chief Secretary for Ireland. In that post, he attempted to end corruption in Irish government by trying to stop the practice of selling public offices and the dismissal of civil servants for their political views. Eventually, he became seen as one of the leading opponents to Catholic Emancipation. In 1814, he established a military-type "peace preservation" force in Ireland that eventually evolved into the Royal Irish Constabulary (RIC). In 1818, he resigned his post in Dublin and returned to London.

He became Home Secretary from 1822 to 1827. Distressed over the problems of law and order in London, he persuaded the House of Commons to pass the *Metropolitan Police Act* in 1829. The first Metropolitan Police patrols went onto the streets September 29, 1829.

He was prime minister twice, from 1834 to 1835 and from 1841 to 1846. Peel died in 1850 as the result of injuries he sustained in a fall from his horse while riding up Constitution Hill in London. Many have called him among the most important statesman in the history of England.

Because of Peel's connection with the creation of both the modern Irish and English police, the Irish police were known as "peelers" and the English police as "bobbies," thus magnifying Peel's role in the development of modern policing.

SOURCES: Thomas A. Reppetto, *The Blue Parade* (New York: Free Press, 1978), pp. 16 to 22; and The Victorian Web, retrieved October 23, 2006, from http://www.victorianweb.org/history/pms/peel/peel10.html.

4. The degree of co-operation of the public that can be secured diminishes proportionately to the necessity of the use of physical force.

5. Police seek and preserve public favour not by catering to public opinion but by constantly demonstrating absolute impartial service to the law.

6. Police use physical force to the extent necessary to secure observance of the law or to restore order only when the exercise of persuasion, advice and warning is found to be insufficient.

7. Police, at all times, should maintain a relationship with the public that gives reality to the historic tradition that the police are the public and the public are the police, the police being only members of the public who are paid to give full-time attention to duties which are incumbent on every citizen in the interests of community welfare and existence.

8. Police should always direction their action strictly towards their functions and never appear to usurp the powers of the judiciary.

9. The test of police efficiency is the absence of crime and disorder, not the visible evidence of police action in dealing with it.[8]

Peel's Principles were concerned with the preventive role of the police and positive relationships and cooperation between the police and the community it served. Consider the similarity between Peel's Principles and the concepts of *community policing* that have influenced policing during our past few decades. See Chapter 12, "Community Policing: The Debate Continues," for a complete discussion of community policing.

As a result of the formation of the new police force, the patchwork of private law enforcement systems in use at the time was abolished. Many believe that the English model of policing eventually became the model for the United States.

The Metropolitan Police was organized around the "**beat system,**" in which officers were assigned to relatively small permanent posts and were expected to become familiar with them and the people residing there, thereby making the officer a part of neighborhood life. This system differed from the patrols of the Paris police, which consisted of periodic roving surveillance of areas. Paris police patrols were never assigned to the same area on successive nights, thus not encouraging a close familiarity between the police and the public.

The main job of the new English police was suppressing mob disorder, winning support from the public, and developing a disciplined force. The development of a professional and disciplined force was difficult, as Thomas Reppetto tells us:

> On September 29, 1829, the force held a muster of its first 1,000 recruits. It was a rainy day, and some of the men broke out very un-military umbrellas, while others, carrying on the quite military habit of hard drinking, showed up intoxicated. The umbrella problem was eliminated by an order issued that day, but drinking was not so easily handled. In the first eight years, 5,000 members of the force had to be dismissed and 6,000 resigned. After four years only 15 percent of the 3,400 original recruits were left.[9]

Rowan, a former army colonel and a veteran of the Battle of Waterloo, was responsible for the efforts to instill military discipline on the new police department.

Unfortunately, the new police were not immediately well received. Some elements of the population saw the police as an occupying army, and open battles between the police and citizens occurred. The tide of sentiment turned in favor of the police, however, when an officer was viciously killed in the Cold Bath Fields riot of 1833. At the murder trial, the jury returned a not guilty verdict, inspiring a groundswell of public support for the much-maligned police. Eventually, Peel's system became so popular that all English cities adopted his idea of a civil police department.

In an interesting recent article in the *British Journal of Criminology*, Lucia Zedner explores the similarities between law enforcement in England before the creation of the London Metropolitan police to policing today in our post–9/11 world. As evidence of this, he points out the generalized insecurity and mounting demands for protection common to then and now. Also, he writes that the trend toward community participation in protective efforts in today's era reflects patterns of enlisting individuals and community organizations in voluntary activities of self-protection in the pre-Peel era before Peel's government-sponsored police concept. Zedner writes that today we are using private security companies in policing neighborhoods, businesses, and commercial areas, similar to the practice in the eighteenth century. He concludes, "Although the state can no longer claim a monopoly over policing [today], it must retain responsibility for protecting the public interest in policing measures and the maintenance of civil rights in the context of security measures being used."[10]

American Policing: The Colonial Experience

The North—The Watch

The American colonists did not have an easy life.[11] They were constantly at risk from foreign enemies, their brother and sister colonists, and Native Americans. Their only protection was their own selves and, at times, the military or militia. By the seventeenth century, the northern colonies started to institute a civil law enforcement system that closely replicated the English model. The county sheriff was the most important law enforcement official. In addition to law enforcement, however, he collected taxes, supervised elections, and had much to do with the legal process. Sheriffs were not paid a salary but, much like the English thief-taker, were paid fees for each arrest they made. Sheriffs did not patrol but stayed in their offices.

In cities, the town marshal was the chief law enforcement official, aided by constables (called schouts in the Dutch settlements) and night watchmen. Night watch was sometimes performed by the military. The city of Boston created the first colonial night watch in 1631 and three years later created the position of constable. In 1658, eight paid watchmen replaced a patrol of citizen volunteers in the Dutch city of Nieuw Amsterdam. The British inherited this police system in 1664 when they took over the city and renamed it New York. By the mid-1700s, the New York night watch was described as follows: "a parcel of idle, drinking, vigilant snorers, who never quell'd any nocturnal tumult in their lives; but would perhaps, be as ready to joining in a burglary as any thief in Christendom."[12]

The South—Slave Patrols

Protection against crime and criminals in the southern American colonies was mainly the responsibility of the individual citizen, as it had been

County Sheriff's Departments: Working in Relative Anonymity

LORENZO BOYD

Lorenzo Boyd is a former deputy sheriff in Suffolk County, Massachusetts. He has taught at Old Dominion University and the College of William and Mary in Virginia and North Carolina Central University in Durham, North Carolina. He is currently an assistant professor on the faculty of the University of North Texas.

Although Sir Robert Peel is credited with establishing the precursor to the modern municipal police department, the office of the sheriff has origins that date back to the ninth century and England's King Alfred the Great. The office of sheriff is the oldest law enforcement office known within the common-law system, and it has always been accorded great dignity and high trust.

The role of the sheriff has changed and evolved over time. Today, as in the past, the sheriff is the lead law enforcer in the county, entrusted with the maintenance of law and order and the preservation of "domestic tranquility." Sheriffs are also responsible for a host of other criminal justice functions and related activities, including law enforcement, jail administration, inmate transportation, court services, and civil process. The responsibilities of the sheriff cover a wide range of public safety functions that vary based on jurisdiction.

Sheriffs are the only elected law enforcement officials in most states. Today, for instance, sheriffs in Massachusetts are elected in each of the 14 counties, and sheriffs in Virginia are elected in each of the 95 counties and 28 major cities. The sheriff in the county that contains the state capital is called the "high sheriff" and is the ranking sheriff in the state.

In Massachusetts, the primary function of the sheriff's department is administration of the county jail and house of correction (in Massachusetts, jail is pretrial only, and the house of correction is short-term postconviction). The law enforcement function, though important, is secondary to the jail function. Because "care, custody, and control" of inmates is paramount, many sheriff's deputies function more as corrections officers than as police officers. In spite of the rich, long law enforcement history of the sheriff's department, often deputies acquiesce to a support role in dealing with municipal police departments. Long before sheriff's deputies can hone their skill on the streets of Boston, they must first serve a significant amount of time working in the county jail.

In most cities, the city police handle day-to-day police work, and the sheriff's department patrols county and rural areas that do not have a municipal police force. Sheriff's deputies handle many prisoner transport functions to and from court and jails, police raids, and "sting" operations. Sheriff's departments also employ a tactical emergency response team, similar to that of police SWAT teams. These tactical teams in the sheriff's department are referred to as Sheriff's Emergency Response Team (SERT). Inside the jail and house of correction, the SERT team is responsible for quelling cellblock riots, hostage situations, gang rivalries, and forced cell moves.

When I was first deputized in 1988, I was under the impression that I was poised to help save the world. "Fighting crime and saving lives" was the motto that I thought I would adopt. Little did I know that I had a lot to learn about the criminal justice system in general and the sheriff's department in particular. I quickly learned that being proficient at the behind-the-scenes, less glorious duties makes the sheriff's department so important.

Training for sheriff's deputies includes both tactical police training and training for correctional settings.

in early England. There was little law and order as we understand it now in the early southern colonies. When immediate action was needed, people generally took matters into their own hands, which led to an American tradition of vigilantism and lynching.[13]

Many police historians and scholars indicate that **slave patrols** in the American South were the precursor to the modern American system of

policing. Studies of this early form of policing in the South indicate that the southern colonies developed a formal system of social control, particularly in rural areas, to maintain the institution of slavery by enforcing restrictive laws against slaves. Slave patrols were prominent in many of the early colonies as a means of apprehending runaway slaves and of protecting the white population from slave insurrections or crimes committed by slaves.

Deputies have to be able to react to situations both in the jail and on the streets at a moment's notice. In the academy, I endured 80 hours of firearms training, 60 hours of criminal law, 40 hours of constitutional law, 20 hours of patrol procedures, 10 hours of self-defense, and a host of other seemingly peripheral topics. My time in the training academy, although critical, did little to prepare me mentally for my first assignment.

Once the academy was over, I donned a pressed uniform and a freshly polished pair of military-style boots and was ready to assume my position in the criminal justice system. I then reported for duty at the Suffolk County Jail in downtown Boston and awaited my new assignment. One thing that I will never forget happened on my first day of work. When I walked into the jail for the first time, the large steel door slammed behind me with a sound that was unnerving. That sound separated freedom from incarceration.

When I reported for duty on that first day, I was given handcuffs, a set of keys, and a radio, and I was assigned to run an inmate housing unit in the county jail. The jail is divided into different inmate housing units, which are treated as separate self-contained jails. I was assigned, on my first day, to what is often called the worst unit in the jail: the homicide unit. In this unit, over 40 men were housed, each facing a trial for murder. It is in situations like these that you find out what you are really made of, mentally. It was a bit intimidating standing face-to-face with the people that I had read about in the newspapers or seen on the evening news accused of having committed the most heinous of crimes. These are the people that I had to interact with for 8 hours per day, every day, in the jail. This is where I was sent to hone my skills, in relative anonymity. If I were good at my job, no one would ever talk about it. Only when things get out of control does the media shine a spotlight on the sheriff's department.

Every problem that occurs in municipal police departments also is present in the sheriff's department. There are power struggles, codes of silence, corruption, and intradepartmental strife. These problems are exacerbated due to the close quarters of the jail. Most of the deputies are struggling to get out of jail duty and move on to patrol, transportation, warrant-management teams, SERT teams, or other glorious assignments. Getting out of the jail onto the streets is something that both deputies and inmates strive for, sometimes with equal fervor.

Often it is the city or state police who make the big arrests in sting operations or on the streets, usually with back up from, or transportation provided by, the sheriff's department. Sheriff's deputies still tend to do the dirty work of transportation, classification, and custody when the city or state police are conducting press conferences. The sheriff's deputies have to deal with the housing, classification, control, and transportation of offenders long after the city or state police have closed their cases. Much of the work of the sheriff's department goes on behind the scenes, with little or no public accolades; nevertheless, the work of the sheriff's department continues in its professional manner often unnoticed by the public.

In retrospect, I have asked myself time and time again if my time in the sheriff's department was a positive one. Overall, I am happy with my experiences, both good and bad, because those experiences helped to mold a view of the criminal justice system. The sheriff's department operates in the best (or worst) of both worlds. Deputies get to patrol the streets as well as learn the inner workings of corrections. I think the sheriff's department is the backbone of criminal justice, even though the deputies tend to work in relative anonymity.

Policing experts, such as Carl B. Klockars and James A. Conser and Gregory D. Russell, actually conclude that the patrol function and concept was first accepted as a police practice by slave patrols in the South.[14]

Police historian Samuel Walker wrote, "In some respects, the slave patrols were the first modern forces in this country."[15] M. P. Roth, in his *Crime and Punishment: A History of the Criminal Justice System,* writes that slave patrols were an important stage in the development of American policing and "the evolution of the southern slave patrols in the early 1700s marked the first real advances in American policing."[16]

Robert C. Wadman and William Thomas Allison discuss the history of slave codes and slave patrols in the American southern colonies in their well-researched recent history of police in America,

To Protect and to Serve: A History of Police in America. They indicate that Maryland and Virginia developed slave codes as early as the 1660s. These codes defined the black slave and his or her family as pieces of property that were indentured to their masters for life and forbid them to engage in many activities that whites engaged in. Slave masters were given the legal authority to control their property—slaves—through physical discipline and punishment.[17]

These slave codes were laws enforced by developing southern police departments to directly support slavery and the existing economic system of the South. These codes were adopted by colonial and, later, state legislatures. Slave patrols became the police mechanism to support the southern economic system of slavery. The codes were designed to ensure the economic survival of southern society—the use of slave labor to produce goods. Slaves were valuable property, and the codes were designed to prevent them from running away or engaging in insurrection. Very simply, these early slave codes were designed to preserve the social order in which whites dominated and subjugated blacks.[18]

The southern slave codes mandated that slaves had no rights as citizens because they were considered property. Even the U.S. Supreme Court, in its infamous **Dred Scott decision,** *Dred Scott v. Sandford* (1857), held that Dred Scott, a black slave, could not sue in court for his freedom because he was not a citizen—he was a piece of property.[19]

Researcher Sally E. Hadden in her book, *Slave Patrols, Law and Violence in Virginia and the Carolinas,* reported that the first slave patrols were authorized in South Carolina to protect white families from slaves. Members of the slave patrols (free white men and some women) could enter, without permission any homes of blacks or whites suspected of harboring slaves who were violating the law. The colonial assembly in South Carolina developed specific rules, guidelines, and duties for the slave patrols that were in effect until the Civil War.[20]

Slave patrols became commonplace by the early eighteenth century and were often combined with local militia and police duties. These patrols varied in size but generally were small. Each well-armed patrol, operating on horseback, was generally required to inspect each plantation within its district at least once a month and to seize any contraband possessed by slaves. North Carolina's slave patrol system was developed in the 1700s under the local justice of the peace, and the patrols were required to visit each plantation in their districts every two weeks. They were allowed to flog or whip any slave caught in a minor violation of the slave codes.

Tennessee's slave patrol system began in 1753 and was administered through county courts, which required the patrollers to inspect all plantations within the county four times a year. Kentucky used its slave patrol system as a traditional police mechanism. It patrolled for runaway slaves, highwaymen (robbers), and other threats to the peace. In some Kentucky counties, the patrol worked 24 hours a day, 7 days a week.

American Policing: Eighteenth and Nineteenth Centuries

Historically, American policing attempted to control crime and disorder in an urban and frontier environment. Although the urban and frontier experiences differed in many ways, both could be classified as brutal and corrupt.

The Urban Experience

During the eighteenth century, the most common form of American law enforcement was the system of constables in the daytime and the watch at night. Crime, street riots, and drunkenness were very common, and law enforcement personnel were incompetent.

From 1790 to 1845, New York City's population grew from 33,000 to 370,000 people, and most were new immigrants. The increased population and poverty dramatically increased crime. An 1840 New York newspaper reported,

> Destructive rascality stalks at large in our streets and public places, at all times of day and night, with none to make it afraid; mobs assemble deliberately. . . . In a word, lawless violence and fury have full dominion over us.[21]

In 1842, a special citizens' committee of New Yorkers wrote,

> The property of the citizen is pilfered, almost before his eyes. Dwellings and warehouses are entered with an ease and apparent coolness and carelessness of detention which shows

You Are There!

First Urban U.S. Police Departments

Boston

1838	Boston Police Department is created with eight officers who only worked in the daytime.
1851	Boston Police Department assumes the night watch.
1853	First Boston police chief is appointed.
1854	First Boston police stations are built.
1859	Boston police officers receive first uniforms.

New York

1845	New York City Police Department is created—with officers on the job 24 hours a day, 7 days a week.
1853	New York City police are required to wear uniforms.
1857	Police "civil war" erupts at New York City Hall.

Philadelphia

1854	Philadelphia Police Department is created.

You Are There!

You Decide: How Did the Term "Cops" Come About?

Did "cops" refer to the copper stars worn by the first New York City police officers?

When the first members of the NYPD began to patrol in the summer of 1845, they only wore badges on their civilian clothing. The badges were eight-pointed stars (representing the first eight paid members of the old Watch during Dutch times) with the seal of the city at the center and were made of stamped copper. The newspapers of the time referred to the new force as the "Star Police" but people, seeing the shiny copper shields, began to call them "Coppers" which was later shortened to "Cops"

or

Was "cops" a shortened way of saying Constables on Patrol (COPs)?

There is also a British police term, Constable On Patrol, which may account for the use of the term "cops" in England as well.

---

that none are safe. Thronged as our city is, men are robbed in the street. Thousands that are arrested go unpunished, and the defenseless and the beautiful are ravished and murdered in the daytime, and no trace of the criminals is found.[22]

Early Police Departments The tremendous migration to large American cities and the poverty and discrimination these new residents encountered led to enormous social problems, including crime and disorder. In response, many large cities began to create formal police departments using the Peelian model. The first organized American police department in the North was created in Boston in 1838. In addition to police duties, the Boston police were charged with maintaining public health until 1853. The first Boston Police Department consisted of only eight members and worked only in the daytime. By 1851, the night watch was assumed by the Boston Police Department. In 1853, the office of police chief was created, and in 1854, police stations were constructed. The Boston police force was not fully uniformed until 1859, when members were required to wear blue jackets and white hats.

In 1844, the New York State legislature authorized communities to organize police forces and gave special funds to cities to provide 24-hour police protection. In New York City, under the leadership of Mayor William F. Havermeyer, a London-style police department was created on May 23, 1845. The first New York City police officers were issued copper stars to wear on their hats and jackets but were not allowed to wear full uniforms until 1853. Actually, the first New York cops did not even want to wear their copper stars because doing so made them targets for the city's ruffians. The New York City police were also in charge of street sweeping until 1881.

Philadelphia started its police department in 1854. By the outbreak of the Civil War, Chicago, New Orleans, Cincinnati, Baltimore, Newark, and a number of other large cities had their own police departments. The new police departments replaced the night watch system. As a result, constables and sheriffs were relieved of much of their patrol and investigative duties. However, they performed other duties in the fledgling criminal justice system, such as serving court orders and managing jails.

Politics in American Policing Nineteenth-century American policing was dominated by local politicians and was notorious for brutality, corruption, and ineptness: "In addition to the pervasive brutality and corruption, the police did little to effectively prevent crime or provide public services. . . . Officers were primarily tools of local politicians; they were not impartial and professional public servants."[23] In his book, *Low Life: Lures and Snares of Old New York,* Luc Sante writes, "The history of the New York police is not a particularly illustrious one, at least in the nineteenth and early twentieth centuries, as throughout the period the law enforcement agents of the city continually and recurrently demonstrated corruption, complacency, confusion, sloth and brutality."[24]

In 1857, political differences between the Democrats, who controlled New York City, and the Republicans, who controlled New York State, caused a full-scale police war. The corrupt New York City police, the Municipal Police, under the control of New York Mayor Fernando Wood, was replaced by the Metropolitan Police, created and controlled by Governor John A. King. Wood, however, refused to disband the Municipals. Thus, the city had two separate police departments, each under the control of one of the two enemies.

On June 16, 1857, the two police departments clashed at New York's City Hall. Fifty Metropolitan police arrived at City Hall with a warrant to arrest Wood. Almost 900 members of the Municipal Police attacked the Metropolitans, causing them to retreat. As the Metropolitans were retreating, the state called in the Seventh Regiment of the National Guard under the command of General Sandford. The members of the National Guard marched on City Hall and raised their weapons as if to fire at the Municipals and City Hall. Eventually Wood surrendered to arrest, and no shots were fired. In court, the mayor was released, and the judge decided that the Metropolitan Police would be the official New York City police.

The primary job of nineteenth-century police was to serve as the enforcement arm of the political party in power, protect private property, and control the rapidly arriving foreign immigrants. In the late 1800s, police work was highly desirable because it paid more than most other blue-collar jobs. The average factory worker earned $450 a year, whereas a police officer was paid, on average, $900.

Politics dominated police departments, and politicians determined who would be appointed a police officer and who would be promoted to higher ranks. Job security for police officers was nonexistent because when a new political party gained control of city government, it would generally fire all police officers and hire new ones.

Regarding the influence of politics on the hiring of police officers, Walker wrote,

> Ignorance, poor health, or old age was no barrier to employment. An individual with the right connections could be hired despite the most obvious lack of qualifications. Recruits received no formal training. A new officer would be handed a copy of the police manual (if one could be found) containing the local ordinances and state laws, and sent out on patrol. There he could receive on-the-job training from experienced officers who, of course, also taught the ways of graft and evasion of duty.[25]

Robert M. Fogelson wrote about the political impact of politicians on the police:

> Most patrolmen who survived for any length of time quickly . . . learned that a patrolman placed his career in jeopardy more by alienating his captain than by disobeying his chief and more by defying his wardman, who regulated vice in the precinct, than by ignoring [his sergeant].[26]

According to one researcher, "They [the police] knew who put them in office and whose support they needed to stay there. Their job was to manage their beat; often they became completely enmeshed in the crime they were expected to suppress. Corruption, brutality, and racial discrimination, although not universal, were characteristic of most big city departments."[27]

The Early Police Officer's Job Police work was primitive. The role of the American urban police in the eighteenth and nineteenth centuries was varied and often not limited to law enforcement. The early police performed many duties they do not have today, including cleaning streets, inspecting boilers, caring for the poor and homeless, operating emergency ambulances, and performing other social services.

American police in the North, in the English tradition, were not issued firearms. However, this changed quickly. In 1858, a New York City police

You Are There!

New York City Police Museum

The New York City Police Department (NYPD) has protected the city for more than 150 years. Its period of development to its modern-day structure dates back to the seventeenth century. The New York City Police Museum is located at 100 Old Slip in Manhattan's financial district within view of the Brooklyn Bridge and the Fulton Fish Market. The building was built in 1909 as the new home for the First Precinct. It was considered a model police facility when built and chiefs of police throughout the country visited the new station house looking to copy some of its features in their own buildings.

The museum captures the history of the NYPD as well as providing a present-day look at the world of law enforcement through the eyes of its officers. Its exhibits include an array of weapons, police shields, fingerprinting and forensic art stations, a drug awareness display, and a tactics simulator.

The museum collects, preserves, and interprets objects related to the history of the NYPD and provides information about its history through exhibitions, lectures, the Internet, publications, school events, and other educational programs. It houses one of the largest collection of police memorabilia in the United States, as well as an extensive photo collection and some police records dating back to the inception of the NYPD in 1845.

SOURCE: New York City Police Department at http://www.nycpolicemuseum.org.

officer shot a fleeing felon with a personal weapon. The case was presented to a grand jury, which did not indict the officer. Police officers in New York then began to arm themselves. A similar incident in Boston led to the arming of that police force. By the early 1900s, cities commonly issued revolvers to their police officers. Officers patrolled on foot with no radios, backup, or supervision. They relied on brute force and brutality to avoid being beaten up or challenged by local toughs.

Citizens had a tremendous hatred for nineteenth-century police officers and saw them as political hacks. The police were subjected to frequent abuse by street gangs, and suspects often had to be physically subdued before arrest. Commenting on this lack of respect by citizens, Walker notes, "A tradition of police brutality developed out of this reciprocal disrespect. Officers sought to gain with their billy clubs the deference to their authority that was not freely given."[28] Regarding this brutality, the social reformer Lincoln Steffens wrote, "He saw the police bring in and kick out their bandaged, bloody prisoners, not only strikers and foreigners, but thieves too, and others of the miserable, friendless, troublesome poor."[29]

Corruption, mismanagement, and brutality were rampant. Consequently, between 1860 and 1866, the police forces of Baltimore, Chicago, Cleveland, Detroit, Kansas City, and St. Louis were placed under state control.

Boston was the first city to form a detective division to investigate past crimes. However, early detectives were as corrupt as their uniformed counterparts, private thief-takers, or bounty hunters.

In the latter part of the nineteenth century, we begin to see some practical and technological advances in policing. The public health and social welfare responsibilities that formerly were the province of the police, including sweeping sidewalks and housing the homeless, were transferred to newly created municipal agencies. In the 1850s, precincts began to be linked to central headquarters by telegraph machines. In the 1860s, telegraph signal stations were installed, first in Chicago and then in Cincinnati. These enabled officers, using Morse code, to check with their precincts for instructions or to call for assistance. In 1881, the Morse code signal system was replaced by telephone call boxes in Cincinnati. A police officer could now call from his beat for a patrol wagon to transport prisoners. A red light on the top of a call box could summons officers for messages from their precinct headquarters.

The Southern Experience

As indicated earlier, slave patrols were an early form of American southern policing and perhaps the first police departments in the United States.

Wadman and Allison, evidencing their disbelief that Peel's London police were the major influence in creating American police departments, indicate that the largest law enforcement organization in the United States in 1837, before the widespread creation of police departments in the North, was in Charleston with a slave patrol that had about 100 members. Also, the Savannah Police Department was organized in 1852, had 86 officers, and operated day and night watches. In 1850, the Mobile, Alabama, Police Department had 30 officers. During the Civil War, the Richmond, Virginia, Police Department had 11 day patrolmen and 72 night patrolmen. However, crime increased so much in Richmond that Confederate President Jefferson Davis declared martial law in 1862.[30]

The Atlanta, Georgia, Police Department, a major railroad hub and supply center for Confederate forces that had troops and refugees flooding into and out of the city from late 1861 through the end of the Civil War in 1865, was challenged by the problems brought by the war, as well as by having to maintain the traditional social order through the slave code at the same time. However, the most serious crime problem in Atlanta was white rowdyism, vandalism, and theft. The Fulton County court dealt with cases involving more whites than bonded slaves and black refugees. Larceny and burglary were the most popular crimes in Atlanta and often involved Confederate soldiers on post in Atlanta. As a result of the crime, "Atlanta had a police force made up of the poor, elderly, and the not-so-honest element."[31]

The Atlanta force doubled in size during the war, from 14 to 28. The largest obstacle facing police leaders was finding qualified, trustworthy men to serve. Although the force never exceeded 30 men at any one time during the war, 48 policemen were found guilty of misconduct and 22 were dismissed. Charges ranged from drunkenness while on duty to extortion and illegal arrest. In 1864, the city hired a city marshal to organize patrol and assist the police, but the attempt failed.[32]

After the Civil War, from 1867 to 1877, law enforcement duties were provided by the military in the military districts created from the Confederacy. U.S. marshals in occupied Southern states often called on federal troops to form a posse to enforce local laws. Also, the army guarded polling places and curbed the actions of the Ku Klux Klan. Once Southern states regained representation in Congress, they tried to prevent such practices.

After the war, many police departments across the South reorganized to meet Reconstruction standards. However, in many cases, police officials under the pre-war system simply returned to their posts and the militia-like nature of slave patrols and volunteer companies survived the war in the newly reorganized police departments. In addition to maintaining public order, police continued to be the upholders of white supremacy in their communities.

Some police departments reluctantly hired blacks on their forces to satisfy demands brought on by Reconstruction. Montgomery, Alabama, and Vicksburg, Mississippi, hired large numbers of blacks on their police departments for a brief time, but most places, like Norfolk, Virginia, had only a token few. These black officers made whites extremely nervous, and whites taunted black police officers and often paid them no heed.[33]

The Frontier Experience

Life on the American frontier was not easy.[34] Early settlers faced tremendous problems from the weather, the terrain, Native Americans, and the criminals within their own ranks. Formal law enforcement on the frontier was rare. What little law enforcement existed in the Old West consisted mainly of the locally elected county sheriff and the appointed town marshal, and sometimes the U.S. marshal, the U.S. Army, or the state militia.

Sheriffs and Town Marshals The locally elected county sheriffs and the appointed town marshals (appointed by the mayor or city council) were usually the only law enforcement officers available on the frontier. Most of the sheriff's time was spent collecting taxes and performing duties for the courts.

If a crime spree occurred or a dangerous criminal was in an area, the sheriff would call upon the **posse comitatus**, a common law descendent of the old hue and cry. (The term posse comitatus, in Latin, means "the power of the county.") No man above the age of fifteen could refuse to serve as a member of a legally constituted posse. The posse was often little more than a legalized form of vigilantism. Vigilantism and lynch mobs were common in the Old West because of the lack of professional law enforcement. Many famous town marshals, such as James Butler (Wild Bill) Hickok of Hays City, Kansas, and later, Abilene, Kansas, and Wyatt Earp of Dodge City, Kansas, were really semireformed outlaws. There was little to distinguish between the good guys and bad guys in the American frontier's criminal justice system.

Federal Marshals Federal marshals played a role in frontier law enforcement. The *Federal Judiciary Act of 1789*, which created the office of the U.S. marshal, also gave the marshals the power to call upon the militia for assistance, a power formalized under federal posse comitatus legislation in 1792. The members of the militia were technically members of the federal marshal's posse and aided him in performing his civil duties. In 1861, Congress passed a law empowering the president to call upon the militia or regular army to enforce the law when ordinary means were insufficient.

The Military In both the North and the South, the military was also used by civilian authorities. In the North, the army was used to suppress labor disturbances. Excesses by the military in enforcing the law resulted in Congress passing the *Posse Comitatus Act of 1879*, forbidding the use of the military to enforce civilian law except where expressly authorized by law. Some of these exceptions applied in the Old West to prevent trespassing on Native American reservations or to enforce unpopular federal decisions regarding territories such as Arizona and New Mexico. The use of the military in the Old West ended around the last quarter of the nineteenth century.

State Police Agencies Some states and territories created their own police organizations. In 1823, Stephen Austin hired a dozen bodyguards to protect fellow "Texicans" from Native Americans and bandits. Austin's hired guns were officially named the Texas Rangers upon Texas's independence in 1835. The Texas Rangers served as a border patrol for the Republic of Texas, guarding against marauding Native Americans and Mexicans. When Texas was admitted to the Union in 1845, the Texas Rangers became the first U.S. state police agency.

Unlike present-day state police, the Texas Rangers and their counterparts, the Arizona Rangers (1901) and the New Mexico Mounted Patrol (1905), were primarily border patrols designed to combat cattle thievery and control outlaw activities on the Rio Grande. With Pennsylvania leading the way in 1905, nonsouthwestern and other states began to create their own state police agencies.

Private Police Private police were much more effective than public law enforcement agencies on the frontier. Allan Pinkerton, a native of Scotland, was a former police detective who established a detective agency in Chicago in 1850. The Pinkerton Agency first gained notoriety just before the Civil War when it thwarted the alleged "Baltimore Plot" to assassinate President-Elect Abraham Lincoln. By the 1880s, Pinkerton's National Detective Agency had offices in nearly two-dozen cities. In the West, Pinkerton's customers included the U.S. Department of Justice, various railroad companies, and major land speculators. The agents arrested train robbers and notorious gangsters, including the James Gang in the 1880s and Robert Leroy Parker (Butch Cassidy) and Harry Longbaugh (the "Sundance Kid") in the early 1900s. The agents also arrested John and Simeon Reno, who organized the nation's first band of professional bank robbers. Pinkerton's agents were also hired in the East by mining and manufacturing companies to suppress labor organizations, such as the Molly Maguires in 1874 to 1875, as well as to suppress the Homestead Riots in Pittsburgh in 1892. The Pinkertons employed informants throughout the United States and its territories and offered cash rewards for information. The Pinkertons mainly protected the interests of the railroads, wealthy eastern bankers, and land speculators.

In competition with the Pinkerton Agency during the latter part of the nineteenth century was the Rocky Mountain Detective Association, which pursued and apprehended bank and train robbers, cattle thieves, murderers, and the road agents who plundered highways and mining communities throughout the Southwest and Rocky Mountain area.

Also in competition with the Pinkertons was Wells, Fargo and Company, started in 1852 by Henry Wells and William G. Fargo as a banking and stock association designed to capitalize on the emerging shipping and banking opportunities in California. Wells Fargo operated as a mail-carrying service and stagecoach line out of more than a hundred offices in the western mining districts. Because the company carried millions of dollars in gold and other valuable cargo, it created a guard company to protect its shipments. The Wells Fargo private security employees were effective in preventing robberies and thefts; moreover, specially trained and equipped agents relentlessly hunted down criminals who held up its banks and carriers.

American Policing: Twentieth Century

The first half of the twentieth century saw such dramatic negative events as the Boston police strike, National Prohibition, and the issuance of the *Wickersham Commission Report*. However, innovation and an increase in professionalism grew to characterize the American police partly through the efforts of such early police professionals as August Vollmer, O. W. Wilson, and J. Edgar Hoover.

Policing from 1900 to 1960

As we have seen, American policing has historically been characterized by ineptness, corruption, and brutality.[35] At the start of the twentieth century, serious attempts were made to reform the police.

Even earlier, Theodore Roosevelt attempted reform as one of the New York City Board of Police Commissioners between 1895 and 1897. Roosevelt raised police recruitment standards and disciplined corrupt and brutal officers. Roosevelt, often called TR by the press, was a colorful and proactive leader who traveled through the streets watching the actions of his police.[36]

However, despite much publicity and some superficial changes, Roosevelt's efforts failed when the corrupt Tammany Hall political machine was returned to power in 1897. Reppetto tells us, "Roosevelt was a man of dash and vigor, but his influence on the police, like his military career, was more form than substance, and things soon returned to normal."[37]

During the progressive era of American government, 1900 to 1914, attempts at reforming the police were originated outside police departments by middle-class, civic-minded reformers. For the most part, however, these attempts failed.

Technology In the twentieth century, the use of technology grew phenomenally in American police departments. By 1913, the police motorcycle was being used by departments in the Northeast. The first police car was used in Akron, Ohio, in 1910, and the police wagon was first used in Cincinnati in 1912. By the 1920s, the patrol car was in widespread use. The patrol car began to change police work by allowing the police to respond quickly to crimes and other problems, as well as by enabling each officer to cover much more territory.

The widespread use of the one-way radio in the 1930s and the two-way radio in the 1940s, combined with the growing use of the patrol car, began to revolutionize police work. A person could call police headquarters or a precinct, and a police car could be dispatched almost immediately, providing rapid response to calls for service and emergencies. Although police administrators greeted this innovation with great joy, motorized patrol eventually forced a separation of the police from the community and played a part in the serious problems in policing that arose in the 1960s.

The Boston Police Strike The Boston police strike of 1919 was one of the most significant events in the history of policing, and it increased interest in police reform. While other professions were unionizing and improving their standards of living, police salaries lagged behind, and the police were becoming upset with their diminished status in society. The fraternal association of Boston police officers, the Boston Social Club, voted to become a union affiliated with the American Federation of Labor (AFL). On September 9, 1919, 70 percent of Boston's police officers—1,117 men—went on strike. Rioting and looting immediately broke out, and Governor Calvin Coolidge mobilized the state militia. Public support went against the police, and the strike was broken. All the striking officers were fired and replaced by new recruits. The strike ended police unionism for decades. Coolidge became a national hero and went on to become president of the United States. Many say that his action in firing the Boston police propelled him to the presidency.

National Prohibition Another significant event in twentieth-century policing, and one that stirred up another police reform movement, was the experiment with the prohibition of alcohol in the United States. The **Volstead Act** (National Prohibition) was passed in 1919 and became law in 1920 with the adoption of the **Eighteenth Amendment** to the Constitution. It forbade the sale and manufacture of alcohol, attempting to make America a dry nation. Traditional organized crime (TOC) families received their impetus during this period as gangsters banded together to meet the tremendous demand of ordinary Americans for alcohol. When the Eighteenth Amendment was repealed in 1933 with the adoption of the Twenty-first Amendment, the organized crime families funneled the tremendous amount of capital that they had received in the alcohol trade into other vice crimes, such as illegal gambling, prostitution, loan sharking, labor racketeering, and later, drug dealing.

Local law enforcement was unable to stop the alcohol and vice operations of organized crime and became even more corrupt as many law enforcement officers cooperated with organized crime. As a result, between 1919 and 1930, 24 states formed crime commissions to study the crime problem and the ability of the police to deal with crime.

The Wickersham Commission In 1929, President Herbert Hoover created the National Commission on Law Observance and Enforcement with George W. Wickersham as its chair. The commission was popularly known as the **Wickersham Commission** and conducted the first national study of the U.S. criminal justice system.

The commission issued a report in 1931, popularly known as the *Wickersham Commission Report.* The report criticized the Volstead Act, which created Prohibition, saying it was not enforced because it was unenforceable. National Prohibition was repealed in 1933.

© Topical Press Agency/Getty Images

Alice Stebbins Wells, who became one of the first policewomen in the United States when she joined the Los Angeles California Police Department in 1910.

The commission found that the average police commander's term of office was too short and that responsibility to politicians made the position insecure. The report indicated that there was a lack of effective, efficient, and honest patrol officers and no efforts to educate, train, or discipline officers or to fire incompetent ones. The commission found further that police forces, even in the biggest cities, did not have adequate communication systems or equipment.

Two volumes of the *Wickersham Commission Report, Lawlessness in Law Enforcement* (volume 2) and *The Police* (volume 14), concerned themselves solely with the police. *Lawlessness in Law Enforcement* portrayed the police as inept, inefficient, racist, and brutal, and accused them of committing illegal acts. The volume concluded, "The third degree—the inflicting of pain, physical or mental, to extract confessions or statements—is extensively practiced."[38]

The *Wickersham Commission Report* blamed the shortcomings of the police on a lack of police professionalism. *The Police,* written primarily by August Vollmer, discussed methods that could be used to create a professional police force in the United States. The methods the commission advocated included increased selectivity in the recruitment of officers, better pay and benefits, and more education for police officers.

The *Wickersham Commission Report* angered citizens and started another groundswell for police reform. With the onset of the Great Depression, however, police reform became less important than economic revival, and another attempt at police reform failed.

Professionalism An early attempt at police reform was the creation in 1893 of a professional society, the International Association of Chiefs of Police (IACP). Its first president was the Washington, D.C., chief of police, Richard Sylvester. The IACP became the leading voice of police reform during the first two decades of the twentieth century by consistently calling for the creation of a civil service police and for the removal of political influence and control over the police. The IACP remains a significant force in policing today.

Eventually a federal law, the **Pendleton Act,** was passed in 1883 to establish a civil service system that tested, appointed, and promoted officers on a merit system. The civil service system was later adopted by local governments, and political influence slowly evaporated from police departments. Today, however, not all U.S. police agencies are governed by civil service rules. Furthermore, despite civil service systems, politics continued to play some part in American law enforcement.

Several people were pioneers in modern policing, and two men, Vollmer and Wilson, stand out in the twentieth century as the founders of police professionalism.

August Vollmer From 1905 to 1932, Vollmer was the chief of police in Berkeley, California. Vollmer instituted many practices that started to professionalize the U.S. police. Among those practices was incorporating university training as a part of police training. Vollmer also introduced the use of intelligence, psychiatric, and neurological tests to aid in the selection of police recruits and initiated scientific crime detection and crime solving techniques. In addition, Vollmer helped develop the School of Criminology at the University of California at Berkeley, which became the model for programs related to law and criminal justice throughout the United States. In addition to authoring the *Wickersham Commission Report's* volume *The Police,* Vollmer trained numerous students who went on to become reform-oriented and progressive police chiefs. Vollmer can certainly be considered the father of modern American policing.

O. W. Wilson A disciple of Vollmer's, Wilson pioneered the use of advanced training for police officers when he took over and reformed the Wichita, Kansas, police department in 1928. While there, Wilson conducted the first systematic study of the effectiveness of one-officer squad cars. Despite officers' complaints about risks to their safety, his study showed that one-officer cars were more efficient, effective, and economical than two-person cars. Wilson developed modern management and administrative techniques for policing. He was the author of the first two textbooks on police management: the International City Management Association's *Municipal Police Administration* and his own text, *Police Administration,* which became the bible of policing for decades.

Wilson was dean of the School of Criminology at the University of California at Berkeley from 1950 to 1960 and the superintendent of the Chicago police from 1960 to 1967. The core of Wilson's approach to police administration was managerial efficiency. He believed that police departments should maximize patrol coverage by replacing foot patrols with one-person auto patrols. He advocated rapid response to calls for service as a key criterion by which to judge the effectiveness of police departments.

Almost every U.S. police department since the 1950s has been organized around the principles espoused in Wilson's books. He developed workload formulas based on reported crimes and calls for service on each beat. Wilson's 1941 workload formula remained unchanged for decades.

Raymond Blaine Fosdick and Bruce Smith Other early pioneers in the movement toward police professionalism were Fosdick and Smith. Neither was a police officer. Fosdick is noted for the first scholarly research regarding the police. In 1915, he published *European Police Systems*, which examined the police structures and practices of Europe. In 1920, he published *American Police Systems* after studying the police of 72 U.S. cities.

Smith, a researcher and later manager of the Institute of Public Administration, also contributed to our early knowledge of the police. His efforts in surveying and researching police departments in approximately 50 leading American cities in 18 states led to his noteworthy 1940 book, *Police Systems in the United States;* a second edition was published in 1949.

John Edgar Hoover One cannot discuss law enforcement in the twentieth-century United States without mentioning Hoover, more popularly known as J. Edgar Hoover. In 1921, Hoover, an attorney working for the U.S. Department of Justice, was appointed assistant director of the Bureau of Investigation, the forerunner of the Federal Bureau of Investigation (FBI) by President Warren G. Harding.

In 1924, President Calvin Coolidge, upon the retirement of the bureau's director, appointed Hoover as the director. During the next 48 years, Hoover was reappointed as director of the FBI by each succeeding U.S. president and remained director until his death in 1972.

Under Hoover's leadership, the FBI changed from an inefficient organization into what many consider the world's primary law enforcement agency. Among his major contributions were the hiring of accountants and lawyers as special agents; the introduction of the FBI *Uniform Crime Reports,* which since 1930 has been the leading source of crime and arrest statistics in the United States; the development of the National Crime Information Center (NCIC); the development of the FBI's Ten Most Wanted Criminals Program, otherwise known as Public Enemies; the development of the FBI Academy at Quantico, Virginia; and the popularizing of the FBI through the media as incorruptible, crime-fighting G-men.

During the past few decades, however, Hoover's reputation has diminished. Revelations have surfaced about his use of the media to build a myth about the FBI, his single mindedness about Communism, and his domestic surveillance operations over prominent Americans.

Kefauver Committee In 1950, in response to fear about crime and the corruption of law enforcement officers, the U.S. Senate's Crime Committee, chaired by Senator Estes Kefauver, was created. The Kefauver Committee held televised public hearings that led to the discovery of a nationwide network of organized crime, a syndicate that has commonly been called the Mafia or Cosa Nostra. The hearings also revealed that many law enforcement officers nationwide were on the syndicate's payroll. The public was shocked over these tales of corruption, and another attempt at police reform began. David R. Johnson wrote about this decade:

> The 1950s marked a turning point in the history of professionalism. Following major scandals, reformers came to power across the nation. Politicians had real choices between the traditional and new models of policing because a number of professional police reformers were available for the first time. With an enraged middle class threatening their livelihoods, the politicians opted for reform.[39]

Policing in the 1960s and 1970s

The 1960s and 1970s, times of great tension and change, were probably the most turbulent era ever for policing in U.S. history. Numerous social problems permeated these decades, and the police were in the middle of each problem. In this era, the struggle for racial equality reached its height, accompanied by marches, demonstrations, and riots. These riots burned down whole neighborhoods in U.S. urban centers. The Vietnam War was reaching its height, soldiers were dying, and students across the United States were protesting the war and governmental policies. The Supreme Court decided in case after case to protect arrested persons from oppressive police practices. The police seemed to be more the targets of radical groups than the respected protectors of the people. In short, during this time of dramatic social change in the United States, the police were not only right in the middle of it all, but often were the focus of it all.

The police, because of their role, were always in the middle—between those fighting for their civil rights and the government officials (the employers of the police) who wanted to maintain the status quo, between demonstrating students and college and city administrators. The police received much criticism during these years. Some of it was deserved, but much of it was beyond their control.

James Q. Wilson perhaps described the decade of the 1960s best when he wrote, "It all began about 1963, that was the year, to over dramatize a bit, that a decade began to fall apart."[40]

Supreme Court Decisions The 1960s saw the Warren Court at its height, a U.S. Supreme Court that focused dramatically on individual rights. Police actions, ranging from arrests to search and seizure and custodial interrogation, were being declared unconstitutional. (Chapter 13, "Police and the Law," will focus on these decisions.) The Court made dramatic use of the exclusionary rule, a Supreme Court ruling in 1914 that declared that evidence seized by the police in violation of the Constitution could not be used against a defendant in federal court, thus leading to the possibility that a guilty defendant could go free because of procedural errors by the police.

Many important police-related cases were decided in this era. *Mapp v. Ohio* (1961) finally, after much warning, applied the exclusionary rule to all states in the nation.[41] *Escobedo v. Illinois* (1964) defined the constitutional right to counsel at police interrogations.[42] *Miranda v. Arizona* (1966) required the police to notify a person who is in police custody and who is going to be interrogated of his or her constitutional rights.[43]

The Civil Rights Movement Legal segregation of the races finally ended with the landmark Supreme Court case of *Brown v. Board of Education of Topeka* (1954),[44] which desegregated schools all over the nation. However, equal treatment of the races did not occur overnight. Numerous marches and demonstrations occurred before the Civil Rights Act of 1964 was passed.

In the 1960s, African Americans and other civil rights demonstrators participated in freedom marches throughout the United States, particularly in the South. Because the police are the enforcement arm of government, they were used to enforce existing laws, which in many cases meant arresting and inhibiting the freedom of those marching for equality.

In 1960, the Freedom Riders left Washington, D.C., by bus to confront segregation throughout the South. The buses and protesters were harassed and were temporarily halted and attacked by violent white mobs in Anniston and Birmingham, Alabama. The police were again used to inhibit these marches for equality.

During the 1960s, the Reverend Martin Luther King, Jr., was at the forefront of the civil rights marches. In 1962, there were mass arrests of civil rights demonstrators in Albany, Georgia. Also in 1962, James Meredith became the first African American to enroll at the University of Mississippi. President John F. Kennedy was forced to send U.S. marshals and the armed forces into Mississippi to protect Meredith against attacks by segregationists because the local police were unable or unwilling to protect him.

In 1963, King led 25,000 demonstrators on a historic march on Washington that culminated in his "I have a dream" speech. During this speech, a defining moment of the movement, a white uniformed police officer stood behind King in a highly visible position, perhaps as a symbolic representation of the new role of the police in America's social history. Officers were to act as defenders rather than oppressors.

Also in 1963, in Birmingham, Alabama, four African American girls were killed when a bomb exploded during a church service at the 16th Street Baptist Church. In the same year, King led a peaceful march against segregation in Birmingham, Alabama, while Birmingham Public Safety Commissioner Bull Connor unleashed hoses and police dogs against the demonstrators. The actions of police personnel like Connor caused the police much negative press and have affected police–minority group relationships ever since.

In 1965, African Americans and other civil rights demonstrators attempted a peaceful march to Selma, Alabama. During the march, Alabama state police, under directions from state officials, stopped the marchers at the Edmund Pettus Bridge in Selma, where a Boston minister was murdered and white toughs beat many others. A massive civil rights march then proceeded from Selma to Montgomery, Alabama, under the protection of the National Guard.

The civil rights movement continued and succeeded partly by enrolling more minorities as voters, outlawing forms of government-sanctioned segregation, and ensuring that more minorities participated in government. Today, many of our large-city mayors and politicians are members of minority groups. The civil rights movement led efforts to increase the recruitment and hiring of blacks and other minorities in our nation's police departments and other agencies of the criminal justice system.

Although the civil rights movement was necessary in the evolution of our nation, the use of the police by government officials to thwart the movement left a wound in police-community relations that has still not healed. The 1991 beating of Rodney King in Los Angeles and the 1992 jury verdict acquitting the four Los Angeles police officers who were charged in King's beating (described later) angered people across the United States. The resultant riots in Los Angeles and other cities seemed to bring the United States back to the same strained racial conditions that existed in the 1960s.

Assassinations In the 1960s, three of the most respected leaders in the United States were assassinated: President Kennedy in 1963 in Dallas, his brother Robert Kennedy in 1968 in Los Angeles, and Dr. Martin Luther King, Jr., also in 1968 in Memphis. These assassinations clearly reflected the turbulence of the decade.

Many say that the person who assassinated President Kennedy as he rode in a Dallas motorcade is still unknown. Lee Harvey Oswald was captured and charged with Kennedy's murder after shooting and killing a Dallas police officer, J. D. Tippit, an hour after the president was killed. Several days later, Oswald was shot and killed by Jack Ruby as Oswald was led out of a Dallas police station. The debate over these incidents continues.

Anti–Vietnam War Demonstrations The Vietnam War was another turbulent, heartrending experience in American history, and again the police were used in a manner that tarnished their image. There were numerous and violent confrontations between opponents of the Vietnam War and the government's representatives—the police—on college campuses and city streets.

In 1967, hundreds of thousands of people using civil disobedience tactics marched in antiwar demonstrations in New York City, Washington, D.C., San Francisco, and numerous other cities around the nation, often clashing with the police, whose job it was to enforce the law and maintain order.

At the Democratic Party presidential convention in Chicago in 1968, police-citizen violence shocked the nation and the world. With information that 10,000 protesters organized by antiwar groups, including the Youth International Party (Yippies), were coming to Chicago for the 1968 National Democratic Convention, Chicago's mayor, Richard J. Daley, mobilized the National Guard and the Chicago police. On August 28, the protesters attempted to force their way into the convention. Police and the National Guard chased the crowd through downtown Chicago. Many report that the police command structure broke down and that the police became a mob that ran through the streets and assaulted protesters, reporters, and bystanders. A study subsequent to the convention, the *Walker Report,* called the actions of the police a police riot.

There are many different viewpoints of the chaotic disturbances that occurred on the U.S. streets during this period. What some perceived as a police riot, others perceived as the police doing their job. Many stress that the Yippies and other protesters were attempting to break up a lawfully gathered assembly by illegal means.

Eight members of the Yippies were charged with conspiracy for starting the disturbances in Chicago and were dubbed the "Chicago Eight." In 1969, the Chicago Eight trial began (it was later called the Chicago Seven trial due to the severance from the trial of Bobby Seale, the co-founder of the

Black Panther Party). A Students for a Democratic Society (SDS) splinter group, the Weathermen, organized the Days of Rage in Chicago, which resulted in violent rampaging in the streets and more confrontation with the police. In 1970, all of the Chicago Eight were acquitted of conspiracy charges; convictions on lesser charges were later overturned as well.

Campus Disorders In addition to the civil rights movement of the 1960s, demonstrations, marches, and civil disobedience also took place on college campuses across the nation. These events protested a perceived lack of academic freedom, the Vietnam War, the presence of Reserve Officers' Training Corps (ROTC) units on campuses, and many other issues. Again, the police were used to enforce the law.

In 1960, the Student Nonviolent Coordinating Committee (SNCC) was organized to coordinate student civil rights protests. In 1961, the SDS held its first national convention in Port Huron, Michigan. These two groups had a tremendous impact on the 1960s. Teach-ins, rallies, student strikes, takeovers of campus buildings, and the burning of draft cards were some of the tactics used on the campuses.

The protests on the campuses caused college administrators to call in local police departments to maintain order. That, in turn, caused students to complain about the actions of the police. Again, the police became the focus of anger and attention.

In 1968, a state of civil disorder was declared in Berkeley, California, following recurring police-student confrontations. Protests, riots, and violent clashes between students and the police replaced education on many college campuses in the United States.

Probably the most widely publicized campus protest of the 1960s was the student takeover at Columbia University, in New York City, in spring 1968. Students employed every tactic that had been used in earlier campus protests, including teach-ins, rallies, picketing, sit-ins, a student strike, and the takeover of university buildings. As negotiations between the college administration and the student rebels broke down, the administration decided to call in the police.

In the early morning of April 30, 1968, after students had taken over many college buildings, 2,000 police officers moved onto the campus and methodically cleared five occupied buildings. The effort to clear the remaining buildings became violent. Finally, the police were able to secure all buildings by arresting 692 students. In late May, the students again took over two buildings on Columbia's campus. The administration again called the police. The Cox Commission, formed to investigate the violence at Columbia University, reported on the police action that followed:

> Hell broke loose. One hundred students locked arms behind the barricades at Amsterdam Avenue. Hundreds more crowded close to the gate. The police swiftly dismantled the obstruction. The hundred broke and ran. But 2,000 students live in dormitories facing South Field. Many of them and hundreds of other people were crowded on the campus. For most, the character of the police action was a profound shock; neither they nor others in the Columbia community appreciated the extent of the violence which is the probable concomitant of massive police action against hundreds, if not thousands, of angry students. As police advanced, most students fled. . . . Some police first warned the students; others chased and clubbed them indiscriminately. But not all students went to their dormitories and some who fled came back out to attack the police. Bottles and bricks were hurled by students. A number of police were injured. The action grew fierce. . . . By 5:30 AM the campus was secured.[45]

The campus antiwar riots reached their height in 1970. The firebombing of a University of Wisconsin ROTC building began a wave of some 500 bombings or arsons on college campuses. Students rampaged through Cambridge's Harvard Yard, two students were killed and nine wounded by police gunfire at Jackson State College in Mississippi, and four students were killed by the National Guard at a protest at Kent State University, causing many U.S. colleges and universities to close for the year. Again, clashes between the police and students caused wounds that were hard to cure.

Urban Riots Major riots erupted in the ghettos of many U.S. cities during the 1960s. Most started directly following a police action. This is not to say that the riots were the result of the police; rather, a police action brought to the surface numerous underlying problems, which many say were the actual causes of the riots.

In summer 1964, an off-duty white New York City police lieutenant shot an African American youth who was threatening a building superintendent with a knife. This shooting precipitated the 1964 Harlem riot. Riots also occurred that summer in Rochester, New York; Jersey City, New Jersey; and Philadelphia. In 1965, riots occurred in Los Angeles (the Watts district), San Diego, and Chicago. In 1966, riots again occurred in Watts, as well as in Cleveland, Brooklyn, and Chicago. In 1967, major riots occurred in Boston's Roxbury section, in Newark, and in Detroit.

The riot in Detroit was responsible for 43 deaths, 2,000 injuries, and property damage estimated at more than $200 million; 7,000 persons were arrested. The Watts riot was responsible for the deaths of 34 people, more than 1,000 injuries, and the arrests of nearly 4,000 people. The Newark riot was responsible for 26 deaths and 1,500 injuries.

In 1968, riots occurred in cities all over the United States—including Baltimore, Boston, Chicago, Detroit, Kansas City, Newark, New York City, Washington, D.C., and scores of other cities—following the murder of Dr. King. The worst riot occurred in Washington, D.C., with 12 people killed, 1,200 people injured, 7,600 people arrested, and nearly $25 million in property damage. Nationwide, 55,000 federal troops and National Guards members were called out. Forty-six deaths resulted from the riots, and 21,270 people were arrested.

Again, the efforts of the police to maintain order during these massive shows of civil disobedience and violence caused wounds in police-community relations that have yet to heal. Problems between the minority communities and the police continued, as did the riots. Several radical groups, including the Black Panther party and the Black Liberation Army, waged urban warfare against the police, resulting in many deaths among their members and the police.

Creation of National Commissions In the wake of the problems of the 1960s, particularly the problems between the police and citizens, three national commissions were created. The first was the **President's Commission on Law Enforcement and Administration of Justice,** which issued a report in 1967 entitled *The Challenge of Crime in a Free Society* and a collection of task force reports covering all aspects of the criminal justice system.

The second national commission was the **National Advisory Commission on Civil Disorders (Kerner Commission),** which released a report in 1968 that decried white racism and a rapidly polarizing society. The report stated, "Our nation is moving toward two societies, one black, one white, separate and unequal." The commission concluded, "Abrasive relationships between police and Negroes and other minority groups, have been a major source of grievance, tension, and, ultimately, disorder."[46]

The third was the President's Commission on Campus Unrest. Its report, issued in 1970, called the gap between youth culture and mainstream society a threat to U.S. stability. These commissions are mentioned often in this text.

Corruption The corruption that has historically permeated American policing in the past has continued into the present. Approximately every 20 years, the nation's largest and most visible police department, the New York City Police Department (NYPD), has been the subject of a major scandal involving police corruption and resulted in governmental hearings: the Seabury Hearings in the 1930s, the Gross Hearings in the 1950s, and the Knapp Commission in 1970.

The Knapp Commission resulted from allegations made by New York City plainclothes police officer Frank Serpico and New York City police sergeant David Durk. Serpico was a Bronx officer (assigned to enforce antigambling laws) who was aware of widespread graft and bribe receiving in his unit. He took his tales of corruption to major police department officials, including the second-highest ranking officer in the department; to the city's Department of Investigation; and eventually even to the mayor's office. When Serpico finally realized that no one was taking his claims seriously, he and Durk went to a *New York Times* reporter, who wrote a series of stories about corruption in the department that shocked the public. The *Times* articles forced the mayor, John Lindsey, to appoint a commission to investigate police corruption, which popularly became known as the Knapp Commission. Chapter 8, "Police Ethics and Police Deviance," will focus on the Knapp Commission and police corruption and misconduct. The revelations of the Knapp Commission regarding widespread, systemic, organized corruption in the NYPD led to sweeping changes in the department's organization, philosophy, operations, and procedures.

Police Research The decades of the 1960s and 1970s saw tremendous research into policing, which brought about sweeping changes in thinking about how police work is done in the United States. One of the most significant developments in modernizing and professionalizing the police was the creation of the Law Enforcement Assistance Administration (LEAA) within the U.S. Department of Justice through Title 1 of the *Omnibus Crime Control and Safe Streets Act of 1968*. The LEAA spent more than $60 million in its first year alone, and between 1969 and 1980, the LEAA spent more than $8 billion to support criminal justice research, education, and training.

LEAA required each state to create its own criminal justice planning agency, which in turn was required to establish an annual, comprehensive, statewide criminal justice plan to distribute LEAA funds throughout the state. One of LEAA's primary benefits to police officers was its Law Enforcement Education Program (LEEP), which provided funds for the college education of police officers.

An independent organization, the Police Foundation, joined LEAA as a funding source for research on innovative police projects. The most significant of these projects were the Kansas City Preventive Patrol Experiment, the Rand Corporation's study of the criminal investigation process, the Police Foundation's study of team policing, and the Newark Foot Patrol Experiment. These innovative studies began to change the way we thought about policing in the United States.

As we will see later in Chapter 9, "Patrol Operations," traditional policing involved three major strategies: (1) routine random patrol, (2) rapid response to calls by citizens to 911, and (3) retroactive investigation of past crimes by detectives. Academic research, starting in the 1960s and 1970s and continuing, has indicated that these three strategies have not worked. This research has led police administrators to implement the innovative approaches to policing that will be discussed in Chapter 10, "Investigations."

Policing in the 1980s and 1990s

The tremendous turmoil that permeated society and policing during the decades of the 1960s and 1970s gave way to somewhat more peaceful times in the 1980s and 1990s. The police, as always, were confronted by a myriad of issues and events that severely tested their professionalism and ability. Prominent among those events were the first terrorist bombing of New York City's World Trade

ON THE JOB

History Is All Relative

I remember when I started at the police department in 1977. I finished the police academy and went on to eight weeks of field training with a more senior officer. The department didn't have a formalized program at the time, they simply put rookie officers with more experienced officers who they felt could teach them how our department did things.

Besides my training officer, I met lots of other officers eager to share their knowledge with me on how to "really do the job." I had some "old timers" tell me about how different it was when they started with the department. "They handed me a badge and a gun and told me to go out and enforce the laws . . . we didn't have any of this training stuff" one told me. This was hard for me to imagine as I thought of all the information I had learned in the academy and was learning during training—not to mention the liability involved. "We never had air-conditioned cars," another told me as I cringed at the thought of driving around in the south Florida heat and humidity without the benefit of air conditioning. "There was no such thing as backup," another said, "we just broke up the fights in the projects and threw 'em in the drunk tank to sober up for a few hours." Again, the thought of detaining people for drunkenness with no real reason to deprive them of their liberty made me nervous. I chalked it up to "the old days" and smiled smugly at how far we'd come and how advanced we were now.

Now I teach my classes, and as we talk about the "history" of law enforcement and how police officers actually relied on car radios and worked without the luxury of portable radios, and how we used .38 revolvers and were ecstatic when speed loaders became part of our equipment, they are shocked to realize I worked that way. They are shocked to learn we used pay phones as a means of communication when we didn't want to use the radio. They can't imagine life without everyone having cell phones. Their jaws really hit the desks when I talk about our early use of "cell phones." I was a lieutenant in charge of the midnight shift when we got our first portable phone. The shift commanders carried the phone in their cars for use in emergency situations where we did not want the press or others to hear our radio transmissions or we had to call "the brass" at home to brief them on situations. This "portable" phone (and I use the term loosely) was mounted in a briefcase and weighed over 15 pounds. If a situation occurred where we were setting up at a scene, I would take the briefcase out of the car, lay it on the trunk, and screw antennas into the phone assembly. Then I hoped the bad guys couldn't hear me pushing the numbers (it sounded loud at 3 AM in the quiet streets) or see all the lights associated with the phone, and most of all, I hoped it worked. Sometimes, I just felt it wasn't worth all the trouble to use it. If nothing else, these stories make students appreciate the ease of communications that law enforcement enjoys today.

—*Linda Forst*

Center in 1993 and the bombing of the Federal Building in Oklahoma City, Oklahoma, in 1995. In these cases, police agencies from all over the nation performed numerous heroic and successful actions that saved lives and resulted in the eventual criminal prosecution of the offenders.

Some of the many positive developments of the 1980s and 1990s included the development of a computer revolution in policing involving communications, record keeping, fingerprinting, and criminal investigations; a drastic reduction in violent crime; and the birth of two major new concepts of police work: community policing and problem-solving policing. Community policing and problem-solving policing can be seen either as new approaches to policing or as a return to the policing of the past—the cop on the beat. Chapter 12, "Community Policing: The Debate Continues," covers these concepts. The computer and technology revolution in policing is covered in Chapter 14, "Computers, Technology, and Criminalistics in Policing."

Some believe that the highlight of recent developments in policing is the significant crime reductions that occurred throughout the nation in the late twentieth century. In 1997, the FBI reported that serious crime for 1996 had declined 3 percent, the fifth annual decrease since 1992. Violent crime, including homicide, robbery, rape, and aggravated assault, dropped 7 percent from the previous year. This decrease in violent crime was the largest in 36 years. The homicide rate was the lowest it had been nationwide since 1969.[47] These crime decreases continued throughout the decade and into the twenty-first century.

Some criminologists attributed this decline to a series of factors, including community policing, problem-solving policing, and aggressive zero-tolerance policing. Other factors mentioned were increased jail and prison populations, demographic changes in the numbers of crime-prone young people, and community efforts against crime.

The explanation, however, that has gained the most popularity among some law enforcement officials, politicians, and criminologists is that the reduced crime rates are the result of aggressive police tactics like those introduced in New York City by its former commissioner, William J. Bratton. Bratton completely reengineered the NYPD to make reducing crime its primary objective.[48] The keynote behind Bratton's reengineering was a process known as CompStat.[49]

CompStat was originally a document, referred to as the "CompStat book," that included current year-to-date statistics for criminal complaints and arrests developed from a computer file called Compare Stats—hence, CompStat. Central to CompStat are the semiweekly crime-strategy sessions conducted at police headquarters. At each CompStat meeting, sophisticated computer-generated maps addressing a seemingly unlimited variety of the latest crime details confront and challenge the precinct commanders. The commanders are held responsible for any increases in crime and must present innovative solutions to address their precincts' crime problems. In these sessions, crime-fighting techniques are developed for implementation. The four-step process that is the essence of CompStat is

1. Timely and accurate intelligence
2. Use of effective tactics in response to that intelligence
3. Rapid deployment of personnel and resources
4. Relentless follow-up and assessment

One writer summed up the essence of NYPD's new policing strategy as follows:

> The multifaceted CompStat process is perhaps best known to law enforcement insiders for its high-stress, semiweekly debriefing and brainstorming sessions at police headquarters, but it is far more. . . . CompStat is enabling the NYPD to pinpoint and analyze crime patterns almost instantly, respond in the most appropriate manner, quickly shift personnel and other resources as needed, assess the impact and viability of anti-crime strategies, identify bright, up-and-coming individuals from deep within the ranks, and transform the organization more fluidly and more effectively than one would ever expect of such a huge police agency.[50]

Only history will tell if the crime reductions of the mid-1990s can continue, and no one can attribute them solely to the police, but Bratton seems convinced: "We've changed course, and the course will be changed for all time."[51]

Despite all the successes of the police in the 1980s and 1990s, many of the problems of earlier decades carried over into this time. Some of the negative issues and problems confronting the police in our generation were the continuing debate about misconduct by the police and the continuing occurrence of riots in our communities.

The endemic corruption that has always characterized U.S. policing seemed to have subsided somewhat during the 1980s and 1990s, although there were sporadic corruption scandals. The most noticeable of these included the Miami River Cops scandal of the 1980s, involving murders, extortions, and drug violations, and New York City's 77th and 32nd Precincts and "Cocaine Cops" scandals, involving drug corruption. Many other police departments throughout the nation also suffered embarrassing corruption and misconduct scandals. Chapter 8, "Police Ethics and Police Deviance" covers this area in detail.

In 1991, the **Rodney King incident** in Los Angeles shocked the public and may have set the police back 30 years in the progress they had made in improving relationships with the community. A citizen captured the police beating of Rodney King, an African American, on videotape. King had taken the police on a 115-mile-per-hour chase throughout Los Angeles and, when finally stopped by the police, allegedly lunged at one of the officers. The

Lessons Learned

videotape shows four Los Angeles police officers beating King with 56 blows from nightsticks while a dozen other officers stood by and watched. King seemed to be in a defenseless, prone position on the ground. Four of the officers were arrested and charged with the assault of King. They were originally acquitted in a criminal trial but were subsequently convicted in a federal trial.

To add a different perspective on this case, some argue that the officers used many different types of nonlethal force against King, who had refused commands to stop his aggressive and threatening behavior toward the officers, instead of using deadly force against him, which could have resulted in his death. They struck him with two 50,000-volt stun-gun discharges, which did not seem to stop his erratic behavior, and used baton procedures taught at the Los Angeles Police Department (LAPD) academy. The supervising officer at the scene, Sergeant Stacey C. Koon, wrote a book about the case, *Presumed Guilty: The Tragedy of the Rodney King Affair.*[52]

The Rodney King incident was followed in 1997 with allegations that at least two police officers from New York City's 70th Precinct assaulted a Haitian American prisoner, Abner Louima, by placing a wooden stick into his rectum and then shoving the blood- and feces-covered stick into his mouth. This incident shocked the world as the King incident did.[53] One officer was eventually convicted and imprisoned for the assault on Louima.

In 1994, a criminal trial also brought negative attention to the police. Former football star Orenthal James (O. J.) Simpson was charged by the Los Angeles police with the brutal murder of his former wife, Nicole Brown, and her friend Ronald Goldman. The trial was covered on national television and captured the attention of the world. Two hundred and fifty days and 126 witnesses later, the jury, despite overwhelming scientific evidence to the contrary, voted to acquit Simpson of all charges.

Many said the verdict was jury nullification; others said it was an indictment of the Los Angeles Police Department. The LAPD was accused of gross incompetence in its handling of the crime scene and forensic evidence, and one of its main witnesses, Detective Mark Fuhrman, later pled guilty to charges that he had lied while testifying in the trial.

In 1997, the Justice Department's inspector general reported that the FBI's renowned crime laboratory was riddled with flawed scientific practices that had potentially tainted dozens of criminal cases, including the bombings of the Federal Building in Oklahoma City and the World Trade Center in New York. The inspector general's findings resulted from an 18-month investigation that uncovered extremely serious and significant problems at the laboratory that had been a symbol of the FBI's cutting-edge scientific sleuthing.[54] The dramatic series of problems associated with the FBI and their alleged bungling of scientific evidence and criminal investigations led the national magazine *Time* to produce a cover article entitled, "What's Wrong at the FBI: The Fiasco at the Crime Lab."[55]

Riots again scarred our sense of domestic tranquility. The city of Miami experienced two major riots in its Overtown district in the 1980s. New York City experienced riots in the 1990s in Crown Heights and Washington Heights. Many other cities witnessed racial and civil unrest and skirmishes between the police and citizens.

Perhaps the worst riot in our nation's history occurred in 1992 following the not-guilty verdicts against the officers in the Rodney King case. The riot began in Los Angeles and spread to other parts of the country.

By the second day of the riot, at least 23 people had been killed, 900 injured, and 500 arrested. Hundreds of buildings burned as the violence spread from south-central Los Angeles to other areas. Entire inner-city blocks lay in ruin. The riot quickly spread to Atlanta; San Francisco; Madison, Wisconsin; and other cities. Fighting between African Americans and whites was reported at high schools in Maryland, Tennessee, Texas, and New York. By the end of the second day, more than 4,000 National Guard troops had entered Los Angeles, as well as more than 500 U.S. Marines. Less than a week after the riot started, calm began to appear. The final toll of the Los Angeles riot revealed that 54 people were killed; 2,383 people were injured; 5,200 buildings, mostly businesses, were destroyed by arson; and more than $1 billion in property damage occurred. The riot resulted in the loss of approximately 40,000 jobs. Almost 17,000 arrests were made.

The following is a vivid newspaper description of the events of the first days of the riot:

> A gunfight broke out this afternoon between Korean merchants and a group of black men in the Korea-town section, a sharp escalation in the tensions that have divided the groups in recent months. Tall plumes of smoke rose from

burning shops in the neighborhood, just north of South-Central.

As fires, police sirens and pockets of violence spread, most of the city shut down, with offices and shops closing and public transport scaling back its operations early. As the guard members were taking up positions in the badly battered South-Central area, convoys of cars carrying young men headed out into affluent West Los Angeles and Beverly Hills, shouting, brandishing hatchets, crowbars and bottles, beating passersby and looting shops.[56]

A special commission under the direction of William H. Webster (the former director of both the Federal Bureau of Investigation and the Central Intelligence Agency), created to study the causes of the Los Angeles riots, issued a report highly critical of the LAPD.[57]

Policing in the 2000s

As the world welcomed a new millennium, some of the same myriad of issues that influenced policing since the creation of the first organized police forces in the early nineteenth century continued to dominate the police landscape. Among these issues were police misconduct, corruption, and brutality. There were also many positives for the police as the crime rate decline that started to occur in the 1990s continued into the 2000s, and local, state, and federal law enforcement agencies reorganized and reengineered themselves to address the concerns of the new millennium. The CompStat program developed in New York City was adopted by numerous departments throughout the nation. Crime in New York City, in particular, dropped to levels not seen since the 1960s.

The *Beltway Sniper case* caught the attention of the United States public in 2002 and engendered tremendous fear. For 23 days in October 2002, the Washington, D.C., and central Virginia regions were terrorized by a team of snipers who used a high-powered rifle to pick off victims indiscriminately. They shot 14 people, 10 of them fatally. The killing spree involved 6 homicides in one 24-hour period, followed by a series of shootings over a 3-week period. The incidents and investigations spanned 8 jurisdictions and involved more than 1,000 investigators. The investigators, working under the command of Police Chief Charles Moose of Montgomery County, Maryland, formed the

Sniper Task Force, which involved federal, local, and state law enforcement officials. This task force had to simultaneously conduct criminal investigations of the incidents, try to prevent more from occurring, and respond to the scenes of new shootings as they occurred. "It's almost like changing the tire of a car while it's moving," said Chuck Wexler, the executive director of the Police Executive Research Forum (PERF).[58]

The task force's performance set positive standards for interagency cooperation among all levels of law enforcement and positive communication with citizens. The two snipers were apprehended on October 24, 2002, at a highway rest stop in Myersville, Maryland, based on a tip from a citizen.

In 2005, the NYPD continued its use of innovative automated crime technology when it opened its *Real Time Crime Center*. The center's real-time (instantaneous) database contains 120 million city records of criminal complaints, warrants, and 911 calls dating back 10 years. It also contains 5 million state criminal and parole records, including mug shots and identifying details such as tattoos and street names, and about 35 billion property and other public records. The center uses satellite imaging and computerized mapping systems to identify geographic patterns of crimes and to pinpoint possible addresses where suspects might flee. Information from the center is relayed to investigators on the street via phone or wireless laptop computers. Detectives who once needed days or weeks to knock on doors, work the phones and informants, and analyze data by shifting through paper records, now have instantaneously access to computerized records.[59]

As we approached 2006, crime reductions continued to occur in many cities, including New York, Los Angeles, and Chicago (Chicago homicides dropped to levels not seen since the early 1960s), as the police adopted or continued aggressive crime-fighting techniques. Some examples follow:

In 2006, in Prince George's County, Maryland, crime decreased sharply after police intensified their patrols and reconfigured beats to increase police presence in neighborhoods and implemented strategies that addressed violent and other crime.[60]

In Compton, California, the Los Angeles County Sheriff's office successfully reduced violence and crime by doubling the numbers of deputies, detectives, and other personnel assigned to Compton. (Compton had disbanded its own police department and now pays the county for police services).

The sheriff's office has also aggressively tracked specific gangs, gang leaders, and gun suppliers. Residents reported seeing a major difference in the area, and one is quoted as saying, "There's a lot more cops out there now. Before, it seemed like nobody was out there patrolling. The sheriff's all around now."[61]

However, crime increased in some other cities. In Philadelphia, despite law enforcement crackdowns, murders and violence continued unabated.[62] Also, in Boston, despite the success of its Operation Ceasefire of the late 1990s that reduced murders by bringing together police, clergy, courts, and citizens to attack youth homicide, the city was alarmed by a resurgence of homicides and shootings concentrated in the city's poorer neighbors. Boston's 2005 murder rate was the highest it has seen in a decade.[63]

The latest FBI statistics revealed that violent crime increased 2.5 percent in 2005 from the previous year and murder increased 4.8 percent.[64] The biggest increases in murder occurred in medium-size cities and in the Midwest. Murder rates increased significantly in St. Louis, Houston, Philadelphia, and Milwaukee, but New York, Los Angeles, and Miami saw a drop in murders. The statistics show that cities with populations of 100,000 to 250,000 residents had the greatest increase in murders with 12.5 percent. Alfred Blumstein of Carnegie Mellon University said the increase could be the result of police efforts being diverted to fighting terrorism among other factors.[65]

The LAPD was involved in a major corruption scandal involving its anti-gang unit operating out of the department's Rampart division. Many of the unit's members were accused of framing hundreds of people, planting evidence, committing perjury, and brutalizing people and forcing confessions through beatings. Officers were also accused of several illegal shootings. One officer, caught stealing $1 million worth of cocaine from the police property room, turned informant and cooperated with the prosecutors. After this scandal surfaced, hundreds of falsely obtained convictions were thrown out of court and numerous civil lawsuits ensued against the department. The informing officer was eventually convicted and sentenced to five years in prison. Other officers were convicted and went to prison.

The periods of civil unrest that dominated earlier times did not end with the new millennium. In 2001, a four-day riot occurred in Cincinnati, Ohio,

after a white police officer was charged with shooting and killing an unarmed man. The American legacy of violence after sporting events and controversial police shootings continued. In October 2004, a Boston police officer fired two shots from a pepper-pellet gun in the direction of a crowd of disorderly college students surrounding Boston's Fenway Park after a Boston Red Sox baseball game. A 21-year old student in the crowd was struck and died from her injuries. Several police commanders were suspended or demoted, and the incident caused tremendous criticism of the Boston Police Department.

Paramount to the new issues facing the police were the tragic **terrorist attacks against the United States of America on September 11, 2001.** Chapter 15, "Homeland Security," will cover these attacks in detail.

As the twin towers of New York City's World Trade Center's Buildings 1 and 2 were struck by planes within minutes of each other, caught on fire, and then imploded, a massive emergency response that included the New York City Police Department, the New York City Fire Department, the police and rescue operations of the Port Authority of New York and New Jersey, and the city's emergency medical service was immediate. These people entered the buildings in an attempt to rescue those within them. Many of these brave rescuers were lost forever, including much of the high command of the fire and Port Authority departments. Medical, law enforcement, and emergency response personnel from around the world responded. Triage centers went into operation, and ordinary residents passed out bottled water to the responding emergency personnel. By the evening of September 11, Buildings 5 and 7 of the World Trade Center had also collapsed, and many buildings began to tremble and show signs of imminent collapse. The fires, smoke, and eerie ash continued blowing through the streets. Almost 3,000 innocent persons were murdered that day. Twenty-three New York City Police Officers, 37 Port Authority of New York and New Jersey officers, 3 New York City Court Officers and more than 300 New York City firefighters paid the ultimate price to their professions that day.

Within minutes of the attacks on the World Trade Center, another plane slammed into one of the five-sided, five-story, concrete-walled structures of the U.S. Pentagon in northern Virginia—the headquarters and command center of the U.S. military forces.

The swiftness, scale, and sophisticated coordinated operations of the terrorists, coupled with the extraordinary planning required, made most people realize that terrorism and mass murder had hit New York City, the United States, and indeed, the world. September 11, 2001, had indeed changed the world.

Following the tragic events of 9/11, many large police departments throughout the nation started specialized antiterrorism units and trained their members in disaster control and antiterrorism duties. As one example, the New York City Police Department started a counter-terrorism bureau under the command of a deputy commissioner who is a retired general with the U.S. Marine Corps. The counterterrorism bureau, consisting of more than 1,000 officers, is under the command of a three-star chief and consists of a counterterrorism section and investigating units.

An article in *Law Enforcement News* reports,

In the three years since 9/11, law enforcement in America on both the local and national levels continue to be dominated and guided by the effects of the terrorist attacks. Terrorism continues to soak up both attention and resources. Some police executives have deemed it "the new normal," others talk about "terror-oriented policing."[66]

Additionally, a major reorganization of the federal government created the massive **Department of Homeland Security.** Chapter 2, "Organizing Public and Private Security in the United States," and Chapter 15, "Homeland Security," will address the enormous organization and operational changes in federal and state law enforcement as a result of the terrorist attacks.

Also, after the terrorist bombings of 9/11, congress passed Public Law No. 107–56, the USA Patriot Act—Uniting and Strengthening America by Providing Appropriate Tools Required to Intercept and Obstruct Terrorism. Popularly termed the **USA Patriot Act,** the new law gives law enforcement new ability to search, seize, detain, or eavesdrop in their pursuit of possible terrorists. The law has proven controversial and has caused many Americans to believe that the law threatened their civil liberties. Chapter 15 will also discuss the Patriot Act.

The new antiterrorism focus of U.S. law enforcement was seen clearly as the United States began war against Iraq in March 2003. The counterterrorism units of law enforcement agencies in the United States matched the dramatic preparations of the military forces abroad:

As the United States waged war on Iraq, New Yorkers and others across the region are witnessing an extraordinary state of heightened security. Police officers are armed like assault troops outside prominent buildings, police boats are combing the waterfronts and trucks are being inspected at bridges and tunnels.[67]

The NYPD's war contingency plan, *Operation Atlas,* described as the most comprehensive terrorism-prevention effort the city had ever conducted, cost at least $5 million a week in police overtime alone, including expanded patrols on the streets, focusing on government buildings, tourist attractions, financial institutions, hotels, and houses of worship, and in the subways, on the waterways, and in the harbor. The plan also strengthened checkpoints at bridges and tunnels and on the streets. There were extra patrols in Jewish neighborhoods deemed to be terrorist targets, 24-hour police coverage of Wall Street, harbor patrols to protect commuter ferries, and bomb-sniffing dogs on the Staten Island Ferry. Officers were also posted outside television news outlets to prevent possible takeovers by terrorists who were feared to want to broadcast anti-American messages. The NYPD also opened its command center at Police Headquarters in Lower Manhattan as well as a backup command center.[68]

These precautionary measures were not limited to New York City as random car searches were reinstated at many airports throughout the nation. In Ohio, weight stations on highways stayed open around the clock for inspections; in South Dakota, six satellite parking lots at Mount Rushmore were shut down, and park rangers, brandishing shotguns, screened each vehicle. In San Francisco, California Highway Patrol officers, some on bikes, joined National Guard troops stationed at the Golden Gate Bridge.[69] Washington State Troopers rode on ferries and questioned passengers, and the boats themselves were shadowed by Coast Guard cutters with .50-caliber machine guns mounted on the sterns and bows.[70]

The war efforts of 2003 also brought back memories of the massive social protests of earlier decades. Reminiscent of the antiwar protests of the 1960s, protesters again took to the streets in March 2003 in response to the U.S. invasion of Iraq. There were street marches and skirmishes with the police in New York City, San Francisco, Washington, D.C., and Madison, Wisconsin, on March 20, 2003.

San Francisco was the epicenter of the antiwar movement's efforts and more than 1,000 protesters were arrested in the financial district on March 20. Demonstrators blocked the San Francisco–Oakland Bay Bridge and about 40 intersections during the morning rush hour. Demonstrators also set fire to bales of hay near the Transamerica Building, opened fire hydrants, and smashed police car windows. They vomited on the pavement outside a federal building and linked themselves with metal chains, forcing firefighters to use circular saws to separate them.[71]

Similarly, in Washington, D.C., protesters forced the police to close Potomac River crossings during the morning commute. In Chicago, protesters shut down Lake Shore Drive during the evening rush hour. Protesters in Atlanta and Boston also shut down major streets. About 100 protesters were arrested in Philadelphia and 8 in Los Angeles; in New York City, 21 people were charged with disorderly conduct after a crowd of several thousand lay down in Times Square. In Madison, Wisconsin, protesters smashed the windows of the state Republican Party headquarters, splattering red paint that they said symbolized blood.[72] In Chicago, police arrested 543 antiwar protesters for civil disobedience that closed downtown streets for hours. A top-ranking police official denounced the demonstrators as anarchists.[73]

In New York City, on March 22, 2003, during a protest by almost 200,000 marchers, 89 persons were arrested. Someone in the crowd had released a canister of pepper spray, injuring 14 officers, including several who were taken to the hospital.[74]

Similar to the 1960s, the police seemed in be again "in the middle" between officials conducting the official policies of government and citizens protesting these polices.

As we reached the second half of the first decade of the twenty-first century, concerns about terrorism and protests were temporarily replaced by a natural disaster, Hurricane Katrina, which hit the Gulf Coast states of Louisiana, Mississippi, and Alabama. The disaster caused by Katrina led to the realization that our local, state, and federal government agencies, despite the creation of the Department of Homeland Security, were ill equipped to handle a major disaster. It also brought to public attention the heroic efforts of our National Guard forces, our U.S. Coast Guard, and police officers

throughout the United States who aided the victims and evacuees of the tragedy. The events of Katrina also brought shame to some members of the New Orleans Police Department (NOPD), who were reported in the press to have abandoned duty when Katrina hit their city and who were reported to have watched looters without taking action.

As Katrina's storm surge caused catastrophic damage along the coasts of Louisiana, the levees separating the city of New Orleans from Lake Pontchartrain were breached by the storm and about 80 percent of New Orleans was flooded. Most of the residents of the affected area, primarily in the city of New Orleans and in Jefferson Parish, were forced to flee their flood-raved homes and neighborhoods and to abandon all their belongings. Thousands of these victims sought refuge at the New Orleans Convention Center and the huge New Orleans Superdome, the football stadium used by the NFL team, the New Orleans Saints. These victims were abandoned there for several days.

The problems for the criminal justice system were devastating. Police stations and courthouses were flooded, and records and files were lost to the floodwaters. Evidence from about 3,000 criminal cases in New Orleans was submerged in toxic floodwaters that swamped police headquarters and the courthouse. About 6,000 prisoners in prisons and jails were evacuated because of flooding. Basic functions of government ceased during and in the aftermath of the storm, including most public safety record keeping. The city's 911 operators were reported to have left their phones when water began to rise around their building. Police headquarters was damaged during the flooding, and the entire police department was temporarily based at a hotel on Bourbon Street, steps away from a group of strip clubs. Shots were fired at rescue and repair workers, including police officers, firefighters, and construction and utility workers.

When normalcy somewhat returned to the area, Katrina was estimated to have been responsible for more than $115 billion in damage, and the death toll of the storm has been estimated at 1,800 people, mainly from Louisiana and Mississippi. Many people remain missing. As of the publication of this textbook, two years after the storm, less than 45 percent of the former residents of the city have returned.

It has been reported that shortly after the hurricane ended, thousands of people who had remained in the city began looting stores, particularly in the French Quarter and along the city's major commercial street, Canal Street. Drug, convenience, clothing, and jewelry stores were among the major businesses looted. Looting also occurred in other towns throughout the disaster area. One looter insisted that she wasn't stealing from the Winn-Dixie supermarket and was quoted as saying, "It's about survival right now. We got to feed our children. I've got eight grandchildren to feed."[75]

Thousands of National Guard and federal troops were mobilized and thousands of police officers from around the United States volunteered to travel to the area to aid in the evacuation of the remaining residents and to restore order. Adding to the problems of Katrina for residents and rescue workers were the rancid, polluted floodwaters throughout the streets that were also laden with human bodies and human waste and sewage. Oil slicks and household chemicals floated out of the abandoned businesses and homes in the area, in addition to the remains of chemical plants, oil facilities, and gas facilities.

NOPD Superintendent Eddie Compass, who was criticized for his department's actions during Katrina, announced his retirement at the end of September 2005 and was replaced by Deputy Superintendent Warren Riley. Riley announced that he was conducting an immediate investigation of the reported misconduct by members of the department. He immediately suspended four officers without pay and put more than a dozen others on report for reported misbehavior after hurricane Katrina. He also reported that he was investigating 249 officers who did not report for active duty during the storm or immediately after it. In support of his department, however, Riley said he did not know how many of his officers had actually abandoned their posts and how many simply could not get to work because of lost spouses and other family problems and destroyed homes. It was later discovered that many officers had lost their homes to the storm as well as not being able to find members of their families among the chaos and destruction.

Riley said,

> Those officers should not be branded quitters or cowards either. This department is not dysfunctional. The more than 2,000 men and women of this agency stand united in not letting a very small segment of members tarnish the great reputation of their department."[76]

Perhaps some of the best descriptions of the stress and the reasons for it affecting the NOPD and its officers came from former Superintendent Compass, while commenting to reporters on the frustration and morale of his officers,

> If I put you out on the street and made you get into gun battles all day with no place to urinate and no place to defecate, I don't think you would be too happy either. Our vehicles can't get any gas. The water in the street is contaminated. My officers are walking around in wet shoes.[77]

> We had no food. We had no water. We ran out of ammunition. We had no vehicles. We were fighting in waist-deep water.[78]

As we have seen in this chapter, the history of policing from early times to today shows that policing is a demanding and unique occupation.

Summary

- The word *police* comes from the Latin word *politia*, which means "civil administration." Etymologically, the police can be seen as those involved in the administration of a city.

- The police represent the civil power of government, rather than the military power of government.

- The concept of preserving the peace and enforcing the law has moved from primitive forms like the watch and ward to highly organized, professional police departments. The history of policing has included brutality, corruption, incompetence, innovation, research, heroism, and professionalism.

- At about the time of Christ, special, highly qualified members of the military formed the Praetorian Guard and could be considered the first police officers. Their job was to protect the palace and the emperor.

- In 1285 C.E., the *Statute of Winchester* established a rudimentary criminal justice system in which most of the responsibility for law enforcement remained with the people themselves. The statute formally established (1) the watch and ward, which required all men in the town to serve on the night watch and was the most rudimentary form of policing; (2) the hue and cry, which required all citizens to assist the watchmen; (3) the parish constable; and (4) the requirement that all males keep weapons in their homes for use in maintaining the public peace.

- In 1828, Sir Robert Peel, England's home secretary, drafted the first police bill, the *Act for Improving the Police in and near the Metropolis* (the *Metropolitan Police Act*), which established the first large-scale, uniformed, organized, paid, civil police force in London. Thus, the police as we know them today were, from their very beginning, ultimately responsible to the public. Peel has become known as the founder of modern policing, and the early police were guided by his nine principles.

- The London Metropolitan Police was organized around the "beat system," in which officers were assigned to relatively small permanent posts and were expected to become familiar with them and the people residing there. This system differed from the patrols of the Paris police, which consisted of periodic roving surveillance of areas.

- In U.S. colonial society, despite the presence of law enforcement officials, law enforcement was still mainly the responsibility of the individual citizen, as it had been in early England. There was little law and order on the colonial frontier. In the southern states, slave patrols were the dominant form of policing.

- During the eighteenth century, the most common form of American law enforcement in the North was the system of constables in the daytime and the watch at night.

- The first organized American police department was created in Boston in 1838, followed by New York City, Philadelphia, Chicago, New Orleans, Cincinnati, Baltimore, and Newark.

- In the nineteenth century, the locally elected county sheriffs and the appointed town marshals were usually the only law enforcement officers available on the American frontier. In the American South, the former slave patrols eventually evolved into formal local police departments.

- The 1960s and 1970s were probably the most turbulent era ever for policing in U.S. history. Numerous social problems permeated these decades, and the police were right in the middle of each problem.

- Academic interest in policing began in earnest in the 1960s with programs in police science, which later were expanded to include the entire criminal justice system and renamed criminal justice programs.

- Police departments have been totally revamped since the 1960s. Human relations training has been implemented. Better recruitment efforts and hiring practices have made police departments better reflect the communities they serve.

- As the world welcomed a new millennium, some of the same issues continued to dominate the police landscape: police misconduct, corruption, and brutality. There were also many positives for the police as the crime rate decline that started to occur in the 1990s continued into the 2000s, and local, state and federal law enforcement agencies reorganized and reengineered themselves to address the concerns of the new millennium.

- The September 11, 2001, terrorist attacks on the United States have changed policing to a degree that we cannot yet imagine. The demands on the police to confront the serious crime and disorder problems they face on the streets, as well as to attempt to ameliorate all the social problems they confront there have been increased with the new duties to protect citizens from terrorist attacks.

- The disaster caused by Hurricane Katrina led to the realization that our local, state, and federal government agencies, despite the creation of the Department of Homeland Security, were ill equipped to handle a major disaster.

Learning Check

1. Discuss the primary means of ensuring personal safety before the establishment of formal, organized police departments.

2. Discuss the watch and ward.

3. Talk about the influence of the English police experience on American policing.

4. Discuss the influence of slave patrols on American policing.

5. Compare and contrast the urban and frontier experiences in eighteenth- and nineteenth-century U.S. policing.

6. Discuss the contributions of Allan Pinkerton to U.S. law enforcement.

7. Identify at least four people instrumental in the development of twentieth-century U.S. policing, and list some of their accomplishments.

8. Explain how the turbulent times of the 1960s and the early 1970s affected U.S. policing.

9. Discuss the Rodney King incident.

10. How did the terrorist attacks of September 11, 2001 affect U.S. policing?

Key Terms

beat system System of policing created by Sir Robert Peel for the London Metropolitan Police in 1829 in which officers were assigned to relatively small permanent posts.

CompStat Weekly crime strategy meetings, featuring the latest computerized crime statistics and high-stress brain storming; developed by the New York City Police Department in the mid-1990s.

constable An official assigned to keep the peace in the mutual pledge system in England.

Department of Homeland Security Federal cabinet department established in the aftermath of the terrorist attacks of September 11, 2001.

Dred Scott decision Infamous U.S. Supreme Court decision of 1857 ruling that slaves had no rights as citizens because they were considered to be property.

hue and cry A method developed in early England for citizens to summons assistance from fellow members of the community.

mutual pledge A form of community self-protection developed by King Alfred the Great in the later part of the 19th century in England.

National Advisory Commission on Civil Disorders (Kerner Commission) Commission created in 1968 to address the reasons for the riots of the 1960s.

Peel's Nine Principles Basic guidelines created by Sir Robert Peel for the London Metropolitan Police in 1829.

Pendleton Act A federal law passed in 1883 to establish a civil service system that tested, appointed, and promoted officers on a merit system.

posse comitatus A common law descendent of the old hue and cry. If a crime spree occurred or a dangerous criminal was in the area, the U.S. frontier sheriff would call upon the posse comitatus, a Latin term meaning "the power of the county."

Praetorian Guard Select group of highly qualified members of the military established by Roman emperor Augustus to protect him and his palace.

President's Commission on Law Enforcement and Administration of Justice Commission that issued a report in 1967 entitled *The Challenge of Crime in a Free Society.* The commission was created following the problems of the 1960s, particularly the problems between police and citizens.

Rodney King incident The 1991 videotaped beating of an African American citizen by members of the Los Angeles Police Department.

shire-reeve Early English official placed in charge of shires as part of the system of mutual pledge; evolved into the modern concept of the sheriff.

slave patrols Police-type organizations created in the American South during colonial times to control slaves and support the southern economic system of slavery.

terrorist attacks against the United States of America on September 11, 2001 The terrorist attacks committed by al Qaeda.

thief-takers Private English citizens with no official status who were paid by the king for every criminal they arrested. They were similar to the bounty hunter of the American West.

Vigiles Early Roman firefighters who also patrolled Rome's streets to protect citizens.

USA Patriot Act Public Law No. 107–56 passed in 2001 giving law enforcement new ability to search, seize, detain, or eavesdrop in their pursuit of possible terrorists; full title of law is USA Patriot Act—Uniting and Strengthening America by Providing Appropriate Tools Required to Intercept and Obstruct Terrorism.

Volstead Act (National Prohibition, Eighteenth Amendment) Became law in 1920 and forbade the sale and manufacture of alcohol.

watch and ward A rudimentary form of policing, designed to protect against crime, disturbances, and fire. All men were required to serve on it.

Wickersham Commission Published the first national study of the U.S. criminal justice system, in 1931.

Organizing Public and Private Security in the United States

© Mitch Wojnarowicz/Amsterdam Recorder/The Image Works

GOALS

- To acquaint you with the many and diverse local, tribal, and state public agencies that enforce the law and ensure public safety in the United States
- To introduce the numerous federal law enforcement agencies that enforce federal laws and regulations and assist local and state police departments
- To describe the size, scope, and functions of law enforcement agencies in the public sector
- To acquaint you with the number and type of jobs available to you in public and private policing
- To alert you to the many changes made in U.S. public and private law enforcement following the September 11, 2001, terrorist attacks against the United States

Introduction

The tragic events of September 11, 2001, the terrorist attacks against New York City's World Trade Center and the U.S. Pentagon, brought the issues of safety and security to the immediate attention of most people in the United States and indeed, the world.

The public and private security industry—those institutions and people who maintain law and order and enforce the law in the United States—is enormous. We can almost say that it is a growth industry, expanding every year. Since September 11, 2001, this industry has expanded even more.

The U.S. security industry spends an immense amount of money and provides jobs for millions of people. The industry operates on all governmental levels: the local level (villages, towns, counties, tribes, and cities), the state level, and the federal level. The public agencies are funded by income taxes, sales taxes, real estate taxes, and other taxes. The security industry is served by the private sector, which hires more people and spends more money than all the public agencies put together. Students interested in a career in policing will find a vast number and many different types of law enforcement jobs from which to choose.

This chapter will discuss the U.S. public security industry, including local, state, and federal law enforcement, as well as international police, Interpol. We will also discuss private security, private investigations, and the private employment of public police.

The U.S. Public and Private Security Industry

Ensuring the safety of U.S. citizens by providing law enforcement services is an extremely complex and expensive undertaking. In 2006, the Bureau of Justice Statistics (BJS) of the U.S. Department of Justice (DOJ) reported that, for the latest reporting year, local, state, and federal agencies spent approximately $185 billion for criminal justice agencies including police, corrections, and judicial services—an increase of 418 percent from 20 years ago. Local, state, and federal criminal justice agencies employed about 2.4 million people, 58 percent at the local level, 31 percent at the state level, and 11 percent at the federal level. Police protection spending amounted to about $83.1 billion of the total national criminal justice budget, up 240 percent from 20 years ago, and local policing expenditures, alone, accounted for about 45 percent of the nation's entire criminal justice budget.[1]

Law enforcement is primarily the responsibility of local governments—77 percent of the nation's police employees worked at the local level, 14 percent of police employees worked for the federal government, and state governments employed the remaining 10 percent.[2]

The U.S. approach to law enforcement is unique when compared with the rest of the world. Japan and some western European countries—for example, Denmark, Finland, Greece, and Sweden—have a single national police force.[3] The United States does not have a national police force, although many people think of the Federal Bureau of Investigation (FBI) as one. We will see later in this chapter that the FBI is an investigative agency, rather than a police agency.

U.S. law enforcement has developed over the years based on a philosophy of **local control**, the formal and informal use of local or neighborhood forms of government and measures to deter abhorrent behaviors. To understand why, remember that the U.S. was built on the fear of a large central government, as had existed in England when the colonists came here. The primary responsibility for police protection still falls to local governments (cities, towns, tribes, and counties). Although we have state and federal law enforcement agencies, they are minuscule in size and importance when compared with the law enforcement agencies of local government.

Because of the tremendous number of law enforcement agencies and their employees in the United States and the lack of a unified system for reporting police personnel, it is very difficult to get a perfect picture of the U.S. law enforcement industry. Every few years the BJS attempts to do this as part of its Law Enforcement Management and Administrative Statistics (**LEMAS**) program.

TABLE 2.1 Employment by General Purpose State and Local Law Enforcement Agencies in the United States, 2003

| Type of agency | Number of agencies | Number of employees | | | | | |
| | | Full-time | | | Part-time | | |
		Total	Sworn	Civilian	Total	Sworn	Civilian
Total	15,766	933,442	683,599	309,843	75,958	35,152	40,806
Local police	12,656	580,749	451,737	129,013	51,281	25,614	25,667
Sheriff	3,061	330,274	174,251	156,022	23,884	9,498	14,386
Primary state	49	82,419	57,611	24,808	793	40	753

Note: Data are for the pay period that included June 30, 2003. Sworn employees are those with general arrest powers.
Source: Matthew J. Hickman and Brian A. Reaves, *Local Police Departments, 2003* (Washington, D.C.: Bureau of Justice Statistics, 2006), p. 1.

Discuss needs (pros/cons) for various levels of L.E. City, County, State, etc

In 2003, state and local governments in the United States operated almost 15,766 full-time law enforcement agencies. These included 12,656 general-purpose local police departments (mostly municipal and county departments), almost 3,061 sheriff's offices, and 49 primary state police departments. (See Table 2.1.) There are also approximately 1,400 special district police departments, including park police, transit police, constable offices, and other specialized state and local departments, not included in the numbers reported earlier.[4]

In addition to state and local law enforcement agencies and personnel, 2006 statistics regarding employment for federal law enforcement agencies indicate that the federal government employed about 156,600 persons dedicated to police protection.[5]

Statistics can sometimes be cumbersome and confusing. When we translate them into words, however, we can make some generalizations about the U.S. law enforcement industry:

1. The size and scope of the U.S. law enforcement industry is enormous.
2. The U.S. law enforcement industry is tremendously diverse and fragmented.
3. The U.S. law enforcement industry is predominantly local.
4. There are many employment opportunities in U.S. law enforcement at the federal, state, local, and private levels.

The U.S. Department of Labor's Bureau of Labor Statistics reported that the employment of police and detectives is expected to increase faster than the average for all occupations through the year 2010. A more security-conscious society and concern about drug-related crimes contribute to the increasing demand for police services.[6]

By 2003, California had the most full-time state and local law enforcement employees, followed by New York, Texas, Florida, and Illinois. The states with the lowest number of state and local law enforcement agencies were Vermont and North Dakota.

Nationwide, there were 362 full-time state and local law enforcement employees for every 100,000 residents for a nationwide **law enforcement employee average** of 3.62 (law enforcement employees per 1,000 citizens). The states with the highest law enforcement averages were the District of Columbia, 8.59; Louisiana, 5.27; and New York, 5.0. The states with the lowest were West Virginia, 2.29; Kentucky, 2.37; and Vermont, 2.4. The nationwide **sworn law enforcement employee average** was 2.52 (sworn law enforcement officers per 1,000 citizens), with the District of Columbia, with 6.93, as the highest; next were Louisiana, 4.15; New York, 3.84; New Jersey, 3.45; and Illinois, 3.21. The states with the lowest sworn law enforcement averages were Vermont, with 1.70; and West Virginia, with 1.74.

The issue of sworn law enforcement employee averages is a very imprecise science and a very sensitive issue for politicians, citizens, and some police officers. How many officers are enough? Jerome H. Skolnick, a law professor at New York University who has written extensively on criminal justice issues and policing says, "There's no formula for that. Nobody knows what the precise proportions should be."[7] It is generally conceded that the size police department a city requires can be affected by many issues including poverty, crime, geography, population density, and even politics. Comparing New York City to Los Angeles is an interesting study. New York City has about 36,000 officers, a sworn law enforcement employee average of 4.5 officers for every 1,000 residents. Los Angeles, on the other hand, has a sworn law enforcement employee average of 2.4 officers for every 1,000 residents.[8]

The Los Angeles police chief since 2002, and former New York City police commissioner, William J. Bratton says, "We are one of the smallest police departments in the country when it comes to ratio of officers to population. Boston, on a Friday night, for its 48 square miles, put out more cars that I put out in my whole city."[9] Washington, D.C., is also an interesting example—it has a very high sworn law enforcement employee average of nearly 7, three times that of Los Angeles, but for decades has had among the highest rates of violent crime of any large city.

According to Franklin E. Zimring of the University of California at Berkeley, "It is very good politics to ask for increases. It is an area of municipal expenditure which has more of a political halo effect than almost any other. It would be very nice if we had independent estimates of what adding a cop would do to the crime rate in other places than New York. You can't do that. The science isn't there."[10] David M. Kennedy, the director of the Center for Crime Prevention and Control at John Jay College of Criminal Justice agrees, "If your current operations aren't terribly effective, simply adding more officers is almost certainly not going to make a difference."

The issue of sworn employee averages also affects many officers. According to Peter C. Moskos, professor at John Jay College and a former police officer in Baltimore,

> When cops don't like their job, a huge part of it is understaffing. When it's chronic, cops can't get days off, they're forced to work more overtime and it hurts family life. An unhappy cop is a bad cop.[11]

In addition to the work done by individual local, state, and federal law enforcement agencies,

these agencies often cooperate and work together to enforce the law and protect and serve the public. As an example, at Super Bowl XXXIX, the premier annual event in football, held in 2006 in Jacksonville, Florida, more than 40 law enforcement agencies and public safety agencies, including the FBI, U.S. Customs and Border Protection (CBP), and the U.S. Coast Guard, under the coordination of the Jacksonville Sheriff's Office (JSO), the lead agency in the event, and the Florida Department of Law Enforcement (FDLE), the primary investigative agency in the event, jointly participated in safeguarding the security of the game and the surrounding events.[12]

A controversial issue in current law enforcement, however, is the cooperation and escalating involvement of local police with federal immigration officials in enforcing immigration laws. Immigration advocates and some local officials fear that this cooperation will further erode an already tense relationship between minority and immigrant communities and local officers entrusted with serving local residents. It has become routine for some police agencies to assist immigration authorities during arrests and to call immigration officials if a criminal suspect appears to be an undocumented alien. Also, some local police have been deputized as immigration agents at the request of federal authorities under signed agreements. Many of these agreements are in effect among some jurisdictions in Alabama, Arizona, California, Florida, and North Carolina. On the other hand, some departments generally prohibit officers from asking people they stop about their immigration status.[13]

As an example, during the Department of Homeland Security's U. S. Immigration and Customs Enforcement's (ICE) weeklong Operation Phoenix in April 2006, when 183 people were arrested in the state of Florida, ICE credited Miami–Dade County Police, Miami police, Hialeah police, the Broward sheriff's office, and the Palm Beach County sheriff's office among others, for their involvement.

In addition to the publicly funded federal, and state, and local law enforcement agencies, the enormous private security industry in the United States employs 1.5 million people and spends about $100 billion yearly. Private policing is growing at a much faster rate than public policing.[14]

You Are There!

Some Interesting Facts about Local Police Departments Today

- 59 percent of departments use foot patrol routinely.
- 38 percent use regular bicycle patrol.
- 92 percent participate in a 911 emergency system compared with 32 percent in 1987, and 73 percent use enhanced 911. (See Chapter 14, "Computers, Technology, and Criminalistics in Policing," for a description of 911 and enhanced 911 systems.)
- 18 percent assign full-time officers to a special unit for drug enforcement, and nearly a quarter assign officers to a multi-agency drug task force.
- 14 percent maintain a written community policing plan, and 58 percent use full-time community policing officers.
- 60 percent have problem-solving partnerships or written agreements with community groups.

- 43 percent use full-time school resource officers.
- Nearly all departments have a written policy on pursuit driving, and 60 percent restrict vehicle pursuits according to specific criteria.
- 99 percent have a written policy on the use of deadly force, and 90 percent have a policy on the use of nonlethal force.
- 39 percent have a written plan specifying actions to be taken in a terrorist attack.
- 99 percent authorize use of chemical agents such as pepper spray, up from 51 percent in 1990.
- 55 percent use video cameras in patrol cars.
- 62 percent have written policies about racial profiling by officers.

SOURCE: Matthew J. Hickman and Brian A. Reaves, *Local Police Departments, 2003* (Washington, D.C.: Bureau of Justice Statistics, 2006), p. iii.

Local Law Enforcement

When we use the term *local law enforcement,* or *local police,* we are talking about the vast majority of all the law enforcement employees in the United States, including metropolitan police and sheriff's offices. Metropolitan police departments are operated by cities, certain very large counties, villages, and towns and are generally led or managed by a police commissioner or police chief who is appointed by the executive of the locality. Sheriff's offices are generally operated by counties and are led or managed by a popularly elected sheriff. Officers in police departments are generally called *police officers,* whereas officers in sheriff's offices are generally termed *deputy sheriffs* or *deputies.* Jobs in these agencies increase yearly. Police protection is primarily a local responsibility—local governments spent 69 percent of the total police expenditures in the United States for the latest reporting year, and local police spending represented about 45 percent of the nation's total justice expenditures. Local expenditures for police protection increased by 305 percent in the past 20 years, for an average annual increase of 6.6 percent.[15]

For the latest reporting period, LEMAS reports that local police departments employed about 581,000 full-time employees, including about 452,000 sworn personnel (see Chapter 3 for an explanation of "sworn personnel"). The number of sworn personnel increased about 11,000 from three years earlier. Local departments also employ about 51,000 people on a part-time basis, about half of whom are sworn officers.[16]

Most local law enforcement agencies are very small. Only 4.7 percent of departments employed 100 or more full-time officers, and about 46 percent of the departments employed fewer than 10 officers, including 561 departments with just one police officer. Eighty-seven percent of police departments have 25 or fewer officers, and they serve in rural and small-town law enforcement.[17]

Racial and ethnic minorities constituted 23.6 percent of full-time sworn personnel in local departments, up from about 14.6 percent in 1987, and women constituted about 11.3 percent,

TABLE 2.2 Local Police Departments and Sheriff's Departments, by Gender and Race, 2003

Local Police Departments		Sheriff's Offices	
Total	100%	Total	100%
Total Male	88.7%	Total Male	87.1%
Total Female	11.3%	Total Female	12.9%
Total Whites	76.4%	Total Whites	81.2%
White Males	69.4%	White Males	72.0%
White Females	7.0%	White Females	9.2%
Total Black/African American	11.7%	Total Black/African American	10.0%
Black/African American Males	9.0%	Black/African American Males	7.5%
Black/African American Females	2.7%	Black/African American Females	2.5%
Total Hispanic/Latino	9.1%	Total Hispanic/Latino	6.9%
Hispanic/Latino Males	7.8%	Hispanic/Latino Males	6.0%
Hispanic/Latino Females	1.3%	Hispanic/Latina Females	0.9%
Total Other	2.8%	Total Other	1.9%
Other Males	2.5%	Other Males	1.7%
Other Females	0.3%	Other Females	0.2%

Other category includes Asians, Native Hawaiians or other Pacific Islanders, American Indians, Alaska Natives, and any other race.

Other category includes Asians, Native Hawaiians or other Pacific Islanders, American Indians, Alaska Natives, and any other race.

SOURCES: Matthew J. Hickman and Brian A. Reaves, *Local Police Departments, 2003* (Washington, D.C.: Bureau of Justice Statistics, 2006), p. 7 and Matthew J. Hickman and Brian A. Reaves, *Sheriffs' Offices, 2003* (Washington, D.C.: Bureau of Justice Statistics, 2006), p. 7.

up from 7.6 percent in 1987.[18] In particular, the number of black or African American local police officers increased by 3 percent during the past 3 years, Hispanic or Latino officers by 13 percent, officers from other minority groups by 7 percent, and female officers by 9 percent.[19] See Table 2.2.

Turnover, attrition, or officer separations from duty are significant in local policing. Sixty-one percent of all U.S. local police departments had officer separation during 2003. Of the approximately 32,100 officers who separated, about 16,000 were resignations, 9,400 were retirements, and 2,600 were dismissals. Also, 21 percent of local police departments had officers called-up as full-time military reservists in 2003—about 7,500 officers. During 2003, also, 60 percent of departments hired new officers—about 34,500.[20]

Metropolitan Law Enforcement

Municipal or city governments operate most of the nearly 12,656 general-purpose local police departments in the United States. The rest are operated by county, tribal, or regional (multijurisdictional) jurisdictions.[21]

Most metropolitan local officers primarily perform patrol duties, whereas others primarily perform criminal investigations, administrative, training, and technical support services.

The largest local department is the New York City Police Department (NYPD) with about 36,000 sworn officers. The next largest local police department is Chicago, with nearly 13,500 sworn employees; followed by Los Angeles, with 9,300;

Philadelphia, with about 6,900; and Houston, with 5,300.[22] About 1 of every 6 full-time local police officers in the United States works for one of these five largest forces.

The largest county police departments (not sheriff's offices) in the United States are the Miami–Dade County, Florida, Police Department with about 3,200 officers; the Suffolk County, New York, Police Department with more than 2,800 sworn members; the Las Vegas–Clark County, Nevada, Police Department with about 2,600 officers; the Nassau County, New York, Police Department with about 2,500 officers, the Baltimore County, Maryland, Police Department with almost 1,800 officers; and the Jacksonville–Duval County, Florida, Police Department with 1,600 officers.[23]

Most police officers today work for these metropolitan police departments. Metropolitan police departments generally provide the duties and services we typically associate with the police. These include arresting law violators, performing routine patrol, investigating crimes, enforcing traffic laws (including parking violations), providing crowd and traffic control at parades and other public events, and issuing special licenses and permits. Since September 11, 2001, many metropolitan departments have been spending more time on antiterrorism duties.

Many larger metropolitan areas have overlapping police jurisdictions. For example, in New York City, the NYPD is assisted by other federal, state, and local police and law enforcement agencies that police the city's public schools, colleges, hospitals, buildings, social service centers, parks, bridges, tunnels, airports, and the like. As another example, in Washington, D.C., many separate local and federal departments have concurrent jurisdiction throughout the city.

Among municipal police departments, the sworn law enforcement employee average was 2.5. Departments serving 25,000 to 99,000 residents had the lowest average 1.8.[24] Recall the earlier discussion of sworn law enforcement employee averages. Big-city mayors and police chiefs are always trying to increase the amount of officers in their departments. New York City Mayor Michael R. Bloomberg announced in 2006 that he was adding 800 officers and 400 civilians to the NYPD, in the largest city-financed expansion of the force since 1993, and Los Angeles Mayor Antonio Villaraigosa announced in 2006 that the city council unanimously approved his plan to hike garbage rates to help fund a major expansion of the Los Angeles Police Department

(LAPD). His plan will double the trash bills of most LA residents. Villaraigosa plans to use the increased funds to bring the LAPD to about 10,200 officers by 2010. He believes that about 3,000 officers will have to be hired over the next four years to overcome attrition and reach his hiring goal.[25] The police chiefs of Denver and Dallas also recently complained about their staffing and have called for major expansion of their departments.[26]

Most academic and professional studies of policing focus on municipal departments because this is where "the action" is in the law enforcement world. This action includes problems with crime, budgeting and funding, politics, and population changes, as well as social problems, including homelessness, unemployment, drug addiction, alcoholism, and child abuse. Additionally, after the terrorist bombings of September 11, 2001, these metropolitan departments have also had to deal increasingly with the problems of terrorism facing their cities. Also, large municipal departments are highly visible because of their size, complexity, budgets, and innovative programs. In addition to attempting to control crime, municipal police have significant problems maintaining public order and solving quality-of-life problems that bother neighborhood residents. The police handle social problems that other public and private agencies either cannot or will not handle. In a big city, when there is a problem, citizens generally do not call the mayor's office; they call 911.

In many geographic areas, metropolitan police are supplemented by special jurisdiction police agencies. In the latest reporting period, nearly 1,400 state and local law enforcement agencies with special geographic jurisdictions or special enforcement responsibilities were operating in the United States with more than 43,400 full-time sworn personnel. About 68 percent of the full-time sworn personnel handled patrol duties, and 17 percent were criminal investigators. Approximately 1 percent was responsible for court-related duties. These agencies performed such duties as guarding government buildings and facilities; enforcing conservation, agricultural, and parks and recreation laws; performing special criminal investigations; patrolling transportation systems and facilities; and engaging in special enforcement duties relating to various functions such as alcohol enforcement, gaming or racing law enforcement, business relations enforcement, or drug enforcement.[27]

The largest special jurisdiction agency in the United States, with more than 1,200 sworn, full-time personnel, is the Port Authority of New York and New Jersey Police Department (PAPD), which polices the facilities owned and operated by the bi-state Port Authority of New York and New Jersey, which includes the area's major airports, tunnels, bridges, and transportation systems, as well as New York City's former World Trade Center. (Thirty-seven PAPD police officers were killed in the September 11, 2001, terrorist attacks against the World Trade Center). The next largest special jurisdiction agencies are the Florida Game and Fresh Water Fish Commission with more than 670 full-time sworn officers, the California Department of Parks and Recreation with about 560 sworn officers, and the Texas Parks and Wildlife Department with about 485 sworn employees.

County Law Enforcement

Most counties in the United States are patrolled by a sheriff's department under the leadership of an elected sheriff (several very large counties in New York, California, Nevada, Florida, and other states have county police departments).

The role of sheriff has evolved in several stages since the early English sheriff (shire-reeve). During the development of the West in the United States and until the development of municipal departments, the sheriff often served as the sole legal authority over vast geographical areas.

Today, the duties of a county sheriff's office vary according to the size and urbanization of the county. The sheriff's office may perform the duties of coroners, tax assessors, tax collectors, keepers of county jails, court attendants, and executors of criminal and civil processes, as well as law enforcement officers.

According to an impressive article by Lee P. Brown, a former big-city police commissioner, there are several different types of sheriff's departments. Some are oriented exclusively toward law enforcement; some carry out only court-related duties; some deal exclusively with correctional and court matters and have no law enforcement duties; others are full-service programs that perform court, correctional, and law enforcement activities.[28]

In the latest reporting year, sheriffs' offices had about 330,000 full-time employees (174,000 sworn). This represents an increase of about 9,500 sworn and 26,900 nonsworn since 2000.[29]

Racial and ethnic minorities composed almost 19 percent of full-time sworn personnel, up from about 13.4 percent in 1987. Women constituted about 12.9 percent, about the same as in 1987. The number of black or African American deputy sheriffs increased by 13 percent between 2000 and 2003; Hispanic or Latino deputies by 20 percent; deputies from other minority groups by 20 percent; and female deputies by 5 percent.[30]

Turnover, attrition, or officer separations from duty are significant among sheriffs' offices. Sixty-nine percent of all U.S. sheriffs' offices had officer separation during 2003. Of the approximately 13,500 deputies who separated about 7,900 were resignations, 2,700 were retirements, and 1,200 were dismissals. Also, 31 percent of sheriff's offices had officers called-up as full-time military reservists in 2003—about 2,800 officers. During 2003, also, sixty-one percent of offices hired new officers—about 13,900.[31]

Nearly all sheriffs' offices are responsible for responding to citizen calls for service. In addition to handling calls for service, about 76 percent of the offices operate one or more jails and nearly 98 percent were responsible for the serving of civil process and 94 percent for court security.[32]

The largest sheriff's office in the nation is the Los Angeles County, California, Sheriff's Department, which employs over 8,600 full-time sworn personnel followed by the Cook County, Illinois, Sheriff's Office, which employs 5,555 full-time sworn personnel.[33] The Los Angeles County Sheriff's Office provides contract patrol services to many local areas that do not have their own departments. As an example, Compton, California, a high crime and gang area, disbanded its own police department and contracted the LA Sheriff's Department for services and has seen a dramatic decrease in crime and an increase in police presence and citizen satisfaction.

Rural and Small-Town Law Enforcement

Eighty-seven percent of police departments have 25 or fewer officers, and they serve in rural and small-town law enforcement. Often, rural and small-town police face the same problems as large metropolitan and county police. They also face other serious problems because of their size. The state of Wyoming, for example, has the lowest population in the United States and has vast open areas where one can drive over 100 miles between small towns.

You Are There!

Some Interesting Facts about Sheriff's Offices Today

- 25 percent of departments use foot patrol routinely.
- 10 percent use regular bicycle patrol.
- 94 percent participate in a 911 emergency system compared with 28 percent in 1987, and 71 percent employ enhanced 911. (See Chapter 14, "Computers, Technology, and Criminalistics in Policing," for a description of 911 and enhanced 911 systems.)
- 36 percent have officers assigned full time to a special unit for drug enforcement, and nearly a quarter assign officers to a multi-agency drug task force.
- 10 percent maintain a written community policing plan, and 51 percent use full-time community policing officers.
- 60 percent have problem-solving partnerships or written agreements with community groups.

- 47 percent use full-time school resource officers.
- Nearly all have a written policy on pursuit driving, and about half of them restrict vehicle pursuits according to specific criteria.
- 97 percent have a written policy on the use of deadly force, and 89 percent have a policy on the use of nonlethal force.
- Nearly half have a written plan specifying actions to be taken in a terrorist attack.
- 96 percent authorize use of chemical agents such as pepper spray, up from 52 percent in 1990.
- Two-thirds use video cameras in patrol cars.
- 63 percent have written policies about racial profiling by officers.

Source: Matthew J. Hickman and Brian A. Reaves, *Sheriffs' Offices, 2003* (Washington, D.C.: Bureau of Justice Statistics, 2006), pp. iii, iv.

The law enforcement officers in this state must routinely face the problem of not having immediate backup in most situations. As Mike Roy, the lead instructor at the Wyoming Law Enforcement Academy, says,

> We deal with great distances out here and there is a different mentality. Every other pickup truck you stop out here has a rifle in a gun rack or a pistol in the glove box. Most of the problems we have in law enforcement centers around people—where you have people you will have problems.[34]

Regarding the lack of readily available backup, Roy says, "Everyone completing our academy is instructed not to get stupid by acting alone in known volatile situations. Officers are instructed to get used to waiting for the closest help to arrive even if it's 60 miles away."[35]

Although everyone seems aware of the drug problems and dangers to police in our large urban communities, many are not aware of the many drug problems and dangers to the police in the many small towns throughout America's heartland. Police officers searching a modest home on the outskirts of Kansas City, Missouri,

encountered a perverse vision of middle-American domesticity:

> In the living room sat the computer where Dad had just been forging driver's licenses, while in another room Mom kept their towheaded children, 8 and 4 years old, away from the family's sawed-off shotgun and a crude laboratory that turned out methamphetamine from ingredients bought in local stores. Toxic waste from the illegal drugmaking had been dumped down the drain. When officers looked in the kitchen, . . . a police detective [said], "we found several jars of meth in the freezer next to the children's Popsicles."[36]

Authorities say that locally made methamphetamine, long popular on the West Coast, has become the small-town Midwest's drug of choice, similar to the scourge that crack or rock cocaine has been to the inner city. Methamphetamine is a stimulant variously called meth, crank, ice, and speed. For years, it was made and distributed by outlaw motorcycle gangs, but today in the Midwest, it is a "Mom and Pop" operation. Medical experts and some users say meth delivers a stronger, cheaper psychoactive kick than crack cocaine, unleashing aggression and leading to long binges that end with physical collapse.

In 1997, more than 60 clandestine methamphetamine laboratories were seized by the Jackson County drug task force, whose officers are drawn from seven towns from western Missouri. In 1996, more than 300 labs were seized in the Drug Enforcement Administration (DEA) field office covering small towns in Missouri, Kansas, Iowa, Nebraska, South Dakota, and southern Illinois. (In contrast, no labs were seized in New York and only one in New Jersey for the same period.)

In addition to the violence associated with meth users, their labs also prove dangerous to the police. A Missouri detective told of finding an overhead light bulb in a dark basement laboratory in Independence that was filled with tiny lead pellets and gunpowder, rigged to explode when the switch was turned on. He has also found a couple of pipe bombs and rattlesnakes, as well as toxic gasses in his raids on the labs.[37]

Gangs are also becoming a problem in rural areas and small towns. Research reported in 2005, by the National Youth Gang Center, indicated that many small towns and rural areas were experiencing gang problems for the first time. During the period of the study, gang-problem patterns were recorded for 1,066 agencies representing rural counties and smaller cities (populations between 2,500 and 25,000). The study revealed that gangs and gang-related problems tend to emerge from larger social and economic problems in the community and are as much a consequence of these factors as a contributor. The report also indicates that changing demographics in some small towns and rural areas may contribute to the emergence or escalation of gang problems and may be related to the immigration of newly arrived racial or ethnic groups into an area.

The study reports that in most cases the gang problem is short-lived and dissipates quickly because small towns and rural areas do not provide the necessary population base to sustain gangs and any disruption (arrest, members dropping out) may weaken the gang.[38] The study also indicates that a balanced and carefully developed collective community effort and strategy involving the following three areas can be more effective than undue media attention and overreliance on and excessive use of law enforcement suppression strategies that may provide cohesiveness to the gang:

■ Prevention programs that aim to prevent youth from developing problem behaviors and later becoming delinquent and joining gangs.

■ Intervention programs that aim to rehabilitate delinquents and divert gang-involved youths from gangs.

■ Suppression activities that include targeting of the gangs with the most high-rate offenders by law enforcement, prosecutors, and courts.

In an excellent recent article in the FBI *Law Enforcement Bulletin,* Supervisory Special Agent Dennis Lindsey, a senior instructor in the International Training Center, Sensitive Investigations Unit, at the DEA and Lieutenant Sean Kelly of the Durham, New Hampshire, Police Department, discuss the issues of officer stress in small-town policing and indicate that these officers are subject to the same stress that big-town police and deputies face, and often additional different types of stress also.[39]

Lindsey and Kelly cite a 40-year study released in 2002 that determined that the average age of death of officers with 10 to 19 years of service was 66, while the average age of death for nonpolice was 74 years for men and 80 years for women. This research found a significantly increased risk of digestive and hematopoietic cancers among officers; as well as maladaptive behaviors such as alcohol and tobacco use, significantly high mortality risk of esophageal cancer and cirrhosis of the liver.[40] The researchers note that officers, after the dangers and rigors of a tour of duty must try to "come down" and return to a normal family and social life, but point out that small-town and rural police constantly face the inability to come down from a hypervigilant state (acting as a police officer), causing their bodies to deteriorate further and faster.[41]

Lindsey and Kelly write,

Police officers who live and work in small towns almost never have an opportunity to decompress. Being well known to the residents, business owners, and others in the community, officers cannot separate on-duty and off-duty time. Essentially small town police officers live in a fishbowl. Off-duty trips to the store frequently become job related because everyone seems to know the officers and their family vehicles. Spouses often come under close observation because residents may think "that cop" is driving past or, simply, because they are the spouse of a police officer. Taking their children to school becomes complicated when other parents wonder out loud why officers are not at work or when a school administrator asks for advice about an unruly child or parent. All of this "off-duty" interaction disallows decompression and contributes to stress and the deterioration of the small town police officer's body. . . . Or, when at a party with their spouses' friends, they must respond to questions about a police officer's conduct in an agency 3,000 miles away. An event that is supposed to be fun, that is supposed to invigorate them, and that is supposed to be enjoyable becomes another time when they must put on the shield and wear their "cop hat."[42]

Rural and small-town law enforcement agencies engage in mutual assistance programs with neighboring agencies and come to one another's aid when necessary.

Limited resources, rising crime trends, and geographic barriers severely impair the ability of rural law enforcement agencies to effectively combat crimes in their communities. To ensure that they can meet the challenge of law enforcement in the twenty-first century rural executives are increasingly seeking opportunities to provide more education and training for their staffs and to maximize their effectiveness through new and improved technology. This attention to the needs of rural law enforcement agencies gave birth to the National Center for Rural Law Enforcement (NCRLE), a part of the Criminal Justice Institute, University of Arkansas, located in Little Rock, Arkansas. To assist law enforcement officials throughout the United States, the NCRLE provides management education and training courses ranging from principles of supervision to detailed courses on the legal aspects of domestic violence. NCRLE also provides research and Internet assistance. The NCRLE brings sheriffs, police chiefs, citizens, and social service agency representatives together to discuss the needs of rural communities and explore the process of creating a community coalition.[43]

Indian Country and Tribal Law Enforcement

Laurence French, professor at the University of New Hampshire, writes that policing American Indians in the United States has always been contentious especially from the tribal perspective. First, American Indians were regulated by the U.S. Army and the Department of War, and then later by the Bureau of Indian Affairs and the Department of the Interior. Today the controversy continues with federal, state, and local jurisdictions attempting to intervene in tribal policing.[44] This has caused jurisdictional confusion, tribal discontent, and litigations, in Indian country.[45]

M. Wesley Clark, a senior attorney in the U.S. Drug Enforcement Administration (DEA), says "Policing in and adjacent to land within Indian country is often a complex and, at times, confusing jurisdictional puzzle. Solving this puzzle depends on a variety of factors, including whether the crime is a felony or misdemeanor, whether the subjects and victims are Indians, and whether the crime violates tribal, state, or federal law."[46]

A 2005 report for the National Institute of Justice offers detailed information gathered on tribal law enforcement agencies, tribal courts and services, and criminal records systems from continental American Indian jurisdictions. More than 92 percent (314) of the 341 federally recognized American Indian tribes in the continental 48 states responded to the census.

Relative to policing, the report reveals that 165 of the responding 314 tribes employed one or more full-time sworn officers with general arrest powers; almost all (99 percent) had cross deputization agreements with another tribal or public agency; and 56 percent of the tribes that employed one or more full-time sworn officers with general arrest powers were also recognized by their state governments to possess arrest authority.[47]

The governmental power to make or enforce laws in Indian country is divided among federal, state, and tribal governments. Jurisdiction in a specific incident depends on the nature of the offense, whether the offender or victim was a tribal member, and the state in which the crime occurred. Public Law 83-280 (commonly called PL 280) conferred criminal jurisdiction in Indian country to six state governments (mandatory PL 280 states) and the federal government—California, Minnesota, Nebraska, Oregon, Wisconsin, and Alaska. It also permitted other states to acquire jurisdiction at their option (Optional PL 280 states). The optional PL 280 states—Nevada, Idaho, Iowa, Washington, South Dakota, Montana, North Dakota, Arizona, and Utah assumed jurisdiction either in whole or in part over Indian country within their boundaries. In states where PL 280 does not apply, the federal government retains criminal jurisdiction for major crimes.

The 1994 Crime Act expanded federal criminal jurisdiction in Indian country in such areas as guns, violent juveniles, drugs, and domestic violence. Thus, law enforcement in Indian country is dispersed among federal, state, local, and tribal agencies. The tribes have inherent powers to exercise criminal jurisdiction over all tribal members and the authority to arrest and detain non-Indians for delivery to state or federal authorities for prosecution. These tribal police powers are generally limited to the reservation. The work of tribal police is often critical to resolving criminal cases referred to state and federal agencies because tribal police usually discover the crime, interview witnesses, and investigate the circumstances involved in the crime. Often tribal police refer cases to U.S. attorney's offices for investigation because tribal courts generally hear only misdemeanor cases.[48]

Cross-deputization agreements have been used to enhance law enforcement capabilities in areas where state and tribal lands are contiguous and intermingled. Under some agreements, federal, state, county/local, and/or tribal law enforcement officers have the power to arrest Indian and non-Indian wrongdoers whenever a violation of law occurs. States, in some cases, have recognized tribal police to have peace officer authority to arrest tribal offenders off the reservation or detain nontribal offenders on the reservation. About 45 percent of the tribes with law enforcement personnel had arrest authority over tribal members off the reservation. About 62 percent of the tribes with at least one sworn officer reported having arrest authority over non-Indians on tribal reservations.

The *Tribal Census* revealed that the largest Indian law enforcement agency was the Navajo Nation in Arizona with 321 full time officers with arrest powers. Next were the Seminole Tribe of Florida—Dania, Big Cypress, Brighton, Hollywood, and Tampa reservations—with 67 sworn officers, followed by the Oglala Sioux Tribe in South Dakota with 58.[49]

Very real problems affect tribal police as they provide law enforcement services in the country's most remote and undeveloped areas. These tribal police officers are stretched thin over large and diverse geographical territories. As an example, in Arizona, the Hualapai Nation has only 1 chief and 10 commissioned officers to cover the reservation's one million acres and population of 2,800 residents. The Stillaguamish Tribal Police of Arlington, Washington, have only seven patrol officers to cover 650 square miles of fish and game territory, as well as a casino. They also face severe community problems and high unemployment making drugs and substance abuse one of their greatest challenges. They also experience a lack of funding to build the type of infrastructure to accomplish the mission of policing.[50]

State Law Enforcement

Forty-nine of the 50 U.S. states have a primary state law enforcement agency. The only state without a primary state police agency is Hawaii, although it has several law enforcement agencies with statewide jurisdiction. (This may surprise those who are familiar with the television series *Hawaii 5-0*, which was based on the fictional Hawaiian State Police.)

In the latest reporting year, the 49 primary state law enforcement agencies had about 82,500 full-time employees and more than 57,600 full-time sworn personnel. Of the full-time sworn personnel, about 69 percent were patrol officers, 11 percent were investigators, and the rest were ranking officers.[51] State expenditures for police protection increased nearly 293 percent from 20 years ago with an average annual change of 6.4 percent.[52]

The largest state law enforcement agency is the California Highway Patrol, which has about 9,700 employees; the next two largest are the Texas Department of Public Safety with 7,000 employees, and the Pennsylvania State Police with over 5,600 employees. The smallest state police agencies are the North Dakota Highway Patrol with 126 sworn employees; the Wyoming Highway Patrol, with 148 sworn personnel; and the South Dakota Highway Patrol, with 153 sworn employees.

Historically, state police departments were developed to deal with growing crime in nonurban areas of the country, which was attributed to the increasing mobility of Americans, the proliferation of cars, and the ease of travel. The state police agencies were formed by governors and legislators to lessen reliance on metropolitan and county police departments, which were more closely linked with politics and urban and county corruption.

Generally, state police patrol small towns and state highways, regulate traffic, and have the primary responsibility to enforce some state laws. The state police also carry out many duties for local police agencies, such as managing state training academies, criminal identification systems, and crime laboratories.

At the state level, there are two distinct models of law enforcement agencies. The **centralized model of state law enforcement** combines the duties of major criminal investigations with the patrol of state highways. The centralized state police agencies generally assist local police departments in criminal investigations when requested and provide the identification, laboratory, and training functions for local departments.

The second state model, the **decentralized model of state law enforcement,** has a clear distinction between traffic enforcement on state highways and other state-level law enforcement functions. The states that use this model—many southern and midwestern, and some western, states—generally have two separate agencies, one a highway patrol and the other a state bureau of investigation. California, for example, has the California Highway Patrol and the California Division of Law Enforcement.

Although the duties of the various state-level police departments may vary considerably, the most common duties include highway patrol, traffic law enforcement, and the patrol of small towns.

Federal Law Enforcement

Although the U.S. Constitution created three branches of government—executive, legislative, and judicial—it did not create a national police force but did give the national government power over a limited number of crimes.

Traditionally in the United States, the creation of laws and the power to enforce them have been matters for the states. The states have given much of their enforcement powers to local police agencies. Policing has largely been local. In recent years, however, the number of crimes included in the U.S. Criminal Code has multiplied greatly, as has the number of people assigned to enforce these crimes. By the latest reporting year, there were about 156,600 full-time federal law enforcement employees.[53] These numbers do not include officers in the U.S. Armed Forces (Army, Navy, Air Force, Marines, and Coast Guard) and do not include federal air marshals and Central Intelligence Agency (CIA) security protective service officers because of classified information restrictions.[54] With the increased attention to border security and homeland defense following the terrorist attacks of September 11, 2001, the number of federal law enforcement officers increases daily.

The total number of criminal justice system employees in the nation grew 86 percent between 1982 and 2003 (the latest reported year), and the federal criminal justice employees increased the most with a 168 percent increase of employees. Also, federal expenditures increased 692 percent with an annual increase of 9.9 percent. Additionally, federal expenditures for police protection increased 708 percent for an annual percentage increase of 10 percent.[55]

Four major U.S. cabinet departments administer most federal law enforcement agencies and personnel: the Department of Justice, the Department of the Treasury, the Department of Homeland Security, and the Department of the Interior. Numerous other federal agencies have law enforcement functions. Each of the agencies discussed in this section have a presence on the web, and students are urged to access these sites to obtain information regarding these agencies, their duties, and the many jobs they have available.

This text pays special attention to federal law enforcement agencies because many of these agencies require a four-year college degree for appointment.

Department of Justice

The U.S. Department of Justice is the primary legal and prosecutorial arm of the U.S. government. The Department of Justice is under the control of the U.S. Attorney General and is responsible for (1) enforcing all federal laws, (2) representing the government when it is involved in a court action,

18 USC ——

and (3) conducting independent investigations through its law enforcement services. The department's Civil Rights Division prosecutes violators of federal civil rights laws, which are designed to protect citizens from discrimination on the basis of their race, creed, ethnic background, or gender. These laws apply to discrimination in education, housing, and job opportunity. The Justice Department's Tax Division prosecutes violators of the tax laws. The Criminal Division prosecutes violators of the *Federal Criminal Code* for such criminal acts as bank robbery, kidnapping, mail fraud, interstate transportation of stolen vehicles, and narcotics and drug trafficking.

The Justice Department also operates the **National Institute of Justice (NIJ)** as its research arm. The National Institute of Justice maintains the **National Criminal Justice Reference Service (NCJRS)** as a national clearinghouse of criminal justice information.

The NCJRS is one of the most extensive sources of information on criminal justice in the world. Created by the NIJ in 1972, the NCJRS contains specialized information centers to provide publications and other information services to the constituencies of each of the U.S. Department of Justice, Office of Justice Programs (OJP), bureaus, and to the Office of National Drug Control Policy. Each OJP agency has established specialized information centers, and each has its own 800 telephone number and staff to answer questions about the agency's mission and initiatives.

The NIJ also conducts the National Crime Victimization Survey (NCVS), a twice-yearly survey of a random sample of the American public that polls citizens about their criminal victimization. Finally, the Justice Department also maintains administrative control over the Federal Bureau of Investigation (FBI), the Drug Enforcement Administration (DEA), the U.S. Marshals, and the Bureau of Alcohol, Tobacco, Firearms and Explosives (ATF).

Federal Bureau of Investigation The FBI is the best known of the federal law enforcement agencies. By 2006, the FBI had more than 12,515 special agents and is the primary agency charged with the enforcement of all federal laws not falling under the purview of other federal agencies. The main headquarters of the FBI is in Washington, D.C., but it also has field offices in major American cities and abroad. The head of the FBI is known as the director and is appointed by the president of the United States, subject to confirmation by the Senate.[56]

In addition to the special agents, the FBI employs almost 18,000 support nonenforcement personnel such as intelligence specialists, language specialists, scientists, information technical specialists, and other staff who perform such duties as fingerprint examinations, computer programming, forensic or crime laboratory analysis, and administrative and clerical duties.

All special agents must attend the FBI Academy, located in Quantico, Virginia. In addition to the special agents, other law enforcement officers and officers from some foreign governments attend the Academy.

The FBI Academy also runs the Leadership Development Institute (LDI), a one-year program to enhance the leadership skills of individuals in law enforcement command-level positions and broaden their exposure to both the domestic and international policing communities. Fellows spend six months at the academy and the remaining six months at their respective agencies or at Quantico for additional research and study.[57]

Contrary to popular opinion, the FBI is not a national police force. Rather, it is an investigative agency that may investigate acts that violate federal law. The FBI may also assist state and local law enforcement agencies and investigate state and local crimes when asked to do so by those agencies.

The FBI was created in 1908, when President Theodore Roosevelt directed the attorney general to develop an investigative unit within the Justice Department. It was first named the Bureau of Investigation; in 1935, it was renamed the Federal Bureau of Investigation. Its most prominent figure and longtime director from 1924 to 1972 was J. Edgar Hoover.

The FBI has had a colorful history. It captured the attention of the media during the Great Depression with nationwide searches and the capture of such notorious criminals as George "Machine Gun" Kelly in 1933, John Dillinger in 1934, and Charles "Pretty Boy" Floyd in 1934.

Critics, however, allege that the FBI under Hoover's regime ignored white-collar crime, organized crime, and violations of the civil rights of minority groups. After Hoover's death in 1972, it was discovered that under his direction, the FBI had committed many violations of citizens' constitutional rights, including spying, conducting illegal wiretaps, and burglarizing premises. These violations were mostly aimed at individuals and groups because of their political beliefs.[58]

Hoover's successors reoriented the mission of the bureau and put more emphasis on the investigation of white-collar crime, organized crime, and political corruption.[59]

In addition to its investigative capacity, the FBI today provides many important services.

Identification Division The FBI's Identification Division, created in 1924, collects and maintains a vast fingerprint file. This file is used for identification purposes by the FBI, as well as by state and local police agencies.

National Crime Information Center The National Crime Information Center (NCIC) is a tremendous computerized database of criminal information. It stores information on stolen property that has identifying information, such as serial numbers or distinctive markings. The NCIC also contains information on outstanding warrants and criminal histories.

FBI Crime Laboratory The FBI Crime Laboratory, created in 1932, provides investigative and analysis services for other law enforcement agencies. It is the world's largest forensic, or criminalistic (scientifically crime related), laboratory and provides microscopic, chemical, and DNA analyses, as well as spectrography and cryptography. Skilled FBI technicians examine such evidence as hairs, fibers, blood, tire tracks, and drugs.

Uniform Crime Reports The Uniform Crime Reporting (UCR) Program is an annual compilation that includes information on crimes reported to local police agencies, arrests, and police killed or wounded in the line of duty, along with other data. The UCR is the result of a nationwide, cooperative statistical effort by most of the nation's city, county, and state law enforcement agencies voluntarily reporting data on crimes brought to their attention by the public and is published once a year as *Crime in the United States*. Since 1930, the FBI has administered the program and issued periodic assessments of the nature and type of crime in the nation. Although the program's primary objective is to provide a reliable set of criminal statistics for use in law enforcement administration, operation, and management, over the years its data have become one of the leading social indicators for the United States. The American public looks to the UCR for information on fluctuations in the level of crime. Criminologists, sociologists, legislators, municipal planners, the press, and students of criminal justice use the statistics for varied research and planning purposes.

The specific crimes measured by the UCR are called Part I—Index crimes. They are murder and nonnegligent manslaughter, forcible rape, robbery, aggravated assault, burglary, larceny-theft, arson, and motor vehicle theft. One of the latest additions to the UCR is the collection of hate crime statistics, mandated by the Hate Crime Statistics Act. This collection of data is being used to study crimes motivated by religious, ethnic, racial, or sexual orientation prejudice.

LEOKA

National Incident-Based Reporting System (*NIBRS*) In response to law enforcement's need for more flexible, in depth data, the UCR formulated the NIBRS, which presents comprehensive, detailed information about crime incidents to law enforcement, researchers, governmental planners, students of crime, and the general public. NIBRS is still not fully implemented throughout the United States, and the data is still not pervasive enough to make broad generalizations about crime in the United States.[60]

Investigatory Activities The FBI investigates more than two hundred categories of federal crimes and has concurrent jurisdiction with the DEA over drug offenses under the Controlled Substances Act.

It was reported in 2006 that over the past two years, FBI investigations have led to corruption convictions for more than 1,000 government employees.[61]

An August 2005 article by Special Agents Leonard G. Johns, Gerard F. Downes, and Camille D. Bibles of the FBI's Critical Incident Response Group shows how the FBI's National Center for the Analysis of Violent Crime (NCAVC) offers consultative services on cold case serial homicides as well as several other types of cases. In this article, the authors described a series of three murders of a suspect's wives from 1978 to 1993. The NCAVC led to the arrest of the subject with the cooperation of investigators from the U.S. Department of Interior and the National Park Service and police from Coconino and Arapahoe counties in Colorado.[62]

In another article, Special Agents Eugene Rugala and James McNamara, also of the NCAVC, and George Wattendorf, a prosecutor and police officer for the Dover, New Hampshire, Police Department, discuss the assistance the NCAVC can render in stalking cases. This is an important issue because research suggests a strong connection between stalking and domestic violence—81 percent of women stalked by husbands or cohabitating partners also suffered a physical assault from that person.[63]

Traditionally, the FBI focused its investigations on organized crime activities, including racketeering, corruption, and pornography; bank robbery; and white-collar crime, including embezzlement, and stock and other business fraud. The FBI is also at the forefront of our government's efforts against domestic terrorist activity and trains special antiterrorist teams to prevent and respond to terrorist attacks. The FBI also maintains surveillance on foreign intelligence agents and investigates their activities within this country.

Realizing that both international and domestic terrorism were serious national concerns, the federal government took several law enforcement measures to deal with terrorism even before September 11, 2001. However, in May 2002, following massive criticism that the FBI had failed to properly handle information that could have led to the prevention of the September 11th attacks, Director Robert S. Mueller issued a press release outlining its complete reorganization and creating a new strategic focus for the agency. The FBI's new focus placed the following as its three priorities: (1) protecting the United States from terrorist attack, (2) protecting the United States against foreign intelligence operations and espionage, and (3) protecting the United States against cyber-based attacks and high-technology crimes. The main organizational improvements Mueller enacted were a complete restructuring of the counterterrorism activities of the bureau and a shift from a reactive to a proactive orientation; the development of special squads to coordinate national and international investigations; a reemphasis on the Joint Terrorism Task Forces; enhanced analytical capabilities with personnel and technological improvements; a permanent shift of additional resources to counterterrorism; the creation of a more mobile, agile, and flexible national terrorism response; and targeted recruitment to acquire agents, analysts, translators, and others with specialized skills and backgrounds.[64]

In a 2006 article, Special Agent Lesley G. Koestner, of the FBI's Criminal Justice Information Services Division, writes that in today's age of terrorism as the FBI evolves from its traditional focus on law enforcement to its post–September 11 mission, which includes the homeland security priorities of counterterrorism, counterintelligence, and cybercrime, its Law Enforcement Online (LEO) Program, a conduit for intelligence information that forms a cornerstone for the bureau's information sharing initiative by providing links to federal, state, local, and tribal law enforcement agencies nationwide is fully operable and assisting all registered law enforcement users nationwide.[65]

LEO provides communication, information, expertise, and full-time access needed by first responding public safety officers facing the initial onslaught of an emergency. LEO contributes to the intelligence, investigative, and safety function in law enforcement and has become the national communications system for all levels of the law enforcement community, and its electronic interfaces enables users to access it with a single log-on and provides them a secure e-mail system. A virtual command center (VCC) runs a software program that provides the capability to maintain an awareness of evolving situations for crisis management, allowing LEO members to track, display, and disseminate information in real time about street-level and tactical activities. This system also enables FBI headquarters to monitor events and resources in an affected area and to help provide federal, state, and local support to the first responders. LEO is a multifaceted tool to enhance the greater law enforcement community's situational awareness. The LEO also serves the investigation of crimes and terrorist threats by allowing users to obtain more comprehensive investigative information and track trends of specific crimes and multiple criminal offenses throughout the country.

The National Alert System (NAS), introduced in 2003, can deliver secure message boxes containing law enforcement sensitive information to 20,000 online members within 5 minutes and simultaneously transmit them to all members' LEO e-mail accounts. An alert message contains a short synopsis and directs the recipient to additional information posted on a secure LEO site. The NAS also can send up to 160,000 notifications to pagers, cell phones, and other wireless devices to advise users of the alert.

The VCC and NAS features of LEO have been called "a one-stop shop" for the law enforcement community for FBI intelligence information, providing a central hub for information sharing to support investigative programs.

In May 2006, Suzel Spiller, an intelligence analyst at FBI Headquarters in Washington, D.C., indicated that in 2003 the FBI created Field Intelligence Groups (FIGs) in all of its 56 field offices. These groups work closely with the Joint Terrorism Task Forces, various field office squads, and other agency components to provide valuable service to law enforcement personnel at the state and local levels by sharing intelligence gathered about transnational terrorism to maximize the sharing of information. The FIGs also produce and disseminate intelligence pertaining to cyber, counterintelligence, and criminal programs.[66]

See Chapter 15, "Homeland Security," for a full description of the FBI's new role in counterterrorism and homeland security.

Drug Enforcement Administration (DEA)

The DEA is at the vanguard of the nation's "war on drugs" by engaging in drug interdiction, conducting surveillance operations, and infiltrating drug rings and arresting major narcotics violators. The agency also tracks illicit drug traffic; registers manufacturers, distributors, and dispensers of pharmaceutical drugs and controlled substances; tracks the movement of chemicals used in the manufacture of illegal drugs; and leads the nation's marijuana eradication program.[67]

U.S. Marshals Service

The U.S. Marshals service performs many functions. Its primary functions are the transportation of federal prisoners between prisons and courts and the security of federal court facilities. The marshals also protect witnesses at federal trials, apprehend federal fugitives, execute federal warrants, operate the Federal Witness Security Program, and are in charge of the federal government's asset seizure and forfeiture programs, handling the seizure and disposal of property resulting from criminal activity.

©Reuters/Corbis

Armed U.S. Marshals patrol a security checkpoint at Logan Airport in Boston, Massachusetts, on September 17, 2001. How has the role of federal law enforcement changed since 9/11?

Bureau of Alcohol, Tobacco, Firearms and Explosives (ATF)

The ATF is the nation's primary agency for enforcing federal laws relating to alcohol, tobacco, firearms, and explosives violations. The ATF enforces laws pertaining to the manufacture, sale, and possession of firearms and explosives; attempts to suppress illegal traffic in tobacco and alcohol products; collects taxes; and regulates industry trade practices regarding these items.

The ATF assists other domestic and international law enforcement agencies as the nation's primary agency for tracing of weapons and explosives. The ATF traces these weapons through its records of manufacturers and dealers in firearms. The ATF also investigates cases of arson and bombing at federal buildings or other institutions that receive federal funds, as well as investigating arson-for-profit schemes.

Department of the Treasury

The Department of the Treasury has administrative control over the Internal Revenue Service— Criminal Investigation Division and several very important offices related to the financial aspects of crime, drug trafficking, and terrorism.

Internal Revenue Service (IRS)

The IRS, the nation's primary revenue-collection agency, is charged with the enforcement of laws regulating federal income tax and its collection. The investigative arm of the IRS is its Criminal Investigation Division (CID). CID agents investigate tax fraud, unreported income, and hidden assets.

In its efforts against organized crime figures and major drug dealers, the federal government often uses the CID to target these individuals with the goal of prosecuting them for tax evasion. Also, many other law enforcement agencies solicit the help of the CID in an attempt to prosecute major drug dealers and other criminals who are in possession of large amounts of undeclared income.

Executive Office for Asset Forfeiture (EOAF) The EOAF administers programs involving applying the forfeiture laws to the infrastructure of criminal enterprises, limiting the ability of these organizations to continue their illegal activities. The EOAF primarily directs its efforts against drug cartels, criminal syndicates, and terrorist organizations by removing their assets and minimizing their profits.

Executive Office for Terrorist Financing and Financial Crime (EOTF/FC) The EOTF/FC develops and implements U.S. government strategies to combat terrorist financing domestically and internationally. It also develops and implements the National Money Laundering Strategy.

Office of Foreign Assets Control (OFAC) The OFAC administers and enforces economic and trade sanctions based on U.S. foreign policy and national security goals against targeted foreign countries, terrorists, international narcotics traffickers, and those engaged in activities related to the proliferation of weapons of mass destruction.

Financial Crimes Enforcement Network (FinCEN) The FinCEN coordinates information sharing among law enforcement agencies to deal with the complex problem of money laundering.

Department of Homeland Security (DHS)

After much study following the terrorist attacks of September 11, 2001, the cabinet-level DHS was established in March 2003.[68] See Chapter 15, "Homeland Security," for a complete description of the DHS and other government and private efforts to prevent terrorism and ensure homeland defense.

The new agency merged 22 previously disparate domestic agencies into one department to protect the nation against threats to the homeland. The new agency consists of more than 170,000 employees, and its creation was the most significant transformation of the U.S. government since 1947 when President Harry S Truman merged the various branches of the U.S. Armed Forces into the Department of Defense to better coordinate the nation's defense against military threats.

The DHS represents a similar consolidation, both in style and substance. The DHS assumed the former duties of the U.S. Coast Guard, the U.S. Customs Service, the Secret Service, the Immigration and Naturalization Service, the Transportation Security Administration, and numerous other federal communications, science, and technology agencies. The DHS does not include the FBI, CIA, or National Security Agency.[69] Each of the separate units of the DHS and their functions will be fully discussed in Chapter 15.

The department's major priority is the protection of the nation against further terrorist attacks. The department's units analyze threats and intelligence, guard our borders and airports, protect our critical infrastructure, and coordinate the responses of our nation to future emergencies. The U.S. Secret Service was also placed under the administration of the DHS in 2003.

U.S. Secret Service The U.S. Secret Service has as its primary mission the protection of the president and his or her family, and other government leaders and foreign dignitaries, as well as the security of designated national events. The Secret Service is also the primary agency responsible for protecting U.S. currency from counterfeiters and safeguarding Americans from credit card fraud, financial crimes, and computer fraud. The Secret Service provides security for designated national events and preserves the integrity of the nation's financial and critical infrastructures. It uses prevention-based training and methods to combat the cybercriminals and terrorists who attempt to use identity theft, telecommunications fraud, and other technology-based crimes to defraud and undermine American consumers and industry.

In its role of protecting the president, vice president, and other government officials and their families, along with former presidents, and presidential and vice presidential candidates, the Secret Service coordinates all security arrangements for official presidential visits, motorcades, and ceremonies with other federal government agencies and state and local law enforcement agencies. The Secret Service has uniformed and non-uniformed divisions. The uniformed division provides protection for the White House complex and other presidential offices, the Main Treasury Building and Annex, and foreign diplomatic missions.

Department of the Interior

The Department of the Interior's myriad law enforcement agencies provide law enforcement services for the property under its purview using the National Park Service, the U.S. Park Police, the Bureau of Indian Affairs, the Fish and Wildlife Service, the Bureau of Land Management, and the Bureau of Reclamation. The agencies are responsible for protecting most of the nation's historic icons, such as Mount Rushmore, the Washington Monument, the Hoover and Grand Coulee Dams and 350 other dams, and millions of acres of uninhabited wilderness in national parks, preserves, and other lands controlled by the federal government.

Enforcement agents for the National Park Service are known as commissioned park rangers. They are responsible for law enforcement, traffic control, fire control, and search and rescue operations in the 30 million acres of the National Park Service. Additional rangers serve seasonally as part-time commissioned rangers. In addition to park rangers, the Park Service also uses park police officers, mainly in the Washington, D.C., area. Enforcement agents for the Department of the Interior's Fish and Wildlife Service are called wildlife law enforcement agents. They investigate people who are illegally trafficking in government-protected animals and birds, such as falcons.

Department of Defense

Each branch of the U.S. military has its own law enforcement agency. The military police agencies are organized in a manner similar to the civil police, using uniformed officers for patrol duties on military bases and investigators to investigate crimes. The Army's investigative arm is the Criminal Investigation Division (CID); the investigative arm of the Navy and Marines is the Naval Criminal Investigative Service (NCIS); and the Air Force's is the Air Force Office of Special Investigations (OSI).

U.S. Postal Service

The Postal Inspections Division of the U.S. Postal Service is one of the oldest of the federal law enforcement agencies, having been created in 1836. Postal inspectors investigate illegal acts committed against the Postal Service and its property and personnel, such as cases of fraud involving the use of the mails; use of the mails to transport drugs, bombs, and firearms; and assaults upon postal employees while exercising their official duties. Postal Inspectors are responsible for criminal investigations covering more than 200 federal statutes related to the postal system. Postal police officers provide security for postal facilities, employees, and assets; escort high-value mail shipments; and perform other protective functions.

Other Federal Enforcement Agencies

Many other federal agencies have law enforcement responsibilities. The Department of Agriculture has enforcement officers in its U.S. Forest Service, and its Office of Investigation investigates fraud in the areas of food stamps and subsidies to farmers and rural home buyers. The Department of Commerce has enforcement divisions in its Bureau of Export Enforcement and the National Marine Fisheries Administration. The Department of Labor has the Office of Labor Racketeering as an enforcement division.[70]

The Food and Drug Administration (FDA) oversees the enforcement of the laws regulating the sale and distribution of pure food and drugs. Criminal law enforcement divisions are also found in the Securities and Exchange Commission (SEC), the Interstate Commerce Commission (ICC), the Federal Trade Commission (FTC), the Department of Health and Human Services, the Tennessee Valley Authority (TVA), the Environmental Protection Agency (EPA), and the Library of Congress. The Department of State has the Diplomatic Security Service to investigate matters involving passport and visa fraud. The U.S. Supreme Court has its own police department.

TABLE 2.3   Major Federal Law Enforcement Agencies

Department of Justice

Federal Bureau of Investigation

Drug Enforcement Administration

U.S. Marshals Service

Bureau of Alcohol, Tobacco, Firearms and Explosives

Department of the Treasury

Internal Revenue Service—Criminal Investigation
    Division

Executive Office for Asset Forfeiture

Executive Office for Terrorist Financing and Financial
    Crime

Office of Foreign Assets Control

Financial Crimes Enforcement Network

Department of Homeland Security (*See Chapter 15*)

Department of the Interior

National Park Service

Fish and Wildlife Service

U.S. Park Police

Bureau of Indian Affairs

Bureau of Land Management

Bureau of Reclamation

Department of Defense

Army Criminal Investigation Division

Naval Criminal Investigative Service

Air Force Office of Special Investigations

U.S. Postal Service

Postal Inspections Service

Department of Agriculture

U.S. Forest Service

Department of Commerce

Bureau of Export Enforcement

National Marine Fisheries Administration

Department of Labor

Office of Labor Racketeering

Department of State

Diplomatic Security Service

Other Federal Law Enforcement Agencies

Amtrak Police

Bureau of Engraving and Printing Police

U.S. Capitol Police

U.S. Mint Police

U.S. Supreme Court Police

Library of Congress Police

National Gallery of Art Police

Even the National Gallery of Art has its own law enforcement unit.

The U.S. Capitol Police employs more than 1,200 officers to provide police services for the U.S. Capitol grounds, buildings, and area immediately surrounding the Capitol complex. The U.S. Mint has a police department that provides police and patrol services for U.S. Mint facilities, including safeguarding the nation's coinage and gold bullion reserves. The Bureau of Engraving and Printing has a police department providing police services for their facilities including those where currency, stamps, securities, and other official U.S. documents are made. The National Railroad Passenger Corporation, better known as Amtrak, has officers who provide police response, patrol, and investigative services for the railroad. See Table 2.3.

Joint Federal and Local Task Force Approach to Law Enforcement

In the 1970s, federal enforcement agencies implemented an innovative approach to law enforcement by using **joint federal and local task forces** involving local, state, and federal law enforcement officers acting as a team. In these task forces, investigators from local police departments and state police agencies are temporarily assigned to a federal law enforcement agency to work with federal agents in combating particular crimes. The local and state officers provide knowledge of the area, local contacts, informants, and street smarts, and federal agents provide investigative experience and resources. The DEA has been using joint drug enforcement task forces in many areas of the country since the early 1970s. The joint task force approach has also been used successfully in ongoing programs to investigate bank robbery, arson, kidnapping, and terrorism.[71] See Chapter 15, "Homeland Security," for a complete description of the Joint Terrorism Task Forces.

International Police

Interpol, the International Criminal Police Organization, is a worldwide organization established for the development of cooperation among nations regarding common police problems. Interpol was founded in 1923, and the United States became a member in 1938. The mission of Interpol is to track and provide information that may help other law enforcement agencies apprehend criminal fugitives, thwart criminal schemes, exchange experience and technology, and analyze major trends of international criminal activity. Interpol attempts to achieve its mission by serving as a clearinghouse and depository of intelligence information on wanted criminals. Interpol's main function is informational; it is neither an investigative nor an enforcement agency. Police officials of any member country may initiate a request for assistance on a case that extends beyond their country's jurisdiction. Interpol headquarters are in France, and its U.S. representative is the U.S. Treasury Department.

Private Security

The preceding sections of this chapter showed the tremendous size and scope of the public law enforcement industry on the local, state, federal, and international levels. However, that was only the tip of the iceberg. Another cast of players is associated with providing safety and security in the United States. The private security industry is the vast

©Tony Savino/The Image Works

The private security industry has grown tremendously in recent years and is one of the nation's expanding industries. Here a private security guard stands watch at a commercial shipping dock on the Miami River in Miami, Florida. What do you think is fueling the growth of private security?

industry that provides security to much of corporate America and, increasingly, to much of public America.

Since September 11, 2001, security has been a rising star in the corporate structure. The people responsible for security have become much more visible to the top of the business and much more important to the business itself. The shift in business attitudes is also evident in a recent market report on the security industry by Lehman Brothers in which the analyst writes that the global security industry "has moved from a peripheral activity to center stage."[72]

What Is Private Security?

As early as 1974, the National Advisory Commission on Criminal Justice Standards and Goals, in its *Report of the Task Force on Private Security*, defined the industry as follows:

> Those self-employed individuals and privately funded business entities and organizations providing security-related services to specific

You Are There!

Major Security Occupational Areas

- *Educational Institution Security*—The primary objective of an educational institution security program is to educate the campus community about the potential for crime, both on and off campus. The central theme of a campus crime prevention program is awareness, self-protection, and prevention. The level of violence on and around educational institutions has brought about a need for security at public and private educational institutions at both the elementary and secondary school levels. Educational institutions may operate a commissioned police department or contract out this responsibility to a security provider.

- *Financial Services Security*—This area deals with banking, stock brokerages, insurance companies, and other financial institutions. This area is regulated by various government agencies. Professionals in this area deal with concerns that can result in losses for their organizations.

- *Gaming and Wagering Security*—In this area, security personnel are employed to secure and protect the facilities of the gaming and wagering industry and the customers utilizing these facilities.

- *Government Industrial Security*—This area is concerned with the classification, declassification, and protection of national security information in the custody of industry. Government industrial security professionals protect special categories of classified information, including restricted data, formerly restricted data, intelligence sources, and related data.

- *Healthcare Security*—This area deals with premise and personal protection in hospitals, long-term care facilities, clinics, and nursing homes.

- *Information Systems Security*—In this area, security employees safeguard administrative and organizational measures designed to ensure the loyalty and reliability of personnel and information. It includes securing hardware, software, and communication networks, as well as the security specialties of computer security, telecommunications security, and Internet security.

- *Lodging Security*—This area is concerned with safeguarding the visitors and possessions of hotels, motels, resorts, and other similar facilities.

- *Manufacturing Security*—In this area, security personnel protect the plants, products, and interests of those participating in this industry.

- *Retail Security*—This area is concerned with preventing the loss of inventory and ensuring the integrity of employees. It is also involved in the investigation of all types of fraud, including credit card and check fraud.

- *Security Sales, Equipment, and Services*—Persons in this area are involved in the selling, equipping, and servicing of products used to enhance premise and personal security for industry and society.

- *Transportation Security*—This security specialty includes all security efforts in airports, airplane hangers, trucking, and land or sea transportation operations.

- *Utilities Security*—Utility security employees are involved in the protection of personnel, property, equipment, and other corporate resources of public and private utility companies and providers.

Source: ASIS Online, *Professional Development: Security Specialty Areas*, retrieved on April 18, 2000 from http://www.asisonline.org.

---

clientele for a fee, for the individual or entity that retains or employs them, or for themselves, in order to protect their persons, private property, or interests from various hazards.[73]

Perhaps, the best way to describe the differences between public and private law enforcement or policing is to say that both are concerned with the prevention of crime and the apprehension of criminals, but public law enforcement personnel are generally paid by public (tax) funds, whereas private security personnel are generally paid by the private sector, either private corporations or private persons.

In the 1980s and 1990s, the U.S. National Institute of Justice (NIJ) hired Hallcrest Systems, Inc., a group of highly experienced security consultants to study the role and resources of the private security industry in the United States, including its nature, extent and growth. These first comprehensive studies of the U.S. private security industry, known collectively as the *Hallcrest Reports,* demonstrated the growing and superior role of private security compared with public law enforcement.[74]

Hallcrest believed that four interrelated factors largely explained the greater employment and expenditure shift from public to private protection and the increasing growth of private security compared with the public police during the 1980s and 1990s: an increase in crimes in the workplace, an increase in fear (real or perceived) of crime, the limitations on public protection imposed by the "fiscal crisis of the state," and an increased public and business awareness and use of the more cost-effective private security products and services.

Hallcrest II identified nine distinct categories of the private security industry[75]:

■ Proprietary (in-house) security. **Proprietary security** means that a particular company has its own security department.

■ Contract Guard and patrol services. **Contract security** services are services that are leased or rented to another company.

■ Alarm services.

■ Private investigations.

■ Armored car services.

■ Manufacturers of security equipment.

■ Locksmiths.

■ Security consultants and engineers.

■ Other—including categories such as guard dogs, drug testing, forensic analysis and honesty testing.

As you can see, the duties and responsibilities of the private security industry are numerous and diverse.

Some recent examples of the increasing use of private security at large-scale events are the 2002 Olympic Winter Games in Salt Lake City, Utah, where almost $213 million was spent for security arrangements and more than 40,000 private security personnel were employed, and the 2004 Summer Olympic Games in Athens, Greece, where the Greek government spent more than $1.2 billion for security.

It is generally believed that the cost of private security is paid for by corporate America, but the consumer also pays for it. The cost of the private guard standing in front of or inside the corner jewelry store will necessarily be reflected in the price we pay for a bracelet we buy in that store.

The cost of the undercover security agent who tries to apprehend shoplifters in Sears, K-Mart, Wal-Mart, or Montgomery Ward is reflected in the cost of everything we purchase in those stores.

Many of the major private security firms, as well as many small ones, have a presence on the Internet. Students are urged to access these sites to find the many jobs and career opportunities in this area. Also, several professional organizations in this industry have a presence on the Internet.

Despite lower crime rates in the 1990s and 2000s, private security expenditures and hiring have kept increasing significantly.

Size and Scope of the Private Security Industry

David H. Bayley and Clifford D. Shearing, in their 2001 study, *The New Structure of Policing: Description, Conceptualization and Research Agenda,* reported that policing is being restructured and transformed in the modern world by the development of private protective services as important adjuncts to public law enforcement. They report that numerous nongovernmental agencies have begun to provide security services, and, in most countries, private police outnumber public police.[76]

It is very difficult to estimate the total size and scope of the private security industry and to compare it with the public security industry. As Samuel Walker, professor at the University of Nebraska at Omaha, reports, "The size of the private security industry is difficult to determine because it involves many small, private agencies, part-time employees, and security personnel that are employed by private businesses."[77] According to *The Economist,* "The most visible and fastest-growing parts of the private security business are in areas that were once the preserve of the public police. Since the functions of private security firms are much wider than those of the public, the equivalent numbers of private security guards and public police are not strictly comparable."[78]

Some estimates reveal that the private security industry has three times more employees than the public police have, with approximately 1.8 million private security personnel and specialists in the United States; private security responds to 50 percent of all crimes committed on private property; there are 60,000 private security firms in the

TABLE 2.4   U.S. Department of Labor Statistics Regarding Private Security Employment, 2005

Category	Employment	Projected employment
Private guards and gaming surveillance officers	1 Million	Faster than average
Private detectives and investigators	48,000	Faster than average
Security and fire alarm systems installers	46,000	Faster than average

SOURCE: Bureau of Labor Statistics, U.S. Department of Labor, *Occupational Outlook Handbook, 2004–05 Edition,* retrieved October 5, 2005, from http://www.bls.gov/oco.

United States, and Americans spend $90 billion a year on private security.[79] Generally, we can say that the size of the U.S. private security industry is enormous, and it has grown by almost exponential rates in the past several decades. It is one of the fastest growing industries in the United States and has tripled the public law enforcement industry in terms of money spent and persons employed; a tremendous number of jobs are available in the industry.

The 2004 *Occupational Outlook Handbook* produced by the U. S. Department of Labor, Bureau of Labor Statistics contains information on several occupational categories related to the private security industry: security guards and gaming surveillance officers; private detectives and investigators; insurance claim investigators; and security and fire alarm system installers. (See Table 2.4.) The following is a synopsis of the current employment statistics and job outlook for the major occupations in the private security industry.[80]

Security Guards and Gaming Surveillance Officers   Security guards and gaming surveillance officers held more than 1 million jobs in the latest reporting year. More than half of the jobs for security guards were in contract security guard and armored car agencies that provide security services on a contract basis, assigning their guards to buildings and other sites as needed. The other security officers were employed directly by proprietary organizations.[81]

Employment of security guards and gaming surveillance officers is expected to grow faster than the average for all occupations through 2012

as concern about crime, vandalism, and terrorism continue to increase. Casinos will continue to hire more surveillance officers as more states legalize gambling and as the number of casinos increases in states where gambling is already legal. Additionally, casino security forces will employ more technically trained personnel as technology becomes increasingly important in thwarting casino cheating and theft.

Private Detectives and Investigators   Private detectives and investigators held about 48,000 jobs in the latest reporting year. About a third of these were self-employed; almost a fifth of the jobs were found in investigations and security services, including private detective agencies, while another fifth were in department stores or other general merchandise stores. The rest of the jobs were primarily in state and local government, legal services firms, employment services, insurance carriers, and credit intermediation and related activities, including banks and other depository institutions.[82]

Keen competition is expected for these positions because they attract many qualified people, including relatively young retirees from law enforcement and military careers. The Department of Labor projects that employment in this field is expected to grow faster than the average for all occupations through 2012.

Insurance Claims Investigators   These employees are part of the larger Department of Labor's category of claims adjusters, appraisers, examiners, and investigators. Insurance claims investigators generally work for property, auto, and casualty insurance companies and deal with claims where there is a question of liability or when fraud or criminal activity is suspected. Their main role is to investigate claims, negotiate settlements, and authorize payments to claimants. Generally, when insurance adjusters or examiners suspect fraud, they refer the claim to an investigator. This fraud usually involves fraudulent or criminal activity, such as arson cases, false workers' disability claims, staged accidents, or unnecessary medical treatments. Some of the investigations can involve complicated fraud rings responsible for many claimants supported by dishonest doctors, lawyers, and even insurance personnel.[83]

Insurance investigators, along with adjusters, appraisers, and examiners, held about 241,000 jobs in the latest reporting year. Many insurance companies require that investigators have a college degree, and many prefer to hire former law enforcement officers, military personnel, private investigators, or experienced claims adjusters or examiners. The Department of Labor reports that this occupation is expected to grow about as fast as the average for all occupations until 2012 and that competition for these jobs will remain keen because it attracts many qualified people.

Security and Fire Alarm Installers These employees install, program, maintain, and repair security and fire alarm wiring and equipment and ensure that work is in accordance with relevant codes. This category excludes electricians who do a broad range of electrical wiring. For the latest reporting year, employment was 46,000 and is expected to rise faster than the average for 2002 through 2012.

Why Do We Have Private Security?

Considering the size and activity of the public police, why do we also have an enormous private security industry that is triple the size of the public police in personnel and money spent? Let us consider some of the many reasons.

Limited Jurisdiction of the Public Police Although the public police have legal police power and jurisdiction in the entire nation, they generally only exercise this power on public streets and thoroughfares, and in public places. They generally do not enter private premises unless citizens call them for an emergency or for some other police service.[84]

Legal Jurisdiction of the Public Police Many of the duties of the private security industry are beyond the legal scope of the public police. For example, the police cannot follow a spouse suspected of cheating on his or her spouse. The spouse must hire private security personnel, specifically a private investigator, to do this. Also, the police cannot escort every business owner to the bank when he or she has a large amount of money to deposit. These are duties for private security personnel. The police jurisdiction is the welfare of all citizens, not the welfare of just a few citizens.

Reactive Role of the Police Generally, the role of the police is reactive. They concentrate on arrests and investigations of past crimes. They also perform general patrol of public places and respond to emergencies. Generally, the role of private security is more proactive than that of the public police. Private security is more concerned with maintaining a sense of security by preventing crime and ensuring a feeling of safety rather than responding to past crimes and invoking the sanctions of the criminal law against offenders.[85] According to Robert J. Fischer and Gion Green, public law enforcement functions are society- or community-oriented, whereas private security functions are essentially client-oriented.[86] In other words, public law enforcement's primary obligation is to society because that is who pays them. On the other hand, private security's obligation is to the client who has hired them and who pays their salary.

Workload and Duties of Police The police are too busy responding to emergencies, arresting offenders, and providing all the duties we, as a society, ask them to do. We cannot expect them to provide services to every business or person requiring them. As a result of the heavy workload and duties of the public police, many in the business community believe that the public police are not doing the proper job for the business community. A survey by the U.S. Chamber of Commerce revealed that half of 446 business executives interviewed believed that law enforcement and the criminal justice system do a poor job of fighting crimes against business.[87]

Private Security Standards Today

Historically, the private security industry, primarily at the entry and nonmanagerial level, has suffered from a lack of professional standards and training. Lately, through the efforts of professional associations, members of academia, and government regulating agencies, we have seen significant improvement in this important area. In 2006, the Washington, D.C., Council passed a new law requiring training for the 11,000 private security guards in the D.C. area. The training will include building evacuation, emergency medical response, security procedures, and other important subjects.[88]

The U.S. Department of Labor reports that most states require guards to be licensed.[89] Recently, rigorous hiring and screening programs consisting of background, criminal record, and fingerprint checks and drug testing are becoming the norm in the occupation. In most states, applicants are expected to have good character references, no serious police records, and good health.[90]

There has been no legislation passed mandating federal regulation of licensing, regulating, hiring, and training standards. However, in December 2004, President George W. Bush signed Senate Bill 2845, popularly known as the Intelligence Reform Bill and the 9-11 Implementation Bill. The bill included the **Private Security Officer Employment Authorization Act of 2004,** giving employers the ability to request criminal background checks from the FBI for applicants and holders of security positions. It covers both contract and propriety security personnel and gives employers the opportunity, if the applicant or employee consents, to send fingerprints or other positive identification to the FBI for a criminal background check.[91]

Professionalization of Private Security

In 1955, a number of private security professionals developed a professional association to improve the image of private security—the American Society for Industrial Security (ASIS). Over the years, membership has increased greatly and the society has indeed improved the image of private security.

By 2005, ASIS International has more than 33,000 members and is the preeminent international organization for professionals responsible for security, including managers and directors of security. In addition, corporate executives, other management personnel, consultants, architects, attorneys, and federal, state, and local law enforcement become involved with ASIS International to better understand the constant changes in security issues and solutions. ASIS International provides educational programs and certifications that address broad security concerns.[92] It is dedicated to increasing the effectiveness and productivity of security professionals by developing educational programs and materials that focus on both the fundamentals and the most recent advancements in security management. ASIS International is headquartered in Alexandria, Virginia, and publishes a monthly magazine and an academic journal.

It offers three certification programs:

■ *Certified Protection Professional (CPP).* This certification designates individuals who have demonstrated competency in all areas constituting security management. Nearly 10,000 individuals have received the CPP certification since its inception in 1977.[93]

■ *Professional Certified Investigator (PCI).* Holders of the PCI certification have demonstrated education and/or experience in the fields of case management, evidence collection, and case presentation.

■ *Physical Security Professional (PSP).* The PSP designation is the certification for those whose primary responsibility is to conduct threat surveys; design integrated security systems that include equipment, procedures, and people; or install, operate, and maintain those systems.

These certifications are offered to individuals meeting specific criteria of professional knowledge and recognize them for having shown a high level of competence by improving the practices of security management. Candidates must meet certain basic standards of experience and formal education and must pass stringent comprehensive written examinations. These certifications are highly coveted by members of the security industry.

The ASIS International websites, *ASIS Online* and *Security Management Online,* first inaugurated in the mid-1990s, have become the repositories of the wealth of knowledge available in the industry.

College Education and Private Security

In 1976, only 5 colleges in the United States offered a bachelor's degree in private security, and no master's programs were available. By 1990, 46 colleges offered a bachelor's degree and 14 offered a master's degree.[94] Many professional and educational institutions and associations have assisted progressive thinking leaders in the private security industry in creating college level courses and programs specific to the industry.

Today, PhD programs in security are increasing, and academic and professional certifications are more prevalent and more attainable, particularly using online options. The American Military University (AMU) has collaborated with ASIS International to deliver an abundance of online degree programs. AMU offers certificates and degrees at the undergraduate and graduate levels focusing on such topics as homeland security, intelligence, information technology, and counterterrorism.[95]

Enrollment in academic security programs and internships is on the rise, both at the undergraduate and graduate level, says Robert McCrie, professor of security management, at John Jay College of Criminal Justice: "Those going into security see a correlation between the private sector and serving the country as a whole. They see private security as a part of homeland security."[96] According to McCrie, "The statistics paint a bright future for private security and those students looking to enter the market. It also looks bright for those looking to make a career change."[97]

This continuing attention paid to college education is starting to affect salaries. Security executives responding to the *ASIS International Employment Survey* reported that they earned on average 26 per cent more if they held four-year college degrees and 15 percent more if they held master's degrees.[98]

The increased demand for quality security education since the terrorist attacks of September 11, 2001, has altered course content and stimulated the development of many new degree programs. Also, since the September 11, 2001, attacks, more than 100 private and state colleges have rushed to create counterterrorism, disaster management, and homeland security courses, and thousands of students are pursuing degrees in that area, including emergency and disaster management, making them some of the fastest-growing fields in academia. These new programs include certificate programs, as well as bachelors, masters, and doctoral programs. They use an interdisciplinary approach, teaching students various social science and practical theories and techniques, and are directed at local officials, first-responders, and corporate managers who have the main responsibility for dealing with problems connected with disasters and terrorism. North Dakota State University in Fargo and George Washington University in Washington, D.C., have introduced doctoral programs.

In 2004, the Federal Emergency Management Agency (FEMA) reported that there were 115 colleges offering these programs and that 100 more colleges are considering adding these types of courses.[99]

In 2004 alone, the DHS gave about $70 million in grant money to colleges and universities to assist in developing new courses.[100] In 2004, the American Association of Community Colleges (AACC) announced it would appoint a 21-member task force on homeland security training for first responders.

The study of terrorism and emergency management has grown out of traditional disaster studies, which were once the domain of community colleges and focused on managing "first responders"—the police, fire, and paramedic departments that respond to hurricanes and riots. These new courses seek to educate local officials and corporate managers who have the major duty of mitigating disasters.

Homeland Security and Private Security

The status and size of the private security industry has increased exponentially since the terrorist attacks of September 11, 2001. Private security employees perform most of the homeland security jobs in our nation, and the private security industry is responsible for most of the protection provided to our nation's people, businesses, and critical infrastructure. A significant proportion of the billions of dollars in taxpayer monies spent by the DHS and local, state, and federal agencies go to the private security industry to protect the homeland.

The events of September 11, 2001, intensified the importance of security in the workplace. According to the Business Roundtable, an association of chief executive officers of leading American corporations, "Security is now a rising star in the corporate firmament. The people responsible for security have become much more visible to the top of the business and much more important to the business itself."[101]

Today, members of corporate executive protection departments and others concerned with personal protection pay constant attention to terrorist possibilities and develop plans to deal with these eventualities in this country and abroad.[102] Most multinational corporations have detailed executive protection plans, crisis management teams, and threat assessment strategies. Companies without security departments or those with smaller security departments often hire large contract security companies to provide corporate, executive, and homeland security services. These companies emphasize strategic prevention and conduct a threat assessment before establishing a prevention plan.

Private Investigations

A major area of private security is private investigations. The Bureau of Labor Statistics of the U.S. Department of Labor reported that private detectives and investigators held about 39,000 jobs in 2000 and that employment of private detectives and investigators is expected to grow faster than the average for all occupations through 2010. Median annual earnings were $26,750 in 2000.[103]

Given the academic studies of detective operations (see Chapter 10, "Investigations") that revealed that much of what detectives do is unproductive work and does not lead to solving crimes, many police departments drastically cut the number of persons they assigned to detective units. Today, generally only 10 percent of a department's personnel are assigned to detective duties. If you are the victim of a crime that does not merit an investigation, your only recourse may be to hire a private investigator if you want the crime solved.

We need private investigators because police power and resources are limited. In some areas of criminal and noncriminal activity, conventional law enforcement is either ill equipped or otherwise prohibited from getting involved. In cases of suspected insurance fraud, for example, most public police agencies have neither the personnel nor the financial resources to undertake intensive investigations. The search for runaway children is also too large a problem for public agencies, and the surveillance of unfaithful spouses is beyond the authority and jurisdiction of any public service agency.

A review of popular magazines and newspapers reveals that private investigators are involved in the following broad areas: investigating art thefts,[104] investigating terrorism cases,[105] investigating kidnapping cases,[106] following lovers and spouses,[107] helping Hollywood stars clear their names of damaging gossip,[108] conducting financial investigations for corporations and foreign governments,[109] checking prospective mates (with the threat of AIDS this could be very important),[110] attempting to free wrongly convicted convicts,[111] exposing defense fraud,[112] investigating business fraud,[113] working for corporate clients, investigating corporate drug rings, tracing stolen goods, tracking lost assets,[114] finding lost pets,[115] investigating insurance fraud, and serving subpoenas.[116]

The fundamental difference between the private investigator and public investigator is the investigative objective. Police and public investigators are primarily concerned with the interests of society, whereas the private detective serves organizational and individual interests.

Generally, there are no formal education requirements for most jobs as private investigators, although many have college degrees. Private detectives and investigators typically have previous experience in other occupations. Some work initially for insurance or collections companies or in the private security industry. Many investigators enter the field after serving in law enforcement, the military, government auditing and investigative positions, or federal intelligence jobs.

Former law enforcement officers, military investigators, and government agents often become private detectives or investigators as a second career because they are frequently able to retire after 20 years of service. Others enter from such diverse fields as finance, accounting, commercial credit, investigative reporting, insurance, and law. These individuals often can apply their prior work experience in a related investigative specialty. A few enter the occupation directly after graduation from college, generally with associate or bachelor's degrees in criminal justice or police science.

Most states and the District of Columbia require private detectives and investigators to be licensed. Training in subjects such as criminal justice is helpful to aspiring private detectives and investigators.

Similar to the public investigation, the private investigation may overlap into a criminal area. However, the private investigator has no authority by state law to investigate a legally proscribed crime and should inform the appropriate law enforcement agency in all cases involving criminal violations.

Private Employment of Public Police

Many public police officers **moonlight** (work on their off-duty hours) as private security guards. Almost all police departments require an officer to obtain the department's permission before obtaining private security employment. In some departments, the officers must find their own private employer; in others, the police department itself or a police organization serves as a broker in assigning off-duty officers to private employers. One department reported that 47 percent of its police officers had security work permits (department permission to work as private security officers while off duty); another department reported that 53 percent of its officers had work permits and worked a total of 20,000 off-duty hours in uniform, earning an average of $1,333 per officer.[117]

Three-quarters of the police departments that permit officers to perform private security on their off-duty hours allow the officers to wear their uniforms. Many departments also permit the off-duty use of other department equipment, including radios and vehicles.[118]

The use of public police as private security guards can lead to obvious problems. To whom is the officer responsible—the primary employer (the police department) or the private company? Who is responsible for the officer's liability in the event he or she makes a mistake? Should a police department continue to pay an officer who is out on sick report because of injuries sustained while working for a private firm? If an officer is guarding a local business and he or she observes a crime on the street, which obligation comes first—the obligation to the private business for security or the obligation to his or her oath of duty?[119]

Some are concerned that there are basic equity problems in the process of buying one's own private protection. As Walker has written,

> There are equity problems. Wealthy neighborhoods are able to purchase additional protection, whereas poor neighborhoods receive less protection because financially strapped city governments are unable to hire more police.[120]

Similarly, although the practice of using regular police officers to supplement private security has generally been permitted by state law, the use of private money to pay for public police has raised questions.[121] Some also argue that the use of public police at private shopping malls is also a problem. However, some police officials say that having public officers at private malls is just an extension of the community policing concept and insist that this practice does not raise questions of equity because everyone benefits. One public official said, "Our responsibility is to provide safety and security for the city of Stamford, period."[122] Another says it makes sense to send officers to malls, "This is where the people are."[123]

Some say that private security by itself violates democratic values because it is not generally under the control of the government as the public police are. For example, Marcia Chaiken and Jan Chaiken, in a National Institute of Justice report, warn that private security officers are not accountable because they are not bound by the decisions of the U.S. Supreme Court regarding civil liberties issues, such as *Miranda*.[124] Walker also refers to this issue: "Supreme Court decisions such as *Miranda* apply to public police . . . private security officers are not bound by these decisions."[125]

Some say that moonlighting can create conflicts of interest—for example, an off-duty officer moonlighting for a private security firm may be caught between the duty to enforce the law and the interest of his or her temporary employee. As an example, in the wealthy towns of Southampton and Easthampton, on Long Island, New York, off-duty police officers face few restrictions on working for private security firms. For decades, this region has been a popular site for high-priced fund-raisers, invitation-only movie premiers, extravagant corporate promotions, and fashion shoots. Some residents point a finger at the local police officers, who, when in uniform, are responsible for maintaining law and order but, when moonlighting as security guards, are protecting the very parties creating chaos. Many think the officers and departments allowing these officers to work as private guards are involved in a conflict of interest—who do they work for, the public or the private hosts. In July, 2004, at hip-hop promoter Sean (P. Diddy) Combs' riotous July Fourth extravaganza in Bridgehampton, New York, neighbors were infuriated by the pounding music, the rowdiness of the 1,500 guests, and the estimated 400 illegally parked cars clogging their streets. Combs had hired a security firm owned by a town police officer and his wife. There was a delay in shutting down the party by on-duty officers responding to complaints by the neighbors. Police were first called at 5 PM, but didn't start towing cars or writing parking tickets until 8 PM, and didn't shut down the party until 10:30 PM when security guards were forced to link arms to hold back a horde of party crashers. The town board had only issued a permit for no more than 400 guests to attend a 45-minute musical performance, cocktail party, and movie premiere. Town officials say they were sandbagged by Combs.[126]

Summary

- For the latest reporting year, local, state, and federal agencies spent approximately $185 billion for criminal justice agencies including police, corrections, and judicial services—an increase of 418 percent from 20 years ago.

- Local, state, and federal criminal justice agencies employed about 2.4 million people, for the latest reporting period—58 percent at the local level, 31 percent at the state level, and 11 percent at the federal level.

- Police protection spending amounted to about $83.1 billion of the total national criminal justice budget, up 240 percent from 20 years ago, and local policing expenditures, alone, accounted for about 45 percent of the nation's entire criminal justice budget.

- Law enforcement is primarily the responsibility of local governments—77 percent of the nation's police employees worked at the local level, 14 percent of police employees worked for the federal government, and state governments employed the remaining 10 percent.

- The United States does not have a national police force, unlike most other countries.

- U.S. law enforcement has developed over the years based on a philosophy of local control, the formal and informal use of local neighborhood forms of control to deter abhorrent behaviors.

- Every few years, the Bureau of Justice Statistics (BJS) attempts to paint a picture of law enforcement personnel and practices in its Law Enforcement Management and Administrative Statistics (LEMAS) program.

- For the latest reporting period, state and local governments in the United States operated almost 15,766 full-time law enforcement agencies, which included 12,656 general purpose local police departments, almost 3,061 sheriff's offices, and 49 primary state police departments. There are also approximately 1,400 special district police departments, and federal law enforcement agencies employed more than 156,600 full-time federal law enforcement personnel authorized to make arrests and carry firearms.

- The size and scope of the U.S. law enforcement industry is enormous and tremendously diverse and fragmented, and predominantly local.

- The federal government, in particular, responded to September 11th by creating the huge cabinet-level Department of Homeland Security, which merged and improved the many disparate federal agencies concerned with terrorism, homeland defense, and response to catastrophic emergencies. Local, state, and private agencies also reengineered themselves to address the need for homeland defense.

- The size of the U.S. private security industry is enormous. The private security industry has three times more employees than the public police, with approximately 1.8 million private security personnel and specialists in the United States; private security responds to 50 percent of all crimes committed on private property; there are 60,000 private security firms in the United States, and Americans spend $90 billion a year on private security.

Learning Check

1. Describe how extensive the safety industry is in the United States relative to personnel and money spent.

2. Most police in the United States are local, rather than state and federal. Discuss why this is so.

3. Discuss the issue of sworn law enforcement employee averages and give some examples of them.

4. Describe some major problems affecting metropolitan law enforcement.

5. Discuss some major problems affecting rural and small-town law enforcement.

6. Discuss the jurisdictional confusion in Indian country and tribal law enforcement.

7. Discuss how state police differ from local police.

8. Explain how federal law enforcement agencies differ from local and state police.

9. Discuss the scope of the private security industry in the United States.

10. Discuss some of the problems involved with using public police as private security guards.

Key Terms

centralized model of state law enforcement Combines the duties of major criminal investigations with the patrol of state highways.

contract security Private security services offered by industrial security firms and guard agencies to private employers or individuals on a contract basis.

decentralized model of state law enforcement A clear distinction between traffic enforcement on state highways and other state-level law enforcement functions.

Hallcrest Reports Two comprehensive reports commissioned by the National Institute of Justice on the private security industry in the United States.

joint federal and local task force Use of federal, state, and local law enforcement agents in a focused task force to address particular crime problems.

law enforcement employee average Number of law enforcement employees for each 1,000 residents.

LEMAS reports Statistical reports on law enforcement personnel data issued by the National Institute of Justice under its Law Enforcement Management and Administrative Statistics program.

local control The formal and informal use of local or neighborhood forms of government and measures to deter abhorrent behaviors.

moonlight Term for police officers working in private security jobs during their off-duty hours.

National Criminal Justice Reference Service (NCJRS) A national clearinghouse of criminal justice information maintained by the National Institute of Justice.

National Institute of Justice (NIJ) The research arm of the U.S. Justice Department.

Private Security Officer Employment Authorization Act of 2004 Federal law giving employers the ability to request criminal background checks from the FBI for applicants and holders of security positions.

proprietary security Security services provided by the organization or company itself.

sworn law enforcement employee average Number of sworn law enforcement employees for each 1,000 residents.

Organizing the Police Department

© Mark Reinstein/The Image Works

GOALS

- To acquaint you with the organizational and managerial concepts necessary to organize and operate a police department and to introduce you to alternative organizational models
- To acquaint you with the complexities of modern police organizations
- To show you how police departments are organized on the basis of personnel, area, time, and function
- To introduce you to the major ranks in a police department and to the responsibilities connected with those ranks
- To introduce you to the major units of a police department and the functions they perform

Introduction

Some of you reading this text want to become members of a police or other law enforcement department or some of you are just interested in what the police do and how they do it. Reading this chapter will give you a good insight into how a police department actually works.

This chapter deals with organizing a police department. Although we use the term *police department,* this is used as a generic term and includes other law enforcement agencies, such as federal, state, and county law enforcement agencies, including sheriffs' offices. In any organization, someone must do the work the organization is charged with doing, someone must supervise those doing the work, and someone must command the operation. Certain commonly accepted rules of management must be followed to accomplish the goals of the organization. This chapter will include a discussion of leadership and some organizational concepts such as division of labor, managerial definitions, manager or supervisors versus leaders; organizational model and structure, chain of command or hierarchy of authority, span of control, delegation of responsibility and authority, unity of command, and

rules and regulations and discipline. We also will offer alternatives to the traditional organizational model of policing, and then discuss the organization of the police department by personnel (rank), area, time, and function or purpose. We will look at the various ranks in a police department and examine the responsibilities of the people holding those ranks. Then we will discuss how a police department allocates or assigns its personnel by area, time, and function or purpose. Different organizations have very different words to describe the division of the department by personnel, area, time, and function, so the terminology here attempts to be generic rather than specific.

This chapter is designed to give you an awareness of the complexities involved in policing 7 days a week, 24 hours a day. Not all police organizations are as complex as what is described here. Actually, as we saw in Chapter 2, most police departments in the United States are small. The intent of this chapter, however, is to cover as many complexities of the police organization as possible to give you the broadest possible view of policing in the United States—what the police do and how do they do it.

Organizing the Department: Managerial Concepts

Before discussing the organization of a police department, some managerial concepts common to most organizations should be understood. These concepts include division of labor; managerial definitions; leadership; organizational model or structure; chain of command (hierarchy of authority); span of control; delegation of responsibility and authority; unity of command; and rules, regulations, and discipline.

Division of Labor

All the varied tasks and duties that must be performed by an organization must be divided among its members in accordance with some logical plan.

In police departments, the tasks of the organization are divided according to personnel, area, time, and function or purpose. Work assignments must be designed so that similar (homogeneous) tasks, functions, and activities are given to a particular group for accomplishment. In a police department, patrol functions are separate from detective functions, which are separate from internal investigative functions. Geographic and time distinctions are also established, with certain officers working certain times and areas. The best way to think of the division of labor in an organization is to ask the question, "Who is going to do what, when, and where?"

The division of labor should be reflected in an organization chart, a pictorial representation of reporting relationships in an organization (Figure 3.1). A good organizational chart is a snapshot of the organization. Workers can see exactly where they stand in the organization (what functions they perform, who they report to, and who reports to them).

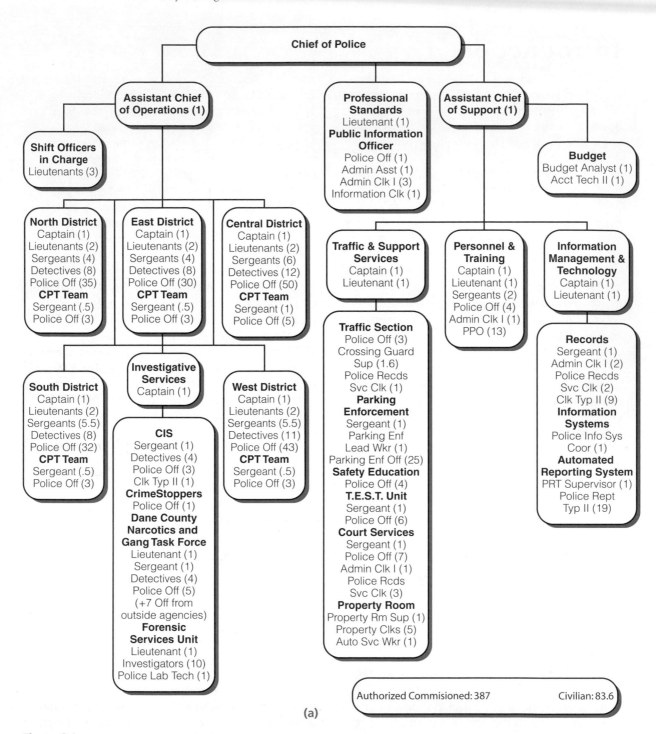

Chief of Police

Assistant Chief of Operations (1)

Professional Standards
Lieutenant (1)
Public Information Officer
Police Off (1)
Admin Asst (1)
Admin Clk I (3)
Information Clk (1)

Assistant Chief of Support (1)

Shift Officers in Charge
Lieutenants (3)

Budget
Budget Analyst (1)
Acct Tech II (1)

North District
Captain (1)
Lieutenants (2)
Sergeants (4)
Detectives (8)
Police Off (35)
CPT Team
Sergeant (.5)
Police Off (3)

East District
Captain (1)
Lieutenants (2)
Sergeants (4)
Detectives (8)
Police Off (30)
CPT Team
Sergeant (.5)
Police Off (3)

Central District
Captain (1)
Lieutenants (2)
Sergeants (6)
Detectives (12)
Police Off (50)
CPT Team
Sergeant (1)
Police Off (5)

Traffic & Support Services
Captain (1)
Lieutenant (1)

Personnel & Training
Captain (1)
Lieutenant (1)
Sergeants (2)
Police Off (4)
Admin Clk I (1)
PPO (13)

Information Management & Technology
Captain (1)
Lieutenant (1)

Investigative Services
Captain (1)

South District
Captain (1)
Lieutenants (2)
Sergeants (5.5)
Detectives (8)
Police Off (32)
CPT Team
Sergeant (.5)
Police Off (3)

West District
Captain (1)
Lieutenants (2)
Sergeants (5.5)
Detectives (11)
Police Off (43)
CPT Team
Sergeant (.5)
Police Off (3)

Traffic Section
Police Off (3)
Crossing Guard
Sup (1.6)
Police Recds
Svc Clk (1)
Parking Enforcement
Sergeant (1)
Parking Enf
Lead Wkr (1)
Parking Enf Off (25)
Safety Education
Police Off (4)
T.E.S.T. Unit
Sergeant (1)
Police Off (6)
Court Services
Sergeant (1)
Police Off (7)
Admin Clk I (1)
Police Rcds
Svc Clk (3)
Property Room
Property Rm Sup (1)
Property Clks (5)
Auto Svc Wkr (1)

Records
Sergeant (1)
Admin Clk I (2)
Police Recds
Svc Clk (2)
Clk Typ II (9)
Information Systems
Police Info Sys
Coor (1)
Automated Reporting System
PRT Supervisor (1)
Police Rept
Typ II (19)

CIS
Sergeant (1)
Detectives (4)
Police Off (3)
Clk Typ II (1)
CrimeStoppers
Police Off (1)
Dane County Narcotics and Gang Task Force
Lieutenant (1)
Sergeant (1)
Detectives (4)
Police Off (5)
(+7 Off from outside agencies)
Forensic Services Unit
Lieutenant (1)
Investigators (10)
Police Lab Tech (1)

Authorized Commisioned: 387   Civilian: 83.6

(a)

Figure 3.1
Organizational Chart of Two Police Departments: (a) Large Department—Madison, Wisconsin; (b) Small Department—Hanson, Massachusetts
Source: Courtesy of the City of Madison Police Department, Madison, Wisconsin.

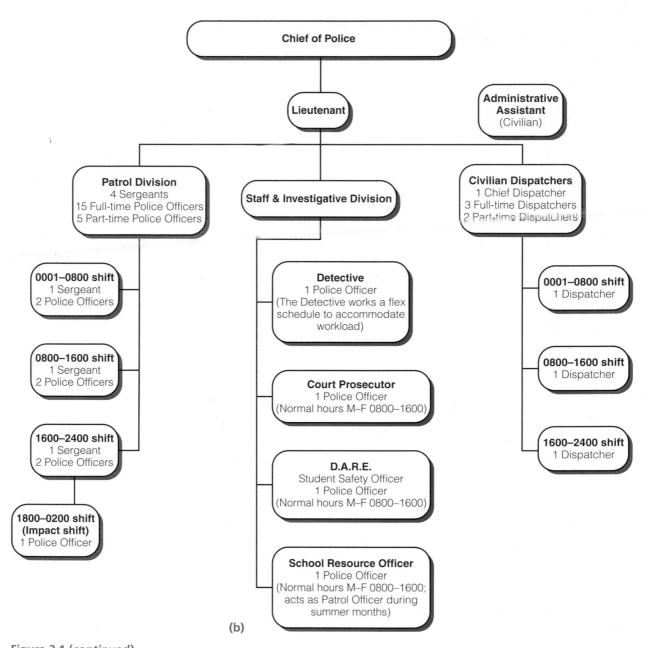

Figure 3.1 (*continued***)**

Source: Courtesy of the Town of Hanson Police Department, Hanson, Massachusetts.

Managerial Definitions

To understand the contents of this chapter, readers should know several managerial concepts.

Organization Nicholas Henry of Georgia Southern University, in the ninth edition of his classic text *Public Administration and Public Affairs,* gives us two definitions of **organization:** "a highly rationalized and impersonal integration of a large number of specialists cooperating to achieve some announced specific objective," and "a system of consciously coordinated personal activities or forces of two or more persons."[1] In 2005, Patrick O'Hara, in *Why Law Enforcement Organizations Fail: Mapping the Organizational Fault Lines in Policing,* gives us a simpler, but no less useful, definition:

> Organizations consist of a deliberate arrangement of people doing specific jobs, following particular procedures in order to accomplish a set of goals determined by some authority.[2]

Bureaucracy Max Weber, who many call "the father of sociology," gave us the classic features of the bureaucracy:

- Hierarchy
- Promotion based on professional merit and skill
- The development of a career service
- Reliance on and use of rules and regulations
- Impersonality of relationships among career professionals in the bureaucracy and with their clientele[3]

Nicolas Henry further explains the principles of bureaucracy as he tells us that the closed model of organizations goes by many names, including bureaucratic, hierarchical, formal, rational, and mechanistic and reports that *bureaucratic* theory or **bureaucracy** is one of the most common permutations, schools, or theories that has thrived. He says that the closed model of organizations has several characteristics, including the following: routine tasks occur in stable conditions; task specialization or division of labor is central; the proper ways to do a job are emphasized; conflict within the organization is adjudicated from the top; one's formal job description is emphasized; responsibility and loyalty is to the subunit to which one is assigned; structure is hierarchical (like a pyramid); one takes orders from above and transmits orders below, but not horizontally; interaction is directed toward obedience, command, and clear superior-subordinate relationships; loyalty and obedience to one's superior and the organization are emphasized, sometimes at the expense of performance; and personal status in the organization is determined largely by one's formal office and rank.[4] Henry says,

> Bureaucracy is in our bones. Prehistoric evidence unearthed at archeological digs suggests that the rudiments of a bureaucratic social order were in place 19,000 years ago. Bureaucracy predates, by many millennia, *Homo sapiens'* earlier experiments with democracy, the emergence of the globe's great religions, and the dawn of civilization itself. Bureaucracy may not be basic to the human condition, but it is basic to human society.[5]

Surely, as you will find in this chapter, modern police organizations can be considered bureaucracies.

Management What is management? Who are managers? **Management** is the process of running an organization so that the organization can accomplish its goals. The traditional principles of management have been described using the acronym **PODSCORB**, which stands for planning, organizing, directing, staffing, coordinating, reporting, and budgeting. Traditionally, managers and supervisors are the people tasked with the duty of managing—getting the functions of the organization accomplished through the members of the organization.

Managers/Supervisors or Leaders?

Leadership is an essential element to any organization. Are managers and supervisors leaders? Are the terms *manage* and *supervise* analogous to the word *lead*? Think of some of the supervisors or bosses you have worked for. Did they merely tell you what to do and how to do it, and then discipline you if you did it poorly? Or, did they motivate you to see the value of the work you were performing, to see how you fit into the broader mission of the organization, and to inspire you to perform your job to the very best of your ability?

Consider and think about these descriptions of leadership.

- Scholar William Arthur Ward wrote, "Leadership is based on inspiration, not domination; on cooperation, not intimidation.[6]
- The Chinese philosopher Lao Tzu wrote, "A good leader inspires people to have confidence in the leader; a great leader inspires people to have confidence in themselves."[7]
- John C. Maxwell, entrepreneur and author wrote, "A leader is one who knows the way, goes the way, and shows the way."[8]
- Former Chairman of the U.S. Joint Chiefs of Staff, and U.S. Secretary of State, Colin Powell, described the absences or failure of leadership: "The day soldiers stop bringing you their problems is the day you have stopped leading them. They have either lost confidence that you can help them or concluded that you do not care. Either case is a failure of leadership."[9]
- Even former professional football quarterback Joe Namath, the winner of Super Bowl III, gave us an example of leadership: "To be a leader, you have to make people want to follow you, and nobody wants to follow someone who doesn't know where he is going."[10]

As you can see, many people from diverse occupations agree on certain aspects of leadership, including motivation, teaching, team coordination, communication, inspiration, and example. Police departments need leaders, not merely managers and supervisors. You, by reading this textbook, are certainly learning about policing. We hope you will take advanced courses that will teach you about leadership. The accomplishments of the police are brought about by leaders and their personnel; the failures of the police are brought about by managers and supervisors who are not leaders, and the performance of their personnel reflect that lack of leadership.

Leadership is essential in police management and leaders, by teaching and setting example, develop new leaders. Many law enforcement agencies are providing leadership training for their supervisors and managers, and this training is creating better agencies and better delivery of services to the communities they serve.[11]

Traditional Organizational Model and Structure

The U.S. police are a civil, as opposed to a military organization. Despite this, our police departments are **quasi-military organizations** (organizations similar to the military). Like the military, the police are organized along structures of authority and reporting relationships; they wear military-style, highly recognizable uniforms; they use military-style rank designations; they carry weapons; and they are authorized by law to use force. Like the military, police officers are trained to respond to orders immediately.

Despite similarities, however, the police are far different from the military. They are not trained as warriors to fight foreign enemies but instead are trained to maintain order, serve and protect the public, and enforce the criminal law. Most important, the power of the police is limited by state laws and by the Bill of Rights.

Recall the formation of the London Metropolitan Police from Chapter 1. Although Sir Robert Peel wanted his police to be a civil agency rather than a military one, he ensured that they would be under strict military-like discipline as evidenced by the selection of veteran military leader Colonel Charles Rowan as one of the first London Metropolitan Police commissioners. Also, European police models used military organizational structures that were separate from local politics and were supervised by the state.

Robert C. Wadman and William Thomas Allison in their *To Protect and to Serve: A History of Police in America* discuss the history of the military model of police organization. They tell us that one of the interesting aspects of police reform in the Progressive Era of American government was the trend toward military models of police organizations. Progressives tended to apply the ideas of scientific management and corporate organizational models to running city governments, but they believed that the "military model" seemed more fitting to what the police were supposed to be doing—fighting a war against crime. They likened American police to a military force. Police departments had organized according to military structure and ranks, uniforms, weapons, insignia, salutes, and other symbols reflected the military analogy. The progressives continued this organizational model because they felt it was a way to separate the police from partisan politics and political machines. In this era, many departments organized or were reorganized along military lines and searched for former military officers to lead their departments. Departments continued to be or were remolded to become more centralized, specialized, and staffed with more administrative and operational support, much like a military unit.[12]

As one example, in 1923 a renowned U.S. Marine Corps general, Smedley Butler, a veteran of the Spanish-American War, the Boxer Rebellion, and other campaigns, was given leave from the Marines to become director of public safety in the corruption-laden and politically connected Philadelphia Police Department. "Within forty-eight hours, 75 percent of the thirteen hundred saloons in Philadelphia had been closed." He organized a special "bandit squad" armed with armored cars and sawed-off shotguns to raid prostitution houses and suspected crime dens. He was quoted as saying, "The only way to reform a crook is to kill him."[13]

Wadman and Allison report that the military analogy did prove effective as it helped further the separation between politics and police and made the administrative and operational aspects of police organization more efficient and effective.[14]

Todd Wuestewald and Brigitte Steinheider tell us that police administration gravitated toward a military orientation during a period of intensive reform early in the twentieth century. They agree with Wadman and Allison by writing that a paramilitary model of policing evolved in response to the widespread corruption and political interference that threatened the credibility of U.S. policing. In an effort to instill discipline, police leaders used authoritarian hierarchy as a tool against both political cooptation and low-level corruption. The scientific management principles of Frederick Taylor were applied to professionalize the police and this management philosophy continues to persist. This control-oriented supervision did succeed in bringing a degree of professionalism.[15]

Chain of Command (Hierarchy of Authority)

The managerial concept of chain of command (also called hierarchy of authority) involves the superior-subordinate or supervisor-worker relationships throughout the department, wherein each individual is supervised by one immediate supervisor or boss. Thus, the chain of command as pictured in the organizational chart shows workers which supervisor they report to; the chain of command also shows supervisors to whom they are accountable and for whom they are responsible. All members of the organization should follow the chain of command. For example, a patrol officer should report to his or her immediate sergeant, not to the captain. A captain should send his or her orders through the chain of command to the lieutenant, who disseminates the directions to the sergeants, who disseminates the information to the patrol officers (see Figure 3.2). Chain of command may be violated, however, when an emergency exists or speed is necessary.

Span of Control

The number of officers or subordinates that a superior can supervise effectively is called the span of control. Although no one can say exactly how many officers a sergeant can supervise or how many sergeants a lieutenant can supervise, most police management experts say the chain of command should be 1 supervisor to every 6 to 10 officers of a lower rank. Nevertheless, it is best to keep the span of control as limited as possible so that the supervisor can more effectively supervise and control. The number of workers a supervisor can effectively supervise is affected by many factors, including distance, time, knowledge, personality, and the complexity of the work to be performed.

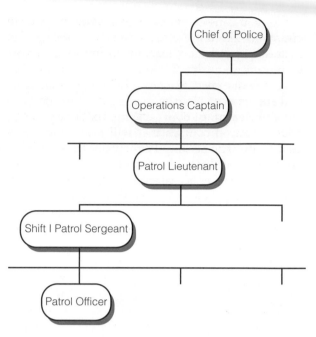

Figure 3.2
Chain of Command from Chief to Patrol Officer

Delegation of Responsibility and Authority

Another important managerial concept in police organizations is delegation of responsibility and authority. Tasks, duties, and responsibilities are assigned to subordinates, along with the power or authority to control, command, make decisions, or otherwise act to complete the tasks that have been delegated or assigned to them.

Unity of Command

The concept of unity of command means that each individual in an organization is directly accountable to only one supervisor. The concept is important because no one person can effectively serve two supervisors at one time. Unity of command may be violated in emergency situations.

Rules, Regulations, and Discipline

Most police organizations have a complex system of rules and regulations designed to control and direct the actions of officers. Most departments have operations manuals or rules and procedures designed to show officers what they must do in most situations they encounter. Rule books are often complex and detailed. In some major police departments, the police rule book can be 1-foot thick.

Police departments have disciplinary standards that are similar to, but less stringent than, the military's. Violation of department standards in dress, appearance, and conduct can lead to sanctions against officers in terms of reprimands, fines, or even dismissal from the department.

Managing problem employees is a common problem in policing as it is in every occupation. Thomas Q. Weitzel, an assistant chief who heads the Riverside, Illinois, Police Department's Administrative Division, writes,

> Identifying and managing problem employees can prove difficult. However, it is crucial that departments identify such individuals and handle them efficiently, objectively, and fairly. These workers can have a negative impact both inside and outside the department. Supervisors may find situations involving problem employees intimidating. However, they can follow effective procedures to identify who these individuals are and to work with them to improve their performance or, if this is not possible, to take more drastic measures.[16]

Alternative Organizational Models and Structures

In the face of continued scandals, police administrators have tended to maintain their almost phobic preoccupation with accountability and conformity. But according to Wuestewald and Steinheider, these control-oriented approaches fail to recognize that police work is, and always has been highly discretionary. The basic paradox of police hierarchy, they wrote, is that discretionary authority tends to be greater at the bottom of the police organization, where officers apply laws, policy, and regulations to situations that do not fit neatly into the rule book. Further, these discretionary choices are made in the field, far removed from the direct scrutiny of managers and supervisors. Many have lamented the apparent disjuncture between historically autocratic police management approaches and the requirements of community policing.[17]

A 2002 national survey of police departments revealed that although 70 percent of agencies had decentralized some operations in support of community police, only 22 percent have reduced bureaucratic hierarchy or pushed authority and decision making down in the organization to any significant degree.[18] A five-year study of police in Australia and New Zealand found that officers felt their organizations were not supportive of them and did not exhibit trust, respect, or recognition of their experience in decision-making processing.[19] As we will see later in Chapter 12, "Community Policing: the Debate Continues," community-oriented policing calls for more decision-making processes by frontline patrol officers.

For many years, the corporate world has been moving toward more democratic processes such as shared leadership and participative management models in workplaces as they try to improve their competitiveness by tapping the knowledge, talents, and creativity of their employees. In this process, organizational hierarchies have tended to flatten as autonomous work teams have replaced managerial levels. Scientific management theories have been replaced by more participative approaches such as employee empowerment, job involvement, and shared leadership. These methods of participative management have greatly improved organizations in productivity, quality, and worker satisfaction.[20] However, these power-sharing methods have found little acceptance in police organizations. At this time when police have been emphasizing proactive, community-oriented approaches to crime reduction and service providing, employee empowerment and shared leadership may offer significant advantages over traditional top-down police administration.

Shared leadership is known by many names: participative management, employee empowerment, job involvement, participative decision-making, dispersed leadership, total quality management (TQM), quality circles (QC), and others. These basic concepts involve any power-sharing arrangement in which workplace influence is shared among individuals who are otherwise hierarchical unequals. Such arrangements may involve various employee involvement schemes resulting in codetermination of work conditions, problem solving, and decision making.[21]

Shared leadership attained renewed interest in the 1980s and 1990s in response to the success Japanese industry seemed to be having with empowerment strategies such as TQM and QC.

Research in both the public and private sector have revealed that participative leadership has resulted in many improvements in job satisfaction, increased productivity, organizational citizenship behavior, labor-management relations, and overall organizational performance. The following are some recent examples of shared leadership programs in policing.

In 2006, Todd Wuestewald, chief of the Broken Arrow, Oklahoma, Police Department (BAPD), a 164-person, full-time department that provides a full spectrum of police services to a metropolitan community of 91,000 in northeastern Oklahoma, and Brigitte Steinheider, the director of Organizational Dynamics at the University of Oklahoma, reported on a program designed to incorporate frontline personnel into the important decision making processes of the BAPD. Since 2003, the BAPD has had participative management in the form of a steering committee called the *Leadership Team,* composed of 12 members of the BAPD who represent the police union, management, and most of the divisions, units, ranks, and functions in the department. The *Leadership Team* is an independent body with authority to make binding decisions on a wide range of policy issues, working conditions, and departmental strategies. The chief's office is not represented on the team, and all decisions are made democratically. The chief retains control of the team's agenda, but once an issue is referred to the team, its decisions are final and binding on all concerned. The team was trained by experts in organizational dynamics to facilitate team interactions and communication. An independent evaluation of the effects of the Leadership Team on departmental functioning, using quantitative and qualitative comparison of the department before and after the establishment of the team, revealed a dramatic improvement in employee relations in such areas as discipline, promotions, hiring, recognition, rewards, and incentives, as well as employee organizational commitment, pride, morale, motivation, productivity, leadership development, and the acceptance of community policing methods. The productivity of the BAPD also improved with increases in arrests of all types, traffic citations, field interview reports, and crime clearance rates.[22]

As another example, Vincent E. Henry, former New York City Police Department (NYPD) sergeant and 2003 Rhodes scholar describes the shared leadership features of the NYPD's *CompStat* program, a management process through which it identifies problems, devises problem-solving strategies, and then measure the results of these problem solving activities. *Many police departments around the world have adopted CompStat.* Henry writes that this program's key strategy is to decentralize an organization's management structure by increasing the authority, responsibilities, and accountabilities of frontline officers and mid-level managers. In reflecting community policing concepts and its problem-oriented focus, the officers on the street and their immediate supervisors work with community leaders and residents to identify their public safety concerns, analyze crime problems specific to each precinct, and develop proactive strategies for addressing them.[23]

As another example, in a 2006 article, Gregory P. Rothaus, chief of police in San Carlos, California, discussed team-building and team-building workshops (TBW). He asserts that no management fact is more obvious and more critical than the operations of the team. In organizations, members depend on each other for support, ideas, leadership, and encouragement. In law enforcement, this is especially critical because often lives are at sake.[24]

■────────────────────────────

Organizing by Personnel

A police department faces the same organizational challenges as any organization, and a major challenge is personnel. The civil service system plays a large role in police hiring. This section will describe that role, along with the quasi-military model of police, sworn versus nonsworn personnel, rank structure, and other personnel issues.

The Civil Service System

The **civil service system** is a method of hiring and managing government employees that is designed to eliminate political influence, favoritism, nepotism, and bias. Civil service rules govern the hiring, promoting, and terminating of most government employees. The **Pendleton Act** created a civil service system for federal employees in 1883, following the assassination of President James Garfield, who was killed in 1881 by someone who had been rejected for appointment to a federal office. Eventually, many state and local governments adopted their own civil service systems.

Wadman and Allison discuss the history of political influence, patronage, and corruption in police departments before the civil service system saying, "Police became one of the plums of boss patronage as well as a sure means to economic security for the individual policeman."[25] The corruption of police organizations and officers are central themes to police history. Before civil service, the competition for police jobs was intense and required the blessing of the local political machine. As an example, appointment to the New York City Police Department required the blessing of the local Tammany Hall (Democratic Party machine) block boss plus a $300 bribe.[26]

Samuel Walker suggests that the pre-civil service nineteenth century beat cop was more a "political operative" than a professional policeman serving the public good.[27] As some examples: Cincinnati dismissed 219 of its 295 police officers in 1880 after an election brought in a new political machine; in 1887, the Democratic victory over the Republicans in Chicago resulted in many native-born Americans being replaced by an influx of Irish Americans; in 1889, in Los Angeles, Republicans defeated the Democratic machine, then dismissed most of the Spanish American officers from the police department.[28] Although many cities adopted civil service reforms relatively quickly, many did not. In 1907, in Louisville, Kentucky, a change of political parties in an election resulted in the demotion of all Democratic captains to patrolman, replacing them with Republican ones. In 1917, the Democrats resumed power in City Hall and eliminated 300 patrol officers from the force of 491. In Salt Lake City, Utah, changeover in police personnel ran as high as 85 percent with each change of political party in power.[29]

Civil service regulations regarding hiring, promoting, and firing helped to remove the police from the partisan control of corrupt city political machines. By 1920, only ten of the sixty-three cities in the United States with a population of over one hundred thousand did not have a civil service system in place.[30]

Today, a vast majority of all government employees at the federal, state, and local levels are covered by the civil service system. Civil service has reduced political interference and paved the way for merit employment, a system in which personal ability is stressed above all other considerations. However, some civil service systems seem to guarantee life tenure in the organization and provide an atmosphere of absolute employee protection instead of stressing the merit that the system was initially designed to emphasize.

Today, most police departments, particularly larger departments, are governed by civil service regulations. Some complain that the civil service system creates many problems for police administrations because a chief or commissioner cannot appoint or promote at will but must follow the civil service rules and appoint and promote according to civil service lists. Additionally, it is often difficult to demote or terminate employees under the civil service system.[31] Although many criticize civil service rules, they help to reduce political influence and eliminate the autocratic power of a supervisor to hire, fire, or transfer employees on a whim.

An example of a noncivil service police department is the Hanson, Massachusetts, Police Department whose 26 sworn and 6 nonsworn members are hired on the local level without a civil service process.[32]

Sworn and Nonsworn (Civilian) Personnel

People who work for police departments fall under two major classifications: sworn members of the department, or police officers, and nonsworn members of the department, or civilians.

Sworn Members   **Sworn members** are those people in the police organization we usually think of as police officers, troopers, or deputy sheriffs. They are given traditional police powers by state and local laws, including penal or criminal laws and criminal procedure laws. Upon appointment, sworn members take an oath to abide by the U.S. Constitution and those sections of state and local law applicable to the exercise of police power.

The best example of police power is the power to arrest. Police officers need only to have probable cause (not definite proof) to make arrests for any crimes or offenses committed in their presence or not. *Probable cause* is a series of facts that would indicate to a "reasonable person" that a crime is being committed or was committed and that a certain person is committing or did commit it. A good example of facts leading to probable cause follows:

1. At 3 AM, screams from a female are heard in an alley.
2. An officer sees a man running from the alley.
3. Upon the officer's command, the man refuses to halt and rushes past the officer.

This gives the officer probable cause to stop the man, even though there is no "proof" yet of a crime. If it later turns out that no crime was committed, the officer has done nothing wrong because he or she acted under probable cause.

Citizens, in contrast, cannot use probable cause, and the crime must have actually happened. (Actually, this leaves citizens open for false arrest lawsuits). Additionally, citizens can only arrest for offenses actually committed in their presence, unless that offense was a felony.

In addition to the power of arrest, the police officer has the power to stop temporarily and question people in public places, to stop vehicles and conduct inspections, and to search for weapons and other contraband. The police officer has significantly more power to use physical force, including deadly physical force, than does the citizen.

These arrest and stopping issues are covered in more detail in Chapter 5, "The Police Role and Police Discretion," and in Chapter 13, "Police and the Law."

Nonsworn (Civilian) Members Nonsworn (civilian) members of police departments are not given traditional police powers and can exercise only the very limited arrest power given to ordinary citizens. Thus, they are assigned to nonenforcement duties in the department. They serve in many different areas of a police organization and in many roles. When we think of nonsworn members, we usually think of typists, 911 operators, and police radio dispatchers. However, nonsworn members serve in many other capacities as well, including clerical, technical, administrative, and managerial jobs. Their rank structure is generally not as vertical as that of sworn officers.

Rank Structure

Sworn members generally have a highly organized rank structure (chain of command). The lowest sworn rank in the police organization is usually the police officer (or in sheriff's offices—deputy sheriff), although many organizations have lower-ranked sworn officers, such as cadets or trainees, who generally perform duties similar to nonsworn members or assist sworn members in performing nonenforcement duties. Many cadets or trainees aspire to an eventual sworn position or are in training for one. In most organizations, those in training at the police academy are known as recruits or cadets and generally have the same legal authority as regular officers, except that they are generally not assigned to enforcement duties while still in training.

To say the police officer is the lowest rank in a police department may sound demeaning to the rank. However, it only refers to the relative rank in the organizational chart, not to the police officer's power or to the quality and importance of the service performed.

The following sections describe the various ranks in the police organization using generic terms. Most departments use the titles police officer, detective, sergeant, lieutenant, and captain. However, some organizations, such as state police departments and county sheriff's offices, use different terms to describe their members. In a state police force, the rank of trooper is almost identical to the rank of police officer. In a sheriff's office, the rank of deputy sheriff is synonymous with the rank of police officer.

The police officer/trooper/deputy sheriff is the most important person in the police organization. He or she is the person who is actually working on the streets, attempting to maintain order and enforce the law. A police agency is only as good as the quality of the men and women it employs.

Police Officer Police officers serve as the workers in the police organization. The average police officer is assigned to patrol duties (See Chapters 9 and 10, "Patrol Operations" and "Investigations," for a complete discussion of the activities of patrol officers.) Police officers perform the basic duties for which the organization exists. They are under the control of supervisors, generally known as ranking officers or superior officers. Ranking officers are generally known as sergeants, lieutenants, and captains. At the highest level in most police organizations are chiefs or commissioners. In some state police organizations, military ranks such as major or colonel are used. In federal law enforcement organizations, nonmilitary terms are used to

ON THE JOB

We're All Working Together

In many police departments, a disparity arises between the sworn and nonsworn personnel. Our department was no different. Smart police officers realize how important the support personnel are to their mission. The help you get when you need it from these essential areas of the department can make an officer's life much easier or harder.

I think of the difference it can make when you're running late for a court appearance and need to pick up some crucial evidence or paperwork and the individual who supplies that evidence or paperwork is very busy with lots of people before you. You didn't plan ahead and allow the time for the request that the department requires. If you're on good working terms with that employee, he or she might go out of the way and make the extra effort to help you out so you don't get in trouble. But if, on the other hand, you have treated that employee as a second-class citizen, that will be remembered, and you will wait your turn; no special effort will be made.

During my career, I had a few officers who didn't see the relationship between the jobs we were all doing and treated some of the support personnel in a less

than equal manner. If I ever saw this behavior, I would sit the officer down, and we'd have a chat about human relations and how we all work together and how these coworkers can make officers look good or bad. Officers usually heeded this advice, but some had to learn the hard way.

I know when I became a patrol captain and went from five years of the midnight shift to working days with 100 people in my division and the politics and events involved with day shift, I relied very heavily on my secretary, Lori. She had been working as the uniform division secretary for many years and had a great depth of knowledge and command of the history of the department. Perhaps she spoiled me, but for any question I asked, she was able to go to the files and pull out a file with all the backup documentation I needed to understand and plan. She was a crucial part of the working of the department, and luckily I had realized her expertise early in my career when I was a sergeant and appreciated all she did. She greatly eased my transition to uniform division captain and contributed to my success in that role.

—Linda Forst

reflect rank structure, such as agent, supervisor, manager, administrator, and director.

Corporal or Master Patrol Officer Many police departments have established the corporal or master patrol officer rank as an intermediate rank between the police officers and the first-line supervisor, the sergeant. Often this intermediate rank is given to an officer as a reward for exemplary service or for additional services performed, such as training or technical functions.

Detective/Investigator Some police officers in a department are designated as detectives, investigators, or inspectors. (The various names for ranks may be confusing because investigators in the San Francisco Police Department are called inspectors, whereas in the NYPD, and many others, the rank of inspector is that of a senior manager. In either case, their role is to investigate past crimes. (See Chapter 10, "Investigations," for a

complete discussion of the role and activities of the detective.) Detectives exercise no supervisory role over police officers except at a crime scene (the location where a serious crime occurred and where possible evidence may be present), where they are in charge and make most major decisions. In many departments, the assigned, case, or primary detective or investigator is the senior ranking officer at crime scenes and even outranks uniformed supervisors.

The role of the detective is generally considered more prestigious than that of police officer. Detectives generally receive a higher salary and do not wear uniforms. They are usually designated detectives by appointment, generally for meritorious work, rather than through the typical civil service promotional examination. Often detectives do not possess civil service tenure and can be demoted back to the police officer rank without the strict civil service restrictions applicable to the other ranks in a police organization.

Sergeant The first supervisor in the police chain of command is the sergeant. The sergeant is the first-line or front-line supervisor and, as many will say, the most important figure in the police supervisory and command hierarchy. To most police officers, the sergeant is the Boss. The sergeant has two main responsibilities in police operations. First, the sergeant is the immediate supervisor of a number of officers assigned to his or her supervision. This group of officers is generally known as a **squad.** (Generally, 6 to 10 officers make up a squad, and several squads may work on a particular tour of duty). The sergeant is responsible for the activities and conduct of members of his or her squad. Second, the sergeant is responsible for decisions made at the scene of a police action until he or she is relieved by a higher-ranking officer.

The sergeant is responsible for getting the job done through the actions of people. Thus, he or she must possess numerous important personal qualities, such as intelligence, integrity, and dedication. The sergeant also draws on numerous organizational, motivational, and communication skills.

Promotion to sergeant generally results in a pay raise and an increase in prestige, but it also is often a difficult adjustment from police officer and often is a very difficult job. As Scott Oldham, supervisory sergeant with the Bloomington, Indiana, Police Department says, "As sergeants, it is incumbent upon us to set the standards for our shifts."[33] Sergeants must make decisions, whether they are popular or not. That is their job. Oldham tells other sergeants, "It is up to the sergeants to teach others the right way to do things and to pass along the knowledge that has been gained from those that have gone before. Yes, doing things this way is hard. Making unpopular decisions is hard, but it is something that must be done for the good of everyone."[34]

Lieutenant Just above sergeant in the chain of command is the lieutenant. Whereas the sergeant is generally in charge of a squad of officers, the lieutenant is in charge of the entire platoon. The **platoon** consists of all of the people working on a particular tour (shift or watch). The lieutenant is in charge of employees and all police operations occurring on a particular tour.

Recall that the terms *squad, tour, shift, platoon,* and *watch* are used in this textbook as generic terms, and many departments use different terms to identify these same concepts.

Captain Next in the chain of command above the lieutenant is the captain. The captain is ultimately responsible for all personnel and all activities in a particular area, or for a particular unit, on a 24-hour-a-day basis. The captain must depend on the lieutenant and sergeants under his or her command to communicate his or her orders to the officers and to exercise discipline and control over the officers.

The captain's role however, is not merely administrative. According to Captain Robert Roy Johnson, a 35-year veteran of the Chicago Police Department and an adjunct professor in the Law Enforcement Management Program at Calumet College of Saint Joseph in Chicago, captains must always be cognizant of what is going on in their commands. He indicates that they should have an "open door policy" in which officers feel comfortable in knowing that they can stop in and talk to the captain and that captains need to step out and mingle with their officers. He says that interpersonal interaction with the rank and file is the key to being accurately informed and that a captain who holes up in the office tending to administrative duties only soon loses touch.[35]

Ranks above Captain Many larger municipal agencies have a hierarchy of ranks above the rank of captain. Inspectors generally have administrative control over several precincts or geographic areas, whereas assistant chiefs or chiefs have administrative control of major units, such as personnel, patrol, or detectives.

Chief of Police/Police Commissioner The head of the police agency is usually termed the *chief of police* or the *police commissioner.* Chiefs of police and police commissioners are generally appointed by the top official of a government (mayor, county executive, or governor) for a definite term of office. Generally, commissioners and chiefs do not have civil service tenure and may be replaced at any time.

Chiefs of police must take an active role in their agencies and properly communicate with employees, including labor representatives. John M. Collins, general counsel, Massachusetts Chiefs of Police Association, writes that in states with collective bargaining, police chiefs intending to implement a new rule or to make material changes to an existing set of rules and regulations should involve the union or unions representing various officer bargaining units before the effective date of

Chief Richard Adriaens stands in front of the Gillette, Wyoming police station after moving there from Royal Oak, Michigan when he was named chief. Many officers who attain rank often move to other departments to assume positions of chief of police.

such rules and regulations. Collins also says that even in organizations without bargaining units, chiefs should involve employees in the development and implementation of rules and regulations. He says that involving employees helps to ensure a sense of teamwork and recognition of the values of input and experience and can produce a sincere commitment to the rules and regulations.[36]

Other Personnel

Police departments are increasingly using nonsworn employees and civilians to perform tasks in the police department. This effort can increase both efficiency in the use of human resources and cut costs. Community service officers and police auxiliaries also help some departments operate more efficiently.

Civilianization The process of removing sworn officers from noncritical or nonenforcement tasks and replacing them with civilians or nonsworn employees is **civilianization.** Civilians with special training and qualifications have been hired to replace officers who formerly did nonenforcement

jobs (traffic control, issuing parking tickets, taking past-crime reports, and so on). Additionally, civilians with clerical skills have been hired to replace officers who were formerly assigned to desk jobs. Approximately one-quarter of all local police department employees are civilians.

The replacement of sworn officers by civilians in nonenforcement jobs is highly cost effective for police departments because civilian employees generally earn much less than sworn officers. This strategy also enables a department to have more sworn personnel available for patrol and other enforcement duties.

A study of civilianization programs found that managers and officers were favorably impressed with the use of civilians for nonenforcement duties. Many officers observed that civilians performed some tasks better than the sworn officers they replaced. Additionally, many officers tended to consider some of the noncivilianized jobs as confining, sedentary, a form of punishment, and not proper police work. Others in the study felt that civilians want careers in police work, and a sizable number of officers recommended that more be hired.[37]

© Andy Nelson/The Christian Science Monitor via Getty Images

Community Service Officers The President's Commission on Law Enforcement and Administration of Justice recommended that three distinct entry-level police personnel categories be established in large and medium-size police departments: (1) police agents, (2) police officers, and (3) **community service officers (CSOs)**.[38] Police agents would be the most knowledgeable and responsible entry-level position. They would be given the most difficult assignments and be allowed to exercise the greatest discretion. The commission suggested a requirement of at least two years of college and preferably a bachelor's degree in the liberal arts or social sciences. Some departments have adopted this recommendation and give these officers the title of corporal or master patrol officer.

Police officers would be the equivalent of the traditional and contemporary police officer. They would perform regular police duties, such as routine preventive patrol and providing emergency services. The commission recommended that a high school degree be required for this position.

CSOs would be police apprentices, youths 17 to 21 years of age, preferably from minority groups. They would have no general law enforcement powers and no weapons. The commission reasoned that because of their social background and greater understanding of inner-city problems, community service officers would be good police-community relations representatives. The commission suggested that the CSOs work with youths, investigate minor thefts, help the disabled, and provide community assistance. The commission also recommended that the lack of a high school diploma and the existence of a minor arrest record not bar the CSOs from employment. It also recommended that the CSOs be allowed to work their way up to become regular police officers.

Police Reserves/Auxiliaries Personnel shortcomings in police departments may be perennial or seasonal, depending on the jurisdiction. Some resort communities face an influx of vacationers and tourists during a particular season that can more than double the normal size of the population. In response to this annual influx, some communities employ "summertime cops."

The use of the term *reserve officer* has been very confusing. In many jurisdictions, reserve officers are part-time employees who serve when needed and are compensated. In other jurisdictions, reserves are not compensated. The key element regarding the reserve officer is that he or she is a nonregular but sworn member of the department who has regular police powers. Other volunteer officers, sometimes referred to as auxiliaries, do not have full police power. Perhaps the best definition of a reserve officer has been provided by the International Association of Chiefs of Police (IACP):

> The term "reserve police officer" usually is applied to a non-regular, sworn member of a police department who has regular police powers while functioning as a department's representative, and who is required to participate in a department's activities on a regular basis. A reserve officer may or may not be compensated for his or her services, depending on each department's policy.[39]

Reserve officers augment the regular force in police departments throughout the nation. Whether paid or not, they have full police powers. Many augment the traditional police force by providing law enforcement services, including patrol, traffic control, assistance at natural and civil disasters, crime prevention, dispatch operations, and numerous other functions.[40]

Each state varies in its requirements for becoming a reserve officer. South Carolina, for example, requires a minimum of sixty hours of police instruction and a firearms qualification conducted by a certified firearms instructor. The reserve candidate must then pass a rigid examination conducted by the South Carolina Criminal Justice Academy. The reserve officer in South Carolina cannot be paid. In North Carolina, however, a reserve candidate must receive the same training as a full-time officer. He or she must attend the Basic Law Enforcement Training Course, which consists of 488 hours of instruction at a host of community colleges or at the central North Carolina Justice Academy at Salemburg, North Carolina. Upon completion of the basic training, the student must pass a state board examination. Reserve officers in North Carolina can receive a salary from their employer.

In some cities, auxiliary officers are unpaid volunteers. Although they wear police-type uniforms and carry nightsticks, these auxiliaries are citizens with no police powers and they do not carry firearms. They usually patrol their own communities, acting as a deterrent force and providing the police with extra eyes and ears. Chapter 11, "Police and the Community," provides coverage of police volunteer programs.

Some Personnel Issues

Like all organizations with employees, police departments have a distinct set of personnel issues. Some important issues are lateral transfers, police unions, and other police affiliations (for example, fraternal organizations and professional organizations).

Lateral Transfers **Lateral transfers**, or lateral movement, in police departments can be defined as the ability and opportunity to transfer from one police department to another. Some states allow lateral transfers from one department in the state to another department and allow lateral transfers from out-of-state departments. Some states allow only in-state lateral transfers, and some states do not allow lateral transfers at all.

The major problem with lateral transfers is that many police pension systems are tied into the local government, and funds put into that fund cannot be transferred into other funds. Thus, lateral transfers in those departments can cause officers to lose all or some of their investments.

The President's Commission on Law Enforcement and Administration of Justice recommended developing a national police retirement system that would permit the transfer of personnel without the loss of benefits. A few experiments with portable police pensions have been tried.[41]

Police Unions Unions exist to harness the power of individual workers into one group, the union, which can then speak with one voice for all the members. Unions in the private sector have been on the decline, but public-sector unionism is growing, particularly among police. Police unions have become increasingly political, endorsing and actively campaigning for candidates at the local, state, and federal level. National umbrella police organizations tend to advocate adversarial tactics and rely on formal, legal redress of grievances.[42] Police unions are predominantly local organizations that bargain and communicate with the local police department and the mayor's or chief executive's office. Local unions often join into federations on a state or federal level to lobby state and federal legislative bodies. Some of the major national federations of local police unions are the International Union of Police Associations (IUPA), the Fraternal Order of Police (FOP), the International Conference of Police Associations (ICPA), and the International Brotherhood of Police Officers (IBPO). Some officers are also members of national federations of civil service workers, such as the American Federation of State, County and Municipal Employees (AFSCME).

As an example, all 55 sworn members of the town of South Kingstown, Rhode Island, Police Department, with the exception of the chief, are members of the IBPO and their contracts are negotiated with the town.[43]

By 1988, more than 70 percent of all American rank-and-file officers were covered by some form of collective bargaining agreement and that trend toward formal recognition will continue to grow in the future.[44] According to a 1997 article, the existence of a collective bargaining mechanism in large police agencies was significantly correlated with supplemental pay benefits such as hazardous duty pay, differential shift pay, education incentive pay, and merit pay.[45]

Police unionism has a long and colorful history. Police employee organizations first arose as fraternal associations to provide fellowship for officers, as well as welfare benefits (death benefits and insurance policies) to protect police families. In some cities, labor unions began to organize the police for the purpose of collective bargaining, and by 1919, 37 locals had been chartered by the American Federation of Labor (AFL). The Boston police strike of 1919, as we saw in Chapter 1, was triggered by the refusal of the city of Boston to recognize the AFL-affiliated union. In response to the strike, Calvin Coolidge, then the governor of Massachusetts, fired all the striking officers—almost the entire police department. Because of the Boston strike, the police union movement stalled until the 1960s, when it reemerged. During the 1960s, Patrolman's Benevolent Associations (PBAs) in major cities, using their rank-and-file officers, increased their lobbying and job actions, which ultimately weakened and reversed the political pressure against union recognition leading to a major victory scored by the New York City's PBA in 1964. Since then, the PBAs and the FOP have transformed from pressure groups into labor unions.[46]

The ultimate bargaining tool of the union has traditionally been the strike. Members of many organizations, such as the telephone company, the department store, the factory, and so on, strike to win labor concessions from their employers. Should police officers be allowed to strike? Many feel that police officers are special employees and should not have the right to strike. In fact, most states have laws that specifically prohibit strikes by public employees.

Despite the presence of laws against strikes, there have been strikes by police employees. In 1970, members of the New York City Police Department staged a wildcat strike, for which all officers were fined two days' pay for each day they participated in the strike. Police strikes have also been staged in Baltimore, San Francisco, and New Orleans.

New Orleans' police officers went out on strike twice in February 1979. The first walkout lasted for 30 hours and was designed to gain recognition of the union, bring the city to the bargaining table, and force agreement on selected economic demands. It was successful. The strike emboldened officers to seek additional concessions and to use the approaching Mardi Gras festivities as a bargaining chip. This walkout was also intended to include ranking officers in the bargaining unit and to compel the city to enter into a collective bargaining agreement with the union. The second strike, which forced the cancellation of Mardi Gras, lasted 16 days and was unsuccessful.[47]

W. J. Bopp writes that states lacking collective bargaining agreements for public employees are creating a climate in which strikes flourish. Even in cities that voluntarily negotiate with their police employees in the absence of enabling legislation, confusion and misunderstanding are likely to occur. Trouble is also likely to result when hostility, bitterness, distrust, and cynicism become dominant characteristics of the relationships between police labor and management.[48]

To avoid the penalties involved in a formal police strike, police union members occasionally engage in informal job actions to protest working conditions or other grievances felt by the officers. These job actions include the **blue flu** (where officers call in on sick report) and a refusal to perform certain job functions, such as writing traffic summonses.

Other Police Affiliations   Police officers affiliate on levels other than unions. The two major types of affiliations are fraternal and professional.

Police fraternal organizations generally focus on national origin, ethnic, or gender identification. Some examples in a specific very large urban police department include the Emerald Society (Irish American officers), the Columbian Society (Italian American officers), the Guardian Association (African American officers), the Schomrin Society (Jewish officers), the Policewoman's Endowment Society (female officers), and the Gay Officers Action League (gay, lesbian, and transgender officers).

The two major professional organizations for police officers, designed as a forum to exchange professional information and provide training, are the International Association of Chiefs of Police (IACP) and the Police Executive Research Forum (PERF), a research-oriented organization.

Organizing by Area

Police departments must be organized by personnel functions and by the geographic area they serve. Each officer and group of officers must be responsible for a particular well-defined area. Geographic areas may be beats or posts, and precincts, or stations or districts. Different organizations have very different words to describe these geographic groupings, so note that our terminology here is generic rather than specific. Figure 3.3 shows a map of the geographic breakdown of a precinct into beats or sectors.

Beats

The **beat** is the smallest geographic area that a single patrol unit—one or two people in a car or on foot—can patrol effectively. A beat may be a foot beat, patrol car beat, mounted beat, motorcycle or scooter beat, or even bicycle beat. Patrol car beats can be much larger than foot beats.

The beat officer ideally should know everyone living or doing business on his or her beat, as well as conditions and problems on the beat that require police assistance or concern. For this reason, a beat should be as geographically limited as possible, without being so small that it is nonproductive or boring to the officer.

Precincts/Districts/Stations

A **precinct/district/station** is generally the entire collection of beats in a given geographic area. In a small department, generally only one precinct serves as the administrative headquarters for the entire department.

The building that serves as the administrative headquarters of a precinct is generally called a precinct house or station house. The station house

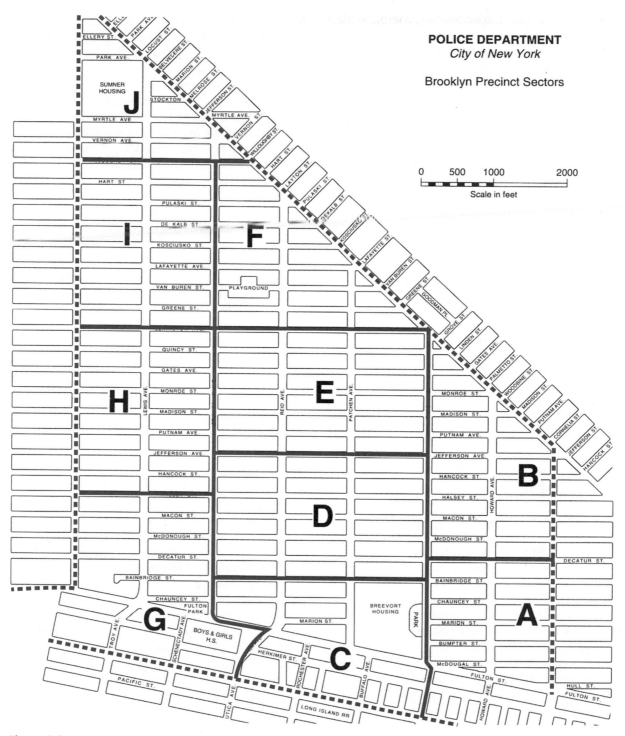

POLICE DEPARTMENT
City of New York

Brooklyn Precinct Sectors

0   500   1000   2000
Scale in feet

Figure 3.3
Map Dividing Precinct into Beats

usually contains detention cells for the temporary detention of prisoners awaiting a court appearance after an arrest, locker rooms in which officers can dress and store their equipment, administrative offices, meeting rooms, and clerical offices.[49]

Often in large urban departments, particularly in the Northeast, the *desk* serves as the centerpiece of the precinct/station/district. The desk is usually an elevated platform near the entrance of the station house, where all major police business is carried on. Prisoners are booked at the desk, and officers are assigned to duty from it. A ranking officer, generally a sergeant or lieutenant, is assigned as the *desk officer* and supervises all activities in the station house. The desk officer is usually in charge of the police blotter, a record in chronological order of all police activities occurring in a precinct each day. The blotter traditionally has been a large bound book in which all entries are handwritten by the desk officer. Although some departments still maintain the classic handwritten blotter, that term is now used more generically as the written record of all activity in a precinct. The blotter can include typed and computerized reports.

Organizing by Time

In addition to being organized by personnel and by area, a police department must organize its use of time. The following discussion will describe the tour system, including the common three-tour system, tour conditions, and steady (fixed) tours. Again, remember that different organizations have very different words to describe these groupings of schedules, so our terminology here is generic rather than specific.

The Three-Tour System

Common sense dictates that police officers, like other workers, can work only a certain number of hours and days before fatigue sets in and they lose their effectiveness. Tradition and civil service rules have established the police officer's working day as 8 hours. The traditional police organization separates each day or 24-hour period into three tours (also called shifts, platoons, or watches): a midnight or night tour, which generally falls between the hours of 12 midnight and 8 AM; a day tour, which generally falls between the hours of 8 AM and 4 PM; and an evening tour, which generally falls between the hours of 4 PM and 12 midnight. Shifts, tours, or watches do not necessarily have to fall between these exact hours; tours can be between any hours, as long as all 24 hours of the day are covered. Some departments have shifts that last longer than 8 hours, and they use the overlapping time as training time. Also, some departments use variations of the three-tour system, including two 12-hour tours a day or four 10-hour tours a week. An example of a department using 12-hour tours is the Nassau County, New York, Police Department, which uses a 7 AM to 7 PM and a 7 PM to 7 AM tour system. This department and others like them who use 12-hour tours thus have only two platoons rather than using the traditional three-platoon system.

Using the traditional three-tour system, it takes three officers to cover each day, one on the night tour, one on the day tour, and one on the evening tour. When days off, vacation time, and sick time are factored into the three-tour system, approximately five officers are required to cover each beat 24 hours a day, 7 days a week, 365 days a year. (Formulas to allocate personnel are available in police organization and management texts.)

Historically, police officers have been allocated evenly during the three tours of duty each day, with equal numbers of officers assigned to each of the tours. However, the academic studies of the police beginning in the 1960s discovered that crime and other police problems do not fit neatly into the three-tour system. Studies indicated that the majority of crime and police problems in the United States occurred during the late evening and early morning hours. Many police departments began to change their methods of allocating police personnel. Most now assign their personnel according to the demand for police services, putting more officers on the street during those hours when crime and calls for police officers are highest.

Tour Conditions

Each of the three shifts in the three-tour system has its own characteristics, as any police officer will tell you.

The midnight tour is sometimes called the overnight or the graveyard shift. Most people are sleeping during this time, although in some large cities a good deal of commerce and business occurs. The most common problems for police officers during this tour are disorderly and intoxicated people at home and on the street, domestic violence, disorderly tavern patrons, commercial burglaries, prostitution, and drug sales. In addition to handling these specific problems, the police provide their normal duties, such as routine patrol, response to emergency calls, aiding the sick and injured, and solving disputes.

The day tour occurs during the normal business hours in the United States. Stores and offices are open, highway and construction crews are working, and children are in school and at play. The most common activities for police officers during this tour are facilitating the traffic flow and ensuring the safety of those traveling to and from work by enforcing parking and moving violations, ensuring the safety of children walking to and from school and entering and leaving school busses, preventing robberies and other property thefts in commercial areas, and providing other normal police services.

The evening tour is generally the busiest for the police. The workday and school day are over, the sun goes down, and the hours of darkness are here. During the evening hours, normal adherence to acceptable ways of behavior often gives way to alcohol and drug abuse, fights, and disputes. The most common activities of the evening tour are facilitating traffic for the homeward-bound commuter; dealing with bar fights, violence at home, and violence on the streets; preventing and dealing with street and commercial robberies; and providing normal routine police services. The largest amount of police activity occurs on this tour, and the majority of officers are assigned to it.

Roll call or briefing is a crucial function in a police agency. Briefings occur at shift change and provide the officers coming on duty with information about what has occurred since their last tour of duty.

Steady (Fixed) Tours

Traditionally, some police departments have assigned their officers to rotating tours of duty: one or several weeks or months or other periods of night tours, one or several weeks or months or other periods of day tours, and one or more weeks or months or other periods of evening tours. Officers' days off are rotated to accommodate the three-tour system. This practice has caused tremendous problems for police officers in both their on-duty and off-duty lives. The strain of working different shifts repeatedly has a negative effect on eating, living, sleeping, and socializing and creates tremendous levels of stress.

There has been a move in recent years, therefore, to place officers on steady, or fixed, tours of duty, much like most other workers in the United States. Today, officers in many jurisdictions are assigned to steady night tours, day tours, or evening tours based on seniority or the officer's own choice. Police administrators hope that these steady tours will make officers' on-duty and off-duty lives more normal, thus eliminating the many problems created by shift work.

Organizing by Function or Purpose

The best way to organize a police department in this way is to place similar functions performed by the police into similar units. Thus, all members of the department performing general patrol duties are placed into a patrol division, whereas all officers performing detective duties are placed into a detective division. Again, remember that different organizations have very different words to describe functions or units, so note that our terminology here is generic rather than specific.

Line and Staff (Support) Functions

Police departments, like all organizations, must be organized by function or purpose. The simplest grouping of units or divisions of a department differentiates between line functions and staff (support) functions. Line functions are those tasks that directly facilitate the accomplishment of organizational goals, whereas staff (support) functions are those tasks that supplement the line units in their task performance.

One of the organizational goals of a police department is order maintenance. Thus, the patrol officers who actually patrol the streets to preserve order would be grouped under a patrol unit or

You Are There!

What Cops Do, as Told by Cops

The police department is a service organization, open for business 24 hours a day, 7 days a week. Dial their number, and somebody has to answer, no matter what it is you want. As one officer put it, "People'll [sic] call us for everything. If their toilet runs over, they call the police before they call the plumber." A police officer deals with the desperate, the disturbed, and all those people out there who are just plain lonely in the middle of the night. Their duties put them on intimate terms with the bizarre things people are doing to each other and to themselves behind all the closed doors and drawn shades in the community. While the rest of us look the other way, they cart away the societal offal we don't want to deal with—suicides, drunks, drug addicts, and derelicts. We call it keeping the peace, but the police officer often thinks of him- or herself as society's garbage collector. All smart cops carry a pair of rubber gloves in the car for handling dirt, disease, and death. They use their gloves much more than they use their guns.

Here are some stories cops tell.

The woman who opened the door for me was just a medium-sized female. The thing unique about her was that I could not see either one of her eyes. Her nose no longer existed. And she had a cavernous opening where there would have been a mouth and teeth. Her cheekbones were broken. In my entire career, I had never seen anybody who was so thoroughly battered. I asked her what the problem was and she said, "My husband beat me up." . . . I'm holding him by his left arm, escorting him down in handcuffs. As we stepped through the front door of the building, she tried to bury a twelve-inch butcher knife right between my shoulder blades. Kachunk! She hit me right in the old bulletproof vest. . . . It's human nature. When I walked in there she was upset because he beat her up so bad. When she saw her true love going out the door with the big bad police hauling him off, then no longer is he the villain. The police is the villain. It just tears your mind up. In spite of all that damage he did to her, she still loved him so much that she wanted me dead as opposed to taking him away.

So it goes, each shift ticked off by one stomach-curdling cup of coffee after another, enlivened only by the knowledge that something hairy just might happen. In those dead hours on the underbelly of the night when the orange glare of streetlights slowly gives way to the dawn, when the worst bar brawler is home in bed or sleeping it off in a cell and the ugliest hooker has made her quota, the hardest part of the job is staying awake until quitting time. By then the cop is running on residual adrenaline alone, struggling to remember that the next wife beater might have a deer rifle, that the next empty warehouse might not be empty after all, that the next underaged driver he stops for speeding might just be crazy enough to poke a pistol in a policeman's face and pull the trigger.

Police work is basically 99 percent pure bull___t, because there is just not that much going on. But it is punctuated by one percent of just sheer terror. And it happens just that quick. That's the reason a lot of policemen keel over from heart attacks, because of all that adrenaline pumping all of a sudden all of the time. Ulcers, too. You ride around for five or six shifts in utter boredom, worried to death about when the next time is going to happen.

SOURCE: From Mark Baker, *Cops: Their Lives in Their Own Words* (New York: Simon & Schuster, 1985), pp. 41–44.

patrol division. Another organizational goal of a department is to investigate past crime. Thus, the detectives charged with investigating past crimes would be grouped together under a detective unit or detective division. Patrol and detective units directly facilitate the accomplishment of the organizational goals of a police department; thus, they perform line functions.

Staff (support) functions are those functions of the police department that are not directly related to the organizational goals of the department but nevertheless are necessary to ensure the smooth running of the department. Investigating candidates for police officers, performing clerical work, and handing out paychecks are examples of staff (support) functions.

TABLE 3.1   Organizing a Police Department by Function or Purpose

Operations	Administration	Auxiliary services
Patrol	Personnel	Records
Traffic	Training	Communications
Criminal investigations	Planning and analysis	Property
Vice	Budget and finance	Laboratory
Organized crime	Legal assistance	Detention
Juvenile services	Public information	Identification
Community services	Clerical/secretarial	Alcohol testing
Crime prevention	Inspections	Facilities
Community relations	Internal affairs	Equipment
	Intelligence	Supply
		Maintenance

SOURCE: Used with permission from *Introduction to Police Administration,* 2d ed., pp. 114–115. Copyright 1998 Matthew Bender & Company, Inc., a member of the LexisNexis Group. All rights reserved.

Police Department Units

The late Robert Sheehan and Gary W. Cordner provided an excellent and comprehensive description of the basic tasks of a police department.[50] They describe 30 tasks or duties the police must perform to have an effective police department. They state that in very large police departments, separate units may be established to perform each task. In smaller departments, the tasks may be grouped together in various ways to be performed by certain units or people. Sheehan and Cordner divided the 30 tasks into three subsystems, which are similar to the previously mentioned division of line and staff functions. Their three task subsystems are operations, administration, and auxiliary services. Table 3.1 summarizes the Sheehan and Cordner system of organizing a police department by function or purpose.

Operational Units Operations are activities performed in direct assistance to the public. These are the duties most of us think about when we think of police departments, including crime fighting, crime detection, and providing service. Operational units include patrol, traffic, criminal investigations, vice, organized crime, juvenile services, community services, crime prevention, and community relations.

The *patrol* unit performs the basic mission of the police department: maintaining order, enforcing the law, responding to calls for assistance, and providing services to citizens. Patrol officers, who are usually on auto or foot patrol, are the backbone of the police service. They are the most important people in police service.

The *traffic* unit performs traffic control at key intersections and in other heavily traveled areas, enforces the traffic laws, and investigates traffic accidents. The *criminal investigations* unit investigates past crimes reported to the police in an effort to identify and apprehend the perpetrators of those crimes. The *vice* unit enforces laws related to illegal gambling, prostitution, controlled substances and other illegal drugs, pornography, and illegal liquor sales. The *organized crime* unit investigates and apprehends members of criminal syndicates who profit from continuing criminal enterprises, such as the vice crimes just mentioned, extortion, loan sharking, and numerous other crimes. The *juvenile services* unit provides a multitude of services to juveniles, including advice and referral to appropriate social agencies designed to assist youth, particularly youthful offenders. This function also investigates cases of child abuse and neglect.

The *community services* unit provides a multitude of services to the community, including dispute resolution, crime victim assistance, counseling, and other routine and emergency services. It also coordinates relationships between the police and the community, including numerous partnership programs between the police and the community. The police *crime prevention* unit attempts to organize and educate the public on methods people can take alone and with the police to make themselves at less risk to crime. Some techniques include target hardening, neighborhood watch programs, and operation identification programs. The *community relations* unit attempts to improve relationships between the police and the public so that positive police-community partnerships can develop to decrease crime and improve the quality of life in U.S. neighborhoods.

Administrative Units Administration in a police department is defined as those activities performed not in direct assistance to the public but for the benefit of the organization as a whole, usually from 9 AM to 5 PM, five days a week. Administrative units include personnel, training, planning and analysis, budget and finance, legal assistance, public information, clerical/secretarial, inspections, internal affairs, and intelligence.

The *personnel* unit performs the duties generally associated with corporate personnel departments, including recruiting and selecting candidates for police positions and assigning, transferring, promoting, and terminating police personnel. The *training* unit provides entry-level training to newly hired recruits and in-service training for veteran officers. The *planning and analysis* unit conducts crime analyses to determine when and where crimes occur so they can be prevented. This unit also conducts operational and administrative analysis to improve police operations and the delivery of police services. The *budget and finance* unit of the police department is involved in the administration of department finances and budgetary matters, including payroll, purchasing, budgeting, billing, accounting, and auditing. The *legal assistance* unit provides legal advice to members of the department, including patrol officers. The *public information* unit informs the public, through the news media, about police activities, including crime and arrests. This unit also informs the public about methods people can take to reduce their chances of becoming crime victims. The *clerical/secretarial* unit prepares the necessary reports and documents required to maintain police record keeping. The *inspections* unit conducts internal quality control inspections to ensure that the department's policies, procedures, and rules and regulations are

being followed. The *internal affairs* unit investigates corruption and misconduct by officers. Finally, the *intelligence* unit conducts analyses of radical, terrorist, and organized crime groups operating in a police department's jurisdiction.

Auxiliary Services Units Auxiliary services are defined as activities that benefit other units within the police department, but on a more regular and frequent basis than do administrative activities. Auxiliary services functions are usually available to assist the police officer 24 hours a day. Auxiliary services units include records, communications, property, laboratory, detention, identification, alcohol testing, facilities, equipment, supply, and maintenance.

The *records* unit of a police department maintains department records, including records of crimes and arrests, statistics and patterns regarding criminal activity, and records of traffic accidents. The *communications* unit answers incoming calls to the department's 911 telephone lines and assigns police units to respond to emergencies and other requests for police services. The *property* unit inventories and stores all property coming into the custody of the police, including evidence, recovered property, and towed and recovered vehicles. The *laboratory* unit examines and classifies seized evidence, including drugs, weapons, and evidence found at crime scenes (for example, fingerprints, fibers, and stains). The *detention* unit provides temporary detention for prisoners awaiting their appearance in court. The *identification* unit fingerprints and photographs criminals, classifies prints, and maintains identification files. The *alcohol-testing* unit administers driving-while-intoxicated tests for court prosecution.

The *facilities* unit of a police department maintains buildings designed for police use, such as station houses, offices, and detention facilities. The *equipment* unit maintains the numerous types of equipment necessary for the department's effective operation. The numerous supplies necessary for the proper operation of the department are purchased by the *supply* unit. Finally, the *maintenance* unit keeps all facilities and equipment serviceable.

Table 3.2 shows the breakdown, by rank and assignment, of a police department. By reading the top line of the chart and following it down to the bottom line ("Total"), one can easily see that there are a total of 165 employees in this department, with 82 police officers, 19 ranking officers (1 chief,

TABLE 3.2 Staffing of a Police Department by Function and Time

	Chief	Captain	Lieutenant	Sergeant	Police officer	Civilian	Coordinators	Crossing guards	Total
Office of the Chief	1					1			2
Operations Division		1				½			1½
Patrol Bureau									
8–4			1	3	21				25
4–Midnight			1	3	23				27
Midnight–8			1	3	15				19
Detective Bureau									
8–4			1		4				5
4–Midnight					1				1
6–2					1				1
Juvenile Bureau									
8–4			1		2				3
6–2					1				1
Traffic Bureau									
8–4				1	3		2	57	63
4–Midnight					3				3
Midnight–8					2				2
Prosecutions Unit					2				2
Fingerprint and Photography Unit					None full-time				
Administration and Services Division		1	1			½			2½
Planning and Records Bureau					1	2			3
Payroll, Billing and Budget Unit					1				1
Community Services and Training Unit					2				2
Custodial Services						1			1
Total	1	2	6	10	82	5	2	57	165

SOURCE: Used with permission from *Introduction to Police Administration,* 2d ed., p. 38. Copyright 1998 Matthew Bender & Company, Inc., a member of the LexisNexis Group. All rights reserved.

2 captains, 6 lieutenants, and 10 sergeants), 5 civilians, 2 coordinators, and 57 crossing guards.

By reading the details under "Police Officers" from the top line down, one can easily see that 59 of the officers are assigned to the Patrol Bureau (21 to 8 AM-to-4 PM tours, 23 to 4 PM-to-midnight tours, and 15 to midnight-to-8 AM tours); 6 to the Detective Bureau; 3 to the Juvenile Bureau; 8 to the Traffic Bureau; 2 to the Prosecutions Unit; 1 to the Planning and Records Bureau; 1 to the Payroll, Billing, and Budget Unit; and 2 to the Community Services and Training Unit.

Summary

- Organizations consist of a deliberate arrangement of people doing specific jobs and following particular procedures to accomplish a set of goals determined by some authority.

- The major managerial concepts common to most organizations are managerial definitions, organizational model or structure, division of labor, chain of command (hierarchy of authority), span of control, delegation of responsibility and authority, unity of command, and rules, regulations and discipline.

- There is a drastic difference between mere managers or supervisors and leaders. In addition to managing and supervising, leaders motivate, teach, coordinate, communicate, inspire, and set examples.

- Most police originations use quasi-military or military models of organization, which has led to the professionalization of the police but resulted in a lack of participation by the rank and file. This has also caused a paradox of leadership in policing because most decisions in policing are actually made by police officers acting autonomously on the street.

- Power-sharing methods have found little acceptance in police organizations. Police have been emphasizing proactive, community-oriented approaches to crime reduction and service providing, and employee empowerment may offer significant advantages over traditional top-down police administration.

- The civil service system has eliminated much political influence, favoritism, nepotism, and bias in police employee management.

- Sworn members of police organizations are those given traditional police powers by state and local laws, such as arrest and the ability to stop, question, and search. Nonsworn members are those without these traditional police powers who perform managerial, administrative, technical, and clerical duties in police organizations.

- Civilianization is the process of removing sworn officers from noncritical or nonenforcement tasks and replacing them with civilians or nonsworn employees.

- Unionization has a long and colorful history in policing. Today, most police unions are local and most American rank-and-file officers are covered by some form of collective bargaining agreement.

- The size of the geographic area many police agencies cover forces them to subdivide the area into smaller areas of responsibility, such as beats.

- Because of the responsibility of being available 24 hours a day, 7 days a week, the police often employ a three-tour system.

- The functions the police are charged with performing are complex and diverse: maintain order, enforce the law, and provide services to citizens. These functions are generally charged to a department's operational units—primarily patrol, criminal investigations, traffic, and community services units. The police also perform administrative duties and auxiliary services.

Learning Check

1. Identify the major managerial concepts that must be considered when organizing a police department.

2. Discuss some of the essential elements of a bureaucracy.

3. Discuss some of the qualities of a leader.

4. Discuss how police departments exercise their quasi-military nature.

5. What is "shared leadership"? Describe and discuss some recent examples of it in policing.

6. Compare and contrast the benefits and drawback of civil service regulations in policing.

7. Describe the differences between sworn and nonsworn or civilian police department members.

8. Name some ways in which civilianization can benefit a police department.

9. Discuss the special problems that must be dealt with in organizing a police department that operates 7 days a week, 24 hours a day.

10. Identify the backbone of the police department, and tell why this is the most important person in police service.

Key Terms

beat The smallest geographical area an individual officer can patrol.

blue flu Informal job actions by officers in which they refuse to perform certain job functions in an attempt to win labor concessions from their employers.

bureaucracy An organizational model marked by hierarchy, promotion on professional merit and skill, the development of a career service, reliance on and use of rules and regulations, and impersonality of relationships among career professionals in the bureaucracy and with their clientele.

chain of command Managerial concept stating that each individual in an organization is supervised and reports to only one immediate supervisor.

civilianization The process of removing sworn officers from noncritical or nonenforcement tasks and replacing them with civilians or nonsworn employees.

civil service system A method of hiring and managing government employees that is designed to eliminate political influence, favoritism, nepotism, and bias.

community service officers (CSOs) A level of entry-level, police employee without general law enforcement powers suggested by the President's Commission on Law Enforcement and Administration of Justice.

lateral transfers The ability and opportunity to transfer from one police department to another.

leadership An influence relationship among leaders and followers who intend real changes that reflect their mutual purposes.

management The process of running an organization so that the organization can accomplish its goals.

nonsworn (civilian) members Police employees without traditional police powers generally assigned to noncritical or nonenforcement tasks.

organization A deliberate arrangement of people doing specific jobs, following particular procedures to accomplish a set of goals determined by some authority.

Pendleton Act A federal law passed in 1883 to establish a civil service system that tested, appointed, and promoted officers on a merit system.

platoon All of the people working on a particular tour or shift.

PODSCORB Acronym for the basic functions of management including planning, organizing, directing, staffing, coordinating, reporting, and budgeting.

precinct/district/station The entire collection of beats in a given geographic area; the organizational headquarters of a police department.

quasi-military organization An organization similar to the military along structures of strict authority and reporting relations.

reserve officer Either part-time compensated or non-compensated sworn police employees who serve when needed.

shared leadership Power sharing arrangement in which workplace influence is shared among individuals who are otherwise hierarchical unequals.

span of control The number of officers or subordinates that a superior can supervise effectively.

squad A group of officers who generally work together all the time under the supervision of a particular sergeant.

sworn members Police employees given traditional police powers by state and local laws, including penal or criminal laws and criminal procedure laws.

unity of command A managerial concept that specifies that each individual in an organization is directly accountable to only one supervisor.

The Personal Side
of Policing

© Royalty-Free/Corbis

Becoming a Police Officer

© Joel Gordon

GOALS

- To show you where you can find information on jobs in law enforcement
- To make you aware of the police selection process
- To acquaint you with the standards that must be met to be accepted for employment as a police officer
- To give you a sense of the type of individuals police departments are interested in employing
- To acquaint you with the police academy training, field training, community policing training, and probationary periods required in many police departments

Introduction

Becoming a police officer is very different from obtaining most other jobs in the United States. The men and women applying for police jobs in the United States must be carefully screened to determine if they have the necessary attributes for this challenging position. Why? Because we trust these individuals with our liberty and safety. We give them guns and enormous discretion.

Many reading this textbook are interested in becoming police officers. Some want to become officers because it is a secure job with a good salary and good benefits. Some are attracted to police work because they find the work exciting or because of the opportunity to help others. When police officer candidates are asked why they are looking for a police officer position, they often cite these reasons. Researchers have found, however, that the new generation of police recruits' work values have shifted. These new candidates value their active participation in the workplace. They are less compelled by loyalty to a company or organization and do not want to be limited to taking orders and adhering to strict job duties. They want to actively participate in their work roles and want work that is meaningful and in which they feel valued. They want to be actively involved in the decision-making processes at the work place.[1] Many are realizing that the police role can fill these requirements.

There are also students who may want to go into the criminal justice field for the same reasons but aren't sure they want to be sworn police officers carrying guns and making arrests. In recent years, many agencies have increased the use of civilians in their departments. Roles traditionally filled by sworn officers have been turned over to civilians when departments analyzed these jobs and determined that it wasn't necessary to have an officer with a badge and a gun performing these jobs. When faced with budgetary challenges and unfilled police officer positions, this allowed the departments to put more police officers on the street. Though it varies from department to department depending on size and location, these civilian positions may include crime analysts, community service officers, telecommunicators, crime prevention specialists, evidence technicians, accident investigators, victim liaisons, records clerks and managers, and crime scene technicians.

The Largo, Florida, Police Department took this idea one step further. The department is reaching out to "people with abilities" a term that those with disabilities use to remind others that they possess talents and capabilities to fill many positions. Individuals interested in the criminal justice field but physically unable to perform the job of a police officer can be "reasonably accommodated" as defined by the **Americans with Disabilities Act** and serve their communities by filling a role behind the scenes and freeing sworn officers to work on the street. For example, a criminal justice student who was paralyzed in a car accident was hired to work in the planning and research division and contribute in a valuable way to the department's mission.[2]

Civilianization of positions within police agencies opens opportunities to individuals wanting to serve their community and be involved in an exciting profession but not necessarily in an enforcement capacity. This movement has been encouraged by the Federal Community Oriented Policing Services (COPS) grants that funded increased use of technology and civilians to put sworn police officers on the street. This trend also allows the department to employ "people with abilities" as well as older workers and make the workplace more representative of the community. However, because of the sensitive nature of the positions, these civilian positions are subject to most of the same requirements, standards, and hiring procedures as the police officer position.

This chapter is designed to show how the average person begins a police career. We will discuss the recruitment process, the job analysis, standards (necessary qualifications to become a police officer), the selection process, the police training process, and the probationary period. The chapter also contains some examples of standards, testing procedures, and requirements for selected police departments.

Today's officer is better educated, better trained, and more representative of the entire community than ever before. Educational levels have risen; training programs, both pre-service and in-service, have improved; and department personnel are more diverse than ever before.

Finding Information on Jobs in Policing

Where do you find information about available jobs in policing or criminal justice in general? Many traditional sources have been used for years, including media advertising, as many police departments today are recruiting through radio, television, and newspapers.

All government entities have human resource or personnel departments that have job postings for both police officer and civilian positions. You can also usually obtain information regarding the next police examination or other information regarding the police by visiting or calling the local police station or headquarters. Many police departments, in an effort to recruit college-educated men and women, participate in college job fairs, and many high school career days include representatives from local police departments or other criminal justice agencies.

In recent years, the Internet has arisen as a favorite choice among employers to get the message out about their job openings because it is a preferred place for applicants to seek information. Searching the Internet for "law enforcement job opportunities" results in numerous websites with links to job listings. The U.S. Department of Labor site also provides job descriptions and responsibilities for various law enforcement positions.

Most police departments have their own sites on the web that include employment information among other information provided to the public. These websites provide a wealth of information and can even allow potential officers to get an idea of the department's organizational culture to help determine whether they feel they would "fit" with a particular department. Most departments also provide information about their requirements and the hiring process. Many address frequently asked questions, give advice on training for the physical agility portion of the test, and provide contact information for further clarification. The Internet provides a time-saving and nonthreatening way of obtaining information about a law enforcement career. There are also websites for private enterprises that have assumed the testing role for many smaller law enforcement agencies in various regions of the country. They also provide current information regarding their process and requirements.

You Are There!

Indiana State Police Qualifications

Basic Eligibility Requirements
1. Must be a U.S. citizen
2. Must be at least 21 and a maximum of 40 years old when appointed as a police employee
3. Vision correctable to 20/50
4. Must possess a valid driver's license
5. Applicants must possess a high school diploma or GED

Selection Process
1. Submission of completed application form
2. Written test
3. Physical ability test
4. Oral interview
5. Polygraph/psychological tests
6. Background investigation
7. Fitness examination/psychological evaluation
8. Superintendent's review

SOURCE: Indiana State Police website, 2006, www.in.gov/isp/career

Word-of-mouth advertising by family members and friends is a common way people receive information about jobs in policing and criminal justice. Many police departments view their current officers as effective recruiters with an accurate perception of the job and what it entails. Through their daily interactions with citizens, officers come into contact with individuals who could be good officer candidates. These recruiters can informally provide valuable information to interested individuals and encourage them to consider a law enforcement career. With the increased competition among departments in the last few years for qualified candidates, some departments are providing financial incentives to officers who recruit successful candidates, including bonuses or paid time off.

An added bonus for college students is the intern program that is required in many criminal justice programs. Students work for a local government agency for a semester while earning college credit. These programs are valuable for two reasons: (1) Students see firsthand what working in a particular agency is like and thus are better equipped to make well-informed decisions regarding future career plans; and (2) students may obtain inside information regarding job opportunities that may not be available to the general public.

Standards in Police Selection

Each police department sets standards, or necessary qualifications, that it requires in selecting its prospective police officers. In recent years, these standards have changed to allow a greater number of females and minorities to become police officers, but they are still more stringent than standards in most other professions. The police standards cover physical, age, and education requirements, as well as criminal record restrictions.

Physical Requirements *PT examples*

At one time, the main requirement for becoming a police officer was the size of a young man's body and his physical strength and courage. Over the years, we have come to realize that brains are more important than brawn in police work. Also, the former physical requirements discriminated against women and minorities. Today, physical requirements are still stringent, but departments are under pressure to demonstrate that the physical requirements are job related and not arbitrary. With the passage of the Americans with Disabilities Act, departments are required to make "reasonable accommodations" for physically challenged employees. The changing role of police officers coupled with rapid technological advances makes it incumbent upon police administrators to examine whether their physical requirements for police candidates are valid in today's environment or whether they are actually keeping excellent potential candidates out of the process.

Height and Weight Requirements Height and weight requirements for police department applicants have changed dramatically in recent years. Only a few decades ago, most departments required officers to be at least 5 feet 8 inches tall. This is no longer a requirement; consequently, women and minorities can enter the police ranks more easily.

In 1977, in *Dothard v. Rawlinson*, the Supreme Court threw out a 5-foot 2-inch, 120-pound minimum height and weight hiring qualification for a correctional officer, stating that the employer failed to demonstrate this requirement as necessary for performance of the job.[3] Courts typically do not support minimum height and weight requirements but do support the need for maximum weight standards or the weight and height relationship.

Vision Requirements Many police departments require an applicant to have very good uncorrected vision that must be correctable to 20/20 vision with eyeglasses or contact lenses, as well as to be free from color blindness. These requirements have created a roadblock for many otherwise qualified candidates. Some contest this requirement, because many police officers wear glasses, and police work does not require perfect uncorrected vision. In recent years, most agencies require vision that is correctable to 20/20, as illustrated by the Madison, Wisconsin, vision requirement as described on its website of "binocular vision correctable to 20/20; normal peripheral vision & no significant eye disease."[4]

It has been long thought that a police officer should have relatively good vision because of the potential for officers to lose their glasses during an altercation with a suspect or have their glasses get fogged up or spotted with rain, which could limit the officer's abilities to see sufficiently. The popularity of contact lenses makes this even less of a problem. With the increased utilization and success of vision correction surgery, vision is less of a concern for applicants today than it was even five years ago.

Smoking

Though over the years many police departments have prohibited smoking in public because of concerns for a professional appearance, health and monetary considerations have now become issues for law enforcement agencies. In an effort to respond to rising medical costs for personnel and to keep officers healthy and productive for a longer time, many departments have implemented no-smoking policies. Generally, current officers are grandfathered in, but new hires must sign affidavits stating they have not smoked tobacco for a year and will not smoke tobacco once employed by the agency. This prohibition applies on or off duty, and it is a condition of employment. Some departments are afraid of the civil rights implications in these types of rules but prohibit smoking in police facilities and vehicles in an effort to reduce smoking and to minimize exposure for other employees to secondhand smoke. Some departments have had no-smoking policies in place for more than 10 years, and so far, they have withstood court challenges. Courts have traditionally upheld that public safety employers have a legitimate interest in the health and fitness of their employees.[5]

Age Requirements

Until recently, most police departments required that an officer be between the ages of 21 and 29 at the time of appointment. Anyone over the age of 29 was considered too old for employment. Sometimes, exceptions were made for those with previous military or police experience. The number of years a candidate served in the military or in previous police employment were added to the maximum age limit. The percentage of departments with maximum age limits has dropped significantly in recent years, largely because of age discrimination issues. Many police departments, however, still do not want to accept candidates past a certain age.

A few years ago, several applicants who took a New York City Police Department (NYPD) police officer examination when they were under the age limit weren't called until much later but still expected to be hired. However, on May 31, 1997, a Manhattan Supreme Court justice upheld the NYPD's policy of limiting new officers to applicants under age 35. The judge said that age limits on public-safety jobs are acceptable exceptions to laws against age discrimination. The applicants had passed the necessary physical, psychological, and educational tests but were denied appointment just before they were to be appointed. A city law setting a maximum age of 34 for new recruits expired in 1993 and was not renewed, but the city argued that police work is stressful and physically demanding and therefore better left to people younger than 35. Eighty passing applicants were denied appointment.[6]

Despite this court ruling, most departments do not have an official upper age limit. Their concerns in hiring revolve around pensions and health issues and the related medical costs. Some departments will hire officers retiring after 20 years with another department, and it is not unusual to see officers enjoy two lengthy police careers in two different departments. Actually, many law enforcement agencies have come to value the more mature and experienced candidate. They have had positive experiences with the older officers that they have hired, leading them to be open to this valuable part of the work force. Some departments noticed an increase in older applicants after September 11, 2001, perhaps fueled by a feeling of patriotism. Many of the older applicants are retired from the military and are particularly well-suited to the discipline and demands of a law enforcement career. The Mobile, Alabama, Police Department recently had two 51-year-old recruits perform notably in the academy—one received the Chief's Award and one was elected class president. The Mobile Department believes the recruits will have no problem meeting the challenges of the job after making it through the academy.[7]

Education Requirements

Among local law enforcement agencies, as reported by the Bureau of Justice Statistics (BJS) in 2006, 81 percent of local departments required a high school diploma, 17 percent had some type of college requirement, and only 1 percent required a four-year college degree in 2003. This was a slightly higher education requirement than in 2000 when 15 percent had some type of college required and 1 percent required a four-year degree. However, the same report indicated that the percentage of officers employed by a department with some type of college requirement was 33 percent in 2000—three times as many as in 1990. The minimum high school diploma requirement may not necessarily reflect actual selection practices because many departments favor applicants who meet more than the minimum standards and do value education for their officers. According to the BJS local police report, 32 percent of departments offer educational incentive pay and 35 percent provide **tuition reimbursement** to their officers.[8]

In reviewing requirements nationally, it appears that most departments with college requirements have major universities nearby, perhaps giving them a larger pool of candidates to draw from as well as providing access to higher education for in-service personnel. As we saw earlier in the text, most federal law enforcement agencies require a four-year college degree for employment. The more sought-after departments, with better pay and benefits, are more likely to require college degrees.

The development of college programs for the police was first stimulated by the recommendations of the National Commission on Law Observance and Enforcement (*Wickersham Commission Report*) in 1931,[9] which discussed, among other police problems, the poor state of police training in the United States. The idea of proper training can be traced back to Sir Robert Peel when he advocated good training as a way to decrease crime. However, the real impetus behind the relatively high levels of police education in recent decades was the **Law Enforcement Education Program (LEEP)**, a federal scholarship and loan program operated by the U.S. Department of Justice between 1968 and 1976. LEEP spent more than $200 million in grants and loans to students in "law enforcement–related" college programs. LEEP funds supported more than 500,000 "student years" of college education. About 90 percent of the students in the program were in-service sworn officers.[10]

Considerable debate has arisen over the desirability of college education for police officers. Many experts believe that all police officers should have a college degree. As early as 1967, the President's Commission on Law Enforcement and Administration of Justice recommended, "The ultimate aim of all police departments should be that all personnel with general enforcement powers have baccalaureate degrees."[11] Though almost 40 years have passed, this goal is far from becoming a reality. This debate about whether a college education makes an individual a better police officer continues. When coupled with the current problem of finding enough candidates to provide for a healthy selection process, most departments are reluctant to impose a higher education requirement. Despite the years and the increased number of police officers with college degrees, there can still be tension between officers who have degrees and those that do not. This issue can affect officers' ability to be promoted and, consequently, their financial status, so it is an emotional issue.

The ideal of an educated workforce in general has taken hold, and society extends that concept to include desiring more education for their police officers.[12] But, within the law enforcement community, there is an ongoing debate and subtle teasing about whether "book smarts" or "street smarts" are most important and of most benefit to police officers. It is sometimes questioned whether well-educated police officers will be happy and satisfied with a law enforcement career.

Over the years, police officers have gone from being minimally trained and poorly equipped to being highly trained in the latest technology, and the public expects police officers to be professional, educated, and up-to-date. This overall perception has been exaggerated by the current popularity of the CSI shows with what has been referred to in law enforcement circles as the CSI effect. The public expects local law enforcement to have all the knowledge, skills, and abilities that the CSI stars seem to possess.

As police officers confront complex social issues and, in this era of community policing, are expected to be problem solvers rather than reactive agents, higher education is valuable. The officers will be better able to understand and analyze cultural issues and societal problems and communicate these with the community and government leaders.[13]

Most of the information about the importance of a higher education for police officers is anecdotal. The studies to date have been inconclusive and contradictory. Some studies have found a positive correlation between higher education and job performance and a negative correlation with citizen complaints.[14] Others have found no relationship between education levels and job performance, commendations, or complaints.[15]

The report of the National Advisory Commission on Higher Education for Police Officers, often called the Sherman Report, stated that some evidence shows that officers with more education become dissatisfied with policing as a career more often than do officers with less education. The report also said that the lack of career opportunities for the educated and ambitious officer is a serious problem in law enforcement agencies, and that new officers with college degrees are often resented by veteran officers with no college experience. The report concludes that evidence indicates that some departments punished officers with more education by denying them career opportunities.[16] The Sherman Report criticized current police higher education programs for "servicing the status quo." It suggested that higher-education programs for the police should offer them a "broadening" experience, which would enable them to expand their abilities to deal with their professional problems. The Sherman Report also recommended recruiting college-educated young people, rather than sending recruits to college and argued that police departments should recruit students from liberal arts programs rather than law enforcement programs.[17]

An interesting study in St. Paul, Minnesota, found that having a four-year degree didn't necessarily correlate with positive work habits, but those with a bachelor of arts degree (rather than a bachelor of science degree) are excellent employees who use less sick time, receive more commendations, and are disciplined less often. The bachelor of arts degree might increase an individual's comfort level with ambiguity and frequently changing conditions. Bachelor of science degree programs tend to emphasize collecting verifiable facts and drawing conclusions based on these facts.[18]

A major concern for law enforcement agencies recently is the ability to have a high-quality applicant pool from which to select their candidates. Administrators feel that the higher the education requirement, the smaller their applicant pool will be. There is also a concern for possibly discriminating against minorities when a higher education requirement is imposed. There is anecdotal evidence to back this up as well as some empirical evidence to support this theory. L. K. Decker and R. G. Huckabee report in their study of 190 police officers over five years that increased education requirements would reduce the pool of minority applicants and that it would eliminate 75 percent of the officers who failed to complete the probationary period.[19]

Department administrators feel they're in a quandary as they strive to have both a large, diverse, and high-quality applicant pool as well as a highly educated police force. The Indiana State Police reluctantly dropped its college requirement for applicants in December 2005 in an effort to increase its applicant pool, including minorities.[20]

Other departments are strongly behind their educational degree requirements. The Arlington, Texas, Police Department is one of the nation's most highly educated departments and has required a bachelor's degree since the late 1980s. They have the benefit of having a university with a highly regarded criminal justice program in Arlington. Administrators there as well as the *Police Association for College Education* at Mineral, Virginia, believe that college-educated police officers are better able to use their brains over brawn when solving problems and understand the legal issues governing their behavior.[21]

This issue is unlikely to go away. Overall, society, police administrators, and police officers see the value in having an educated police force. At times, the real world problems and practical matters of recruitment and selection might interfere with the desired goal of more education. The demands placed on officers as our society rapidly changes will necessitate educational requirements being constantly reassessed by departments and state Peace Officer Standards and Training commissions (POSTs) and perhaps more and better incentives and requirements being put in place to speed the realization of the goal for a fully college educated police force.

Prior Drug Use

Departments have continually faced the problem of a candidate's prior drug use. Should a candidate be disqualified because of prior drug use? Is experimentation with marijuana enough to dismiss a candidate? What about cocaine? How many prior uses of drugs are acceptable?

Recently, many departments around the country have liberalized their policies regarding drug use because of a smaller applicant pool as well as societal changes. According to John Firman, the research director for the International Association of Chiefs of Police (IACP), the most common restriction is 10 years for hard drugs and 5 for marijuana.[22] A recent study found a lot of flexibility in department policies on police applicants and marijuana use. The most important issues to departments were the number of times and when it was used. There is no consensus among departments, but 35 percent of the departments surveyed did not reject outright candidates who had used marijuana. Outright rejection of otherwise suitable candidates for smoking marijuana is felt to be counterproductive to recruiting efforts. They may have guidelines in writing, but there is a considerable amount of flexibility in the policies, and the word used is often "may" regarding whether marijuana use will disqualify an applicant. Applicants are usually given an opportunity to explain their drug use, and the circumstances, how many times, and when are examined by the hiring agency. The agencies prefer to look at the totality of the process rather than a single criterion, taking into consideration the individual and the organization's reputation as well as community expectations and desires.[23] Drug restrictions vary widely from agency to agency and will require research by interested applicants for whom this is an issue. A policy or action that is too liberal can raise issues of liability for agencies. Most departments also have random drug testing, and officers can be fired and stripped of their state certificate if found to be using drugs.

Criminal Record Restrictions

People wishing to become police officers must respect the rules of our society and must adhere to these rules. The lack of a significant criminal record is a requirement for becoming a police officer. However, many police departments recognize that people may make mistakes, especially when young, that might result in an arrest. Police departments also distinguish between arrests and convictions. A Justice Department survey discovered that 99 percent of all police departments conduct criminal records checks for all applicants and 98 percent conduct background investigations.[24] Most departments will reject a candidate with a felony conviction, but a misdemeanor conviction does not necessarily prohibit a person from employment. Like drug use, the severity and violence of the crime, the circumstances surrounding the crime, the time lapse since the crime, and the age of the individual when the crime was committed will be examined. Applicants who have concerns should check the websites of the agencies they are interested in. Most of them will post exactly what the disqualifying crimes are. Agencies have an interest in not wasting the applicant's or the agency's time and want to make that information available. Remember that in the U.S. criminal justice system, a person is not considered guilty until convicted in court.

Along with the issue of criminal records is undetected criminal activity. This will be explored during the background investigation, polygraph exams, and interviews.

The Recruitment Process

According to Gary W. Cordner and Robert Sheehan, police departments seem to discourage applicants from applying. Sheehan and Cordner also point to the low esteem in which police are held in some communities and the fictitious television image of the police as other factors that discourage qualified applicants from applying for police jobs.[25]

Some potential candidates may have negative images of police, whereas others may perceive the physical attributes as being beyond their reach. Since September 11, 2001, the law enforcement occupation has been more favorably viewed and, as the media focused on the heroes who served on 9/11, many realized they were everyday people with a desire to help and contribute to society. With dedication and hard work, these individuals had attained their goals.

In recent years, recruiting adequate numbers of qualified police candidates has become increasingly challenging. The U.S. war on terror means that many potential police officer recruits are serving their country overseas. In their 2004 report *Hiring and Keeping Police Officers,* the National Institute of Justice found that since 2000, more than half of small agencies (population less than 50,000) and two-thirds of large agencies (population greater than 50,000) reported a lack of qualified candidates make it difficult to fill vacancies.[26] Some possible explanations cited by the report as well as others include the following:

- The strong economy luring candidates into the private sector
- Increased education requirements
- High attrition because of retiring baby boomers
- The deployment of qualified candidates in Iraq and Afghanistan
- The booming homeland security industry after 9/11 luring officers and candidates away from law enforcement

More than 80 percent of the nation's 17,000 law enforcement agencies are facing vacancies they're unable to fill.[27]

Successful police recruiters recruit in high schools and colleges, among other places. In an effort to attract minorities, many departments recruit at predominantly minority colleges in their region. Recruiters also often attend church gatherings, women's shows, and women's athletic events to reach others who may not have considered a law enforcement career. Numerous departments throughout the United States use the local media (especially television and radio) to recruit for their examinations.

Rapid changes in U.S. demographics have made recruiting minorities for police careers more essential than ever before. The U.S. Census Bureau predicts that by 2050, minority populations will be 49.9 percent of the population. Hispanics will constitute approximately 25 percent, African Americans 15 percent, and Asians 8 percent of the population.[28]

The age of the U.S. population is also changing, and the percentage of the population between the ages of 16 and 24 (the ages traditionally recruited from for police jobs) is declining. According to the U.S. Census Bureau, by 2050 the percentage of Americans age 65 and over will increase from 12 to 21 percent.[29]

Despite some of the challenges faced by departments in recruiting recently, in the long term, law enforcement is a very good choice of a career for many people. It is an opportunity to serve the public and offers a good, steady income despite the ups and downs of the economy over 20 years. Individuals who choose to progress up the ranks have an opportunity to make a very good salary and, ultimately, an excellent pension. In positions of leadership, they will also have an opportunity to shape law enforcement policies into the future. Currently, individuals entering the job market might not be closely examining these issues and, consequently, turning their attentions elsewhere.

In recent years, law enforcement agencies around the country have found themselves in the unusual position of having to compete among themselves as well as with the private sector to fill vacancies. This has led to departments reexamining their employment requirements as well as employing new and smarter recruitment techniques. These techniques include signing bonuses to obtain new recruits and increased salaries to keep officers and reduce turnover. Agencies are conducting more targeted advertising as well as making recruiting trips across the country, targeting lateral transfers and emphasizing the benefits as well as the quality of life in their jurisdictions. Members of the North Las Vegas Police Department travel the country recruiting officers and distributing the city's "Community Report," which emphasizes the benefits of living and working in North Las Vegas—"your community of choice"—in addition to their police department brochures. In Boca Raton, Florida, the "Guess Who's Coming to Dinner?" campaign received national attention and response after announcing that the chief or another high-ranking police official would bring dinner and a pitch for the job to the candidate's home. The campaign was paid for by donations from a business in town. Boynton Beach, Florida, advertised heavily in the northeast United States in ads that included pictures of the "Boynton Beach Snowman," which was a puddle of water on the beach.[30] Duane L. West, of the Tallahassee, Florida, Police Department writes of the new procedures used by his department in aggressively recruiting a diverse group of officers who meet the highest standards both personally and educationally and who are representative of the community they may serve. He reports that hiring benchmarks have been established based on both race and gender to ensure that the department mirrors the community's ethnic and gender demographics.[31] The Baltimore Police Department traveled to Puerto Rico to recruit bilingual candidates,[32] and recruiters are traveling around the country when word spreads of layoffs such as the automotive industry in Detroit.

Recruiters are being encouraged to think "outside the box" in their efforts to reach qualified candidates. This may mean improving benefits and incentives such as salary, signing bonuses, uniform allowances, training dollars, educational incentive, overtime opportunities, take-home vehicles, and so forth. They can also make their process more "user friendly" and convenient to the applicant by continually accepting applications and explaining the testing process on their website and offering help throughout various stages of the process.[33] Others examined why recruits are attracted to law enforcement careers and build on that. The New York State Police (NYSP) found that two issues affect this decision: the ability to help others and the ability to serve their community. The NYSP stresses these elements in their vision and mission statements as well as in their recruitment efforts.[34]

This recruitment challenge is leading departments to "work smarter" in various ways, including **"civilianization,"** which involves using civilian personnel to fill nonhazardous positions in an effort to put more sworn officers on the street. This will increase the availability of jobs for individuals seeking public service positions in law enforcement but not as police officers. The NYPD announced in summer of 2006 they have a goal of hiring 800 new police officers and 400 new civilians, which will free up an additional 400 officers who will then go on the street. These 400 civilian positions are spread throughout the department.[35] Civilianization is also seen as a way to assist departments in increasing staffing to help combat the temporary vacancies caused by police officers who have been called up for military duty.

The Job Analysis

Before the selection process for new members can actually begin, a police department must know what type of person it is interested in hiring.

To determine this, the department must first decide what type of work is done by officers and then determine the type of person who would be most qualified to do that type of work. This job analysis identifies the important tasks that must be performed by police officers and then identifies the knowledge, skills, and abilities necessary to perform those tasks.

In the past, women and members of minority groups were rejected from police departments because they didn't meet certain standards, such as height, weight, and strength requirements. A good job analysis can avoid that situation by measuring what current police officers in a department actually do. From this study, the department then can establish the standards and qualifications necessary for its officers to perform the needed duties.

If a competent job analysis is performed, the knowledge, skills, and abilities necessary for performance in that department are judged to be job related. If a certain qualification is deemed to be job related, that requirement can withstand review by the courts, and the specific test measuring for that knowledge or those skills or abilities is nondiscriminatory.

The case of *Guardians Association of New York City Police Department v. Civil Service Commission of New York* (1980) is a landmark appellate court decision regarding the job analysis.[36] In this case, the federal courts accepted the job analysis of the New York City Department of Personnel and the New York City Police Department. Two researchers have outlined these departments' procedures in preparing the job analysis, which were considered nondiscriminatory.

First, the Department of Personnel identified 71 tasks that police officers generally perform; the department based the choice of tasks on interviews with 49 officers and 49 supervisors. Second, a panel of 7 officers and supervisors reviewed the list of tasks to add any tasks that might have been omitted and to eliminate duplicate tasks and tasks not performed by entry-level officers. Certain tasks were combined, and some were added or deleted. This process resulted in a final list of 42 tasks commonly performed by entry-level police officers. Third, a questionnaire was sent to 5,600 officers requesting them to rate each of the 42 tasks on the basis of frequency of occurrence, importance, and the amount of time normally spent on performing the task. The 2,600 responses received were analyzed by computer to yield a ranking of the 42 tasks. The ranking was confirmed by observations made by professors from the John Jay College of Criminal Justice in New York City. Next, the Department of Personnel divided the list of 42 ranked tasks into clusters of related activities. Each one of the clusters was then analyzed by a separate panel of police officers to identify the knowledge, skills, and abilities (KSAs) for the cluster as a whole.[37] KSAs are a shortened way to indicate the knowledge, skills, and abilities needed to do police work. Candidates are not expected to know how to do police work, but they must have the KSAs to learn how to perform the duties of the profession. Some KSAs are the ability to read, write, reason, memorize facts, and communicate with others. Additional KSAs include physical ability, such as physical agility and endurance. The fact that this job analysis and the entrance examination based on it successfully passed the court's examination of job relatedness shows that a police department must carefully construct its entrance examinations based on the duties actually performed by police officers.

The Selection Process

The police selection process is lengthy, difficult, and competitive. It involves a series of examinations, interviews, and investigative steps designed to select the best candidate to appoint to a police department from the many who apply. Practitioners relate that in many agencies only 1 out of 100 applicants makes it into the employment ranks. This process can appear very intimidating to young applicants. The number of steps and all the rules and expectations can make them very apprehensive. They don't know what to expect. Reading texts like this will help to educate and prepare candidates about what to expect.

According to the Bureau of Justice Statistics, municipal police agencies used the following screening procedures[38]:

- Written aptitude testing (43 percent)
- Personal interview (98 percent)
- Physical agility (50 percent)
- Polygraph exam (25 percent)
- Voice stress analyzer (4 percent)
- Psychological evaluation (67 percent)
- Drug testing (73 percent)
- Medical exam (85 percent)
- Background investigation (98 percent)

The report also indicated that the percentage of departments using the screening methods increased significantly as the size of the department increased. In perusing police department websites, it is clear that this protocol is widespread among all types of law enforcement agencies. Typically a candidate has to pass every step before going on to the next step in the process and must pass each and every step to become a police officer. The order of the steps in the selection process varies by department depending on its philosophy and financial and personnel resources. However, it is fairly universal that the written and physical agility test will come at the beginning of the screening process and the psychological and medical evaluations will be the last screening procedures, after a conditional offer of employment has been made to the applicant.

A crucial element of the police selection process is that each step is court defensible and has validity to the job performance of a police officer. Under the U.S. Equal Employment Opportunity Commission (EEOC) guidelines, **"adverse impact"** or a different rate of selection occurs when the selection rate for any gender, race, or ethnic group is less than 80 percent of the selection rate for the group with the highest selection rate. If "adverse impact" is noted and the test or selection criteria cannot be shown to be valid, the EEOC would classify the test as impermissible discrimination and this could result in legal problems for a police agency.

In addition to sworn or uniformed members of law enforcement agencies, nonsworn or civilian members of many departments—for example, 911 operators, community service officers, crime scene technicians, and so on often receive preemployment screening similar to that of police officers.

According to its website, the Madison, Wisconsin, Police Department has numerous recruiting and hiring goals. The department seeks men and women who reflect the diversity of their community. They want to recruit applicants who can communicate effectively both verbally and in writing. They also seek individuals who are committed to improving the quality of life and who can enforce the law while protecting the constitutional rights of all.[39] Though positions are open to individuals over 18 by state law, Madison finds that the most successful applicants tend to have an average age of 27 or 28 and have previous work experience in various professions.

Applicants fill out an extensive application form, and after it is reviewed, they are invited to take a written exam testing reading comprehension, vocabulary, and the ability to organize thoughts and communicate them on paper. After the successful completion of the written test, an internal review panel will determine which applicants will proceed further in the process. These candidates will continue on to the physical agility exam, and the internal panel will then meet again and determine which applicants will proceed to the oral interview in front of a panel. The remaining steps include a thorough background investigation, an interview with the chief of police, a ride along with a field training officer, a personality assessment, and other interviews with departmental personnel. Eventually, a conditional job offer will be made to the selected candidates, which will be followed by a thorough medical exam conducted at city expense. For out-of-town applicants, Madison tries to condense some of these steps to minimize the cost and time to the applicant.

Timothy N. Oettmeier, of the Houston, Texas, Police Department, recently discussed the selection process in view of the increasing adoption of the community policing philosophy throughout the United States. He warned that departments must not radically change existing approaches to selecting the right personnel to adapt to this innovative policing philosophy; a commitment to community policing does not necessarily mean a department must make radical changes to its selection procedures. Actually, before implementing any changes, department members should reach consensus about an officer's role and responsibilities in a community-based department.[40] Oettmeier recommends departments take the following four general steps before restructuring the selection process for community policing:

1. Redefine the role of the officer.
2. Reevaluate knowledge, skills, and abilities.
3. Place a new emphasis on marketing police positions.
4. Proceed with caution.

The Community Policing Consortium addresses this issue on its website (www.communitypolicing.org). The consortium believes efforts can be undertaken by agencies that will facilitate hiring individuals with talents geared toward community policing and that these efforts will benefit overall police hiring as well. The organization believes that education and experience should be stressed. This would include having educational requirements in place, providing tuition reimbursement, recruiting more mature applicants, and removing artificial boundaries such as residency requirements. The organization emphasizes the use of psychological exams coupled with thorough background investigations and the use of good job analysis and assessment centers to screen applicants. The more an applicant can be evaluated based on performance in realistic situations, the better the chance of hiring individuals with the desired flexibility and interpersonal skills. This would be good for law enforcement in general and community policing specifically.

Characteristics of Good Police Officers

What are the "right" characteristics police administrators should look for when selecting future police officers? A number of efforts have been made to determine the specific criteria that predict future police performance, but in many respects, the results have been inconclusive. With the changing demands placed on police officers in our rapidly changing society and the changing demographics of the officers themselves, defining what makes a good officer can be difficult and challenging.

One of the first issues to be examined would have to be "what exactly is a good police officer?" This issue has confronted police supervisors and administrators for years as they struggled with performance evaluations. Is the officer who writes lots of tickets the good officer or is it the officer who gives more warnings than citations and builds community relationships? Should officers be encouraged to make arrests, whether or not it solves the problem or to solve the problem regardless of whether an arrest is made? Exactly what an agency and community wants its officers to do is the first thing that has to be determined.

The second consideration would be the type of individual who could best fill this role. A former Harvard Business School professor, Hrand Saxenian, advocated the theory that the selection process should emphasize the "person" and select the most mature, intelligent, stable applicant without concern for exactly what the job is. The individual could then be taught the particular tasks needed for the job. He felt that maturity was the most important criterion and attempted to measure maturity by looking at the ability of a person to express his or her feelings and convictions while considering the thoughts and feelings of other people. Saxenian interviewed police recruits at the start of a police academy and ranked them for maturity level. At the end of the 12-week academy, the recruits were ranked in performance by the academy staff. The rankings were statistically correlated. Follow-up studies also verified that the more mature recruits were the top performers.[41]

Police administrators seem to agree with the importance of maturity in a police recruit. Many agencies have tended toward hiring the more mature applicants in recent years. With the removal of upper age limits and the desire not to discriminate against someone because of age, many departments are hiring older recruits and are very pleased with the performance of these recruits. They have more maturity and life experience, which aids them in making well thought-out decisions when faced with difficult issues on the street.

Other characteristics often mentioned by police administrators include a high ethical standard and integrity, the ability to communicate well with all types of people, the ability to make good decisions and think on their feet.

It is hard to define and measure—and consequently defend in court—personal characteristics such as judgment and decision-making abilities. To assist in this area and to further embrace the community policing philosophy, some agencies are systematically seeking input from the community about what types of police officers citizens are looking for in their community. This is a radical change in the process and, if it continues and spreads, could significantly affect the selection process. It would also have the potential to enhance the relationship between the community and the police.[42]

The Department of Justice Office of Community Oriented Policing Services (COPS) published a report in 2006 presenting the findings from the *Hiring in the Spirit of Service* project. This federally funded project involves the community in the recruiting and hiring of service-oriented law enforcement personnel. Five agencies of various sizes, locations and facing various challenges were chosen to participate; Sacramento, California, Police Department; Burlington, Vermont, Police Department; Hillsborough County, Florida, Sheriff's Office, Detroit Police Department; and King County, Washington, Sheriff's Office.

These agencies employed advisory committees to participate in activities and provide feedback regarding the recruiting and hiring process. They also used focus groups to engage community support and vision. The objectives of the *Hiring in the Spirit of Service* strategy include developing an agency image, revising the screening process, and incorporating hiring practices that coincide with the new trends in police service. It was a common finding across all sites that including the community in the recruitment and hiring process is not easy, nor is identifying service oriented traits that all stakeholders can agree upon.[43]

The Sacramento Police Department is committed to the process they have started. The department feels it is a fresh approach to attracting qualified minorities into policing. The department identified community leaders and educated them about what the police job was like, what the requirements were, and what the selection process involved is. The department encouraged these leaders to identify and then "sponsor" a recruit by meeting with the recruit and his or her family regularly as well as attending the police academy graduation. As soon as the officers successfully complete the field training process, they are assigned back to their community so the community members can see their officer patrolling in their community. This program has resulted in quality candidates who successfully complete probation and have good relationships with the community, and it has served as a tremendous learning opportunity for the police department.[44]

Hillsborough County, Florida, found in its implementation of this process that the community, deputies, and supervisors agreed on the top five attributes (from Hilson's Job Analysis Questionnaire) that service-oriented deputies should possess: communication skills, admission of shortcomings, lack of procrastination, work patterns, and "frustration tolerance." This would indicate that police agencies and the community can agree on some of these desired attributes.[45]

Written Entrance Examination

With large numbers of individuals needing to be screened in this first step of the selection process, written tests are often used to minimize the time and cost to the agency. These tests are often conducted on a regular basis so there is a list of candidates from which to choose when an opening occurs. The tests are often held at schools, community buildings, and military bases for the applicants'

convenience. Sometimes, these tests are contracted out to private enterprise, with the cost to be born by the applicant. Because large numbers are screened out at this stage, the exams are often subject to litigation. To this point, cognitive tests are most commonly used and have been found to be correlated with successful job performance.[46] But departments are looking to improve testing and find the individual best suited to law enforcement and looking beyond cognitive skills. Assessment centers have been found to be excellent tools in predicting job performance,[47] and they ensure that candidates will be fairly and objectively evaluated based on their performance of the tasks needed in their potential position.[48] Unfortunately, assessment centers tend to be costly in human and dollar resources, and although many departments use them for promotional exams, most do not use them for hiring selection.

A written exam can be fair and unbiased when developed from a job analysis that incorporates the expertise of law enforcement practitioners in an effort to determine the KSAs required for the police position. Fairness is the degree to which all ethnic and gender groups are evaluated fairly and consistently.[49]

Many departments use tests specifically developed for the police selection process. Most of these new tests are administered through the use of computer simulations or assessment centers. Law enforcement agencies either purchase these systems, contract with private providers, or turn the testing or certain aspects of the testing over to a private enterprise with the cost to be absorbed by the applicant. Many departments have found the testing process to be costly, time consuming, and legally challenging. They have also found that applicants are willing to absorb the cost of testing, especially when it results in less inconvenience to the applicant. Consequently, private enterprises have arisen to fill this niche and provide legally defensible consolidated testing for many agencies (typically smaller agencies) within a region. One such company, Public Safety Testing (www.publicsafetytesting.com), provides written and physical agility testing for many agencies throughout Washington and Idaho. Its website stresses the convenience for applicants, including convenient testing venues with one application, one written test, and one physical agility test, which may be accepted by more than one agency. The company will then send the applicant's scores to all the agencies the applicant wants to pursue.

You Are There!

Sample Agility Tests

Arlington, Texas, Police Department
1. Rapid-acceleration agility course (includes hurdles, walls, and actions simulating low hedges, fences, storm drains, bridges, and running through crowds)
2. Trigger squeeze
3. Dummy drag
4. Ladder climb with shotgun
5. Endurance run

Arlington also provides tips and guidelines on its website about preparing for the test.

Fort Lauderdale, Florida, Police Department
1. Trigger pull
2. Long jump
3. Vehicle push
4. Half-mile run
5. Job task course (15-station obstacle course)
6. Swim test

SOURCES: Arlington, Texas, http://www.arlingtonpd.org/; Fort Lauderdale, Florida, http://ci.ftlaud.fl.us/police/

Physical Agility Test

Police departments are interested in police candidates who are physically fit. During the past 20 years, **physical agility testing** has been criticized for discriminating against some candidates, particularly women and physically small members of certain minority groups. Some argue that the tests relate to aspects of the police job that are rarely performed. Others argue that, although these aspects of the police job are not routinely and frequently performed, they are critically important. Not possessing the strength, endurance, or flexibility needed for the job could result in injury or death to the officer or a citizen. It also may increase the likelihood of an officer having to resort to deadly force.

Sometimes, candidates don't adequately prepare for the exam and assume they can pass it. Other candidates simply have a problem with a particular area of the physical agility test. Rather than lose an otherwise quality candidate, departments often provide training or guidance before the agility test. The Dayton, Ohio, Police Department goes further

by providing applicants who fail the physical agility a membership in a fitness club and encouraging them to test again.[50]

The question that law enforcement needs to answer is how fit officers must be, and then law enforcement has to prove job relatedness to the standards, or the courts will find against them. A recent study, conducted over 15 years and collecting data from 34 physical fitness standards validation studies performed on more than 5,500 officers from federal, state, and local law enforcement, enables law enforcement to document that fitness areas underlie specific task performance. Using several police officer job scenarios, the authors were able to tie in the need for aerobic power (1.5-mile run), anaerobic power (300-meter run), upper-body absolute strength (bench press), upper-body muscular endurance (pushups), abdominal muscular endurance (sit-ups), explosive leg power (vertical jump), and agility (agility run) to the police job.[51]

A related issue that is often raised by officers, applicants, unions, and scholars is maintaining fitness once someone is employed as a police officer. How can an agency justify having rigorous agility tests for hiring if nothing is done to follow through on this stated job qualification once the officer is hired? Traditionally, police officers have had no standards to adhere to once they were hired. With the inherent physical demands that can be placed on an officer in a moment's notice, this is a recipe for disaster. This is slowly changing, but it is a complicated issue involving standards, discipline, incentives, compensation for time, and liability regarding injuries.

Most officers keep themselves in top shape, motivated by personal pride and a desire to be healthy, minimize their chance for injury, and better serve the community. This effort is facilitated by departments providing on-site workout facilities or contracts with fitness facilities, on-duty time to work out, and various incentives for maintaining certain levels of fitness. Some employ fitness coordinators to guide employees in their efforts.

In most cases, civilian or nonsworn personnel would not be required to take a physical agility test.

Polygraph Examination

The **polygraph,** often called the lie detector, is a mechanical device designed to ascertain whether a person is telling the truth. It was first used by the Berkeley, California, Police Department in 1921.

The polygraph records any changes in such body measurements as pulse, blood pressure, breathing rate, and galvanic skin response. The effectiveness of the polygraph is based on the belief that a person is under stress when telling a lie. Therefore, if a person lies, the machine will record that stress in the body measurements. The polygraph's accuracy depends on the subject, the equipment, and the operator's training and experience. In some cases, the polygraph may fail to detect lies because the subject is on drugs or is a psychopathic personality. The polygraph was used extensively within private industry for screening job applicants and preventing employee theft. The use of the polygraph in preemployment screening was severely limited in the Employee Polygraph Protection Act (EPPA) signed into law in June 1988. The EPPA prohibited random polygraph testing by private sector employers and the use of the polygraph for preemployment screening. However, the law exempts the U.S. government or any state or local government from its provisions and restrictions. Although the results of polygraph tests may not be admissible in court, they are still used in the police selection process. The results are inadmissible in court because of doubts about their reliability. However, many experts believe there is value in the polygraph in that people believe they work and make admissions.[52]

Some departments have switched from the polygraph to the voice stress analyzer because they find it to be easier to administer and less intrusive to the candidate. It operates under a similar theory that stress will be registered in an individual's voice. According to the BJS 2006 report on local police departments, 25 percent of all local police departments use the polygraph in the screening process, and an additional 4 percent use the voice stress analyzer.

Oral Interview

Oral boards can be used to examine a candidate's characteristics that might be otherwise difficult to assess including poise, presence, and communication skills. The oral interview in the police selection process can be conducted by a board of ranking officers, a psychologist, the police chief, or an investigator. There often are multiple oral boards or interviews conducted by numerous representatives of the department. Stakeholders in the process may include representatives of other city, county, or state departments such as personnel or community development that may also actively participate on the board. As mentioned earlier, members of the community may also serve on the oral board when the department is engaged in the process of *Hiring in the Spirit of Service* or the community policing philosophy. The goal is to solicit input from many stakeholders in the organization and to minimize the chance of a personality conflict that might result in an applicant being kept out of the selection pool. The oral interview may merely discuss the candidate's application and background or may be used to test the candidate's ability to deal with stressful situations. In the "hypotheticals" presented, board members can observe the candidates' decision-making process and watch them prioritize and defend their choices. An officer could face these scenarios on the street. The candidate's demeanor while under pressure can be assessed. The oral board is a more structured and court defensible process than an unstructured one-on-one oral interview. Generally, the oral board will consist of three to six members who develop specific, standardized questions. All candidates are asked the same questions and rated on their responses.

Background Investigation

In an effective **background investigation,** a candidate's past life, past employment, school records, medical records, relationships with neighbors and others, and military record are placed under a microscope. The investigator looks for evidence of incidents that might point to unfavorable traits or habits that could affect the individual's ability to be a good police officer. Such factors are poor work habits, dishonesty, use of alcohol or drugs, or a tendency to violence. Thorough background investigations by a hiring agency are critical to avoid hiring the wrong person for the job. Investigators are looking for officially documented incidents as well as unreported or undetected questionable activity and deception. Though the process may vary between agencies, a good solid investigation will include the following:

1. *Background interview.* The investigator advises the applicant about the process and meets the candidate for an initial impression.

2. *Background investigation form.* Applicants are provided a detailed form to fill out regarding their entire lives, including residences, schools, jobs, driving, military experience, and criminal activity—detected and undetected.

ON THE JOB

Some Advice to Police Candidates

Here is some good advice to candidates taking the police test or meeting their background investigator:

Make a test run. A few days before your appointment, go to the location where you are scheduled to appear. Know how long it will take you to get there. Learn where you can park, where to get coffee or a bite to eat, where you can find a public bathroom. If you are late, you may not be allowed to take the test. If you are late meeting your investigator, it will give him or her a very bad impression of you.

Whenever you are scheduled to meet your investigator, wear proper business attire. For a man,

that is a conservative suit and tie. For a woman, it is a simple dress or business suit. Select conservative colors—gray, blue, or black. Polish your shoes. Be neat. Take off the earring. You can always put it back after the interview. Accessories that are appropriate for the club scene are not appropriate for an interview. Men and women should eliminate jewelry of any type except for a functioning watch.

And remember: Always call your investigator or anyone else you encounter in candidate processing, "Sir" or "Ma'am."

—*John S. Dempsey*

3. *Release of Information Form (waiver).* A form signed by the applicant and notarized, allowing individuals to share information with the investigator.

4. *Photos and fingerprints.* These are used for identification purposes and criminal records checks.

5. *Educational records.* These records are used to verify completion and degree and determine attendance and disciplinary issues.

6. *Employment records.* These are used to verify or examine jobs, titles, absenteeism, job performance, honesty, initiative, and work relationships.

7. *Credit check.* To verify past behavior of fulfilling obligations as well as determining the risk of being susceptible to graft. The credit check is also helpful for investigating the possibility of addictions.

8. *Criminal history.* Every law enforcement agency that has jurisdiction over areas in which the candidate lived, went to school, or worked is contacted.

9. *Driving record.* The applicant's record of accidents and traffic infractions are reviewed.

10. *Military history.* This is used to determine any discipline issues while in the military as well as the discharge type.

Though it can be costly, the investigator will usually travel to the applicant's previous areas of residence for the background. Conducting these interviews in person results in more detailed and honest information.

Psychological Appraisal

The preemployment psychological evaluation is an invaluable tool in the selection process and aids in assessing an individual's current level of functioning as a potential police officer. The psychological appraisal can assist in identifying individuals who may not adjust well to the law enforcement profession. This evaluation is typically done after a conditional offer of employment and evaluates many factors including personality disorders that might affect an individual's functioning in a law enforcement agency and/or interacting with the public. This evaluation also considers issues such as substance abuse, self-management skills (anger management, team functioning abilities, impact of prior experiences and traumas), and intellectual abilities.[53]

In recent years, the trend has been away from using general psychologists and psychiatrists and toward using those in the field who specialize in law enforcement hiring and fitness-for-duty exams. Because of their expertise, as well as open communication with the agencies hiring them, these specialists understand the unique requirements of law enforcement personnel and the major issues involved in fitness for duty as well as the constraints of conforming to the requirements of the Americans with Disabilities Act (ADA).[54] These psychologists will typically make one of three recommendations to a law enforcement agency regarding an applicant—"recommended," "recommended with reservations," and "not recommended"—or rate them from A to E, with A being the best recommendation. The agency will then choose whether to follow this recommendation. There could be legal problems in the future if an agency hires an individual against the psychologist's recommendation and that officer becomes involved in a questionable situation.

Medical Examination

Police departments generally want candidates who are in excellent health, without medical problems that could affect their ability to perform the police job. There are long-range and short-range reasons for using medical examinations in the police selection process. The short-range purpose is to ensure that candidates can do the police job. The long-range purpose is to ensure that candidates are not prone to injuries that may lead to early retirement and an economic loss to the department. Individuals who are unfit tend to have less energy and might not be able to work the sometimes-demanding hours and assignments required of the police job. Drug testing is also part of the medical exam because departments want to ensure the candidates are drug free.

The ADA, signed into law in 1990, extended the basic protection of the Rehabilitation Act of 1973 to government and private industry. This law took effect in 1992 and mandated that discrimination on the basis of disability is prohibited by all governmental entities and all but the smallest private employers. The ADA prohibits discrimination against disabled persons who can perform the essential functions of the job despite their disabilities. If a police agency rejects a disabled person for employment, it must show that the disabled person cannot adequately perform the job. The law provides an affirmative duty for employers to reasonably accommodate qualified disabled persons unless doing so would create an undue hardship. Areas covered by ADA include physical agility tests, psychological tests, and drug testing.[55]

The Police Training Process

Once an individual has been chosen to be a member of a police department, he or she begins months of intensive training. Recruit training and in-service training programs vary from department to department, and, in reality, police training never ends. Veteran police officers continue their education and training in many areas to keep up with the latest trends in fighting crime as well as to keep up with changing laws and procedures. Police officers also receive specialized training in preparation for serving in specialized units or managerial positions.

Recruit Training

Recruit training is the initial training a police officer receives. It teaches officers the state laws and state procedures and educates them in the goals, objectives, and procedures of their state and later their individual department. It provides them with the knowledge, skills, and abilities to do the job. Recruit training starts with the police academy, moves on to field training, and ends with the completion of the probationary period.

The Police Academy

The recruit **police academy** provides most of the average police officer's formal career training. It is often the beginning of the socialization process for the new officer. This will be discussed in a later chapter.

Most big cities in the United States have their own police academies. Although only 3 percent of departments operate their own academies, approximately 90 percent of the agencies serving populations greater 250,000 do so.[56] Localities without their own academies often use a nearby state or regional police academy. Many academies are also based at colleges, community colleges, or technical schools or universities. Academies are residential in nature where the students only go home on weekends or commuter facilities where the students commute on a daily basis from their homes. The instructors may be full time academy instructors or police officers on loan from their agencies to the academy for a pre-determined amount of time. There is debate about which type of academy, residential or commuter, is the better

ON THE JOB

The Oral Interview

When students ask me for advice, I give them advice similar to that Professor Dempsey gives them. I will add a couple of examples and pieces of advice gathered over my many years of participating in oral boards and conducting background investigations.

1. The number one piece of advice is, *"Don't lie,"* and that includes exaggerating facts and leaving information out. You will be found out. Investigating is law enforcement's strong point. I was constantly amazed by applicants who would lie in interviews or about their backgrounds, sometimes about trivial things that would not have affected their chances and sometimes about big things that were very easy to verify. Once a candidate lies, he or she is out of the game. No second chances.

2. As Professor Dempsey stated, dress appropriately. I remember participating on oral boards (as a lieutenant) with a male captain who frequently was heard to exclaim to a candidate, "Look how I'm dressed, and I have a job!" The common perception (and in my experience, accurate perception) among law enforcement executives is that the candidate's demeanor, appearance, and attitude are likely to be the best they will ever be during the hiring process. If it is not top notch at that time, the future is bleak. How will the applicant dress for court appearances?

3. To add to Professor Dempsey's comments, showing respect for the position of the interviewers is an excellent idea. I have been called both "sir" and "ma'am." In the case of the former, the applicant either had a vision problem, was extremely nervous, or, in the worst-case scenario, was a sexist trying to make a point. Personally, I never liked to be referred to as "ma'am" because it made me feel old. I've heard other female executives make the same comment. I believe if it is at all possible, the preferred method is making note of the interviewer's rank or title and using that. It shows respect for the time and effort required to attain the rank and shows a basic understanding of police organizations and the rank structure.

4. I also recommend you prepare. Know the organization. Research the jurisdiction and the agency on the Internet. Be aware of the vision of the agency as well as specific goals and initiatives the department is involved in. This preparation will allow you to ask good questions of the interviewers (most oral boards will allow you to ask them questions at the end of the interview) as well as illustrate your understanding of the agency and its challenges and philosophies and to show your initiative. The board will view this positively.

5. Lastly, "be yourself." Trying to project an image or persona that you think they want to see, but is not you, will result in a less than positive interview process. Better to let your true personality come through and thereby determine if it is a fit or not with the agency.

—*Linda S. Forst*

option for new officers. The residential academy is generally more militaristic in nature and often has more physical and discipline emphasis. Some recruits may view this as a more stressful academy that often places more of a hardship on the recruit's family. The commuter program is more "college-like" and not as stressful on the recruits or their families. The officer does generally not devote any evenings or weekends to the program.

Currently, there are 626 police academies nationwide; 274 county, regional, or state academies; 249 college, university, or technical school based academies; and 103 city or municipal academies.[57] In the last decade, another option has grown more popular. Some states (approximately 37 states offer some variation of this academy) are allowing aspiring police officers to complete their physical and classroom training in an academy they pay for and then taking those credentials with them to the selection process. There is debate about whether this is a good option. Some agencies view it as a way to keep their costs down (academy costs as well as the salary of an officer for the many months in the academy) and expedite filling a vacancy. The newly hired officer is ready to go on the street much sooner.[58] Considerations that need to be examined are the background investigations being conducted to get into this academy—whether they conform to what the agencies are doing—as well as the cost of the academy and its possible affect on the diversity of the candidates able to afford this type of program and not work for several months.

Education and training for police officers does not end after the academy. New officers rely on more experienced officers during the field training process and for mentoring once they are on their own on the streets.

Some programs address part of this concern by offering a part-time program.

During the last four decades, there has been a dramatic increase in the quality and quantity of police training, and departments are paying more attention to curriculum, training methods, and the development of training facilities. Perhaps the improvement in police training can be traced to the 1967 recommendation by the President's Commission on Law Enforcement and Administration of Justice that police departments provide "an absolute minimum of 400 hours of classroom work spread over a 4- to 6-month period so that it can be combined with carefully selected and supervised field training." The commission also recommended in-service training at least once a year, along with incentives for officers to continue their education.[59] The number of hours devoted to recruit training since then has increased dramatically.

In 2003, new police officers in cities across the nation averaged 628 hours of academy training. In general, the larger police departments had the most academy hours. Most states have mandated a minimum number of hours for their academies, but most academies exceed this number in an effort to provide the most comprehensive training possible to their new officers.[60]

The basic law enforcement academy in the state of Washington is representative of what is being offered around the country. Recruits are provided with 720 hours of instruction, including criminal law and procedures, traffic enforcement, cultural awareness, communication skills, emergency vehicle operator's course, firearms, crisis intervention, patrol procedures, criminal investigation, and defensive tactics.

Field Training

Field training is on-the-job training for recently graduated recruits from the police academy. The training is provided by specially selected patrol officers and is designed to supplement the theory taught at the police academy with the reality of the street. The length of field training can vary greatly among departments. The average number of hours of field training is 326 hours, with the smallest departments averaging 199 hours and the largest departments averaging 513 hours. The departments with the largest number of hours are those serving populations of 250,00 to 500,000, which average 654 hours of field training.[61]

The San Jose, California, Police Department created a field training program as early as 1972 that has been adopted by many police departments across the country. The San Jose program consists of two phases of training: (1) 16 weeks of regular police academy classroom training and (2) 14 weeks of field training. During the field training phase, a recruit is assigned to three different **field training officers (FTOs).** Recruits receive daily evaluation reports by their FTOs and weekly evaluation reports by the FTO's supervisor. Many departments continue to use the San Jose program or a variation of it. However, in 1996, at a conference on field training held in Boulder, Colorado, the issue of reexamining the San Jose program was raised because the trainers felt it hadn't kept up with changing times. Police chiefs were looking for ways to implement community policing into their agencies and felt the FTO program was a logical time to do so. After a study funded by the COPS office and conducted by the Police Executive Research Forum (PERF) and the Reno Police Department, the "Reno Model" was born. The objectives of the Police Training Officer (PTO) program are to provide learning opportunities for the officer that meet or exceed the needs of both the police agency and the community, and the program was designed so that it could be modified to fit individual organizations. The program uses an adult-learning and problem-based learning model that teaches transferable skills to the recruit. The Reno model is designed to produce graduates capable of providing customer-centered, responsible, community-focused police services. The PTOs stress community involvement in all of the training activities. The evaluations are primarily narrative and are worked on as teams during the 15-week program. There are four modes of policing (emergency response, non-emergency response, patrol activities, and criminal investigations) around which outcomes were developed and officers are instructed and evaluated in these areas. The program is seen as an important innovation in police training and has the support of the National Association of Field Training Officers (NAFTO), which also continues to support the San Jose model. The Reno model is intended to be used as a variation of the San Jose model or in addition to it. The Reno model would not benefit all departments, and the San Jose model is still an important one in the field training process.[62]

NAFTO held its first annual conference in Monterey, California, in 1992. The organization was chartered for the purpose of furthering and representing the interests of law enforcement, corrections, and communications field training officers. This organization strives to keep the field training process relevant for all new officers.

Firearms Training

In the 1960s, most police firearms training in the United States consisted of firing at bull's-eye targets. Later, training became more sophisticated, using more realistic silhouette targets shaped like armed adversaries. The FBI's Practical Pistol Course began to modernize firearms training; the course required qualification from different distances and from different positions, such as standing, kneeling, and prone positions. As firearms training progressed, shoot/don't shoot training was introduced using **Hogan's Alley** courses. Targets depicting "good guys" and "bad guys" would pop up, requiring officers to make split-second decisions. Today, many agencies have replaced Hogan's Alley programs with computer-controlled visual simulations.[63] These simulations such as Firearms Training Systems (FATS) allow the officer to shoot at a target, and a laser indicates where the shot went. Some of these computer simulations allow the officer to interact verbally in the scenario, and the situation can be altered accordingly. These simulations provide enlightening and realistic training for officers new to the position as well as for those that have been working the street for some time.

Departments nationwide are reviewing actual shooting incidents and, in an attempt to increase officer safety and minimize litigation, are attempting to make their training as realistic as possible and incorporate stressors that occur in street situations. Administrators have realized that shootings rarely occur with warnings in sterile and controlled situations involving stationary targets, so inclement weather, realistic dress, flashing lights, blaring sirens, other distractions, and multiple individuals or targets involved in the scenarios have been included. Administrators have found that training in this manner, together with stressing the decision to shoot or not shoot, is better equipping officers when they confront situations on the street.

In-Service, Management, and Specialized Training

Police training generally does not end at the recruit level. In many departments, **in-service training** is

The Learning Process Continues

MICHELLE BENNETT

Michelle Bennett has worked for the King County Sheriff's Office in Washington State since 1990. She has been a patrol officer, detective, and a sergeant supervising school programs and community police centers. She is currently the Chief of Police in a suburb near Seattle. She has a master's degree in psychology and is currently finishing her doctorate in education.

March 25, 1991, was my first day on patrol, and as a brand new deputy, I was really excited. I'd spent three months in the basic academy, then a month in a posta-cademy class learning about our department, and finally a week sitting on my hands riding with a seasoned vet-eran officer, observing what I could. Now, after months of training, I was ready to get into a patrol car and inflict my newfound knowledge of the law on unsuspecting citizens. Little did I know I would be the one learning most of the lessons on that day.

I walked into the precinct roll-call room and was greeted by my first field-training officer, another female deputy. "Hi, I'm Diana," she said and suddenly paused, "How old are you anyway?"

"Twenty-one," I replied excitedly.

She groaned, "Great," then said, "C'mon let's go; it's getting busy out there." I got into the passenger seat of her patrol car. As a first-month deputy, I was told I was not allowed to drive yet. We were immediately dis-patched to help an apparently disoriented senior citizen who was wandering around a residential neighborhood. We arrived, and Diana explained that I was to handle this; she would jump in if I needed any help. I put on my best professional face and proceeded to try out my best problem-solving skills as I began to ask this elderly gentleman a series of questions in order to determine where he lived. He ignored me and continued rambling on, not listening to a word I said. He finally turned to look me in the eye. Raising a craggy, wrinkled finger, he

pointed to my face and said, "I think you're a little too young to be troubleshooting, Missy!" Diana began laughing behind me as my facade of composure began to fade. Diana finished the questioning, and she was able to locate the man's family.

Okay, so it was my first call. Overall, it could have been worse. I could not help my youth; I would just show them all that it was not the age, but the sea-soning that mattered. Our second call was an area check for criminal activity in a local park. We walked through a construction site to get into the park and were greeted by the construction workers, "Hey Cagney, Lacey, come arrest me!" "No, come arrest me, will you handcuff me?" "No, come over here and search me!" I was embarrassed and shocked that any person would address a police officer in such a way. We arrived on the scene to find nothing but were greeted on our way back out by another construction worker. "Would you like to share my cupcakes with me, cupcake?" he said as he pulled some Hostess cupcakes out of his lunch box. Diana ignored him and continued walking. "No, thank you," I said politely and ran to catch up with my trainer. "You had better get used to this," she said. "It will get worse."

Next, we took a tour of the precinct area. We drove down the main highway, a street laced with seedy motels, strip bars, and taverns. We came upon a group of juveniles jaywalking across the highway. They turned away quickly when they saw us. "Let's go talk to them," Diana said. "You start, and I'll jump in if you need help." No problem, I thought—two years of college and four months of training, I can handle a group of misguided kids. I began speaking to the youth I felt was the ring-leader. He largely ignored what I was saying and began mouthing off to me in an apparent attempt to impress his peers. "Don't you be flippant with me, young man," I said, pointing my finger in his face. Diana interrupted me at that point and finished the questioning, satisfied that we could find nothing on them. We got back into the car, and she turned to me with an incredulous look on her face and said, "'Don't be flippant with me, young man?' Look, I don't even know what 'flippant'

used to regularly update the skills and knowledge base of veteran officers. Because laws and devel-opments in policing are constantly changing, offi-cers need to be kept up-to-date. Many states have

chosen to mandate a required number of in-service training hours for officers to maintain their state certification. Primarily, this was done as a way to ensure departments were keeping their officers means, how in the hell is that kid going to know what it means? You've really got to dumb down, or this isn't going to work! I need a break. Let's get lunch."

We drove to the nearest cozy diner, and I sat immersed in thought about my first day. It was nothing like I thought it was going to be. Respect had to be earned. I had no idea how to talk to people. All of my logical, pragmatic thought processes and problem-solving abilities seemed lost upon the public. To make matters worse, my new bulletproof vest was so tight and uncomfortable that it was hard to breath. I voiced this last concern to Diana. "Well," she said, "you need to get one with boobs built into it." After some clarification, I realized that I had received a male fitted vest from our property management unit, and the female vests actually had a curved chest allowing the female wearer to breathe.

"I'll take care of this first thing tomorrow," I thought to myself. We sat down to eat, and I noticed that it seemed as though everyone in the restaurant was staring at us. Then people started coming up to us, asking questions while we were trying to enjoy the meal. "This is why I usually get food to go and sit behind a building somewhere," Diana said. I thought about that for a minute . . . wow, here we were public servants, yet we were hiding from the people we were supposed to be serving? It would take me years to understand that concept.

Our next call was a three-car accident blocking the roadway. Upon our arrival, I learned the importance of multitasking at a scene. Who needs aid? Who will block the roadway? Who will call the tow trucks? When do we get the driver's information, and how do we write the report? As all of these things were running through my mind, things got even worse when I realized the driver who caused the accident was intoxicated. I performed field sobriety tests and decided to take the driver into custody. I told her she was under arrest. I soon realized it was a big mistake (and was duly chastised) not to handcuff her first. Suddenly, the fight was on. I could not believe someone would actually fight with a police officer. Weren't we there to protect the public? Were we not there to help and serve? Did we not command the respect of all those we dealt with?

After all, we had guns! I utilized my newly learned defensive tactics and techniques to put the woman into custody as we struggled. Diana yelled for me to call for backup, and I did as I was instructed. A few days later I was given a private speech from a male officer warning me about how it sounds when female officers call for backup. He told me to not do it too often, as the men will think I can't handle myself (another lesson it took me years to un-learn). However, before backup arrived, Diana and I were able to subdue the extremely drunk and agitated woman. The woman hurled every nasty name in the book at me . . . another huge shock. "Get used to it," Diana said. "Drunk women always want to fight female officers." Over the course of my career, I realized how true her statement was. In my years of police work, approximately 85 percent of all of my physical confrontations have been with women; and, of those, approximately 84 percent of those women were under the influence of an intoxicating substance.

We drove back to the precinct and finished the case report and booking information on our arrested female. It was then I learned another important fact about police work. For every two minutes of excitement on the job, there are at least two hours of paperwork. We spent the rest of our shift completing all of the paperwork from our DUI accident, and I ended up staying late trying to get things done. "I'm going home," Diana said. "See you tomorrow, and we'll start all over again."

I could barely sleep that night, just thinking about the day's events. I wrote everything down in a journal just to get my thoughts out on paper. I was excited about the job, but it was so different from what my perceptions had been. It was so real and exciting, yet at times so tedious, difficult, embarrassing, and dangerous. To me, as a woman, it seemed like there was a whole set of unwritten rules and lessons that I had yet to learn. I have learned and will continue to discover many of those lessons for years to come. I started my first day thinking about all the things I had to teach people and all the knowledge I could impart about the law. In the end, I discovered little of what the job had to do with the law; it had to do with people, emotion, respect, and wisdom. The learning process continues . . .

updated on the latest laws and procedures and ensure some degree of uniformity from jurisdiction to jurisdiction. The average annual number of hours required for in-service officers was 47 hours in 2003, which included an average of 24 annual state-mandated hours.[64] Some popular topics for in-service training around the country include ethics, use of force, cultural awareness, stress, domestic violence, workplace harassment, critical incidents, hate crimes, victim assistance, hostage situations, pursuits, interviews and interrogations, fraud, identity theft, and computer crime.

In addition to in-service training, many departments use management training programs to teach supervisory and management skills to newly promoted supervisors and managers. Some of them send supervisors and managers to regional or state sites for this training in supervision or management. There are several well-known law enforcement administrative officers' courses around the country that departments may use to improve the managerial skills of their mid- and upper-level managers. These include the FBI Academy in Quantico, Virginia; the Southern Police Institute at the University of Louisville, Kentucky; the Center for Public Safety at Northwestern University in Illinois; the Senior Management Institute for Police in Boston; the Management Institute at the Federal Law Enforcement Training Center in Glynco, Georgia; the Institute of Police Technology and Management at the University of North Florida in Jacksonville; and the Southwestern Law Enforcement Institute in Texas. Typically, administrators attend these schools for anywhere from 8 to 13 weeks and are paid a salary while they attend. The managers obtain the latest information concerning law enforcement practices and network with other managers from around the country. This is a valuable source of information and subsequent resources for mid- and upper-level managers who often spend their entire careers in one department.

Many departments also offer specialized training programs for officers assigned to new duties. These may be conducted on site or at other locations. Recently, many of these training opportunities have been offered online. Training units can be developed that can be worked around an officer's schedule. They can be anywhere from 10-minute training segments to use during or after roll-call or several hours for a more in-depth discussion of a topic. The attraction for agencies is that the training can be worked in around an officer's schedule, and transportation costs as well as time away from duty are minimized or eliminated when the training is done at the station instead of having to drive to a training facility, which is particularly beneficial in the more rural areas of the country.

This also minimizes the cost of overtime for officers working the night shift if they can fit training in around their work, rather than having to go during the day and get overtime or fill in their work shift at night with an officer on overtime. This training can also increase consistency of training across the particular state or region.

These opportunities are often located at and facilitated by the state or regional training academy. In Florida, community colleges are the site of these regional training opportunities. They routinely host in-service training for officers who need to learn new skills to specialize in new assignments. These include drug investigations, traffic homicide investigations, radar, surveillance, investigation, DARE, School Resource Officer, Firearms Instructor, Crowd Control, Instructor Certification, Crime Scene Investigation, Child Abuse, Sex Crimes, Robbery Investigations, Interview and Interrogation, and other classes that chiefs request.

Training for the Police Corps

The Police Corps is a federally funded program designed to address violent crime by increasing the number of police officers on the street with advanced education and training. Scholarships of as much as $3,750 per year are provided on a competitive basis to students who agree to complete their bachelors degrees, Police Corps training, and then serve four years on patrol with law enforcement agencies in areas of great need. This program models training after the military's successful Reserve Officer Training Corps (ROTC). As part of the 1994 federal anticrime law, $10 million was appropriated for six states to develop these programs. The Police Corps reduces costs to agencies by providing funds to the states to provide 16 to 24 weeks of rigorous residential Police Corps training for each participant. In 2003, 27 states actively participated in the Police Corps program. Because of budgetary constraints, no new states have been accepted since then. By the end of 2003, the program had 1,597 participants. Proponents of the Police Corps say it will transform policing, not just by attracting college graduates, but by having these older, better-educated recruits trained in a different way. They will have a new curriculum focusing on the community and emphasizing leadership, sensitivity, and social skills as tools to break down the friction and distrust that officers often encounter. To deal with these problems, recruits will learn the demographics of neighborhoods and communication and note-taking skills in addition to regular police procedures. Role play will also be a major part of training. In 2003, the PERF evaluated the program and found the Police Corps graduates perform at a high level pertaining to skills, legal, leadership, ethics, problem solving, communication, and wellness that the Police Corps training emphasizes. Further information on the Police Corps program can be found on the Department of Justice website (http://www.ojp. usdoj.gov/opclee/).

Jacksonville, Illinois, police academy students role play a domestic violence call. Why is role play being used increasingly in preservice training?

Community Policing Training

Numerous departments throughout the United States have begun to develop low-cost and effective local and regional community policing training to inculcate community awareness into their recruits and in-service personnel. In 2003, 39 percent of local departments provided at least eight hours of training in community policing to new recruits and 48 percent provided at least eight hours of training in community policing to their in-service officers.[65] The U.S. Department of Justice, Office of Community Oriented Policing Services (COPS), funds training provided by the Community Policing Consortium, a group of five of the leading policing organizations in the United States: the International Association of Chiefs of Police (IACP), the National Organization of Black Law Enforcement Executives (NOBLE), the National Sheriffs' Association (NSA), the Police Executive Research Forum (PERF), and the Police Foundation. This consortium delivers free community policing training to all recipients of COPS grants under the 1994 Crime Bill in the form of regional training. Sessions include community policing orientation, sheriff-specific training, cultural diversity/building community partnerships, problem solving, personnel needs and managing calls for service, and train-the-trainer courses. Information is available on the Community Policing Consortium website (http://www.communitypolicing.org).

Probationary Period

A **probationary period** is the period of time that a department has to evaluate a new officer's ability to perform his or her job effectively. Generally, a probationary officer can be dismissed at will without proof of specific violations of law or department regulations. Once officers are off probation, civil service rules often make it very difficult to dismiss them. Probationary periods can last anywhere from 6 months to 3 years. Today, the average probationary period ranges from 12 to 18 months. It has lengthened in recent years because of the increased length of time devoted to academy training and field training. Agencies want to have enough time to evaluate officers' performance while they are performing on the street on their own.

Summary

- Many jobs are available in policing in the federal, state, and local level, including a growing number of civilian positions.

- The most convenient way to find out about law enforcement jobs, department standards, and the testing process is through law enforcement websites.

- The standards for hiring police officers have changed in recent years to facilitate the inclusion of more females, minorities, and older candidates.

- The percentage of departments with maximum age limits has declined and police departments are finding the older, more mature candidates to be excellent police officers.

- A job analysis will be conducted by the law enforcement agency to determine the knowledge, skills, and abilities (KSAs) needed for the job, and these will be incorporated into the selection process.

- In an effort to have the largest possible applicant pool, many departments are not requiring a college degree, however, education is valued, encouraged, and often required for promotion.

- The selection process is lengthy and usually includes a written exam, physical agility test, polygraph, oral board, background investigation, psychological evaluation, and a medical evaluation.

- In the past, physical agility tests were often found to keep minorities or women out of law enforcement and consequently departments have worked hard to make the tests more job related and less discriminatory.

- The background investigation that candidates go through is extensive in an effort to screen out candidates with undetected criminal behavior, deception, or unfavorable traits or habits that might affect their ability to be good police officers.

- Recruit training consists of training in a police academy followed by field training.

- Recruits will then complete a probationary period usually lasting from 12 to 18 months.

- Police training will continue throughout an officer's career and include mandatory in-service training, specialty training, supervisory and management training.

Learning Check

1. When looking for a job in law enforcement, where would you look for information on job opportunities and information regarding departments and their requirements and testing process?

2. Discuss why the job analysis is such a vital phase in the police hiring practice.

3. Explain the typical selection process most police departments use to identify and select qualified police officers.

4. What type of physical agility test do you think is most relevant to the police job? What physical tests should the candidate be asked to do?

5. Explain the standards most police departments use to select qualified police officers.

6. How much education should a police officer be required to have and why?

7. What rules or standards are department using regarding drug usage and police applicants?

8. What is the background investigation composed of?

9. Discuss why field training programs and probationary periods are vital phases in the police training practice.

10. In your own words, describe the average newly hired U.S. police officer, given the police recruitment and selection process.

Key Terms

adverse impact A form of de facto discrimination resulting from a testing element that discriminates against a particular group, essentially keeping them out of the applicant pool.

Americans with Disabilities Act Signed into law in 1990, the world's first comprehensive civil rights law for people with disabilities. The act prohibits discrimination against people with disabilities in employment, public services, public accommodations, and telecommunications.

background investigation The complete and thorough investigation of an applicant's past life, including education, employment, military, driving, criminal history, relationships, and character. This includes verification of all statements made by the applicant on the background form and the evaluation of detected and undetected behavior to make a determination if the candidate is the type of person suited to a career in law enforcement.

civilianization Replacing sworn positions with civilian employees. Some positions that are often civilianized include call takers, dispatchers, front desk personnel, crime analysts, crime prevention specialists, accident investigators, crime scene technicians, public information officers, and training personnel.

field training An on-the-job training program that occurs after the police academy under the direction of an FTO.

Guardians Association of New York City Police Department v. Civil Service Commission of New York A landmark appellate court decision on the issue of job analysis.

field training officer (FTO) Experienced officer who mentors and trains a new police officer.

Hogan's Alley A shooting course in which simulated "good guys" and "bad guys" pop up, requiring police officers to make split-second decisions.

in-service training Training that occurs during a police officer's career, usually on a regular basis and usually within the department; often required by department policy or state mandate.

job analysis Identifies the important skills that must be performed by police officers, and then identifies the knowledge, skills, and abilities necessary to perform those tasks.

job relatedness Concept that job requirements must be necessary for the performance of the job a person is applying for.

knowledge, skills, and abilities (KSAs) Talents or attributes necessary to do a particular job.

Law Enforcement Education Program (LEEP) A federal scholarship and loan program operated by the DOJ between 1968 and 1976. LEEP put money into developing criminal justice programs in colleges and provided tuition and expenses to in-service police officers to go to college.

physical agility test A test of physical fitness to determine if a candidate has the needed strength and endurance to perform the job of police officer.

police academy The initial formal training that a new police officer receives to learn police procedures, state laws, and objectives of law enforcement. The academy gives police officers the KSAs to accomplish the police job.

polygraph Also called the lie detector test; a mechanical device designed to ascertain whether a person is telling the truth.

probationary period The period in the early part of an officer's career in which the officer can be dismissed if not performing to the departments standards.

recruitment process The effort to attract the best people to apply for the police position.

selection process The steps or tests an individual must progress through before being hired as a police officer.

tuition reimbursement The money a police department will pay officers to reimburse them for tuition expenses while they are employed by the police department and are pursuing a college degree.

The Police Role and Police Discretion

© Lori C. Diehl/Photo Edit Inc.

GOALS

- To explore the police role and its many interpretations
- To introduce you to the goals and objectives of policing
- To explore various operational styles of the police
- To introduce and explore the concept of police discretion, seeking to understand how and why discretion is exercised and the methods that have been used to control it
- To explore the concept of discretion and police force, including police shootings and deadly force

Introduction

The role of the police and the exercise of police discretion are among the most important issues in policing. Who are the police? What do they do? How do they do what they do? What should they do instead?

This chapter will look at the role of the police in society, including the crime-fighting role, the order maintenance role, the ambiguity of the police role, and the effects of the September 11, 2001, terrorist attacks on the United States. It will discuss the goals and objectives of the police, as well as various police operational styles discovered by researchers who study the police. The chapter will also discuss police discretion. It will examine what discretion is, how and why discretion is exercised, what factors influence discretion, and how discretion can be controlled by police administrators. It will also discuss the concept of discretion and police use of force, including police shootings and deadly force.

The Police Role

What is the **police role?** Who are the police in the United States? What do they do? What should they do? These are very difficult questions to answer. The scholar Herman Goldstein warns, "Anyone attempting to construct a workable definition of the police role will typically come away with old images shattered and a newfound appreciation for the intricacies of police work."[1]

Two major views of the role of the police exist:

1. The police are crime fighters concerned with law enforcement (crime fighting).

2. The police are order maintainers concerned with keeping the peace and providing social services to the community **(order maintenance).**

Crime-Fighting Role

Movies and television shows about the police emphasize the police **crime-fighting role.** If we believe these stories, the police engage in numerous daily gunfights, car chases, and acts of violence, and they arrest numerous people every day. Fictional books about police work also emphasize the crime-fighting role. Even the news media emphasize this role; television news shows and newspaper headlines dramatize exciting arrests and action by the police.

The police themselves also emphasize their role as crime fighters and play down their job as peacekeepers and social service providers. As a former professor turned police officer, George L. Kirkham, states,

The police have historically overemphasized their role as crime fighters and played down their more common work as keepers of the peace and providers of social services, simply because our society proffers rewards for the former (crime fighting) but cares little for the latter (peace-keeping and providing services). The public accords considerable recognition and esteem to the patrol officer who becomes involved in a shoot-out with an armed robber or who chases and apprehends a rapist, and therefore so do the officer's peers and superiors."[2]

At first glance, there appears to be some truth to the belief that police are primarily crime fighters. Statistics for the latest reporting year reveal that the U.S. police made more than 14 million arrests for all criminal infractions, excluding traffic violations.[3]

An analysis of the arrests, however, shows a different perspective. About 2.21 million of the arrests were for the FBI's Index or Part I crimes, of these arrests, about 604,000 were for violent crimes (murder, forcible rape, robbery, and aggravated assault) and about 1.61 million of the arrests were for property crimes (burglary, larceny/theft, motor vehicle theft, and arson). However, the following accounted for the other 12.28 million arrests:

1. Driving under the influence (DUI) or driving while intoxicated (DWI)—about 1.37 million arrests.

2. Drug abuse violations—about 1.85 million arrests.

3. Misdemeanor assaults—about 1.3 million arrests.

4. Liquor law violations, drunkenness, disorderly conduct, vagrancy, and loitering—about 2 million arrests.

5. A large variety of lesser offenses excluding traffic offenses.

Though officers do not spend the majority of their time as crime fighters, it is an important role for them. Procedures and safety are important considerations even when officers have K-9 backup.

TABLE 5.1 Arrests in the United States, by Crime Committed 2005

Total*	14,094,186	Stolen property: buying, receiving, possessing	133,856
Part 1 Crimes		Vandalism	279,562
Murder and nonnegligent manslaughter	14,062	Weapons: carrying, possessing, etc	193,469
		Prostitution and commercialized vice	84,891
Forcible rape	25,528	Sex offenses (except forcible rape and prostitution)	91,625
Robbery	114,616	Drug abuse violations	1,846,351
Aggravated Assault	449,297	Gambling	11,180
Burglary	298,835	Offenses against the family and children	129,128
Larceny-theft	1,146,696	Driving under the influence	1,371,919
Motor vehicle theft	147,459	Liquor laws	597,838
Arson	16,337	Drunkenness	556,167
Violent Crime**	603,503	Disorderly conduct	678,231
Property Crime***	1,609,327	Vagrancy	33,227
Other Assaults	1,301,392	All other offenses	3,863,785
Forgery and Counterfeiting	118,455	Suspicion	3,764
Fraud	321,521	Curfew and loitering law violations	140,835
Embezzlement	18,970	Runaways	108,954

*Does not include suspicion. Because of rounding, the figures may not add to total.
**Murder, forcible rape, robbery, and aggravated assault.
***Burglary, larceny-theft, motor vehicle theft, and arson.
SOURCE: Federal Bureau of Investigation, *Uniform Crime Reports, 2005*. Retrieved November 3, 2006, from http://www.fbi.gov.

From the analyses of the arrests made by police, we can see that the vast majority of the arrests are not serious Index crimes but, rather, what we might call crimes of disorder or actions that annoy citizens and negatively affect their quality of life (for example, offenses involving drugs and alcohol). Even the vast majority of crime fighting the police do is related to order maintenance rather than serious crime.

Furthermore, the 2005 report, *Contacts between Police and the Public: Findings from the 2002 National Survey*, revealed that approximately 45 million citizens had contacts with the police during the previous reporting year. Most of the contacts involved motor vehicle or traffic related issues. Only about 1.5 percent of all contacts involved the use of or threat of force by the police.[4]

Order Maintenance Role

If police are not primarily crime fighters, then, what are they? In an effort to determine the proper role of the police, researchers have conducted numerous studies to determine what it is that police do and why people call on their services. As far back as 1965, Elaine Cumming and her colleagues reported that the ordinary work routines of police officers included relatively little law enforcement and comprised a large variety of other activities that came to be known as peacekeeping and order maintenance.[5] Since then researchers have consistently reinforced Cumming's findings. A summary of some key studies follows.

In a classic study of patrol activities in a city of 400,000, John Webster found that providing social service functions and performing administrative tasks accounted for 55 percent of police officers' time and accounted for 57 percent of their calls. Activities involving crime fighting took up only 17 percent of patrol time and amounted to about 16 percent of the calls to the police.[6]

Robert Lilly found that of 18,000 calls to a Kentucky police department made during a four-month period, 60 percent were for information, and 13 percent concerned traffic problems. Less than 3 percent were about violent crime, and about 2 percent were about theft.[7]

In the Police Services Study (PSS), a survey of 26,000 calls to police in 24 different police departments in 60 neighborhoods, researchers found that only 19 percent of calls involved the report of a criminal activity.[8] Similar studies were conducted by Michael Brown in California, Albert J. Reiss in Chicago, and Norman Weiner in Kansas City with similar results.[9] Additionally, Steven Meagher analyzed the job functions (duties) of 531 police officers in 249 municipal departments and found that regardless of their size, most police agencies and police officers have similar functions and do pretty much the same thing.[10]

The academic studies clearly indicate that what the police do is maintain order and provide services. People call the police to obtain services or to get help in maintaining order.

Ambiguity of the Police Role

The police role is extremely diverse, **ambiguous**, and dynamic. Egon Bittner has stated that from its earliest origins, police work has been a "tainted occupation," "The taint that attaches to police work refers to the fact that policemen are viewed as the fire it takes to fight fire, that in the natural course of their duties they inflict harm, albeit deserved, and that their very existence attests that the nobler aspirations of mankind do not contain the means necessary to insure survival."[11]

Carl B. Klockars, in *Idea of Police*, broadly defines the basic function of the police as dealing with all those problems that may require the use of coercive force. He emphasizes that democratic societies give the police the right to use morally dangerous, dirty, and illegal means to achieve good ends because in most cases, noble institutions do not contain the means to ensure their survival.[12]

We must remember that England's Sir Robert Peel, who arranged for the organization of the first paid, full-time, uniformed police department, conceived the police role as a conspicuous community-oriented patrol designed more for prevention and deterrence than for enforcement. Peel designed the police to be an alternative to the repression of crime and disorder that could have been achieved through military might and severe legal sanctions. See Chapter 1, "Police History."

The early American settlers brought Peel's ideas on the role of the police to our shores. As Alan Coffey tells us, however, as the United States began to pass increasingly statutory laws, the police role expanded from maintaining order to enforcing the law. Coffey states, "It is this combination of role expectations that generates controversy, particularly with those who emphasize the peace-keeping segment of police work as opposed to actual enforcement."[13]

One way of defining the police role may be to say that it is whatever the community expects the police to be. However, we must remember that most communities consist of many diverse groups with different goals and interests. One group in the community may expect police to do something entirely different from what another group expects. For example, older people in a community or store owners may want the police to hassle teenagers hanging on the street, yet the teenagers, for their part, may feel that if the police do hassle them, the officers are abusing them. Parents in a community may want the police to search and arrest drug dealers and drug users yet not want the police to search their own children. In these and many other ways, the police are often in no-win situations.

One researcher, George Pugh, writing on the expansive and varied role of the police, states that a good police officer must have the qualities of common sense and mature judgment, and must react quickly and effectively to problem situations. A good police officer, Pugh says, must be able to adopt the appropriate role of policing to the situation he or she encounters. Common roles include law enforcer, maintainer of social order, and public servant. Finally, a good police officer must have the appropriate concepts of policing that guide and prioritize the role the officer should employ in particular situations. These concepts governing police work, Pugh says, are the following: (1) an effort to improve the welfare of the community and (2) a respect for the individual's rights, worth, and dignity.[14]

Robert Sheehan and Gary W. Cordner, using the work of previous scholars, offer the following synopsis of the police role:

1. The core of the police role involves law enforcement and the use of coercive force.
2. The primary skill of policing involves effectively handling problem situations while avoiding the use of force.
3. Skillful police officers avoid the use of force primarily through effective, creative communication.[15]

In summing up the police role, we might agree with Joseph J. Senna and Larry J. Siegel. They say that the police role has become that of a social handywoman or handyman called to handle social problems that citizens wish would simply go away.[16]

The Police Role in the Aftermath of September 11, 2001

The ambiguous role of the police has been further complicated by the September 11, 2001, terrorist attacks against the United States. Since 9/11, many have seen the police as the frontline of homeland defense against further terrorist attacks, and many police departments and officers are viewing themselves similarly. Police departments have responded to this by forming specialized, military-like antiterrorist units that appear in public as a strong deterrent force against would-be terrorists. This has concentrated attention on the law enforcement role of the police.

The order maintenance role and social service role of the police has also been reemphasized because the police are the first responders to all emergencies and unusual occurrences in the nation and are tasked with the many duties that this entails, including crowd control, emergency medical response and treatment, and maintenance of public order in often catastrophic conditions.

See Chapter 15, "Homeland Security," which discusses the new duties placed on the police for homeland defense.

Goals and Objectives of Policing

Much study and research has gone into determining the proper goals and objectives of a police department. This topic can be discussed more easily by thinking in terms of primary goals and objectives and secondary goals and objectives.

Primary Goals and Objectives

The two primary goals and objectives of police departments, according to Sheehan and Cordner, are maintaining order and protecting life and property.[17] These are among the most basic roles of government, and government hires the police to perform these services. To achieve these goals, the police perform a myriad of duties. As Senna and Siegel say,

> Police are expected to perform many civic duties that in earlier times were the responsibility of every citizen: keeping the peace, performing emergency medical care, and dealing with civil emergencies. Today, we leave those tasks to the police. Although most of us agree that a neighborhood brawl must be broken up, that the homeless family must be found shelter, or the drunk taken safely home, few of us want to jump personally into the fray; we'd rather "call the cops."[18]

Secondary Goals and Objectives

Sheehan and Cordner also list six secondary goals and objectives toward which police resources and activities are used to meet the primary two objectives:

1. Preventing crime
2. Arresting and prosecuting offenders
3. Recovering stolen and missing property
4. Assisting the sick and injured
5. Enforcing noncriminal regulations
6. Delivering services not available elsewhere in the community[19]

The police attempt to prevent crime by trying to create a sense of **omnipresence** (the police are always there) through routine patrol, responding to calls by citizens to deal with problems that may cause crime, and establishing and participating in police-citizen partnerships designed to prevent crime.

Arresting offenders and assisting prosecutors in bringing charges against defendants is one of the primary methods used by the police to maintain order and protect life and property.

When people find property on the street, they often bring it to a police officer or to a police station. The police then attempt to find the owner. If that is not possible, they store the property in the hopes that the rightful owner will come in to claim it. When people lose property, they generally go to the police station in the hopes that someone has turned it in. Besides all of their other duties, then, the police serve as society's foremost lost and found department.

Because they are available "twenty-four/seven," 7 days a week and 24 hours a day, and because they are highly mobile, the police generally are the closest government agency to any problem. In many jurisdictions, the police are called to emergency cases of sickness and injury to assess the situation before an ambulance is dispatched, or they are called to assist ambulance, paramedical, or other emergency response personnel.

In the absence of other regulatory personnel or during the times they are not available, the police enforce numerous noncriminal regulations, including traffic and parking regulations, liquor law regulations, and many others.

The police are generally the only government officials available every day, around the clock. When government offices close, the police become roving representatives of the government who assist people with problems no one else is available to handle. When the lights go off in an apartment building, people call the police. When the water main breaks, people call the police. When your neighbor's dog barks all night and keeps you awake, who do you generally call? You call the police. After all, who else can you call at 3:00 in the morning? The police respond and take whatever action they can to ameliorate problems and to deal with emergencies. They direct traffic, evacuate residents, and decide who to call for assistance.

■─────────────────────

Police Operational Styles

People who research the police write about **police operational styles**—styles adopted by police officers as a way of thinking about the role of the police and law in society and how they should perform their jobs. The findings of several leading researchers, including John J. Broderick, James Q. Wilson, William Muir, Ellen Hochstedler, John Van Maanen, and others will be discussed here.

The concept of operational styles is useful in analyzing the police role and police behavior.

However, no officer conforms solely to one of these styles to the exclusion of the others. Many officers show characteristics of several of these styles. (See Figure 5.1.)

Siegel and Senna tell us that several studies have attempted to define and classify police operational styles into behavioral clusters. These classifications or typologies attempt to categorize officers by groups, each of which has a unique approach to police work. They report that the purpose of these classifications is to demonstrate that the police are not a cohesive, homogeneous group but, rather, individuals with differing approaches to their work.[20] Siegel and Senna present four basic styles of policing or typologies they call the crime fighter, the social agent, the law enforcer, and the watchman. Borrowing from the work of Wilson and Muir, Siegel and Senna define the four basic styles as[21]

- *Crime fighter*—Investigating serious crimes and apprehending criminals
- *Social agent*—Performing a wide range of activities without regard for their connection to law enforcement
- *Law enforcer*—Enforcing the law "by the book"
- *Watchman*—Maintaining public order

Broderick, in his *Police in a Time of Change,* also presents four distinct police operational styles: enforcers, idealists, realists, and optimists.[22]

- *Enforcers*—Their major role is maintaining order on their beat, keeping society safe, and protecting society by arresting criminals.
- *Idealists*—Similar to enforcers, yet they place a higher value on individual rights and the adherence to due process as required by the U.S. Constitution
- *Realists*—Relatively low emphasis on both social order and individual rights; they concentrate their efforts on the concept of police loyalty and the mutual support of their fellow officers.
- *Optimists*—Place a relatively high value on individual rights and see their job as people oriented, rather than crime oriented.

In his seminal work, *Varieties of Police Behavior: The Management of Law and Order in Eight Communities,* Wilson described three distinct styles of policing that a police department can deploy in maintaining order and responding to less serious violations of law, the watchman style, the legalistic style, and the service style. (Within each style, the police treat serious felonies similarly.)[23] He found that the political culture of a city, which reflects the socioeconomic characteristics of the city and its organization of government, exerts a major influence on the style of policing exercised by the police.

- *Watchman style*—Primarily concerned with order maintenance—maintaining order and controlling illegal and disruptive behavior. Officers in a watchman-style department exercise a great deal of discretion and ignore many minor violations, especially those involving juveniles and traffic. Officers use persuasion and threats, or even "hassle" or "rough up" disruptive people, instead of making formal arrests. This style, Wilson says, is generally found in working-class communities with partisan mayor–city council forms of government.

- *Legalistic style*—Enforce the letter of the law strictly by issuing many citations and making many misdemeanor arrests. They proceed vigorously against illegal enterprises. This style of enforcement, Wilson says, occurs in reform administrations' government styles. Furthermore, this style often occurs in the aftermath of a scandal in a watchperson-type of department that results in the hiring of a "reform" police chief.

- *Service style*—Stress servicing the needs of the community. The officers see themselves more as helpers than as soldiers in a war against crime. The service style, Wilson says, is generally found in more affluent suburban areas.

Muir, in *Police: Streetcorner Politicians,* observed the behavior of 28 young police officers in an American city during the 1970s to attempt to explain how police adjust to their coercive role in society and how they cope with society's irrationality and violence. Based on his observations, he theorized that an officer becomes a good officer to the extent that he or she develops two virtues: intellectually, he or she has to grasp the nature of human suffering, and morally has to resolve the contradiction of achieving just ends with coercive means. He proposed a typology of four general types that police officers can be grouped into, including the professional, the enforcer, the reciprocator, and the avoider. These

The Police Role

    Crime fighting (law enforcement)

    or

    Order maintenance (peacekeeping)

Police Operational Styles

Larry J. Siegel and Joseph J. Senna

    Crime fighter

    Social agent

    Law enforcer

    Watchman

John J. Broderick

    Enforcers

    Idealists

    Realists

    Optimists

William Muir

    Professional

    Enforcer

    Reciprocator

    Avoider

Styles of Policing

James Q. Wilson

    Watchman style

    Legalistic style

    Service style

Policing Ideals

Claudia Mendias and
E. James Kehoe

    Law enforcement

    Peace maintenance

    Procedural compliance

    Protagonist acceptance

Figure 5.1
The Police Role, Police Operational Styles, Styles of Policing, Policing Ideals

SOURCES: Larry J. Siegel and Joseph J. Senna, *Introduction to Criminal Justice,* 10th ed. (Belmont, Calif.: Thomson/Wadsworth, 2005), p. 211. Siegel and Senna cite in this regard, John J. Broderick, *Police in a Time of Change,* 2nd ed. (Prospect Heights, Ill.: Waveland Press, 1987); Claudia Mendias and E. James Kehoe, "Engagement of Policing Ideals and Their Relationship to the Exercise of Discretionary Powers," *Criminal Justice and Behavior* (February 2006), pp. 70–92; William K. Muir, Jr., *Police: Streetcorner Politicians* (Chicago: University of Chicago Press, 1977); and James Q. Wilson, *Varieties of Police Behavior: The Management of Law and Order in Eight Communities* (Cambridge, Mass.: Harvard University Press, 1968).

types represented combinations of the officer's view of the nature of humankind and the officer's view of the moral justification of the use or threat of coercion. The typologies were designed to address the need to find police personnel who can perform their duties in a democratic yet efficient manner.[24] However, Hochstedler, in her doctoral dissertation at the State University of New York at Albany, failed to support Muir's typology, reporting that Muir's dimensions did not predict the types he proposed and that it was impossible to identify types that conformed to Muir's four types. She concluded that his typology has not yet been shown to describe anything beyond mere logical possibilities and cannot yet be considered for practical applications. She further noted that the types Muir describes might not

exist. Hochstedler's study included attitudinal and behavioral items of 1,134 police officers. She chose 45 criterion variables to indicate the officers' job satisfaction, attitudes about the parameters of their task, the role of the officer, and personal conduct.[25]

In his classic article, "Asshole," Van Maanen describes the interactional origins and consequences of the label "asshole," as it is used by officers as they perform their daily tasks. He writes that the "asshole" is a distinct type of person who is familiar to the police and with whom they deal on a regular basis. He also writes that the label arises from a set of conditions largely unrelated to the formal, social mandate of the police (that is, to protect life and property, arrest offenders, and preserve the peace) but, rather, in response to some occupational and personal concerns shared by most officers. His article describes certain understandings shared by officers about what is involved in their work, and deals with the concept of street justice as it is meted out to the "asshole." The article implies that there is an implicit license granted by society to the police, by virtue of which certain police actions taken against this type of person are not governed.[26]

Also, Van Maanen, in "Kinsmen in Repose: Occupational Perspectives of Patrolmen," writes that police officers view themselves as performing society's dirty work and, therefore, as being isolated from the mainstream culture and stigmatized. Police work, he writes, is characterized by drudgery, danger, and dogma and that these structural strains and contradictions lead to high levels of tension. Police recruits come under heavy pressure to bow to group standards of adherence to general axioms of police work and to the ground rules of the everyday work world. He describes two distinct occupational perspectives that together form the officer's personal identity. These include the officer's unique role in the social world and her or his outsider position in the community, and the survival dictums that stem from the unique nature of the officer's work.[27]

Claudia Mendias and E. James Kehoe discuss four policing ideals—law enforcement, peace maintenance, procedural compliance, and protagonist acceptance of responsibility. In a 2006 study, they reported that 66 percent of participating police officers, from 12 police stations in Sydney, Australia, employed two combinations of policing ideals to justify decisions to arrest: keeping the peace/procedural compliance and law enforcement/procedural compliance ideals.[28]

Removal of 3 Freedoms

Police Discretion

The use of discretion is one of the major challenges facing U.S. police today. The following sections will discuss the meaning of police discretion, how and why it is exercised, what factors influence discretion, and how it can be controlled. The use of discretion by police clearly affects other crucial areas covered in this textbook, including biased-based policing; police misconduct, brutality, and corruption; and the liability of the police for their conduct, as indicated in Chapter 8, "Police Ethics and Police Deviance."

What Is Discretion?

Discretion means the availability of a choice of options or actions one can take in a situation. We all exercise discretion many times every day in our lives. At a restaurant, we have discretion in selecting a steak dinner or a fish dinner. At the video store, we have discretion in picking a mystery or a comedy to view. Discretion involves making a judgment and a decision. It involves selecting one from a group of options.

The criminal justice system involves a tremendous amount of discretion. A judge exercises discretion in sentencing. He or she can sentence a defendant to a prison term or to probation. A judge can release a defendant on bail or order the defendant incarcerated until trial. Prosecutors exercise discretion: they can reduce charges against a defendant or drop the charges entirely. Parole boards exercise discretion: they can parole a person from prison or order him or her to serve the complete sentence. The entire criminal justice system is based on the concept of discretion.

Why is there so much discretion in the U.S. system of criminal justice? In our system, we tend to treat people as individuals. One person who commits a robbery is not the same as another person who commits a robbery. Our system takes into account why the person committed the crime and how he or she committed it. Were there any mitigating or aggravating circumstances? The U.S. system is interested in the spirit of the law, in addition to the letter of the law.

When a judge, a prosecutor, or a parole board member exercises discretion, each generally has sufficient time and data necessary to make a careful, reasoned decision.

The judge can read the presentence report prepared by the probation department or consult with the probation department staff member preparing the report. The judge can also consult with the district attorney or the defense attorney. The prosecutor and parole board member also have sufficient data and time in which to decide what action to take in a case.

However, most crucial decisions made in the criminal justice system do not take place as described in the previous paragraph. The most important decisions do not take place within an ornately decorated courtroom or a wood-paneled conference room. They take place on the streets. They take place any time of the day or night, and generally without the opportunity for the decision makers to consult with others or to carefully consider all the facts. These split-second decisions are often based on little information. They take place at the very lowest level in the criminal justice system. The police officer is generally the first decision maker in the U.S. criminal justice system and is often the most important.

Wilson described the police officer's role in exercising discretion as being "unlike that of any other occupation . . . one in which sub-professionals, working alone, exercise wide discretion in matters of utmost importance (life and death, honor and dishonor) in an environment that is apprehensive and perhaps hostile."[29]

Two researchers state, "The police really suffer the worst of all worlds: they must exercise broad discretion behind a facade of performing in ministerial fashion; and they are expected to realize a high level of equality and justice in their discretionary determinations though they have not been provided with the means most commonly relied upon in government to achieve these ends."[30] Kenneth Culp Davis, an expert on police discretion, says, "The police make policy about what law to enforce, how much to enforce it, against whom, and on what occasions."[31]

Not much happens in the U.S. criminal justice system without the use of discretion by the police. How does a police officer exercise discretion on the street?

Before we look at how discretion is exercised, it is important to understand police-committed and police-uncommitted time. Police are often directed by the police dispatcher (911) to crimes, emergencies, and other calls requesting police services. Often supervisors will assign police during particular hours to specific areas to perform duties. These are examples of committed time. However, most of police patrol time is spent doing whatever the individual officers want to do; this is uncommitted time.

In his pioneering work, "Police Patrol Work Load Studies: a Review and Critique," Gary W. Cordner stated,

> Patrol officers have the opportunity to determine what their workload will be during the uncommitted portion of their patrol time. [This proactive] component of patrol work is also largely ambiguous, because the conduct and effect of preventive patrol are not clear, and many of the self-initiated activities undertaken are not strictly crime—or noncrime-related.[32]

In 2005, Christine N. Famega of California State University–San Bernardino, James Frank of the University of Cincinnati, and Lorraine Mazerolle of Griffith University confirmed Cordner's early work. They found that more than three-quarters of a patrol officer's shift is unassigned. Their study concerned three districts of the Baltimore Police Department. During this time, officers primarily self-initiated routine patrol, or backed up officers on calls to which they were not dispatched.[33] In another 2005 report, Famega writes that a literature review of 11 studies of police workload published between 1970 and 2001, using data from either dispatch records or systematic social observation of patrol officers, indicate that patrol officers "clearly had a lot of downtime."[34]

Most of the research literature concerning police workload has involved large, municipal police agencies; in 2006, however, John Liederbach and James Frank produced a study concentrating on a comparison of the use of patrol time by county deputy sheriffs and small-town municipal police officers. This study included observations of county deputy sheriffs and a group of five small-town municipal police agencies located in an Ohio county. In examining the activities and citizen interactions of both the deputy sheriffs and the small-town municipal officers, Liederbach and Frank discovered that the deputy sheriffs spent an extremely large percentage of their time formally handling crime-related problems, whereas small-town municipal officers tended to engage citizens much more informally.[35]

How Is Discretion Exercised?

The police exercise discretion to perform the following crucial actions:

- To arrest
- To stop, question, or frisk
- To use physical force
- To use deadly force
- To write traffic summonses
- To use certain enforcement tactics (harassment, moving loiterers, warning, and so on)
- To take a report on a crime
- To investigate a crime

Some of the extent of police discretion is indicated by the following research findings. Donald

You Are There!

You Decide
Think about what you would do as a police officer under the following circumstances. This is a perfect example of a case calling for the exercise of police discretion.

Facts
You receive a call to respond to a boy who is bleeding on the street. You arrive at the location, and you find a 14-year-old Asian boy, naked and with blood on his buttocks; a male in his late 20s or early 30s; and two women. The two women tell you that the man must be trying to kill the boy. The boy is too dazed to respond and remains mute. The man tells you that he and the boy are homosexual lovers and were having an argument.

What Would You Do?
If you were the police officer at the scene, which of the following actions would you take?

- Further question all parties at the scene.
- Bring all parties to the station house for further investigation.
- Request that your supervisor or the detectives meet you at the scene.
- Arrest the man for assault and sexual relations with a minor.

- Ignore the situation and let these people solve their own problems.

The Actual Case
The previous facts are from an actual case you probably recognize. Shortly after midnight on May 27, 1990, two women saw a man chasing a 14-year-old Asian boy, naked and with blood on his buttocks, down an alley behind the Oxford Apartments in a low-income area of Milwaukee, Wisconsin. The women called the police. Two police officers arrived in a patrol car. The man told the police officers that he and the boy were gay lovers having a spat. The officers told all parties to go home and resumed patrol.

The boy was later identified as Konerak Sinthasomphone after his remains were found amid the carnage at Apartment 213 of the Oxford Apartments in 1991. The man was later identified as Jeffrey Dahmer. When the police searched Dahmer's apartment, they found parts of at least 11 bodies. These included three severed heads in the refrigerator; decomposed hands and a genital organ in a lobster pot; five full skeletons; and the remains of six other bodies, three of which were in a chemical-filled, 57-gallon plastic drum in the basement. Dahmer later confessed to the murder of 17 males.

Black found that only 58 percent of adults suspected of felonies were arrested.[36] John A. Gardiner found that Dallas police officers wrote traffic tickets at a rate 20 times higher than that of Boston police.[37] The Police Foundation noted that the police in Birmingham, Alabama, shot and killed citizens at a rate of 25 per 1,000 officers, compared with 4.2 per 1,000 in Portland, Oregon.[38]

Why Is Discretion Exercised?

Discretion is an extremely necessary part of police work. Sheehan and Cordner tell us that the police exercise discretion for seven reasons:

1. If the police attempted to enforce all the laws all the time, they would be in the station house or court all the time and would not be on the street maintaining order and protecting life and property.

2. Because of political realities, legislators pass some laws that they do not intend to have strictly enforced all the time.

3. Lawmakers pass some laws that are vague and ill-defined, making it necessary for the police to interpret these laws and decide when to apply them.

4. Most violations of the law are minor (for example, traffic violations) and do not require full enforcement.

5. The complete enforcement of all the laws all the time would alienate the public from the police and the entire criminal justice system.

6. The full enforcement of all the laws would overwhelm the courts, jails, and prisons.

7. The police have so many duties to perform and such limited resources that good judgment must be exercised in when, where, and how they enforce the law.[39]

What Factors Influence Discretion?

We know that officers practice discretion, and we know that discretion is necessary. Are there factors, however, that cause the police to exercise discretion in a certain way? Scholars have been studying this issue for quite a while.

Herbert Jacob wrote that four major factors influence police officers in determining the exercise of discretion:

1. *Characteristics of the crime.* A serious crime leaves the police less freedom or ability to ignore it or exercise discretion regarding it.

2. *Relationship between the alleged criminal and the victim.* Generally, the police tend to avoid making arrests when a perpetrator and a victim have a close relationship. In recent years, however, many departments have limited discretion in domestic violence or family assault cases and have adopted pro-arrest policies. Domestic violence will be discussed in Chapter 11, "Police and the Community."

3. *Relationship between police and the criminal or victim.* Generally, a respectful, mannerly complainant is taken more seriously and treated better by the police than an antagonistic one. In the same way, a violator who acts respectfully to the police is also less likely to be arrested than is an antagonistic one.

4. *Department policies.* The preferences of the police chief and city administration, as expressed in department policy, generally influence the actions of the officer.[40]

In *Varieties of Police Behavior,* Wilson found that an officer's discretion varied depending on the type of situation he or she encountered. Wilson found that police have wide latitude in self-initiated situations, such as the enforcement of traffic or drug violations, because there is usually no complainant or victim demanding police action. However, in citizen-initiated situations, an officer has less discretion, and the preferences of the citizen will often influence the officer's decision to arrest or not to arrest.[41]

Research has identified other specific factors that could influence police discretion to arrest, including the subject's offense, attitude, race, socioeconomic status, gender, officer race, and police peer-group pressure. Many studies considering these factors are discussed in this chapter.

Studies of police discretion have shown that the most significant factor in the decision to arrest is the seriousness of the offense committed. This factor is supplemented by other information, such as the offender's current mental state, the offender's past criminal record (when known to the arresting officer), whether weapons were involved, the availability of the complainant, and the relative danger to the officer involved.[42]

Irving Pilavin and Scott Briar found that the subject's attitude greatly influenced an officer's discretion to arrest. With the exception of offenders who had committed serious crimes or who were wanted by the police, the disposition of juvenile cases depended largely on how a youth's character was evaluated by the officer. This evaluation and the decisions that followed from it were limited to information gathered by police during their encounter with the juveniles.[43]

In a 2005 article, John D. McCluskey, of the University of Texas at San Antonio, William Terrill, of Northeastern University, and Eugene A. Paoline, III, of the University of Central Florida found that collective peer group attitudes toward aggressive patrol does not influence police use of force behavior. The researchers examined almost 1,500 police-suspect encounters.[44]

Numerous studies have looked at discretion to arrest as it relates to race. Wilson has reported that the influence of race on police discretion varies from jurisdiction to jurisdiction and may be a function of the professionalism of the individual department.[45] A number of studies have produced data indicating that racial bias does not influence the decision to arrest and process a suspect.[46]

A 2005 study by Arrick L. Jackson of Southeast Missouri State University in Cape Girardeau, Missouri, and Lorenzo M. Boyd, formerly a deputy sheriff in Suffolk County, Massachusetts, and presently a professor of criminal justice at the University of North Texas, in Denton, Texas, found a significant direct relationship between the numbers of black residents in a community and lenient policing (ignoring minor crimes for more serious crimes). Using a sample of 353 police officers from a midwestern police agency and census tract data, the researchers discovered that patrol divisions with more minority residents are less likely to be lenient than officers in districts that have a majority of white residents. Jackson and Boyd also found that as the percentage of minorities increased in the population police were less likely to use lenient policing.[47]

In a 2004 study, Robin Shepard Engel of the University of Cincinnati and Jennifer Calnon, a doctoral candidate at Pennsylvania State University, using data from the *1999 Police-Public Contact Survey*[48] (a nationwide survey of citizens that explores police-citizen interactions) wrote that their research found that young black and Hispanic males are at increased risk for citations, searches, arrests, and uses of force than are whites. Engel and Calnon indicate that additional analyses show that minority drivers are not, however, more likely to be carrying contraband than are white drivers.[49]

Numerous other studies have looked at discretion to arrest as it relates to the race of the offender. Dennis Powell found that a community's racial makeup can influence police discretion. Powell studied five adjacent police jurisdictions and found that the police in predominantly African American, urban communities demonstrated a higher use of discretion and were more punitive toward whites than toward African Americans, whereas police in predominantly white areas were significantly more punitive toward African-American offenders than toward white offenders.[50] Dale Dannefer and Russel Schutt found that racial bias was often present in the patrol officer's decision to arrest juveniles and bring them to juvenile court.[51]

In 2005, the Bureau of Justice Statistics (BJS) issued its *Contacts between Police and the Public: Findings from the 2002 National Survey* reporting on 45.3 million contacts between police and citizens. The BJS reported that the likelihood of being stopped by the police while driving did not differ significantly between white (8.7 percent), black (9.1 percent), and Hispanic (8.6 percent) drivers. However, the survey disclosed that during the traffic stop, police were more likely to carry out some type of search on a black person (10.2 percent) or Hispanic person (11.4 percent) than on a white person (3.5 percent).[52]

The report also indicated that about 1.5 percent of all of the contacts involved the police use or threat of force. Blacks (3.5 percent) and Hispanics (2.5 percent) were reported to be more likely than whites (1.1 percent) to experience police threat or use of force.[53]

Some studies have indicated that the victim's race rather than the criminal's race was the key to racial bias in the use of discretion. One study discovered that the police were more likely to take formal action when the victim of a crime was white than when the victim was a minority group member.[54] Another study found that police were more likely to report child abuse involving white families than African American families.[55]

Some research has also been done on the effect of the race of an officer on police discretion. A 2006 article by Robert A. Brown of Indiana University in Indianapolis and James Frank of the University of Cincinnati disclosed a study that found that officer race had a direct influence on arrest outcomes and that there were substantive differences between white and black officers in the decision to arrest. In this study, based on systematic social observations of police-citizen encounters in Cincinnati, Ohio, white officers were more likely to arrest suspects than were black officers, but black suspects were more likely to be arrested by a black officer.[56]

As for discretion and a subject's gender, there is also much conflicting evidence. Douglas Smith and Christy Visher found that males and females were equally likely to be arrested and formally processed for law violations when encountered by the police.[57] However, Visher later found in a reanalysis of the data that demographic variables were more important in arrest decisions for females than males. She found that police were more likely to arrest women whose attitude and actions deviated from the stereotype of "proper" female behavior. Visher also found that older white female suspects were less likely to be arrested than were younger African American women.[58] In another study, Richard J. Lundman found that, in confrontations with juveniles and for public drunkenness encounters, gender played no role in the decision to arrest[59]; and in another study, David Klinger found that gender had no effect on the arrest decision.[60]

Contrary to the previous findings, other studies suggest that being male significantly increased the likelihood of arrest.[61] In 2003, Lundman and R. L Kaufman suggest that women were significantly less likely than men to report being stopped by the police but were more likely than men to report that they were stopped for legitimate reasons and that the police acted properly during the stop.[62] And in 2004, Engel and Calnon found that gender played an important role in citations, searches, arrests, and use of force. They say that being male increased the odds by 23 percent of respondents reporting a traffic citation, 300 percent for a search, 180 percent for an arrest, and 230 percent for force.[63] The 2005 study based on the 2002 National Survey of contacts between the police and the public revealed that men were more likely to be subject to vehicle stops than

ON THE JOB

The Changing View

The issue of the police culture and the police role really hit home with me when I was a road patrol lieutenant working the midnight shift. I had been working the midnight shift for several years. As we know, the types of police work you do can vary somewhat depending on the shift you work, the district you work, and the assignment you have.

On the midnight shift, you spend a lot of time working with "bad guys," because most average citizens are home in bed. Obviously, there are exceptions to this, but, overall, officers on midnights are dealing with people on the street who are up to no good. This observation or feeling starts to ingrain itself in an officer's head, and he or she becomes suspicious of everyone encountered. What are they really doing? Are they lying? Why? The officer develops a protective attitude physically and mentally when approaching and talking to people during the shift. He or she will assume the worst. This is not necessarily a negative trait when looking at it in terms of officer safety and survival, but it can have an impact on the officer's interactions with people he or she encounters.

I remember one night seeing a car driving in an area of warehouses where we had numerous burglary problems during the midnight shift hours. I watched the vehicle for a few minutes and then pulled it over. I approached the young male driver and asked him what he was doing out here at this time of day—in other words, what was he really up to? He looked at me quizzically and replied that he was just going to work. He was able to produce paperwork that documented this (which of course doesn't necessarily mean he wasn't doing burglaries in the area). I allowed him to go on his way and thought about the encounter. Though it was still dark, it was just after 6 AM, and good, hardworking people were in fact getting up and going to work, but I was still thinking of "bad guys" being out and about and up to no good.

—Linda Forst

were women and were more likely to be subject to the use of force.[64]

In a 2006 study, Michael R. Smith, a former police officer and currently a professor at the University of South Carolina, Geoffrey P. Alpert of the University of South Carolina, and Matthew Makarios, a PhD student at the University of Cincinnati, drawing on more than 66,000 traffic stop records from the Miami–Dade County Police Department, suggest that police may develop unconscious, cognitive schemas that make them more likely to be suspicious of population subgroups that they repeatedly encounter in street-level situations involving crime and violence. In this study, police were found to be significantly more suspicious of men than of women in traffic-stop encounters and that this suspicion was strongly associated with the decision to arrest.[65]

Studies on factors influencing police discretion and police decision making continue. A literature review points to the tremendous complexity of the issue and the concern we all should have regarding it.[66] To add to the confusion, in 2006, Alpert, Roger G. Dunham, and their colleagues discussed their 2004 study based on observations and debriefings of police officers in Savannah, Georgia, regarding factors causing officers to make stops of individuals and vehicles. They made the following observations[67]:

- Characteristics of the person stopped were not a significant factor in why an officer decided to make the stop. Officers were equally likely to stop individuals who were male or female, black or white, or of low or high socioeconomic status based on appearances.

- In most of the cases where stops were made, the behavior of the suspect was what concerned the officer.

- Appearances of individuals and vehicles only became important in stops when they matched descriptions of suspects for traffic violations or crimes that had been reported.

- Officer observation of a traffic violation, obvious efforts to avoid the officer, and acting nervous in the officer's presence were common behaviors that caused officers to stop individuals.

- Time and place were not significant in officers' decisions to make stops. Officers did not make stops impulsively based upon initial notice of an individual or vehicle. They were not usually made until after continued observations confirmed an initial suspicion that a stop might be required.

Thus, as you can see, the discussions of factors leading to the use of police discretion continue to be complex.

How Can Discretion Be Controlled?

In recent years, much attention has been given to the need to prepare police for the appropriate use of discretion. Most experts believe that discretion itself is not bad, but that the real problem is uncontrolled or unregulated discretion. The experts feel that discretion cannot and should not be abolished but believe that police departments should attempt to control or regulate it.[68]

Most researchers believe that discretion should be narrowed to the point where all officers in the same agency are dealing with similar issues in similar ways. They feel there should be limits on discretion that reflect the objectives, priorities, and operating philosophy of the department. The limits on discretion should be sufficiently specific to enable an officer to make judgments in a wide variety of unpredictable circumstances in a proper, unbiased manner that will achieve a reasonable degree of uniformity in handling similar incidents in the community.[69]

One approach to managing police behavior involves requiring obedience to a formal set of policies or guidelines that can ensure the just administration of the law. Many police departments established written policies regarding the use of deadly force as far back as the early 1970s, even before the U.S. Supreme Court decision *Tennessee v. Garner*[70] that will be discussed later in this chapter. These policies dramatically reduced the number of shootings of civilians by the police and reduced the number of officers shot by civilians. Since the 1980s, many departments have established formal procedures for dealing with emotionally disturbed persons, police pursuits, and other critical issues discussed in this text.

One way of controlling discretion, particularly improper application of discretion, is the establishment of employee early warning systems. These automated systems detect significant events in an officer's statistics, such as a high number of use of force incidents, vehicle pursuits, sick days, involvement in significant events, or low numbers of arrests or citizen contacts. These systems provide a warning to managers and supervisors, who can then investigate any irregular patterns. The Phoenix, Arizona, Police Department has had such a system in place for several years.[71]

Most important, however, Wilson tells us that controlling discretion involves more than just establishing policies and ensuring that they are obeyed. Managing discretion involves an effort by management to instill a proper value system in officers. According to Wilson, controlling discretion "depends only partly on sanctions and inducements; it also requires instilling in them a shared outlook or ethos that provides for them a common definition of the situations they are likely to encounter and that to the outsider gives to the organization its distinctive character or 'feel.'"[72]

■ ─────────────────────────────

Police Discretion and Police Shootings and the Use of Deadly Force

Police shootings or the use of **deadly force** by the police might be the ultimate use of discretion by the police. Sometimes, officers are forced into making a split-second decision about whether to use deadly force. If they hesitate, they run the risk of being killed or seriously injured themselves, or allowing an innocent citizen to be killed or seriously injured. If their split-second decision later is found to be wrong and that they misused their discretion, they face public and legal criticism and perhaps arrest itself. They are also criticized by the press and the community. Worse still is that they may have to live with this mistaken decision for the rest of their life. Being a police officer and using necessary discretion is not an easy job. Sometimes government officials understand this. Mayor John F. Street of Philadelphia, in a 2006 press conference, expressed indignation about those who "second-guess" officers who have fatally shot civilians and said that in some cases their criticism was "unconscionable":

> When we ask people to put on a uniform and to go out and fight crime and to go out into some of the most difficult and the most

ON THE JOB

The Public's Perception

It is difficult to know at the outset of a call how people are going to respond to your commands. We constantly need to adjust our perception of the situation and the amount of force that may be necessary to solve the problem. We also need to be aware that we are always being watched and that citizens may perceive things differently than we do.

I remember handling a call on a Friday evening during the height of tourist season in Boca. We received a call at a local restaurant/lounge advising of an elderly female threatening to "slash" the bartender with a knife. I was the first officer on the scene and contacted the bartender. He told me that the woman had left. He briefly described her and said that she did in fact show a kitchen knife and threaten to slash his face if he didn't serve her another drink. He felt she was unstable.

As I was talking to him, we got a similar call at the restaurant a few blocks away. This was a large chain-type bistro, and there was an elderly female in the restaurant yelling, acting irrationally, and stating she had a knife. I hopped in my car and drove to the restaurant. The restaurant was packed with families and tourists. I spoke with the manager who directed me to the woman in the back of the restaurant. By this time, two other officers had arrived. Two of us walked to the back and talked to the woman while the third officer waited by our cars. The woman was agitated but agreed to come out front with us to discuss the

situation. While we were talking, she became increasingly irrational and started screaming that she was going to "slash" us. I patted her down and was attempting to take her knife from her when she went nuts and started fighting with us and screaming. This woman was only about 5'4" and 65 to 70 years old and frail looking. We didn't want her to get hurt, and we didn't want one of us to get hurt, and we felt that by using three officers, we could handcuff her and minimize the chance of injuries by each officer taking an arm and another one doing the cuffing. She struggled and fought us but we got her cuffed without hurting her. We were standing by the back of one of the police cars right in front of the big plate glass window of the restaurant, and lots of people were watching. We used only as much force as we needed; even though she was old and frail, she was a danger to herself and others, but we knew it didn't look good— three officers in uniform handcuffing one elderly female. In fact, one individual leaving the restaurant made a comment to the effect that we were bullies. But we knew we had done the best we could under the circumstances and, despite outward appearances, were able to keep anyone from getting hurt. Officers are always going to be questioned about the amount of force they use in any given situation.

—Linda Forst

troubling areas of our community, under circumstances that most of us really wouldn't want to even think about, it is unfair for people to second-guess everything they do, every time they do it.[73]

Police Use of Force

In 2005, the Bureau of Justice Statistics, in its *Contacts Between Police and the Public: Findings from the 2002 National Survey,* reporting on 45.3 million contacts between police and citizens, noted that only about 1.5 percent of all of the contacts involved the police use or threat of force. About 14 percent of those who experienced force were

injured because of the police action. About 87 percent of the persons experiencing the threat or use of force felt that the police acted improperly, and about 24 percent of the persons involved in a police force incident reported that they argued with, cursed at, insulted, or verbally threatened the officers during the incident. The police force most reported was "pushed or shoved," (42 percent), and 19 percent involved police pointing a gun at someone.[74]

Statistics clearly indicate that police officers do not overuse force. In a 2002 report, covering research in six law enforcement agencies, it was disclosed that officers used some physical force in about 17 percent of the adult custody arrests they made, and suspects used some physical force in about 12 percent of their arrests. The researchers found that the officers' use of force was low—weapons were used in only 2.1 percent of all arrests (the weapon most often used was pepper spray).[75]

Number of Citizens Shot by the Police

Historically, the shooting of a citizen by the police has been a major problem facing the police. Police shootings have had a serious negative impact on police-community relations. Numerous incidents of civil unrest have followed police shootings of civilians. Wilson stated, "No aspect of policing elicits more passionate concern or more divided opinions than the use of deadly force."[76]

Police shootings receive tremendous media attention. However, the late James J. Fyfe, a former New York City police lieutenant and deputy commissioner for training and one of the leading experts on the police use of deadly force in the United States, reported that the systematic examination of the use of deadly force was largely neglected until a series of police shootings and other police problems precipitated the urban violence of the 1960s.[77]

According to the latest comprehensive report on police shootings, in 2001, an average of 373 people per year were killed justifiably by police officers during the latest 22 years.[78] In 99 percent of these incidents, police used a firearm. Ninety-eight percent of the subjects were males, and 98 percent of the officers were male. From 1976 to 1998, the officers involved in 84 percent of justifiable homicides were white, and 15 percent were African American. This percentage is in keeping with their average percentage in the police ranks across the nation (approximately 87 percent of police officers are white). In 65 percent of justifiable homicides by police, the officer's race and the offender's race were the same. Although the U.S. population, age 13 and older, had increased by 47 million in this time, and the number of police officers had increased by approximately 200,000, the number of felons justifiably killed by police did not significantly increase.[79] Perhaps the police are becoming more judicious with their use of deadly force. This may be the result of better training, better procedures, or the expansion of less-than-lethal alternatives.

Do Police Discriminate with Their Trigger Fingers?

Numerous studies have been conducted to determine if there is, in fact, racial discrimination in the police use of deadly force. If one considers only total numbers, the overwhelming difference in the percentage of African Americans shot over the percentage of whites shot could lead to the conclusion that discrimination does indeed exist. The 2001 report mentioned earlier indicates that a disproportionate number of African Americans are justifiably killed by police officers. During the years covered by the study, African Americans made up 12 percent of the population, aged 13 and older, but were 35 percent of felons killed by police. However, this percentage is similar to that of African Americans (40 percent) arrested by police for violent crime. It was also reported, however, that the rate at which African Americans were fatally shot by the police declined from 1976 to 1998, whereas the rate for whites killed has remained steady.[80]

In one of the first studies of police shootings, Gerald Robin, in 1963, found that Chicago police, over a 10-year period, shot and killed African Americans at a rate of 16.1 per 100,000 citizens, compared with 2.1 whites per 100,000 citizens. Other cities had even greater disparities. In Boston, the police shot and killed African Americans 25 times more often than they shot and killed whites.[81]

Fyfe's analysis in the late 1970s of citizens shot and killed by the Memphis police over a five-year period found a pattern of extreme racial disparity, particularly with respect to unarmed citizens. Overall, 26 of the 34 people shot and killed in that period (85.7 percent) were African American. In the category of nonassaultive and unarmed people, the Memphis police shot and killed 13 African Americans and only one white. Half of all the African Americans shot and killed were nonassaultive and unarmed. The data suggest that the Memphis police were much more likely to shoot unarmed African Americans than unarmed whites. Fyfe wrote, "Blacks and Hispanics are everywhere overrepresented among those on the other side of police guns."[82]

There is another side, however, to the analysis of race and police shootings. Two studies indicate that people who engage in violent crime or who engage the police in violent confrontations are much more likely to be the victims of police shootings. In one study, participation in violent crime was used as a relevant variable in police shootings because participation in crime generally places a person at risk of being confronted by the police and being shot by the police. The Chicago Law Enforcement Study Group examined shootings by Chicago police during a five-year period. The group first analyzed the rate at which whites, African Americans, and Hispanic Americans were shot and killed relative to their number in the population and then the rate at which the same groups were shot and killed while participating in violent crimes. The data indicated that African Americans were shot and killed six times as often as whites relative to the total population, but the disparity disappeared when participation in violent crimes was a factor. Whites were shot and killed at a rate of 5.6 per 1,000 arrests for forcible felonies, compared with 4.5 African Americans shot and killed per 1,000 arrests for the same category of crime.[83]

In the other study—Fyfe's pioneering PhD dissertation, "Shots Fired," a study of New York City police shootings during a five-year period in the 1970s—Fyfe found that police officers are most likely to shoot suspects who are armed and with whom they become involved in violent confrontations. Fyfe found that if factors such as being armed with a weapon, being involved in a violent crime, and attacking an officer are considered, the racial differences in the police use of deadly force became nonsignificant.[84]

David Lester, pointing to the jurisdictional variation of police use of deadly force, reported that police officers kill more people in communities with high violence rates and during years in which the homicide rates were highest.[85]

In a 2004 study Michael D. White reported that many factors are involved in the quick decision-making process involved in a police shooting, including the victim's actions, the officer's actions, the type of assault against the officer, and the type of weapon involved, as well as other options available to the officer in addition to deadly violence. These are in addition to the environmental factors such as community characteristics and organizational factors such as the department's policies and organizational climate.[86]

An interesting study involving ordinary citizens was conducted by researchers at the University of Washington in 2003. A psychology professor showed 208 shooting scenarios to 106 undergraduate psychology students on computers. They had one second to either "shoot," send a "safety signal" that they saw a police officer, or do nothing.

The students were told before the scenario that the criminal, who was always armed, was either African American or white. In the scenarios, African Americans were found to be mistaken more often for the criminal than were whites. African Americans were "wrongly shot" 35 percent of the time and whites 26 percent of the time. A sergeant with the State of Washington Criminal Justice Training Commission does not believe this translates to police recruits because of their training. In training more than 2,000 recruits on simulators, he found they were likely to err on the side of not shooting and are actually more focused on the weapon and often aren't aware of the race of someone they had just "shot."[87] The Department of Justice's statistics mentioned earlier tend to back up this sergeant's observation.

Departure from the "Fleeing Felon" Rule

Before the great amount of attention given to police shootings in the wake of the civil disorders of the 1960s, most U.S. police departments operated under the common-law "fleeing felon" doctrine, which held that law enforcement officers could, if necessary, use deadly force to apprehend any fleeing felony suspect. This doctrine evolved from the common-law tradition of medieval England, when all felonies were capital offenses (liable for the death penalty). Because there was very little official law enforcement in those days, and very few escaping felons were apprehended, the law allowed a person who had committed a felony to be killed while fleeing the scene.

The fleeing felon rule, like most of England's common law, came to the United States. Today, however, there is little need for the fleeing felon rule in the United States because we have sufficient armed police and modern communications systems to aid in the apprehension of fleeing felons. Also, the legality and morality of the fleeing felon rule is challenged because of the U.S. legal concept of presumption of innocence. Most U.S. states, however, maintained the fleeing felon rule well into the 1960s and 1970s. In 1985, the fleeing felon rule was declared unconstitutional by the U.S. Supreme Court in the landmark case *Tennessee v. Garner*.[88]

Although many agreed with the Garner decision (the use of deadly force on an unarmed fleeing felon is unconstitutional unless it is necessary

You Are There!

Tennessee v. Garner

The *Garner* case finally ended the fleeing felon rule. On October 3, 1974, at about 10:45 PM, two Memphis police officers, Elton Hymon and Leslie Wright, responded to a prowler run (a report of "prowler inside"). Upon reaching the location, they were met by a neighbor, who told them she had heard someone breaking into the house next to hers. Officer Wright radioed for assistance as Officer Hymon went to the rear of the house. As the officer approached the backyard, he heard a door slamming, and he observed someone running across the backyard. The fleeing person stopped at a 6-foot-high chain-link fence at the end of the yard. The officer shone his flashlight and saw what appeared to be a 17- or 18-year-old youth about 5 feet 7 inches tall. The officer yelled, "Police! Halt!" However, the youth began to climb the fence.

If You Were Officer Hymon, What Would You Do?

The officer, thinking that the youth would escape, fired a shot at him, which struck him in the back of the head. The youth later died on the operating table. Ten dollars and a purse taken from the house were found on his body. The dead youth was later identified as Edward Garner, a 15-year-old eighth grader. At the trial, the officer admitted that he knew that Garner was unarmed and was trying to escape. The officer testified that he was acting under the provisions of Tennessee law that stated that an officer may use all the necessary means to effect an arrest if, after notice of the intention to arrest, the defendant either flees or forcibly resists.

The U.S. Supreme Court ruled 6 to 3 that the use of deadly force against apparently unarmed and nondangerous fleeing felons is an illegal seizure under the Fourth Amendment. The Court ended the common law fleeing felon rule by stating,

> The use of deadly force to prevent the escape of all felony suspects, whatever the circumstances, is constitutionally unreasonable. It is not better that all felony suspects die than they escape. Where the suspect poses no immediate threat to the officer and no threat to others, the harm resulting from failing to apprehend him does not justify the use of deadly force to do so. It is no doubt unfortunate when a suspect who is in sight escapes, but the fact that the police arrive a little late or are a little slower afoot does not always justify killing the suspect. A police officer may not seize an unarmed, nondangerous suspect by shooting him dead.

If you had been a member of the Court, would you have agreed with this ruling?

SOURCE: Based on *Tennessee v. Garner*, 471 U.S. 1 (1985).

to prevent the escape and the officer has probable cause to believe that the suspect poses a significant threat of death or serious physical injury to the officers or others), one critic argued that the standard is much too restrictive, ambiguous, and unrealistic, in that it imposes an impossible burden on an officer to determine in a split second whether a fleeing felon is dangerous to the officer or to others.[89]

Before the Garner case, and subsequent to the urban riots of the 1960s, many states replaced the fleeing felon rule with new state laws, internal rules of police departments, and court decisions. During the 1970s, many police departments developed an alternative to the fleeing felon doctrine, based in part on recommendations by the American Law Institute and the Police Foundation. This rule used the **"defense of life" standard,** which allowed police officers to use deadly force against people who were using deadly force against an officer or another person, as well as in certain violent felony situations. The replacement of the common-law fleeing felon rule by the defense of life standard changed the incidence of police shootings. Lawrence O'Donnell found that police departments with effective deadly force rules showed sharp decreases in citizen deaths and in officer deaths. In Kansas City, Missouri, for example, after the department adopted a rule that prohibited police from shooting juveniles except in self-defense, the number of youths younger than 18 shot by the police dropped dramatically.[90]

Fyfe found that the number of police shootings dropped sharply following the New York City Police Department (NYPD)'s adoption of a strict deadly force rule (defense of life standard). He also found that the average number of shots fired by New York City police officers was reduced by

You Are There!

Alternatives to the Fleeing Felon Rule

In the 1970s, the American Law Institute proposed a Model Penal Code, which included new policies on the use of deadly force. Many states replaced their existing penal codes with this model code. During the same period, the Police Foundation proposed its own policies regarding the use of deadly force, which were adopted by many police departments.

Model Penal Code

The Model Penal Code, developed by the American Law Institute, permits the use of deadly force by police officers if an officer believes that (1) the felony for which the arrest is made involved the use, or the threatened use, of deadly force; or (2) there is a substantial risk that the suspect will cause death or serious bodily injury if not immediately apprehended; and (3) the force employed creates no substantial risk of injury to innocent people.

The Police Foundation Standard

After studying the deadly force policies of numerous police departments, including those of Birmingham, Alabama; Detroit, Michigan; Indianapolis, Indiana; Kansas City, Missouri; Oakland, California; Portland, Oregon; and Washington, D.C., the Police Foundation recommended that police departments develop rules governing the use of deadly force after consultation with citizens and police line officers. It recommended that officers be allowed to shoot to defend themselves and others, as well as to apprehend suspects in deadly or potentially deadly felonies. The Police Foundation also recommended several internal police policies that could lead to an improved use of deadly force by the police. These policies included carefully screening recruits to eliminate both unstable and violence-prone officers, dismissing probationary officers who demonstrate instability or propensity to violence, and providing more meaningful training in the rules of deadly force.

The Police Foundation proposed the following deadly force rules that departments might adopt: Officers might use deadly force to defend themselves or others from what the officers reasonably perceive as an immediate threat of death or serious injury, when there is no apparent alternative. Officers also might use deadly force to apprehend an armed and dangerous subject when alternative means of apprehension would involve a substantial risk of death or serious injury, and when the safety of innocent bystanders would not be additionally jeopardized by the officers' actions. Any of the following could make an armed subject dangerous enough to justify the use of deadly force: (1) the subject has recently shot, shot at, killed, or attempted to kill someone, or has done so more than once in the past; (2) the subject has recently committed a serious assault on a law enforcement officer acting in the line of duty; and (3) the subject has declared that he or she will kill, if necessary, to avoid arrest.

SOURCE: Adapted from American Law Institute, *Model Penal Code,* section 307(2)(b); and Catherine H. Milton, Jeanne Wahl Halleck, James Lardner, and Gary L. Abrecht, *Police Use of Deadly Force* (Washington, D.C.: Police Foundation, 1977).

---

30 percent. The greatest reduction occurred in fleeing felon situations. Fyfe found, moreover, that the number of police officers shot also dropped. Hence, Fyfe concluded, stricter deadly force rules appear to reduce police and citizen fatalities and woundings.[91] Fyfe observed, "Reductions in police shooting frequency and changes in police shooting patterns have followed implementation of restrictive administrative policies on deadly force and weapon use."[92]

In 1995, after tremendous negative publicity and after detailed investigations into the actions of federal agents at the deadly siege of the Branch Davidian compound in Waco, Texas, and at the home of antigovernment separatist Randy Weaver, in Ruby Ridge, Idaho, the federal government announced that it was refining the deadly force policy used by federal agents and adopted the "imminent danger" standard, basically the same "defense of life" standard that law enforcement agencies have been following for years. It restricts the use of deadly force to only those situations where the lives of agents or others are in imminent danger. The revised policy also permits deadly physical force against a prisoner attempting escape who was being held in or sentenced to a high-security prison. The new policy also forbids the firing of warning shots and shooting at moving vehicles in an attempt to disable such vehicles.[93]

Realizing how important this issue is and the need for guidance for officers, 95 percent of all local police departments and 97 percent of all sheriff's officers have a written policy on use of deadly force—see Chapter 2, "Organizing Public and Private Security in the United States."[94]

Firearms Training

During the 1970s and 1980s, police departments came to the realization that officers needed more realistic firearms training and weapons at least equal to the criminals on the street. By 1990, 73 percent of all local departments had authorized the use of some type of semiautomatic weapon, and by 2000, that number had increased to almost all local police departments and sheriff's offices.[95]

In 1970, the NYPD began using a "Firearms Discharge Report" to document all gunshots by NYPD officers. By compiling this data, they were hoping to document where, when, and under what conditions officers were firing their guns. Over the years, other departments followed suit to analyze shooting incidents and address training needs in an effort to keep officers safe. This included studies by Metro-Dade Miami and Los Angeles Sheriff's Departments. The old style of standing or kneeling at a range and firing at bull's-eye targets 25 or 50 yards downrange clearly wasn't preparing officers for the real-life conditions they encountered on the street.[96]

Most departments are now attempting to incorporate real-life conditions such as low light, noise, sirens, flashing lights, and weather conditions into their training. They are also stressing the "shoot–don't shoot" aspect of shooting as much as accuracy. As much as agencies strive to make firearms training as realistic as possible, it will be difficult to simulate randomly moving targets and the emotional, life-threatening dynamics of the real thing, but the effort must continue.[97]

Most police departments now train their officers in the use of force using the "use of force continuum" in which police officers are taught to escalate their force to the same extent that the subject is using, and to only use deadly force as a final option and only when the subject is using deadly force against the officer or a third party. Special Agent Thomas D. Petrowski of the FBI criticizes this practice, claiming that it results in hesitation in the officer to use force. He writes that such hesitation by the officer is the cause of many officer injuries and deaths.[98] He argues further that policies and training must focus on overcoming instinctive hesitation in using force, rather than encouraging it, that the cornerstone of use of force training should be threat assessment, and that officers must

be trained to respond to the threat of violence and not to the actual violence itself.[99]

Less-Than-Lethal Force

In 2005, the U.S. Government Accountability Office, in a report to the U.S. Congress, reported that the growing popularity of **less-than-lethal weapons** (LTLW) by police officers in the United States virtually ensured their increased use in the law enforcement community.[100]

In 2006, the Department of Justice reported that 90 percent of all local departments and 89 percent of all sheriff's departments had a policy regarding nonlethal force and almost all departments authorized the use of one or more nonlethal weapons.[101]

- 99 percent of local police departments and 96 percent of sheriff's offices authorized the use of chemical sprays

- 95 percent of local police departments and 92 percent of sheriff's offices authorized use of batons of some type

- 23 percent of local departments and 30 percent of sheriff's departments authorized electronic devices (stun guns or Tasers) of some type

- 13 percent of local police departments and 11 percent of sheriff's offices authorized choke holds, carotid holds, or neck restraints.

Departments have turned to some of these less-than-lethal weapons in an effort to give officers options other than deadly force when faced with a combative subject. Various forms of chemical sprays have been in the police arsenal for years. Electronic devices have also given officers an alternative to deadly force, allowing a subject to be temporarily subdued without a gun. There have been several deaths in Taser or stun-gun situations, though none have been blamed on the Taser itself. Most of the time, drugs were found to be the primary cause of death. Supporters of these weapons believe that the use of the Taser or stun gun has saved many lives. The International Association of Chiefs of Police (IACP) has a model policy regarding the use of Tasers and other electronic devices and states their purpose is to save lives.[102] A spokesman for Taser International, which makes the Taser, reported that more than 8,000 law enforcement agencies in the United States use it and that in Cincinnati, Ohio, where the Taser was used 1,000 times, police officials noted a 56 percent drop in injuries to officers and a 35 percent drop in injuries to suspects.[103]

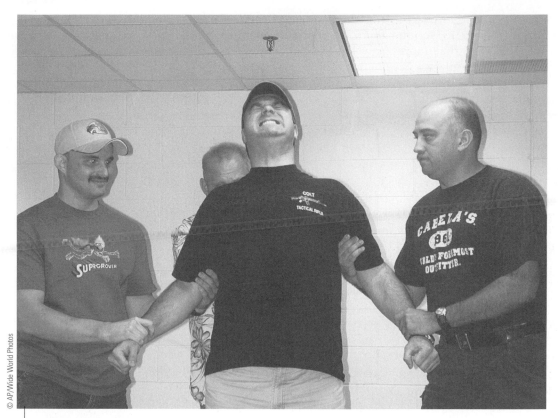

© AP/Wide World Photos

Officers have discretion in making the decision to use a weapon or not. In an effort to aid in this decision making process, officers are required to experience a taser shock before they are issued a taser to carry on duty. Here, an officer in Iowa is supported by other officers as he is shocked with a taser during training.

Choke holds, carotid holds, or neck restraints became a source of controversy after some deaths were associated with their use. Many departments have removed this option for officers from their policies. Some also consider the use of K-9s to be less-than-lethal force, and there is a concern by some that they are used in a biased manner. Twenty-nine percent of local departments used dogs for law enforcement purposes; the bigger the department, the more likely it is to use dogs, with 94 percent of departments serving more than 100,000 people using dogs. Fifty-five percent of sheriff's offices use canines.[104]

Many less-than-lethal weapons—including the baton, oleoresin capsicum (OC), and the Taser or stun gun—are not control and restraint techniques; for example, a person sprayed with OC must still be controlled and then handcuffed. These weapons are useful in temporarily distracting a subject long enough for control and handcuffing to be achieved.[105] Stun guns or Tasers shoot two barbs that are attached to wires that reach up to 35 feet.

The barbs deliver a five-second electrical jolt that seizes the body's major muscle groups and temporarily incapacitates the person, allowing the police to approach a dangerous suspect more closely.

Despite concerns about safety to the target person and to the officer of OC use, Charles S. Petty, M.D., of the University of Texas Southwestern Medical Center, in a 2002 report for the U.S. Department of Justice, reported on the pathological and toxicological information on 63 deaths occurring after the use of OC. Petty's analysis found drugs, disease, and drugs and disease combined with confrontational situations. His results showed that there is no evidence that OC, as used by law enforcement officers, in these confrontational situations was a total or contributing cause of death. He wrote that the use of OC is relatively innocuous.[106]

However, the use of Tasers or stun guns is gaining in controversy. In June 2006, the U.S. Department of Justice reported that it is reviewing the deaths of as many as 180 people who died after law enforcement officers used stun guns or other electro-shock devices to subdue them. Amnesty International reports that more than 150 people have died after being hit by a Taser since 2001 and that it was officially ruled at least a contributing factor in 23 deaths nationwide.[107]

Glenn Schmitt of the National Institute of Justice said that the review was prompted after law enforcement authorities, including the IACP, expressed concern about the increasing numbers of deaths of subjects when stun guns were used against them by the police. He said that the review will enlist the help of the National Association of Medical Examiners, the American College of Pathologists, the Centers for Disease Control and Prevention, and the IACP.[108]

Summary

- The two major ways of looking at the police roles are the crime-fighting role (law enforcement) and the order maintenance role (peacekeeping and providing social services).

- The police role is very ambiguous, but thinking about the role of the police has increased since September 11, 2001.

- The two primary goals and objectives of police departments are maintaining order and protecting life and property. Secondary goals include preventing crime, arresting and prosecuting offenders, recovering stolen and missing property, assisting sick and injured people, enforcing noncriminal regulations, and delivering services not available elsewhere in the community.

- Many researchers suggest that police officers adopt a police operational style in thinking about their role in society and how they should do their jobs.

- An important aspect of a police officer's job is the exercise of discretion, what it means, how and why it is exercised, what factors influence the use of discretion by the police, and how police departments can attempt to control discretion.

- Research has identified many factors that can influence police discretion to arrest, including characteristics of the crime; relationship between the alleged criminal and the victim; relationship between police and the criminal or victim; department policies; the subject's offense, attitude, race, socioeconomic status, and gender; the officer's race; and police peer group pressure.

- In recent years, much attention has been given to the need to prepare police for the appropriate use of discretion.

- Despite common perceptions, police rarely use force. Police shootings or the use of deadly force by the police, might be the ultimate use of discretion by the police.

- In 1985, the U.S. Supreme Court in *Tennessee v. Garner* declared the fleeing felon rule unconstitutional. Current law generally only allows the police to use deadly force against those using it against them or another person.

- Almost all local police departments and sheriff's officers use less-than-lethal weapons, most commonly chemical sprays, batons, or electronic devices, such as stun guns or Tasers.

Learning Check

1. Explain the basic difference between the crime-fighting role and the order maintenance role of the police.

2. Discuss the ambiguity of the police role.

3. Discuss the effect on the police role of the September 11, 2001, terrorist attacks on the United States.

4. List the major goals and objectives of the police.

5. What are police operational styles? Discuss some of them.

6. Define discretion. Discuss some of the major ways police exercise discretion.

7. Identify some of the major factors that influence police discretion.

8. What do the latest statistics reveal about the use of force by the police?

9. Explain the fleeing felon rule and why it existed.

10. Discuss the extent and use of less-than-lethal weapons by the police.

Key Terms

ambiguous The concept that the police role is very diverse and dynamic.

crime-fighting role A major view of the role of the police that emphasizes crime fighting or law enforcement.

deadly force Force that can cause death.

defense of life standard Doctrine allowing police officers to use deadly force against individuals using deadly force against an officer or others.

discretion Freedom to act or decide a matter on one's own.

fleeing felon doctrine Doctrine widely followed before the 1960s that allowed police officers to use deadly force to apprehend a fleeing felon.

less-than-lethal weapons Innovative alternatives to traditional firearms, such as batons, bodily force techniques, chemical irritant sprays, and Tasers or stun guns.

omnipresence A concept that suggests that the police are always present or always seem to be present.

order maintenance Major view of the role of the police that emphasizes keeping the peace and providing social services.

police operational styles Styles adopted by police officers as a way of thinking about the role of the police and law in society.

police role The concept of "what do the police do."

Tennessee v. Garner U.S. Supreme Court case that ended the use of the fleeing felon rule.

6

Police Culture, Personality, and Stress

©HO/AFP/Getty Images

GOALS

- To acquaint you with the research indicating the existence of a distinct police culture or subculture and to familiarize you with studies of the police personality, including attempts made to define the police personality
- To present studies of police cynicism and to familiarize you with the Dirty Harry problem. Do good endings justify the use of bad means to achieve those endings?
- To discuss one of the most serious police problems—police stress—and to see why it occurs, how it is exhibited, and what means can be taken to deal with it
- To discuss the serious and sad problem of police officer suicide and how it is frequently caused by stress
- To increase awareness of dangers facing the police, including being killed and injured in the line of duty and dealing with contagious diseases, such as AIDS

Introduction

On September 11, 2001, police officers throughout New York City, many responding while off duty, raced through the streets to respond to a 911 call reporting that a plane had crashed into New York City's World Trade Center. The rest is history. Many rushed into the building to help citizens get out. They rushed in while regular citizens rushed out. Thirty-seven Port Authority of New York/New Jersey police officers, 23 New York City police officers, and 3 New York court officers lost their lives in their valiant effort to protect and serve. In 1995 in Oklahoma City, officers rushed courageously into the Federal Building to help others get out. In fact, every day, in cities and towns all over the United States, law enforcement officers put their own safety and lives at risk to protect and serve. Are these brave officers displaying the traits of the police culture?

Many experts and researchers studying the police write about such concepts as a distinct police culture or subculture and a distinct police personality. Are the police different from most other people? Much research indicates that they are.

This chapter will discuss such concepts as the police culture or subculture, the police personality, police cynicism, the Dirty Harry problem, police stress, "suicide by cop," and police danger. Police stress is a very serious issue facing the police. Therefore, this chapter will attempt to define it and to show why it occurs, how it exhibits itself, and how police agencies can deal with it.[1]

The Police Culture or Subculture

Numerous academic studies have indicated that the nature of policing and the experiences officers go through on the job cause them to band together into their own subculture, which many researchers call the police culture or police subculture.[2] For example, if someone who was not a police officer walked into a bar at 1:00 AM and overheard a group of men and women engaged in animated conversation using such words as *collars, mopes, skells, perps, vics, edps,* and *shoeflies,* he or she would have great difficulty understanding. However, to the off-duty police officers having a few drinks and talking about their previous tour of duty, each word has a precise meaning.

The word *culture* generally refers to patterns of human activity or the way of life for a society. It generally includes informal codes or rules of manners, dress, language, behavior, rituals, and systems of belief.[3] The key components of culture consist of values, norms, and institutions. Values comprise ideas about what in life seems important. These values tend to guide the rest of the culture. Norms consist of expectations of how people will behave in various situations, and each culture has methods (sanctions) for enforcing its norms. Institutions are the structures of a society within which values and norms are transmitted.[4]

Large societies often have subcultures, or groups of people with distinct sets of values, attitudes, behavior, and beliefs that differentiate them from a larger culture of which they are a part. Sometimes subcultures can be defined by religious, occupational, or other factors. Many researchers point to a separate police culture or subculture. This does not mean that the police in most important respects do not share the dominant values of the larger culture. The **police culture** or **police subculture** is a combination of shared norms, values, goals, career patterns, life styles, and occupational structures that is somewhat different from the combination held by the rest of society. The police subculture, like most subcultures, is characterized by clannishness, secrecy, and isolation from those not in the group. Police officers work with other police officers during their tours of duty. Many socialize together after work and on days off, often to the exclusion of others—even old friends and family. When socializing, off-duty officers tend to talk about their jobs.

Working strange shifts of duty, especially 4 to 12s (4:00 PM to 12:00 midnight) and midnights (12:00 midnight to 8:00 AM) and working weekends and holidays make it difficult for the police officer to socialize with the average person, who works a 9-to-5 job Monday through Friday. Many

Courtesy of Linda Forst

Due to challenging work schedules, police officers often socialize more frequently with other officers than with the average citizen. Though this might increase isolation, in some cases it can be beneficial for stress reduction by providing a healthy opportunity to ventilate and exercise.

police officers find it difficult to sleep after a tense, busy evening tour. If officers want to socialize or relax after work instead of going home to a house whose inhabitants have to get up at 6:00 AM to go to regular jobs, many tend to socialize with their comrades from the job. When officers work weekends, their days off fall during the average person's workweek, so again, many tend to socialize with other officers. Police spouses tend to socialize with other police spouses, and police families tend to associate with other police families. After a while, the police world (the Job) is the only world for many officers.

Michael Brown, in *Working the Street,* tells us that police officers create their own culture to deal with the recurring anxiety and emotional stress that is endemic to policing. Brown believes that the

police subculture is based on three major principles: honor, loyalty, and individuality.[5]

Honor is given to officers for engaging in risk-taking behavior. (An example of risk-taking behavior is being the first one in the door to challenge an armed adversary when taking cover and waiting for backup would have been the more prudent course of action.)

Loyalty is a major part of the police subculture, and police loyalty is extremely intense. The word *backup* occurs often in police officer conversations. Backup involves assisting other officers in emergency situations and coming to their aid when they are challenged, criticized, or even charged with wrongdoing. Brown explains the importance of backup by pointing out that the violence that police must deal with and the strong bonding that occurs among police officers "places the highest value upon the obligation to back up and support a fellow officer."[6]

The ideal officer, then, according to the police subculture, takes risks (honor), is first on the scene to aid a fellow police officer (loyalty), and is able to handle any situation by doing it her or his own way (individuality).

The idea of danger permeates the police subculture. George L. Kirkham, a college professor who became a police officer to better understand his police students, discusses the police mistrust of civilians and police reliance on their own peer group support to survive on the streets: "As someone who had always regarded policemen as a 'paranoid lot,' I discovered in the daily round of violence which became part of my life that chronic suspiciousness is something that a good cop cultivates in the interest of going home to his family each evening.[7] (See Table 6.1.)

Egon Bittner, a police researcher, also has said that an esprit de corps develops in police work as a function of the dangerous and unpleasant tasks police officers are required to do. Police solidarity, a "one for all, and all for one" attitude, Bittner says, is one of the most cherished aspects of the police occupation.[8]

John M. Violanti, a former police officer and expert on police suicide, focuses on the police subculture and suicide. He writes that entry into law enforcement involves a process of abrupt change from citizen to police officer. This process is very strong in basic police training and continues to dominate officers' lives throughout their careers. Police officers can become addicted to excitement and danger, which can decrease their

TABLE 6.1	Traits of the Police Culture/Subculture

- Clannishness
- Isolation from the public
- Secrecy
- Honor
- Loyalty
- Individuality

ability to assess the nature of current challenges and interfere with rational decision processes. Police officers, through psychological and physiological mechanisms, become ingrained in police work and isolated from other life roles such as family, friendships, or community involvement.[9]

Eugene A. Paoline III, in his *Rethinking Police Culture: Officers' Occupational Attitudes,* discusses the ways in which police officers perceive and cope with aspects of their working environments in contemporary police departments. He says that the occupational attitudes associated with police culture include distrust and suspiciousness of citizens, assessing people in terms of their potential threat, a "we versus they" attitude toward citizens, and loyalty to the peer group.[10]

The police personality is reflected in the many coping strategies officers use to deal with stress, including humor and keeping an emotional distance from themselves and stressful events.[11] Often, officers tend to use "gallows humor" or appear disinterested in the suffering of others. Sometimes, citizens wrongly assume that this attitude of appearing disinterested indicates that the police are uncaring.

In 2003, Paoline produced another study on the police culture. He wrote that the conventional wisdom about police culture rests on descriptions of a single occupational phenomenon in which the attitudes, values, and norms of members are homogenous. He believes however, that as departments continue to diversify and as community policing becomes part of the philosophy of policing, there will be more cultural variations. He urges researchers to focus their efforts on studying this increased cultural variation of the traditional police culture and how it expresses itself.[12]

A student interested in studying the police culture might be interested in seeing some police officer homepages on the Internet where active and retired police officers from all over the nation and abroad have created their own homepages. Often, retired officers will contact former colleagues through the Internet.

The Blue Wall of Silence

Studies of the police culture indicate that police officers protect one another from outsiders, often even refusing to aid police superiors or other law enforcement officials in investigating wrongdoing by other officers. Many believe that this part of the police culture or the police subculture produces a protective barrier known as the **blue wall of silence.**[13]

Writing about the police subculture and the blue wall of silence, Bittner says, "Policing is a dangerous occupation and the availability of unquestioned support and loyalty is not something officers could readily do without."[14]

Robert Sheehan and Gary W. Cordner write about how this aspect of the police subculture can destroy the reputation and integrity of a police department, "The influence of dominant police subcultural role expectations can have a devastating effect on a police department. Actually, the existence of such unofficially established, negative, institutionalized role expectations is the primary reason that so many police departments are held in such low esteem by the public."[15]

Sheehan and Cordner give two examples of how the police subculture can create a "blue wall of silence" and adversely affect a police department in two fictional cities, Cod Bay and Tulane City.[16] In Cod Bay, a police sergeant is dealing with an irate motorist whose car was towed because it was parked illegally. As the sergeant talks to the officer who wrote the summons that caused the car to be towed, the sergeant realizes that the motorist's car was indeed parked legally, and the towing was in error. The sergeant, however, following the dominant police subcultural expectation that he must back the officer whether he was right or wrong, tells the motorist that to get his car back, he must pay the towing charge.

In Sheehan and Cordner's other fictional city, Tulane City, politics rules the police department. A police chief who is appointed by local politicians accepts corruption, incompetence, and brutality by his officers because he realizes that when another mayor takes office, that mayor will select his own police chief, and he himself will return to the

High-ranking San Francisco law enforcement officials pled innocent after being indicted in March 2003 for allegedly covering up a street fight that involved off-duty officers. What message does this type of incident send to the public?

that this personality is thought to include such traits as authoritarianism, suspicion, hostility, insecurity, conservatism, and cynicism.[18] (See Table 6.2.)

What Is the Police Personality?

Jerome Skolnick coined the term "working personality of police officers."[19] Skolnick stated that the police officer's "working personality" is shaped by constant exposure to danger and the need to use force and authority to reduce and control threatening situations.[20] Skolnick wrote,

> The policeman's role contains two principal variables, danger and authority, which should be interpreted in the light of a "constant" pressure to appear efficient. The element of danger seems to make the policeman especially attentive to signs indicating a potential for violence and lawbreaking. As a result the policeman is generally a "suspicious person." Furthermore, the character of the policeman's work makes him less desirable as a friend since norms of friendship implicate others in his work. Accordingly the element of danger isolates the policeman socially from that segment of the citizenry whom he regards as symbolically dangerous and also from the conventional citizenry with whom he identifies."[21]

department in a lower rank. If he had tried to reform the police department while chief, he would be ostracized by officers when he returned to a lower status. Failing to adhere to the existing police subculture would have been dangerous to the chief in the future.

Another example of the police subcultural blue wall of silence is William Westley's classic study of the Gary, Indiana, Police Department, in which he found a police culture that had its own customs, law, and morality. Westley says these values produce the **blue curtain**—a situation in which police officers only trust other police officers and do not aid in the investigation of wrongdoing by other officers. Westley calls the blue curtain a barrier that isolates police officers from the rest of society.[17]

The Police Personality

The police culture or subculture leads to what scholars call the **police personality**, or traits common to most police officers. Scholars have reported

Elizabeth Burbeck and Adrian Furnham identified three important features of an officer's working personality: danger, authority, and isolation from the public.[22] They reviewed the literature comparing the attitudes of police officers with those of the general population and found that police officers place a higher emphasis on terminal values (such as family security, mature love, and a sense of accomplishment) than on social values (such as equality).

One example of the studies Burbeck and Furnham looked at was the Rokeach study. Social psychologist Milton Rokeach and his colleagues studied police officers in Lansing, Michigan. He

© Frederic Larson/San Francisco Chronicle/Corbis

TABLE 6.2	Traits of the Police Personality

- Authoritarianism
- Suspicion
- Hostility
- Insecurity
- Conservatism
- Cynicism

compared their personality traits with a national sample of private citizens and concluded that police officers seemed more oriented toward self-control and obedience than does the average citizen. Also, police were more interested in personal goals, such as "an exciting life," and less interested in social goals, such as "a world of peace." Rokeach also compared values of veteran officers with those of recruits and discovered no significant differences. Rokeach believed police officers have a particular value orientation and personality before they start their police careers.[23]

Many social scientists have attempted to duplicate the Rokeach study to see if the recruit police officer has values that differ from those of the ordinary citizen. The results have been mixed and inconclusive. Some researchers have found that police officers are actually psychologically healthier, less depressed and anxious, and more social and assertive than the general population.[24]

Are They Born Like That, or Is It the Job?

Two opposing viewpoints on the development of the police personality exist. One says that police departments recruit people who by nature possess those traits that we see in the police personality. The second point of view holds that officers develop those traits through their socialization and experiences in the police department.[25]

Edward Thibault, Lawrence M. Lynch, and R. Bruce McBride tell us that most studies have found that the police working personality derives from the socialization process in the police academy, field training, and patrol experience.[26] John Van Maanen also asserts that the police personality is developed through the process of learning and doing police work. In a study of one urban police department, he found that the typical police recruit is a sincere individual who becomes a police officer for the job security, salary, belief that the job will be interesting, and the desire to enter an occupation that can benefit society.[27] He found that at the academy, highly idealistic recruits are taught to have a strong sense of camaraderie with follow rookies. The recruits begin to admire the exploits of the veteran officers who are their teachers. From their instructors, the recruits learn when to do police work by the book and when to ignore department rules and rely on personal discretion.[28]

Van Maanen says that the learning process continues when the recruits are assigned to street duty and trained by field training officers. The recruits listen to the folklore, myths, and legends about veteran officers and start to understand police work in the way that older officers desire them to. By adopting the sentiments and behavior of the older officers, the new recruits avoid ostracism and censure by their supervisors and colleagues.[29]

A recently completed longitudinal study of attitudes of police over time as they were exposed to police work certainly showed an effect. The study tested police recruits during the first week of the academy and then at several follow-up periods up to almost four years after the academy. The testing included the Minnesota Multiphasic Personality Inventory (MMPI), standard demographic questions, questions concerning the respondent's physical exercise program and tobacco use, an alcohol consumption assessment, and Arthur Niederhoffer's cynicism scale. Clear evidence indicated that the personality characteristics of the officers started to change shortly after their induction into the policing environment. With rare exceptions, officers tended to become more cynical, more paranoid, more depressed, angrier, more dominant, and more hostile the longer they were in the policing environment. White females were the least affected group, and black females were the most affected group. Black males were more affected by their exposure to policing than were white males.[30]

Conversely, several researchers have found little evidence that a "typical" police personality actually exists. Studies by sociologists Larry Tifft, David Bayley and Harold Mendelsohn, and Robert Balch indicate that even experienced police officers are quite similar to the average citizen.[31] Nevertheless, the weight of existing evidence generally points to the existence of a unique police personality that develops from the police socialization process.

Police Cynicism

Police cynicism is an attitude that there is no hope for the world and a view of humanity at its worst. This is produced by the police officer's constant contact with offenders and what he or she perceives as miscarriages of justice, such as lenient court decisions and plea bargaining.

Niederhoffer described police cynicism as follows:

> Cynicism is an emotional plank deeply entrenched in the ethos of the police world and it serves equally well for attack or defense. For many reasons police are particularly vulnerable to cynicism. When they succumb, they lose faith in people, society, and eventually in themselves. In their Hobbesian view, the world becomes a jungle in which crime, corruption and brutality are normal features of terrain.[32]

Niederhoffer, a former NYPD lieutenant and then professor at John Jay College of Criminal Justice, wrote what is one the best-known studies of the police personality, *Behind the Shield: The Police in Urban Society.* Niederhoffer examined the thesis that most police officers develop into cynics as a function of their experience as police officers.[33] Niederhoffer tested Westley's assumption that police officers learn to mistrust the citizens they are paid to protect as a result of being constantly faced with keeping people in line and believing that most people are out to break the law or injure a police officer.[34] Niederhoffer distributed a survey measuring attitudes and values to 220 New York City police officers. Among his most important findings were that police cynicism increased with length of service in the police department, that police officers with a college education became quite cynical if they were denied promotion, and that quasi-military police academy training caused new recruits to become cynical about themselves quickly. For example, Niederhoffer found that nearly 80 percent of first-day recruits believed that the police department was an "efficient, smoothly operating organization." Two months later, less than a third held that belief. Also, half the new recruits believed that a police superior was "very interested in the welfare of his subordinates." Two months later, that number declined to 13 percent.[35]

Cynicism may hurt the relationship between the police and the public, but it may help advance an officer in his or her career within the department. In a longitudinal study of police officers in Georgia, Richard Anson, J. Dale Mann, and Dale Sherman found that the officers with the most cynical attitudes were the ones most likely to get high supervisory ratings. The researchers concluded, "Cynicism is a valued quality of the personality of the police officer and is positively evaluated by important individuals in police organizations."[36]

The Dirty Harry Problem

Police officers are often confronted with situations in which they feel forced to take certain illegal actions to achieve a greater good. Indeed, one of the greatest and oldest ethical questions people have ever faced is, Do the good ends ever justify the bad means?[37]

Carl B. Klockars has dubbed this moral dilemma of police officers as the **Dirty Harry problem,** from the 1971 film *Dirty Harry,* starring Clint Eastwood as Detective Harry Callahan. In the film, a young girl has been kidnapped by a psychopathic killer named Scorpio, who demands $200,000 in ransom. Scorpio has buried the girl with just enough oxygen to survive a few hours. Harry eventually finds Scorpio, shoots him, and tortures him to find out where the girl is. Finally, Scorpio tells Harry where the girl is. Harry finds her, but she has already died from lack of oxygen.

Let's change the plot of the movie and say that Harry's action resulted in his finding the girl and saving her life. This would be a great Hollywood ending, but think about it. Harry had a good end in mind (finding the girl before she dies), but what about the means (torturing Scorpio and not giving him his constitutional rights before interrogation)?

Harry was wrong, right? He violated police procedure. He violated the precepts of the Fifth Amendment to the U.S. Constitution, which he swore an oath to obey. He has committed crimes, the most obvious of which is assault.

Harry was wrong, right? If Harry had used proper police procedure, had not violated the law, had not violated the Constitution of the United States, and had advised Scorpio of his right to an attorney, and if Scorpio had availed himself of one, there is no doubt the attorney would have told him to remain silent, and the little girl would have died.

Which is more wrong morally? Is it more wrong to (1) torture Scorpio, thereby violating the police oath of office and legal obligations but therefore finding the girl and saving her life, or

(2) act in accordance with the rules of the system and not make every effort, illegal or not, to force Scorpio to talk and thus permit the girl to die?

Sure, this is only Hollywood. You would never be faced with this dilemma as a police officer, would you? As Klockars writes,

> In real, everyday policing, situations in which innocent victims are buried with just enough oxygen to keep them alive are, thankfully, very rare. But the core scene in *Dirty Harry* should only be understood as an especially dramatic example of a far more common problem: real, everyday, routine situations in which police officers know they can only achieve good ends by employing dirty means. Each time a police officer considers deceiving a suspect into confessing by telling him that his fingerprints were found at the scene or that a conspirator has already confessed, each time a police officer considers adding some untrue details to his account of probable cause to legitimate a crucial stop or search . . . that police officer faces a Dirty Harry Problem.[38]

We can sympathize with Harry Callahan, and surely we can sympathize with the plight of the little girl about to die. However, despite Hollywood portrayals, police officers must operate within the boundaries of the law, because the law is what the people, through their representatives, want to be governed by. The police cannot make their own laws. Harry Callahan, although he attempted to save the life of the child, was wrong. In our system of law, we cannot use unlawful means to achieve worthy goals. Police work is a tough business. Tough choices must be made. As Klockars says,

> Dirty Harry Problems are an inevitable part of policing. They will not go away. The reason they won't is that policing is a moral occupation which constantly places its practitioners in situations in which unquestionable good ends can only be achieved by employing morally, legally, or politically dirty means to their achievements.

> The effects of Dirty Harry Problems on real police officers are often devastating. They can lead officers to lose their sense of moral proportion, fail to care, turn cynical, or allow their too passionate caring to lead them to employ dirty means too readily or too crudely. They make policing the most morally corrosive occupation.[39]

Can the Dirty Harry or Dirty Harriet problem lead to a serious ethical problem facing our police? The results of the Dirty Harry or Dirty Harriet problem certainly can result in ethical problems for the police. Police officers must be always alert to the fact that bad means never justify good ends. The police swear allegiance to their oath of office and the U.S. Constitution and their state constitution. Although it may be tempting, police cannot solve all the problems of this world and they certainly cannot solve them by violating their oath of office and their dedication to the Constitution of our land. Much more will be discussed regarding ethics in Chapter 8, "Police Ethics and Police Deviance."

Police Stress

Police officers are faced with stressful situations often during a routine tour of duty. The dispatcher assigns them to respond to a "gun run." (A gun run is a dispatcher's order to patrol units to respond to a certain location because of a report over 911 that a person has a gun in his or her possession. These calls receive immediate police response.) Citizens stop them to report a crime or dangerous condition. Officers find an open door to a factory and search for a possible burglar. They wait in a stakeout for an armed felon to appear. Police officers are always ready to react. Their bodies' response to these stressful situations is good in that it prepares them for any emergency, but the stress response takes its toll on officers' physical and mental states.

What Is Stress?

Stress is the body's reaction to internal or external stimuli that upset the body's normal state. A stimulus that causes stress (stressor) can be physical, mental, or emotional. The term *stress* is used to refer to both the body's reaction and the stimuli that caused it.

The body's reaction to highly stressful situations is known as the **flight-or-fight response.** Under stressful circumstances, quantities of adrenaline, a hormone produced by the adrenal glands, are released into the bloodstream. This stimulates the liver to provide the body with stored carbohydrates for extra energy. It also results in quickened heartbeat and respiration, as well as increased blood pressure and muscle tension. The body is getting

TABLE 6.3	**Mental and Physical Problems Associated with Stress**

- Psychiatric problems
  Posttraumatic stress syndrome
  Neuroses
  Transient situational disturbances
- Immunology problems
  Reduced resistance to infection
  Tumors
- Cardiovascular problems
  Heart attacks
  Coronary artery disease
  Hypertension
  Stroke
- Genitourinary problems
  Failure to menstruate
  Impotence
  Incontinence
- Gastrointestinal problems
  Ulcers

SOURCE: Adapted from Edwin S. Geffner, ed., *The Internist's Compendium of Patient Information* (New York: McGraw-Hill, 1987), sec. 30.

prepared for extraordinary physical exertion; this is good. However, if the need for this extraordinary exertion does not materialize, the frustrated readiness may cause headache, upset stomach, irritability, and a host of other symptoms.[40]

Some experts say that stress alone probably does not cause illness, but it contributes to circumstances in which diseases may take hold and flourish. Stress weakens and disturbs the body's defense mechanisms and may play a role in the development of hypertension, ulcers, cardiovascular disease, and as research indicates, probably cancer.[41] (See Table 6.3.)

Nature of Stress in Policing

Although most people have stress in their careers or lives, studies have found evidence of particularly high rates of stress in certain professions. Some have called policing the most stressful of all professions.

The American Institute of Stress ranked police work among the top-10 stress-producing jobs in the United States.[42]

A reporter riding with the police addressed the stress that officers experience:

> The world inside the patrol car is a world of its own, two officers who are slave to the dispatcher on the crackling radio who can send them speeding into adrenaline overdrive racing to catch a suspect with a gun and then can order "slow it down" after enough cars are already at a crime scene. The result is an emotional up and down in just six blocks.[43]

Some studies indicate that police have higher rates of divorce, suicide, and other manifestations of stress than do other professions.[44] One writer said, "It would be difficult to find an occupation that is subject to more consistent and persistent tension, strain, confrontations and nerve wracking that that of the uniformed patrolman."[45]

Researchers have identified four general categories of stress with which police officers are confronted: external, organizational, personal, and operational.[46]

External Stress Stress produced by real threats and dangers, such as responding to gun runs and other dangerous assignments and taking part in auto pursuits.

A recent study of police stress in Canada involving full shift ride-alongs with randomly selected officers from 12 municipal departments in British Columbia found significant levels of physical stress among police officers. Using heart rate, coupled with observed physical-activity data, researchers found the highest physical stress to occur during officers' physical enforcement activities; marked psychosocial stress when responding to critical incidents, particularly during the interaction with a suspect both during the critical incident and then during each subsequent interaction with suspects for the remainder of the shift. The average heart rate of those involved in a critical incident remained elevated for the remainder of the shift for all tasks including report writing in the last hour of the shift. The evidence also suggests that officers anticipate stress as they conduct their work, experiencing anticipatory stress at the start of each shift.[47]

Consider also, the external stress faced by members of the New Orleans Police Department (NOPD) in the aftermath of Hurricane Katrina. Many of them were flooded out of their own homes and separated from their families and loved ones, and they had to face constant attacks by armed assailants looking to loot and plunder the little that was left in New Orleans.[48]

Organizational Stress Stress produced by elements inherent in the quasi-military character of the police service, such as constant adjustment to changing tours of duty, odd working hours, working holidays, and the strict discipline imposed on officers. Organizational stress also results from workplace conditions, the lack of influence over work activities, and workplace bias.

In a 2006 study, Merry Morash, Robin Haarr, and Dae-Hoon Kwak found that several workplace conditions cause police stress. They found that the most predictive stressors were lack of influence over work activities and biases against one's racial, ethnic, or gender group. Their findings also indicated that a lack of influence on how police work is accomplished is a considerable stressor.[49]

In a 2006 article, Dr. James D. Sewell, formerly an assistant commissioner of the Florida Department of Law Enforcement, wrote that, unfortunately, some management practices also create stress in the lives of officers. He notes that although contemporary leadership and supervisory courses foster effective management techniques, some managers, often trained in traditional policies or management practices or, perhaps more interested in their own advancement, forget that their actions can create a stressful work environment and affect the success and well-being of a work unit or organization.[50]

Personal Stress Stress produced by the interpersonal characteristics of belonging to the police organization, such as difficulties in getting along with other officers.

Operational Stress Stress produced by the daily need to confront the tragedies of urban life:

©AP/Wide World Photos

A San Antonio Police Officer helps a young Hurricane Katrina evacuee from New Orleans find her mother at a shelter set up at the old Levi Strauss plant in San Antonio. Though police officers are often involved in stressful situations, it can be a stress relief when an officer is able to help someone.

the need to deal with derelicts, criminals, the mentally disturbed, and the drug addicted; the need to engage in dangerous activity to protect a public that appears to be unappreciative of the police; and the constant awareness of the possibility of being legally liable for actions performed while on duty.

Most research on police stress has focused primarily on large, urban and suburban officers and scant research has been done on rural and small-town police. Some researchers assert that the public's and scholars' views of rural and small-town officer concerns merely as a "small" version of the urban problem are wrong and that the tendency to extrapolate findings has led to questions about the ability to generalize them. Also some researchers argue that an urban bias in our society is perpetuated in academic research.[51]

In 2004, to bridge this gap, Yolanda M. Scott of Roger Williams University in Rhode Island, produced a study of 135 rural and small-town officers employed in 11 Pennsylvania municipal police agencies and their stress experiences. Her research suggests that the widespread public assumption of rural and small-town officers resembling media portrayals of "Mayberry" law enforcement grossly misrepresents the level and types of stress experienced by these officers. Officers in these agencies were indeed distressed by several factors. She found that organizational stress was among the most problematic for officers and that their perceptions of the organizational setting, specifically administrative changes, were significantly predictive of all forms of officer stress. These officers perceived that changes to the department's top administrative positions would interrupt every part of their lives and work, including their treatment within the department, situations of danger or violence, and the impact of the job on their families. She also found that media criticism was linked to officer stress and that this is particularly upsetting to officers because it disrupts their creditability with the community to which they are a part. She explains that they are recognizable people in the community and have difficulty finding privacy whether on or off duty. As Scott says, "In contrast to many of their urban counterparts, rural and small-town officers' service area is also the place they call 'home.'" Overall, her findings suggest that rural and small-town police officers would benefit from and likely respond to stress intervention programs such as peer support and mental health counseling.[52]

Scott has also studied coping mechanisms in response to stress among rural and small-town police officers and found that they tend to use a variety of healthy or adaptive coping mechanisms, such as physical exercise, activities or hobbies, and sharing their problems. However, a substantial proportion of the officers used maladaptive or unhealthy forms of coping, including absenteeism, avoiding discussion with supervisors, sleeping, drinking alcohol, and tobacco use.[53]

Factors Causing Stress in Policing

According to researchers, many factors lead to stress in police work including poor training, substandard equipment, poor pay, lack of opportunity, role conflict, exposure to brutality, fears about job competence and safety, and lack of job satisfaction. Researchers also say that the pressure of being on duty 24 hours a day leads to stress and that the police learn to cope with that stress by becoming emotionally detached from their work and the people they are paid to serve.[54] Fatigue can also affect officers' stress. Working long hours and overtime produces fatigue and, consequently, stress in officers[55] (see Table 6.4).

One researcher attributed stress problems to a lack of emphasis on physical fitness once an officer leaves the police academy, "Without police fitness standards, a police department has too many 'loose wires' to account for. It is unfair to place the burden of quality effectiveness on each individual without presenting a plan that will achieve these goals."[56]

Does officer race and gender matter in police stress? This is the subject of several recent studies. In 2005, Ni He, Jihong Zhao, and Ling Ren studied more than 1,100 police officers from each of Baltimore's nine police precincts and police headquarters to determine the effects of officer race and gender on police stress. For the purposes of the study, the sample of officers was divided into four subgroups: white males, African American males, white females, and African American females. They were compared on stressors, coping mechanisms, and multiple psychological symptoms of stress. The researchers discovered that white males reported higher levels of physical symptoms of stress, anxiety, and depression than did their African American male counterparts. Levels of psychological stress reported by females were higher than were those reported by males. There was no statistically significant difference between white and African American female officers. Both male and female African American officers were more likely to use constructive coping than were their white counterparts.[57] Another recent study revealed that female officers had higher levels of depression compared with male officers, but that male and female police officers did not differ statistically in clinically developed measures of anxiety.[58]

TABLE 6.4 Sources of Law Enforcement Stress

■ **External stressors**

Lack of consideration by courts in scheduling officers for court appearances

Public's lack of support

Negative or distorted media coverage

■ **Internal stressors**

Policies and procedures that are offensive

Poor or inadequate training and inadequate career development opportunities

Lack of identity and recognition

Poor economic benefits and working conditions

Excessive paperwork

Inconsistent discipline

Perceived favoritism

■ **Stressors in law enforcement work itself**

Rigors of shift work

Role conflict

Frequent exposures to life's miseries

Boredom

Fear

Responsibility for protecting other people

Fragmented nature of the job

Work overload

■ **Stressors confronting the individual officer**

Necessity to conform

Necessity to take a second job

Altered social status in the community

SOURCE: Adapted from Richard M. Ayres and George S. Flanagan, *Preventing Law Enforcement Stress: The Organization's Role* (National Sheriff's Association, Bureau of Justice Assistance, 1990).

Other research has disclosed that in the general population, women exhibit a greater lifetime prevalence of posttraumatic stress (PTSD); men have a greater risk than do women for developing PTSD symptoms of irritability and impulsiveness, but women are twice as likely as men to have depression and anxiety disorders associated with PTSD.[59]

Some recent research also suggests that female officers' baseline rate of work-related stress may compound their trauma reaction to events such as the 9/11 attacks; women officers may experience added work stress from working in a male-dominated environment where they are constantly exposed to the belief that female officers perform less effectively than male officers do; women officers are particularly reluctant to seek counseling in the management of stress, because of the fear that this would reinforce male officers' belief that women are not tough enough to handle police work.[60]

Suicide by Cop Compounding the stress problems of police officers is the phenomenon known as **suicide by cop,** in which a person wishing to die deliberately places an officer in a life-threatening situation, causing the officer to use **deadly force** against that person.

In 2006, for example, in St. Charles, Missouri, a man pointed what police believed to be a real gun at them, and they fatally shot him. It was later discovered that the man's gun was a pellet gun and that the man had earlier had a discussion with his brother about provoking the police to kill him. He also had a history of alcohol abuse and had tried to commit suicide previously.[61]

Perhaps the classic case of "suicide by cop," occurred on a Long Island, New York, expressway, when a 19-year-old man, despondent over a gambling debt, drove recklessly causing the police to pull him over. He then pulled a "very real-looking gun" (the "gun" was actually a $1.79 toy revolver) on them. Police fatally shot him. Inside the youth's auto were good-bye cards for his friends and a chilling suicide note addressed "To The Officer Who Shot Me," in which he apologized for getting the police involved.[62]

The effect on police officers involved in these cases is devastating. According to David Klinger, a former police officer, now a professor at the University of Missouri at St. Louis, "Police find out after the fact that they did not need to shoot to protect themselves. It angers them that they hurt or killed someone." Klinger said even though police officers are trained to use deadly force, actually using it on someone, especially someone who has a death wish, can be life-altering for the officers involved. "Police officers generally can develop a bit of a thick skin about dealing with individuals who have killed themselves, but when you are the instrument of that death, it can take quite a toll."[63]

In addition to leaving the police with feelings of guilt and of being tricked into using deadly force, these feelings are often compounded by media accounts that depict the deceased as the victim. In the St. Charles case mentioned earlier, the daughter of the man who had caused the police to shoot him, questioned the officers' use of force because he never fired at them. She said that the police should have wounded him. St. Charles Police Chief Tim Swope determined that the officers' actions were justified. He said, "These officers have families; they want to go home at the end of the day. It's unfortunate that they had to do this, but that's part of the job." St. Charles County Sheriff Tom Neer agreed saying, "We are trained to eliminate the threat. I know it sounds cold, but we aren't trained to wound people because wounded people kill others."[64]

The "suicide by cop" phenomenon became widely reported in 1996 by a Canadian police officer, Richard B. Parent, in a landmark report on victim-precipitated homicide. Parent, who interviewed cops after they were involved in such incidents, said many quit the police department, got divorced, and abused drugs or alcohol after the killings.[65]

A study that appeared in the *Annals of Emergency Medicine,* an analysis of 437 deputy-involved shootings that occurred in the Los Angeles County, California, Sheriff's Department, disclosed that "suicide by cop" incidents accounted for 11 percent of the shootings and 13 percent of all deputy-involved justifiable homicides. The victims in these cases enacted elaborate schemes, including doing something to draw officers to the scene; disobeying commands to put down the weapon; continuing to threaten officers and other individuals; and escalating the encounter to the point where police felt that they had to use deadly force to protect themselves, their partners, and civilians. The study indicated that most of the subjects in these cases were male and had a history of domestic violence, suicide attempts, and alcohol and drug abuse. Police officers involved in these incidents experienced emotions ranging from shock and remorse to shame, anger, and powerlessness. The report concluded that suicide by cop constitutes an actual form of suicide.[66]

A study of the psychological effects of suicide by cop on involved officers revealed that the short-term effects of these incidents seemed to involve the same psychological impacts experienced by officers involved in most critical incidents, including replaying the event repeatedly, disruption of sleep, feelings of irritability and detachment, being hypercritical, sensory disturbance, and hypervigilance.

The most dominant emotion experienced by the officers was anger toward the subject for controlling the situation and forcing the officer to use deadly force. Some long-term effects were feelings of vulnerability, being more protective of family, and being less trusting of the general public. More than half of the officers interviewed seriously considered retiring or quitting the department. Often these thoughts were reinforced by family members, who experienced intensified fears of their loved one being killed in the line of duty. Officers reported that psychological debriefing was particularly important in helping them through the impact of the suicide by cop incident.[67]

Anthony J. Pinizzotto, senior scientist and clinical forensic psychologist in the FBI's Behavioral Science Unit (BSU), Edward F. Davis, a retired police officer and instructor at the BSU, and Charles E. Miller III, a retired police captain, and coordinator and instructor in the FBI's Criminal Justice Information Services Division recommended that there should be a national reporting process for suicide by cop incidents, similar to the UCR reporting process, which was expanded in 1990 to include the category of hate crimes.[68]

Effects of Stress on Police Officers

Too much stress affects health. Police officers face the stress created by always being ready for danger day in and day out. In addition, the working hours of police officers and the resultant living conditions have a further negative effect on their health. One writer reports that police officers may be among those with the most unhealthy diets in the United States because of a very high rate of consumption of fast food and junk food.[69] In fact, Dorothy Bracey, in a study, found that because of a poor diet and lack of exercise, a significant sample of U.S. police possessed a body composition, blood chemistry, and general level of physical fitness greatly inferior to that of a similarly sized sample of prison convicts.[70]

A recent National Institute of Justice report has listed the following as consequences of job related stress commonly reported by police officers[71]:

- Cynicism and suspiciousness
- Emotional detachment from various aspects of daily life
- Reduced efficiency

- Absenteeism and early retirement
- Excessive aggressiveness (which may trigger an increase in citizen complaints)
- Alcoholism and other substance abuse problems
- Marital or other family problems (for example, extramarital affairs, divorce, or domestic violence)
- Posttraumatic stress disorder
- Heart attacks, ulcers, weight gain, and other health problems
- Suicide

An early study of 2,300 police officers in 20 U.S. police departments revealed that 37 percent had serious marital problems, 36 percent had health problems, 23 percent had problems with alcohol, 20 percent had problems with their children, and 10 percent had drug problems.[72] Other researchers estimate that between 20 and 30 percent of all police officers have alcohol problems. The typical drinker was described as single, older than 40 years of age, with 15 to 20 years of police experience.[73]

In an extremely important 2004 article, Chad L. Cross, a research scientist, and Larry Ashley, an internationally recognized expert on combat trauma and addictions, both faculty members at the University of Nevada, Las Vegas, write that studies have estimated that nearly 25 percent of law enforcement officers are alcohol dependant as a result of on-the-job stress and indicate that this estimate probably falls well below the true number because of incomplete reporting.[74]

A study of 852 police officers in New South Wales, Australia, found that almost 50 percent of male and 40 percent of female officers consumed excessive amounts of alcohol (defined as more than 8 drinks per week at least twice a month, or more than 28 drinks a month for males, and more than 6 drinks per week at least twice a month, or 14 drinks a month for females), and that nearly 90 percent of all officers consumed alcohol to some degree.[75] Recent reports indicate that drug use also is on the rise in law enforcement agencies.[76]

Cross and Ashley assert that the unique subculture of the law enforcement profession often makes alcohol use appear as an accepted practice to promote camaraderie and social interaction among officers. They write that what starts as an occasional socializing activity, however, later can become a dangerous addiction as alcohol use evolves into a coping mechanism to camouflage the stress and trauma experienced by officers on a daily basis and that when the effects of the alcohol wear off, the stress or trauma that led to the drinking episode still exists.[77]

Other studies indicate that police officers are 300 percent more likely to suffer from alcoholism than is the average citizen[78]; the average life expectancy of a police officer is 57 years, compared with 71 for the general public; and officers rank at the top among professions in rates of heart disease, hypertension, and diabetes.[79]

Critical incidents and critical incident responses, particularly police shootings, are extremely stressful. Two recent studies revealed the prevalence of acute traumatic dissociate responses in officers who have been involved in these critical incidents.[80] Professors at Michigan State University have found that officers who have had to kill someone in the line of duty suffer postshooting trauma that may lead to severe problems, including the ruin of their careers. Studies indicate that 70 percent of these officers leave the police force within seven years after the shooting.[81] However, in a 2006 report, David Klinger explored the emotional, psychological, and physical reactions of 80 officers and sheriffs' deputies during and after 113 incidents in which they shot someone, he found evidence that most suffer few long-term negative emotional or physical effects after shooting a suspect.[82]

Stress and Police Families

Police work not only affects officers, it also affects their families, loved ones, and friends, "police work . . . affects, shapes, and at times, scars the individuals and families involved."[83] Studies of stress in the immediate families of police officers reveal that between 10 and 20 percent of all police wives are dissatisfied with their husband's job and would like to see their husbands leave the police department.[84] In addition, rotation shift work interferes with planning and celebrating holidays and important family events, such as birthdays and anniversaries. Rotating shifts also makes it difficult for a spouse to pursue another career.[85]

Ellen Scrivner, the director of the Psychological Services Division of the Prince George's County, Maryland, Police Department and president of the Psychologists in Public Service Division of the American Psychological Association, identified a number of job-related issues that contribute to family dysfunction in police families[86]:

1. *Family disruption because of rotating shifts.* Problems caused by rotating shifts include providing child care, unavailability on holidays and at other family events, and physical problems caused by overtime and shift work, which causes irritability and increased tension.

2. *Unpredictable work environment.* The constantly changing work setting of the police officer leads to crisis and emergency responses, as well as fear of death or injury and of being the target of internal investigations.

3. *Job-related personal change and family relationships.* An officer is forced to see much human tragedy and is always personally affected. Changes in the officer's personality and attitudes, in turn, affect the family.

4. *Community expectations and demands.* The public seems to hold police officers to a higher standard of behavior in comparison with other workers. Neighbors often expect their police officer neighbors to take care of neighborhood problems and be available for emergencies.

5. *Intrusion into family life.* The police officer may have to carry parts of his or her job home. For example, police officers generally carry weapons, which they must secure in a safe place at home. Officers also must be available 24 hours a day.

Additionally, as indicated earlier by Professor Scott, officers in small towns and rural areas are particularly affected by stress because they live and work in the same area.[87]

Police Departments Dealing with Stress

A 1981 report by the U.S. Commission on Civil Rights emphasized the need to provide stress management programs and services for police. The commission noted that most police departments lack such programs, despite the recent emphasis on stress as "an important underlying factor in police misconduct incidents." The commission recommended the following: "Police officials should institute comprehensive stress management programs that include identification of officers with stress problems, counseling, periodic screening and training on stress management."[88]

Since then, however, many police departments around the nation have developed stress programs for their officers. For example, in 1986, the NYPD responded to the problem of police suicides by training 100 officers as peer counselors. The NYPD also established telephone hotlines in four precincts; officers needing help in stressful situations could call for help 24 hours a day, 7 days a week.[89] A 1998 summary report on this program revealed a reduction in the number of police suicides, numerous telephone calls on the help line, referrals to mental health clinicians, and families participating in family support seminars.[90]

Stress management has a physical as well as a psychological component. The FBI's Training Division Research and Development Unit mailed a training-needs survey packet to 2,497 police agencies across the nation. The survey results indicated that handling personal stress and maintaining an appropriate level of physical fitness ranked first and second in programs most requested by police officers. In another survey, 90 percent of the nearly 2,000 officers questioned reported that they were in favor of a department-sponsored physical fitness program.[91]

Some departments have instituted health and fitness programs to ensure their officers' physical and emotional well-being. For example, the Ohio State Patrol has implemented a mandatory health and fitness program for all its officers. The Ohio program is designed to ensure a "high quality of life during the troopers' active career period and into retirement."[92]

Speaking of the need for physical fitness, James J. Ness and John Light state,

> The adverse effects of the lack of fitness are overwhelming, while the positive benefits of fitness are often overlooked. Being physically fit diminishes stress, promotes self-esteem, improves firearms accuracy, increases an officer's confidence in confrontations, makes him more effective with impact weapons and defense tactics, and generally improves his quality of life.[93]

Following the terrorist attacks of September 11, 2001, the NYPD ordered all 55,000 of its employees to attend mental health counseling to deal with the stress brought about by this event.[94] A similar program of mental health counseling was implemented to help Oklahoma City rescue workers in 1995 following the terrorist attack in that city.[95]

The Worcester, Massachusetts, Police Department has used peer counselors as "stress responders" to assist other officers in dealing with stressful incidents for more than 20 years. A 2002 book describes the work of police peer counselors and presents their history, describes their strategies and tactics, and identifies the obstacles they face in their work.[96] High among the counselors' recommendations is immediate response to critical incident stress events and the necessity to conduct immediate critical incident stress debriefings (CISDs) for officers who have been exposed to potentially traumatic circumstances. The counselors report that this can help minimize or eliminate the secondary trauma that often occurs and that the counselor can be an understanding listening ear and often a strong bond may be forged between the officer and the counselor that can foster follow-up care.[97]

The National Institute of Justice has created the Corrections and Law Enforcement Family Support program (CLEFS) to deal with some of the problems of police stress. It has sponsored research and program development in some 30 agencies and related organizations (labor unions and employee professional organizations, for example). These projects include developing innovative treatment and training programs as well as research into the nature and causes of stress.[98]

Today, there are numerous training programs and support groups for police officers and their families. Many of them have a presence on the web. In 2006, Laurence Miller reviewed the literature on police psychology and law enforcement behavioral science, as well as his own clinical and practical experiences.[99] Also in 2006, Samuel Walker, retired professor of criminal justice at the University of Nebraska at Omaha, Stacy Osnick Milligan, a criminal justice consultant, and Anna Berke, a research assistant for the Police Executive Research Forum (PERF) produced a comprehensive report regarding strategies for intervening with officers through early intervention systems. The report stresses the need for counseling by the immediate supervisor, training, professional counseling on personal or family problems, peer support programs, crisis intervention teams, and reassignment and relief from duty.[100]

However, it has been reported that some officers avoid using Employee Assistance Programs (EAPS) because they feel such programs do not provide enough confidentiality, staff do not

understand law enforcement, and that stigma is attached to using an EAPS.[101]

Some researchers believe that the highest amount of stress for the officer is organizational stress—stress from the organizational and management policies and procedures of the agency and its supervisors and managers. Scott writes that this problem is compounded for rural and small-town officers because their departments often lack adequate economic and social services resources to address officers' stress. She adds that efforts must be made to fund programs to address these officers' specific needs, particularly to cope with change to administration and management of stigmatization resulting from media criticism.[102]

Ronnie Garrett writes that an organization that runs well smoothly, confidently, and consistently can reduce stress for its employees. He writes that police organizations can cultivate the need to change and provide organizational health to change the stress culture. Ways to do this include the following[103]:

- Run things efficiently by handling things effectively, quickly, and confidently
- Place people in command who are clear in their goals, in their com_____who are highly support
- Pay close attenti____ after an incident a____ feelings of stress a____

In a 2002 article,____ matter what else may____liorate stress, organi____ key to improving the lives of police ____

■—————————————

Police Suicide

Closely associated with the problem of stress in policing is the problem of **police suicide.** The problem of police suicide seems to worsen over the years. Despite all the programs existing to deal with officer problems that may cause suicide, the toll continues to mount. Studies indicate that the suicide rate among police officers is much higher than that of the general population and the rate of police suicides doubled in the 1990s.[105]

Miller, in 2006, wrote that the suicide rate for police officers is three times that of the general population, and three times as many officers kill themselves than are killed by criminals in the line

ON THE JOB

Losing a Good Friend

Suicide is something that happens to other people. You never think it is going to happen to someone you know and never anticipate experiencing suicidal thoughts. Over my police career and through my interactions with the families of suicide victims as well as people experiencing thoughts of suicide or who attempt suicide, I sadly found this was not true.

One of the saddest times of my career was when a friend and coworker committed suicide. Bernie was in his mid-40s when I joined the department. He was a detective and highly respected within the agency and throughout our local criminal justice system. He was known as a great investigator and interviewer and worked relentlessly to get to the truth and then pursue the case to its conclusion. He had the highest ethical standards and never took shortcuts.

I was very fortunate, as Bernie took me under his wing and became my mentor when I joined the department. He said he saw a lot of potential and wanted to help me in any way he could. He worked "crimes against persons" and had become our resident expert in sex crimes. He called me out whenever he was called in for a sex crime. We worked together regularly, and I learned a tremendous amount from Bernie. The strongest impact he made on me was how to interact with people. He had an unassuming and compassionate style that made people feel comfortable and encouraged them to talk. This resulted in many confessions to sex crimes that other officers were surprised were obtained.

I can only guess that though Bernie was able to encourage others to talk, he was not as able to open up to others. We spent some off-duty time together, and I knew that he was divorced and his children were up north. But he was dating someone and seemed well adjusted to his lifestyle.

After I had been in the department five years, Bernie took some leave time for minor surgery and a friend took care of taking him to and from the hospital. I talked to the friend; Bernie didn't want any visitors while he was home recuperating and would see us when he got back to work. A week later, that friend (a detective bureau supervisor) came to my door in the evening. I could tell by the look on his face that something was wrong, but I assumed it was an official visit. We sat down, and he told me that Bernie was dead. Sometime that day Bernie had shot himself with his service weapon.

I had the feelings of guilt that survivors often experience. I should have seen something, I should have visited him even though he didn't want visitors, I should have spent more time with him, I should have encouraged him to talk more . . . all the things you wish you'd done.

Bernie had a lasting impact not only with all the victims and families he worked with but with all the many officers he trained and the officers they went on to train. I have taught many investigators Bernie's techniques and philosophies, so he lives on in the efforts of many.

—*Linda Forst*

of duty. According to Miller, "This makes officer suicide the most lethal threat in police history."[106]

In 2006, based on data from the Centers for Disease Control and Prevention, Robert Douglas of the National Police Suicide Foundation estimated that police officers commit suicide at a rate of 300 to 400 a year.[107]

John M. Violanti, a professor in the Criminal Justice Department of the Rochester Institute of Technology in Rochester, New York, and a member of the Department of Social and Preventive Medicine, University of New York at Buffalo, works on the problem of police suicide. Violanti, who also served 23 years with the New York State Police, notes that the police culture and the reluctance of police officers to ask for help complicates the problem of police suicide. His research revealed that police are at higher risk for committing suicide for a variety of reasons, including access to firearms, continuous exposure to human misery, shift work, social strain and marital difficulties, drinking problems, physical illness, impending retirement, and lack of control over their jobs and personal lives. Violanti's work indicates that police commit suicide at a rate up to 53 percent higher than other city workers.[108]

Violanti reports that police officers become ingrained in police work and isolated from other life roles such as family, friendships, or community involvement; tend to view reality as a "black and white" situation; and are inflexible in their thinking. Violanti writes that good adjustment involves being able to view frustrating life situations from many angles, rather than simply as black and white. Police officers tend to have problems with personal relationships, and these problems may increase their potential for suicide.[109]

Leonard Territo and Harold J. Vetter have attempted to explain the high rates of suicide among police officers. The stressors they identify shed a light on the particularly stressful nature of police work[110]:

1. Police work is a male-dominated profession, and men have higher suicide rates than women.

2. The use, availability, and familiarity with firearms by police in their work make it fairly certain that suicide attempts will be successful.

3. There are psychological repercussions to being exposed to potential death on a constant basis.

4. Long and irregular working hours do not promote strong friendships and strain family ties.

5. There is constant exposure to public criticism and dislike toward the police.

6. Judicial contradictions, irregularities, and inconsistent decisions tend to negate the value of police work in officers' lives.

Traditionally, no matter what their problems, police officers refrain from asking for help. There are various reasons for this reluctance. The primary reason, however, is that officers do not want to appear weak or vulnerable in front of their peers. Individuals who perceive themselves as problem solvers often have great difficulty admitting that they have problems of their own. As a result, some officers who feel that they can no longer tolerate psychological pain choose to solve the problem themselves through suicide rather than by asking others for help.[111]

Daniel W. Clark and Elizabeth K. White, in 2003, wrote that the factors that may interfere with an officer seeking help include the stigma of suicide, confidentiality concerns, job impact worries, personality traits, the stigma of emotional problems, alcohol, mistrust of the psychological field, and the negative perception of taking medication as treatment.[112]

Miller, noting that the risk of suicide is greatest in officers with prior histories of depression and those who have recently faced debilitating stressors linked to feelings of hopelessness and helplessness, has said that much can be done by law enforcement agencies to counter and prevent officer depression and suicide including these[113]:

1. The severity of the problem must be acknowledged and openly addressed by both command and line officers through instruction in occupational stress, signs of impairment, and how to cope with stress in positive ways.

2. Officers should receive training in crisis intervention skills that they can use with fellow officers.

3. Supervisors must be alert to signs of depression and other problems that may signal the possibility of suicidal thoughts.

4. There must be a convenient and nonstigmatizing system for referring distressed officers for psychological help.

5. When the acute crisis has passed, referral to a mental health clinician is crucial in determining the officer's fitness for duty and in helping the officer build mental and emotional resources to prevent subsequent crises.

In a 2006 article, Patricia Kelly and Rich Martin suggest that if law enforcement agencies spend time and money equipping and training officers to protect themselves while on duty, they should be equally, if not more, committed to doing what is required to prevent officer suicides. Kelly and Martin argue that agency personnel who observe warning signs in fellow officers and family members of officers at risk should be encouraged to contact the officer's supervisor. They write that a clear indication of the intent to commit suicide warrants immediately taking the officer to a hospital emergency room for a full psychological evaluation.[114]

Police Danger

How often are police officers killed or injured in the line of duty? What are the specific threats to the police regarding personal safety? No one would disagree with the statement that police work is dangerous. Unfortunately, its dangers are increasing, too. Each year many officers are injured or killed in the line of duty. The chances of

LEOKA

contracting life-threatening diseases, such as AIDS, are increasing as more of the general population is affected. This section puts these dangers into perspective.

Police officers perform necessary and often dangerous tasks. They deal constantly with what may be the most dangerous species on this planet—the human being—often in the most stressful and dangerous situations. They regularly respond to people shooting at each other, stabbing each other, and beating each other. In a typical tour of duty, officers can deal with the full range of human emotions. They also respond to calls where they may meet armed adversaries such as robberies in progress and hostage situations. Most frequently officers respond to "unknown problems" or "unknown disturbances" types of calls, where someone is calling for help, but the officers are unable to gather further information and really don't know what they're walking into. The dangerous conditions facing U.S. police officers are compounded by the irrationality produced by alcohol and drugs. The urban drug business since the 1980s has been characterized by an emphasis on tremendous inflows of cash and instant gratification. The proliferation of young, urban, uneducated, and unemployable males, armed with a plethora of weapons (including military-like automatic assault weapons), makes officers increasingly fearful for their safety. As Barbara Raffel Price of the John Jay College of Criminal Justice wrote, "It would be foolish not to recognize that the violence associated with the drug business puts the police and citizens in greater jeopardy and that it makes the job of policing almost impossible."[115]

Also, the risk of exposure to dangerous chemicals in police work is always present. Deputies and police officers are always subject to the possibility of contamination from a variety of toxic chemicals, such as lye, iodine, and lithium when they must enter methamphetamine (meth) labs to place offenders under arrest or while processing those under arrest who are contaminated themselves.[116] Other risks constantly threaten police officers. In 2006, in Minneapolis, it was reported that felons are increasingly donning body armor in the form of bullet-resistant vests when they hit the streets. Some factors could explain this—body armor, although expensive, is becoming cheaper and available on the Internet; and criminals are getting more violent. According to Minneapolis Captain Rich Stanek, "Wearing it is almost a fashion statement to some of these guys."[117]

Officers Killed in the Line of Duty

The FBI (which maintains records of law enforcement officers murdered, accidentally killed, and injured in the line of duty each year) reported that 55 state and local law enforcement officers were feloniously slain in the line of duty in 53 incidents for the latest reporting year, 2005. Of these officers, 8 were killed in arrest situations (4 while responding to robberies in progress or pursuing robbery suspects, 1 while responding to a burglary in progress or pursuing burglary suspects, and 3 while attempting other types of arrests). Eight officers were ambushed by their assailants, with 4 being victims of unprovoked attacks and 4 victims of premeditation. Seven officers were killed while investigating disturbance calls (5 in domestic cases, and 2 while investigating bar fights or persons with firearms). Seven officers were murdered investigating suspicious persons or circumstances, and 15 were slain in the course of stopping vehicles for violations or the resulting vehicle pursuit. Three officers were killed while working to resolve hostage situations or other high-risk tactical situations; 2 were slain while handling mentally deranged individuals; and 1 was killed while handling a prisoner. Four officers were murdered while conducting investigative activities such as surveillance, searches, and interviews. Fifty of the 55 officers murdered were slain with firearms.[118] One federal law enforcement officer was killed in the line of duty in 2004, and 2 were murdered over the last five reporting years.[119]

Thirty of the 50 officers murdered with firearms in 2005 were wearing body armor at the time of their deaths In some of these cases, the bullets entered the officers' bodies in areas not covered by the body armor, and in some case, the bullets penetrated the armor.[120]

An examination of data from the last 10 reportable years showed that 575 officers were feloniously killed in the line of duty during that period. Over this decade, firearms (particularly handguns) were responsible for most of the killings: 394 officers were killed with handguns, 103 with rifles, and 35 with shotguns. Vehicles were used as the murder weapon in 31 killings; 1 officer was killed by a bomb blast, and 6 were killed with knives or other cutting instruments. Personal weapons (hands, fists, or feet) were used in 3 of the incidents, and blunt force instruments were used in 2 of the murders.[121]

Accidents killed 67 law enforcement officers in 2005, with 39 dying in automobile crashes, 4 in motorcycle crashes, and 11 struck by vehicles. Additionally, 4 officers were accidentally shot, 2 died in aircraft accidents, 2 drowned, 3 fell to their deaths, and 2 were killed in other situations. Data for the latest 10-year period shows that 725 officers died from accidents: 410 were killed in auto accidents, 121 when struck by vehicles, 61 in motorcycle accidents, 37 in aircraft accidents, 30 were mistakenly shot, 22 drowned, 21 died from falls, and 23 died in other situations.[122]

The 1970s were the deadliest decade for American law enforcement when an average of 226 officers were killed in the line of duty each year, compared with the average of 162 line-of-duty deaths per years between 1995 and 2005.[123]

Other studies over the years give us information regarding the murder of police officers. William Geller and Michael S. Scott's study revealed that in 1971 police were feloniously killed at a rate of 38 per 100,000 officers, but this rate decreased steadily until it reached 12 per 100,000 officers in the 1990s.[124] (As indicated earlier the 1970s were the most dangerous for police in the terms of officers being killed). David Lester's study of the characteristics of cities that have high rates of police officer fatalities indicated that these cities were mainly located in the South. The cities had low population densities, high murder rates, and a high proportion of gun ownership.[125] Geller has shown that off-duty police officers and plainclothes officers have high rates of shooting fatalities.[126] His explanation for these high rates was that off-duty officers, who are usually armed, are expected to take appropriate action when they encounter criminal situations. However, they suffer from the lack of normal tactical advantages, such as communication, cover, and backup. Geller indicated that plainclothes officers may often be mistaken for perpetrators in criminal situations.

The **National Law Enforcement Officers Memorial (NLEOM)** is located in Washington, D.C., and has the names of about 17,500 slain officers inscribed on its walls. Its website is visited by more than 200,000 people each year and enhances public knowledge of and appreciation for law enforcement officers and the dangers they face. The National Law Enforcement Memorial Fund (NLEOMF) collects and catalogs information on law enforcement fatalities in an effort to educate the public about officer safety and with the goal that no officer slain in the line of duty will ever be forgotten.[127]

The organization Concerns of Police Survivors Inc. (COPS) started in 1984 to provide resources to survivors of law enforcement officers killed in the line of duty. Its website provides information to survivors and police agencies. COPS also provides training and assistance to departments in how to respond to a law enforcement death in their department in the hopes of reducing the trauma suffered by coworkers. COPS states on its website, "There is no membership fee to join COPS, for the price paid is already too high."[128]

When one looks at the number of police officer-citizen contacts each year—about 45 million, according to the Bureau of Justice Statistics[129]—and the dangerous situations they often find themselves in, the police have relatively low murder rates. What accounts for the relatively low murder rates of police officers despite the constant possibility of violence with which they are faced? There are several explanations.

People who would not think twice about shooting a fellow citizen might hesitate in shooting a police officer, knowing that society places a special value on the lives of those they depend on for maintaining law and order on the streets. People also know that the criminal justice system reacts in a harsher way to a "cop killer" than to an ordinary killer.

Also contributing to the relatively low level of officer killings is the fact that professional criminals, including organized crime members and drug dealers, know that killing a police officer is "very bad for business." Such a killing will result in tremendous disruption of their business while the police hunt for, and prosecute, the killer.

Another reason for the relatively low number of killings of police officers is their awareness of the dangers they face every day and the resultant physical and mental precautions they take to deal with such dangers. The discussion of the police personality earlier in this chapter characterized it as suspicious, loyal, and cynical. Most experts believe that the police personality is caused by the dangers of police work. It's possible that the negative aspects of the police personality keep officers relatively safe. Also, advances in medical science, and improved training and equipment have helped to save the lives of police officers. Officers are now trained not to blindly rush into situations but to obtain as much information as possible (aided by improved records systems) while en route and upon arrival. Obtaining cover and waiting for backup are also stressed.

In the Line of Duty

DAVID H. SWIM

David H. Swim is a retired captain from the Stockton, California, Police Department, having spent 22 years with that agency. While with that department he worked the street as a police officer, sergeant, and lieutenant. He was also assigned to SWAT, serving 6 years as the SWAT unit's commander. He received his doctorate in public administration from the University of Southern California and is currently an associate professor of criminal justice administration and leadership, with California State University–Sacramento. He teaches upper-division courses in police administration, critical issues, and leadership, and two graduate courses in the history of criminal justice in America and collective bargaining.

In front of the Stockton Police Department stands a 10-foot high gray granite monument. It stands as a sentinel, to acknowledge those officers of our community who gave their all for law enforcement, in the line of duty. The 14 names etched into the granite will endure as long as the granite. They are enduring in the sense that the absence of these officers and their untimely deaths echo eternally; enduring in the sense that spouses, children, parents, and siblings will constantly feel their absence; enduring in the fact that each day, as officers arrive at work, they pass by this solemn sentinel, reminding them that they, too, could fall, in the line of duty.

The chiseled reality of loss is softened by a plaque occupying the top portion of the obelisk. The police officer holding a small child in his arms contrasts the kindness of the calling of police officer with the harshness of reality. Death in the line of duty is not attended by some euphoric national pride or sense of mission. In fact, silently, over 100 officers are killed annually, simply doing their job. While we are not paid to die, it is a harsh reality of police work.

During my 22 years at the Stockton PD, seven of those names were added to that monument. Five were killed by gunfire, one was beaten to death, and one died during a foot pursuit. All were friends, some more so than others. Each had a family, most that I personally knew. Each death weathered my soul, extracted tears not cried, and demanded resolution of my shortcomings. Each death reminded me of my own mortality, but, most of all, my inadequacy to properly return to my maker.

One was killed during the exchange of gunfire at the end of a vehicle pursuit. Two were SWAT members whom I had trained to be the "best of the best"; the assailant's bullet pays no respect to training, skill, and finesse. One was ambushed from inside a residence with a rifle that no body armor could stop. One was shot in the face during an exchange of gunfire that also killed his assailant. At the hospital three of us stood around a gurney, silently weeping, knowing that, in the line of duty, real cops cry.

Another possible explanation for decrease in officer murders is the increased use of body armor. The latest statistics released in 2006 indicate that most departments today require their field officers to wear protective body armor—74 percent of local police departments, compared with 30 percent in 1990, and 76 percent of sheriff's offices, compared with 30 percent in 1990.[130] Recall, however, that the majority of officers murdered by people with firearms were wearing body armor at the time of their death. Also, some of the slain officers wearing body armor died from torso wounds caused by bullets entering despite wearing the armor.[131] This reinforces the fact that body armor is not "bullet proof."

In an interesting article, Claire Mayhew, an Australian criminologist, discussed the risk of death, homicide, assault, communicable disease, stress and fatigue, injuries, and illnesses to officers. Mayhew notes the relatively constant rate of police homicides in a time of increased availability of firearms and illicit drugs suggests that body armor, medical technology, and training strategies have kept pace with the threats. She notes the risk of assaults far exceeds fatalities and is probably increasing. Assaults on officers in Australia are relatively common, and approximately 10 percent of officers are assaulted each year.[132]

Officers Assaulted in the Line of Duty

As we have seen, police officers have relatively low murder rates, but how often are officers injured

Two were narcotics officers killed on search warrants, by bullets that went over the top of or through the nonexistent side panel of body armor of the 1970s. One of these narcotics officers was the son of our chief of police, who responded to the hospital to find his pride and joy expired on the gurney. As we wept together, how does one console a father, let alone the chief of police? The other narcotics officer's father was working as a reserve the day of his death and expired of a heart attack when he heard of his son's death.

During a several-block foot pursuit of a fleeing suspect, a rare and undiagnosed heart malady stopped the heart of the pursuing officer, making him the sixth of those added to the list during my years with the department. Death was instantaneous, yet absolutely confusing to his attending officers, until the post mortem. A night time traffic stop of a parolee, bulked up by prison yard weight lifting, resulted in a beating with the seventh officer's own flashlight, so severe that the officer expired days later, never recovering from his comatose state.

Of the seven deaths, six were instant and finality came over us as immediately as the summer sun is eclipsed by clouds. The expiration of the beaten officer took days as the family and officers anticipated the eventuality of death. Each day was torture as we were literally or figuratively part of the death watch. Ironically, finality brought peace, commensurate with the immense pain.

Each of these deaths left widows and orphans. Each of these deaths tore the heart out of parents, whereas no parent should have a child precede him or her in death. Each left a community shocked, at least for the moment. Each created an atmosphere where spouses felt the visceral impact and fear for their loved one, in the line of duty. Each reminded us that we were mortal.

Seven viewings with the attendant honor guard in Class A uniforms at each end of the casket. Seven funerals with their respective masses or services. Seven funeral processions with hundreds of marching officers, with labor and management, for the moment, united in step and purpose. Miles of police vehicles with emergency lights beaconing heaven that another chosen servant is on his way. Seven postfuneral receptions where officers attempt to absorb some of the pain and loss of the family of the deceased and yet are confused as they sort out their own personal loss. I was asked by family to speak at two of those funerals. How does one comfort the family, his fellow officers, and express any justification at all for an officer's life being cut short, in the line of duty? Notwithstanding the nobility of the calling, the price is too high.

Policing is a noble calling. It is true, "and on the eighth day God created cops." The heroism of the many and the sacrifice of these few is tarnished by any who accept this calling and do not live up to the ethic required of this noble profession. We live in an era when our profession is under the greatest scrutiny and oftentimes disdain from an ambivalent public, due to the actions of those that disrespect their oath of office. Nonetheless, as with the centurions of old, the world is a better place, because the noble are willing to be in the line of duty.

by criminal assaults in the line of duty? In 2005, almost 58,000 assaults were committed against state and local police officers in local, state, and tribal agencies. The assaults resulted in injuries to almost 16,000 officers (27.4 percent of the officers assaulted). The assaults most commonly involved personal weapons such as hands, feet, and fists. Firearms were used against officers in 3.7 percent of assaults and knives or cutting instruments in 1.8 percent of the assaults.[133]

About 31 percent of the assaults occurred while officers were responding to disturbance calls; 17 percent while attempting arrests; 13 percent while handling, transporting, or otherwise having custody of prisoners; 14 percent while performing other duties; 11 percent while conducting traffic stops or pursuits; almost 10 percent while investigating suspicious persons or circumstances; 2 percent while handling mentally deranged persons; 1.4 percent while investigating burglaries in progress or pursuing burglary suspects; 1.3 percent while policing civil disorders, and 0.9 percent while responding to robberies in progress or pursuing robbery suspects. Only 0.3 percent of the assaults were ambush situations.[134]

In 2005, 1,882 federal law enforcement officers were the subjects of assaults in the line of duty, and 309 of these assaults resulted in injuries: 1,159 of the officers were from the Department of Homeland Security; 528 from the Department of the Interior; 162 from the Department of Justice; 18 from the U.S. Postal Inspection Service; 12 from the U.S. Capitol Police; and 3 from the Department of the Treasury. Nearly half of the officers assaulted were performing patrol or guard duties when assaulted. A study of data covering the latest five-year reporting period revealed that 3,964 federal officers were injured.[135]

Despite the murders and assaults of police officers discussed in this chapter, it might be interesting to note that the actuality of these events may be relatively low when one considers that the police generally have face-to-face contact with more than 45 million persons a year, sometimes in extremely tense and stressful encounters.[136]

Perhaps these statistics do not tell the complete story, according to Rich Roberts, a former police officer and spokesman for the International Union of Police Associations, "Police are a stoic breed. Often they take their lumps and don't make a big deal about it. They limp around for a couple of days. But no one's charged, and they don't miss any work."[137]

Police and AIDS

Since the 1980s, human immunodeficiency virus (HIV), acquired immune deficiency syndrome (AIDS), and hepatitis B and C have become sources of great concern to U.S. police officers, as well as to everyone else. **AIDS,** a deadly disease, is transmitted mainly through sexual contact and the exchange of body fluids. Although AIDS was formerly associated mainly with male homosexuals, intravenous drug users, and prostitutes, it is now known that anyone could be subject to infection by this disease.

The impact of HIV/AIDS is readily apparent. According to the Centers for Disease Control (CDC), the estimated cumulative number of AIDS diagnoses in the United States through 2004 was 944,305, with 9,443 of those being children younger than 13. The estimated cumulative number of deaths from AIDS in the United States through 2004 was 529,113, including 5,515 children younger than 13. In 2004 in the United States alone, the estimated deaths from AIDS totaled 15,798, including 61 children younger than 13. Worldwide, the statistics are even more frightening, with more than 40 million people believed to be living with HIV/AIDS by 2003. During 2003, the disease was acquired by 5 million people and caused the deaths of 3 million people worldwide.[138]

These figures do not include individuals infected with HIV who may carry the disease for years before any symptoms of AIDS appear. These individuals are still contagious. Though there is no cure for AIDS, advances have been made in the treatment of the disease, allowing infected individuals to live longer lives.[139]

Police officers frequently encounter all types of people—including those having infectious diseases—and officers often have contact with blood and other body fluids. Therefore, officers are at special risk for catching communicable diseases. They must take precautionary measures during searches and other contacts with possible carriers of infectious diseases, as well as at crime scenes, where blood and other body fluids may be present.[140]

The International Association of Chiefs of Police (IACP) model policy on HIV/AIDS prevention defines an exposure as "any contact with body fluids including, but not limited to, direct contact with skin, eyes, nose and mouth, and through needle sticks." The policy stresses prevention of HIV/AIDS exposure and recommends behaviors and procedures to minimize the chance of becoming exposed. It also addresses the supplies that departments should have on hand and procedures to be used for cleanup in the event of a body fluid spill or deposit in a patrol vehicle or booking area. The policy also discusses the importance of documenting and following through on an exposure for educational purposes and to ensure the officers are covered if the disease has been contracted. It stresses education and the use of "universal precautions" or generic precautionary rules. This is the practice of treating all body fluids as potentially hazardous, routinely using gloves and plastic mouthpieces for CPR, and adopting policies and behaviors that minimize the chance of being exposed to HIV/AIDS. Universal precautions mitigate the fact that, because of confidentiality issues in most states, officers will not know who is or is not infected with a communicable disease.[141]

The FBI has published numerous recommendations about how to collect and handle evidence that might be infected with the viruses, bacteria, and germs of infectious diseases.[142] The National Institute of Justice has also published recommendations on dealing with possibly infected evidence.[143] Despite serious medical risks, police officers may not refuse to handle incidents involving persons infected with the AIDS virus or with other infectious diseases. Failing to perform certain duties—such as rendering first aid, assisting, or even arresting a person—would be a dereliction of duty, as well as discrimination against a class of people.[144]

Summary

- The police culture or police subculture is a combination of shared norms, values, goals, career patterns, life styles, and occupational structures that is somewhat different from the combination held by the rest of society, and is characterized by clannishness, secrecy, and isolation from those not in the group.

- Police officers protect one another from outsiders, often even refusing to aid police superiors or other law enforcement officials in investigating wrongdoing of other officers, producing a protective barrier known as the blue wall of silence.

- The police subculture leads to the police personality, or traits common to most police officers, such as authoritarianism, suspicion, hostility, insecurity, conservatism, and cynicism.

- Police cynicism is an attitude that there is no hope for the world and a view of humanity at its worst.

- The Dirty Harry problem refers to the reality that police officers are often confronted with situations in which they feel forced to take certain illegal actions to achieve a greater good.

- Stress is the body's reaction to internal or external stimuli that upset the body's normal state. The body's reaction to highly stressful situations is known as the flight-or-fight response.

- Police have higher rates of divorce, suicide, alcoholism and other manifestations of stress than do other professions.

- Police officers are confronted with four general categories of stress: external stress, organizational stress, personal stress, and operational stress.

- Many factors lead to stress in police work, including poor training, substandard equipment, poor pay, lack of opportunity, role conflict, exposure to brutality, fears about job competence and safety, lack of job satisfaction, the pressure of being on duty 24 hours a day, and fatigue. Police officers learn to cope with that stress by becoming emotionally detached from their work and the people they are paid to serve.

- The phenomenon of "suicide by cop" is a very serious problem for police officers. Many officer-involved shootings are the result of suicide by cop incidents.

- The suicide rate for police officers is three times that of the general population, and three times as many officers kill themselves compared with the number of officers killed by criminals in the line of duty.

- In 2005, 55 state and local law enforcement officers were feloniously slain in the line of duty in 53 incidents. 50 of them were slain with firearms.

- In the last 10 reportable years, 575 state and local officers were feloniously killed in the line of duty. Firearms, particularly handguns, were responsible for most of the killings.

- The 1970s were the deadliest decade for American law enforcement—an average of 226 officers were killed in the line of duty each year, compared with the average of 162 line-of-duty deaths per years between 1995 and 2005.

- In 2005, almost 58,000 assaults were committed against state and local police officers. One federal officer was killed in the latest reporting year, and 1,882 were the subjects of assaults. During the last five reporting years, 2 federal officers were murdered.

Learning Check

1. Explain what the police culture or subculture is and how it expresses itself.

2. Define the police personality and discuss how it expresses itself.

3. List some reasons for the existence of a police subculture and a police personality.

4. Give some reasons why police officers experience high levels of stress.

5. Discuss what police departments can do to deal with the high levels of stress present in their officers.

6. What is "suicide by cop"? Give some examples.

7. Describe and discuss some of the reasons that police work is seen as a dangerous job.

8. Discuss killings of police officers. What are the trends in the killing of police officers during the past three decades?

9. Discuss the role of firearms in the killings of police officers.

10. What are some of the precautions police take to avoid being infected by AIDS?

Key Terms

AIDS Acquired immune deficiency syndrome.

blue curtain A concept developed by William Westley that claims that police officers only trust other police officers and do not aid in the investigation of wrongdoing by other officers.

blue wall of silence A figurative protective barrier erected by the police in which officers protect one another from outsiders, often even refusing to aid police superiors or other law enforcement officials in investigating wrongdoing of other officers.

deadly force Force that can cause death.

Dirty Harry problem A moral dilemma faced by police officers in which they may feel forced to take certain illegal actions to achieve a greater good.

flight-or-fight response The body's reaction to highly stressful situations in which it is getting prepared for extraordinary physical exertion.

National Law Enforcement Officers Memorial (NLEOM) A memorial in Washington D.C. established to recognize the ultimate sacrifice of police officers killed in the line of duty.

police culture or police subculture A combination of shared norms, values, goals, career patterns, life styles, and occupational structures that is somewhat different from the combination held by the rest of society.

police cynicism An attitude that there is no hope for the world and a view of humanity at its worst.

police personality Traits common to most police officers. Scholars have reported that this personality is thought to include such traits as authoritarianism, suspicion, hostility, insecurity, conservatism, and cynicism.

police suicide The intentional taking of one's own life by a police officer.

suicide by cop The phenomenon in which a person wishing to die deliberately places an officer in a life-threatening situation, causing the officer to use deadly force against that person.

Minorities in Policing

© Dennis MacDonald/Photo Edit Inc.

GOALS

- To describe the history and problems of minorities in policing
- To illustrate how discrimination affects minorities in obtaining employment and promotions in policing
- To discuss the provisions of the U.S. legal system that enabled minorities to overcome job discrimination
- To introduce the academic studies showing the performance of minorities in police work
- To portray a sense of the problems minorities still face in law enforcement, even in the twenty-first century

Introduction

Female police officers on uniformed patrol duty are common today, as are officers who are African American or members of other minority groups. In fact, all races and ethnic groups are represented in U.S. police departments. However, this was not always the case. Until quite recently, white males dominated the ranks. African Americans were traditionally excluded from U.S. police departments. As just one example among many, there was not a single black police officer in the deep south, including Alabama, Louisiana, Georgia, Mississippi, and South Carolina, in the 1930s and early 1940s, even though these states had most of the black population in the United States.[1] This underrepresentation of minorities in police departments has not been limited to southern cities. Northern jurisdictions also had a history of discriminating against African Americans and limiting their job responsibilities in law enforcement.[2] Although the United States has had organized, paid police depart-

ments since the 1840s, the first female police officer was not appointed until 1910 when Alice Stebbins Wells was hired by Los Angeles Police Department (LAPD) as the "first policewoman" in the United States.[3] As the entry of women into police departments progressed, women were given only clerical duties or duties dealing with juveniles or female prisoners. Women were not permitted to perform the same patrol duties as men until the late 1960s.[4]

This chapter will focus on the roles of minority groups in U.S. police departments. We will review their experience and the methods they used to secure the same job opportunities as white men. The chapter will also show the extent to which minorities have influenced today's police departments and explore the capabilities of women in performing what has traditionally been viewed as a male occupation. Finally, we will examine the status of minorities in U.S. law enforcement today.

Discrimination in Policing

The United States has a long history of job **discrimination** against women and minorities. Discrimination is the unequal treatment of persons in personnel decisions (hiring, promotion, and firing) on the basis of their race, religion, national origin, gender, or sexual orientation. Only in the past several decades have women and minorities been able to share the American dream of equal employment. Their treatment in police departments was not much different from their treatment in other jobs and in society in general. The federal government admitted this fact in 1974 in an affirmative action guidebook for employers: "American law guarantees all persons equal opportunity in employment. However, employment discrimination has existed in police departments for a long time. The main areas of discrimination are race/ethnic background and gender."[5]

Discrimination against Women

Women have faced an enormous uphill struggle to earn the right to wear the uniform and perform the same basic police duties that men have performed for years. Why were women excluded from performing regular police work? Until the 1970s, it was presumed that women, because of their gender and typical size, were not capable of performing the same type of patrol duty as men. Other social forces also contributed to the discrimination against women. If women could do the "police" job, that challenged the macho image of the job. Men did not want to have their behavior inhibited in any way by the presence of women on the job. They did not want to be overshadowed by, or to take orders from, women, and they did not want to be supported by women in the performance of potentially dangerous work. The issue of jealousy of male police officers' wives was also brought up at times. The most commonly heard comment by male police officers during the 1970s as women entered the patrol arena had to do with the fear of female officers being beaten up and their guns taken. This would endanger the female officer, citizens, and the male officers who would be backing up the women. The men feared that law enforcement would be forever changed and the world as they knew it would come to an end![6]

Until 1967, women constituted only a very small percentage of U.S. police officers. The early women were restricted to issuing parking tickets or performing routine clerical tasks. In the early days of female policing, women were normally used in only three actual police-related jobs: vice, juvenile work, and guarding female prisoners.[7] Even O. W. Wilson, writing in his *Police Administration* text, considered by many to be the "bible" of law enforcement managers, proposed that women were an asset in certain police positions, but not all. Through all four editions of his text, from 1950 to 1977, he conceded that women had value as juvenile officers and in other limited areas but that they did not have what it took to be leaders. Men had more experience and were "less likely to become irritable and overcritical under emotional stress, than women."[8] In the late 1960s and early 1970s, the role of women in U.S. police departments began to change. To some degree, this was facilitated by the 1964 Civil Rights Act, which barred discrimination on the basis of sex. The change can also be attributed to the woman's rights movement and to the efforts by female officers themselves to gain the right to perform patrol duty to achieve equality with male officers.[9] Even as late as the mid-1970s, however, female officers in some jurisdictions experienced different sets of rules as their administrations and coworkers fluctuated between endorsing their full equality and wanting to "protect" them.

Discrimination against African Americans

The first African American police officer was appointed to the Washington, D.C., Police Department in 1867. Within 10 years, numerous other cities began appointing blacks to police departments, and just after the turn of the twentieth century, significant appointments began taking place in St. Louis, Dayton, Berkeley, and Atlanta.[10]

By 1910, African Americans had all but disappeared from southern police forces. In 1910, the U.S. Census Bureau reported 576 blacks serving as police officers in the United States, most in northern cities. Though Houston, Austin, Galveston, San Antonio, and Knoxville continued to employ African American police officers, they often had no uniforms, couldn't arrest whites, and worked exclusively in black neighborhoods. Until the 1940s, not a single black police officer worked in the Deep South—including South Carolina, Georgia, Louisiana, Mississippi, and Alabama—yet in the 1930s and 1940s, these states had most of the black population in the United States.[11] Most blacks were eliminated because they posed a threat to white supremacy.

Even in the north, African Americans faced discrimination in assignments and promotions. Police officers felt their issues were not addressed by their administrations and took matters into their own hands. Though not identified at the time, an early form of double marginality (which will be discussed shortly) led the black officers to socialize with each other and teach each other how to successfully deal with the discrimination and the dual system of law enforcement. It also led to increased camaraderie and organization within their group. Black officers formed the Texas Negro Peace Officers Association in 1935. This first formal police association organized by black officers in the United States, was followed by others in the 1940s and 1950s. In 1943, the Guardians Association was organized by black New York City officers to "recognize the views and ideals of black policemen in New York City."[12]

In his classic study of African American police officers in the New York City Police Department (NYPD) in 1969, *Black in Blue: A Study of the Negro Policeman*, Nicholas Alex discovered that African Americans were excluded from the department's detective division. Alex also found that African American officers were usually accepted by white officers as fellow police officers but were socially excluded from the white officers' off-duty activities.[13] Alex's major finding was that African American police officers had to suffer **double marginality**—the simultaneous expectation by white officers that African American officers will give members of their own race better treatment and hostility from the African American community that black officers are traitors to their race. The African American officers were also subjected to racist behavior of white cops. Alex found that African American officers, to deal with this pressure, adapted behaviors ranging from denying that African American suspects should be treated differently from whites to treating African American offenders more harshly to prove their lack of bias. Thus, African American cops, Alex found, suffered from the racism of their fellow officers and were seen to be rougher on African Americans to appease whites. In a repeat of his study in 1976, *New York Cops Talk Back,* Alex claimed to have found a more aggressive, self-assured African American police officer. The officers he studied were less willing to accept any discriminatory practices by the police department.[14]

Stephen Leinen, in his book *Black Police, White Society,* found significant discrimination in the NYPD until the 1960s. African American police officers were assigned only to African American neighborhoods and were not assigned to specialized, high profile units. Leinen also noted that disciplinary actions against African American officers were inequitable when compared with those against white officers. He found, however, that institutional discrimination had largely disappeared in subsequent years. He attributes this to the legal, social, and political events of the civil rights era, along with the efforts of African American police officer organizations, such as the NYPD's Guardians.[15]

National Commissions to Study Discrimination In the 1960s and early 1970s, the U.S. government recognized the problems caused by the lack of minorities in policing. Various national commissions were established to study, and make recommendations toward improving, the criminal justice system.

The National Advisory Commission on Civil Disorders stated that discriminatory police employment practices contributed to the riots of the middle and late 1960s. It found that in every city affected by the riots, the percentage of minority group officers was substantially lower than the percentage of minorities in the community. The commission noted that in Cleveland, minorities represented 34 percent of the population but only 7 percent of the sworn officers, and in Detroit, minorities represented 39 percent of the population but only 5 percent of the sworn officers. The commission also noted that although African Americans made up at least 12 percent of the U.S. population, they represented less than 5 percent of police officers nationwide. The commission also reported that minorities were seriously underrepresented in supervisory ranks in police departments. Another commission formed at this time, the President's Commission on Law Enforcement and Administration of Justice, commented on the low percentage of minorities in police departments: "If police departments, through their hiring or promotion policies, indicate they have little interest in hiring minority group officers, the minority community is not likely to be sympathetic to the police."[16] Another group, the **National Advisory Commission on Criminal Justice Standards and Goals,** realized the need to recruit more minorities into U.S. police departments. This presidential commission, which was formed to study the criminal justice system, issued standards to which police agencies should adhere to reduce job discrimination. Among these were standards on the employment of women and minority recruitment. On the employment of women, the commission stated that every police agency should immediately ensure that no agency policy discourages qualified women from seeking employment as sworn or civilian personnel or prevents them from realizing their full employment.[17] Minority recruiting was discussed:

> Every police agency immediately should insure that it presents no artificial or arbitrary barriers (cultural or institutional) to discourage qualified individuals from seeking employment or from being employed as police officers.
>
> Every police agency should engage in positive efforts to employ ethnic minority group members. When a substantial ethnic minority population resides within the jurisdiction the police agency should take affirmative action to achieve a ratio of minority group employees in approximate proportion to the makeup of the population.[18]

The **National Advisory Commission on Civil Disorders,** also known as the **Kerner Commission,** recommended among other things that police departments "intensify their efforts to recruit more Negroes" and examine their promotional policies and increase the use and visibility of integrated patrol in ghetto areas.[19] This report together with increased pressure from the public led to more aggressive recruiting efforts in police agencies during the 1970s and 1980s.

How Did Women and Minorities Strive for Equality?

Despite pronouncements by national commissions, minorities were forced to take their cases to the U.S. courts in an attempt to achieve equality with white men in U.S. police departments. The primary instrument governing employment equality, as well as all equality, in U.S. society is the Fourteenth Amendment to the U.S. Constitution. This amendment, passed in 1868, guarantees "equal protection of the law" to all citizens of the United States:

> Section 1. All persons born or naturalized in the United States, and subject to the jurisdiction thereof, are citizens of the United States and of the State wherein they reside. No State shall make or enforce any law which shall abridge the privileges or immunities of citizens of the United States; nor shall any State deprive any person of life, liberty, or property, without due process of law; nor deny to any person within its jurisdiction the equal protection of the law.

More than the Fourteenth Amendment was needed, however, to end job discrimination in policing (or any government agency). In addition to the Fourteenth Amendment, the path to equality had as milestones the Civil Rights Act of 1964, Title VII of the same law, the Equal Employment Opportunity Act of 1972 (EEOA), the Civil Rights Act of 1991, federal court cases on discrimination, and government-mandated affirmative action programs.

The Civil Rights Act of 1964

Despite the existence of the Fourteenth Amendment, discrimination by U.S. government agencies continued. In an effort to ensure equality, the **Civil Rights Act of 1964** was passed by Congress and signed into law by President Lyndon B. Johnson in 1964.[20] Title VII of this law was designed to prohibit all job discrimination based on race, color, religion, sex, or national origin. It covered all employment practices, including hiring, promotion,

You Are There!

The Path to Equality— Court Cases

1971	*Griggs v. Duke Power Company*
1973	*Vulcan Society v. Civil Service Commission*
1976	*Mieth v. Dothard*
1979	*Vanguard Justice Society v. Hughes*
1979	*United States v. State of New York*
1980	*Guardians Association of New York City Police Department v. Civil Service Commission of New York*

compensation, dismissal, and all other terms or conditions of employment.

The Omnibus Crime Control and Safe Streets Act of 1968

The **Omnibus Crime Control and Safe Streets Act of 1968** was enacted with the goal of assisting local governments in reducing the incidence of crime by increasing the effectiveness, fairness and coordination of law enforcement and the criminal justice system. Legislators felt that to prevent crime and ensure greater safety of people, the law enforcement efforts would be better coordinated and intensified at the local level as crime is a local problem. Legislators wanted the federal government to give assistance through grants but not interfere in the efforts. The Law Enforcement Assistance Administration (LEAA) was created to assist with this process. Grants would be awarded in many areas, including the recruitment of law enforcement personnel and their training of these personnel. Money was also allocated to the area of public education relating to crime prevention and encouraging respect for law and order, including education programs in schools and programs to improve the understanding of and cooperation with law enforcement agencies.[21] A major goal of this act (after the trials of the 1960s) was improved community relations and the involvement of the community in crime prevention and public safety. This act encouraged the recruitment of minority personnel to better represent and improve relations with minority communities.

The Equal Employment Opportunity Act of 1972

The **Equal Employment Opportunity Act of 1972 (EEOA)** extended the 1964 Civil Rights Act and made its provisions, including Title VII, applicable to state and local governments.[22] The EEOA expanded the jurisdiction and strengthened the powers of the Federal Equal Employment Opportunity Commission (EEOC). The EEOA allowed employees of state and local governments to file employment discrimination suits with the EEOC, strengthened the commission's investigatory powers by allowing it to document allegations of discrimination better, and permitted the U.S. Department of Justice to sue state and local governments for violations of Title VII. The EEOA stated that all procedures regarding entry and promotion in agencies—including application forms, written tests, probation ratings, and physical ability tests—are subject to EEOC review, in order to determine whether there has been any unlawful act of discrimination.

The Civil Rights Act of 1991

The Civil Rights Act of 1991, also administered by the EEOC, allows for the awarding of punitive damages regarding civil rights violations under certain conditions based on the number of employees a company has. Though this act does not apply to governmental agencies, it is a significant development in the civil rights movement and influences behavior throughout the community.

Federal Courts and Job Discrimination

Job discrimination may take several forms. The most obvious, of course, is where there is a clear and explicit policy of discrimination—for example, separate job titles, recruitment efforts, standards, pay, and procedures for female or minority employees. The second, and probably most prevalent, form of job discrimination is **de facto discrimination.** De facto discrimination is discrimination that is the indirect result of policies or practices that are not intended to discriminate but do, in fact, discriminate.

Under EEOC guidelines, discrimination in testing occurs when there is a substantially different rate of selection in hiring, promotion, or another employment decision that works to the disadvantage of members of a particular race, sex, or ethnic group. Let us say that a substantially different rate of passing a particular examination occurs for different racial or ethnic minority groups or members of a certain gender and that this works to the disadvantage of a particular group. For example, if a certain examination results in almost all women failing that test and almost all men passing it, the particular examination is said to have an **adverse impact** on women. Adverse impact can be seen as a form of de facto discrimination. In the 1970s and 1980s, women and minorities began to use Title VII and the courts (particularly the federal courts) to attempt to achieve equality.

Job Relatedness The first important job discrimination case was *Griggs v. Duke Power Company* in 1971, which declared that the practices of the Duke Power Company were unconstitutional because they required that all of its employees have a high school diploma and pass a standard intelligence test before being hired.[23] The court ruled that these requirements were discriminatory unless they could be shown to measure the attributes needed to perform a specific job. The decision in *Griggs v. Duke Power Company* established the concept that job requirements must be job related—they must be necessary for the performance of the job a person is applying for.

De facto discrimination or adverse impact was found to be most prevalent in employment standards and entrance examinations. These standards and tests discriminated against certain candidates, particularly women and minorities. To eliminate the discriminatory effect of recruitment and testing practices, the EEOC required that all tests and examinations be job related. To prove that a test or standard is job related, an agency must provide evidence that the test, examination, or standard measures qualifications and abilities are actually necessary to perform the specific job for which an applicant is applying or being tested. In the words of the EEOC, to be job related, a test must be "predictive or significantly correlated with important elements of work behavior which comprise or are relevant to the job or jobs for which candidates are being evaluated."[24]

How did all these regulations apply to police departments? Candidates who formerly were denied acceptance into police departments because they could not meet certain standards (height and weight) or could not pass certain tests (strength) began to argue that these standards were not job related—that is, the standards did not measure skills and qualifications needed to perform police work.

The requirement that officers not be less than a certain height (height requirement) was probably the strongest example of discrimination against women candidates. With very few exceptions, police departments lost court cases involving the height requirement. In *Mieth v. Dothard* (1976), a lawsuit against the Alabama Department of Public Safety, the court ruled

> Evidence failed to establish . . . that tall officers hold an advantage over smaller colleagues in effectuating arrests and administering emergency aid; furthermore, the contention that tall officers have a psychological advantage was not, as a measure of job performance, sufficient constitutional justification for blanket exclusion of all individuals under the specified height."[25]

In another court case regarding height, the court in *Vanguard Justice Society v. Hughes* (1979) noted that the Baltimore Police Department's height requirement of 5 feet, 7 inches was a prima facie case of sex discrimination because it excluded 95 percent of the female population, in addition to 32 percent of the male population.[26] (*Prima facie* is from the Latin, "at first sight." It refers to a fact or evidence sufficient to establish a defense or a claim unless otherwise contradicted.)

Previous forms of physical ability testing were also challenged and found discriminatory by the courts. Newer tests, known as physical agility tests, were developed to reduce adverse impact. These newer physical agility tests required much less physical strength than the former tests and relied more on physical fitness. Some researchers who have studied these physical agility tests have found that some still had an adverse impact on women. One study discovered that women were four times more likely than men to fail physical agility testing for deputy sheriff positions.[27] Another study concluded that these physical agility tests did not represent realistic job samples because they related to aspects of the job that were rarely performed.[28] In cases in which the courts decided that these tests still discriminated against females, the police departments were ordered to create new ones. This issue is still being examined throughout the country.

While most recognize that it is crucial for police officers to be fit, law enforcement administrators have struggled with exactly how to define *fit* and how fit officers should be. A recent study conducted during the past 15 years that examined validation studies from more than 5,500 police officers from federal, state, and local law enforcement allowed job-related fitness areas to be documented. This study and the results are discussed in Chapter 4 on becoming a police officer.

The Job Analysis Today, as indicated in Chapter 4, to ensure that entry and promotion examinations are job related, police departments perform a job analysis for each position. An acceptable job analysis, declared constitutional by the courts, includes identification of tasks officers generally perform. This identification is based on interviews of officers and supervisors; reviews by another panel of officers and supervisors; computer analyses of questionnaires to determine the frequency of tasks performed; and analyses of the knowledge, skills, and abilities needed to perform the task.

The courts have issued numerous rulings regarding testing and the job analysis. In *Vulcan Society v. Civil Service Commission* (1973), the court rejected personnel tests because of the lack of a job analysis.[29]

However, in the case of *Guardians Association of New York City Police Department v. Civil Service Commission of New York* (1980), which is considered a landmark ruling, the court actually accepted the job analysis of the New York City Department of Personnel and the New York City Police Department as being nondiscriminatory.[30] This ruling showed that police departments had begun to follow the mandates of the federal courts without being ordered to do so.

Affirmative Action Programs

The most controversial method of ending job discrimination is the concept of **affirmative action**. In 1965, in Executive Order 11246, President Lyndon B. Johnson required all federal contractors and subcontractors to develop affirmative action programs. Subsequent orders have amended and expanded the original executive order. In essence, the concept of affirmative action means that employers must take active steps to ensure equal employment opportunity and to redress past discrimination. It is an "active effort" to improve the employment or educational opportunities of members of minority groups. This differs from equal opportunity, which ensures that no discrimination takes place and that everyone has the same opportunity to obtain a job or promotion.

Affirmative action must be result oriented—it must focus on the result of employment practices. It is not enough for an agency merely to stop discriminating; the agency must take steps to correct past discrimination and give jobs to those against whom it has discriminated in the past.[31] Basically, affirmative action is designed to make up for, or to undo, past discrimination. Affirmative action programs involve several major steps. First, the agency must study its personnel makeup and determine a proper level of minority and female representation. If it does not meet that level, the agency must establish goals, quotas, and timetables to correct female and minority representation. It must make every effort to advertise job openings and actively seek out and encourage female and minority applicants. All tests and screening procedures must be validated as being job related, and any potentially discriminatory procedures must be eliminated.

The major concept behind affirmative action, and possibly the most disturbing concept to many, is the establishment of **quotas.** To implement affirmative action plans, departments incorporate goals and objectives involving numbers and timetables to correct past underrepresentation. These plans do not necessarily involve rigid quotas, just hiring and promotion goals to strive for. Some feel that affirmative action plans and quotas lead to **reverse discrimination.** Under a quota arrangement, a certain percentage of openings are reserved for particular groups, and some agencies may have separate promotional lists for different minorities and hire or promote alternately off each list. Individuals hired or promoted off one list might have scored lower than someone who does not rank high enough on another list to be hired or promoted. The argument is that this involves reverse discrimination against whites or males in violation of the 1964 Civil Rights Act and the equal protection clause of the Fourteenth Amendment. In a recent publication by the Department of Justice, the researchers advocated police departments direct their efforts into attracting larger numbers of qualified minorities into the applicant pool rather than implementing quotas or changing hiring requirements to reach goal numbers desired.[32] A survey of 281 police agencies also found that affirmative action plans had only a minor impact on the number of African American officers employed and the most important determinant was the size of the African American population within the community.[33] In the late 1990s and early 2000s, the concept of affirmative action was under attack on numerous fronts, ranging from U.S. Supreme Court cases to state and local laws.

White Male Backlash

As more police jobs and promotions began to go to minorities, fewer white males received these jobs and promotions. White males were passed over on entrance and promotion examinations by minorities, some of whom had received lower test scores. This resulted in turmoil and angry white males voicing anger and resentment, and counter lawsuits followed.

Though the EEOC prohibits all discrimination and consequently does not use the theory of "reverse discrimination," majority individuals often label the preferential treatment received by minority groups as "reverse discrimination."[34] They argue that selecting police officers based on their race or gender actually violates the 1964 Civil Rights Act and is discriminatory. Critics also argue that selecting officers who have scored lower on civil service tests lowers the personnel standards of a police department and will result in poorer performance by the department. It is viewed as a threat to their job security.

Even in law enforcement, with the loyalty that generally exists and where officers depend on each other when responding to calls, tensions can arise between various groups in the workplace. In Chicago, white officers intervened on the side of the city when an African American police officer organization filed suit to change promotion criteria.[35] In Detroit, the Detroit Police Officers Association filed suit to prevent the police department from setting up a quota plan for hiring African American police sergeants.[36]

In 1995, a sergeant with the Los Angeles County Sheriff's Department formed the Association of White Male Peace Officers to protect the rights of white male officers through zero discrimination in hiring, promotion, or assignment. The Sheriff's Department said it cannot prevent officers from joining the group but reported that it does not sanction the group or understand the reason for its formation.

Also in 1995, 18 white Dallas police officers filed a $1.8 million lawsuit alleging they were passed over for promotion to senior corporal in favor of minority officers who scored lower on a promotional exam. The lawsuit called for an order barring the city from imposing quotas to implement its affirmative action plan.[37]

The continued need for affirmative action programs is under renewed challenge from critics who contend that they have achieved their original goals of ending discrimination against minorities and providing parity with white males. In April 1995, Maryland State Police agreed to provide approximately $250,000 in back pay to 99 white male troopers who claimed they were unfairly passed over for promotions in 1989 and 1990.[38]

In March 2005, a jury ruled against former Milwaukee Police Chief Arthur Jones, charging he was discriminating against 17 white male lieutenants when he used his own subjective criteria to promote allegedly less-qualified blacks and females to the rank of captain. Jones was the first African American to head the Milwaukee Police Department and took over the agency just before the end of a consent decree imposed by the courts in 1984 that imposed a hiring quota: 40 percent of new officers had to be minorities and 20 percent had to be female. Before that, only 8 percent had been black, and none were above the rank of sergeant. When Jones took command, 22 of 25 captains were white males, but now just 9 of 24 are white. This led to allegations of reverse discrimination. The chief's supporters state he did nothing differently from previous chiefs, and the suit is going to cost the City of Milwaukee, both monetarily (over $5 million to promote 13 of the plaintiffs and pay damages) and socially because of morale issues.[39]

Can Minorities Do the Job?

Much of the discrimination against women in police departments was based on a fear that they could not do police work effectively because of their gender and size. Much of the discrimination against minorities was based on a fear that they would not be accepted by nonminority citizens. The academic studies and anecdotal evidence presented in this section show that minorities do indeed make effective police officers.

Academic Studies

In the 1970s, many police officials argued that female officers could not handle the tasks of patrol duty effectively. According to this traditional, macho perspective, policing required physical strength and a tough, masculine attitude. Two important academic studies, however—one by the Police Foundation and the other by the Law Enforcement Assistance Administration (LEAA)—found that women were just as effective on patrol as comparable men.[40] The latter study was performed for the Law Enforcement Assistance Administration, the precursor of the National Institute of Justice.

The study performed for the Police Foundation, *Policewomen on Patrol: Final Report,* evaluated and compared the performance of female recruits during their first year on patrol in Washington, D.C., with that of a matched group of new male officers in the same department. This was the first time a police department had integrated a substantial number of women into the backbone of the department. This research project was designed to determine: (1) the ability of women to perform patrol work successfully, (2) their impact on the operations of a police department, and (3) their reception by the community. The study found that women exhibited extremely satisfactory work performance. The women were found to respond to similar types of calls as men, and their arrests were as likely as the men's arrests to result in convictions. The report also found that women were more likely than their male colleagues to receive support from the community, and they were less likely to be charged with improper conduct.[41]

The LEAA study was titled *Women on Patrol: A Pilot Study of Police Performance in New York City* and involved the observation of 3,625 hours of female police officer patrol in New York City, and it included 2,400 police-citizen encounters. The report concluded that female officers were perceived by citizens as being more competent, pleasant, and respectful than male officers. This study found that women performed better when serving with other female officers and that women, when serving with male partners, seemed to be intimidated by their partners and were less likely to be assertive and self-sufficient.[42]

Thus, the first two large-scale studies of female patrol officers dispelled the myth that they were not able to do the job. Follow-up anecdotal evidence

In most jurisdictions police officers work in one-officer units. The officer must be able to take control of situations immediately and conduct preliminary investigations in an effort to determine whether a crime was committed. Numerous studies have shown that female officers can indeed handle the tasks of patrol effectively.

and empirical studies further bolstered the assertion that women make effective patrol officers.

In addition to the studies cited earlier, numerous other academic studies of job performance by women police officers were conducted, with similar results. James David studied the behavior of 2,293 police officers in Texas and Oklahoma and found that the arrest rates of men and women were almost identical, despite the stereotype that women make fewer arrests than men. David also found that women were more inclined to intervene than were their male counterparts when violations of the law occurred in their presence.[43] A study of police perceptions of spouse abuse, by Robert Homant and Daniel Kennedy, concluded that women were more understanding of, and sympathetic to, the victims of spouse abuse than were men, and women were more likely than men to refer those victims to shelters.[44]

Loretta Stalans and Mary Finn supported this finding when their study revealed that though there was no difference between men and women in arrest rates on domestic violence calls, experienced female officers were more likely to recommend battered women's shelters and less likely to recommend marriage counseling than were their male counterparts. This difference did not occur among rookie officers. Is this variation the result of their experience over the years with domestic violence calls or because they were willing to act contrary to the men's norms?[45]

In an analysis of the existing research on female police officers, Merry Morash and Jack Greene found that the traditional male belief that female officers could not be effective on patrol was not supported by existing research. Morash and Greene concluded that evidence existed showing that women make highly successful police officers.[46]

Former New York City police detective Sean Grennan's study of patrol teams in New York City found no basic difference between the way men and women, working as a patrol team, reacted to violent confrontations. Grennan also found that female police officers, in most cases, were far more emotionally stable than their male counterparts. Women also lacked the need to project the macho image, which, Grennan believes, seems to be inherent in the personality of most of the men he studied. He found that the female officer, with her less aggressive personality, was more likely to calm a potentially violent situation and less likely to cause physical injury. She was also less likely to use a firearm and no more likely to suffer on-the-job injuries.[47]

The Christopher Commission found similar results in 1991 while conducting a review of the practices of the Los Angeles Police Department after the Rodney King incident. The commission reported that, of the 120 officers with the most allegations concerning the use of force, all were men.[48]

A councilman for the city of Los Angeles introduced five motions following the Christopher Commission report that would encourage the hiring of more women and substantially decrease police violence in the LAPD. These included making the police department and the police commission more gender balanced and making this an important issue in the selection of the new chief of police. He believed that true change in the philosophy of the department would result from achieving more gender balance.[49]

This was supported by a study conducted in a large police department in the Southeast in which 527 internal affairs complaints of misconduct over a three-year period were examined. These incidents translated into 682 allegations of wrongdoing (more than one officer was involved in some incidents). The analysis revealed that men were overrepresented in these complaints. Women accounted for 12.4 percent of those employed by the agency, but they accounted for only 5.7 percent of the allegations.[50]

Recently, a study was conducted in which 40 patrol officers (20 men and 20 women) were observed during a 10-week period while working the 3-to-11 shift in Syracuse, New York. Their attitudes were also assessed by using surveys and scenarios. Results indicated there were no differences in how the officers viewed or performed their jobs.[51]

Despite these indications that women are performing no differently than men—or perhaps better, in some situations—resistance or lack of acceptance still exists, though to a lesser degree, among the public and fellow police officers. Kristen Leger found that there is a growing acceptance by the public for women in the law enforcement role. Especially noteworthy is that the unfounded skepticism concerning women's ability to handle violent encounters, which is often raised, no longer exists among most citizens. The public attitude toward women in law enforcement is changing, and police officers and administrators should take note of that.[52]

Although citizens are more accepting, they do also have certain preconceived notions about men's and women's strong and weak areas within law enforcement. These stereotypes affect citizen expectations and, consequently, their reactions to police officers. When college students were given three scenarios (domestic violence, shoplifting, and a noisy party) and the gender of the officer was manipulated, students rated the officers differently based on what they expected the officer's strengths to be. (In this case, it was expected that women would be extremely knowledgeable and capable in the area of domestic violence.) Officers who didn't live up to these preconceived stereotypes were rated as being less effective. This phenomenon could lead to unrealistic expectations and inappropriate judging of women's performance.[53]

The International Association of Chiefs of Police (IACP) conducted a study of 800 police departments in 1998. The researchers found that law enforcement administrators felt overwhelmingly that women possess exceptional skills in the area of verbal and written communications as well as outstanding interpersonal skills in relating to all types of people and being sensitive to their needs whether they are victims, witnesses, or suspects.[54]

The National Center for Women and Policing agrees that women offer unique advantages to the contemporary field of law enforcement with its emphasis on community policing and the high volume of calls involving diversity issues and violence against women and the strengths that will prevail in these situations.[55] An examination of use of excessive force as related to officer gender found that women were significantly underrepresented compared with men in both citizen complaints and sustained allegations of excessive force. Women also cost their departments significantly less than men in civil liability payouts involving excessive force. In the Los Angeles Police Department between 1990 and 1999, when the men outnumbered the women on patrol by a ratio of 4 to 1, the payouts for excessive force for males exceeded those for females by a larger ratio of 23 to 1.[56]

Although women have been assigned to patrol duties for only three decades, evidence exists that they are very effective as patrol officers. The former belief that they lacked the size, strength, and temperament to do the job has given way to a realization that being a patrol officer requires more than size, strength, and a tough attitude.

Unlike the situation for women, there have been no studies regarding the ability of African Americans to do police work. Anecdotal evidence, however, suggests that they perform as well as any other group. This lack of study seems somewhat unusual given their controversial history. What research was done is old and tended to involve a

You Are There!

The Walls Come Tumbling Down

Throughout the years, numerous lawsuits involving affirmative action were filed by and on behalf of women and minorities. The judicial findings and consent decrees (agreements between parties before, and instead of, a final decision by a judge) did much to ease the way for women and minorities into U.S. police departments. A sampling of these cases follows.

A lawsuit filed against the San Francisco Police Department resulted in a federal court order establishing an experimental quota of 60 women as patrol officers. The department also revised the height and weight requirements that had barred women from patrol jobs. In response to a lawsuit filed by the Department of Justice, Maryland agreed to recruit more female state police officers.

Similarly, the New Jersey State Police agreed to establish, within a year of the court's ruling, hiring goals for women in both sworn and nonsworn positions.

A rejected female applicant filed suit against the California Highway Patrol, charging that its male-only standards unlawfully discriminated against women under Title VII of the Civil Rights Act. Following the results of a two-year feasibility study, a decision was made in the plaintiff's favor. As a result, the California Highway Patrol officially began accepting qualified women for state trooper positions, ending a 46-year tradition of using only men as traffic officers.

With the threat of a lawsuit in the offing, the New York City Police Department ended its height requirements, unfroze its list of female applicants, and increased its female officers on patrol to 400 in a brief period of time.

The Los Angeles Police Department signed a consent decree with the Justice Department awarding $2 million in back pay to officers who were discriminated against, agreeing that 45 percent of all new recruits would be African American or Hispanic American and that 20 percent of all new recruits would be women.

A consent decree required that one-third of all promotions in the Miami Police Department be given to women and minorities.

Sources: Adapted from Anthony V. Bouza, "Women in Policing," *FBI Law Enforcement Bulletin* (September 1975), pp. 4–7; Glen Craig, "California Highway Patrol Officers," *Police Chief* (January 1977), p. 60; *Criminal Justice Newsletter* (December 1980), p. 6; *New York Times* (September 14, 1976), p. 8; *New York Times* (October 8, 1975), p. 45; and Dianne Townsey, "Black Women in American Policing: An Advancement Display," *Journal of Criminal Justice,* 10 (1982), pp. 455–468.

---

small number of patrol officers in New York City.[57] There have been some inquiries regarding the attitudinal beliefs of African American officers as well as examinations of the early career experiences of current black police administrators. Attitudinal studies seem to indicate that African American officers have very different attitudes than white police officers do. African American officers tend to believe that police use excessive force against racial and ethnic minorities and poor people and consequently are supportive of citizen oversight. They often speak out regarding brutality, and the National Black Police Officers Association published a pamphlet urging its members to report misconduct by other officers. Black officers are also more supportive of innovation and change within the policing occupation and are generally more supportive than are white officers of community policing.[58]

In his study of African American police executives, R. Alan Thompson reports some common experiences these executives went through in their earlier careers and how many of these correlate with some common assumptions held because of anecdotal evidence whereas others do not. Thompson found that most black police executives perceived a lack of social acceptance by white officers and felt that white officers viewed them as "tokens" and not equals during the first five years of their career. He also found that the police culture, professionalism, and loyalty issues overcame these perceived differences when the chips were down. Most officers believed that their coworkers would come to their aid and would respond when needed regardless of race. Almost half felt resentment by the white community, but on the positive side, just over half felt that they were fully accepted by the white citizens. There was more confusion regarding the relations with the black community. Most black executive officers felt there was ambiguity within the black community regarding support of the police and the acknowledging of the black police officer's authority. More than 80 percent of these executives felt that black police officers experienced a unique form of tension between their roles as members of the black community and as an enforcer of the laws, exemplifying the "double marginality" issue. Despite some of these troubling findings, most of the executives felt that interracial working relations within law enforcement have improved during the past decade, though gradually. Many cite the fact that old-time police officers with more prejudiced views have retired over the years and that newer, younger officers do not share these negative attitudes toward black officers, making the workplace more comfortable.[59]

Minorities in Policing Today

As this chapter has shown, during the past three decades, U.S. police departments have attempted to better reflect the communities they serve. Police administrators have intensified the recruitment of minorities to have more balanced police departments. They've also directed their efforts toward the retention of these officers. Many departments have links on their websites for the targeted population that provide additional information and outreach as well as mentoring services.

Departments have altered their entry requirements and training curriculums—sometimes willingly, and sometimes under court mandate—to facilitate the hiring and training of minority officers. Today minorities serve in all aspects of police work and in all neighborhoods of towns and cities across the United States.

Female Representation

A 2006 Bureau of Justice Statistics (BJS) publication reports that 11.3 percent of all full-time sworn officers in local law enforcement were women in 2003, up from 10.6 percent in 2000 and 7.6 percent in 1987. Numbers ranged from 17 percent in departments serving populations of 1 million or more to approximately 6 percent in departments serving fewer than 10,000.[60] To put these percentages into perspective, although the presence and status of women in law enforcement have risen, the percentage of women officers falls below 44.7 percent, the percentage of the labor force that women currently occupy. Women in policing appear to be lagging behind women in other traditionally male professions.

More women are now attaining the length of service and breadth of experience typically associated with command positions. Consequently, recent years have seen a significant increase in the numbers of women in administrative positions and serving as chiefs and sheriffs. The numbers of female police chiefs and sheriffs doubled from 1994 to 2004 compared to the previous 10 years.[61] These women have come to their leadership positions in various ways. Some have stayed with the department where they began their careers and moved up through the ranks. Others have changed departments, particularly in states with liberal lateral transfers. Others have left law enforcement for brief stints in school or in law and returned to law enforcement in upper administration. Women have been or are currently executives in all sizes of municipal agencies, sheriffs departments, state police, campus police, transit police, and federal agencies. Elizabeth Watson became the first woman to lead a police department in a city of greater than a million population when she headed the Houston, Texas, Police Department from 1990 to 1992; upon leaving Houston, she became the first woman to head the Austin, Texas, Police Department. Paula Meara headed the Springfield, Massachusetts, Police Department starting in 1996 after working her way up the ranks of that department. Annette Sandberg was appointed to head the Washington State Patrol in 1995 after leaving the agency for a time to practice law. She ultimately retired in 2002 leaving Anne Beers as the head of the Minnesota State Patrol as the only female head of a state agency at the time.[62] African American women have also headed major agencies even in the South. These include Beverly Harvard who headed the Atlanta Police Department from 1994 to 2002, Annetta Nunn who was sworn in as the Chief of Birmingham, Alabama, Police Department in 2003, and Ella Bully-Cummings who was named as chief of the Detroit Police Department less than a year later.[63] Anne Kirkpatrick, current chief of police in Spokane, Washington, has moved between departments. She began her career at the Memphis, Tennessee, Police Department and moved to the Redmond, Washington, Police Department. After obtaining her law degree and spending time as a professor in a community college, she became the head of the Ellensburg, Washington, Police Department and later the director of Public Safety in Federal Way, Washington. Colleen

Wilson was named the chief of police in Monroe, Washington, in 1993 after rising through the ranks. In 2004, she was named chief of the Sumner, Washington, Police Department.[64]

In 2002, Connie Patrick became the director of the Federal Law Enforcement Training Center in Glynco, Georgia, after a long and distinguished law enforcement career. In 2003, Nannette H. Hegerty became the first female chief in the history of the Milwaukee Police Department. In 2004, Heather Fong was named chief of police in San Francisco; soon after Kathleen O'Toole was appointed chief of the Boston Police Department. In 2006, O'Toole left the Boston Police Department to accept a chief inspector position in the Irish National Police.[65] In late June 2006, Rosie Sizer was permanently appointed as chief of police in Portland, Oregon, where she had been the acting chief for several months. The mayor had intended to conduct a nationwide search for a new chief but after obtaining feedback from the community and noting the dramatically improved morale within the department, decided to appoint her permanently.[66] Another groundbreaking event that occurred in 2006 was the swearing in of Chief Marianne Viverette of Gaithersburg, Maryland, Police Department as the president of the International Association of Chiefs of Police. Reports are also being received of mothers and daughters serving in the same police departments and perhaps these kinds of reports may lead to the tradition of women following in other family members' footsteps in a police career as men have traditionally done.

A recent study found that consent decrees over the last couple of decades have been very effective in increasing the numbers of women in law enforcement. A consent decree is an agreement that in this situation binds the agency to a particular course of action in regard to hiring and promoting women in law enforcement. The study reported that the representation of female officers in agencies with a consent decree was substantially higher than in agencies without consent decrees and higher than the national average for that type of department. Municipal agencies were found to employ 17.8 percent sworn females (25 percent higher than the national average for municipal agencies), county agencies 12 percent (9 percent higher than the national average for counties), and state police agencies 7.2 percent females (23 percent higher than the national average for state police agencies). Unfortunately, the report states that once the consent decree ends, the progress for women tends to slow in the agency. The authors believe the consent

decree may be a worthwhile tool to stick with until agencies progress on their own in this area.[67]

Others believe this is unnecessary. Though the percentages of women in law enforcement today are nowhere near the 50 percent that women represent in society, many argue that this is a result to some degree of self-selection and that law enforcement is simply not a career for everyone. The current numbers of women in law enforcement are a big improvement, considering they have been actively engaged in the profession for only a few decades. There is some concern, however, that the growth appears to have slowed in the last decade. Some attribute these stagnant advances to bias in the hiring and selection process (in particular the physical fitness training), as well as inadequate recruitment policies and the image of police officers and agencies as macho and militaristic.

It is encouraging, however, that these are all issues that law enforcement executives are currently addressing in a desire to recruit and retain more women. Some innovative strategies are discussed later in this chapter. The slow, steady increase in numbers already seen, coupled with new efforts to eliminate bias in the hiring process and with proactive police administrators, will help increase the numbers of women in law enforcement. This will be greatly aided by women attaining rank in agencies, as mentioned earlier, and becoming more visible as well as having increased input regarding policies and procedures.

African American Representation

In the 1970s and 1980s, African Americans were appointed as police commissioners or chiefs in some of the nation's biggest city police departments. Among them were William Hart, Detroit; Lee P. Brown, Atlanta, Houston, and New York City; and Benjamin Ward, New York City.

In the 1990s, this trend continued with Willie Williams in Los Angeles in 1992. In 1997, Melvin H. Wearing was named police chief of New Haven, Connecticut, the first African American to hold that post. Also in 1997, Mel Carraway became the first African American to be appointed to head the Indiana State Police.

By 2004, many police departments had African Americans in their command staff or serving as chiefs of police. These include the notable and progressive agencies of Arlington, Texas, with

Dr. Theron Bowman as chief of police; Madison, Wisconsin, with Chief Noble Wray; and Atlanta, Georgia, with Chief Richard Pennington. In 2005, John Batiste was appointed as the head of the Washington State Patrol after having retired from that agency to be an assistant chief in another agency. Several African American females are also heading major agencies, as mentioned in the last section.

According to a Bureau of Justice Statistics Report, in 2003, 23.6 percent of full-time local law enforcement officers were members of a racial or ethnic minority, an increase from 14.6 percent in 1987. African American officers represented 11.7 percent of all law enforcement officers, which was an increase of 35 percent compared with 1990. Their representation is highest in agencies serving more than 250,000 people, where they compose over a third of all officers.[68]

Progress is occurring in the representation of African Americans in U.S. police departments, but it has been a slow, gradual process from the 1960s into the twenty-first century, and the progress has sometimes been accompanied by failures. Strides are being made, however, and police departments are becoming more representative of the people they serve.

Hispanic Representation

The number of Hispanic American officers has increased significantly in the last two decades, as has their percentage in the general population. According to the Department of Justice, Hispanic or Latino officers accounted for 9.1 percent of police officers nationwide in 2003. The highest percentage of Hispanic officers was in departments serving populations of greater than 1 million, in which they represented 19.3 percent of the officers. This was an increase over the year 2000 in which 8.3 percent of officers were Hispanic and 1987 in which only 4.5 percent of police officers were Hispanic.[69]

Though there is little empirical research regarding Hispanic officers, these officers are extremely valuable to law enforcement agencies. The diversity of the department is a plus, the officers' ability to relate to the Hispanic community is an asset, and they can help bridge the language and cultural barrier. These officers serve as ambassadors to the large Latino population and greatly facilitate the communication process in emergency situations and when members of the community request assistance.

A major issue regarding Hispanic officers both in counting their numbers and in determining their role and fit in the community, is simply determining what is meant by Hispanic. The Hispanic culture can include many cultural groups, including Mexicans, Cubans, South Americans, Central Americans, and Puerto Ricans. These groups are not homogeneous; there are many cultural differences, and in some cases, there are tensions between the groups. Considering all these groups as one does a disservice to both the ethnic communities and the officers. Different groups will predominate in different parts of the country. South Florida is dominated by Cubans, but there are also increasing numbers of Mexicans and South and Central Americans. The Mexicans are the largest group of Hispanics in the states that border Mexico, including California, Arizona, and Texas.

Among officers, many Hispanic officers are not bilingual and many do not necessarily share the cultural experiences of many of the residents. To assume all Hispanic officers are the same is inaccurate. So, what makes someone Hispanic when we're looking at classifications and numbers? Is it an individual of Hispanic background but born and raised in the United States and not bilingual? Is someone of mixed parentage Hispanic? Is an officer born in another country but raised and educated in the United States and not bilingual considered a Hispanic officer? Or is it only an officer born and raised in another country (and bilingual) that is truly considered a Hispanic officer? There appears to be no clear consensus, and it is usually up to the officer to declare. According to some officers, it can make a difference in the way they perceive their job and their community and in the way their community perceives them. Consider the border states of California, Texas, and Arizona where Mexican Americans predominate. There is a definite difference among officers and their ability to relate to the community and the community's trust in them based on the three types of Hispanic officers. First are the officers who are of Hispanic descent but were born and raised in the United States but are not fluent in Spanish and do not share the culture and experience of having lived in Mexico in their formative years. Second are Hispanic officers who are bilingual and were born in Mexico but raised in the United States.[70] These officers have the ability to communicate but may not have the cultural awareness that the third group of Hispanic officers has. This third group was born and

Hispanic officers can also experience a type of double marginality as African American officers do. Hispanic officers sometimes feel pressure to behave in a different manner because they are Hispanic or of a specific ethnicity such as Mexican. For instance, newly arrived Mexicans may expect to be given a break or treated more leniently when interacting with a Mexican American officer.

© Bob Daemmrich/Photo Edit

raised in Mexico, recently came to the United States, and became citizens. They share the cultural knowledge and experience of having lived in Mexico with the newly arrived resident. These officers are often best able to build a relationship of trust with residents.

Hispanic officers can also experience a type of double marginality as African American officers do. Hispanic officers sometimes feel pressure to behave in a different manner because they are Hispanic or of a specific ethnicity such as Mexican. Newly arrived Mexicans may expect to be given a break or treated more leniently when interacting with a Mexican American officer. The officers can experience role conflict and emotional challenges when interacting with newly arrived hardworking immigrants who are looking for a better life and trying to get ahead. As one officer stated, "I see my parents in their early, struggling days when I stop an old beat up pick-up truck with red tape over the brake light, and I really don't want to write them a ticket and add to their financial troubles."[71]

Hispanic officers' assimilation has not been without controversy. They have also been involved in discrimination issues and affirmative action plans. Several organizations have arisen to serve as support groups for Hispanic officers and to facilitate communication between those officers around the country. The Hispanic American Police Command Officers Association (HAPCOA) is a national organization that was established in 1973, with goals of meeting the challenge of selecting, promoting, and retaining Hispanic American men and women in criminal justice agencies. They support applicants and offer agencies guidance and support to address the concerns of Hispanic officers and improve community relations within the Latino community. The National Latino Peace Officers Association was established in 1972, and one of its major goals is recruiting Latinos into law enforcement and promoting equality and professionalism in law enforcement. Both of these organizations have websites with additional information. These organizations are not common among smaller departments, and many officers can be hesitant to start or join organizations such as these because they often prefer to blend in with fellow officers.

There does not usually appear to be overt discrimination against Hispanic officers but many feel that commonly held stereotypes impede their progress in doing their job or assimilating within the department. Some Hispanic officers appear Caucasian and can be privy to these stereotypes when comments are made by other officers and or citizens who are not aware of the officer's ethnicity.[72] Issues can sometimes arise that similarly appear in the discussions with African American officers. Hispanic officers may or may not feel discriminated against when asked to patrol certain areas of their city simply because they are Hispanic, or they may similarly feel discriminated against when frequently called away from their duties to translate for other officers, simply because they are bilingual. This second issue has led many jurisdictions to provide additional enhancement pay to officers who are bilingual. This makes it easier for the organization to consider it part of their job to translate and should minimize any resentment that may exist among officers constantly called to translate. Enhancement pay is also a way for the department to let prospective candidates know that their skills are solicited and valued and that they will be fairly compensated for these skills, as well as to ensure a ready supply of officers able to communicate with the Spanish-speaking community.

Hispanics are the fastest growing ethnic group in the United States, increasing at a rate of more than 55 percent every 10 years. The Census Bureau predicts that Hispanics will constitute 20 percent of the U.S. population by 2010 and 45 percent by 2050. As the Assistant Attorney General of the United States stated in her speech to the HAPCOA training conference, rather than being viewed as a minority, Hispanics should be seen as an "emerging majority group."[73] With this prediction, police organizations must develop recruitment programs within the Hispanic community. This can present challenges, as with other minorities, some Hispanics have had negative interactions with police in their native lands. In Mexico and some other Central American and South American countries, the police are corrupt and abusive. There is often no mechanism in place to make a complaint or even to get help from local law enforcement. Consequently, the newly arrived immigrants do not trust police in the United States and will not contact the police when they need help and will not assist police officers when asked for help. In the border states that deal with numerous Mexican immigrants, officers see the barriers start to come down when the officer speaks Spanish and a desire to assist becomes apparent when the Mexican American finds out the officer is also from Mexico. Typically, these residents will call specific officers that they know are Mexican rather than call the police department. A major challenge is and will continue to be to reach out to these communities to educate them about what the police in the United States are like and what they do and encourage immigrants to pursue law enforcement as an occupation to help make their communities safer and to help serve their fellow Mexican Americans.[74]

Though Hispanic officers are far more common in most agencies than 20 years ago, issues still arise regarding discrimination. Recently 29 complaints were filed by the Denver Police Latino organization against the Denver Police Department and the city's Civil Service Commission. These complaints were filed with the EEOC and the Department of Justice and include a complaint in which a female officer claims she was sexually assaulted by a white male police officer on the job; the case was never resolved by Internal Affairs and the male officer was allowed to retire. Not all of the complainants in these cases were Latino officers, but the organization was willing to step forward on behalf of the others. These cases are pending.[75]

Asian Representation

Though their numbers have increased slightly during the last few years, Asian Americans are poorly represented in police departments across the country. According to the latest statistics, minorities—including Asians, Pacific Islanders, and Native Americans—constituted 2.8 percent of local police officers in 2003. This compares with 2.7 percent in 2000 and .8 percent in 1987.[76] The biggest challenge concerning Asian Americans in law enforcement appears to be recruitment. Despite dramatic increases in the Asian population across the nation, most departments have few if any Asian officers. According to police administrators, Asians are just not applying for the jobs. It seems to be a cultural issue. Parents are not encouraging their children to seek this type of employment. In some homelands, police officers are looked upon as corrupt, brutal, or uneducated. *— Professions which require education*

Police departments are making efforts to overcome these cultural barriers. Their goal is to have their departments mirror their communities and to facilitate trust in the police and encourage the exchange of information. In 2000, the U.S. Census reported that Asians composed 4.2 percent of the U.S. population but only 1.6 percent of officers and deputies across the United States. In New Jersey, where Asians make up 7.1 percent of the population, they are only 1.1 percent of the State troopers. The New York City Police Department has managed to double its Asian representation to 3.5 percent of the department. Of the Asians who do pursue law enforcement careers, most experience no blatant bias from colleagues. One Asian FBI agent comments he doesn't note any discrimination from coworkers or the public but often does encounter surprise, especially in smaller towns, by people who have never before encountered an Asian FBI agent.[77]

California agencies tend to lead the way with the employment of Asian Americans in law enforcement. A recent recruit class in Sacramento is almost evenly split between white males and minorities and includes the department's second Hmong American man, first Hmong American woman, and first Chinese American woman.[78] The agencies are reaching into their ethnic communities to improve communication and build credibility. Because a law enforcement career is not generally part of many Asians' culture, recruiting seems to occur when the potential candidate is a student or through police-community interactions.

This type of effort was instrumental in leading San Francisco's current chief, Heather Fong, to choose a law enforcement career. As mentioned earlier, she was named chief of the San Francisco Police Department in 2004. She was recruited to the department by San Francisco's first Asian American Chief, Fred Lau, who lived near her and mentored her career. While an undergraduate at the University of San Francisco, she took the police exam and worked as a cadet. Her parents supported her career choice partly because Chief Lau stressed the importance to the city of women and minorities joining the police department.[79]

This effort toward recruitment should prove more successful as Asian Americans become more visible in departments and are able to reach into the community for qualified recruits.

Muslim Representation

A small but increasingly visible group that has experienced discrimination is the Muslim officers. Since September 11, 2001, this group has received increased attention from the media, the public, and their coworkers. Recently, cases have arisen in which Muslim officers have claimed they've been discriminated against. These claims usually involve grooming issues, including the wearing of untrimmed beards by male public safety personnel and the wearing of head coverings by Muslim females. These conventions are an important part of Muslim religious and cultural tradition. However, departments usually back their policies, claiming it's a safety and discipline issue. It is believed to be most important for the community and the citizens who encounter their police officers that they have a uniformed appearance. Police officers have worn uniforms for most of their history because it is critical that the public readily identify them. Although it is beneficial for the public to see officers as part of other communities, their role as public servants to protect and serve citizens takes priority. There should be no hesitation or doubt about who is or is not a police officer.

Recently, cases of bias have arisen in New York, Washington D.C., Detroit, and Decatur, Georgia. Researchers who track Muslim and Arab Americans in law enforcement say that if the cases are valid, they are isolated incidents because there has been no evidence of widespread discrimination in police agencies.[80]

Gay and Lesbian Representation

Another group with a challenging history in law enforcement is gay officers. Police departments have had a history of discriminating against job applicants because of their sexual orientation. Until the beginning of the focus on equal employment opportunity, many police departments discriminated against homosexuals in employment decisions, and the International Association of Chiefs of Police (IACP) maintained a policy of opposing the employment of gay officers. In 1969, the IACP rescinded its policy of opposing the employment of gay officers. By 1990, an estimated 20 percent of the sworn officers in the San Francisco County Sheriff's Department and perhaps 10 percent of officers in the Los Angeles Police Department were gay men or lesbians.[81] The percentage of gay and lesbian officers is a difficult number to determine. Many departments are not asking about sexual orientation, and, because of a fear of making their sexual orientation known to their coworkers, many police officers hide the fact that they are gay or lesbian. Police work has traditionally been thought of as a "macho" occupation, and the perception was that gay officers didn't fit the mold.

Many police administrators have decided not to make an issue of sexual orientation in the background investigation. It's believed that this decision may reflect an overall change in society's social and sexual mores, as well as a concern by police administrators that if they do not voluntarily take the lead, the federal courts may be called upon to intercede on the behalf of the gay community, as the courts have already done in the case of other minorities. This, coupled with the Federal Government's "don't ask, don't tell" policy with the military, the rise of gay and lesbian police officer groups, and the rescinding of the IACP policy opposing the hiring of gays, contributed to police departments' laissez faire attitudes.[82]

Some cities are recruiting openly gay officers in an attempt to bridge a perceived gap with their gay community. The Key West Police Department has the largest number of openly gay officers in south Florida (seven) relative to the city's population. Sergeant Alan Newby, an openly gay officer with Key West and also the president of the Florida chapter of *Law Enforcement for Gays and Lesbians,* states that though officers may receive training in diversity and sexual orientation, "The important thing is that the agency support gay and lesbian police officers and let that officer know he is going to be judged on work product, not sexual orientation." Though Newby sees no need for publicizing officers' sexual orientation, he believes that gay officers are needed in any city with a significant gay population. A gay officer may be more sensitive to issues that arise in the gay community. In advising other departments that are interested in actively recruiting openly gay officers, Newby relates that more internal preparations will need to be made if a gay man rather than a lesbian joins the department: "Police work traditionally is viewed as a macho job, and departments are usually more accepting of lesbian officers than gay officers."[83]

Gay officers in law enforcement say it's one of the last civil rights battles being fought. Most states provide no special job protection for gay workers, but some departments are providing benefits to same sex partners. In the 1970s, gay officers in California started the Golden State Peace Officers Association (GSPOA). Another of the nation's first gay officers' associations was the New York City Police Department's Gay Officers Action League (GOAL), which was established in 1981, and, as explained on their website, holds yearly conferences and provides links with 10 U.S. and 8 international gay and lesbian police organizations. Law Enforcement Gays and Lesbians (LEGAL) and similar support groups around the country also offer support to gay, lesbian, bisexual, and transgender workers in the criminal justice system. They hope to improve the environment within law enforcement agencies for gays and ultimately improve the relationship between the police and the gay community. Organizations such as GOAL and LEGAL serve as support groups and advocates for gay and lesbian officers.[84] Some departments believe that providing a welcoming climate for gay officers is important but recruitment isn't necessary. Miami Beach Police Department Detective Bobby Hernandez states they've hired their openly gay officers by doing what they always do: "We hire the most qualified applicants. It's not an issue, and quite frankly, it's none of our business." Perhaps an openly gay citizen in Wilton Manors, Florida, a town looking to actively recruit openly gay officers, summed it up best: "It does not matter to me whether a police officer is openly gay, closeted, or straight, as long as the police department keeps my neighborhood safe."[85]

Problems Persist for Minorities in Policing

Problems for Women

Burnout!

Women in law enforcement have progressed tremendously during the last three decades, but challenges remain. These include recruiting and hiring, acceptance of the women, workplace harassment, dating, pregnancy, and family issues. The IACP believes the recruitment of women is an important issue for law enforcement today. The IACP has become involved in investigating the climate in law enforcement regarding women and have actively educated departments on recruiting and retaining female officers. Departments are also addressing these challenges themselves on their own.

The first challenge encountered is the recruitment and hiring issue. Agencies need to reach out to females and provide an opportunity for women to see themselves in the role of police officer. As Detroit Police Department Chief Ella Bully-Cummings says, visibility of female police officers is important. "If you can't see it, you can't dream it."[86] Many departments do this through their websites where they profile female officers and women's issues are addressed. Fort Lauderdale, Florida, has a particularly informative "women's gateway" on its site. Los Angeles Police Department has similar biographies of female officers on its website and has implemented programs to support females such as the Candidate Assistance Program, Academy Trainer Program, and the Women's Coordinator.

Once they decide to apply, female applicants have also been challenged by the physical agility part of the testing process. Agencies are addressing this issue by examining their requirements and providing information and training to assist the female in developing the necessary competencies.

Acceptance is important to women in law enforcement. The police culture and socialization is important to new recruits. It is a constant balancing by female officers between their more feminine characteristics, which have been encouraged by their socialization process, such as compassion, warmth, and accommodation, and their more masculine traits such as assertiveness, competitiveness, and no-nonsense approaches. Sometimes it seems like a no-win situation, and women can be and are criticized by male coworkers regardless of which traits they emphasize. Women are either perceived as too soft, weak, and feminine for the job or as overbearing, bossy, and pushy if behaving in a more "male" fashion. It can be a fine line as females discover what works best for them. Many successful female officers recommend developing good communication skills, a strong work ethic, flexibility, the ability to be a team player, a good sense of humor, and a "thick skin."[87]

Sometimes a female employee can be a target for workplace harassment. This can occur as a personal issue where a particular employee is the target, but other times it can be an organizational, pervasive sense of an "unwelcoming" atmosphere toward female employees. This can include inappropriate cartoons, jokes, and posters. There also can be subtle harassment occurring in ways including job, shift, or zone assignment; vehicle or equipment assignment; or even grooming or uniform policies. To work on this issue, departments are clarifying their working conditions and writing policies concerning workplace harassment, which includes gender, racial, ethnic, or sexual orientation. These policies are disseminated and training is conducted for all personnel so that employees, supervisors, and administrators are well versed in what is acceptable behavior and what is not.

The next two issues challenging departments concern workplace romances and pregnancy. Many departments do not address these issues at all, resulting in some lawsuits. Other departments are feverishly drafting policies in an attempt to insulate themselves from such litigation.[88] Policies on pregnancy and job assignment are issues that need to be addressed by police agencies for legal reasons as well as for the message these policies send to the female officers. Departments have to offer the same benefits to pregnant officers as to officers with other conditions, such as a temporary back injury or recovery from surgery. If officers in those situations are allowed to work limited or light-duty assignments, then pregnant officers must be allowed the same choice. Policies and benefits must be equitable. The Pregnancy Discrimination Act (PDA), which amended Title VII of the Civil Rights Act of 1964, states that discrimination on the basis of pregnancy constitutes a type of sex discrimination.

Many departments are allowing the pregnant officer to choose whether to take light or limited duty or to stay in her job assignment. This is the policy of the San Diego County Sheriff's Department (SDCSD), and the administrators make sure supervisors know and adhere to the policy. Chief Vicky Stormo of the University of Washington Police Department and president of the National Association of Women Law Enforcement Executives (NAWLEE), agrees that the officer should make the decision and the department shouldn't dictate when or if an officer will go on limited duty.[89] Some officers elect to remain in their job assignments throughout the pregnancy, whereas some assume limited duty after the first trimester and others wait until the last trimester. It depends on what their job assignment is and how they feel physically. Some departments even provide maternity uniforms for officers who will be in the public eye.

In the past, some agencies have forced pregnant officers to take sick leave or to go to a limited-duty assignment despite their desires. Besides the potential liability if this differs from what is offered to an officer who is injured in another way, this action also sends a message to the officer and her female coworkers. Administrators interested in recruiting and retaining females have noticed that many left after giving birth, not necessarily because they wanted to stay home with their babies but, rather, because of the atmosphere and workplace culture. They felt unwelcome and as if they were a burden to the agency.

A recent case illustrates the challenges involved in the pregnancy issue. The Suffolk Police Department's policy of not giving limited duties to officers who can't patrol because of nonwork related injuries was found to be unfair to pregnant officers, a jury decided in Federal Court. Officers filed suit after a policy was enacted in 2000 causing pregnant officers to either work their regular assignment while pregnant or use their sick time. Though this was the policy for men with nonduty related injuries, the jury felt it placed an unfair burden on pregnant women forcing them to make this difficult decision between potential danger to their unborn child and economic security.[90]

There is a concern among chiefs and sheriffs for the safety of the unborn child. This issue is a bit murky, according to Sam Marcosson, professor at the Brandeis School of Law at the University of Louisville, who served as a litigator in the Appellate Division of the Equal Employment

Opportunity Commission. He believes that in a circumstance where a department has to allow a pregnant officer to continue at her job until such time that she or her doctor requests limited duty, the courts will probably not hold the department liable for job-related injuries. However, many departments are taking a conservative approach regarding exposure to lead, which results from firearms qualifications exercises. Many departments allow pregnant officers to forego firearms training until they come back from maternity leave.[91] Having a fair and equitable policy in place will aid the department in creating a supportive and welcoming atmosphere for women and is likely to lead to more applicants and a higher rate of retention for female officers.

Workplace dating is another murky area that some agencies are trying to address. Some sexual harassment cases have arisen from relationships that have soured, leading some departments to want to prohibit fraternization. Though this situation is not unique to the law enforcement workplace, it can be a bit more problematic because of lack of supervision and the variety of locations and situations in which law enforcement can place officers. The issue is complicated by the police culture and the need to socialize with coworkers, regardless of gender. Departments are struggling with this tough issue in an effort to forestall bad situations.

In the last few decades, state, regional, national, and international organizations have been started to lend support to female officers and to address and present a unified voice on issues that affect females in law enforcement. The International Association of Women Police (IAWP) is committed to several goals in striving to achieve its mission, including serving as a support system and source of info and referral and providing networking and training opportunities. Many states and regions around the country also have women police officer organizations. More recently (since 1995), the National Center for Women and Policing has been working to educate criminal justice policy makers, the media, and the public about the impacts of increasing the representation of women in policing.

Family issues and conflicts between personal and professional demands also pose a challenge for women and the advancement of their careers. Time taken off for maternity leave and choice of job assignment to better accommodate family life may detract from an officer's active career and put such officers on the "mommy track," which may impede their rise through the ranks. Dual policing

careers, having a husband on a police department, especially if it's the same department can also provide unique challenges. These are all issues that police leaders are recognizing should be discussed and addressed.

Real change will occur as more women move into the policy-making positions in law enforcement and have the ability to substantively affect the working conditions women face. Addressing the issues that are retarding recruitment and retention will encourage more women to enter and remain in the profession. Increased visibility as these women are seen on the street and in the media will further the recruitment effort as women discount some of the previous myths they held and relate to the women they see in the public domain. Realistic books (even fiction), movies, and news and magazine articles will also respond to the curiosity that women may have about the profession. Books such as Marion Gold's *Top Cops: Profiles of Women in Command* and *Women Police: Portraits of Success* by Patricia Lunneborg portray women who have risen to the top in the law enforcement culture and provide their perspective on law enforcement as a career. A former police officer and now college professor, Donna Stuccio, turned her talent for playwriting into a way to spread the word about women in law enforcement. Her play *Blue Moon,* which has been produced on stage, takes place predominantly in the women's locker room of a police department and brings out some of the issues and challenges women face.[92]

Despite the problems women still experience in police departments, they have shown that they will do all that is necessary to attain the job, and they have shown that they can do the job. Many have given the ultimate sacrifice, their lives. There are currently 210 women's names included among the 14,000 law enforcement officers killed, listed on the National Law Enforcement Memorial in Washington, D.C. As women continue to serve and contribute to law enforcement in this country, the face of law enforcement will evolve, and their future in policing will be dynamic and interesting.

Problems for African Americans

As with females, recruitment of qualified candidates is the first challenge to be faced, and it is as formidable as ever. In recent years, there has been

ON THE JOB

We've Come a Long Way!

While in college at Florida Atlantic University (FAU), I participated in a "field experience" at the Boca Raton Police Department. I was impressed with the individuals I met there and the progressive chief, Charles McCutcheon, who also taught at FAU. I knew that going into law enforcement as a female in the mid-1970s would be a challenge and I would not be uniformly welcomed. But I felt that Boca with its high percentage of college-educated officers and a progressive, educated chief would be less of a hurdle than many other departments. It was the only department I applied to. After graduating from the Police Academy, I was assigned a Platoon and Field Training Officer. It was common knowledge that I would be going to C Platoon, as there were already three female officers in the department, one on every platoon except C. The consensus was that they wanted to evenly distribute the female officers. I was happy with the way this worked out as I knew a lot of the guys on C Platoon, and we'd become friends. My Field Training Officer was chosen because he was the only married officer on the platoon, and the administration didn't want two young, single officers riding around together for eight hours a day . . . who knew what might happen? The chosen officer had no training in being a training officer, didn't particularly want to be one, and in fact, seemed to not be very much in favor of female officers on the road.

During my first couple of years, I was touched and propositioned by a couple of superiors, had a snake put in my patrol car and a rat in my briefcase, and was locked in the men's restroom and the back of a patrol car. These were things I put up with to be "one of the guys."

I watched as the department grew and more females came to the job. I met personally with each one to offer support and a shoulder if they needed it. I offered to serve as a "mentor" in any way that I could and always

encouraged them to apply for new assignments and take promotional exams. When I became the Uniform Division Captain in 1991, there were many women working the road among the 100 or so personnel in the division. One of my proudest moments came one day when I was looking at the deployment of personnel and realized some squads had 50 percent females and even higher, while others had lower percentages—someone's race or gender had ceased to be an issue. Everyone was simply an officer choosing a schedule by seniority, and gender, race, or ethnicity was never brought up by anyone in the process.

We also had a "workplace harassment" policy in place that was strictly adhered to. Employees were disciplined and even fired for inappropriate comments or behavior, depending on the severity of the offense. There were department representatives designated for employees who had harassment issues, and each incident was investigated. We strived to make all employees feel safe, and we educated all employees on what constituted harassment in the workplace. Employees didn't have to quietly go through what I did in my early career.

Later in my career, when I was involved in the hiring process and did a report regarding female and minority representation, I realized we had greatly diversified our employees with our major efforts aimed simply at hiring the best employees possible. We had female FTOs, supervisors, and specialists in all areas. I was proud of the fact that someone could drive down the streets of Boca, go into a DARE classroom, walk into a community policing outreach center, or get pulled over by an officer on a motorcycle, and be likely to see a female or a person of color. We've come a long way!

—Linda Forst

less of a problem with African Americans seeing themselves as police officers and even police executives as there are significant role models out there. The problem lies with the extensive competition for these talented African Americans, not only within law enforcement but from the private sector, which offers less media scrutiny, safer working conditions, and more money.[93]

Another issue that arises with African American police officers more than other officers is the issue of friendly fire shooting incidents. These officers are often in the undercover or off-duty capacity and intervening in a situation with their weapons. As they are taking action or detaining a suspect with the aid of their weapons, they are often mistaken for an offender by responding on-duty uniformed personnel. This typically occurs in large organizations or when the off-duty officer is outside his jurisdiction and unknown by responding officers. Several officers have been killed in this manner, which is devastating for all concerned. The FBI reports that 43 police officers have been killed by friendly fire from 1987 to 2005, some of which fit this description. Though the number is small, it is unnecessary and preventable. Police departments are examining their policies that require officers to always be armed and ready to respond because of these tragedies. A woman has filed a civil rights lawsuit in Rhode Island after her son was killed. She alleges that the rookie officer who shot her son had not received adequate training to recognize plainclothes or off-duty colleagues. The IACP also recommends off-duty officers who witness a crime call for assistance rather than pull a weapon.[94] *FLETC Scenario*

Another problem that persists for African American officers is the perception of "tokenism" by themselves, their coworkers, and the public. With departments' efforts to promote diversity and enhance recruiting, they will often use African Americans in recruiting literature or at recruiting events where it's hoped their visibility will help African Americans see themselves in the job and wearing the uniform. Unfortunately, this can lead to the perception that black officers are getting particular assignments because they are African American. This may feel like "tokenism." Their various assignments may lead to excessive publicity or attention in a desire by the administration or media to promote role models. Recently, basketball great Shaquille O'Neal was sworn in as a reserve officer with the Miami Beach Police Department, which garnered national publicity. He made it clear to the department, however, that he "didn't want to just be a poster boy for photo ops, he wanted to get down and dirty and do the job—he's here to conduct investigations and to make arrests," according to the department's spokesperson.[95]

This apparent quest for publicity can cause the feeling among white officers that the department's goal is improved public relations with the minority community rather than the department's interests. In the past, this has led white officers to believe that black officers didn't deserve to be on the job but that they were "tokens" to appease the community.[96] The normal competition for limited promotional opportunities can cause conflicts between groups even in the best of situations. African American police executives

interviewed by Thompson note that overall working relationships with white officers have improved, but they still believe that some white coworkers continue to hold negative views about them and their abilities.[97]

As these stories indicate, problems persist for police officers who are African American. The National Organization of Black Law Enforcement Executives (NOBLE) is trying to address some of these problems and further the status of blacks in law enforcement. Their motto is "Justice by Action." NOBLE aggressively pursues its goals by conducting research, speaking out, and performing outreach activities. NOBLE plays a major role in shaping policy in areas of importance to minorities and the law enforcement community including recruiting, retaining, and promoting minority officers. It is hoped that efforts of organizations such as NOBLE, individual police organizations' efforts, and the minority officers' increased visibility in uniform will help to improve the situation for minorities in law enforcement.

Problems for Other Minorities

Other minority groups seem to face the same problems. As their rise in law enforcement is relatively more recent than that of African Americans and women, other minorities face the challenge of getting more representation in the command structure of police departments. That comes with time on the department and time in rank and should continue to grow especially within the Hispanic officer population, which has big numbers in the rank and file.

Recruitment is an issue related to this issue of representation and particularly command representation in the department. The minority officers need to get out in the community and establish relationships of trust with community members and help them to realize that law enforcement is a viable career for them and their children and that police in the United States are different than what the police may have been like where they came from. Minority officers need to show residents that programs, policies, and protections are in place to assist community members who may have felt wronged and that police officers follow rules, guidelines, and laws when doing their jobs. The community policing philosophy is a valuable tool in this undertaking. One Mexican American police officer in a border city felt one of his most important roles was to "build bridges" with the Mexican-American community, educate them about the police in the United States, and to "mentor" youth to become police officers.[98]

Minority groups continue to be faced with stereotypes that people, both other officers and community members, hold and don't vocalize. These are generally not overt, and minority officers may not even be aware that they are held by particular people, making challenging these stereotypes difficult. As with past practice, minority groups are hesitant to make waves and challenge issues that they might not agree with, particularly when they are small in number or new to their careers. Though it is rare that any type of retribution takes

place, most don't want to be labeled as troublemakers and do not want to stand out. In keeping with the police culture, they want to be known as team players and want to attain their advancement through their hard work, job performance, attitude, and accomplishments.[99] Most minorities do not want anyone to believe or comment that they are where they are because they are a minority; they want to make it clear it is on merit. As is often the case with minorities who can be closely scrutinized, they know they are under the microscope and often any error they make may be generalized to their minority group. They usually have to work longer and harder to get ahead, but they are generally very devoted to their chosen profession and serve as great role models for the community.

Summary

- The law enforcement agencies in the United States have a long history of discrimination against minorities.

- This discrimination has occurred in the hiring process as well as after minorities were employed in their job assignments or promotions.

- Though employed in law enforcement in the early 1900s, women were not given full patrol duties until the 1970s.

- Though the first African American police officer was hired in 1867, African Americans officers were often restricted in the types of functions they could perform.

- The fight for equality was facilitated by the 1964 Civil Rights Act, which barred discrimination on the basis of gender, race, color, religion or national origin.

- Though it might not be intentional, discrimination can occur as a result of adverse impact.

- The Kerner Commission made many recommendations including the increased recruiting of African American officers as a way to minimize or avoid the civil disturbances that occurred in the 1960s.

- Despite recommendations by national commissions, minorities were forced to take their cases to the U.S. courts.

- Affirmative action programs are one of the most controversial methods of ending job discrimination.

- Affirmative action programs and quotas gave rise to white male backlash.

- Academic studies indicated that females could perform the duties involved in the patrol function.

- The representation of Hispanic officers across the country has increased significantly in the last 20 years as has the Hispanic population

- Minorities are now making their way into administrative positions in law enforcement agencies.

- Challenges remain to achieve appropriate representation of underrepresented groups in law enforcement.

- Great progress has been made by minorities in law enforcement, and we hope that discrimination in U.S. police departments will soon be completely eliminated.

Learning Check

1. Describe the role the federal government played in removing equal employment opportunity barriers to minorities in policing.

2. Identify the various minority groups and the issues involved in the recruitment of these groups.

3. Describe the issues and challenges faced by African American police officers in the past.

4. Describe the impact of the police testing process on certain minority groups.

5. Describe how affirmative action policies have affected white males in hiring and promotional policies.

6. Talk about how effective women are as patrol officers, as compared with their male counterparts.

7. Identify ways in which women and minorities still face problems in policing.

8. Identify the challenges faced by Hispanic police officers in today's culturally diverse society.

9. Identify the challenges faced in recruiting Asian American officers and discuss strategies to address these challenges.

10. Describe the challenges involved in the recruitment of gay and lesbian officers and whether or not departments should address these issues, and if so, how.

Key Terms

adverse impact When there is a significantly different rate of selection in hiring or promotion, a type of de facto discrimination.

affirmative action An active effort to improve employment or educational opportunities for minorities. This includes ensuring equal opportunity as well as redressing past discrimination.

Civil Rights Act of 1964 Prohibits job discrimination based on race, color, religion, sex, or national origin.

consent decree An agreement binding an agency to a particular course of action for hiring and promoting minorities.

de facto discrimination The indirect result of policies or practices that are not intended to discriminate, but do, in fact, discriminate.

discrimination Unequal treatment of persons in personnel decisions on the basis of their race,

religion, national origin, gender, or sexual orientation.

double marginality The simultaneous expectation by white officers that African American officers will give members of their own race better treatment and hostility from the African American community that black officers are traitors to their race.

Equal Employment Opportunity Act of 1972 (EEOA) Extended the 1964 civil Rights Act and made it applicable to state and local governments.

Fourteenth Amendment Amendment to the U.S. Constitution passed in 1868 that guarantees "equal protection of the law" to all citizens of the United States; frequently used to govern employment equality in the United States.

National Advisory Commission on Civil Disorders (Kerner Commission) Formed to examine the civil disorders of the 1960s and recommended, among other things, that police agencies intensify their efforts to recruit more African Americans.

National Advisory Commission on Criminal Justice Standards and Goals Presidential commission formed to study the criminal justice system and recommend standards to adhere to for police agencies to reduce discrimination.

Omnibus Crime Control and Safe Streets Act of 1968 Enacted to aid communities in reducing the crime problem and created the Law Enforcement Assistance Administration, which provided grants for recruitment, training, and education.

quota Numbers put into place as part of goals and objectives in affirmative action plans.

reverse discrimination The label often attached to the preferential treatment received by minority groups.

Police Ethics and Police Deviance

© Syracuse Newspapers/Mike Greenlar/The Image Works

GOALS

- To acquaint you with the various definitions, the types, and the extent of police corruption
- To explore various reasons for police corruption
- To acquaint you with forms of police misconduct other than police corruption, including drug-related corruption, police deception, sex-related corruption, and domestic violence
- To discuss the definition, types, and extent of police brutality
- To explore various responses to police brutality, including citizen complaint review boards
- To discuss the issue of liability and the effects of lawsuits on police officers and police agencies

Introduction

Police officers in the United States are given tremendous authority and wide latitude in using that authority. In addition, to the average citizen, the police are the most visible symbol of not only the U.S. criminal justice system but also the U.S. government.

Many police officers complain that the press overdoes coverage of corrupt or brutal police officers. The 1991 Rodney King tape (the home videotape of the beating of African American motorist Rodney King by four white Los Angeles police officers) was broadcast over every television network in the United States for weeks. The 1997 Abner Louima case (in which a New York City police officer allegedly inserted a stick into the rectum of a prisoner and then put the feces- and blood-covered stick into the prisoner's mouth) was worldwide news. Sometimes it can seem like the media is only covering the bad things and ignores all the good work that police officers do on a daily basis.

We must remember that the media operate under the following philosophy: If a dog bites a person, that is not news. Dogs bite people every day of the week. But if a person bites a dog, that's news. The news is that which is different and not normal. Police officers across the United States do hundreds of thousands of good acts a day. They arrest lawbreakers, find lost children and people suffering from Alzheimer's, walk the elderly across the street, bring the sick and injured to the hospital, deliver babies, stop fights and arguments, and counsel the confused. That is their job, and they do it well, but that is not news. But when the very people we trust to uphold our law—to serve as the model of what our law is and what it stands for—violate that law, that is news. That is the person biting the dog. It is healthy that police misconduct is news. Imagine if this misconduct were so common that it did not qualify as news.

It must be remembered, before reading this chapter, that the vast majority of the over 800,000 men and women in our nation's law enforcement agencies are extremely ethical. Unfortunately, a few are not. Therefore, this chapter must exist. However, it is, indeed, about the person biting the dog, not the dog biting the person. This chapter will discuss ethics; police deviance, including police **corruption** and other misconduct such as police sexual violence, domestic violence in police families, police deception, and police brutality.

Ethics and the Police

What is ethics? **Ethics** is defined as the study of what constitutes good or bad conduct. The term is often used interchangeably with morals, which is understandable because they came from similar root meanings pertaining to behavioral practices or character. Applied ethics is concerned with the study of what constitutes right and wrong behavior in certain situations.[1] Basic ethics are the rather broad moral principles that govern all conduct, whereas applied ethics focuses these broad principles upon specific applications. For example, a basic ethical tenet assumes that lying is wrong, and applied ethics would examine under what conditions such a wrong would occur.

Aristotle defined virtue as what he called the Golden Mean or *Nicomachean Ethics*. This philosophy suggests that life circumstances trigger a natural range of response that includes a mean between excessive and defective responses. A person's "character traits" are their habitual ways of responding, and those individuals that are the most admirable are those that find the norm between the two extremes regularly. The virtues cited by Aristotle more than 2,000 years ago include courage, self-control, generosity, high-mindedness, gentleness, truthfulness, and modesty.[2] These traits are still looked upon as evidence of good character.

There has been a growing interest in ethics in the academic and law enforcement literature over the past few decades, including textbooks, studies, journal articles, and media articles. Many departments and law enforcement organizations are promoting in-service training in the area of ethics. The International Association of Chiefs of Police (IACP) offers courses in ethics, including "Ethical Standards in Police Service, Force Management, and Integrity Issues" and "Value-Centered Leadership: A Workshop on Ethics and Quality Leadership." The IACP and the Office of Community Oriented Policing Services (COPS) have made a resource available on their website for increasing awareness of law enforcement ethics, called the "Ethics

Toolkit." Some departments, such as the Santa Monica, California, Police Department, have facilitated ethics training as part of their commitment to community policing. These departments recognize that trust is a vital element of community policing and that ethical people inspire trust but unethical people do not. They realize that ethics training will help departments recognize their full potential.[3]

It is important for police officers to study ethics for many reasons. Police officers use a lot of discretion and one of their duties is the enforcement of the law. At the same time, it is their duty to protect the Constitutional safeguards that are the basis of our system, due process and equal protection. Lastly, they are public servants and their behavior involves the public trust.[4] The importance of these reasons have been compounded by the feelings of fear and vulnerability that have emerged since the events of September 11, 2001, and the Iraq war. As judicial guidelines become more complex and criminal operation more skilled, the temptation toward unethical conduct could increase. Accordingly, education and training that address the issue of ethical decision making will aid officers in the decision-making process. As mentioned, IACP and police departments across the nation have recognized this importance and ethics training takes place in academies as well as a part of in-service training.

How do we measure police ethical standards? What standards have been established to determine how police officers should act? Joycelyn Pollock, in her excellent book, *Ethics in Crime and Justice: Dilemmas and Decisions,* identified some of these standards:

- Organizational value systems or codes of ethics designed to educate and guide the behavior of those who work within the organization
- An oath of office, which can be considered a shorthand version of the value system or code of ethics
- The Law Enforcement Code of Ethics, as promulgated by the International Association of Chiefs of Police (IACP)[5]

Other standards governing police ethics are the U.S. Constitution and the Bill of Rights, case law as determined by appellate courts and the U.S. Supreme Court, and federal and state criminal laws and codes of criminal procedure.

Although these standards appear to set a perfect example for police officers and mandate exemplary performance by them, how widely accepted and followed are they by individual officers and departments? As Pollack explains, the police subculture often works against these official ethical precepts:

> It is apparent that the formal code of ethics or the organizational value system is quite different from subculture values. Violations of formal ethical standards such as the use of force, acceptance of preferential or discriminatory treatment, use of illegal investigation tactics, and differential enforcement of laws are all supported by the subculture. The police subculture has an ethical code of its own.[6]

Perhaps it is the police subculture, or perhaps the individual actions of officers or groups of officers create police deviance. Whatever the reason, deviance certainly occurs in policing. However, remember, as most officers know, and apparently the public knows, most of our nation's police officers are highly ethical. Albert Cantara, a psychologist for the Austin, Texas, Police Department, addresses some of these issues in his article entitled "An Open Letter from a Police Psychologist to All Officers." He states that training and education in ethics can be very beneficial and helpful to the officer in putting the "code of honor" before the "code of silence." He also emphasizes the role of the organization and supervisors in protecting their personnel—especially those in "high-risk" specialties. He stresses proper selection techniques, mandatory periodic counseling, and proactive supervisors who are quick to take action if they observe any potential problems arising.[7]

Evidence exists that the U.S. public believes to a great extent that our police are good, ethical, and do the right thing. In a 2005 Gallup poll asking respondents to rate the honesty and ethical standards of various occupations, the police came in with 61 percent of respondents rating them either very high or high in honesty and ethical standards. Ranking lower than police officers in honesty and ethical standards were bankers, clergy, journalists, business executives, stockbrokers, lawyers, labor union leaders, insurance salespeople, advertising practitioners, and members of Congress. Only nurses, doctors, pharmacists, and high school teachers were rated higher.[8]

In fact, in a report prepared by the Administration of Justice Program at George Mason University for the IACP in October 2001, the authors found that not only do the police consistently rank among the institutions and occupations in which the public expresses the highest confidence and trust, but most citizens are satisfied with police service in their own neighborhoods. Interestingly, most citizens have not had face-to-face contact with police, and therefore, their opinions are primarily based on second-hand information and media accounts.[9]

The Dilemma of Law Versus Order

Police corruption and police brutality have always been part of policing. The names, places, and times change, but corruption and brutality remain. There has always been an inherent conflict in the role of the police in maintaining law and order in U.S. society.[10] It would be very easy to maintain law and order by ensuring that our cops were bigger, meaner, and tougher than our criminals, and by letting the cops just beat up all the criminals to ensure a safe society. Of course, we cannot do that. We must have our police comply with the same law they are paid to enforce.

Police officers face ethical dilemmas everyday. They make difficult decisions on a daily basis using discretion. Every situation is different, and circumstances surrounding an incident may determine whether an arrest is made. Officers have to weigh many variables and sometimes contemplate accomplishing the most good for the greatest number of people. Whenever they do this, they are open to questioning and criticism. If they considered the wrong factors (race, ability to gain influence, payoffs) in making these decisions, they could be on the slippery slope to corruption. The slippery slope concept suggests that when people begin to deviate they do it in small ways. But once they have deviated, they begin to slide down a slope that leads to greater and more pronounced types of deviance. Therefore, there is no such thing as "minor" unethical behavior.[11]

Review of the Police

Possibly because of the dilemma of law versus order, the police are constantly under review by government agencies, including federal, state, and local agencies; the courts; academics; the media; and the general public. Numerous national commissions have looked into the operations of the police. Among the most noteworthy were the

You Are There!

National Commissions Overseeing the Police

1931	National Commission on Law Observance and Enforcement (Wickersham Commission)
1967	President's Commission on Law Enforcement and Administration of Justice
1968	National Advisory Commission on Civil Disorders
1973	National Advisory Commission on Criminal Justice Standards and Goals
1982	Commission on Accreditation for Law Enforcement Agencies

National Commission on Law Observance and Enforcement, more popularly known as the Wickersham Commission (1931); the President's Commission on Law Enforcement and Administration of Justice (1967); the National Advisory Commission on Civil Disorders, commonly referred to as the Kerner Commission (1968); the National Advisory Commission on Criminal Justice Standards and Goals (1973); and the Commission on Accreditation for Law Enforcement Agencies (1982).[12] In addition to the national commissions, numerous state and local commissions, panels, and hearings have looked into the behavior and operations of the police. The most notable was the Knapp Commission to Investigate Allegations of Police Corruption in New York City known as the **Knapp Commission**.[13] The Knapp Commission was created in 1970 by New York City mayor John V. Lindsay in response to a series of articles in the *New York Times* detailing organized, widespread police corruption in New York City. The Knapp Commission held public hearings, and its findings caused widespread changes in the policies and operations of the New York City Police Department (NYPD).

The police are also under constant review by the U.S. judicial system through the process of judicial review. **Judicial review** is the process by which the actions of the police in such areas as arrests, search and seizure, and custodial interrogation are reviewed by the U.S. court system at various levels to ensure the constitutionality of those actions. Judicial review has resulted in such landmark Supreme Court cases as *Mapp v. Ohio* (1961) and

You Are There!

The Knapp Commission Discovers Corruption

The Knapp Commission was created in 1970 by New York City Mayor John V. Lindsay in response to allegations brought by New York City police officers Frank Serpico and David Durk of widespread corruption in the New York City Police Department. These allegations were detailed in several articles in the *New York Times* and received national attention. The hearings conducted by the commission also received national attention in the media. The committee's final report was issued in 1972, and its findings were responsible for widespread changes in the policies and operations of the NYPD. The types of corruption in the NYPD discovered by the Knapp Commission through its hearings, investigations, and informants were so many and so varied that they could fill volumes. The Knapp Commission discovered corruption in the following areas:

1. *Gambling.* Officers assigned to plainclothes (antigambling) units received regular monthly payments from the operators of illegal book-making, policy, and other gambling operations. The regular monthly payments were called "the pad." Other payments that involved onetime-only payments were called "scores."

2. *Narcotics.* Officers assigned to narcotics units extorted money and other bribes, including drugs, from drug addicts and dealers. The officers also conducted illegal wiretaps and used other unlawful investigatory techniques.

   Officers engaged in flaking people (claiming someone was in possession of narcotics when he or she was not—the drugs used for evidence were from the officer's own supply) and padding arrests (similar to flaking, but involving adding enough extra narcotics, or felony weight, to the defendant's total to raise the charge to a felony).

3. *Prostitution.* Officers involved in plainclothes units had maintained pads and received scores from houses of prostitution, prostitute bars, and prostitutes.

4. *Construction.* Uniformed officers received payoffs from contractors who violated city regulations or who did not possess proper licenses and permits.

5. *Bars.* Officers received payoffs from licensed and unlicensed bars to overlook crimes and violations.

6. *Sabbath law.* Officers received payoffs from food store owners to allow the owners to violate the Sabbath law, a former New York City law that required certain food stores—such as delicatessens, groceries, and bodegas—to close down on Sundays.

7. *Parking and traffic.* Officers received payoffs from motorists who wanted to avoid traffic summonses, as well as from business establishments to discourage officers from issuing summonses for illegal parking in front of their businesses.

8. *Retrieving seized automobiles from the police.* Officers at city automobile storage yards received payments from owners to retrieve their automobiles.

9. *Intradepartmental payments.* Certain officers received payments for doing paperwork for other officers and for temporary assignments, permanent assignments, and medical discharges.

10. *Sale of information.* Officers received payments for the sale of confidential police information to criminals and private investigation firms.

11. *Gratuities.* Officers received free meals, drinks, hotel rooms, merchandise, Christmas payments, and other gifts and tips for services rendered.

12. *Miscellaneous.* Officers received payments from fortune-tellers, loan sharks, automobile theft rings, hijackers, and peddlers. Officers stole money and property from dead bodies (DOAs) and their apartments. They burglarized stores and other premises.

The Knapp Commission's report distinguished between two types of corrupt officers: grass eaters and meat eaters. Grass eating, the most common form of police deviance, was described as illegitimate activity that occurs from time to time in the normal course of police work, such as taking small bribes or relatively minor services offered by citizens seeking to avoid arrest or to get special police services. Meat eating, in contrast, was a much more serious form of corruption involving the active seeking of illicit moneymaking opportunities. Meat eaters solicited bribes through threat or intimidation, whereas grass eaters made the simpler mistake of not refusing those that were offered.

SOURCE: Adapted from Knapp Commission, *Report on Police Corruption* (New York: Braziller, 1973), pp. 1–5.

Miranda v. Arizona (1966). In addition, the police are reviewed daily by the media: newspapers, magazines, radio, and television. Finally, they are under constant review by citizens, many of whom do not hesitate to report what they consider to be deviant conduct to the media, to the police themselves, or to other legal authorities. Officers' high visibility often puts them under the microscope.

The police today act in many types of situations, and it is difficult for courts or police administrators to predict every possible situation that could arise. This, coupled with the fact that the legal authority of the police and the interpretation of the constitutional limitations of the police by the courts are constantly changing, leads to a dynamic and challenging situation.[14]

Police Corruption

Police corruption has many definitions. Herman Goldstein defines it as "acts involving the misuse of authority by a police officer in a manner designed to produce personal gain for himself or others."[15] Carl B. Klockars defines it as the abuse of police authority for personal or organizational gain.[16] Michael J. Palmiotto explains that police officers involved in corruption gain economically by providing services they should already be performing, or by failing to perform services that are required by their position.[17]

Richard J. Lundman defines police corruption as "when officers accept money, goods, or services for actions they are sworn to do anyway. It also exists when police officers accept money, goods, or services for ignoring actions they are sworn to invoke legal procedures against."[18]

Although these definitions differ, we can find enough commonalities to define corruption for our purposes as follows: A police officer is corrupt when he or she is acting under his or her official capacity and receives a benefit or something of value (other than his or her paycheck) for doing something or for refraining from doing something.

Is giving an officer a free cup of coffee or a sandwich an act of corruption? It can be difficult to distinguish between genuine gifts (such as Christmas gifts), gratuities, bribes, and corruption. At times, however, accepting any kind of gift is the beginning of the slippery slope syndrome where it becomes easier to accept other, larger gratuities in the future and eventually bribes.

Corruption Makes Good Books and Films

Police corruption is a popular topic in literature and film. Does life imitate art, or does art imitate life? This eternal question is easily answered when we discuss police corruption: Art imitates life.

As an example, the novel *Serpico*, by Peter Maas, and the movie starring Al Pacino were great successes.[19] *Serpico* tells the true tale of an honest NYPD plainclothes officer, Frank Serpico, who roams the police department and city government for a seemingly endless time in an attempt to report that there is corruption in his plainclothes division in the Bronx. Serpico tells his supervisors, his commanders, the chief of personnel, an assistant to the mayor, and the city's Department of Investigation his tale, and nothing is done; corruption remains rampant. Finally, frustrated in his efforts, Serpico and a friend, Sergeant David Durk, report their allegations to a reporter for the *New York Times*. This leads to the formation of the Knapp Commission and widespread changes in the NYPD's policies and procedures initiated by Commissioner Patrick V. Murphy, who was appointed soon after the allegations were made.

The novel, *Prince of the City: The Story of a Cop Who Knew Too Much*, by Robert Daley, and the movie of the same name starring Treat Williams also were great successes.[20] *Prince of the City* tells the true story of a corrupt, experienced narcotics detective, Robert Leuci, assigned to the elite Special Investigations Unit of the NYPD's Narcotics Division. Leuci was a corrupt cop who, to save his own skin, worked as a federal informer to obtain evidence to put his partners behind bars.

The book *Buddy Boys: When Good Cops Turn Bad*, by Mike McAlary, was a best seller.[21] *Buddy Boys* is also a true tale of 13 corrupt police officers in Brooklyn's 77th Precinct who stole drugs from drug dealers, sold drugs and guns, and committed other nefarious crimes.

The movie *L.A. Confidential*, which was released in 1997, portrays life in the 1940s in Hollywood. Police corruption, and other types of corruption, is portrayed throughout the story. Some of the factors that contribute to or facilitate police corruption can be seen throughout the movie, including power, financial gain, and job advancement. In 2001, *Training Day*, written by David Ayer was released. Denzel Washington stars as a cop in Los Angeles who becomes involved in corruption on the street level of

© AP/Wide World Photos

Los Angeles Police Chief William Bratton, left, speaks during a news conference regarding police corruption. A renegade gang, including five former officers, broke into homes and businesses dressed in police uniforms, often threatening and assaulting occupants while conducting illicit searches for drugs, money, and weapons.

the organization. Ayer wrote another film released in 2003, *Dark Blue,* which stars Kurt Russell. This film examines morality and corruption and is set during the time of the King riots. The movie focuses a bit more on the internal corruption of the agency. The many current TV shows and cable shows concerning crime and police also frequently involve "crooked" cops to add an interesting twist to the story. It makes for good TV.

Examples of Police Corruption

Despite all the attention police corruption has received and the efforts by police administrators to detect and eradicate it, there are still numerous recent examples of serious police corruption.

During the 1980s and 1990s, many large-scale corruption cases occurred around the country, in some cases fueled by Americans' thirst for drugs. Officers in cities including Miami, New York, and

New Orleans were involved in and later charged with drug dealing, robberies, batteries, and even murder, including the infamous "Miami River Cops."

By February 2000, more than 70 Los Angeles Police Department (LAPD) officers were investigated in what came to be known as the "Rampart" scandal. These officers either committed crimes or covered up unjustified beatings and shootings, planted evidence, and committed perjury. It started as an aggressive policing effort to clean up the gangs, lower the crime rate, and make the streets safe. It was behavior that took hold after officers were commended by the department and the community for their efforts and results in cleaning up the streets. The officers were working hard to put bad guys in jail and turn the streets over to the law-abiding citizens. The officers began to circumvent the law to accomplish their noble purpose.[22]

In 2003, a Hackensack, New Jersey, police officer who was also the union treasurer pled guilty to stealing $180,000 from the union to support his gambling habit. Most of the money came from the union's death benefits fund, meant to help deceased officers' families.[23]

In 2003, a federal jury convicted three Miami officers of conspiracy for covering up questionable shootings that occurred from 1995 to 1997. Eleven officers had been indicted, two had previously pled guilty and testified at the trial, three were found not guilty, and mistrials were declared for the remaining three officers. The officers received sentences ranging from 13 months to 37 months in prison coupled with 3 years of supervised release.[24]

After Hurricane Katrina in 2005 in New Orleans, there were allegations that New Orleans police officers participated in the large-scale looting spree that overtook the city. News reports indicated officers were at the scene of some of the heaviest looting in the city, and some witnesses stated that officers were taking items from the shelves of a Wal-Mart. Though this allegation reportedly involved fewer than 20 officers, more than 200 officers abandoned the city during the hurricane and were fired or suspended.[25]

In 2006, the "Mafia Cops," as they were branded, were found guilty of betraying their city of New York and the NYPD by joining with the mob in the commission of crimes. These cops were convicted of eight gangland slayings and leaking confidential information about mob informants to the Luchese crime family. Detectives Louis Eppolito and Stephen Caracappa joined the mob for cold, hard cash. They worked for organized crime for more than a decade and in the meantime, Caracappa was instrumental in setting up the NYPD's Organized Crime Homicide Unit and possessed vast amounts of intelligence information in this area. The detectives were reportedly on retainer for $4,000 a month beginning in the late 1980s and were paid as much as $65,000 to carry out one murder. After retiring from the NYPD, they both moved to Las Vegas, and Eppolito wrote an autobiography, *Mafia Cop,* about his life as a police officer growing up in a mob family. Information leading to their arrest in 2005 did not become available until many years after their retirement.[26]

Corruption is not limited to rank-and-file police officers. In 2001, a city manager in Miami who had previously been the police chief was charged with taking almost $70,000 from a youth anticrime group while he was police chief during the 1990s. He was on the charity's board of directors for nine years. He served a year in prison, was ordered to repay the money, and lost his police pension.[27] In

June 2006, the former chief deputy in the Allegheny county Sheriff's office, Dennis Skosnik, was sentenced to five years in prison for taking bribes to direct county business to his friends. He also forced his subordinates to contribute to election campaigns, and he advised a witness how to lie in front of the grand jury. A four-year investigation revealed that Skosnik forced deputies to contribute to the sheriff's re-election campaign to receive better job assignments and those who didn't contribute received less desirable shifts and less opportunity for overtime. Skosnik also used deputies to perform landscaping work at his home and drive his son to and from law school.[28]

Bernard Kerik, the former New York City police commissioner and brief nominee to the cabinet post of head of the Department of Homeland Security in 2004 is currently involved in arranging a plea agreement regarding some abnormalities that occurred while he was on the city payroll. Kerik was a familiar face to Americans immediately following 9/11 as he flanked then Mayor Rudolph Giuliani at press conferences, as the Police Commissioner of NYPD. Shortly after being nominated by President Bush to head Homeland Security, he was forced to withdraw because of some tax problems with the family's nanny. Later investigation revealed that Kerik failed to report that he accepted $200,000 in renovations to his Bronx apartment from a New Jersey company long accused by the city of having ties to organized crime. He also intervened and attempted to help that company get a New York City license, and his brother was given an $85,000 a year job with the company.[29]

In 2006, the Tennessee Highway Patrol totally revamped its hiring and promotional system after a long-standing culture of cronyism and political influence was exposed by investigative reporting and confirmed by a state and consultant's investigation. The goal is to erase the political influence that plagued the department for decades and plunged it into political scandal in 2005. Previously, hiring and promotions were hidden in a veil of secrecy, and the individuals who were hired or promoted were usually those that had made significant campaign contributions or received recommendations by politically powerful patrons. This set the stage for unfair enforcement of the law within the state of Tennessee. Particularly disturbing to the hardworking personnel in the department is that no one ever knew exactly how these promotional decisions were made or where troopers stood in the process. Now the lists will be published and available on the Internet and rules will govern how the administrator can pick the individuals to promote. Promoting staff based on merit and a fair testing process should allow the most talented leaders to rise to the top in the agency. Despite the outcome of the tests and processes, troopers are encouraged that at least they will know where they stand in the process, good or bad.[30]

Federal law enforcement agents have also succumbed to this temptation of corruption and misconduct. A customs agent is awaiting sentencing, which could be as much as life in prison and a $4 million fine, after looking the other way and allowing drug smugglers to cross the border from Mexico to the United States with large loads of marijuana. Investigators believe he took more than $1 million in bribes while waving through more than 50 tons of drugs. When Customs Inspector Lizandro Martinez came under suspicion in 2003, investigators found he lived way beyond his means. Though they declared bankruptcy in 2000 and essentially had no assets, Martinez and his wife were spending more than $400,000 a year in cash with only his $55,664 yearly salary reported as income in 2003. Their purchases included expensive jewelry, a car dealership, 10 classic muscle cars, and payments toward a very luxurious home in Texas.[31] Another embarrassing case for the federal government occurred in April 2006 when a Homeland Security Department spokesman was arrested on 23 felony counts of trying to seduce what he thought was a 14-year-old girl on the Internet. Apparently, during the contacts that occurred before the meeting, he was very open about who he was, giving his name and job title during his first chat with the detective posing as a 14-year-old girl.[32]

Recently, several books have focused specifically on the issues of police deviance as this continues to be a challenge for law enforcement. These books will all provide a more in-depth opportunity to study the subject of police corruption and deviance.[33]

Reasons for Police Corruption

Numerous theories attempt to explain corruption in law enforcement agencies. Frank Schmalleger offers an interesting theory about the reason some police officers become corrupt by tying Edwin H. Sutherland's theory of differential association to police corruption. Sutherland's theory of differential association holds that crime is basically "imitative"—we learn crime the same way we learn other behavior. We tend to imitate the behavior that surrounds us. Schmalleger asks us to consider a police officer's typical day—associating with and arresting petty thieves, issuing traffic citations and other summonses to citizens who try to talk their way out of the tickets, dealing with prostitutes who feel hassled by the cops, and arresting drug users who think what they are doing is not wrong. Schmalleger asks us to combine these everyday experiences with the relatively low pay officers receive and the sense that police work is not really valued to understand how officers might develop a jaded attitude toward the double standards of the civilization they are sworn to protect. Such a jaded attitude, Schmalleger says, may entice officers into corruption. Today's drug scene, similar to the Prohibition era, also provides strong financial and social pressure on police officers.[34]

When we consider the enormous authority given to our police officers, the tremendous discretion they are allowed to exercise, and the existence of the police personality and police cynicism, it is easy to see that police work is fertile ground for the growth of corruption. Add to this environment the constant contact police have with criminals and unsavory people, the moral dilemma they face when given the responsibility of enforcing unenforceable laws regarding services people actually want (illegal drugs, gambling, alcohol, and prostitution), and the enormous amount of money that can be made by corrupt officers. Based on all these factors, it is little wonder that corruption emerges in police departments.

Samuel Walker and Charles Katz cite several possible explanations for corruption:

■ *Individual officer explanations:* The blame for corruption is placed on the "rotten apple" in the department. This is the most convenient for the agency but not widely accepted because hiring has improved and because some departments seem to experience more corruption than others do.

■ *Social structural explanations:* Certain social structures in America tend to encourage and sustain corruption including the criminal law (regulations prohibiting activities many consider legitimate and ordinances that serve conflicting purposes), cultural conflict (some outlawed behavior is considered appropriate in certain cultures), and local politics (if the local government and community is corrupt, the police department will also tend to be corrupt).

■ *Neighborhood explanations:* Neighborhoods with social disorganization have higher levels of poverty, lower levels of social control, and higher levels of corruption.

■ *The nature of police work:* Police work takes place with officers working alone or in pairs and with little or no supervision, and the conditions of work often cause the officer to become cynical. Constant exposure to wrongdoing can lead the officer to believe that everyone is doing it.

■ *The police organization:* Corruption flourishes in departments in which the organizational culture tolerates it and the departmental integrity and expectations of being disciplined for certain acts are low.

■ *The police subculture:* The police subculture's emphasis on loyalty and group solidarity can lead to lying and cover-ups.[35]

Any or all of these explanations can be at work in influencing the existence and extent of corruption in police agencies.

Types and Forms of Corruption

Corruption is not limited to the present day. Lawrence W. Sherman reports, "For as long as there have been police, there has been police corruption."[36] Goldstein says, "Corruption is endemic to policing. The very nature of the police function is bound to subject officers to tempting offers."[37] Schmalleger says, "Police corruption has been a problem in American society since the early days of policing. The combination of power, authority, and discretion in police work produces great potential of abuse. In today's society, the personal and financial benefits of having the police 'on your side' are greater than ever."[38]

When the Knapp Commission reported on the police corruption in New York City in the early 1970s, it distinguished two primary types of corrupt police officers. "**Grass-eaters**" are more passive and will accept what is offered to them. "**Meat-eaters**" are more aggressive and search out opportunities to exploit for financial gain. Most officers who accept bribes are grass-eaters.[39]

Walker and Katz describe four general types of police corruption: taking gratuities, taking bribes, theft or burglary, and internal corruption.[40]

Gratuities are small tips or discounts on goods purchased. In many communities, taking gratuities is not considered corruption but merely the showing of good will to the police (with, of course, the hope that the police might perform their duties a little better for the person who shows them goodwill). Pollack defines gratuities as items of value received by someone because of his or her role or job rather than because of a personal relationship.[41] Whether to define the acceptance of gratuities as corruption has been and continues to be hotly debated by both police professionals and the community. The concern by those who feel it is corruption is that it may be the beginning of that slippery slope and make it easier for officers to justify participating in more serious acts of wrongdoing. It may lead officers to feel they are entitled to special privileges. It may also lead the public or the person providing the gratuity to expect differential treatment. The opposing argument that many businesses provide, especially 24-hour businesses or businesses in more crime-prone areas, is that if providing an officer with a free cup of coffee causes them to hang around their business a little longer or a little more frequently, it is a form of preventative patrol. Some view it as an enhancement of the community policing philosophy with officers spending time in the business and finding out about the issues and problems of the area. Though many departments have policies against the acceptance of gratuities, many do not. The policies are often not clear and often are ignored by the rank and file, often with the knowledge of the administration.

Police corruption also may involve taking **bribes**—the payment of money or other consideration to police officers with the intent to subvert the aims of the criminal justice system. This is a far more serious form of corruption and often involves payment for nonenforcement of laws or ordinances. According to Walker and Katz, bribes may take two forms: (1) the pad (formal, regular, periodic payments to the police to overlook continuing criminal enterprises) and (2) the score (a one-time payment to avoid arrest for illegal conduct). The pad is the type of bribe that would be used by meat-eaters after identifying good targets. Grass-eaters would most commonly be involved in the acceptance of one-time payments that come their way.[42]

Theft or burglary—the taking of money or property by the police while performing their duties—is another form of police corruption, according to Walker and Katz. The police have access to numerous premises, including warehouses and stores, while investigating burglaries, open doors, or alarms. They also have access to homes while on official business. This is especially true and tempting at narcotics investigations. There are often huge amounts of cash or drugs lying around, and often no one, not even the suspects, knows exactly how much is there. Until an official cash count or drug inventory is done (which can be hours), exact amounts of contraband are unknown. A corrupt police officer has plenty of opportunity to take property from others.

Walker and Katz's final type of police corruption is internal corruption. Officers pay members of their departments for special assignments or promotions.

Sherman discusses three general levels of police corruption based on the pervasiveness of the corruption, the source of the bribes, and the organization of the corruption.[43] The first is the "**rotten apples** and rotten pockets" theory of police corruption, which holds that only one officer or a very small group of officers in a department or precinct is corrupt. At first thought, this may not seem very serious. If only one officer or a handful of officers is corrupt, a department needs only to arrest the officer or group and use the arrest as an example to other officers of what might happen to them also, if they were to become corrupt. The dangerous part of this theory is that if police commanders believe that only a few officers are bad, they will not take the tough, proactive measures necessary to uncover and eradicate corruption in the entire precinct or department. New York City's Commissioner Patrick V. Murphy, in the wake of the Serpico allegations, faced a dilemma. He could accept the rotten apple theory, or he could admit that the entire barrel might be rotten. To his credit, and for the betterment of the NYPD, Murphy chose the latter and took the steps necessary to correct the situation.

The second level of corruption that Sherman found might exist in a police department was pervasive, unorganized corruption, where most of the officers are corrupt but are not actively working with one another on an organized or planned basis.

Sherman's third level of corruption was pervasive, organized corruption, where almost all members of a department or precinct are working together in systematic and organized corruption.

Several stages of the moral decline of police officers have been identified. Sherman tells us about certain stages in an officer's moral career. The first stage involves the acceptance of minor gratuities, such as free meals. Peer pressure from other officers is extremely important at this stage. The second and third stages involve accepting gratuities to overlook regulatory offenses, such as accepting money to allow bars to remain open past regular closing hours or accepting money from a motorist instead of giving him or her a summons. Peer pressure from other officers is also very important at this stage. The final stage involves changing from passively accepting gratuities to actively seeking bribes. As the corruption continues, it becomes more systematic. It involves larger amounts of money and includes numerous types of crimes, ranging from gambling violations and prostitution to dealing in narcotics.[44]

Noble Cause Corruption

Noble cause corruption refers to situations where a police officer bends the rules to attain the "right" result. This is also often referred to as the "Dirty Harry" syndrome. In the extreme situation, an officer might justify violating a suspect's rights to save someone's life. More commonly, the rights violation would be justified in the officer's mind by the ultimate good of putting the bad guy in jail where he belongs. These behaviors involve police officers misusing their legal authority but they are not doing it for personal gain. They rationalize the behavior to get the bad guys behind bars and consider it a noble cause type of corruption.[45]

According to Michael A. Caldero and John P. Crank in their book *Police Ethics: the Corruption of Noble Cause,* noble cause corruption is a more significant problem than economic corruption is, and noble cause corruption is increasing in United States police departments today. In our past reforms targeting corruption, we have some safeguards in place to minimize the chances of "rotten apples" obtaining law enforcement careers. Today's officers are morally committed to their work and making their community a better place. They believe in enforcing the law and putting criminals in jail. The professionalism movement with this commitment to the police mission may have unintentionally contributed to the growth of noble cause corruption: The corruption of belief from caring about police work too much.[46]

In this ends-oriented view of policing, officers will do what it takes to get "bad guys" off the street, including the use of the "magic pencil" in which officers write up an incident in such a way as to criminalize a subject or make the incident more serious. This is sometimes referred to as "creative report writing." This type of action will do more harm to the "bad guy" than hitting him in some manner and leaving marks.[47]

Caldero and Crank speak of the "golden apple" rather than the "rotten apple" in the police department. Traditionally, we have looked to the rotten apple—the officer rotten to the core—as being responsible for incidents of police corruption. This is an easy issue for us to solve—just throw them out. Actually, our screening process has kept most of these individuals out. In keeping with their theory of the prevalence of noble cause corruption, Caldero and Crank speak of the golden apple, who is an intelligent, hardworking officer who is committed to the noble cause and values efficiency and effectiveness. These officers become too focused on the good ends and break the law or violate policy to "do something about the crime problem." These apples are more difficult for agencies or chiefs to deal with because it is a more complicated issue and departmental policies may be involved.[48]

Caldero and Crank revisit the slippery slope model in the venue of noble cause corruption. The model acts out what the officers have been psychologically prepared for in the academy and through their early socialization process. It is primarily a test of loyalty to the group. Caldero and Crank call the initial step the "Mama Rosa's" test: A new rookie officer is out to dinner with his training officer and other officers and at the end of the meal takes out his money, asking the others how much he should leave. The other officers tell him to put away his money and be quiet. The cops have been eating at Mama Rosa's for free for years, and it has never been robbed, unlike the other establishments in the area. Mama Rosa is very appreciative. Now the recruit is tested—if he goes along he is tainted, but if he does not, he will not be trusted as a team player. If he goes along, he will be tested again in the field. This is a test for loyalty to the field and the "good" they are accomplishing by keeping Mama Rosa's safe. The second test will involve backing up another officer's version of events, another test of loyalty. The stakes will now be higher. Loyalty to each other and commitment to the noble cause are viewed as intertwined. Caldero's and Crank's view of the slippery slope model can be summarized as follows:

1. Free meals (a test of loyalty)
2. Loyalty backup (loyalty with higher stakes such as false testimony, finding evidence in plain sight that had originally been found in an unlawful search, or making a false call of a crime)
3. Physical violence against citizens (much more serious)
4. Flaking drugs (planting drugs or adding drugs to make it a more serious crime—very serious and generally very limited)

Noble cause corruption then becomes a gateway for material reward or financial corruption.[49]

If noble cause corruption is the most prevalent type of corruption in law enforcement today, then this is where our efforts should be directed in an effort to educate officers and intervene early in the socialization process.

Effects of Police Corruption

For the past few decades, police misconduct has made headlines far too often. This gives a black eye to officers who have never, and would never, consider any type of misconduct, as well as to agencies with similar standards. Police misconduct also affects the reputations of police officers and police agencies in general. Misconduct committed by an officer affects that officer, the department that the officer works for, the community he or she serves, and every police department and police officer in America.[50] It also affects the police community relationship in general and can and will undermine the public's trust in the police.

Law enforcement has come to the realization that it can be far more effective in its mission with the help of the community. Citizens won't help the police if they don't trust the police. Citizens must feel that they will be treated fairly and treated with respect.

Morale within the department will suffer as the officers may feel they are "painted with the same wide brush." This happens even with incidents that happen in other jurisdictions and even other states. Many officers will tell you they were questioned by citizens for months after the Rodney King incident, regardless of what state or what type agency they worked for.

An incident that occurs within an officers' organization is often complicated by rumors and lack of official information. During an investigation, it is quickly common knowledge that an investigation is occurring, and rumors fly. Departments typically do not release any information or discuss the investigation before the conclusion of the investigation. Officers are left with rumors as their source of

ON THE JOB

Deviance and the Job

Police departments strive to hire the most ethical individuals that they can. In my opinion, they do an outstanding job. When you realize the vast opportunities officers have to do the "wrong thing" and look at the fact that very few choose to follow that path, that says something about the quality of the individual working the street. Officers are confronted on a daily basis with ethical issues.

I remember as a police officer working the street being constantly challenged by citizens and business owners who wanted to show their appreciation for the job we were doing. The crime rate was very high, and citizens were grateful when we gave them the service they deserved even in matters they may have perceived as minor.

Half-price meals or free coffee were fairly common offerings. The arguments that ensued over payment were embarrassing and usually resulted in my leaving the full price of the meal on the table or counter; they could use it as a tip if nothing else. Unfortunately, it sometimes resulted in my avoiding that restaurant and going elsewhere, which of course was the exact opposite of what the business owner wanted.

In this book, we mention that studies find that often the biggest complaint citizens had about officers' behavior toward them was abusive or derogatory language rather than excessive force. Though I feel that everyone should be treated with respect, I was also concerned with the safety of the community and my own safety as well as that of other officers. There were times when people I encountered on the street did not respond to my requests. There were times when I resorted to crazy language, bad language, or harsh orders to avoid the need for a physical confrontation. One time I spotted an unarmed robbery suspect while I was patrolling the edge of town. I confronted him, and the chase was on. Because I was out in the woods on

the edge of town, I knew there would be no backup anywhere close. I yelled all sorts of things at this guy, because I wanted him to think I was crazy and might not "play by the rules." It worked. He stopped and put his hands up, and I was able to cuff him and take him in.

I also feel that public education can help in these complaint situations and aid in smoothing misunderstandings between the police and the community. I remember as a road patrol captain, I used to get calls from angry citizens complaining about the harsh treatment they received from an officer. I explained the officer's point of view and police procedure, including the officer's need to control the situation. I also explained that the officer encounters all types of people during the day and that many officers get killed or injured during car stops. I found that after being made aware of these factors, the citizen usually no longer wanted to make a complaint.

Lastly, I think it is critical that departments make it as difficult as possible for officers to be tempted to deviate from their good ethical conduct. They need to have good, solid policies and procedures in place to protect the officers from temptation and to protect the officers from any possible allegations of wrongdoing. I went to many scenes as a road supervisor where the narcotics unit had made some arrests. There were often bags of money and/or drugs all around with no one sure exactly how much was there. Once there was half a million dollars in duffle bags. How tempting it might be for an officer having trouble paying the mortgage to take some cash from bad guys that no one would even miss—or how easy for someone to make that accusation. There must be policies in place to provide checks and balances and protections for the officers on the scene. Police departments owe it to their organization and their officers.

—*Linda Forst*

information, and everyone is nervous about what is going on, what will happen next, who else is involved, and whether or not they will be questioned. Officers don't know whom to trust, and morale plummets. The air of suspicion can last for months while the investigation is conducted. This type of atmosphere is emotionally draining for

officers and will greatly contribute to the stress they experience.

An incident of corruption can result in an organization writing a policy or implementing training that might have prevented this particular incident from occurring but is not a realistic policy or training session nor needed for most of the personnel. Officers may find their work lives or personal lives made more difficult or complicated in an inappropriate manner for an incident involving someone else.

Just one or two incidents of corruption can ruin a department's reputation and destroy the trust the community has in the department. It can take years to overcome this bad publicity. It will affect the department in many ways. There will be a lack of trust, resulting in a lack of cooperation and information from the community. The department will be less attractive to highly qualified police officer candidates as well as to police administrators. Consequently, the department will stagnate for years under this perception unless drastic and highly visible changes are made.

Other Police Misconduct

Police corruption and police brutality are the most serious forms of police deviance. Police brutality will be discussed later in the chapter. Other types of police deviance also exist. Chief among them are drug-related corruption, sleeping on duty, police deception, sexual violence, and domestic violence.

Drug-Related Corruption

Drug-related corruption is also a concern to modern law enforcement agencies. In theory, drug-related corruption is similar to other types of corruption, but it is an added concern because of the frequency with which these incidents can occur. Drug users and dealers make good targets for corrupt officers because they are less likely to report being victimized. There is also an opportunity to make a lot of money simply by looking the other way. In a report to the U.S. House of Representatives, the General Accounting Office (GAO) found that there was no central data source from which to gather this information, but the report was able to provide some valuable insight through research and interviews. Although finding that most police officers are honest, the GAO noted a potential for drug-related police corruption in cities where drug dealing was a concern. Typically, this involves small groups of officers who assist and protect each other in criminal activities, including protecting criminals or ignoring their activities, stealing drugs or money from drug dealers, selling drugs, and lying about illegal searches. Profit was the most frequent motive.[51]

The report also cited four management-related factors associated with drug-related corruption, including a culture characterized by a code of silence and cynicism, officers with less education and maturity, ineffective supervision, and a lack of emphasis on integrity and internal oversight within the department.

Without the proper procedures in place, close supervision, and oversight, it will be easier for officers to fall victim to the lure of the quick buck around the drug trade or to use their power and opportunities to steal from those they feel will never report it. In 2002, a West Palm Beach, Florida, officer was indicted on money-laundering charges after being paid by a cocaine distributor to use his cash to pay the construction costs of three houses, and two officers in Hialeah, Florida, were sentenced to more than 20 years in connection with federal robbery, narcotics, and firearms charges. Some of these incidents occurred while the officers were on duty, using their marked police vehicles as escape vehicles after robberies.[52]

Sleeping on Duty

Fatigue is an issue for all involved in police work, and consequently, sleeping on duty intentionally or unintentionally is an issue. With officers working the night shift and the rest of the world functioning on a day shift schedule, conflicts arise. Officers attend court and meetings during the day when they should be sleeping. Their sleep is interrupted by phones, delivery personnel, repair people, children, and family responsibilities. Because of the nature of police work and the lack of activity and supervision during the early morning hours, it can be easy for an officer to find a "hiding place" and attempt to sleep for a while. This is clearly inattention to duty and is hazardous for the officer and his or her coworkers.

Most departments have policies in place to minimize the fatigue issue, including restrictions on the number of hours of extra-duty jobs that an officer can work and attempts to streamline court procedures, particularly traffic court. This misconduct can arise if officers decide to work as many extra-duty jobs as possible or maximize their overtime hours for economic reasons with the expectation that they will catch a little sleep while working the street. If an officer is involved in activity that is in any way questioned, such as a shooting, pursuit, or violent confrontation, the issue of impaired judgment because of fatigue may be raised. The fatigue issue and the resulting liability is part of the police culture, and professional departments are making every effort to address it.

Police Deception

Another form of police misconduct is **police deception,** which includes perjury while testifying in court and attempts to circumvent rules regarding searches and seizures of evidence, and falsifying police reports.

Skolnick states that police deception, if it occurs, usually occurs at three stages of the police detection process: investigation, interrogation, and testimony in court. "Particularly objectionable," says Skolnick, "is the idea that a police officer would not be truthful when testifying under oath in court. However, much evidence suggests that there are 'tolerable' levels of perjury among police officers when testifying in court."[53]

Columbia University law students analyzed the effect of the landmark U.S. Supreme Court case *Mapp v. Ohio* (1961) on police practices in the seizure of narcotics. This case severely restricted the power of the police to make certain searches of persons or premises. The students found that before *Mapp v. Ohio,* police officers typically testified that they found narcotics hidden on the defendants' persons. After the *Mapp* case, police officers testified that the narcotics they found were dropped on the ground by the defendants. This became known as dropsy (from "drop-see testimony"). Before the *Mapp* case, narcotics evidence obtained from suspects by police, even when illegally seized, was admissible in court. After *Mapp,* this was no longer so. Hence, the researchers said, police officers began to commit perjury to circumvent the illegal seizure of evidence rule and to ensure that their testimony and the evidence would be admissible against defendants charged with narcotics possession.[54]

The FBI was involved in numerous deceptive practices while J. Edgar Hoover was its head. Tony G. Poveda, in *Lawlessness and Reform: The FBI in Transition,* details the illegal conduct engaged in by the FBI, which included disrupting political groups, performing illegal burglaries, maintaining secret files, and attempting to deceive the public. There have also been cases of police officers fabricating stories for more unusual reasons, believing their status as officers will lead them to be believed. An officer in Toledo, Ohio, was found guilty of tampering with evidence after producing false documents and staging incidents in an attempt to make it appear she was being stalked. She was trying to gain sympathy from fellow officers.[55] In 2003, in San Jose, California, an eight-year veteran officer concocted a story about a robbery to cover up an alleged drunken driving accident. While off duty and calling the emergency dispatcher, he identified himself as an officer and stated he'd been robbed by two black males. Though his story quickly unraveled, the description of the offenders as black caused concern and hurt in the community.[56]

In the last decade or so, increased attention has fallen on departments altering some of their crime statistics. There have been scandals in large and small cities around the country. In some cases, officers or supervisors have lost their jobs. Generally, this is part of the organizational culture, and there is a desire to make the city appear safer or possibly more dangerous than it is. Transferring crime statistics into Uniform Crime Reports (UCR) data is not always a precise science. Officers and administrators within a department may elect to err on a particular side when making these decisions. Often these errors or discrepancies are good faith errors, but sometimes they are an effort to make the city appear safer for tourism or business reasons. On occasion, cities have wanted to make it appear their crime problem was more severe so they could qualify for federal grants to implement a crime-fighting program or initiative. In June 2006, it became known that the Washington, D.C., Police Department had 119 cases in 2005 that were not properly classified as robberies or other crimes but, rather, were classified as incidents that were not crimes. This exposure occurred after a *New York Times* reporter was robbed and murdered, and prior robbery victims indicated the suspects could have been arrested had the previous reports been properly investigated as crimes. To put things in perspective, however, the 119 cases were less than 1 percent of the district's felonies.[57] Recently, there was a major scandal in Broward County, Florida, in which many deputies were clearing cases that should not have been cleared. This was done to make the clearance rate of the sheriff's office look extremely high in comparison with other jurisdictions with whom the sheriff was negotiating contracts for service. These actions made the sheriff's office as well as the individual detectives look good. Some officers in these cases now face criminal charges because reports were falsified, confessions made up, and people charged with the crimes who could not have been involved.[58]

Sex-Related Corruption

Police sexual violence incorporates many behaviors and involves "those situations in which a citizen experiences a sexually degrading, humiliating, violating, damaging or threatening act committed by a police officer, through the use of force or police authority."[59] These are very serious offenses against the public trust. Most police officers detest this behavior by the few who perpetrate it. The community is shocked to think an officer would use his position of trust to violate some of the most vulnerable citizens. The average officer has a hard time believing this type of abuse occurs, but a perusal of newspapers across the country indicates that it does occur.

Police administrators need to be aware of this type of violation and be vigilant in looking for warning signs. Often, behavior can signal a potential problem; if that behavior is handled quickly and effectively, administrators could avert a bigger problem or give the organization documentation of behavior for a discipline case.

Examples of warning signs might include a male officer who pulls over female drivers, spends a lot of time outside bars at closing time, spends an inordinate amount of time at any place women tend to congregate, or conducts inappropriate follow-ups that he wouldn't conduct for the average citizen. Most of these activities can be explained away in the context of performing good police service, but together they could be a pattern of behavior worth watching.

Male police officers using their position of authority to sexually abuse females occurs more often than one would expect given the serious nature of this offense. In El Paso, Texas, two deputies were arrested; one was sentenced to 10 years and another was wanted for failure to appear for depriving a woman of her civil rights after raping her when she was stranded with a flat tire.[60] In Margate, Florida, an officer had sex with a 16-year-old girl in the backseat of his patrol car after arresting her for DUI after an accident.[61] In Lakewood, Ohio, a seven-year police veteran pled guilty to sexual battery for having sex with a woman in the backseat of his patrol car. He took the woman into custody on Christmas Eve, though he never charged her. He didn't use physical force, but his position of authority, not to mention his gun, made

the sex illegal.[62] In Los Angeles, an officer referred to by the prosecutor as a "Wolf in LAPD clothing" was sentenced to three consecutive 25-years-to-life terms for three rapes he committed while on duty. He was armed with a gun each time, and two of his victims were bound or tied. He was convicted of 14 felony counts, including forcible rape, sexual penetration by a foreign object, sodomy by use of force, and sodomy under color of authority.[63]

Domestic Violence in Police Families

Some studies indicate that domestic violence may be more prevalent in police families than in the general population.[64] It has traditionally been a hidden problem because victims are hesitant to report it. Domestic violence is only beginning to be addressed, and it is an uphill battle. If the victim is a spouse of a police officer, then the offender has friends and supporters in the department who may not believe the allegations, the offender has a gun, and the offender knows the system and knows where the shelters are. A victim who is a police officer must deal with all sorts of psychological issues as to why he or she can't handle this problem alone. The victims fear for their safety and for the economic future of their family because an act of domestic violence could cost the officer his or her job.

Many departments that get a report of this kind choose to handle it informally in an effort to protect the officer. This has resulted in tragedy. How departments handle domestic violence has been found to be inconsistent between departments and even within departments. A 1994 survey of 123 police departments documented that 45 percent had no specific policy for handling officers involved in domestic violence, and the most common form of discipline for sustained allegations was counseling.[65] The International Association of Chiefs of Police (IACP) has developed a model policy regarding police-involved domestic violence, and some departments are building on that policy and becoming proactive. However, a survey indicated that after the issuance of the IACP model policy, of 282 agencies that were contacted in the Midwest, only 21 percent had heard of the IACP model policy and only 11 percent had implemented a policy for police involved domestic violence. Out of a random sample of 100 large agencies a couple of years later, less than 29 percent had a police domestic violence policy.[66] The 1996 Federal Law (18 U.S.C. 925) that prohibits anyone convicted of a misdemeanor from owning or using a firearm further complicates the law enforcement issue. Some argue that an abusive police officer shouldn't lose his or her job (which being prohibited from carrying a gun would effectively accomplish), but others feel the law as written is ineffective and are challenging the constitutionality of it. They feel it is too harsh a punishment for an incident that may be nothing more than a misdemeanor battery (such as touching or grabbing) on an incorrigible teen.[67]

In 1997, a task force studying the LAPD found that 91 of 227 cases of alleged domestic violence cases investigated between 1990 and 1997 were sustained. In more than 75 percent of the 91 cases, the sustained allegations were not mentioned in the officer's yearly evaluations, and in fact, 26 of these officers were promoted.

Tragically, a case that exemplifies this type of response happened in Tacoma, Washington. On April 26, 2003, David Brame, the Chief of Police in Tacoma, Washington, fatally shot his wife and then himself in front of his children in a parking lot in a neighboring community. This came several days after allegations of abuse and the divorce paperwork became public, despite his wife's efforts to minimize his anger and embarrassment by filing the divorce papers in a neighboring county. His wife, Crystal, had filed for divorce and moved out of the home with the children in February, alleging that her husband was abusive and possessive. Brame was assistant chief and a 20-year veteran of the department when he was named chief in December 2001. There are allegations that the city manager knew of rumors of abuse and an acquaintance rape issue in Brame's past but did not investigate them thoroughly before appointing him chief. The state of Washington concluded an investigation of the incident in November 2003 and found no grounds for criminal charges but significant evidence of mismanagement within the city of Tacoma. Relatives of Crystal Brame have filed a $75 million wrongful-death civil suit, with the belief that the city's inaction or inappropriate actions ultimately led to Crystal's death.[68]

Biased-Based Policing

Biased-based policing has emerged as an important issue in communities in the last two decades. But, in reality, the government has faced this issue or topic since *Plessy v. Ferguson* (1896) and *Brown v. Board of Education of Topeka* (1954). Providing equal protection and equal opportunity is a critical issue to the American people. The behavior that has led to the coining of the phrase *biased-based policing* has existed for years. When it increased in frequency and severity in the 1980s and 1990s, in an attempt to fight the rising crime rate and escalating drug problem, the community began to notice and speak out. The issue of whether this was proper police procedure or ethical police behavior was raised.

Racial profiling, the term commonly used for bias-based policing, is generally defined as any police-initiated activity that relies on a person's race or ethnic background rather than on behavior as a basis for identifying that individual as being involved in criminal activity. Police may not use race or ethnicity to decide whom to stop or search, but they may use it to determine whether an individual matches a specific description of a suspect.[69]

The difficulty arises in the validity of stops when police are investigating a crime committed by a group of individuals who may share ethnic or racial characteristics. Some criminal enterprises are composed of persons with similar ethnic or racial or national origins, but under this definition using this characteristic as a determining factor could be interpreted as racial profiling.[70]

During the 1990s, racial profiling became a hot topic in the media. New terms were coined, such as "driving while black" (DWB). The media attention brought the topic up for discussion in communities. A survey indicated that 53 percent of Americans believed that police engaged in racial profiling, and 69 percent disagreed with the practice.[71] This perception of the prevalence of the problem varied slightly by race, with 56 percent of whites and 77 percent of African Americans responding that racial profiling was widely used by police. Six percent of whites and 42 percent of African Americans felt they'd been stopped by the police because of their race, and a staggering 72 percent of African American males between 18 and 34 believed they'd been stopped because of their race. This perception of racial profiling correlates with animosity toward police in a community. According to the same Gallup poll, African American respondents had a lower opinion of police (58 percent had a favorable opinion of local police, and 64 percent favorably viewed state police versus 85 percent and 87 percent, respectively, by white residents). Fifty-three percent of African American males between 18 and

34 said they'd been treated unfairly by police.[72] In fact, the Department of Justice found that nationwide, among traffic stops of young male drivers in 2002, 11 percent were physically searched or had their vehicles searched, but blacks (22%) and Hispanics (17%) were searched more frequently than whites (8%).[73]

Most people believe that police do engage in racial profiling, but most police chiefs do not believe their personnel engage in this behavior.[74] Regardless of whether it occurs, the mere perception of its existence, can result in problems with the community. Departments and states realize this so many states have instituted legislation requiring the gathering of data and the implementation of racial profiling policies. In fact, 96 percent of police academies in the country addressed racially biased policing as part of their basic training program,[75] and according to the Department of Justice's Survey of Local Police Departments, 62 percent of departments had written policies about racial profiling by officers.[76]

Police officers have a lot of discretion in their jobs, and this is particularly evident in traffic stops. First, officers decide whether or not to stop a car; then, they decide how to handle the stop, that is, remove occupants from the vehicle, call a drug dog, ask for a consent search, and so on. Citizens have questioned how officers make these discretionary decisions, and some allege decisions are based on race or ethnicity. Many members of minority groups feel they are being stopped for petty traffic violations such as failure to use a traffic signal or an equipment violation so that the officers can use the opportunity to question occupants or search vehicles.

Recent research on bias-based policing or racial profiling has been used in lawsuits. John Lamberth of Temple University analyzed police searches by Maryland State Police along I-95. He found that 74 percent of speeders were white, and 17.5 percent were African American, yet African Americans made up 79 percent of the drivers searched. He was also asked to analyze New Jersey data when there were complaints that African American drivers were being stopped disproportionately by state troopers. He analyzed data from 1988 through 1991 and found that African Americans constituted 13.5 percent of New Jersey Turnpike traffic and 15 percent of the drivers speeding, yet they represented 35 percent of those stopped and 73.2 percent of those arrested. Lamberth concluded African Americans were much more likely to be stopped and arrested than were whites. The Superior Court

of New Jersey used these data when it suppressed evidence seized by troopers and agreed that troopers were relying on race in stopping and searching vehicles. In April 1999, the Attorney General of New Jersey issued a report indicating New Jersey troopers had participated in racial profiling on the Jersey Turnpike; people of color were 40.6 percent of those stopped on the turnpike and 77.2 percent of the people searched. The report also found that 80 percent of consent searches involved minority motorists.[77]

The New York attorney general analyzed New York City's stop-and-frisk practices and, in December 1999, released the results, which indicated that African Americans and Latinos were much more likely to be stopped and searched. This phenomenon has also been documented in Britain.[78]

The state of Missouri found that statewide there was a disparity in car stops in 2005, when blacks were stopped at a rate 42 percent higher than would be expected by their numbers in the population. The report went on to say that African American drivers who were stopped were 78 percent more likely to be searched than were white drivers. Hispanics were less likely to be stopped than their proportion in the population; however, those who were stopped were almost twice as likely to be searched as white drivers.[79]

Recently, Jim Ruiz and Matthew Woessner conducted a study of Louisiana in an effort to examine the profiling issue. They reviewed arrest statistics of the Louisiana State Police–Criminal Patrol Unit and some St. Martin Parish Sheriff's deputies and observed significant discrepancies consistent with demographic and racial profiling when compared with the baseline group, the Louisiana State Police–Traffic patrol. The researchers believe that those officers were conducting focused traffic stops on targeted populations in a drug interdiction effort along I-10.[80]

These limited studies together with anecdotal evidence have helped criminal justice practitioners as well as community activists understand what is happening. More data are needed to better determine if there is a specific problem in various cities and states across the country. In response to the community outcry, most states have implemented some type of data collection system. By 2000, most states had taken steps to address the problem, from California requiring cards with complaint numbers be given out to everyone stopped, to Arizona having more than 100 police chiefs sign a declaration stating that racial profiling will not be tolerated, to Colorado collecting ethnicity data and providing

© AP/Wide World Photos

Though some departments are under court order to collect data regarding traffic and pedestrian stops, most are taking a proactive approach to address the issue of racial profiling. Agencies are training their officers in the area of racial profiling and ensuring that data regarding stops is collected and analyzed to determine if there is a problem.

anti-bias training to all certified officers. Though California failed to pass a measure mandating the collection of ethnicity data, more than 60 percent of the departments in the state voluntarily track and analyze that data. Missouri has gone so far as to pass a law on racial profiling (which will be monitored by an 18-member task force), which requires police to keep data on motorists pulled over and allows the governor to withhold money from agencies failing to comply.[81] In many states, the American Civil Liberties Union (ACLU) has been distributing profiling packets to residents to advise them of what the laws or policies of local agencies require.

Collecting these data will either help the community to see there is no problem with the activities of their police or help the police and community to understand the scope of the problems. This data collection will also send a message to all concerned that racial profiling is unacceptable. Analyzing the data and initiating an early warning system can also help identify particular officers or squads who may be prone to inappropriate stops. There is a likelihood of initial resistance from officers asked to compile these data, but many have come to accept this

collection process, especially when the data were used to examine trends, rather than target individual officers. The data should be looked at as part of a big picture, however. Characteristics of a particular jurisdiction can skew the data—major highways, large shopping centers, and large employers can affect the amount of nonresidential population traveling to or through a jurisdiction. How departments collect the information varies. Some departments have officers record information regarding ethnicity and other factors regarding their stops; others radio it in to dispatchers, who log the information for administrative review, as in "Operation Vanguard" in a couple of cities in Kansas.[82] Some agencies may not be pleased with the analysis of their data, but others will be reassured. The Washington State Patrol conducted a study of their stops and found that whites and African Americans were stopped more frequently than Native Americans or Asians. Whites make up 88.8 percent of the population and account for 92.2 percent of stops, African Americans are 3.4 percent of the population and 4 percent of the stops; Asian Americans are 5.9 percent of the population and 2.9 percent of the stops; and Native Americans are 1.9 percent of the population and .9 percent of the stops. They did discover, however, that Hispanic and African American drivers were arrested or ticketed more frequently than were whites after being stopped.[83]

If analysis of these data reveals a problem, it can be addressed. New procedures, training, or counseling can be employed to make changes. Some departments are reassured when they find there is not a bias-based policing problem, and the data can help them counter allegations of unfair treatment. Having the data available is a starting point toward improvement, if there is a need for it, and documentation to defend the department's practices, if no problem is detected. This recently served to law enforcement's advantage when Congresswoman Cynthia McKinney from Georgia alleged she was the victim of biased-based policing, excessive force, and "being in Congress while black." She was stopped by a capitol police officer after she walked past a security checkpoint. The media made this front-page news for a couple days. When the investigation was completed and it was determined that McKinney was not wearing the proper identifying badge that was required to bypass the security and had responded physically when the officer attempted to detain her to obtain identification, and that in fact, everything had been handled according to policy, the incident was quickly out of the papers. The officer had not exhibited bias or used excessive force.[84] Most citizens believed the officer's actions to be appropriate. Community support and relationships can be enhanced when the community has faith in the unbiased behavior of their police officers. A community that trusts its department is more likely to work with its department in making the community safe, and this is a good thing for all concerned.

Police Brutality

Use of force is a necessary part of police work. Officers are allowed to use the level of force necessary to counter a suspect's resistance and get the suspect to comply with a lawful order. Use of force can range from a loud, commanding voice to deadly force. The use of force must be reasonable and it must be appropriate. When officers exceed this necessary level of force to achieve compliance, they are using excessive force. Excessive force occurs when an officer uses more force than is necessary to counter a sub-

ject's resistance. It occurs when force is necessary, but an officer uses a greater amount than is needed. Police brutality is more severe and represents a significant disparity between the level of compliance by the citizen and the level of police force used.[85] When an officer uses physical violence against citizens, it is a significant occurrence. When it is excessive and not warranted and qualifies as brutality, it is further along on the slippery slope of corruption. Police brutality involves significant risk, including injury or death to the suspect, officer, or other officers, as well as the risk of citizen retaliation.

Police brutality has existed as long as there have been organized police departments. In 1931, the Wickersham Commission noted the problem of police lawlessness and abuses to obtain confessions. Subsequent commissions in the 1940s and 1960s also raised the issue of police brutality.[86] Claims of police brutality were common during the civil disorders of the 1960s and 1970s. Incidents of police brutality continued to be significant in the 1980s and 1990s. Shootings of African American men in Miami between 1980 and 1989 resulted in three race riots. The last riot in 1989 resulted when an unarmed African American motorcyclist was shot by a Hispanic American police officer. As recently as the 1990s, people in the United States were stunned by the use of excessive force by police officers in the Abner Louima and Rodney King cases. In fact, the 1992 Los Angeles riots came on the heels of not-guilty verdicts in the trials of the four LAPD officers accused of beating Rodney King.

Police brutality still exists. According to the Department of Justice, 26,556 complaints of excessive force were reported in 2002 with state and local law enforcement agencies that have at least 100 full-time officers. A year after the complaints were lodged, 94 percent had a final disposition and among them,

- 25 percent were unfounded (they did not occur).
- 23 percent of the complaints exonerated the officers (they performed lawfully).
- 34 percent turned up insufficient evidence to prove the allegation.
- 8 percent were sustained (there was sufficient evidence to justify disciplining the accused officers).
- The remainder had some other type of disposition, such as withdrawal of the complaint.

This is an average of 1 incident per 200 full-time officers. Interestingly, the rate was higher for agencies with a civilian complaint review board

(11.9 versus 6.6) per 100 officers. Advocates of civilian review boards have long maintained that citizens are more willing to bring abuse complaints forward to civilians than to officers.[87]

Caldero and Crank believe that a lot of the brutality that occurs is because of noble cause corruption and the ends-oriented thinking. Officers involved in chases with subjects who run from them or try to fight them often believe that these individuals need to be taught a lesson to make the streets safer for everyone else. The officer believes he or she is doing a good thing for society. But, what happens when this is caught on tape and aired on the evening news? Now the officer is seen as the bad guy, the bad guy is seen as the victim, more harm has been done for the larger society, and the bad guy gets the benefit. The noble cause corruption with the ends justifying the means has backfired.[88]

Responses to Police Corruption

Investigations

The most important step in eliminating or reducing police corruption is to admit that corruption exists. The need for candor, Goldstein argues, is paramount. Police officials have traditionally attempted to ignore the problem and deny that it exists.[89] Many police departments have established **internal affairs divisions** as their major department resource to combat corruption. Internal affairs divisions or units are the police who police the police department. Though it can vary by department, depending on the organizational climate in the agency, sometimes internal affairs investigators are not very popular with other members of the department because many officers see them as spies who only want to get other officers in trouble.

In understanding both the negative connotations of the "internal affairs" title and the need for systematic preventive initiatives regarding corruption, many departments have implemented "professional standards" units, "compliance" units, or "integrity" units. These divisions within the police department will investigate allegations of wrongdoing but will also be actively involved in developing and implementing policies and procedures that will minimize the chances of corruption occurring. This unit will conduct audits and inspections to ensure these safeguards are in place

and procedures are being adhered to. Good record keeping is essential in preventing corruption, or, if it occurs, helpful in the investigative process.

Internal affairs divisions can attack corruption in two ways, reactively and proactively. In a reactive investigation, the investigator waits for a complaint of corruption from the public and then investigates that specific complaint using traditional investigative techniques. In a proactive investigation into police corruption, investigators provide opportunities for officers to commit illegal acts, such as leaving valuable property at a scene to see if officers follow normal procedures regarding found property. Proactive investigations are often called **integrity tests.** Newark and Clarksburg

Police corruption can also be investigated by local district attorneys, state and federal prosecutors, and special investigative bodies, such as the Knapp Commission (New York City police corruption, 1970s), the Mollen Commission (New York City police corruption, 1990s), and the Christopher Commission (Los Angeles police brutality, 1991). In addition, the FBI has jurisdiction to investigate police corruption, and these investigations have had a major effect on several police departments, including the Philadelphia and the New Orleans departments.

The recent gun and conspiracy scandal in Miami was the biggest corruption scandal since the famous Miami River Cops scandal of the 1980s. The recent convictions came in the third month of the new chief, John Timoney, who was brought in to clean up the department. "He cleaned house at the police department and moved the internal affairs office out of headquarters to strengthen its ability to operate independently and began an extensive review of the department's policies."[90]

Discipline and Termination

When corruption has been discovered in an agency, discipline is in order. This will start with any individuals directly involved and move up the chain to "clean house." Typically, anyone who could have or should have known there was a problem (and perhaps chose to look the other way, ignore it, or was just simply an ineffective leader) will be terminated. This usually will include the chief. At times, this can be problematic. Officers, like everyone, are entitled to due process. With civil service protections and union representation, what can appear as a clear violation worthy of discipline or termination to administrators (especially in the case of noncriminal misconduct) can be ultimately overturned by arbitrators, civil service boards, or courts. Departments can be in a state of limbo as these cases work through their various appeals. Often the department will not be able to fill the apparent vacancy because if the individual is granted his job back on appeal, the department would not want to demote or lay off the individual they filled it with.

Departments often choose to put the officers on administrative leave, in administrative assignments, or allow them to continue in their assignments while awaiting the final outcome of their discipline. Agencies may also allow the officer to resign rather than be fired to save the costs of going through expensive litigation. Both of these options allow the officer to continue to benefit from tax dollars in salary or pension benefits, which can greatly anger taxpayers. King County, Washington, had a deputy awaiting the disciplinary outcome for allegedly beating his girlfriend and during that time he took advantage of extra-duty work offered and earned enough overtime to almost double his salary qualifying him for a $63,000 pension. Another deputy drove his unmarked vehicle while intoxicated and then conducted an unauthorized drug sting and vandalized a woman's vehicle. He was suspended but allowed to keep his job, and though he went on to accumulate many complaints over the years, he now has retired on a decent pension. These were two cases of several brought to light by investigative reporting.[91]

Decertification is also an option for law enforcement agencies. This is an administrative action coordinated through the state police standards organization that will determine if cause exists to strip an officer of his or her state certification to be a police officer. This will keep problem officers from going from agency to agency. In the past, some smaller agencies didn't conduct thorough background investigations and were unaware or unconcerned with an officer's past wrongdoing. States want to ensure some uniformity in who continues to wear a badge in the state.

San Francisco suffered negative publicity as allegations were made of widespread corruption in the department regarding cover-ups. It started over a police brawl involving off-duty officers in November 2002. The three junior officers involved were indicted on assault and battery charges, and seven command officers, including the chief of police and an assistant chief whose son was one of the junior officers involved, were indicted on charges of conspiracy to obstruct justice. The chief went on medical leave after he was indicted and announced his retirement several days after he was cleared of conspiracy in August 2003.[92] Although charges against the top brass were dropped, the case has brought attention to the code of silence that exists in police organizations.

Preventative Administrative Actions

The ideal way for police agencies to handle the deviance and corruption issue is through prevention. The hiring and screening process is the first step in preventing police corruption and misconduct. By screening applicants out of the process who might be prone to violence, have a quick temper, hold inappropriate attitudes, show a tendency to be "badge heavy," or already have committed criminal acts, many problems can be avoided. This is accomplished through the use of the polygraph, the psychological evaluation, the background investigation, and if necessary, the field training process and probationary period. Hiring the wrong person can have disastrous results for an agency both monetarily and morale wise. Because of the difficulty in terminating employees, these "problem employees" can cause problems, work, and receive payouts for years before the agency has enough documentation to terminate.

Another administrative tool to prevent corruption or misconduct is a good policy and procedure manual. This way, officers, supervisors, administrators, and the public know what behavior is allowed and what is not acceptable. Some agencies have gone one step further and in addition to having the policies printed in a book (which of course every officer should read), may choose certain "high liability" policies to discuss verbally one-on-one with the officers early in their careers. This is usually built in to the orientation and training process systematically, and the officer will have an opportunity to clarify any questions regarding the policy and often will sign that they have read and understood the policy. These policies should all be written as clearly as possible so everyone knows what is expected. Officers may view them as a way to "hang" the officer if they are too vague or too much is left to the discretion of the supervisor. It is an ongoing challenge for agencies to develop policies relevant to every possible contingency.

In addition to being knowledgeable about the department's policies and procedures, citizens should also be informed of the procedure for making a complaint against a department employee. They should be allowed to make the complaint via phone, by mail, or in person. The department should have a procedure in place to govern these complaints to make sure they all are investigated and that a determination is made regarding the validity of the complaint. There should be a system for tracking cases. It can cause problems and bad press when citizens bring up former complaints that were made and claim that nothing was done; if a complaint was not properly documented or recorded, the department or officers can't properly defend themselves, even though the officers might have been cleared or the behavior was justified. Proper documentation and tracking shows the community that the department is not afraid to examine allegations and then take disciplinary action when an officer is wrong. This will promote a feeling of trust between the police and the community.

Training is a follow-up to the development of good policies. Ongoing training is necessary as laws and policies change. Officers need to be aware of the latest policies and changes in the law and review these policies and role-play particular scenarios or problem-solve situations. This will assist officers in making decisions as situations arise on the street.

Adequate supervision can help prevent misconduct that may occur during slow times of the shift or in certain areas of town or on particularly problematic types of calls. The knowledge that a supervisor will or could show up may keep an officer from making the wrong decision, and the knowledge that they will have to explain their actions will also help officers "do the right thing" on their calls. If officers feel their behavior is not being monitored or that certain actions do not receive discipline, they may determine that misdeeds will not be caught or that they are condoned. This is of particular importance with new officers or with officers assigned to a particularly sensitive and discretionary assignment such as narcotics. These days, a reminder that a video or still camera could be rolling from overhead, an apartment balcony, or a person in the crowd's cell phone may help officers make the right decision.

The organizational culture can help prevent corruption and misconduct. If a department takes a proactive stance toward promoting integrity throughout the entire agency, the environment will not be conducive toward the development of corruption or deviance. If officers know where the chief stands and the chief models ethical behavior, officers will know which behavior will not be tolerated. The late Carl Klockars and his associates found that an agency's culture of integrity may be more important in shaping the ethics of police officers than is the hiring of the right officers. This culture is defined by clearly understood and implemented policies and rules. If unwritten rules conflict with the written rules, the confusion that results undermines the department's integrity-enhancing efforts. The officers will gauge the integrity of the department by the department's diligence in detecting and disciplining those who engage in misconduct.[93] First-line supervisors are also critically important in modeling ethical behavior because they are the personnel who interact most frequently with road officers on a daily basis. Even officers acknowledge this importance.[94] This, together with rewarding good officer behavior, including officers that may report wrongdoing by others, will help establish an ethical climate in the agency. Administrators must work to ensure that officers who report or confirm misconduct do not suffer retribution or alienation by their coworkers.

Computerized early warning systems have made it easier in the last few years to identify officers who might have a problem. These are generally now referred to as early intervention systems. Early warning systems typically use computer programs that flag officers who may be prone to "problems" when interacting with the public. Typically, in most agencies, only a small percentage of officers cause most of the problems and generate the most complaints from citizens. The paradigm has shifted somewhat now, and early intervention systems look at any number of criteria, including use of force and citizen complaints, that a department deems appropriate to determine which officers can benefit from early intervention before they become "problem" officers. Early intervention systems have also become a routine part of the supervision and evaluation process.[95] The department can intervene through counseling or training and can monitor the officer's performance in the future. These systems are particularly valuable in larger agencies, where supervisors may not be as familiar with individual officers and their personalities, work habits, and reliability. These systems must be coupled with the common sense of supervisors and management. For example, officers with more aggressive assignments and generally working the nighttime shifts or areas of town with high crime rates will generate the most complaints because their assignment is to be proactive and prevent crime.

When a department incorporates all these preventative methods, works to promote integrity, and consequently, works with the community to solve problems and reduce crime, this leads to an improved environment for all. Former Attorney General Janet Reno called attention to the inscription on the side of the Justice Department building in Washington, D.C., which reads "The common law is derived from the will of mankind, issuing from the people, framed through mutual confidence, sanctioned by the light of reason." She followed this, in concluding her introduction to the U.S. Department of Justice (DOJ) report on integrity, with the comment, "Policing at its best can do more than anything to frame that confidence and bring together all of the people, in the knowledge that the law speaks fairly to them."[96]

Citizen Oversight

Citizen oversight (also referred to as civilian review, citizen complaint boards, or external review) is a method designed to allow for independent citizen review of complaints filed against the police through a board or committee that independently reviews allegations, monitors the complaint process, examines procedures, and makes recommendations regarding procedures and the quality of the investigations in the department. Citizen oversight has generally been implemented when the community was unhappy with its police department and believes that citizens have not had adequate input into how the department is operated. When the community feels that internal affairs is not doing its job, citizen's rights groups have demanded some type of citizen oversight to ensure that complaints against the police are adequately investigated. Though they have existed for several decades, citizen review boards rose in popularity after the civil disturbances of the 1960s and 1970s. Today, most major cities have some type of citizen oversight in place. The DOJ recommends using an open complaint process as a "best practice" for enhancing integrity in a department and advocates a process in which it is convenient for citizens to file complaints against members of the organization and have confidence that the complaints will be fairly investigated.[97]

There are four basic models of oversight systems:

- Citizens investigate allegations of misconduct and make recommendations to the head of the agency.
- Officers conduct the investigations and develop findings that the citizens then review,

recommending to the head of the agency to approve or reject the findings.
- Officers investigate misconduct and render recommendations, but citizens can appeal the findings to citizens who make recommendations to the head of the agency.
- An auditor investigates the process the department uses to investigate misconduct and reports on the fairness and thoroughness of the process to the community.[98]

A citizen's review board can play several general roles:

- The board can provide an independent review of complaints. The belief is that an independent review board with no ties to the police will provide a more fair and unbiased investigation and the mere perception of this will provide greater public confidence in the complaint process.
- This board can monitor both the complaint process and general police department policies and practices.
- The board can provide policy review for the department when looking into the underlying problems that resulted in the citizen's complaint.[99]

In general, citizens are in favor of the citizen review process. Police can be somewhat resistant regarding the use of civilian review boards, but often come to see the value when they realize the effect the process can have on the community's perception of their department. However, most departments like to have the final say in the discipline, policies, and training the department implements. The concept of individuals who know nothing about police work making such important decisions and recommendations for departments makes administrators and officers alike nervous. Depending on the model used, the board can also duplicate the work of internal affairs and cause unnecessary expense and time to the community. On the other hand, citizens may question a review board's power when they are only advisory and have no real clout, but generally feel that community input into the running of their police organization will help to make the department more representative of the community.

Despite the valid arguments on both sides of the issue of citizen oversights, processes involving citizens are widely used. Seventy-five percent of the largest U.S. cities have established some form of review in which citizens participate. Therefore, the

The Message

JEFF MAGERS

Dr. Jeffrey S. Magers is an assistant professor in the Law and Public Policy Program at California University of Pennsylvania. He retired as a captain with the Jefferson County Police Department in Louisville, Kentucky (now called the Louisville Metro Police Department). Dr. Magers is a Lieutenant Colonel in the U.S. Army Reserve (retired). He attended the Southern Police Institute Administrative Officers Course and the FBI National Academy.

The criminal justice system relies upon the credibility, integrity, and professional conduct of police officers under the supervision of ethical police leaders. Police leaders often underestimate the influence they have on the ethical climate of an organization and the ethical conduct of individual police officers under their command. This essay will present a true story illustrating how much influence a single, determined, ethical police leader can have when he or she takes the opportunity and demonstrates the conviction of strong moral character and ethical leadership.

Early in my police career I was a detective in the violent crime unit of a 450-officer county police department. At that time, I worked the evening shift with four other detectives and a sergeant. One evening, early in the shift, I was sitting at my desk writing reports. The other detectives with whom I worked were doing the same. I looked up from my report for a moment and saw our lieutenant walking in the squad room with a determined look on his face. Visits from the lieutenant were not unusual; he worked the day shift and often visited us in the squad room before departing for the day. This evening, with no greeting, he walked directly to the chair in front of my desk. Without prelude, the lieutenant immediately began a speech that I will never forget. He said, "I hate liars, I will not tolerate liars under my command, and anyone under my command whom I catch lying, I will personally do everything I can to see to it that they are terminated." Good evening LT, how are you today! Needless to say the lieutenant had my attention, because he was sitting directly across from my desk. I immediately wondered,

"Is he talking to me?" I quickly discerned that he had not focused on me alone. His gaze was scanning the room. I realized he was making a blanket statement to all who could hear, and without a doubt he had our undivided attention. He continued to elaborate by saying he would not tolerate lying to him, the sergeant, the captain, to other officers, to the media, to prosecutors, and I expected him to say and to our parents, spouses, and children, but he left them out of this speech. He continued speaking on this theme for several more minutes. He was not happy about something, and it was apparent he felt that someone in his command had lied. He was angry and disappointed.

To this day I think he suspected that someone had lied about some aspect of a politically sensitive case we had been working on. I suspect he did not know who the culprit was, because no one lost their job that day. The lieutenant finished his tirade, lifted himself from the chair, and left the room abruptly. I remember the general comments in the room after he left focused on what had the LT bent out of shape. That was not what I was thinking. I had just heard the most definitive, firm stance on police ethics that I had ever heard in my relatively short police career. He left no doubt in my mind as to his expectations of ethical conduct for his detectives and for all police officers in general. As impressive a speech as it had been, at that moment I did not fully realize how much it would influence my career.

Months later, I was assigned a particularly difficult investigation. It was an unusual case because it was one that to my knowledge no one in our unit had ever tried to investigate and prosecute. Because this was an extraordinary case for which no one had any experience in how to proceed, I was investigating the case without much help or guidance. During the course of the investigation I made a serious mistake. The mistake was one I should not have made, but I had not intentionally done so. I came to work one day as the investigation of this case was nearly complete, and we were beginning the prosecution phase. I was confronted with my error by the lieutenant. He informed me of my mistake in no uncertain terms and asked me to explain. I could have lied that day and told the LT a story that maybe would have shifted the blame, but I was looking into the eyes of the man who just a few months earlier had given the "speech." My parents had taught me not to lie, and this was reinforced by an honor code as a commissioned officer in the U.S. Army (my first job after college), but under pressure, the temptation to lie is intense. If we are truthful with ourselves, we know this temptation all too well. Looking at the LT I realized lying was not an option, as well it should never have been. I told the lieutenant the truth about my error, because when presented with the facts, I realized, I had to be responsible for my actions involving this investigative mistake. I know you want to know what the mistake was, but that is irrelevant to this story. It was not criminal; it was just a procedural error that could have jeopardized the case and certainly caused everyone working on the case more work. I still obtained a conviction in the case.

After I had confessed my error, the LT gave me a vigorous oral reprimand, as did the captain, the major, and the deputy chief of police. Thank goodness the chief was off that day and I was spared that nightmare, although I must admit I was undeserving of a break that day. When the ordeal was over I went about the task of correcting my error. It was only days later that I realized that I had faced a crucial moment in my career. Had I lied that day, I truly believe it would have been the end of my police career. Without the lieutenant's speech, I may have had the strength of character to tell the truth that day, but maybe I would not have. I will never know. I do know the words of the LT echoed in my head, setting the standard for ethical policing. The lieutenant's definitive ethical message was the support I needed at that critical moment. Later when I reflected on the situation, I realized how important the lieutenant's words were to me and to my young career. I do not know if the other detectives in the squad room heard the message in the same way I did, but the influence it had on me was profound.

After this incident I thought about the three officers in my recruit class who had been terminated for separate ethical lapses. If they had heard this same message, would they have heeded the warning and lived up to the ethical expectations so effectively expressed by my lieutenant, a police leader who took the time to clearly set the standard for ethical conduct of the police officers in his command? We will never know. Years later, as a sergeant, I was selected for an assignment by that same lieutenant, who by then was a major and the commander of a joint city–county narcotics unit. He chose me to be the asset forfeiture manager for the unit. After I was with the unit for a while, I asked him why he chose me for the job. He said I was the one sergeant he knew he could trust for this highly sensitive position, involving the handling of considerable amounts of cash.

While still working as a police officer I returned to college to earn a doctorate in leadership education. A considerable amount of my coursework concerned ethics and leadership. I began teaching basic and in-service training ethics classes for police officers and police supervisors in my department, the state, and various venues throughout the country. In every class I have told this story, repeating the lieutenant's message each time. All police leaders, police officers, police recruits, and criminal justice students in college must hear the same message. Because ethical decision-making for police officers is such an important issue, I chose to complete my doctoral dissertation on the topic of how police supervisors influence police officers to lie to cover up unethical behavior. Needless to say my research indicated what the lieutenant intuitively knew: Police supervisors have a significant effect on the ethical behavior of police officers.

The burden to create an ethical police environment rests not just with police leaders. Individual officers are responsible for their conduct. Leaders can set the tone, but each officer must make a conscious decision to accept or not accept the wise counsel of ethical police leaders. So, in this era where people often blame others for their crimes or ethical lapses, one should not shift the blame entirely to supervisors for the ethical conduct of their subordinates. Police leaders providing clear ethical messages certainly help those who would choose to make sound, ethical decisions in the course of their daily police lives. Ultimately it is an individual decision. It is your decision to hold yourself accountable and to hold other officers accountable for their actions when police leaders are not physically present.

I retired from policing; I now teach in a masters program at a regional state university in Pennsylvania and provide seminars for police officers and leaders. Every time I tell this story, I hope there are those who hear the same clear, concise, ethical message I heard from the lieutenant to whom I owe so much.

issue may have been settled from the public's point of view about the value of these reviews. The only decision to be made is what type of review system to incorporate. The issue, as viewed from the police perspective, is that these types of boards are most often implemented after a highly publicized and emotionally charged incident has occurred. Consequently, they are sometimes hastily put together and may not be the system best designed to serve the particular police department. To have more time and input in choosing the system that best complements the police organization, many departments are taking a proactive approach and putting a system in place before a crisis erupts. Ultimately, this may contribute to the success of the system for all concerned.[100]

▪

Police Civil and Criminal Liability

Misconduct by police officers can lead to civil and criminal liability. Police officers may be held legally liable—that is arrested, sued, and prosecuted for their conduct. This concept of police legal liability comes in many different forms. Police **civil liability** means that a police officer may be sued in civil court for improper behavior, using such civil law concepts as negligence and torts. Civil liability is a relatively new approach to correcting improper actions by the police through lawsuits and the resultant monetary judgments. Officers may also be sued under the provisions of a state civil rights law for violation of a person's civil rights.

Rolando V. del Carmen has identified several major sources of police legal liability: Under state law, police are subject to (1) civil liabilities, including state tort laws and state civil rights laws; (2) criminal liabilities, including state penal code provisions applicable only to public officials and general state penal law provisions; and (3) administrative liabilities. Under federal law, police are subject to (1) civil liabilities, including three sections of Title 42 of the U.S. Code; (2) criminal liabilities, including three sections of Title 18 of the U.S. Code; and (3) administrative liabilities.[101]

State Liability

Police may be sued in state civil courts for torts. A tort is a private wrong, as opposed to a crime that is considered a public wrong. Torts can be classified as intentional torts or negligence torts. As for criminal liability, many states have provisions in their penal codes that make certain actions by police officers or other public servants a crime. Police officers, like everyone else, are also subject to being charged with violations of the state penal law, such as murder, assault, or larceny.

Police officers are also subject to administrative liability: They are liable for the rules and regulations established by their department to govern the conduct of its officers. Officers charged with violations of a department's internal rules and regulations may be subject to discipline in the form of fines, demotions, and even dismissal from the department.

Federal Liability

In recent years, an increasing number of lawsuits against police officers have been brought to federal courts on civil rights grounds. These federal suits are known as 1983 suits, because they are based on Section 1983 of Title 42 of the U.S. Code (Civil Action for Deprivation of Civil Rights):

> Every person who, under color of any statute, ordinance, regulation, custom, or usage, of any State or Territory, subjects or causes to be subjected, any citizen of the United States or other persons within the jurisdiction thereof to the deprivation of any rights, privileges or immunities secured by the Constitution and laws, shall be liable to the party injured in an action at law, suit in equity, or other proper proceeding for redress.

This law was passed in 1871 by Congress to ensure the civil rights of individuals. It requires due process of law before any person can be deprived of life, liberty, or property and provides redress for the denial of these constitutional rights by officials acting under color of state law (under the authority of their power as public officials).[102] Section 1983 of Title 42 of the U.S. Code was originally know as Section 1 of the Ku Klux Klan Act of April 20, 1871, enacted by Congress as a means of enforcing the Fourteenth Amendment guarantee of rights to the newly freed slaves. This law originally was given a narrow interpretation by the courts and was seldom used. Between 1871 and 1920, only 21 cases were decided under Section 1983.[103] Police officers who violate a person's civil rights by unlawfully searching or detaining a person can be sued under this law. It can also be used in abuse-of-force cases. Two other sections of Title 42 of the U.S. Code also apply to police officers. Section 1985 (Conspiracy to Interfere with Civil Rights) can be used against two or more officers who conspire to deprive a person of the equal protection of the law. Section 1981 (Equal Rights under the Law) can also be used against officers. In addition to being sued by a plaintiff civilly for violation of a person's civil rights, a police officer can face criminal charges by the government, using Title 18 of the U.S. Code, Section 242 (Deprivation of Rights Under Color of Law), and in conspiracy cases, Title 18 of the U.S. Code, Section 241 (Conspiracy Against Rights). Title 18 of the U.S. Code, Section 245 (Federally Protected Activities), may be used against officers who interfere with certain activities such as voting, serving as a juror in a federal court, and other federally regulated activities.

Federal law enforcement officers are also subject to administrative liability—to the rules and regulations of their agencies—just as state officers are subject to the rules and regulations of their departments. The violation of these regulations may lead to such disciplinary action as fines, demotions, or dismissal.

Reasons for Suing Police Officers

Schmalleger identifies the major sources of police civil liability: failure to render proper emergency medical assistance, failure to aid private citizens, false arrest, excessive force or inappropriate use of deadly force, malicious prosecution, patterns of unfair and inequitable treatment, negligence in the care of suspects in police custody, failure to prevent a foreseeable crime, lack of due regard for the safety of others, false imprisonment, violations of constitutional rights, and racial profiling.[104] Typically, the issue of excessive force is the most widely publicized and well-known basis for civil liability because of the media attention it receives.

In *Civil Liabilities in American Policing: A Text for Law Enforcement Personnel*, del Carmen includes chapters on the following types of liabilities affecting law enforcement personnel: liability for nondeadly and deadly use of force; liability for false arrest and false imprisonment; liability for searches and seizures; liability for negligence, specific instances of negligence in police work; liability for jail management; liabilities of police supervisors for what their subordinates do; and liabilities of police supervisors for what they do to their subordinates.[105]

In his text *Critical Issues in Police Civil Liability*, Victor Kappeler addresses the issue of negligence and discusses areas of concern to law enforcement officers. These areas of potential liability include negligent operation of emergency vehicles; negligent failure to protect; negligent failure to arrest; negligent failure to render assistance; negligent selection, hiring, and retention; negligent police supervision and direction; negligent entrustment and assignment; and negligent failure to discipline and investigate. Some of these issues are of more concern to law enforcement administrators, but many should be of concern to the street officer.[106]

Kappeler further discusses areas of concern to officers on the liability associated with excessive force, high-risk drug enforcement, abandoning citizens in dangerous places, failure to arrest intoxicated drivers, and negligence at accident scenes.

The following are some examples of civil lawsuits against the police. In *Biscoe v. Arlington* (1984), Alvin Biscoe, an innocent bystander who was waiting to cross the street, was struck by a police car that had gone out of control while involved in a high-speed automobile pursuit. The accident caused Biscoe to lose both legs. Biscoe was awarded $5 million by the court.[107] *Kaplan v. Lloyd's Insurance Company* (1985) was another lawsuit involving an accident that resulted from a high-speed police chase. The officer driving the police car, who drove 75 miles per hour in a 40-mile-per-hour zone, was found to be negligent and was held liable for damages.[108]

The city of Boston agreed to pay $500,000 to the parents of a teenager who was shot to death by a police officer, even though the youth was in a stolen car involved in a high-speed chase with the police.[109] In *Prior v. Woods* (1981), a Detroit police officer mistakenly shot and killed a man, David Prior, in front of his home because the officer suspected Prior of being a burglar. A $5.7 million judgment was imposed against the Detroit Police Department.[110]

In 1996, Drewey and Mona Scarberry were awarded $950,000 by the city of Tacoma, Washington, as the result of a car crash that left Drewey Scarberry partially paralyzed. The couple's car was broadsided by a carload of gang members being pursued by the police.[111]

In 2006, Los Angeles reached a tentative agreement of at least $1.5 million with the mother of a 13-year-old boy shot and killed by the police. The 13 year old backed a stolen vehicle toward a police car at 4 AM after a brief pursuit. He had been driving erratically and police suspected he was drunk. The officer fired 10 shots, hitting the youth 7 times.[112]

That same year, the city of Oakland, California, agreed to pay $2 million to antiwar protesters injured three years earlier by police use of "less than lethal" force. The police fired less than lethal rounds (rubber and wooden bullets) at the demonstrators, some of whom had thrown rocks at the police, which resulted in 58 people being injured.[113]

Effects of Lawsuits on Police Departments and Officers

The use of civil lawsuits against the police has been increasing at a rapid rate and is having a dramatic effect on the treasuries of some counties and cities. Advocates of police civil damage lawsuits see these lawsuits as a vehicle for stimulating police reform. They assume that the dollar cost of police misconduct will force other city officials to intervene and force improvements in the police department through discipline, policy change, or training.

Increased media attention, coupled with some high judgments and out-of-court settlements, have encouraged individuals and lawyers to go after the most visible arm of the criminal justice system—the police. Seminars are held around the country instructing attorneys on how to sue police departments, and there are seminars for government entities and police managers on how to avoid or protect themselves against lawsuits. In New York City, trends show suits against police are steadily increasing. They are a "growth industry" and in 1998 to 1999, the city of New York paid $40 million to settle cases, 40 percent more than the year before.[114] Some also have the perception that the government has "deep pockets" and the ability to pay these judgments and settlements. Early estimates indicated that only 4 percent of the cases alleging police wrongdoing resulted in a verdict against the police, but more recently, police have lost approximately 8 percent of cases reported. This number seems small, but departments feel a significant impact financially and in the area of morale.[115]

The cost to taxpayers for civil suits is extremely high when factoring in the cost of liability insurance, litigation, out-of-court settlements, and punitive damage awards. A recent study of police liability cases handed down by the federal district courts from 1978 to 1995 indicated the average reported award and attorney fees against police departments was $118,698, with judgments ranging from $1 to $1.6 million.[116] It is unfortunate, but because of the high costs, many governments pay minimal out-of-

court settlements to get rid of the case and avoid the costs of litigation. This angers police officers, who feel they did nothing wrong and that the government should always defend them and stand up for what is right, rather than just looking at the least expensive way to resolve the situation. Police also fear that settlements encourage frivolous lawsuits.

This issue of settling lawsuits is often viewed by rank and file and even police administrators as an additional ethical issue. Cities or counties often settle lawsuits simply because it makes sense financially because of the high cost of employing specialist lawyers and beginning a defense strategy. When officers and supervisors believe that everything was done correctly, yet the city agrees to settle with an accuser, it sends the wrong message—that the officers were wrong and the accuser is right. This is usually far from the truth. Officers note that they are held to high ethical standards and encouraged to do the "right thing," and this standard should also hold for the governing entity, which should not "settle" cases just to save money. The government should back their officers when they have behaved appropriately in the performance of their job.

So many suits have been filed against the police that the U.S. Supreme Court, in *Canton v. Harris* (1989), made it more difficult for victims to sue for damages. The Court ruled that to be liable, police departments must be deliberately indifferent to the needs of the people with whom police come in contact.[117]

Officers and administrators need to be aware of the issue of civil liability and the police. Sometimes the threat of civil suits and large penalties proves to be an effective deterrent to excessive force, but unrealistic fears of civil liability have a number of negative effects, including morale problems, alienation from the public, and sometimes misunderstandings. Some officers may develop a reluctance to take action that should be taken as part of their job because of the fear of being sued. This could result in an ineffective police agency with many officers just doing enough to "get by" and stay out of trouble. The increase in litigation does have a positive side in that it allows for proper redress of police wrongdoing and promotes better police training and more responsible police practices; it also sets the standard for police behavior.[118] Officers should be as educated in this area as possible to have a realistic view and accurate understanding of the issue. Kappeler's text, *Critical Issues in Police Civil Liability*, is a good place to begin that education.

The Emotional Toll

The emotional toll that internal affairs investigations can cause is a subject often ignored by academics. Although it is important to receive, document, and track complaints against the police for many reasons, people have all sorts of reasons for complaining about police officers. Many mistakenly hope to get out of whatever charges they face from traffic tickets to arrests. Often the person charged is not even the one to make the complaint. He or she tells someone about it, and that third party may decide to make an issue of it. These complaints can generate a lot of media attention. The media love to report on "bad cops," sometimes even without the facts all being in.

The public reads about it in the paper or hears about it in the news, and the statement is often made that "Officer Smith would not comment," which the public may view negatively. The press does not usually mention that most of the time department policy, and sometimes state law prevents an officer from discussing an ongoing investigation. This results in the citizen complainant getting to tell his or her story, often repeatedly, with that account not being disputed by the police until the conclusion of the investigation. Unfortunately, this procedure can take weeks or months, depending on how involved the investigation is, by which time the public or the press no longer cares about the case.

This has a drastic impact on the psychological well-being of the officers involved, as well as their families, as they see their names trashed in the papers and on the news. Sometimes fellow officers may unintentionally distance themselves from an accused officer, wanting to avoid any negative publicity or association. Command staff and supervisors may also avoid contact with the officer in hopes of not contaminating the investigation, and the involved officer is often placed on administrative leave. This leads to the officer feeling abandoned and alone, with no one to talk to about the incident. Departments often don't consider this because their most pressing concern becomes distancing the department and its policies from the officer's behavior if necessary. Police administrators and officers need to remind themselves that police officers go into law enforcement to serve the public and do the right thing. If by being wrongly accused or by making a mistake, they are now vilified, the effects can be devastating. The worst-case scenario is the officer who commits suicide as his or her world crumbles, and lesser problems include turning to alcohol, marital problems, or extreme cynicism for the remainder of his or her career. Police administrators need to be cognizant of the emotional toll of internal investigations and have some procedures in place to help minimize those effects.

Summary

- Police deviance, which has a long tradition in U.S. police departments, appears to be intractable.

- The media highlights incidents of police corruption or misconduct.

- Ethics is defined as the study of what is good or bad conduct and is critical in understanding and confronting police misconduct.

- Police behavior is governed by the U.S. Constitution, the Bill of Rights, the Supreme Court, case law, state laws, department policies and procedures, the Law Enforcement Code of Ethics, and an oath of office.

- Police corruption has been around for many years, and several high-profile incidents have lead to the formation of commissions to study the problem.

- *Noble cause corruption* refers to situations where officers bend the rules to attain the "right" result.

- There are many different responses to police corruption, including investigations, discipline, and preventative actions.

- Preventative actions used to minimize the occurrences of corruption and misconduct include hiring processes, policies and procedures, training, supervision, promoting integrity within the department, and early intervention systems.

- Other forms of police misconduct include drug-related corruption, sleeping on duty, police deception, sex-related corruption, domestic violence in police families and biased-based policing.

- Although use of force is a necessary part of the job, it must be reasonable and appropriate. When officers cross the line, force becomes excessive, and brutality is even more severe with a significant disparity between the level of compliance and the amount of force used.

- Citizen oversight is often demanded by the community when citizens believe the police department is not being responsive to their concerns and investigations are not being fairly conducted.

- Police may be held liable for their actions through the state courts or the federal courts.

- Only a very small percentage of officers are involved in misconduct, and though it would be nice if we could eliminate all police deviance, it will probably never occur. Nevertheless, police departments must do all that they can to prevent police deviance.

Learning Check

1. Define police corruption. Identify some of the forms it takes.
2. Explain why some police officers become corrupt.
3. Discuss whether something about police work makes police corruption and other police deviance more likely than in other professions.
4. Define police brutality. Identify some of the forms it takes.
5. Identify and discuss forms of police deviance other than corruption and brutality.
6. Define noble cause corruption and give some examples.
7. List some ways that agencies can combat corruption.
8. Describe the effects of allegations of corruption on the officer, the agency, law enforcement in general and the community.
9. Do you feel the acceptance of gratuities is corruption? Should it be allowed? Explain or defend your answer.
10. Discuss the challenges involved in the exposure of and investigation of the crime of domestic violence in police families.

Key Terms

biased-based policing Any police-initiated activity that relies on a person's race or ethnic background rather than on behavior as a basis for identifying that individual as being involved in criminal activity.

bribe Payment of money or other contribution to a police officer with the intent to subvert the aim of the criminal justice system.

citizen oversight Also referred to as civilian review or external review. A method that allows for the independent citizen review of complaints filed against the police through a board or committee that independently reviews allegations of misconduct.

civil liability Potential liability for payment of damages as a result of a ruling in a lawsuit.

corruption Acts involving misuse of authority by a police officer in a manner designed to produce personal gain for the officer or others.

criminal liability Subject to punishment for a crime.

ethics The study of what constitutes good or bad conduct.

gratuities Items of value received by someone because of his or her role or job rather than because of a personal relationship.

grass-eaters Police officers who participate in the more passive type of police corruption by accepting opportunities of corruption that present themselves.

integrity test Proactive investigation of corruption in which investigators provide opportunities for officers to commit illegal acts.

internal affairs division The unit of a police agency that is charged with investigating police corruption or misconduct.

judicial review Process by which the actions of the police in areas such as arrests, search and seizure, and custodial interrogation are reviewed by the court system to ensure their constitutionality.

Knapp Commission Commission created in 1970 to investigate allegations of widespread, organized corruption in the New York City Police Department.

meat-eaters Officers who participate in a more aggressive types of corruption by seeking out and taking advantage of opportunities of corruption.

noble cause corruption Stems from ends-oriented policing and involves police officers bending the rules to achieve the "right" goal of putting a criminal in jail.

police deception Form of misconduct that includes perjury and falsifying police reports.

"rotten apple" theory Theory of corruption in which it is believed that individual officers within the agency are bad, rather than the organization as a whole.

Police Operations

© Royalty-Free/Corbis

Patrol Operations

© Michael Newman/Photo Edit Inc.

GOALS

- To acquaint you with the three traditional methods of doing police work and examine their effectiveness
- To introduce the academic studies of police patrol
- To discuss how law enforcement has responded to the academic studies
- To acquaint you with police traffic operations and special operations
- To discuss some of the innovative ways of performing the patrol function
- To make you aware of methods of resource allocation
- To discuss new tactical approaches to patrol operations
- To explore the various vehicles law enforcement is using for patrol activities
- To discuss police automobile pursuits
- To address new efforts to combat the drunk driving problem and efforts targeting aggressive driving
- To discuss special operations, including SWAT teams, emergency service units and K-9 units

Introduction

This chapter is about police operations: what the police do and how they do it. It covers police patrol operations, responding to 911 calls, allocation of resources, alternative crime-fighting strategies, traffic operations, and other police operational units.

The chapter will discuss the academic studies of the 1960s and 1970s, particularly the Kansas City study, which has changed our understanding of the effectiveness of the traditional methods of doing police work. The Kansas City study, as well as other studies, forced academics and progressive police administrators to look closely at their operations to see if there were better, more effective ways to do police work. We will examine some of the changes that have taken place as a result of these studies and some of the new, more effective ways of policing.

Most of this chapter will be related to police patrol operations, the core of policing. Patrol operations involve the activities and role of the patrol officer and the various methods of doing patrol work, including motorized and foot patrol. Additionally, the chapter will discuss traffic operations and special operations, including SWAT teams and emergency service units.

Traditional Methods of Police Work

The three cornerstones of traditional police work include: (1) random routine patrol, (2) rapid response to calls by citizens to 911, and (3) retroactive investigation of past crimes by detectives.[1]

The average U.S. police officer arrives at work at the beginning of his or her shift and receives the keys and the patrol car from the officer who used it on the previous tour. The officer then drives around a designated geographic area (**random routine patrol**). When the officer receives a call from the police dispatcher, he or she responds to the call and performs whatever police work is required—an arrest, first aid, breaking up a fight, taking a crime report, and so on (**rapid response to citizens' calls to 911**). If the call involves a crime, the officer conducts a preliminary investigation and often refers the case to a detective, who conducts a follow-up investigation of the crime (**retroactive investigation of past crimes by detectives**). As soon as the officer is finished handling the call, he or she resumes patrol and is ready to respond to another call.   *Cold Case*

These are the methods of traditional police work. However, are random routine patrol, rapid response to citizens' calls to 911, and retroactive investigation of past crimes by detectives the proper ways for the police to safeguard our communities? Are these methods effective? Is this combination of methods the only way to do police work? This chapter will address these issues, and retroactive investigation of past crimes will be examined in depth in Chapter 10.

Police Patrol Operations

When we think of the police, our first image is that of the man or woman in uniform driving a police car, at rapid speeds with lights and siren, to the scene of a crime or an accident. We also may think of the uniformed officer on foot patrol ("walking a beat") in a downtown business area, moving a drunk and disorderly citizen away from a group of ordinary shoppers. (**Foot patrol** is a method of deploying police officers that gives them responsibility for all policing activity by requiring them to walk around a defined geographic area.) We may think of a police officer on horseback or one on a motorcycle. All these officers have one thing in common: They are patrol officers.

Since the time of Sir Robert Peel (the promoter of the first organized, paid, uniformed police force in London in 1829), patrol has been the most important and visible part of police work to the public. Peel's major innovation and contribution to society was the idea of a continuous police presence throughout a community that is organized and delivered by means of regular patrol over a fixed beat by uniformed officers. Patrol is the essence of policing.

Activities of the Patrol Officer

Patrol is known as the foundation of the police department. Patrol officers are the uniformed officers who respond to calls for service, emergencies, and all sorts of disturbances that occur. They are the most visible arm of the criminal justice system as well as the gatekeepers to the system. Almost without exception, all police officers begin their career in patrol, and this is where they garner the bulk of their police experience. Patrol is where most sworn personnel are assigned and carry out the mission of the police agency. According to the U.S. Justice Department, 61 percent of sworn personnel in municipal law enforcement are in uniform and assigned to respond to calls for service.[2]

According to Samuel Walker and Charles Katz, the basic purpose of patrol has not changed since 1829. Patrol has the following purposes:

1. The deterrence of crime
2. The maintenance of a feeling of public security
3. Twenty-four-hour availability for service to the public[3]

Traditionally, the primary services provided by the patrol function include enforcing laws, deterring crime, maintaining order, keeping the peace, enforcing traffic laws and keeping traffic flowing, investigating accidents, conducting preliminary investigations, responding to calls for assistance and assisting those who cannot help themselves.

The patrol officer is the police department's generalist and foremost representative to the public. He or she performs numerous and varied duties in and for the community. Patrol officers face numerous complex problems on a daily basis and see things that most people never see. Patrol officers respond to calls about overflowing sewers and lights being out, reports of attempted suicides, domestic disputes, neighborhood disputes, dogs running loose, reports of Martians trying to gain entry to people's homes, reports of people banging their heads against brick walls, requests to check on the welfare of elderly people who haven't been seen for a few days, requests to check out strange smells, requests to "do something about" the aggressive person on the street corner, and requests for information and help with almost anything you can think of. When citizens don't know whom to call or other businesses or services are not available, they call the police.

The Legacy of O. W. Wilson

Until the 1970s, most of what we knew about patrol was written by O. W. Wilson, former dean of the School of Criminology at the University of California at Berkeley and a former police chief in Wichita, Kansas, and Chicago, and his associate, Roy Clinton McLaren, in the classic *Police Administration*. Wilson called patrol "the backbone of policing" and stated that patrol is designed to create "an impression of omnipresence," which will eliminate "the actual opportunity (or the belief that the opportunity exists) for successful misconduct."[4] The word omnipresence can be defined as "the quality of always being there." Thus, if the police are always there or seem to be always there, criminals cannot operate. Wilson's patrol ideas were designed to make the police appear to be as omnipresent as possible.

Wilson defined the distribution of patrol officers as the "assignment of a given number of personnel according to area, workload, time or function."[5] Under Wilson's theory, some police officers work the day shift, some work the evening shift, and others work the night shift. Officers are assigned to certain areas based on the workload (number of crimes, arrests, and calls for service) in a particular area. Patrol officers are also assigned according to the type of work they perform—foot, radio car, traffic, canine, or some other type of patrol function. Professional police management has consistently followed Wilson's ideas emphasizing the rational distribution of patrol officers according to a workload formula.

Implicit within Wilson's concept of random routine patrol by marked police vehicles was his insistence that the cars should contain one officer, rather than the two officers that were commonly used earlier. This was quite controversial at the time and remains so. Wilson believed that one-officer patrols could observe more than two-officer patrols could, that one-officer patrols would respond more quickly to calls for service, and that officers patrolling by themselves were actually safer than were officers patrolling in pairs. In a 2003 study of police officer attitudes toward one-officer versus two-officer patrol, officers generally agreed that they would perform the same regardless of whether they were in a one or two-officer patrol car; however, they believed that two-officer units should be used during the evening or midnight shift as well as in areas of the city where people mistrust the police and that two-officer patrols were generally more effective.[6] As chief of police in Wichita, Wilson popularized many of the innovations he had observed at Berkeley, including the use of the polygraph, marked police cars, and a crime laboratory.

By the 1960s, Wilson had become a giant in the field of policing, and his recommendations were taken as gospel. His *Police Administration* was the first textbook for police executives and continues to be used. Wilson firmly believed in honest law enforcement. He believed that corruption was the by-product of poor organization, lack of planning, and tangled lines of command. He developed the concept of preventive patrol, coined the term *crime analysis,* and believed that an aggressive omnipresent patrol force could thwart criminal behavior by reducing the opportunity for crime.[7]

Evaluating the Effectiveness of Police Work

Evaluating the effectiveness of police work is very difficult. If a city has a high crime rate, does it follow that its police department is not effective? If a city has a low crime rate, does it follow that its police department is an effective one? When we talk about crime, we are talking about many different and complex variables. The police cannot control all the variables that might produce crime, such as social disorganization; anger; poverty; hostility; revenge; psychological, social, or biological problems; and the desire to commit crime as an alternative to the world of work.

Despite the difficulties and problems associated with conducting academic and scientific research in policing, the research has been influential in the development of policing strategies during the last three decades. Although systematic research on policing is relatively new, it has influenced how police departments operate and public perceptions of policing. Changes in policy and practice around the country suggest that research has had particularly important conceptual and operational effects in patrol operations. Most of all, the research that has been conducted, though somewhat limited, has caused law enforcement personnel to reexamine their beliefs about crime and preventing crime and to consider more creative ways to address the crime issue.

One of the problems in conducting scientific studies of policing involves attempting to set up controlled experiments. When scientists conduct academic studies of the effects of a variable on something—for example, to see if a particular drug cures a particular illness—they conduct a controlled experiment. In a **controlled experiment,** two categories of groups are used. One group is the **experimental group,** and the other is the **control group.** The experimental group, in the drug example, is given the drug, whereas the control group is not given the drug. If the drug is effective, the experimental group will recover from the illness, and the control group will not.

Another example of a controlled experiment could be changing the packaging of a particular product sold in a store to see if putting a product in a red package results in more people buying the product than when the same product is offered in a blue box. The new red packages would be the experimental group, and the old blue packages would be the control group. If we leave all other variables the same (the price, where the packages are located in the store, and so on), and the red boxes sell at a better rate than the blue boxes, it can be said that the red boxes make a difference.

Can we have controlled experiments to see if a police department is effective? Can we eliminate police patrols from one neighborhood and compare the crime rate in that neighborhood with the crime rate in the neighborhood where there are police patrols? A myriad of problems accompany controlled experiments with crime. Is such experimentation ethical? Is it legal? This chapter will look at several controlled experiments with crime and see how they have affected our traditional concepts of doing police work.

Random Routine Patrol: The Kansas City Study

Random routine patrol, otherwise known as preventive patrol, involves a police officer driving around and within a community when he or she is not on an assignment from the radio dispatcher or a supervisor. Tradition has held that random routine patrol creates a sense of omnipresence and deters crime because a criminal will not chance committing a crime if a police officer might be just around the corner. Random routine patrol was believed to enable police officers to catch criminals in the act of committing their crimes. Just how effective is random routine patrol? The **Kansas City Patrol study** was the first attempt to actually test the effectiveness of random routine patrol.

The Kansas City Study in Brief

During 1972 and 1973, the Kansas City Police Department, under the leadership of Police Chief Clarence Kelly (who later became the director of the FBI) and with the support of the Police Foundation, conducted an experiment to test the effects of routine preventive patrol. This yearlong experiment has been both influential and controversial.

Fifteen patrol beats in Kansas City's South Patrol Division were used for the study. Five of these beats were assigned to a control group with no changes in normal patrol staffing or tactics. Five other beats were chosen as reactive beats, and all preventive patrolling was eliminated. Outside patrol units handled calls in the reactive beats, and units left the beats once they had handled the calls. The final five beats in the experiment were proactive beats, in which two to three times the usual level of preventive patrolling was provided. Thus, the reactive beats (with all routine patrol eliminated) and the proactive beats (with routine patrol increased) were the experimental groups. If random routine patrol is an effective way of policing our communities, we should expect to see changes in the reactive and proactive beats.

Before the outset of the experiment, researchers collected data on reported crime, arrests, traffic accidents, response times, citizen attitudes, and citizen and business victimization for each of the 15 beats. The researchers collected similar data after the conclusion of the yearlong experiment. During the experiment, the activities of the police officers assigned to the beats were observed and monitored. No one in the community was advised of the experiment.[8]

Results of the Kansas City Study

When the Kansas City study was finished, the researchers concluded, "Decreasing or increasing routine preventive patrol within the range tested in [the] experiment had no effect on crime, citizen fear of crime, community attitudes toward the police on the delivery of police service, police response time or traffic accidents."[9] In effect, the study failed to demonstrate that adding or taking away police patrols from an area made any difference within the community.

At the end of the experiment, no one in the community had any idea that an experiment regarding policing had been conducted in their community.

The conclusions of the Kansas City study shocked many people and differed from all the assumptions we had always made regarding police patrol. It had been commonly believed that putting more officers on patrol would cause a decrease in crime, and taking away police would cause an increase in crime. The Kansas City study told us that this basic assumption about police work was wrong. Or did it?

Critiques of the Kansas City Study

In an evaluation of the Kansas City study, James Q. Wilson cautions that the results should not be misinterpreted: "The experiment does not show that the police make no difference and it does not show that adding more police is useless in controlling crime. All it shows is that changes in the amount of random preventive patrol in marked cars does not, by itself, seem to affect over one year's time in Kansas City, how much crime occurs or how safe citizens feel." Wilson says that very different results might have occurred if changes had been made in how the police were used and not merely in the number of marked patrol cars placed in one area.[10]

Joseph D. McNamara, who succeeded Kelly as chief of the Kansas City Police Department in 1974 and later served as chief of the San Jose, California, Police Department, warned, "A great deal of caution must be used to avoid the error that the experiment proved more than it actually did. One thing the experiment did not show is that a visible police presence can have no impact on crime in selected circumstances." McNamara stressed the fact that the experiment seemed to show that police officers' uncommitted time (time they are not responding to 911 calls or doing self-initiated police work)—approximately 50 percent of their time—could be used more effectively. Uncommitted time probably should be devoted to activities with more specific objectives than routine patrol.[11]

Richard C. Larson, in contrast, reported that he found serious flaws in the research design of the experiment. He noted that when police cars in the reactive beats entered the area in response to calls, they made a visible police presence. In the eyes of citizens and potential criminals, this was the same as routine patrol. Larson also pointed out that police vehicles from other specialized units (who were not part of the experiment) operated in the reactive beats, thereby creating a visible police presence. Larson found other differences in the reactive beats. Officers undertook a higher rate of self-initiated activities (such as vehicle stops), and they used sirens and lights more often in responding to calls. Furthermore, there was a higher incidence of two or more cars responding to a call for service.[12]

The major proponent of the effectiveness of patrol, O. W. Wilson, and his associate McLaren, argued that despite the conclusions of the researchers, the value of police patrol cannot be measured by a statistical study like the Kansas City study alone and must be evaluated based on historical experience. Wilson and McLaren stated, "The fact remains that in the few situations in recent history in which police response was obviously not immediately available . . . wholesale looting and lawlessness have been the result."[13]

Wilson made that statement in the 1970s. In 2005, the absence of police patrols by the New Orleans Police Department was considered a significant factor in the looting and lawlessness in the city in the aftermath of Hurricane Katrina. Was Wilson prophetic? It must be remembered, however, that a myriad of factors in addition to the lack of police presence led to the disturbing results regarding human behavior following Katrina.

To date, only one attempt has been made to replicate the Kansas City experiment. A similar study in Albuquerque, New Mexico, reached essentially similar conclusions.[14] Another analysis revealed that the relationship between crime and the time police spend on patrol may be more complex than previously recognized. For example, in some instances, the rates of reported robbery have actually increased when police patrol has increased. This may be because citizens are more likely to report robberies when they know that police are concentrating more time and effort on detecting that crime.[15]

Value of the Kansas City Study

Gary W. Cordner, Kathryn E. Scarborough, and Robert Sheehan describe the value of the Kansas City study by saying that the study did not result in the elimination of preventive or random routine patrol but, rather, set the stage for further experimentation with alternative patrol strategies and tactics. Because of the study, police executives realized that they could try alternative patrol tactics without fearing that reduced random routine patrol would result in calamity.[16] It paves the way for using some, if not all, of the time that had previously been used in preventive patrol in the pursuit of more innovative and creative methods of addressing the crime problem.

In summary, the Kansas City study indicated that our traditional three cornerstones of policing might not be the most effective way to do police work. The Kansas City study definitely set the stage for the academic study of policing, which in turn has caused tremendous changes in our thinking about policing. A later section of this chapter will further explore police patrol—what patrol officers do and how they do it. In this chapter and the next, we will also look at new approaches to police work that resulted from the Kansas City study.

Rapid Response to Citizens' 911 Calls

Rapid response to citizens' calls to 911 has traditionally been thought of as a way in which the police could catch criminals while they were in the act of committing their crimes or as they were escaping from their crimes. The ideal scenario is this: A citizen observes a person committing a crime and immediately calls 911. The police respond in seconds and arrest the perpetrator. This sounds great, but it rarely works that way.

Another scenario follows: A citizen is mugged and, just after the mugging, immediately calls 911 and reports the crime. The police respond in seconds and catch the perpetrator as he or she is at the crime scene or in immediate flight from it. This also sounds great, but again, it rarely works that way. The traditional approach of rapid response to 911 calls was based on unexamined assumptions

© AP/Wide World Photos

Many areas of the country have gone to regional dispatch centers in an effort to provide more efficient communications services. 911 centers aid in the documentation of many facets of emergency response, allowing departments to use their resources in the most effective manner.

about police patrol. Research during the past 20 years has pointed out that we cannot depend on this television portrayal of police work.

Early Studies of Rapid Response

In 1967, the President's Commission on Law Enforcement and Administration of Justice, in its *Task Force Report: Science and Technology,* found that quick response to a citizen's report of a crime to 911 made an arrest more likely. However, the commission emphasized that only extremely quick response times were likely to result in arrest. The commission discovered that when police response time was one or two minutes, an arrest was likely, and improvements in the response time of even 15 to 30 seconds greatly improved the likelihood of an arrest. In contrast, when response time exceeded three or four minutes, the probability of an arrest dropped sharply.[17]

In 1973, the National Advisory Commission on Criminal Justice Standards and Goals recommended, "Urban area response time . . . under normal conditions should not exceed 3 minutes for emergency calls and 20 minutes for non-emergency

calls." The commission stated, "When the time is cut to 2 minutes, it can have a dramatic effect on crime."[18]

Later Studies of Rapid Response

In time, further studies of rapid response to citizens' calls to 911 were carried out. These studies took into account the complexity of response time, which the earlier research by the two commissions had failed to do. Total response time (from the moment of the crime to the arrival of the first police officer) consists of three basic components:

1. The time between when the crime occurs and the moment the victim or a witness calls the police (this element of response time is outside the police department's control)

2. The time required for the police to process the call (answer the phone, obtain details from the citizen, and dispatch a patrol car)

3. Travel time from the time the patrol car receives the call from the dispatcher until it arrives at the scene

Two studies looked even more carefully at response time and at the different types of situations that spur calls to 911 for police assistance. These studies found that victims often delay calling the police after a crime or other incident occurs. Sometimes no phone is available; sometimes the victims are physically prevented from calling by the perpetrator. Often, victims of crime are temporarily disoriented, frightened, ashamed, or even apathetic. Some people in one study reported that they first called parents, insurance companies, or their doctors. The later studies reported that the average citizen delay in calling the police for serious crimes was between five and ten minutes. The discovery that citizens often wait several minutes before calling the police puts response time in a different light and suggests that rapid response may not be as significant as was once thought.[19]

The later studies also made an important distinction between involvement crimes and discovery crimes. In involvement crimes, the victim is actually present when the crime occurs. Rapid response might be productive if the citizen has not delayed too long before calling 911. In discovery crimes, a citizen comes home (from work or vacation, for example) and discovers that a burglary has occurred. In this case, rapid police response is unlikely to matter because the crime probably occurred a long time before the call to the police. Frequently, then, the actual time of occurrence may be hours or days earlier, making even instantaneous police arrival irrelevant.[20]

The emphasis on rapid response time (one or two minutes) makes no sense for several reasons. First, citizens generally cannot or do not report crimes immediately. Second, it is unlikely that a police car can get to a given location in one or two minutes. Consider the delay in calling the police, the time involved in processing the call by the 911 operator, and the distance the available police car has to travel and the traffic with which the car's driver has to contend.

We will always need some type of rapid police response to citizens' calls to 911, even though we have to realize that a one- or two-minute response is highly unrealistic. We will always need rapid response to injury accidents, violent arguments and fights, in-progress calls, calls where someone is in danger or being hurt, as well as to those crimes where rapid response may be effective (the victim or witness calls immediately, and the perpetrator is still on the scene or is in immediate flight from it). Also, quick response improves the chances for finding and interviewing possible witnesses and securing and retrieving physical evidence for analysis. However, as the academic studies have indicated, alternative strategies to rapid response to citizens' calls to 911 are needed to make better use of police officers.

Later, we will discuss an alternative to rapid response, differential response to calls for service in which the police carefully screen all calls to 911 and only provide immediate response to serious crimes, crimes in progress, or other emergencies. In other types of calls, the police may provide a delayed response, take the report on the telephone, or advise the reporter to come into the station house to report the crime.

Academic Studies of the Police Patrol Function

Before the 1960s, there was little study of the police patrol function—what patrol officers do and how they do it. For years, O. W. Wilson's writings were the bible of policing. It took many years of study to realize that much of what Wilson had taught us about police patrol was wrong and was based on faulty assumptions. Despite the fact that many of Wilson's ideas were replaced by new ideas and concepts based on the subsequent research revolution in policing, we still owe a tremendous thanks to him as the first researcher to really study and write on police operations. As three of the leading police researchers since the 1980s, James J. Fyfe, Jack R. Greene, and William F. Walsh, said in their 1997 revised edition of Wilson's classic *Police Administration*:

> Other materials in this edition also are new and, in some cases, actually in conflict with information included in past editions. These conflicts, however, do not indicate that Fyfe, Greene, and Walsh are in disagreement with the Wilson/McLaren tradition. The Wilson/McLaren tradition is to present readers with the state of the art of police administration, rather than to perpetuate information that may be time-locked in earlier years. The fact is that the state of the art has changed since 1976: It is our honor to continue in the tradition of O. W. Wilson and Roy C. McLaren by attempting to present the state of the art as it exists at this writing.[21]

George L. Kelling and Mary A. Wycoff, in their 2001 *Evolving Strategy of Policing: Case Studies of*

ON THE JOB

Rushing to the Scene

When I entered policing, responding to calls with lights and siren was not that uncommon. We did it a lot more frequently than officers do today. I can remember responding to bar fights with lights and siren, as was the procedure at the time. After responding to many of these calls in this manner, I began to question the rationale of running red lights and driving over the speed limit with cars pulling over in every direction to get out of my way. I began to wonder why I was risking my life and the lives of other motorists as very rarely was there still a fight going on when I got there. Most of the time, friends had separated the individuals involved, and it was usually a situation of mutual (drunk) combatants. It didn't seem to be a call worth risking lives over. Over the years, police departments looked at this situation and came to similar conclusions. Our department started to strictly limit which calls we could respond to in an emergency mode because of the potential for injuries and death and the liability involved.

But early in my career we were very cognizant of police response times, and a bar fight was a call with potential injuries; we wanted to have a good response time. We were not considering the fact that often the fight had been going on for a while or might even be over before someone—usually management—decided to call the police. It was often a threat made by management when the subjects wouldn't leave the lounge. When the subjects didn't leave, the management picked up the phone and called police, the subjects saw they were serious and left, and consequently, they were often gone or leaving when we got there.

When police departments started examining the philosophy of immediate response and response time, it became apparent there were other factors that determined whether our response was in fact immediate. Often there was a delay before the call was even made so our "immediate" response lost a lot of its value. When departments weighed the issues of danger to the public and officers, departments severely restricted the types of calls that required an emergency response.

It took a long time, and officers still like to respond as an emergency vehicle and would like to do it more often. They may argue it's better to get to most situations earlier rather than later, but with streets increasingly more crowded at all hours of the day, it just isn't safe.

—Linda Forst

Strategic Change, write that during the era dominated by O. W. Wilson and his colleagues, roughly the 1920s through the 1970s, police strategy and management emphasized bureaucratic autonomy, efficiency, and internal accountability through command and control systems that focused on countering serious crime by criminal investigation, random preventive patrol by automobile, and rapid response to calls for service.[22] During the 1970s, however, research into police practices challenged the core competencies of police preventive patrol and rapid response to calls for service.

What do the police hope to accomplish through the use of patrol? William Gay, Theodore H. Schell, and Stephen Schack define the goals of patrol as follows: "crime prevention and deterrence, the apprehension of criminals, the provision of noncrime related service, the provision of a sense of community security and satisfaction with the police and the recovery of stolen property." They then divide routine patrol activity into four basic functional categories:

1. *Calls for services.* Responding to citizens' calls to 911 relative to emergencies or other problems accounts for 25 percent of patrol time.

2. *Preventive patrol.* Driving through a community in an attempt to provide what O. W. Wilson described as omnipresence accounts for 40 percent of patrol time.

3. *Officer-initiated activities.* Stopping motorists or pedestrians and questioning them about their activities account for 15 percent of patrol time.

4. *Administrative tasks.* Paperwork accounts for 20 percent of patrol time.[23]

James Q. Wilson's pioneering work, *Varieties of Police Behavior: The Management of Law and Order in Eight Communities,* attempted to study what police officers do. Wilson concluded that the major role of the police was "handling the situation" and believed that the police encounter many troubling incidents that need some sort of "fixing up." He says that enforcing the law might be one tool a patrol officer uses; threats, coercion, sympathy, understanding, and apathy might be others. Most important to the police officer, Wilson says, "is keeping things under control so that there are no complaints that he is doing nothing or that he is doing too much."[24]

For many years, the major role of police patrol was considered to be law enforcement. However, research conducted in the 1960s and 1970s by academics showed that very little of a patrol officer's time was spent on crime-fighting duties.

Patrol Activity Studies To determine what police actually do, researchers have conducted patrol activity studies. This research involved studying four major sets of data: data on incoming calls to police departments (calls to 911), calls radioed to patrol officers, actual activity by patrol officers, and police-citizen encounters.

The nature of incoming calls to police departments reveals the kinds of problems or conditions for which citizens call 911. Data from these calls can usually be retrieved from telephone logs or from recordings of conversations between callers and 911 operators. The nature of the calls radioed to patrol officers, or assignments given to police patrol units by 911 dispatchers, reveals the types of problems for which people call the police and the types of problems the police feel deserve a response by patrol units.

The collection of data regarding the actual activity of patrol officers during each hour of their tours is probably the best answer to the question, "What do police officers do?" This information includes activities the police are directed to perform from the 911 dispatcher, as well as the officers' self-initiated activities. These data can usually be retrieved from officers' activity reports and observations by researchers riding with police patrol officers.[25] Data on what occurs when an officer encounters a citizen—either when the officer is on assignment from the dispatcher or is on self-initiated activities—can best be retrieved from observations by researchers riding with police patrol officers.

The following sections summarize findings by researchers in each of the categories just described.

Robert Lilly found that of 18,000 calls to the Newport, Kentucky, Police Department made during a four-month period, 60 percent were requests for information and 13 percent concerned traffic problems. Only 2.7 percent of the calls were about violent crime; 1.8 percent of the calls concerned theft.[26] In a survey of 26,000 calls to the police in 21 different jurisdictions, George Antunes and Eric Scott found that only 20 percent of the calls involved the report of criminal activity.[27] James Q. Wilson conducted a study of all calls to the Syracuse, New York, Police Department during a six-day period. He discovered that only one-tenth of the calls involved incidents in which the police would have to perform a law enforcement function.[28]

Albert J. Reiss monitored all calls to the Chicago Police Department during a 28-day period. Of all the calls, 58 percent were regarding criminal or potentially criminal matters. Of these calls, 26 percent involved breaches of the peace, 16 percent were offenses against property, 6 percent were offenses against persons, 5 percent were violations regarding automobiles, and 3 percent involved suspicious persons. Reiss noted that the Chicago police themselves categorized as noncriminal some 83 percent of the incidents reported to them.[29] Lawrence W. Sherman analyzed more than 300,000 dispatches in Minneapolis and discovered that approximately 33 percent involved conflict management; 28 percent, property crime; 19 percent traffic problems; 13 percent, service; 5 percent, miscellaneous; and 2 percent, stranger-to-stranger crime.[30]

Summarizing these studies of calls to 911, Cordner reports that most of the calls to police departments are requests for information, requests for services, and reports of disputes and disturbances.[31] He also points out that sizable portions of patrol workload are calls regarding order maintenance, traffic, and service responsibilities. Reiss found that the average police officer's typical tour of duty does not involve a single arrest.[32] Egon Bittner found that patrol officers average about one arrest per month and only three Index crime arrests per year.[33] Finally, Kelling and his associates in the Kansas City study found that 60 percent of patrol time in Kansas City was uncommitted.[34]

Cordner, commenting on these studies, writes that most patrol work involves not doing anything very specific but, rather, taking breaks, meeting with other officers, and engaging in preventive patrolling. He states that administrative duties are the most common in police patrol, and the remaining time is divided among police-initiated activities

(33 percent) and calls from the police dispatcher (67 percent). Cordner says the police-initiated activities are mostly related to law enforcement (particularly traffic enforcement). The calls from the dispatcher involve a blend of crimes, disputes, traffic problems, and service requests, with crimes and disputes being the most common.[35]

The Police Services Study examined patrol work in 60 different neighborhoods. Observers accompanied patrol officers on all shifts in 24 different police departments. The observers collected information on each encounter between a police officer and a citizen, detailing nearly 6,000 encounters. The study found that only 38 percent of all police-citizen encounters dealt primarily with crime-related problems. Most of these were nonviolent crimes or incidents involving suspicious circumstances. The next most common kinds of encounters were disorder problems and traffic-related matters, each accounting for 22 percent of the total. Finally, 18 percent of the police-citizen encounters were primarily of a service nature. The Police Services Study data also indicated that the police invoked the law relatively rarely, making arrests in only 5 percent of the encounters and issuing tickets in less than 10 percent of the encounters.[36]

Jack R. Greene and Carl B. Klockars have described a survey of a full year's worth of computer-aided dispatch (CAD) data for the Wilmington, Delaware, Police Department. Their survey has given us a more recent look at police activity.[37] Greene and Klockars also describe many of the previous studies regarding police activity and note that most of these studies, as we have seen, reveal that much of police work deals with problems that are not related to crime.

The study revealed that the police spent 26 percent of their time on criminal matters, 9 percent on order maintenance assignments, 4 percent on service-related functions, 11 percent on traffic matters, 2 percent on medical assistance, and 12 percent on administrative matters. Five percent of their time, they were unavailable for service, and almost 30 percent of the time was clear or unassigned, when the officers performed random routine patrol.

Two of the significant findings of this study follow. First, when the percentage of time involved in unavailable, administrative, and clear time is excluded from the data, the data indicate that the police spent almost 50 percent of their time on criminal matters, 16 percent on order maintenance, 8 percent on service, 21 percent on traffic, and

4 percent on medical assistance. Second, 47 percent of the officers' time was spent on activities other than actual assignments.

In 2005, the National Institute of Justice reported the results of a national survey of contacts between the police and citizens, the Police-Public Contact Survey (PPCS). The report revealed that about 21 percent of the total population, age 16 or older, have face-to-face contacts with the police each year. Almost half of these contacts involve some form of motor vehicle or traffic-related issue, about 26 percent contact the police to report a crime, and about 3 percent of the contacts occur because the police suspected them of involvement in a crime. Fifty-nine percent of these contacts were initiated by police with the remaining 41 percent initiated by the citizen or other interested party.[38] It would appear from this survey that police officers do spend a good portion of their time on crime-related calls.

Observations on the Studies We have seen that the police spend their time performing numerous types of duties. They spend significant time on criminal matters, but the measurement of this time varies depending on the study.

Looking at all the police activity studies, it is obvious why most experts today agree that the great bulk of police patrol work is devoted to what has been described as random routine patrol, administrative matters, order maintenance, and service-related functions. Sheehan and Cordner state that, although the studies performed a valuable function by challenging the crime-fighting image of police work, by the late 1970s many police chiefs and scholars carried them too far and began to downplay and deemphasize the crime-related and law enforcement aspects of police work.[39] James Q. Wilson noted that he would "prefer the police to act and talk as if they were able to control crime."[40]

Sheehan and Cordner sum up all the studies on "what do cops do" as follows:

> Taking all of these studies into consideration, we think a middle of the road position is advisable. It is obvious now that police work is not so completely dominated by crime fighting as its public image and media misrepresentations would suggest. However, it is equally clear that crime-related matters occupy an appreciable portion of the police workload. The available research conclusively demonstrates

that those who have been arguing that police work has little or nothing to do with crime know little or nothing about police work.[41]

A former police chief gives a vivid description of police patrol work that may point more to the truth of the matter than can academic studies:

Cops on the street hurry from call to call, bound to their crackling radios, which offer no relief—especially on summer weekend nights. That is the time when the ghetto throbs with noise, booze, violence, drugs, illness, blaring TVs, and human misery. The cops jump from crisis to crisis, rarely having time to do more than tamp one down sufficiently and leave for the next. Gaps of boredom and inactivity fill the interims, although there aren't many of these in the hot months. Periods of boredom get increasingly longer as the night wears on and the weather gets colder.[42]

From the Foot Beat to the Patrol Car

Patrol allocation models give the police answers as to where and when to assign officers. Over the years, however, different methods of deploying police officers have been used. The two major deployments are motorized patrol and foot patrol.

Police patrol, as we saw in Chapter 1, is a historical outgrowth of the early watch system. The first formal police patrols were on foot, and the cop on the beat became the symbol and very essence of policing in the United States. Furthermore, the cop on the beat became the embodiment of American government to most citizens. However, as early as the 1930s—even before the automobile had become an integral part of American life—foot patrols were beginning to vanish in favor of the more efficient and faster patrol car.[43]

By the late 1930s and 1940s, police management experts stressed the importance of motorized patrol as a means of increasing efficiency, and the number of cities using motorized patrol grew.

By the 1960s, the efficiency of the remaining foot patrols was being challenged. Foot patrols were considered geographically restrictive and wasteful of personnel. Foot officers, who at the time had no portable radios (these did not become available until the 1970s), were not efficient in terms of covering large areas or being available to be signaled and sent on assignments. Thus, to management experts, foot patrols were not as efficient as the readily available radio cars.

In 1968, the District of Columbia Crime Commission, criticizing the District of Columbia's continued use of foot patrol, stated, "The department's continued reliance on foot patrol is an inefficient and outdated utilization of manpower resources. . . . As long as the Department uses foot patrol as the primary method of patrol, however, available economics will not be realized and the city will not be provided the best possible police service."[44]

At about this time, many cities—including Kansas City, Missouri; Dallas, Texas; Phoenix, Arizona; Omaha, Nebraska; Oklahoma City; Birmingham, Alabama; and other large cities—had shifted almost totally away from foot patrols, replacing them with more deployable two-person car patrols. However, as a report of the Kansas City, Missouri, Police Department pointed out, in 1966, the number of foot patrol beats per shift in Boston, Baltimore, Pittsburgh, and other major urban centers remained in the hundreds.[45]

At almost the same time these reports from Kansas City and the District of Columbia were prepared, the International Association of Chiefs of Police (IACP) went one step further, strongly advocating a conspicuous patrol that conveyed a sense of police omnipresence. The association felt that this could be best achieved using a highly mobile force of one-person cars:

The more men and more cars that are visible on the streets, the greater is the potential for preventing a crime. A heavy blanket of conspicuous patrol at all times and in all parts of the city tends to suppress violations of the law. The most economical manner of providing this heavy blanket of patrol is by using one-man cars when and where they are feasible.[46]

The change from foot to motor patrol revolutionized U.S. policing. It fulfilled the expectations of the management experts by enabling police departments to provide more efficient patrol coverage—that is, covering more areas more frequently and responding more quickly to calls for service. However, one major unforeseen consequence of the shift to motorized patrol continues to haunt us. Motorized patrol tended to isolate police officers from the community as they quickly drove through the streets to respond to the calls for service, and the personal contact with the officer on the foot beat was lost.

Motor patrol was very efficient in coverage, but it involved a trade-off in the relationship between the police and the community. Now police officers had few contacts with ordinary citizens in normal situations; most calls involved problems, either crime or order maintenance problems. A growing rift began to develop between the police and the public. Few people noticed this change in policing until the riots of the 1960s dramatized the problem of police–community relations.[47]

As early as 1968, experts began to realize the problems created by the emphasis on the efficiency of the patrol car and by the absence of the foot officer's closeness to the community. The *Task Force Report* of the President's Commission on Law Enforcement and Administration of Justice noted, "The most significant weakness in American motor patrol operations today is the general lack of contact with citizens except when an officer has responded to a call. Forced to stay near the car's radio, awaiting an assignment, most patrol officers have few opportunities to develop closer relationships with persons living in the district."[48] Despite the drawbacks, by 1978, the *Police Practices Survey* found that more than 90 percent of all beats were handled by motor patrol. Foot patrol accounted for less than 10 percent.[49]

Return to Foot Patrol

Police officers on motorized patrols are more efficient than foot officers. Cars get to locations much more quickly; they can cover much larger areas; and they provide the officers more comfort in inclement weather. Cars also allow the transport of all the equipment that officers of today have in their arsenals. However, as we have seen, some police managers and other experts feel that automobile patrolling had led to a distancing of police officers from the community that they serve.

In the mid-1980s, in an attempt to get the police closer to the public and to avoid the problems caused by the alienation of radio car officers from the community, an emphasis on foot patrol began to return to many cities. By 1985, foot patrol had returned to Newark, New Jersey; Oakland and Los Angeles, California; Detroit and Flint, Michigan; Houston, Texas; Boston; New York City; Atlanta, Georgia; Tampa, Florida; Minneapolis; Cincinnati; and many other cities. A 1984 survey revealed that approximately two-thirds of medium-sized and large police departments used foot patrol in some form. Researchers arrived at the following conclusions about the reinstitution of foot patrol in Newark and Flint:

1. When foot patrol is added in neighborhoods, levels of fear decrease significantly.

2. When foot patrol is withdrawn from neighborhoods, levels of fear increase significantly.

3. Citizen satisfaction with police increases when foot patrol is added in neighborhoods.

4. Police who patrol on foot have a greater appreciation for the values of the neighborhood residents than do police who patrol the same area in automobiles.

5. Police who patrol on foot have greater job satisfaction, less fear, and higher morale than do officers who patrol in automobiles.[50]

A thorough study conducted in Newark regarding foot patrols was unable to demonstrate that either adding or removing foot patrol affected crime in any way. However, Newark citizens involved in this study were less fearful of crime and more satisfied with services provided by officers on foot patrol than services by officers on motorized patrol. Also, Newark citizens in this study were aware of additions and deletions of foot patrol from their neighborhoods, in contrast with the Kansas City study, where citizens did not perceive changes in the level of motorized patrol. Thus, the **Newark foot patrol study** does not prove that foot patrols reduce crime but, rather, that foot patrols actually make citizens feel safer. Experience indicates that citizens want to see a return to the old "cop on the beat."[51]

The best evidence that citizens want foot patrols may have been shown in Flint. Despite the highest unemployment rate in the nation, citizens there voted in 1982 and 1985 to increase their taxes to extend foot patrol to the entire city.[52]

Interviews over a four-year period disclosed that the Neighborhood Foot Patrol program in Flint improved relationships between the police and the community. Residents of the community indicated their belief that the police on foot patrol were more responsive to their needs than had been the case before the experimental program.[53]

Citizens want and like foot patrol officers. Why does this more expensive form of policing seem more effective than traditional radio car patrol? It's not necessarily the implementation of foot patrol itself but, rather, the relationship that develops between the officer and the community because of the officer's increased accessibility. Through relationships with the community members, the officer will feel a part of the community and work to address the true underlying issues affecting the community, and the citizens will feel an improved sense of safety when they feel they can trust their police officers.

Patrol Innovations: Working Smarter

These studies and the resulting challenging of long-term beliefs regarding policing in general and patrol in particular, has caused law enforcement to examine traditional ways of doing things. If random patrol produces no real benefit, how can that time be better spent? Is there another type of patrol activity that might prove more productive? If responding immediately and in emergency mode is not necessarily beneficial, how can we organize our response so that it is appropriate to the call for service and reduces the potential danger to the officer and the public? Can we couple the two issues and come up with blocks of time to spend in other ways in an effort to address crime problems?

In the overall realization that the crime problem is not entirely under the control of law enforcement, the importance of involving the community in the crime-fighting effort has become clear. Much of the police role involves order maintenance and service activities. Developing a partnership and a working relationship with the community can help address these issues and make the law enforcement mission successful. This is the driving force behind community policing, which will be more thoroughly discussed in Chapter 12.

Evidence–Based Policing

The revelation that some experimentation could be conducted and could possibly challenge long-held beliefs led some researchers to stress that using scientific research could provide great information for improving police response and tactics to various situations. To the extent that relevant scientific research can be conducted without endangering the community or raising ethical issues, it could provide an excellent scientific basis for future activities and programs. Noted criminologist Lawrence W. Sherman proposed this concept in 1998 and calls it **evidence-based policing** (EBP). He defines it as "the use of the best available research on the outcomes of police work to implement guidelines and evaluate agencies, units, and officers" ("evidence" refers to scientific evidence not criminal evidence). To successfully make use of evidence-based policing, departments will have to let go of the traditional wisdom that has become part of department history and be willing to deviate from "the way we've always done it." Sherman recommends departments access the "best practices" from the literature and adapt them to their specific laws, policies, and community. He then advocates monitoring and evaluating the project to determine if it is working and if it could be improved. The sharing of the information with other agencies will continue to add to the knowledge available.[54] This philosophy can be used in most areas of patrol in which police are looking to improve effectiveness.

Modern Response to Citizens' 911 Calls

The current popular alternatives to random routine patrol and rapid response to citizens' 911 calls are directed patrol, split-force patrol, and differential response to calls for service. These innovative approaches to policing are designed to make better use of officers' patrol time, as well as to make better use of a department's resources.

Directed Patrol

An alternative to random routine patrol is **directed patrol**, in which officers are given specific directions to follow when they are not responding to calls. The directed patrol assignments are given to officers before they begin their tour and are meant to replace uncommitted random patrol time with specific duties that police commanders believe will be effective. Directed patrol assignments can be based on crime analysis, specific problems, or complaints received from the community. In departments using the community policing philosophy, patrol officers are often given the freedom of determining where and when their directed patrol efforts should be directed based on crime analysis and their experiences.

Several studies present some evidence that target crimes were reduced by directed patrol. By basing directed patrol assignments on statistical studies, many of the inadequacies of random, unstructured patrol may be overcome. The data suggest that citizen satisfaction and crime control efforts increase when patrol is based on a systematic analysis of crime. A significant recent example of a directed patrol program that achieved positive results was the "Kansas City Gun Experiment." Working with the University of Maryland, the Kansas City, Missouri, Police Department focused extra directed patrol attention to gun crimes in a "hot spot" area that was determined by computer analysis. The goal was to determine whether vigorously enforcing gun laws could reduce gun crimes. A special unit was assigned to the area (they did not respond to radio calls), and guns were removed from citizens following searches incident to arrest for other crimes and other valid stop and frisk situations. During the 29-week experiment, the gun patrol officers made thousands of car and pedestrian checks, traffic stops, and more than 600 arrests. The gun patrol efforts did affect crime rates. There was a decrease of 49 percent in gun crimes in the target area compared with a slight increase in a nontargeted area. Drive-by shootings and homicides decreased significantly. Interestingly, none of the seven contiguous beats showed a significant increase in gun crime, indicating that there was little crime displacement effect.[55]

Community surveys conducted before and after the program was initiated indicated that citizens in the target area were less fearful of crime and more satisfied with their neighborhood than were residents in companion areas. After the extra directed patrols were ended, crime rates went back to their normal levels.

Joseph J. Senna and Larry J. Siegel indicated that the Kansas City gun patrol experiment suggests that a modest police patrol effort targeting a specific crime problem can produce dramatic effects on the crime rate.[56] Success could be attributed to taking violent offenders off the street or a deterrence effect. Whether such efforts should be made part of general police policy remains to be seen. They could produce risks to officer safety, provoke hostile reactions from citizens, and make people subject to police searches hostile and angry. These risks may be acceptable if aggressive police action could significantly reduce the threat of gun violence.

Split-Force Patrol

As we have just seen, directed patrol is designed so officers can pay particular attention to specific crimes and disorder while they are not on assignment from the police dispatcher. One of the problems with directed patrol, however, is that calls for service often interrupt the performance of directed patrol assignments. **Split-force patrol** offers a solution to this problem. One portion of the patrol force is designated to handle all calls dispatched to patrol units. The remaining portion of the officers working that tour are given directed patrol assignments with the assurance that except for serious emergencies, they will not be interrupted. The most extensive test of the split-force strategy was conducted in Wilmington, Delaware. The evaluation of the experiment found that this patrol improved both call-handling productivity and patrol productivity, while enhancing patrol professionalism and accountability.[57]

The Houston Police Department, faced with a spiraling crime rate, implemented a form of split-force patrol called the high-intensity patrol (HIP). HIPs were an effort to put more officers on the streets in different parts of the city during peak crime hours. The HIP officers performed highly visible patrol in specific areas to emphasize the police presence but were directed not to answer 911 calls and to remain patrolling in their assigned areas. Critics of the Houston program state that it was mismanaged and calls were allowed to accumulate because not enough officers were assigned to handling calls. The program garnered the nickname, "the drive-by-and-wave program." One officer stated, "The regular officers were really upset because they are running from one call to another while the other guys weren't doing anything.[58] This can sometimes be a complaint heard in departments employing this strategy, particularly if the program hasn't been thoroughly explained or the rank and file does not buy into the program and its goals.

As of 2004, the Houston Police Department continued to emphasize directed patrol as a strategy in addressing crime issues as well as nuisance calls. Although the department could not credit a slight reduction in crime to this strategy, the administrators do believe these patrols have led to a decrease in fear of crime and an increase in citizen satisfaction with the police. Department representatives meet regularly with citizens' groups to discuss issues of importance and develop plans to address these issues. Approximately 30 percent of the patrol force is devoted to specialty units working directed patrols, and, though there is still some resistance among officers, it has declined dramatically. This decline can be attributed partly to the fact that commanders are now allowing these specialty units to handle calls for service at peak times, particularly during shift changes. This has minimized the problem of calls stacking up at busy times for the patrol units handling calls for service.

Differential Response to Calls for Service and the 911 System

Differential response to calls for service is a policy that abandons the traditional practice of responding to all calls for service. In differential response, responses to citizens' calls to 911 for service are matched to the importance or severity of the calls. Reports of injuries, crimes, or emergencies in progress, as well as reports of serious past crimes, continue to receive an immediate response by sworn police. However, less serious calls are handled by alternative methods. Conditions for which delayed or alternative responses are appropriate include the following: delayed burglaries, thefts, vandalisms, lost property, and insurance reports.

Differential response alternatives can replace sending a patrol unit to investigate a past crime. A patrol unit can be sent later, when there are fewer calls for service. The caller can be asked to come into the precinct headquarters to report the crime. The call can be transferred to a nonsworn member, who then takes the report over the phone. In some departments, the report can be made online. Finally, the dispatcher can make an appointment for a nonsworn member to respond to the caller's home to take a report. Differential response to calls for service is designed to reduce and better manage the workload of patrol officers. It gives patrol officers more time to devote to directed patrol, investigations, or crime prevention programs.

The idea of differential response for calls arose from the studies that looked at the value of rapid response for police officers. This program also makes sense when looking at the overall use of resources, including both personnel and equipment (such as the police vehicle and fuel). Perhaps rapid response is good for police public relations—"See how fast we respond when you call!"—but the allocation of scarce patrol resources should depend on police effectiveness rather than on public relations. Research has shown that most citizens will accept explanations of alternative police responses if the explanations are politely and logically presented. Departments have different ways of presenting this information and educating the public about their policies, and the Internet can increase the available options. The Arlington, Texas, Police Department explains on its web page about the policy regarding response to 911 calls and how and why the department prioritizes calls.

Departments suffering from financial difficulties that prevent them from hiring additional officers may benefit most from differential response. They can spread out the workload while ensuring that all emergency calls are responded to and all reports to past crimes and incidents are recorded and investigated. They also make use of less-expensive civilian personnel and perhaps even volunteers in some of this report taking by stacking nonpriority calls until the zone car is available, rather than sending an adjacent zone car immediately. This saves department resources and identifies a need to realign the zones if a disparity in workload becomes apparent. Studies also indicate that, in addition to the benefits to the departments, citizens are not unhappy with delayed response from police departments even when they must wait an hour or more for a police response.[59] This is especially true when the citizen is aware there will be a delay, and the rationale is explained. Many citizens find the new options, including online reporting, phone reporting, and referrals, more convenient for their busy schedules.

An example of this process includes the trend for most cities to minimize the time and resources spent responding to false alarm calls. By legislating ordinances and working with alarm companies, most departments have been able to decrease or at least keep the number of alarm calls constant even though the use of alarm systems has risen greatly. These efforts include ordinance development, registration of alarms, graduated fine structure, new equipment standards, suspension of response to chronic abusers, and the use of enhanced call verification where the alarm company makes numerous phone calls before calling the police agency with what appears to be a needed response. Not that long ago law enforcement responded to every alarm that went off, whether it was one of 20 going off during a thunderstorm or the residence that has a faulty alarm system that is set off on a daily basis by the family pet. In an effort to manage the police resources, as well as enhance officer safety (officers can develop a "false alarm" mentality that leads to injury or death on the "real" call), cities saw the necessity to change their response methods.[60]

The 911 and 311 systems have evolved over the years to make police departments more effective and to assist their efforts to manage their resources. Traditionally, the 911 call has determined the police department priorities. Before undertaking the efforts to employ differential response to calls, citizens more or less made the decision of what call was handled when, by what they said when they called in and when they called in. When the 911 number was introduced by AT&T in 1968, the concept was very exciting. By 1993, more than 90 percent of police departments with populations greater than 50,000 had 911 in place, and calls to 911 had skyrocketed because of the promotion and advertising regarding this number.[61] Police departments strive to educate their citizens to only use 911 in true emergencies, and that is often the first question the call takers ask the caller. Unfortunately, when someone needs help but doesn't know who to call, 911 is often the number that person remembers. Recently, a movement to use a 311 system to take some of the demand off the 911 lines and keep it available for true emergencies has been undertaken. A 311 system allows non-emergency calls to be redirected or referred to other referral agencies or government agencies, either by citizens directly calling 311 or by 911 operators quickly rerouting the appropriate calls to 311.

In the mid to late 1990s, jurisdictions began to introduce the 311 system to relieve overburdened 911 systems. Baltimore, Maryland, and Dallas, Texas, were studied to determine how the addition of a 311 system affected the 911 system as well as officer workload. The study found that accompanied by an effective public awareness campaign, a 311 system can greatly reduce the 911 call burden by removing non-emergency calls for service or information from the queue and sending them to more appropriate agencies. In these two cities, even though it appeared to free time for police officers, most officers did not notice an increase in

discretionary time. The researchers believe it can affect officers' free time but to have that occur, recommends that departments not have officers respond to 311 calls but simply make the referral to an alternate referral agency.[62]

■——————————————————

Allocation of Resources

Personnel

Personnel are the most expensive part of a police department's budget. In this day of shrinking budgets, agencies must allocate their personnel in the most efficient way possible and consider other than traditional ways of doing things. Qualified candidates for police officer are not as plentiful as they have been at other times in the past. Most departments have reexamined their roles and tasks and are questioning whether certain jobs need to be done, how they might be better done—say, over the phone or online—and who should do them. Many departments have increased their use of civilians for nonhazardous jobs such as evidence technician, accident investigator, property technician, call taker, and front-desk attendant. This allows the sworn officers to be used for the more hazardous duties. This can help a department put more officers on the street in an effort to combat crime and keep the residents safe.

Scheduling officers is also a big issue. You don't want to have too many officers on duty at one time so they are climbing all over each other to respond to calls nor do you want to be understaffed should a significant emergency occur. Unfortunately, law enforcement is a very unpredictable field. You never know what is going to happen and it can be extremely quiet and boring one minute, but in the second it takes for an alert tone to come over the radio, the day or night can become crazy. This is especially important if the department wants to conduct directed patrol activities to address certain crime problems.

Traditionally, departments commonly used equal staffing for every shift. In other words, there were 10 officers on days, 10 officers on evenings and 10 officers on midnights. Officers and administrators alike knew the workload wasn't the same, but it was difficult to quantify before computers. Now there is plenty of data available as long as departments know how to collect it and analyze it. Departments can determine workload by types of call and areas of the city by the hour. This can help to design beats or zones so that the workload is more evenly divided between officers. Departments can also determine what kind of calls are happening at what hours of the day, how much time the particular calls take, and whether they are and can be handled by one officer, two officers, or perhaps even more.

A zone or beat with a big mall in it might be extremely busy during the day with shoplifter calls, stolen vehicles, vehicle burglaries, robberies, and so on. This might require one, two, or even three officers during certain hours of the day but during the midnight shift could be made part of another zone or handled by an officer who is also handling the adjacent zone. Likewise, in certain areas of town the calls for service will increase significantly at night because of local drinking establishments, people hanging out on the street, or gang activity. These beats or zones may require more than one car or possibly two-officer cars.

Departments have also gone to staggered shift changes and briefings. Beside the obvious issue of the criminal element quickly figuring out when shift change occurs by all the patrol cars heading in at the end of the shift, there is also the issue of responding to emergency calls that come in around shift change. How this is handled will affect the overtime budget and personnel costs. If the patrol cars are all close to or in the station at a particular time, the response time will be delayed even if a car responds immediately. Besides that issue, the determination would have to be made for a crime that occurs for example, 20 minutes before shift change. Should an officer due to get off be held over to handle the call on overtime, should an oncoming unit be sent out early, or should the call be held for the oncoming beat car after briefing. If a few of these calls come in, conceivably most of units from a new shift could be tied up as soon as they hit the street. By staggering shifts and briefings for half the force by an hour, this problem could be solved. Cars would be scattered around the city to respond to emergencies and overtime costs could be minimized as well as the tying up of all the oncoming units. The concern in the past was often the idea of conducting more than one briefing per shift but with the use of computers and mobile digital terminals, this concern is lessened because officers can brief themselves if necessary.

Departments that want to employ directed patrol or encourage officers to conduct initiated activity need to be knowledgeable about what kind of time an officer has available. The studies that have been conducted on officers' use of time are fairly limited and dated. Times have changed, and every city or jurisdiction is different. With computers and the knowledge of what type of information they want to collect, departments can conduct their own studies on a yearly or quarterly basis and have exactly the information they need for their particular circumstances. In general, officers working the day and evening shifts are going to have more time devoted to calls for service and little "free time" in which to conduct activity aimed at discovering suspicious activity or individuals. During the midnight shift when most residents are asleep, there will be far fewer calls for service received through dispatch and much more officer-initiated activity as officers drive their beats looking for suspicious activity and checking on their businesses, and so forth. These officer-initiated activities also frequently involve arrests that can be time consuming and keep an officer tied up for several hours on paperwork and possibly transporting prisoners. If a city wants officers to conduct proactive efforts, they need to make sure enough people are working so that there is enough discretionary time for an officer to do so.

A city that correctly analyzes all this data will have a better working knowledge of how many officers are needed per shift and by the day of the week, and so on. It is a very complicated issue, however, because this information and these needs must be tempered by proper or humane work schedules and contract or collective bargaining restrictions. If officers like particular shifts—say the 12-hour shift—they will often try to get it in the union contract so that it can't be changed arbitrarily. Another issue to contend with is how officers choose their schedules. Is it by seniority, where perhaps the most senior officers all end up working days with weekends off and all rookies work midnights on the weekends? Should officers work fixed schedules for a certain amount of time—for example, midnight shift with Sunday, Monday, and Tuesday off for six months—or should squads rotate together—work a month of days followed by a month of midnights—in an effort to make it more fair?

Scheduling of personnel is very challenging and complicated with many competing factors to be considered. Studies are being conducted to look at the health ramifications of shift work in general and whether it is better to rotate forward or backward or have two days or three days off. But in a 24/7 service as law enforcement is, there is no getting around the fact that all shifts must be appropriately covered. Fortunately, computer programs and models can now accommodate 8-, 10-, and 12-hour shifts to help administrators with this task.

Vehicles

Most departments use fleet vehicles—that is, patrol vehicles that are used by different officers around the clock. This allows the jurisdiction to get the most use of its vehicles and have the fewest number of vehicles needed to patrol the streets. This is viewed as an efficient use of resources especially, when all officers report to the same location for the start and end of their shift. Agencies that cover a bigger geographical area, such as sheriff's departments and state patrols, often find this impractical. They issue officers their own vehicles, which the officers then take home with them at the end of every shift. This allows officers to go in service from their homes and start responding to calls immediately. Officers also have all of their equipment already loaded and stowed in the vehicle. The vehicle loading and inspection time is greatly reduced for these officers and maximizes their in-service time.

Some cities with a central shift change area have also looked at and implemented take-home vehicle plans. Although initially significantly more expensive than fleet programs, these patrol vehicles last longer because they receive less wear and tear and abuse that comes from 24-hour usage. It is also believed that officers take better care of these vehicles when they are "theirs" and maintain them well and drive them more carefully. The added incentive for cities to undertake programs like these are the ability to attract quality candidates with the lure of the extra benefit of a take-home vehicle and the increased police visibility while these vehicles are driven around town, to and from work, and parked in neighborhoods. Some also believe there might be a benefit in improved community relations as citizens see their officers (with vehicles) at the park running the fitness trail or coaching a little league team and realize officers are just like everyone else and are actually part of the community.

The allocation of police vehicles is a significant part of the police budget and, consequently, how to best accomplish this task is a big decision. Motor vehicles are a major part of most police

departments' operations, so many policies and procedures govern usage and maintenance and so forth of the vehicles, regardless of which plan the department may elect to follow.

Alternative Strategies

Police departments are using varying strategies to combat the crime problem. These include tactical operations, decoy vehicles, and various types of vehicles for the officers to patrol on.

Uniformed Tactical Operations

Uniformed tactical operations involve the use of traditional patrol operations in a more aggressive manner. The two basic kinds of uniformed tactical operations are aggressive patrol tactics and saturation patrol. Uniformed tactical units are officers who are relieved of routine patrol responsibilities, such as random routine patrol and handling calls for service, so they can concentrate on proactive crime control. Uniformed tactical units often saturate an area that is experiencing a serious crime problem. The tactical units are aggressive and make numerous pedestrian and vehicle stops to increase the likelihood of encountering offenders. These specially assigned officers make numerous field interrogations. A field interrogation or interview is a contact with a citizen initiated by a patrol officer who stops, questions, and sometimes searches a citizen because the officer has reasonable suspicion that the subject may have committed, may be committing, or may be about to commit a crime. These contacts are valuable because they let law enforcement know who was present in a given area at a given time and may be a suspect should a crime be discovered. It also lets the people contacted know the police are aware of their presence, which may deter them from committing illegal acts.

Some bigger cities have large tactical units able to aggressively patrol many areas of the city, but most departments have smaller tactical units that may be full-time units or they may be assembled on a temporary basis in response to a particular crime problem. Typically, these units work flexible schedules and employ varying techniques depending on the particular problem they're addressing. For example, the Santa Barbara,

California, Police Department has a tactical patrol force composed of one sergeant and four officers.[63] Their primary responsibility is street crime in the central and beachfront business districts. These officers do not handle calls; working closely with community policing units and crime analysis, they proactively address street crime and quality-of-life issues. Their goal is to reduce crime and the perception of crime. They often use bicycle patrol and foot patrol in their efforts.

Aggressive Patrol Uniformed tactical operations make use of aggressive patrol tactics: stopping numerous people and vehicles in an attempt to find evidence that they may have committed a crime or may be committing a crime. Aggressive patrol tactics using field interrogations can be very effective in reducing crime. However, they often cause problems with the community because of their potential for abusing citizens' rights.

A study in San Diego tested the effects of field interrogations. In this study, field interrogation activity was suspended for nine months in one experimental area but maintained at normal levels in two control areas. Crime in the area where field interrogations were suspended increased by a substantial amount, but it remained about the same in the control areas where field interrogations continued to be used. With the resumption of field interview activity in the experimental area, crime decreased to about the same level it had been before the experiment.[64]

Researchers James Q. Wilson and Barbara Boland found that proactive, aggressive law enforcement styles may help reduce crime rates. They found that jurisdictions that encourage patrol officers to stop motor vehicles to issue citations and to aggressively arrest and detain suspicious persons experience lower crime rates than do jurisdictions that do not follow such proactive policies.[65] Robert Sampson and Jacqueline Cohen found that departments that more actively enforced disorderly conduct and traffic laws also experienced lower robbery rates.[66]

Some of the innovative aggressive tactics regarding crime are based on research that indicates that a great deal of urban crime is concentrated in a few "hot spots." Lawrence Sherman, Patrick Gartin, and Michael Buerger have found that a significant portion of all police calls in Minneapolis came from a relatively few locations: bars, malls, the bus depot, hotels, and certain apartment buildings. They believed that concentrating police resources on these hot spots of crime could appreciably reduce crime.[67]

Many claim that the drastic drop in crime rates in the mid-1990s, particularly in cities like New York, were the results of aggressive, zero-tolerance anticrime policies. During this period, New York City's crime rates dropped to 30-year lows under the administration of Police Commissioner William J. Bratton. As part of his crime-fighting strategy, he ordered his officers to crack down on such minor offenses as public urination, loitering, loud radios, and unlicensed street vending to improve the city's quality of life. He told his uniformed street officers to resume making low-level drug arrests and not leave them to specialized units, which the NYPD had done for many years for fear of corruption scandals. Under his policies, all minor offenders were frisked for guns and checked for outstanding warrants. Computer-plotted maps were made daily to track crime in every block in the city. Bratton said, "I want to challenge the old idea that policing can't make a substantial impact on social change. American policing has been swatting at mosquitoes for 20 years. In New York we've learned how to drain the swamp."[68]

In growing numbers, police executives are convinced that effective policing can decrease crime, and even a growing cohort of criminologists is conceding that police work is responsible for the recent notable decline in crime. Nationwide, there are clear signs of departments reorganizing and implementing anticrime strategies, targeting problems and attacking them.

The evidence seems to suggest that proactive, aggressive police strategies are effective in reducing crime, at least in target areas. However, many believe that aggressive patrol tactics breed resentment in minority areas; citizens there often believe they are the target of police suspicion and reaction. This leads to a serious conflict for police administrators. Do they reduce crime rates by using effective yet aggressive police techniques and therefore risk poor relationships with lawful members of the community? It must be stated, however, that, despite the credit paid to the police in reducing crime, many criminologists and other students of crime and criminal justice point to other possible reasons for crime reduction, including the aging of the criminal-age-prone population, the increased prison and jail populations, the increased commitment of community groups in addressing crime conditions, and other such issues.

Gang Investigations

CLAUDIA LEYVA

Claudia Leyva is a sergeant with the Yuma, Arizona, Police Department. She has been with the department for 14 years, spending much of it working with the gang unit. She is currently working in Internal Affairs. She graduated as a Dean's Scholar from the 115th Administrative Officer's Course at Southern Police Institute.

Gang investigations were handed over to me soon after I became a detective. It was an assignment no one really wanted, including me. I quickly learned these types of cases could be time-consuming and challenging. I didn't have enough seniority to be a homicide detective but soon found that gang investigations were going to bring a wide variety of cases my way, including high-profile cases. I worked graffiti cases, assault cases, and narcotics cases, as well as shootings and stabbings. The assignment that nobody wanted and the one that I was unsure of soon became one I was grateful to have.

A simple case can be magnified in complexity once you determine more than one gang member participated in the event. In a nongang case, you usually have a victim and a suspect. The victim reports the circumstances of how he was victimized and when the suspect is located, we try to get his version of the events, with the goal of developing probable cause for an arrest.

In a gang-related investigation, there are often two or more opposing groups involved in an offense in an attempt to promote their gang. Generally, we call the group on the losing end of the incident the "victims," but there may not be any true victims in gang-related cases. These "victims" won't readily report all the circumstances surrounding their "victimization," even if they are lying in a pool of their own blood. They may give us bits and pieces of the facts but rarely tell us everything up front. They aren't forthcoming often because they have usually committed a crime themselves, during the event or in the past, to contribute to the gang rivalry.

The next step is usually trying to find a witness. We try to find one that is not afraid of retaliation, one that will tell us what the "victim" wouldn't. We hope to learn enough about the incident to lead us to the suspects.

During the course of identifying and interviewing everyone, we often learn new information that will necessitate reinterviewing everyone. This sometimes happens more than once, and this helps explain why these cases are so time-consuming and complicated.

In a simple nongang-related case, you may need to obtain and serve a search warrant on a home or vehicle. In a gang case, the number of search warrants to be served is multiplied by the number of suspects *and* "victims." Because the "victims" in these cases are often suspects as well, properly articulated search warrants could grant you access to all participants' homes in search of gang indicia and any other evidence of the crime. This is part of the complexity of the case but can also be invaluable to the case, especially when evidence of other crimes, such as narcotics or stolen property, is found.

During the course of one case, I wrote an affidavit for search warrants on 21 homes. It took two days and the assistance of over 70 officers from many different law enforcement agencies in the area. It made my case, and I was also happy with the message sent to the citizens, which made clear we were addressing the widespread gang issue.

In another case, my co-workers and I were at a home serving a warrant and were amazed to find graffiti carved into furniture and painted or marked on items throughout the house. It was difficult for me to understand why a gang member would do that to their own home. I saw two toddlers playing with a toy covered in graffiti and noticed a three-dot tattoo on the mother's hand and a teardrop tattoo on her face. I then realized just how challenging the fight would be. How could we make a gang member believe the gang lifestyle was wrong when his family members lived it and accepted it? And when would we be dealing with those toddlers as gang members?

Gang investigations are complicated and challenging. Being a female investigator dealing mostly with young Hispanic males was part of the challenge. I was able though to use it to my advantage by getting them to identify with me as their sister, aunt, or even mother. I have had some successes in getting the bad guys off the streets and some successes in luring some young people away from the gang lifestyle. On the bad days, it was these successes that motivated me to continue my efforts and to be grateful for the assignment.

Saturation Patrol Another kind of uniformed tactical operation is **saturation patrol.** A larger number of uniformed officers than normal is assigned to a particular area to deal with a particular crime problem. The results of this type of strategy are mixed, according to several studies involving saturation patrol. In a study of a New York City precinct, researchers concluded that a 40 percent increase in patrol personnel resulted in 30 to 50 percent decreases in street crime.[69] A study that analyzed New York subway robberies in relation to increased patrol over an eight-year period also found that saturation patrol reduced crime. In this instance, the deployment of substantially more subway patrol officers in the evening hours resulted in a decrease in subway robberies during the hours of the patrols. After a brief decrease, however, daytime robberies increased steadily.[70]

In a study of saturation patrol in Nashville, Tennessee, three patrol areas experiencing high burglary incidences during daylight hours were given increased patrols between 8:00 AM and 4:00 PM. The level of saturation raised the number of patrol cars per area from one to between four and eight. During the five weeks of the study, the number of burglary arrests increased, but there were no changes in the incidence of burglary. A year later, in Nashville, four high-crime areas were given increased patrol, two during daytime hours and two during evening hours. Patrol in all areas during the saturation times was increased from one to five cars. The results indicated that daytime saturation patrols had no effect on crime, but that evening saturation patrols did decrease crime.[71]

One of the most effective tactical operations employed by the New York City Police Department during the 1980s was Operation Pressure Point. Located in the city's Lower East Side, Operation Pressure Point involved using numerous young rookie officers on foot patrol. The officers were encouraged to use aggressive field interrogation techniques and undercover operations to combat the sale and possession of drugs, which had ravaged the neighborhood for years.[72] Operation Pressure Point was so successful that real estate prices began to skyrocket, turning the Lower East Side into a gentrified, high-rent section of the city. Although crime was reduced in the target area, it was merely displaced to adjoining neighborhoods.

Other initiatives have had mixed results. Programs evaluated by M. Kleiman in 1988 that were similar to Operation Pressure Point had little effect on street drug sales in Harlem; slightly improved crime statistics in Lynn, Massachusetts; and did improve crime statistics in Lawrence, Massachusetts. A program in Jersey City examined by Weisburg and Green in 1995 found a reduction in drug trafficking, rather than merely displacement, with a neighborhood crackdown coupled with police surveillance in high-crime and drug-trafficking locations.[73]

Decoy Vehicles

Though using individuals as decoys has been done for years, typically by investigations units but sometimes by and with the assistance of patrol, another type of decoy operation has been used recently with success. It involves no danger to officers, and its primary goal is preventing crime violations, rather than catching criminals. This decoy operation involves using unoccupied marked police vehicles in strategic locations to give the perception of omnipresence. This tactic has been used successfully to address less serious yet demanding crime problems and traffic violations. It is a way of addressing issues that are a problem in the least resource-intensive way.

Sometimes police agencies park a marked vehicle on a roadside where there is a problem with speeding. Drivers see the unit in the distance and slow down. Even if they see that the vehicle is unoccupied, it serves as a reminder that it could have been occupied and they could have gotten a ticket. It helps drivers become more aware of their driving habits and slows them down. Some agencies have taken this a step further and placed inflatable dummies in the driver's seat. This serves as a technique to increase awareness and educate drivers, much like the portable radar devices that post the speed limit and measure and show drivers their speed. This technique allows police agencies to address traffic problems without tying up an officer for extended periods.

This idea can be and has been expanded upon. When faced with numerous and persistent "smash and grabs" at exclusive women's clothing stores, the Boca Raton, Florida, Police Department had a problem. There was no discernable pattern to these burglaries, which were occurring throughout Dade, Broward, and Palm Beach Counties, yet store owners were outraged by repeat victimization that occurred over many months. With a limited number of midnight shift officers, many square miles of territory, and a high number of women's clothing stores, the police department had to come up with a method to address this problem and reassure the community that they considered this problem a priority. They started parking unoccupied marked vehicles in front of some of the more vulnerable targets. The hope was that the offender driving on the main roadways looking for a target would bypass these stores thinking either that there was an officer in the car, in the store, or in the area. Unfortunately, as is common with law enforcement efforts at crime prevention, it was difficult to measure success. However, businesses with police vehicles in the area were not broken into and store owners appreciated police efforts.

Although this strategy alone would not solve the crime, if a surveillance effort were put into effect at the remaining stores, the criminals might be displaced to those establishments, and an arrest could result. At the least, it was a preventive technique for the businesses and led to displacement of the crime to another area or town. Unfortunately, as with "target hardening" prevention techniques, this sometimes can be all we hope to do.

Alternative Vehicle Deployment

Most police patrol today is performed by uniformed officers in radio-equipped patrol cars or on foot. Police also patrol on motorcycles, scooters, boats, planes, helicopters, horses, and bicycles. Officers also patrol in golf carts, in all-terrain vehicles, and on roller skates. In 1997, the city of Philadelphia actually started a patrol unit using officers on in-line skates.[74] In 2003, many police departments began experimenting with patrols using the battery-operated self-balancing vehicle, the Segway.[75] Departments are willing to explore new ways of providing their services, especially when the method will assist them in being among the people, responding more quickly, and in this time of escalating fuel costs, saving money on the cost of fuel.

A 2003 article explains the versatility of certain specialized patrol vehicles for patrol:

- The police motorcycle's maneuverability and acceleration make it ideal for traffic enforcement, escort details, and crowd control.

- Bicycles are quiet and efficient and provide a bridge between motorized vehicles and foot patrol. They provide efficient transportation to areas that are normally available only by walking, such as parks, public housing developments with limited street access, tourist areas, college campuses, business plazas, and sports arenas.

- Electric bikes provide all of the advantages of the pedal bicycle but require less physical effort by the rider.

- Scooters are more maneuverable than cars, yet offer many of the features of a car in a compact space. They also provide shelter from the weather and enable officers to carry more equipment than bicycles do. They are especially suited for parking enforcement and specialized patrol on college campuses and business premises.

- Multi-terrain vehicles are useful when officers are required to travel into remote areas such as mountains and beaches. Their low-pressure, high-flotation tires and motorcycle-type engines and handlebar steering provide maneuverability in traversing rough terrain. They can often be used for search and rescue missions.

- Mobile substations or precincts can be driven to a specific area to provide a base of operations for beat officers and to facilitate community interaction. They can function as self-contained community policing headquarters and be used in daily community policing programs. They can also be used as a command center at the scene of a crime or disaster.[76]

A common method of transportation used by police officers in many different jurisdictions around the country is the bicycle. It's hard to imagine that as recently as just over two decades ago, police officers were rarely seen on bicycles. Now there are "police packages" recommended for officers using bikes to patrol and training programs that are conducted around the country to teach new bike officers techniques for policing and ways to stay safe. It is believed that the movement got its start in 1987, when former Seattle police officer, Paul Grady, was sitting in traffic unable to respond to a call when he observed bike messengers weaving their way through the traffic jam to get to their destination. He thought that might work for patrolling downtown and approached his commander, who approved. Grady and his partner, Mike Miller, began to patrol downtown Seattle on their personal mountain bikes, and a movement was born. The idea quickly spread, and bicycle patrols are now used across the country.[77]

They are used for downtown congested areas, major sporting events and community gatherings, beach and park properties, and even residential areas. They are very adaptable and can be moved around town on bike racks on the back of patrol vehicles. They consume no fuel, emit no pollution, are quiet, and give the officers time to interact with the public. This method can even enhance the officer's fitness and health. They seem an ideal solution for many situations.

Bicycles are also a tool employed by many departments, including Santa Barbara, California, in their tactical policing efforts. They can be used in covert surveillance by plainclothes officers who will have a better ability to blend in with their surroundings on bicycles. They can also prove valuable for officers in uniform, allowing them to maneuver in crowded conditions such as parades, street fairs, and crowded downtown streets when workers are arriving or leaving work, and to quietly and quickly approach individuals they suspect are involved in suspicious activity. Officers on the midnight shift can also use bicycles to check businesses in areas where they are having a burglary problem. In the quiet of the early morning hours, approaching police vehicles are easily identified, but an officer on a bike can get around quickly and quietly and surprise the criminals.

As mentioned earlier in the chapter, foot patrol is a popular option for citizens and consequently police departments. It appears to make citizens feel safer and enhances the police-community relationship. Many departments believe strongly in this benefit and in fact, in 2003, 59 percent of all municipal departments, including 75 percent of departments serving 250,000 residents or more, routinely used foot patrol.[78] This relationship is a philosophy behind the community policing movement, which will be discussed later in Chapter 12.

Police Traffic Operations

Though some may underestimate the importance of the traffic function in policing, it always ranks high as an area of concern among the public. Being able to get where you need to go in a fluid manner as well as having the confidence that drivers are driving through your neighborhood in a responsible manner are important. Feeling safe in your vehicle as you go about your daily lives is part of what defines the concept of "quality of life." Controlling the movement of vehicular traffic and enforcing the traffic laws is another one of the important activities the police engage in. Most law enforcement agencies have traffic units that are able to spend most of their time on traffic education and enforcement, but this is also seen as one of the primary tasks of patrol officers. The traffic unit is typically assigned to the same bureau or division as patrol, so they work closely with the uniformed patrol officers. There are usually not enough traffic officers to handle all traffic incidents, but they can lend expertise and handle the more complicated and serious incidents. Traffic incidents can place a significant demand on officers' time; consequently, departments are always exploring better ways of handling them as well as ways to prevent incidents from occurring. Working with city departments to improve traffic engineering and signage can help prevent accidents, and working with the public information office, if there is one, or community groups directly, to educate the public, can also help reduce accidents. Using new techniques and equipment to address traffic issues can make things work more smoothly and efficiently. The International Association of Chiefs of Police (IACP) realizes the importance of this function as well as the importance of sharing information among police agencies. The IACP has a highway safety committee that works closely with National Highway Traffic Safety Administration (NHTSA) and offers numerous publications. The chair of the IACP Highway Safety Committee recently wrote an article entitled, *The Top Ten Trends in Traffic Enforcement,* which lists the following concerns for law enforcement in 2005[79]:

1. *Speed enforcement:* Speed is involved in one of every three fatalities in the United States.

2. *Dangerous work zones:* Every year highway workers are needlessly killed or injured because of inattentive drivers.

3. *Fatigued or distracted drivers:* Many drivers are sleep deprived and many others are multitasking, using driving time to talk on cell phones, read the paper, put on lipstick, or eat chili dogs. Part of this mission includes keeping rest areas safe with high visibility patrol, so drivers view this as an alternative when tired.

4. *Sleep-deprived officers:* Because of court, overtime, and extra jobs, police officers are often sleep deprived. Combating this would include policies and procedures restricting the amount of overtime officers can work.

5. *Safer traffic stops:* Many officers are injured or killed while writing citations, speaking with drivers or working accidents—departments must educate officers in the newest techniques to minimize their chances of being hurt.

6. *New laws and tactics:* Keeping up to date on court decisions and the newest techniques and procedures for safe and legal enforcement is challenging and time-consuming.

7. *New types of vehicles:* Hybrids and electric vehicles pose new safety concerns.

8. *Drugged drivers:* A significant number of drivers that police encounter are under the influence of drugs or alcohol. Departments should have an adequate number of officers certified as drug recognition experts (DRE).

9. *Traffic officers and homeland security:* Officers must know how to recognize suspicious activities or information while on traffic stops.

10. *Incident clearance:* Interdisciplinary traffic teams should be formed with all agencies involved in traffic incidents in order to develop protocols for responding quickly and effectively and minimizing the disruption to the public.

The proliferation of automobiles, motorcycles, and trucks in the United States has been accompanied by a tremendous amount of traffic fatalities, injuries, and property damage. For the latest reporting year, 2005, 43,200 persons died, 2.68 million persons were injured, and $230.6 billion dollars in economic loss occurred as a result of traffic accidents. Alcohol-related fatalities were up 1.7 percent since 2004, and 55 percent (a decrease of 4 percent since 2002) of those who died in 2005 were not wearing safety belts. Currently, the NHTSA estimates seat belt compliance to be approximately 82 percent nationwide.[80]

The states have enacted numerous laws dealing with vehicle use, and it falls upon the police to enforce those laws. Police investigate accidents and identify their causes, identify traffic hazards and attempt to neutralize them, and strive to educate the public. States and police agencies use the statistics that NHTSA gathers to determine where their efforts would best be directed. The effort in many states is on seat belt enforcement as the data indicates that increased seat belt usage can decrease the numbers of fatalities. The state of Washington highly publicizes its "Click it or Ticket" campaign to increase public awareness of the penalty for violating the law and to let the public know it is a priority.

In recent years, states have also changed their laws regarding new drivers after being frustrated by the high numbers of unnecessary deaths among teen drivers. Most states have various forms of graduated licensing, which restricts the hours that teen drivers can operate a motor vehicle as well as restrictions on who and how many people may be in the vehicle with a new driver. Efforts in this area appear to be paying off. Recently, Wisconsin reported that 4 years after adopting a graduated driver's license law, accidents among teenage drivers are at their lowest point in 10 years. The average number of 16 year olds involved in all accidents decreased 17 percent from 2000 to 2004 (the years the new restrictions have been in effect) compared with the 4 years before the change in the law. The number of 16-year-old drivers involved in fatal or injury accidents dropped even more—22 percent. Researchers at the Johns Hopkins School of Medicine recently analyzed the data around the country and found that the graduated licenses have decreased the number of fatalities involving teens by an average of 11 percent, and in the states with the strictest laws, these fatalities dropped approximately 20 percent.[81]

Most local and state law enforcement agencies have the responsibility of enforcing state and local traffic laws and ordinances. Some states have a state highway patrol, whose primary duties are the enforcement of traffic laws. Many police departments create a special unit, such as a traffic division, to pay special attention to traffic problems. However, the enforcement of traffic regulations is generally the duty of all officers in a department. In some municipalities, nonsworn officers or civilians are hired for traffic control and enforcing local parking regulations.

Police Automobile Pursuits

The police practice of using high-powered police vehicles to chase speeding motorists (**police pursuits**) has resulted in numerous accidents, injuries, and deaths to innocent civilians, police officers, and the pursued drivers.

Geoffrey Alpert and Patrick R. Anderson characterize the police high-speed automobile pursuit as the most deadly force available to the police and define high-speed pursuits as "an active attempt by a law enforcement officer operating an emergency vehicle to apprehend alleged criminals in a moving motor vehicle, when the driver of the vehicle, in an attempt to avoid apprehension, significantly increases his or her speed or takes other evasive action." Alpert and Anderson point out several outcomes of such chases:

■ The pursued driver stops the car and surrenders.

■ The chased vehicle crashes into a structure, and the driver and occupants are apprehended, escape, are injured, or are killed.

■ The chased vehicle crashes into another vehicle (with or without injuries to the driver and other occupants in the chased vehicle or another vehicle).

■ The vehicle being chased strikes a pedestrian (with or without injuries or death).

■ The police use some level of force to stop the pursued vehicle, including firearms, roadblocks, ramming, bumping, boxing, and so on.

■ The police car crashes (with or without injuries to officers or civilians).[82]

Not all of these possible outcomes are acceptable for the police or innocent civilians. A current debate questions whether the police should pursue fleeing vehicles, especially when such a pursuit could risk injuries to the police or innocent civilians. Certainly, no one wants officers or civilians injured. According to the NHTSA, about 520 people nationally who were not the subject of a chase died as a result of police pursuits from 1997 to 2001.[83] However, people on the other side in the debate say that if the police do not pursue fleeing drivers, they are sending a message to violators that they can get away with traffic violations by fleeing.

Studies Involving Police Pursuits

Studies have been conducted to determine what happens in a rapid pursuit. This information may help police administrators establish policies on rapid pursuits. A review by the California Highway Patrol of nearly 700 pursuits on its highways during a six-month period revealed the following about the typical pursuit:

■ It starts as a traffic violation.

■ It occurs at night.

■ It covers only a mile or so.

■ It takes approximately two minutes to resolve.

■ It involves at least two police cars.

■ It ends when the pursued driver stops his or her vehicle.

■ It results in the apprehension of more than three-fourths of the pursued drivers.

■ It ends without an accident 70 percent of the time.

The California Highway Patrol Study also revealed that drivers failed to stop for the following reasons, based on the judgment of the pursuing officer:

■ To avoid driving while intoxicated (DWI) or drug arrest (19 percent)

■ To avoid a summons for a traffic infraction (14 percent)

■ Because the driver was driving a stolen vehicle (12 percent)

■ To avoid an arrest for a law violation (11 percent)

■ Because of unknown or miscellaneous reasons, such as the driver's being afraid of the police, disliking the police, or enjoying the excitement of the chase (44 percent)[84]

The California Highway Patrol study concluded that although there are risks in high-speed pursuits, the pursuits are worth the risks:

Attempted apprehension of motorists in violation of what appear to be minor traffic infractions is necessary for the preservation of order on the highways of California. . . . One can imagine what would happen if the police suddenly banned pursuits. Undoubtedly, innocent people may be injured or killed because an officer chooses to pursue a suspect, but this risk is necessary to avoid the even greater loss that would occur if law enforcement agencies were not allowed to aggressively pursue violators.[85]

Alpert and Roger G. Dunham studied 952 pursuits in Dade County, Florida, by the area's two major police departments, the Metro-Dade Police Department and the City of Miami Police Department. The researchers found that 38 percent of the pursuits resulted in an accident, 17 percent in injury, and 0.7 percent in death. Of the 160 pursuits with injury, 30 involved injury to the police officer, 17 involved injury to an innocent bystander, and

A gunman hijacked this bus in Los Angeles after a shooting incident and then led police on a high-speed chase through downtown streets, killing one person and injuring seven. Many departments are instituting restrictive policies due to the extreme risks that pursuits pose and allowing them only in cases of violent offenses such as this one.

© David McNew/Newsmakers/Getty Images

113 involved injury to the fleeing driver, the passengers, or both. Alpert and Dunham also concluded that 54 percent of the pursuits were initiated for traffic offenses, 2 percent for reckless driving or impaired driving, 33 percent for serious criminal activity, and 11 percent for "be on the lookout" (BOLO) alarms.[86]

A study conducted in Minnesota indicated that 44 percent of pursuits resulted in accidents, and 24 percent resulted in injuries. The causes of the pursuits included traffic (76 percent), suspicion of driving under the influence (DUI) (6 percent), and suspicion of a felony (16 percent).[87] The NHTSA has attributed 3,000 deaths to pursuits in the last decade and states that 40 percent of police chases end in crashes.[88]

In 2004, the University of Washington released a study conducted by two researchers at the Harborview Medical Center's Injury Prevention and Research Center. The researchers examined all traffic fatalities in the nation from 1994 through 2002 and found 2,654 fatal crashes with 3,146 deaths resulting from police pursuits. Of those deaths, 1,048, or one-third, were of people not in fleeing vehicles. They were drivers or occupants of other vehicles, pedestrians, or bicyclists; 40 were police officers. The report did not determine how many police chases don't end in deaths or analyze the reasons for the pursuits but did state that police chase fatalities make up 1 percent of all motor vehicle related deaths in the United States.[89]

An article in the *FBI Law Enforcement Bulletin* indicates that as many as 40 percent of all motor vehicle police pursuits end in collisions, and these collisions end in the deaths of 300 officers, offenders, and innocent bystanders a year.[90] Clearly, this is a serious safety issue for police and citizens and requires much further study.

The Evolution of Pursuits

Departments are examining their long-standing policy of actively pursuing anyone that fails to stop for a police officer. As the studies discussed earlier mention, these pursuits cause a lot of injury, death, damage and emotional pain and economic costs. With today's technology, the offender can often be apprehended in safer ways.

The number of accidents and injuries resulting from police high-speed pursuits has led many U.S. police departments to establish formal **police pursuit policies** (policies regulating the circumstances and conditions under which the police should pursue or chase motorists driving at high speeds in a dangerous manner). Some departments are even telling their officers to discontinue a pursuit under certain circumstances.

Most departments have examined this issue closely over the last few years, and many have come to the conclusion that the dangers to officers, citizens, and even the individual being pursued often determine that pursuits are not an effective

Goodnight headlights   sip Chase N
on 79
mike Lynch

tactic and the dangers far outweigh the benefits. Policies give clear guidelines to officers and supervisors about what their roles are. In 2003, nearly all departments had pursuit policies, 60 percent of local police agencies had a restrictive pursuit policy (restrictions based on speed, type of offense, and so on); 25 percent of departments had a judgmental pursuit policy leaving it to the officer's discretion; and 6 percent discouraged all vehicle pursuits.[91] In 2003, major cities such as Los Angeles, Chicago, and Seattle joined the ranks of big-city departments using a restrictive policy. Seattle's policy dictates officers should chase drivers "only when the need for immediate capture outweighs the danger created by the pursuit itself." Officers are "allowed to chase drivers who have committed serious crimes, displayed weapons, or are creating a clear danger to others."[92] Sergeants complete special reports every time there is a pursuit, and the administration will analyze these reports on a yearly basis.

A small study on pursuit outcomes in Hillsboro, Oregon, determined that implementing a restrictive pursuit policy encouraging officers to call off a pursuit and seek other alternatives to apprehend the suspect neither encouraged drivers to flee nor resulted in offenders getting away. The department used a three-pronged approach: updated the policy putting the responsibility for ending the pursuit on the officer, provided pursuit-related training including realistic scenarios on a regular basis, and required review of all pursuits—terminated or not. Part of the training also includes stressing officers recording other identifying characteristics of the fleeing vehicle to assist in later apprehension and the "flooding" of the area with other units to be available for apprehension when the pursuit was terminated. The department found a common reaction after termination was for the offenders to slow down and resume normal driving or abandon the vehicle, which increased opportunities for apprehension.[93]

Pursuit policies can also cause conflicts between neighboring towns or counties when their policies differ; one jurisdiction may initiate a pursuit that crosses a boundary into another jurisdiction where officers won't pursue. The agencies need to communicate their policies and plan how they will handle the conflicts that may arise.

Considering the widely televised beatings of individuals after pursuits, a proposal by Alpert, a professor of criminology at the University of South Carolina, seems to make a great deal of sense. In a 1996 study of police pursuit policies, Alpert recommended that suspects be apprehended by officers other than those who led the chase. Alpert found that officers chasing suspects experience an adrenaline high that can lead to the use of excessive force once they've caught up with the fleeing suspects.[94]

One of the best alternatives that departments are exploring is the use of technology. Law enforcement air units commonly assist in pursuits and track the offender to a stopping place, often with the added element of video. Many departments also have good working relationships with the TV media where they may request the same kind of monitored assistance. Many departments have been using tire deflation spikes in appropriate situations, and another weapon was introduced in 2006 and is currently being tested in Los Angeles—the StarChase system. Patrol cars will be equipped with compressed air launchers that fire a miniature GPS receiver in a sticky compound resembling a golf ball, which sticks to the offender's vehicle and emits a radio signal to police.[95] This potential alternative has law enforcement officers excited and awaiting the results of the field study.

Efforts against Drunk Drivers

During the 1990s, much attention has been paid to the tremendous damage done on our highways by drunk drivers. Efforts by such groups as Mothers Against Drunk Driving (MADD) and Students Against Drunk Driving (SADD) have caused the police to pay particular attention to the problem. The worst-ever year for alcohol-related fatalities was 1986, when 24,045 deaths occurred.[96] According to the NHTSA, the United States experienced the largest percentage of increase in alcohol-related traffic deaths in 2000 when 17,380 people were killed in alcohol-related crashes—one every 30 minutes. The number continued to go up, with 17,400 people killed in 2001 and 17,419 killed in 2002. In 2002, this accounted for 41 percent of people killed in traffic crashes nationally, according to MADD's website. However, in 2003, there was a 3 percent reduction in alcohol-related traffic deaths, and NHTSA attributes this decline to a strategy that was implemented in 2002 in 13 states that emphasizes high-visibility enforcement. High-visibility enforcement consistently shows the greatest immediate impact on reducing impaired driving.

The goal of this strategy is to create general deterrence by increasing the numbers of citations and arrests.[97] Patrol officers cannot be expected to deal effectively with the problem of drunk drivers, because so much of the officers' time is occupied by other duties but there are things they can do. To enforce the laws against DWI or DUI, the police have resorted to sobriety checkpoints. The following describes the typical DWI checkpoint or roadblock: Officers conducting a roadblock may stop all traffic or after a set number, such as every fifth vehicle. After a vehicle is directed to the side of the road, an officer may request to see an operator's license, registration, and insurance card. The officer may ask several questions to observe the driver's demeanor and if the officer detects signs of inebriation, the motorist may be directed to move the vehicle to a secondary area and submit to a roadside sobriety test or Breathalyzer test. The failure to pass either test constitutes sufficient probable cause for arrest. Police are also using saturation patrol to combat the drunk driving problem. Officers will saturate a pre-designated area with roving police officers to monitor traffic for signs of impaired driving. They also emphasize speeding and seat belt violations.

Studies indicate that laws establishing administrative license revocation (ALR) have reduced alcohol-related crashes by almost 40 percent.[98] Police can continue to work with legislative bodies to implement these types of drivers' license sanctions.

NHTSA supports all these efforts targeting impaired drivers. In an effort to assist departments in running saturation patrols and sobriety checkpoints, NHTSA provides guidelines on its website and issues that need to be addressed to successfully run checkpoints.[99]

Recently, MADD has expanded its previous efforts in the DUI battle. With the approach of the holidays in December 2006, MADD announced a new campaign in its fight against drunk driving. An integral strategy in this campaign is the push for states to enact laws requiring breath-test interlock devices in the vehicles of all those convicted of drunk driving, including first time offenders. This would prevent the car from starting if alcohol is detected on the driver's breath. Though some states allow this device for repeat offenders, New Mexico is the only state that has such a law for first offenders. MADD is encouraging other states to implement similar laws, which are currently being considered in several states.[100]

The Department of Justice (DOJ) has recently published a guide for law enforcement to address the drunk driving problem using the problem-oriented approach, which is available on the DOJ website. The guide advocates that law enforcement personnel analyze their community's DUI problem: Where and when are people drinking, who is doing the drinking, and what approach is the best to address these specifics. It may be through legislation, enforcement, training, education, sanctions, environmental design, or a combination of some or all of these techniques. Law enforcement personnel should monitor and evaluate the effectiveness of these strategies and follow-up appropriately. This is also an example of Sherman's evidence-based policing. The challenge will be isolating the effectiveness of the various strategies independently, if that was desired. However, using the scientific method to address a problem lends itself most effectively to determining what is successful.[101]

Fighting Aggressive Driving

In recent years, road rage and aggressive driving have become problems. People have been assaulted and even murdered in road rage incidents. Sometimes this road rage takes the form of aggressive driving, and innocent people have died because of the reckless driving of aggressive drivers. Aggressive driving is not necessarily defined as a specific offense but, rather, is a combination of several violations including speeding, tailgating, driving on the shoulder, and not signaling when changing lanes. NHTSA defines aggressive driving as "the commission of two or more moving violations that is likely to endanger other persons or property, or any single intentional violation that requires a defensive reaction of another driver." According to the Washington State Patrol website, the state of Washington defines road rage as "an assault with a motor vehicle or other dangerous weapon by the operator or passenger(s) of one motor vehicle on the operator or passenger(s) of another motor vehicle caused by an incident that occurred on a roadway."[102]

The frustration caused by heavy traffic, traffic jams, and drivers who make errors because of inattention results in some individuals resorting to driving behavior to "get back" at the other driver. These actions may include passing a vehicle and then stopping suddenly or tailgating a vehicle the driver perceives as moving too slowly. If the other driver buys into this behavior, it can result in a verbal or physical confrontation at a traffic light. The Washington State Patrol describes symptoms of road rage and aggressive driving on its website.[103]

Sometimes drivers are just frustrated with slow-moving traffic or traffic jams and will do whatever they feel will help them move faster, such as passing cars, quickly changing lanes, or tailgating to intimidate other drivers into changing lanes. When this behavior includes inappropriately passing vehicles, it has resulted in fatal head-on crashes. Many states are targeting this aggressive driving in an effort to reduce crashes and make the roads safer.

The Colorado State Patrol has an aggressive driving program known as Aggressive Drivers Are Public Threats (ADAPT), which uses unmarked vehicles, motorcycles, and aircraft for enforcement coupled with an extensive media campaign. There is a designated phone number to call to report aggressive driving. If the reported incident requires police response, a unit will be sent; if not, the incident will be logged in the computer database and the complainant allowed to vent his or her frustration. The system can track the vehicles with repeated aggressive behavior; with three logged offenses, the owner of the car is notified. In their media campaign to educate the public, the Colorado State Patrol advocates motorists to use the two-finger "peace" or "victory" sign to mean "thank you," "sorry," or "excuse me."[104]

The Washington State Patrol has formed the "Aggressive Driver Apprehension Team," which uses unmarked vehicles armed with cameras in the windshield to record traffic stops. In 2002, officers pulled over approximately 29,000 drivers for aggressive driving, more than twice the number stopped in 2001, and are viewed as having a successful program.[105]

Other Police Operational Units

One type of police work that has increased greatly in recent years includes special weapons and tactical teams (SWAT) and emergency service units (ESUs). SWAT teams and ESUs address specific emergency and lifesaving situations that regular officers on routine patrol do not have the time or expertise to handle. K-9 units are a supplement to the patrol force that greatly enhance police response and efforts to keep citizens and officers safe.

SWAT Teams

SWAT teams were created in many cities during the 1960s, generally in response to riots and similar disturbances. The first SWAT team was the Philadelphia Police Department's 100-officer SWAT squad, which was organized in 1964 in response to the growing number of bank robberies throughout the city.[106] SWAT teams are commonly used around the country but sometimes have other names. Some believe that the name SWAT sounds a little too aggressive and militaristic, and some cities have chosen other variations of the title for the same type of team such as special response unit (SRU) or special response team (SRT).

Members of SWAT teams are carefully chosen and trained in the use of weapons and strategic invasion tactics. SWAT teams are used in situations involving hostages, serious crimes, airplane hijackings, and prison riots, as well as in other situations requiring specialized skills and training. In the last decade, more and more departments are using them when serving search warrants and arrest warrants. It is safer to use these highly trained officers to make the entry than using the narcotics investigators who may be working the case and getting the warrants, and it means that the unit can be better trained. Most departments are too small to have a full-time SWAT team, however, so will have a SWAT team composed of officers with varying assignments throughout the department. Officers have their regular assignments, but when a SWAT call-out occurs, they will respond from wherever they are. Unless a city is very large and very busy, there just aren't enough SWAT calls to justify a full-time unit. Some departments have difficulty justifying their own SWAT team even when it is composed of officers on other job assignments. In these situations, departments in an area may collaborate to form a regional SWAT team with officers coming from several departments. The most important issue in this situation is determining who has control of the unit and who is in charge. There can be no confusion regarding this on a SWAT call.

No matter how the SWAT team is formed, the most important consideration is training. Deploying a SWAT team is expensive, primarily because of the training requirements. The units must be constantly training and working together so that any action they take will be appropriate and court defensible.

Emergency Service Units

Police departments provide numerous emergency services, including emergency first aid to sick and injured citizens, rescues of people trapped in automobiles at accident scenes, rescues of those trapped in burning or collapsed buildings, and often rescues of people attempting to commit suicide by jumping from buildings and bridges. These duties involve specialized training and, often, sophisticated rescue equipment. The first aid and rescue services are often provided by patrol officers as part of their routine services. Many larger cities or counties, however, provide special patrol units whose primary responsibility is to respond to these emergencies. Often these emergency duties are merged into a department's SWAT operations or are provided by specialized emergency service units with sophisticated rescue and lifesaving equipment. Some of these services, especially search and rescue services may be provided by the fire department. Some agencies have smaller versions of these units, and they often have names such as Critical Incident Teams.

The New York City Police Department has had its ESU since 1930. This unit spends most of its time on rescue missions, as well as on performing traditional hostage and SWAT operations. An emergency service volunteer recruit described his training:

> [The ESU recruit] is schooled in a staggering syllabus of skills. He is trained as a marksman so he can play a key role when an armed perpetrator takes cover or a terrorist takes hostages. Then he is taught the psychology of barricaded criminals so he can avoid using his marksmanship talents. He is certified as an emergency medical technician and can administer cardiopulmonary resuscitation and oxygen to victims of coronaries, respiratory ailments, smoke inhalation

and asphyxiation. He is versed in the art of extrication and rescues people trapped in not only elevators but also vehicles, heavy machinery and cave-ins. He knows how to secure dangerous cornices and scaffolds, repair downed electrical wires and poles . . . and navigate an armored personnel carrier for rescuing people pinned down by gunfire.[107]

K-9 Units

Most departments today employ K-9 units. These talented dogs have been used for many years, but during the last few years, their role has expanded and the need for them has grown. Traditionally, K-9 units have supplemented the patrol function by responding to burglary calls or open doors where a premises search is needed. These dogs can do it more safely and accurately than human officers particularly when the area to be searched is large or difficult to reach such as a crawl space. This aids in the effort to keep officers safe. The dogs have also been used for tracking when crimes have just occurred. They can help officers know the direction of travel of a suspect or if the suspect got in a vehicle, and if so, where the vehicle was parked. In the best-case scenario, the dog will lead officers to the suspect's home or vehicle or hiding place. K-9s can also assist in convincing a suspect to surrender. People know they can't reason with a dog, so when they know the dog is being set loose to apprehend them, they might be more likely to give up peacefully. This saves an officer from getting injured trying to take a noncompliant suspect into custody. Dogs have also been a big asset in the war on drugs for years, sniffing vehicles and packages and signaling if drugs are present.

Since September 11, 2001, there has been an increase in the demand for dogs that sniff bombs and explosives. These dogs are used routinely at airports, train stations, ferry terminals, ports, subways, highways, bridges, and tunnels.

The dogs are also a public relations asset and a great tool at bridging the gap between the community and the officers at special events. Departments that cannot justify having their own dog will often have an arrangement with other local agencies or the county or state to have a dog respond when needed.

Summary

- The three cornerstones of traditional police work include random routine patrol, rapid response to calls by citizens to 911, and retroactive investigation of past crimes by detectives.

- Before the academic studies of the 1960s and 1970s—particularly the Kansas City study—most of what we knew about police work, and most of the way police work was done in the United States, relied on untested assumptions.

- The Kansas City study forced academics and progressive police administrators to look closely at police operations to see if there were better, more effective ways to do them. This self-examination occurred after the Kansas City study indicated that the amount of random patrol had no effect on crime or the citizens' fear of crime.

- Rapid police response to calls was found to be not as critical as once thought because of delays outside the police control. When it was determined that there was often a delay between a crime's occurrence and when the citizen reported it, any advantage of a quick police response was negated.

- After moving from foot patrol to vehicle patrol, law enforcement has realized the value of foot patrol and is once again using it. Reactions by both police officers and the community indicate that foot patrol enhances the relationship between the police and the community and leads to improved exchange of information.

- Departments should use Evidence-based policing to determine which methods to employ in solving the problems they encounter.

- Officers and departments can better use discretionary time to fight crime through directed patrol activities.

- Police can better manage their resources by responding to calls based on the severity and importance of the calls and employing differential response alternatives.

- Police officers can use a variety of methods to fight crime and serve their community including vehicle patrol, foot patrol, bicycle patrol, mounted patrol, and other innovative methods, such as scooters, multi-terrain vehicles and mobile substations.

- Police departments are restricting the use of pursuits and using alternative methods to catch the individuals who attempt to elude police officers.

- Law enforcement is using more innovative techniques in an effort to attack the DUI and aggressive driving problem.

- SWAT teams, ESUs, and K-9 units also supplement the patrol mission in fighting crime.

Learning Check

1. Name the three basic methods used by the police to fulfill their mission.

2. Discuss whether the three basic methods used by the police to fulfill their mission are effective. If they are effective, why? If they are not effective, why not?

3. Identify the major value of the Kansas City study.

4. Explain what the academic studies regarding police patrol revealed about what the police do while on patrol.

5. Discuss the value of evidence-based policing.

6. Identify some of the benefits associated with foot patrol and bicycle patrol.

7. Explain how directed patrol differs from the traditional random patrol.

8. Identify and describe some alternative responses to crime that law enforcement can use rather than rapid response to calls.

9. Discuss some of the issues that should be examined when deciding how to schedule personnel in road patrol.

10. Explain what the research says about police pursuits and how law enforcement is responding to this information.

Key Terms

bike patrol Officers patrol an assigned area on bicycle rather than in a patrol car.

control group The group that is not acted upon, nothing is changed.

controlled experiment An experiment or study using a control group and an experimental group.

differential response to calls for service The police response to calls for service varies according to the type and severity of the call.

directed patrol Officers patrol specific locations at specific times to address a specific crime problem.

evidence-based policing Using available scientific research on policing to implement crime-fighting strategies and department policies.

experimental group The group that receives the changed conditions.

foot patrol Police officers walk a beat or assigned area rather than patrolling in a motor vehicle.

Kansas City Patrol study The first study conducted to test the effectiveness of random routine patrol.

Newark foot patrol study A study conducted to determine the effectiveness of foot patrol officers in preventing crime.

omnipresence The impression of always being there.

police pursuits The attempt by law enforcement to apprehend alleged criminals in a moving motor vehicle when the driver is trying to elude capture and increases speed or takes evasive action.

police pursuit policies Policies regulating the circumstances and conditions under which the police should pursue or chase motorists driving at high speeds in a dangerous manner.

random routine patrol Officers driving around a designated geographic area.

rapid response to citizens' calls to 911 Officers being dispatched to calls immediately, regardless of the type of call.

retroactive investigation of past crimes by detectives The follow-up investigation of crimes by detectives that occurs after a crime has been reported.

saturation patrol Assigning a larger number of uniformed officers to an area to deal with a particular crime problem.

split-force patrol A method in which the patrol force is split and half respond to calls for service and the other half performs directed patrol activities.

Investigations

© AP/Wide World Photos

GOALS

- To discuss traditional detective operations
- To introduce you to alternatives to retroactive investigation of past crimes by detectives
- To acquaint you with the most recent proactive tactics being used by investigators, including tactical operations, decoy operations, sting operations, civil liability and code enforcement teams, and multijurisdictional task forces
- To acquaint you with undercover operations, including police, federal, and private security operations, and undercover drug operations
- To define entrapment and show how it relates to police tactical and undercover operations

website

Introduction

After an unprecedented crime decrease in the 1990s, crime rates across the country remained relatively flat from 2000 to 2004. In 2005, the FBI reported an increase in violent crime in its preliminary 2005 crime report.[1] The Preliminary Uniform Crime Report indicates that nationally the violent crime rate is up 2.5 percent compared with 2004 figures. Included in the violent crime rate are the crimes of murder, forcible rape, robbery, and aggravated assault. The property crime rate fell 1.5 percent in 2005 compared with 2004.[2] Though experts hesitate to overstate the issue, stating it could be a one-year blip, most believe the issue needs to be seriously examined to keep it from signaling a trend. Murder rates were up 4.8 percent nationally, which is the largest increase in 15 years. The interesting observation is that although the murder rates are down in some big cities, and overall are about the same in these cities, cities with smaller populations saw a much sharper increase in murders. Birmingham, Alabama, experienced a murder rate 76 percent higher than 2004; Milwaukee, Wisconsin, was up 40 percent; and Kansas City, Missouri, was up 42 percent. Overall, cities with populations of 100,000 to 250,000 showed a murder rate increase of 12.5 percent.[3]

Smaller cities have felt immune to big-city problems and perhaps never put programs into place to combat the crime problem as the bigger cities did. The last big crime surge of the late 1980s and early 1990s was largely attributed to the spread of crack cocaine and guns on the street. Big cities launched various initiatives to address the issue, and the crime rate declined during the 1990s. Experts cite many possible causes for this recent increase—from budget cuts to police and social services, the number of guns on the street, the increase in meth use and production, the spread of violent ideas through media and music, and the diversion of police attention and tax dollars to terrorism and homeland security.[4] The difficult challenge that police departments face is determining why exactly their violent crime rate went up and developing ways to combat it and keep their citizens safe. Crime rate increases in "middle America" will attract the attention of the community. If citizens don't feel safe in their hometowns, they will let their elected officials know and will demand tactics and solutions. The issue has and will continue to receive media attention. James Alan Fox of Northeastern University in Boston states that even though the increased rate is not necessarily an epidemic, "It does suggest it could be a cause for concern unless we get back to fighting crime the way we did in the 90s. When we started to see a reduction in crime, we shouldn't have been cutting programs, we should have been reinforcing them."[5] On the positive side, perhaps taxpayers will be more likely to fund initiatives that cities develop to address the crime problem.

Police departments throughout the nation have learned that they must be more specific and focused in addressing crime and disorder problems. Departments have created new policies, procedures, and units to address these concerns. This chapter will discuss and examine some of these innovations. Traditional detective operations have been modified in response to academic studies that have indicated that new methods can be used in the investigation of past crimes and the apprehension of career criminals. Improved investigations of past crimes include changes made in detective operations in response to research conducted by the Rand Corporation and other think tanks, as well as the use of cold-case squads. Increased attention to career criminals has led to a proliferation of repeat offender programs (ROPs) throughout the United States. Information management and information sharing, such as through the use of multi-agency investigative task forces, has been facilitated. New tactics and operations have been developed over the past two decades in an attempt to provide more effective crime investigation. This chapter will discuss some of these newer innovations as well as the more tried and true methods including decoy operations, stakeout operations, sting operations, and code enforcement teams.

We also discuss the major types of undercover operations, including police, federal, and private security undercover operations. The chapter concludes with a discussion of the legal aspects of entrapment and how it relates to undercover work and other law enforcement tactics.

Bureau of Justice Statistics (handwritten)

Retroactive Investigation of Past Crimes by Detectives

Cold Case (handwritten)

Before the Rand study, *The Criminal Investigation Process,* it was common for police departments to have policies and procedures in place that emphasized the retroactive investigation of past crimes by detectives. The investigation of almost all felonies and of some misdemeanors was the sole responsibility of the detective division of a police department.[6] The patrol officer merely obtained information for a complaint or incident report and referred the case to the detectives for follow-up investigation. Theoretically, detectives would interview complainants and witnesses again, respond to the scene of the crime, and search for clues and leads that could solve the crime.

In 1975, the Rand Corporation think tank found that much of a detective's time was spent in nonproductive work—93 percent of a detective's time was spent on activities that did not lead directly to solving previously reported crimes—and that investigative expertise did little to solve cases. The Rand report said that half of all detectives could be replaced without negatively influencing crime clearance rates:

> The single most important determinant of whether or not a case will be solved is the information the victim supplies to the immediately responding patrol officer. If information that uniquely identifies the perpetrator is not present at the time the crime is reported, the perpetrator, by and large, will not be subsequently identified. Of those cases that are ultimately cleared but in which the perpetrator is not identifiable at the time of the initial police incident report, almost all are cleared as a result of routine police procedures. . . .
>
> Our data consistently reveal that an investigator's time is largely consumed in reviewing reports, documenting files and attempting to locate and interview victims on cases that experience shows will not be solved. For cases that are solved (i.e., a suspect is identified), an investigator spends more time in post-clearance processing than he does in identifying the perpetrator.[7]

The effectiveness of detectives was also questioned by a Police Executive Research Forum (PERF) study in 1981. Data from the study disclosed that if a crime is reported while it is in progress, police have about a 33 percent chance of making an arrest. However, the probability of arrest declines to about 10 percent if the crime is reported one minute later and to 5 percent if more than 15 minutes elapse before the crime is reported. In addition, as time elapses between the crime and the arrest, the chances of a conviction are reduced, probably because the ability to recover evidence is lost. Once a crime has been completed and the investigation is put into the hands of detectives, the chances of identifying and arresting the perpetrator diminish rapidly.[8] Mark Willman and John Snortum duplicated the Rand and PERF findings in a study of detective work in 1984. The researchers analyzed 5,336 cases reported to a suburban police department and found that most cases that were solved were solved when the perpetrator was identified at the scene of the crime; scientific detective work was rarely necessary.[9]

These early studies of detective operations indicate that detectives are not very successful in the criminal investigation process. This chapter will explore some better techniques that police departments have developed to investigate past crimes.

Detective Operations

Most of the activities of a police department involve police patrol operations. As we saw in earlier chapters, however, the police engage in numerous other activities. Detective operations and investigations are an important part of police work.

What Detectives Do

The detective division of a police department is charged with solving, or clearing, reported crimes. In traditional detective operations, detectives conduct a follow-up investigation of a past crime after a member of the patrol force takes the initial report of the crime and conducts some sort of preliminary investigation.

According to police tradition, a detective or investigator re-interviews the victim of the crime and any witnesses there may be, collects evidence,

Give examples of Investigations; petty theft Vandalism
Arrest of Speas

and processes or oversees the processing of the crime scene (searches the scene of a crime for physical evidence, collects the evidence, and forwards it to the police laboratory for analysis). The detective or investigator also conducts canvasses (searches areas for witnesses), interrogates possible suspects, arrests the alleged perpetrator, and prepares the case, with the assistance of the district attorney's or prosecutor's office, for presentation in court.

The detective generally begins an investigation upon receipt of an incident report (complaint report) prepared by the officer who conducted the initial interview with the victim. The incident report contains identifying information regarding the victim, details of the crime, identifying information regarding the perpetrator(s) or suspect (s), or a description of them, and identifying information regarding any property taken.

As the detective begins the investigation, he or she maintains a file on the case, using follow-up reports for each stage of the investigation. The incident report and the follow-up reports are generally placed in a case folder and serve as the official history of the crime and its investigation. This information or report is then used by the prosecutor to prosecute the case in court. (To prosecute means to conduct criminal procedures in a court of law against a person accused of committing criminal offenses. The people performing this duty are generally called prosecutors. They are also called, in various jurisdictions, district attorneys, state attorneys, or U.S. attorneys.) The incident report and the follow-up reports may also be subpoenaed by a defendant's defense attorney under the legal process known as discovery, which allows a defendant, before a trial, to have access to the information the police and prosecutor will use at the trial.

Detective units may be organized on a decentralized or centralized basis. In a decentralized system, each precinct in a city has its own local detective squad, which investigates all crimes occurring in the precinct. Detectives or investigators in a decentralized squad are considered generalists.

In a centralized system, in contrast, all detectives operate out of one central office or headquarters and are each responsible for particular types of crime in the entire city. These detectives are considered specialists. Some departments separate centralized or specialty squads into crimes against persons squads and crimes against property squads. Some departments operate specialized squads or units for most serious crimes—for example, they may have a homicide squad, sex crime squad, robbery squad, burglary squad, forgery squad, auto theft squad, and bias crimes squad (which investigates crimes that are motivated by bigotry or hatred of a person's race, ethnic origin, gender, or sexual orientation), and most recently, computer crimes squads.

Some cities use both decentralized and centralized investigatory units. The decentralized squads operate out of a local precinct and refer some of their cases to the specialized centralized squads, such as sex crime, homicide, or arson squads. The decentralized squads then investigate less serious cases themselves. In smaller departments, detectives tend to be generalists. There may be one detective with expertise and special training in sex crimes, juvenile crimes, cybercrimes, and homicide crimes. Or, one or two detectives may receive all of this training and conduct all major investigations in their jurisdiction. In some cities, the police department may call for assistance from county or state law enforcement when confronted with a homicide or rash of sex crimes. It really doesn't matter which approach the jurisdiction uses as long as the individuals who investigate the major crimes have the latest training available and have current information about the legal issues. It is also helpful to work closely with the prosecutor's office as early in the investigation as possible.

The Detective Mystique

Detectives work out of uniform, perform no patrol duties, and are sometimes paid at a higher rate than regular uniformed officers. The assignment to detective duties has in the past been a promotion that an officer attains through a promotional exam process. That has changed during the last couple of decades for several reasons, though in larger, big-city departments, it is still a promotion with higher pay. In most small and mid-sized departments, a detective is a plainclothes police officer. They are the same rank as a police officer, but through a competitive process have attained an assignment in the detective bureau or division. They may be paid more in the form of assignment pay or clothing allowance required by their union or collective bargaining contract. The important distinction between the detective as a plainclothes police officer versus as a promotional rank is that when the position is not a rank, it is a temporary assignment. If it doesn't work out or the department needs to downsize the detective division, the officer can be transferred back to the road without being demoted or violating the contract. Often, officers are chosen for transfer to the detective bureau based on their performance as a patrol officer. There is no guarantee that the individual chosen will be the same high performer as a detective, and most departments prefer the flexibility of being able to assign them back to the road. Though the jobs are very similar, some different skill sets are needed, and the work conditions vary enough that the fit may not be right. Conversely, an officer may love the job of patrol officer and conducting the occasional investigation and the preliminary investigations that come his or her way, but not like doing it every day. Sometimes, patrol officers don't realize exactly what the detective job involves before they actually do it. They may miss the day-to-day contact with citizens and being able to help them in small ways. They may miss the excitement of responding at the time of the crime. Most noticeably, new detectives may tire of the constant stress of conducting investigations and never feeling as if they have finished their job. As a road officer, most officers start their shift with a clean slate, whereas at the start of each tour, detectives find themselves facing the cases and work that they left the day before. They tend to take their cases home with them and think about them at night and sometimes even dream about them. This doesn't create a problem for many or most detectives who learn to cope in their own ways, but it makes some prefer to go back to the patrol division. When the positions are the same rank, this can be done with minimal embarrassment and a minimal impact to their career or financial status. Why would there be embarrassment? Even in police departments, not to mention in the general community, detectives generally enjoy much greater status and prestige than patrol officers do. Detectives have historically been seen as the heroes of police work in novels, television, and the movies—consider Sherlock Holmes, Cagney and Lacey, Andy Sipowicz, Crockett and Tubbs, Dirty Harry Callahan, and other fictional detectives. Are real-life detectives as heroic, smart, individualistic, tough, hardworking, and mysterious as their fictional counterparts? Or is there a mystique attached to the detective position?

The **detective mystique** is the idea that detective work is glamorous, exciting, and dangerous, as it is depicted in the movies and on television. In reality, however, detectives spend most of their time filling out reports and re-interviewing victims

on the telephone. Commenting on the detective mystique, Herman Goldstein has written,

> Part of the mystique of detective operations is the impression that a detective has difficult-to-come-by qualifications and skills, that investigating crime is a real science, that a detective does much more important work than other police officers, that all detective work is exciting and that a good detective can solve any crime. . . . [In] the context of the totality of police operations, the cases detectives solve account for a much smaller part of police business than is commonly realized. This is so because in case after case, there is literally nothing to go on: no physical evidence, no description of the offender, no witness and often no cooperation, even from the victim.[10]

Before the Rand Study of the Criminal Investigation Process, the detective mystique was considered an accurate representation of reality. It was believed that each crime was completely investigated, that all leads and tips were followed to their logical conclusion, and that each case was successfully solved. This was not true, as we will see when we discuss the Rand study. The reality of detective work usually has little in common with its media representations. Much of what detectives do consists of routine and simple chores and it is somewhat boring; it is arguable as to whether any special skills are required to be a detective according to Herman Goldstein.[11]

Because of the Rand study and other studies, police administrators can now make some generalizations about detective operations. First, the single most important determinant of whether or not a crime is solved is not the quality of the work performed by the detectives but the information the responding officers obtain from the victim and witnesses at the scene.[12] Next, detectives are not very effective in solving crimes. Nationally, police are only able to clear (solve) 46.3 percent of all violent crimes (murder, forcible rape, robbery, aggravated assault) and 16.5 percent of property crimes (burglary, theft, and motor vehicle theft) reported to them. These figures are relatively consistent from year to year. The difference between the clearance rates for violent versus property crimes is because of the vigorous investigation put forth in the more serious cases and because the violent crimes often have a victim or witness available to assist police with information.[13] Furthermore, because not all cases are reported to the police, the clearance rate is actually even lower. (Police cannot clear crimes not reported to them.) Finally, patrol officers, not detectives, are responsible for the vast majority of all arrests, which they generally make at the scene of the crime.

Alternatives to Retroactive Investigation of Past Crimes by Detectives

Current popular alternatives to retroactive investigation of past crimes by detectives are improved investigation of past crimes and repeat offender programs. These innovative techniques are designed to concentrate investigative resources on crimes that have a high chance of being solved.

Improved Investigation of Past Crimes

The National Advisory Commission on Criminal Justice Standards and Goals has recommended the increased use of patrol officers in the criminal investigation process. The commission recommended that every police agency direct patrol officers to conduct thorough preliminary investigations and recommended that agencies establish written priorities to ensure that investigative efforts are spent in a manner that best achieves organizational goals. The commission further recommended that investigative specialists (detectives) only be assigned to very serious or complex preliminary investigations.[14] As a consequence of the Rand study and other studies, the Law Enforcement Assistance Administrative (LEAA) funded research that led to the publication and wide dissemination of a new proposal regarding methods that should be used to investigate past crimes.[15]

Managing Criminal Investigations (MCI)

The proposal that resulted from the LEAA research, **Managing Criminal Investigations (MCI)**, offers a series of guidelines that recommend (1) expanding the role of patrol officers to include investigative responsibilities and (2) designing a new method to manage criminal investigations by including **solvability factors,** case screening, case enhancement, and police and prosecutor coordination.[16] Under an MCI program, the responding patrol officer is responsible for a great deal of the follow-up activity that used to be assigned to detectives. These duties include locating and interviewing the victim and witnesses, detecting physical evidence, and preparing an initial investigative report that will serve as a guide for investigators. This report must contain proper documentation to indicate whether the case should be assigned for continued investigation or immediately suspended for lack of evidence.[17] The other major innovation under MCI involves the use of a managerial system that grades cases according to their solvability; detectives then work only on cases that have a chance of being solved. Though it can vary by department, the road supervisor will often make the decision about whether the case will be followed up by the road officer or a detective or whether the case will be "inactivated" based on these solvability factors. Some solvability factors include the following:

1. Is there a witness?

2. Is a suspect named or known?

3. Can a suspect be identified?

4. Will the complainant cooperate in the investigation?

Each solvability factor is given a numerical weight. In the next process, case screening, the total weight of all solvability factors—the total score—determines whether the case will be investigated or not.[18] The MCI method of managing investigations is designed to put most of an investigator's time and effort into only very important cases and into cases that actually can be solved. Research conducted by numerous police departments has demonstrated that scoring systems using checklists and point scores successfully screen out cases with a low probability of being solved and identify promising cases.[19]

Over the years, departments using the MCI approach have redesigned their crime reports to highlight these solvability factors. An education component aids the success of the program. Detectives and patrol officers must be educated about the philosophy and the goals of the program as well as the techniques to employ. This can be a difficult hurdle to overcome generations of the expectation of detectives "solving" all crimes. Citizens must also be informed by the responding officer about what to expect to happen to their case. Because most cases (especially property crimes) have little or no significant evidence, the percentage screened out for no follow-up would be considerable.[20] Sometimes the solvability factors may be disregarded, and a case will be investigated that does not meet the numerical criteria because of officers' concern, political reasons, or public safety. Some cases are so important or serious that they demand a follow-up regardless of their potential solvability based on the solvability factors. The MCI approach gives investigators a more manageable caseload and an opportunity to be more organized and methodical in their efforts. Investigators will be more efficient when they are working 15 to 20 cases a month with strategic investigative activities than when they are carrying 40 to 50 cases a month, many of which are not solvable and there isn't much they can do other than keep looking at them and hoping something will appear. Even with all the changes recommended by the Rand and other studies, and even though police departments have implemented many changes in the investigatory process, the police are still not very successful in clearing crimes reported to them. The improved methods of investigation, however, have resulted in less waste and more efficiency in police detective operations and have allowed departments to use personnel in more proactive policing.

Mentoring and Training

Training for investigators or detectives has long been viewed as a way to improve their productivity. Specialized investigations require specialized training. This includes homicide investigation, sex crime investigation, juvenile crime and juvenile offenders, cybercrime, white-collar crime, and even auto theft. Detectives or investigators are usually sent to these specialized schools as soon as practical or perhaps even before they are appointed as investigators.

Informal **mentoring** programs have gone on for years as experienced detectives have taught new detectives what they know. Often detectives would see potential in a patrol officer, then mentor or work with that officer, even when he or she is still a patrol officer. These patrol officers may come in when they're not on shift to work a case with detectives or manage to talk their road supervisors into freeing the patrol officers to work with detectives on an investigation, thereby gaining experience.

Some departments have also implemented formal mentoring programs. Typically, a mentor is a role model, teacher, motivator, coach, or advisor who invests time in facilitating another person's professional job growth. A mentor program allows a non-investigator to be paired with an experienced investigator to become familiar with the investigative process. It strengthens non-investigators' preliminary investigation skills, eases the transition should they become detectives, and allows them to "try out" the role of investigator to see if they would like it. Overall, mentoring improves the quality of investigations throughout the department and improves the skills of all personnel involved.[21] This also helps to keep the knowledge pool current to prepare for the inevitable job turnover. When police detectives retire, they take a wealth of information with them. A good mentoring program allows that information to be shared with others.[22] *Agent - Unabomber 20 yrs*

Crime Analysis and Information Management

Crime Analysis

Crime analysis has grown tremendously in the last two decades. Crime analysis is the process of analyzing the data collected in a police organization to determine exactly what the crime problem is and where, when, and possibly even why it is happening. Crime analysis goes hand in hand with community-oriented policing and problem-oriented policing. Analysis allows the smarter use of information and, consequently, the smarter use of personnel and resources to address the true crime problem. Many departments employ full-time civilian crime analysts, but others have their investigators do the crime analysis as part of their investigative responsibility. The goal of crime analysis is to determine crime patterns and problems.[23] It begins with collating the information that comes in to the police department. This includes the information from dispatch, the police reports, and intelligence information, as well as information gathered from parking citations, traffic citations, and field interviews. Crime analysis allows police to make links between incidents that have occurred

Modus Operandi

IACP PERF NA

and people and vehicles passing through town. This is especially critical for bigger departments where various shifts and beats may not know what the other is doing. Historically, before computers and formal crime analysis, officers often did this function on their own. They knew who on their beats did burglaries and what their modus operandi (MO) was and whether they were in or out of jail. As crime increased and cities and towns grew, it became more difficult for officers to do this on their own. With the advent of computers, it became possible to formally perform this function to allow better deployment of police resources. With incident reports and citations formatted to collect the relevant data, data can then be retrieved to look for trends or patterns. For instance, when burglaries increase, analysts can look at the reports and query via the computer to see where in town they are occurring, what time they are occurring, what is being taken, and how the burglars are gaining entry. Analysts may also be able to come up with possible suspects based on past burglaries or vehicle description and can put out reports detailing this information and telling patrol officers what to look for. This information can help the agency, and the beat officer in particular, know how to direct their efforts in directed patrol activities on particular shifts. It can also help shift supervisors know how to allocate their personnel and help the appropriate division determine the best strategy to address a particular crime pattern, such as decoys, stings, or public notification and education. This means "working smarter" with the resources at hand. Ultimately, this information can also be used for budgetary purposes to request more personnel or equipment as the particular crime patterns and trends may dictate.

Information Management

The key to police work, and in particular investigations, is information and obtaining good information. Whether it is information from complainants, victims, witnesses, the suspect, or all the various files of data that are kept, it can all enhance and strengthen the investigation. In this computer age, we have a lot of information at our fingertips. Sometimes, it may seem that there may be too much information, and we may experience information overload. Although this increased information generally helps with solving crimes, it can

also require many hours of work to go through the information and discern which information is valuable and pertinent to the case. The computer age has allowed law enforcement agencies to share information with each other, which has enhanced investigations and assisted with detecting patterns and similar MOs.

Detectives can obtain information from a number of sources and share it in several ways. The Internet provides an opportunity for police personnel to research topics and to share knowledge with other officers through internal e-mail lists, expert directories, professional organizations, and outside e-mail lists that pertain to certain areas of interest. Journals, trade magazines, and newspaper articles that may be available online can be a wealth of information regarding what strategies are being used in other departments and also alert investigators to crime trends in neighboring communities.[24] This has traditionally been done and continues to be done in person as well. Investigators will hold monthly meetings with investigators who work similar types of crime (such as sex crimes, auto thefts, and so forth) from other agencies and compare and share information. Information on the Internet and through e-mail is often more current than a meeting is. Do these methods of sharing information over the computer help law enforcement be more efficient? In a recent study, the officers using an automated information system in the San Diego area strongly believed that information sharing made them more productive. They participated in a web-based network of criminal justice agencies called the *Automated Regional Justice Information System* (ARJIS) that allowed them to gather information for tactical analysis and investigations. The system could be requested to notify them when information they need about a person or vehicle or location becomes available from another agency or officer. Though they felt the information system made them more productive compared with the control group in an area of the country without an automated regional system, the data didn't indicate this. The investigators with the regional system had lower clearance rates and arrest rates than did the control group without the automated regional system. However, the control group was using CompStat as part of its management system so that might have accounted for the higher clearance and arrest rate.[25]

Whereas crime analysis addresses routine crime, intelligence analysis tends to emphasize organized

Information vs Intelligence

crimes (usually involving narcotics, human smuggling, gambling, and terrorism). This intelligence can be obtained from many sources, as with crime analysis, evaluated for reliability and validity, and used in a proactive manner.[26] Police in Kansas City, Missouri, created a task force to see if there were any common threads among the increased number of murders that occurred in 2005. They analyzed all the data available on the 127 murders and found that 85 percent of the victims had some type of criminal record and that the use of guns in homicides is up (105 of the homicides were shootings). In response to this information, they doubled the numbers of detectives assigned to investigate assaults with the goal of stopping them before they become homicides, and in 2006, the rate of murders is down 28 percent for the first half of year.[27] The FBI has recently updated its information technology given the weaknesses recognized after the terrorist attacks of September 11, 2001. The goal of this undertaking is to make sure that the dots are connected next time. These updates include deploying a high-speed, secure network that allows FBI personnel around the country to share data, and audio, video, and image files and an information technology (IT) infrastructure that allows secure communication with FBI intelligence community partners including designated local law enforcement officers. In addition, the FBI deployed several new investigative and information-sharing capabilities to make accessing investigative information and uncovering potential links between information bits easier than the previously labor-intensive and time-intensive systems.[28]

It is hoped that by being better able to record, analyze, share and disseminate information to the needed parties, more crimes can be solved, more offenders jailed, and more incidents prevented.

Multi-Agency Investigative Task Forces

In recent years, there has been an increase in the use of multi-agency **investigative task forces.** With the realization that criminals know no boundaries, and often intentionally cross jurisdictional lines to commit crimes, the importance of sharing information and working together has been increasingly recognized. With some areas of the country experiencing record-breaking crime rates and

violence, they are willing to try new approaches to solve the crimes, including cooperative investigative efforts. Recently, Palm Beach County, Florida, instituted the 13-member Palm Beach County Violent Crime Task Force, which consists of 7 full-time and 6 part-time detectives from various agencies in the county as well as the sheriff's office and the school district police (public schools are organized in a county wide school district which has its own police department). A full-time prosecutor is assigned to the task force and investigators from the FBI, the U.S. Marshals Service, the federal Bureau of Alcohol, Tobacco, Firearms and Explosives, and the Florida Department of Law Enforcement are available to assist. Local agencies call on the unit when they have difficulty solving a homicide, drive-by shooting, violent home invasion, or armed robbery that appears to involve gangs or career criminals. The unit consists primarily of veteran violent-crime and gang detectives who are actively involved in each other's cases. With the free flow of information about these individuals and gangs, detectives are often able to make connections they were unable to make before instituting this unit. Detectives gather information from their informants and use it to solve these cases, regardless of jurisdiction. It has also proved beneficial to have a prosecutor involved from the beginning, helping investigators build stronger cases to get and keep these offenders off the street.[29]

One of the largest multi-agency task forces involved the Washington, D.C., area sniper investigation during fall 2002. This manhunt and investigation, which led to the capture of 2 individuals, involved more than 20 local, 2 state, and at least 10 federal law enforcement agencies. This investigation spanned 23 days in October 2002 while the Virginia, Maryland, and D.C. areas were terrorized by snipers with high-powered rifles shooting at people indiscriminately. John Allen Muhammad and Lee Boyd Malvo were arrested at a rest area in Myersville, Maryland, but not before shooting 14 people, 10 of whom died. In 2004, Muhammad was sentenced to death and Malvo (a teenager) was sentenced to life in prison.[30] The Police Executive Research Forum (PERF) issued a report entitled *Managing a Multijurisdictional Case: Identifying Lessons Learned from the Sniper Investigation,* which identified the challenges faced by law enforcement personnel in this particular incident, including having to conduct criminal investigations

© Wally McNamee/Corbis

Investigations can be very complex and involve many agencies. During the 1996 Summer Olympic Games in Atlanta, the investigation into the bombing in Centennial Olympic Park involved the Atlanta Police Department, the FBI, and ATF as well as other state and county agencies.

with the public. This was probably enhanced in this particular area because the federal agencies work with the state and local law enforcement more than they might in other parts of the country. PERF recommends having a plan for investigations or incidents such as this, and though it might not exactly apply to each situation, it can be tweaked and put in place. One of the crucial aspects is defining roles and responsibilities. The agencies involved in this case did an exemplary job considering the unprecedented nature of the incident, though there was some room for improvement. Crucial to an investigation like this is providing a daily briefing to staff to curtail rumors and regular and honest communication among the leaders of the agency. This was accomplished via a daily or more frequent conference call with the leaders of the organizations and daily briefings within their organizations. An automated and efficient way of receiving tips (they received almost 10,000 tips a day) is critical to minimize duplication of effort and to make sure a crucial lead is not lost. There also have to be regular conversations regarding what information will be released to the public to allow citizens to protect themselves and possibly contribute to the investigation, yet not panic and succumb to mass hysteria. Overall, it was felt that organizational barriers and power and control issues that might ordinarily have arisen were overridden by the seriousness of the crimes and everyone's desire to do whatever it took to solve the crime, arrest the offenders, and make the public safe.[33] This incident and response as well as the report can serve as an important guide to agencies to have a plan in place for any similar situation that might arise. In today's extremely mobile society and with copycat crimes as well as individuals wanting their 15 minutes of fame, a well thought-out plan for law enforcement can greatly enhance the likelihood of a quick resolution to a serious incident.

simultaneously on each incident, trying to prevent more from occurring, and responding to the scenes as new ones occurred.[31]

PERF identified information management and teamwork or relationships as being the most critical issues in a major investigation such as this. The difference between a quick apprehension and a prolonged frustrating effort, said the report, lay in the development of an effective information management system.[32] The communication included communicating between leaders of the agencies, communicating with the rank and file and people on the street, and communicating

Repeat Offender Programs (ROPs)

U.S. criminologist Marvin Wolfgang discovered that only a few criminals are responsible for most of the predatory street crime in the United States. Most Americans do not commit street robberies; only a relatively small group of people does, but they commit a tremendous amount of crime each year. Borrowing from Wolfgang's research, police started to address their investigative resources to the career criminal using repeat offender programs (ROPs). These programs can be conducted in two major ways.

First, police can identify certain people to be the target of investigation. Once a career criminal is identified, the police can use surveillance techniques, follow the criminal, and wait to either catch the person in the act of committing a crime or catch him or her immediately after a crime occurs. These target offender programs are labor intensive.

The second way police can operate a ROP is through case enhancement. Specialized career criminal detectives can be notified of the arrest of a robbery suspect by other officers and then determine from the suspect's conviction or arrest rate whether or not the arrest merits enhancement. If the case is enhanced, an experienced detective assists the arresting officer in preparing the case for presentation in court and debriefs the suspect to obtain further information. A major tactic behind case enhancement is liaison with the district attorney's office to alert the prosecuting attorney to the importance of the case and to the suspect's past record. Such information helps ensure zealous efforts by the prosecutor. Houston Police Department's Targeted Offender program uses a pre-arrest targeting and post-arrest case enhancement to get violent career criminals off the street.[34] The Maricopa County, Arizona, attorney's office targets repeat offenders for special prosecution with the belief that 10 percent of known offenders are responsible for 90 percent of crime.[35]

A study in Washington, D.C., found that a proactive repeat offender unit was successful in arresting targeted offenders. In addition, those offenders who were apprehended had much more extensive and serious prior records than other arrested offenders. The tactics of this unit included conducting surveillances of active offenders, locating wanted serious offenders, acting on tips from informants, and employing decoy and sting methods.[36]

Marcia Chaiken and Jan Chaiken, in their report *Priority Prosecutors of High-Rate Dangerous Offenders*, distinguished between persistent offenders (those who commit crimes over a long period of time), high-rate offenders (those who commit numerous crimes per year), and dangerous offenders (those who commit crimes of violence).[37]

Chaiken and Chaiken suggest that the most accurate way to identify high-rate dangerous offenders is using a two-stage screening process. The first stage, they say, should look for evidence of a serious previous felony conviction, failure to complete a previous sentence, arrests while in pretrial release, or a known drug problem. The authors state that defendants falling into three of these categories have a 90 percent chance of being high-rate dangerous offenders and should be further screened. The second screening involves looking for evidence of the following: use of a weapon in the current crime, one or more juvenile convictions for robbery, or status of wanted for failure to complete a previous sentence.[38] The presence of any of these aggravating factors would cause the defendant to be considered a high-rate dangerous offender. The authors suggest that any defendant considered a high-rate dangerous offender should receive special attention by investigators and prosecutors.

The Chicago Police Department implemented a program targeting repeat offenders in Englewood, a 4-square-mile section of the city in which more than 700 people have been murdered in the last decade, including 61 in 2002.[39] The Repeat Offender Geographic Urban Enforcement Strategies (ROGUES) project will assign a Cook County prosecutor to the police districts that have a lot of narcotics trafficking taking place around schools and churches. When law enforcement identifies an individual as a problem due to gang membership, violent history, or being a repeat offender, the ROGUES team will be notified, and the assigned prosecutor will follow the case to its conclusion.

Working from the belief that 10 percent of criminals commit as many as half of the crimes, the Los Angeles Police Department (LAPD) has implemented a program in which the department seeks the stiffest possible penalties for the most frequent repeat offenders, even for relatively minor crimes. This is called the "10 percenter" program, and the LAPD hopes to reduce crime on the streets by keeping repeat criminals behind bars as long as possible. According to Chief William J. Bratton, "This gives us the maximum bang for the buck by focusing on that 10 percent."[40] Boston implemented a program that will markedly increase around-the-clock physical surveillance of dozens of hard-core criminals on the city streets in an effort to forestall what officials and community leaders feared would be a particularly bloody summer. The police indicate that summers are generally the more violent time of year, and in 2006, violent crime was alarmingly high. The police were monitoring the criminals believed responsible for the significant increase in gun violence. The goal is to catch the criminals in the act if they commit a crime and to otherwise gather intelligence information.[41] A pilot program involving the federal government and local agencies called the *Violent Crime Impact Teams* (VCIT) has found that during the first 6 months of operation, 13 of the 15 pilot programs have reported decreases in homicides committed with firearms. This program was designed to identify, target, disrupt, arrest, and prosecute the worst criminal offenders in high crime areas throughout the country. The strategy relies heavily on a team effort between the federal, state, and local law enforcement agencies in the area and it's believed to be the most crucial factor to the long-term success of the initiative. Overall, the VCIT areas reported a 17 percent decrease in firearm-related homicides, 500 targeted individuals were arrested, 3,000 firearms were confiscated, more than $2 million was seized, and 2,500 other criminals were arrested. The initiative appears to be a success, and additional cities are being added.[42]

Internet Registries

Some jurisdictions are enacting laws requiring the registration of various types of criminals. For years, sex offenders have been tracked in most states. This primarily serves as a public notification system, to allow parents to know if there are any sex offenders living in their neighborhood. This allows parents to take the proper precautions to keep their children safe and notifies local law enforcement of individuals residing in their community with a past in this particular type of crime. If a crime occurs, the officers have individuals they can contact or investigate as part of their investigation into a particular crime, possibly increasing the chances of a successful investigation. Some states have added the information they provide on the registry. The state of Florida recently added vehicle information (and boat information) as well as more detailed crime information to its sex offender website. This is to assist citizens in more accurately

assessing their risk.[43] Recently, some states have created a similar registry for meth offenders. The governor of Minnesota signed an executive order creating a new online registry for people convicted of making or selling methamphetamine. It is modeled after a similar registry in Tennessee. The governor stated, "When you have public awareness of the presence of these individuals, there will be further accountability by neighbors, by people who are interested in making sure that their areas of work or residence are safe." Georgia, Oklahoma, Washington, and West Virginia have similar bills pending, and Montana and Illinois have laws in place. In Illinois, the purpose of the law is to expedite law enforcement's research regarding conviction records rather than inform the public, but the public isn't barred from accessing the information.[44] The hope is that these neighbors and citizens would be extra vigilant and perhaps help in investigations, allowing law enforcement to get these offenders off the streets for longer periods.[45] Washington, D.C., approved an emergency bill in July 2006 in an effort to fight the surge in violent crime and help investigators in their investigations of violent crimes that occur. In addition to imposing a curfew for all youths younger than 18, the bill gives police immediate access to some confidential juvenile records. Under the bill, family court is required to report the release of juveniles with multiple and violent offenses and their location within 48 hours to the police. This is currently provided on a case-by-case basis when requested. Washington, D.C., Police Chief Charles H. Ramsey believes the information will help detectives solve cases and reduce crime.[46]

Global Positioning System (GPS) Technology

Surveillance of offenders is extremely labor intensive and costly. Today, technology has improved to a degree to allow law enforcement to track offenders without having them physically followed 24 hours a day. Global Positioning System (GPS) technology has allowed many states to implement programs monitoring offenders. It costs between 5 and 10 dollars a day to track each offender, and many states require offenders to pay unless they are indigent. Though some states are using it to monitor paroled gang members, most are using it to monitor sex offenders. Some states have named their laws after Jennifer Lunsford, a 9-year-old Florida

CHAPTER 10 ■ Investigations **273**

girl who was kidnapped, raped, and killed in February 2005, by a man who was a convicted sex offender who hadn't reported that he lived across the street from her family. He fled after her murder, and it took a month to find him. Many states have passed laws, and others have bills pending because it appears to have tremendous support among elected officials. At least 23 states have implemented programs to monitor sex offenders by satellite. Most are reporting success with their programs. In California, in just under a year, 45 offenders (out of 130) have been arrested for violating parole and no new crimes have been committed. Massachusetts has arrested 8 of its 192 high-risk offenders in the same period. A study by Florida State University released in February 2006 found that offenders tracked by GPS were 90 percent less likely to abscond or re-offend than were those not monitored. Most states plan to continue and possibly expand their programs.[47]

Closed-Circuit TV

Surveillance cameras are everywhere today, and despite some challenges, most courts have upheld their use, stating that they are not a violation of individuals' rights because there is no expectation of privacy in most of these locations. Although these cameras have been touted as a crime prevention tool, they have been critical in solving some major cases in the last few years. Many cities across the country, large and small, are allocating budget dollars to install surveillance cameras, including New York City, Louisville, Cincinnati, Seattle, Baltimore, Chicago, and Philadelphia. Some dispute their value in crime fighting and crime prevention and even their constitutionality.[48] However, it is hard to dispute the contribution they have made in some high-profile cases recently that may not have been solved had it not been for surveillance cameras that had been installed by property owners. When 11-year-old Carlie Brucia was reported missing in Sarasota, Florida, on February 1, 2004, there were few leads other than where she had been and that she was believed to be heading home. Detectives obtained a surveillance video from a car wash located along Carlie's route home. The video showed Carlie walking along the rear of the car wash and a man was seen approaching her and forcibly walking her out of view of the camera. This video was released to the media and an "Amber Alert" system was activated. Numerous phone calls were received

identifying the suspect, Joseph Smith, and he was subsequently arrested[49] and convicted[50] of raping and murdering Carlie.

A surveillance tape that showed three teens beating a homeless man with a baseball bat in Fort Lauderdale, Florida, led to the arrest of the teens for first-degree murder and attempted first-degree murder. The attack was linked to other attacks, one of which ended in the death of the victim. The teens were identified by TV news viewers after the tape was aired and the public was asked for help.[51] Other videotapes have captured robbers, burglars, and vandals on tape and, when aired on TV, have resulted in some arrests. A surveillance camera in a convenience store and the persistence of a concerned citizen who made the video known to law enforcement led to a little girl being found in the company of a convicted sex offender.

These cases would most likely not have had a successful conclusion if not for the public coming forward in response to images captured on tape.

Cold-Case Squads

The advances of DNA technology have led to the increase in the use of cold-case squads to solve crimes. **Cold-case squads** reexamine old cases that have remained unsolved. They use the passage of time coupled with a fresh set of eyes to help solve cases that had been stagnant for years and often decades.

Over time, relationships change. People may no longer be married, may no longer be friends, or may no longer be intimidated or afraid of the same people. Someone who was reluctant to talk because of fear or loyalty may decide to tell the truth years later. Individuals may have found religion or changed their lifestyles, and years later realize that what they did, witnessed, or knew about was bad and they want to set the record straight. Cold-case detectives re-interview all individuals involved and hope someone has had a change of heart over the years or forgotten what was said initially, allowing police to uncover new information.

Cold-case detectives also use the passage of time in another way. They take advantage of the tremendous advances in forensic science, especially DNA testing. Much smaller samples are necessary now to get a more definitive match through DNA than even a couple of years ago. Cold-case detectives are able to solve many cases solely by

© AP/Wide World Photos

Mike Evanoff, owner of Evie's Car Wash, testifies about this security video footage from his business which was used in the trial of Joseph Smith. Smith was charged in the death of 11-year-old Carlie Brucia after he was identified in the security video footage approaching Brucia and taking her forcibly by the arm.

reexamining the evidence. In 1977, a 6-year-old girl was reported missing in Reno, Nevada; 23 years later, the detectives had her clothes retested, finding previously undetected DNA evidence, tying the crime to a convicted felon.[52] In 2003, an individual was arrested in Miami for a 10-year-old, previously unsolved murder in Seattle after he was arrested for another crime, and his DNA was obtained and compared with DNA from the victim's body resubmitted by investigators. This had been a random sexual assault and murder by an individual with no known connection to the victim. The investigation revealed that the suspect had in fact lived in Seattle for a brief period of time, during which the murder occurred. Another case that caused a lot of fear in the community of Wichita, Kansas, was solved in 2005. The BTK (a name the killer gave himself many years ago stood for bind, torture, kill) killer who was believed responsible for 10 murders from 1974 to 1991 was arrested. The BTK killer had taunted the police and media over the years with letters, but the po-

lice were never able to solve the murders. The killer had apparently been inactive for almost 13 years when the *Wichita Eagle* published a 30-year anniversary story about the BTK killer in 2004. Dennis Rader came to the attention of the police, and he was pinpointed as the killer based on DNA evidence obtained from his daughter's medical records.[53] The community was shocked because the killer, Dennis L. Rader, was a long-term, active community member with a wife and two children and very involved with the Boy Scouts and his church, but relieved at his capture.[54]

Investigators who make up the cold-case squad must not be afraid to use whatever means may help their case, including the media. Some use shows such as *America's Most Wanted* to help bring a suspect or a crime back into the mind of the public. Detectives use innovative ideas to obtain evidence they may need for comparison purposes. A man from New Jersey was recently arrested for a decades-old murder of a teenage girl in Seattle, when he too was a teen. He had been a prime suspect, but investigators had no evidence linking him to the crime. In 2003, they sent him a form to fill out to participate in a suit regarding parking fines in Seattle. He filled out the form, put it in the envelope, licked the envelope, and mailed it back to Seattle. Detectives were able to match the DNA from his saliva to that found on evidence, and he was arrested. That case has also withstood several challenges by his attorneys, and the defendant is in prison.

Cold-case squads are providing great hope and comfort to families of victims of old, unsolved crimes and a sense of justice to the community when detectives are able to solve these long-unsolved cases and bring defendants to justice.

New Proactive Tactics

Decoy Operations

One of the primary purposes of police patrol is to prevent crime by creating a sense of omnipresence; potential criminals are deterred from crime by the presence or potential presence of the police. Omnipresence does not work well, however. We have crime both on our streets and in areas where ordinary police patrols cannot see crime developing, such as the inside of a store or the hallway of a housing project. We have also seen that retroactive investigations of crimes, with the intent to identify and arrest perpetrators, are not very effective.

During the past three decades, an innovative proactive approach to apprehending criminals in the course of committing a crime has developed—**decoy operations.** Decoy operations take several forms, among them blending and decoy. In **blending,** officers dressed in civilian clothes try to blend into an area and patrol it on foot or in unmarked police cars in an attempt to catch a criminal in the act of committing a crime. Officers may target areas where a significant amount of crime occurs, or they may follow particular people who appear to be potential victims or potential offenders. To blend, officers assume the roles and dress of ordinary citizens—construction workers, shoppers, joggers, bicyclists, physically disabled persons, and so on—so that the officers, without being observed as officers, can be close enough to observe and intervene should a crime occur.

In decoy, officers dress as, and play the role of, potential victims—drunks, nurses, businesspeople,

tourists, prostitutes, blind people, isolated subway riders, or defenseless elderly people. The officers wait to be the subject of a crime while a team of backup officers is ready to apprehend the violator in the act of committing the crime. Decoy operations are most effective in combating the crimes of robbery, purse snatching, and other larcenies from the person; burglaries; and thefts of and from automobiles.

Descriptions of decoy operations in major cities contain numerous successful applications.[55] A successful decoy operation was begun by the Miami Police Department in 1991 with the establishment of an undercover decoy operation targeting tourist robberies, known as Safeguarding Tourists Against Robberies (STAR). Members of this 12-officer unit pose as tourists sitting in parked rental cars near busy areas. When robbers strike, a backup team moves in to assist in the arrest. STAR has resulted in a 33 percent decrease in tourist robberies.[56]

The New York City Police Department's (NYPD) Street Crime Unit (SCU) has been extremely successful and has served as a model for numerous other police agencies. The SCU consists of experienced volunteer officers who are aggressive and street smart. The SCU members, who receive extensive training in decoy techniques, are assigned to high-crime areas.[57] Each of New York City's 76 patrol precincts has its own decoy unit, called an anticrime unit, composed of volunteer officers with high arrest records.

Among the more effective decoy and blending operations was another NYPD unit, the Taxi-Truck Surveillance Unit, which was organized to combat the growing number of nighttime assaults on truck and cab drivers. For a period of five years, specially equipped officers from both patrol and detective units were selected to play the roles of cabbies and truckers. This undercover approach ultimately reduced assaults and robberies of cabbies and truckers by almost 50 percent.[58] Police officers around the country have responded creatively to crime problems by playing many roles. Some have filled in as coffee shop employees or as baristas at espresso stands. They've worked at convenience stores, nail salons, and video stores in an effort to catch robbers in the act. Many successful arrests have been made in such situations, and the surrounding publicity creates uncertainty for criminals about whether their intended victim might be a police officer. A man who had posted a fraudulent ad for "models" and "actresses" in a South Florida newspaper and even rented a phony

ON THE JOB

Jogging on the Job

Decoy work varies tremendously in challenge and desirability. In large departments, it can be an officer's regular assignment, but in most mid-sized and smaller departments, it will be used as necessary depending on crime issues that arise. In these cases, it will usually be a break from an officer's regular assignment. Over my police career, I had many occasions to work decoy assignments in which females were targeted victims. I found these assignments to be a challenge and a welcome break to my routine, whether I was assigned to patrol or the detective bureau at the time.

One June we had a couple of incidents of indecent exposure at a popular but somewhat isolated jogging trail. We then had an incident where a female was grabbed at 8:00 AM and pulled into the bushes along this jogging trail. She fought her attacker off and managed to get away, but it was clearly an attempted rape. We decided that for two weeks, we would put a female out jogging this same trail in the early morning hours. Since I was known to be a runner, I was chosen for the assignment. It sounds pretty cool, get paid to run and work out on duty, but the conditions were less than ideal.

June in South Florida is *very* hot and humid, and this trail was in a scrub area with lots of bushes but not many trees; consequently, there was little shade. I put on a wire so that I had voice communication when I was out of sight of the two backup officers along the three-mile course. I had to be covered up enough to hide the wire, which meant I would be even warmer. I ran and walked for about two hours a day around this course; and, as I sweated profusely, jumped over and avoided snakes, and was bitten by the biggest horseflies I had ever seen, I started singing Helen Reddy's song "Ain't No Way to Treat a Lady" for the entertainment of my backup officers (and perhaps to make a point). We saw nothing of interest during the two weeks, and there were never any more attacks there, so the offender must have moved on or been arrested for something else. Or maybe he heard me singing and got scared off?

—*Linda Forst*

office and then proceeded to fondle and molest female applicants was shocked after one of his "applicants" came back to the office wearing a badge and reading him his rights.

Anticrime and decoy strategies focus on reducing serious and violent street crimes, apprehending criminals in the act, making quality arrests, and maintaining a high conviction record. In achieving successful prosecutions in their cases, decoy operations overcome the problem police encounter when witnesses and victims are reluctant to cooperate with police and prosecutors because of fear, apathy, or interminable court delays.[59]

A San Francisco police sergeant successfully defined the goals and operations of a decoy program: "The underlying theory . . . is that the type of criminal that is responsible for the most violent street crime is an opportunist. The criminal walks the streets looking for a victim that is weaker than himself, looking for an opportunity to make a 'score' without any danger to himself, or any danger of apprehension. The decoy program is intended to respond to this type of criminal."[60] There has been some criticism of decoy operations. As one former police commander says, "Decoy operations are often seen as entrapment, even though they rarely come close to it."[61] Also, decoy programs, in which officers dress and assume the roles of victims, can be dangerous to the officers involved.

As mentioned in Chapter 9, Patrol Operations, decoy vehicles can often be used to prevent crimes. They can also assist in solving crimes and enhancing investigations. When an agency has a lot of vehicles being broken into in a particular place, say a mall or hospital parking lot, they can set up a decoy vehicle with similarities to the vehicles that appear to be the target. Investigators can watch the vehicle and when the perpetrator breaks in, they can quickly make an arrest.

Stakeout Operations

Many crimes occur indoors, where passing patrol officers cannot see their occurrence. A stakeout consists of a group of heavily armed officers who hide in an area of a store or building waiting for an impending holdup. If an armed robber enters the store and attempts a robbery, the officers yell "Police!" from their hidden areas. If the perpetrators fail to drop their weapons, the officers open fire. Stakeouts are effective in cases in which the police receive a tip that a crime is going to occur in a commercial establishment or in which the police discover or come upon a pattern. A typical pattern would be a group of liquor stores in a certain downtown commercial area that have been robbed at gunpoint in a consistent way that indicates it might happen again. Stakeouts are extremely expensive in terms of police personnel. They are also controversial because they can be dangerous for all involved. The situations are always dynamic and officers have to decide how far to let the incident progress. There are so many variables that police can never know when violence may erupt in even a previously nonviolent pattern of crimes, and law enforcement personnel don't want to risk standing by and having innocent people get hurt.

Sting Operations

Sting operations, which have become a major law enforcement technique in recent years, involve using various undercover methods to apprehend thieves and recover stolen property. For example, the police rent a storefront and put the word out on the street that they will buy any stolen property—no questions asked. The police set up hidden video and audio recorders that can be used to identify "customers," who are then located and placed under arrest several months later. The audio and video recorders make excellent evidence in court. There are numerous examples of successful stings.

An FBI-run high-tech electronics store in Miami was used by drug traffickers to purchase beepers, cellular phones, and computers. The 17-month operation resulted in 93 arrests.[62] Another FBI sting in New Jersey, in which agents posed as fences who bought 170 stolen trucks and luxury cars worth $9 million during a 2-year period, netted 35 arrests.[63] Another type of sting operation is directed against people wanted on warrants. These wanted persons are mailed a letter telling them that they have won an award (such as tickets to an important ball game) and that they should report to a certain location (usually a hotel) at a certain time to pick up the prize. When the person appears, he or she is arrested.

Studies of sting operations have found that they account for a large number of arrests and the recovery of a significant amount of stolen property. However, the studies have failed to demonstrate that the tactic leads to reductions in crime.[64] A major drawback to sting operations is that they can serve as inducements to burglary and theft because they create a market for stolen goods. Sting operations can also lead to questions regarding ethics. Consider the congressional Abscam operations. Abscam was a 1978 to 1980 sting conducted by FBI agents against members of Congress. The agents, posing as Arab sheikhs, offered bribes to members of Congress in return for receive favors. The sting resulted in the conviction of seven members of Congress and other officials, as well as harsh criticism (by some) of the FBI for its undercover methods.

Recently, police departments have expanded their definition of stings. Frustrated with increasing gun violence and the perception that the federal government wasn't taking any action, New York City decided to take on gun dealers in other states. New York City sent teams of private investigators posing as gun buyers to stores in 5 states and caught 15 dealers making illegal sales. These businesses had been the source of 500 guns that were used in the commission of crimes in New York City. The operatives went into the stores with hidden cameras. One investigator looked at the guns, talked with the sales staff, and made the decision. This investigator then called the second investigator over (usually a female) who had not been involved in any way, to fill out the background paperwork, and then the first investigator would pay for the gun. This practice is referred to as using a "straw buyer," someone with no criminal record, to fill out the background paperwork to purchase a gun from a dealer.

One of the gun shops was in Orangeburg, South Carolina, and officials had traced 98 guns connected to crimes in New York City, including one death, to the shop. New York City sued this shop as well as the other 14 officials investigated. The lawsuit seeks monetary damages from the 15 dealers and the appointment of a special master to monitor sales closely, and city officials are debating whether to ask the court to shut the businesses down.[65] Within three months, two Georgia dealers had settled and agreed to monitoring. New York Mayor Michael Bloomberg had backed the investigation, which angered many in Congress and the gun industry, and is hopeful that the settlement will influence the other dealers involved and all dealers around the country.[66] Other cities around the country are following New York's lead, including Minneapolis, which discovered that some of its gun dealers were selling many guns to the same "straw buyers" repeatedly. Local gangs were using female "straw buyers" for the purchases.[67] This may be a way to increase accountability among gun dealers and sellers and help to bring down the violent crime rate.

Law enforcement has also been working with the media in operating child pornography stings. Since 2004, *Dateline* on the NBC TV network has been airing "To Catch a Predator" where a sting is set up in a rented home. *Dateline* staff members worked with an organization from Portland, Oregon, called Perverted Justice, whose volunteer members pose as young boys and girls in Internet chat rooms and wait to be contacted by adult men seeking sex with minors. The volunteers lure the men to the rented house, where they are confronted by a *Dateline* reporter on camera. Some of these men were subsequently arrested. In many situations, NBC did not notify local law enforcement. Citizens became outraged because these men were not arrested and law enforcement had to explain that they need a certain standard of proof and an investigation had to be conducted. After seeing the popularity of the show, NBC formalized its relationship with Perverted Justice, compensating their members financially, and started working more closely with law enforcement, which resulted in police making more arrests after the confrontations. These relationships and operations are not without controversy as roles and relationships have become blurred.[68] The public seems hungry for this type of story and eager to put these pedophiles behind bars. Legal outcomes and court challenges will help determine whether these types of arrangements and stings continue.

Civil Liability and Code Enforcement Teams

"Vacant apartments have become a maze of traps, meant to block out drug dealers' rivals and the police. Electrified wires have been stretched across window frames. Holes have been smashed in the walls and floors to provide easy escape routes. And hallway floors have been smeared with Vaseline to trip unwary intruders."[69] The hallways are spray-painted with directions to where the drugs are sold, and with a warning that informers will be killed.[70] This is a graphic example of the squalid and dangerous conditions that cities and their residents have had to face. Many have turned to **civil liability (or code) enforcement** to attempt to deal with local problems that have a negative effect on the quality of life in their communities. These cities use civil, as well as criminal, laws to force property owners and others in control of premises to correct illegal conditions. These cities have established code enforcement teams, which consist of a number of agents from different municipal agencies working together using local ordinances and codes, as well as the criminal law, in an attempt to solve particular problems.

Fort Lauderdale, Florida, has established a code enforcement team with members representing the police, fire, building, and zoning departments. In a three-year period, Fort Lauderdale's code enforcement team demolished 124 crack cocaine houses and boarded up another 587. The team collected $600,000 in fines from 300 property owners and property managers of substandard housing. Team members also pressured property owners into spending $5.7 million on repairs to deteriorating properties. Drug activity in the code enforcement team's targeted area dropped 57 percent.[71] By 2003, the team had six members, and the command issue that arose had been addressed by forming a steering committee. Executives from the affected departments as well as the assistant city manager serve on the steering committee to handle policy issues. The code team works closely with the community policing unit and has an extensive range of enforcement options to deal with quality-of-life issues, which has led to success.[72] Milwaukee, Wisconsin, formed an interagency team to combat crack houses in the city. Representatives from the city's police department, building inspection department, city attorney's office, and Community Outreach joined forces to attack drug houses in the community. In its first year, the team closed 264 drug houses. A key component to Milwaukee's success is the input from the public. The website has a link to "Report a Drug House" that explains how to identify a "drug house" as well as the negative ramifications of a drug house in the neighborhood. The site clearly

You Are There!

The Legality of Police Undercover Drug Investigations:
Gordon v. Warren Consolidated Board of Education

High-school officials had placed an undercover officer into regular classes to investigate student drug use. After the investigation, several students were arrested and convicted of participating in the drug trade. They appealed their convictions claiming that the actions of the school officials violated their rights under the First Amendment of the United States Constitution. Their appeal was dismissed by appellate court ruling that the presence of the police officer working undercover

did not constitute any more than a "chilling" effect on the students' First Amendment rights, because it did not disrupt classroom activities or education and it did not have any tangible effect on inhibiting expression of particular views in the classroom.

SOURCE: Based on *Gordon v. Warren Consolidated Board of Education,* 706 F.2d 778 6th Cir. (1983).

---

proclaims, "Milwaukee Police Department needs your help in identifying suspected drug houses in your neighborhood" and offers several ways that a citizen can report this information.[73]

In 1997, a zero-tolerance program targeting drug houses in Worcester, Massachusetts, was so successful that it had rid neighborhoods of locations where drug activity flourished. At least 60 drug houses were driven out of business, and police made hundreds of arrests in the interagency effort. The city put pressure on property owners to clean and make repairs to their properties. The owners were also put on notice that they could lose their properties under the city's nuisance laws if criminal activity reoccurs.[74] Worcester uses very aggressive methods to conduct its zero-tolerance program. Uniformed and undercover police officers flood the streets of the target areas, making arrests and maintaining a high-profile presence that keeps potential drug buyers away from the area. Worcester Police report that their partnerships with the Department of Housing and Urban Development (HUD) and the Worcester Housing Authority (WHA) have led to a continued reduction of crime and the fear associated with crime in the neighborhoods.[75]

Undercover Operations

An **undercover investigation** may be defined as one in which an investigator assumes a different identity to obtain information or achieve another

investigatory purpose. The undercover investigator generally plays the role of another person. In an undercover investigation, the investigator can be doing many things, including merely observing or performing certain actions that are designed to get other people to do something or to react to or interact with the investigator in a certain way. The primary function of the investigator in these cases is to play a role without anyone realizing that he or she is playing a role. In policing, the primary purpose of the undercover operation most often is the collection of evidence of crimes.

There are several general types of undercover investigations, including police undercover investigations, federal undercover investigations, and private security undercover investigations. This section will discuss these types of investigations and operations and will pay particular attention to the drug undercover investigation.

Police Undercover Investigations

These investigations generally include drug undercover investigations; stings, including warrant stings and fencing stings that involve the buying and selling of stolen goods and other contraband; decoy operations targeted against the crimes of robbery, burglary, and assault; anti-prostitution operations; and operations involving the infiltration and arrest of people involved in organized crime, white-collar crime, and corruption. Police undercover officers have a dangerous yet often rewarding job. It can be rewarding as well as a relief when the undercover officer gets to arrest the offender at the end of the investigation. Offenders are often very surprised when they realize the role an undercover officer played in their arrest. Undercover investigations can present some significant challenges to police officers and police organizations. Officers who infiltrate that lifestyle are living a lie. They spend their working hours in a role quite contrary to who they are. The difficulty involved in this will vary with the assignment and the length of the assignment. Hanging around with criminals and attempting to become their friends and fit in with the lifestyle can lead to a socialization process very different from what they experienced growing up and preparing for the police job. Their bonds to other officers and even family and friends may be cut or weakened depending on the assignment. This has contributed to some officers becoming deviant, adhering to the subculture, ending up breaking the law, and ending their careers. This is further complicated because undercover officers receive little supervision and often little training in preparation for their roles. This is a real tragedy for all concerned.

Realizing the difficult challenges and conditions that undercover officers face, departments are implementing policies to minimize the chance of officers going astray and to protect them and the department. The Commission on Accreditation for Law Enforcement Agencies (CALEA) requires departments to have policies and procedures in place concerning undercover and decoy operations as well as vice and drug surveillance and investigations.[76]

Federal Undercover Investigations

These investigations generally include efforts at detecting and arresting people involved in political corruption, insurance fraud, labor racketeering, and other types of organized conspiracy-type crimes. Perhaps the classic case of a successful undercover investigation was the work of FBI Special Agent Joseph D. Pistone, who assumed the cover identity of Donnie Brasco. Pistone began his infiltration of La Cosa Nostra (the American Mafia) in 1976 and continued it for six years. Pistone was so completely accepted by the Mafia that he was able to move freely among all the Mafia families and learn their secrets. He was so effective that he had

to terminate his undercover operations because he was about to be inducted into the Mafia as a "made man" and was expected to kill another Mafioso. As a result of Pistone's work, more than 100 federal criminal convictions were obtained, dealing a severe blow to Mafia operations throughout the United States.

An FBI undercover investigation shows the success of the undercover investigation concept. For two years, FBI agents conducted Operation Road Spill, in which they established a bogus company, Southern Leasing Systems of South Kearny, New Jersey. The agents posed as shady business people who were willing to pay cash for stolen BMWs, Acura Legends, and other luxury cars. During the investigation, they bought 120 stolen cars for a fraction of their value.[77]

The federal agencies, including the Drug Enforcement Administration (DEA), Customs, and the Bureau of Alcohol, Tobacco, Firearms and Explosives (ATF), often form joint task force investigations with local, county, and state law enforcement agencies. Some of the agents work undercover and others work surveillance. This allows them to pool resources and expertise. This approach has been particularly successful in South Florida. Many major drug or arms smuggling operations were broken up, arrests were made, and millions of dollars worth of property confiscated.

Private Security Undercover Investigations

Undercover security operations generally involve inventory losses, pilferage, willful neglect of machinery, unreported absenteeism, employee attitudes, and workplace harassment issues. Like the rest of society, violence has penetrated into the workplace. Employees' domestic troubles have followed them to the workplace and shootings and killings have occurred in the workplace because of issues regarding divorces, child custody, and other civil matters. There have been shootings in attorney's offices and at courthouses by individuals unhappy with the outcome of civil or criminal cases. Unfortunately, these violent incidents are often a surprise and shock, but sometimes there were signs that the business might have noticed. If there is a long-standing issue or problem, private security investigators can infiltrate the workplace to try to determine if a threat exists and if it can be mitigated before reaching the violent stage. This section will address the more common **private security industry** undercover operations: shopping services, anonymous reporting programs, internal intelligence programs, and the store detective.

Shopping Services Most larger corporations will have their own staff of "shoppers" who will travel from store to store as needed or randomly to check on employee integrity as well as service. Integrity analysis of employees is a very important aspect of undercover investigations. This test of employees' honesty is performed by "shoppers" (undercover agents) posing as customers and is designed to act as a deterrent to inventory shrinkage, detect dishonest employees, and provide evidence for prosecuting employees caught stealing. Private investigation firms will also provide the same service when a commercial outlet is too small to have its own department or employees are too well known to the employees being tested.

Anonymous Reporting Programs Wackenhut Corporation is a global private security and investigations firm offering many varied and far-reaching services in post–9/11 society. According to its website,[78] Wackenhut has a "Safe2Say" hotline that allows employees to report suspected incidents of wrongdoing in the workplace to highly trained, multilingual communications specialists. The hotline has a global reach and is available 24 hours, 7 days a week, toll free. This hotline gives employees a confidential, anonymous outlet to report concerns of fraud, theft, violence, and other workplace issues. Wackenhut reports that it created the program because of its belief that most employees are honest and that they are disturbed by the threat of illegal activities to their employer, their jobs, and themselves but are often afraid to speak out. This program can be customized to fit particular businesses. Wackenhut also offers an "Anything2Say" exit interview program for garnering similar information when employees leave the organization or business for any reason.

Internal Intelligence Program Private investigative firms offer corporations undercover internal intelligence programs in which they plant undercover agents into a corporation's business operations to make observations and report to the company. These programs have been used successfully in combating theft of funds and merchandise, use of alcohol or drugs on the job, gambling, sabotage, and other crimes or incidents that compromise the business's ability to continue to do business. Wackenhut also assists businesses with undercover investigations. It describes its undercover operations in the following way: Skilled investigators posing as employees are placed into an unsuspecting workforce to gather information on workplace problems.[79] They prepare a written report and make recommendations to the business regarding remedial action and prevention steps that can be taken. The net result of an effective investigation should be an objective and unbiased assessment of employee behavior, morale, and supervisory competence.

The Store Detective One of the most common types of undercover private investigations is the store detective (also known as a loss prevention specialist). Shoplifting is one of the most common crimes in the United States. Statistics available through the U.S. Department of Justice reveal that shoplifting is the fastest-growing crime in the larceny-theft category, with more than one million arrests reported each year since 1989. However, these figures may be only the tip of the iceberg; some experts speculate that for every shoplifter caught, as many as 10 to 20 others go undetected. Many individuals consider shoplifting a relatively safe crime with little likelihood of being caught. Coupled with many businesses that are reluctant to report and prosecute shoplifting, especially when the offender offers to pay, "forgot to pay," or is sorry and remorseful, it is difficult to determine exactly how much shoplifting is occurring.

Shrinkage is a major problem for retailers. The term *shrinkage* is used by retailers to describe the difference between inventory on hand at the beginning of the year and inventory on hand at year's end, taking into account the year's sales. It includes employee theft and vendor theft. In a national retail security survey, the average shrinkage for surveyed department stores was 1.7 percent. The total loss is estimated at $33 billion a year. This is the highest source of property crime annually in the United States. The average family of four spends $440 a year more in higher prices because of inventory theft.[80] A major portion of inventory loss is employee theft and the National Survey indicates that it is increasing: 48.5 percent of this loss is employee theft, up from 46 percent, costing retailers a record $15 billion a year.[81]

The goal of the store detective is to apprehend persons stealing property from the store. After apprehending the shoplifter, the store detective retrieves the stolen property. In many cases, the police are called to arrest the violator and process him or her through the criminal justice system. Some stores use sophisticated camera equipment to scan the store for people stealing merchandise, whereas other stores rely on a store detective "roaming" the store, appearing to look like an ordinary shopper.

Drug Undercover Investigations

Most law enforcement agencies have devoted resources to drug enforcement. Nine of 10 local law enforcement agencies performed drug enforcement functions. Although only 18 percent of all local departments operate a special unit for drug enforcement with one or more full-time officers assigned, most departments serving populations of greater than 50,000 had a full-time drug enforcement unit. Nationally, approximately 12,212 local police officers are assigned full-time to drug enforcement, for an average of 6 officers per department.[82] What do these officers do? What type of drug enforcement do they do?

Undercover drug operations can be very dangerous. The drug dealers are usually armed, it may be a rip-off and not an actual deal, and the dealers may be in a paranoid state or under the influence of narcotics at the time of the deal. Caution also needs to be taken to make sure that the deal is not being done between two law enforcement agencies. That has happened in the past, and most agencies now have procedures in place to check that out before the deal goes down.

At least three general methods can be used in conducting drug undercover investigations. The first involves infiltrating criminal organizations that sell large amounts of drugs. The method is to buy larger and larger amounts of drugs so the buyer can reach as high as possible into the particular organizational hierarchy. Lower members of the criminal hierarchy have access only to a fixed quantity of drugs. To obtain larger amounts, they have to introduce the investigator to their source or connection, who is generally someone in the upper echelon of the organization or a member of a more sophisticated organization. These operations generally require sophisticated electronic surveillance measures and large sums of money. Also, they can be very lengthy and dangerous to undercover investigators.

The next method that can be used to attack drug syndicates or drug locations is the process of "staking out" (a fixed surveillance) a particular location and making detailed observations of the conditions that indicate drug sales, such as the arrival and brief visit of numerous autos and people. These observations are best if recorded on video to establish probable cause for obtaining a search warrant. If a judge agrees with the probable cause, he or she can issue a search warrant, which can then be executed against a particular person, automobile, or premises. These investigations can be very lengthy and involve extensive sophisticated electronic surveillance.

The third method is the undercover "buy-bust," an operation in which an undercover police officer purchases a quantity of drugs from a subject, then leaves the scene, contacts the backup team, and identifies the seller. The backup team, in or out of uniform, responds to the location of the sale and arrests the seller, based on the description given by the undercover officer. The legal basis of the arrest is probable cause to believe that a crime was committed and that the subject is the perpetrator of the crime. Based on the legal arrest, the backup team can search the subject and seize any illegal drugs. If the arrest occurs inside the premises, the backup team can seize any illegal substances that are in plain view. The undercover officer then goes to the police facility the subject was brought to and makes a positive identification of the subject from a hidden location, generally through a one-way mirror or window. By viewing the suspect through the one-way mirror or window, the undercover officer cannot be seen and can be used again in the same role. The buy-bust is generally used in low-level drug operations that receive numerous complaints from the community. The purpose is to take the person into custody as quickly as possible to relieve the quality-of-life problem in the neighborhood. A sufficient number of officers is extremely important in undercover "buy-bust" operations. The basic players in the game are

1. *The undercover officer (U/C).*
2. *The ghost officer.* This officer closely shadows or follows the U/C as she or he travels within an area and approaches the dealer.

3. *The backup team.* This should consist of at least five officers, if possible, who can watch from a discreet location to ensure the safety of the U/C and ghost and who can move in when ready to arrest the dealer.

4. *The supervisor.* This critical member of the team plans and directs the operation and makes all key decisions.

Often, the undercover officer will make numerous purchases over time and then obtain an arrest warrant for the dealer, and a team will go in and make the arrest. This is a good strategy because the dealer is less likely to make a connection to the buyer/officer, and it allows the officer to build probable cause and a stronger case.

Sometimes, law enforcement may then conduct a reverse-sting operation. This is where after the buy-bust, an officer then poses as the drug dealer and arrests the buyers that come to purchase drugs. This is usually done in areas that readily attract buyers. As soon as an exchange is made, the back-up team makes the bust. This type of operation can often lead to accusations of entrapment, so officers must be thoroughly versed in their state laws and court rulings regarding entrapment.

Entrapment

Often people believe that undercover operations by the police are entrapment. What is entrapment? **Entrapment** is defined as inducing an individual to commit a crime he or she did not contemplate, for the sole purpose of instituting a criminal prosecution against the offender.[83] Entrapment is a defense to criminal responsibility that arises from improper acts committed against an accused by another, usually an undercover agent. *Inducement* is the key word; when police encouragement plays upon the weaknesses of innocent persons and beguiles them into committing crimes they normally would not attempt, it can be deemed improper as entrapment and the evidence barred under the exclusionary rule. Entrapment is an affirmative defense and easily raised at trial. It is based on the principle that people should not be convicted of a crime that was instigated by the government and it arises when "government officials 'plant the seeds' of criminal intent."[84]

The police, by giving a person the opportunity to commit a crime, are not guilty of entrapment. For example, an undercover officer sitting on the sidewalk, apparently drunk, with a 10-dollar bill sticking out of his or her pocket, is not forcing a person to take the money but giving a person the opportunity to take the money. A person who takes advantage of the apparent drunk and takes the money is committing a larceny. The entrapment defense is not applicable to this situation. However, when the police action is outrageous and forces an otherwise innocent person to commit a crime, the entrapment defense may apply.

In *Jacobson v. United States* (503 U.S. 540, 1992), the U.S. Supreme Court ruled that the government's action of repeatedly, for two and a half years, sending a man advertisements of material of a sexual nature, causing the man to order an illegal sexually oriented magazine, constituted entrapment. It ruled that law enforcement officers "may not originate a criminal design, implant in an innocent person's mind the disposition to commit a criminal act, and then induce commission of the crime so that the government may prosecute." The issue of entrapment is a contentious one with the defendant's predisposition being evaluated against the government activities. The defendant's predisposition is very subjective but the government activities are more objective and easier to evaluate. The American Law Institute's Model Penal Code looks at the entrapment defense in this way: "If the government employed methods of persuasion or inducement which create a substantial risk that such an offense will be committed by persons other than those who are ready to commit it," then the defense is available despite the offender's predisposition.[85] The Supreme Court, however, has predominantly focused on the predisposition of the defendant and ruled the entrapment defense did not apply.[86] Although in the Hampton case[87] the Court held that the defendant's predisposition matters regarding the entrapment defense rather than government conduct, justices did state in a concurring opinion that if government behavior "shocks the conscience," it could violate due process. Certainly, such behavior as instigating robberies or beatings to gather evidence would cross the line. The Supreme Court has failed to identify specific actions, but some lower courts have. If officers "use violence, supply contraband that is wholly unobtainable or engage in a criminal enterprise," defendants often succeed with an entrapment defense.[88]

You Are There!

Jacobson v. United States, 1992

In February 1984, a 56-year-old Nebraska farmer (hereinafter the defendant), with no record or reputation for violating any law, lawfully ordered and received from an adult bookstore two magazines that contained photographs of nude teenage boys. Subsequent to this, Congress passed the Child Protection Act of 1984, which made it illegal to receive such material through the mail. Later that year, the U.S. Postal Service obtained the defendant's name from a mailing list seized at the adult bookstore, and, in January 1985, began an undercover operation targeting him.

Over the next two and a half years, government investigators, through five fictitious organizations and a bogus pen pal, repeatedly contacted the defendant by mail, exploring his attitudes toward child pornography. The communications also contained disparaging remarks about the legitimacy and constitutionality of efforts to restrict the availability of sexually explicit material, and finally, offered the defendant the opportunity to order illegal child pornography. Twenty-six months after the mailings to the defendant commenced, government investigators sent him a brochure advertising photographs of young boys engaging in sex. At this time, the defendant placed an order that was never filled. Meanwhile, the investigators attempted to further pique the defendant's interest through a fictitious letter decrying censorship

and suggesting a method of getting material to him without the "prying eyes of U.S. Customs." A catalogue was then sent to him, and he ordered a magazine containing child pornography. After a controlled delivery of a photocopy of the magazine, the defendant was arrested. A search of his home revealed only the material he received from the government and the two sexually oriented magazines he lawfully acquired in 1984. The defendant was charged with receiving child pornography through the mail in violation of 18 U.S.C. 2252(a)(2)(A). He defended himself by claiming that the government's conduct was outrageous, that the government needed reasonable suspicion before it could legally begin an investigation of him, and that he had been entrapped by the government's investigative techniques. The lower federal courts rejected these defenses, but, in a 5–4 decision, the Supreme Court reversed his conviction based solely on the entrapment claim. In *Jacobson,* the Supreme Court held that law enforcement officers "may not originate a criminal design, implant in an innocent person's mind the disposition to commit a criminal act, and then induce commission of the crime so that the government may prosecute."

SOURCE: Based on *Jacobson v. United States,* 503 U.S. 540 (1992); and Thomas V. Kukura, J.D., "Undercover Investigations and the Entrapment Defense: Recent Court Cases," *FBI Law Enforcement Bulletin* (April 1993), pp. 27–32.

An interesting case that recently went through the court system occurred in South Florida. An appeals court overturned a judge's ruling from a 2002 drug sting case letting the defendant off based on his defense of entrapment. The defendant sold drugs to an undercover officer in a gay nightclub in Fort Lauderdale. The defense argued that the defendant, a gay man, was attracted to the officer and the officer kept asking for drugs. The defendant said he couldn't find cocaine but he could get crystal meth. The officer gave him 60 dollars and he went to the restroom and returned with the drugs. The defendant had no prior history,

but according to his attorney, the officer's looks and the defendant's desire for sex were what caused him to purchase drugs. During trial, Judge Susan Lebow agreed, stating if the officer hadn't been so good looking, the defendant may have never committed the crime, and she dismissed the charges. The Fourth Circuit Court of Appeals ruled that law enforcement's conduct was "not so outrageous that dismissal was warranted." They ruled that a jury should be allowed to determine "if the defendant is not guilty due to subjective entrapment," after hearing the facts of the case.[89]

Summary

- Traditionally, investigations have been conducted by detectives.

- The Rand Study of the Criminal Investigation Process revealed that a lot of detectives' time was spent unproductively and consequently investigations were not being efficiently conducted.

- Alternatives to traditional retroactive investigation of past crimes by detectives include improved case management, mentoring and training of detectives, and improved crime analysis and information management.

- Multi-agency task forces, repeat offender programs, cold-case squads, and the use of closed-circuit TV or surveillance cameras have lead to improved case clearance.

- Repeat offender programs may identify certain individuals to be the target of an intensified investigation through surveillance and other strategies or may seek case enhancement by working closely with the prosecutor in the hopes of obtaining stronger sentences.

- Global Positioning System technology and closed-circuit TV allow investigators to obtain information for their investigations without having to be physically present.

- With the tremendous advances in technology during the last couple of decades, cold-case squads have had significant success in investigating old, dormant cases.

- New proactive tactics in police investigations include decoy operations, stakeout operations, sting operations, and code enforcement teams.

- Other traditional proactive techniques include undercover operations, including police, federal, and private security undercover operations.

- The legal concept of entrapment and how it affects undercover operations and proactive tactics is an important concept for officers to understand.

Learning Check

1. Discuss the innovations to police detective operations motivated by the Rand study and other studies.

2. Describe how "managing criminal investigations" programs work and their impact on the detectives' job.

3. List some examples of solvability factors.

4. Discuss some of the strengths and weaknesses involved in the use of multi-agency task forces.

5. Discuss the rationale behind repeat offender programs (ROPs) and give some examples.

6. Describe two of the new technologies that assist law enforcement in investigations. Explain how they help and describe any constitutional concerns.

7. Describe the approach that cold-case squads take toward investigations and how they achieve success.

8. Name some of the new proactive tactics employed by investigators.

9. List some of the types of investigations conducted by private security.

10. Define entrapment and give some examples.

Key Terms

blending Plainclothes officers' efforts to blend into an area and attempt to catch a criminal.

civil liability or code enforcement teams Teams used in jurisdictions to address the crime problem through the enforcement of civil laws and building and occupational codes.

cold-case squads Investigative units that reexamine old cases that have remained unsolved. They use the passage of time coupled with a fresh set of eyes to help solve cases that have been stagnant for years and often decades.

crime analysis The use of analytical methods to obtain pertinent information on crime patterns and trends that can then be disseminated to officers on the street.

decoy operations Operations in which officers dress as and play the role of potential victims in the hope of attracting and catching a criminal.

detective mystique The idea that detective work is glamorous, exciting, and dangerous, as it is depicted in the movies and on television.

entrapment A legal defense that holds that police originated the criminal idea or initiated the criminal action.

investigative task forces A group of investigators working together to investigate one or more crimes. These investigators are often from different law enforcement agencies.

Managing Criminal Investigations (MCI) Proposal recommended by the Rand Study regarding a more effective way of investigating crimes, including allowing patrol officers to follow up cases and using solvability factors in determining which cases to follow up.

mentoring Filling a role as teacher, model, motivator, coach, or advisor in someone else's professional growth.

private security industry The industry that provides private and corporate security programs in the United States.

retroactive investigation of past crimes by detectives Follow-up investigations of past crimes.

repeat offender programs (ROPs) Enforcement efforts directed at known repeat offenders through surveillance or case enhancement.

solvability factors Factors considered in determining whether or not a case should be assigned for follow-up investigation.

sting operations Undercover police operations in which police pose as criminals to arrest law violators.

undercover investigations Covert investigations involving plainclothes officers.

Police and the Community

© Dennis MacDonald/Photo Edit Inc.

GOALS

- To illustrate the meaning of police community relations and their importance to the safety and quality of life in a community
- To explore public attitudes regarding the police and efforts undertaken around the nation to improve public perceptions
- To describe various minority populations and some of their issues regarding police interactions
- To explore the challenges various populations, including the aging population, youth, crime victims, victims of domestic violence, the mentally ill, and the homeless, face when interacting with the police
- To identify efforts being made to better serve these populations
- To describe some innovative community crime prevention programs that focus on crime reduction and improving the quality of life in communities

Introduction

This chapter deals with relationships between the police and the citizens they are paid to protect: the community. This chapter, along with Chapter 12, forms the focus of the police and community section of this text. Chapter 12 will deal with the philosophies of community policing and problem-solving policing, and this chapter will discuss the relationships between the police and the public. We will describe numerous programs being implemented by police agencies to better serve these populations.

The chapter emphasizes the need for proper relationships between the police and the community and presents definitions of police human relations, police public relations, and police-community relations. We also explore public opinion of the police, the challenges presented by an increasingly diverse population, and the relationships between the police and minority communities (including African Americans, Hispanic Americans, Asian Americans, Native Americans, Arab Americans, Muslims, and Jews; women; gays and lesbians; new immigrants; and the physically challenged). It will also look at relationships between the police and some special populations, including senior citizens, young people, the homeless, crime victims, domestic violence victims and physically and mentally challenged individuals.

The chapter also discusses community crime prevention programs, including Neighborhood Watch programs, National Night Out, citizen patrols, citizen volunteer programs, home security surveys and Operation Identification, police storefronts or ministations, Crime Stoppers, mass media campaigns, chaplain programs, citizen police academies, and other police-sponsored crime prevention programs and police and citizen initiatives.

The Need for Proper Police Community Relationships

The police are needed to handle emergencies, maintain order, regulate traffic, and promote a sense of security within the community. To accomplish this, the police must be part of the community. They cannot be viewed as mercenaries or as an army of occupation. When the police see themselves as an occupying army or are seen as one by the community, urban unrest results. The police can best serve the community when they are regarded as part of the community both by the residents and themselves.

The police and community need each other to help communities to be as vibrant and safe as possible. Police-community relationships must be two-way partnerships. In a democratic society, the legitimacy of the police depends on broad and active public acceptance and support. Police chiefs or police commissioners have the responsibility and obligation to educate the public about the many causes of crime and the inability of the police, acting alone and on their own, to control crime. Former New York City Police Commissioner

Lee P. Brown (also former police chief of Houston and Atlanta) has said that the police chief must "take the lead in addressing broadened local social service needs that could, if neglected, produce greater crime problems."[1] The more educated a community is concerning the role of the police and the challenges the police face in meeting multiple demands, the more supportive and helpful they can be.

The leadership of the chief in reaching out to the community is essential. As R. C. Davis says, "Initiating positive interaction with the community generally results in increased citizen support, higher morale in the work force, protection against or insulation from many hostile external forces, and increased resources."[2] Although it is very important for a chief to seek the support and cooperation of the public to improve efforts to police the community, the most important person in the police department, in terms of improving police community relations, is the individual police officer. Patrol officers, traffic officers, and detectives are the individuals within the department who come into contact with the public on a regular basis. Most people receive their impression of a particular police department through the actions of the police officers they encounter. A person who has a bad experience with a particular officer may believe that the entire department mirrors that officer. Because of the high visibility of uniformed officers, many citizens will form opinions based on behavior they may observe in restaurants, stores, on car stops, or at scenes, or even by police driving their marked police vehicles. The officer most likely won't even be aware he or she is being scrutinized in these situations. Officers are constantly serving as ambassadors for their departments. The Police Foundation has stated, "It is imperative that every . . . officer see a great deal of community relations as part of his daily patrol or investigative assignment."[3]

© Spencer Grant/PhotoEdit Inc.

In order to strengthen their relationships with people they serve, police departments are striving to make themselves more diverse and representative of their communities. Their commitment to communication may be paying off: The approval rating of police by younger people has risen in the past few years.

Human Relations, Public Relations, Community Relations

A tremendous emphasis on police community relations has arisen since the civil disorders of the 1960s. Numerous textbooks and courses exist on police community relations and police human relations. What do these terms mean? Are they interchangeable? Are community relations and human relations the same as police public relations? Steven M. Cox and Jack D. Fitzgerald perhaps best define these terms. They define police **human relations** as follows: "In the most general sense, the concept of human relations refers to everything we do with, for, and to each other as citizens and as human beings."[4] Human relations thus connotes treating others with respect and dignity and following the Golden Rule—acting toward others as you would want others to act toward you. Cox and Fitzgerald define **police public relations** as "a variety of activities with the express intent of creating a favorable image of themselves . . . sponsored and paid for by the organization." Then, using these two definitions, they define **police community relations** as follows:

Community relations are comprised of the combined effects of human and public relations. Police community relations then encompass the sum total of human and public relations, whether initiated by the police or other members of the community. . . . Police community relations may be either positive or negative, depending upon the quality of police interactions with other citizens (human relations) and the collective images each holds of the other (which are derived from public as well as human relations).[5]

In 1967, the President's Commission on Law Enforcement and Administration of Justice reported, "Police relations with minority groups had sunk to explosively low levels." The commission defined police community relations in its summary report, *The Challenge of Crime in a Free Society*:

A community relations program is not a public relations program "to sell the police image" to the people. . . . It is a long-range, full-scale effort to acquaint the police and the community with each other's problems and to stimulate action aimed at solving these problems.[6]

Louis A. Radelet, a pioneer in studying the role of the police in the community, traced the development of the **police community relations (PCR) movement** to an annual conference begun in 1955.[7] However, some believe that the PCR movement grew out of the riots and civil disorders of the 1960s. The PCR movement should not be confused with today's community policing. The PCR movement involved assigning a few officers in a department as community affairs or community relations specialists. These officers attended community meetings and tried to reduce tensions between members of the department and the public. Some of the programs were shams or merely public relations attempts. The PCR movement had no real effect on the philosophy or culture of most police departments. Egon Bittner has said that for PCR programs to be effective, they need to reach to "the grassroots of discontent," where citizen dissatisfaction with the police exists.[8] In short, police human relations skills are needed.

Since the urban disorders of the 1960s, training in human relations has become part of the police academy and in-service training in many departments. Sensitivity training—sometimes referred to as T-groups, or encounter groups—is designed to provide participants an opportunity to learn more about themselves and their impact on others, as well as to learn to function more effectively in face-to-face situations. In a typical encounter group, officers may engage in a role-play face to face with a group of minority citizens, teenagers, or others who have had problem relationships with the police. The police officers play the role of the other group, and the members of the other group play the role of the police. The goal of this training is to facilitate the ability of police officers to understand the perceptions and behaviors of the citizen group.

The **International Association of Chiefs of Police (IACP)** understands the importance of public relations and the interactions between the police and the community. In recent years, the IACP has issued training keys on managing anger, police-citizen contacts, dealing with the mentally ill, elderly victimization, and hate crimes. There is also an understanding that crucial to police-community relations is the community's faith in the police department to police itself. It must be understood by all that allegations of police misconduct will be thoroughly and fairly investigated. The IACP has issued several training keys on this topic.

Public Opinion and the Police

Although it's well known the police have a difficult job, the role of the police has always been somewhat ambiguous. The perception of the police mission by police leaders as well as the

community leaders has varied during the last few decades. With the adoption of the community policing philosophy (discussed in the next chapter), many law enforcement agencies have seen their roles expand to include activities that previously were not viewed as police functions. In the fiscally challenged times since September 11, 2001, agencies have found it necessary to turn some previous police duties over to other entities. These methods include privatization, the use of volunteers, and civilianization within the department. Despite this reassessment, the police role continues to be viewed in three primary areas—crime fighters, order maintainers, and service providers. Though views differ, it is a common refrain from police and citizens alike that there are not enough police officers on the streets.

Given the difficult job the police have, it is easier for them to perform their duties if they have the support of the public. The media often portray a police force that is not liked by the public. However, this is a false perception.

In a nationwide poll asking people how much respect they have for the police, 61 percent answered "a great deal," 29 percent answered "some," and 7 percent answered "very little," and 1 percent answered "none" (see Table 11.1). With regard to

TABLE 11.1 Reported Confidence in the Police, 2005

	A great deal	Some	Very little	None
Nationwide	63%	29%	7%	1%
By gender				
Male	65%	27%	7%	1%
Female	61%	31%	7%	1%
By race				
White	66%	28%	5%	1%
Nonwhite	53%	31%	14%	2%
African American	49%	37%	14%	0%
By age				
18–29	52%	31%	14%	3%
30–49	66%	29%	4%	1%
50 & older	64%	29%	7%	<.5%

SOURCE: Adapted from *Sourcebook of Criminal Justice Statistics Online, 2005.* http://www.albany.edu/sourcebook/pdf/t2122005.pdf, retrieved December 12, 2006.

TABLE 11.2 Reported Confidence in Selected U.S. Institutions 2005

Question: "I'm going to read you a list of institutions in American society. Please tell me how much confidence you, yourself, have in each one—a great deal, quite a lot, some, or very little?"

Institution	Percent answering "a great deal" or "quite a lot"
Banks	49%
Big business	22%
Church/organized religion	53%
Congress	22%
Criminal justice system	26%
Medical system	42%
Military	74%
Newspapers	28%
Organized labor	24%
Police	63%
Presidency	44%
Public schools	37%
TV news	28%
U.S. Supreme Court	41%

SOURCE: The Gallup Organization, Inc., The Gallup Poll (online), cited by http://www.albany.edu/sourcebook/pdf/t2102005.pdf, retrieved December 12, 2006.

police in their areas, the numbers were similar, with 60 percent of respondents having "a great deal" of respect for police in their area.[9]

The public's opinion of the police has remained relatively constant over time, with most of the public giving favorable ratings to the police. Whites and older citizens generally give the police better ratings than do African Americans and younger people.

Interestingly, the approval ratings of police by younger people have risen slightly. In a 1991 national poll, 49 percent of people aged 18 to 29 had a "great deal" of respect for police, whereas in 2005, 52 percent of the same age group felt that way.[10] Perhaps this reflects the efforts police agencies have made regarding the youth in their communities.

In a nationwide poll conducted by the Gallup organization in 2005,[11] citizens were questioned regarding how much confidence they had in some American institutions. The percentage reporting

they had a "great deal" or "quite a lot" of confidence in the police was 63 percent, slightly outscoring the presidency (44 percent). It was less than the military (74 percent), but more than organized religion (53 percent), Congress (22 percent), the medical system (42 percent), TV news (28 percent), and the U.S. Supreme Court (41 percent). (See Table 11.2.)

James Q. Wilson has said, "The single most striking fact about the attitudes of citizens, black and white, toward the police is that in general these attitudes are positive, not negative." The polls mentioned here clearly indicate that Wilson was right. Generally, however, the police feel that the public does not like them or support them. Wilson, acknowledging the fact that most police officers feel that the public does not like or appreciate them, concluded that the police "probably exaggerate the extent of citizen hostility."[12] Perhaps one reason many officers believe the public does not like them is that officers, particularly in high-crime areas, spend a significant proportion of their time dealing with criminals and unsavory-type people. Further confusing perceptions, any conflicts or negative issues that arise are played out repeatedly in the media and the community.

Police and Minority Communities

One of the most significant problems facing the police during the past three decades has been the tension, and often outright hostility, between the police and minority group citizens. Most of this tension has focused on relationships between African Americans and the police. However, tension has existed between police and Hispanic Americans, Native Americans, Asian Americans, and other minority groups, including women and the gay community. One of the best ways to improve relationships between the police and minority groups is to ensure that minority groups are adequately represented in a jurisdiction's police department. Recently, minority representation has increased significantly in U.S. police departments. This should improve relationships between the police and minority communities. However, as Chapter 4 on hiring discussed, African Americans, Hispanic Americans, and other minorities (including women) are still seriously underrepresented in U.S. police departments.

Although increasing diversity within the law enforcement workforce will facilitate cultural awareness and understanding with various minority populations, law enforcement can make other efforts. Having and conveying respect for these cultures is critical. Opening the lines of communication with the informal leaders of these communities to discuss their issues and their needs will result in greater cooperation.

Officers should be trained in the background and cultures of the various communities to aid in understanding. If language is a barrier, the identification of reliable, honest translators within the community will be helpful. In turn, education of the community in police goals and operations will increase residents' understanding and lessen their fear. The Community Relations Service (CRS) of the Department of Justice has published a guide, "Avoiding Racial Conflict," that may help improve and maintain good relations between the police and the various minority groups.[13]

Multiculturalism

The 2000 U.S. Census reports that 11.1 percent of the total U.S. population is foreign born, accounting for 32.5 million people. Of these, 52 percent were born in Latin America, 26 percent in Asia, and 14 percent in Europe, with the remainder coming from other areas of the world, including Africa. Significantly, more than 20 percent of these foreign-born residents have less than a ninth-grade education. Almost 18 percent of American households now report that they speak a language other than English at home.[14] These factors have implications for police officers responding to calls involving these residents. Not only is there likely to be a communication problem, but there may be a lack of trust and understanding of police, possibly resulting in fear.

An abbreviated census survey was conducted for the first time in 2005. It revealed that the U.S. is very rapidly becoming even more diverse and this is no longer limited to border and southern states. The immigration issue has affected every state in the union. Minority groups make up an increasing share of the population in every state except West Virginia, possibly because of its struggling economy and lack of history in attracting immigrants. "This is just an extraordinary explosion of diversity all across the United States," said William Frey, a demographer at the Brookings Institution, a Washington think tank. "It's diversity and immigration going hand in hand."[15] Non-Hispanic whites are now a minority in four states, Hawaii, New Mexico, California, and Texas as well as the District of Columbia and are below 60 percent in Maryland, Georgia, and Nevada. Nationally, the percentage of non-Hispanic whites has declined from 70 percent in 2000 to 67 percent in 2005. The immigrants have shown they will go where the jobs are, and for the first time have moved to many states not typically challenged with immigration issues. South Carolina's immigrant population increased 47 percent since 2000, and the Hispanic population increased 48 percent in Arkansas.[16] This rapid increase has led to some backlash and some challenges for law enforcement in communities that had not previously faced this issue. Numerous training programs have been developed to address the issues of cultural diversity. Law enforcement is aggressively looking for, developing, and implementing relevant training programs for officers as well as outreach programs for the minority communities to increase multicultural understanding. It is believed that increasing the understanding of the culture of the various minority groups will facilitate improved relations with them.

African Americans

The face of the U.S. population is changing as it has continued to become more diverse year after year. Whereas in 1950 Caucasians represented approximately 87 percent of the U.S. population, by 2030 they will make up only 59 percent of the American population. African Americans currently are 13 percent of the population, compared with 10 percent in 1950. Their percentage of the population is expected to remain relatively constant with projections of 13 percent in 2030.[17] In fact, the 2005 census found blacks represent 12.8 percent of the population, and they have been surpassed by Hispanics as the country's largest minority group.[18]

African Americans have historically faced discrimination in U.S. society. Not until 1954, with the landmark Supreme Court case of *Brown* v. *Board of Education of Topeka*, was legal segregation of the races officially declared unconstitutional.[19] This case overturned the old "separate but equal" doctrine regarding race and public schools. A decade later, Congress passed the Civil Rights Act of 1964, which strengthened the rights of all citizens regardless of race, religion, or national origin.

Access to equal rights did not come easily. The 1950s and 1960s saw demonstrations, marches, and protests by minority groups to win these rights.

Often the police, being the official agents of government bodies seeking to block equality for all people, were forced to enforce laws against minority groups, sometimes by arresting them and breaking up their gatherings. The police were also forced to confront protests by people opposing equality for all. The police were constantly in the middle between those striving for equality and those expressing "white backlash."

Although some might disagree, police contacts with African Americans were not the only—and perhaps not even the major—cause of the urban riots in the 1960s. However, police actions generally were the immediate precipitators or the precipitating events of these riots. The riots in Harlem, Watts, Newark, and Detroit were all precipitated by arrests of African Americans by white police officers.[20]

Following the 1960s riots, police departments throughout the United States established community relations programs designed to improve relationships with minority members of the community. Police departments increased their recruitment and hiring of African American officers. The 1980s, 1990s, and early twenty-first century saw the election of African American mayors and other officials in many large cities, as well as the appointment of African American police commissioners in many of the largest U.S. police departments.

Despite the elimination of legal racism and the increased acceptance of minorities into mainstream society, however, the problems of African Americans did not disappear. Racism and hatred still exist in our society. Many African Americans in the inner cities remain unemployed or underemployed. Many live below the poverty level and remain in a state of chronic anger or rage. Many say this rage led to the 1992 Los Angeles riots.

Cox and Fitzgerald, writing in 1992 (before the Los Angeles riots), seem to have been prophetic. After discussing the urban riots of the sixties, they state,

> We have the distinct impression that the horrors of the 1960s have receded into the backs of the minds of many police administrators; the same appears to be true of the general public. There is little doubt in our minds, however, that the same tensions that found temporary release on the streets of the urban centers of our country still exist. The growing "underclass" of minority-group members presents a real and present problem that we cannot afford to ignore. Well-thought-out, well-planned police minority

relations programs are essential if the mistakes of the 1960s are not to be repeated.[21]

If police administrators had heeded the advice of Cox and Fitzgerald, they might have been more prepared for the 1992 Los Angeles incident. Serious problems remain between the police and the African American community. In a 1996 survey by the Joint Center for Political and Economic Studies, about 43 percent of the African Americans polled said police brutality and harassment were serious problems where they live, whereas only 13 percent of the general population responded similarly. A 1995 report by the Sentencing Project, a public-interest group that advocates sentencing reform, reported that one in every three young black men in the United States is imprisoned, on probation, or on parole. A similar study in 1991 had found that one out of every four young black men was under some type of criminal justice supervision. The new figure represents an increase of 31 percent.[22]

There continues to be a concern among individuals in the African American community about unfair treatment by law enforcement and the criminal justice system. The terms *racial profiling* and *driving while black* have become commonplace. Racial profiling is a "form of discrimination and singles out people of racial or ethnic groups because of a belief that these groups are more likely than others to commit certain types of crimes. Race-based enforcement is illegal."[23] This issue was discussed in Chapter 8.

The controversy regarding racial profiling has resulted in many states passing legislation requiring officers to document the race and ethnicity of individuals being stopped by police as well as requiring sensitivity training for police officers.[24] One of the goals of this legislation is to ensure that individuals are not stopped based on their race or ethnicity and to document for the public that this is not occurring or what steps have been taken if statistics indicated it was perhaps being done. These statistics, documentation, and efforts will go a long way to smoothing relations between minority community members, in particular African Americans, and the police, but other areas also need to be addressed.

When examining perceptions of police brutality in respondents' area, the Gallup Organization found that although 25 percent of whites believed there was a problem with police brutality in their area, a much higher 67 percent of blacks felt there was a problem.[25] Furthermore, when asked about racial profiling, 67 percent of blacks felt racial profiling was widespread and only 23 percent felt it was ever justified, whereas only 50 percent of whites believed it was widespread and 31 percent felt it was sometimes justified.[26] Clearly, the relationship between police and African Americans remains an area that needs to be addressed. Police officers must make efforts to understand these attitudes of all community members and work with the community members for fair law enforcement and to protect all community members regardless of race or ethnicity from the criminals that victimize the law-abiding citizens.

Hispanic Americans

The Hispanic community is composed of many different cultures. The Census Bureau uses the term *Hispanic* for people with ethnic backgrounds in Spanish-speaking countries. Hispanics can be of any race, and most in the United States are white.[27] (To differentiate between white Hispanics and Caucasians, the term *non-Hispanic whites* is often used.) Officers must understand and acknowledge this diversity. In 1950, Hispanics comprised approximately 3 percent of the U.S. population. By 2030, this proportion is projected to be approximately 20 percent.[28] The 2000 U.S. Census reports that 11.1 percent of the U.S. population was born outside of the United States. Of these, almost 52 percent were born in Latin America (including South America, Central America, Mexico, and the Caribbean).[29] In 2005, Hispanics surpassed blacks as the largest minority group at 14.5 percent of the population.[30] Officers can't assume that all of the Hispanic groups share the same culture and beliefs. Though there are similarities, each is unique. If police officers group all Hispanics together because of a lack of understanding or knowledge, this can lead to resentment within the community.

Hispanic Americans have suffered discrimination, and many are also handicapped by language and cultural barriers. Their relationships with the police have often been as tense as the relationships between the police and the African American community.

Considerable attention has been given to recruiting and hiring Hispanic Americans as police officers. In addition, affirmative action programs have been used to appoint and promote Hispanic Americans to higher ranks, and many police departments offer courses to teach their employees how to speak Spanish. Many provide differential pay to officers who are able to translate for community members, though the community itself differentiates between Spanish-speaking officers, American officers of Hispanic background, and officers born in various countries who have become naturalized citizens and know the culture of their country of origin. Though knowing Spanish may ease the communication process, it does not necessarily do anything to facilitate a deeper relationship with the community, except perhaps show community members that the officers and department are willing to put forth an effort to learn their language. Many departments do attempt to provide basic "Police-language" training to police officers to minimize the problems that might occur because of a lack of understanding of rudimentary commands.

Many departments are looking at more inclusive programs in an effort to address the issue on many fronts. Durham, North Carolina, has implemented a program called Hispanic Outreach and Intervention Team (HOIST) designed to bridge the gap between municipal services, particularly law enforcement, and the growing Hispanic community. Part of the program provides direct victim services to members of Durham's Latino population in an effort to reduce the rate of crime and victimization in the Hispanic community. Other initiatives in the program include the Spanish-Speaking Citizens Police Academy, cultural awareness training for all police officers, increased employment opportunities for Hispanics, and free Spanish classes during city employees' lunch breaks. The liaisons within the department also work closely with the domestic violence unit in an effort to educate the Hispanic community about the domestic violence laws and their rights. Liaisons also work with various recreational programs to build relationships with Hispanic youth. The city leaders of Durham believe the last few years have shown their program to be a success based partly on the numbers of Hispanic community members actively involved in planning programs, implementation, and broader participation.[31]

Spanish or Latino citizen police academies and victims liaisons programs have exploded across the country as the Hispanic population has increased. Fueled by the belief in the success and value of these popular academies, many cities chose to build on this success. Some Citizens Police Academies, especially those targeting newer immigrants, have included information on the U.S. government and history and governmental procedures and rules. This has also led law enforcement to learn of some of the obstacles that inhibit the immigrants' assimilation and understanding of U.S. government. Though some of these items may not be directly related to the law enforcement mission, they do help to improve the quality of life for the community members.[32]

Asian Americans

According to the 2000 U.S. Census, of the 11 percent of the population born outside the United States, 26.4 percent were born in Asia.[33] These Asian Americans include many distinct and separate cultures—China, Japan, Korea, Vietnam, Laos, Cambodia, Thailand, and other countries of the Far East. Chinese Americans are among the most visible of the Asian American community, with Chinatowns in many large U.S. cities. Pockets of Koreans, Vietnamese, and Cambodians have also grown in certain areas of the country and become strong economic and cultural forces in certain cities and towns.

Many departments are strengthening their relationships with the Asian population by reaching out to the community and educating Asian Americans about the role of police in the United States. There are often misperceptions and misunderstandings about what the police do and why they do it, especially given what the various cultures have experienced in their homelands. Police departments have also made concerted efforts to recruit more Asian Americans, as discussed in Chapter 7 on minorities in policing.

Opening the lines of communication with the various groups and understanding their history, beliefs, and culture go a long way toward facilitating an open relationship. Particularly important for officers to understand are the political culture of the native countries, including the police role, both formal and informal. This will help officers understand reactions they are encountering on the street and minimize the opportunity for misunderstandings.[34]

Establishing a liaison program between the police department and community leaders with the

© Joel Gordon

Many police departments have found it difficult to recruit Asian American officers, but with increased exposure and visibility, these officers will aid in improving relations with the community and also serve as role models and mentors for youth.

goal of educating both the residents and police officers will have a positive affect on the relationship. For example, the Minneapolis, Minnesota, Police Department has established an initiative to reach out to their Asian communities, the Southeast Asian Community Leaders Forum. This forum has had positive effects, including increased communication and information sharing and enhanced recruiting efforts. The schools have also noticed benefits from this increased community investment in the Asian students.[35]

Native Americans

In the 2000 Census, Native Americans numbered almost 2.4 million, or a little under one percent

The trend in recent years is for tribes to assume their own police responsibilities. Officer Carlis G. Yazzie, a Native American officer in the Navajo Tribal Police, is on patrol in Chinle, Arizona.

© Joel Gordon

or law enforcement. These beliefs also influence how Native Americans interact with others, including law enforcement, and may result in misunderstandings if officers aren't aware of these cultural differences. For the Navajo, for example, a direct statement that sounds like a warning, such as "you better wear your seatbelt or you could get killed," is likely to be interpreted as the speaker wishing that event on the person being addressed.[39]

Law enforcement in tribal areas is typically very complex. There are overlaps as well as gaps in law enforcement, depending on whether the officer is a Native American or Anglo and whether the individual involved is a tribal member or an Anglo. This, coupled with the alarming statistics regarding an increased crime rate involving American Indians, spurred the IACP to address this issue with tribal communities through the summit "Improving Safety in Indian Country."[40]

Two recent Bureau of Justice Statistics studies indicated a high victimization rate and offender rate for Native Americans in the 1990s when the crime rate in the rest of the U.S. population was declining. Problems that are being addressed outside Indian country are not being adequately addressed inside.[41] The summit was held to develop some ideas about how to reverse this trend. Recommendations include cross-jurisdictional cooperation, elimination of jurisdictional authority issues that impede law enforcement, improved crime prevention programs and funding, training for law enforcement working in or near tribal country regarding Native American culture, improved data collection and information sharing, and improving victims' services to minimize re-victimization. Considering the fact that Native Americans are victims of violent crimes at greater than twice the national average, issues can arise frequently, and consequently, police officers will have regular contact with Native Americans.[42]

Many reservations employ both Native Americans and non-Native Americans as police officers.

of the U.S. population.[36] Native American nations, reservations, colonies, and communities with criminal jurisdiction have traditionally been policed in two ways: by federal officers from the Bureau of Indian Affairs (BIA) or by their own police departments, like any other governmental entity. Currently, American Indian tribes operate 171 law enforcement agencies and employ 2,303 full-time, sworn officers.[37]

Throughout the United States, there are more than 500 different tribal groups, all with different beliefs. They have distinct histories, cultures, and often a separate language.[38] The various cultural beliefs will filter the residents' perceptions of information they receive from governmental personnel

Some prefer Native American officers because of the cultural issues, but many agencies have found that with training and communication on both sides, ethnic background shouldn't be a factor. Many are also involved in community relations programs in an outreach effort to residents of the tribal lands.

The Menominee Tribal Police Department in Wisconsin has found a way to reach out to the residents and increase communications—with softball. The department sponsored a series of co-ed softball games and found that this program allowed members of the community to interact with police officers in a nonthreatening arena. The officers and community have both benefited from the improved communications.[43] Law enforcement is continuing to examine issues involving Native Americans and what efforts can be undertaken to address those issues.

Arab Americans and Muslims

Since September 11, 2001, there has been an increased awareness of the needs and issues of the Middle Eastern community. After it was revealed that the 9/11 terrorists had lived, worked, and gone to school in many South Florida communities without arousing any suspicion, many residents became alarmed at any individual of Middle Eastern descent living in their neighborhoods. The Muslim community has raised concerns for their civil rights and the suspicion that seems to have been generated within their communities.

Many Muslims have asked law enforcement for extra protection because they fear hate crimes being perpetrated because of their ethnicity. The Community Relations Service of the Department of Justice has written a guide to help law enforcement respond to this issue.[43] The guide recommends conducting a community assessment to determine the vulnerable targets. Increasing high-visibility patrol in those areas is one strategy, as is opening the lines of communication with the Muslim community to determine Muslims' fears, concerns, and tensions. A proactive approach by the police department, speaking out against hate crimes and promising vigorous investigation and prosecution, will set the tone for the community. The guide also recommends initiating dialogues via task forces or committees among representatives of the various ethnic and religious groups within the community. This will help to break down barriers and stereotypes among residents. Training for police officers and education for community residents in the Muslim beliefs and traditions is also advocated for spreading the truth and minimizing misunderstandings. Having access to community leaders and good translators will help the communication process. (AT&T has a service if there are no local individuals available; 1-800-628-8486). In 2006, the June arrest of seven men in Miami for allegedly planning a terrorist attack on the Sears Tower, the thwarted terrorist plot out of Heathrow Airport in August, and the shooting by a Muslim American inside the Jewish Federation in Seattle in July have all led to increased concerns among the Muslim population about being targeted by police as well as the community. The fear is more of being "profiled" by the police and the community rather than of being victims of hate crimes. Law enforcement is under pressure to be proactive in the fight on terror.

From 2003 to 2005, the Vera Institute of Justice conducted a study funded by the Justice Department, that involved interviewing both law enforcement personnel and members of the Arab American community. Both groups felt the primary problem was a lack of trust between law enforcement and the Muslim community and the events of September 11, 2001, had considerably derailed the relationships that had been built during the last two decades to encourage new immigrants to trust the police. Both groups expressed dismay at the reporting of false information in the form of anonymous tips that were actually the result of petty disputes, business competition, and dating rivalries. The police often feel as victimized as the community when placed in the middle of these "tips." The primary recommendation coming out of the study was that the best way to maintain or enhance relationships will be the continued use of the community policing philosophy and the partnerships between the Muslim community and law enforcement being used to address the homeland security mission.[45]

In addition, for the long term, increasing recruiting efforts within these ethnic minorities will facilitate understanding. All these efforts should help members of the community of Middle Eastern descent feel less threatened and less ostracized.

Jews

Since September 11, 2001, there has been fear among the Jewish population of being a "soft" terrorism target. In cities with large Jewish populations, this is particularly dramatic. These fears and concerns for the safety of the Jewish residents, synagogues, temples, schools, and group homes can cause a surge in demand for police protection. The American public was reminded of this with the shooting in the Jewish Federation of Greater Seattle offices in July 2006. A Muslim gunman killed one, injured five, and shattered the peace and tranquility of many. He told the dispatcher during the incident, "These are Jews and I'm tired of getting pushed around and our people getting pushed around by the situation in the Middle East," referring to the fighting between the Israelis and Hezbollah occurring on the border with Lebanon then.[46] Afraid of copycat crimes and increased violence aimed toward the Jewish population, demands for protection from law enforcement increased in the Seattle area as well as around the country.

Some innovative programs are being put in place in areas with large Jewish populations to make the community feel safer and make police officers and other non-Jewish residents of the community more sensitive to the needs of the Jewish population. The Metropolitan Police Department in Washington, D.C., has implemented a police training program for police recruits. Through a partnership with the Anti-Defamation League (ADL) and the U.S. Holocaust Memorial Museum (USHMM), Chief Charles Ramsey has mandated that all police recruits attend a tour of the museum as part of the "hate crimes" component of their training.[47] Following the tour, the recruits engage in educational sessions emphasizing case studies from the Holocaust. This program was a 2001 IACP award-winner in the education and training section.

The Boca Raton, Florida, Police Department has teamed up with the American Jewish Committee to create a program called Safe Community Initiative.[48] The program, which is viewed as a model for the nation, will instruct leaders of the local Jewish community about how to respond to terrorism threats and other emergencies. It will take "crime prevention" a step farther because of the "times" and the "current war" and the possibility of Jewish facilities being considered "soft" targets. The attendees will learn how to react to a gun threat, to deal with suspicious packages and threatening phone calls, and to respond to catastrophic events. They will learn how to respond in the time before police and rescue workers arrive to assume control. A woman that many, including Seattle Police Chief Gil Kerlikowski, consider to be a hero in the Seattle incident, credited training that

she had received in crisis intervention as helping her keep a cool head during the shooting rampage at the Jewish Federation. (She had managed to calm the suspect down and, despite his orders not to do so, called 911 and convinced the suspect to speak with the dispatcher.) The Safe Community Initiative program is modeled after one in England in which Jewish leaders work with Scotland Yard.

Women

Women make up approximately 50 percent of the population, so police officers will have frequent interactions with women. Unfortunately, law enforcement often becomes involved with women when they are victims of crimes. In the last few years, however, officers' contact with women offenders has increased as statistics indicate there are more of them. Although women are often victims of the same types of crimes as men, they also are more vulnerable to certain crimes that men often don't have to be overly concerned about. It can be difficult for men to understand what it feels like to feel vulnerable and to sometimes fear 50 percent of the population. That doesn't happen to men under ordinary living conditions. Although men can be victims of sex offenses, it is far more common for women to be sexually assaulted or raped. Women are involved in domestic violence cases but most frequently as the victim of an assault rather than as the offender. Police officers will encounter them as victims and will need to be aware of the psychological aspects of this victimization. Women have often been critical of police methods of handling domestic violence cases and have often complained of insensitivity by the police in rape and other sexual assault cases. As we will discuss shortly, the police have heeded complaints regarding the handling of domestic violence cases by the increasing adoption of pro-arrest policies in these cases. During the past three decades, the police have also been much more sensitive to women in rape and sexual assault cases. Numerous police departments have formed special investigating units to handle sex crimes (often using women investigators). Many departments conduct sensitivity sessions to help officers understand the concerns of women. Also, today, much of the prior discrimination against women in hiring and promotions in police departments has been officially eliminated, and women are active members of law enforcement agencies throughout much of the nation. However, as we saw in Chapter 4 on becoming a police officer, women still face problems in law enforcement agencies.

With the increased numbers of women in law enforcement and the slowly increasing number in the upper administration of police organizations, the policies and procedures in place are more reflective of the female perspective than ever before. As the women officers become more visible in the community, the perception of the police as being more supportive of women should increase.

This extends to the support of victim/witness services that exist in many departments around the country. These individuals or units receive specialized training in crime victimization, including domestic and sexual violence. Police departments are using these units within their own agencies to better serve the victims and witnesses of crime, many of whom are women. This effort also represents an effort to be more receptive to women's needs within the criminal justice system.

Recently, there has also been an increase in women as offenders. They are committing more crimes than in the past, they are committing different crimes than they traditionally have been involved in, and often more violence is involved in their crimes. Information also seems to indicate that they sometimes are more violent in domestic assault cases. A report released by the Women's Prison Association indicates that the number of women inmates serving sentences of more than a year grew by 757 percent from 1977 to 2004, which is almost twice the 388 percent for men. At the end of 2004, 96,125 women were in prison compared with 11,212 in 1977.[49] In addition, according to the Annual Probation Survey and the Annual Parole Survey, in 2004, about 1 of 8 adults on parole were women and almost 2 of every 4 adults on probation were women. And, according to the Department of Justice, women represented 23.2 percent of all arrests across the country.[50] Several risk factors have been identified as contributing to women's criminal behavior, including substance abuse, mental illness, spousal abuse, and most significantly, prior victimization.[51] Anecdotally, women inmates generally agree that substance abuse, in particular meth abuse, is a primary risk factor. According to some inmates in Arizona, "meth is cheap, easy to get and very addictive. A terrible combination."[52] The addicts will then turn to prostitution or theft to get money to support their children (who they are often raising alone) or fuel their habit. Maricopa County, Arizona, Sheriff Joe Arpaio concurs and states that 42 percent of women booked

into the county jail system test positive for meth compared with 30 percent of men. Even more frustrating, the recidivism rate for these offenders is 60 percent. But on a hopeful note, the recidivism rate for inmates who go through their jail-sponsored self-help programs is only 15 percent.[53] The issue of women as offenders can best be dealt with if these underlying issues and challenges are examined. Perhaps by addressing these issues and intervening with drug rehabilitation and support services for offenders in jail or on probation, or diverting offenders into other programs, law enforcement can work with the rest of the criminal justice system to stem this increase in offending.

Some evidence indicates that women have expanded the variety and seriousness of crimes that they commit. More women have been involved in bank robberies—for example, the "cell phone" robber who was seen on TV talking on her cell as she obtained her money from tellers at several banks, and the 15-year-old girl who was arrested in Lima, Ohio, because the police found her book bag in the get-away car. "We're seeing women really taking a more aggressive role in bank robberies than in years past, women are more involved in violent crimes and bank robbery goes hand in hand with that," stated the FBI agent that coordinates bank robbery investigations in the area. "Bank robbery is a predominantly male-oriented field. Traditionally, if a woman was involved, it was usually in a support role like getaway driver. Now, they're going into banks with more frequency."[54]

Another crime that has traditionally been associated with men but recently has seen more women involved is sexual abuse of minors. Women in Florida, Georgia, New Jersey, Washington, and Michigan have faced charges in the last couple of years involving having consensual sex with males under the age of consent. Many of these women were teachers. In Saginaw, Michigan, a middle-school band teacher admitted having sex with six of her students from November 2004 to March 2005. In Farmington Hills, Michigan, a 41-year-old married mother of three had more than 20 sexual encounters with a friend of her 14-year-old son. According to the Department of Justice, 96 percent of all sexual assaults reported to police nationwide are committed by men, but women, who are often in the caretaker roles, sometimes take advantage of their access to children. Women tend to romanticize these affairs rather than being serial pedophiles as men often are. The issue came into the spotlight in 1996 when Mary Kay Letourneau, then 34, admitted having sex with her 13-year-old student in Washington State. She spent 7½ years in prison, and she and her young, now husband, have two children who were raised by her boyfriend's mother while Letourneau was in prison. It is believed that this crime is significantly underreported and investigated, but with the increased public awareness and the increased numbers of women police officers and prosecutors, this crime will continue to get more attention.[55]

Gays and Lesbians

In cities with large gay populations, there have been numerous verbal and physical attacks on members of the gay community (sometimes called "gay bashing"). Police departments across the United States have created bias units to investigate crimes that are the result of racial, religious, ethnic, or sexual orientation hatred. Earlier in the text, we discussed the efforts to recruit gay police officers. These efforts have certainly improved relationships between the police and the gay community. Publicized efforts of police departments to recruit homosexuals have reduced fears of reporting crimes among many members of the gay community. The gay and lesbian unit of the Washington, D.C., Metropolitan Police Department was the only law enforcement program to be named a finalist for the "Innovations in American Government" award in 2005, an award presented each year by Harvard University's Kennedy School of Government. The unit investigates crimes committed by and against homosexuals, bisexuals, and transgendered individuals and advises the police chief on issues affecting D.C.'s gay residents.[56]

Despite these efforts, some members of the gay community still believe they are viewed as easy crime targets. An international gay and lesbian gun advocacy group was started in Boston in 2000 called the Pink Pistols and now has 43 chapters throughout the United States and Canada. Their motto is "Armed gays don't get bashed." They want to be able to defend themselves if targeted by gay bashers.[57]

The murder of Matthew Shepard made it clear that hate-motivated violence is still a problem for the gay community. The Lambda Legal Defense and Education Fund—a legal organization dedicated to the civil rights of lesbians, gay men, people with HIV and AIDS, and the transgendered community—proposes increased prevention efforts to target antigay attitudes and violent tendencies that start at a young age.[58] Hate crime legislation seeks to appropriately punish individuals perpetrating such crimes, but it is felt that if attitudes and socialization issues can be changed, we could reduce the number of these types of crimes and allow these minority populations to live free of fear.

Law Enforcement Gays and Lesbians (LEGAL) and other similar support groups around the country also offer support for gay, lesbian, bisexual, and transgendered workers in the criminal justice system. LEGAL members hope to improve the environment within law enforcement agencies for gays and ultimately improve the relationship between the police and the gay community.

New Immigrants

A great proportion of new immigrants, particularly in larger cities and border states, are Mexicans, Chinese, Haitians, and Cubans. The numbers of people arriving on Florida shores seeking political asylum and improved economic conditions have proven challenging for the local governments and schools. These immigrants often bring strong religious and cultural beliefs with them that law enforcement is unfamiliar with. These beliefs and rituals can affect police services and have presented challenges to police, resulting in the desire to learn as much as possible about these cultures to minimize misunderstandings and danger to officers or to the immigrants. These new immigrants, seeking to make a new life for themselves, also must shed their ingrained beliefs concerning police officers. The police in their native lands often operate much differently than do the police in America; to gain their trust, law enforcement personnel need to educate these new immigrants in the U.S. system.

Large cities and border states are not the only places confronting the immigrant issue any more. Census data shows the most dramatic increase in new immigrants to be in the South and Midwest. This is affecting smaller towns in a dramatic way. The immigrant population in these new immigrant growth states is disproportionately new arrivals, which correlates with them having a limited ability to speak English.[59] In addition, the Census Bureau reports that almost 18 percent of the U.S. population speaks a language other than English at home. Nearly 30 percent of Spanish speakers and 25 percent of Asian and Pacific Island language speakers identify themselves as "limited English proficient" or LEP.[60] Consequently, one of the most important issues that law enforcement needs to address is the language barrier. Language barriers make police officers less effective and could prove fatal in a crisis. To maintain the integrity of the criminal justice system, it is important to ensure defendants gets all the rights they are entitled to as well as documenting that they got all their rights and the investigation and arrest were conducted correctly, thereby enhancing prosecution. The federal government also requires that speakers of other languages have access to all the governmental services under Title VI of the Civil Rights Act of 1964. Every department should have a language plan in place, customized to its needs, so officers are prepared to deal with the situation when it arises. The department leaders will consider their size, the composition of their staff, location, and the population the department serves. The plan should indicate if and when a translator is used and who the translators are and how to get in contact with them, language training for officers, and so forth. Though implementing a plan and ensuring adequate resources are involved could be expensive, it could save the city money in the form of civil suits.[61]

Law enforcement procedures have evolved over the years as immigrants have arrived in larger numbers. Police strive to serve the new arrivals better and to minimize the impact on police services. Law enforcement agencies are addressing the challenge of newly arrived immigrants from all over the world who do not speak English nor understand the culture of the United States. Police strive to educate immigrants about what the police do in the United States compared with their countries of origin and to build a relationship between the community and the police.

A program called "Talking with the Police" was implemented in Monterey Park, California, to help nonnative English speakers improve their English skills, learn about American law enforcement, and overcome their fear of police. The program was developed by the police department and the library, and there are many activities in which learners interact with police officers. The program seems to be successful, and it has been found to motivate adults to practice English, promotes public confidence, and increases public understanding of law enforcement practices within the community. The Monterey Park Police Department has made this program available for other law enforcement agencies to implement.[62]

In Broward County, Florida, the sheriff's office began a Brazilian Leadership Academy designed to introduce Brazilian immigrants to the workings of the sheriff's office, after launching similar successful programs with larger new immigrant groups. Working through a couple of churches to spread the word, officers spent time educating the attendees about how American law enforcement works and how it differs from in Brazil where corruption, graft, and complicity are commonplace. Police also use the opportunity to recruit employees.[63] In Minneapolis, the police are working with the Somali immigrants to curtail the emerging gang problem among their youth. Working through a translator, law enforcement listened as the Somali elders expressed their concern for their youth who are learning about the U.S. culture from gang members as the elders are working all day to build a life. To improve the flow of information, a Ramsey County deputy and Minneapolis, Minnesota, police officer are attending community meetings with the group to address their concerns.[64]

South Florida police agencies and police academies have developed similar programs targeting the rapidly growing Haitian population and have experienced success with improved understanding and communication between the groups. Qualified Haitian Americans are also eagerly recruited as police officers. Non–Haitian American officers are also assigned to these communities with the goal of being highly visible and getting to know the residents. All these officers are able to assist in bridging the gap between the community and the police.

The Cuban immigrants arriving on the Florida shores tend to stay in South Florida where there is a large support group of Cuban Americans ready to render any kind of assistance that is needed. Cuban Americans in South Florida are a powerful group and a strong political force. The Cuban immigrants have used anything available to escape Cuba and travel the 90 miles to Florida, from inner tubes and rickety fishing ships, even to Cuban-owned vessels. The immigrants then scramble to the shore and have been seen kissing the sand and smiling widely, knowing they had "made it" and would be allowed to stay. The Cuban community in residence in South Florida has helped integrate the newcomers into the community, and relations with the police do not seem to be an issue.

The rate of new immigrants, including many illegal immigrants, has increased tremendously from 2000 to 2005, which has resulted in many challenges to law enforcement. There has also been some backlash in towns and cities around the country. Hazelton, Pennsylvania, a small city of 31,000, has passed some tough new immigration laws that target employers and property owners rather than

Risking All for the American Dream

I was a police officer in Boca Raton, Florida, when Haitians started to arrive on our shores. I was a sergeant on the road when the issue first presented itself in the mid-1980s. It was something we had never dealt with before, and we had no idea how to address this new challenge. The first time it happened was around 4 or 5 in the morning; we got a call from a citizen that there was a group of blacks who were soaking wet, walking up to State Road A1A from the beach.

Previously, we had been confronted with drug dealers using boats to smuggle marijuana and cocaine to the beaches. At times, their boats broke up, and people and drugs scattered; other times, the drugs were dumped offshore as the occupants of the vessel were scared by the possibility of law enforcement being in the area, either on the water or in the air. When word got out of drugs washing up, there was often a response by locals trying to gather up some of the drugs.

Because this had been my previous experience, that was my assumption regarding the call as I responded to back up the zone officer. When we arrived, we found about eight black men and women walking in two different directions on A1A. We stopped them and attempted to communicate with them. None of us knew Creole, and the Haitians did not speak English. One Haitian knew a little English, and we were able to ascertain that they had come from Haiti on a small boat that had broken up a few hundred yards offshore, and that they had swum and then walked to shore. These people were wet, cold, tired, hungry, and scared. We tried to talk to them as best we could, but, in addition to the language barrier, they would not look us in the eye, which made us suspicious that they were perhaps lying to us.

We ended up using several police vehicles to transport them to the police station. Once at the station, we searched all of them (there were those drug smuggling fears again) and ultimately ended up transporting them to Miami where U.S. Immigration and Naturalization Services (INS) took custody of them.

This began to happen with increased regularity, and the numbers got larger and larger. Tragedy also resulted on several occasions with people drowning on their way to shore. We also saw pregnant women and children arriving with these groups. We learned some things about these new arrivals with each group that came, and we sat down as a police organization and with other groups such as the INS to decide how these situations should be handled.

We found that economic conditions in Haiti were deplorable, and people were fleeing to the United States for an opportunity to work. Others were persecuted by the dictatorship in Haiti and in fear of their lives. The police were different in Haiti and often shot citizens for no reason. Knowing this, I was surprised these people were so docile and cooperative when we stopped them. I can only attribute it to fear. In fact, their reluctance to look us in the eye was a cultural sign of respect.

For the most part, reports of them sailing the ocean in the rickety boats they were getting off were false. Most were transported most of the way by smugglers and then placed on the old boats to go the rest of the way, or they were simply forced to jump off the smugglers' boats, often resulting in death.

When I searched the women early on in this process, I found that they were wearing several layers of clothing in an effort to bring as many clothes with them as possible. They carried nothing. They literally came to this country with just the clothes on their backs.

Our procedures changed as this became a more regular occurrence and with larger groups. We stopped bringing them to the station and searching them and began calling INS to respond directly to the beach. We often had groups of more than 100 Haitians, and we would have officers stay with them in a designated area on or near the beach and await buses that INS sent. Most of these arrivals spent months in the Krome Detention Center in Miami waiting for their cases to be heard and decided by Immigration.

South Florida has a large population of Haitians, and as a police officer, I frequently interacted with them. They quickly went to work at any job they could find. Overall, I found them a very hardworking, peaceful group of people. They were happy to be able to work and send money home to Haiti to their families and often spent their nonworking time studying English. They also brought some unique cultural beliefs, in particular concerning voodoo, that were new to me as well as other officers. It was something we learned about and had to be aware of when we were investigating crimes. The department did provide us with training regarding the Haitian culture as well as some basic Creole to facilitate communication. It was an eye-opening experience for me to witness these people risking everything, including their lives, for an opportunity to work at (usually) very menial positions. The situation reminded me how lucky we are here in the United States.

—Linda Forst

the immigrants. The elected officials believe that they have to do it to protect the quality of life in their community, which has seen a drastic increase in new immigrants, many of which are believed to be illegal. A similar law was passed in Riverside, New Jersey, and several are in various draft stages in Palm Bay, Florida; Allentown, Shenandoah, and Mount Pocono in Pennsylvania; Gadsden, Alabama; Kennewick, Washington; and Escondido, California. These towns range in size from 3,000 to 134,000. Community leaders state they are doing this because of inaction by the federal government in enforcing immigration laws. Several states, including Utah, Georgia, Louisiana, Colorado, and Pennsylvania, have also drafted immigration related laws. They believe it is legal because "states and localities bear a significant amount of the burden for dealing with illegal aliens, but the Federal government bears the brunt of enforcing the law, and when they don't states and local governments pay the price."[65] The American Civil Liberties Union (ACLU) and other groups have filed suit against Hazelton, stating Hazelton is intruding on the federal government's role and discriminating against minorities. Law enforcement has been thrown into the middle of this controversy because towns and cities want something done and the federal government is unresponsive. When cities write new laws, it will fall to law enforcement personnel to enforce them and probably also intervene in disturbances that arise over their implementation.

The Physically Challenged

Depending on the definition of physically challenged, there are between 40 million and 70 million physically challenged people in the United States. According to the Census Bureau, among the 53 million adults with disabilities in the United States in 1997, 33 million had a severe disability and 10 million needed assistance in their daily lives. In 1997, almost 1 in 5 adults had some type of disability and the likelihood of a disability increased with age.[66] Those with disabilities include the deaf and hard of hearing; those who use wheelchairs, walkers, canes, and other mobility aids; the blind and visually impaired; those with communication problems; the mentally ill; and the retarded.

As is true in working with new immigrants, the deaf community can present a difficult challenge to law enforcement, particularly in a crisis situation. Communication is always a vital part of

police response, so being unable to communicate with a member of the deaf community can be a significant hurdle.

The Washington, D.C., police encountered such a hurdle after a Gallaudet freshman was found bludgeoned to death in his dorm room in September 2000. The crime resulted in panic at the famous college for the deaf and hard of hearing. The police missed some clues and arrested a student who admitted fighting with the victim, because police interpreted this to be a confession to murder. The student was released, and ultimately another suspect was arrested.

District police have installed teletypewriter (TTY) telephones for the deaf in their seven stations, given cultural training to the officers, and provided training in sign language to interested officers. Officer Myra Jordan has proposed establishing a liaison unit for the deaf community, as has been provided for other minority communities, and has offered to lead the unit. She learned sign language at a young age and attends Gallaudet.[67]

Many departments across the country have implemented training for police officers to increase the understanding of the hurdles of the deaf community and conduct informational sessions for the deaf community.

Diabetics also have significant problems of which the police should be aware. Because of the prevalence of drug abuse in our society, officers frequently confront people who are in possession of hypodermic syringes and needles or are actually using a hypodermic needle. Some, however, may be people suffering from diabetes, treating themselves by injecting insulin. Diabetics often wear easily recognizable identification alerting first responders and police that they have insulin-treated diabetes. Officers might also encounter diabetics who appear to be suffering from drug- or alcohol-related impairment, are unconscious, or are suffering from seizures.[68] With education and awareness, officers will be able to summon the necessary medical assistance for these individuals.

Police and Special Populations

As we have seen, the community the police serve is extremely diverse. Special populations offer unique challenges for police departments. Some of the groups with special needs are senior citizens, young people, crime victims, victims of domestic violence, the mentally ill, the homeless, and the disabled.

The Aging Population

America is getting older. Nationally, the median age—the age at which half the population is older and half is younger—increased from 35.3 in 2000 to 36.4 in 2005.[69] By the year 2030, there will be 66 million older people in our society. Senior citizens experience particular problems that necessitate special attention from the police. Although seniors have the lowest criminal victimization rates of all age groups, they experience a tremendous fear of crime, often refusing to leave their homes because of the fear of being a victim. Many senior citizens are infirm and require emergency services. Police often provide special programs and services for senior citizens.[70]

Also of concern to older Americans is the desire to retain their independence. An AARP (originally, the American Association of Retired Persons) study found that 85 percent of people over the age of 60 want to remain living independently as they age. Only one in eight lives with other relatives.[71]

Although there are many innovative programs to assist the aging population, law enforcement leaders have realized that education and training of their officers must occur for officers to foster a good relationship with this segment of the population. As has been mentioned earlier, the patrol officer is the ambassador for the department. The way these officers treat older people will affect what the seniors think of the department.

It is important for officers to understand the physical, emotional, and social challenges that people face as they age. Officers can then adapt some of their procedures to minimize the affect of some of the physical challenges (changes in vision, hearing, and mobility) on their interactions with older people.[72] An officer who understands the psychological and social issues will be able to understand an unexpectedly emotional reaction to what he or she perceives as a routine event. An example would be an overreaction by an older person to being involved in an automobile crash. To the person involved, this accident could be seen as a threat to his or her independence. A citation could affect a senior's ability to keep his or her license and consequently to remain independent. The social issues confronting older Americans include adjusting to retirement, loosing family and friends to death,

coping with illness and impairments, and perhaps facing a terminal illness. To have these things happen in close proximity to each other enhances the effects.[73]

Line officers also need to be aware of special issues facing the older person, including driving, fraud, self-neglect, and elder abuse. Increased awareness will help the officer to take action or make the proper referrals as well as helping the department to develop appropriate programs to address these issues.

Many departments are realizing what a valuable resource their retired citizens can be. According to the U.S. Census in 2000, there were 25 million men and 31 million women aged 55 and older. These individuals make up a major consumer market as well as a strong political force. If these people are knowledgeable about police resources and programs, they can be valuable political allies at budget time. Today's older citizen is wealthier, healthier, and better educated than ever before. Many of these residents strongly believe in contributing to the community and "giving back" and have a strong desire to stay active. What they need are ways to contribute in meaningful ways. Smart police departments assess their needs and determine areas in which these residents can contribute. The use of volunteers will be discussed in a later section. Currently, many special programs that are offered by police departments can be found on their websites. If older people have access to computers and are computer literate, this information (as well as crime statistics) is at their fingertips. It is a good avenue of outreach for police departments.

Today, police departments have created numerous special programs to deal with the problems of seniors. One such program is **Triad,** a partnership between the police and senior citizens to address specific problems seniors encounter with safety and quality-of-life issues. Triad was started by the International Association of Chiefs of Police (IACP) in cooperation with the AARP and the National Sheriffs' Association (NSA). The three associations have designated members to serve as a national Triad policy board, which is responsible for providing guidance and technical support to local Triads.[74] One example of a Triad program involves the plight of some seniors in personal care homes in Columbus, Georgia. The local Triad council devised a strategy to investigate elder abuse with the assistance of the sheriff's office and the police and health departments. They obtained a search warrant for the homes, arranged for proper lodging and care for those seniors living in unhealthy and unsafe conditions, and planned for more careful monitoring of such homes.[75] Triads are also involved in training police officers to interact with seniors and advising departments on various programs.

Some examples of programs that offer assistance to older residents include the following:

■ The Colorado Springs, Colorado, Police Department has the Senior Victim Assistance Team (SVAT). The SVAT provides assistance to victims of crime over 60 years of age, immediate crisis intervention, reassurance, support and referral, and services to older adults seeking special assistance from Colorado Springs Police Department.[76]

■ The Waltham, Massachusetts, Police Department has a comprehensive Triad program that stresses crime prevention and quality of life for the senior residents. Like all Triad programs, the Waltham program stresses cooperation and coordination with many other government and community organizations and protective services. One of the components of this program is the "file of life," a magnetized card placed on the resident's refrigerator with his or her medical information. There is also a Postal Carrier Alert program in which residents fill out an information card with emergency contacts that can be used when postal employees notice mail accumulating.

■ Seattle, Washington, has a coordinated program called Protecting Our Elderly Together (POET) that involves the domestic violence unit of Seattle Police Department, the city attorney's office, and victims' advocates and caseworkers from Family Protective Services, Geriatric Mental Health Services, and Aging and Disability Services. A lawyer representing a legal assistance organization also participates in the meetings. They have monthly meetings during which they review cases and look for solutions to difficult cases, making sure all necessary services are used and coordinated.[77]

AARP has cooperated with law enforcement by publishing several brochures on crime prevention for the elderly. The brochures contain practical advice about how to reduce criminal opportunity. Crime prevention information as well as driving information for elders is available through the AARP website.

Alzheimer's is a disease that does and will continue to affect police officers' jobs as they encounter Alzheimer's victims wandering or receive reports from concerned family regarding missing family members. Symptoms of Alzheimer's include memory loss, disorientation, loss of language skills, impairment of judgment, and personality changes. Patients have been known to wander aimlessly. Because of these factors, law enforcement personnel frequently encounter Alzheimer's sufferers. There are about 4 million Alzheimer's victims in the United States. Most victims are older than 65, but this disease can strike people in their 40s and 50s. As our population ages, it has been estimated that the number of people affected will reach 14 million by the middle of this century unless a cure or treatment is found.

There is help for law enforcement agencies in dealing with Alzheimer's. In 1994, the Alzheimer's Association developed the Safe Return program, which provides a national registry for people with Alzheimer's or who suffer memory impairment for other reasons. Through Safe Return, caregivers register their loved ones or patients through the Alzheimer's Association, providing the name, address, phone number, characteristics, distinguishing features, and other information, as well as names and phone numbers of contact persons. The registrant receives an identity bracelet or necklace, wallet cards, and clothing labels with his or her Safe Return ID number and Safe Return's 24-hour toll-free number. If a registrant is found, Safe Return is contacted and, through the ID number, his or her information is provided. Also, if a registrant is reported missing, Safe Return notifies the National Crime Information Center (NCIC) so law enforcement agencies are alerted about the missing person and his or her medical condition. More information on this program as well as training provided for law enforcement is available on the Alzheimer's Association website.[78]

Young People

Young children are a special target of police community relations programs because they are impressionable, and it is believed that if children learn something early enough in life, it will stay with them forever. The problem of crime and young people has been a concern for decades. During the 1980s and early 1990s, crime involving juveniles soared. The nation responded by implementing many different types of programs to try to

Community Policing with the Aging Population

ANDREW SCOTT

Andrew J. Scott III began his career in law enforcement in 1978 at the North Miami Police Department in Miami/Dade County. After several years, Chief Scott moved to the North Miami Beach Police Department. He remained there until 1998 and ascended to the rank of Assistant Chief of Police. He was appointed as the Chief of Police of the city of Boca Raton in 1998 and served in that capacity until 2006. He is now employed in the private sector. Chief Scott earned a master of science degree in management from St. Thomas University in Miami in 1993 and a bachelor of arts degree in psychology from Florida International University in 1977. He is a graduate of the FBI National Academy.

The city of Boca Raton has an interesting demographic makeup—over 30 percent of our population is over the age of 60. As in the United States as a whole (according to the 2000 U.S. Census), the 85 and older citizenry is currently the fastest growing segment of the population. Moreover, this population is comprised overwhelmingly of women, many of whom have outlived their spouses, their financial resources, and, in some cases, their children and other relatives.

As calls for service increased among the elder population, officers looked for resources to assist residents but often did not know how to help. Concerned neighbors and family living out of state also contacted our agency. Though in most cases no actual crime occurred, quality of life issues such as failing health, isolation, depression, and competency arose repeatedly. Social service agencies, both public and nonprofit, also alerted our attention to the aging population phenomenon as they sought assistance in aiding these citizens.

An Alzheimer's or dementia diagnosis further complicates domestic situations, as officers are increasingly responding to victims who are abused by their caregivers or to caregivers who are incapable of taking care of their loved ones and are battered by the patient. We soon discovered that there is a tremendous gap in services for frail and vulnerable adults, unless they are in extreme poverty and qualify for services through the Department of Children and Families.

As a result, it became apparent that the city's increased elder population were vulnerable adults, at an increased risk to become victims of crime. In response, the Boca Raton Police Services Department wanted to augment the current social services provided and implement proactive measures to this underserved population. Although bridging the gap between state legal protection and social service providers is difficult, the Boca Raton Police Services Department (BRPSD) endeavored to establish an in-house position to assist elders who fall through the cracks.

The Elder Crime Specialist position is a relatively new addition to the Boca Raton Police Services Department, initiated in February 2002. Most notably, it is a position that did not exist within any other Palm Beach County law enforcement agency. This civilian position was added to address the increased victimization of the elder population in Boca Raton. In recent years, we have seen an increase in elder crime, especially consumer fraud and financial exploitation. In 2001, 10 percent of crimes committed in the city were against the elderly. In 2002, the percentage jumped to almost 13 percent.

The primary objective in designating an Elder Crime Specialist was to reach out to the senior community and provide a police department liaison to the elders in the city. In this way, law enforcement becomes proactive in identifying and targeting particular issues that affect city residents. Another goal was to educate elders, focusing on crime awareness and prevention. Telemarketing fraud is the most prevalent crime committed against elders, with other types of white-collar crimes following a close second. Making elders aware of their own vulnerabilities and the types of crimes that most affect them is the first step in reducing their risk level.

In the summer of 2002, Boca Raton Police initiated the first-ever Elder Education Seminar. The program educates seniors on county and state agencies providing free services to people over the age of 60. Over 25 state agencies and nonprofit organizations covered topics such as Medicare fraud; consumer fraud; Alzheimer's and dementia diagnosis and care; elder abuse, neglect, and exploitation; health care facility and health care professional licensing requirements; transportation; fixed incomes; assisted living facilities and nursing home standards; and volunteer opportunities. Two seminars have been completed, with over 50 attendees at each eight-week session. Education is a crucial piece in crime prevention, and the Elder Education Seminars seek to provide elders with the information they need to protect themselves and each other.

In the winter of 2002, Boca Raton Police initiated a free cellular telephone program for city seniors to ensure constant access to 911. Area businesses and high schools have been an integral part of this program by collecting and donating used phones. The Boca Raton Police Explorers (a high school student group) clean and program the phones, preparing them for distribution to the elder community. The Elder Crime Specialist meets with each phone recipient to instruct and educate the elder about the phone.

The state-operated Long Term Care (LTC) Ombudsman Council has partnered with the agency to train staff members and residents at assisted living facilities and nursing homes. The state of Florida is currently experiencing a significant nursing shortage, affecting staffing ratios at many long-term care facilities. Unfortunately, crimes such as elder abuse and neglect are on the rise in these facilities, as staffing shortages continue and traditional nursing positions are filled with unlicensed certified nursing assistants. Educating the staff about resident rights is imperative, as many caregivers in these facilities are unaware of the special rights that protect residents. Further, staff often is uneducated about behaviors that not only violate these special rights but also can be prosecuted by state law under the elder abuse, neglect, and exploitation chapter. The Elder Crime Specialist and LTC Ombudsman representative conduct both staff and resident training at 12 facilities in the city.

Home visits to frail and vulnerable elders by our Elder Crime Specialist provide intervention and situation assessment. As law enforcement becomes aware of these individuals, either through calls for service or a phone call made to our agency by a concerned friend or neighbor, we can mitigate potentially dangerous circumstances. Identifying elders at risk gives us an opportunity to protect an elder and possibly prevent a future crime from occurring. Further, we can actively participate in making certain that quality of life measures are upheld. Sometimes that means a simple phone call to an out-of-state relative. Many times it is as easy as making sure the elder has meals delivered to his or her home. More complicated cases involve elders with no family or means of supporting themselves.

Participation in committees such as the State Attorney's Crimes Against the Elderly Task Force enables the department to interface with other law enforcement agencies and various state and county agencies to share information, discuss prevention and intervention techniques, and troubleshoot difficult cases. BRPSD in-service training is held in conjunction with agencies such as Adult Protective Services, the Legal Aid Society, and the state attorney's office to educate road patrol officers about crimes against the elderly and the importance of detailed incident reports.

The Elder Crime Specialist regularly speaks about crimes against the elderly to homeowner association meetings, civic organizations, and assisted and independent living facilities. Educating and warning elders about recent telemarketing scams and other fraud schemes empowers them to be aware of common ploys to exploit them or their friends.

Community partners include state, county, and nonprofit agencies charged with providing services to vulnerable adults in Palm Beach County and the city of Boca Raton. They include the Department of Children and Families division of Adult Protective Service, the Area Agency on Aging, the Long Term Care Ombudsman Council, the Department of Elder Affairs, Alzheimer's Community Care, the Mae Volen Senior Center, and the Center for Information and Crisis Services, to name a few. These agencies engage in collaborative efforts with local law enforcement to share information and provide resources for elder residents of our city.

Partnerships with agencies such as Alzheimer's Community Care and the Legal Aid Society division greatly assisted our agency in mitigating the magnitude of elder abuse, neglect, and exploitation occurring in our city. These agencies have aggressively fought to assist vulnerable adults by responding in unconventional ways, including making home visits to victims.

Local businesses have responded with tremendous generosity, both financially and by donating their valuable time. Key contributors include Publix Supermarkets and Florida Power and Light, who combined to make the holiday food and gift basket drive an overwhelming success. Additionally, several local merchants donated cell phones that ultimately were distributed to city elders.

Community input also comes from Boca Raton Police Department volunteers, most over the age of 65. Their role serves two primary purposes: to identify and prioritize concerns of the elderly and, more importantly, to retain their independence by giving back to the city.

address this issue. Programs were implemented addressing family issues and living conditions, educational and school programs were started, and law enforcement implemented programs. Factors studied included educational attainment, substance abuse, mentors and role models, supervision, and others. Police felt that if the American public cared about the crime program, then programs targeting children and youth needed to be undertaken. The arrests of juveniles for violent crime have decreased steadily since 1994 and are currently at a level not seen since the 1970s. In 1990, 2,232 juveniles were arrested for homicide across the country, but in 2003 that number was down to 928. The concern is that the female proportion of juvenile violent crime has increased, especially for assault. This presents some of the issues discussed earlier. The other significant finding is that most crime involving juveniles happens in the hours after school, which may assist in directing the efforts of some of the juvenile programs.[79]

Antidrug Programs For Young People Currently, the most popular antidrug program aimed at children is **Drug Abuse Resistance Education (DARE)**. In DARE programs, police officers teach students in their own classrooms about the dangers of drug abuse. The program is designed to help youths (1) build self-esteem, (2) build self-confidence, (3) manage youthful stress, (4) redirect behavior to viable alternatives, and (5) see police officers as positive role models.

The DARE curriculum is organized into 17 classroom sessions conducted by a police officer, coupled with suggested activities taught by the regular classroom teacher. The course includes classroom lectures, group discussions, role-plays, workbook exercises, and questions and answers.[80]

DARE is the single largest and most widely used substance abuse prevention program in the world. It is being used in all 50 states and in 54 countries around the world; it benefits more than 36 million school children each year.[81] It operates in 80 percent of all school districts around the country and reaches 36 million students per year.[82]

A 1994 study confirmed the popularity of DARE and revealed that its appeal cuts across racial, ethnic, and socioeconomic lines. The study indicated considerable support for expansion of the program, yet reported that DARE had little, if any, statistical impact on drug use by young people.[83]

A 1999 study of 3,150 high school juniors in Ohio found that students who completed two or more semesters of DARE in elementary school were 50 percent less likely to become high-risk abusers of drugs and alcohol than were students not exposed to DARE. The program also strengthened peer resistance skills regarding drugs and alcohol.[84]

A 2000 study conducted in Houston, Texas, reported increased awareness of drug, alcohol, tobacco, weapons, and theft problems on their campus among middle and high school students who took the program; parents strongly supported its continuance.[85] There is generally great support for the program as a community relations tool.

Although DARE has been popular, some believe that it is not an effective use of resources in combating drug use among young people and point to other programs that are more effective. The national research strongly supports the short-term efforts of DARE, but the long-term success relative to drug avoidance is mixed. Researchers believe DARE's effects can be strengthened when it is part of a more comprehensive effort by communities. Recently, a study indicated that DARE students were five times less likely to start smoking.[86]

In a continuing effort to improve its program and address concerns regarding benefits, DARE has developed some new curricula and joined forces with the University of Akron to conduct further research.[87]

Despite the mixed reviews, many parents and teachers believe such programs are crucial if children are to learn to resist peer pressure and stay away from drugs. Researchers seem to believe that the programs can't be one-size-fits-all and can't condemn outright legitimate medications and in moderation, alcohol, which may confuse the students and conflict with what they learn at home.[88] It will take more time and more study of DARE and other similar programs to determine what components of the program are most effective and in what way.

severly! Collapsed or dysfunctional family

Other Programs for Young People Police programs for young people exist to address concerns other than drugs. In this section, we discuss some of the most popular programs.

The **Gang Resistance Education and Training (GREAT)** program is modeled after DARE but specifically addresses the issues of gangs. GREAT is a confidence-building class with the emphasis on resisting peer pressure regarding gangs and what they offer. It differs from other gang programs in that it does not target gang members but, rather, is presented to entire classrooms without attempting to predict which students are most likely to become involved with a gang. The program is provided for middle school students to reduce their involvement in gangs and delinquent behavior, teach them the consequences of gang involvement, and help them develop positive relations with law enforcement. Recently, a five-year longitudinal study showed that GREAT has modest positive effects on adolescents' attitudes and delinquency risk factors (peer group associations, and attitudes about gangs, law enforcement, and risk-seeking behaviors) but no effect on their involvement in gangs and actual delinquent behaviors. It fulfilled one of its program objectives in steering the youths toward law enforcement and increasing their awareness of gang involvement. Parents, teachers, and officers also viewed the GREAT program very favorably.[89]

Youth Crime Watch of America is a youth-led movement to create a crime-free, drug-free, and violence-free environment in the schools and neighborhoods.[90] The program offers a variety of components based on the "watch out, help out" philosophy, which can be tailored to fit different communities. These include crime reporting; youth patrols; drug, crime and violence education; bus safety; mentoring; conflict resolution; mediation; peer and cross-age teaching; and action projects. The program also provides a monthly newsletter and online chats.

Anti-bullying programs are becoming more prevalent. In the wake of recent school violence, many schools and communities are addressing the area of bullying in their schools with various education and prevention programs. State legislatures are also addressing this issue. Bullying and being bullied have been correlated with violence and with lack of student success. It's been found that the more invested a student is in the school, the better he or she performs academically.

Oak Harbor High School in Washington State implemented an anti-bullying program in 1999 that was a joint effort involving the police, a youth advocate from Citizens Against Domestic and Sexual Abuse, and school personnel. The goal and slogan emphasized catching verbal assaults and intervening to prevent physical assaults. Data indicate that bullying, harassment, and intimidation have decreased.[91]

Youth hate crime prevention programs have grown as many schools have also recognized that hate crimes are a problem in the community and that a significant proportion involves young people. It is believed that these crimes are caused by attitudes that are learned and that, by providing educational materials to prevent or change these prejudiced attitudes and tendencies toward violence, the problem can be greatly reduced. These programs also hope to enable young people to resist recruiting efforts by hate groups.[92]

Community Emergency Response Team (CERT) training has been made available to high school students in many schools throughout the country. After September 11, 2001, there was increased awareness of the importance of civilians being trained in basic emergency response, first aid, and search and rescue. It was also realized that students would be a great asset to improving safety in their schools in the event of a disaster. Students view this as an opportunity to learn valuable skills that could enhance their chances of obtaining employment in police and fire departments. Successful programs have been launched in many schools, including Los Altos High School in Los Altos, California; Northport High School in Sarasota, Florida; Glencoe High School in Hillsboro, Oregon; and Grants Pass High School in Grants Pass, Oregon.[93]

Officer Friendly and other programs designed to help children see and talk to police officers are popular with schools and police administrators alike. The intent of the Officer Friendly programs is to encourage young children to view police officers as friends by getting to know some. Some officers dress up as clowns or old-time police officers and perform clown-type tricks with balloons. This has proven to be popular with young children. Police officers have also been involved in literacy programs at schools where they read with or to young students. K-9 demonstrations have also proven to be beneficial in building relationships with children. Some departments use music to reach out to young people and have officers that perform together in rock bands, jazz groups, or singing groups.

The **Police Explorer** program is part of the Boy Scouts and is a popular program available around the nation. Police Explorer programs are a win-win for all concerned. They give young people an opportunity to explore the law enforcement field. The explorers receive training in various areas of law enforcement either through their sponsoring agency or sometimes through regional or state training opportunities. They are also sometimes involved in competitions with other posts. The explorers help to supplement the workforce of the department and can assist with community

Police Exploring

Students can find out firsthand what police work is all about in several ways. If your school has an intern program with the local government, try to get into it and request to work with the police department. If your police department has an auxiliary program that allows you to contribute your time to the department, try that out. If your police department has a ride-along program, take advantage of it. Being a Police Explorer will make students more aware of the needs and problems of their community. The program can strengthen or clarify your decision to become a police officer.

The Law Enforcement Exploring program involves young men and women, ages 14 through 20 years, in a hands-on look at law enforcement as a potential career. Youths interested in Law Enforcement Exploring join posts sponsored by a law enforcement agency. The law enforcement agency provides a sworn officer as the post leader. Liability insurance is provided by the Boy Scouts of America (BSA), which offers Law Enforcement Exploring as a program for older youths. The BSA also operates regional and national events for Explorers. In a

typical post, Explorers are required to work approximately 20 hours a month to maintain their eligibility, but they may work more hours if they wish. Some of the ways in which Explorers work with the police include assisting the police in crowd, traffic, and parking control at parades and festivals; staging crime prevention programs for neighborhood associations and assisting with Operation Identification by marking citizens' valuables; assisting the police in performing clerical functions; and serving as role models for younger children and assistants for officers teaching DARE. Explorers can attend regional events in which they compete in pistol shooting, crime scene searches, hostage negotiations, report writing, traffic accident investigations, and other events based on aspects of law enforcement. Every other year, a national conference with interpost competition is held. According to the BSA, approximately 40 percent of Explorers become either law enforcement officers or lawyers.

—*John S. Dempsey*

festivals, parades, and emergencies in areas such as directing traffic and assisting the public. Recently, they have been found to be valuable in emergency preparedness. Being an Explorer is a great way to determine if a law enforcement career is right for a young person, and the department gets an opportunity to look at a potential candidate. These Explorers will provide for a future work force that is well-trained and educated in the law enforcement field. Most Police Explorer units have web pages attached to their police department's site with information regarding their post.

Police trading cards are another popular youth program. Trading cards are in the format of baseball cards that feature the photographs and personal information of officers in the department. Young people often go to the police station to find officers from whom they want a card or autograph. Some officers use them as their business cards. Officers may provide their favorite quote or inspirational saying on the backs of the cards as well as their professional background. Some agencies will

have cards for particular units, such as the bicycle unit, motor unit, or K-9s, in addition to individual cards. Some police departments feature a "card of the week" or "card of the month," which will be printed in the local paper and available at the front desk for pick-up. Police administrators are often surprised at the number of youths responding to add to their collection. The cards provide a good icebreaker for officers as well as the youth to initiate conversations.

The school resource officer, a position designed to combat the increase of juvenile crime and improve relationships between school children and the police, has proven to be effective. Nationally, 43 percent of local police departments used full-time school resource officers in 2003.[94] This program assigns uniformed police officers to schools, generally junior and senior high schools, to provide a wide variety of services. These officers build bridges and become friendly with the students. They provide someone who is available and familiar to go to with problems or to give advice that might help the student make good choices. The school resource officer also functions as a good resource person for the teachers and administrators and in an emergency can serve as a first responder with a good working knowledge of the school, its personnel, and its layout.

Anti-child abduction programs are also very popular. The U.S. Department of Justice estimates that approximately 19 out of every 1,000 children are missing, but less than 10 percent of those are abducted. Most are runaways or throwaways living on the streets.[95] Many law enforcement agencies provide parents with free photo ID documents and crucial information about safety for their children. Recently, some departments have begun to facilitate the collection of DNA from children via a swabbing kit. The parents then retain the specimen. In 2003, President Bush signed the Protect Act of 2003. Although many states have had Amber Alert systems in place since this program originated in Texas in 1996, the Protect Act formally established the federal government's role in the Amber Alert system. The goal is to get entire communities involved in the search for missing children by joining the efforts of law enforcement and the media. Using the media to quickly alert the public to the descriptions of individuals endangering children has already had a number of successes.[96] In conjunction with these efforts, many departments offer Internet safety brochures and programs to guide parents in keeping their children safe on the computer. Schools are also providing the information directly to the teens via school assemblies. This is an emerging safety issue because online predators seem to be multiplying and naïve pre-teens are posting too much personal information on sites such as My Space, making themselves easy targets.

Police athletic programs or **Police Athletic Leagues (PALs)** have long been one of the most popular programs involving the police and youth. These programs include boxing, baseball, football, and basketball leagues (including midnight basketball) and summer camps. Some prominent former members of PALs around the nation include boxers Mohammed Ali and Evander Holyfield and entertainer Bill Cosby. PAL is the largest organization of law enforcement agencies using athletics, recreation, and education to instill positive life principles and character-building tools to deter crime and violence. By 2004, there were more than 350 chapters serving more than two million youths nationwide.[97]

Police department–college intern programs are also common throughout the nation. Most programs span the duration of an academic quarter or semester. Generally, interns participate for 200 to 300 hours and prepare a research project or paper on a topic approved by the college and the department. Students usually spend part of their internship doing some administrative work—perhaps a project the department normally does not have the personnel to handle—and the remainder working within different areas of the department, including patrol. Interns can work various shifts and see the flavor of law enforcement at different times of the day and the work in various units (including investigations, traffic, crime lab, and jails) allows them to observe the work of the units as well as how it all fits together as part of the greater mission. This is a valuable part of the college experience, helping the criminal justice student to narrow their area of interest and providing exposure to a particular department. It also allows the department to observe potential employment candidates.

Crime Victims

"Victim issues and concerns are becoming an integral part of policing in the 21st century. We have to prioritize this in our law enforcement mission," according to Chief Frank Winters, Chairman of the IACP Victim Services Committee.[98]

There are as many as 31 million victims of violent or property crime in the United States annually.[99] Many efforts have been undertaken to assist victims of crime, including victims' rights laws, victim assistance programs, and crime compensation funds. Recently, law enforcement has realized that by working more closely with these victims, they can better serve the victims and enhance community support, and they can also help advance the law enforcement mission and goal of reducing and solving crime and reducing fear of crime.

Victims have traditionally been considered law enforcement clients because they receive law enforcement services. Recently, the criminal justice system has recognized that victims are powerful and resourceful stakeholders in the system; by working more closely with them and incorporating their assistance, police can have a greater impact on crime and the perception of community safety.[100] Many departments around the country have established victim's services units within their agency and have found this to be a very positive undertaking. Victim's services staff can have a more rapid response and consequently obtain more and better information regarding the crime and the victim's needs than they would by reading the report the next day or even later. Crisis counseling can be initiated earlier, and police time can be devoted to investigation. This supportive atmosphere may also encourage citizens to report more crime, cooperate more fully, and consequently, increase conviction rates.

The city of Austin, Texas, has initiated a comprehensive program. The Victim Services Division within the Austin Police Department provides crisis and trauma counseling to victims, families, witnesses, and others and assists street officers and investigators on cases. Austin is a large department with a large Victim Services Division. In the 20 years since its implementation, this division has grown to 35 full- and part-time staff and 300 volunteers. They see 14,000 victims a year.[101] Smaller departments can implement similar programs on a smaller scale. One victim/witness coordinator or victim advocate may be enough to serve a smaller community but still make a valuable contribution to the community.

Police also have instituted special investigative units during the past decades and use special tools to make the investigative process less threatening to victims of crime. Police try to minimize the number of times a victim or witness has to talk to someone and to make any meetings as convenient as possible for the victims and witnesses, and they strive to keep victims informed of the status of the case. This has proven especially critical among homicide victims' families. Often, the detective is working very hard on a homicide case but does not have the time and in the past did not consider it a priority to keep the family informed. The family frequently perceived this as the investigator either not caring or not working on their loved one's case. Many departments have initiated programs where they regularly exchange information with the family or loved ones of homicide victims. This has proven to be very successful and has greatly improved relationships within communities. Washington, D.C., has recently implemented an "open house" gathering following the suggestion of an activist who had suffered through the murder of two sons. The first open house targeted the homicides that had occurred since 2004, which included 266 unsolved cases among the total of 450 homicides. More than 200 people attended and although some left as angry as they arrived, most were pleased to discover their cases had not been forgotten and were actually being followed up. This event allowed the families to see how difficult the investigations are and the challenges involved in obtaining witnesses and leads. On the other hand, it was also a reminder to the detective or investigator about what was important to the community and the victim's families, and though a homicide case may be 1 of 20 cases the investigator is working, it is a major, significant, life-altering trauma to the family.[102] Philadelphia Police are also holding monthly meetings with murder victim's families. These meetings were facilitated by a support group (Mothers in Charge) that helps families who lost loved ones to homicides.[103]

Victims of Domestic Violence

There has also been increased demand on law enforcement to be responsive to the needs of domestic violence victims.[104] Family violence is one of the most frequent types of violence that police encounter and though it is not necessarily considered the most dangerous police call (because of improved training and procedures), it is one filled with danger and emotional trauma for all concerned. Although police once dismissed it as a "civil matter," the latest statistics indicate the seriousness of this violence. According to the 1998 Commonwealth Fund survey of women's health, "One of 6 women experienced physical and/or sexual abuse during childhood. The equivalent of 3 million women nationwide reported experiencing domestic abuse in the past year. One in 5 said she's been raped or assaulted in her lifetime."[105] Female murder victims are far more likely than are male murder victims to have been killed by an intimate. Three out of four women murder victims were attributed to intimate partner violence.[106] Though this is a troubling situation with troubling numbers, the good news is that the rate of domestic violence is not increasing. According to the Department of Justice, the rate of intimate partner violence (violence committed by a current or former spouse, boyfriend, or girlfriend) declined from 1994 to 2004 and did not change between 2003 and 2004.[107] Results from a self-report study conducted by Group Health Cooperative released in 2006 indicated that approximately 44 percent of 3,500 randomly surveyed women with the cooperative indicated they had been physically, psychologically, or sexually assaulted by a partner in their lifetimes. Many of these women are socially isolated by their partners, so a doctor's visit may be the only opportunity these women have to get help or talk about the issue. Group Health's purpose was to alert doctors to this issue and emphasize the role they could play in these women's physical and emotional health and facilitate doctors assisting these women to get needed help.[108]

Despite the sometimes-harsh criticism toward women reluctant to leave abusive partners, it is a dangerous time. A woman is most at risk to be murdered when she tries to break off an abusive relationship.[109]

A 1997 University of Michigan study found that violence between intimate couples of opposite gender may start very early. In a survey of 635 suburban, middle-class high school students, about 36 percent of girls and 37 percent of boys said they had experienced physical abuse from a date. Half of the girls—and just 4 percent of the boys—had said their worst abusive experience "hurt a lot." Among the other key findings were that 44 percent of the girls stayed with boys after moderate violence, including slapping, and 36 percent stayed after severe abuse, including choking and punching.[110]

Traditional Police Response to Domestic Violence
Traditionally, the criminal justice system took a hands-off policy toward domestic violence, treating it as a private affair that should be handled within the family and police didn't make arrests even when it qualified as a felony. Two assumptions prevailed: (1) that the arrest would make life worse for the victim, because the abuser might retaliate, and (2) that the victim would refuse to press charges. Most police departments had no formal policies regarding domestic violence, and officers used many different techniques to deal with the problem when called to the scene, including attempts to calm down both parties, mediating the conflict, and referring the participants to social service agencies for assistance in dealing with their problems. Often officers would escort abusive spouses out of the residence and advise them not to return until the next day or until things calmed down. Two important lawsuits—brought forward by women's groups in New York City (*Bruno v. Codd*, 396 N.Y.S. 2nd 974, 1977) and Oakland, California (*Scott v. Hart*, C-76-2395 N.D. Cal, 1976)—began to change the police response in domestic violence cases. The suits charged that the police departments had denied women equal protection of the law by failing to arrest people who had committed assaults against them. As a result of the lawsuits, both departments formulated official written policies mandating arrests in cases of felonious spousal assault.[111]

Minneapolis Domestic Violence Experiment
Subsequent to these lawsuits, the Police Foundation conducted the **Minneapolis Domestic Violence Experiment** (1981 to 1982). This experiment was designed to examine the deterrent effect of various methods of handling domestic violence, including mandatory arrest. During this experiment, officers called to incidents of domestic violence were required to select at random one of a group of instructions to tell them how to deal with the incidents. The officers' forced choice required them to do one of the following: (1) arrest the offender, (2) mediate the dispute, or (3) escort the offender from the home. Repeat violence over the next six months was measured through follow-up interviews with victims and police department records of calls to the same address. The findings indicated that arrest prevented further domestic violence more effectively than did separation or mediation. Repeat violence occurred in 10 percent of the arrest cases, compared with 19 percent of the mediation incidents and 24 percent of the separation incidents. The actual sanction imposed by arrest involved little more than an evening in jail; only 3 of the 136 people arrested were ever convicted and sentenced.[112] Lawrence Sherman and Richard Berk made three recommendations when concluding their Minneapolis Domestic Violence Experiment: First, the arrest would probably be the preferred response in domestic violence cases; second, that the experiment should be replicated to see if the results hold up; and third, that mandatory arrest should not be employed until more data were in, especially to avoid stifling future research into the topic.[113] Despite Sherman's concerns, mandatory arrest laws were adopted around the country, fueled by women's rights groups and battered women's advocates.

The Minneapolis experiment has been replicated in a number of other localities around the country to determine whether the results would be the same. These studies have had inconsistent results. In some areas, arrest provided no deterrence; in others, only certain types of offenders were deterred. Sherman and others have called for mandatory arrest laws to be repealed, and others feel a more holistic approach should be taken toward the issue of family violence, including close coordination with other criminal justice agencies and victim service providers. A recent review of these replication studies indicates that mandatory arrest is still the preferred method of handling domestic violence and that it aids the individuals

Trooper Lint ER Domestic Suicide Attempt — 45 min most Crucial

involved in getting into the system and getting help as well as educating the public that domestic violence is a crime.[114]

Police Response to Domestic Violence Today

Despite the lack of a clear consensus regarding the effectiveness of arrest in domestic violence cases, police departments nationwide have begun to establish new police guidelines for domestic violence cases. Currently, 87 percent of departments have special policies regarding domestic disputes. This statistic is somewhat skewed by smaller departments. Almost all categories (sizes) of departments have almost 100 percent of the agencies in that category with a domestic policy except for departments serving populations of less than 2,500 people. Only 78 percent of those departments have a domestic policy.[115] Mandatory arrests for domestic violence, however, are still controversial even though most states have laws and departments have policies that are pro-arrest. Arguments against arrest include the arguments previously used for keeping it a civil matter, including that it may deter women victims from calling the police in the first place; and that arresting an abusive spouse might make him angrier and cause him to commit further violence against his spouse.

It has been found that officers are often making double arrests at scenes of domestic violence. They cite the pressure to make arrests coupled with an inability to determine for sure which party is telling the truth. The feeling is that it is preferable to arrest both parties, get them in the system, and give them access to services rather than not making an arrest, with the individuals not receiving the services they need and the officers possibly facing departmental criticism. This alternative is frowned upon by victim's advocates because victims are often afraid to call the police for fear of being arrested along with the partner, especially when they know the partner is particularly good at presenting his or her side of the story and perhaps "conning" others.

In response to the demands placed on law enforcement because of domestic violence calls and the desire to be more sensitive to the needs of the victim, many police departments throughout the country employ domestic violence specialists or coordinators to oversee the domestic violence cases the department handles. Depending on the size of the department and the size of the unit, they may or may not personally follow up on every domestic violence call. The specialist will ensure that all victims are aware of the services available and assist them

in obtaining these services. The specialist will attempt to make sure that no cases slip through the cracks because of inaccurate reporting and assist the officers in handling these situations when requested. Women's perception of how they were treated by police affects whether or not they will call the police again. Researchers Eve Buzawa and the late Gerald Hotaling, as cited in the *National Institute of Justice Journal,* interviewed 353 women and found that in 55 percent of the cases, women were generally satisfied with the outcome of the case and in 17 percent, they were dissatisfied. These dissatisfied women indicated they might not call the police again in similar situations. The researchers found that the main factor regarding victim satisfaction in these cases was the extent of control the women felt over the outcome: the lower their sense of control was, the lower was their satisfaction with the system and the police.[116] The IACP is committed to devoting resources to the issue and ending violence against women. In late 2004, the IACP announced a new initiative: Police Response to Violence Against Women and the National Law Enforcement Leadership initiative being facilitated by the National Violence Against Women Advisory Group.[117]

The trend is to deal with domestic violence as part of the bigger picture involving family violence and provide a coordinated effort to all members of a family plagued by violence. It is no longer desirable or efficient for agencies to work independently, and there is increased communication and coordination, with use of liaisons and even task forces to deal with the issue of family violence. The impact of violence on our society, especially when witnessed or experienced at a young age, is becoming apparent, and service providers and criminal justice practitioners see the importance of intervening as early as possible.

The Mentally Ill

Police officers frequently encounter people with mental illness, which poses a significant challenge for law enforcement. Approximately 10 to 15 percent of jail inmates have severe mental illness. In jurisdictions with populations greater than 100,000, approximately 7 percent of police contacts involve the mentally ill.[118] The calls involving people with mental illness can be some of the most dangerous that officers face. Often the calls come from family members who have tried to handle the situation themselves but find they are unable to do so. Often, this is an ongoing problem; they have been able to handle it many times in the past but do not wish to involve the police if they don't have to. If, however, they start to fear for their safety or the safety of the mentally ill person, they will call the police. The other way that officers encounter mentally ill persons is when they are causing some type of disruption in public and a citizen or businessperson observes this odd or threatening behavior and calls police. Sometimes officers encounter individuals acting strangely out in public and believe they need to take some type of action. Often, the mentally ill person is in the process of committing a crime. Officers have several difficult decisions to make. First, they decide if the person needs to be restricted in some way. If they feel they have calmed an individual down and so the individual is not a danger to himself or herself or to others, officers may leave the individual where that person is or with family. If the individual cannot safely be left, the officer can take the person to jail or a mental health facility. This decision will depend on what mental health facilities are available. If the community doesn't have competent mental health facilities or if they are full and refusing any new patients, an officer may find a way to make an arrest to keep the person safe and get some mental health care in jail.[119] Police officers are limited in what they can do with people who are acting strangely and, consequently, frequently use creative problem solving when nothing else seems available. Officers were using and are using a form of problem-oriented policing even before the term was popularized. However, in the most serious and dangerous cases, officers believe they need to take action. Unless they can adequately document that the individual is a danger to self or others, they cannot involuntarily commit the individual. Sometimes, it can be difficult to define exactly when that occurs, but officers encounter these decisions frequently and often respond repeatedly to the same individuals and locations. Many officers become frustrated as they attempt to bring someone to the mental health crisis facility only to have the crisis center staff will say they are full or that the person doesn't meet the facility's criteria, or they may take the individual in and conduct an evaluation, only to release the person within a few hours. Two Fairfax County, Virginia, officers were shot to death in the restricted section of their parking lot of their police facility in May 2006 by a man with an AK-47 style assault rifle, 5 handguns, and extra clips of ammo who fired off more than 70 rounds. He was known to have severe psychiatric problems and despite arrests and some treatment, failed to get the help he

needed.[120] A 36-year-old father of two was shot dead in Fort Lauderdale, Florida, by police after threatening several neighbors with a metal saw and screaming that he would kill them. He ignored police commands to drop his weapon and was shot as he made "hostile and aggressive movements" toward police. The man had undergone court-ordered mental health treatment the year before after being ruled incompetent to stand trial regarding criminal traffic charges. Neighbors were angry and demanded a public hearing over what they perceived as excessive force.[121]

Though mental health issues are not a police job per se, it has become one because these individuals are in the community and get involved in disturbances, assaults, suicide attempts, or other criminal actions. Confrontations with these people who may be delusional often ends with the individual, the officer, or a bystander being injured or killed. Police departments have worked hard to develop policies and procedures and weapons or technology to minimize this outcome. Three problems that are closely related to the challenge of people with mental illness include homelessness, drug abuse, and alcohol abuse.[122] Society needs to have all sectors of the community that deal with these issues work together to develop proactive solutions to these problems.

Huffer @ East Gate / Diabetic @ East

The Homeless

Police departments are generally the only agency available 24 hours a day, 7 days a week. Therefore, the police are frequently called to deal with alcoholics, the mentally ill, and the homeless (street people). Large numbers of people live on the streets today. Many of these people are often in drug or alcoholic stupors or frenzies, or they exhibit wild and chaotic behavior. The roots of the homeless problem include the policy in the 1960s and 1970s of releasing the institutionalized mentally ill, today's jail overcrowding, the decriminalization of public intoxication, and the lack of affordable housing.

Community residents often call the police and insist they remove homeless people from the streets. Residents do not realize, do not understand, and perhaps do not care that the police have very few options for dealing with these unfortunate members of the community.

A 1990 U.S. Supreme Court case, *Zinermon v. Burch,* added another barrier to those already impeding the treatment of the mentally ill.[123] In this ruling, the Court held that all patients must be "competent" to sign themselves voluntarily into a mental hospital. Because of this ruling, patients who are marginally competent may have to be admitted involuntarily and have their treatment validated by the courts.

Today's homeless population, compared with the homeless before the 1990s, has special problems, as pointed out by Alan Coffey. Coffey writes, "The homeless are no longer the group of vagrants that police have traditionally encountered. Although hobos are still among the homeless in America, many urban areas are witnessing the inclusion of women and children, even whole families, in this group."[124]

Who are the homeless? The National Institute of Justice (NIJ) reported that 25 to 45 percent of the people living on the streets are alcoholics, and that about 30 percent of all homeless people suffer from severe mental disorders. Many more homeless suffer from less severe psychological disorders that may prevent them from holding stable jobs. The NIJ also reports that a surprising number of homeless people are military veterans. Runaways also account for many of the homeless. Others are neither alcoholic nor suffering from mental illness, but they have instead experienced economic hard times or cannot afford housing.[125]

Nationally, 49 percent of homeless people are homeless for the first time, 28 percent of the homeless have been homeless for three months or less, but 30 percent have been homeless for more than two years.[126] The homeless are no longer living just in subways, along railroad tracks, or in urban downtown areas. They are in suburban and rural towns, living along rivers, in wooded areas, and in business districts. They live almost anywhere in cars, trucks, tents, and tarps. It can be difficult to locate these individuals to even offer various available services.

Many of the homeless who come to the attention of the police do so as a result of committing a crime or being the victim of a crime. Typically, these incidents include drinking in public, disturbing the peace, fighting, thefts, panhandling, and more serious offenses including sex crimes, robberies, and murders.

Businesses frequently call the police to remove these members of the population because business owners believe the homeless are keeping customers away from their businesses because of begging, harassment, odors, urine or excrement in the area, noise, litter, and narcotics usage. Business owners feel that this population poses a health

and public safety concern to themselves and the community.

The homeless issue today is a multifaceted one and requires many organizations working together to attempt to solve the underlying problems. Many police departments have realized this and have taken a proactive approach. Police leaders differ in their beliefs about how to best address the situation. Police leaders may want to restrict the ability of the homeless to gather and arrest them for any possible violation or work with local government leaders to enact laws that will outlaw camping, sleeping, and such in a way to drive the homeless out of the area. Generally, the courts don't look favorably on these types of laws and only allow them if they are narrow in scope such as during certain hours or for a particular area of town and for good reasons. The outright banning of the homeless is unconstitutional. Other departments try to address the issue and look at what the underlying causes are and see if they can work with social service agencies to put programs together to address these underlying problems.

The Fort Lauderdale, Florida, Police Department has a homeless outreach program that has proven to be successful. Instead of making arrests, the officers are trained to provide aid and referrals to the homeless population. After taking a three-hour training session on homeless issues, they are more sensitive to the needs and rights of these people. The police are in partnership with a homeless assistance center that provides help with social services and educational and employment programs, as well as a place to sleep and eat. Staff of both organizations meet monthly to discuss issues regarding their efforts.[127] The Los Angeles and Baltimore police departments also have active homeless outreach programs that include officer training, communication, and referrals.

The Seattle Police Department has initiated a new training requirement for all new officers—a one-week immersion in the city's social services. Officers spend time in several city crisis centers, the Union Gospel Mission, and homeless shelters and talk with service providers and clients. One goal of the program is to assist officers in being more open-minded and compassionate about this population that they will interact with on a daily basis when they hit the streets.[128]

The vulnerability of this population has been more evident recently after several high-profile attacks on the homeless. Several homeless men were beaten and one killed in and around Fort

Lauderdale, Florida, in January 2006, and one of the attacks was caught on video. Another man was set on fire in Boston, and another was beaten in San Francisco, which was caught on video. The viciousness of this attack shocked the public as well as law enforcement. Most of these attacks involve teens and young adults. Homeless advocates are not sure if these are "copycat crimes or it's just open season on the homeless," but the National Coalition for the Homeless is sending homeless and formerly homeless people to speak in schools and to youth groups in an effort to fight this crime.[129]

Community Crime Prevention Programs

Police expert George L. Kelling has written that citizens have "armed themselves, restricted their activities, rejected cities, built fortress houses and housing complexes both inside and outside the cities, and panicked about particular groups and classes of citizens."[130] Surely, citizens are worried about crimes and have taken measures to isolate or protect themselves against it. However, the police have an obligation to help citizens protect themselves against crime. It is obvious that the police cannot solve the crime and disorder problems of the United States by themselves, and they cannot let citizens take the law into their own hands. To address these problems, the police must turn to the public for its support and active participation in programs to make the streets safer and improve the quality of life. Community crime prevention programs include Neighborhood Watch, National Night Out, citizen patrols, citizen volunteer programs, home security surveys and Operation Identification, police storefronts, Crime Stoppers, mass media campaigns, chaplain programs, Citizen Police Academies, and other police-sponsored programs.

Neighborhood Watch Programs

Citizen involvement in crime prevention programs has increased greatly during the past three decades. The idea behind these various programs goes back to the early days of law enforcement in the United States where citizens were the eyes and ears of the community and worked with their neighbors to keep it safe. Community-based crime prevention programs require strong, committed leadership, and the partnership between the citizens and the community will empower the citizen with an active role in crime prevention activities. The IACP Crime Prevention Committee encourages police agencies to base this crime prevention strategy on the organizational philosophy and policy of the department.[131] Boca Raton, Florida, followed this advice when beginning a new crime prevention initiative in March 2005. The department obtained a letter of commitment from the mayor and then 500 citizens at a large city festival. The participants who commit to the crime prevention effort in writing then receive a blue wristband (inspired by the Lance Armstrong "Live Strong" campaign) and explain the wristband when asked. Street officers carry a supply of commitment letters and blue wristbands with them on duty.[132]

Crime prevention programs in which community members participate have different names in various parts of the country. Examples are Crime Watch, Block Watch, Community Alert, and, most commonly, **Neighborhood Watch.** Neighborhood Watch was launched in 1972 and is sponsored by the National Sheriffs' Association (NSA). In this organization, citizens organize themselves and work with law enforcement personnel to keep trained eyes and ears on their communities. Within 10 years of its beginnings, Neighborhood Watch programs involved more than 12 percent of the population nationally.[133] These groups engage in a wide range of specific crime prevention activities, as well as community-oriented activities. Citizens watch over activities on their block and alert the police to any suspicious or disorderly behavior. Neighborhood Watch blocks have clear signs alerting people that the block is protected by a Neighborhood Watch group.

In some jurisdictions, regular service providers have gotten involved in various crime watch programs. Providers such as postal employees, power company employees, and delivery personnel who are routinely out in residential areas are trained in identification of suspicious activity. They radio or call in this activity to their dispatchers, who in turn notify the police.

It has been reported that Neighborhood Watch programs can produce at least short-term reductions in certain crimes—particularly house burglaries—and are more likely to be effective when they are part of general purpose or multi-issue community groups rather than when they only address crime problems.[134]

Voluntary community organizations are often more successful in middle-class or high-income neighborhoods and neighborhoods with a strong sense of community and a certain degree of stability. One of the keys is the transient nature of the community. The more rooted the residents feel, the more they have invested in the community. Their tendency would be to get involved to maintain the highest level of quality of life. If the residents envision living there for only a few months, they don't care about the long-term future of the area. Therefore, the more stable the residents, the more successful a program will be.

National Night Out

Every year citizens are encouraged to turn on all outside lighting and step outside their homes between 8:00 PM and 9:00 PM on a well-publicized, designated night, called National Night Out. Though the exact date may vary by community, National Night Out is generally held during the first week in August. In addition, a growing number of residents are expanding their participation by staging parades and concerts and securing corporate sponsors for the annual event. One of the program's primary objectives is to enable neighbors to get to know one another so suspicious people and activities can be detected and reported as soon as possible. Other objectives include generating community support for, and participation in, local anticrime efforts, strengthening community spirit, and placing criminals on notice that neighborhood residents are watching them.

Citizen Patrols

Citizen patrols are very popular around the nation. They involve citizens patrolling on foot or in private cars and alerting the police to possible crimes or criminals in the area, thus being the eyes and ears of the police. One of the best-known citizen patrols is the Guardian Angels. The group, begun by Curtis Sliwa in 1977 to patrol New York City subway cars and stations, now has chapters in many other parts of the United States. The Angels are young people in distinctive red berets and T-shirts who patrol on buses, subways, and streets. Their main function is to act as an intimidating force against possible criminals or potentially disruptive people. Many people report that the mere

presence of the Guardian Angels reassures them. Despite their popularity with citizens, however, the Guardian Angels have not been welcomed by police executives, who argue that only well-trained officers can maintain order.[135] In 1996, however, the Guardian Angels finally received official acceptance by the New York City Police Department (NYPD) when the department announced it would train 12 Guardian Angels in civilian crime-fighting techniques and make them part of a police-sponsored rollerblade patrol to improve safety in New York City's famed Central Park.[136]

Researcher Susan Pennell evaluated the Guardian Angels' impact on crime in San Diego and 20 other localities in the United States. The impact of the Angels on crime was inconclusive. However, the study revealed that most citizens knew that the Guardian Angels were patrolling their neighborhood, and most of those who knew about the Angels felt safer as a result of their presence.[137] Recently, the Guardian Angels have developed an academy, which is licensed in New York and is working in conjunction with the U.S. Department of Homeland Security to make the nation more secure.[138] The Guardians rely on their attitude of intimidation and perception of toughness to disarm troublemakers without physical contact. Their goal is to defuse the violence, subdue troublemakers, and call the police. They try to avoid any type of physical violence and feel that stopping the violence is the responsibility of the entire community.[139]

Many police departments are now using citizens as observers in more formal ways. Volunteers with training (often graduates of the Citizens' Police Academy) are uniformed and drive in department vehicles. These vehicles are marked but carefully painted differently than police cars. These citizens patrol in teams and are another set of eyes and ears for the police guided by strict policies on noninvolvement and instructions how to report suspicious activity.

The Nashville Police Department has an active "Be on the Lookout" (BOLO) patrol. Citizens are trained to make observations in their neighborhoods and report suspicious activity to patrol officers. When they are out patrolling, they wear special insignias designating they are with the BOLO program. They address quality-of-life issues including things such as graffiti or lights out. In a business-community partnership, GTE Wireless donated 100 phones and service to the BOLO program.[140]

Citizen Volunteer Programs

Citizen volunteer programs—in which citizens volunteer to do police jobs, thus freeing police officers to return to patrol duties—have become numerous and popular. Citizens perform such jobs as crime analysis, clerical work, victim assistance, crime prevention, patrolling shopping centers, vacant house checks, and fingerprinting children. The program and services provided should be tailored to the department and community.

The use of volunteers in police departments has increased tremendously in the last fifteen years. Departments have realized the value of using the talents of their residents from many perspectives. A police department that doesn't actively seek to recruit volunteers is not practicing good management. Volunteer programs can help a department accomplish its duties more effectively, maximize existing resources, enhance public safety and services, and improve community relations. It allows police officers to focus on patrol work and investigations while providing services that citizens may want.

The volunteers feel a vested interest in their police department and can often be counted on for support when departments are trying to expand, start new programs, or hire additional personnel. The police officers have increased involvement with the citizens at times other than crisis situations. Administrators can redirect sworn employees to more hazardous duties when volunteers assume nonhazardous jobs. The department may be able to try new programs they wouldn't ordinarily be able to attempt because of a lack of personnel. The city or county government benefits from reduced or flat expenditures and the ability to not raise taxes in these budget-strapped times. The community benefits with a more educated citizenry and an increased feeling of safety. It is a win-win situation for all involved. Though there is no salary to pay, there are costs associated with using volunteers, including costs for salary and benefits for the program coordinator, screening, training, workspace requirements, supplies, equipment, uniforms, and recognition. Most departments that have launched successful programs have found the value of volunteer hours contributed far exceeds the costs associated with the program.[141]

Use of volunteers is limited only by the imagination of police managers and volunteers. Nationwide, departments use volunteers for parking enforcement, help at special events, as crime prevention specialists, for telephone follow-ups and pawnshop investigations, and as receptionists and in clerical positions, as well as tour guides of the facility. Citizens may volunteer with PAL, at communitywide safety fairs conducting fingerprinting, and even for role-play situations in police training. Riding on the wave of the popularity of the CSI TV programs, some departments are using volunteers in some of the less sensitive areas of those units.[142]

Some retirees have special talents that prove extremely valuable to police departments such as computer expertise, printing know-how, writing abilities (for brochures or notices), photographic or video expertise, or even cooking or catering skills to supply refreshments for special occasions.

Departments are actively recruiting volunteers and have web pages devoted to the volunteer effort, including application forms. For instance, the Nashville, Tennessee, Police Department site has a page entitled "Get Involved: Help make a difference in your community." It then lists the various ways community members can get involved in their department.[143]

Home Security Surveys and Operation Identification

Target-hardening programs have become very popular in the last few decades. Target hardening involves installing burglar alarms, installing protective gates, and using other devices and techniques to make it more difficult for criminals to enter premises to commit crime. To facilitate target hardening, numerous police departments offer home security surveys and business security surveys free of charge.

Operation Identification programs involve engraving identifying numbers onto such property as bicycles, televisions, and other personal electronic items with the goal of returning the property to owners if it is stolen and then recovered by the police. The program also involves displaying decals on windows announcing that a house is equipped with an alarm or has participated in an Operation Identification program.

Police Storefront Stations or Ministations

In an effort to get closer to the public, many police departments operate **police storefront stations** or

ministations. In these programs, a small group of police officers is assigned to patrol in the immediate area of a ministation or storefront station and to engage in crime prevention programs with members of the community. Although they would not be considered ministations, many businesses, such as 7-Eleven, McDonald's, and the pharmacy chain CVS, are opening their stores for the local police to use as temporary community police stations by reserving workstations for them at a table near the front of the store.

Many jurisdictions have consolidated services in their police storefronts or ministations. Their goal is to use their tax dollars more efficiently and make city services as accessible as possible for their taxpayers. They may be able to conduct minor water department or zoning business or obtain various city forms at the station. Paramedics often host "wellness fairs" at these facilities, where health information is distributed along with blood pressure tests and the like.

Crime Stoppers

Crime Stoppers originated in 1975 in Albuquerque, New Mexico, and quickly spread across the country. In the typical Crime Stoppers program, the police ask television and radio stations to publicize an "unsolved crime of the week." Cash rewards are given for information that results in the conviction of the offender.[144] By 2004, there were an estimated 911 Crime Stoppers programs in the United States. Based on information from 433 of the 911 known programs, Crime Stoppers USA has resulted in 316,724 arrests, recovered more than $3 billion in property and narcotics, and paid out more than $47 million in rewards.[145] The successful Virginia Beach, Virginia, program recovered more than $603,000 in property and narcotics in 2003 and paid out more than $29,000 in rewards. Since its inception in 1982, Virginia Beach's program has received more than 22,500 calls, resulting in more than 6,000 arrests and the recovery of more than $24 million in property and narcotics.[146]

Similar to Crime Stopper programs are programs that provide citizens the opportunity to leave anonymous tips regarding crimes and criminals for the police. Along the same lines, some television shows focus on locating wanted persons. One show that has enjoyed great success is *America's Most Wanted,* hosted by John Walsh. The show precipitated one of its highest-profile captures on March 12, 2003. Information aired by the show led to citizens calling the police when they spotted Elizabeth Smart and her kidnappers. That call, together with good police work by the officers who responded, led to a happy conclusion. Elizabeth was a 14-year-old girl kidnapped from her bedroom as she slept at home in Salt Lake City, Utah. She had been missing for many months, and her captors had many contacts with people who didn't recognize them. The show put the information back in people's minds, and the country rejoiced when she was safely reunited with her family. This capture was the 747th influenced by the show. This is an example of the public and private sector working together for the good of the community.

Mass Media Campaigns

Mass media campaigns, such as the "Take a Bite Out of Crime" advertisements in newspapers, magazines, and on television, provide crime prevention suggestions for citizens. The "Take a Bite Out of Crime" national media campaign features the crime dog McGruff, a trench-coated cartoon figure. McGruff advises readers or viewers of actions they should take when they witness criminal activity.

The media has taken on a greater role in fighting crime during the last two decades. The media are able to respond quickly to calls they hear over police frequencies and are quick to set up their cameras. A good working relationship with the press and the media is essential to get their cooperation and not release particular information they may obtain or locations or photos that they may be recording in real time, such as in a hostage or tactical situation. There have been many occasions where media helicopters have followed suspects and assisted law enforcement in catching them. Media also have taken on active roles in helping to solve crimes, especially in the case of child abductions. Since the implementation of the Amber Alert system, the media broadcast information regarding suspects and vehicle descriptions has facilitated the safe return of many children and the arrest of their abductors.

The media can also be asked to assist with a particular crime problem a community is experiencing by covering it and letting the public know this crime is occurring and what steps citizens can take to minimize their chances of becoming a victim.

The media wield a lot of influence, as was seen during Hurricane Katrina. There was a lot of reporting from various venues in New Orleans and Mississippi, and some of the information obtained from sources was erroneous and broadcast around the world. Because of an extreme breakdown in official communications, unverified, second- and third-hand information was being spread. One tragic result was that response decisions were based on this erroneous information. Paramedics were barred from entering Slidell, Louisiana, for almost 10 hours based on information that a mob of armed people had commandeered boats and were dangerous, and some rescue missions were postponed after erroneous reports of helicopters being shot at.[147]

Overall, the media can be a great asset to law enforcement, but this depends on relationships that are developed. The more law enforcement can learn about journalists and the more journalists can learn about law enforcement, the more successful the partnership will be. The Poynter Institute (a training institute for journalists) recommends that journalists spend time riding with officers and learning their culture and jargon. Conversely, law enforcement should spend time learning what the goals of the news industry are and ways in which they can work together for mutually successful outcomes. This can be a very fruitful relationship that will aid in making the community safer.

Chaplain Programs

Departments around the country have discovered the benefits of having an active, involved chaplains program. These volunteers serve as liaisons with various religious institutions in the community. They are indispensable in the event of a tragedy. They can provide counseling and referral services to victims, families, and police officers as needed. When they show up to assist at a suicide or homicide scene, they can help to free up officers from the emotional demands of the scene to concentrate on their investigation.

A well-rounded chaplains program will attempt to have representatives from all religious groups in the community. In the event of disharmony in the community, these volunteers can also provide calming voices to their constituents and help solve problems within the community. The faith community concept is believed to be an essential ingredient in making law enforcement more sensitive to the needs of the community.[148]

In Oklahoma, law enforcement has taken the role even further. A 36-hour academy for police chaplains has been implemented. It is felt that this academy better prepares chaplains for the role they find themselves frequently filling in the community. That role is as an advocate for issues facing law enforcement personnel; chaplains find themselves increasingly in the role of mediator between law enforcement personnel and the community. The academy also reassures the public that they are being served by well-trained, qualified, and motivated individuals.[149]

Citizen Police Academies

Many police departments have established **citizen police academies**. Through these academies, police agencies seek to educate community members about the roles and responsibilities of police officers and to familiarize the public with the departments and how they work within the community. The goal of most citizen police academies is not to provide civilians trained in law enforcement but, rather, to create a nucleus of citizens who are well informed about a department's practices and services.

Many departments use their citizen police academy as a form of training and preparation for their volunteer pools. The academy gives the volunteer an excellent overview of the police department. At times, departments may tailor their citizen academies to meet the needs of a specific group, such as older residents or high school students. The academy also may be held off-site to facilitate attendance by groups with transportation problems. Websites often describe the course and provide application forms online.

The Boca Raton, Florida, Police Department instituted one of the first citizen's academies in Florida and has run a successful citizen police academy three times a year since 1992. This has helped provide a resource of informed citizens in the community.

This concept has spread rapidly throughout the country. Typically, a citizen police academy is held 1 night a week for 8 to 10 weeks, and each major function of the department will be addressed. The key is that the department uses the specialists to teach about their areas of expertise, sharing their passion and enthusiasm with the students. Most officers involved in this endeavor, love it. The participants get to meet many officers in the department and learn how the various divisions function. They can be taught why police can and can't do certain things, resulting in realistic expectations within the community. Departments have recently begun to conduct these classes for minority populations, particularly new immigrants, to enhance relations and educate them about police in the United States.

Other Police-Sponsored Crime Prevention Programs

To allow citizens to get an inside look at how the police perform their jobs and to help them understand the police better, many police departments offer such programs as ride-alongs and tours of precincts and other police facilities. In the ride-along programs, citizens actually ride in patrol cars with police officers and respond to calls for police services with the officers. Citizens get a firsthand look at the activities the police perform and the special problems they encounter. Police departments providing ride-along programs require participants to sign a waiver freeing the jurisdiction from civil liability if a participant is injured. Many departments also provide tours of police stations, police headquarters buildings, shooting ranges, and other facilities to allow citizens to see how their tax dollars are spent. Some may also allow citizens to participate in their shoot/don't shoot programs using the computer simulator programs to enhance understanding of the complex situations officers face on the street.

In recent years, police agencies have facilitated the forming of **Community Emergency Response Teams (CERT).** The team members undergo training to help them act in the event of an emergency or disaster. The training enables them to respond before emergency services arrive on the scene and to assist the emergency service personnel when they do arrive. Many larger departments address this role on their websites and have links to the organization conducting the training. This training provides communities with a pool of trained civilians able to respond in disaster situations. It also encourages a feeling of teamwork in the community.

■——————————————————

Police and Business Cooperation

Businesses throughout the United States have become increasingly involved in assisting their local police departments in the last couple of decades. It becomes more pronounced in times of tight budgets for governments that don't allow police to offer programs they may wish to provide, attend training they may find beneficial, or buy equipment that could improve the effectiveness of the police department. Businesses may provide vehicles for DARE or crime prevention, buy advertising on marked vehicles, donate computers, donate printing for trading cards or brochures, donate food for police-community meetings, provide and outfit bikes for a bicycle unit, provide prizes for children for safety contests such as helmet safety or bike rodeos, fund police dogs or equipment for them, or provide bullet proof vests for officers. As with volunteer opportunities, the ideas are endless. The problem is that like gratuities, it is a "slippery slope" and departments and businesses have to be aware of how a donation might look to the public as well as how it is perceived within the department and the business community. Many cities and towns address this ethical issue for businesses (as well as individuals) that want to donate money or equipment to the police department through the formation of a private foundation. This must be accomplished by the citizens involved, but concerned citizens and businesses can join to form a charitable foundation that raises money to assist the police department in various ways. It is up to the foundation board how the money is spent. Often they will hold fund raisers for people to donate and raise funds for things like K-9's and their equipment, bikes, funds for training, expenses for officers hurt or killed in the line of duty, and so on. These foundations can be very successful and very helpful to law enforcement agencies as well as individual officers without particular individuals or businesses being the source of the funding. They also allow the citizens and businesses to have a positive impact on their communities.

On the positive side of the business-police partnership, business often has the personnel and resources and the know how to get things done, sometimes more quickly and with less red tape than governments can. Coupled with the view that crime is a community issue, businesses and corporations want to get involved and do their part to contribute to the community good. There is a trend in corporate donations being directed at solving societal problems. The retailer Target is an active partner to law enforcement applying some of their state of the art technology to various problems. Target employees run a forensics lab in Minneapolis; work with Customs on monitoring the integrity of cargo shipments; contribute money for prosecutors to combat repeat criminals; provide police with remote control surveillance systems; link city, county and state databases to keep track of repeat offenders; and give training to FBI and police leaders.

A program called "Target and Blue" helps define its approach to partnership with law enforcement.[150] Certainly, Target has had an impact on crime issues and the safety of the community in a way that might not have been possible without the company's support and financial backing. Critics might question what Target gets out of it. Does the company expect some kind of preferential treatment? Will police respond more quickly to calls for assistance at Target stores?

These are issues that law enforcement and the corporate community must grapple with and clarify before getting involved in these partnerships. This issue was raised with the 2006 IACP conference being held in Boston in October. The conference has "raised eyebrows . . . because corporate sponsors have been asked to pony up exorbitant donations to pay for it."[151] The solicitations sent to 200 area businesses offer sponsorship packages ranging from $100,000 for "title sponsors" to $10,000 for "bronze sponsorships." Several of these sponsorships include having dinner with the Boston police commissioner as well as other law enforcement leaders across the country. A high-ranking police official from New York said, "It's not corrupt, but it's tacky. It gives the appearance of selling influence with police commanders. The events smell of corporate CEOs buying face time with Boston police officials."[152] The Boston police commissioner responded, "There is no influence for sale in Boston, the businesses involved are trying to be good citizens here. They are investing in an event that will be great for the city."[153]

Overall, there is great potential in the police-business relationship. However, it is incumbent on government to scrutinize the partnership in terms of ethics, fairness, and public perception.

Summary

- This chapter discussed the importance of positive relationships between the police and the public.

- Public opinion and the police and the relationships between the police and minority communities and special groups were covered.

- Partnerships and outreach have occurred between police departments and African Americans, Hispanic Americans, Asian Americans, Arab Americans, Muslins, Jews, women, and gays and lesbians.

- With the increase in immigrant populations and their movement around the country, police agencies are implementing programs to facilitate communication.

- The many groups that make up our communities have specific and varying needs that the police need to be aware of and make efforts to address to build and strengthen their relationships.

- With the aging of the baby boomers, programs directed at and involving the older population are extremely important.

- Police agencies are training their officers so they are better able to serve communities with special needs, such as the physically challenged, crime victims, the homeless, and the mentally ill.

- Police programs involving young people appear to have the greatest potential for success in creating positive relationships with the police and causing youths to develop positive ways of behaving that will lead to future success.

- Community crime prevention programs, including Neighborhood Watch, National Night Out, citizen patrols, citizen volunteer programs, home security surveys, police storefront stations, Crime Stoppers, mass media campaigns, chaplain programs, citizen police academies, and other programs are designed to assist in the fight against crime and improve the quality of life in U.S. communities.

- The expanded use of volunteers, which in many situations may pull from the aging baby boomer population, is a wise and effective goal for police agencies.

- The business community is a valuable asset and partner in the crime fight, though not one without controversy.

Learning Check

1. Explain why it is essential that the police maintain positive relationships with the community.

2. How are the police perceived by the community? How is this related to other organizations?

3. Discuss why there has been a tradition of negative relationships between the police and the African American community.

4. Discuss some of the efforts law enforcement is making to reach out to various segments of communities.

5. Explain the rationale behind DARE programs.

6. Describe some of the youth programs being used around the country in addition to the DARE program.

7. Describe how police agencies are working with crime victims and how this may improve services.

8. Discuss why it is important for police to work with the homeless population and describe what types of things are being done.

9. Identify some special populations and how the police help them with their problems.

10. List some ways that volunteers can be used in police departments.

Key Terms

citizen police academies Academies provided by the police department for the citizens of the community to enhance their understanding of the workings of their police department.

citizen patrols A program that involves citizens patrolling on foot or in private cars and alerting the police to possible crimes or criminals in the area.

Community Emergency Response Team (CERT) A program in which civilians are trained in basic emergency response, first aid, and search and rescue.

Crime Stoppers A program where a cash reward is offered for information that results in the conviction of an offender.

Drug Abuse Resistance Education (DARE) The most popular antidrug program in which police officers teach students in schools about the dangers of drug use.

Gang Resistance Education and Training (GREAT) An educational program designed after DARE which addresses the issue of gangs.

human relations Everything done with each other as human beings in all kinds of relationships.

International Association of Chiefs of Police (IACP) An organization composed of police leaders from across the country that is very influential in setting standards for police departments throughout the country. IACP publishes *Police Chief* magazine, conducts research, and writes publications to assist law enforcement around the country.

Minneapolis Domestic Violence Experiment An experiment conducted in Minneapolis, Minnesota, to determine the deterrent effect of various methods of handling domestic violence, including mandatory arrest.

Neighborhood Watch Crime prevention programs in which community members participate and engage in a wide range of specific crime prevention activities, as well as community-oriented activities.

Operation Identification Engraving identifying numbers onto property that is most likely to be stolen.

Police Athletic League (PAL) A large sports program involving police officers and youth.

police community relations The relationships involved in both human relations and public relations between the police and the community.

police community relations (PCR) movement The assigning of officers to a special community relations unit or public relations unit to interact with the public and attend community meetings.

Police Explorers A program for young adults between the ages of 14 and 20 in which they work closely with law enforcement and explore the police career.

police public relations Activities performed by police agencies designed to create a favorable image of themselves.

police storefront station or ministation A small satellite police station designed to serve a local part of the community and facilitate the community's access to the police officers.

Triad A joint partnership between the police and senior citizens to address specific problems seniors encounter with safety and quality-of-life issues.

Community Policing:
The Debate Continues

© Bob Daemmrich/The Image Works

GOALS

- To acquaint you with the most current thinking about corporate strategies for policing, including strategic policing, community policing, and problem-solving policing
- To explore the philosophy and genesis of the current corporate strategies of community policing and problem-solving policing
- To discuss the effect of community policing and problem-solving policing on current policing
- To discuss the implementation of community policing strategies, including the most recent methods, the role of the federal government, and some recent community policing successes
- To explain why some scholars and practitioners do not agree with the implementation of community policing strategies
- To discuss how community policing strategies can be useful in the fight against terror

Introduction

Chapter 11 discussed police and the community. Specifically, we explored the concepts of police community relations, public relations, and human relations; public opinion and the police; and problems and relationships between the police and many specific populations, including minority groups and such special populations as senior citizens, young people, the homeless, the disabled, and crime victims. That chapter also discussed numerous forms of crime-prevention services the police offer the community and numerous partnerships between the police and the community to deter crime and improve the quality of life in our communities.

This chapter continues discussing relationships between the police and the community but deals with more philosophical and strategic issues about reducing crime and improving our quality of life. It addresses the concepts of community policing and problem-solving policing, concepts that many consider new strategies of policing. Others feel these concepts are not new strategies but, rather, a return to the policing of the past. In 1988, the scholar George L. Kelling stated,

> A quiet revolution is reshaping American policing. Police in dozens of communities are returning to foot patrol. In many communities, police are surveying citizens to learn what they believed to be their most serious neighborhood problems. Many police departments are finding alternatives to rapidly responding to the majority of calls for service. Many departments are targeting resources on citizen fear of crime by concentrating on disorder. Organizing citizens' groups has become a priority in many departments. Increasingly, police departments are looking for means to evaluate themselves on their contribution to the quality of neighborhood life, not just crime statistics. Are such activities the business of policing? In a crescendo, police are answering yes.[1]

By 1998, many said the face of policing had changed dramatically. Community policing and problem-solving policing had been practiced for more than a decade and had proven to be tremendously popular with some citizens, academics, politicians, and police chiefs. Many believe that community policing and problem-solving policing could be the best strategies to use in policing our nation. These two ideas emphasize community involvement and the building of partnerships between the police and the community. In many areas where community policing and problem-solving policing have been implemented, crime rates have gone down, quality of life has been improved, and people have felt safer.

By 1999, state and local law enforcement agencies had almost 113,000 full-time sworn personnel who served as community policing officers or were involved in community policing activities. In addition, 64 percent of departments, representing 86 percent of the U.S. population served by local police, had full-time officers engaged in community policing activities.[2] Many, however, are not enthusiastic about this new philosophy and argue about its definition and implementation. The discussion of and study of community policing continues. Even though numbers indicate that in 2003 the numbers of officers devoted to full-time community policing activities were down slightly from 2000, most departments around the country are committed to the community policing philosophy. Though the numbers formally assigned to community policing are down, the agencies have incorporated the community policing philosophy into their policies and procedures and their mission statements.[3]

This chapter is intended to present the facts, explore the issues, and continue the debate. We will discuss three corporate strategies for modern policing: strategic policing, community policing, and problem-solving policing. We will also discuss the underlying philosophy and the genesis of the thinking about community policing and problem-solving policing and then discuss some examples of how these concepts can be translated into action.

The chapter will also cover the federal government and its influence over community policing, including the 1994 Crime Bill, the Office of Community Oriented Policing Services, and the Community Policing Consortium. We will present some empirical and anecdotal evidence of the accomplishments of community policing but will also show how some scholars and practitioners do not agree with these policing strategies.

It is hoped that, by presenting the issues and exploring them, we may continue the process begun by Sir Robert Peel in 1829 of making the police an essential part of life in the community.

Corporate Strategies for Policing

For several decades, police chiefs and academics throughout the United States have discussed changes in the traditional methods of policing and have explored new ways of accomplishing the police mission. Many of these strategies have been discussed in this text. Since the mid-1980s, Harvard University's prestigious John F. Kennedy School of Government has held periodic meetings to discuss the current state of policing in the United States. These Executive Sessions on Policing were developed and administered by the Kennedy School's Program in Criminal Justice Policy and Management. At these sessions, leading police administrators and academics gathered at Harvard to focus and debate on the use and price of such strategies as strategic policing, community policing, and problem-solving policing.

Beginning in 1988, the National Institute of Justice and Harvard produced a series of monographs that have shaped the current state of police thinking. These monographs discussed community policing, problem-oriented policing, police values, corporate strategies of policing, crime and policing, policing and the fear of crime, the history of policing, police accountability, and drugs and the police.[4]

Harvard's Executive Sessions on Policing identified three corporate strategies for policing that are presently guiding U.S. policing: (1) strategic policing, (2) community policing, and (3) problem-solving policing.[5] Strategic policing involves a continued reliance on traditional police operations, but with an increased emphasis on crimes that are not generally well controlled by traditional policing (for example, serial offenders, gangs, organized crime, drug distribution networks, and white-collar and computer criminals).

Strategic policing represents an advanced stage of traditional policing using innovative enforcement techniques, including intelligence operations, electronic surveillance, and sophisticated forensic techniques. Much of this textbook, particularly the chapters on police operations and technology, deals with strategic policing issues.

Community policing is an attempt to involve the community as an active partner with the police in addressing crime problems in the community. It involves a true trusting partnership with the community and a willingness to accept and use input from the community.

Problem-solving policing emphasizes that many crimes are caused by underlying social problems and attempts to deal with those underlying problems rather than just responding to each criminal incident. Problem-solving or problem-oriented policing seeks to solve problems and have an outcome.

Community policing and problem-solving policing are very similar approaches to the crime and disorder problems in our communities. Most departments adopting a community policing program also follow many of the tenets of problem-solving policing. These two philosophies or strategies tend to go hand in hand.

The Philosophy of Community Policing and Problem–Solving Policing

In the 1960s, increases in crime, technological advances, and changes in police management thinking led to the abandonment of police foot patrols and their resultant ties to the community. Foot patrols were replaced by highly mobile police officers who could drive from one incident to another in minutes.

At about the same time, many urban communities were experiencing drastic demographic changes. Longtime community residents were moving from the inner city to newly opened suburbs and being replaced by newly arrived people from rural areas and Caribbean and Latin American countries. These people were not used to urban life and the culture, norms, and mores of their adopted neighborhoods. Often, there was a language barrier between the immigrants and older members of the community. These changes brought severe social problems to our cities and, of course, problems to our police. In addition, the heroin epidemic hit the United States in the 1960s, causing crime, social disorganization, and fear and mistrust. Recall the descriptions of the urban riots of the late 1960s described in Chapter 1.

© Jay Noble/The Image Works

In the community policing philosophy the police and community work toward the ultimate goal of reducing the fear of crime as well as the crime rate. This crack house in Philadelphia was shut down in an effort to address both the crime and disorder issues in the neighborhood.

had been; the police were increasingly seen as an invading army or an army of occupation. As a result, many police departments began to establish community relations units to address problems between themselves and the community. The units were part of what was called the police community relations (PCR) movement.

The PCR units were supposed to address this communication gap. These units were not effective, however, because they usually appeared only after an ugly incident. Although the community relations units were well intentioned, they could not work in reality. The real responsibility for proper police community relations, as any professional, experienced police officer knows, rests with every police officer, not with a select, small group of community relations officers. Today's community policing is completely different from the earlier PCR movement and should not be confused with it.

Modern community policing, as compared with the PCR movement, entails a substantial change in police thinking. It expands the responsibility for fighting crime to the community as a whole and, through a partnership with the community, addresses the community's concerns and underlying problems that lead to crime. The police and community work toward the ultimate goal of reducing the fear of crime as well as the crime rate.[6]

Many believe that the modern stage of community policing began with the seminal 1982 article in the *Atlantic Monthly* by **James Q. Wilson and George L. Kelling,** "'Broken Windows': The Police and Neighborhood Safety." Theirs has come to be known as the **broken windows model** of policing.[7] Wilson and Kelling made several very critical points.

First, disorder in neighborhoods creates fear. Urban streets that are often occupied by homeless people, prostitutes, drug addicts, youth gangs, and the mentally disturbed, as well as regular citizens, are more likely than are other areas to have high crime rates. Second, certain neighborhoods send out "signals" that encourage crime. A community in which housing has deteriorated, broken windows are left unrepaired, and disorderly behavior is ignored may actually promote crime. Honest and good citizens live in fear in these areas, and predatory criminals are attracted. Third, community policing is essential. If police are to reduce fear and combat crime in these areas, they must rely on the cooperation of citizens for support and assistance. Wilson and Kelling argued that

Many problems developed between the police and the newly arrived residents as rapidly moving police mobile units, with flashing lights and roaring sirens, arrived in a community to answer someone's request for assistance or report of a crime. A lack of communication and mistrust often ensued because of the police officers' need to take quick action and get violent people off the street as soon as possible and then to return to more serious emergencies. The police were no longer seen as members of the community, as the old beat cops community preservation, public safety, and order maintenance—not crime fighting—should become the primary focus of police patrol. From this concept, many believe, the modern concept of community policing began. Expanding on the work of Wilson and Kelling, Wesley G. Skogan surveyed numerous neighborhoods and identified two major categories of disorder that affect the quality of life in the community: human and physical disorder. The human behaviors found to be extremely disruptive to the community were public drinking, corner gangs, street harassment, drugs, noisy neighbors, and commercial sex. The physical disorders that Skogan found extremely destructive to the community were vandalism, dilapidation and abandonment, and rubbish.[8]

Using the Wilson and Kelling and Skogan ideas as a philosophical and practical framework, many scholars and progressive police chiefs jumped onto the community policing bandwagon.

Community Policing

Community-oriented policing is an approach toward crime that addresses the underlying causes of crime and endeavors to apply long-term problem solving to the issue through improved police-community partnerships and communication. **Robert C. Trojanowicz** founded the National Center for Community Policing in East Lansing, Michigan, in 1983 and was the director until his death in 1994. Trojanowicz believed that community policing can play a vital role in reducing three important kinds of violence in the community: (1) individual violence, ranging from street crime to domestic abuse to drug-related violence; (2) civil unrest, which can often include gang violence and open confrontations among various segments of society, specifically the police; and (3) police brutality.[9]

Community policing is not a new concept. As we saw in Chapter 1, policing, from its early English roots, has always been community oriented. As one officer reminded us in 1997, the concept of community policing goes as far back as London's Sir Robert Peel, when he began building his public police in 1829. In his original principles, he said, "The police are the public and the public are the police; the police being only members of the public who are paid to give full-time attention to duties which are incumbent on every citizen in the interests of community welfare and existence."[10]

David L. Carter, of Michigan State University, explains that community policing did not suddenly materialize as a new idea; rather, it evolved from research conducted by a wide range of scholars and police research organizations. Beginning primarily in the early 1970s, a great deal of research was conducted on police patrol.[11]

Community policing seeks to replace our traditional methods of police patrol with a more holistic approach. Some scholars liken it to the medical model. Traditional law enforcement held the belief that the "experts" would save us and over the years has moved to the holistic concept where we are all partners in the health of our communities as in the health of our bodies in the medical model. Although there is a need for experts to save us in the emergency room or operating room as in making arrests, there is also a need to maintain our health and prevent certain illnesses or crimes from happening, or to intervene before they reach the "emergency" or critical stage. In this approach, a community policing officer working a particular neighborhood fills a role similar to that of a family physician, and the street officer responding to the emergency call is fulfilling the role of society's emergency room physician. The community policing officer acts as a problem solver and an ombudsman to other social service agencies that can assist in addressing the problem.[12] This model supports Trojanowicz's belief that "community policing is a philosophy of full service personalized policing, where the same officer patrols and works in the same area on a permanent basis, from a decentralized place, working in a proactive partnership with citizens to identify and solve problems."[13]

Some examples of very early attempts at community policing involved the experiences of Detroit, New York City, and Houston.

In Detroit, one innovative approach developed by community policing advocates was the development of decentralized neighborhood-based precincts that serve as "store-front" police stations. One well-known program is the Detroit Mini-Station Program, which established more than 36 such stations around the city. At first, the community did not accept the program because the officers assigned to the mini-stations seemed to lack commitment. Later, however, officers were chosen for mini-station duty on the basis of their community relations skills and crime prevention ability, and since then the program has met with much greater community acceptance.[14] A study in

Community Policing in the Bronx

When I first started as a police officer in the 41st Precinct in the Bronx, in 1966, I was a foot patrol cop, as were most of us. During my first two years there, there were only four Radio Motor Patrol (RMP) sector cars in the entire precinct, plus the sergeant's car. Our foot patrol beats generally covered five or six blocks. Early in my career there, the precinct earned the nickname Fort Apache because of the wild conditions and crime that permeated the precinct. It was considered the busiest and most dangerous precinct in the City of New York, and probably the world, in the 1960s and 1970s. Later, a movie was made, starring Paul Newman, called *Fort Apache—The Bronx,* detailing life as a police officer in the days I was there. You can still see the movie on TV or get it from your video store. Believe me, the movie made the place seem too tame. It was much crazier than that.

My foot patrol post, Post 28, covered all of Westchester Avenue from Southern Boulevard to Kelly Street, both sides of the streets and all of the side streets including Simpson Street, Fox Street, Tiffany Street, and Kelly Street. Westchester Avenue, under the el, was the commercial hub of the area, and all of the side blocks were covered by wall-to-wall five-story tenements. It was the height of the heroin crisis in New York City, and crime and disorder were rampant. I patrolled this post alone without the portable radio you see officers carry today. I loved it. I made hundreds of collars [arrests], mostly gun collars and junk [drug] arrests. I also broke up fights, delivered babies, brought kids home to their parents, directed traffic, gave comfort and advice, and helped as many people as I could. Whatever the time, day or night, whenever I was working, people knew they could talk to me. Whenever they had a problem, they could come to me. The good people on my post loved me—they called me their amigo. The people who wanted to annoy the good people on my post learned to avoid me—they went someplace else. The criminals . . . well, they didn't like me too much. I put them in jail. In summary, I was the *cop.*

Everyone knew me. I was part of the life of that community, part of the life of that little spot of the world—Patrol Post 28 of the 41st Precinct. We didn't have a concept known as community policing then. We were all just cops, doing our job. As the years went by, the number of patrol car sectors assigned to the precinct increased and increased until by 1970 we had over 14 sectors, almost four times the number we had when I started. I guess this was due to new management thinking in the department: A radio motor patrol unit can cover so much more territory than a foot cop, thus officers in a car are more economical, cost effective, and efficient. Also, 911 had taken over the NYPD by then. We would race from one 911 call to another—handle one incident after another—do what we had to do and then do it all over again, time after time. No longer did we deal with problems. We just dealt with incidents. Although this change from foot patrol to the more cost-effective motorized patrol may have been necessary because of 911, I think it was a big mistake. Most of us were assigned to regular seats in the radio cars and never walked our foot beats again. What we gained in efficiency, we lost in closeness to the community. Many of the people on my beat felt they had lost their amigo—I was always busy running around the entire precinct handling 911 jobs.

Today's community police officer, I believe and hope, is a return to the past, a return to the cop on the beat who knows, and is known by, everyone. The major difference between today's community officer and the beat cop of my day is structure. Today, the officers receive training and support from the department and other city agencies. They have offices and answering machines and fill out paperwork. I hope they also become what I was on Post 28 in the 41st Precinct— part of life in that little part of the world—the good people's amigo.

—*John Dempsey*

Houston that involved patrol officers visiting households to solicit viewpoints and information on community problems reported both crime and fear decreases in the study area.[15]

The New York City Police Department began a Community Patrol Officer Program (CPOP) in 1984. CPOP officers did not respond to calls from 911 but instead were directed to identify neighborhood problems and develop short- and long-term strategies for solving them. Each officer kept a beat book in which he or she was expected to identify major problems on his or her beat and list strategies to deal with them. Officers thus were encouraged to think about problems and their solutions.[16]

Regarding community policing, Joseph E. Braun, of the U.S. Department of Justice, wrote in 1997,

> The traditional role of law enforcement is changing. . . . Community policing allows law enforcement practitioners to bring government resources closer to the community. Hence, participation and cooperation are key . . . we cannot expect law enforcement to solve crime and social disorder problems alone. Community involvement is imperative. . . . With the implementation of community policing practices, officers and deputies still retain their enforcement duties and powers. Community policing does not mean that authority is relinquished; rather, its proactive nature is intended to reduce the need for enforcement in the long term as problems are addressed up front and much earlier. This can only occur with the cooperation and participation of the community.[17]

Community policing mandates that the police work with the community, rather than against it, to be effective. The foot patrol experiments described earlier in the text are examples of the community policing model suggested by Wilson and Kelling in their "broken windows" approach to policing.

In *"Broken Windows" and Police Discretion*, Kelling notes that the community policing model expands and encourages the use of discretion among officers at all levels of the organization. The traditional method of telling officers what they can and can't do, as is commonly found in police manuals, will not greatly improve the quality of policing. He advocates teaching officers how to think about what they should do, do it, and then review their actions with coworkers. With time, this should lead to improved practices and the sharing of values, knowledge, and skills that will prove valuable in the performance of their job.[18] Kelling supports "guideline development" in police agencies to facilitate the discretionary behavior of police officers and enable them to better work with the public in enhancing the quality of life.

Herman Goldstein offers the following list of the most important benefits of community policing:

1. A more realistic acknowledgment of police functions
2. A recognition of the interrelationships among police functions
3. An acknowledgment of the limited capacity of the police to accomplish their jobs on their own and of the importance of an alliance between the police and the public
4. Less dependence on the criminal justice system and more emphasis on new problem-solving methods
5. Greatly increased use of the knowledge gained by the police of their assigned areas
6. More effective use of personnel
7. An increased awareness of community problems as a basis for designing more effective police response[19]

Though not a new phenomenon, the community policing philosophy has grown tremendously in the last few years. Departments are expanding their efforts to work with their communities, including incorporating new technology and developing new policies and procedures. In some cases, departments are examining the characteristics that make for a good community policing officer and are incorporating those characteristics into their hiring and evaluation practices. The public seems to like this community policing trend.

The Department of Justice conducted a study of residents in 12 cities across the country. The percentage of residents who were "very satisfied" or "satisfied" with the police ranged from 97 percent in Madison, Wisconsin, to 78 percent in Washington, D.C. More than 50 percent of these residents knew what community policing was, and 54 percent said their departments practice community policing in their neighborhood.

According to U.S. Deputy Attorney General Eric Holder,

> The high degree of citizen support for America's neighborhood police officers is a testament to the dedicated men and women who work day in and day out to establish relationships with the residents in their communities. These relationships help citizens and police work together to promote community safety.[20]

In 1999, 64 percent of departments had full-time community policing officers. By 2003, that percentage had decreased to 58 percent. This may cause some to question law enforcement's support of the community policing concept, but it should actually be interpreted in a positive manner. As mentioned earlier, community policing differs from the police community relations concept in that it is a philosophy that runs throughout the department. It must be believed, supported, and practiced by all levels of the department, especially the line officers. They are the ones in contact with the public on a regular basis. Having a special unit devoted to community policing can enhance the departments' efforts but cannot be the basis of the department's efforts. For smaller departments where dollars and personnel are more limited, it would be difficult and highly unlikely that they would be able to allocate full-time personnel to community policing. Because community policing promotes the use of organizational strategies to address the causes of crime and social disorder through problem-solving and police-community partnerships, there are other trends worth examining. More interesting is the indication of departments' interest in providing training in the area of community policing and incorporating problem solving into how they do business. Thirty-nine percent of local departments provided community policing training to new recruits, and 48 percent provided such training to in-service officers. Most departments serving populations greater than 10,000 assigned officers by geographic area, which is a major tenet of the community policing philosophy. Twenty-five percent of all local departments encourage officers to engage in problem-solving projects in their beats, and most departments serving populations greater than 50,000 have such a policy. The partnership with the community is demonstrated by departments that reach out and encourage input from the community. In 2003, 60 percent of departments had problem-solving partnerships with community groups or others, 37 percent of departments partnered with citizen groups to solicit input and develop community policing strategies, 18 percent of departments offered training in community policing to the public, and 17 percent of departments offered citizen police academies. Some departments are also institutionalizing community policing into personnel issues, and 27 percent of agencies assessed new recruits' analytical and problem-solving abilities and 14 percent of the departments assessed the recruits' understanding of diverse populations.[21]

Community policing is also more easily facilitated with the technology available today. Departments are taking advantage of that, using computers and the Internet to maximize their outreach to the community. Most departments today have an Internet home page. A presence on the Internet with a high-quality interactive web page can be a highly successful way of sharing the department's philosophy, beliefs, and practices with the community, as well as sharing information about the law enforcement personnel, aiding in familiarity with employees, facilitating a relationship, and encouraging a partnership. Sharing procedures, resources, and crime statistics with the community in an open way can show the community the department's commitment to a partnership and to providing citizens with as much information as possible in an effort to meet their needs. Communication is further enhanced with links, e-mail, and the availability to make reports online. Departments realize this is a crucial element to their outreach and are devoting dollars and personnel to this effort.

Problem-Solving Policing

The idea of problem-solving policing can be attributed to Herman Goldstein, a law professor at the University of Wisconsin, who spent a great deal of time in the trenches with different police departments. The problem-solving approach to policing was first mentioned by Goldstein in a 1979 article calling for a new kind of policing, which he termed problem-oriented policing.[22]

In traditional policing, most of what the police do is incident driven—they respond to incident after incident, dealing with each one and then responding to the next. Problem-solving policing, or problem-oriented policing, however, forces the police to focus on the problems that cause the incidents. Goldstein's central theory is that the broad types of police roles (crime, order maintenance, and service) can be further broken down; for example, murder, drunk driving, auto theft. Each of these can be addressed and specific strategies or responses can be developed, depending on the underlying social or criminal issues for each one. Instead of the strategy of the reactive 911 system of responding to each incident and resolving it, the problem-oriented approach involves officers examining the underlying problems and developing responses to address these problems. The power within the department must be decentralized and the line officer empowered to take action.[23]

With incident-driven policing, officers tend to respond to similar incidents at the same location numerous times—burglaries in a certain housing project—car thefts in a certain parking lot. Because the police have traditionally focused on incidents, rarely have they sought to determine the underlying causes of these incidents. Problem-oriented policing tries to find out what is causing citizen calls for help and what the underlying issues are. Historically, beat officers had naturally seen crime on their beats in terms of patterns: they were responsible for all incidents on their turf, and a rash of burglaries or overdoses signaled a burglar or a dealer who needed to be dealt with. With the advent of mobile response, officers, tied to their radios, saw crime as an endless string of isolated incidents. Several burglaries in the same general vicinity might draw several different officers.

The problem-oriented policing strategy consists of four distinct parts: scanning, analysis, response, and assessment. Problem-oriented policing practitioners call this process by the acronym SARA. In the scanning process, groups of officers discuss incidents as "problems" instead of as specific incidents and criminal law concepts, such as "robberies" or "larcenies." Problems are defined as two or more incidents, similar in nature (through such things as location, suspects, targets, or modus operandi [MO]), capable of causing harm and about which the public expects the police to do something.[24] For example, a robbery, which used to be thought of as a single incident, in the scanning process is thought of as being part of a pattern of robberies, which in turn might be related to another problem, such as prostitution-related robberies in a particular area of the city.

After defining the problem, officers begin analysis. They collect information from a variety of sources, including non-police sources, such as members of the business community, other city agencies, or local citizens. The officers then use the information to discover the underlying nature of the problem, its causes, and options for solutions.

After scanning and analysis, the police begin response. They work with citizens, business owners, and public and private agencies to prepare a program of action suitable to the specifics of the particular problem. Solutions may include arrest

but also may involve action by other community agencies and organizations. Responses are developed through brainstorming sessions to come up with plans, followed by determining what needs to be done before the plan can be implemented, who is responsible for these preliminary actions and then outlining and implementing the plan. Examining what other communities have done to respond to a similar problem is a valuable part of the process. There are several viable expectations for the plan, including eliminating the problem, reducing the problem, reducing the harm, and moving the problem.[25]

In the assessment process—after the police make their response to the problem—they evaluate the effectiveness of the response. They examine the following: Was the plan implemented? What was the goal? Was the goal attained and how do you know? What will happen if the plan is removed or remains in place? What new strategies can be implemented to increase effectiveness and how can the response be monitored in the future? Police may use the results to revise the response, collect more data, or even to redefine the problem.[26]

In summary, the SARA process is

Scanning: Identifying the neighborhood crime and disorder problems

Analysis: Understanding the conditions that cause the problems to occur

Response: Developing and implementing solutions

Assessment: Determining the impact of the solutions

Problem-oriented policing involves officers' thinking, not just responding to yet another call for duty. It involves officers dealing with the underlying causes of incidents to prevent those incidents from happening again, and it encourages the wide use of resources (not just police resources) by officers to engage in the developing of solutions. This process necessitates improving various skill sets including communication (agreement to share thoughts and ideas with various groups), coordination (networking), cooperation (two or more parties agreeing to assist each other), and collaboration (a formal sustained commitment to work together to accomplish a common mission). There are many new tools available to law enforcement today to assist with this problem analysis. Goldstein defined problem analysis as "an approach/method/ process conducted within the police agency in which formal criminal justice theory, research methods, and comprehensive data collection and analysis procedures are used in a systematic way to conduct in-depth examination of, develop informed responses to, and evaluate crime and disorder problems."[27]

It is hoped that this problem analysis occurs within the department, using the latest research to develop appropriate procedures to successfully address problems in the community. Developing partnerships with local universities may prove to be a win–win solution for police organizations. By understanding the underlying factors leading to the problems, the most realistic solutions can be developed.[28]

New technology enhances law enforcement's ability to analyze crime and geography and consider factors such as repeat victimization, repeat offending, and MOs and therefore obtain the data that will facilitate their successfully addressing the crime problem. This can be accomplished with improved technology, despite recent budgetary constraints, and, together with criminological theories and up-to-date research, the new technologies may lead to innovative ways to reduce crime.

Successful Examples of Problem-Oriented Policing

The concepts of community policing and problem-solving policing have merged in the past decade and are sometimes looked at as one philosophy. This philosophy has been given several names in addition to community policing and problem-solving policing, including community-oriented policing. Whatever the name given to this philosophy, the concept is the same—the involvement of the community as a partner in the policing process and an emphasis on proactive, problem-oriented policing rather than incident-driven policing. The community policing concept is a philosophy of policing that emphasizes a partnership with the community, problem-solving, and organizational transformation.[29] Although the two philosophies are close and go hand-in-hand, there are differences. Community policing is concerned with the relationship between the police and the community, and problem-oriented policing is more concerned with solving a particular problem and having an outcome.

It involves making efforts to solve problems and have positive results. This process will clearly be more successful when there is a good relationship with the community and a partnership exists that promotes dialogue and teamwork. This section will address several of the methods, techniques, or ways of implementing community-oriented policing and using problem-oriented policing to solve problems.

The California Highway Patrol (CHP) recently implemented a program to keep the thousands of farm laborers who are hired to work the fields safe while being transported to work sites. There had been a large number of collisions with fatalities and injuries, and in the Central Division during peak months, the traffic fatalities were 42 percent higher than nonpeak months. In examining why there were such high numbers of injuries and fatalities, CHP observed that there were statutory and regulatory shortcomings regarding vehicle safety in California. For instance, farm labor vehicles were exempt from the mandatory seat belt law and because of language barriers the outreach and education efforts were less than optimal. CHP worked with the California State Legislature to get two bills passed to enhance the safety of farm workers and vehicles. The mandatory use of seat belts, stronger safety and inspection programs for the farm vehicles, increased staff within CHP to handle inspections, enforcement of these issues, and an increased public education effort had a significant impact on the issue. For the first time in eight years, there were no fatalities resulting from farm labor vehicle collisions and the number of collisions involving farm labor vehicles dropped 73 percent.[30]

The Charlotte-Mecklenburg Police Department used problem-oriented policing to address an increasing domestic violence rate. Analysis revealed that the average domestic violence victim had filed nine previous police reports, most involving the same suspect and some crossing district boundaries. In analyzing the situations, the officers determined it would be desirable to regard the victim and suspect as "hot spots," rather than as traditional fixed locations, and developed a detailed database allowing this to be done. In addition, the officers instituted a zero-tolerance program, the use of other criminal justice agencies and social service agencies, and a Police Watch Program and Domestic Violence Hotline voice mail system for victims. Repeat calls for service were reduced by 98.9 percent at seven target locations. Domestic assaults decreased 7 percent in the district targeted while the rest of the city experienced a 29 percent increase.[31]

The Charlotte-Mecklenburg Police Department also used problem-oriented policing to address an increase in robbery victimization among the Hispanic population. When officers analyzed the situation, they found the majority at a particular apartment complex and met with the residents. Police found most occurred in the parking lot and near the laundry facilities, that the residents were doing their socializing in the parking lots, and that they frequently had large sums of money because they didn't trust banks. The police also found the victimization was more than previously thought because the residents rarely called police, and the offenders were from outside the area. Officers worked with the complex management and improved the safety, access, and lighting. They shared information gathered with the robbery unit and arrested several suspects and worked to build relationships with the Hispanic residents. Officers partnered with the local banking industry to educate the residents and facilitate banking activities. These efforts produced a 72 percent decline in robbery rates in the apartment complex and overall calls for service also declined. Police replicated the strategy in five other areas and produced an average decrease of 8 percent in robberies. In addition, residents have reported increased trust in police and greater use of bank accounts.[32]

El Monte, California, is a city of 120,000 in which 33 percent of the households have incomes below the poverty level. City leaders wanted to improve the quality of life for residents. The city implemented a program called Improving and Maintaining Public Awareness and Community Teamwork (IMPACT), which brings several city programs under one umbrella and is designed as a long-term connection with the police and other city departments. The city is divided into 65 reporting districts with an officer assigned to each. The officer is responsible for the district and empowered to use whatever resources are needed to solve problems. Officers have regular meetings with residents and businesses to identify problems and determine solutions. Residents are encouraged to call their officer on a city cell phone to report any problems or gang activity. The police department has a strong tradition in gang prevention, has a job placement program, and has partnered with a hospital to aid in tattoo removal. The officers target properties in their district that need

to be cleaned up and brought up to code compliance. These efforts were complemented by implementing a citizens academy from which volunteers to the department are then recruited for the Volunteers Caring and Patrolling (VCAP) program. The results from these combined efforts were impressive: a 21 percent decrease in calls for service regarding transient-related activity; a 7 percent overall reduction in calls for service; 78 graffiti vandals were identified; a 17.4 percent decrease in crimes against persons; and clean-up efforts included 5,344 shopping carts returned to stores, 915 abandoned vehicles towed from city streets; and 2,175 graffiti locations were painted over or repaired. Much work remains, but with the increased cooperation between the community and the city, continued progress is anticipated.[33]

Though hesitant to attribute all the success to community policing efforts, the chief of Lawrence, Massachusetts, Police Department was ecstatic to report that 2005 was the first year since 1972 without recording a single homicide and that there was a significant decline in the overall crime rate. At the same time, Boston was experiencing the highest homicide rate in 10 years. In addition to having some improved criminal data availability, the Lawrence department's chief and officers regularly attend community meetings throughout the city to build relationships with the community and be available for citizens to talk to. The chief targeted domestic violence, gangs, and drugs—three areas that lead to homicides. He also recruited more bilingual officers to interact with the predominantly Latino city. Residents and police alike report that the residents have taken ownership in their city and are joining with the police department to improve the quality of life in their city and feel things are "changing for the best."[34]

Community Policing Today

Many of the programs and outreach efforts discussed in Chapter 11 are examples of community policing strategies. When departments use store-front substations, ministations or kiosks, they are seeking to allow the citizens to interact with them on a more frequent basis. The hope is that by decentralizing police operations and making officers and information more available, the residents will

Courtesy of the Boca Raton Police Department

Bicycle patrol is a strategy that enhances community policing while at the same time effectively fights crime. It allows officers to get out in the community without the barrier of a car. It also allows officers to patrol in situations that might be difficult for motor vehicles.

All the programs aimed at working with various populations to serve them better are examples of community policing. The youth programs, including Police Athletic League (PAL), the recreation and tutoring programs, Drug Abuse Resistance Education (DARE), Gang Resistance Education and Training (GREAT), and the wilderness programs for at-risk youth all seek to actively involve the youth and their families in improving quality of life in the community and address and minimize various risk factors. Police work with the senior population in an effort to empower seniors and minimize their fear of crime as well as to enhance their ability to contribute to their community and police department in a positive manner. The outreach that law enforcement provides to the various segments of the diverse community makes those groups feel part of the community and gives them a voice, and the work that is done with crime victims helps empower them and makes the police department more responsive to the needs of crime victims. Most departments today use a multitude of programs to express and demonstrate their community policing philosophy. Citizens can visit their department's website and see the various community policing efforts. Just having a website and allowing the reporting of information, asking of questions or contacting the correct people in the organization is a community policing strategy. The Boston Police Department recently started a new program as a result of a business partnership with the retailer Bread and Circus Markets and that led to the creation of the GREAT cooking class. Students participating in GREAT have a weekly cooking session in a fully stocked cooking demonstration kitchen. The students learn how to prepare the chosen recipes, and they learn the national customs surrounding the food being prepared. They are expanding their knowledge of foods, tastes, cooking skills, and customs and histories of the various foods. This program also shows them that teamwork and learning can give them alternatives to a criminal lifestyle.[35]

become more involved with their police department and local government. Using various modes of transportation such as bicycles, scooters, all-terrain vehicles (ATVs), and horses also gets the officer into the community, especially at community events with the goal of enhancing relationships. Citizen police academies, new resident information sessions, police officer trading cards, informational brochures in other languages, and police department tours are all examples of community policing efforts. Implementing Neighborhood Watch programs, Community Emergency Response Team (CERT) training programs and volunteer programs are all efforts to give residents more opportunity to participate in their department and their community in a positive manner. The message is that the quality of life in the community, and consequently, the crime rate and fear of crime is also partially a responsibility of the residents and when working together with the police and supplementing law enforcement's efforts, real impacts can be made.

Elgin, Illinois, a community of more than 77,000 people, located 35 miles northwest of Chicago, has focused its department on numerous products that have supported a comprehensive, innovative community policing philosophy. This philosophy emphasizes that policing is done by everyone in the community and that police officers are the paid professionals who facilitate it. The strategy includes many of the programs discussed in the police and the community chapter and the philosophies discussed in this chapter. Among the Elgin programs are

© AP/Wide World Photos

Police departments are realizing what a valuable resource and ally older residents can be. Many are expanding their outreach efforts with their older citizens and developing ways that they can contribute to the community. Sgt. Eric Lawrence shares a laugh with a resident in Boca Raton, Florida.

- The Resident Officer Program of Elgin (ROPE), in which officers live and work in distressed neighborhoods of the city
- The Neighborhood Officer Program of Elgin (NOPE), through which officers are assigned to particular neighborhoods within the city
- A "Crime-Free Housing Unit," in which officers work closely with all constituents (renters, managers, owners, neighbors) in rental communities in an effort to decrease crime and improve the quality of life
- An informative website with newsletters, monthly and yearly crime statistics, internal affairs investigations statistics, and crime reporting information
- A liaison officer who works with senior services and the local crisis center to enhance services through better criminal investigation, information, and education and Cellular Assistance for Seniors (CASE), in which seniors can obtain free cell phones that are programmed for 911 calls
- School liaison officers who provide support for the schools, teach gang resistance education and awareness training programs, and attend students' social and sporting activities
- A social services coordinator who offers immediate assistance to victims of crime and domestic violence
- Community outreach workers who offer special services to the city's Laotian and Hispanic population
- A phone line for reporting crime anonymously

- Crime prevention and community relations programs, including Neighborhood Watch, citizen patrol, and other volunteer activities
- Police officer involvement on numerous community boards and committees that are working to prevent crime, drug use, and gang activity
- Use of an AT&T language line that provides translation of more than 200 foreign languages

The keystone, perhaps, of the Elgin program is ROPE, in which an officer is assigned to live and work in a neighborhood that has been identified as needing direct police attention because of criminal and social issues. Elgin's was the first such program in the United States. Resident officer programs are becoming very popular throughout the nation, as we will see later in this chapter.

The Elgin Police Department website explains its philosophy by making the mission statements of the department, the ROPE unit, and the "Crime-Free Housing Unit" available. All speak to the issue of the necessity of the police and the community working together to solve the community's problems. They also warn that it is not a quick fix. Neighborhoods had deteriorated and crime rose over the years and reversing the situation will take a long-term investment in time and personnel.[36]

Chicago's Alternative Policing Strategy (CAPS), one of the nation's most ambitious community policing initiatives, also embodies the philosophies discussed earlier in this chapter. In an average month, some 6,000 Chicagoans connect with their beat officers through the 230 community meetings held throughout the city. The purpose of the beat officer is to identify and resolve problems of crime and disorder in Chicago's neighborhoods. Both the police and community members have been trained in problem solving and partnership building, resulting in the formation of meaningful partnerships. Other city agencies have been brought into the process to address quality-of-life issues. Beat officers work the same neighborhood and watch for one year to ensure they become a familiar presence in the community.[37]

According to a CAPS press release provided on the Northwestern University website, Chicago's program has made strides in involving the public in securing neighborhood safety. The majority of the city's population (79 percent) knows about the program, largely because of the TV campaign, and participation has been maintained in the communities that need it most. Though participation in community meetings appears low, those who do attend feel positive about the process. One criticism is that it appears to be the police who propose solutions to the problems rather than the community. Community policing training in the police department is ongoing, and progress has been made, but the department is looking to address the concerns and weaknesses in their program.[38]

Although most of the academic and professional writing about policing centers on our nation's big cities, many crime and disorder problems occur in small towns and mid-size suburban departments. Community-oriented policing strategies have proven successful and are also widely used in these cities and towns. The true community policing philosophy is one that permeates the department and is put into action by all officers and personnel who have contact with the public. But, as the following examples will show, successful community policing initiatives can be undertaken in any size community.

In 2005, Estes Park, Colorado, received the Community Policing award from the International Association of Chiefs of Police (IACP) for police departments serving populations less than 20,000. This small resort community hosts three million visitors a year who enjoy the downtown area. However, there were problems with loud music, illegal drug use, underage drinking, tourists being accosted, assaults, graffiti and vandalism, and

threats against business owners who intervened. The police department worked with the community and built a skate park, instituted new park rules, implemented a foot patrol assignment downtown, developed a restorative justice program, and developed a "constitutional law" course in the high schools. Their efforts proved a success as evidenced by a decrease in calls for service of 92 percent, a drop in juvenile arrests of 100 percent, and an increase of 81 percent in overall satisfaction with the police department—which was an all-time high.[39]

The Draper Police Department in Utah received the Community Policing award for cities serving a population between 20,000 and 50,000. The Draper PD was a newly formed police department charged with patrolling a rugged, mountainous area that was growing rapidly. There were many problems of damage to the recreation areas including overuse, littering, damage to the waterways, and erosion. The department partnered with community groups, business owners, and church groups to recruit volunteers for a grant-funded Mobile Neighborhood Watch. There were an overwhelming number of volunteers who were trained to patrol the area using ATVs, horses, mountain bikes, and foot. The negative impact to the land has decreased by 82 percent, juvenile problems have decreased by 40 percent, and thefts have decreased by 70 percent.[40]

In the next largest categories, cities serving populations from 50,000 to 100,000, the North Little Rock Police Department in Arkansas received the award from IACP. Gangs, violence and drugs had been a long-standing problem in North Little Rock, and the town had deteriorated, residents and business owners were fearful and property values had declined. The police department formed a partnership with the community and other city departments called Support, Abatements, Fines and Enforcement (SAFE). The city offered incentives to property owners to improve their properties and take legal action against noncomplying tenants. They also worked together to update their ordinances and improve the working relationships between the property owners and police. As a result of their efforts, 95 percent of property owners cooperated and evicted problem tenants, crime decreased, property values increased, and new homes were built for the first time in 50 years.[41]

The Irvine, California, Police Department (IPD) has built itself around the community policing philosophy since its inception in 1975. In 2002, the IACP recognized Irvine's efforts to promote safety in the community in response to some blatant gang-related violence the city was experiencing. The department initially found that the stakeholders in the youth violence issue in the city were more concerned with protecting themselves from blame than in working together to come up with solutions. In response, the department formed the Safe Community Task Force, comprising many community partners, which was charged with researching the issue of community safety and making recommendations for solutions.

The primary goals were to reduce the use of alcohol, tobacco, and drugs and the level of violence among youth; increase attendance in school; and ensure that all students feel connected to their schools and their homes. Many innovative programs were eventually developed. These included the IPD Youth Services Unit, a discrete youth crimes investigation unit to consistently be present around the schools; Operation Safe Campus, an interagency organization that regularly meets to discuss emerging trends and issues around school safety; Alternative to Suspension; a School Attendance Review Board; a High-Risk Youth Interagency Intervention Team; an interagency team to manage high-risk students; FOR Families, providing free information and short-term support to needy residents; Families Forward, serving families with a food bank program and transitional housing; Human Options, serving victims of domestic violence; Pennies for Prevention, collecting pennies in the schools to support prevention efforts; Pizza Night, designed to promote block parties throughout the community; Community Education, providing cross-training opportunities; and Youth Development, hosting teen forums.

Though prevention is difficult to measure, Irvine experienced a 39.8 percent decrease in violent crime as a result of these activities and is a leader in developing partnerships to prevent problems.[42]

The Louisville, Kentucky, Division of Police was also recognized by the IACP for a community policing initiative developed to improve success on calls involving mental illness. In consulting with mental health professionals in the community, the Louisville police developed a 24-hour proactive citywide crisis intervention team based on a program in place in Memphis, Tennessee, composed of specially trained crisis intervention team (CIT) officers. The primary objective of the program included increased training for all officers

in the area of mental health issues and a reduction in the use of force as well as an increase in options involving less-than-lethal force in the handling of these calls.

The program seems to be successful; in a three-month period, CIT officers responded to 503 calls. Of those, 401 of these individuals were hospitalized for evaluation or treatment, 11 were charged with offenses, and force was used in only three cases, and that was "empty-hand control" only. The program continues to be closely monitored and evaluated by the CIT committee initially formed to implement the plan.[43]

University Police agencies and University communities can also be involved in community policing efforts. The University of Vermont Department of Public Safety was also given recognition for its community policing initiative, designed to address poor relations with students resulting in tension, lack of reporting of crime, and lack of trust. The primary goal was to improve communications and work with the students to solve the problems of the campus community. The department appointed liaison officers for various groups and solicited input from the students, faculty, and staff via surveys regarding issues on the campus. Police Services also became more involved in university-wide staff development and training regarding safety issues. Evaluation continues, but initial survey results found that 57.4 percent of the campus community was either very satisfied or satisfied with police services.[44]

Resident Officer Programs— The Ultimate in Community Policing?

Numerous initiatives generally known as **resident officer programs** have sprung up around the nation since the early 1990s. Supporters of these programs believe resident officer programs capture the essence of community policing: improved relationships between police and their neighbors, who team together to fight crime and address quality-of-life conditions that contribute to crime.

Elgin's ROPE, which started in 1991 with three officers, grew to eight officers by 1997. One of the original locations closed after three years in 1993 because of its success and a sustained decrease in crime. The ROPE officers, living in donated or subsidized homes or apartments, normally work an eight-hour day, but, for all

ON THE JOB

Community Policing in Florida

My experience with community policing began when we got a new chief of police from outside the agency in the early 1980s. He used the term *team policing,* but the philosophy was similar to community policing.

I was a road sergeant at the time and was given supervisory responsibility for everything that happened in a particular sector of the city. The chief had divided the city into three sectors, and the supervisory staff was responsible for everything occurring in all the zones within that sector; the lieutenants and captain were accountable for everything that occurred in that sector whether they were on duty or not.

Personnel were assigned to sectors, and this assignment never changed. Staffing was the responsibility of the sector supervisors, and they did not get help from the other sectors. The lieutenants were most affected by this change in philosophy, and some did not like it, but they seemed to accept it well. The new chief also implemented changes in the detective bureau that appeared to diminish some of their authority and autonomy. Patrol officers were following up minor crimes, and some detectives were reporting to sector supervisors. That chief didn't last too long, because of other issues, but some of his philosophies and changes remained.

When a new chief was appointed who had risen through the ranks, he continued with many of these ideas but also expanded further and implemented various strategies to address problems within our community. He put together various task forces to address certain problems and instructed them to work with the community to attempt to come up with solutions. He recognized the need for training when implementing these changes and PERF came to the department to provide training in problem-oriented policing. The training started with the supervisors and then progressed to the officers. We used real problems

in our community to practice the steps in problem solving. Later we would actually implement some of these ideas. Most importantly, this training got us thinking "outside the box" in addressing some of our persistent problems.

My experience as well as that of a lot of other officers and supervisors was that a lot of the strategies that community policing stressed were in fact things we were already doing and enjoyed doing. Getting out of my police vehicle and talking with business owners, residents, and tourists was something I loved to do. I had found it was also a great way to develop relationships and obtain information. I preferred to work the same zone so that I could get to know the comings and goings of the people living and working in the zone. Most supervisors also believed in this and assigned people to the same zone for extended periods whenever they were able to. The response of some officers and supervisors to this training was, "What else is new? We already know this and already do this . . . they're just giving it a new name." Most went along with the change and encouraged their coworkers to try new things.

We had a particular section of town called Pearl City, a lower socioeconomic area that was experiencing crime and drug problems. The neighborhood was centrally located along main highways and railroad tracks and had been splintered by road expansion as the city grew. A minority police officer was assigned to foot patrol in this predominantly minority-populated section of town. He spent all his time in the neighborhood and established relationships with the community. He became a friend to older and younger residents, someone they knew and could come to with problems. He worked with them in addressing the problems the community was facing. In 1987, he established the Children and Teens Service (CATS) program in the community. He worked with other resources in the

practical purposes, they are on 24-hour-a-day call, because residents call them at all hours for assistance. The officers listen and work closely with the residents to creatively address the community's problems and challenges. They are also the liaison with government resources. Everyone understands that community policing is not a

"quick fix," and the whole community engages in long-term problem solving to achieve mutually agreed-upon goals. The mission statement for ROPE is, "By working and living in a distressed neighborhood, we will provide police service and be the stimulus that empowers the residents to problem-solve, improve their quality of life and

community to provide positive role models, mentors, after-school and summer activities, and educational opportunities. He worked with other city agencies to clean up the neighborhood. He was a charismatic officer and was good at marketing his program and getting community leaders to donate effort, time, and money. This program grew and became successful in many ways and ultimately was used as a model in other neighborhoods in the city. These programs became known as the Neighborhood Improvement Programs and encompassed various programs under that heading. Educational funding for college was guaranteed for students maintaining certain standards in school, computer labs were built and staffed by high school and college students, tutoring and recreational programs were available in an effort to provide wholesome activities and even the playing field in school for some of these children from less affluent homes. These programs were successful and gained national recognition. There were TV documentaries, magazine articles, and national awards.

This was of course great news for the organization, right? Yes, but the fame and attention that this one officer received caused some resentment in other officers. Some officers felt that their efforts at aggressive law enforcement, conducted in addition to these "softer" methods to clean up the area, were ignored. They felt they had risked injury and worked hard to clean up the area, and only one officer was getting the credit. They believed these were good programs but also felt the one officer couldn't have accomplished what he did without other officers backing him up and covering the calls for service that he would have been handling had he not had this special assignment. Luckily, this resentment was small-scale and didn't grow, because most officers realized that the ultimate goal was to improve the quality of life for the residents of that community as well as everyone else in the city and to minimize our repeat responses to

problems. Those goals were being accomplished, and most knowledgeable people would realize that it took a coordinated effort throughout the department.

One of the most significant changes within the department occurred when supervisors allowed officers to take risks in addressing problems in unconventional ways. When supervisors truly allowed officers to "fail" without marking them down on their evaluations, this encouraged officers to try new things. One of the most difficult issues to deal with in our department and probably any department was that some officers and some supervisors just don't want to do the thinking or work involved in problem solving. They would rather just continue to do law enforcement the traditional way and then just throw their hands up and blame other conditions or factors when they can't solve a problem.

The other philosophy that I have carried with me since leaving law enforcement, and look for in other law enforcement agencies and personnel, is the realization that the police department belongs to the community and is an extension of the community. Police organizations need to be responsive to the residents and realize the residents are actually their "bosses." The effort to improve the quality of life for all residents, not just lower socioeconomic populations, should be ongoing. Making it easier for residents to file reports, obtain reports, understand the department, obtain information, and speak with employees should always be a concern. Whether through the various strategies we have mentioned, such as online reporting, telephone reporting, web pages, ministations throughout the community, citizen academies, or public forums, or just the philosophy of always giving the citizens the best service possible, we must be willing to go the extra mile to build the partnership between the police and community.

—*Linda Forst*

independently take ownership of the neighborhood."[45]

The program's effectiveness can be seen by the change in answers to a survey distributed to one area's residents. When ROPE first started in the neighborhood, a questionnaire asked what problems concerned the residents. "Drugs and gangs"

were the major problem then; two years later, the same residents answered that loud stereos and speeding cars were now their biggest concerns.

The Macon, Georgia, Police Department implemented a resident officer program in 1995 in which officers agree to live in rent-free, city-owned housing in exchange for working with at-risk youths for

24 hours a month. Macon's Youth Enrichment Services (Project YES) is a collaborative effort with the Economic and Community Development Department to place resident police officers in inner-city neighborhoods to strengthen relationships with the communities. More specifically, they serve as role models and mentors for at-risk youth between the ages of 10 and 14 by leading them in enrichment activities including academic, social, recreational and cultural events.[46]

The city of Phoenix, Arizona, has a Police Officer Placement Solutions (POPS) program. According to the department, the purpose of the POPS program is to enable the city to assist neighborhoods in recruiting police officers to become residents in their community. The program is an element of an overall commitment between the city and its neighborhoods related to a community-based policing philosophy with a goal of reducing crime and fear of crime. The intended goal is to enhance the quality of life in the neighborhoods by making them safe enough for people to live without fear of crime. The officers become familiar with the neighborhood and function as an avenue of communication as well as a deterrent to crime. The officers benefit with financial incentives regarding rent and utilities and the opportunity to drive a marked take-home police vehicle. The officers are expected to be good neighbors and act as resources for the community, with police service and 911 calls being handled by on-duty personnel. This program was started in 1993; in 2006, it was still going strong with guidelines for participation and application procedures available on the department's website.[47]

In 1997, President Clinton joined the resident officer bandwagon when he announced a plan to give 50 percent discounts to 2,000 police officers to buy federally foreclosed homes in 500 low-income neighborhoods nationwide. Participants must agree to live in the homes for at least three years. This program, called **Officer Next Door (OND)**, is part of a wide-ranging Urban Homestead Initiative designed to reduce crime and make low-income neighborhoods more attractive to homeowners. The OND is under the Good Neighbor Next Door program. Teachers, firefighters, and emergency medical technicians have been added to the program in recent years. The programs were suspended for several months in 2001 after fraud and criminal convictions involving some of the participants. According to its website, the U.S. Department of Housing and Urban Development (HUD) has reopened its OND and Teacher Next Door

programs after implementing corrective actions to eliminate abuse and allow these winning programs to continue to benefit and strengthen the communities involved. HUD states that having these public safety personnel living in these communities makes American communities stronger and helps to build a safer nation. The OND program helps make this goal a reality by encouraging public servants to become homeowners in these revitalization areas.[48]

Other communities are adopting resident officer programs with the belief that resident officers provide a high-profile presence that helps to prevent crime.

The Federal Government and Community Policing

In the 1992 presidential race, Bill Clinton championed the concept of community-oriented policing and promised to add 100,000 more police officers to the nation's streets. After the election, the federal government made tremendous contributions to the state of community policing strategies throughout the nation. This section will discuss the 1994 Crime Bill, the Department of Justice's Office of Community Oriented Policing Services, and the Community Policing Consortium (CPC).

The Crime Bill

After much political debate, the Violent Crime Control and Law Enforcement Act (the **Crime Bill**) was signed into law by President Clinton in 1994. The provisions of this bill authorized the expenditure of nearly $8 billion over six years for grants to law enforcement agencies to reduce crime.

Office of Community Oriented Policing Services (COPS)

As the research and evaluation arm of the Department of Justice, the National Institute of Justice (NIJ) has mounted a broad agenda to study changes in policing. In the wake of the passage of the Crime Bill, Attorney General Janet Reno established the **Office of Community Oriented Policing Services (COPS).**[49] The COPS office was established to administer the grant money provided by the Crime Bill and to promote community-oriented policing.

The mission statement reflecting the values and goals of the COPS office states the mission of the organization is to "Advance the practice of community policing as an effective strategy in communities' efforts to improve public safety." The program has four primary goals: increasing the numbers of officers on the street, encouraging partnerships between police and the community, promoting innovation in policing, and developing new technologies to help reduce crime and its consequences. As the director, Carl R. Peed is quoted on the website, the COPS program "is considered to be a critical component in responding to crime, gang activity and homeland security."[50]

COPS allocated the funds in three ways. The first was for three-year grants to hire police officers to work in community policing initiatives. The second method was to award grants for improved productivity through acquiring technology or hiring civilians to free sworn-officer time, which could then be devoted to community policing activities. The third approach was to award grants to agencies for special programs attacking specific crime issues.

To maximize participation by the agencies that needed the resources and to facilitate the most equitable distribution of funds throughout the nation, the act establishing COPS required simplified application procedures and equal distribution of funds between jurisdictions with more and less than 150,000 population.

The COPS program appears to be a success. Though falling short of its original goal to put "100,000 new cops on the beat," it did greatly increase the numbers of police officers out in the field. In examining the data, we can see that there are many more officers on the street than there would have been without the federal funding, which has greatly aided the fight against rising crime rates. This includes the numbers of police officer hires and the full-time equivalents gained through increased productivity because of technology use or the implementation of new programs. Though it is difficult to document, it is also believed that the effort facilitated the growth of community policing in the country. Because nongrant recipients also initiated community policing initiatives, it's difficult to conclusively link the two. It was noted, however, that most departments were pleased with the simplified application process and the technical support available from the COPS office.[51]

The COPS office has continued to expand its services over the years. Between 1994 and 2005, COPS awarded more than $11.3 billion in total to local, state, and tribal agencies to hire and redeploy more than 118,000 law enforcement officers. COPS has supported other law enforcement community policing initiatives, including $10.9 million in antigang initiatives, $21.7 million in training since 1999 for "COPS in Schools," and $69.6 million for community policing initiatives to combat domestic violence. In March 2004, the COPS website announced that $20.7 million in grants had been awarded to hire 194 new police officers in schools across the nation.[52]

COPS is examining the character of police officers, including exploring changes in how law enforcement officers are recruited and hired through its program Hiring in the Spirit of Service, started in 2000. COPS has also allocated $35 million since 1997 through its Police Integrity Training Initiative.

In responding to issues deemed community problems, COPS has allocated financial backing to law enforcement agencies developing innovative community policing responses to problems created by methamphetamine, through grants that have reached $223 million since 1998. COPS members believe that a strong relationship between law enforcement and the community can help to combat the methamphetamine problem. In 2004, COPS allocated 4.6 million in funding to combat meth through the "Methamphetamine Training Initiative" assisting law enforcement in developing and enhancing comprehensive methamphetamine eradication strategies that emphasize training and technical assistance. The COPS program has also recently funded the development of interoperable communication networks, and awarded $59.6 million to its Homeland Security Overtime Program (HSOP) in an effort to keep our homeland safe.[53] In examining the community problems in 2006, and prioritizing funding, COPS allocated money to the meth problem ($63 million), law enforcement technology (almost $130 million), and interoperable communication technology ($10 million).[54]

COPS also supports the **Regional Community Policing Institutes (RCPIs),** which consist of partnerships across a variety of police agencies, community groups, and organizations to create a delivery system for training police officers in community-oriented policing. Each of the more than

30 RCPIs develops innovative, region-specific curricula for community policing training as well as providing technical assistance opportunities for policing agencies and community members. The RCPI network is facilitating the growth of community policing throughout the United States. The COPS program is also active in publishing articles, researching strategies, and conducting training (either through the RCPI or nationally) for law enforcement. Many of its publications can be downloaded from the website.

COPS funding is helping to continue to encourage police-community partnerships. One successful program was developed in Phoenix, Arizona, to facilitate the collaborative partnership between the police and the citizens. The Phoenix Neighborhood Patrol (PNP) empowers neighborhood residents to be the eyes and ears of the Phoenix Police Department. The PNP participants receive eight hours of training in patrol procedures, observation skills, the 911 system, reporting techniques, confrontation avoidance, and safety practices. They also have the opportunity to ride along with a patrol officer. After this training, they are issued an identification card and an official shirt so they are easily identifiable in their communities. Participants patrol their own community with which they're very familiar and report any suspicious activity to the police. Some have also been trained to patrol schools and shopping centers, as well as assist in finding missing persons and Alzheimer's patients. This program, in addition to others the Phoenix PD has employed, has allowed officers and the residents to keep the lines of communication strong.[55]

Using a COPS methamphetamine grant, Salt Lake City established a task force involving more than 30 government agencies working together to prevent the use and production of methamphetamine. One result of the initiative, the Drug Endangered Children Program (DEC), succeeded in changing the child endangerment statutes to better protect drug-exposed children.[56] The COPS office continues to respond to the changing needs of law enforcement and the American community. After September 11, 2001, COPS reassessed some of law enforcement's processes and decided to address the information-sharing aspect of law enforcement. COPS funded a project by the IACP to determine ways to improve information sharing between federal, state, local, and tribal law enforcement agencies. The result was a report entitled "Criminal Intelligence Sharing: A National Plan for Intelligence-Led Policing at the Local, State and Federal Levels." Among other things, the report recommends the creation of a Criminal Intelligence Coordinating Council (CICC) to help the Department of Homeland Security share criminal intelligence.[57] COPS members view community policing as a strong weapon in the fight against terror, so they will continue to address the issue.

In viewing the success of the COPS program, the weak area appears to be the problem-solving and relationship-building initiatives. Relationship building is somewhat dependent on the community and citizens' willingness to participate in the process. In some communities, the residents have been reluctant or unable to participate. Problem solving as a methodology spans a wide continuum. Some departments are truly practicing problem solving as Goldstein defined it. In other agencies, problem solving may occur in name only as things are done in the same traditional law enforcement manner with some additional steps added.[58]

With the tightening of budget dollars because of the Iraq war and the fight on terror, some COPS programs have been scaled back in recent years and more of the money is targeted toward programs in homeland security. The programs do continue, however, and successes can be seen around the country. Though law enforcement strives to stay out of politics, it is impossible. When a program is a federally funded program and parties change, politics can be evident. The Government Accounting Office (GAO) was asked to prepare a report for Congress about the success of the COPS program. This report indicated that the crime rate fell by 26 percent from 1993 to 2000 but only attributed 1.3 percent of the drop to the COPS program, concluding that factors other than COPS funds accounted for most of the decline. Despite the widely repeated contention that 100,000 new cops were put on the street, the number was actually closer to 88,000. The GAO did state, however, that there may have been other intangible results of the grants.[59] However, the biggest study conducted so far was conducted by Jihong "Solomon" Zhao and Quint Thurman, who found that the COPS program was very effective. They examined almost 6,000 cities during a seven-year period that had been the recipients of the grant funding through COPS. Zhao and Thurman found that COPS hiring and innovative grant programs are related to significant reductions in local crime rates for cities with populations of greater than 10,000 in both violent and nonviolent offenses.[60]

Community Policing Consortium

The **Community Policing Consortium** comprises five of the leading policing associations in the United States: the International Association of Chiefs of Police (IACP), the National Organization of Black Law Enforcement Executives (NOBLE), the National Sheriffs' Association (NSA), the Police Executive Research Forum (PERF), and the Police Foundation. The consortium, funded by COPS, issues a bimonthly publication, *Community Policing Exchange,* dedicated to reporting the newest developments in community policing partnerships. Its statement of purpose reads, "*Community Policing Exchange* strives to assist law enforcement practitioners in bridging the distance between communities, facilitating the exchange of information, and giving voice to all involved in the implementation of community policing."[61]

The Community Policing Consortium maintains a website that provides information and links regarding community policing. Its primary mission is to deliver community policing training and technical assistance to police departments and sheriff's offices that are designated COPS grantees. The website provides information, resources, tools, publications, and a chat room regarding community policing.

Some Accomplishments of Community Policing

As reports of overall crime rate decreases hit the presses in the mid- and late-1990s, some police officials associated this decrease to closer relationships with their communities through community policing, as well as the addition of new community policing officers. Some examples:

- Fort Worth, Texas, police attributed a 7 percent decrease in overall crime and a 50 percent drop in homicides to a closer relationship between the department and the community.
- Wichita, Kansas, police attributed an 11 percent decease in crime to community policing and its different way of looking at the crime issue.

- Los Angeles police attributed a 4 percent crime decline to police-community participation and emphasis on problem solving.
- Baton Rouge, Louisiana, experienced three straight years of crime rate decreases and gave much of the credit to the community.
- Denver, Colorado, police officials noted a 13 percent decrease in crime and attributed it to community participation in the crime fight.
- Police officials in Austin, Texas, also credited increased citizen involvement for a 23 percent drop in crime and the ability of residents and police to reclaim a city park that had become a haven for drug deals.
- New Orleans police reported that a community policing plan had helped cut the murder rate by 18 percent and led to a homicide rate decrease in three public housing developments where police deployed community-oriented police teams.[62]

Newark, New Jersey, has been using the broken windows theory for nearly 10 years with startling results. Violent crime has been cut by nearly 73 percent and property crime is down 58 percent. There have been blips, homicide and car thefts have increased, and even the broken windows proponents admit other factors may also be at work. But overall, the strategy is a success and people are headed back into the city. Newark had adopted Kelling's ideas after seeing the success that New York City had.[63]

Denver, Colorado, recently instituted the broken windows theory after years of increasing crime and decreasing arrest rates. Though it is early, Denver police are attributing crime decreases and increased public perception to the strategy. Criminal offenses have dropped by 7.4 percent for the first five months of 2006 compared with the same time in 2005, and arrests had increased more than 10 percent. The police department cracked down on crimes of disorder including graffiti and increased aggressive patrols. Residents noticed the increased cleanup of graffiti and the increased police presence and decrease in car burglaries. The city government and residents are encouraged by the new police tactics and the resulting crime drops.[64]

The biggest success often cited is that of New York City. In the mid-1980s New York's crime rate was escalating and the quality of life was dismal in many areas of the city with panhandlers intimidating tourists and residents, graffiti was all over the city, vagrants were sleeping on the street, subways overwhelmingly smelled of urine, and peep shows and sex shops took over the streets as more legitimate businesses left town. After some particularly horrendous homicides, New Yorkers had had enough. Mayor Rudolph Giuliani launched an effort to restore public confidence and take back the city. The city condemned property, enforced new ordinances, removed graffiti, pursued con artists and loiterers as well as violent criminals. Business associations also got involved to provide assistance to the police effort. Judges and courts cooperated, and new counseling, rehabilitation and community service programs were implemented. Violent and property crime rates are way down in New York and business investors as well as residents and tourists are flocking to Times Square and Grand Central Station as the city flourishes with new investment and business and a perception of safety.[65]

Surveys indicate that the public supports community policing and strategies that are indicative of community policing. One survey found that when citizens were queried about strategies that are part of community policing, they overwhelmingly supported the increased use of community meetings with the police as well as the increased use of police programs in schools.[66] Some studies have shown that community policing initiatives led to not only decreases in crime but also to an increase in residents' confidence in policing and feelings of safety and the belief that police were successfully addressing community problems.[67] Although many attribute crime reduction to community policing strategies, many do not. Some believe that these new philosophies are merely rhetoric. Many others attribute the drastic decrease in crime rates in the mid- and late 1990s to more aggressive, strategic, and legalistic law enforcement, similar to that practiced in New York City and other metropolitan areas, as discussed in Chapter 1.

■

Not All Agree with Community Policing

Research on the effectiveness of community-oriented policing has yielded mixed results. Many experts are not overly enthusiastic over the idea of community policing. One of the problems faced in community policing is to define what is meant by *community*. In many community policing projects,

the concept of community is defined in terms of "administrative areas" traditionally used by police departments to allocate patrols, instead of in terms of "ecological areas" defined by common norms, shared values, and interpersonal bonds. If the police are using administrative areas instead of ecological areas, they lose the ability to activate a community's norms and cultural values. Some administrators are also uncomfortable with dividing a community up into "parcels" and possibly having those areas competing against themselves for funding, attention, and service. Though it is important for various sections of town to have their say, it is important for cities or towns to work on problems that affect the entire population communitywide rather than just the neighborhood working on them. Community members should be able to come together and discuss issues and challenges and prioritize action plans to address them.[68]

Many feel that community policing can actually have a negative effect on certain people. An analysis of a victim callback program established by the Houston Police Department found that the program, which was originally designed to help victims, had a generally negative effect on some minority groups (Asian Americans and Hispanic Americans), whose members may have been suspicious of the department's intentions.[69]

A concern that has been raised by some law enforcement leaders is questioning whether the activities that officers are engaging in under the umbrella of community policing (recreational roles, tutoring roles, social work roles) are the type of activities that law enforcement officers should be doing. Departments need to address that issue on a continuing basis.

Another concern is the debate about community policing and reverting to the older foot patrol model of close interactions with the community. As discussed earlier in the text, there is always a concern for corruption and unfair influence when officers get too involved or too close to community groups. Are the community policing strategies placing officers in an ambiguous position and perhaps enhancing relationships and consequently influence with one group over another? This also leads to the discussion earlier about zero-tolerance policies and aggressive patrolling to clean up the streets, make community groups happy, and improve the quality of life. Can this desire to please and be successful lead to overly aggressive techniques and possibly cross the line to abuse? These concerns need to be continually considered and examined. A reassuring report is from New York City, one of the success stories regarding broken windows. The city saw the crime rate plunge—including murders, which decreased from 2,262 in 1990 to 629 in 1998—and concurrently, complaints against police and police shootings declined. In fact, police shootings reached their lowest level since the 1970s when the data was first recorded.[70]

An audit of the Houston Police Department by a consulting firm criticized the department's neighborhood-oriented policing (NOP) approach. The audit concluded that although "well-conceived," NOP faced a number of difficulties and had not produced any comprehensive improvements in police services. The report acknowledged that NOP has the potential to enhance the quality of police services without adding costs but claimed that the Houston program did not have tangible effects on citizens' security and quality of life. The report said that the program, which had been implemented at the expense of more proactive law enforcement functions, such as arresting criminals, had resulted in mediocre performance in response time to emergency calls for service.[71]

Some believe the empirical evidence for community policing's effectiveness in solving the crime problem is both limited and contradictory.[72] Other researchers admit there are a number of documented successes of community policing programs, but there is also an indication that community policing may displace crime. Indeed, several studies indicate there has been an increase in crime in the areas surrounding the community policing impact area.[73]

The debate continues to rage regarding community policing, sometimes even among officials of the same agency. Different departments may define community policing in different ways. They may label certain programs as community policing when they are just the traditional methods with a new name. A thorough commitment to community policing involves new structures and new responsibilities for the officers in engaging the community in problem solving rather than just using the rhetoric or titles.[74] To effectively use the community policing philosophy, departments need to tailor their responses to their community—it is not "one size fits all." To evaluate community policing initiatives correctly, the initiatives must be examined closely to separate true community policing from "pretenders."[75] In many agencies, police administrators have used specialization to create special units and call them community policing squads,

units, or officers. These officers typically are relieved of regular patrol duties to devote their time to "community policing" efforts. This is despite the general agreement of law enforcement leaders that community policing should be the responsibility of all personnel.[76] Although these units can be part of a community policing effort in a department, street officers will have different opportunities to engage in community policing and different options for those initiatives depending on what part of town they work in and what hours they work. To effectively evaluate community policing efforts, everyone needs to clearly understand what we are defining as community policing as well as what is defined as "success" and how it is measured. A concern for agencies implementing and using community policing is that it may necessitate the development of new hiring guidelines, evaluation guidelines, and promotional standards. Departments need to define what type of qualities they are looking for in officers so they can maximize their success in the community policing environment. This may seem like an overwhelming duty for agencies entrenched in traditional evaluation methods and possibly constrained by union or collective bargaining agreements.

Researchers who traveled to St. Petersburg, Florida, to observe changes occurring in police roles and police community relations after the implementation of community policing found that the citizens seemed satisfied with community policing. The researchers also found high levels of cooperation in everyday police-citizen contact and found that 85 percent of those interviewed were "very" or "somewhat" satisfied with neighborhood policing services. The department seems to be attaining the goal of high visibility because approximately one-third of those surveyed said they had seen the police in the previous 24 hours. Of more interest, the perception of police officers toward community policing had improved, although the researchers noted distinctions between community policing officers and road officers. Generally, community policing officers were more supportive of the importance of assisting citizens and enforcing minor laws than were the officers handling calls for service. An interesting finding was that, among all the police officers, a still rather high 25 percent said they have reason to distrust most citizens.[77]

Recently, the success of broken windows was challenged by Bernard Harcourt, a professor in the University of Chicago Law School. Harcourt and Jens Ludwig, an associate professor at Georgetown

University, reanalyzed Northwestern University Professor Wesley Skogan's *Disorder and Decline: Crime and the Spiral of Decay in American Neighborhoods,* originally presented in 1990. As Bratton and Kelling note, Skogan's original findings supported the link between disorder and serious crime, fortifying support for the broken windows theory.[78] Harcourt and Ludwig argue the "popular crime fighting strategy is, well, wrong," and it doesn't work in practice.[79] Harcourt states that the targeted areas chosen for the initiative were also the areas most affected by the crack cocaine epidemic and that when the epidemic ebbed so did the crime rate, which would have happened with or without the broken windows policing. He and Ludwig concluded, "In our opinion, focusing on minor misdemeanors is a diversion of valuable police funding and time from what really seems to help—targeted police patrols against violence, gang activity and gun crimes in the highest-crime 'hot spots' . . . it's not about being pro-cop or anti-cop. It's about using police officer time and limited resources intelligently."[80] William J. Bratton and George L. Kelling criticized Harcourt's analysis charging that he had eliminated two areas from the study that showed strong relationships between disorder and crime. Bratton was the New York City Police commissioner at the time and now heads the Los Angeles Police Department (LAPD) where he has employed similar strategies: in three years, crime has gone down 26 percent and homicides have decreased 25 percent.[81] Bratton stands firmly behind the broken windows strategy, as do many law enforcement leaders who are employing it.

An initial concern in the early stages of the COPS grants was whether departments would permanently retain the police officers hired through the grants and absorb the costs locally. In September 1997, it was reported that the first cycle of U.S. Justice Department grants, begun in 1994 and mentioned earlier in this chapter, were ending. This would require agencies throughout the nation to fund all of the new officers added since the 1994 Crime Bill without the help of the federal government, which had been funding 75 percent of the cost. It was reported that local officials might be tempted to scrap community policing programs or shift officers around to avoid retaining COPS hires.[82]

This fear seems to be unfounded. In mid 1999, after the first round of grants was expiring, 98 percent of respondents indicated they had kept the COPS-funded officers or quickly filled any vacancies that arose. In addition, 95 percent reported

that the officers were or would be part of the department's budget by the time grant funding ended.[83] This was a stipulation that the federal government required before granting the money to departments. The grant required the department to gradually take over funding for the officers in the three-year grant period and totally assume the cost at the end. Department leaders and government leaders had to sign off on that stipulation. Some were uncomfortable with doing that, and some departments are experiencing hurdles in this area. As an example of problems now being faced by departments, consider the example of Toledo, Ohio. The city was originally awarded $10 million to add 125 new officers to its police department but refused some of the money and hired fewer officers. According to its police chief,

> All of a sudden, they [the federal government] gave us 75 officers in one crack, for a total award of $5.6 million. The cost for one officer in Toledo, with benefits, is $150,000. The city has to match $75,000, and that $5.5 million bill has come out of the general fund. There's no way we can fund that.[84]

Toledo is not alone. According to the chief of the South Pasadena, California, Police Department, "Every police chief I've talked to is worried about how to keep the officers hired with federal money once the grant runs out."[85]

The biggest recent threat to community policing and, consequently, the biggest criticism of the initiatives that have taken place concern the current inability to keep police departments fully staffed and to keep the money flowing to these initiatives. Bratton spoke at a conference and declared that community policing had caused a downward trend in crime nationally in the 1990s, but that crime is beginning to rebound because less money and attention is being devoted to community policing since September 11, 2001. Many of the resources previously devoted to community policing have been siphoned to prevent terrorism. He believes local jurisdictions as well as states and the federal government need to reexamine this issue.[86] This isn't just affecting the big cities. Stamford, Connecticut, is cutting back on its community policing efforts because of a lack of funding and a lack of personnel. With lower numbers of officers, increased residents, and the loss of federal and state funding since 9/11, the chief can no longer afford to devote the resources to the more labor-intensive community efforts.[87] On many fronts, the debate continues.

Policing in the Sphere of Illegal Immigration

ADOLFO GONZALES

Dr. Adolfo Gonzales is the chief of police for the National City Police Department in California and an adjunct professor in Organizational Leadership for Chapman University College in San Diego. Dr. Gonzales earned his EdD from the University of San Diego School of Education in 1996. His research interests include evaluating police performance and organizations, leadership in a diverse community, community policing, police administrative reform, and policy review.

Immigrants, whether legal or illegal, are a defining part of our nation's past, present, and future. U.S. policymakers and the public often question how the new immigrant population will impact social service systems like the educational and health care systems.

Policies shape how we police the streets in National City, California. We are located in San Diego County, about seven miles north of the U.S.–Mexico international border. Though the city is only about nine square miles large, illegal immigration is something residents and officers must deal with on a daily basis. As we police our streets, we often see two things in terms of illegal immigration: (1) undocumented persons who are victims of crimes, and (2) undocumented people responsible for committing various crimes. Some proportion of our city's criminals and victims are in the United States illegally, but it is difficult to gauge the percentage of victims or criminals that are undocumented. Undocumented people are less likely to report crimes, so crime data on undocumented victimization rates likely underreport the true level of crimes against undocumented people. Similarly, the true number of undocumented criminals may be undervalued. To uphold our respect for individuals and to prevent the propensity to engage in racial profiling, NCPD's policy is to *not* collect data on the immigration status of victims or suspects. Most of our data is based on the individual voluntarily telling us their immigration status.

We, like all law enforcement agencies, are responsible for the enforcement of all laws and for the safety and protection of all persons. In National City, our officers will not detain undocumented persons for U.S.

Customs and Border Protection (USBP), if the persons are victims or witnesses of crime, unless they are needed as material witnesses. Additionally, our officers will not detain undocumented persons during family disturbance calls, while on minor traffic enforcement, and if the persons are seeking medical treatment.

Our officers have a duty to contact any person(s) when there is a "reasonable suspicion" to believe they are involved in criminal activity. Officers will arrest a person if the probable cause to arrest exists, regardless of what immigration status the person is perceived to hold. If the arrested individual is found to be in the country illegally, a "hold" will be placed on the person for U.S. Customs and Border Protection. This means that before the individual is released from jail, the U.S. Border Patrol is called and the person is turned over to them for deportation.

As officers in the field, we also see that federal policies often have very real impacts on the local level. Following Operation Gatekeeper, an effort by the United States Border Patrol in the 1990s to reduce the number of undocumented persons crossing into the United States, we saw an influx of people attempting to cross into the United States through the mountains and deserts. Attempting to cross through more dangerous terrain, many of these people never survived their journey. Operation Gatekeepers' efforts managed to curtail the flow of people over land, but we saw an increase of underground tunnels. These tunnels are believed to be used by major narcotic traffickers to smuggle drugs into the United States. Moreover, human traffickers also utilize these same tunnels.

In a post–September 11, 2001 era, controlling our borders and stopping the flow of undocumented persons is often touted as a critical strategy for homeland security and combating the war on terror. Since the September 11th terrorist attacks, the United States has tripled spending on border enforcement. Despite increased funding, illegal immigration doubled and an estimated 21 million undocumented immigrants are now in the United States . . . This just goes to show that even with new laws, programs, and funding, we can't always be sure that the outcome will be what we hoped for or expected. Sometimes solving one problem may incite another. As officers, we must always be prepared to adapt to shifts in crime and security trends.

Homeland Security and the Future of Community Policing

Since September 11, 2001, some have made increased efforts to get back to essential police services. Budget dollars are at a premium and "extra" programs may be viewed as nonessential. Some feel that by going back to more traditional law enforcement with more militaristic tactics is the only way to fight the war on terror.

In examining the events leading up to 9/11 and in an effort to prevent these types of informational gaps from happening in the future, community policing could fill a vital role. In an article posted on the COPS website, "Community Policing: Now More Than Ever," Rob Chapman and Matthew Scheider illustrate the strengths of community policing and how they would prove beneficial in the war on terror.

One of the primary goals would be the prevention of terrorist acts. Through partnerships with other agencies and the community, "hard" and "soft" targets can be identified, vulnerability assessed, and responses planned. Additionally, with established, positive, trusting relationships, members of the community will be more likely to come forward with good intelligence information allowing law enforcement to "connect the dots" before it is too late.[88]

If such an incident were to occur again, knowing the community and neighborhood would prove beneficial. Community leaders—possibly already CERT trained (as discussed in Chapter 11, "Police and the Community")—could be called to assist with response. Previous relationships and knowledge of the neighborhood would facilitate response. Police officers used to making decisions and not having to rely on superiors to make decisions would be an advantage in a crisis situation where events are unfolding, communication challenged, and innovative responses needed.[89]

Police agencies are joining with federal law enforcement and state and county agencies to integrate responses to significant events and working to train personnel from all areas of life to recognize and share appropriate information to facilitate "connecting the dots" in a timely basis. The assistant director of the FBI stated, "The FBI fully understands that our success in the fight against terrorism is directly related to the strength of our relationship with our state and local partners."[90] To facilitate this, the Department of Justice Office of Community Oriented Policing Services (COPS) and the Police Executive Research Forum (PERF) have produced a guide for law enforcement entitled "Protecting Your Community from Terrorism: Strategies for Local Law Enforcement," which addresses partnerships to promote homeland security.[91] As another way of recognizing efforts in this area, the International Association of Chiefs of Police (IACP) began giving Community Policing awards in the Homeland Security category in 2004. In 2005, Tempe, Arizona, was recognized for its efforts after partnering with community members representing business, education, faith, police, elected officials, utility companies, Neighborhood Watch, emergency services, health care, and the local university to form the Citizen Corps Council. The council is the bridge connecting all the groups and created the Assistance in Disaster (AID) program to organize and mobilize a community response in the event of a natural disaster or terrorist attack. They pre-screened and trained volunteers in evacuations, searches, traffic control, evidence preservation, and missing persons.[92] Departments take this need seriously and are devoting personnel, time, and money to this endeavor. The Massachusetts Law Enforcement Technology and Training Support Center is researching the integration of the homeland security mission into community policing. This is funded through a COPS grant and brought together first responders to develop a homeland security plan. They have developed training programs, addressed the approachability issue, and explored outreach efforts and communication issues. They came up with many community information sources who can be trained in recognizing and reporting suspicious actions to the appropriate agency. These sources include Neighborhood Watch, hotel personnel, real estate agents, storage facility employees, transportation center and tourist attraction employees, custodians, public works and sanitation workers, meter readers, and vehicle rental employees among others.[93] Homeland security efforts can be greatly enhanced by training these community members to know what constitutes possibly threatening behavior and what to do with this information.

Community policing is an excellent vehicle for addressing homeland security and the value of the partnership and the trusting relationship with the community will prove to be invaluable as the entire community—in the largest sense—contributes to keeping our homeland safe.

Though the debate continues, research continues to add to the literature, and police administrators are looking to using the community policing philosophy to address new issues that arise. Though more time may be needed to examine the initiatives more closely and over longer periods, some preliminary research has indicated success. The state of California has conducted statewide research in an effort to answer the big question, "Does community policing work at reducing the crime rate?" The results indicate that "broken windows" law enforcement strategies can be effective in reducing more serious crime and agencies that are exploring the issue can be reassured that these strategies are likely to work.[94]

Summary

- Community policing and problem-solving policing have been practiced for longer than one decade, and some say it has been tremendously popular and successful.

- Others have disagreed, so the debate continues, which is good for policing.

- The three corporate strategies for modern policing include strategic policing, community policing, and problem-solving policing.

- Problem-oriented or problem-solving policing involves the process of scanning, analysis, response, and assessment (SARA).

- The problem-oriented policing method can be used for almost any type of problem an agency faces to determine what the underlying causes of problems are and how best to address them.

- There are many ways to implement community policing; it is flexible and can be implemented to address the particular problems that an agency faces.

- The resident officer program is one particular form of community policing that many cities are using.

- The chapter also discussed the federal government and its current role in community policing, including the 1994 Crime Bill, the Office of Community Oriented Policing Services, and the Community Policing Consortium.

- We presented some empirical and anecdotal evidence of the benefits of COPS but also showed how some scholars and practitioners do not agree with community policing strategies.

- The evolving nature of community policing as it is used to address new issues was examined.

- The future of community policing in particular in the areas of terrorism was discussed as well as the role that community policing can play in homeland security.

Learning Check

1. Define community policing and problem-solving policing and give three actual examples of each.

2. Discuss the importance of the research of scholars James Q. Wilson and George L. Kelling to the concept of community policing.

3. What does the broken windows model say?

4. Discuss the medical model as it pertains to law enforcement and the crime fight.

5. How is the community policing philosophy best exemplified in a police department?

6. Discuss the contributions of Herman Goldstein to the concept of problem-solving policing.

7. How does problem-oriented policing differ from traditional methods of policing?

8. Define a resident officer program and give three actual examples.

9. Discuss some of the programs administered and supported by the Office of Community Oriented Policing Services (COPS) of the U.S. Department of Justice.

10. Discuss some of the ways community policing is being or can be used in the fight against terror.

Key Terms

broken windows model Theory that unrepaired broken windows indicate to others that members of the community do not care about the quality of life in the neighborhood and are unlikely to get involved; consequently, disorder and crime will thrive.

community policing Philosophy of empowering citizens and developing a partnership between the police and the community to work together to solve problems.

Community Policing Consortium An organization reporting on and encouraging the latest community policing activities that comprises the International Association of Chiefs of Police (IACP), the National Organization of Black Law Enforcement Executives (NOBLE), the National Sheriffs' Association (NSA), the Police Executive Research Forum (PERF), and the Police Foundation.

Crime Bill of 1994 The Violent Crime Control and Law Enforcement Act, signed by President Clinton in 1994.

James Q. Wilson and George L. Kelling The authors of the seminal article in 1982 in the *Atlantic Monthly* entitled "Broken Windows: The Police and Neighborhood Safety," which came to be called the broken windows model of policing.

Herman Goldstein First mentioned the concept of "problem-solving or problem-oriented policing" in 1979.

Officer Next Door (OND) program A plan initiated in 1997 allowing police officers to receive 50 percent discounts and low-cost loans to purchase homes in "distressed" areas nationwide. It is under the umbrella Good Neighbor Next Door program, which also includes teachers, firefighters, and emergency medical technicians.

Office of Community Oriented Policing Services (COPS) Established to administer the grant money provided by the 1994 Crime Bill and to promote community policing.

problem-solving policing Analyzing crime issues to determine the underlying problems and addressing those underlying problems.

Regional Community Policing Institutes (RCPIs) Part of the COPS program, the 30 RCPIs provide regional training and technical assistance to law enforcement around the country regarding community policing.

resident officer programs Programs through which officers live in particular communities to strengthen relations between the police and the community.

Robert C. Trojanowicz Founded the National Center for Community Policing in East Lansing, Michigan.

strategic policing Involves a continued reliance on traditional policing operations.

Police and the Law

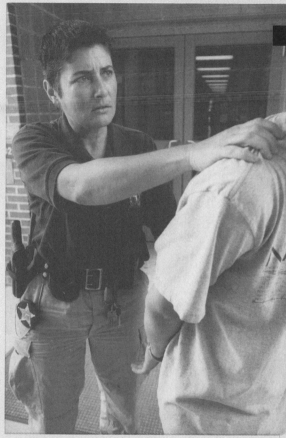

© Joel Gordon

GOALS

- To acquaint you with the amount and type of crime in the United States, as well as the number and type of arrests made by the police
- To apprise you of the role of the Bill of Rights and the U.S. Supreme Court in regulating the actions of the police
- To explain the role of the police in making arrests, searching people and places, and stopping automobiles
- To make you aware, through the exploration of case law, of the changing philosophy of the U.S. Supreme Court in areas regarding arrests, search and seizure, custodial interrogation, and identification procedures
- To make you aware, through the exploration of case law, of current standard police procedures in arrest, search and seizure, custodial interrogation, and identification procedures

Introduction

When people think about the police, they generally think about the power of the police to arrest someone, about the power of the police to issue a citation for driving violations, or about some other enforcement activity. People think of the police in terms of the law. As this text has shown, the police do much more than enforce the law. Although the police role is not limited to law enforcement, that is definitely a major part of the police role.

This chapter will discuss the amount and types of crime in the United States, along with the amount and types of arrests made by the police. It will also discuss the U.S. Constitution and the Bill of Rights, focusing on the relationship between the police and the Bill of Rights as interpreted by the U.S. Supreme Court over the years. We will explore significant areas of police power, including the power to arrest people, to stop people and inquire about their conduct, to search people and places and seize property, and to question people about their participation in a crime. Landmark Supreme Court cases will be used to show how the police have altered their procedures to comply with the provisions of the U.S. Constitution. The chapter provides the fact pattern behind some of the cases. A *fact pattern* is the events in a criminal case that led to the arrest, as well as the facts of the investigation and arrest. The fact pattern is considered by the courts in adjudicating a case. Reading these fact patterns will help you see that law is not abstract principles but, rather, the result of personal and dynamic events.

This chapter is perhaps the most important one in this text. The role of the police is a very special one in our society. The police enforce the law. When enforcing the law, they sometimes have to arrest people. By arresting people, the police take away what Americans value most highly—their freedom and their liberty. The police must know the law and must apply it correctly.

Crime in the United States

Crime is part of life in the United States. We read about crime in our newspapers, and often details of the crimes are the lead stories on our television news broadcasts. The following sections will discuss how we measure crime in the United States, how much crime occurs, and how many arrests are made.

How Do We Measure Crime?

Two major methods are used to measure crime in the United States. They are (1) the *Uniform Crime Reports* and (2) the National Crime Victimization Survey.

Uniform Crime Reports The **Uniform Crime Reports** (UCR) are collected and published by the FBI based on reports of crimes made to the police across the United States. The FBI publishes a yearly report entitled *Crime in the United States* based on all reports made to the police for the year and forwarded to the FBI. The UCR has four major sections, the Crime Index, Crime Index Offenses Cleared, Persons Arrested, and Law Enforcement Personnel.

The FBI's *Crime Index* consists of data regarding the major Index crimes (murder and nonnegligent manslaughter, forcible rape, robbery, aggravated assault, burglary, larceny-theft, motor vehicle theft, and arson). The Crime Index section of the yearly UCR generally comprises several hundred pages of tables and graphs regarding the Index crimes. Included on these pages are five-year analyses of each of the crimes using numerous variables, such as the relationship between perpetrator and victim, weapons used, age, race, and gender; crime trends; and crime rates for all offenses reported to the police for the previous year for each of the reporting cities, towns, universities/colleges, and suburban and rural counties.

The *Crime Index Offenses Cleared* section lists the clearance rates (rates of crimes solved by arrest) for the Index crimes according to certain variables, such as population group and geographic region of the country.

The section on *Persons Arrested* lists all arrests in the United States for the Index crimes and other crimes according to certain variables. These include geographic area, age, race, and gender.

The *Law Enforcement Personnel* section lists the number of all uniformed and civilian law enforcement employees for each reporting town, city, and county.

Before 1972, the UCR was the only nationwide measure of crime in the United States. Scholars, however, became skeptical of the crime report data in the UCR because it was based solely on reports made to the police and did not recognize the fact that many crimes are not reported to the police. To get a truer account of crime, the National Crime Victimization Survey was started.

National Crime Victimization Survey The **National Crime Victimization Survey (NCVS)** is prepared by the National Institute of Justice (NIJ), the research arm of the U.S. Department of Justice. The NCVS, as the name implies, is a survey of a random sample of U.S. households, asking them if a crime was committed against anyone in the household during the prior six months. It also asks them certain questions about the incident. Data from the NCVS is published by the NIJ yearly as *Criminal Victimization in the United States.* The NIJ also issues periodic reports regarding trends in particular crimes.

How Much Crime Occurs in the United States?

Crime information for the latest year available for each of the Index crimes is shown in Table 13.1. The data in the UCR are easy to read. For example, when we look at the figures for murder we see that there were 16,692 murders, which amounts to 5.6 murders for every 100,000 Americans. Table 13.2, the UCR's crime clock, is a graphic representation of the relative frequency of criminal occurrences.

The other crime measure, the NCVS, reports the crime data shown in Table 13.3. Notice that the number of incidents for each crime is quite different in the two reports. The UCR data only include incidents actually reported to the police, whereas the NCVS data are based on results of interviews with people, many of whom did not report their criminal victimization to the police. Note that the figures for motor vehicle theft (auto larceny) are closest in both reports. This is because most people in the United States are covered by automobile insurance

TABLE 13.1 Uniform Crime Reports Data, 2005

Index Crime	Amount	Crime rate per 100,000 residents
Violent Crime	1,390,695	469.1
Murder and nonnegligent manslaughter	16,692	5.6
Forcible rape	93,934	31.7
Robbery	417,122	140.7
Aggravated assault	862,947	291.1
Property Crime	10,166,159	3,429.7
Burglary	2,154,126	726.7
Larceny/Theft	6,776,807	2,286.3
Motor vehicle theft	1,235,226	416.7

NOTE: Regarding arson: Because of the limited reporting of arson offenses by law enforcement agencies, the UCR does not estimate for arson; therefore arson offenses are not included in this table.
SOURCE: Federal Bureau of Investigation, *Uniform Crime Reports, 2005,* Table 1. Retrieved September 19, 2006, from: http://www.fbi.gov.

TABLE 13.2 UCR Crime Clock, 2005

Every 22.7 seconds: One violent crime
Every 31.5 minutes: One murder
Every 5.6 minutes: One forcible rape
Every 1.3 minutes: One robbery
Every 36.5 seconds: One aggravated assault
Every 3.1 seconds: One property crime
Every 14.6 seconds: One burglary
Every 4.7 seconds: One larceny/theft
Every 25.5 seconds: One motor vehicle theft

NOTE: The Crime Clock should be viewed with care. It is the most aggregate representation of the annual reported crime experience and shows a relative frequency of occurrence; it should not be taken to imply a regularity in the commission of crime. The Crime Clock portrays an actual ratio of crime to fixed time intervals.
SOURCE: Federal Bureau of Investigation, *Uniform Crime Reports, 2005,* Crime Clock. Retrieved September 19, 2006, from http://www.fbi.gov.

TABLE 13.3 Crime Victimization, Numbers and Rates, 2005

Type of Crime	Number of Victimizations	Victimization rate (per 1,000 persons age 12 or older or per 1,000 households)
All Crimes	23,440,720	—
Violent Crimes	5,173,720	21.2
Rape/sexual assault	191,670	0.8
Robbery	624,850	2.6
Assault	4,357,190	17.8
Aggravated	1,052,260	04.3
Simple	3,304,930	213.5
Personal Theft	227,070	0.9
Property Crimes	18,039,930	154.0
Household burglary	3,456,220	29.5
Motor vehicle theft	978,120	8.4
Theft	13,605,590	116.2

NOTE: The NCVS is based on interviews with victims and therefore cannot measure murder.
SOURCE: Shannan M. Catalano, *Criminal Victimization, 2005*. (Washington, D.C.: National Institute of Justice, 2006), p. 2.

and thus report an automobile theft to the police so they can make a claim with their insurance company.

Arrests in the United States

For the latest reporting year, the U.S. police made about 14 million arrests for all criminal infractions except traffic violations. About 2.1 million of these arrests were for the FBI's Index or Part 1 crimes. Of these crimes, about 604,000 were for violent crimes (murder, forcible rape, robbery, and aggravated assault) and about 1.61 million were for property crimes (burglary, larceny/theft, motor vehicle theft, and arson).

The remaining 12.28 million arrests were for various other offenses. The major categories of these arrests and their approximate totals follow: misdemeanor assaults, 1.3 million; drug abuse violations, 1.85 million; driving under the influence, 1.37 million; liquor-related, disorderly conduct, vagrancy, and loitering, 2 million; and other offenses 3.9 million.[1]

The Police and the U.S. Constitution

The United States is a nation governed by law. The primary law regulating life in the United States is the U.S. Constitution, including its many amendments. The following sections will discuss the first ten amendments to the Constitution (the Bill of Rights), the Fourteenth Amendment, the role of the U.S. Supreme Court in regulating the police, and the exclusionary rule and its impact on the police.

It must be remembered that the U.S. Constitution is a continuing, dynamic document constantly being reviewed by the U.S. Supreme Court. This chapter discusses hundreds of Supreme Court decisions, "landmark cases," which have affected the police and the entire criminal justice system, as well as our society. As this judicial review process of the Court is constantly reinterpreting the Constitution and constantly changing the rules that govern police behavior, all officers must constantly review their own organization's rules and directives with the realization that the law is always changing.

The Bill of Rights and the Fourteenth Amendment

The U.S. criminal justice system is based on the Bill of Rights, the first ten amendments to the U.S. Constitution. Five of the first ten amendments specifically address freedoms or rights that people possess when involved with the criminal justice system. See Table 13.4 for the amendments that specifically affect the U.S. criminal justice system.

To understand the U.S. system of criminal justice, we must go back to the birth of the United States. The early colonists came to escape persecution by the English king and to seek freedom. The colonists, however, continued to be persecuted and to be denied freedom. They rebelled, wrote the Declaration of Independence, fought for independence from England, and were able to defeat the British troops. As newly freed people, the former colonists wrote the U.S. Constitution to govern themselves. They then wrote the first ten amendments to the Constitution, which form the basis of our criminal justice system—the rights and freedoms we possess that can be used against government tyranny.

TABLE 13.4 U.S. Constitution: Amendments Governing the U.S. Criminal Justice System

First Amendment

RAPPS

Congress shall make no law respecting an establishment of religion, or prohibiting the free exercise thereof; or abridging the freedom of speech, or of the press; or the right of the people peaceably to assemble, and to petition the government for a redress of grievances.

Fourth Amendment

The right of the people to be secure in their persons, houses, papers, and effects, against unreasonable searches and seizures, shall not be violated, and no warrants shall issue, but upon probable cause, supported by oath or affirmation, and particularly describing the place to be searched, and the persons or things to be seized.

Fifth Amendment

No person shall be held to answer for a capital, or otherwise infamous crime, unless on a presentment or indictment of a grand jury, except in cases arising in the land or naval forces, or in the militia, when in actual service in time of war or public danger; nor shall any person be subject for the same offense to be twice put in jeopardy of life or limb; nor shall be compelled in any criminal case to be a witness, against himself, nor be deprived of life, liberty, or property, without due process of law; nor shall private property be taken for public use, without just compensation.

Sixth Amendment

In all criminal prosecutions, the accused shall enjoy the right to a speedy and public trial, by an impartial jury of the State and district wherein the crime shall have been committed, which district shall have been previously ascertained by law, and to be informed of the nature and cause of the accusation; to be confronted with the witnesses against him; to have compulsory process for obtaining witnesses in his favor, and to have the assistance of counsel for his defense.

Eighth Amendment

Excessive bail shall not be required, nor excessive fines imposed, nor cruel and unusual punishments inflicted.

Fourteenth Amendment (Section 1)

All persons born or naturalized in the United States and subject to the jurisdiction thereof, are citizens of the United States and of the State wherein they reside. No State shall make or enforce any law which shall abridge the privileges or immunities of citizens of the United States; nor shall any State deprive any person of life, liberty, or property, without due process of law; nor deny to any person within its jurisdiction the equal protection of the laws.

The Fourteenth Amendment also has an effect on the U.S. criminal justice system. The Supreme Court, over the years, has extended the Bill of Rights to the states through the due process clause of the Fourteenth Amendment. The due process clause is that section of the Fourteenth Amendment that protects all citizens of the United States against any state depriving them of life, liberty, or property except through the proper legal processes guaranteed by the U.S. Constitution. The section has been the vehicle through which much of the Bill of Rights has been interpreted to apply to state courts as well as federal courts.

The Role of the Supreme Court in Regulating the Police

The U.S. Supreme Court, through its policy of **judicial review,** has made a significant impact on the way the police do their job. As early as 1914, in *Weeks v. United States,* the Court influenced the police by regulating how officers should conduct their searches and seizures.[2] In 1936, in *Brown v. Mississippi,* the Court began to affect the police by ruling certain methods of police interrogation unconstitutional.[3]

Most Supreme Court cases regarding criminal justice try to strike a balance between the rights of the individual and the rights of society. But what do we mean by the rights of the individual and the rights of society? A simple example, which could have occurred today in your classroom, might explain it. You and your fellow students want a safe classroom. You do not want a student walking into class with an illegal gun that could be used to shoot you (rights of society). However, which of you would like the police to be at the classroom door each morning searching you for illegal guns without just cause (rights of the individual)?

The Supreme Court has the difficult task of bringing balance between these two often-conflicting goals. There is an inherent inconsistency between protecting the rights of the individual and the rights of society. To have unlimited individual rights risks the chance of limiting the rights of society to be safe from crime. To have unlimited rights of society to be safe from crime risks giving up individual rights. It falls upon the Supreme Court to balance these two precious rights.

ON THE JOB

Law is History—Know Your Facts

Many landmark U.S. Supreme Court cases are described in this chapter. You should know the facts of these cases.

The law is not mere theory or the application of reason to problems. U.S. law is as much history as it is reason and logic. To paraphrase Justice Oliver Wendell Holmes, Jr., "There is more law in a page of history than in a volume of logic." This means that the law is dynamic. It changes over time, and it changes because it is responsive to the thoughts, feelings, and needs of society.

The law—specifically, case law—is based on real experiences of real people. (Case law is the body of law that results from court interpretations of statutory law—law written by the legislative or executive branch of the government—or from court decisions).

In discussions of case law, one often hears the names Dollree Mapp, Danny Escobedo, Ernesto Miranda, and even Donald (or Don) King, Mike Tyson's former boxing promoter. Sure, they were people who were often on the "other side of the law," but as Justice Felix Frankfurter once observed, "The safeguards of liberty have frequently been forged in controversies involving not very nice people." (Fred W. Friendly and Martha J. H. Elliot, *The Constitution: That Delicate Balance* [New York: McGraw-Hill, 1984], p. vii). Sure, Dollree Mapp was a small-time gambler and was hiding a man wanted by the police, Danny Escobedo was a murderer, and Ernesto Miranda was a rapist. But they influenced legal history, and they did it by exercising their rights under the U.S. Constitution—those very rights that also apply to all of us.

As you further your studies in criminal law, or if you enter law school, a text or a professor might refer to a "*Terry* stop" or say, "as the Court ruled in *Chimel*," and assume that you know these concepts. And you should know these concepts.

—*John S. Dempsey*

In police matters, the Supreme Court hears cases, on appeal, from people who have been the subject of police actions, including arrest, search and seizure, and custodial interrogation. The justices then decide whether the police action violated the person's constitutional rights. In most cases, they do this by interpreting one of the amendments to the Constitution. Supreme Court decisions can bring about changes in police procedures. Certain significant cases, such as *Mapp v. Ohio* and *Miranda v. Arizona*, are known as landmark cases.[4] The major method used by the Supreme Court to ensure that the police do not violate people's constitutional rights is the use of the exclusionary rule.

The Exclusionary Rule

The **exclusionary rule** is not a part of the U.S. Constitution. It is an interpretation of the Fourteenth Amendment by the Supreme Court that holds that evidence seized in violation of the U.S. Constitution cannot be used in court against a defendant. Such evidence is suppressed (not allowed to be used in court).

The exclusionary rule evolved in U.S. law through a series of Supreme Court cases. Since at least 1914, the Supreme Court has been concerned with the use of illegal means by the police to seize evidence in violation of the Constitution, and then using that evidence to convict a defendant in court. Because the Bill of Rights, when written, only applied to agents of the federal government—not those of local governments—the Court first applied the exclusionary rule only to federal courts and federal law enforcement officers. The Court continually warned state courts and law enforcement agencies that they must amend their procedures to comply with the U.S. Constitution or risk the exclusionary rule's being imposed on them as well. By 1961, the Supreme Court, noting that states had not amended their procedures to

You Are There!

Weeks v. United States (1914)

Freemont Weeks was arrested at his place of business and charged with using the U.S. mail to conduct an illegal lottery. The police then searched Week's house and turned over articles and papers to a U.S. marshal. The marshal, then, together with the police, searched Weeks's room and confiscated other documents and letters. All the searches were conducted without a warrant.

Weeks was convicted based on the evidence seized from his home. On appeal to the U.S. Supreme Court, his conviction was overturned, and the exclusionary rule was established.

SOURCE: Based on *Weeks v. United States*, 232 U.S. 383 (1914).

conform to the Constitution, applied the exclusionary rule to state courts and law enforcement agencies, as well as federal ones. The following four landmark cases show how the exclusionary rule developed in this country.

Weeks v. United States *Weeks v. United States* (1914) was the first case in which the exclusionary rule was used.[5] It involved federal law enforcement personnel entering an arrested person's home and seizing evidence without a warrant. The evidence was used against him in court, and he was convicted based on it.

On appeal, the Supreme Court overturned the man's conviction and established the exclusionary rule. Expressing the opinion of the Court, Justice William R. Day wrote the following:

If letters and private documents can thus be seized and held and used in evidence against a citizen accused of an offense, the protection of the Fourth Amendment, declaring his right to be secure against such searches and seizures, is of no value, and so far as those thus placed are concerned, might as well be stricken from the Constitution. The efforts of the courts and their officials to bring the guilty to punishment, praiseworthy as they are, are not to be aided by the sacrifice of these great principles established by years of

endeavor and suffering which have resulted in their embodiment in the fundamental law of the law.

The exclusionary rule provided that any evidence seized in violation of the Fourth Amendment could not be used against a defendant in a criminal case. The exclusionary rule, as enunciated in the *Weeks* case, applied only to evidence seized in an unconstitutional search and seizure by a federal agent and used in a federal court. It did not apply to state courts.

The exclusionary rule gave rise to another form of police misconduct that has been called the **silver platter doctrine**. Under the silver platter doctrine, federal prosecutors were allowed to use "*tainted*" evidence obtained by state police officers seized through unreasonable searches and seizures, provided that the evidence was obtained without federal participation and was turned over to federal officers. In *Silverthorne Lumber Co. v. United States* (1920) the Court ruled that this *tainted* evidence is essentially the *fruit of the poisoned tree* and is illegal to use in court.[6] In its colorful language, the Court compared the illegal search to be the "poisoned tree" and any evidence resulting from the illegal search as the "fruit of the poisoned tree."

Wolf v. Colorado Another case that involved the exclusionary rule was *Wolf v. Colorado* in 1949.[7] Mr. Wolf was suspected of being an illegal abortionist. A deputy sheriff seized his appointment book without a warrant and interrogated people whose names appeared in the book. Based on the evidence from these patients, Wolf was arrested, charged with committing illegal abortions, and convicted in court.

On appeal, the Supreme Court issued what could be seen as a rather strange decision. It ruled that although the Fourth Amendment did bar the admissibility of illegally seized evidence, it would not impose federal standards (the exclusionary rule) on state courts. The Court directed that the states create stronger state rules that would prevent illegally obtained evidence from being admitted into state courts. At the time of the *Wolf* decision, 31 states had rejected the exclusionary rule, and the Court had accepted this, respecting states' rights. By 1961, when *Mapp v. Ohio* reached the Supreme Court, many states had accepted the exclusionary rule.

You Are There!

Rochin v. California (1952)

On July 1, 1949, based on information received that Mr. Rochin was selling narcotics, three Los Angeles County deputy sheriffs entered Rochin's house without a warrant and forced open the door to his apartment within the house. When the police entered Rochin's bedroom, they saw two capsules on his bedside table and asked him what they were. Rochin picked up the capsules and swallowed them. A struggle ensued between Rochin and the police, and the police attempted to open Rochin's mouth to get to the capsules. Failing to do this, they handcuffed him and forcibly took him to a hospital. At the hospital, under the direction of one of the police officers, a doctor forced an emetic solution through a tube into Rochin's stomach against his will. The stomach pumping caused Rochin to vomit. In the vomited matter were found two capsules, which proved to be morphine.

Source: Based on *Rochin v. California*, 342 U.S. 165 (1952).

In *Wolf,* Justice Felix Frankfurter, speaking for the Court, wrote, "We hold, therefore, that in a prosecution in a State Court for a State crime the Fourteenth Amendment does not forbid the admission of evidence obtained by an unreasonable search and seizure."

Rochin v. California In *Rochin v. California* (1952), another landmark case in the development of the exclusionary rule, the police entered Mr. Rochin's home without a warrant and, upon seeing him place what they believed to be narcotics into his mouth, forcefully attempted to extract the narcotics from him.[8] Failing this, they brought Rochin to a hospital, where his stomach was pumped. The stomach pumping produced two capsules as evidence of illegal drugs. Rochin was convicted in court and sentenced to 60 days' imprisonment. The chief evidence against him was the two capsules.

The Supreme Court overturned Rochin's conviction, considering the forcible seizure of evidence as a violation of the Fourteenth Amendment's due process clause. Speaking for the Court, Justice Felix Frankfurter wrote,

This is conduct that shocks the conscience. Illegally breaking into the privacy of Rochin, the struggle to open his mouth and remove what was there, the forcible extraction of his stomach's contents—this course of proceedings by agents of government to obtain evidence is bound to offend even hardened sensibilities. They are methods too close to the rack and screw to permit of constitutional differentiation.

In the *Rochin* case, the Court did not make the exclusionary rule applicable in all state cases, but only in those cases of extremely serious police misconduct—misconduct that, in Justice Frankfurter's words, shocks the conscience. The Court again urged the states to enact laws prohibiting the use of illegally seized evidence in state courts and threatened that if the states did not enact those laws, the Court might impose the exclusionary rule upon the states.

Mapp v. Ohio *Mapp v. Ohio* (1961) was the vehicle the Supreme Court used for applying the exclusionary rule to state courts.[9] The case involved the warrantless entry of police into a woman's home to search for a man in connection with a bombing. While in her home, the police searched it and found "obscene materials," for which she was arrested and ultimately convicted in court.

Speaking for the Supreme Court, Justice Tom C. Clark wrote the following:

The ignoble shortcut to conviction left open to the State tends to destroy the entire system of constitutional restraints on which the liberties of the people rest. Having once recognized that the right to privacy embodied in the Fourth Amendment is enforceable against the States, and that the right to be secure against rude invasions of privacy by state officers is, therefore constitutional in origin, we can no longer permit that right to remain an empty promise. Because it is enforceable in the same manner and to like effect as other basic rights secured by the Due Process Clause, we can no longer permit it to be revocable at the whim of the police officer who, in the name of law enforcement itself,

You Are There!

Mapp v. Ohio (1961)

On May 23, 1957, three Cleveland police officers went to the home of Dollree ("Dolly") Mapp to search for a man named Virgil Ogletree, who was wanted in connection with a bombing at the home of Donald King. (Donald King was the well-known boxing promoter who promoted former heavyweight champion Mike Tyson, among other fighters.) The police knocked at the door and demanded entry. Mapp telephoned her lawyer and, on his advice, refused to allow the police to enter without a warrant.

Three hours later, the police again arrived with additional officers. The police then forced their way into the house. At this point, Mapp's lawyer arrived but was not allowed to see his client or to enter the house. As the police were rushing up the stairs to Mapp's second-floor apartment, Mapp was halfway down the stairs, rushing the police and demanding to see the warrant. In response to Mapp's demand, one of the officers held up a piece of paper purported to be a warrant. Mapp grabbed the piece of paper and stuffed it down the front of her clothing. A struggle ensued, during which the officers retrieved the piece of paper and then handcuffed Mapp because she was acting "belligerent." The officers then forcibly took her to her bedroom, where they searched a dresser, a chest of drawers, a closet, and some suitcases. They also looked through a photo album and some of Mapp's personal papers. The police also searched the living room, dining area, kitchen, and Mapp's daughter's bedroom. They then went to the basement and searched it and a trunk located there. During the search, the police found an unspecified amount of pornographic literature.

Mapp was charged with possession of "lewd and lascivious books, pictures and photographs" and subsequently convicted in court for possessing obscene materials. The warrant was never produced in court.

On appeal, the Supreme Court reversed Mapp's conviction based on the police's violation of the Fourth Amendment. It then extended the exclusionary rule to all state courts and law enforcement personnel.

Note: Do you know what happened to Dollree Mapp after this case?

In 1970, Dollree Mapp was arrested by New York City police for the possession of drugs. Suspecting that Mapp was dealing in stolen property, the police obtained a search warrant. While executing it, they found 50,000 envelopes of heroin and stolen property valued at over $100,000. Mapp was convicted and sentenced to a term of 20 years to life. On New Year's Eve in 1980, the New York governor commuted her sentence.

SOURCE: Based on *Mapp v. Ohio*, 367 U.S. 643 (1961); James A. Inciardi, *Criminal Justice*, 3rd ed. (Orlando, Fla.: Harcourt Brace Jovanovich, 1990), p. 280.

TABLE 13.5   **Landmark U.S. Supreme Court Decisions: Exclusionary Rule in Police Search and Seizure Cases**

Case	Decision
Weeks v. United States (1914)	Exclusionary rule applies to federal law enforcement agents
Rochin v. California (1952)	Exclusionary rule applies in shocking cases
Mapp v. Ohio (1961)	Exclusionary rule applies to all law enforcement agents

---

chooses to suspend its enjoyment. Our decision, founded on reason and truth, gives to the individual no more than that which the Constitution guarantees him, to the police officer no less than that to which honest law enforcement is entitled, and to the courts, the judicial integrity so necessary in the true administration of justice.

See Table 13.5 for a list of landmark cases regarding the exclusionary rule in search and seizure cases.

ON THE JOB

Crime and the Community

The law and enforcing the law are not always cut and dried. Politics and community values and priorities will influence what police officers do in their jurisdiction. They are two of the factors that influence officer discretion.

I remember that, when I was a detective, we had a robbery go down in our business district. It was a time of very high crime rates; the public was fed up with "bad guys," and they wanted them arrested and punished. Citizens wanted to feel safe in their community and be able to walk the streets without fear of being robbed or of going home and finding their house broken into.

This robbery, in fact, was similar to many we'd been having throughout the city. There was no weapon involved—just physical force. Two young men walked into a jewelry store in a crowded strip mall. It was around 1 PM on a beautiful day in the middle of December, the height of both the tourist season and the busy holiday shopping season. These two young men asked to look at some gold chains and were shown several by the employees. Leery because they had been victimized on several prior occasions by "snatchers," the employees showed only a couple at a time and didn't stray far from the counter.

After a few minutes of looking at chains and discussing pros and cons, the two "customers" grabbed several and ran out the door. The owner pulled a gun and told them to stop. They did not. They ran out the door, and the owner followed. He let off some rounds and hit one of the subjects in the butt as he exited the store. The owner continued running after the other subject and fired off two more rounds but missed him. Shoppers were diving for cover, and the two rounds lodged in the wall of an adjacent store (the strip mall was L-shaped, with several stores perpendicular to the jewelry store).

When I got to the scene, the injured offender was still there. Though he wasn't seriously injured, he was transported to the hospital where the bullet was removed, and he was released. The second subject was apprehended not far from the scene. It turned out these two subjects were juveniles—big juveniles (about 6') but only 16 years old. They were charged with their crime and sent to the detention center. I wanted to charge the store owner with firing his weapon, because it was not a case of self-defense and there was a significant potential for harming innocent bystanders. I consulted with the state attorney's office, and the ultimate decision was that we would present the case to a grand jury. The state attorney recognized the political nature of this case (as did I) in this time of soaring crime rates and citizens' anger and impatience with "bad guys." He didn't think it would be a good move politically to charge the owner outright but rather to let a grand jury of 21 citizens make the decision.

We took the case to the grand jury; after listening to the testimony, they decided not to charge the owner. With many of the jurors having been crime victims or knowing crime victims, they could relate to the frustration of the business owner. They felt he was justified in doing what he did because he had been victimized so many times and was just trying to protect his business and livelihood. I'm just glad no one got hurt in this reckless action.

—*Linda S. Forst*

Impact of the Exclusionary Rule on the Police

Many police officers and citizens feel that the exclusionary rule is unfair—that it is procriminal and antipolice. They feel that the rule allows hard-ened criminals the chance to escape justice and be released "on a technicality." Since the *Mapp* and *Miranda* decisions, many have claimed that the Supreme Court has "handcuffed" the police and that the police no longer have the tools to fight crime. (The *Miranda* case will be discussed later in this chapter). Academic studies of the effect of the exclusionary rule have not confirmed these fears. One study revealed that the exclusionary rule is overwhelmingly used with drug offenses, rather than violent crimes, and that the rule was responsible for evidence being suppressed in less than 1 percent of all criminal cases in the study.[10] Another study—a review of 7,500 felony cases in nine counties in three states—found that only .6 percent were dismissed because of the exclusionary rule.[11]

The remainder of this chapter will deal with constitutional limitations on the police in the areas of arrest, search and seizure, custodial interrogation, and identification procedures.

The Police and Arrest

The police authority to **arrest** is restricted by the Fifth Amendment, which forbids depriving citizens of life, liberty, or property without due processes of law. An arrest is also controlled by the Fourth Amendment's restrictions on searches and seizures because an arrest is the ultimate seizure—the seizure of one's body. A state's criminal procedure law defines an arrest and directs who can make an arrest, for what offenses, and when. Most states define an arrest as "the taking of a person into custody, in the manner authorized by law for the purpose of presenting that person before a magistrate to answer for the commission of a crime."

In 2001, in *Atwater v. City of Lago Vista*, the Supreme Court ruled that custodial arrests are reasonable seizures under the Fourth Amendment regardless of the possible punishment for the crime that resulted in the arrest.[12] In this case, police in Lago Vista, Texas, arrested Gail Atwater for driving her vehicle with her two children, ages 3 and 5, in the front seat, without seat belts, which is a misdemeanor in Texas punishable by a maximum fine of $50. (Neither Atwater nor the two children were wearing seat belts.) Texas law permits police to make warrantless arrests for **misdemeanors.** Atwater was handcuffed, transported to the police station for booking, and placed in a cell for an hour before being seen by a magistrate. Atwater, after pleading no contest to the seat belt violation and paying a $50 fine, sued the police and the city of Lago Vista for being subjected to an unreasonable Fourth Amendment seizure. She argued that her offense carried no jail time and there was no need for her immediate detention. In this case, the Supreme Court ruled that Atwater's arrest satisfied constitutional requirements because it was based on probable cause to believe that Atwater had committed a crime in the arresting officer's presence. Many commentators have criticized this decision by the Court saying that it gave new unprecedented power to the police. They argue that Atwater could merely have been given a traffic citation or traffic ticket for her offense—no seat belts. However, the decision actually only confirmed the Court's long-standing opinion that the police can make an arrest for any offense committed in their presence, and traffic tickets or citations are only options in lieu of physical arrest. Atwater's actions were a misdemeanor under Texas law and an actual arrest, rather than a traffic citation, was justified in this case.

Arrests can be made with or without a *warrant* (a writ, or formal written order, issued by a judicial officer that directs a law enforcement officer to perform a specified act and affords the officer protection from damage if he or she acts according to the order). In general, police officers can arrest a person (1) for any crime committed in the officers' presence, (2) for a **felony** not committed in the officers' presence if they have probable cause to believe that a felony has occurred and that the person they have arrested committed the felony, or (3) under the authority of an arrest warrant. As an example of the first circumstance, officers can arrest a man they observe committing a robbery with a gun. An arrest can also be made in the following scenario: an officer is called to a scene where there is a dead body and is told by witnesses that a woman in a black leather jacket was engaged in an altercation with the deceased and took out a gun and shot him. The officer searches the area around the crime scene and finds a woman in a black jacket; she is hiding under a staircase. Upon searching the woman, the officer finds a gun. In the event the officer does not find the woman after the crime, but witnesses positively identify her, the officer can go to court and obtain an arrest warrant for the woman and a search warrant to search her house for the gun.

However, if a routine arrest is to be made in a suspect's home an arrest warrant is necessary unless the suspect gives consent or an emergency exists. In *Payton v. New York* (1980), New York City police were attempting to arrest Payton based on probable cause for a murder. They attempted to gain entrance to Payton's apartment but there was no response to their knocks. Officers then went into the apartment by breaking down the door. Upon entering the apartment, they observed in plain view a .30 caliber shell casing that was used as evidence of the murder. The Supreme Court ruled that this was a routine arrest and the police had ample time to gain a warrant before entry.[13] See Table 13.6 for a sample state code defining a police officer's power to arrest.

<table>
<tr><td>**TABLE 13.6**</td><td>**A Police Officer's Power to Arrest**</td></tr>
</table>

The Tennessee Code, Section 40.803, reads as follows:

Grounds for arrest by officer without warrant—An officer may, without a warrant, arrest a person:

1. For a public offense committed or a breach of the peace threatened in his presence.

2. When the person has committed a felony, though not in his presence.

3. When a felony has in fact been committed, and he has reasonable cause for believing the person arrested to have committed it.

4. On a charge made, upon reasonable cause, of the commission of a felony by the person arrested.

Probable Cause

Most of the arrests made by the average police officer do not involve a warrant because most crimes an officer becomes aware of on the street necessitate immediate action and do not allow the officer the time necessary to go to court to obtain a warrant. Most of the arrests made by the police are based on the probable cause standard.

Probable cause can be defined as evidence that may lead a reasonable person to believe that a crime has been committed and that a certain person committed it. Probable cause is less than *beyond a reasonable doubt*, which is the standard used by a court to convict a person of a crime. Probable cause is more than **reasonable suspicion,** which is a standard of proof that would lead a reasonable person (a police officer) to believe a certain condition or fact (that a crime is, will be, or has occurred) exists. This is the standard necessary for police officers to conduct stop and frisks.

The evidence needed to establish probable cause must be established before arrest. For example, if an officer sees a man, walking down a block, adjust his jacket to the extent that a gun can be seen protruding from his waistband, the officer has reasonable suspicion to stop and question the man. If the possession of the gun is illegal, the officer has probable cause to make an arrest. Because the arrest is legal, the search that produced the gun is legal; therefore, the gun can be entered into evidence. In contrast, if an officer stops all people walking down the street and searches them without sufficient justification, any arrest for possession of a gun would be illegal, and the gun would be suppressed in court.

The U.S. Supreme Court has made numerous important decisions on the legality and requirements for arrests. In 1959, *Henry v. United States* set the precedent that an arrest must be made on firmer grounds than mere suspicion and that the Fourth Amendment applies to searches and arrests.[14] The Supreme Court, in *Brinegar v. United States* (1949), ruled that relaxations of the fundamental requirements of probable cause, as it relates to the power of arrest, would leave law-abiding citizens at the mercy of police officers' whims.[15] *Draper v. United States* (1959) held that the identification of a suspect by a reliable informant may constitute probable cause for an arrest, where the information given is sufficiently accurate to lead the officers directly to the suspect.[16]

In 1991, in *County of Riverside v. McLaughlin,* the Court ruled that a person arrested without a warrant must generally be provided with a judicial determination of probable cause within 48 hours after arrest, including intervening weekends and holidays, meaning that weekends and holidays could not be excluded from the 48-hour rule.[17]

In *Maryland v. Pringle* (2003), the Supreme Court addressed the constitutionality of arresting a group of companions when the officer has reason to believe that at least one or more of them is involved in criminal activity but does not have information to identify with certainty who is the actual person or persons in the group responsible for the criminal activity.[18] In this case, an officer stopped a car occupied by three men for speeding. The officer requested and was given consent to search the vehicle. During the search, he found five plastic bags of cocaine and more than $700 rolled-up cash. The three occupants of the vehicle denied any knowledge of the money and drugs, and the officer arrested all three, including Pringle. Pringle later confessed that the cocaine belonged to him and that the others were not aware that drugs were in the car. At trial, Pringle challenged the use of his confession, arguing that his arrest was not supported by probable cause. The trial court agreed and held that without specific factors establishing Pringle's dominion and control over the drugs, the officer's mere finding that it was in a car occupied by Pringle was insufficient to justify probable cause to arrest. Upon, appeal, the U.S. Supreme Court reversed the trial court and ruled that the officer had sufficient probable cause to arrest Pringle based on the information known to the officer at the time of

| TABLE 13.7 | Landmark U.S. Supreme Court Decisions: Arrests by Police |

Issue	Cases
Probable cause	*Brinegar v. United States* (1949), *Draper v. United States* (1959), *Henry v. United States* (1959), *Atwater v. City of Lago Vista* (2001), *Maryland v. Pringle* (2003)
48-hour rule	*County of Riverside v. McLaughlin* (1991)
Must identify self	*Hiibel v. Sixth Judicial District Court of Nevada, Humboldt County* (2004)

arrest and the reasonable inferences the officer could draw therefrom. It held that the officer could reasonably infer that one or all of the three occupants of the car had knowledge of, and exercised dominion and control over the cocaine because all three were riding together in a small vehicle and appeared to be engaged in a common enterprise. The Court noted that a standard higher than probable cause is to be applied later in the criminal justice process and does not apply to the decision to arrest someone. See Table 13.7 for a list of landmark cases regarding police arrests.

Reasonable and Deadly Force in Making Arrests

The amount of force an officer can use when making an arrest is called **reasonable force.** Reasonable force is that amount of force necessary to overcome resistance by the person being arrested by the police. For example, if a person is punching the officer in an effort to avoid the arrest, the officer may use similar force in an attempt to subdue the person and control him or her. As an attacker's force escalates, an officer may escalate his or her use of force.[19]

The best way to define reasonable force may be to define unreasonable force. Punching, kicking, or otherwise using force against a person who is not resisting and who is willingly submitting to an arrest would be the unreasonable use of force. Continuing to strike at a person after he or she is subdued, handcuffed, and under the officer's physical control would be an unreasonable use of force. The **Rodney King incident** (1991) discussed in Chapter 8 would appear to be an excellent example of unreasonable force, even though the jury

You Are There!

Delaware v. Prouse (1979)

On November 30, 1976, at about 7:30 PM, a New Castle County, Delaware, police officer stopped an automobile owned by William Prouse. Another man was driving Prouse's car, and Prouse was an occupant. As the officer approached the vehicle, he smelled the odor of marijuana. He then observed marijuana on the floor of the automobile. Prouse was arrested and later went on trial. At the trial, the officer testified that his stop of Prouse's car was "routine." He stated that he saw the car, and because he was not answering any other calls, he decided to stop the car. He further testified that he saw no traffic violations or vehicle equipment violations.

The trial court ruled that the stop and detention had been capricious and was a violation of Prouse's Fourth Amendment rights. The state of Delaware appealed the case to the Supreme Court, which affirmed the opinion of the trial court. The Supreme Court ruled that random spot checks of automobiles are a violation of citizens' Fourth Amendment rights.

SOURCE: Based on *Delaware v. Prouse,* 440 U.S. 648 (1979).

apparently saw it differently in the first trial. In the video, King does not appear to be resisting, yet the officers continue to hit him with their batons.

The use of deadly force (force sufficient to cause a person's death) has long been a controversial topic in policing. The use of deadly force by the police is generally permitted (1) when an officer's life or another's life is at peril from the person against whom the deadly physical force is directed, (2) where the officer has probable cause to believe the suspect has committed a crime involving serious physical harm to another, or (3) in other serious felony cases. The landmark U.S. Supreme Court case relative to use of deadly force by the police is *Tennessee v. Garner* (1985).[20]

Police Traffic Stops

"It was a routine traffic stop," many officers used to testify in court regarding summonses and arrests for drivers of automobiles. The routine traffic stop came to an end, however, in 1979, with the case of *Delaware v. Prouse.*[21] In this case, the Supreme Court ruled that the police cannot make capricious car

© Bill Bachmann/The Image Works

A motorist performs a roadside sobriety test after being stopped for suspicion of drunk driving. The motorist's performance on this test, together with the driving witnessed by the officers, will determine whether he is taken into custody for drunk driving.

stops and that "random spot checks" of motorists are a violation of a citizen's Fourth Amendment rights.

The Court, however, stated that police may still stop automobiles based on reasonable suspicion that (1) a crime was being committed or (2) a traffic violation occurred. The Court also said that the police can establish roadblocks as long as (1) all citizens are subject to the stop or (2) a pattern is set such as every third car is stopped.

Can a police officer legally order a driver or a passenger out of the vehicle after he or she has stopped it? Yes, ruled the Supreme Court in two cases. In *Pennsylvania v. Mimms* (1977), the Court ruled that the Fourth Amendment allows a law enforcement officer who has made a lawful routine stop of a vehicle for a traffic offense to order the driver to exit the vehicle without requiring any additional factual justification.[22] In this case, the defendant was stopped for driving with an expired license plate. The officer then ordered the defendant to exit the vehicle. The officer later testified that he routinely ordered all drivers to exit vehicles following routine traffic stops out of a concern for his safety. When Mimms stepped out of the vehicle, the officer noticed a bulge in his jacket, prompting the officer to conduct a limited search

for weapons and leading to the discovery of a handgun.

In *Maryland v. Wilson* (1997), a Maryland state trooper pulled over a vehicle for speeding.[23] The trooper, out of concern for his safety, directed the defendant, Wilson, a passenger in the vehicle, to step out of the vehicle. As the man exited the car, the trooper observed a bag of cocaine fall to the ground.

In both cases, the Court recognized the inherently dangerous nature of the traffic stop. In fact, in *Maryland v. Wilson*, the Court cited statistics showing that in the year in which the *Mimms* stop occurred, almost 6,000 officers were assaulted and 11 were killed during traffic pursuits and stops.[24]

In 1990, the Supreme Court, in *Michigan Department of State Police v. Sitz*, ruled that brief, suspicion-less stops at highway checkpoints for the purpose of combating drunk driving, were legal.[25] However, in 2000, in *City of Indianapolis v. Edmond*, the Court ruled that when the purpose of the checkpoint is to locate illegal drugs, the seizure involved is unconstitutional.[26] Thus, highway checkpoints for DWI enforcement are constitutional, but for drug enforcement, they are not legal. In this case, the Court reasoned that the drunk driving checkpoint was clearly aimed at reducing the immediate hazard posed by drunk drivers on the highways, but general crime control (such as drug enforcement) stops needed some quantum of individualized suspicion.

In 2004, in *Illinois v. Lidster,* the Supreme Court clarified its *Edmond* decision ruling that *Edmond* did not condemn all highway checkpoints.[27] In this case, police established a highway checkpoint to locate witnesses to a previous hit-and-run death of a bicyclist. Police stopped all vehicles approaching the checkpoint and asked the occupants whether they knew anything about the accident. As Lidster approached the checkpoint, his vehicle nearly struck an officer. The officer approached the vehicle and smelled alcohol on Lidster's breath. Lidster subsequently failed a field sobriety test and was arrested and then convicted for driving under the influence of alcohol. Lidster appealed his conviction claiming that the information leading to his arrest was derived from an unlawful seizure, asserting that the checkpoint violated the Fourth Amendment based on the *Edmond* ruling. The appellate court agreed with Lidster and suppressed the evidence against him. The U.S. Supreme Court, however, reversed the appellate court and concluded that the use of the checkpoint in *Lidster* differed greatly from the one in *Edmond,* noting that its purpose was to solicit information about a fatal accident rather than general crime control.

In *Whren v. United States,* in 1996, the Supreme Court ruled that pretextual traffic stops, also known as pretext stops (the temporary detention of a motorist upon probable cause to believe that he has violated the traffic laws even if another reasonable officer may not have stopped the motorist absent some additional law enforcement objective) do not violate the Fourth Amendment. In this case, plainclothes vice officers were patrolling a high drug activity area in an unmarked car when they noticed a vehicle with temporary license plates and youthful occupants waiting at a stop sign. The truck remained stopped at the intersection for what appeared to be an unusually long time while the driver stared into the lap of the passenger. When the officers made a U-turn and headed toward the vehicle, it made a sudden right turn without signaling and sped off at an "unreasonable" speed. The officers overtook the vehicle when it stopped at a red light. When one of the officers approached the vehicle, he observed two large plastic bags of what appeared to be crack cocaine in Whren's hands. He was arrested. At trial, Whren sought to suppress the evidence, saying that the plainclothes officer would

not normally stop traffic violators and that there was no probable cause to make a stop on drug charges; therefore, the stop on the traffic violation was merely a pretext to determine whether Whren had drugs.[28] Despite his argument, the Court ruled that Whren's stop was not unconstitutional.

■

The Police and Search and Seizure

Search and seizure is the search for and taking of persons and property as evidence of crime by law enforcement officers. Searches and seizures are the means used by the police to obtain evidence that can be used by the courts to prove a defendant's guilt. Police searches are governed by the Fourth Amendment, which prohibits all unreasonable searches and seizures and requires that all warrants be based on probable cause and that they particularly describe the place to be searched and the persons or things to be seized.

The sanctity of one's home is very important in U.S. legal tradition, and it is commonly assumed that *a person's home is his or her castle.* The U.S. Supreme Court has consistently ruled that the police must use due process to enter one's home. In *Payton v. New York* (1980), discussed earlier in this chapter, the Court ruled that the police need a warrant to enter a person's home to make a routine arrest absent consent or emergency situations.[29] In *Minnesota v. Olson* (1990), the Supreme Court held than an overnight guest had a sufficient expectation of privacy in a host's dwelling and is entitled to the Fourth Amendment protection against unreasonable searches and seizures.[30] In *Minnesota v. Carter* (1998), however, the Court refused to extend Fourth Amendment protections to a person who is merely present with the consent of the householder.[31]

In 2002, in *Kirk v. Louisiana,* the Court reaffirmed its previous ruling in *Payton* that the police may not enter a person's home without a warrant, unless emergency or exigent circumstances are present. In this case, police had entered Kirk's apartment after observing what they believed to be drug purchases therein and then stopping one of the apparent buyers on the street to verify the drug sales. Officers testified that "because the stop took place within a block of the apartment [they] feared that evidence would be destroyed and ordered the apartment be entered." They immediately knocked on the

You Are There!

Katz v. United States (1967)

Mr. Justice Stewart delivered the opinion of the Court.

The petitioner was convicted in the District Court of the Southern District of California under an eight-count indictment charging him with transmitting wagering information by telephone from Los Angeles to Miami and Boston, in violation of a federal statute. At trial the Government was permitted, over the petitioner's objection, to introduce evidence of the petitioner's end of telephone conversations, overheard by FBI agents who had attached an electronic listening and recording device to the outside of the public telephone booth from which he had placed his calls. In affirming his conviction, the Court of Appeals rejected the contention that the recordings had been obtained in violation of

the Fourth Amendment, because "there was no physical entrance into the area occupied by the petitioner." We granted certiorari in order to consider the constitutional questions. . . .

Wherever a man may be, he is entitled to know that he will remain free from unreasonable searches and seizures. The government agents here ignored "the procedure of antecedent justification" . . . that is central to the Fourth Amendment, a procedure that we hold to be a constitutional precondition of the kind of electronic surveillance involved in this case. Because the surveillance here failed to meet that condition, and because it led to the petitioner's conviction, the judgment must be reversed.

It is so ordered.

Source: Based on: *Katz v. United Sates,* 389 U.S. 347 (1967).

---

door of the apartment, arrested Kirk, searched him and found a drug vial in his underwear and then observed contraband in plain view in the apartment. The Court ruled that police officers need either a warrant or probable cause plus exigent circumstances to make a lawful entry into a home.[32]

A good example to explain the meaning of a legal Fourth Amendment search is the 2000 U.S. Supreme Court landmark case *Bond v. United States*.[33] In this case, Dewayne Bond was a passenger with carry-on luggage on a bus. When the bus stopped at a Border Patrol checkpoint, a Border Patrol agent boarded the bus to check the passengers' immigration status. In an effort to locate illegal drugs, the agent began to squeeze the soft luggage, which some passengers had placed in the overhead storage space above their seats. The agent squeezed the canvas bag above Bond's seat and noticed that it contained a "brick-like" object. Bond admitted that the bag was his and consented to its search. When the agent looked inside the bag, he discovered a "brick" of methamphetamine. Bond was arrested and then indicted and convicted for federal drug charges. Upon appeal, the Supreme Court reversed the conviction and ruled that the agent's manipulation of the bag was an unreasonable search and that it violated the Fourth Amendment.

In *Bond*, the Court ruled that the agent did in fact conduct a search and that the search was

unreasonable because he conducted it without a warrant and the search did not fall under any of the recognized exceptions to the warrant requirement. Although Bond consented to a search of his bag, his consent was not an issue. The agent's squeezing of Bond's bag was at issue—Bond argued and the Court agreed that the agent's squeezing of his bag was an illegal search and occurred before any consent given by Bond.[34]

In explaining the legality of a search and seizure, the Court's reasoning in this case was that the search was in violation of the Fourth Amendment in that according to *Katz v. United States* (1967) a search is a government infringement of a person's reasonable expectation of privacy and that a search must be reasonable to comply with the Fourth Amendment. The Court has ruled that any government search conducted without a warrant is *per se* unreasonable, unless the search falls under a few recognized exceptions to the warrant requirement (for example, consent searches, emergency searches, motor vehicle searches, inventory searches, searches incident to arrest, and the like).[35]

In a recent case, *Kyllo v. United States* (2001), the Supreme Court again refined its definition of "what is a search." *Kyllo* was a federal drug prosecution that began in 1992, when two federal agents trained a new thermal imaging device, called an Agema Thermovision 210, on a home in

TABLE 13.8	Landmark U.S. Supreme Court Decisions: Police Traffic Stops and Canine Sniffs

Issue	Cases
Police traffic stops	
Routine traffic stops	*Delaware v. Prouse* (1979)
Ordering driver out of vehicle	*Pennsylvania v. Mimms* (1977)
Ordering passenger out of vehicle	*Maryland v. Wilson* (1997)
DWI checkpoints	*Michigan Department of State Police v. Sitz* (1990)
Drug checkpoints	*City of Indianapolis v. Edmond* (2000)
Pretext stops	*Whren v. United States* (1996)
Non-DWI or drug checkpoints	*Illinois v. Lidster* (2004)
What is a search?	*Katz v. United States* (1967), *Bond v. United States* (2000), *Kyllo v. United States* (2001)
Canine sniffs	
Not a search under Fourth Amendment	*U.S. v. Place* (1983), *Illinois v. Caballes* (2005)

Florence, Oregon, where, on the basis of tips and utility bills, they believed marijuana was being grown under high-intensity lamps. Although the thermal imager cannot see through walls, it can detect hot spots, and in this case disclosed that part of the roof and a side wall were warmer than the rest of the building and the neighboring houses. The agents used that information to get a warrant to enter and search the home, where they found more than a hundred marijuana plants growing under halide lights. The resident of the home, Danny Kyllo, was arrested. He contested the validity of the search to the U.S. Supreme Court. The government strongly defended use of thermal imagers on the grounds that in detecting heat loss, the devices neither reveal private information nor violate the "reasonable expectation of privacy" that is the Court's test under the Fourth Amendment. The issue in the case was whether the thermal-imaging device aimed at a private home from a public street, constitutes a search under the Fourth Amendment. The Court ruled in *Kyllo* that the use of the surveillance device was a search and a warrant should have been obtained before its use. It further ruled that a warrant would also be necessary before the use of other new sophisticated devices in use or in development that let the police gain knowledge that in the past would have been impossible without a physical entry into the home. The Court applied this rule only to homes and didn't address warrantless

imaging of other locations.[36] See Table 13.8 for a list of landmark cases relative to police traffic stops and canine sniffs.

Canine Sniffs

The U.S. Supreme Court has consistently ruled that canine sniffs by a trained drug dog are not actual search and seizures controlled by the Fourth Amendment. In 1983, in *United States v. Place*, the U.S. Supreme Court ruled that exposure of luggage in a public place to a trained drug canine did not constitute a search within the meaning of the Fourth Amendment.[37] The Court explained that the dog's alert to the presence of drugs created probable cause for the issuance of a search warrant for drugs. It explained that the dog's sniff is nonintrusive and reveals only the presence of contraband. Many cases have ruled that a dog's positive alert alone generally constitutes probable cause to search a vehicle under the motor vehicle exception to the search warrant requirement.[38]

Special Agent Michael J. Bulzomi, a legal instructor at the FBI Academy writes that drug detection dogs remain extremely important in drug interdiction. They represent a highly efficient and cost-effective way to establish quickly whether probable cause exists to execute a search for contraband. The use of drug detection dogs has met with few real legal challenges in the courts. The only notable area that has been challenged is a

© Gary I Rothstein/Reuters/Corbis

A bomb-sniffing K-9 named Chance from Palm Beach County Sheriff's Office checks packages outside a meeting venue. Canine sniffs represent a highly efficient and cost-effective way to establish quickly whether probable cause exists to execute a search for contraband.

dog's reliability. Drug detection dog handlers should be prepared to establish a dog's reliability by providing prosecutors with a complete record of the dog's training, success rate, and certification in drug detection.[39] Jayme S. Walker, in a 2001 article in the *FBI Law Enforcement Bulletin,* shows many examples of court decisions declaring dog sniffs not searches under the Fourth Amendment in cases involving luggage, packages, warehouses or garages, busses, trains, motel rooms, apartments, and homes.[40]

In an extension of *United States v. Place,*[41] the U.S. Supreme Court in *Illinois v. Caballes* (2005) held that a dog sniff of the exterior of an automobile conducted during the course of a lawful vehicle stop is not a search and may be performed without any suspicion that the vehicle's occupants are engaged in criminal activity.[42] In *Caballes,* an Illinois state trooper stopped Caballes for speeding and radioed his stop in to dispatch. A second trooper overheard the radio transmission and drove to the scene with his narcotics-detection dog. While the first trooper was writing Caballes a warning ticket, the second trooper walked the dog around the vehicle. When

the dog alerted to the trunk, both officers searched it and found marijuana. Caballes was then arrested and later convicted on drug charges. The U.S. Supreme Court affirmed the conviction ruling that the use of the narcotics-detection dog to sniff around the exterior of the vehicle did not constitute any additional infringement on Fourth Amendment rights. The Court ruled that in this case, the traffic stop was not extended beyond the time necessary to issue a warning ticket. It ruled that the use of a well-trained dog "does not expose noncontraband items that otherwise would remain hidden from public view."[43]

The Warrant Requirement and the Search Warrant

In the United States, the general rule regarding search and seizure is that law enforcement officers obtain a search warrant before any search and seizure. (However, there are many exceptions.) A search warrant is an order from a court, issued by a judge, authorizing and directing the police to search a particular place for certain property described in the warrant and directing the police to bring that property to court. Generally, to get a search warrant, a police officer prepares a typed affidavit applying for the warrant and then personally appears before a judge. The judge reads the application; questions the officer, if necessary; and signs the warrant if in agreement with the officer that there is probable cause that certain property that may be evidence of a crime, proceeds from a crime, or contraband (material that is illegal to possess, such as illegal drugs or illegal weapons) is present at a certain place.

Generally, a warrant can be executed only during daylight hours and within a certain time period. However, there are many exceptions. Officers executing a warrant generally must announce their presence before entering. At times, judges may add a "no knock" provision to the warrant, which allows the officers to enter without announcing their presence.[44]

Most searches by police officers are not made with warrants because they are made on the street, where there is no time for an officer to proceed to court to obtain a warrant. Most searches are made in accordance with one of the exceptions to the search warrant requirement-situations involving **exigent circumstances** (emergency situations). Exceptions to the warrant requirement will be discussed at length in the next section.

Often, the cases in which search warrants are generally used are lengthy investigations in which immediate action is not required. Warrants are often used in organized crime and other conspiracy-type investigations.

One of the major uses of warrants is after an informant provides information to the police that certain people are engaged in continuous illegal acts, such as drug dealing. For example, a man tells the police that a certain person is a drug dealer and sells the drugs from her house. The police get as much information as they can from the informant and then dispatch a team of plainclothes officers to make undercover observations of the house. The officers do not see actual drug dealing, because it is going on inside the house, but they see certain actions that go along with the drug trade, such as cars stopping at the house and people entering the house for a short time and then leaving and driving away. Based on these observations, the police can then go to court and request that a judge issue a search warrant. If a search warrant is issued, the police can enter and search the house.

The Supreme Court has had several standards by which to determine what evidence would constitute probable cause for a judge to issue a warrant. The first standard was a two-part (two-pronged) test that mandated that the police show (1) why they believed the informant and (2) the circumstances that showed that the informant had personal knowledge of the crime. This standard was articulated in two major Supreme Court cases, *Aguilar v. Texas* (1964) and *Spinelli v. United States* (1969).[45] There were problems with this standard. To show why the police believed the informant and how the informant obtained the information, the police would have to identify the informant or show how the informant was trustworthy in the past, or both. Identifying the informant and the description of past tips could put the informant in danger.

In *Illinois v. Gates,* the Supreme Court in 1983 reversed the *Aguilar-Spinelli* two-pronged test.[46] The Court replaced it with the *totality of circumstances test,* which holds that an informant could be considered reliable if he or she gives the police sufficient facts to indicate that a crime is being committed and if the police verify these facts.[47]

In *Michigan v. Summers* (1981),[48] the Supreme Court ruled that officers serving a search warrant for drugs could detain the occupants of the premises during their search to prevent their flight in the event that incriminating evidence is found; to minimize the risk of harm to the officers; and to facilitate the search because the occupants' "self-interest may induce them to open locked doors or locked containers." The court ruled that a warrant to search for contraband carries with it the limited authority to detain occupants of the premises while a search is conducted.

In 1990, in *Maryland v. Buie,* the Court, considering officers' safety, extended the authority of the police to search locations in a house where a potentially dangerous person could hide (protective sweeps), while an arrest warrant is being served.[49] In a similar vein, in 2001, in *Illinois v. McArthur,* the Court held that a police officer's refusal to allow residents to enter their homes without a police officer until a search warrant was obtained did not violate the Fourth Amendment.[50]

In *Muehler v. Mena* (2005),[51] the Court expanded on *Summers,* concluding that an officer's authority to detain occupants incident to the execution of a search warrant for contraband or evidence was absolute and unqualified and did not require any justification beyond the warrant itself. In this

You Are There!

Illinois v. Gates (1983)

The Bloomingdale, Illinois, Police Department received by mail the following anonymous handwritten letter:

> This letter is to inform you that you have a couple in your town who strictly make their living on selling drugs. They are Sue and Lance Gates, they live on Greenway, off Bloomingdale Rd. in the condominiums. Most of their buys are done in Florida. Sue his wife drives their car to Florida, where she leaves it to be loaded up with drugs, then Lance flys [*sic*] down and drives it back. Sue flys [*sic*] back after she drops the car off in Florida. May 3 she is driving down there again and Lance will be flying down in a few days to drive it back. At the time Lance drives the car back he has the trunk loaded with over $100,000.00 in drugs. Presently they have over $100,000.00 worth of drugs in their basement.
>
> They brag about the fact they never have to work, and make their living on pushers. I guarantee if you watch them carefully you will make a big catch. They are friends with some big drugs dealers who visit their house often.
>
> "Lance & Susan Gates"
>
> "Greenway"
>
> "in Condominiums"

The *Aguilar-Spinelli* two-pronged test could not apply to this case. The writer was anonymous; the police could not produce the writer and prove his or her reliability.

Based on this letter, however, the police performed the following investigatory actions:

1. They verified the Gates's address.
2. They obtained information from a confidential informant about Lance Gates.
3. They obtained information from an O'Hare Airport police officer that "L. Gates" had made a reservation on Eastern Airlines to West Palm Beach, Florida, departing Chicago on May 5 at 4:15 PM.
4. They arranged for the Drug Enforcement Administration to conduct a surveillance of the May 5 Eastern Airlines flight.

The surveillance resulted in the information that Lance Gates arrived in West Palm Beach and went to a Holiday Inn room registered to one Susan Gates, as well as other information verifying the information in the letter. A judge issued a search warrant for the Gates's apartment and automobile. Using the warrant, the police seized approximately 350 pounds of marijuana, weapons, and other contraband.

The Gateses were arrested and indicted for violation of state drug laws. The evidence however, was suppressed in a pretrial motion, as the judge ruled that the affidavit submitted in support of the application for the warrant was inadequate under the *Aguilar-Spinelli* standard. Upon appeal, the U.S. Supreme Court replaced the *Aguilar-Spinelli* standard with the totality of circumstances standard.

SOURCE: Based on *Illinois v. Gates,* 462 U.S. 213 (1983).

---

case, police in California obtained a warrant in connection with a drive-by shooting to search a suspected gang member's house for weapons, ammunition, and gang paraphernalia. Because of the high-risk nature of the case, a police special weapons and tactics (SWAT) team made the initial entry. Four occupants, including Iris Mena, were handcuffed at gunpoint and taken to a garage on the premises, where they were detained for the two to three hours it took to finish the search. Mena brought a civil action against officers alleging a violation of her Fourth Amendment rights. The Supreme Court rejected the civil action.

In *United States v. Banks* (2003), the U.S. Supreme Court provided guidance to law enforcement officers is assessing how much time they are required to wait before making a forcible entry after knocking and announcing their presence and demanding entry in a warrant case.[52] In this case, officers obtained a search warrant based on information that cocaine was being sold from an apartment. Officers at the front door of the apartment knocked and announced loudly enough to be heard by officers located in the back. After waiting 15 to 20 seconds with no response, officers forcibly entered the apartment using a battering ram. They encountered the defendant walking out of the shower after he heard them enter. Evidence of drug dealing was found during the search, which the defendant sought to suppress, arguing that the

> **TABLE 13.9** Landmark U.S. Supreme Court Decisions: Warrants

Issue	Cases
Two-pronged test	*Aguilar v. Texas* (1964), *Spinelli v. United States* (1969)
Totality of circumstances test	*Illinois v. Gates* (1983)
Time to wait before forcible entry	*United States v. Banks* (2003)
Authority to detain, handcuff, question	*Muehler v. Mena* (2005)
Can detain occupants during search	*Michigan v. Summers* (1981), *Illinois v. McArthur* (2001)
Need warrant to enter home to arrest	*Payton v. New York* (1980), *Minnesota v. Olson* (1990), *Kirk v. Louisiana* (2002)
Violation of "knock and announce" rule does not require suppression of evidence	*Hudson v. Michigan* (2006)

officers failed to wait a reasonable time before the forcible entry. The federal Ninth Circuit Court of Appeals agreed with the defendant and suppressed the evidence. The U.S. Supreme Court, however, on appeal, rejected the appellate court's decision and re-allowed the evidence and ruled that the delay of 15 to 20 seconds in *Banks* was sufficient given that a reasonably objective law enforcement officer could conclude that the danger of disposal of the drugs had ripened.

In 2006, in what some saw as a controversial decision, the Court, in *Hudson v. Michigan*, ruled that violation of the common-law principle that law enforcement officers must announce their presence and provide residents an opportunity to open a door (knock-and-announce rule) does not require the suppression of evidence found in a search (exclusionary rule). In this case, Detroit police were executing a search warrant for narcotics and weapons and entered Booker T. Hudson's home. When the police arrived to execute the warrant, they announced their presence, but waited only a short time—perhaps "three to five seconds"—before turning the knob of the unlocked front door and entering Hudson's home. They discovered large quantities of drugs, including cocaine rocks in Hudson's pocket and a loaded gun lodged between the cushion and armrest of the chair in which he was sitting.[53] In the Court's decision, Justice Antonin Scalia wrote,

> The social costs of applying the exclusionary rule to knock-and-announce violations are considerable; the incentive to such violations is minimal to begin with, and the extant deterrences against them are substantial—

comparably greater than the factors deterring warrantless entries when *Mapp* was decided. Resort to the massive remedy of suppressing evidence of guilt is unjustified.[54]

See Table 13.9 for a list of landmark cases regarding search warrants.

Exceptions to the Warrant Requirement

Many exigent circumstances arise in which the police cannot be expected to travel to court to obtain a search warrant. The evidence might be destroyed by a suspect, the suspect might get away, or the officer might be injured. The following are the major exceptions to the search warrant requirement and the rules established by the Supreme Court that govern these exceptions.

Incident to Lawful Arrest In *Chimel v. California* (1969), the U.S. Supreme Court established guidelines regarding searches at the time of arrest.[55] In this case, the Court ruled that incident to (at the time of) an arrest, the police may search the defendant and only that area immediately surrounding the defendant for the purpose of preventing injury to the officer and the destruction of evidence. This has become known as the "arm's reach doctrine."

On September 13, 1965, three police officers from the Santa Ana, California, Police Department arrived at Ted Chimel's house with a warrant to arrest him for the burglary of a coin shop. The police showed Chimel the arrest warrant and asked him if they could "look around." Chimel objected, but the

You Are There!

Terry v. Ohio (1968)

Detective Martin McFadden, a veteran of the Cleveland Police Department's robbery squad, was on routine stakeout duty in a Cleveland downtown shopping district when he observed two men acting suspiciously on the street in the vicinity of Huron Road and Euclid Avenue. One of the suspects looked furtively into a store, walked on, returned to look at the same store, and then joined a companion. The companion, another man, then went to the store, looked in it, and then rejoined his companion. The two men continually repeated these actions and looked into the store numerous times. The two men then met with a third man.

McFadden suspected that the men were casing the store for a stickup and believed that they were armed. He approached the three men, identified himself as a police officer, and asked the men their names. The men mumbled something, whereupon McFadden patted them down (frisked them, or ran his hands over their outer clothing). His frisk and subsequent search revealed that one of the men, Terry, was in possession of a gun. Another frisk and subsequent search revealed that one of his companions, Richard Chilton, also had a gun.

Terry and Chilton were arrested for possession of a gun and were convicted. Upon appeal, the Supreme Court ruled that McFadden's actions were constitutional.

SOURCE: Based on *Terry v. Ohio*, 392 U.S. 1 (1968).

---

officers told him they could search the house on the basis of the lawful arrest. The officers then searched the entire three-bedroom house for 45 minutes. They seized numerous items, including some coins. The coins were admitted into evidence, and Chimel was convicted at trial of burglary.

Upon appeal, the U.S. Supreme Court ruled that the warrantless search of Chimel's home was a violation of his constitutional rights. The Court thus established the "arms reach doctrine."

In 1973, in *United States v. Robinson*, the Court ruled that because a probable cause arrest is a reasonable Fourth Amendment intrusion, a search incident to that arrest requires no additional justification.[56]

In *Knowles v. Iowa* (1998), the Supreme Court considered the right of the warrantless search incident to arrest to the search of a motor vehicle stopped by the police incident to a traffic citation. In *Knowles,* Patrick Knowles was stopped for speeding by a police officer in Newton, Iowa. The officer issued Knowles a citation and then conducted a thorough search of Knowles's car without his consent and found a bag of marijuana and a "pot pipe" and arrested and charged him with violation of the controlled substances statutes. The Court ruled that when the police officer stopped Knowles, he had probable cause to believe Knowles had violated traffic laws. He could have arrested Knowles for that violation, but chose instead to issue a citation.

The Court ruled that the search incident to an arrest exception does not apply to a traffic citation.[57]

Field Interrogations (Stop and Frisk) In 1968, the Supreme Court established the standard for allowing police officers to perform a **stop and frisk** (pat down) of a suspect in *Terry v. Ohio*.[58] A stop and frisk is the detaining of a person by a law enforcement officer for the purpose of investigation (**field interrogation**), accompanied by a superficial examination by the officer of the person's body surface or clothing to discover weapons, contraband, or other objects relating to criminal activity. In *Terry v. Ohio*, the Court ruled that a police officer could stop a person in a public place to make reasonable inquiries about the person's conduct. It ruled that when the following five conditions exist, a police officer is justified in patting down, or frisking, a suspect:

1. Where a police officer observes unusual conduct which leads him reasonably to conclude in light of his experience that criminal activity may be afoot . . .

2. . . . and that the person with whom he is dealing may be armed and dangerous . . .

3. . . . where in the course of investigating this behavior he identifies himself as a policeman . . .

4. . . . and makes reasonable inquiry . . .

5. . . . and where nothing in the initial stages of the encounter serves to dispel his reasonable fear for his own or other's safety . . . he is entitled to conduct a carefully limited search of the outer clothing of such persons in an attempt to discover weapons which might be used to assault him. Such search is a reasonable search under the Fourth Amendment and any weapons seized may properly be introduced in evidence against the person from whom they were taken.[59]

In *Hiibel v. Sixth Judicial District Court of Nevada, Humboldt County* (2004), the Supreme Court approved a state statute requiring individuals to identify themselves as part of an investigative detention or field interrogation, ruling that it was not a violation of the Fourth or Fifth Amendment.[60] In this case, a deputy sheriff responding to a call reporting an assault lawfully detained a man who later turned out to be Hiibel based on reasonable suspicion of his involvement in the crime. After numerous attempts to determine the man's identity, the deputy arrested him for failing to identify himself during an investigative detention pursuant to the Nevada's stop and identity statute. Hiibel was convicted and appealed, challenging the constitutionality of the statute. The Supreme Court rejected Hiibel's appeal and ruled that if a stop is justified at its inception (based on reasonable suspicion) and the request for identity is reasonably related to the purpose of the stop, it is justified.

In 1993, in *Minnesota v. Dickerson,* the Court placed new limits on an officer's ability to seize evidence discovered during a pat down search conducted for protective reasons when the search itself is based merely upon suspicion and fails to immediately reveal the presence of a weapon.[61] In this case, Timothy Dickerson was stopped by Minneapolis police after they noticed him acting suspiciously while leaving a building known for cocaine trafficking. The officers decided to investigate and ordered Dickerson to submit to a pat down search. The officer testified that he felt no weapon but did feel a small lump in Dickerson's jacket pocket, which he believed to be a lump of cocaine upon examining it with his fingers. Dickerson was arrested and convicted of drug possession. Upon appeal, the U.S. Supreme Court ruled that the search was illegal, saying, "While *Terry* entitled [the officer] to place his hands on respondent's jacket and to feel the lump in his pocket, his continued exploration of the pocket after he concluded that it contained no weapons

was unrelated to the sole justification for the search under *Terry.*"

In *Illinois v. Wardlow* (2000), the Court held that a police officer's initial stop of a suspect was supported by reasonable suspicion if the suspect was both present in an area of expected criminal activity and fled upon seeing the police.[62] In this case, two police officers were investigating drug transactions while driving in an area known for heavy drug trafficking. They noticed Mr. Wardlow holding a bag. When Wardlow saw the officers, he fled. The officers pursued and stopped him. One of the officers conducted a protective pat down search for weapons because in his experience, it was common for weapons to be in the vicinity of drug transactions. During the pat down, the officers squeezed Wardlow's bag and felt a heavy, hard object in the shape of a gun. When the officer opened the bag, he did in fact discover a handgun with ammunition. Wardlow was arrested. Upon appeal that the arrest was illegal because the officers did not perform a lawful stop and frisk, the Court held that the initial stop was reasonable and supported by reasonable suspicion and cited *Terry v. Ohio,* "Under *Terry,* an officer may, consistent with the Fourth Amendment, conduct a brief, investigatory stop when the officer has a reasonable, articulable suspicion that criminal activity is afoot."[63] Thus in *Wardlow,* the Court ruled that several factors can be used to determine whether an officer has reasonable suspicion to make a *Terry* stop, including (1) whether the stop occurred in a high crime area, (2) a suspect's nervous, evasive behavior, and (3) a suspect's unprovoked flight upon noticing the police.[64]

Regarding field interrogations and anonymous tips to the police, the Supreme Court has ruled that if an officer is relying on an anonymous tip to make a *Terry* stop, then the tip must be sufficiently reliable to provide the officer with reasonable suspicion to make the stop. Generally, an anonymous tip alone is not sufficiently reliable. The Court explained that an anonymous tip that is suitably corroborated may be sufficiently reliable to provide the officer with reasonable suspicion to make a *Terry* stop, considering two factors: (1) what the officers knew—either by their own observations, their experience, or prior knowledge of the suspect or area—before they conducted their stop; and (2) whether the anonymous tip showed that the informant had predicted accurately the suspect's movements or had knowledge of concealed criminal activity. A tip that merely identifies a specific person is not reliable enough to show knowledge of concealed criminal activity.

In *Florida v. J. L.* (2000), the Court held than an anonymous tip that a person is carrying a gun, without more information, does not justify a police officer's stop and frisk of that person. In this case, an anonymous caller reported to the police that a young black man standing at a particular bus stop and wearing a plaid shirt was carrying a gun. There was no audio recording of the tip and nothing was known about the informant. Officers went to the bus stop and saw three black men. One of the men, J. L., was wearing a plaid shirt. Aside from the tip, the officers had no reason to suspect the three of illegal conduct. The officers did not see a firearm or observe any unusual movements. One of the officers frisked J. L. and seized a gun from his pocket.[65]

Exigent Circumstances Although the general rule on searches within a home without a warrant is that they are presumptively unreasonable,[66] the Supreme Court has established a few narrowly crafted exceptions to the warrant requirement. These exceptions allow the police to act when "the public interest requires some flexibility in the application of the general rule that a valid warrant is a prerequisite for a search."[67] The Court has recognized the following "exigent" or emergency circumstances as those in which there are insufficient time to obtain a search warrant:

1. To prevent escape
2. To prevent harm to the officers or others
3. To prevent the destruction of evidence
4. While in hot pursuit of a criminal suspect
5. To render immediate aid to a person in need of assistance[68]

As some examples, in *Warden v. Hayden* (1967), the Court approved the warrantless search of a residence after reports that an armed robber had fled into a building[69]; in *Mincey v. Arizona* (1978), the Court held that the Fourth Amendment does not require police officers to delay an investigation if to do so would gravely endanger their lives or others[70]; in 1990, in *Maryland v. Buie*, the Court extended the warrantless authority of police to search locations in a house (protective sweep) where a potentially dangerous person could hide while an arrest warrant is being served[71]; and in *Wilson v. Arkansas* (1995), the Court ruled that officers need not announce themselves while executing

a warrant if evidence may be destroyed, officers are pursuing a recently escaped arrestee, or officers' lives may be endangered.[72] Also, in 2001, in *Illinois v. McArthur,* the Court ruled that officers with probable cause to believe that a home contains contraband or evidence of criminal activity may reasonably prevent a suspect found outside the home from reentering it while they apply for a search warrant.[73]

A call to 911, even an anonymous one, is an example of a possible exigent circumstance. In these situations, however, to make a lawful warrantless, nonconsensual entry and search to render aid, the police must reasonably believe that an emergency situation exists requiring immediate police intervention, the search must not be motivated primarily by intent to arrest and seize evidence, and there must be some reasonable basis, approximating probable cause, to associate the emergency with the area or place to be searched.

Michael L. Ciminelli, in a 2003 *FBI Law Enforcement Bulletin,* while acknowledging that officers should not hesitate to act reasonably to preserve life and protect others in potentially dangerous situations, says officers can follow the following guidelines to help support the legal justification to enter a home when answering an anonymous 911 call:

■ Take reasonable steps to identify the caller before making the entry if circumstances permit; however, in certain cases—for example, screams for help, sounds of a struggle, or shots fired—this may not always be possible.

■ Where safe and feasible, take reasonable steps to investigate and corroborate the anonymous call before acting by speaking to neighbors and other persons in the vicinity.

■ Where safe and feasible, attempt to obtain a valid consent to enter.

■ Accurately document the information given by the anonymous caller.

■ Accurately document conditions found at the scene that may corroborate the anonymous call.[74]

Consent Searches A police officer can also search without a warrant if consent is given by a person having authority to give such consent. Consent searches have some limitations. The request cannot be phrased as a command or a threat; it must be a genuine request for permission. The police must receive an oral reply; a nod of the head is not consent. Also, the search must be limited to the area for which consent is given.[75]

The following are some of the most important consent search decisions made by the Supreme Court.

In *Schneckloth v. Bustamonte* (1973), the Supreme Court ruled that a search conducted pursuant to lawfully given consent is an exception to the warrant and probable cause requirements of the Fourth Amendment; however, because a consensual search is still a search, the Fourth Amendment reasonableness requirement still applies. The court ruled that to determine whether an individual voluntarily consented to a search, the reviewing court should consider the totality of the circumstances surrounding the consent.[76] In *United States v. Matlock* (1974), the Court ruled that for a consent search to be constitutionally valid, the consent must be voluntarily given by a person with proper authority. In this case, the Court ruled that a person sharing a room with another person had the authority to allow the police to search the room.[77]

An example of a search that was considered unconstitutional occurred in *Bumper v. North Carolina* (1968), in which the police searched a defendant's house by getting the permission of the defendant's grandmother, who also occupied the house.[78] To get the grandmother's permission, the police told her that they had a lawful search warrant, which they actually did not have. During the search, the officers found a gun in the house, which was used as evidence in a rape case against the defendant Bumper. The Court ruled that the government has the burden of proving that an individual voluntarily consented to the search, and in this case, the government did not. The Court ruled that the officers' assertion that they had a search warrant was "coercive-albeit colorably lawful coercion," and the gun was suppressed as evidence.

In 1990, in *Illinois v. Rodriguez*, the Court declared constitutional the actions of the police in entering the defendant's Chicago apartment with his former girlfriend's consent and key after she claimed he had seriously assaulted her.[79] Upon entry, the police found the defendant, Rodriguez, and a quantity of cocaine and drug paraphernalia. Rodriguez's claim that his former girlfriend had no control over the apartment since she had moved out at least a month earlier did not sway the Court.

In 1991, in *Florida v. Bostick*, the Supreme Court reinterpreted consent searches by ruling that police requests to a person to look into his or her luggage

do not require that the officer have reasonable suspicion that the person is violating the law.[80]

The Supreme Court has also established a "consent once removed" exception to the search warrant requirement. Under that exception, officers are permitted to make a warrantless entry to arrest a suspect based on the consent to enter given earlier to an undercover officer or informant.[81] An example is the 2000 case of *United States v. Pollard*, in which an informant and an undercover officer entered a residence to purchase four kilograms of cocaine. Upon seeing the cocaine in the apartment, the informant gave the arrest signal. In response to the arrest signal, approximately six officers, without knocking or announcing, immediately broke down the front door and arrested the defendants. The U.S. Court of Appeals for the Sixth Circuit ruled that the entry by the backup officers to arrest the defendants was lawful under the consent once removed doctrine. The court found that once the defendants gave the undercover officer and the informant permission to enter, the entry by the arrest team did not create any further invasion of privacy.[82]

In 2006, the Court ruled, in *Georgia v. Randolph*, that consent to search a residence was not constitutional when one co-occupant, who was present at the time, refused to consent.[83] This case was substantially different than *United States v. Matlock* (1974) and *Illinois v. Rodriguez* (1990) because in those two cases the co-occupants were not present.[84] See Table 13.10 for a list of landmark cases regarding exceptions to the warrant requirement.

Plain View   Plain view evidence is unconcealed evidence inadvertently seen by an officer engaged in a lawful activity. If an officer is at a location legally doing police work and observes contraband or other plain view evidence, its seizure without a warrant is legal, according to the U.S. Supreme Court in *Harris v. United States* (1968).[85] In *Arizona v. Hicks* (1987), the Court ruled that the evidence must indeed be in plain view without the police moving or dislodging objects to view the evidence.[86]

Many people think that there is a **crime scene** exception to the search warrant. This is not so. In *Mincey v. Arizona* (1978), the Court refused to recognize a crime scene search as one of the well-delineated exceptions to the search warrant requirement. As a result, crime scenes are given no special consideration under the Fourth Amendment. If a crime occurs in an area where there is a reasonable expectation of privacy, law enforcement officers are

TABLE 13.10 Landmark U.S. Supreme Court Decisions: Exceptions to the Warrant Requirement in Police Search and Seizure Cases

Issue	Cases
Abandoned property	*Abel v. United States* (1960), *California v. Greenwood* (1988), *California v. Hodari, D.* (1991)
Automobile exception	*Carroll v. United States* (1925), *New York v. Belton* (1981), *United States v. Ross* (1982), *California v. Acevedo* (1991), *Florida v. Jimeno* (1991), *Pennsylvania v. Labron* (1996), *Maryland v. Dyson* (1998), *Florida v. White* (1999), *Wyoming v. Houghton* (1999); *Thornton v. United States* (2004)
Border searches	*United States v. Martinez-Fuerte* (1976)
Buses	*Florida v. Bostick* (1991)
Computer error	*Arizona v. Evans* (1995)
Consent	*Bumper v. North Carolina* (1968), *Schneckloth v. Bustamonte* (1973), *United States v. Matlock* (1974), *Illinois v. Rodriquez* (1990), *United States v. Pollard* (2000), *Georgia v. Randolph* (2006)
Exigent circumstances	*Warden v. Hayden* (1967), *Mincey v. Arizona* (1978), *Wilson v. Arkansas* (1995), *Bond v. United States* (2000), *Illinois v. McArthur* (2001), *Kirk v. Louisiana* (2002)
Good faith	*Massachusetts v. Sheppard* (1984), *United States v. Leon* (1984), *Illinois v. Krull* (1987), *Maryland v. Garrison* (1987), *Groh v. Ramirez* (2004)
Incident to arrest	*Chimel v. California* (1969), *United States v. Robinson* (1973), *Knowles v. Iowa* (1998)
Inventory	*Colorado v. Bertine* (1987)
Open fields	*Hester v. United States* (1924), *Oliver v. United States* (1984), *California v. Ciraola* (1986), *Florida v. Riley* (1989)
Motor homes	*California v. Carney* (1985)
Plain view	*Coolidge v. New Hampshire* (1971), *Harris v. New York* (1971), *Arizona v. Hicks* (1987)
Protective sweep	*Maryland v. Buie* (1990)
Stop and frisk, field interrogations	*Terry v. Ohio* (1968), *Minnesota v. Dickerson* (1993), *Illinois v. Wardlow* (2000), *Florida v. J. L.* (2000), *Hiibel v. Sixth Judicial District Court of Nevada, Humboldt County* (2004)
Watercraft	*United States v. Villamonte-Marquez* (1983)

compelled to obtain a search warrant before the crime scene search.[87] To obtain a valid search warrant, officer must meet two critical requirements of the Fourth Amendment. First, they must establish probable cause to believe that the location contains evidence of a crime, and second, they must particularly describe that evidence. It is very simple to justify the granting of a search warrant for a crime scene because by its very nature a crime scene establishes the probable cause for obtaining the warrant. Descriptions of the evidence believed to be present at the scene are generally relatively generic; for example, blood, a weapon, and the like.[88]

Yet, despite the general requirement to obtain a search warrant, it is very common that most crime scenes do not permit the police sufficient time to obtain a search warrant before making

initial entries onto the scene. Consequently, they are forced to rely on exceptions to the warrant requirement to justify these searches. The most common justifications in these cases are consent, emergencies (exigent circumstances), public place, and plain view.

The consent exception can apply to many crime scenes because often the person who has summoned the police to the scene is someone who can consent to the search. However, for the crime scene search to be constitutional, consent must be given voluntarily by a person reasonably believed by law enforcement officers to have lawful access and control over the premises.[89]

The emergency exception also applies to many crime scenes. Traditionally, courts have recognized three different types of emergencies: threats to life or safety, destruction or removal of evidence, and escape. It is indeed difficult to imagine a crime scene that would not automatically present officers with the necessary belief that at least one of these exigent circumstances exists. However, once officers are inside the premises, and have done whatever is necessary to resolve the emergency, the emergency is over. The officers must have a warrant or one of the other exceptions to the warrant requirement to either remain on the premises or to continue their search.

Although officers cannot conduct a full-scale search of a crime scene under the emergency exception, there are certain investigative steps that may lead to the discovery of evidence that fall well within its scope. For instance, officers arriving on the scene of a violent crime unquestionably can sweep the premises in an effort to locate other victims or the suspect if they reasonably suspect that either is present. If a body is found at the scene, taking the medical examiner to view and collect the body is deemed a reasonable step. If officers have probable cause to believe a crime scene contains evidence that will be destroyed if not quickly recovered, that evidence may be retrieved as part of the emergency. Officers may also secure doors and control people on the premises, to guarantee that the scene is not *contaminated*. Finally, if the crime scene is in a public place or evidence is in plain view, a warrant is not required.[90]

Abandoned Property In *Abel v. United States* (1960), the U.S. Supreme Court established a standard regarding police searches of abandoned property.[91] A hotel manager gave an FBI agent permission to search a hotel room that had been previously occupied by Abel. The agent found incriminating evidence in a wastepaper basket. Abel was arrested and convicted based on this evidence. On appeal to the U.S. Supreme Court, the Court ruled that once Abel vacated the room, the hotel had the right to give law enforcement agents the right to search it.

In *California v. Greenwood* (1988), the Supreme Court extended the abandoned property rule to include garbage left at the curb.[92] In this case, the police in Laguna Beach, California, received information from an informant that Billy Greenwood was engaged in drug dealing from his house. They made observations of the house and found numerous cars stopping there at night. The drivers would leave their cars, enter the house for a

short time, and then leave. The police arranged with the local garbage collector to pick up Greenwood's trash, which he left in brown plastic bags in front of his house, and to take it to the station house. The police searched the garbage and found evidence indicating a drug business, including razor blades and straws with cocaine residue and discarded telephone bills with numerous calls to people who had police records for drug possession. Using this evidence, the police obtained a search warrant. When they executed the warrant, they found hashish and cocaine, and they arrested Greenwood.

The U.S. Supreme Court ruled that searches of a person's discarded garbage were not violations of the Fourth Amendment. Speaking for the Court, Justice Byron White stated, "It is common knowledge that garbage bags left on or at the side of a public street are readily accessible to animals, children, scavengers, snoops and other members of the public. Requiring police to seek warrants before searching such refuse would therefore be inappropriate."

In 1991, in *California v. Hodari, D.*, the Court ruled the police were proper in arresting a defendant who fled from the police and threw away (abandoned) evidence as he retreated.[93] In this case, a group of youths in Oakland, California, fled when they saw the approach of two police officers. The officers retrieved a rock of crack cocaine thrown away by one of the youths.

Inventory In *Colorado v. Bertine,* the Supreme Court ruled in 1987 that the police may enter a defendant's automobile, which they impounded for safekeeping and were going to return to the defendant after initial police and court processing, and inventory its contents without a warrant to ensure that all contents were accounted for.[94] In this case, Bertine had been arrested for driving while intoxicated. Upon making an inventory of his van's contents, the police found canisters of drugs. Bertine was additionally charged with violation of the drug laws. The Supreme Court ruled that the police action did not violate Bertine's constitutional rights.

Open Fields In *Hester v. United States* (1924), the Supreme Court established an "open fields exception" to the warrant requirement.[95] The Court said that fields not immediately surrounding a home did not have the protection of the Fourth Amendment and that no warrant was required to enter them and search. Justice Oliver Wendell Holmes, Jr., speaking for the Court, wrote,

> The special protection accorded by the Fourth Amendment to the people in their "persons, houses, papers, and effects," is not extended to the open fields. The distinction between the latter and the house is as old as the common law.

In *Oliver v. United States,* the Supreme Court was asked in 1984 to reexamine its open fields exception under the following circumstances:

> Acting on reports that marijuana was being raised on the farm of petitioner Oliver, two narcotics agents of the Kentucky State Police went to the farm to investigate. Arriving at the farm they drove past petitioner's house to a locked gate with a "No Trespassing" sign . . . The officers found a field of marihuana over a mile from petitioner's house.[96]

Speaking for the Court, and reaffirming the open fields exception, Justice Lewis F. Powell, Jr., wrote the following: "We conclude that the open fields doctrine, as enunciated in *Hester* is consistent with the plain language of the Fourth Amendment and its historical purpose."

Two additional cases in the 1980s expanded the power of the police to watch over citizens without a warrant. In 1986, in *California v. Ciraola,* the Court ruled on the actions of the police who had received a tip that marijuana was growing in the defendant Ciraola's backyard.[97] The backyard was surrounded by fences, one of which was 10 feet high. Police flew over the yard in a private plane at an altitude of one thousand feet in an effort to verify the tip. On the basis of their observations, the police were able to secure and execute a search warrant, which resulted in the seizure of marijuana. Ciraola was convicted on the drug charges, and on appeal, the Court ruled that the police actions were not unconstitutional.

In 1989, in *Florida v. Riley,* the police flew a helicopter four hundred feet over a greenhouse in which Riley and his associates were growing marijuana plants.[98] Based on their observations, the police arrested Riley on drug charges. On appeal, the Court ruled that the police did not need a search warrant to conduct such a low-altitude helicopter search of private property because the flight was within airspace legally available to helicopters under federal regulations.

You Are There!

Carroll v. United States (1925)

On September 29, 1921, during Prohibition, two federal agents were in an apartment in Grand Rapids, Michigan, when George Carroll and John Kiro entered. The agents arranged to buy a case of whiskey from them. Arrangements were made for the two men to deliver the whiskey the next day, but they never returned. A few days later, on October 6, 1921, the agents observed Carroll and Kiro driving an automobile on a highway. They pursued them but lost them. Two months later, on December 15, 1921, the agents again observed them on the same highway and were able to overtake them and stop them. The agents searched the car and found 68 bottles of whiskey within the upholstery of the seats. Carroll and Kiro were arrested for violation of the Prohibition laws. Upon appeal, the Supreme Court established the automobile exception to the Fourth Amendment.

SOURCE: Based on *Carroll v. United States,* 267 U.S. 132 (1925).

The Automobile Exception Many students complain about the actions of police officers who search their automobiles. "Don't we have Fourth Amendment rights when we are in our cars?," they ask. "Yes," the professor answers, "but less than in your house."

The automobile exception to the search warrant requirement goes all the way back to 1925, in *Carroll v. United States.*[99] In this case, the Supreme Court ruled that distinctions should be made between searches of automobiles, persons, and homes, and that a warrantless search of a vehicle, which can be readily moved, is valid if the police have probable cause to believe that the car contains evidence they are seeking. This decision has become known as the **Carroll doctrine.**[100]

In 1981, in *New York v. Belton,* the Supreme Court ruled that a search incident to a lawful arrest of the occupant of an automobile can extend to the entire passenger compartment of the automobile, including the glove compartment and luggage boxes or clothing found in them.[101] This extended the Chimel "arms reach doctrine," but only in the case of automobiles.

In *United States v. Ross* (1982), the Supreme Court held that if probable cause exists to believe that an automobile contains criminal evidence, the police may make a warrantless search of the automobile.[102] In 1983 in *United States* v. *Villamonte-Marquez,* the Court extended the *Carroll* doctrine to include watercraft, and in 1985 in *California v. Carney,* the Court extended the doctrine to include motor homes.[103]

In 1991, the Supreme Court further extended police rights in vehicle searches. In *California v. Acevedo* and a similar case, *Florida v. Jimeno,* the Court ruled that the automobile exception not only covers vehicles but also permits warrantless searches of immobile packages that have been placed in cars.[104] In the *Acevedo* case, the police had observed the defendant leaving his house and carrying a brown paper bag the size of marijuana packages they had seen earlier. The defendant placed the bag in the car's trunk. As he drove away, the police stopped the car, opened the trunk, and seized and opened the bag.

In 1996, the Court reaffirmed the *Carroll* doctrine in *Pennsylvania v. Labron* by ruling that in probable cause cases, there is no need for a warrant in vehicle searches if the vehicle is readily mobile, even if there is time to obtain a warrant.[105]

The Supreme Court has provided further clarification of the constitutionality of searching a motor vehicle without a warrant in other cases. In *Maryland v. Dyson,* the Court remained consistent with its prior rulings by ruling that a warrantless search of a vehicle is permitted when officers have probable cause that a motor vehicle contains evidence or contraband, even in the absence of exigent circumstances.[106] In *Florida v. White,* a forfeiture case, the Court ruled that the police do not have to obtain a warrant before seizing a vehicle while it is parked in a public place.[107] In *Wyoming v. Houghton* (1999) the Court held that when an officer has probable cause to search a vehicle, the officer may search objects belonging to a passenger in the vehicle provided the item(s) the officer is looking for could reasonably be in the passenger's belongings.[108]

In 2004, in *Thornton v. United States,* the U.S. Supreme Court expanded the *Houghton* decision and held that police can search the passenger compartment of a vehicle incident to arrest when the arrestee was a recent occupant of the vehicle.[109] In this case, police became suspicious of Thornton's driving because he appeared nervous and attempted to avoid contact with the officer. The officer checked the license plate and discovered that it belonged to a different vehicle. Before being stopped by the officer, Thornton turned his vehicle into a parking lot, parked, and began walking away. The officer confronted him and asked whether he had any weapons or drugs on him, which Thornton denied. Thornton consented to a limited search of his person, which revealed a suspicious item that he admitted to contain drugs. He was arrested and placed in the back of a police car. The officer then searched Thornton's vehicle incident to the arrest and found a handgun. The Supreme Court rejected the defendant's appeal that the seizure of the gun was unconstitutional and held that the search was done incident to the arrest to safeguard the officer and to prevent the destruction of evidence.

Border Searches A border search can be made without probable cause without a warrant, and indeed, without any articulable suspicion at all.[110] In *United States v. Martinez-Fuerte,* the Supreme Court ruled in 1976 that border patrol officers do not have to have probable cause or a warrant to stop cars for brief questioning at fixed checkpoints.[111]

Good Faith The Supreme Court established a "good faith" exception to the exclusionary rule in *United States v. Leon* (1984). It waived the exclusionary rule in cases in which the police act in reasonable reliance and good faith on a search warrant that is later ruled faulty or found to be unsupported by probable cause.[112]

Speaking for the Court, Justice Byron R. White stated,

> In the absence of an allegation that the magistrate abandoned his detached and neutral role, suppression is appropriate only if the officers were dishonest or reckless in preparing their affidavit or could not have harbored an objectively reasonable belief in the existence of probable cause. . . ."

During the 1980s, the Court continued its emphasis on "good faith" exceptions to the Fourth Amendment, in *Massachusetts v. Sheppard* (1984), *Illinois v. Krull* (1987), and *Maryland v. Garrison* (1987).[113]

In 1995, in *Arizona v. Evans,* the Court extended the "good faith" exception by creating a "computer errors exception." In this case, the police arrested Evans for a traffic violation. A routine computer check reported an outstanding arrest warrant for Evans. He was arrested, and a search of his vehicle revealed possession of a controlled substance. Later, it was determined that the arrest

You Are There!

United States v. Leon (1984)

In August 1981, Officer Cyril Rombach, an experienced and well-trained narcotics investigator, prepared an application for a search warrant to search the homes and automobiles of several suspects in a drug investigation. In September 1981, a search warrant was issued by a state superior judge. The officer executed the search warrant and found large quantities of drugs at three residences and in two automobiles listed on the warrant. Rombach arrested several people, including Alberto Leon, for drug violations.

The defendants were indicted by a grand jury and charged with conspiracy to possess and distribute cocaine. The defendants filed motions to suppress the evidence, and the district court granted the motions to suppress in part. It concluded that the affidavit was insufficient to establish probable cause. The court

recognized that Rombach had acted in good faith, but it rejected the government's suggestion that the Fourth Amendment exclusionary rule should not apply where evidence is seized in reasonable good faith reliance on a search warrant.

Upon appeal, the Supreme Court overruled the district court and established the "good faith doctrine." It ruled that evidence obtained in good faith, where the officers reasonably believed they had sufficient probable cause to get a warrant, is admissible in court. The Court said that the exclusionary rule should be applied only in cases in which the police purposely, recklessly, or negligently violate the law.

SOURCE: Based on *United States v. Leon,* 468 U.S. 897 (1984).

warrant should have been removed from the computer a few weeks earlier. However, the Court reasoned that officers could not be held responsible for a clerical error made by a court worker and did, in fact, act in good faith.[114]

In 2004, in *Groh v. Ramirez,* however, the Supreme Court rejected a "good faith" exception in a case involving a warrant to search a residence.[115] The warrant application and affidavit (paperwork presented to the Court to obtain the warrant) contained a particular description of the items to be seized. However, the warrant itself did not contain such a description as required by the Fourth Amendment. Although the warrant was reviewed, signed by a judge, and executed, the Supreme Court concluded that it was unconstitutional because any reasonable officer would have concluded from just a cursory look at the warrant that it was invalid.

Searches by Private Persons In *Burdeau v. McDowell* (1921), the Supreme Court ruled that the Bill of Rights applies only to the actions of government agents; it does not apply to private security employees or private citizens not acting on behalf of, or with, official law enforcement agencies.[116] The fact that private security personnel are not bound by the tenets of the Constitution and cannot obtain warrants, however, does not mean that they can indiscriminately violate the rights of offenders. If they

do, they can be sued at civil law and suffer severe financial damages.

The Police and Custodial Interrogation

FBI legal instructor Kimberly A. Crawford has written that the U.S. Supreme Court has recognized two constitutional sources of the right to counsel during interrogation. One source is the Court's interpretation in *Miranda v. Arizona*[117] of the Fifth Amendment right against self-incrimination; the other is contained within the language of the Sixth Amendment. The impetus for the creation of the *Miranda* rights was the Supreme Court's concern that **custodial interrogations** are intrinsically coercive. The right to counsel contained within *Miranda* applies only when the subject of an interrogation is in custody.[118]

In English common law, the lack of a confession was often viewed as a serious deficiency in the government's case, enough to cause a judge or jury to acquit an accused person. Although not required to prove guilt, the emphasis on securing a confession from a suspect remains today.[119]

You Are There!

Brown v. Mississippi (1936)

On March 30, 1934, Raymond Steward was murdered. On that night, Deputy Sheriff Dial went to the home of Ellington, one of the defendants, and requested him to accompany him to the house of the deceased, and there a number of white men were gathered, who began to accuse the defendant of the crime. Upon his denial, they seized him and hanged him by a rope to the limb of a tree, twice. When they took him down the second time, they tied him to a tree and whipped him. The trial record showed that the signs of the rope on his neck were plainly visible during the trial. He was again picked up a day or two later, and again severely beaten until he confessed. The other two defendants, Ed Brown and Henry Shields, were also arrested and taken to jail. To obtain the confession, the defendants were "made to strip and they were laid over chairs and their backs were cut to pieces with a leather strap with buckles on it and they were likewise made by the said

deputy definitely to understand that the whipping would be continued unless and until they confessed, and not only confessed, but confessed to every matter of detail as demanded by those present."

The defendants made their confession on April 1, 1934, were indicted on April 4, went on trial on April 5, and were convicted and sentenced to death on April 6, 1934. The deputy sheriff who administered over the beatings, Deputy Sheriff Dial, testifying in court, responded to an inquiry as to how severely a defendant was whipped by stating, "Not too much for a negro; not as much as I would have done if it were left to me."

On appeal, the Supreme Court ruled that the actions against the three men were violations of their due process rights.

SOURCE: Based on *Brown v. Mississippi*, 297 U.S. 278 (1936).

Louis DiPietro, a special agent and legal instructor at the FBI Academy, states that a confession is probably the most substantiating and damaging evidence that can be admitted against a defendant. To be admissible, due process mandates that a confession be made voluntarily. In addition, it mandates the investigator's scrupulous compliance with the U.S. Supreme Court's requirements emanating from the landmark *Miranda* case and other constitutional rights of an accused. DiPietro warns that if the government obtains a nonvoluntary confession, the resulting confession will be excludable on the grounds of denial of due process of law.[120]

This section will pay particular attention to cases leading to the *Miranda* ruling, the *Miranda* case and its ruling, cases that seem to have led to the erosion of the *Miranda* rule, the *Dickerson* ruling and cases subsequent to *Dickerson,* and surreptitious recording of suspects' conversations.

The Path to *Miranda*

The police have many crimes to investigate and often not enough resources to accomplish their mission. In many cases, there is not enough physical evidence or there are no eyewitnesses to assist the police in their investigation. Thus, police must

seek to gain a confession from a defendant, particularly in murder cases, to gain a conviction.

The history of methods used by the police to obtain confessions from suspects has been sordid, including beatings and torture by the police that came to be known as the third degree. From 1936 until 1966, the Supreme Court issued a number of rulings to preclude this misconduct and ensure compliance with due process as guaranteed by the Bill of Rights. The following landmark cases show the development of rules regarding custodial interrogation during those three decades. See Table 13.11 for a list of landmark cases leading to the *Miranda* decision.

End of the Third Degree In *Brown v. Mississippi* (1936), the Supreme Court put an end to the almost

TABLE 13.11 The Path to *Miranda*

Brown v. Mississippi (1936)

McNabb-Mallory Rule (1957)

Escobedo v. Illinois (1964)

Miranda v. Arizona (1966)

The *Miranda* Rules (1966)

You Are There!

McNabb v. United States (1943) and *Mallory v. United States* (1957)

The McNabb family consisted of five Tennessee mountain people who operated an illegal moonshine business near Chattanooga. During a raid on their business by federal agents, a police officer was killed. The five were arrested and subjected to continuous interrogation for two days. Two of the McNabbs were convicted based on their confessions, and each was sentenced to 45 years in prison for murder. In *McNabb v. United States,* the Supreme Court ruled that these confessions were in violation of the Constitution because they violated the Federal Rules of Criminal Procedure, which required that defendants must be taken before a magistrate without unnecessary delay.

In *Mallory v. United States,* the defendant was a 19-year-old male of limited intelligence who was arrested for rape in Washington, D.C. He was arrested the day after the crime, taken to the police station, and questioned over a 10-hour period. He confessed under interrogation by the police officer administering the polygraph examination. The Supreme Court again ruled that the delay in bringing the defendant before a magistrate was a violation of the Federal Rules of Criminal Procedure.

In both of these cases, the Court did not even consider the question of voluntariness. The new standard that the Court adopted was called the *McNabb-Mallory* rule and considered only the time element between the arrest and the first appearance before a judge. This rule applied only to actions of federal law enforcement officers.

SOURCE: Based on *McNabb v. United States,* 318 U.S. 332 (1943) and *Mallory v. United States,* 354 U.S. 449 (1957).

"official" practice of brutality and violence (the **third degree**) used by the police to obtain confessions from suspects. The case involved the coerced confessions, through beatings, of three men. The Supreme Court suppressed the confessions and emphasized that the use of confessions obtained through barbaric tactics deprived the defendants of their right to due process under the Fourteenth Amendment. The Court, in effect, said that coerced confessions were untrustworthy, unreliable, and unconstitutional.[121]

Speaking for the Court, Chief Justice Charles E. Hughes wrote the following:

> Because a State may dispense with a jury trial, it does not follow that it may substitute trial by ordeal. The rack and torture chamber may not be substituted for the witness stand. The State may not permit an accused to be hurried to conviction under mob domination—where the whole proceeding is but a mask—without supplying corrective process. . . . The due process clause requires "that state action, whether through one agency or another, shall be consistent with the fundamental principles of liberty and justice which lie at the base of all our civil and political institutions." . . . It would be difficult to conceive of methods more revolting to the sense of justice than

those taken to procure the confessions of these petitioners, and the use of confessions thus obtained as the basis for conviction and sentence was a clear denial of due process.

The Prompt Arraignment Rule *McNabb v. United States* (1943) and *Mallory v. United States* (1957) were cases that involved confessions obtained as a result of delays in the "prompt arraignment" of the defendants before a federal judge.[122] The Court did not address whether or not the confessions were voluntary, the previous standard for admitting them into evidence. Instead, it considered how long it took for law enforcement agents to bring the suspects before a judge and whether the confessions should be admissible because of this delay.

Entry of Lawyers into the Station House In 1964, the Supreme Court ruled in *Escobedo v. Illinois* that the refusal by the police to honor a suspect's request to consult with his lawyer during the course of an interrogation constituted a denial of his Sixth Amendment right to counsel and his Fifth Amendment right to be free from self-incrimination—rights made obligatory upon the states by the Fourteenth Amendment.[123] The decision rendered any incriminating statement elicited by the police during such an interrogation inadmissible in court. The Court ruled that once a

You Are There!

Escobedo v. Illinois (1964)

On the evening of January 19, 1960, Danny Escobedo's brother-in-law, Manual, was shot to death. The next morning the Chicago police arrested Escobedo and attempted to interrogate him. However, his attorney obtained a writ of habeas corpus, requiring the police to free him.

On January 30, Benedict DiGerlando, who was then in police custody, told the police that Escobedo had fired the fatal shots at his brother-in-law. The police then rearrested Escobedo and brought him to police headquarters. Escobedo told the police he wanted to consult his lawyer. Shortly after the arrest, Escobedo's attorney arrived at headquarters and attempted to see him but was denied access to Escobedo. During their stay at headquarters, the police caused an encounter between Escobedo and DiGerlando during which Escobedo made admissions to the crime. Later, a statement was taken from Escobedo. He was never advised of his rights. He was convicted of the murder of Manual based on his statements.

The Supreme Court reversed Escobedo's conviction based on the fact that the police violated Escobedo's Sixth Amendment rights, rights made obligatory on the states through the Fourteenth Amendment.

Subsequent to his landmark Supreme Court case, Escobedo was arrested for burglary and selling drugs. He was sentenced to prison and paroled in 1975. In 1984, he was again sentenced to prison on sex crime charges involving a 13-year-old girl. While free on bond pending an appeal on that conviction, he was arrested in Chicago for attempted murder. He pled guilty.

SOURCE: Based on *Escobedo v. Illinois* 378 U.S. 478 (1964); and James A. Inciardi, *Criminal Justice,* 3rd ed. (Orlando, Fla.: Harcourt Brace Jovanovich, 1990), pp. 280–281.

suspect becomes the focus of a police interrogation, is taken into custody, and requests the advice of a lawyer, the police must permit access to the lawyer.

The *Miranda* Ruling

The well-known case of *Miranda v. Arizona* (1966) was the culmination of many Supreme Court decisions focusing on the rights of individuals during police interrogations.[124] The *Miranda* decision was actually a combination of cases involving four persons: Ernesto Miranda, arrested in Phoenix, for kidnapping and rape; Michael Vignera, arrested in New York City for robbery; Carl Westover, arrested in Kansas City for robbery; and Roy Stewart, arrested in Los Angeles for robbery. What we now call the *Miranda* rules could have been called the Vignera, or Westover, or Stewart rules, but the Court decided to issue their ruling under Ernesto Miranda's case.[125]

In *Miranda,* the Supreme Court ruled that confessions are by their very nature inherently coercive and that custodial interrogation makes any statements obtained from defendants compelled and thus not voluntary. The Court felt that interrogations violate the Fifth Amendment, which guarantees that no one shall be compelled to be a witness against himself or herself in a criminal case, and that this guarantee is violated anytime a person is taken into custody and interrogated.

The Court then established the well-known *Miranda* **rules** or *Miranda* **warnings,** which state that before any interrogation of a person in custody the police must do the following:

- Advise the suspect that he or she has the right to remain silent
- Advise the suspect that anything he or she says can and will be used in court against him or her
- Advise the suspect that he or she has the right to consult a lawyer and to have the lawyer present during questioning
- Advise the suspect that if he or she cannot afford an attorney, an attorney will be provided, free of charge

The Court further ruled that if before or during the interrogation, the suspect, in any way, indicates a wish to remain silent or to have an attorney, the interrogation may no longer proceed.

The *Miranda* rule applies to all custodial interrogations; however, this does not mean every police interview requires the warnings. The Supreme Court has made it clear that *Miranda* applies only when the suspect is *both* in custody and subject to interrogation.[126] Even interrogations taking place at

You Are There!

Miranda v. Arizona (1966)

On March 2, 1963, in Phoenix, Arizona, an 18-year-old woman walking to a bus stop after work was accosted by a man who shoved her into his car and tied her hands and ankles. He then took her to the edge of the city where he raped her. The rapist drove the victim to a street near her home and let her out of the car. On March 13, the Phoenix police arrested a 23-year-old, eighth-grade dropout named Ernesto Miranda and charged him with the crime. Miranda had a police record dating back to when he was 14 years old, had been given an undesirable discharge by the army for being a Peeping Tom, and had served time in federal prison for driving a stolen car across a state line.

Miranda was placed in a lineup at the station house and positively identified by the victim. He was then taken to an interrogation room where he was questioned by the police without being informed that he had a right to have an attorney present. Two hours later, police emerged from the interrogation room with a written confession signed by Miranda. At the top of the statement was a typed paragraph stating

that the confession was made voluntarily, without threats or promises of immunity and "with full knowledge of my legal rights, understanding any statement I make may be used against me."

At trial, Miranda was found guilty of kidnapping and rape, and sentenced to 20 to 30 years in prison. Upon appeal, the Supreme Court ruled that Miranda's confession was inadmissible.

Ernesto Miranda was subsequently given a new trial. He was convicted of rape and kidnapping after his common-law wife, Twila Hoffman, testified that he had admitted kidnapping and raping the victim. He was sentenced to a 20- to 30-year prison term and was paroled in 1972. In 1974, he was arrested for the illegal possession of a gun and drugs. In 1976, at age thirty-four, Miranda was murdered in a Phoenix skid row bar during a quarrel over a card game.

SOURCE: Based on *Miranda v. Arizona,* 384 U.S. 436 (1966); and James A. Inciardi, *Criminal Justice,* 3rd ed. (Orlando, Fla.: Harcourt Brace Jovanovich, 1990), pp. 280–281.

---

the police station may not fall within the meaning of custodial interrogation. For example, in *Oregon v. Mathiason* (1977), the Court held that a suspect who was invited to come to the police station, voluntarily arrived unaccompanied by the police, and was told before the interrogation that he was not under arrest was not in custody for the purpose of *Miranda*.[127] The Court has also found that routine traffic stops and questioning at the suspect's home are noncustodial situations.[128]

When giving the *Miranda* warnings, officers must ensure that a suspect makes a knowing, intelligent, and voluntary waiver of his rights as a prerequisite to questioning. Also, if a suspect clearly indicates unwillingness to answer questions and invokes the right to silence, police must scrupulously honor that request. Where a suspect makes a clear request to consult with an attorney, police must immediately cease any further questioning and may not contact the suspect about any crime unless a lawyer is present or unless the suspect initiates the contact with the police.[129] The Court has also ruled that persons who cannot understand the

Miranda warnings because of their age, mental handicaps, or language problems, cannot be legally questioned without an attorney being present.[130] In *Arizona v. Roberson* (1988), the Court held that the police may not avoid a suspect's request for a lawyer by beginning a new line of questioning, even if it is about an unrelated offense.[131]

The Erosion of *Miranda*

In the aftermath of the *Miranda* decision, there was tremendous confusion in the legal community over its exact meaning. Consequently, a large number of cases were brought to the Court challenging and questioning it. Eventually the Supreme Court of the 1970s and 1980s under Chief Justice Burger began to impose a series of exceptions to the *Miranda* decision. These decisions led noted civil liberties lawyer and Harvard law professor Alan M. Dershowitz to write an article in 1984 entitled, "A Requiem for the Exclusionary Rule," in which he said, "The Burger Court has chipped away at the exclusionary rule—carving out so many exceptions that it is falling of its own weight."[132] Dershowitz added,

> Our twenty-five year experiment with the exclusionary rule may well be coming to an end. We have learned precious little from it, because the exclusionary rule was never really given a chance. The public, spurred by politicians' rhetoric, closed its eyes and ears to facts like the following: that only a tiny fraction of defendants (less than half of one percent, according to a federal study) are freed because of the exclusionary rule; and that there has been a marked improvement both in police efficiency and in compliance with the Constitution since the exclusionary rule was established.[133]

Despite Dershowitz's thoughts, the *Miranda* rule still stands and defendants in custody must still be advised of their constitutional rights before any interrogation. However, the Court does recognize certain exceptions to *Miranda*. A sample of post-*Miranda* cases that have led to its weakening follow.

Harris v. New York In *Harris v. New York* (1971), the Court ruled that statements that are trustworthy, even though they were obtained without giving a defendant *Miranda* warnings, may be used to attack the credibility of a defendant who takes the witness stand.[134] The prosecutor accused Harris of lying on the stand and used statements obtained by the police, without *Miranda* warnings, before the trial to prove it.

Justice Warren E. Burger, speaking for the Court relative to the *Miranda* rule, wrote, "The shield provided by *Miranda* cannot be perverted into a license to use perjury by way of a defense, free from the risk of confrontation with prior inconsistent utterances. We hold, therefore, that petitioner's credibility was appropriately impeached by use of his earlier conflicting statements."

Michigan v. Mosley In *Michigan v. Mosley* (1975), the Court ruled that a second interrogation, held after the suspect had initially refused to make a statement, was not a violation of the *Miranda* decision. In the second interrogation, which was for a different crime, the suspect had been read the *Miranda* warnings.[135]

Brewer v. Williams In *Brewer v. Williams*, decided in 1977, the Supreme Court seemed to extend the meaning of the word *interrogation* by interpreting comments made by a police detective as "subtle coercion."[136] This case affirmed *Miranda* but is presented here because of a second decision in the case of *Nix v. Williams* (1984).[137] In this case, the state of Iowa continued to appeal the decision reached in *Brewer v. Williams*. In 1984, the Supreme Court, in *Nix v. Williams*, promulgated the "inevitability of discovery rule." Victim Pamela Powers's body would have been discovered inevitably, so it should be allowed as evidence in the trial despite the subtle coercion of the police.

Rhode Island v. Innis In *Rhode Island v. Innis* (1980), the Supreme Court clarified its definition of interrogation by ruling that the "definition of interrogation can extend only to words or actions on the part of police officers that *they should have known* [court's emphasis] were reasonably likely to elicit an incriminating response."[138] In this case, a man told the police where he had left a shotgun he had used in a shooting after the police had made remarks about the possibility of a disabled child finding it. (There was a home for disabled children nearby).

New York v. Quarles In *New York v. Quarles* (1984), the Supreme Court created a "public safety" exception to the *Miranda* rule.[139] In this case, a police officer, after handcuffing a man wanted in connection with a crime, and after feeling an empty shoulder holster on the man's body, asked him where the gun was without giving the man the *Miranda* warnings. The gun was suppressed as evidence because the officer's question was not preceded by the warnings. The Supreme Court, however, overruled the state court and said the officer's failure to read the *Miranda* warnings was justified in the interest of public safety.

The Court wrote,

> We conclude that the need for answers to questions in a situation posing a threat to the public safety outweighs the need for the prophylactic rule protecting the Fifth Amendment's privilege against self-incrimination. We decline to place officers such as Officer Kraft in the untenable position of having to consider, often in a matter of seconds, whether it best serves society for them to ask the necessary questions without the *Miranda* warnings and render whatever probative evidence they uncover inadmissible, or for them to give the warnings in order to preserve the admissibility of evidence they

You Are There!

Brewer v. Williams (1977) and Nix v. Williams (1984)

On Christmas Eve, 1968, 10-year-old Pamela Powers was at a Des Moines, Iowa, YMCA with her parents to watch her brother participate in a wrestling match. Pamela told her parents that she was going to use the bathroom. She was never seen alive again. At about the time of Pamela's disappearance, a young boy saw a man, later identified as Robert Williams, walking out of the YMCA carrying a bundle wrapped in a blanket to his car. The boy told police that he thought he saw two legs under the blanket. Robert Williams was a resident of the YMCA, a religious fanatic, and an escaped mental patient. On Christmas Day Williams's car was found abandoned near the city of Davenport, Iowa, 160 miles from Des Moines. On the day after Christmas, Williams walked into the Davenport police station house and surrendered to the police. The Davenport police notified the Des Moines police, who arranged to pick up Williams.

When Detective Leaming arrived at the Davenport police station to pick up Williams, Williams's lawyer, Henry McKnight, said that he did not want Williams to be the subject of any interrogation during the trip from Davenport to Des Moines. Leaming agreed to the lawyer's request.

In the car on the way back to Des Moines, Detective Leaming, knowing that Williams was a religious fanatic, addressed him as "Reverend" and made what has become known as the "Christian Burial Speech":

> I want to give you something to think about while we're traveling down the road. . . . Number one, I want you to observe the weather conditions. It's raining, it's sleeting, it's freezing, driving is very treacherous, visibility is poor, it's going to be dark early this evening. They are predicting several inches of snow for tonight, and I feel that you yourself are the only person that knows where this little girl's body is, that you yourself have only been there once, and if you get a snow on top of it you yourself may be unable to find it. And, since we will be going right past the area on the way into Des Moines, I feel that we could stop and locate the body, that the parents of this little girl should be entitled to a Christian burial for the little girl who was snatched away from them on Christmas Eve and murdered. And I feel we should stop and locate it on the way in rather than waiting until morning and trying to come back out after a snowstorm and possibly not being able to find it at all.

After this speech, Williams directed the police to the young girl's dead body. Williams was convicted of her murder.

On appeal to the Supreme Court, the Court voted 5–4 that Leaming's "Christian Burial Speech" constituted custodial interrogation and that the evidence, the body, was illegally obtained and therefore not admissible in court.

But, the state of Iowa continued to appeal the *Brewer* decision, and in 1984 the Supreme Court in *Nix v. Williams* promulgated the "inevitability of discovery rule," saying in effect that Pamela Powers's body would have been discovered inevitably, thus it should be allowed to be used as evidence in a trial.

SOURCE: Based on *Brewer v. Williams*, 430 U.S. 387 (1977); and *Nix v. Williams*, 467 U.S. 431 (1984).

might uncover but possibly damage or destroy their ability to obtain that evidence and neutralize the volatile situation confronting them.

Oregon v. Elstad In *Oregon v. Elstad* (1985), the Supreme Court ruled that the simple failure of the police to warn a suspect of his *Miranda* rights (with no indication of misbehavior or coercion on the part of the police) until after obtaining an incriminating statement or confession was not a violation of *Miranda*.[140] In *Elstad,* law enforcement officers went to the home of a burglary suspect, Elstad, to take him into custody. The suspect's mother answered the door and led the officers to the suspect who was in his bedroom. Before the arrest, one of the officers waited for the suspect to get dressed and accompanied him to the living room while the other officer asked the suspect's mother to step into the kitchen where he advised her that they had a warrant for her son's arrest on a burglary charge. The officer who remained with Elstad asked him if he was aware of why they were at his home to arrest him. Elstad replied that he did not know. The officer then asked

You Are There!

Rhode Island v. Innis (1980)

On the night of January 12, 1975, John Mulvaney, a Providence, Rhode Island, cabdriver, disappeared after being dispatched to pick up a fare. His body was discovered four days later buried in a shallow grave in Coventry, Rhode Island. He had died from a shotgun blast to the back of his head.

Five days later, shortly after midnight, the Providence police received a phone call from a cabdriver who reported that he had just been robbed by a man with a sawed-off shotgun. While at the police station the robbery victim noticed a picture of his assailant on a bulletin board and informed a detective. The detective prepared a photo array, and the complainant identified the suspect again. The police began a search of the area where the cabdriver had brought the suspect. At about 4:30 AM, an officer spotted the suspect standing in the street. Upon apprehending the suspect, the officer, Patrolman Lovel, advised him of his *Miranda* rights. A sergeant responded and advised the suspect of his *Miranda* rights. A captain responded and also advised the suspect of his constitutional rights. The suspect stated that he understood his rights and wanted to speak with an attorney. The captain directed three officers in a caged wagon, a four-door police car with a wire screen mesh between the front and rear seats, to bring the suspect to the police station. While en route to the police station two of the officers engaged in conversation. One, Patrolman Gleckman, testified at the trial:

> At this point, I was talking back and forth with Patrolman McKenna stating that I frequent this area while on patrol and (that because a school for handicapped children is located nearby) there's a lot of handicapped children running around in

this area, and God forbid one of them might find a weapon with shells and they might hurt themselves.

Patrolman McKenna testified:

> I more or less concurred with him that it was a safety factor and that we should, you know, continue to search for the weapon and try to find it.

The third officer, Patrolman Williams, didn't participate in the conversation but testified as to the conversation between the two officers:

> He (Gleckman) said it would be too bad if the little—I believe he said a girl—would pick up the gun, maybe kill herself.

According to police testimony, the suspect then interrupted the conversation, stating that the officers should turn the car around so he could show them where the gun was located. When they reached the crime scene, the suspect was again advised of his *Miranda* rights and the suspect said he understood his rights but that he "wanted to get the gun out of the way because of the kids in the area in the school." The suspect then led the police to the area where the shotgun was located.

The defendant Innis was convicted, but upon appeal, the gun was suppressed. However, in 1980, the United States Supreme Court heard the case and reversed the Rhode Island appeal court, ruling that the officers' statements were not interrogation, and the gun was allowed to remain in evidence.

SOURCE: Based on *Rhode Island v. Innis,* 446 U.S. 291 (1980).

---

him if he knew a person by the name of Gross (the subject of the burglary), and Elstad replied that he did and added that he heard that there was a robbery at the Gross house. The officer then told Elstad that he believed that he (Elstad) was involved in the burglary. Elstad then stated to the officer, "Yes, I was there."

The police then brought Elstad to the police station where he was advised of his *Miranda* rights and subjected to custodial interrogation. Elstad waived his rights and gave a full confession admitting to his

role in the burglary. In court, Elstad's attorney made a motion to suppress his confession arguing that the confession was "tainted" by the unwarned statement made in Elstad's living room. The trial court agreed and held that once the initial *Miranda* violation occurred, all that followed was tainted, including the station house confession, and therefore, it was inadmissible. Upon appeal to the U.S. Supreme Court, the Court rejected the lower court's ruling and held that a simple failure to administer the *Miranda* warnings to a suspect, with no indication

You Are There!

New York v. Quarles (1984)

At 12:30 AM, police officers Frank Kraft and Sal Scarring were on routine patrol in Queens, New York, when a young woman approached them and told them that she had been raped by a black man, approximately 6 feet tall, who was wearing a black jacket with the name "Big Ben" printed in yellow letters on the back. She then told the officers that the man had just entered an A&P supermarket located nearby and that the man had a gun. The officers put the woman into the police car and drove to the A&P, where Officer Kraft entered the store while his partner radioed for backup. Kraft observed the suspect, Mr. Quarles, approaching a checkout counter. On seeing the officer, Quarles turned and ran toward the rear of the store. Kraft took out his revolver and chased Quarles. When Quarles turned the corner at the end of an aisle, Kraft lost sight of him for several seconds. On regaining sight of Quarles, Kraft apprehended him and ordered him to stop and put his

hands over his head. Kraft then frisked Quarles and discovered that he was wearing an empty shoulder holster. After handcuffing him, Kraft asked him where the gun was. Quarles nodded in the direction of some empty cartons and said, "The gun is over there." Kraft then retrieved a loaded .38 caliber revolver from one of the cartons and then formally arrested Quarles and read him his *Miranda* warnings. At trial the judge suppressed Quarles's statement, "The gun is over there," and suppressed the gun because Kraft had not given Quarles his *Miranda* warnings before asking, "Where's the gun?"

On appeal from the prosecutor to the United States Supreme Court, the Court reversed the New York ruling and created a "public safety" exception to the requirement that police give a suspect his *Miranda* warnings before interrogation.

SOURCE: Based on *New York v. Quarles,* 104 S.Ct. 2626 (1984).

of behavior by the law enforcement officer that could be interpreted as coercion, compulsion, or an effort to undermine the suspect's ability to exercise his free will, should not keep out a statement that the suspect makes that otherwise is voluntary.

Moran v. Burbine In *Moran v. Burbine* (1986), a murder case, the Supreme Court ruled that the police failure to inform a suspect undergoing custodial interrogation of his attorney's attempts to reach him does not constitute a violation of the *Miranda* rule.[141] The Court reasoned that events that are not known by a defendant have no bearing on his capacity to knowingly waive his or her rights.

Speaking for the Court, Justice Sandra Day O'Connor, commenting on the actions of the police in lying to the lawyer, Munson, wrote,

> Focusing primarily on the impropriety of conveying false information to an attorney, he [Burbine] invites us to declare that such behavior should be condemned as violative of canons fundamental to the "traditions and conscience of our people." . . . We do not question that on facts more egregious than those presented here police deception might rise to a level of a due process violation. . . .

We hold only that, on these facts, the challenged conduct falls short of the kind of misbehavior that so shocks the sensibilities of civilized society as to warrant a federal intrusion into the criminal processes of the States.

Illinois v. Perkins In *Illinois v. Perkins* (1990), the Supreme Court further clarified its *Miranda* decision.[142] In the *Perkins* case, police placed an informant and an undercover officer in a cellblock with Lloyd Perkins, a suspected murderer incarcerated on an unrelated charge of aggravated assault. While planning a prison break, the undercover officer asked Perkins whether he had ever "done" anyone. In response, Perkins described at length the details of a murder-for-hire he had committed.

When Perkins was subsequently charged with the murder, he argued successfully to have the statements he made in prison suppressed because no *Miranda* warnings had been given before his conversation with the informant and undercover officer. On review, however, the Supreme Court reversed the order of suppression.

Rejecting Perkins's argument, the Supreme Court recognized that there are limitations to the

You Are There!

Moran v. Burbine (1986)

On March 3, 1977, Mary Jo Hickey was found unconscious in a factory parking lot in Providence, Rhode Island. Suffering from injuries to her skull apparently inflicted by a metal pipe found at the scene, she was rushed to a nearby hospital. Three weeks later, she died from her wounds.

Several months after her death, the Cranston, Rhode Island, police arrested Brian Burbine and two others for burglary. Shortly before the arrest, Detective Ferranti of the Cranston police had learned from a confidential informant that the man responsible for Ms. Hickey's death lived at a certain address and was also known by the nickname "Butch." On learning from the arresting officer that Burbine went by the nickname Butch and that he gave his address as the same one previously given by the informant, Ferranti advised Burbine of his constitutional rights. Burbine refused to speak to the detective. Ferranti spoke to Burbine's two associates and obtained more incriminating information. Ferranti then called the Providence police, who sent three detectives to Cranston to interrogate Burbine.

That evening Burbine's sister called the Providence Public Defender's Office to obtain legal assistance for her brother. A lawyer from the office, Allegra Munson, called the Cranston detective division. The conversation went as follows:

> A male voice responded with the word "Detectives." Ms. Munson identified herself and asked if

Brian Burbine was being held; the person responded affirmatively. Ms. Munson explained to the person that Burbine was represented by attorney and she would act as Burbine's legal counsel in the event that the police intended to place him in a lineup or question him. The unidentified person told Ms. Munson that the police would not be questioning Burbine or putting him in a lineup and that they were through with him for the night. Ms. Munson was not informed that the Providence Police were at the Cranston police station or that Burbine was a suspect in Mary's murder.

Less than an hour after Munson's call, Burbine was brought to an interrogation room and questioned about Mary Jo Hickey's murder. He was informed of his *Miranda* rights on three separate occasions, and he signed three written forms acknowledging that he understood his right to the presence of an attorney and indicating that he did not want an attorney called or appointed for him. Burbine signed three written statements fully admitting to the murder. Based on his written statements Burbine was convicted of murder. Upon appeal, the Rhode Island Court of Appeals reversed the conviction.

The U.S. Supreme Court reversed the court of appeals ruling and ruled that Burbine's constitutional rights were not violated.

SOURCE: Based on *Moran v. Burbine,* 475 U.S. 412 (1986).

---

rules announced in *Miranda*. The Court expressly declined to accept the notion that the *Miranda* warnings are required whenever a suspect is in custody in a technical sense and converses with someone who happens to be a government agent. Rather, the Court concluded that not every custodial interrogation creates the psychologically compelling atmosphere that *Miranda* was designed to protect against. When the compulsion is lacking, the Court found, so is the need for *Miranda* warnings.

The Court in *Perkins* found the facts at issue to be a clear example of a custodial interrogation that created no compulsion. Pointing out that compulsion is determined from the perspective of the

suspect, the Court noted that Perkins had no reason to believe that either the informant or the undercover officer had any official power over him, and therefore, he had no reason to feel any compulsion to make self-incriminating statements. On the contrary, Perkins bragged about his role in the murder in an effort to impress those he believed to be his fellow inmates. *Miranda* was not designed to protect individuals from themselves.

Pennsylvania v. Muniz In *Pennsylvania v. Muniz* (1990), the Court ruled that the police use of the defendant's slurred and drunken responses to booking questions (he was arrested for driving under the influence of alcohol) as evidence in his trial was not a violation of *Miranda* rights even thought he was never given his *Miranda* warnings.[143]

Arizona v. Fulminante In 1991, in *Arizona v. Fulminante,* the Supreme Court further weakened *Miranda* by ruling that a coerced confession might be a harmless trial error.[144] In this case, the Court overruled years of precedent to hold that if other evidence introduced at trial is strong enough, the use of a coerced confession could be considered harmless and a conviction upheld. In other words, a coerced confession, by itself, is not sufficient to have a conviction overruled if there is other compelling evidence of guilt.

Minnick v. Mississippi In *Minnick v. Mississippi* (1991), the Court clarified the mechanics of *Miranda* by ruling that once a suspect in custody requests counsel in response to *Miranda* warnings, law enforcement officers may no longer attempt to re-interrogate that suspect unless the suspect's attorney is present or the suspect initiates the contact with the law enforcement agents.[145]

McNeil v. Wisconsin In *McNeil v. Wisconsin* (1991), the Court ruled that an in-custody suspect who requests counsel at a judicial proceeding, such as an arraignment or initial appearance, is only invoking the Sixth Amendment right to counsel as to the charged offense and is not invoking the Fifth Amendment right to have an attorney present during the custodial interrogation.[146]

Withrow v. Williams In *Withrow v. Williams* (1993), the Supreme Court distinguished *Miranda* violations from Fourth Amendment violations with respect to habeas corpus proceedings.[147] The Court held that criminal defendants can continue to raise *Miranda* violations in habeas corpus proceedings, even though it had previously restricted habeas corpus petitions that raised Fourth Amendment issues.

Davis v. United States In *Davis v. United States* (1994), the Court ruled that after law enforcement officers obtain a valid *Miranda* waiver from an in-custody suspect, they may continue questioning him when he makes an ambiguous or equivocal request for counsel during the questioning.[148] The Court stated that although it may be a good law enforcement practice to attempt to clarify an equivocal request for counsel, that practice is not constitutionally required.

In *Davis,* Naval Investigative Service (NIS) agents investigating a murder obtained both oral and written *Miranda* waivers from the defendant. After being interviewed for approximately 90 minutes, the defendant said, "Maybe I should talk to a lawyer." After asking some clarifying questions, the NIS agents continued to interrogate him. The Court ruled that the defendant's statement was not sufficiently unequivocal to constitute an assertion of his *Miranda* right to counsel.

Stansbury v. California In *Stansbury v. California* (1994), the Court reaffirmed the principle that an officer's uncommunicated suspicions about a suspect's guilt are irrelevant to the question of whether that suspect is in custody for purposes of *Miranda.*[149] Thus, custody for *Miranda* purposes is a completely objective determination based on facts and circumstances known to the subject.

In *Stansbury,* the Court reiterated its earlier holding in *Oregon v. Mathiason* (1977),[150] that *Miranda* warnings are required only when a person is in custody, which can be defined as either a formal arrest or a restraint on freedom of movement to the degree associated with a formal arrest. The Court then stated that this determination of custody depends on objective factors and not on the subjective views of the officers or the subject.

The *Dickerson* Ruling and Beyond

In a much-anticipated case, *Dickerson v. United States* (2000), the Supreme Court ruled that *Miranda* was a constitutional decision that cannot be overruled by an act of Congress.[151] In this case, Charles Thomas Dickerson was charged with conspiracy to commit bank robbery and other offenses. Before trial, he moved to suppress a statement he had made to the FBI on the grounds that he had not received *Miranda* warnings before being interrogated. The District Court suppressed the statement. The prosecution appealed, arguing that two years after the Supreme Court's *Miranda* decision, Congress passed a new federal criminal procedure and evidence law, 18 USC 3501, providing that a confession shall be admissible in federal court if it is voluntarily given. The law did not require the giving of *Miranda* warnings to suspects in custody. The prosecution felt that Congress intended to overrule *Miranda* because the new law required merely voluntariness—not the four warnings as per *Miranda*—as the determining factor as to whether a statement or confession will be admissible.

After several appellate decisions the U.S. Supreme Court finally ruled in *Dickerson* that *Miranda* was a constitutional decision—that is, a decision that interprets and polices the Constitution—that cannot be overruled by an Act of Congress, such as 18 USC 3501. Though conceding that Congress may modify or set aside the Court's rules of evidence and procedure that are not required by the Constitution, the Court emphasized that Congress may not overrule the Court's decisions, such as *Miranda,* that interpret and apply the Constitution.

The Court cited various other reasons for reaching its conclusion that *Miranda* is a constitutionally based rule. Among them, the Court noted that *Miranda* had become part of our national culture because the warnings were embedded in routine police practice. By holding *Miranda* to be a constitutional decision, the Court reaffirmed that *Miranda* governs the admissibility of statements made during custodial interrogation in both state and federal courts. Given the *Dickerson* decision, a violation of *Miranda* is now clearly a violation of the Constitution, which can result in suppression of statements in both federal and state courts.[152]

Before *Dickerson,* some constitutional scholars had expected that the Court might find a way to use the many cases mentioned in the "Erosion of *Miranda*" section to overrule *Miranda*. The Court expressly declined to do so in *Dickerson*. The Court's decision in this case did not attempt to find and defend an underlying rationale that would reconcile *Miranda* with those previous relevant cases that threatened to undermine or erode *Miranda*.[153]

After *Dickerson,* the Supreme Court continued to make significant rulings regarding custodial interrogation and the *Miranda* rule. In *Texas v. Cobb* (2001), the Court ruled that the Sixth Amendment right to counsel only applies to the case for which that right was invoked by the suspect and not other cases affecting the suspect.[154]

In this case, Raymond Cobb, 17, was accused of burglarizing the home of Lindsey Owings. When Owings returned from work, he found his house burglarized and his wife and daughter missing. The police conducted an investigation and eventually questioned Cobb about the incident. At the time of the questioning, Cobb was incarcerated on an unrelated offense. After being advised of and waiving his *Miranda* rights, Cobb admitted to the burglary but denied any knowledge of the whereabouts of

the woman and child. He was indicted on the burglary and invoked his Sixth Amendment right to counsel. After being freed on bond, Cobb confessed to his father that he had killed the woman and the child. The father reported his son's confession to the police, and a warrant was obtained for the boy's arrest on charges of murder.

After the arrest, Cobb was advised of his *Miranda* rights and waived them. He then admitted to the police that he stabbed the wife to death with a knife he had brought with him and then took her body into a wooded area behind the house to bury her. He then returned to the house and found the sixteen-month-old child sleeping on its bed. He took the baby into the woods and laid it near the mother. He then obtained a shovel and dug a grave. Before Cobb had put the mother's body in the grave, the child awoke and began stumbling around, looking for her mother. When the baby fell into the grave, Cobb put the mother's body on top of her and buried them both. Cobb subsequently led police to the grave.

Cobb was convicted of capital murder and sentenced to death. He appealed his conviction on the grounds that the interrogation following his arrest on the murder charges violated his Sixth Amendment right to counsel that had attached and been invoked with respect to the burglary charge. An appellate court agreed and Cobb's murder conviction was reversed. The Supreme Court, however, reversed the appellate court and ruled that the interrogation did not violate Cobb's Sixth Amendment right to counsel and that the confession was admissible. The Court argued that the Sixth Amendment right to counsel is "offense specific," and applied to the burglary charge only and not the murder charge.

In 2003, the U.S. Supreme Court decided two more important cases involving confessions. In *Chavez v. Martinez,* the Court held that questioning alone, unrelated to a criminal case, does not violate the Fifth Amendment self-incrimination clause. The Court ruled that the phrase "criminal case" in the Fifth Amendment's self-incrimination clause, at the very least requires initiation of legal proceedings and does not encompass the entire criminal investigatory process, including police interrogations.[155] In this case, Sergeant Chavez was interviewing Martinez while Martinez was being treated in a hospital emergency room suffering from gunshot wounds inflicted by the police. Martinez was not charged with a crime before the questioning, but during the questioning admitted that he had just used heroin and had stolen a police officer's gun. The Court ruled that Sergeant Chavez's questioning was not a *Miranda* violation.

In another 2003 case, *Kaupp v. Texas,* the Court made a different decision and vacated the conviction of a 17-year-old boy who was awakened late at night by the police, taken to the police station in handcuffs in his underwear, and interrogated.[156] The boy had been awakened at 3 AM, and the officer told him, "We need to go and talk," to which the boy responded, "Okay." The boy was taken to the scene of the crime where the victim's body had just been recovered, and then taken to the police station. All parties agreed that the police, at this point, did not have probable cause to arrest the young man. At the police station, the youth was given his *Miranda* rights and after a brief interrogation, he confessed to some involvement in the murder. He was subsequently convicted and given a 55-year sentence. On appeal, Texas courts affirmed the conviction and held that the boy's response of "Okay" indicated consent, that his failure to protest was a waiver or rights, and that his transport to the police station was simply routine. The U.S. Supreme Court, in vacating the conviction, concluded that a 17-year-old boy being awakened late at night, taken to the police station in handcuffs in his underwear and interrogated, is indistinguishable from a traditional arrest and because he was arrested without probable cause, his subsequent confession must be suppressed absent evidence of intervening events sufficient to purge the taint of the unlawful seizure.

In 2004, the U.S. Supreme Court decided two other very important custodial interrogation cases. In *United States v. Patane,* the U.S. Supreme Court ruled that the failure to provide *Miranda* warnings before engaging in custodial interrogation does not require suppression of physical evidence discovered as a result of the person's unwarned but voluntary statements. The Court held, however, that the unwarned statement itself was inadmissible.[157] In this case, police arrested Patane, sought to question him about his alleged possession of a handgun, and began reading him his *Miranda* rights. The defendant, Patane, interrupted right after he was advised he had the right to remain silent and told the officers that they did not need to read him his rights because he already understood them. In response to the questioning, Patane told the officers where the gun was located and gave them permission to retrieve it. The Supreme Court allowed the gun to remain in evidence.

In another 2004 case, *Missouri v. Seibert,*[158] involving unwarned statements, the U.S. Supreme Court clarified its 1985 *Oregon v. Elstad*[159] decision relative to the admission of unwarned statements given before *Miranda* rulings. Recall that in *Elstad,* the Court had held that a simple failure to administer the *Miranda* warnings, with no indication of behavior by the law enforcement officer that could be interpreted as coercion, compulsion, or an effort to undermine the suspect's ability to exercise his free will, should not keep out a statement that otherwise is voluntary. In *Seibert,* however, there was a different pattern of behavior by the police, and the Supreme Court made a different decision than it made in *Elstad.*

In *Siebert,* the defendant Seibert's young son, Jonathan, who was afflicted with cerebral palsy, died in his sleep, and the defendant feared that she would be charged with the neglect of her son when the death was reported to the police. In concert with two of her other sons and two of their friends, she concocted a scheme to conceal the true cause of Jonathan's death by setting the mobile home in which they lived on fire with Jonathan's body inside. Concerned with how she would explain leaving her ill son alone and unattended, the group decided to also leave Donald Rector, a mentally ill teenager who lived with the Seibert family, in the mobile home when it was set on fire. Upon investigation, Siebert was arrested for her role in the crime and transported to the police station for questioning. Once at the police station, the arresting officer began to question Seibert without advising her of her *Miranda* rights. The officer testified at the trial that he had purposefully refrained from advising Seibert of her rights even though he knew that he was conducting a custodial interrogation and stated that he had learned this interrogation technique ("two-tier interrogation" or "beachheading") during a police training session. He questioned her for about 30 to 40 minutes before advising her of her rights under *Miranda.* During this unwarned time, Seibert admitted that before committing the arson she knew that Donald Rector would die in the fire. Seibert was then given a 20-minute break. The officer then advised Seibert of her rights and obtained a signed waiver of rights from her. During the subsequent custodial interrogation, Seibert admitted to facts of the crime. Based on her statements, she was convicted of second-degree murder. The trial court suppressed Seibert's first statement because she had not been advised of her *Miranda* warnings but allowed her second statement to be used under the precedent of *Oregon v. Elstad.* It held that the admissions during the second interrogation were admissible because she was advised of her rights and she provided a signed waiver. The U.S. Supreme Court however, found that the situation in this case was different from *Elstad* and involved an approach that implicitly encouraged *Miranda* violations. It ruled that the practice of two-tier interrogations, sometimes referred to as "beach-heading," violates the purpose of *Miranda* and is unconstitutional. It held that the officer's intentional omission of a *Miranda* warning was intended to deprive Seibert of the opportunity to knowingly and intelligently waive her *Miranda* rights.

Police and Surreptitious Recording of Suspects' Conversations

Crawford reports that the surreptitious recording of suspects' conversations is an effective investigative technique that, if done properly, can withstand both constitutional and statutory challenges.[160] She cites several cases in which the courts have ruled that the surreptitious recording of suspects' conversations did not violate the custodial interrogation rules decided in *Miranda.*

In *Stanley v. Wainwright* (1979), two robbery suspects were arrested and placed in the back seat of a police car. They were unaware that one of the arresting officers had turned on a tape recorder on the front seat of the car before leaving the suspects unattended for a short period. During that time, the suspects engaged in a conversation that later proved to be incriminating. On appeal, the defense argued that the recording violated the ruling in *Miranda* because the suspects were in custody at the time the recording was made and placing of the suspects alone in the vehicle with the activated recorder was interrogation for purposes of *Miranda.* The appeals court summarily dismissed this argument and found that the statements were spontaneously made and not the product of interrogation.[161]

In *Kuhlmann v. Wilson* (1986), the Supreme Court held that placing an informant in a cell with a formally charged suspect in an effort to gain incriminating statements did not amount to a violation of the defendant's constitutional rights, stating,

> Since the Sixth Amendment is not violated whenever—by luck or happenstance—the State obtains incriminating statements from the

accused after the right to counsel was attached, a defendant does not make out a violation of that right simply by showing that an informant, either through prior arrangement or voluntarily, reported his incriminating statements to the police. Rather, the defendant must demonstrate that the police and their informant took some action, beyond merely listening, that was designed deliberately to elicit incriminating remarks.[162]

In a 1989 case, *Ahmad A. v. Superior Court,* the California Court of Appeals confronted a Fourth Amendment challenge to the admissibility of a surreptitiously recorded conversation between the defendant and his mother. The defendant, a juvenile arrested for murder, asked to speak with his mother when advised of his constitutional rights. The two were thereafter permitted to converse in an interrogation room with the door closed. During the surreptitiously recorded conversation that ensued, the defendant admitted his part in the murder. Reviewing the defendant's subsequent Fourth Amendment challenge, the California court noted that at the time the mother and her son were permitted to meet in the interrogation room, no representations or inquiries were made as to privacy or confidentiality. Finding the age-old truism "walls have ears" to be applicable, the court held that any subjective expectation that the defendant had regarding the privacy of his conversation was not objectively reasonable.[163]

In 2001, in *Belmar v. Commonwealth,* the Virginia Appellate Court, ruling on a case similar to *Ahmad A. v. Superior Court,* wrote that police interrogation rooms are "designed for disclosure, not the hiding, of information."[164]

These cases and others show that the mere placing of a recorder in a prison cell, interrogation room, or police vehicle does not constitute a violation of a suspect's rights. Instead, to raise a successful Sixth Amendment challenge, the defense has to show that someone acting on behalf of the government went beyond the role of a mere passive listener (often referred to by the courts as a "listening post") and actively pursued incriminating statements from the suspect.

Crawford suggests that law enforcement officers contemplating the use of this technique comply with the following guidelines:

■ To avoid a Sixth Amendment problem, this technique should not be used after formal charges have been filed or the initial appearance

TABLE 13.12	Landmark Supreme Court Decisions: Custodial Interrogations
Issue	Cases
Physical torture	*Brown v. Mississippi* (1936)
Prompt arraignment	*McNabb v. United States* (1943), *Mallory v. United States* (1957)
Refusal to allow counsel	*Escobedo v. Illinois* (1964)
Must advise of constitutional rights	*Miranda v. Arizona* (1966)
Inevitability of discovery	*Brewer v. Williams* (1977), *Nix v. Williams* (1984)
Public safety	*New York v. Quarles* (1984)
Use of unwarned statement	*Oregon v. Elstad* (1985), *Kaupp v. Texas* (2003)
Lying to lawyers	*Moran v. Burbine* (1986)
Placing informer in prison cell	*Illinois v. Perkins* (1990)
Harmless trial error	*Arizona v. Fulminante* (1991)
Equivocal request for counsel	*Davis v. United States* (1994)
Suppression of physical evidence in case of unwarned but voluntary statement	*United States v. Patane* (2004)
Use of statements obtained in follow-up interrogation despite an earlier violation of *Miranda* (beachheading)	*Missouri v. Seibert* (2004)
Questioning—not in criminal case	*Chavez v. Martinez* (2003)

in court, unless the conversation does not involve a government actor, the conversation involves a government actor who has assumed the role of a "listening post," or the conversation pertains to a crime other than the one with which the suspect has been charged.

■ To avoid conflicts with both Fourth Amendment and Title III of the Omnibus Crime Control and Safe Streets Act, suspects should not be given any specific assurances that their conversations are private.[165]

See Table 13.12 for a list of landmark cases regarding custodial interrogation.

Police Eyewitness Identification Procedures

Often law enforcement officers apprehend suspects based on descriptions given by victims of violent crimes. To ensure that the apprehended person is actually the perpetrator, the police must obtain assistance from the victim or employ other identification procedures. The following sections discuss procedures to identify suspects properly as the actual perpetrators of crimes.

Lineups, Showups, and Photo Arrays

Lineups, showups, and photo arrays are important parts of the police investigation process, as are procedures requiring suspects to give samples of their voice, blood, and handwriting to be used in identification comparison procedures.

A **lineup** is the placing of a suspect with a group of other people of similar physical characteristics (such as race, age, hair color, hair type, height, and weight) so that a witness or victim of a crime has the opportunity to identify the perpetrator of the crime. Lineups are usually used after an arrest.

A **showup** involves bringing a suspect back to the scene of the crime or another place (for example, a hospital where an injured victim is) where the suspect can be seen and possibly identified by a victim or witness. The showup must be conducted as soon as possible after the crime, and with no suggestion that the person is a suspect. A showup is usually used after an arrest.

A **photo array** is similar to a lineup, except that photos of the suspect (who is not in custody) and others are shown to a witness. Photo arrays are used before arrest.

Could these procedures be construed as violating a defendant's freedom against self-incrimination as provided by the Fifth Amendment to the U.S. Constitution?

The following cases detail the key landmark decisions of the Supreme Court in lineup, showup, and photo array cases.

United States v. Wade In *United States v. Wade,* the Supreme Court in 1967 made two very important decisions about lineups.[166] It ruled that a person can be made to stand in a lineup and perform certain actions that were performed by the suspect during the crime, such as saying certain words or walking in a certain fashion. The Court also ruled that once a person is indicted, that person has a right to have an attorney present at the lineup.

Kirby v. Illinois In 1972, in *Kirby v. Illinois,* the Supreme Court ruled that the right to counsel at lineups applies only after the initiation of formal judicial criminal proceedings, such as an indictment, information, or arraignment—that is, when a person formally enters the court system.[167] An *information* is a formal charging document drafted by a prosecutor and presented to a judge. An *indictment* is a formal charging document returned by a grand jury based on evidence presented to it by a prosecutor. The indictment is then presented to a judge. Indictments generally cover felonies. An *arraignment* is a hearing before a court having jurisdiction in a criminal case, in which the identity of the defendant is established, the defendant is informed of the charge or charges and his or her rights, and the defendant is required to enter a plea. In *Kirby,* the Court reasoned that because a lineup may free an innocent person, and the required presence of an attorney might delay the lineup, it is preferable to have the lineup as soon as possible, even without an attorney.

Thus, in a postarrest, pre-indictment lineup, there is no right to have an attorney present. Many police departments, however, will permit an attorney to be present at a lineup and make reasonable suggestions, as long as there is no significant delay of the lineup.

You Are There!

United States v. Wade (1967)

On September 21, 1964, a man with a piece of tape on each side of his face forced a cashier and a bank official to put money into a pillow case. The robber then left the bank and drove away with an accomplice, who was waiting outside in a car.

In March 1965, six months after the robbery, an indictment was returned against Wade and an accomplice for the robbery. Wade was arrested on April 2, 1965. Two weeks later, an FBI agent put Wade into a lineup to be observed by two bank employees. Wade had a lawyer, but the lawyer was not notified of the lineup. Each person in the lineup had strips of tape on his face, similar to those worn by the robber, and each was told to say words that had been spoken at the robbery. Both bank employees identified Wade as the robber. Wade was convicted based on the identification by the witnesses.

On appeal, the Supreme Court ruled that placing someone in a lineup and forcing that person to speak or perform other acts at the lineup did not violate the Fifth Amendment privilege against self-incrimination. The Court held, however, that because Wade had been indicted and was represented by counsel, the lawyer should have been allowed to be there.

SOURCE: Based on *United States v. Wade,* 388 U.S. 218 (1967).

Stoval v. Denno In *Stoval v. Denno* (1967), the Supreme Court ruled that showups are constitutional and do not require the presence of an attorney.[168] The Court addressed the issue as follows:

> The practice of showing suspects singly to persons for purpose of identification, and not a part of a lineup, has been unduly condemned. . . . However, a claimed violation of due process of law in the conduct of a confrontation depends on the totality of the circumstances surrounding it and the record in the present case reveals that the showing of Stoval to Mrs. Behrendt in an immediate hospital confrontation was imperative.

Subsequent to *Stoval v. Denno,* a federal appellate court established a set of guidelines phrased in the form of questions that could decide the constitutionality of a showup. A careful review of the questions reveals that the court clearly prefers lineups to showups but will permit showups if certain conditions are met:

- Was the defendant the only individual who could possibly be identified as the guilty party by the complaining witness, or were there others near him or her at the time of the showup so as to negate the assertion that he or she was shown alone to the witness?
- Where did the showup take place?
- Were there any compelling reasons for a prompt showup that would deprive the police of the opportunity of securing other similar individuals for the purpose of holding a lineup?
- Was the witness aware of any observation by another or any other evidence indicating the guilt of the suspect at the time of the showup?
- Were any tangible objects related to the offence placed before the witness that would encourage identification?
- Was the witness identification based on only part of the suspect's total personality?
- Was the identification a product of mutual reinforcement of opinion among witnesses simultaneously viewing the defendant?
- Was the emotional state of the witness such as to preclude identification.[169]

United States v. Ash In *United States v. Ash* (1973), the Supreme Court ruled that the police could show victims or witnesses photographic displays containing a suspect's photograph (photo arrays) without the requirement that the suspect's lawyer be present.[170]

Other Identification Procedures

The Fifth Amendment governs any type of testimony. However, in most cases coming before it, the Supreme Court declared that procedures that are not testimonial are not under the purview of the Fifth Amendment. (*Testimonial* refers to oral or written communication by a suspect, rather than the taking of blood or exemplars as indicated in this section). Sample of such cases follow.

Schmerber v. California In 1966, in *Schmerber v. California,* the Supreme Court ruled that the forced

You Are There!

Winston v. Lee (1985)

On July 18, 1982, Ralph E. Warkinson was shot during a robbery attempt at his place of business. Warkinson fired at the shooter and believed he hit the robber in the side. The police brought Warkinson to a local hospital emergency room. Twenty minutes later, the police responded to a reported shooting and found Rudolph Lee suffering from a gunshot wound to the left chest area. Lee said he had been shot during a robbery attempt by two men. When Lee was taken to the hospital (the same one to which Warkinson had been taken), Warkinson identified Lee as the man who had shot him. After a police interrogation, Lee was arrested for the shooting.

In an effort to obtain ballistics evidence, the police attempted to have Lee undergo a surgical procedure under a general anesthetic for the removal of the bullet lodged in his chest. Lee appealed to the courts, which ruled in his favor and against the operation. The Commonwealth of Virginia appealed the case to the U.S. Supreme Court. The Court ruled that such surgical procedure, without Lee's permission, would be a violation of his Fourth Amendment rights.

Based on *Winston v. Lee,* 470 U.S. 753 (1985).

extraction of blood by a doctor from a man who was arrested for driving while intoxicated was not a violation of that man's constitutional rights.[171] Note the difference between *Schmerber* and *Rochin v. California* (1952), mentioned earlier in this chapter. In *Rochin,* the Court held that the police had engaged in behavior that "shocks the conscience" and thus held their actions to be unconstitutional. In *Schmerber,* the Court found no similar shocking behavior and thus held the doctor's actions to be constitutional.

Winston v. Lee In *Winston v. Lee* (1985), the Supreme Court clarified its position on medical provisions regarding prisoners.[172] When the Court decided the Schmerber case, it warned, "That we today hold that the Constitution does not forbid the States' minor intrusions into an individual's body under stringently limited conditions in no way indicates that it permits more substantial intrusions, or intrusions under other conditions.[173] The Rudolph Lee case provided the test of how far the police can go in attempting to retrieve evidence from a suspect's body.

Lee, a suspect in a robbery, was shot by the victim. The police endeavored to have a bullet removed from Lee's body to use it for a ballistics examination.

Justice William J. Brennan, speaking for the Court, wrote the following:

> We conclude that the procedure sought here is an example of the 'more substantial intrusion' cautioned against in Schmerber, and hold that to permit the procedure would violate respondent's right to be secure in his person guaranteed by the Fourth Amendment.[174]

United States v. Dionisio In *United States v. Dionisio,* the Supreme Court ruled in 1973 that a suspect must provide voice exemplars (samples of his or her voice) that can be compared with the voice spoken at the time of the crime.[175]

United States v. Mara In 1973, in *United States v. Mara,* the Supreme Court ruled that it was not a violation of constitutional rights for the police to require a suspect to provide a handwriting exemplar (a sample of his or her handwriting) for comparison with handwriting involved in the crime.[176]

Eyewitness Identification Concerning eyewitness identification, in 2001, the National Institute

TABLE 13.13	Landmark Supreme Court Decisions: Police Identification Procedures
Issue	Cases
Lineups	*United States v. Wade* (1967), *Kirby v. Illinois* (1972)
Showups	*Stoval v. Denno* (1967)
Photo arrays	*United States v. Ash* (1973)
Medical procedures	*Schmerber v. California* (1966), *Winston v. Lee* (1985)

of Justice produced a guide for law enforcement for the collection and preservation of eyewitness evidence that represented a combination of the best current, workable police practices and psychological research. It describes practices and procedures that, if consistently applied, will tend to increase the overall accuracy and reliability of eyewitness evidence. Although not intended to state legal criteria for the admissibility of evidence, it sets out rigorous criteria for handling eyewitness evidence that are as demanding as those governing the handling of physical trace evidence. It outlines basic procedures that officers can use to obtain the most reliable and accurate information from eyewitnesses.[177] See Table 13.13 for a list of landmark cases regarding police identification.

Summary

- Two major methods are used to measure crime in the United States: (1) the *Uniform Crime Reports* and (2) the National Crime Victimization Survey.

- For the latest reporting year, the U.S. police made about 14 million arrests for all criminal infractions except traffic violations.

- The United States is a nation governed by law. The primary law regulating life in the United States is the U.S. Constitution, including its many amendments.

- The U.S. Constitution is a continuing, dynamic document constantly being reviewed by the U.S. Supreme Court.

- The U.S. criminal justice system is based on the Bill of Rights, the first ten amendments to the U.S. Constitution. Five of the first ten amendments specifically address freedoms or rights that people possess when involved with the criminal justice system.

- The U.S. Supreme Court, through its policy of judicial review, has made a significant impact on the way the police do their job. As early as 1914, in *Weeks v. United States,* the Court influenced the police by regulating how they should conduct their searches and seizures. In 1936, in *Brown v. Mississippi,* the Court began to affect the police by ruling certain methods of police interrogation unconstitutional.

- Most Supreme Court cases regarding criminal justice try to strike a balance between the rights of the individual and the rights of society. The Supreme Court has the difficult task of bringing balance between these two often-conflicting goals.

- In police matters, the Supreme Court hears cases, on appeal, from people who have been the subject of police actions, including arrest, search and seizure, and custodial interrogation. The justices then decide whether the police action violated the person's constitutional rights, usually by interpreting one of the amendments to the Constitution. Certain significant cases, such as *Mapp v. Ohio* and *Miranda v. Arizona,* are known as landmark cases and can bring about changes in police procedures.

- The major method used by the Supreme Court to ensure that the police do not violate people's constitutional rights is the use of the exclusionary rule, which is an interpretation of the Fourteenth Amendment by the Supreme Court that holds that evidence seized in violation of the U.S. Constitution cannot be used in court against a defendant. The exclusionary rule evolved in U.S. law through a series of Supreme Court cases. By 1961, the Supreme Court, noting that states had not amended their procedures to conform to the Constitution, applied the exclusionary rule to state courts and law enforcement agencies, as well as federal ones.

- Most of the arrests made by the average police officer do not involve a warrant because most crimes an officer becomes aware of on the street necessitate immediate action and do not allow the officer the time necessary to go to court to obtain a warrant.

- Most of the arrests made by the police are based on the probable cause standard, which can be defined as evidence that may lead a reasonable person to believe that a crime has been committed and that a certain person committed it.

- Reasonable suspicion is a standard of proof that would lead a reasonable person (a police officer) to believe a certain condition or fact (that a crime is, will be, or has occurred) exists. This is the standard necessary for police officers to conduct stop and frisks.

- The U.S. Supreme Court has consistently ruled that canine sniffs by a trained drug dog are not actual search and seizures controlled by the Fourth Amendment.

- Police searches are governed by the Fourth Amendment, which prohibits all unreasonable searches and seizures and requires that all warrants be based on probable cause and that they particularly describe the place to be searched and the persons or things to be seized.

- The major exceptions to the warrant requirement of the Fourth Amendment are: abandoned property, automobile exception, border searches, computer error, consent, exigent circumstances, good faith, incident to arrest, inventory, open fields, plain view, and field interrogations.

- The U.S. Supreme Court has recognized two constitutional sources of the right to counsel during interrogation: the Court's interpretation in *Miranda v. Arizona* of the Fifth Amendment right against self-incrimination and the Sixth Amendment.

- The *Miranda* rules or *Miranda* warnings state that before any interrogation of a person in custody the police must do the following:
  - Advise the suspect that he or she has the right to remain silent
  - Advise the suspect that anything he or she says can and will be used in court against him or her
  - Advise the suspect that he or she has the right to consult a lawyer and to have the lawyer present during questioning
  - Advise the suspect that if he or she cannot afford an attorney, an attorney will be provided, free of charge

- In *Dickerson v. United States* (2000), the Supreme Court ruled that *Miranda* was a constitutional decision that cannot be overruled by an act of Congress.

- The surreptitious recording of suspects' conversations is an effective investigative technique that, if done properly, can withstand both constitutional and statutory challenges.

- Lineups, showups, and photo arrays are important parts of the police investigation process, as are procedures requiring suspects to give samples of their voice, blood, and handwriting to be used in identification comparison procedures.

Learning Check

1. Explain how crime is measured in the United States. Determine how much crime occurs in the United States. Tell how many arrests are made in the United States and what the majority of the arrests are for.

2. Explain how the Bill of Rights and the actions of the U.S. Supreme Court regulate the police.

3. What is the Exclusionary Rule? Discuss its history through several landmark U.S. Supreme Court cases.

4. Discuss the effect of the Exclusionary Rule on the police.

5. Discuss how the Fourteenth Amendment to the U.S. Constitution affects the actions of the police.

6. Discuss the power of the police to stop vehicles.

7. List several of the exceptions to the warrant requirement in search and seizure cases, and cite and discuss several U.S. Supreme Court cases to illustrate the exceptions.

8. Describe the development of the requirement to be advised of one's constitutional rights before police interrogation when in police custody. Cite and discuss several U.S. Supreme Court cases to show the changes in police interrogation procedures over time.

9. Explain the significance of the *Dickerson* decision.

10. Explain the differences between lineups, showups, and photo arrays. Give an example of how each one can be legally used.

Key Terms

arrest The initial taking into custody of a person by law enforcement authorities to answer for a criminal offense or violation of a code or ordinance.

Carroll doctrine The legal doctrine that automobiles have less Fourth Amendment protection than other places. Arose from the landmark 1925 U.S. Supreme Court case *Carroll v. United States.*

crime Any act that the government has declared to be contrary to the public good, that is declared by statute to be a crime, and that is prosecuted in a criminal proceeding. In some jurisdictions, crimes only include felonies and/or misdemeanors.

crime scene The location where a crime occurred.

custodial interrogation The questioning of a person in police custody regarding his or her participation in a crime.

exclusionary rule An interpretation of the U.S. Constitution by the U.S. Supreme Court that holds that evidence seized in violation of the U.S. Constitution cannot be used in court against a defendant.

exigent circumstances One of the major exceptions to the warrant requirement of the Fourth Amendment. Exigency may be translated as "emergency."

field interrogation Unplanned questioning of an individual who has aroused the suspicions of an officer.

judicial review Process by which actions of the police in areas such as arrests, search and seizure, and interrogations are reviewed by the U.S. Court system at various levels to ensure the constitutionality of these actions.

lineup Police identification procedure involving the placing of a suspect with a group of other people of similar physical characteristics so that a witness or victim of a crime can have the opportunity to identify the perpetrator of the crime.

***Miranda* rules (*Miranda* warnings)** Rules established by the U.S. Supreme Court in the landmark case *Miranda v. United States* (1966) that require the police to advise suspects confronting custodial interrogation of their constitutional rights.

misdemeanor A class of criminal deviance that is usually punished by a maximum of $1,000 fine and/or up to one year in a county or city jail. A misdemeanor is less serious than a felony. Different jurisdictions classify misdemeanors and sanctions for violation thereof differently.

National Crime Victimization Survey (NCVS) National Institute of Justice survey of a random sample of U.S. households, asking them if a crime was committed against anyone in the household during the prior six months.

photo array Police identification procedure similar to a lineup, except that photos of the suspect (who is not in custody) and others are shown to a witness or victim of a crime.

plain view evidence Evidence seized by police without a warrant who have the right to be in a position to observe it.

probable cause Evidence that may lead a reasonable person to believe that a crime has been committed and that a certain person committed it.

reasonable force The amount of force an officer can use when making an arrest.

reasonable suspicion The standard of proof that is necessary for police officers to conduct stops and frisks.

search and seizure Legal concept relating to the searching for and confiscation of evidence by the police.

search warrant A written order, based on probable cause, signed by a judge authorizing police to search a specific person, place, or property to obtain evidence.

showup Police identification process involving bringing a suspect back to the scene of the crime or another place (for example, a hospital where an injured victim is) where the suspect can be seen and possibly identified by a victim or witness of a crime.

silver platter doctrine Legal tactic that allowed federal prosecutors to use evidence obtained by state police officers seized through unreasonable searches and seizures.

stop and frisk The detaining of a person by law enforcement officers for the purpose of investigation, accompanied by a superficial examination of the person's body surface or clothing to discover weapons, contraband, or other objects relating to criminal activity.

third degree The pattern of brutality and violence used by the police to obtain confessions by suspects.

***Uniform Crime Reports* (UCR)** Yearly collection of aggregate crime statistics prepared by the FBI based on citizens' reports of crimes to the police.

Critical Issues in Policing

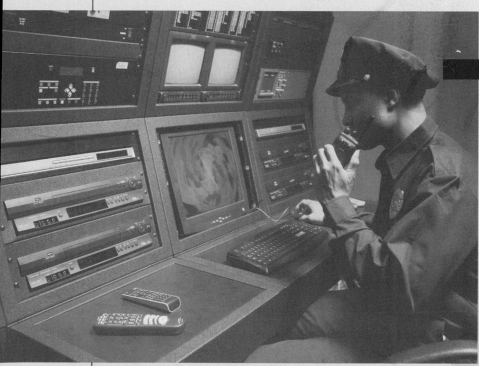

© Andersen Ross/Getty Images

Computers, Technology, and Criminalistics in Policing

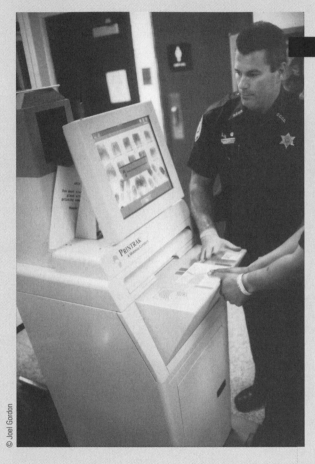

© Joel Gordon

GOALS

- To acquaint you with the latest technological advances in policing
- To show you how the computer and technology are revolutionizing policing
- To acquaint you with the latest uses of computers in police operations, criminal investigations, and police management tasks
- To introduce you to the latest criminalistic and forensic techniques, including DNA profiling
- To alert you to the threat to civil liberties caused by rapidly advancing technology

Introduction

Computers, technology, and modern forensic or criminalistics techniques have revolutionized policing and have made the police more effective in crime-fighting and other duties. As one example, Lee Boyd Malvo, the teen-age sniper responsible for the 2002 Beltway Snipers shootings that shocked the Washington, D.C., metropolitan and suburban areas, was identified as a result of a recent fingerprinting innovation that will be described later in this chapter. As another example, Dennis Rader, known as the BTK (bind, torture, and kill) killer, who murdered at least 10 people in and around Wichita, Kansas, between 1974 and 1991, was identified and arrested in 2005 based on another innovation mentioned in this chapter.

Video cameras, videocassette recorders (VCRs), microcomputers, personal computers, cash machines, cellular telephones, satellites, and the Internet are all very familiar to the students reading this text. However, many might not be aware that little was known of this technology on the day they were born. The past few decades have seen advances in technology that most of us would never have foreseen. The computer chip has revolutionized society. The criminal justice system and the police in particular have benefited greatly from this technological revolution. The terrorist attacks of September 11, 2001, and other cases have heightened public awareness of the police and forensic and scientific evidence to an extent that had never existed before. As you will see in this chapter, policing is adapting to this new technology.

As former U.S. Attorney General John Ashcroft stated in 2001,

> The wave of technological advancement that has changed the lives of almost every individual, business, and institution in the nation has also changed the world of criminal justice—from how we fight crime to how we manage law enforcement resources to the types of crimes we face. New technologies can help law enforcement agencies prevent crime, apprehend criminals, manage offender populations, and protect the public from the threat of terrorism.[1]

This chapter will discuss technology in policing, including computers and their application in record keeping, crime analysis, communications, personnel allocation, investigations, administration, and training. It will also discuss fingerprint technology, including basic categories of fingerprints and automated fingerprint and palm print identification systems. Additionally it will discuss less-than-lethal weapons, including chemical irritant sprays, the Taser and other stun devices, and the safety and effectiveness of these innovative alternatives to the use of deadly force.

The chapter will cover emerging state-of-the-art surveillance technology, including surveillance vans, vehicle tracking systems, night vision devices, global positioning systems, surveillance aircraft, and electronic video surveillance, as well as advanced photographic techniques such as digital photography, mug shot imaging, age progression photographs, and composite sketches. We will also cover forensics and criminalistics such as the CSI effect, modern crime labs, crime lab accreditation, and DNA profiling, which includes the science of DNA, history of DNA in U.S. courts, current DNA Technology, DNA databases, and other current DNA issues.

Biometric identification, videotaping, robotics, and concerns about civil liberties and the increased police use of modern technology will be discussed.

Computers in Policing

In 1964, St. Louis was the only city in the United States with a computer system for its police department. By 1968, 10 states and 50 cities had computer-based criminal justice information systems. Today, almost every law enforcement agency uses computers in many phases of its operations. Computer use in police work has increased exponentially since 1964.

By 2003, 83 percent of local police officers and 81 percent of sheriffs' deputies worked for an agency that used in-field computers or terminals, compared with 30 percent and 28 percent in 1990. Also, 38 percent of local police departments and 33 percent of sheriff's offices used computers and data devices as the primary means to transmit criminal incident data to a central information system (increased from 9 percent and 7 percent respectively from 1997).[2]

Some people may think that computerization has to be an expensive undertaking available only to large police departments, but this is far from the truth. A small department can become computerized with a basic computer system, including easily available database software management programs.

Today, computers have become more geared toward law enforcement, giving agencies more choices and a better ability to tailor the technology to their specific needs. Officers are using laptops, embedded or modular systems, and handheld personal digital assistants (PDAs) for transporting information back and forth between their police vehicle or field assignment and the police station.[3]

The following sections discuss the most commonly used applications of computers in police work.

Computer–Aided Dispatch (CAD)

Before the computer revolution, the police communications system was slow and cumbersome. A citizen would call the police using a seven-digit telephone number. A police telephone operator would take the information, write it on an index card, and put the card on a conveyor belt, where it would travel to the dispatcher's desk. The dispatcher would then manually search maps and records for the police car that covered the area from which the call originated and then call the car, giving the officer all the information from the index card. All records were kept manually.

The 911 emergency telephone number system was introduced by American Telephone and Telegraph (AT&T) in 1968.[4] By 2003, 92 percent of local police departments and 94 percent of sheriff's offices participated in an emergency 911 system. In addition, 73 percent of local police departments and 71 percent of sheriffs' offices had enhanced 911 systems, capable of automatically displaying information such as a caller's phone number, address, and special needs.[5]

According to Scott Freitag, president of the National Academies of Emergency Dispatch, about 500,000 911 calls are placed each day. He said fewer than 1 percent of the calls are prank calls, in which someone is trying to play a trick on the operator, and about 10 to 15 percent are bad calls (hang-ups, misdials, or accidental activation of 911 buttons on cellular phones). About 35 percent of all 911 calls are life-threatening emergencies. Freitag said the three most important rules in handling 911 calls are these: treat each call as legitimate until proven otherwise, follow a script, rather than adlibbing a response, and use a professional and encouraging demeanor.[6]

Today **computer-aided dispatch (CAD)** allows almost immediate communication between the police dispatcher and police units in the field. Numerous CAD system software packages are available for purchase by police departments. With typical CAD systems, after a 911 operator takes a call from a citizen, the operator codes the information into the computer, and the information immediately flashes on the dispatcher's screen. The CAD system prioritizes the calls on the dispatcher's screen, putting more serious calls (such as crimes in progress and heart attacks) above less serious calls (such as past crimes and nonemergency requests for assistance). The system also verifies the caller's address and telephone number, as well as determining the most direct route to the location. The system also searches a database for dangers near the location to which the officers are responding, calls to the same location within the last 24 hours, and any previous history of calls to that location. The CAD system also constantly maintains the status of each patrol unit. In this way, the dispatcher knows which units are available and where all units are located. The system also determines which patrol unit is closest to the location needing police assistance.

Some CAD systems have automatic transponders within patrol units. These enable dispatch personnel to monitor visually all patrol vehicles via a computer monitor and to assign them in coordination with this computer-generated information.

Enhanced CAD (Enhanced 911, or E911) The technology director for the National Emergency Number Association reports that 96 percent of the nation is covered by dispatch centers that have enhanced 911 capabilities. He said that the movement toward 100 percent is slow because the counties that haven't converted yet are typically low population and don't have the money to do so. As an example, 24 rural counties in Kentucky have only basic 911 service. Without enhanced 911, dispatchers have to take the time to get precise directions from callers before they can notify police or other emergency responders.[7]

With an E911 system, when a person calls 911 for assistance, vital information is immediately flashed on a screen in front of the operator. The screen gives the exact address of the telephone being used; the name of the telephone subscriber; whether it is a residence, business, or pay telephone; the police patrol beat it is on; the nearest ambulance; and the closest fire department. This system gives the police the ability to assist people at risk even if they cannot communicate because of illness, injury, or an inability to speak English. For example, if a sick or injured person initiates a call to 911 for assistance and then passes out or can no longer continue the conversation for some other reason, the police, having the information in the computer, are still able to respond with assistance.

Some enhanced CAD and enhanced 911 systems use **mobile digital terminals (MDTs)** in each patrol unit. In systems using MDTs, voice communications are replaced by electronic transmissions that appear on an officer's MDT, a device put into a police vehicle that allows the electronic transmission of messages between the police dispatcher and the officer in the field. Officers receive messages via a computer screen and transmit messages via a keyboard. MDT systems offer the following advantages over voice systems[8]:

1. A direct interface between the patrol unit and local, county, state, and federal criminal justice information system computers, enabling an officer to query names, license plates, and driver's licenses with almost immediate response, and without interfering with radio communications or requesting the services of a dispatcher.

2. The elimination of many clerical duties.

3. The availability of more detailed information, including addresses displayed with the nearest cross streets and map coordinates (and in some cases, even floor plans).

4. Better coordination of all emergency agencies because their movements can be monitored visually by both officers at the scene and dispatchers.

5. Automatic processing of incident information via a preformatted incident form, eliminating the need for the officer to drop off an incident report at the station house and the need for someone to type up a report.

6. A dramatic increase in response time because the entire dispatch process, from call to arrival, is fully automated.

7. The capability for the accumulation of large amounts of data regarding police incidents and personnel, which can be used in crime analysis and staff allocation planning to assign personnel when and where crime is highest or calls for assistance are heaviest. A report on the use of mobile data access to law enforcement databases reveals that officers with in-car data access technology make more than eight times as many inquiries on driving records, vehicle registrations, and wanted persons or property per eight-hour shift than do officers without in-car computers.

Cell Phone Technology Today, nearly half of all 911 calls are placed from a cell phone, and most sophisticated 911 systems have the ability to trace the cell phone or get a location from which the call is coming from. This aids the police greatly. As a recent example, in July 2006, an 18-year-old woman was taken from the deserted streets of lower Manhattan in the early morning hours to a seedy hotel in Weehawken, New Jersey, where she was raped and murdered. The suspect stuffed the victim's body into a suitcase and dumped it in a trash bin behind an apartment building two blocks away. He then drove back to New York City and registered into another hotel. Police were able to find the suspect because he had taken the victim's cell phone and used it to make some calls to his mother and girlfriend. Police started their investigation by tracking her cell phone, which led them to the people the killer had called. The cell phone number appeared on caller IDs on the phones the killer had called. The police were able to take him into custody shortly thereafter.[9]

Unfortunately, it was reported in 2006 that the state of Utah and three other states have yet to provide more than 40 percent of its population with enhanced 911 mobile service. Most emergency call centers in Utah lack the ability to get a fix on the location of callers in distress. In 2004, a man in Provo died in a botched 911 response. Paramedics were sent to a wrong address and had no way to pinpoint the accurate location of the call. The man's body was found four days later. According to Utah's E911 program manager, many rural counties don't have the tax base to sustain their 911 services.[10]

According to M. Wesley Clark, in a 2006 *FBI Law Enforcement Bulletin* article, the legal requirements for acquisition of cell site information by the police for the purpose of identifying the location of a cellular telephone and its user is still uncertain. He says that traditional law does not provide law enforcement with clear-cut guidance in the area of cell phone technology. He writes that traditional law enforcement methods of tracking, whether through the use of a tracking device on a vehicle or other conveyance or placing a device inside a container, fits with the analysis provided by the U.S. Supreme Court in *United States v. Knotts* (1983) and *United States v. Karo* (1984). These cases held that as long as the conveyance or thing to be monitored is out and about on the public thoroughfares, open fields, or even on private property, all instances where the information revealed by the target could be observed by visual surveillance engaged in by third parties, no showing of evidence—let alone probable cause—is required.[11]

Clark says his analysis holds true today as long as the tracking equipment belongs to the government; it does not resolve the issue when third-party assistance from the service provider is required. Cell phone companies with mounting concerns about liability concerns typically will not furnish cell phone location information to law enforcement without a court order.[12]

IP Telephony Telephone technology is constantly growing. **Internet Protocol (IP) telephony** is a collection of new communication technologies, products, and services that can facilitate communication across diverse systems. **Voice over IP (VoIP)** is a subset of IP telephony and is a set of software, hardware, and standards designed to enable voice transmissions over packet-switched networks, which can be either an internal local area network or the Internet. VoIP is not associated with a physical telephone line but, rather, with an IP address that is linked to a phone number.[13] Many police departments are now using IP telephony.

Reverse 911 (R911) R911 is a way for the police to contact the community using the telephone, by a simple digital click, in the event of an emergency or serious situation, more quickly and over a larger area than if the officers had to go door to door to notify residents. This technology was first used in DuPage County, Illinois, in 1996 and has been used by many municipalities since the terrorist attacks of September 11, 2001. It was used very successfully in Arlington, Virginia, following the terrorist attack on the Pentagon and enabling rapid mobilization of off-duty officers.[14]

Automated Databases

As we have come into the twenty-first century, computer technology is doing things previously unthinkable in policing. A simple example of how far we have come is a system in Mesa, Arizona. The Mesa Police Department's Cellular Digital Packet Data (CDPD) technology, an automated database, gives officers immediate access, via mobile computers, to critical information contained in the city's mainframe computer. The department's divisions using this system include homicide, pawn detail, auto theft, public information, gang control, and hostage negotiation.[15] In 2006, a new pocket PC system, the Advanced Ground Information System (AGIS), was developed that allows the rapid exchange of voice, text, photos, video, and other information from emergency personnel from multiple agencies that are responding to the same event on a cell phone.[16]

The availability of automated databases has revolutionized police work. An automated database is an enormous electronic filing cabinet that is capable of storing information and retrieving it in any desired format.

The FBI created a major automated database, the **National Crime Information Center (NCIC)** in 1967. The NCIC collects and retrieves data about people wanted for crimes anywhere in the United States; stolen and lost property, including stolen automobiles, license plates, identifiable property, boats, and securities; and other criminal justice information. The NCIC also contains criminal history files and the status (prison, jail, probation, or parole) of criminals. The NCIC has millions of active records, which are completely automated by computer. The NCIC provides virtually uninterrupted operation day or night, seven days a week. Although the FBI operates the NCIC, approximately 70 percent of its use is by local, state, and other federal agencies.

In 2000, the NCIC was renamed **NCIC 2000** and provided a major upgrade to the services previously described and extended these services down to the patrol car and the mobile officer. With this system, a police officer can identify fugitives and missing persons quickly using automated fingerprint identification system (AFIS) technology, which will be discussed later in this chapter. The officer may place a subject's finger on a fingerprint reader in a patrol car, and the reader will transmit the image to the NCIC computer. Within minutes, the computer forwards a reply to the officer. A

You Are There!

Sample ViCAP Alert—April 2006

On October 24, 2003, deer hunters found the body of a woman lying face down in a wooded area off Devil Dog Road about 1 mile south of Interstate 40 and 6 miles west of Williams, Arizona. This area is a popular entrance into the Grand Canyon National Park. The victim died from a single blow to her head and likely was killed someplace other than where her body was discovered. All attempts to identify this woman have been unsuccessful.

The victim is described as a white female, 60 years of age or older, 5'4" tall, 150 pounds, with blondish-gray hair in a bob style. The victim had brown eyes and no ear piercings or tattoos. Moles are present on the left side of the forehead, on the tip of the right shoulder, over the left clavicle, on the front of the right lower leg, and on the right ankle. Old scars are noted on the back of the left hand, below the right knee, and on the back of the right forearm. There was evidence of heart disease and also a skin condition (senile ecchymosis), likely requiring dermatological intervention.

An examination of the dental records revealed extensive dental work worth $20,000. These restorations included porcelain fused to metal crowns, four root canals, a full gold crown, and two three unit fixed partial dentures (bridges).

Law enforcement agencies should bring this information to the attention of all homicide, missing persons, special victims, and crime analysis units.

SOURCE: "ViCAP Alert, Unidentified Homicide Victim," *FBI Law Enforcement Bulletin,* April 2006, p. 24.

printer installed in patrol cars allows officers to get copies of a suspect's photograph, fingerprint image, signature, and tattoos, along with composite drawings of unknown subjects. The printer can also receive images of stolen goods, including cars. The new system also provides for enhanced name searches (based on phonetically similar names); prisoner, probation, and parole records; convicted sex offender registries; and other services.[17]

In addition, the FBI maintains the National Instant Criminal Background Check System (NICS), which provides access to millions of criminal history records from all 50 states and the District of Columbia to match subject information for background checks on individuals attempting to purchase a firearm.[18]

The FBI also maintains the Violent Criminal Apprehension Program (ViCAP) database, which contains information on unsolved murders. ViCAP has helped local and state law enforcement agencies solve violent crimes for almost 20 years.[19] In addition to these national databases, local law enforcement agencies maintain their own databases. Many agencies use CD-ROMs, which are capable of storing massive files of data. The advantages of CD-ROM technology are that it is inexpensive and has numerous law enforcement applications. Police departments and investigators can store numerous types of archived files onto CD-ROM, such as closed cases, mug shots, fingerprint cards, motor vehicle records, firearm registration information, wanted notices, court decisions, missing person photos and information, and known career criminal files, including photographs and fingerprints.[20]

Automated Crime Analysis (Crime Mapping)

Numerous software application programs aid the police in **automated crime analysis** or crime mapping. Crime analysis entails the collection and analysis of data regarding crime (when, where, who, what, how, and why) to discern criminal patterns and assist in the effective assignment of personnel to combat crime. The most basic use of crime analysis is to determine where and when crimes occur so that personnel can be assigned to catch perpetrators in the act of committing the crime or to prevent them from committing it.

The forerunner in the use of modern sophisticated automated crime analysis was the New York City Police Department's CompStat program, which was discussed in chapter 1. CompStat provides instant statistical updating of all reported crimes, arrests, and other police activities, such as traffic and other citations. This program and its movie screen–type visual displays provide the framework for the weekly crime analysis meetings at the New York City Police Department (NYPD)'s headquarters during which precinct commanders must account for all increases in crime and must provide strategies to combat these crimes. The keynote of the NYPD reengineering program of the mid-1990s and the envy of police departments throughout the world, CompStat is a process that began to evolve in early 1994 when, after changes in the leadership of many of the NYPD's bureaus, disturbing information emerged. It appeared that the NYPD did not know most of its own current crime statistics, and there was a time lag of three to six months in its statistical reporting methods. Upon learning this, the department made a concerted effort to generate crime activity data on a weekly basis. CompStat has been credited with causing crime in New York City to drop to levels not seen since the 1960s.[21] Numerous cities are now using CompStat programs and other forms of automated crime analysis and crime mapping.

Regional Crime Analysis Geographic Information Systems (RCAGIS) Spatial Analysis   Regional Crime Analysis Geographic Information Systems (RCAGIS) Spatial Analysis is another computer program several police departments have added to their arsenal of anticrime programs. Although still an imprecise science, these computer programs have been able to help police locate crime "hot spots," spatially relate a list of potential suspects to actual crimes, profile crime geographically to identify where a serial criminal most likely lives, and even forecast where the next crime in a series might occur. Geographic profiling was developed in the late 1980s. The Baltimore County, Maryland, Police Department uses a RCAGIS program called CrimeStat.[22]

A 2006 article disclosed that numerous law enforcement agencies throughout the nation are using a variety of different GIS or spatial analysis software programs. The police use of special forecasting has been spurred by the development of electronic police records, advances in street maps for crime model specification, and improvement in police management that places an emphasis on performance measures and accountability. Currently, the National Law Enforcement Corrections and Technology Center (NLECTC) and several other research bodies are attempting to find the best one.[23]

The United Kingdom uses GIS-based information sharing systems in its Crime and Disorder Reduction Partnerships (CDRPs).[24]

Although the GIS systems show great promise, they cannot be considered a replacement for the experienced crime analyst and investigator. According to Ronald Wilson, program manager of the Mapping and Analysis for Public Safety (MAPS) program at the National Institute of Justice, "There is a lot of human behavior that cannot be accounted for by mathematical models."[25]

Computer-Aided Investigation (Computerized Case Management)

Computer-aided investigation and **computerized case management** are revolutionizing the criminal investigation process. As early as the 1980s, the NYPD's Detective Division created an automated mug shot file called Computer-Assisted Terminal Criminal Hunt (CATCH). Using CATCH, detectives feed the description and modus operandi (MO) information of an unknown robbery perpetrator into the computer and then receive a computer printout that lists, in rank order, any potential suspects. The detectives can then obtain photographs of possible suspects and show them in photo arrays to victims for possible identification. The Los Angeles Police Department has operated a system similar to that of New York since 1985.[26]

Since the 1990s, British police have operated a computer-aided investigation system called the Home Office Large Major Enquiry System (HOLMES, which is a reference to the legendary fictional detective Sherlock Holmes). It is a sophisticated computer program developed for British investigators to aid them in managing complex investigations. (In Great Britain, an investigation is called an enquiry.) HOLMES is a complete case management system that can retrieve, process, organize, recognize, interrelate, and retrieve all aspects of information on a case. It also keeps track of ongoing progress, or the lack of it, in investigations. The system was created in response to the infamous Yorkshire Ripper case, in which 13 women were killed between 1974 and 1981. When the perpetrator was finally apprehended in 1981, it was discovered that he had been detained and questioned by at least six different police departments in connection with the attacks. Because sharing of information on related cases was so cumbersome for the neighboring forces at that time, the connection was never made.[27]

The St. Petersburg, Florida, Police Department adopted HOLMES. Information on criminal cases is constantly being entered, evaluated, reviewed, processed, and analyzed. Thousands of pages of information are readily available to any investigator working on a case at any time. Every piece of paper in a case is first evaluated by a "receiver and indexer" who decides how it is to be entered into the system so it can be retrieved quickly. Imputers then enter the material into any of the six "indexes" or data classifications in the system. A document may suggest that certain follow-up actions are required, such as interviewing a new lead mentioned. These actions will be brought up by the "statement reader" and sent to the "action allocator." Thus, all potential leads are noted and immediately assigned for follow-up action. These follow-up actions are entered into the computer, and HOLMES enters them into a master progress report. Every time the case manager checks on the progress of a case, he or she knows immediately what has and has not been done by all those connected with the case. Even news releases issued are entered into the computer. Then, if a suspect is questioned later about facts on the case, the investigators know whether any pertinent details were leaked to the press.

Information in the system can be recalled or combined in any desired format. For example, the investigator might ask to see information on anyone whose name has come up more than two or three times during the investigation. If this program had been used in the Yorkshire Ripper case, the suspect's name would have appeared regularly early in the investigation.

HOLMES can locate multiple uses of one name in the records of any one case at the lightning speed of more than one million words a minute. It can also scan all descriptions of people connected in any way to a case and advise if any of them comes close to the description of the main suspect. This description can include such items as the make or color of the car or boat driven or owned.

The system helps investigators follow up on leads, generate new leads, and then piece together seemingly unrelated information by organizing evidence in new ways and by linking scattered leads. Access to all information is so streamlined that it is estimated that thousands of human resource hours are saved on each case.

Investigators in Washington State battle violent crime with the Homicide Investigation and Tracking System (HITS/SMART). HITS/SMART, an electronic investigation system, stores, collates, and analyzes characteristics of all murders and sexual offenses in Washington State. Investigators statewide can then retrieve information from the system on these violent crimes to help them solve related cases. The system relies on the voluntary submission of information by law enforcement agencies throughout the state. These agencies submit data about murders, attempted murders, missing persons (when foul play is suspected), unidentified dead persons believed to be murder victims, and predatory sex offenders.[28]

Based on the information provided by the detectives, HITS/SMART analysts can query the database for any combination of the victim's gender, race, lifestyle, method and cause of death, geographic location of the crime, the absence or presence of clothing on the body, concealment of the body, and the dates of death and body discovery. In this way, analysts can identify other murder cases with common elements. Once the database is accessed, analysts can then supply detectives with the names of similarly murdered victims (if known), investigating agencies, case numbers, and the primary investigator's name and telephone number. Designing the query usually takes only a few minutes, as does the data search.

A database connected to HITS/SMART stores information contained in records from the Washington State Department of Corrections. This file gives HITS/SMART immediate access to the identification of present and former inmates with murder and sexual assault convictions. Their physical descriptions can be checked against the physical descriptions of unidentified suspects in recent sexual assault investigations.

As one example of the success of HITS/SMART, after a brutal rape, a detective made a request to the system for information about offenders having certain physical descriptions and MOs. The system staff provided the investigator with a list of known sexual offenders released from prison during the past five years and the areas to which they had been released. Along with this information, the HITS/SMART staff provided a collection of photographs to the detective, and the victim immediately identified one of the former offenders as her assailant.

Unfortunately, in 2005 the FBI, which faced tremendous criticism over its poorly functioning and outdated computerized case management system after September 11, 2001, was forced to abandon its planned Virtual Case File that was to be part of a billion-dollar effort to overhaul FBI systems.[29]

Despite the computer's influence in the investigative process, it will never replace the investigator. The successful investigation of crimes and other police incidents will always primarily depend on the intelligence and hard work of investigators and police officers. As a prime example, recall the 2002 Beltway Sniper case, a series of random shootings that terrorized Washington, D.C., and its suburbs. The Beltway snipers killed 10 people and wounded another 3. Despite using geographic profiling and other computer models in one of the most intense manhunts in U.S. criminal history, the suspects were identified based on leads provided by one of the snipers about a seemingly unrelated case in Alabama. Moreover, despite the formation of a massive law enforcement dragnet for the suspects, they were caught after an alert motorist saw them sleeping in their car 50 miles from the closest crime scene.[30]

Computer-Assisted Instruction

Computers are valuable teaching tools in police departments. Computer-assisted instruction (CAI) is a learning process in which students interact one-on-one with a computer, which instructs them and quizzes them. One of the most popular CAI systems is the Firearms Training Systems (FATS), a computer-driven laser disk mechanism, to train police officers to make decisions in life-threatening situations. FATS assists both veteran officers and new recruits in making shoot/don't shoot decisions.

Administrative Uses of Computers

Police departments use computers to perform many administrative functions. Management information systems and automated clerical processing systems free personnel to concentrate on serving the public. Software packages can assist police departments in jail and prisoner management. Automated patrol allocation is also possible.

Management Information Systems Police departments, like other U.S. businesses, use management information systems. Robert Sheehan and Gary W. Cordner define management information systems as "those systems that provide information needed for supervisory, allocation, strategic, tactical, policy and administrative decisions."[31] Sheehan and Cordner list the following management information systems found in police departments: (1) personnel information systems, (2) warranty control information systems, (3) equipment inventory systems, (4) evidence and property control systems, (5) booking information systems, (6) detention information systems, (7) case-tracking systems, (8) financial information systems, and (9) fleet maintenance information systems.[32]

Computers are perfect vehicles for management information systems, especially in larger police departments. Computer use eliminates the need to keep handwritten records and conduct manual searches. Many of the management information systems just listed are now computerized in most large, modern police departments. For example, in 1997, the Prince George's County, Maryland, Police Department joined a growing roster of law enforcement agencies nationwide that have instituted computer-aided early-warning systems to identify officers who are experiencing stress or other problems so that positive interventions can be made before the situation becomes career-threatening.[33]

Automated Clerical Processing Systems Policing involves a tremendous amount of paperwork, including arrest reports, incident and follow-up reports, and accident and injury reports. The computer simplifies the report-writing process. Many police departments today used automated clerical processing systems, and many officers use these systems in their patrol cars with portable or laptop computers.

Jail and Prisoner Management Many software packages can assist in jail and prisoner management. This application of computers is useful for police departments and sheriff's offices that are responsible for the lodging of prisoners awaiting appearance in court. These packages perform booking, updating, record inquiry, daily logs and audit trails, medical accounting, classification and pretrial release, inmate cash accounting, and billing.[34]

Patrol Allocation Design Patrol allocation is a very important responsibility for police administrators. Sheehan and Cordner summarize the major issues in patrol allocation as follows[35]:

1. Determining the number of patrol units needed in each precinct, at each time of the day, and for each day of the week

2. Designing patrol beats

3. Developing policies to dispatch and redeploy patrol units

4. Scheduling patrol personnel to match variations in the number of units on duty

Several computerized models are available for automated patrol allocation. These software packages determine the number of patrol units needed by precinct, day of the week, and shift, based on predetermined objectives.

Computer Networks and the Internet

A computer network allows users from many different areas to communicate with one another and to access the network's database. Computer networks are becoming common in policing.

The International Association of Chiefs of Police (IACP) has formed a nationwide computer network for the exchange of semiofficial and informal communications among police departments. Today, a great many police departments, large and small, have created their own websites and home pages on the Internet.

The Internet provides quick and easy access to literally millions of organizations and people around the world, including persons, organizations, businesses, and government and education sources. Millions of people today use the Internet as a form of communication, entertainment, and business. Today, most students are very familiar with the Internet and use it for their personal business and research. Much of the information in this chapter can be accessed through the Internet without taking the time to travel to a library, call a corporation, or look for a book. The Internet has revolutionized society and has revolutionized policing by enhancing the ability of officers and investigators to access tremendous amounts of data at a moment's notice without leaving their workplace. The ability to surf the net through search engines, business, media,

educational, and government websites and by exploring links attached to many websites is becoming essential in policing. As an example of how the Internet can help the police interact with the public, many cities, counties, and states in all regions of the nation are putting their crime maps on the web, which enables citizens to view them.

In 2006, it was reported that the San Francisco Police Department (SFPD), which started taking citizen's crime reports on the web two years ago, now has 10 to 12 percent of its citizen crime reports submitted online. A SFPD spokesperson said, "If we don't have to send an officer out to take a report, the officer is available to respond to more emergency calls." In San Mateo, California, it used to take an officer about 40 minutes to complete a crime report. Taking reports online has saved more than eight officer-workweeks per year. In San Mateo, more than 500 reports were filed by citizens in the first six months after online reporting began.[36]

Fingerprint Technology   *QCP*

Fingerprints have historically offered an infallible means of personal identification. Criminal identification by means of fingerprints is one of the most potent factors in apprehending fugitives who might otherwise escape arrest and continue their criminal activities indefinitely. This type of identification also makes possible an accurate determination of a person's previous arrests and convictions, which results in the imposition of more equitable sentences by the judiciary. In addition, this system of identification enables the prosecutor to present his or her case in the light of the offender's previous record. It also provides probation officers and parole board members with definite information upon which to base their judgment in dealing with criminals in their jurisdiction.[37]

Fingerprints may be recorded on standard fingerprint cards or can be recorded digitally and transmitted electronically for comparison. By comparing fingerprints at the scene of a crime with the fingerprint record of suspect persons, officials can establish absolute proof of the presence or identity of a person.[38]

You Are There!

Some Fingerprint Facts

Three Classifications

Three fingerprint classifications form the basis for all ten-print classification systems presently in use:

- *Loops:* Fingerprints that are characterized by ridge lines that enter from one side of the pattern and curve around to exit from the same side of the pattern. Some 60 percent of fingerprints are loops.
- *Whorls:* Fingerprints that include ridge patterns that are generally rounded or circular in shape and have two deltas. Some 30 percent of fingerprints are whorls.
- *Arches:* Fingerprints characterized by ridge lines that enter the print from one side and flow out of the other side. Some 5 percent of fingerprints are arches.

Three Types

Most people refer to any fingerprint discovered at a crime scene as a latent fingerprint. But there are really three basic types of prints:

- *Visible prints:* Made by fingers touching a surface after the ridges have been in contact with a colored material such as blood, paint, grease, or ink.
- *Plastic prints:* Ridge impressions left on a soft material such as putty, wax, soap, or dust.
- *Latent (invisible) prints:* Impressions caused when body perspiration or oils present on fingerprint ridges adhere to the surface of an object.

SOURCE: Adapted from Richard Saferstein, *Criminalistics: An Introduction to Forensic Science,* 7th ed. (Upper Saddle River, NJ: Prentice Hall 2001), p. 401.

Basic Categories of Fingerprints

There are two basic categories of fingerprints: inked prints or ten-prints and latent prints:

- **Inked Prints or ten-prints** are the result of the process of rolling each finger onto a ten-print card (each finger is rolled onto a separate box on the card) using fingerprinting ink. Inked prints are kept on file at local police departments, state criminal justice information agencies, and the FBI. When a person is arrested, he or she is fingerprinted, and those inked prints are compared with fingerprints on file of known criminals. Inked prints or ten-prints are also taken for numerous other types of investigations such as employment background and licenses applications.

- **Latent Prints** are impressions left on evidence. These prints may be "lifted" and then compared with inked prints on file to establish the identity of the perpetrator. Latent prints are impressions produced by the ridged skin on human fingers, palms, and soles of the feet. Latent print examiners analyze and compare latent prints to known prints of individuals in an

effort to make identifications or exclusions. The uniqueness, permanence, and arrangement of the friction ridges allow examiners to positively match two prints and to determine whether an area of a friction ridge impression originated from one source to the exclusion of others.

A variety of techniques, including use of chemicals, powders, lasers, alternate light sources, and other physical means, are employed in the detection and development of latent prints. In instances where a latent print has limited quality and quantity of detail, examiners may perform microscopic examinations to make conclusive comparisons.

Sometimes, a latent fingerprint found in dust may be the only lead in an investigation. Even though this kind of print was actually caused by some of the dust being removed—because it adhered to the ridges of the skin that touched there—methods of lifting these prints are now available.[39] Lasers can be used to lift prints from surfaces that often defy traditional powder or chemical techniques, including glass, paper, cardboard, rubber, wood, plastic, leather, and even human skin.[40] The use of lasers in fingerprint lifting allowed the FBI to detect a 40-year-old fingerprint of a Nazi war criminal on a postcard.[41] In an article, the special agent in charge of the Forensic Services

You Are There!

How to Find and Develop Latent Fingerprints

- *Carbon dusting powders:* When finely ground carbon powder is applied lightly to a surface with a camel's-hair or fiberglass brush, it will adhere to perspiration residues left on the surface and can render an invisible impression visible. Generally, the print technician will apply powder of a contrasting color to the color of the surface being dusted. The raised print is photographed, lifted off the surface using transparent tape, and then transferred to a card that has a contrasting color to the color of the powder used on the tape.

- *Iodine fuming:* Crystals of iodine are placed in a glass container called a fumer along with the article suspected of containing latent prints. When the crystals are heated, iodine vapors will fill the chamber and make the latent print visible. Iodine prints are not permanent and begin to fade once the fuming process is stopped. The resultant fingerprints must be immediately photographed. This method is particularly useful for obtaining prints from paper or cardboard.

- *Silver nitrate:* A solution of silver nitrate in distilled water is sprayed or saturated on paper believed to have latent prints. When the paper is exposed to light, the print becomes visible.

- *Ninhydrin:* The chemical ninhydrin is sprayed over large cardboard or paper containers, and if a latent print is present, it will become visible.

- *Super glue fuming:* Super glue (cyanoacrylate) treated with sodium hydroxide is placed within a chamber with an object believed to contain latent prints. The resultant fumes from the glue adhere to the latent print, making it visible.

- *Ultraviolet light:* An ultraviolet (UV) lamp (black light) can be effective in a darkened environment to expose latent prints.

- *Laser:* The laser, when directed at a surface, can cause the perspiration forming a latent fingerprint to fluoresce, thus making the print visible.

- *Alternative light sources:* An alternative light source (ALS) operates under the same principle as a laser and can make latent fingerprints fluoresce and become visible. It is much more portable than the laser.

SOURCE: Adapted from Larry Ragle, *Crime Scene* (New York: Avon, 1995), pp. 101–108; Richard Saferstein, *Criminalistics: An Introduction to Forensic Science*, 7th ed. (Upper Saddle River, NJ: Prentice Hall, 2001), pp. 405–413.

Division of the U.S. Secret Service cited numerous cases of the successful use of sophisticated fingerprint technology. He mentioned such high-profile cases as the original bombing of the World Trade Center and the killing of two CIA employees in Langley, Virginia.[42]

Innovations in fingerprint analysis continue, including, by 2006, methods for development of fingerprints on thermal paper, detection of latent fingerprints on fruits and vegetables, obtaining fingerprint impressions using a vacuum box, and improvements in the FBI's latent print processes.[43]

Automated Fingerprint Identification Systems

By the 1980s, **automated fingerprint identification systems (AFIS)** began to be developed. An AFIS system enables a print technician to enter unidentified latent prints into the computer. The computer then automatically searches its files and presents a list of likely matches, which can then be visually examined by a fingerprint technician to find the perfect match. Using AFIS technology, a person's prints can be taken and stored into memory without the use of traditional inking and rolling techniques.[44]

The first locally funded, regional automated fingerprint identification system in the United States was Northern Virginia Regional Identification System (NOVARIS).[45] Since then, numerous police departments have developed AFIS systems, and there are numerous successful examples of automated fingerprint identification systems in Wisconsin, Nevada, Alaska, California, Idaho, Oregon, Utah, Washington, Wyoming, Rhode Island, Maryland, and Canada.[46]

Until recently, AFIS technology has been extraordinarily expensive and therefore procured only

ON THE JOB

Can a Person Change Fingerprints?

It is impossible to change one's fingerprints, although many criminals have tried to obscure them. Perhaps, the most celebrated attempt to obliterate one's fingerprints was the efforts by the notorious 1930s gangster John Dillinger, who tried to destroy his own fingerprints by applying a corrosive acid to them. However, prints taken at the morgue after he was shot to death, compared with fingerprints taken at the time of a previous arrest, proved that his efforts had been a failure.

Richard Saferstein, the noted criminalistics expert, has indicated that efforts at intentionally scarring the skin on one's fingerprints can only be self-defeating, for it would be totally impossible to obliterate all the ridge characteristics on the hand, and the presence of permanent scars merely provides new characteristics for identification.

—*John S. Dempsey*

SOURCE: Adapted from Richard Saferstein, *Criminalistics: An Introduction to Forensic Science,* 7th ed. (Upper Saddle River, N.J.: Prentice Hall, 2001), p. 400.

by the largest agencies. The technology provided excellent high-speed fingerprint matching once fingerprint databases became large enough. Still, a drawback was that each system has been stand-alone—that is, systems could not exchange information rapidly. But there are now software-based systems using open-system architecture. In other words, that means any brand of computer based on the UNIX operating system will work with them.[47] These systems are also designed to exchange fingerprint and other data over the wire with other criminal justice information systems, using the widely accepted Henry System of fingerprint classification.

These systems, designed for use in a booking facility, can use ink and paper fingerprints, or can employ **Live Scan,** an optical fingerprint scanning system, to read a suspect's prints. The scanner uses electronic capture of the suspect's fingerprint pattern, using 500 DPI resolution, electronic quality analysis, and automatic image centering. The booking officer begins with a single-finger or dual-digit search, placing the suspect's finger on the scanner for reading. If the computer finds a possible match, the officer gets news of a "hit" within minutes. The computer selects the most likely matches, which then must be verified by a human operator. If there is no hit, the computer adds the fingerprint to its database automatically.

These systems also have electronic quality checking, image enhancement, and ten-print system capability. They can scan fingerprint cards, reducing them to electronic records, and store them for future reference. They can also print finger-

print cards from electronically scanned Live Scan fingerprints. A latent fingerprint examiner can link separate crime scenes using single latent prints, which can point to a common perpetrator or a pattern.

The use of Live Scan stations allows fingerprints and demographic information to be electronically captured, stored, and transmitted in minutes. Greater use of applicant fingerprints is among the many reasons why the use of ten-print Live Scan stations is increasing nationwide. Built-in quality-control software helps reduce human errors. Because there is no ink, there is no smearing. If a mistake is made, a print can be retaken until one high-quality record is obtained. There is no need to print a person again for local, state, and federal agencies because Live Scan can make copies. Higher quality fingerprints mean a higher likelihood of the AFIS finding a match in its database without human verification.[48]

Integrated Automated Fingerprint Identification System (IAFIS) In 1999, the FBI began its **Integrated Automated Fingerprint Identification System (IAFIS).** This system provides the capability to search latent fingerprints against the largest criminal fingerprint repository in the world, which contains the fingerprints of almost 45 million individuals. This allows the FBI to make identifications without benefit of a named suspect to help solve a variety of crimes.[49]

IAFIS is primarily a ten-print system for searching an individual's fingerprints to determine

You Are There!

DNA Couldn't Find the Suspect, but IAFIS Did

The Georgia Bureau of Identification (GBI) and the Pleasant Prairie, Wisconsin, Police Department (PPPD) were both looking for the same rape suspect in crimes committed in their jurisdictions. The PPPD contacted the GBI because they noted common characteristics in the rapes: The victims all worked as clerks at retail strip malls near interstates. The PPPD sent fingerprint and DNA samples for examination. Through DNA testing, the GBI tied those two rapes to a rape in Florence, Kentucky, but could not identify the suspect.

After exhaustive investigation efforts with the PPPD, including a requested subject analysis by the FBI's Violent Crime Apprehension Program, had yielded no viable leads, the GBI submitted the Wisconsin print for examination by the FBI's IAFIS database. Within minutes, the search produced the name of a suspect.

The man was located in jail at Lawrenceville, Georgia, where he was being held on an unrelated crime. The GBI was granted a search warrant to obtain a blood sample. Although he denied any involvement in the crimes, his blood was matched to DNA samples from the serial rapes. A few days after the sample was taken, he used a bedsheet to hang himself in his jail cell. He implicated himself in other rapes before his death.

The lesson from this investigation is the value of the IAFIS latent search technique. Despite exhaustive investigative efforts, none of the other organizations' efforts were able to identify a suspect for these serial crimes. IAFIS did.

SOURCE: Adapted from "Unsolved Case Fingerprint Matching," *FBI Law Enforcement Bulletin* (December 2000), pp. 12–13.

whether a prior arrest record exists and then maintaining a criminal arrest record history for each individual. The system also offers significant latent print capabilities. Using IAFIS, a latent print specialist can digitally capture latent print and ten-print images and perform several functions with each including enhancing to improve image quality, comparing latent fingerprints against suspect ten-print records retrieved from the criminal fingerprint repository, searching latent fingerprints against the ten-print fingerprint repository when no suspects have been developed, doing automatic searches of new arrest ten-print records against an unsolved latent fingerprint repository, and creating special files of ten-print records to support major criminal investigations.[50]

In 2000, the fingerprint databases of the FBI and the Immigration and Naturalization Service (INS) (now part of the Department of Homeland Security) were merged. Formerly, federal, state, and local law enforcement officials did not have access to all fingerprint information captured by Border Patrol agents, and INS did not have access to the FBI's records when its agents apprehended suspects at the border. The merging of the two systems was prompted by the inadvertent release by the INS in 1999 of Angel Maturino-Resendez, the suspected serial killer—known as the "railroad killer"—who was alleged to have stowed away on trains and murdered eight people near rail lines during a three-state killing spree. Border Patrol agents had picked up Maturino-Resendez for illegal entry into the United States and sent him back to Mexico. The agents were unaware that he was wanted by the Houston police and the FBI for questioning in the murders. Within days of his release, Maturino-Resendez killed four of his victims. Eventually, he surrendered to Texas Rangers in July 1999.[51]

By 2003, IAFIS had almost 45 million records and provides an international standard for providing fingerprints electronically. After a criminal 10-print search is submitted electronically, the FBI guarantees a response within two hours and the prints are compared with those of anyone who has been arrested in the United States since the 1920s. One of the biggest current problems with IAFIS is that 8 states still do not electronically submit standardized criminal fingerprints to the system and 20 states do not submit latent fingerprints. IAFIS was instrumental in the capture of Lee Boyd Malvo, one of the two suspects in the 2002 Washington, D.C., area sniper case. A latent print entered into IAFIS matched Malvo—his prints were in the system because he had been previously arrested by the INS.[52]

ON THE JOB

"What a Difference Technology Makes"

During my police career, I saw some great improvements in technology. Many tasks that took hours to complete and document began to be done by computers. We handwrote reports that had five copies and were turned in to the supervisor who read them, signed off on them, and sent them to records (after perhaps having us rewrite it a few times). A data entry clerk then entered the data so that very basic information could be retrieved for future reference. When it was time to go to court, the officer went back to records and requested a copy of the report to take to court. When I left the department, officers had been using laptops for several years with state-of-the-art programs; they wrote their reports, and the supervisors retrieved and reviewed them electronically and uploaded them to the main computer system. Much more extensive data was thus available for retrieval without the use of a data entry clerk. Reports were generated on a daily basis to gather needed information for units such as Crime Analysis, Press Information Office, and the Detective Bureau.

In my opinion, the most significant improvement I saw over my career was the advent of the automated fingerprint identification system (AFIS). When I started

with the police department, we had a sworn officer, a sergeant in fact, doing fingerprint comparisons. If we arrested a suspect and thought he might have committed some specific crimes, we could request that his prints be compared with the latents lifted at the scenes. If we worked a scene and had some possible suspects, we could request that the latents be compared with the suspect's prints—if we had them. If we had no suspect, the sergeant could compare the prints with those of some local offenders known to have committed similar crimes, but other than that, we were out of luck. This man spent eight hours a day comparing prints with little productive results.

Now, when an officer works a scene, he or she turns in any latents, and they can be compared with all the latents in the database within minutes if not seconds. Clearance rates have been greatly enhanced by this technology. We are also able to put that sergeant position out on the street where it is needed. Dusting for fingerprints is no longer seen as an exercise in futility. This is just one way technology has made law enforcement much more productive and effective.

—*Linda S. Forst*

IBIS A new portable handheld device, Identification Based Information System (IBIS) is available as a handheld tool that delivers on-the-spot positive identification when a suspect has no driver's license or seems to be presenting a false identification. The IBIS captures thumbprints and mug shots and receives text and mug shots from databases with criminal histories, warrants, and images. It even has a silent assist button in the event the investigator requires help from fellow officers. The IBIS offers a high-resolution camera to make images of latent fingerprints at a crime scene, a digital voice recorder, and a GIS. Local agencies can connect with state and federal communications and information systems when the system is fully developed.[53]

Numerous other countries have also made innovations in fingerprinting technology.[54] The International Association for Identification (IAI) is a professional organization for those interested in fingerprint identification, latent prints, and AFIS.

Automated Palm Print Technology

Recent advances in biometrics have made it possible for automated palm print systems to complement standard AFIS technology. The technology works in the same manner as its AFIS counterpart, but instead of fingerprints, it captures the four core areas of the palm and converts them into data for storage in a palm print repository. On arrest, suspects have their palms scanned along with their fingerprints. After a palm print is lifted from a crime scene, it too is scanned and entered into the database for matching. The palm print matching processor will then return a rank-ordered notification of match candidates to the workstation. Before palm print technology, if police didn't have a suspect to compare prints to, the only way they could make a palm print match was to manually compare latent palm prints with hundreds

You Are There!

The Power of Fluorescent Print Detection: The Polly Klaas Case

The power of fluorescent print detection was demonstrated in the Polly Klaas kidnap and murder case in Petaluma, California. The young victim was abducted from her bedroom by an unknown intruder. Police used black powder methods to discover several prints, none of which matched the subsequently identified suspect.

In an effort to locate more evidence, the FBI's Evidence Response Team (ERT) was called upon. ERTs are trained and equipped with the latest forensic technology. Agents from the San Francisco ERT processed the scene using an Omniprint 1000. After the victim's wooden bed frame was dusted with Redwop illumination at 450nm, a clear palm print was revealed.

A suspect was subsequently arrested, but he denied any knowledge of the crime. When learning of the palm print evidence, however, he admitted to the crime and directed investigators to the location of the victim's body. The palm print was the only print that matched the suspect and could not have been found by traditional fingerprint techniques.

Unfortunately, solving the crime did not prevent the death of the victim. The FBI is building a computerized fingerprint database of all convicted sex offenders. It is hoped that rapid matching of any prints found at an abduction scene will lead to the apprehension of the suspect before the victim is physically harmed. Fluorescent print detection is clearly going to be a widely used tool in these efforts.

SOURCE: Adapted from Mary C. Nolte, "The Role of the Photon in Modern Forensics," *Law and Order* (November 1994), pp. 51–54.

---

of thousands of individual prints sitting in repositories. In most cases, for obvious reasons, this simply was not possible.[55]

Automated palm print technology has been in development for some time, but it has only recently come onto the market. One reason for this is the complicated nature of the palm print itself. The palm area contains as many as one thousand minutiae (small characteristics), compared with the approximate one hundred minutiae found in the average fingerprint. This difference in size means that an automated palm print system must actively scan and match a larger area, requiring complex refining of the technology to ensure the highest accuracy rate possible.

Less-Than-Lethal Weapons

Police departments are using technological devices to stop and disable armed, dangerous, and violent subjects without resorting to the use of firearms. The term **less-than-lethal weapons,** or nonlethal weapons, is used to identify innovative alternatives to traditional nonfirearm weapons (such as batons and flashlights) and tactics (such as martial arts techniques and other bodily force techniques, including tackles and choke holds). Nonlethal weapons can be seen as shooting-avoidance tools because these weapons can control unarmed but resisting suspects early in a confrontation, before they have the opportunity to become armed and attack an officer. These weapons can also be used against a subject who is armed with less than a firearm—for example, a knife, club, or other instrument that can cause injury to officers. Among the most popular nonlethal weapons being used by the police are chemical irritant sprays and the Taser and other stun devices.[56]

Chemical Irritant Sprays

Chemical irritant sprays are handheld liquid products that contain the active ingredients of cayenne pepper or CS or CN tear gas. They can be sprayed into the face of a resisting suspect from as far away as fifteen feet to cause discomfort and temporary disorientation. Thus, officers gain the necessary time to subdue the subject safely.

For many years, the aerosol CN tear gas, originally introduced by Smith & Wesson under the name Chemical Mace, was regarded by law enforcement as the closest thing to a perfect nonlethal weapon. Today, however, police are experimenting with other types of aerosol sprays.

Aerosol subject restraints (ASRs), for example, are different from CS or CN sprays in that they do not rely on pain. ASRs cause a subject's eyes to close and double the subject over with uncontrollable coughing. They also cause a temporary loss of strength and coordination. ASRs cause no physical damage and require no area decontamination. Among popular ASRs are oleoresin capsicum (OC, the hot ingredient in chili peppers), Aerko (Punch), Def-Tee (Pepper Mace), Guardian Personal Security Products (Bodyguard), and Zarc (Cap-Stun).[57]

A recent National Institute of Justice (NIJ) study of officer and arrestee injuries in three North Carolina police jurisdictions before and after pepper spray was introduced found a correlation between pepper-spray use and a decline in injuries. The NIJ report also covered another study of 63 cases in which deaths of in-custody suspects followed pepper spray use. The study disclosed that in only two of these cases was pepper spray found to have been a factor in the deaths, but not the cause of the deaths.[58]

The Taser and Other Stun Devices

The Taser, an acronym for Thomas A. Swift's Electric Rifle, is a handheld electronic stun gun that discharges a high-voltage, low-amperage, pulsating current via tiny wires and darts, which can be fired from as far as fifteen feet away. When the darts strike the subject, the electric current causes a temporary incapacitation of the muscles. This gives the officers the necessary time to subdue the subject safely. The electricity can penetrate as much as two inches of clothing. The Taser discharges only a few watts of power and is not harmful to cardiac patients with implanted pacemakers, nor can it be modified to produce a lethal charge.[59]

Another increasingly popular less-than-lethal weapon is the "beanbag" gun. The one-inch square canvas bag, filled with bird shot, has been used by SWAT teams for several years and more recently by regular patrol officers. The beanbag gun produces a velocity of 320 feet per second within a range of a few inches to 30 feet away with nonlethal force.[60] However, in the 2001 *Deorle v. Rutherford* court decision by the U.S. Court of Appeals for the Ninth Circuit, the court decided that firing bean bag rounds at an unarmed suspect without first issuing a verbal warning represented excessive force and ruled that the beanbag round

represented force with a significant risk of serious injury.[61]

Safety and Effectiveness of Less-Than-Lethal Weapons

J. P. Morgan, chief of the Goldsboro, North Carolina, Police Department, points to a possible drawback of the less-than-lethal weapon: "Sometimes . . . it can give a false sense of security, as evidenced by an officer's response to the offer of a back-up. 'I don't need one, I got my OC' [oleoresin capsicum, a pepper spray]."[62]

Just how safe are less-than-lethal weapons? A study of 502 use-of-force incidents not involving the use of firearms attempted to discover the injury rate to officers and subjects from eight specific types of force used by the officers. The force was used to cause a suspect to fall to the ground so that the officers could safely subdue him or her. The types of force studied were (1) striking with a baton; (2) a karate kick; (3) a punch; (4) striking with a flashlight; (5) swarming techniques, or organized tackles by a group of officers; (6) miscellaneous bodily force, including pushing, shoving, and tackling; (7) chemical irritant sprays (CS and CN); and (8) the Taser.[63]

The most used types of force in the study were the baton, miscellaneous bodily force, and the Taser; the least used were chemical irritant sprays, flashlights, and punches. The Taser was used in 102 cases and chemical irritant sprays were used in 21 cases. The Taser was about as effective as the other forms of nonlethal force in subduing a subject, and it resulted in fewer injuries to officers and subjects. The researcher concluded, "Expanded use of nonlethal weapons, along with the concurrent development of the next generation of such devices, will lead to fewer and less severe injuries to suspects and officers, reduced civil liability claims and payments, reduced personnel complaints, reduced disability time out of the field, reduced disability pension payments and an improved public image for law enforcement."[64]

The use of the Taser has been upheld in court. In *Michenfelder v. Sumner,* a federal court found the following: "Authorities believe the Taser is the preferred method for controlling prisoners because it is the 'least confrontational' when compared to the use of physical restraint, billy clubs, mace or beanbag guns. . . . When contrasted to alternative methods for physically controlling inmates, some of which can have serious after-effects, the Taser compared favorably."[65]

However, more recent studies present a less promising picture of less-than-lethal weapons. The Toronto, Canada, Police Service conducted a comprehensive survey in 2001 of less-than-lethal weapons to assist in the reduction of the use of force and deadly force by the police. The study's emphasis was to evaluate the practicality and effectiveness of these devices. Its conclusion was that there are presently no less-than-lethal weapons available that could replace the police firearm in certain life and death situations. Impact projectile launchers, capture nets, and electronic stun devices were determined to be impractical and ineffective, although the report did note that batons or pepper spray were useful in less deadly situations and could sometimes prevent an officer from having to use deadly force.[66] A 2001 report by the Great Britain Home Office discussing the United Kingdom's police need for less lethal weapon technologies, after reviewing all current commercially available weapon possibilities, concluded only that further testing of all the devices will continue to assess their potential use in policing.[67] Furthermore, according to a 2002 article, recent research has found that technological gadgetry, such as beanbag devices and rubber bullets, have caused death and serious injuries over the past years. The author asserts that there is a fear that if common criminals see law enforcement using more force and more lethal trends, they will also, and he concludes that less-than-lethal technologies have not been able to co-exist with lethal force because in most street-level confrontations, they have turned out worse than using lethal force.[68] See Chapter 5, "The Police Role and Police Discretion," for more discussion of the use of less-than-lethal force.

■

Surveillance Technology

Police agencies use surveillance for a variety of reasons. Surveillance might be used to provide cover for an undercover officer and an arrest team in a buy and bust narcotics operation, to gather intelligence, or to establish probable cause for arrest. Today's advances in technology provide us with more surveillance devices than ever before.[69]

Formerly, surveillance equipment consisted of a nearly broken-down undercover van used to store the typical surveillance equipment: a camera and a pair of binoculars. Times have changed. Today's police have high-tech state-of-the-art listening, recording, and viewing devices, high-tech surveillance vans, night vision devices, vehicle tracking systems, global positioning systems, and surveillance aircraft, among other innovations.

Scientific breakthroughs in the areas of surveillance, mobile communications, and illicit drug detection are arming law enforcement agencies with increasingly sophisticated tools in their fight against illegal drug traffickers and other criminals.[70] This section will discuss the latest in surveillance devices.

Surveillance Vans

A vehicle specialist describes today's state-of-the-art surveillance van: "When talking about surveillance vehicles today, . . . we tend to think of a van whose interior looks slightly less complex than the bridge of Star Trek's USS Enterprise." He describes the ideal surveillance van as having the following equipment: power periscopes operated by a video game-like joystick; six cameras to cover 360 degrees of the van's exterior, plus a periscope mounted observer's camera; videotape decks to record everything happening on the street; quick-change periscope camera mounts; portable toilets; video printers; motion detection cameras; night vision cameras; cellular telephones; AM/FM cassette entertainment systems; CB radios, police radios, and police scanners; and other personalized equipment.[71]

Vehicle Tracking Systems

Vehicle tracking systems, sometimes referred to as transponders, bumper beepers, or homing devices, enable officers and investigators to track a vehicle during surveillance. These systems are actually transmitters that can be placed on a subject's vehicle. The tracking system consists of the transmitter on the subject's vehicle and a receiver, which picks up the signal from the transmitter. There are three basic vehicle tracking systems on the market:

■ *Radio frequency (RF) tracking systems* are usually short-range systems that operate on a transmitted signal from a transmitter placed on the target vehicle. The receiver receives the signal using three or four antennas and determines the direction of the target vehicle.

■ *Cellular tracking systems* work similarly to RF tracking systems but use transmitters that link to cellular telephone towers to track the target vehicle. Often, a cellular telephone serves as the transmitter signal that the tracking system employs. Tracking range is limited to the range of towers in the area.

■ *Global Positioning System (GPS) tracking systems* use GPS satellites to pinpoint the location of a target vehicle. GPS technology can locate a target vehicle anywhere in the world. Mapping software allows the target vehicle's location to be displayed on detailed street maps. Global positioning systems will be discussed further in this chapter.

Night Vision Devices

Among the most sophisticated surveillance devices in use today are enhanced **night vision devices,** including monocular devices small enough to hold in one hand, which can be adapted to a camera, video camera, or countersniper rifle. An expert describes the potential of such devices:

> Perhaps an automobile slowly approaches you in the dark with its lights out. With a normal night vision scope you can see it clearly—but you can't see through the windshield to see who's driving the car. Switch on the infrared (IR) laser, and it illuminates a spot through the windshield so you can identify the operator. In another case, at night a man lurks on the porch of a mountain cabin. In normal mode only the cabin and porch are clearly visible. The IR laser illuminates a spot to show the person waiting in the shadows.[72]

As far back as 1800, Sir William Herschel discovered the fact that every object emits thermal energy in the infrared (IR) wavelengths. His son, Sir John Herschel, took the first IR photographs of the sun approximately 40 years later. Infrared surveillance systems appeared toward the end of World War II as a covert way to observe the enemy at night. The Germans were the first to use IR systems as impressive nighttime tank killers. The Soviets developed IR systems in the 1960s and 1970s. Since then, these systems have been used by the United States during the Korean, Vietnam, and Gulf Wars.[73]

A more sophisticated form of infrared technology is thermal imaging (TI), which does not require any light at all. Traditional night vision equipment requires minimal light, such as from the moon. Thermal imaging can also see through fog, mist, or smoke and is especially useful in penetrating many types of camouflaging. TI takes advantage of the IR emission but does it passively, so only the user knows when it is in operation, not the subject.[74]

IR and TI systems can be mounted on police vehicles and pan possible subjects in all directions. Display screens can be mounted in patrol cars or investigators' cars, and joysticks can be used to direct the panning of the cameras.[75]

Law enforcement agents from the U.S. Department of Homeland Security (DHS) make extensive use of thermal imagers. These heat-sensing cameras detect the presence and location of a human; then an image intensifier makes the image clearer so that identification is possible. These tools are used for myriad law enforcement and investigatory purposes, such as search-and-rescue missions, fugitive searches, perimeter surveillance, vehicle pursuits, flight safety, marine and ground surveillance, structure profiles, disturbed surfaces, hidden compartments, environmental hazards, and officer safety. Other emerging uses of TI are obtaining more accurate skid-mark measures at a crash scene and obtaining evidence at a crime scene that cannot be observed with the human eye.[76] DHS officers also uses many other different night vision technologies in their duties, including IR cameras, night vision goggles, handheld searchlights with a band that reaches more than a mile, seismic and infrared sensors, and fiberscopes.[77]

Global Positioning Systems

Global Positioning Systems (GPS) are the most recent technology available to help law enforcement and investigators. The GPS is a network of 24 satellites used by the U.S. Department of Defense to pinpoint targets and guide bombs. The satellites are equipped with atomic clocks and equally accurate position measuring telemetry gear. GPS has been used for everything from helping hikers find their way through the woods to guiding law enforcement officers to stolen vehicles.[78] When GPS is combined with geographic information systems (GIS) and automatic vehicle locations (AVL), officers can tell where they are on a map and the dispatch center can continuously monitor the officers' location. Police departments can determine the location of each patrol vehicle without any communication from the officer who is driving. In a car wreck, such a system could automatically notify the dispatcher of a possibly injured officer at a specific location. Also, if an officer engages in a high-speed chase, such a system would provide the vehicle's location automatically, or if an officer is injured in an encounter with a suspect, it can suggest that help be sent immediately.

GPS is also used by fleet operators in the private sector to track fleets for routing purposes and for rolling emergencies. It can be used to track the route over time and to monitor the vehicle's speed. GPS is also used for crime mapping, tracking, and monitoring the location of probationers and parolees around the clock.[79]

Surveillance Aircraft

Airplanes are being added to law enforcement's arsenal of surveillance devices. These aircraft do not require extensive landing fields and have proved to be very successful in surveillance operations. Fixed-wing aircraft and rotorcraft complement ground-based vehicles in hundreds of police agencies worldwide and aid search and rescue operations, surveillance, and investigative missions. Advanced electronic and computer systems for aircraft now include real-time video downlinks and low-light surveillance.[80]

Electronic Video Surveillance

The use of electronic video surveillance (surveillance and security cameras and closed-circuit television [CCTV] systems) has increased rapidly in both the private security industry and public policing. Electronic video surveillance systems can passively record and play back video at certain intervals, be actively monitored by security personnel, or used in a combination of these methods. Some evidence suggests that video surveillance is successful in reducing and preventing crimes and is helpful in prosecuting criminals.

Electronic video surveillance has several objectives, including reducing crime and disorder, making people feel safer, and providing evidence for police investigations.[81]

British police began using surveillance cameras and CCTV technology in the late 1950s to assist in the one-person operation of traffic lights. In the 1960s, the police began discussing the use of CCTV to prevent crime, and by 1969, 14 different police forces were using CCTV with 67 cameras in use nationwide. Only 4 of the departments were using video recorders at that time.[82] Since then, surveillance cameras have increased exponentially in Great Britain.

Research results in Britain have been somewhat incomplete, confusing, and inconsistent. Instead of discussing each conflicting study in this chapter, we suggest the reader seriously interested in studying this research can access the reports cited in the endnotes of this chapter.[83] The most recent information from the British Home Office in 2005 is that academic studies of the effectiveness of electronic video surveillance are still inconclusive.[84] However, a 2005 survey of British police officers revealed that most viewed CCTV as a cost-effective tool that can facilitate the speed of investigations and encourage offenders captured on CCTV to plead guilty, thus saving police and court time. A 2005 survey of the British public revealed that 80 percent of respondents believed CCTV would reduce crimes in their areas.[85]

Testimony before the U.S. Congress in 2002 revealed that there are more than a million video surveillance cameras in use in the United States (however, a video security firm cited later in this chapter estimated that there were 26 million surveillance cameras in the United States in 2005). Testimony revealed that the reasons for using video surveillance included preventing and detecting crime, reducing citizens' fear of crime, aiding criminal investigations through post-event analysis of surveillance tapes, and countering terrorism.[86]

Some experts feel there is little evidence to date that electronic video surveillance has had a great impact on crime; however, its symbolic impact as a deterrent is believed by police forces to be significant. Further, police favor it because it expands the visual surveillance of the police without having to increase the number of officers.[87]

Eighty percent of 200 U.S. law enforcement agencies that responded to a survey by the International Association of Chiefs of Police (IACP) reported that they have used CCTV technology and the other 20 percent anticipate using it in the future. Sixty-three percent of those using it found it was useful for investigative assistance, 54 percent found in useful for gathering evidence, and 20 percent found it useful in crime reduction.

Ninety-six percent of the agencies did not have a way to measure its crime reduction ability, but of the eight agencies that did, three said it had a great effect in reducing crime.[88]

Electronic video surveillance systems make some law-abiding citizens feel safer whereas they make others very nervous. In 2005, the police commissioner of the Redlands, California, Police Department, which already uses 20 cameras at three sites, reported that the department was planning to install more surveillance cameras throughout the city and anticipates having hundreds of them within a decade. Many citizens reported pleasure at the announcement; however, the mayor said he did not think more cameras are necessary, "This is absolutely crazy. In my opinion, it's Big Brother coming in," and the associate director of the American Civil Liberties Union (ACLU) of Southern California said she had "grave concerns about the proliferation of cameras and the whole Big Brother aspect of every person's movement being captured throughout the day in many locations."[89]

The installation in Washington, D.C., of a network of more than 14 high-tech video cameras caused privacy concerns about the possible misuse of the videotapes by the government, and critics maintain that the cost of installing them can be equal to half of the annual salary of a new police recruit, raising the question of whether it would be more important to hire more police. However, surveillance cameras have been reported to give tourists a feeling of confidence.[90]

In 2005, it was reported that the New York City Police Department (NYPD) monitors 80 surveillance cameras in public places, as well as 3,000 cameras in the city's Housing Authority's 15 public housing developments. The cameras in the housing developments were credited by the NYPD as cutting crime by 36 percent, mostly quality of life crimes such as graffiti and public urination. Other large cities aggressively stepping up surveillance systems include Chicago and Baltimore, financed partly with federal funds. Chicago announced in 2005 that it was linking 2,000 surveillance cameras.[91]

Grant Fredericks, forensic video analyst with the nonprofit Law Enforcement and Emergency Services Video Association, says fingerprints used to have the most important role in crime scene evidence, but that role is now filled by electronic video surveillance systems. "There's more visual evidence at crime scenes today than any other evidence," he says. Surveillance cameras have been useful in solving many types of cases, including terrorism, robberies, kidnappings, murders, thefts, fraud, and burglaries. One video security firm says there are more than 26 million surveillance cameras in the country, including at banks, stores, train stations, schools, highways, and rooftops.[92] The increasing use of video monitoring by law enforcement agencies, public agencies, private businesses, and citizens is providing law enforcement agencies with an unprecedented amount of visual information to aid in investigations. When police are investigating crimes, it is a common practice to view any videotapes that have been captured by businesses or public buildings near the crime scene to retrieve any evidence that may have observed a suspect committing the crime or fleeing the area. In many cases, the video may reveal important leads, such as escape vehicles or accomplices acting as lookouts. Police use evidence and chain-of-custody procedures in these cases and consult with prosecutors.[93]

The proliferation of private surveillance cameras around the nation is transforming police work, and surveillance cameras have become key tools in investigations. "One of the things we do at the scene of any crime is look for cameras, private-sector cameras," said New York City Police Commissioner Raymond W. Kelly. "It was not standard procedure 10 or 15 years ago."[94]

The security tapes can prove more reliable than human witnesses' fuzzy recollections. The improved quality of cameras, recording systems, and digital enhancement means that evidence like a license plate number or face can be easily singled out and enhanced. The objective nature of cameras has been critical in obtaining confessions and gaining convictions. In the 2005 perjury trial of rap performer Lil' Kim, a video shows her standing within a few feet of rap producer Damien Butler, also known as D-Roc, before a shootout, even though she claimed in her grand jury testimony that she did not recall his presence. She was convicted on perjury charges based on her testimony.[95]

Experts say criminals are more likely to make confessions when they realize they have been caught on video. A surveillance video expert from the University of Indianapolis, Thomas C. Christenberry, says, "In the absence of any human witness, the video might be your only witness."[96]

The use of electronic video surveillance has been consistently held by the courts to be constitutional and not a violation of citizens' privacy rights. Although privacy advocates are uneasy about the use of electronic video surveillance to monitor public meetings and demonstrations, courts have generally ruled that people do not have a reasonable expectation of privacy when in public because their actions are readily observable by others.[97] Also, the use of video surveillance on private property is not a violation of the U.S. Constitution.

Despite the complaints of privacy advocates, video evidence can also exonerate a wrongly accused suspect. As an example, a homeless man arrested in New York City in 2000 for a brutal brick attack on a young woman was released after a week in jail, although having been picked out of a lineup by three witnesses, and making a confession of guilt. A review of security tapes at a Virgin Megastore about 20 blocks from the scene revealed that he was in that store at the time of the assault and thus could not have been the attacker. Police reviewed 15 hours of tapes from 31 surveillance cameras inside the store to obtain this exculpatory evidence.[98]

Norman Siegel, former executive director of the New York Civil Liberties Union, wants public hearings on the pros and cons of surveillance cameras, "You are talking about fundamental freedoms: the right to freely travel, the right of anonymity." A NYPD spokesperson claims, however, "There is no privacy issue here at all. They (the cameras) would only be placed in areas where there is absolutely no expectation of privacy."[99]

Advanced Photographic Techniques

Photography has always played a major role in policing. Innovations and advanced techniques have increased this role. This section discusses digital photography, mug shot imaging systems, age-progression photography, and composite sketching.

Digital Photography

Digital photography is being increasingly recognized and used in law enforcement as an efficient tool that enables instant viewing and distribution of images that aid in criminal investigations.

The major concern about digital photography is its admissibility as evidence in court because it can be manipulated with computer software.

Traditional film-based photography can also be manipulated, however, either while taking the original photograph or in developing the film. Under current rules of evidence, parties seeking to introduce a film-based photograph must demonstrate its relevancy and authenticity. Courts generally require the original (the negative or any print therefrom). A 2005 article recommends that to alleviate fears that digital photographs can elude confirmation of authenticity, police agencies should attempt to establish standard operating procedures that include the preservation of and accountability for the original image on a camera chip before processing via computer software and a printer as well as evidence of how the image was processed before admission into evidence.[100]

Mug Shot Imaging

Mug shot imaging is a system of digitizing a picture and storing its image on a computer so that it can be retrieved later. The picture is taken with a video camera and is then transferred to a color video monitor, where it appears as an electronic image. When the image is filed, the operator enters the identifying data such as race, gender, date of birth, and the subject's case number. Using this system, victims of crimes can quickly view possible mug shots on a computer screen.[101]

A good example of mug shot imaging is the Advanced Law Enforcement Response Technology (ALERT) System. This system allows a photo of a subject to be transmitted from one police vehicle to others with the necessary equipment, giving officers an immediate view of a wanted suspect or a missing person.[102]

Automated systems that capture and digitize mug shots can incorporate biometric facial recognition. The Los Angeles County Sheriff's Department installed a system that can take the composite drawing of a suspect or a video image of someone committing a crime and search it against its database of digitized mug shots. The department also searches for suspects on "Megan's Law CD," a photo database of registered sex offenders.[103]

Age-Progression Photographs

One important development in police photography is the **age-progression photo.** The ability to recognize a face may be thwarted by the changes

You Are There!

Finding Missing Children through Age-Enhanced Photos

An investigator from Oakland, California, reached out across the United States and Canada with age-enhanced images of two missing brothers. After exhausting every lead, the investigator turned to the television program *Unsolved Mysteries*.

On the evening of the broadcast, hundreds of calls poured in from the Albuquerque, New Mexico, area. Authorities located the children in a trailer on the outskirts of town, where they lived with their mother and her new husband—a known drug dealer. The boys were returned to their father, who had not seen them in several years. Although the aged images of the boys were very accurate, the relentless determination of the investigator and the assistance of the public ultimately solved the case.

SOURCE: Adapted from Gene O'Donnell, "Forensic Imaging Comes of Age," *FBI Law Enforcement Bulletin* (January 1994), p. 9.

that naturally occur to the face with age. To counter this, two medical illustrators, Scott Barrows and Lewis Sadler, developed techniques in the early 1980s for producing age-progression drawings. Today, thanks to a computer algorithm, the same process that used to take hours using calipers, ruler, and pen can be completed in seconds. Developed by a colleague of Barrows and Sadler, the age-progression program systematizes the knowledge of the anatomy of 14 major bones and more than one hundred muscles, and how they grow. It also shows the change in relationship, over time, of 48 facial landmarks, such as the corners of the eyes and the nose. Computers have enabled the National Center for Missing and Exploited Children to arrange to have thousands of age-progressed pictures printed onto milk cartons and flyers.[104]

The FBI uses its own age-progression program for adult faces. The system allows artists to do such things as thin hair, add jowls, or increase wrinkles while maintaining the basic facial proportions. The FBI's software for aging children's faces allows pictures of parents and older siblings to be fused into photos of missing children to obtain a more accurate image.[105]

Composite Sketches

Police have for many years sought the assistance of forensic artists in preparing **composite sketches.** The FBI began to use composite sketching in 1920; other agencies had been using it even earlier. These portrait-style drawings generally require hours of interview, drawing, and revision. Today, the FBI has converted its book of photographs, used for interviewing witnesses for composites, into hand-drawn images using forensic imaging. The hand-drawn images are entered into a computer, where they form the basis of a database that automatically generates images similar to those that are hand-drawn. Once the witness selects features from the catalog, the composite image appears on the computer screen in just a few minutes.[106]

Computer software can also allow officers to produce a digitized composite photo of a suspect based on the recollections of victims and witnesses. The resulting photo can then be compared with thousands of digital mug shots stored in the growing number of databases in jurisdictions all over the nation, including those states that now issue digitized photos on driver's licenses. Included in this software is a databank of thousands of facial features from which witnesses select the ones that best fit their description of suspects. Software users, who need no formal artistic training, can adjust the composite by using a scanner to adjust the facial features chosen by the witness.[107]

Often, an artist is not even necessary. With practice, investigators can place the features on the screen and modify the image as the witness instructs. The system can be loaded into a laptop computer to further speed up the process by taking it directly to a crime scene. It can also be accessed via a modem hookup or put online, with an artist in another city available to prepare the composite while a witness views and suggests changes.

A CD-ROM program called "Faces, the Ultimate Composite Picture," provides nearly 4 thousand facial features that can be selected to create billions of faces. The designers used photos taken of approximately 15 thousand volunteers, ages 17 to 60, to acquire images of hair, eyes, chins and more. Instead of a police artist trying to coax the memory of an offender's face from a frightened victim, artists and even victims themselves can create photo-quality composites in about 30 minutes.[108]

There remains a controversy, however, about the value of forensic artistry versus the use of digital imaging composite software. Hand-drawn

You Are There!

Criminalistics and Good Old Detective Work Find Suspect in Hit and Run

In January 2001, Marjorie Cordero, the wife of famed jockey Angel Cordero, was struck and killed by an auto driven by a hit-and-run driver as she crossed a road near her home in Greenvale, New York. Among the evidence left at the scene was a headlight and a 2-inch by 3-inch plate of fiberglass from a header panel of the car. Eventually this evidence enabled police to make an arrest in May 2001.

Criminalists from the Nassau County Police Department's Scientific Investigation Bureau analyzed the headlight and the fiberglass and determined that these pieces of evidence came from a 1987 or 1988 black Mercury Cougar. They ran that description through the state Department of Motor Vehicles database and found there were hundreds of cars of that model in the Nassau County and eastern Queens area. During the weeks that followed, investigators looked at more than 300 Mercury Cougars—staking out driveways, glancing at header panels—before zeroing in on the suspect's car. They obtained a warrant to search it, and the piece of black fiberglass recovered at the scene fit into the header panel of the suspect's car like a missing piece of a jigsaw puzzle.

SOURCE: Adapted from: Oscar Corral, "Hit-Run Arrest: Cops Find Suspect in Incident That Killed Marjorie Cordero," *Newsday*, May 2, 2001, p. A3.

---

sketches are seen as having the ability to include subtleties that cannot compare with composite software programs and can increase the number of unique facial features possible. Digital composites, on the other hand, can be made in the field immediately following an incident, printed out, and dispersed to field units almost immediately. Hand-drawn sketches can then be scanned into a digital imaging program.[109] According to a 2006 article, the construction of a composite image based on selections provided by computer graphics software can be useful, but it may be either too limited in its selections or features or provide so many selections that victims or witnesses become confused and frustrated whereas artist-drawn composites can be flexible and responsive to the distinctive memories of victims and witnesses. Also the author indicates that the cost of computer-generated imaging and all the required software and equipment makes the training of a composite artist cost efficient and these artists can also perform other useful functions, such as creating demonstrative evidence for courtroom presentations, age progressions, post-mortem imaging, and facial reconstruction.[110]

Modern Forensics or Criminalistics

The use of scientific technology to solve crime is generally referred to as **forensic science,** or **criminalistics.** The terms *forensic science* and *criminalistics* are often used interchangeably. However, forensic science, the more general of the two terms, is that part of science applied to answering legal questions. According to Richard Saferstein, former chief forensic scientist of the New Jersey State Police laboratory and the author of eight editions of the leading textbook regarding forensic science and criminalistics, *Criminalistics: An Introduction to Forensic Science,* "Forensic science is the application of science to those criminal and civil laws that are enforced by police agencies in a criminal justice system."[111] Regarding the interchangeability of the terms *forensic science* and *criminalistics,* Saferstein says that for all intents and purposes, the two terms are seen as similar and he uses them interchangeably in his text.

Criminalistics is actually just one of several branches of forensic science. Others include forensic medicine, forensic pathology, toxicology, physical anthropology, odontology, psychiatry, questioned documents, ballistics, tool work comparison, and serology.[112] (See Table 14.2.) To simplify the information in this chapter for the nonscience student, however, the word *criminalistics* will be used interchangeably with *forensic science.*[113]

Criminalistics has been defined as "the examination, evaluation, and explanation of physical evidence related to crime."[114] The California Association of Criminalists defines criminalistics as "that profession and scientific discipline directed to the recognition, identification, individualization, and evaluation of physical evidence by the application of the natural sciences to law-science matters."[115] Criminalistic evidence includes such clues as fingerprints, blood and bloodstains, semen stains, drugs and alcohol, hairs and fibers, and firearms and toolmarks. Forensic technicians, forensic scientists, forensic chemists, or the more generic term, criminalists, generally specialize in one or more of the following areas: analysis of trace evidence, serology, drug chemistry, firearms and toolmarks, and questioned documents.

The purpose of criminalistics is to take physical evidence from a crime or a crime scene and to use it to (1) identify the person who committed the crime and (2) exonerate others who may be under suspicion. For example, was the revolver found on a suspect the one that fired the bullet found in the body of a murder victim? If so, did the suspect fire it? Criminalistic evidence also can be used to establish an element of the crime and reconstruct how the crime was committed.

In court, criminalistic evidence is presented via laboratory analysis by an expert prepared to interpret and testify to the scientific results, thus distinguishing forensic evidence from other forms of physical or tangible evidence such as stolen goods, articles of clothing, and other personal property.

In a study of criminalistic evidence and the criminal justice system, the National Institute of Justice discovered that the police are, on average, about three times more likely to clear (solve) cases when scientific evidence is gathered and analyzed, prosecutors are less likely to agree to enter into plea negotiations if criminalistic evidence strongly associates the defendant with the crime, and judges issue more severe sentences when criminalistic evidence is presented at trials.[116]

As indicated in Chapter 1, there has been serious criticism of crimes labs and scientific evidence, particularly in the O. J. Simpson case.

In 1997, the Justice Department's inspector general reported that the FBI's renowned crime laboratory was riddled with flawed scientific practices that had potentially tainted dozens of criminal cases, including the bombing of the Federal Building in Oklahoma City and the original bombing of the World Trade Center in New York. The inspector general's findings resulted from an 18-month investigation that uncovered extremely serious and significant problems at the laboratory that had been a symbol of the FBI's cutting-edge scientific sleuthing.[117] The dramatic series of problems associated with the FBI and its alleged bungling of scientific evidence and criminal investigations led the national magazine *Time* to produce a cover article

entitled, "What's Wrong at the FBI?: The Fiasco at the Crime Lab."[118]

In 2001, an Oklahoma City Police Department forensic scientist was accused of a series of forensic errors involving at least five cases in which she made significant errors or overstepped the acceptable limits of forensic science. In response, Oklahoma's governor launched a review of every one of the thousands of cases the scientist had handled between 1980 and 1993. In 12 of these cases, the defendants were awaiting the death penalty, and in another 11, the defendants had already been put to death.[119]

In 2003, DNA evidence in 64 criminal cases from Marion County, Indiana, was challenged because of concerns that a laboratory technician may have cut corners.[120] In 2006, a special investigator assigned to study the Houston Police Department's crime lab indicated that 43 DNA cases and 50 serology cases dating back to 1980 have "major issues." The investigator said the cases contained problems that raise significant doubt about the reliability of the work performed, the validity of the analytical results, or the correctness of the analysts' conclusions. The DNA division of the Houston crime laboratory was closed in 2002 after an independent audit exposed widespread problems with protocols and personnel. In the years since then, errors have also been exposed in the lab's firearms, serology, and drug units.[121]

A professional society for the professionals dedicated to the application of science to the law is the American Academy of Forensic Sciences (AAFS), whose membership includes physicians, criminalists, toxicologists, attorneys, dentists, physical anthropologists, document examiners, engineers, psychiatrists, educators, and others who practice and perform research in the many diverse fields relating to forensic science.

The CSI Effect

The popularity of the television series *CSI: Crime Scene Investigation,* and its spin-offs *CSI: Miami* and *CSI: New York* and other television shows and movies that romanticize criminalistics work has produced what many call the **CSI effect.** The CSI effect has created challenges to investigators, forensic experts, and juries. According to a Lowell, Massachusetts, police captain, "People are demanding today to see what they see on TV, DNA takes 15 minutes to analyze on TV, but in reality, it takes months." Commenting on the possibility of physical evidence being as prolific as indicated on the *CSI* shows, Lawrence Kobilinsky, a forensic scientist and consultant at John Jay College, said, "Not every case is a case where you've got physical evidence." As an example, in Alabama, hair, fibers, glass, paint, and other trace evidence makes up less than 1 percent of the total number of cases submitted to forensic analysis.[122]

In 2006, one writer argued that because of the CSI effect, the public now expects a 40-minute investigation turnaround, compared with what typically can take months. She says that jurors also expect law enforcement to be using the biggest and best equipment that is shown on the TV shows. This phenomenon affects more than just the court system: those committing the crimes as criminals are becoming better educated about what not to leave behind at a crime scene. On a positive note, however, the CSI effect is leading many high school and college students to take forensic science or criminalistics courses and to prepare for careers in the field.[123]

A very good example of the CSI effect was the 2006 case involving the alleged assault and rape of a 27-year-old exotic dancer in Durham, North Carolina, by a group of 46 Duke University lacrosse players at a team party. The case received national attention because it stirred passions regarding class and race differences. The dancer was black and all but one of the lacrosse players were white. All of the lacrosse players were the subject of DNA tests, which found no matching DNA. The lawyers representing the players claimed that the absence of DNA indicated that his clients were innocent. Others agreed with this assertion. However, the prosecutor dismissed the DNA findings and two of the players were indicted on rape charges.[124]

The true facts are that DNA evidence from an attacker is successfully recovered in less than a quarter of sexual assault cases, that two-thirds of sexual assault cases are solved without DNA evidence, and that tests that pinpoint DNA are often overplayed as a forensic tool. The mere fact that DNA is not present does not indicate that there was no contact between the victim and the players.[125]

The Modern Crime Lab

There are hundreds of public and private crime laboratories in the United States today. There are 351 publicly funded labs, including 203 state or regional labs, 65 county, 50 municipal, and 33 federal labs. By 2002, these public labs employed more than 9,300

Major Section	Function
Ballistics	Examination of guns and bullets
Serology	Examination of blood, semen, and other body fluids
Criminalistics	Examination of hairs, fibers, paints, clothing, glass, and other trace evidence
Chemistry	Examination of drugs and alcohol
Document analysis	Comparison of handwriting

TABLE 14.1 Police Forensic Laboratories

full-time personnel, had total budgets exceeding $750 million, and received nearly 2.7 million new cases. Most very large police departments operate their own police laboratories. Smaller departments may contract with large county crime labs or state police crime labs. Some departments use the services of the FBI lab.[126] The FBI lab reports that it conducts more than one million examinations each year. The FBI opened its new $130 million, 500,000-square-foot laboratory on its campus in Quantico, Virginia, in 2003.[127]

Private (that is, nongovernment) labs are taking on greater importance in the U.S. legal system. Their analyses are increasingly being introduced into criminal and civil trials, often not only as evidence but also to contradict evidence presented by a prosecutor that was analyzed in a police lab.

Most crime labs have the following sections that concentrate on different criminalistics evidence: ballistics, serology, criminalistics, chemistry, and documents analysis. (See Table 14.1.)

By 2004, there were significant problems in the timely processing of criminal cases by crime labs. The American Society of Crime Laboratory Directors (ASCLD) reported that a survey of the 50 largest crime labs revealed that they ended the year with a 134 percent increase in their backlogs. About 80 percent of the backlogged requests involved controlled substances, latent prints, and DNA. Other backlogs involved firearms and toolmarks, toxicology, and trace evidence. The ASCLD reported that the primary need identified by lab managers was personnel. The increased personnel needed to achieve a 30-day turnaround for all requests required more than $36 million, and about $18 million was needed for new equipment.[128]

In 2004, a major summit convened in Washington, D.C., to assess the needs of local and state

TABLE 14.2	Forensic Specialties
Forensic pathology	Dead bodies
Forensic physical anthropology	Skeletal remains
Forensic odontology	Teeth formation
Forensic toxicology	Poisons
Forensic entomology	Insects at death scenes

forensic labs and medical examiners. The four major forensic service organizations—the IAI, the ASCLD, the AAFS, and the National Association of Medical Examiners—all agreed that the primary needs for crime labs were increased personnel and increased education and training for them.[129]

Ballistics The **ballistics** section of the crime lab conducts scientific analysis of guns and bullets. (Ballistics is the science of the study of objects in motion and at rest). Examination of firearms evidence involves the identification, testing, and classification of firearms submitted to the lab. Technicians microscopically examine a bullet, cartridge case, or shotgun shell to determine whether

it was fired from a specific firearm to the exclusion of any other firearm.

The ballistics examination provides the investigator with such information related to shooting cases as comparison of a spent (that is, fired) bullet to a suspect weapon, the type and model of weapon that may have been used in a shooting, the description and operating condition of a suspect weapon, the bullet trajectory of a bullet wound (the line of fire and firing position of the shooter), the possibility of an accidental discharge of a weapon rather than a purposeful discharge, the trigger pull (amount of force required to fire a particular weapon), the shooting distance in possible suicide cases, and restored serial numbers from a weapon in which the original serial numbers were altered or obliterated.

To determine whether a suspect firearm was used in a particular shooting, ballistics experts test fire a bullet from it into a tank of water known as a ballistics recovery tank. The spent bullet is then compared with the bullet taken from a victim or the crime scene using a ballistic comparison microscope. The rationale behind this testing is that bullets fired from a gun receive a mark on them from the lands and grooves of the barrel of the gun. These small individualistic markings are called

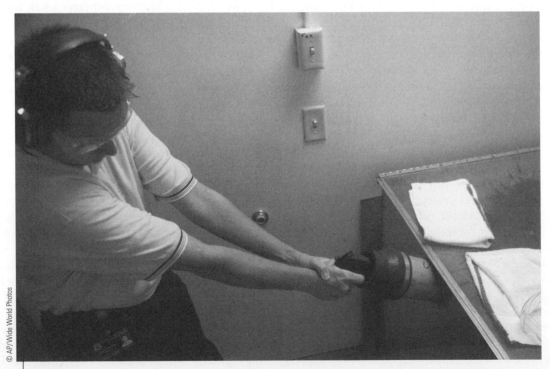

© AP/Wide World Photos

Guns can be tested by firing them into a tank of water. The bullets are collected from the bottom of the tank and then analyzed using microscopes and computers.

striae. Bullets fired from the same gun should have similar markings.

The NYPD's ballistics lab of its Forensics Investigations Division maintains a collection of 720 guns used in previous shootings, including the gun used to kill John Lennon and the one used by the Son of Sam killer, David Berkowitz, that they use for comparison purposes. Everyday, the NYPD collects between 40 and 50 weapons seized or found on the city's streets.[130]

The Federal Bureau of Alcohol, Tobacco, Firearms and Explosives (ATF) maintains the Integrated Ballistics Information System (IBIS). IBIS is a computer identification system that correlates and matches both projectile (bullet) and shell casing ballistic evidence. This unique ballistic comparison system allows firearms technicians to digitize and store bullets and shell casings at a greatly accelerated rate. It stores bullet "signatures" in a database to allow ballistics examiners to quickly determine whether a spent bullet may be linked to a crime. The software-driven system includes a customized microscope, video camera, specimen manipulator, image digitizer, and a series of computers. The video camera and microscope record the unique, telltale markings and grooves made as a soft lead bullet is fired through a gun barrel, then digitally translate the information for computer storage and future analysis. The system alerts the operator if a possible match has already been entered into the database by providing the examiner with a numerically ranked list. The examiner can then retrieve the stored image for a side-by-side visual comparison, eliminating the need to track down the original specimen. It also allows examiners to magnify any portion of the stored images.[131] ATF also maintains the National Tracing Center (NTC), which provides assistance to law enforcement agencies, 24 hours a day, seven days a week. NTC traces firearms recovered in crimes worldwide and has over 100 million firearm records.[132]

By 2000, the various national law enforcement ammunition-tracing databases created since 1993 held more than 800 thousand images of bullets and shell casings. More than 8 thousand matches have been made in over 16 thousand cases. Law enforcement officials say that computer ballistic imaging technology is the most important forensic advancement since the development of the comparison microscope over 70 years ago.[133]

In September 2005, the FBI lab announced it had stopped making comparative bullet lead analyses (data-chaining), a four-decades-old technique

that attempts to link a fired bullet with a particular box of bullets. This action was to the result of a study by the National Academy of Sciences that found significant flaws in the techniques used in this test.[134]

In 2006, the FBI Lab also announced that it will discontinue analyzing gunshot residue (GSR). GSR is made up of the microscopic particles that explode from a gun when it is fired. The particles can be collected from suspects' hands, analyzed, and used as evidence in court. A spokesperson for the lab said that in recent years it had been receiving fewer than 10 requests per year and decided its resources were better used in "areas that directly relate to fighting terrorism." However, there have been indications that contamination studies revealed hundreds of particles consistent with gunshot residue in several areas of the lab that could cast doubts on the origin of residue in a sample. A major problem with GSR is that the particles float like ash and never disintegrate, causing the possibility that it can be contaminated from a police officer's hands to lab work tables and contaminate fresh samples. It has also been claimed that all trace evidence, including GSR, can be presented to jurors with a false degree of certainty.[135]

A professional organization for persons interested in firearms and ballistics examinations is the Association of Firearms and Tool Mark Examiners (AFTE).

Serology The crime lab's **serology** section analyzes blood, semen, and other body fluids found at a crime scene—important evidence in homicide and sexual assault cases. If blood on a suspect's shirt can be matched to the victim's blood, it can place the suspect at the crime scene. If semen found in a rape victim or on her clothing can be matched to a suspect's, it can link the perpetrator to the crime. Certain tests are useful in this process. The hemin crystal test will determine if a particular stain is actually blood. The precipitin test will determine if the blood is human, animal, or a mixture of both. Other tests can determine the specific blood type of the stain. Tests can also detect the existence of semen in stains and match the semen to a particular blood type. Laboratory tests can reveal if a stain is semen, if sperm is present, if the person was a secretor, and, if so, establish blood groups.

The use of the chemical Luminol can produce evidence that blood was at a scene even if the area was meticulously cleaned. When Luminol is sprayed on an area, a luminescence or glow is produced if blood has been present. The development of DNA profiling or genetic fingerprinting (which will be discussed later in this chapter) has revolutionized the serology capacity of the crime lab.

Criminalistics The criminalistics section of the crime lab studies myriad pieces of physical evidence that may connect a suspect to a crime or a crime scene. Often this evidence is crucial to the understanding of the crime scene and the identification of perpetrators. A perpetrator may unknowingly take something from a crime scene (for example, fibers from the victim's carpet may be found on the suspect's clothing) or may leave something at the crime scene (a shoe print in the mud outside the victim's window or marks from a tool used to pry open the victim's window).

The matching of samples of evidence found at the crime scene to a particular subject can be instrumental in the identification and successful prosecution of a suspect. The following are some examples of crime scene evidence that can be of value in an investigation.

Glass Fragments of glass found at a crime scene can give an investigator a great deal of useful information. Traces of blood, clothing, hair, or fingerprints can be found on glass fragments. When a suspect is arrested, these same fragments can conclusively establish the individual's presence at the scene if they are also found on his or her clothing.

Glass can also tell an investigator how a crime was committed. Investigators can study conchoidal fractures, radial fractures, and concentric breaks to determine how the glass was broken, the angle at which a bullet was fired, and even which bullet was fired first through a window with multiple bullet holes.

Glass offers a wealth of information because of differences in the way it is made. It varies widely in physical and chemical composition, and has numerous impurities. Through the use of refractive index analysis, dispersion analysis, densities analysis, and spectrographic analysis, a crime lab can link glass from a suspect's clothing to that collected at a crime scene, or specify the type of vehicle from fragments collected at a hit-and-run accident.

Hairs and Fibers Hairs and fibers can be vital pieces of evidence. They can be found on a victim's clothing and in objects at the crime scene, such as bed linen, carpets, and furniture. Hair can tell the

perpetrator's race and gender. Investigators can tell which part of the body the hair came. They can see whether it was pulled out forcibly or fell out naturally, or if it was smashed with a blunt object or sheared with a sharp instrument.

Fibers are also very specific in the information they reveal. Because they vary dramatically in color, source, shape, and composition, they actually have more identifying characteristics than hair does.

Fingernail Scrapings Two types of evidence can be taken from fingernail scrapings and fingernails at a crime scene. First, when fingernails are trimmed and collected from a victim, scrapings of hairs, fibers, skin, or blood from under the nail can reveal a variety of information about the crime and the perpetrator, especially in cases in which the victim struggled with the perpetrator. Second, when a broken fingernail is left at the scene and later compared with the nails of a suspect, it can include or exclude that person from the list of suspects. Much like fingerprints, nails are unique to each individual and rarely change through a person's life. Fingernails can be examined in much the same way as tool marks, bullets, and casings. Because the striae on nails are on the same scale as that found on fired bullets, the same type of comparison microscope is used.

Impressions and Casts Impressions and casts taken of footprints at a crime scene can be very important to the investigator because no two people will wear shoes in precisely the same pattern or show damage in the same places. Footprints can include or exclude a suspect, as well as tell investigators whether he or she was walking or running, was carrying a heavy object, or seemed unfamiliar with the area, or unsure of the terrain.

Chemistry The chemistry section studies alcohol and possible drugs or controlled substances gathered in investigations and arrests. This section analyzes most of the cases handled by the crime lab.

The most commonly used standard for the degree of intoxication in criminal cases such as driving while intoxicated (DWI) or driving while under the influence (DUI) is the measure of alcohol concentration in the suspect's blood. The alcohol concentration level determined by the lab is instrumental in the eventual prosecution of these alcohol-related crimes.

The chemistry section also tests substances believed to be in violation of the drug laws. Using

TABLE 14.3 Services Provided by the FBI Laboratory

- Chemistry
- Combined DNA Index System (CODIS)
- Computer analysis and response
- DNA analysis
- Evidence response
- Explosives
- Firearms and toolmarks
- Forensic audio, video, and image analysis
- Forensic science research
- Forensic science training
- Hazardous materials response
- Investigative and prosecutive graphics
- Latent prints
- Materials analysis
- Questioned documents
- Racketeering records
- Special photographic analysis
- Structural design
- Trace evidence

SOURCE: Adapted from *FBI Laboratory Services,* retrieved August 1, 2006, from, www.fbi.gov/hq/lab/org/labchart.htm.

chemical and other tests, chemists can identify the type of drug in a substance, as well as the percentage of a drug in a particular mixture.

Document Analysis The document analysis section studies handwriting, printing, typewriting, and the paper and ink used in the preparation of a document to provide investigators with leads to the identity of the writer. The document technician can compare requested handwriting exemplars (samples of the suspect's handwriting requested by the police) with the questioned document. This is a very important type of analysis in investigating ransom notes, anonymous letters, and possible forgeries.

Document analysis can also determine if there were any additions, changes, or deletions made. The paper on which a document is written can provide a number of clues to the investigator, such as the manufacturer, date of production, the pH and fiber composition, trace elements, and chemical elements including fibers, waxes, dyes, fluorescent brighteners, and fillers. By 2006, scientists and technicians were still innovating new improvements in document analysis.[136] (See Table 14.3.)

The American Society of Questioned Document Examiners (ASQDE) is a professional organization for forensic document examiners.

Crime Lab Accreditation

Crime lab accreditation is designed to ameliorate some of the problems raised earlier in this chapter regarding mistakes made by our nation's crime labs.

The American Society of Crime Laboratory Directors (ASCLD) is a nonprofit professional society of crime laboratory directors, devoted to the improvement of crime laboratory operations through sound management practices. Its purpose is to foster the common professional interests of its members and to promote and foster the development of laboratory management principles and techniques. Its Crime Laboratory Accreditation Program is a voluntary program in which any crime laboratory may participate to demonstrate that its management, operations, personnel, procedures, equipment, physical plant, security, and personnel safety procedures meet established standards. The accreditation process is part of a laboratory's quality assurance program that should also include proficiency testing, continuing education, and other programs to help the laboratory give better overall service to the criminal justice system. The ASCLD maintains that the process of self-evaluation is in itself a valuable management tool for the crime laboratory director.[137]

The American Board of Criminalists (ABC) certifies lab employees. Because it ensures that lab personnel are all held to the same standard, certification helps analysts fend off courtroom salvos about their experience, background, and training.

Accreditation and certification is certainly needed in the nation's labs. According to Ron Urbanovsky, director of the Texas Department of Public Safety's statewide system of crime labs, "Part of the Simpson case fallout was that we've seen much longer and stiffer cross-examinations in court. Testimony that used to take two to three hours now takes eight to 12 hours, and it's grueling. We are asked to be perfect in a non-perfect world."[138]

In 2000, the National Institute of Justice created the Technical Working Group on Crime Scene Investigation (TWGCSI) as a multidisciplinary group of experts from across the United States from both urban and rural jurisdictions. TWGCSI produced *Crime Scene Investigation: A Guide for Law Enforcement,* which documents and explains the major steps and processes in working a crime scene.[139]

DNA Profiling/Genetic Fingerprinting

DNA profiling, also called **genetic fingerprinting** or **DNA typing,** has shown exponential progress in the last decade in helping investigators solve crimes and ensuring that those guilty of crimes are convicted in court. According to the U.S. Department of Justice, "DNA evidence arguably has become the most well-known type of forensic evidence, probably because it can be uniquely identifying and because it is the genetic blueprint of the human body. For these reasons, DNA evidence has become a highly influential piece of the crime puzzle."[140] This section will cover the science of DNA, the history of DNA in U.S. Courts, current DNA technology, DNA databases, and current DNA issues. (See Table 14.4.)

The Science of DNA

Deoxyribonucleic acid (DNA) is the basic building code for all of the human body's chromosomes and is the same for each cell of an individual's body, including skin, bone, teeth, hair, organs, fingernails and toenails, and all body fluids, including blood, semen, saliva, mucus, perspiration, urine, and feces. Every cell of the body contains DNA. Because the characteristics of certain segments of DNA vary from person to person, it is possible to analyze certain bodily substances and compare them with a sample from a suspect.

Forensic science consultant Richard Saferstein tells us that portions of the DNA structure are as unique to each individual as fingerprints. He writes that inside each of the 60 trillion cells in the human body are strands of genetic material called chromosomes. Arranged along the chromosomes, like beads on a thread, are nearly 100 thousand genes. Genes are the fundamental unit of heredity. They instruct the body cells to make proteins that determine everything from hair color to susceptibility to diseases. Each gene is actually composed of DNA specifically designed to carry out a single body function. Scientists have determined that

DNA is the substance by which genetic instructions are passed from one generation to the next.[141]

DNA profiling has helped investigators solve crimes and ensure that those guilty of crimes are convicted in court. It is the examination of DNA samples from a body substance or fluid to determine whether they came from a particular subject. For example, semen on a rape victim's jeans can be positively or negatively compared with a suspect's semen.

DNA is powerful evidence. Elizabeth Devine, former supervising criminalist in the Scientific Services Bureau of the Los Angeles County Sheriff's Department says, "The power of what we can look for and analyze now is incredible. It's like magic. Every day we discover evidence where we never thought it would be. You almost can't do anything without leaving some DNA around. DNA takes longer than fingerprints to analyze but you get a really big bang for your buck."[142]

DNA profiling has been used in criminal investigations since 1987, and the FBI has made great progress in improving the technology since opening its first DNA typing laboratory in October 1988.[143]

To show the further utility of DNA profiling, the U.S. Defense Department has established a repository of genetic information for the more than two million members of the U.S. armed forces as a way of identifying future casualties of war. DNA is collected and stored by the Armed Forces Institute of Pathology. Formerly, unidentified dead were identified, if possible, by fingerprints and medical records. However, DNA can now be used to identify people from body parts, such as a single leg.[144]

DNA technology in law enforcement has changed rapidly. The latest procedure—polymerase chain reaction-short tandem repeat (**PCR-STR**)—has several distinct advantages for law enforcement over restricted fragment length polymorphism (**RFLP**), an earlier DNA procedure. The newer PCR-STR requires only pin-size samples, rather than the dime-size samples needed for RFLP. With the PCR-STR process, samples degraded or broken down by exposure to heat, light, or humidity can be analyzed; only two days are needed for laboratory analysis, compared with eight weeks for RFLP, and the entire DNA process can be automated, greatly reducing the possibility of human error.[145]

The DNA Analysis Unit of the FBI Laboratory analyzes body fluids and body fluid stains recovered as evidence in violent crimes. Examinations include the identification and characterization of blood, semen, saliva, and other body fluids using traditional serological techniques and related bio-chemical analysis. Once the stain is identified, it is characterized by DNA analysis using RFLP or PCR-STR techniques. The results of the analyses are compared with results obtained from known blood or saliva samples submitted from the victims or suspects.[146] Technological advances have made DNA more reliable and more efficient as the time needed to determine a sample's DNA profile has dropped from between 6 and 8 weeks to between 1 and 2 days.[147]

The unit also uses **mitochondrial DNA (MtDNA)** analysis, which is applied to evidence containing very small or degraded quantities of DNA from hair, bones, teeth, and body fluids. The results of MtDNA analysis are then also compared with blood or saliva submitted from victims and suspects.

Another current DNA innovation is **Combined DNA Index System (CODIS)** or DNA databases. CODIS contains DNA profiles obtained from subjects convicted of homicide, sexual assault, and other serious felonies. Investigators are able to search evidence from their individual cases against the system's extensive national file of DNA genetic markers.[148]

CODIS provides software and support services so that state and local laboratories can establish databases of convicted offenders, unsolved crime scenes, and missing persons. It allows these forensic laboratories to exchange and compare DNA profiles electronically, thereby linking serial violent crimes, especially sexual assaults, to each other, and to identify suspects by matching DNA from crime scenes to convicted offenders. All 50 states have enacted DNA database laws requiring the collection of a DNA sample from specified categories of convicted offenders. Most currently take samples from convicted felons, but they vary on which types of felons. Some states are trying to pass legislation to take samples from all persons charged with a felony; some are even considering collecting them from people convicted of misdemeanors. Most federal, state, and local DNA analysts have received CODIS training. The FBI laboratory has also provided CODIS software and training to criminal justice agencies in other countries. The National DNA Index System (NDIS) is the final level of CODIS and supports the sharing of DNA profiles from convicted offenders and crime scene evidence submitted by state and local forensic laboratories across the United States.[149]

© Roger Tulley/Stone/Getty Images

DNA sequences taken from a person's body sample can be a means of identification. Areas of DNA are segmented and arranged. Probes mark the segments, and x-ray film is placed on the probes and developed to form a pattern of black bars—the DNA "fingerprint." They are then compared.

The current version of CODIS contains two indexes: a Convicted Offender Index and a Forensic Index. The former index contains DNA profiles from those convicted of violent crimes, and the latter contains DNA profiles acquired from crime scene evidence. The CODIS system is also separated into different segments, from the local to the national level. The system stores the information necessary for determining a match (a specimen identifier, the sponsoring laboratory's identifier,

You Are There!

The Blooding—The First Use of DNA Typing in a Criminal Case

DNA profiling was the subject of *The Blooding* by Joseph Wambaugh. This book describes the case surrounding brutal beating and murder of two young girls in the English county of Leicestershire. Although the police had no clues to the identity of the killer, eventually a young man whom Wambaugh called only the "Kitchen Porter" confessed to the murder of the first girl and was also charged by the police with the second murder. Hoping to get physical evidence to corroborate this confession, the police asked Alec Jeffreys, a young geneticist at nearby Leicestershire University and the man who discovered genetic fingerprinting, to compare DNA samples from the victims with the DNA of the defendant.

After performing his testing, Jeffreys told the police that their suspect definitely did not commit the murders. He also told them that the same one man—not their suspect, however—was responsible for the murders of both girls.

The police decided to embark on a campaign of "blooding" to find the killer. They "requested" that all men within a certain age group who lived, worked, or had business in the area appear at the police station and submit to a venipuncture (the drawing of a vial of blood). The blood was then analyzed using Jeffrey's technique. But even after more than 4,500 men gave samples of their blood, the police had no suspects. Eventually it was discovered, over a few beers in a local pub, that a young man, Colin Pitchfork, had paid another young man, Ian Kelly, to appear and be "blooded" for him. When the police approached Pitchfork, he willingly confessed to both murders. His blood samples were then tested, and the DNA tests revealed that he was, indeed, the murderer of both girls.

The DNA analysis did not solve the case, although it did eliminate a suspect, and it did confirm guilt. Even if DNA profiling is fully accepted by the scientific community, it will never replace regular detective work.

SOURCE: Based on Joseph Wambaugh, *The Blooding* (New York: William Morrow, 1989).

---

the names of laboratory personnel who produced the profile, and the DNA profile). To ensure privacy, it does not include such things as social security numbers, criminal history, or case-related information.[150]

The FBI maintains the national database, whereas each state has one designated database location, and each participating locality maintains its own local database. Thus, it is possible for each locality to cross reference a DNA profile against other DNA profiles across the country. Furthermore, it is likely that an international DNA database may be implemented, allowing law enforcement officials to identify suspects both nationally and internationally. By 2006, it was estimated that the National DNA system has about 3 million offender profiles and about 135,000 from the scenes of unsolved crimes.[151] It has been estimated that the DNA bank is growing by more than 80,000 people every month.[152]

New technologies regarding DNA evidence emerge constantly. One is Low Copy Number (LCN) DNA, which attempts to provide unprecedented levels of detection by obtaining DNA profiles from objects that were simply touched by a suspect. LCN DNA can be obtained from as little as a fingerprint or residue from the lip of a drinking glass. However, there are still some complications and limitations of this technology. The DNA could be transferred from one person to another (for example, through a handshake) and then to an object. This challenges the reliability of placing a person at a crime scene through this type of analysis. More research is being conducted on this promising technology to reduce the dangers of contamination.[153]

History of DNA in U.S. Courts

The use of DNA in U.S. courts has an interesting history. The process has gained popularity at an exponential rate since its introduction in the United States in 1987. It was initially hailed as "foolproof" and 99 percent positive. Most of the positive claims about DNA profiling were based on the testimony of interested parties, such as prosecutors and scientists from companies involved in DNA testing. Defense attorneys were often unable to combat DNA evidence in court or to find experts to testify against it. Generally, defendants, when confronted with a DNA match, pleaded guilty in a plea bargain—until the Castro case.

On February 5, 1987, 23-year-old Vilma Ponce and her 2-year-old daughter were stabbed to death in their apartment in the Bronx, New York. There were few leads until police arrested the building's superintendent, Joseph Castro, and found some dried blood in the grooves of his watch. When questioned, he said the blood was his own. Prosecutors sent the blood from the watch, samples of the victims' blood and a sample of Castro's blood to a firm called Lifecodes for testing.

Lifecodes declared a match between the DNA from the blood on the watch and the DNA from Vilma Ponce's blood. Defense attorneys Barry Scheck and Peter Neufeld located experts who agreed to testify against the admission of the DNA typing evidence. For 12 weeks, the evidence was argued before New York Supreme Court Acting Justice Gerald Sheindlin, who listened to experts from both sides. The experts for the defense were able to uncover such serious blunders committed by Lifecodes in its performance of the tests that the prosecution's expert witnesses recanted their position. In an unprecedented move, two expert witnesses for the defense and two for the prosecution issued a joint statement:

> The DNA data in this case are not scientifically reliable enough to support the assertion that the samples . . . do or do not match. If these data were submitted to a peer-reviewed journal in support of a conclusion, they would not be accepted. Further experimentation would be required.[154]

Ultimately, Justice Sheindlin ruled the evidence of the match inadmissible, and the case against Castro was dismissed. The main problem with DNA profiling at the Castro stage was that it could not pass the **Frye test.** The Frye test was based on the court case *Frye v. United States,* in which the court ruled that novel scientific evidence will not be accepted into evidence until it has gained general acceptance in the particular scientific discipline in which it belongs.[155] Although DNA was accepted by some courts and rejected by others, its reliability had to be held in question until it gained general acceptance by the scientific community.[156]

A 1992 unanimous decision by the U.S. Court of Appeals for the Second Circuit began to change court rulings nationwide on DNA evidence. The court approved the use of DNA evidence and affirmed the kidnapping conviction of Randolph Jakobetz for kidnapping and rape. The evidence on which he was convicted involved an FBI analysis of the DNA from semen recovered from the woman and matched to Jakobetz from a blood test.

Legal experts have said that this decision was the first clear-cut guidance from the federal appellate bench on the use of DNA fingerprinting. Previously, many courts would not allow DNA evidence to be used at a trial unless it was presented first at a pretrial hearing. Under the new ruling, courts could allow DNA evidence without such hearings and let the jury determine the worth of the evidence. In this case, the court seems to have overruled the Frye test by ruling that "scientific evidence was like any other and that it could be admitted if its 'probativeness, materiality and reliability' outweighed any tendency to mislead, prejudice and confuse the jury."[157]

The Jakobetz case was followed by two other important U.S. Supreme Court cases, *Daubert v. Merrell Dow Pharmaceuticals, Inc.* (1993) and *General Electric Co. v. Joiner* (1997), which further undermined the restrictive Frye test by ruling that federal courts should generally allow admission of all relevant evidence. This ruling applied to all evidence in civil and criminal cases, including DNA evidence and other forensic science issues.[158]

In 1992, after a two-year study, a 12-member panel consisting of forensic, legal, and molecular biology experts, endorsed DNA profiling in the identification of suspects in criminal cases. Conducted under the auspices of the National Academy of Sciences, the study concluded that DNA fingerprinting is a reliable method of identification for use as evidence in criminal trials, but found problems with current methods of sampling, labeling, and general quality assurance. The panel of experts recommended that accreditation be required of forensic laboratories performing this work.[159]

The panel also advised the courts to consider the reliability of new DNA typing techniques on a case-by-case basis when determining the admissibility of DNA evidence. The panel's report called for the creation of a national DNA profile databank that would contain DNA samples and document information on the genetic makeup of felons convicted of violent crimes. This report led to the creation of CODIS, described earlier.

The National Commission on the Future of DNA Evidence was created in 1998 at the request of the U.S. attorney general. The commission's mission is to examine the future of DNA evidence and how the Justice Department could encourage its most effective use. One of the duties of the commission is to submit recommendations to the attorney general that will ensure more effective use of DNA as a crime-fighting tool and foster its use through the entire criminal justice system. Other focal areas for the commission's consideration included crime scene investigation and evidence collection, laboratory funding, legal issues, and research and development.[160]

Current Technology

In 2000, the National Commission on the Future of DNA Evidence reported,

> The great variability of DNA polymorphisms has made it possible to offer strong support for concluding that DNA from a suspect and from the crime scene are from the same person. Prior to this . . . , it was possible to exclude a suspect, but evidence for inclusion was weaker than it is now because the probability of a coincidental match was larger. DNA polymorphisms brought an enormous change. Evidence that two DNA samples are from the same person is still probabilistic rather than certain. But with today's battery of genetic markers, the likelihood that two matching profiles came from the same person approaches certainty.[161]

Although the evidence that two samples came from the same person is statistical, the conclusion that they came from different persons is certain (assuming no human or technical errors). As a result of DNA testing, more than 70 persons previously convicted of capital crimes and frequently having served long prison terms have been exonerated.

The commission made the following conclusions and projections for the near future:

- We emphasize that current state-of-the-art DNA typing is such that the technology and statistical methods are accurate and reproducible. . . .

- Methods of automation, increasing the speed and output and reliability of STR methods, will continue. In particular we expect that portable, miniature chips will make possible the analysis of DNA directly at the crime scene. This can be telemetered to databases, offering the possibility of immediate identification. . . . [162]

DNA Databases

Initially, DNA fingerprinting or profiling was used to confirm the identity of an individual already suspected of committing a specific crime; now the use of offender DNA databases has altered the way a criminal investigation can proceed. Very small amounts of DNA recovered from a crime scene can be used to link an otherwise unknown suspect to the crime. The existing offender DNA databases have been upheld over Fourth Amendment challenges because of the minimal privacy expectations offenders have because of their status as offenders.

By 2006, every state had a DNA database statute that allows collection of DNA from specified offenders. All 50 states require DNA from sex offenders and murderers, and 46 states require DNA from all violent convictions (including assault and battery and robbery). Over the past several years, a growing number of states have been expanding their databases to include nonviolent felony convictions; 45 states require DNA from burglary convictions, 36 states require DNA from certain drug convictions, and 31 states require DNA from all felony convictions.[163]

Some believe that the growing practice of using voluntary DNA samples to link the donor to other unsolved crimes should be curbed. However, police and prosecutors defend the strategy, claiming that it allows them to take full advantage of the technology to solve crimes. Darrell Sanders, chief of police in Frankfort, Illinois, says, "If we get someone's DNA legally, how can we justify giving him a free pass on something else he once did?" Defense attorneys, such as Barry Scheck, foresee the potential for abuse, "As it is, there's nothing to stop police from setting up a DNA base of 'the usual subjects'."[164]

Another issue is the implementation of a universal DNA database containing DNA fingerprints from every member of society. Some believe this would not withstand constitutional scrutiny because free persons have no diminished expectations of privacy, as prisoners do. In addition, some feel that allowing a universal DNA database would allow the government to intrude without suspicion on an individual's privacy.[165]

A 2003 report by the Executive Office of the President of the United States praised DNA technology for becoming increasingly vital to identifying criminals, clearing suspects, and identifying missing persons. However, the report acknowledged the current federal and state DNA collection and analysis needs improvement because crime labs are overwhelmed and ill-equipped to deal with the influx of DNA samples and evidence. The president proposed federal funding for improving the use of DNA in these labs. Subsequently, Congress passed a five-year, $1 billion bill, the *Justice for All Act of 2004*.[166] The National Institute of Justice has issued numerous training guidelines regarding DNA and human forensic identification.[167]

In 2006, the FBI reported it plans to uses its national DNA database system to help identify not only criminals, but also missing persons and tens of thousands of unidentified bodies held by local coroners and medical examiners. The FBI will compare genetic profiles taken from unidentified bodies or body parts with DNA submitted by family members of missing persons. The International Homicide Investigators Association estimates that there are more than 40,000 unidentified dead nationally.[168]

Other countries, including Canada, England, and Australia, are making effective use of DNA technology in crime fighting.[169]

Other Current DNA Issues

Backlog A major problem with DNA today is the growing backlog of DNA cases. In a 2006 article in the *Criminal Justice Policy Review,* Travis C. Pratt, Michael J. Gaffney and Nicholas P. Lovrich, professors at Washington State University, and doctoral student Charles L. Johnson, also of Washington State University, revealed that by 2003, there were 169,229 unsolved rape cases and 51,774 homicide cases that might contain biological evidence that had not yet been sent to a forensic laboratory for DNA testing. This means that this evidence is just sitting around in police property rooms. State and local laboratories reported 57,349 backlogged cases of rape and homicide on hand waiting for DNA analysis. Thus, the combined estimate of rape and murder cases that still required DNA review was 278,352 throughout the nation.

The study estimated that as many as 264,371 property crime cases with possible biological evidence had not yet been subjected to DNA analysis. This means that there is a total backlog of 542,723

cases with the possibility of DNA evidence. The authors suggest that one reason that so many unsolved cases had yet to be subjected to DNA analysis is police investigators' belief that forensic laboratories could not process such evidence quickly enough to be helpful. Pratt and colleagues also suggest that local and regional forensic laboratories cannot afford the personnel, equipment, and facilities necessary to increase the volume of DNA analysis.[170]

Edwin Zedlewski and Mary B. Murphy report that three National Institute of Justice (NIJ)–funded pilot programs designed to decrease the backlog of DNA samples waiting for analysis in high-volume property crimes were successful in identifying suspects and also in linking that crime to other crimes. As an example, of 201 DNA samples from New York state burglaries, 86 were matched to offenders already entered in CODIS. The authors write that the success of the project underscores the importance of collecting and analyzing DNA evidence from high-volume property crimes, especially given the high recidivism rates and tendency of these persons to engage in violent crime.[171]

Contamination Another problem with DNA is the possibility of fingerprinting techniques contaminating DNA results. Testing reported in 2005 revealed the possibility that fingerprint brushes can accumulate DNA from surfaces with which they come into contact, and that they can redeposit this DNA-containing material to a number of subsequently brushed objects. The chance of this occurring increases after powdering biological samples, such as blood, saliva, skin, or fresh prints.[172]

Cold Hits A **cold hit** is a DNA sample collected from a crime scene that ties an unknown suspect to the DNA profile of someone in the national or a state's database. During the last 12 years, the FBI DNA database has resulted in more than 30,000 cold hits,[173] California's 2,000 cold hits,[174] and New York's 3,500 cold hits.[175] Ohio's CODIS database has profiles on 127,000 felons and 8,826 crime scenes and since opening has helped in 1,555 investigations.[176] The National Police Services of Canada's National DNA Data Bank contains the DNA profiles of more than 46,000 convicted offenders, and about 1,000 cold hits have been made since the database opened in June 2000.[177]

A cold hit is not enough to close a case—an investigator from the jurisdiction where the original crime was committed has to reopen the case, then locate and apprehend the subject. Often, the subject may be in prison, and the investigator has to go there to process him or her. The investigator also has to confirm the DNA sample and retest the subject to ensure accuracy.

Sometimes, errors can occur in this process. In 2003, the Oakland, California, Police Department processed DNA evidence from a teenage rape victim and subsequently received a cold hit from it. Officers did not follow up the cold hit until May 2006, and the subject is still at large. In another case, a sexual assault against a 10-year-old girl, the police received a cold hit in January 2004 but took a year to arrest the subject; in the interim, he sexually assaulted another 10-year-old. In 2006, it was reported that the Oakland police had 73 unresolved rape or homicide cold-hit DNA cases in which the subject has yet to be apprehended.[178]

In another processing mistake, a Baltimore man entered Maryland's state prison in 2004 on conviction of attempted sale of cocaine to a police officer. A bill had been passed in 2002 requiring the collection of DNA from Maryland's 20,000 state prison inmates serving time for felonies. The man's DNA was never collected despite the law. If proper procedures had been followed, police would have been alerted that his DNA matched two unsolved crimes, a 1999 rape and a 2002 murder. The man escaped in 2004, never having been subjected to a DNA test. During the year he was free, he killed three more persons, assaulted four others, and raped one more woman before being arrested again in 2005. When his DNA was finally taken, it linked him to five murders over six years. A 2004 audit revealed that despite the law, 8,300 inmates had not yet had their DNA collected, and 8,200 samples collected the previous year had not been sent for testing. Numerous similar cases have been reported.[179]

DNA Warrants In 1999, the Milwaukee, Wisconsin, county prosecutor made an innovative legal move regarding DNA in an effort to prevent the statute of limitations from expiring in a case against an unknown person suspected in a series of kidnappings and rapes. The prosecutor filed a "John Doe" warrant, not uncommon in cases where a suspect's identity is unknown. What made this case different was the means used to identify the suspect. The warrant identifies the assailant as "John Doe, unknown male with matching deoxyribonucleic acid (DNA) at five locations."[180] Since then, DNA warrants have been used a great deal.

In 2003, New York City criminal justice officials announced a sweeping, innovative plan, termed the "John Doe Indictment Project," in which prosecutors, investigators, and scientists will seek to match the DNA profiles of unknown sexual offenders in the most serious unsolved sex attacks to specific DNA profiles in the state DNA known-offender databank, then file John Doe warrants before they have linked a name to the DNA or arrested a suspect. The first 600 cases for which evidence will be reviewed concern attacks in 1994. If the indictments are completed before the statute of limitations clock (10 years) runs out, officials can arrest and prosecute the offender anytime in the future.[181]

DNA Dragnets DNA dragnets are requests by the police of persons in an area to give a voluntary DNA sample so that the police can compare their DNA with evidence found at the scene of a crime.[182] DNA lineups give police and grand juries limited authority to test the DNA of small groups of people based on a "reasonable suspicion" standard of probability that each member of the group might be involved in a crime.[183]

Familial DNA Searches Familial DNA analysis from the daughter of Dennis Rader, the BTK killer, was instrumental in his 2005 arrest for at least 10 homicides. Familial DNA searches are common in Great Britain. Some researchers believe that close relatives of criminals are more likely than others to break the law. This technique has proven successful in several cases.[184] In one case, police retrieved DNA from a brick that was thrown from an overpass and smashed through a windshield killing the driver. A near-match of that DNA with someone in Britain's DNA base led police to investigate that offender's relatives, one of whom confessed to the crime when confronted with the evidence. However, Troy Duster, a sociologist at New York University, says familial searches would exacerbate already serious racial inequities in the U.S. criminal justice system because incarceration rates are eight times higher for blacks than they are for whites, so any technique that focuses on relatives of people in the databases will just expand that trend.[185]

Exonerations There have been reports of numerous cases of persons who had been convicted of serious felonies and later exonerated by DNA evidence.[186] In 2003, Janet Reno, former Attorney

TABLE 14.4 Milestones in the Development of DNA Use in Police Work

Date	Development
1900	A, B, O blood groups discovered
1923	*Frye v. United States*
1983	PCR first conceived by Kerry Mullis
1984	First DNA profiling test developed by Alec Jeffreys
1986	First use of DNA to solve a crime and exonerate an innocent subject (Colin Pitchfork case)
1986	First acceptance of DNA testing in a U.S. civil court
1987	First use of DNA profiling in a U.S. criminal court
1987	Castro case
1992	Publication of DNA technology in *Forensic Science*
1992	Jakobetz case
1993	*Daubert v. Merrell Dow Pharmaceuticals, Inc.*
1997	*General Electric Co. v. Joiner*
1998	Creation of the National Commission on the Future of DNA Evidence
2000	Publication of *The Future of Forensic DNA Testing*

SOURCE: Adapted from National Institute of Justice, *The Future of Forensic DNA Testing: Predictions of the Research and Development Working Group* (Washington, D.C.: National Institute of Justice, 2000); Norah Rudin, "Forensic Science Timeline," retrieved May 12, 2001, from http://www.forensicdna.com/Timeline.htm.

General, in a speech to the National Conference on Preventing the Conviction of Innocent Persons, stated that during the past 30 years more than 100 people have been exonerated because of DNA or other tests.[187]

In the early 1990s, Scheck and Neufeld founded the first "Innocence Project" in conjunction with Cardozo Law School in New York. The project began reviewing cases and assisting inmates from across the country who claimed they were innocent. By 2005, it was reported that the project had contributed to the exoneration of 162 persons who had been convicted and sentenced to death or long prison terms.

Biometric Identification

Fingerprints and palm prints are only two of the forms of **biometric identification.** Biometric systems use a physical characteristic to distinguish one person from another. Other systems involve the face, the eyes, the hands, and the voice. A study of the accuracy, applications, costs, legal issues, and privacy issues associated with potential uses concluded that biometric systems have enormous potential for public and private organizations alike.[188]

Biometric systems serve two purposes: identification and authentication. They can help identify criminals, prevent welfare fraud, aid security in corrections, support border control, conduct criminal background checks, and establish identities on driver's licenses. Biometric systems already on the market can identify and authenticate people with a high degree of accuracy. Fingerprints remain the best choice for applications involving large numbers of users. Iris-based systems (which scan the human eye) may equal or exceed fingerprints in accuracy, but the limited number of vendors and lack of precedent for iris recognition make them less attractive. Hand-geometry systems have proven themselves in physical control, particularly in prisons, which require high levels of accuracy and security. Voice recognition proves least accurate but might be the best alternative to verify someone's identity over the phone. Facial-recognition systems create opportunities to identify people unobtrusively and without their cooperation, as in video surveillance, and they can be added to digital photo systems used for mug shots or driver's licenses.[189]

Facial identification technology and its potential impact on crime control were examined in a futures study that focused on the history of identification systems, the nature and status of the technology, and privacy issues. The study noted that facial recognition technology compares a real-time picture from a video camera to digital pictures in a computerized database to identify a person. It has the potential for both access security and the identification and apprehension of criminals.[190]

A project funded by the National Institute of Justice developed a surveillance system using real-time facial recognition technology to increase the usefulness of currently existing CCTV-compatible surveillance software. The system is a state-of-the-art, automated facial recognition surveillance system that could be extremely useful to law enforcement, intelligence personnel, and CCTV control room officers.[191]

British police plan to automatically monitor closed-circuit surveillance video cameras with facial-recognition software. In Britain, more than 200 thousand video cameras are used for surveillance, many watching streets and shopping areas. A computer will monitor video cameras set to watch for known criminals. When the system recognizes someone, it will alert the police.[192]

According to the consulting firm, the Freedonia Group, biometric systems will spur the market for electronic access controls by 10 percent per year through 2007. The Freedonia Group reports that facial recognition, voice recognition, and iris scanning are likely to break out of niche use and join fingerprint and hand-geometry systems as more widely deployed biometrics.[193]

Face-recognition technology, often touted as a promising tool in the fight against terrorism, earned a bad reputation after it failed miserably in some well-publicized tests for picking faces out of crowds. Yet, on simpler challenges, its performance is improving. Major casinos now use facial recognition to spot card counters at blackjack tables. Several states are using face-recognition systems to check for persons who have obtained multiple drivers licenses by lying about their identities. Facial recognition systems use cameras and computers to map someone's facial features, collect the data for storage in databases or on a microchip on documents such as passports. Making the technology work has required nearly perfect lighting and cooperative subjects, conditions that are not present when trying to spot suspected terrorists and criminals in a crowd.[194]

The most damaging publicity for facial recognition came from tests of the face-recognition software and video-surveillance cameras used to spot criminal suspects on the streets of Tampa, Florida, and Virginia Beach, Virginia. The programs did not lead to a single arrest and angered privacy advocates. Another facial recognition system that scanned 100,000 football fans entering the 2001 Super Bowl in Tampa picked out 19 people with criminal records, but none were among those being sought by the authorities.[195]

Analysts and many industry officials say that too much is being expected from the technology, which is still one of the newest methods in biometrics. Advocates of facial recognition have long promoted it as one of the least intrusive biometrics and potentially the most powerful because it can make use of a huge amount of existing data, such as the 1.2 billion digitized photographs of people in databases around the world. Performance in facial recognition plummets in poor lighting, when subjects move past control points without staring directly into the cameras, and when eyeglasses or other objects cover part of the face. Success rates also declined as the databases of potential matches grew and as the photos used got older.[196]

In 2005, the Department of Homeland Security (DHS) announced its first biometric standard for facial recognition. It provides technical criteria vendors can use to design equipment such as cameras and software for facial recognition. The standard is designed to be consistent with international biometric standards for travel documents and other applications.[197]

Videotaping

The use of handheld compact videotaping equipment is an example of the growing use of technology as a policing tool. For many years, the police have also been using videotape in investigations, undercover operations, and recording the confessions of suspects.

By 2003, 60 percent of all local police departments and 66 percent of all sheriffs' offices used video cameras on a regular basis. The most common use of video cameras was in patrol cars, with 55 percent of local police departments and 58 percent of sheriffs' offices using video cameras in this application. Local police departments used 48,800 in-car cameras, and sheriffs' offices used 17,700.[198]

Two examples show the potential of the use of videotaping in police work. The Franklin County, Ohio, Sheriff's Office and the Columbus, Ohio, Police Department were the recipients of several video cameras donated by insurance companies and Mothers Against Drunk Drivers (MADD). The cameras are mounted to the dashboards of police cars. When an officer sees a vehicle that appears to be operated by an alcohol-impaired driver, the officer begins to record the suspect's driving and notes on tape the location and the circumstances raising suspicions of drunk driving. When the vehicle is stopped, the officer approaching the car wears an activated wireless microphone that is

From the Road to the Lab

MICHELLE DUNKERLEY

Michelle Dunkerley is a Laboratory Director with the Michigan Department of State Police. She has been with the department for 20 years, spending the past 17 in the Forensic Science Division. She has a Bachelors Degree from Saginaw Valley State University and was a graduate of the 100th Recruit School.

When I went into the Michigan State Police, forensic science was the furthest thing from my mind. I was a trooper working the road. Writing tickets, handling traffic accidents, and arresting criminals were my primary concerns. Then an opening in the narcotics unit gave me the opportunity to work undercover. I thought that I had found my career path. I really enjoyed buying drugs and arresting individuals. I worked undercover for about a year when I saw a posting for a position in the Forensic Science Division as a Questioned Document trainee. I put in for it and started my career in the field of forensic science. I worked in the Questioned Document Unit for the next 13 years, being promoted from a trooper in training to a sergeant and then to a lieutenant in charge of that unit. When I was promoted to a first lieutenant, I became the director of an entire laboratory.

I am currently the director of the Michigan State Police Lansing Forensic Laboratory. There are six other Michigan State Police regional laboratories in the state: Bridgeport, Grand Rapids, Grayling, Northville, Marquette, and Sterling Heights. I have been the director of the Sterling Heights and Bridgeport laboratories, as well. Each of the laboratories covers a designated area in the state. Lansing is the largest laboratory with 65 employees. The disciplines in the Lansing Laboratory include

- Biology, which includes serology and DNA
- Blood alcohol
- Bomb squad
- CODIS
- Crime scene response
- Drug analysis
- Firearms and toolmarks
- Latent prints
- Micro chemical or trace
- Polygraph

- Questioned documents
- Toxicology

The Blood Alcohol, CODIS, Questioned Document, and Toxicology Units provide statewide services. The Biology Units from the Bridgeport, Grayling, and Marquette laboratories send their DNA casework to Lansing. The remaining units are located in each of the seven laboratories. All seven laboratories have a director. That director is responsible for overseeing the operations of that particular laboratory.

As a laboratory director, I am involved in the selection of personnel. Due to shows like *CSI,* the number of applicants is growing. When I came into the laboratory, there were usually 10 to 20 applicants per position. Now, it is not unusual to get at least 100 applicants for an entry level position.

Once a forensic scientist is hired, they have to be trained. The average training period for a forensic scientist is two years. I oversee the training and education of the staff for professional growth. One of the courses I assist in teaching new forensic scientists is Expert Witness Testimony. Not only do forensic scientists have to be able to explain to a jury what they did and why, but they may have to explain what they didn't do and why not. The forensic scientist is the expert and has to be able to explain the value of the evidence, and what it proves or disproves. In many cases, certain evidence may not be of probative value to the case. Due to the "CSI Effect," juries believe that forensic scientists always find evidence and that the analyses can be completed in a short period of time. In the majority of cases, the investigator brings the evidence to the laboratory and makes a request for the type of analysis to be conducted. The forensic scientist then does the analysis and reports their findings. The forensic scientist is only a small portion of proving a case. Much of the work is completed by the investigator.

However, there are pressures put on forensic scientists. One of the main pressures is to maintain the quality of work while producing a sufficient quantity of cases, at the same time, being aware of your backlog. A forensic scientist is expected to complete a certain number of cases, but there is no room for mistakes. One mistake could be the end of an individual's career.

I know as far as a career is concerned, I couldn't have asked for a better one.

able to record conversations as far as 500 feet from the camera. The videotape provides corroborating evidence to the officer's testimony.[199]

The other example of a promising application of videotaping involves departments equipping its patrol vehicles with video recorders. These cameras automatically record everything said or done within their range. The system was originally intended to aid in drug interdiction cases, in prosecuting alcohol-impaired drivers, and in accident investigations. However, the police discovered that the video cameras provided reliable, unbiased evidence in citizen complaint cases. In one case, a trooper was accused of being rude and using profanity during a traffic stop. The videotape proved that the charges were unfounded. In another case, a trooper was accused of shooting an unarmed motorist. The videotape revealed that the trooper had issued at least 26 warnings for the person to drop his gun before the officer fired. The videotape can also confirm wrongdoing by an officer. In one case in which a trooper was accused of raping a motorist he had stopped for a traffic violation, the videotape was admitted into evidence against him.[200]

There have been numerous cases of officers catching their own assault, and several their own felonious death, on the patrol vehicle's video recorder. One, in 1997, involved Deputy Sheriff Henry Huff, a member of the Walton County, Georgia, Sheriff's Office, who was shot at point-blank range during a traffic stop by a 9mm-wielding 16-year-old. Huff's squad car was equipped with an automatic surveillance camera, and the entire incident was recorded on videotape. Fortunately, despite being shot twice in the chest, Huff was spared serious injury by his bullet-resistant vest and has since returned to duty.[201]

Robotics

Robotics is the science of using robots to perform operations formerly done by human beings. Robots have been available to law enforcement since the early 1970s. However, because of their high cost, they were seldom purchased for law enforcement use. Since the mid-1980s, robots have become very popular in police departments for bomb disposal, or explosive ordinance disposal (EOD).

The bomb robots can be operated by an electric cable or by radio control. They can take X-rays, photographs of packages, search suspect locations,

and place explosive devices into a transport vessel, thus keeping bomb personnel safely away from the immediate area. Robots can have closed-circuit video systems, audio systems, and spotlights. Some of the more sophisticated robots can climb stairs, cross ditches, and knock down doors.[202]

In a series of studies, law enforcement officials indicated that they had other uses for robots, including the functions of small item delivery, passive remote communication, and remote surveillance. The features of the robots considered most important were stair climbing ability, a robust communication link, low cost, and longer battery life. A study by the U.S. Department of Defense's (DoD) Defense Advanced Research Projects Agency (DARPA) indicated that no single robot could meet all of the demand of law enforcement beyond EOD work. DARPA recommended that any robots developed for police work be modular, with application-specific mission packages or tool sets that can be tailored to the needs of a particular user.[203]

Carnegie Mellon University's Robotics Institute has a 4-foot, 160-pound helicopter that can perform search and rescue, surveillance, aerial cinematographing, and mapping functions. It operates with vision-guided systems that can visually lock-on to ground objects and sense its own position in real-time. These vision-guided robot helicopters can be used for law enforcement applications, such as patrol. They can also be used in hostage negotiations or SWAT operations.[204]

Robots were used at Ground Zero in New York City in two basic applications. Small, tethered robots (about the size of a shoebox) were used on the rubble pile for the first two weeks to locate voids where survivors might be found. The next two weeks, the robots focused more on structural inspection. Researchers are currently working on more functions for police robots, such as crawling under closed doors to detect biological chemicals and detecting illegal drugs.[205]

Concerns about Technology and Civil Liberties

Some fear that technological developments, such as improved computer-based files and long-range electronic surveillance devices, will give the police more power to intrude into the private lives of citizens. A Congressional report found reason to believe that DNA fingerprinting may work against a suspect's reasonable expectation of privacy.[206]

Even the magazine *Popular Mechanics* worries about the civil liberties issues of enhanced police technology:

> Along with the advantages, however, has come new potential for abuse. For example, the same computer databases that make AFIS possible could also be used for random searches that might focus suspicion on people because they have stayed in a homeless shelter, or because they fall into certain categories based on age, race or other discriminatory criteria.[207]

The noted civil liberties lawyer Alan M. Dershowitz, of Harvard University Law School, in *Taking Liberties: A Decade of Hard Cases, Bad Laws, and Bum Raps,* comments on the 1986 U.S. Supreme Court case *California v. Ciraolo.*[208] In this case, the Court ruled that evidence obtained by the police flying over and photographing a person's property was not a violation of the person's Fourth Amendment rights. Dershowitz wrote, "You can be sure that our Constitution's Founding Fathers would have been appalled at this breach of privacy. A person's home—whether it be a walled estate, a plantation, or small cottage—was regarded as his castle, free from the intruding eye of government, without a warrant based on probable cause."[209]

Commenting on the call by some for a national registry of every American's DNA profile against which the police could instantly compare crime-scene specimens, many civil libertarians express concern: "These databases are starting to look more like a surveillance tool than a tool for criminal investigation. A universal database will bring us more wrongful arrests and possibly more wrongful convictions," says Tania Simoncelli of the ACLU in New York. "We don't know all the potential uses of DNA, but once the state has your sample and there are not limits on how it can be used, then the potential civil liberty violations are as vast as the uses themselves," says Carol Roses, of the Massachusetts ACLU.[210]

Summary

- Tremendous improvements have been made in the police use of technology in the fields of computers, communications, criminal investigation, surveillance, and criminalistics. Computers have enabled the police to dispatch officers immediately to any calls for service. They have also aided the police in the investigation process by enabling officers to feed descriptions and MOs into the computer and to receive almost instantaneous printouts on possible suspects. Computers have enabled police to maintain better records more easily.

- The computer has also caused a revolution in the processing of fingerprints through automated fingerprint identification system (AFIS) terminals.

- In recent years, the police have also used science to develop less-than-lethal weapons, such as Tasers and chemical irritant sprays, as an alternative to using deadly force.

- Other technology, including improved surveillance devices and improved forensic techniques (such as DNA profiling), is enhancing the ability of the police to solve crime.

- The CSI effect makes the public and jurors believe that the police can do what their television counterparts can.

- DNA profiling, also called genetic fingerprinting or DNA typing, has shown exponential progress in the last decade in helping investigators solve crimes and ensuring that those guilty of crimes are convicted in court. However, significant backlogs exist in DNA testing; more than 542,000 criminal cases with possible biological evidence remain in the hands of law enforcement or have been backlogged at forensic labs.

- Despite the advances that science brings to police work, the key to police work will always be people—the men and women we hire to serve and protect us.

Learning Check

1. Discuss the advantages of computer-aided dispatch (CAD) systems, including enhanced CAD.

2. What are automated databases? Discuss some examples of their use in policing.

3. List and discuss some of the major uses of the computer in police departments today.

4. What are the two basic categories of fingerprints? Discuss them.

5. Discuss automated fingerprint identification systems.

6. Explain the latest advances in fingerprint processing.

7. Discuss the advantages and disadvantages of less-than-lethal weapons in policing.

8. What is the CSI effect? Discuss it.

9. What are the major sections of a police crime lab? Discuss the evidence each examines.

10. Define DNA and talk about the accuracy of the results of genetic fingerprinting (DNA profiling).

Key Terms

age-progression photos Photo systems that show changes that will naturally occur to the face with age; also called age-enhanced photos.

automated crime analysis The automated collection and analysis of data regarding crime (when, where, who, what, how, and why) to discern criminal patterns and assist in the effective assignment of personnel to combat crime.

automated fingerprint identification system (AFIS) Fingerprinting innovation begun in the 1980s in which a print technician can enter unidentified latent fingerprints into a computer. The computer then automatically searches its files and presents a list of likely matches.

ballistics Scientific analysis of guns and bullets.

biometric identification Automated identification systems that use particular physical characteristics to distinguish one person from another; can identify criminals or provide authentication.

cold hit A DNA sample collected from a crime scene that ties an unknown suspect to the DNA profile of someone in the national or a state's database.

Combined DNA Index System (CODIS) Database that contains DNA profiles obtained from subjects convicted of homicide, sexual assault, and other serious felonies.

composite sketches Sketches prepared by forensic artists or automated means of people wanted by the police for a crime.

computer-aided dispatch (CAD) System that allows almost immediate communication between the police dispatcher and police units in the field.

computer-aided investigations (computerized case management) The use of computers to perform case management and other functions in investigations.

crime analysis The use of analytical methods to obtain pertinent information on crime patterns and trends that can then be disseminated to officers on the street.

criminalistics A branch of forensic science that deals with the study of physical evidence related to crime.

CSI **effect** The phenomenon that the popularity of the television series *CSI: Crime Scene Investigation,* and its spin-offs *CSI: Miami* and *CSI: New York* and other television shows and movies makes the public and jurors believe that the police can do what their television counterparts can.

deoxyribonucleic acid (DNA) The basic building code for all of the human body's chromosomes.

DNA profiling, genetic fingerprinting, DNA typing The examination of DNA samples from a body fluid to determine whether they came from a particular subject.

forensic science That part of science applied to answering legal questions.

Frye test Standard to admitting new scientific evidence into U.S. Courts; based on the U.S. Supreme case *Frye v. United States* (1923).

Global Positioning Systems (GPS) A satellite system used to locate any position on the map.

inked prints (ten-prints) Result of the process of rolling each finger onto a ten-print card.

Integrated Automated Fingerprint Identification System (IAFIS) A system for searching an individual's fingerprints against a computerized database of all fingerprints.

IP telephony A collection of new communication technologies, products, and services that can facilitate communication across diverse systems.

latent prints Fingerprint impressions left at a crime scene.

less-than-lethal weapons Innovative alternatives to traditional nonfirearm weapons, such as batons, flashlights, or bodily force techniques; includes chemical irritant sprays and Tasers, among others.

Live Scan The electronic taking and transmission of fingerprints as opposed to traditional ink methods.

mitochondrial DNA (MtDNA) DNA analysis applied to evidence containing very small or degraded quantities from hair, bones, teeth, and body fluids.

mobile digital terminal (MDT) A device put into a police vehicle that allows the electronic transmission of messages between the police dispatcher and the officer in the field.

mug shot imaging A system of digitizing a mug shot picture and storing its image on a computer so that it can be retrieved later.

National Crime Information Center (NCIC) Computerized database of criminal information maintained by the FBI.

night vision devices Photographic and viewing devices that allow visibility in darkness.

polymerase chain reaction-short tandem repeat (PCR-STR) One of the latest DNA technology

systems; requires only pin-size samples rather than dime-size samples needed for RFLP.

Regional Crime Analysis Geographic Information Systems (RCAGIS) Spatial Analysis Computer programs to help police locate crime "hot spots," spatially relate a list of potential suspects to actual crimes, profile crime geographically to identify where a serial criminal most likely lives, and forecast where the next crime in a series might occur.

restricted fragment length polymorphism (RFLP) Traditional method of DNA technology analysis.

robotics The science of using robots to perform operations formerly done by human beings.

serology Scientific analysis of blood, semen, and other body fluids.

vehicle tracking systems Transmitters that enable investigators to track a vehicle during a surveillance; also called transponders, bumper beepers, or homing devices.

Voice over IP (VoIP) A subset of IP telephony that is a set of software, hardware, and standards designed to enable voice transmissions over packet-switched networks, which can be either an internal local area network or the Internet. VoIP is not associated with a physical telephone line but, rather, with an IP address that is linked to a phone number.

Homeland Security

© Spencer Platt/Getty Images

GOALS

- To introduce you to the concept of international and domestic terrorism and its disastrous results
- To alert you to the need for the government and the police to ensure homeland defense
- To familiarize you with the rapid, unprecedented actions taken by the U.S. government and law enforcement to secure the United States in reaction to the terrorist attacks of September 11, 2001
- To acquaint you with the many efforts to prevent and deal with terrorism and ensure homeland security by national, state, and local law enforcement agencies, and private security agencies
- To discuss the issue of security versus civil liberties

Introduction

On September 11, 2001, our world changed.

On **September 11, 2001,** a series of unthinkable and incomprehensible events led to disasters in New York City, Washington D.C., and a grassy field in Pennsylvania. Those events shocked the world and changed world history.

The swiftness, scale, and sophistication of the coordinated operation, coupled with the extraordinary planning required, made most people realize that terrorism and mass murder had hit New York City, the United States, and indeed, the world. In the immediate aftermath of 9/11, it was reported that almost 5,000 people were missing and more than 400 confirmed dead. Eventually, it was determined that the missing persons included 23 New York City police officers, 35 New York and New Jersey Port Authority officers, 3 New York State court officers, and more than 300 New York City firefighters. These attacks shocked us, even though there had been similar events, although not as massive, before. Terrorism was not new to the United States.

For years, most Americans had believed that terrorist attacks only occurred in foreign nations, but events in the past few years have changed American's perceptions. Why?

In 1993, there was the first terrorist attack on New York City's World Trade Center, killing 6 and wounding 1,000. In 1995, there was the bombing of the Alfred P. Murrah Federal Building in Oklahoma City, killing 168 persons and injuring 675 others. Then there was the 1996 bombing at the Olympic Games in Atlanta, Georgia, which killed 1 person and wounded 111 others. During these years, there were also terrorist acts committed against family planning clinics that provide abortions and churches, and many other depraved, senseless incidents. These events awakened Americans to the fact that terrorism had actually come ashore. However, no other day in America's history had been quite like September 11, 2001.

The terrorist attacks of September 11, 2001, jolted Americans out of a sense of complacency, and perhaps lethargy, and made them realize that they were the

© Robert Brenner/Photo Edit Inc

The events of September 11, 2001, were an unprecedented challenge to the rescue personnel who responded. They tried to restore some order and calm, despite their own physical and emotional responses to viewing the tragedy and its effects up close.

targets of terrorism. What really made the terrorism threat hit home to most Americans was that Americans were actually attacked in their homeland. The need for a strong homeland defense has been a primary interest of U.S. law enforcement since then.

This chapter will discuss terrorism directed against Americans and American interests abroad including foreign terrorism and domestic terrorism. We will discuss the immediate aftermath of September 11, 2001 and the rapid, unprecedented efforts made by the U.S. government. The chapter will describe federal, state, local, and private security efforts against terrorism and for homeland security and the issue of security versus individual rights—how we can ensure a safe environment without threatening our civil liberties and individual freedoms granted under the U.S. Constitution.

Terrorism

Founding Fathers

Terrorism has many definitions. The Federal Bureau of Investigation (FBI) defines **terrorism** as "the unlawful use of force or violence against persons or property to intimidate or coerce a government, the civilian population, or a segment thereof, in furtherance of political or social objectives." The U.S. Defense Department defines it as "the unlawful use or threatened use of force or violence against individuals or property to coerce or intimidate governments or societies, often to achieve political, religious, or ideological objectives."[1] Jonathan R. White, professor of criminal justice and executive director of the Homeland Defense Initiative at Grand Valley State University in Grand Rapids, Michigan, sums up terrorism simply, "Terrorism uses violence or threatened violence against innocent people to achieve a social or political goal."[2] The National Counterterrorism Center defines terrorism as "premeditated politically motivated violence perpetrated against noncombatant targets."[3]

Terrorism has a long tradition in world history. Terrorist tactics have been used frequently by radical and criminal groups to influence public opinion and to attempt to force authorities to do their will. Terrorists have criminal, political, and other nefarious motives. Some may remember the terrorist activities that occurred during the 1972 Olympic Games in Munich, Germany, when terrorists attacked and took hostage the Israeli Olympic team and killed all of them; the 1988 explosion of Flight 103 in the air over Lockerbie, Scotland, killing all 270 persons aboard; and the actions of the Unabomber.

Many Americans and most major U.S. firms have been targeted by terrorists in some way. Political extremists and terrorists use the violence and suspense of terrorist acts such as bombing, kidnapping, and hostage situations to put pressure on those in authority to comply with their demands and cause the authorities and public to recognize their power. Extremists and terrorists use their activities to obtain money for their causes, to alter business or government policies, or to change public opinion. Attacks against executives are common in Latin America, the Middle East, and Europe, and they have spread to the United States. Successful terrorist techniques employed in one country spread to others. Governments and corporations have had to develop extensive plans to deal with terrorism.

According to Louis J. Freeh, former director of the FBI,

> Terrorists are among the most ruthless of criminals, but their motivation rarely stems from personal need or a desire for material gain. Unlike the majority of violent criminals, terrorists do not know their victims; in fact, one of the hallmarks of terrorism is its indiscriminate victimization. Also, unlike most serious criminal activity, terrorism invites—and even depends upon—media attention to ensure a maximum yield of terror.[4]

The Terrorism Knowledge Base is operated by the National Memorial Institute for the Prevention of Terrorism (MIPT), a nonprofit organization dedicated to preventing terrorism on U.S. soil or mitigating its effects. The MIPT was established after the 1995 bombing of the federal building in Oklahoma City and is funded by the U.S. Department of Homeland Security (DHS). The Terrorism Knowledge Base is a repository of incidents arranged by type, perpetrator, date, location, and other factors. It also contains overviews of terrorist groups, legal cases involving terrorism, information resources, and other valuable materials for terrorism researchers. Users can create graphs of incidents by group, incident, and other factors, and they can search terrorist organizations by ideology, such as antiglobalization, environmental, right-wing, reactionary and other groups.[5]

According to the Terrorism Knowledge Base, from 1968 through 2004, international terrorists most frequently targeted private citizens, businesses, and property. Of the 19,383 total incidents of terrorism around the world in that period, 3,192 hit private citizens and property. Business targets were a close second, with 3,065 incidents. Among other targets hit, transportation was victimized 831 times, utilities 554 times, and airports and airlines 798 times. After al Qaeda, the most lethal group during these years was Hizballah, causing more than 800 deaths.[6]

The National Counterterrorism Center (NCTC) was created in 2004, under the Intelligence Reform and Terrorism Prevention Act (IRTPA) to serve as the primary organization in the U.S. government for integrating and analyzing all intelligence pertaining to terrorism and counterterrorism and to conduct strategic operational planning by integrating all instruments of national power. It is under the administrative control of the Office of the Director of National Intelligence (DNI).

In 2006, the NCTC reported that there were more than 11,000 terrorist acts worldwide in 2005 that resulted in the deaths of more than 14,500 noncombatants. Attacks in Iraq accounted for 30 percent of the total attacks and 55 percent of the fatalities. American deaths from terrorism totaled 56. Most fatalities were the result of armed attacks and bombings; none occurred in the United States or used weapons of mass destruction. The NCTC report said, "It is likely that we will face a resilient enemy for years to come." For the 2005 report, the NCTC significantly changed the methodology for counting terrorist attacks to reflect the nature of the threat posed by terrorism more accurately. Thus, the new methodology makes it difficult to compare 2005 with previous government efforts to compile terrorist statistics. The NCTC changed its definition of terrorism to "premeditated politically motivated violence perpetrated against noncombatant targets."[7]

International Terrorism

According to John F. Lewis, Jr., retired assistant director of the FBI's National Security Division, the FBI divides the current international threat to the United States into three categories[8]:

First, there are threats from foreign sponsors of **international terrorism.** These sponsors view terrorism as a tool of foreign policy. Their activities have changed over time. Past activities included direct terrorist support and operations by official state agents. Now these sponsors generally seek to conceal their support of terrorism by relying on surrogates to conduct operations. State sponsors remain involved in terrorist activities by funding, organizing, networking, and providing other support and instruction to formal terrorist groups and loosely affiliated extremists.

Second, according to Lewis, there are threats from formalized terrorist groups, such as al Qaeda, the Lebanese Hizballah, the Egyptian Al-Gama'a al-Islamiyya, and the Palestinian Hamas. These autonomous organizations have their own infrastructures, personnel, financial arrangements, and training facilities. They can plan and mount terrorist campaigns overseas as well as support terrorist operations inside the United States. Some groups use supporters in the United States to plan and coordinate acts of terrorism. In the past, these formalized terrorist groups engaged in such criminal activities in the United States as illegally acquiring weapons, violating U.S. immigration laws, and providing safe havens to fugitives.[9]

Third, there are threats from loosely affiliated international radical extremists, such as those who attacked the World Trade Center in 1995. These extremists do not represent a particular nation. Loosely affiliated extremists may pose the most urgent threat to the United States at this time because they remain relatively unknown to law enforcement. They can travel freely, obtain a variety of identities, and recruit like-minded sympathizers from various countries.[10]

In 2005, the DHS reported that the threat of countries facilitating or supporting terrorism had diminished. It said that ideologically driven actors, particularly al Qaeda, are the top terrorist threat against the United States today. The DHS also named several visual symbols such as the White House and the Statue of Liberty as the most likely targets of terrorism and truck bombs and small explosives-laden boats as the most likely terrorism weapons.[11]

Many cases of international terrorism have involved this country primarily by targeting U.S. citizens and interests abroad. Some memorable attacks in addition to the those mentioned earlier include the abduction of hostages in Lebanon in the mid-1980s; the 1996 detonation of an explosive device outside the Khobar Towers in Dhahran, Saudi Arabia, in which 10 U.S. military personnel were killed; the 1998 bombings of the U.S. embassies in Nairobi, Kenya, and Dar es Salaam, Tanzania, which resulted in the deaths of 12 Americans and 200 others; the terrorist attack on the U.S.S. *Cole* in the waters of Aden, which killed 19 U.S. sailors; and the abduction and subsequent murder of *Wall Street Journal* journalist Daniel Pearl in 2002. Before the September 11, 2001, attack, the most recent case of international terrorism occurring on our shores was on February 26, 1993, when foreign terrorists bombed the World Trade Center.

Foreign terrorism continued after September 11, 2001. In 2002, terrorist bombings in Bali, Indonesia, killed more than 200 persons in nightclub bombings. The Indonesian capital of Jakarta was also targeted by suicide bombings during 2003 and 2004.[12] In 2004, Russia lost at least 425 people in terrorist attacks, including a bombing at a Moscow subway station, two bombed passenger jets, and a massacre at an elementary school on the first day of school in which 32 terrorists seized the school, taking at least 1,000 hostages.[13] Also in 2004, terrorist attacks on commuter trains in Madrid, Spain, killed hundreds.

On July 7, 2005, during rush hour, a series of at least six explosions occurred on the London transportation network, including five attacks on the underground system and one on a bus in the city's centre, causing 56 deaths and more than 700 injuries. This was London's worst attack since World War II. The incidents took place on the day after it was announced that the 2012 Olympic summer games were awarded to London. It also coincided with a meeting of the leaders of the G8 (major officials of the major countries) at Gleneagles, Scotland.[14] Four suspects were arrested within a week, three British-born and one Jamaican-born British citizen who were Muslims and Islamic fanatics. Three lived in Leeds, an industrial city in Northern England.[15] A few weeks later, four bombs went off almost simultaneously on London undergrounds trains and a bus again, but only the detonators blew up.[16]

Subsequent to the London bombings, three bombings in the Egyptian resort town of Sharm el-Sheikh, a vacationing hot spot for Europeans, Israelis, and Arabs alike, killed at least 88 and wounded more than 200.[17] Also in 2005, three suicide bombers wearing explosive vests blew themselves up in three crowded restaurants in the tourist resort of Bali, Indonesia, killing about 25 people and wounding 101 others.

In April 2006, suicide bombers killed 24 persons and wounded 100 at a Sinai resort.[18] In June 2006, Canadian police charged 12 men and 5 youths with planning a wave of terrorist attacks, ranging from blowing up the Toronto Stock Exchange to storming the national public broadcaster and Parliament buildings in Ottawa and beheading the prime minister.[19] Also in June 2006, 6 men were arrested in Miami and 1 in Atlanta for plotting to destroy Chicago's Sears Tower. The arrest was the result of an FBI sting involving an informant who posed as an al Qaeda operative.[20] In July 2006, about 190 persons were killed and about 600 were injured when bombs exploded on seven commuter trains during the evening rush hour in Mumbai, India. A few days earlier, a series of grenade explosions struck Srinagar, the summer capital of Indian-administered Kashmir, hitting a tourist bus and killing 8 persons and wounding more than 40.[21] Also in 2006, extreme violence was reported in Somalia by Islamist militias operating under an umbrella group calling itself the Council of Islamic Courts.[22]

In August 2006, British authorities arrested 24 extremists who planned to use liquid explosives to blow up airplanes flying from Britain to the United States. The men were planning to carry the liquids in drink bottles and combine them into explosive cocktails to commit mass murder aboard as many as 10 flights over the Atlantic. The arrests caused massive alerts at airports and new rules regarding what could be brought aboard a plane.[23]

Another significant recent concern that falls under the umbrella of terrorism is bioterrorism or **biological weapons.** The anthrax attacks of 2001 caused numerous deaths and sicknesses, as well as significant panic in our nation. Mailed letters containing alleged anthrax paralyzed the nation's postal system and forced the government to spend billions to install sophisticated detection equipment at postal centers throughout the country.

Four types of biological agents can be weaponized, including natural poisons or toxins that occur without human modification, viruses, bacteria, and plagues. The Centers for Disease Control and Prevention (CDC) classifies the most threatening agents as smallpox, anthrax, plague, botulism, tularemia, and hemorrhagic fever. Smallpox is a deadly contagious virus. Anthrax is a noncontagious bacterial infection, whereas plague is transmitted by insects. Botulism is a food-borne illness, and tularemia is an infectious disease often caused by contact with animals. Hemorrhagic fevers are caused by viruses. One of the best-known hemorrhagic fevers is the Ebola virus.[24]

Fortunately, the U.S. General Accounting Office (GAO) reported in 2004 that the CDC had learned the lessons from the anthrax incidents and had developed databases and expertise on biological agents likely to be used in a terrorism attack.[25] In 2004, the president signed a bill creating *Project BioShield* to help the U.S. purchase, develop, and deploy cutting-edge defenses against biological weapons attacks. The bill authorized the expenditure of $5.6 billion over 10 years for the government to purchase and stockpile vaccines and drugs to fight anthrax, smallpox, and other potential agents of bioterror. Project BioShield also purchased 75 million doses of an improved anthrax vaccine for the Strategic National Stockpile.[26] Fortunately, a major drawback in the use of biological weapons is that they cannot be controlled. For example, if terrorists were to release a weaponized strain of smallpox, the disease might spread to the terrorist group and its allies.[27]

ON THE JOB

Involvement in Major Incidents

I have always felt it was important for everyone in law enforcement to be aware of what was going on in their jurisdiction as well as nationally, to know about crime trends, unusual incidents, and investigations and court rulings.

I was no longer working for the police department when the attacks of September 11, 2001, occurred. Like everyone, I was glued to the TV, and we discussed it quite a bit in class. When the anthrax threat occurred several weeks later and we didn't know whether there was a relationship or not, again I watched events unfold.

The anthrax incidents held particular interest because the American Media building is located in Boca Raton. When an employee died, another went to the hospital, and almost 1,000 lined up in the hot sun at the Health Department to obtain testing and precautionary antibiotics, I also looked at the situation as a former police administrator in that city.

The logistics and cost to the agency to serve in this highly unusual and unexpected situation created a challenge that agency personnel had to meet quickly. Securing the building 24 hours a day, documenting who came and went, interviewing employees, conferencing with other emergency response personnel and federal agencies, maintaining order among the anxious employees waiting for testing in the hot and humid conditions, collating information, and disseminating that information to a demanding press and a concerned public would tax their resources to the maximum. The city still required protection, but clearly all sworn personnel suspended their normal activities except those of an emergency nature. The calls for service were also increased with citizens bringing in "suspicious" packages and substances as well as calling in information regarding "suspicious" individuals who may be accomplices to the terrorists, some of whom had been living in the South Florida area.

These demands required the administration to reassign personnel, change schedules, examine vehicle demands, devise procedures for handling the suspicious substances, define roles among the multiple investigatory agencies, establish procedures for handling the American Media scene, and clarify and disseminate information regarding the health risks to the public. These demands lasted quite a while, and though they eventually de-escalated, the unusual level of activity continued. As the emergency nature of the situation slowly decreased, concern about paying for all these services did not.

It was exciting to watch the coverage and see friends and former coworkers being interviewed, giving press conferences, and walking around at the scene. It would have been an exciting and challenging time to be on the Boca Raton Police Department.

—Linda Forst

Domestic Terrorism

According to Lewis, **domestic terrorism** involves groups or individuals who operate without foreign direction entirely within the United States and target elements of the U.S. government or citizens. He states that the 1995 federal building explosion in Oklahoma City and the pipe bomb explosion in Centennial Olympic Park during the 1996 Summer Olympic Games underscore the ever-present threat that exists from individuals determined to use violence to advance their agendas.[28]

Lewis reports that domestic terrorist groups today represent extreme right-wing, extreme left-wing, and special-interest beliefs. The main themes espoused today by extremist right-wing groups are conspiracies having to do with the New World Order, gun control laws, and white supremacy. Many of these extremist groups also advocate antigovernment, antitaxation, or antiabortion sentiments and engage in survivalist training, with their goal being to ensure the perpetuation of the United States as a white, Christian nation.

Domestic terrorism was responsible for the bombing in Centennial Olympic Park at the Atlanta Olympics Games on July 27, 1996. The media reported that the FBI originally suspected security guard Richard A. Jewell of complicity in the bombing, but later the FBI indicated that there was no evidence that he had any criminal part in it. In

You Are There!

Some Major International Terrorism Cases Affecting the United States

1993 World Trade Center Attack

Six persons were killed and more than 1,000 others were injured in the blast on February 26, 1993, in New York City. In 1994, four men were convicted of bombing the World Trade Center. Abdel Rahman, also known as Omar Ahmad Ali Abdel Rahman, a blind Egyptian religious leader, was charged with being one of the planners of the bombing conspiracy and leading a terrorist organization that sprang up in the United States in 1989. Investigators also say he participated in conversations involving the planned bombing of the United Nations building and the assassination of Egyptian President Hosni Mubarak. Rahman and 11 others were convicted in federal court on charges of trying to assassinate political leaders and bomb major New York City landmarks. In 1995, another man, Ramzi Ahmed Yousef, was arrested as the main plotter behind the World Trade Center bombing.

U.S. Embassy Bombings

On August 7, 1998, simultaneous bombings occurred in the U.S. embassies in Dar es Salaam, Tanzania, and Nairobi, Kenya. These attacks killed more than 200 persons, including 20 Americans. Osama bin Laden—who also uses the aliases of Usama bin Muhammad bin Ladin, Shaykh Usama bin Ladin, the Prince, the Emir, Abu Abdallah, Mujahid Shaykh, Hajj, and the Director—is still wanted by the FBI in connection with these bombings.

Millennium Bomb Plot

On December 14, 1999, as the world was preparing to celebrate the year 2000 millennium, an Algerian terrorist attempted to enter the United States from Canada with the intention of setting off a bomb at the Los Angeles International Airport during the celebrations. The would-be bomber, Ahmed Ressam, was arrested at the border near Seattle with a trunk full of explosives. The FBI started a sweeping search for other suspects and information about the plot. Investigators developed information that the plot was linked to a worldwide network of terrorists orchestrated by Osama bin Laden. Ressam was convicted and sentenced to prison in May 2000.

In July 2001, an Algerian-born shopkeeper, Mokhtar Haouari, age 32, who ran a gift shop in Montreal and as a sideline dealt in false identification documents, as well as check and credit card scams, was also convicted in the conspiracy. A third suspect, Abdel Ghani Meskini, offered testimony against the other plotters in exchange for a reduced sentence. The suspects said they were trained in guerilla camps in Afghanistan run by bin Laden.

Bombing of the U.S.S. *Cole*

On October 12, 2000, two Arabic-speaking suicide bombers attacked the U.S. destroyer *Cole* in the waters off Aden, killing 17 American sailors. The FBI linked the bombing once again to Osama bin Laden, the fugitive Saudi, who had declared a worldwide "holy war" against the United States. Six men were arrested soon after the bombing. Bin Laden remains at large.

June 1997, an FBI task force linked the Olympic bombing to the 1997 bombings at the Sandy Springs Professional Building (housing the Atlanta Northside Family Planning Services clinic—an abortion clinic) and an Atlanta lesbian nightclub.[29]

This case was finally cleared in 2003. The FBI had earlier determined the primary suspect in the bombing at Centennial Olympic Park, as well as the gay bar and abortion clinics in Atlanta and Alabama, to be Eric Rudolph. He was arrested in 2003, after hiding in the mountains of North Carolina for five years. He had defeated all efforts to find him and was found not by an elite squad but by a rookie police officer in Murphy, North Carolina. The concern of the government is that it is doubtful that Rudolph was able to survive and hide in the wilderness unaided for five years. It is believed that he had help, illustrating at the very least that sympathy and support for some of these domestic terrorist groups does exist.[30]

One particularly troubling element of right-wing extremism is the militia, or patriot, movement. Militia members want to remove federal involvement from various issues. They generally are law-abiding citizens who have become intolerant of what they perceive as violations of their constitutional rights. Membership in a militia organization is not entirely illegal in the United States,

You Are There!

Some Major Domestic Terrorism Cases in the United States

Oklahoma City Federal Building

At 9:05 AM on April 19, 1995, an explosion occurred at the Alfred P. Murrah Federal Building in Oklahoma City. The bombing destroyed the structure, killed 168 people, and injured 675. Later that day, an Oklahoma state trooper arrested Timothy McVeigh on Interstate 35 for driving without license plates. Several days later McVeigh was charged with the bombing. He was alleged to have links to white supremacist and patriot groups. McVeigh was convicted for his crimes in 1997 and executed in 2001.

Atlanta Olympic Games

On July 27, 1996, a bombing occurred in Centennial Olympic Park at the Atlanta Olympic Games; a woman was killed and 111 other people were injured. In June 1997, the FBI linked the Olympic bombing to the January 16, 1997, bombing at the Sandy Springs Professional Building, which housed the Atlanta

Northside Family Planning Services clinic (a clinic that provided abortions) and the February 2, 1997, bombing of an Atlanta lesbian nightclub. The FBI claimed that letters mailed to the press by a militant religious cell known as the Army of God connected the group to the bombings.

After a five-year manhunt, Eric Robert Rudolph was arrested in the small town of Murphy, North Carolina, on May 31, 2003, by rookie police officer Jeff Postell. Rudolph was charged with these crimes, which killed and injured hundreds.

SOURCES: "FBI Ten Most Wanted Fugitives: Eric Robert Rudolph," retrieved from http://www.fbi.gov/mostwant/topten/fugitives/rudolph.htm; Kevin Sack, "Officials Link Atlanta Bombings and Ask for Help," *New York Times* (June 10, 1997), p. A1; and Jo Thomas, "McVeigh Guilty on All Counts in the Oklahoma City Bombing," *New York Times* (June 3, 1997), p. A1.

---

but certain states have legislated limits on militias, including on the types of training (for example, paramilitary training) that they can offer. The FBI bases its interest in the militia movement on the risk of violence or the potential for violence and criminal activity.

Experts have traced the growth of the militia movement partly to the effective use of modern communication mediums. Videotapes, computer bulletin boards, and the Internet have been used with great effectiveness by militia sympathizers. Promilitia networks disseminate material from well-known hate group figures and conspiracy theorists. Organizers can promote their ideologies at militia meetings, patriot rallies, and gatherings of various other groups espousing antigovernment sentiments.

FBI Special Agents James E. Duffy and Alan C. Brantley give us this profile of the typical militia member:

> Most militia organization members are white males who range in age from the early 20s to the mid-50s. The majority of militia members appear to be attracted to the movement because of gun control issues. . . . Militia members generally maintain strong Christian

beliefs and justify their actions by claiming to be ardent defenders of the Constitution.[31]

In a 2005 report, terrorism experts noted that the number of paramilitary militia groups in the United States has dwindled substantially since the Oklahoma City bombing in 1995 because of public backlash and intense pressure from law enforcement. They say, however, that the terrorism threat posed by individual "lone wolf" extremists remains strong. By 2005, there were about 150 militia groups in the country compared with about 900 immediately after the Oklahoma City bombing. Terrorism experts also say that far-left environmental and animal-rights groups also pose a serious threat.[32]

Left-wing extremist groups generally profess a revolutionary socialist doctrine and view themselves as protectors of the American people against capitalism and imperialism. They aim to change the nation through revolutionary means rather than by participating in the regular political and social process.

During the 1970s, leftist-oriented extremist groups posed the predominant domestic terrorist threat in the United States. Beginning in the 1980s, however, the FBI dismantled many of these groups

When were you?

You Are There!

Catching the Oklahoma City Bomber, Timothy McVeigh: Feds Took the Credit, but Charley Caught Him

Police Officer Charles J. Hanger of the Oklahoma Highway Patrol was on patrol on Interstate 35 in Oklahoma, 60 miles north of Oklahoma City, on April 19, 1995, when he observed a yellow 1977 Mercury Marquis in the opposite lane of traffic with no license plates. Hanger pursued the auto and stopped it, something he had done thousands of times in his police career.

When the driver reached for his license at the trooper's request, Hanger saw a bulge under his jacket. The bulge reminded Hanger of one of the dangers of his job: the armed felon. He ordered the driver out of the automobile and retrieved a loaded Glock semiautomatic pistol, two clips of ammunition, and a knife from under his jacket. The pistol had a live round in the chamber—a Black Talon bullet. The driver was arrested for driving without license plates, having no insurance, and carrying a concealed weapon. The time of the arrest was approximately 90 minutes after the infamous bombing of the Alfred P. Murrah Federal Building, which killed and injured hundreds of people. Trooper Hanger testified at the driver's trial on April 29, 1997.

The driver, of course, was Timothy J. McVeigh.

We all know how the government cracked the case and charged McVeigh with the worst terrorist attack against the United States of America until that date. But would he have been apprehended if Hanger had not made that routine traffic stop on I-35?

SOURCE: Peter Annin and Evan Thomas, "Judgment Day," *Newsweek* (March 24, 1997), p. 41.

by arresting key members for their criminal activities. The transformation of the former Soviet Union also deprived many leftist groups of a coherent ideology or spiritual patron. As a result, membership and support for these groups has declined.

Special-interest terrorist groups are also domestic threats. They differ from both extreme left-wing and right-wing terrorist groups because their members seek to resolve specific interests rather than pursue widespread political change. Members of such groups include animal rights advocates, supporters of environmental issues, and antiabortion advocates. Although some consider the causes that these groups represent understandable or even noteworthy, they remain separated from traditional law-abiding special interest groups because of their criminal activity. Groups such as the Animal Liberation Front (ALF) and the Earth Liberation Front (ELF) have used violent actions to attempt to force various segments of society, including the general public, to change their attitudes about issues they consider important.

These groups have released caged animals into the wild, targeted buildings where experimentation on animals have been conducted, damaged vehicles they feel are not environmentally friendly, and burned down new residential communities. In August 2003, several car dealerships in Southern California were targeted by ELF members who burned dozens of SUVs, as well as an auto dealership warehouse, and spray painted some vehicles with sayings such as "Fat, Lazy Americans." ELF has claimed responsibility for many arsons against commercial establishments that ELF members say damage the environment.[33]

In December 2005, federal agents made the most extensive arrest of eco-saboteurs in U.S. history, charging seven people with a series of arsons and vandalism that plagued the Pacific Northwest for nearly three years. Agents took six men and one woman into custody from Oregon to New York, tying them to nearly $5 million in arson and vandalism damage from 1998 to 2001. Several were members of ELF and ALF. Agents used a provision of the USA Patriot Act to close in on them by getting search warrants from a U.S. Magistrate in Oregon to search in other states for evidence.[34]

Radical, extremist, and hate groups have long presented a serious problem to society. Throughout a major part of our history, the Ku Klux Klan terrorized and killed thousands of citizens. In the 1960s and 1970s, radical hate groups, such as the Black Panthers and the Black Liberation Army, raged urban warfare against the police, maiming and killing scores of police officers. Also during that period of our history, militant student and antiwar

You Are There!

Agant _____

A Domestic Terrorist: The Unabomber

Thomas J. Mosser, an executive with the Young & Rubicam advertising firm in Manhattan, was killed by a mail bomb on December 10, 1994. The parcel had been mailed to his home.

The explosion and Mosser's murder were attributed to the work of a serial bomber known as the Unabomber, who was believed to be responsible for 14 other bombings or attempted bombings beginning in 1978. The FBI reports that 2 people died and 23 others were injured in these explosions, which occurred over some 16 years, as this man terrorized his fellow American citizens.

The sequence of events related to the Unabomber is

- A bomb exploded at Northwestern University in Illinois, May 25, 1978; a security guard was injured.
- A second person at Northwestern was injured on May 9, 1979, when a bomb exploded in the technical building.
- On American Airlines Flight 444 (Chicago to Boston), 12 persons suffered smoke inhalation injuries on November 15, 1979. This bomb was traced to a mailbag aboard the airliner.
- The president of United Airlines, Percy Wood, was injured by a bomb on June 10, 1980. Again, the bomb was in a package mailed to his home.
- A bomb in a business classroom at the University of Utah exploded on October 8, 1981.
- At Vanderbilt University in Nashville, a secretary was injured on May 5, 1982, when a bomb mailed to the head of the computer science department exploded.
- Two people were injured, one seriously, at the University of California, Berkeley, as a result of bombings: an electrical engineering professor on July 2, 1982, and a student on May 15, 1985.

- Alert employees of the Boeing Company in Washington State had a bomb safely dismantled on May 18, 1985, when they realized a mailed package contained an explosive device.
- On November 15, 1985, the research assistant to a psychology professor at the University of Michigan at Ann Arbor was injured when a bomb received at the professor's home exploded.
- On December 11, 1985, Hugh Campbell, the owner of a computer rental store in Sacramento, California, was killed by a bomb left at his store.
- In Salt Lake City, another employee in the computer industry was maimed by a bomb placed in a bag in the company parking lot on February 20, 1987.
- A geneticist at the University of California at San Francisco sustained injuries when he opened a package received in the mail at his home on June 22, 1993.
- A computer scientist at Yale University opened a package mailed to his office and was injured by a bomb on June 24, 1993.

The FBI was certain that these bombings were related and attributable to one suspect, the Unabomber. The bombs were all built from similar materials and had a comparable, sophisticated design.

In 1996, based on a tip provided by his brother, Theodore Kaczynski was arrested and charged with all the Unabomber attacks. At trial, he was found guilty and sentenced to life imprisonment.

SOURCE: John S. Dempsey, *An Introduction to Public and Private Investigations*, (Minneapolis/St. Paul: West, 1996), pp. 16–17.

---

groups caused tremendous problems for the police. Historically, in our nation, radical groups have been involved in assassinations, bombings, terrorism, and other crimes and acts of violence to protest the policies of the United States and to attempt to impose their views on all members of our society.

One noted extremist group was the Branch Davidians. A 51-day siege of the Branch Davidian compound in Waco, Texas, ended in April 1993 when 80 members of the sect died after a fire and a

shootout with police and federal agents. David Koresh, leader of the group, died of a gunshot wound to the head sometime during the blaze. Another controversial action against an extremist group occurred in 1992 when U.S. marshals tried to arrest white separatist Randall C. Weaver on firearms charges. During the resulting siege in Ruby Ridge, Idaho, Weaver's unarmed wife, Vicki, and his son, Sammy, age 14 (as well as U.S. Marshal William Degan) were killed. In 1995, the

U.S. government, without admitting guilt in the case, agreed to pay $3.1 million to Weaver and his three surviving children.[35] Regarding Ruby Ridge, one news source stated, "Like Waco, Ruby Ridge long ago entered the political mythology of the ultraright. Like Waco, it attests to the emergence of a reckless mentality that sullies the image of the FBI and plays straight into the hands of those who like to demagogue the federal government."[36]

In 2004, Mark Potok of the Southern Poverty Law Center, which tracks domestic hate and extremist groups, says that there are now about 750 virulent hate groups in the United States and the numbers are rising. However, he says that right-wing extremist activity has ebbed since its high-water mark in the 1990s, and there has been an erosion of these groups at the organizational level since the 2002 death of William Pierce, the founder and leader of the neo-Nazi National Alliance and the incarceration of Matt Hale of the World Church of the Creator.[37]

In 2006, furor over the illegal immigration issue in the United States has renewed attention on hate groups. Potok says that the number of racist groups operating in the United States today increased 5 percent compared with last year: "They think they've found an issue with racial overtones and a real resonance with the American public and they are exploiting it as effectively as they can."[38]

Anarchists also keep operating in the United States as they protest global and trade issues. Some of their members advocate violence and destruction of property and travel to trade meetings with the goal of disrupting the meetings and causing chaos and destruction in the streets.

Methods of Investigating Terrorism

As with many types of investigations, there are two primary methods of investigating acts of terrorism: proactive and reactive. In addition, there is the federal-local Joint Terrorism Task Force concept, which is described later in this chapter. These three methods together can help prevent and detect acts of terrorism before they occur, and when that is not possible, investigate their occurrences, determine who was involved in their commission, and bring the offenders to justice.[39]

Proactive Methods

Much of this chapter discusses proactive techniques that are in use constantly to prevent acts of terrorism before they occur. These methods include ongoing and coordinated planning, intelligence gathering, and investigating activity by various agencies.

Reactive Methods

Numerous reactive investigative methods can be used to investigate acts of terrorism after they occur, including response to the incident, crime scene processing and analysis, following up on leads and tips, use of informants, surveillance, and other normal investigative activities.

Response to the Incident The local law enforcement agency is usually the first responder to scenes of terrorist crimes—just as it is on any crime scene. These officers must follow the normal first-responder duties of rendering aid to the injured, arresting suspects, questioning witnesses, and other immediate response and investigatory issues. It is essential that they safeguard the scene and preserve the evidence for processing by laboratory personnel and arson and terrorist specialists. As with the crime of arson, much of the evidence is present in the debris that follows a terrorist explosion.

Crime Scene Processing and Analysis Crime scene specialists and trained personnel from the various federal, state, and local investigating units use their special skills to seek the means used to commit the crime and any evidence that might connect the crime to the persons responsible for it. As an example of the importance of crime scene processing and analysis, two small pieces of evidence were the keys to determining the cause of the Pan Am explosion over Lockerbie, Scotland. Investigators had painstakingly searched a crime scene of more than 845 square miles of debris to find this evidence.

How extensive are terrorist crime scenes? Consider the 2001 World Trade Center attack. When the jumbo jets crashed into the buildings, several things occurred. First, the explosive force of a plane entering the building destroyed much of the immediate internal structure and the victims within. The planes, just refueled for their flights, contained thousands of pounds of fuel. The ensuing fireball, reaching incredibly high temperatures, incinerated all in its path. The fuel then worked its way down to lower floors, continuing its destruction. Shortly after the initial explosion, the weakened building, with some of its steel infrastructure actually melting in the intense heat, collapsed under the weight of the crumbling upper floors. The result: millions of pounds of crime scene material and evidence.

The crime scene investigation was extensive. The first concern of this investigation was to account for and identify as many victims as possible. But before any identifications could be made, the remains had to be recovered. This required the detailed sifting of all the debris and material collected from the crime scene. Sifting was also conducted during the examination of the Oklahoma City bombing incident.

After suspected human remains were recovered from the debris, determinations needed to be made about their origin and identity. Efforts to identify recovered remains included such forensic disciplines as pathology, odontology, biology, and anthropology. For the most part, DNA was used to establish the identity of the deceased. Personal items found at the crime scene—such as jewelry and clothing—were also used for identification, but were considered presumptive in nature, because many of these items are not unique. Still, personal items provided investigators with information on the identity of the missing.

Following Up on Leads and Tips There must be canvasses and recanvasses, and interviews and reinterviews. (*Canvas* is an investigatory term for the search of an area for witnesses to an incident). Anyone with any information at all must be interviewed immediately. All leads must be followed through to their logical conclusions. Tip lines must be established and all tips must be followed up.

Use of Informants Informants can be very important in the investigation of terrorist incidents. A good example of the value of an informant's information was the February 1995 arrest of Ramzi Ahmed Yousef, ranked at the time as number one on the FBI's Most Wanted List and believed to be the main plotter behind the 1993 World Trade Center bombing in New York City. Yousef was the target of an international manhunt spanning several countries and thousands of miles. He was located and arrested based on information provided by an unexpected informer who simply walked into the American Embassy in Islamabad, Pakistan. Authorities believed the informer was seeking to collect the $2 million reward that the U.S. State Department was offering for information resulting in Yousef's arrest. After receiving the informant's information, a team of Pakistani police and American law enforcement officials was assembled and sent to the hotel room where Yousef was believed to be; the team broke down the door and rushed into the room and found Yousef lying on his bed, a suitcase of explosives nearby.[40]

Surveillance Surveillance is used in terrorist investigations to follow suspects identified as involved in the crime. (*Surveillance* is an investigatory term used for covertly following subjects in an investigation and recording their activities.) Other methods of surveillance or information-gathering techniques can also be used for intelligence purposes. Flight recorders in aircraft cockpits provide investigators with a multitude of details about a hijacking. Security cameras in public locations provide details on a terrorist's actions. Timothy McVeigh's truck was recorded on a security camera; terrorists involved in the September 11 attack were recorded on airport security systems. These types of surveillance systems are invaluable for the investigation of terrorist activities.

Post–September 11, 2001, Response to Terrorism and Homeland Defense

In the immediate aftermath of the terrorist attacks of September 11, 2001, strict security procedures were immediately instituted at airports, government buildings, cultural centers, and many other facilities. The FBI advised state and local law enforcement agencies to move to their highest level of alert and be prepared to respond to any further acts of terrorism. Armed National Guard troops supplemented airport security officers and local and state police in many jurisdictions. Military aircraft flew protective patrol over U.S. cities, and the

Coast Guard patrolled coastlines and ports. Some other immediate responses included expanding the intelligence community's ability to intercept and translate messages in Arabic, Farsi, and other languages; fortification of cockpits to prevent access by hijackers; placing federal air marshals on commercial flights; and more intensive screening of luggage.

Approximately 4,000 FBI special agents were assigned to the September 11, 2001, attacks case nationwide, and by early October, the FBI was handling more than a quarter-million potential leads and tips. It sent all law enforcement agencies a list of more than 190 witnesses, suspects, and others the FBI wanted to interview and, in the two months following the attack, the Justice Department had arrested more than 1,000 people suspected of having links to terrorist groups.[41] The 9/11 terrorist acts were attributed to the multinational terrorist group al Qaeda (the Base) operated by Osama bin Laden, a known terrorist residing in Afghanistan, sheltered by the ruling Taliban government.

On October 7, 2001, the United States launched a full-scale military assault—a war—against Afghanistan, the Taliban and its allies, al Qaeda, and Osama bin Laden. As a result of this military action, the Taliban government was replaced in Afghanistan, many members of al Qaeda were killed or arrested, but to the best of our current knowledge, Osama bin Laden remains at large.

Much has been written about the failure of U.S. law enforcement, particularly federal law enforcement, to deal with terrorism. Some report that the failure to follow up leads and analyze information made the efforts of terrorists to commit terrorist attacks against America easier. Others reported that a major flaw of counterterrorism measures was a lack of interagency cooperation and data sharing.[42]

To address these concerns, on October 8, 2001, President Bush signed Executive Order 13228, which established the Office of Homeland Security.[43] The office's mission was to develop and coordinate the implementation of a comprehensive national strategy to secure the United States from threats and attacks. The office coordinated the executive branch's efforts to detect, prepare for, prevent, and respond to terrorist attacks within this country. The president also established a Homeland Security Council that was responsible for advising and assisting him with all aspects of security. The council consisted of the president and vice president, the secretary of the treasury, the secretary of defense, the attorney general, the secretary of health and human services, the secretary of transportation, the director of the Federal Emergency Management Agency (FEMA), the director of the FBI, the director of the Central Intelligence Agency, and the assistant to the president for homeland security.[44]

On October 26, 2001, President Bush signed into law the USA Patriot Act—Uniting and Strengthening America by Providing Appropriate Tools Required to Intercept and Obstruct Terrorism,[45] which gave law enforcement personnel new abilities to search, seize, detain, or eavesdrop in their pursuit of possible terrorists. The law expanded the FBI's wiretapping and electronic surveillance authority and allowed nationwide jurisdiction for search warrants and electronic surveillance devices, including legal expansion of those devices to e-mail and the Internet. The Patriot Act also included money-laundering provisions and set strong penalties for anyone harboring or financing terrorists. It also established new punishments for possession of biological weapons and made it a federal crime to commit an act of terrorism against a mass transit system. The bill also allowed law enforcement agents to detain terrorism suspects for as long as seven days without filing charges against them.[46] The Patriot Act is covered more thoroughly later in this chapter.

In November 2001, the president signed into law the Aviation and Transportation Security Act, which among other things established the Transportation Security Administration (TSA) within the Department of Transportation to protect the nation's transportation systems and ensure freedom of movement for people and commerce. This new agency assumed the duties formerly provided by the Federal Aviation Administration (FAA). The TSA recruited thousands of security personnel to perform screening duties at commercial airports and significantly expanded the federal air marshals program. It also created the positions of federal security directors to be directly responsible for security at airports, developed new passenger boarding procedures, trained pilots and flight crews in hijacking scenarios, and required all airport personnel to undergo background checks.[47]

Polls conducted immediately following the 9/11 attacks revealed that an overwhelming majority of Americans—approximately 75 percent—thought it necessary to give up some personal freedoms for the sake of security.[48]

You Are There!

Seeking a Job with the U.S. Department of Homeland Security (DHS)

Persons interested in applying for Department of Homeland Security positions should visit the USAJobs electronic portal to governmentwide opportunities. From that site, they can search for current DHS employment opportunities job category, location, salary, and more.

DHS job announcements provide important information about job qualifications, duties, salary, duty location, benefits, and security requirements. Persons can view this site to determine if their interests, education, and professional background will make them good candidates for the job.

All DHS jobs require U.S. citizenship, and most require successful completion of a full background investigation. Applicants may also be required to submit to drug tests.

SOURCE: U.S. Department of Homeland Security, *Working with DHS: Job Seekers*, retrieved December 15, 2005, from http://www.dhs.

Later, in June 2002, the president proposed creating a new cabinet-level agency, the U.S. Department of Homeland Security (DHS), to replace the Office of Homeland Security. With the new cabinet agency, duties formerly belonging to other government agencies were merged, including border and transportation security; emergency preparedness and response; chemical, biological, radiological, and nuclear countermeasures; and information analysis and infrastructure protection.[49] The new DHS went into effect in 2003.

In the six months following September 11, 2001, $10.6 billion was spent on creating new mechanisms for homeland security, responding to and investigating terrorist threats, and providing security for likely terrorist targets.[50] In 2002, in response to public demand, the president and Congress appointed a blue ribbon national commission to investigate the attacks. It was called the *National Commission on Terrorist Attacks upon the United States,* and popularly known as the 9/11 Commission. Its charge was to investigate how the nation was unprepared for these terrorist attacks, how they happened, and how the nation could avoid such a repeat tragedy. Its final report, the

9/11 Commission Report: The Final Report of the National Commission on Terrorist Attacks upon the United States, was released in 2004 and will be discussed later in this chapter.[51]

Federal Law Enforcement Efforts for Homeland Security

The major federal law enforcement efforts for **homeland security** involve the Department of Homeland Security, the FBI, and some other federal agencies.

Department of Homeland Security (DHS)

After much debate, study, and planning in the aftermath of the terrorist attacks of September 11, 2001, the cabinet-level U.S. **Department of Homeland Security (DHS)** was established in March 2003.[52] (See Table 15.1.)

The new agency merged 22 previously disparate domestic agencies into one department to protect the nation against threats to the homeland and consists of more than 170,000 employees. The creation of DHS was the most significant transformation of the U.S. government since 1947 when President Harry S. Truman merged the various branches of the U.S. Armed Forces into the Department of Defense to better coordinate the nation's defense against military threats. DHS represents a similar consolidation, both in style and substance. The DHS includes former duties of many agencies, including the Coast Guard, U.S. Customs Service, the Secret Service, the Immigration and Naturalization Service, and the Transportation Security Administration, along with numerous other federal communications, science, and technology agencies. The DHS does not include the FBI, CIA, or National Security Agency, but these agencies are required to share their data with the department's new intelligence center.

The department's first priority is to protect the nation against further terrorist attacks. The department's agencies analyze threats and intelligence, guard our borders and airports, protect our critical

You Are There!

Career Opportunity Areas with the Department of Homeland Security (DHS)

The DHS reports the following career opportunity areas:

- *Office of the Secretary:* Employees work in multiple offices contributing to the overall Homeland Security mission.
- *Office of Management:* Employees work in one of a variety of critical areas, from human resources and administration to budgeting, procurement, and information technology (IT), making certain that the right resources and systems are in place to achieve Homeland Security's mission.
- *Office of Inspector General:* Employees work side-by-side with special agents, attorneys, engineers, and IT experts to prevent and detect fraud, waste, and abuse in Homeland Security programs and operations.
- *Border and Transportation Security (BTS):* These employees secure our nation's air, land, and sea borders. BTS employees also protect our country's transportation systems and official ports of entry, and enforce the nation's immigration laws. Four agencies carry out this mission, including U.S. Customs and Border Protection (CBP) employees who prevent terrorists and terrorist weapons from entering the United States while facilitating the flow of legitimate trade and travel; U.S. Immigration and Customs Enforcement (ICE) employees who enforce immigration and customs laws, safeguard U.S. commercial aviation, and protect federal facilities; U.S. Transportation Security Administration (TSA) employees who help to secure our transportation infrastructure from future terrorist acts in intelligence, regulation enforcement and inspection positions; and Federal Law Enforcement Training Center (FLETC) whose employees develop

the skills, knowledge, and professionalism of law enforcers from over 80 federal agencies.

- *Federal Emergency Management Agency (FEMA):* These employees prevent losses from disasters whenever possible, and assist when they do happen.
- *Information Analysis and Infrastructure Protection (IAIP):* Employees apply their skills and talents to help deter, prevent and mitigate acts of terrorism by identifying and assessing threats, mapping them against our vulnerabilities, issuing warnings and supporting the implementation of protective measures to secure the homeland.
- *Science and Technology (S&T):* Employees plan, fund, and manage research and development programs in technical fields to ensure that federal, state, and local responders have the scientific resources to protect our homeland.
- *U.S. Citizenship and Immigration Services (USCIS):* Employees are responsible for adjudicating and processing the host of applications and forms necessary to ensure the immigration of people and their families to the United States, from initial stages through their transition, to permanent residence, and finally to citizenship.
- *U.S. Coast Guard:* Civilian and military personnel work to save lives, enforce the law, operate ports and waterways, and protect the environment.
- *U.S. Secret Service:* These employees have the dual missions of protecting our nation's leaders, and conducting criminal investigations involving law enforcement, security, information technology, communications, administration, intelligence, forensics, and other specialized fields.

Source: Department of Homeland Security, *Working with DHS: Job Seekers: Career Opportunity Areas.* Retrieved December 4, 2005, from http://www.dhs.gov.

infrastructure, and coordinate the responses of our nation for future emergencies.

To understand the importance of the DHS to our homeland security, consider that 730 million people travel on commercial aircraft each year; more than 700 million pieces of baggage are screened for explosives each year; 11.2 million trucks and 2.2 million rail cars cross into the United States each year; and 7,500 foreign flagships make 51,000 calls in U.S. ports annually.[53]

The DHS controls immigration into the United States through its US-VISIT Program. US-VISIT is

TABLE 15.1 U.S. Department of Homeland Security (DHS) Organization— Major Subunits

Border and Transportation Security (BTS)

    Transportation Security Administration (TSA)

    Customs and Border Protection (CBP)

    Immigrations and Customs Enforcement (ICE)

    Federal Law Enforcement Training Center (FLETC)

Emergency Preparedness and Response (EP&R)

    Federal Emergency Management Agency (FEMA)

Information Analysis and Infrastructure Protection (IAIP)

    Homeland Security Operations Center (HSOC)

    Information Analysis (IA)

    Infrastructure Protection (IP)

Science and Technology (S&T)

    Office of National Laboratories

    Homeland Security Laboratories

    Homeland Security Advanced Research Projects Agency (HSARPA)

Office of Management

U.S. Citizenship and Immigration Services (USCIS)

    U.S. Citizenship and Immigration Services

    Office of Citizenship

    National Customer Service Center

U.S. Coast Guard

U.S. Secret Service (USSS)

SOURCE: U.S. Department of Homeland Security, retrieved August 11, 2006, from http://www.dhs.gov.

You Are There!

Enormous Responsibilities for U.S. Border Protection

- The United States has 5,525 miles of border with Canada and 1,989 miles with Mexico.
- The U.S. maritime border includes 95,000 miles of shoreline and a 3.4 million mile exclusive economic zone with 350 official ports of entry.
- Each year, more than 500 million people cross the borders into the United States, some 330 million of whom are noncitizens.
- More than 730 million people travel on commercial aircraft each year, and more than 700 million pieces of baggage are screened for explosives each year.
- Approximately 11.2 million trucks and 2.2 million railcars cross into the United States each year.
- 7,500 foreign flagships make 51,000 calls in U.S. ports annually

SOURCE: U.S. Department of Homeland Security, retrieved August 18, 206, from http://www.dhs.gov.

part of a continuum of security measures that begins outside U.S. borders and continues through a visitor's arrival in and departure from the United States. The program applies to all visitors entering the United States and is a top priority for DHS because it enhances security for our citizens and visitors while facilitating legitimate travel and trade across our borders. The program helps secure the borders, facilitate the entry and exit process, and enhance the integrity of our immigration system while respecting the privacy of our visitors.[54]

The TSA is on the front lines of the nation's efforts to secure air transportation from terrorism.

Since 2002, federal rules have required that the TSA conduct security inspections of all air passengers and air travel. By 2006, TSA had about 43,000 screeners. TSA air marshals are deployed on flights around the world. The number of marshals is classified. They blend in with passengers and rely on their training, including investigative techniques, criminal terrorist behavior recognition, firearms proficiency, aircraft specific tactics, and close quarter self-defense measures to protect the flying public. Air marshals work in plainclothes, in teams of two, or sometimes more. They board airplanes before passengers, survey the cabin, and watch passengers as they walk toward their seats.[55]

TSA federal air marshals used fatal force for the first time in December 2005 at Miami International Airport when they shot and killed an airlines passenger who claimed to have a bomb and was running out of a plane onto a jet way. The man's wife, who was traveling with him, claimed he was mentally ill.[56]

U.S. Customs and Border Protection (CBP) is responsible for securing our borders while facilitating the flow of legitimate trade and travel. It protects 5,000 miles of border with Canada,

You Are There!

A Typical Day at U.S. Customs and Border Protection (CBP)

On a typical day in 2005, U.S. Customs and Border Protection (CBP):

Processed more than

- 1,181,605 passengers and pedestrians, including 630,976 aliens
- 69,370 truck, rail, and sea containers
- 235,732 incoming international air passengers
- 71,858 passengers/crew arriving by ship
- 333,226 incoming privately owned vehicles
- 79,107 shipments of goods approved for entry
- $81,834,298 in fees, duties, and tariffs
- 493 terrorism-related inquiries

Executed more than

- 62 arrests at ports of entry
- 3,257 apprehensions between ports for illegal entry

Seized an average of

- 2,187 pounds of narcotics in 65 seizures at ports of entry
- 3,354 pounds of narcotics in 20 seizures between ports of entry
- $77,360 in undeclared or illicit currency and $329,119 worth of fraudulent commercial merchandize at ports of entry
- 49 vehicles between ports of entry
- 1,145 prohibited meat, plant materials, or animals products, including 147 agricultural pests at ports of entry

Refused entry of

- 868 noncitizens at our ports of entry
- 45 criminal aliens attempting to enter the United States

Intercepted more than

- 210 fraudulent documents

- 1 traveler for terrorism/national security concerns
- 1 stowaway

Rescued more than

- 4 illegal crossers in dangerous conditions between our ports of entry

Deployed more than

- 1,200 canine enforcement teams
- 13,400 vehicles, 85 aircraft, 75 watercraft, 130 horses on equestrian patrol, and 400 all-terrain vehicles

Utilized

- 265 remote video surveillance cameras
- 11,938 underground sensors

Protected more than

- 5,000 miles of border with Canada
- 1,900 miles of border with Mexico
- 95,000 miles of shoreline

Employed approximately 42,000 employees, including the following enforcement personnel,

- 18,000 officers
- 11,300 Border Patrol agents
- 1,800 agricultural specialists
- 1,150 air and marine officers and pilots

Managed

- 317 ports of entry
- 20 sectors with 33 border checkpoints between the ports of entry

SOURCE: U.S. Customs and Border Protection, *A Typical Day at U.S. Customs and Border Protection (CBP)*, retrieved August 18, 2006, from http://www.cbp.gov

1,900 miles of border with Mexico, and 95,000 miles of shoreline. It employs 42,000 employees, including the following enforcement personnel: 18,000 officers, 11,300 Border Patrol agents, 1,800 agriculture specialists, and 1,150 air and marine officers and pilots.[57] In June 2006, the U.S. National Guard was deployed to the southern border to assist the Border Patrol.[58]

U.S. Immigration and Customs Enforcement (ICE) is responsible for the enforcement of federal immigration laws, customs laws, and air security laws. It targets illegal immigrants; the people, money and materials that support terrorism; and other criminal activities.[59] On the front lines of our efforts in maritime security is the U.S. Coast Guard. The Coast Guard protects ports and waterways.[60]

The Federal Bureau of Investigation (FBI)

The Federal Bureau of Investigation (FBI) has traditionally been the lead federal agency in the response to and investigation of terrorism. In May 2002, in the wake of massive criticism that the FBI had failed to properly handle information that could have led to the prevention of the September 11 attacks, FBI Director Robert S. Mueller completely reorganized the bureau and created a new strategic focus for the agency. The FBI's new focus placed the following on its first three priorities: (1) protecting the United States from terrorist attack, (2) protecting the United States against foreign intelligence operations and espionage, and (3) protecting the United States against cyber-based attacks and high-technology crimes. The main organizational improvements Mueller implemented in a complete restructuring of the **counterterrorism** activities of the Bureau and a shift from a reactive to a proactive orientation were the development of special squads to coordinate national and international investigations; a reemphasis on the **Joint Terrorism Task Forces (JTTF)**; enhanced analytical capabilities with personnel and technological improvements; a permanent shift of additional resources to counterterrorism; the creation of a more mobile, agile, and flexible national terrorism response; and targeted recruitment to acquire agents, analysts, translators, and others with specialized skills and backgrounds.[61]

Possibly the most important unit in investigating terrorism in the United States is the FBI–local JTTF. Before the establishment of these task forces, ad hoc task forces of local and federal authorities would be established to investigate each new terrorist case as they occurred and then disbanded after the investigation. The new concept ensures that the unit remains in place, becoming a close-knit, cohesive group capable of addressing the complex problems inherent in terrorism investigations. Because federal, state, and local law enforcement resources have been combined in these task forces, there is effective maximization of resources, provision of sophisticated investigative and technological resources, and linkage to all federal government resources in the United States and worldwide.[62]

The objectives of these task forces are twofold: to respond to and investigate terrorist incidents or terrorist-related criminal activity (reactive measures), and to investigate domestic and foreign terrorist groups and individuals targeting or operating in the area for the purpose of detecting, preventing, and prosecuting their criminal activity (proactive measures).

The key to the success of the JTTF is the melding of personnel and talent from various law enforcement agencies in a single, focused unit. The local police members bring the insights that come from years of living and working with the people in their area. They have usually advanced through their careers from uniformed precinct patrol to various detective duties before being assigned to the task force. Each of the participating agencies similarly contributes its own resources and areas of expertise to the team. The integration of the many agencies, each bringing its own unique skills and investigative specialties to the task force, makes these units formidable in combating terrorism.

In an article in the *FBI Law Enforcement Bulletin,* Robert A. Martin, former deputy inspector for the New York City Police Department (NYPD) and former member of the

You Are There!

FBI Priorities Post–September 11, 2001

- Protect the United States from terrorist attack
- Protect the United States against foreign intelligence operations and espionage
- Protect the United States against cyber-based attacks and high-technology crimes
- Combat public corruption at all levels
- Protect civil rights
- Combat transnational and national criminal organizations and enterprises
- Combat major white-collar crime
- Combat significant violent crime
- Support federal, state, local, and international partners
- Upgrade technology to successfully perform the FBI's mission

SOURCE: Federal Bureau of Investigation, retrieved August 21, 2006, from http://www.fbi.gov.

Homeland Security

JIM NIELSEN

Jim Nielsen is a lieutenant with the Moorhead Police Department, Moorhead, Minnesota. He has been a police officer for more than 22 years and is a graduate of the Southern Police Administrative Officers Course.

I am a lieutenant employed by the Moorhead Police Department, in Moorhead, Minnesota. The 50 sworn officers in our department serve a population of 33,000 residents within a larger metropolitan area of 175,000 along the borders of Minnesota and North Dakota. Our department is highly service-oriented, and we do not experience a large amount of serious crime.

Our experiences with homeland security have been positive. New initiatives have allowed us to purchase a great deal of needed equipment and to improve communications among our regional emergency service providers. We also receive much more intelligence information than we did prior to 9/11, via two fusion centers. One of these is the Minnesota Department of Homeland Security, which sends us regular e-mail bulletins containing statewide, regional, and national intelligence information related to homeland security, including information from federal law enforcement agencies. We also receive email intelligence bulletins from a regional center encompassing Minnesota, North Dakota, and Manitoba, Canada, that are focused on our immediate region. They contain information specific to the nearby border crossings into Canada, some of it provided by the Royal Canadian Mounted Police (RCMP).

In a broader sense, our officers now realize they cannot take any suspicious activity for granted. Five years ago I do not believe that our city's water supply was a high security issue, but today it obviously is. Our city does not have any installations that have required an increase in our staffing or a significant increase in our calls for service, but we do place an increased emphasis on planning our involvement in major community events since 9/11.

However, the greatest benefit our department has obtained as a result of homeland security efforts is the purchase of radio equipment which allows all emergency personnel in our region to instantly communicate with each other. Through a combination of three grants the Fargo Metropolitan Statistical Area (Fargo MSA) has received over eight million dollars of funding for radio equipment. Our region includes all emergency services provided in Clay County, Minnesota, and Cass County, North Dakota. This includes the cities of Moorhead, Minnesota, and Fargo, North Dakota.

Prior to receiving the grant, some of the area's law enforcement agencies were using VHF radio frequencies, while others were using UHF radio frequencies. VHF radios could not communicate with UHF radios. The region's two full-time fire departments also used radios operating on different radio bands. These grants allowed us to purchase mobile radios, portable radios, and voting repeaters which allow all the region's law enforcement agencies, EMS providers, and fire departments to communicate instantly with each other.

The channels on all mobile and portable radios in our region are now uniformly labeled, allowing officers to easily find the channel they are directed to use in an emergency. The radio system is digital and operates on VHF frequencies. Law enforcement agencies can also send encrypted communications from both their mobile and portable radios. Formerly, there were some small areas of our city where the portable radios we used did not always transmit reliably. We now have clear communication on portable radio throughout the city, because the grants allowed us to replace our existing voting repeaters with new digital voting repeaters, and to add two additional voting repeaters.

Prior to receiving this funding, the Red River Valley SWAT team, the regional tactical team to which our department belongs, had to purchase portable radios just for their team's use. The different agency's radios were not compatible because of their different frequencies, and they could not send encrypted transmissions. Now the team can not only send such transmissions, but use the same portable radios their members use as part of their routine law enforcement functions. They can also use any agency's repeaters to speak directly to any assisting agencies.

Our region already had a joint dispatch center called the Red River Valley Regional Dispatch Center, a shared law enforcement records system, and a joint mobile data computer system. Obtaining the funding for a regional radio system was another step making our regional providers of emergency services better able to routinely work together. In the event of a disaster, this new radio system will dramatically improve our ability to serve the citizens of our region.

FBI-NYPD JTTF, describes the operation of the task force:

> The FBI special agents bring vast investigative experience from assignments all over the world. The FBI legal attachés, assigned to U.S. embassies throughout the world, provide initial law enforcement information on international terrorism cases. Since many terrorist events are committed by suspects from other countries, it is necessary to gain the cooperation of law enforcement agencies from the countries of origin. Interagency cooperation is essential when investigating crimes committed internationally. The FBI will work in tandem with other agencies to develop investigative leads.[63]

Before September 11, 2001, the United States had 35 formal JTTFs. After the attacks, JTTFs were added to each of the FBI's 56 field offices, as well as 10 stand-alone, formalized JTTFs in the FBI's largest resident agencies (resident agencies are maintained in smaller cities and towns across the county).[64]

Other Federal Agencies

In addition to the DHS, the FBI, and the U.S. military, several other federal agencies are involved with crisis activities involving terrorism. One example is the Bureau of Alcohol, Tobacco, Firearms and Explosives (ATF), which has special responsibilities in cases of arson and explosives.

Many argue that the federal government has still not done enough for homeland security. In 2005, it was reported that the government has missed dozens of deadlines set by Congress after 9/11 for developing ways to protect planes, ships, and railways from terrorists. A member of the House Homeland Security Committee stated, "The incompetence we recently saw with FEMA's leadership [Hurricane Katrina] appears to exist throughout the Homeland Security Department. Our nation is still vulnerable." He said that the government has yet to develop a comprehensive plan to protect roads, bridges, tunnels, power plants, pipelines, and dams. He said that a broad plan to protect levies and dams might have helped prevent the New Orleans levies from being breached.[65]

State and Local Law Enforcement Efforts for Homeland Security

Although the previous section of this chapter emphasized the role of our national government in responding to and combating terrorism and homeland defense, we must remember that each act of terrorism is essentially a local problem that must be addressed by local authorities.

D. Douglas Bodrero, former commissioner of public safety for the state of Utah and a senior research associate with the Institute for Intergovernmental Research, writing in 1999, stated, "Every act of terrorism occurring within the United States remains local in nature. . . ."[66] Bodrero, writing again in 2002, reiterated his emphasis that terrorism is primarily a concern for local governments,

> The planning or execution of terrorist acts on U.S. soil are the concern of every law enforcement agency, regardless of size or area of responsibility. Every terrorist event, every act of planning and preparation for that event occurs in some local law enforcement agency's jurisdiction. No agency is closer to the activities within its community than the law enforcement agency that has responsibility and jurisdiction for protecting that community.[67]

Expressing similar concerns in 2002, William B. Burger, chief of the North Miami Beach, Florida, police department and the president of the International Association of Chiefs of Police (IACP), stated,

> State and local law enforcement agencies in the United States—and the 700,000 officers they employ—patrol the streets of our cities and towns daily and, as a result, have an intimate knowledge of those communities they serve. This unique relationship provides these agencies with a tremendous edge in effectively tracking down information related to terrorists."[68]

Even after the 1993 World Trade Center bombing, most state and local law enforcement administrators continued to view terrorism primarily as an international threat. Many administrators believed that metropolitan centers such as New York, Miami, and Chicago remained the most likely targets. A

© Joe Raedle/Getty Images

A Citrus County sheriff's deputy stands guard at the entrance to the Florida Power Corporation's nuclear power plant in Crystal River, Florida. Nuclear power plants around the country have increased security measures since the September 11 terrorist attacks, placing an increased demand upon local law enforcement agencies around the country.

1995 National Institute of Justice (NIJ) study confirmed that state and local law enforcement agencies viewed the threat of terrorism as real, but their response varied widely according to the size and resources of the agency and the nature of the threat in its community. Major cities developed prevention and preparation programs, often in cooperation with the FBI and its JTTF; in contrast, smaller cities and counties usually operated on their own. Antiterrorism resources varied based on the existing threat potential. Some smaller jurisdictions developed regional alliances to address specific extremist groups and organizations operating locally.[69]

These perceptions changed after the 1995 Oklahoma City explosion. Bodrero wrote that since then most jurisdictions have realized the threat presented by extremist individuals and groups and now assess the threat that such groups pose to their respective communities and to related operational planning and readiness issues.[70]

Although the FBI maintains the lead federal role in the investigation and prevention of domestic terrorism, every terrorist act, as Bodrero and Burger wrote, is essentially local. Local law enforcement officers will respond first to a terrorist threat or incident and are the closest to sense the discontent among terrorist movements; they can monitor the activity of extremist causes, respond

to hate crimes, and serve as the foundation for an effective assessment of threatening activities in their own communities.

In 2002, a four-day conference was held on the effect of community policing and homeland security. Conference speakers agreed that the community should be involved in countering any chronic crime problem facing the community including terrorism. In the keynote address, former U.S. Attorney General John Ashcroft noted that the terrorists who committed the atrocities of September 11, 2001, lived in local communities for many months, moving unnoticed in neighborhoods and public places. He emphasized that citizens must become active stakeholders in securing their own safety by being trained by police agencies to become alert observers of dangerous signals, which can result in the supplying of valuable information to law enforcement agencies in their preventive efforts.[71]

In the aftermath of the September 11, 2001, terrorist attacks, state and local agencies are being asked to play a bigger part as first responders to terrorist incidents and in gathering intelligence. Federal funding has been made available to state and local law enforcement for the development and enhancement of law enforcement information systems relating to terrorism with an emphasis on information sharing.[72] Some have even suggested changing our traditional concept of policing because of terrorism. Melchor C. De Guzman of Indiana University South Bend in a 2002 speech at a symposium on the changing role of criminal justice agencies in a time of terror stated that the attacks of September 11th clearly brought to the limelight not only the false sense of security of the United States but also its vulnerability to the violence of terrorism on its domestic soil. He said that our society must reexamine and revise our strategic thinking and paradigms about the way domestic security is maintained and that public policing has to make the necessary adjustments to contribute to the immediate security requirements of the nation. He concluded by stating,

> The roles and strategies of the police are shaped by the need of the times. In this time of terror, police are required to be more vigilant and perhaps more suspicious. They are required to be more proactive both in detecting and investigating acts of terrorism. The community policing roles that they have embraced for the last decade should be examined in the light of its opposing tenets to

You Are There!

They Stopped the Terrorists Before They Could Attack

The police officers who patrol New York City, the NYPD, are called New York's Finest—an accolade they deserve every day. The finest of the Finest has to be NYPD's elite emergency service unit (ESU). These are the men and women who risk life and limb to climb to the tops of the city's myriad bridges and skyscrapers to rescue potential "jumpers" from themselves, enter blazing buildings, and breathe life back into cardiac victims and others who are near death. The NYPD's ESU is also the city's special weapons and tactical (SWAT) team. They are the Marine Corps of the city, called in daily with their automatic weapons to combat armed terrorists and maniacs. Their action on July 31, 1997, was just one of the heroic things cops in New York did that day, but it saved the city from certain disaster.

The events began unfolding with the frantic waving of a man along a darkened Brooklyn street. A Long Island Railroad police officer, on patrol in his radio car, observed the man acting irrationally at 10:45 PM on July 30, 1997. He was repeatedly screaming in Arabic, "Bomba" and cupping his hands and moving them apart to mimic an explosion. The officer took the man to the 88th Precinct station house in Fort Greene, Brooklyn, where an interpreter determined that bombs and plans to blow up New York City subways were at a house at 248 Fourth Avenue in the Park Slope neighborhood.

Just before dawn on July 31, the police closed off scores of blocks in Park Slope and called on the ESU to enter the building. The officers entered the cramped apartment, led by hero cops Joseph Dolan, age 34, and David Martinez, age 38, shouting, "Police! Don't move!" whereupon one man reached for one of the officers' weapons and another reached for one of four toggle switches on a pipe bomb. Officers Dolan and Martinez shot both suspects before any actions against them could be taken. A 9-inch pipe packed with gunpowder and nails and a device in which four pipes had been wrapped together and equipped with toggle-switch detonators were among the explosives removed by the police. Further investigation revealed that the men were Middle Eastern terrorists who had planned to carry out a suicide bombing of the New York City subways on that very day.

The police action came a day after a suicide bombing in a Jerusalem market had killed and injured scores. The lives of over a million New York City commuters and residents were disrupted by the police action and investigation, but no injuries or deaths ensued. Says Officer Martinez, "I felt a little sick when I woke up the next day. I started to realize I almost wasn't here. I started to think of the magnitude of what these people were going to do. They would have killed hundreds of people, little children, mothers, people they don't even know. It's a great feeling to know in some way you helped alter the future."

Mayor Rudolph Giuliani said, "They prevented a major terrorist attack from taking place."

SOURCES: "Heroes of Bomb Scare: Courageous Cops of Emergency Unit Honored," *Daily News,* August 3, 1997, p. 3; Rocco Parascandola, "Hail Storm for City's Finest of Heroes," *New York Post,* August 3, 1997, p. 1; William K. Rashbaum and Patrice O'Shaughnessy, "Raiders Knew Lethal Risk: With Seconds to Spare, Cops Nearly 'Naked' vs. Bomb," *Daily News,* Aug. 3, 1997, p. 2; And "They Saved the City: New York Would Be Counting Its Dead If These Hero Cops Had Not Acted," *New York Post,* August 3, 1997, p. 1.

the demands of providing police service in time of terror. The police should lean toward a more legalistic style and begin to apply their innate talent for sensing danger. This is the philosophical shift that circumstances demand. This is probably the role that the American people demand from their law enforcement officers.[73]

As an example of local efforts to address the problems of terrorism, the New York City Police Department created two new deputy commissioner positions in 2002, a deputy commissioner for intelligence and a deputy commissioner for counterterrorism. It filled these positions with former high-ranking officials from the Central Intelligence Agency and the Marine Corps. The NYPD also created the Counter Terrorism Bureau (CTB) of one thousand officers. The CTB consists of the Counter Terrorism Division as its intelligence and research arm and the JTTF as its investigative arm. New equipment, such as radiation-detection gear

You Are There!

New York City's Counter Terrorism Initiative—Operation Atlas

Since September 11, 2001, the NYPD has instituted numerous counter terrorism initiatives, including Operation Atlas. Core elements of Operation Atlas are as follows:

- Increased personnel deployment
- Transit system security
- Patrol operations/increased coverage
- Intelligence
- Airspace security

Increased Personnel Deployment

- Increased deployments of Harbor, Aviation, and Emergency Service Units.
- COBRA (Chemical, Biological or Radiological Actions) Team deployments.
- SAMPSON team deployments.
- Harbor units increased protection of commuter ferries.
- Bomb sniffing dogs are assigned to the Staten Island Ferry.
- ARCHANGEL teams, composed of Emergency Services Personnel, bomb experts and investigators have been staged strategically in the city.
- HAMMER teams, police and fire department experts in hazardous materials, are deployed jointly.
- Heavily armed HERCULES teams are deployed randomly through the city.
- Counter assault teams in unmarked armored vehicles with heavily armed officers are deployed.

- Counter terrorism inspectors are coordinating mobilization drills.

Transit System Security

- Transportation Bureau is working closely with the Metropolitan Transit Authority and the Port Authority to ensure war-related precautions are in place.
- The National Guard is assisting in patrolling the subway system.
- Train Order Maintenance Sweeps, "TOMS," are deployed to arrest fare evaders and others, whose initial low-level offenses are often precursors of more serious crimes in the subway system. TOMS may discourage or even intercept a terrorist attack.
- Mobile Arrest Processing Centers, MAPC buses, are on standby.
- Additional police officers are patrolling high-density transit locations such as Times Square, Grand Central, and Penn Station.
- Undercover teams are riding the subways.
- Radiation detection is being used in the subways.
- Conducting "surge responses" in which large numbers of officers saturate a given subway station.
- Highway patrol officers are on 12-hour tours.
- Checkpoints are in place along 96th Street and at all bridges and tunnels into the city. Checkpoint locations are subject to unannounced change.
- Vehicles parked in front of sensitive locations are being towed.

and biohazard suits, is now standard issue for all NYPD officers.

By 2005, about 1,000 NYPD employees were still working directly on terrorism-related issues every day, including active investigations. The NYPD also has its own liaison officers working full time in Britain, France, Israel, Canada, Singapore, Jordan, the Dominican Republic, and Australia, filing daily reports on developments there, as well as a group of 80 highly trained civilians working on terrorism. They build profiles of possible terrorists by drawing on confidential informants, surveillance, and links with other law enforcement agencies around the world. The civilians educate the department about terrorist tactics and help search for threats in the city. The NYPD's CTB also has

Arabic and Farsi linguists and dozens of detectives and liaison officers from other city and state agencies. The department's telephone terrorist tip line receives about 150 calls a day.[74]

The following description in the media gives a sense of the security changes in the New York City area a year and a half after 9/11,

As the United States wages war on Iraq, New Yorkers and others across the region are witnessing an extraordinary state of heightened security. Police officers are armed like assault troops outside prominent buildings, police boats are combing the waterfronts and trucks are being inspected at bridges and tunnels. . . . No one can live or

Patrol Operations/Increased Coverage

- Counter Terrorism inspectors are working 12-hour shifts guaranteeing round-the-clock coverage by executive staff.
- Deploying critical response vans to events, or simply to stop at certain locations, like hotels, restaurants, landmarks, or tourist attractions.
- The Financial District is under intense 24-hour coverage.
- The Counter Terrorism Bureau is supplying terrorist-related updates to APPLE, an association of New York City Corporate and Institutional Security Directors.
- Each Patrol Borough commander has stand alone plans in place to act as an autonomous police department should police headquarters command and control become disabled.
- Systematic citywide search for any radioactive material or devices.
- Prepared to use up to 4,000 school safety officers in the event of an emergency. This includes using them to evacuate children, as well as adults, from the schools and to transport police resources throughout the city. They may also be used to staff emergency shelters.

Intelligence

- Daily assessments to determine which synagogues and other houses of worship may merit additional protection.

- Daily assessments to determine which hotels, museums, landmarks, and other attractions merit additional protection.
- Fuel depots in the greater metropolitan area are under greater surveillance.
- Intelligence personnel continue to brief garage owners and attendants about suspect vehicles that might be left at parking lots in Manhattan.
- In cooperation with New Jersey authorities, sites in New Jersey where radioactive material could be stored clandestinely, in close proximity to NYC are being inspected.
- Daily assessment regarding which foreign missions merit additional protection and which dignitaries may need added security.
- Reviewed the security at smaller airports in the metropolitan area to make sure general aviation is not used as a weapon against New York City.

Airspace Security

- The FAA has restricted air traffic over Manhattan.
- The Department of Defense has assigned combat aircraft to protect NYC airspace.

SOURCE: New York City Police Department, "Operation Atlas," retrieved August 12, 2006, from http://www.nyc.gov/html/nypd/html/atlas.html.

work in the region without having noticed the proliferation of armed security guards, surveillance cameras, handbag searches, metal detectors, electronic access cards and bomb-sniffing dogs, all of which have multiplied from Pennsylvania Station to the Metropolitan Museum of Art. Layered atop those are changes hidden from most eyes, like the detectives paying visits to chemical companies that terrorists might contact, the immigration agents demanding credit card numbers from foreign visitors, or the hospital emergency room stockpiles of nerve gas antidotes.[75]

After September 11, 2001, other local governments and local police agencies created new systems to protect their localities against terrorism. Some of these were the following[76]:

- The Pasadena, California, police department created its own threat matrix system to prioritize the continual stream of alerts from federal agencies, with the highest level reserved for those that specifically target Southern California.

- Des Moines, Iowa, police developed an intelligence-sharing system called Cop-Link, which has an artificial intelligence component allowing it to combine data so that municipal and county law enforcement do not have to call each other to find out what information the other might have.

▪ Stafford County, Virginia, developed a Homeland Security Neighborhood Watch to train participants living near railroads, airports, and other key areas to note license-plate numbers, directions of travel, and descriptions.

Local police have continued to pay increased attention to terrorism. In 2005, the Palm Beach County, Florida, Sheriff's Office formed its own homeland security department and has instituted around-the-clock marine patrols, created an intelligence operations center, and added strategic intelligence agents. In 2006, it announced officers will be riding trains and buses, in plainclothes, blending in with riders in an attempt to stop terrorist or any other threats to or from other passengers. Other Florida law enforcement agencies, including the Broward County Sheriff's Office and Miami-Dade police, have uniform and plainclothes officers riding the transit systems.[77]

Miami police adopted the "Miami Shield" program in 2005 to attempt to thwart terrorists by staging random "in-your-face" security operations at so-called "soft targets" such as city buses and sports arenas. For example, a group of officers might surround a downtown bank building checking the identification of each person going in and out.[78]

Since September 11, 2001, the California Highway Patrol (CHP) has spent more than one million hours in homeland security–related activities. Among CHP efforts are aggressive traffic enforcement, visible patrol, and investigations.[79] In a 2006 article, Dennis M. Rees writes that patrol officers have become more aware of and alert to possible terrorist targets and signs of terrorist planning in the communities they serve.[80]

Terrorism also affects officer safety. Michael E. Buerger and Bernard H. Levin wrote that because of the potential scope and deadliness of a terrorist attack, particularly one that involves biological or chemical weapons, concerns for officer safety should focus on prevention and extensive pre-planning for officer protection against the effects of extraordinary weaponry. Buerger and Levin also stated that law enforcement can prevent terrorist attacks by intelligence gathering. Using community liaisons, cultural awareness, and close relationships with immigrant communities, police can develop channels for information sharing that can help police detect terrorists' planning activities.[81]

Buttressing Bodrero's emphasis on the importance of local police in the fight against terrorism, Earl M. Sweeney wrote that terrorists are already in this country and likely moving about on our roads and highways enabling patrol officers to be in a unique position to observe and interdict suspicious vehicles and their occupants during traffic stops. Sweeney stresses that there must be research-based standardized training for all patrol officers in terrorists' tactics.[82]

Major police professional organizations, such as the International Association of Chiefs of Police (IACP), the National Sheriffs' Association (NSA), the National Organization of Black Law Enforcement Officials (NOBLE), the Major Cities Chiefs Association, and the Police Foundation, with the cooperation of the U.S. Department of Justice, have cooperated to form the *Post–9/11 Policing Project* to help bring domestic preparedness to the top of the law enforcement agenda.[83]

A 2005 report from the Rand Corporation, based on a survey of law enforcement preparedness after September 11, 2001, revealed that most state and local law enforcement agencies have conducted terrorism threat assessments; about one third of local law enforcement agencies have collaborated with the FBI's JTTFs; about 16 percent of local law enforcement agencies and 75 percent of states have specialized terrorism units; and local law enforcement agencies have increased their commitment of resources to counterterrorism efforts, usually at the expense of other policing areas.[84]

Some, however, believe that some smaller law enforcement agencies have not yet done enough about terrorism. For example, Patrick Faiella, professor at Massasoit Community College in Massachusetts and a member of the 25-officer Hanson Police Department, says,

> For moderate and small sized departments terrorism has been like the weather. Everyone talks about it and has an opinion but nobody does anything about it. I have not seen any significant contribution toward the readiness or capabilities of small suburban and rural police departments toward recognizing and combating terrorist activities. Training has centered around such things as ICS (Incident Command Systems) but little or no monetary or material contributions in the form of intelligence data sharing systems, defensive

equipment such as detectors, gas masks and decontamination stations, or modernization of existing police weaponry have been forthcoming.[85]

Some officers from mid-size departments question the participation of local departments to homeland security. As one example, Police Officer Richard Martin of the Rochester, New York, Police Department says,

> It seems strange to me how much we keep hearing about homeland security and all of the changes that have resulted from it because it has had no effect on the day to day operations in our department. Perhaps there are more pressing issues at hand or perhaps a feeling that it won't happen in Rochester, New York. With manpower at a premium, it's all we can do to keep up with the volume of calls for service.[86]

On the other hand, some believe that the police are spending too many resources on terrorism and that it soaks up both police attention and resources. Some police executives have deemed it "the new normal," others talk about "terror-oriented policing."[87] In 2006, the FBI reported a nearly 5 percent spike in homicides from 2004 to 2005 (the largest percentage change in 15 years), and the trend seems to have continued into 2006. Some, such as William Pridemore of Indiana University, have said that one possible reason for the rise in crime is the overall shifting of resources from policing, youth programs, and anti-violence initiatives to homeland security and other areas.[88]

Private Security Efforts for Homeland Security

The events of September 11, 2001, intensified the importance of private security in the workplace. According to market research, the global security industry has moved from a peripheral activity to center stage.[89] Private industry owns and operates about 85 percent of America's critical infrastructure and key assets; therefore, it is incumbent on this industry to play a central and aggressive role in protecting these vital economic sectors.[90]

In December 2004, the Congressional Budget Office released a comprehensive special report, *Homeland Security and the Private Sector,* that examined the role of the private sector in responding to the threat of terrorism in the United States since September 11, 2001. The report indicated that the private sector generates the vast majority of the nation's economic output, so it is in the interests of businesses to undertake measures that can help reduce the nation's vulnerability to attack and subsequent potential losses.

The report covers the essential critical industries of nuclear power, chemicals and hazardous materials, electrical service, and food and agriculture. It also discusses security concerns such as vulnerability from attack, potential losses, current programs for safety, and ideas for new approaches.[91]

Governor Mitt Romney of Massachusetts, the leader of a national working group on safeguarding the nation, told homeland security officials in December 2004 that to protect America against terrorists, state and local agencies, as well as private businesses, need to gather intelligence themselves and not just rely on intelligence gathered by the federal government. He said, "Meter readers, EMS drivers, law enforcement, and private sector personnel need to be on the lookout for information which may be useful."[92]

The *9/11 Commission Report: Final Report of the National Commission on Terrorist Attacks upon the United States* emphasized that the mandate of the Department of Homeland Security does not end with the government and stated that DHS is also responsible for working with the private sector to ensure preparedness. The 9/11 Commission emphasized that unless a terrorist's target is a military or other secure government facility, the "first" first responders will almost certainly be civilians and that national preparedness therefore often begins with the private sector.

Some examples of the private security industry's post–9/11 operations for homeland security follow:

■ In 2004, the ASIS International Foundation partnered with the Police Foundation and the Vera Institute of Justice to assess the preparedness of retail mall security to respond to terrorist acts.[93]

■ In 2004, ASIS International created its Chief Security Officer (CSO) Roundtable, an organization of 30 top-level private security executives from some of the nation's largest companies, such as General Dynamics, Fidelity Investments, and Toyota, to lead its homeland security efforts. The Roundtable has direct channels of communication with leaders in government and business, and participates in forming national policy on homeland security. At its inaugural meeting, the assistant secretary of the DHS identified this group as a core element of U.S. homeland security efforts.[94]

■ Many private corporations and businesses are formally training their private security personnel for homeland security threats. For example, the University of Findlay's Center for Terrorism Preparedness (CTP) in Ohio has trained more than 2,000 private security personnel, law enforcement agents, and other first responders since 1999. Other universities across the nation offer similar training to private security personnel. Major courses in these curriculums include vulnerability assessment, threat-assessment management, and actual field operations. As another example, Ross Laboratories (a division of Abbott Laboratories of Chicago) has hosted antiterrorism training for both security personnel and law enforcement.[95]

■ Companies are taking numerous efforts to improve bomb-detection at their facilities. Experts say that bomb-detection technology, perimeter protection, electronic video surveillance, access control, and employee vetting are crucial to organizations' overall antiterrorism strategies.[96]

■ Many companies have spent millions of dollars on scanners, turnstiles, and other security measures. Many large companies have erected security barriers around their buildings, some using concrete barriers, some using huge potted flowerbeds that limit access. As an example, Morgan Stanley, in New York City, ringed its corporate headquarters with 41 dark gray, eight-foot-long concrete planter tubs and 16 cylindrical planters. At some places, the tubs are barely more than one foot apart. According to Peter DiMaggio, of the American Institute of Architects, these standoff barricades are important because one of the most effective tools a designer has against a high-explosive terrorist attack is to force the terrorist to detonate the explosives as far from the building as possible.[97]

■ The 2004 National Policy Summit, Building Private Security/Public Policing Partnerships to Prevent and Respond to Terrorism and Public Disorder, held in Arlington, Virginia, made numerous important suggestions to improve private security and public policing cooperation for homeland security. This summit involved about 140 executive-level representatives of local, state, federal, and other law enforcement agencies; security departments of major corporations; security product and services providers; professional organizations in the law enforcement and private security field; universities; and federal agencies.[98]

In a 2005 article, James F. Pastor emphasized the important of private security and public policing cooperation when he wrote that the threat of future terrorism will change the nature of policing, transitioning it from a community policing model toward alternatives, specifically a private policing model. He writes that this fundamental shift in policing emphasizes tactical methods, technology, and alternative service providers, such as private security personnel. He predicts that the use of private security within public environments is likely to be increased in direct relation to the level of terrorist threats. He warns, however, that in this time of redefining the nature of policing, that the delicate balance between security and liberty cannot be lost.[99]

Some, however, disagree that private security is doing enough for homeland security,

■ The 9/11 Commission noted that it believed that the private sector was still totally unprepared for a catastrophic emergency similar to the 9/11 attacks:[100]

> As we examined the emergency response to 9/11, witness after witness told us that despite 9/11, the private sector remains largely unprepared for a terrorist attack. We were also advised that the lack of a widely embraced private-sector preparedness standard was a principal contributing factor to this lack of preparedness.[101]

■ Thomas E. Cavanagh of the Conference Board spent three years studying how corporations responded to the 9/11 attacks and reported that in a study of 100 midsize companies—including potentially vulnerable industries like transportation, financial services, utilities, and telecommunications—almost half of these corporations had not increased annual spending on security at all after 9/11. Forty percent of the executives said security was an expense that

ON THE JOB

Increased Security since September 11, 2001

Since my retirement from the New York City Police Department, I have continued to live in the metropolitan New York City area, about 25 miles from midtown Manhattan. I travel about the country often to attend conferences and visit colleagues and relatives. I have seen major changes in security since 9/11 and truly appreciate the efforts of our law enforcement agencies and private security professionals. Improved security is extremely important. I have heard some people complain about the many layers of security they now have to endure and the delays it causes them. I don't agree with these people and believe that if we are to prevent another terrorist attack and to ensure our safety, we have to cooperate with these improved security measures and appreciate the efforts of the professionals who are there to protect our security. It might take a few more moments out of one's daily routine to comply with these measures, but they are entirely necessary.

One particular improvement I have noticed is security at the airports. It is completely different than it was before September 11, 2001. I see unformed police and security employees everywhere throughout the airports I travel to and much more professionalism and effectiveness in security and screening processes. Having to go through several layers of security screening may help to prevent the opportunity to commit crimes. I have also noticed that the behavior of passengers has improved greatly since the terrorist acts of 9/11. Before then, I used to notice many passengers making silly comments about security measures and causing inconvenience to other travelers. Since 9/11, I think most people have matured a great deal.

I use local mass transit often in New York and truly appreciate the presence of military, police, and security personnel on these systems. I always go out of my way to say hello and "thanks for being here" to these people when I pass them. They have a tough, but necessary, job to do, and a smile and a hello might make their day a little more bearable.

As a former police officer, I am continually amazed at the current operations of my former department, the NYPD. I sense that the very obvious surge responses and Hercules and Atlas operations involving the massive presence of uniformed officers truly emphasize the importance of local police in our homeland security operations and keep the public aware of the constant possibility of terrorism. Most New Yorkers are used to them by now, but the tourists always seemed awed by them. I think the NYPD is very good for tourism in the city.

Private security is also extremely obvious in the city. I am a big sports fan and often go to ballparks in New York City with my grandchildren from Virginia when they come up to visit us. On the way into Madison Square Garden in the city to attend WNBA, NBA, college games, and other events, all patrons are screened and packages they are carrying are searched. Last year my nine-year old granddaughter, Nikki, was subjected to a search of her pocketbook as she was coming into the Garden with me to attend a WNBA New York Liberty game. After the search was completed, I asked her how she felt about the security officer going through her pocketbook. She said, "I feel safe." That is the whole point of security screening, for people like Nikki to be safe.

—John S. Dempsey

---

should be minimized, and a quarter of the companies said their chief executives had not met in the last year with their security chiefs.[102]

- A recent survey conducted by the American Management Association revealed that most employers fail to train all of their support staff in crisis management and that 90 percent of respondents revealed that those receiving training are only subjected to the material once per year.[103]

9/11 Commission's Review of Efforts for Homeland Security

In 2004, the *9/11 Commission Report: The Final Report of the National Commission on Terrorist Attacks upon the United States* was released by the National Commission on Terrorist Attacks.[104] The members of the commission met for two years, reviewed more than 2.5 million pages of documents, and interviewed more than 1,200 individuals in 10 countries. The commission held 19 days of hearings and took public testimony from 160 witnesses. It made 41 main proposals to improve homeland security and prevent future acts of terrorism against our nation. Some of the commission's recommendations were accepted and implemented by the government.

In December 2005, the former commission, which re-created itself as a private nonprofit organization to pressure Congress and the White House to act on its recommendations, issued a report card as its last official act, giving the federal government largely failing and mediocre marks as well as "incompletes" in its implementation of the panel's 41 main proposals. It gave its highest mark, an A–, for the government's vigorous efforts against terrorist financing, and Bs and Cs for other efforts such as the creation of a director of national intelligence and the ongoing presence in Afghanistan. However, the Commission heavily criticized the government for numerous failures that the Commission claimed were largely caused by political wrangling and bureaucracy. The Commission particularly mentioned the failure of Congress to focus homeland security funding on risk assessments and gave the FBI a C because it was restructuring itself too slowly.[105]

The panel chairperson wrote, "We believe that the terrorists will strike again. If they do, and these reforms that might have prevented such an attack have not been implemented, what will our excuses be?"[106] The chairperson also stated before the release of the report, "It's not a priority for the government right now. More than four years after 9/11 . . . people are not paying attention. God help us if we have another attack." Another former commission member called the country "less safe than we were 18 months ago."[107]

Security versus Civil Liberties

Although no one questions the importance of fighting terrorism, there has been a continuing debate since September 11, 2001, about the tools being used by law enforcement to fight this evil.

Many believe that since 9/11 the government has been given too much ability to affect citizen's constitutional rights and civil liberties while combating terrorism. Recall from Chapter 13, "Police and the Law," the early colonists came to America to escape persecution by the English king and to seek freedom. The colonists, however, continued to be persecuted and to be denied freedom. They rebelled, wrote the Declaration of Independence, fought for independence from England, and were able to defeat the British troops. As newly freed people, the former colonists wrote the U.S. Constitution to govern themselves. They then wrote the first ten Amendments to the Constitution, the Bill of Rights, which form the basis of our criminal justice system—the rights and freedoms we possess that can be used against government tyranny. Our Constitution was based on a fear of unreasonable government power, and our criminal justice system evolved based upon this fear. Americans have a long tradition of attempting to strike a balance between security and individual liberty.

According to Thomas Rossler, a paradigm shift has occurred within the American justice system as a result of the terrorist attacks of 2001, and the ensuing legislation has expanded police and governmental powers. This paradigm shift, according to Rossler, involves a change in perspective from post facto responses to criminal activity to an aggressive stance on preventing criminal activities before they are carried out.[108]

As indicated earlier in this chapter, the **USA Patriot Act** was enacted in the immediate aftermath of the 9/11 attacks. The Act has ten sections or titles outlining new powers for government operations. Titles I, II, III, IV, and VII specifically affect law enforcement's role in antiterrorist activities.[109] See Table 15.2.

One of the main objectives of the Patriot Act was to remedy a lack of communication between the federal law enforcement agencies and intelligence agencies that were individually trying to fight terrorism. The 9/11 terrorist attacks demonstrated how critical inter- and intra-agency communications are to prevent and respond to such attacks. The Patriot Act attempts to establish a coordinating mechanism to combat terrorism by employing the combined efforts of all U.S. law enforcement and intelligence agencies.

According to Jim Ruiz, a professor at the Pennsylvania State University at Harrisburg, and Kathleen H. Winters, a Ph.D. student at Ohio State University, the lack of inter-agency communication

| **TABLE 15.2** | Overview of the USA Patriot Act |

Title I Designed to Enhance Domestic Security. Creates a counterterrorism fund, increases technical support for the FBI, allows law enforcement to request military assistance in certain emergencies, expands the National Electronic Task Force, and forbids discrimination against Muslims and Arabs.

Title II Designed to Improve Surveillance. Grants authority to federal law enforcement agencies to intercept communication about terrorism, allows searches of computers, allows intelligence agencies to share information with criminal justice agencies, explains procedures for warrants, creates new definitions of intelligence, allows for roving wiretaps, and provides for expanding intelligence gathering.

Title III Designed to Stop Terrorism Finances. Grants expanded powers to law enforcement agencies to seize financial records, provides access to financial records, forces transactions to be disclosed, and expands investigative power in money laundering.

Title IV Designed to Protect U.S. Borders. Outlines measures to protect the borders, tightens immigration procedures, allows foreigners to be photographed and fingerprinted, and gives benefits to victims of terrorism.

Title V Designed to Enhance Investigative Powers. Provides a reward program, calls for sharing of investigative findings among law enforcement agencies, extends Secret Service jurisdiction, and forces educational institutions to release records of foreign students.

Title VI Designed to Compensate the Families of Public Safety Officers Killed during a Terrorist Attack.

Title VII Designed to Expand the Information Sharing Network. Provides for the expansion of law enforcement's nationwide information exchange, the Regional Information Sharing System (RISS).

Title VIII Designed to Strengthen Criminal Laws. Defines terrorist attacks, defines domestic terrorism, provides the basis for charging terrorists overseas, criminalizes support for terrorism, criminalizes cyberterrorism, allows investigation of terrorism as racketeering, and expands bioterrorism laws.

Titles IX and X contains miscellaneous addenda.

SOURCE: Jonathan R. White, *Terrorism and Homeland Security,* 5th ed. (Belmont, CA: Thompson/Wadsworth, 2006), p. 294.

was a by-product of multiple federal law enforcement and intelligence agencies gathering information on terrorism but failing to share the intelligence gathered with other departments and even within their respective agencies. The CIA often compartmentalized its information to lessen the likelihood of interception, and the National Security Agency (NSA) exhibited an "almost obsessive protection of sources and methods," thus forcing other agencies to possibly duplicate investigations to obtain information that had already been collected by other federal agencies. Also, "pressure from the Office of Intelligence Policy Review, FBI leadership, and the [*Foreign Intelligence Surveillance Act of 1978*] FISA Court built barriers between agents—even agents serving on the same squads."[110]

Ruiz and Winters also report that the national security strategy upon which the United States had been operating was created in the late 1940s, and because the national and international scene had changed dramatically since the end of the Cold War the nation was in need of a new national security policy, mostly due to the new climate of terrorism.

FBI Special Agent and legal instructor at the FBI Academy Michael J. Bulzomi writes that the USA Patriot Act changed the way foreign intelligence gathering is conducted, allowing intelligence officials to work with law enforcement officials to investigate possible threats to national security. Bulzomi writes, "The government must use its new tools in a way that preserves the rights and freedoms guaranteed by America's democracy, but at the same time, ensure that the fight against terrorism is vigorous and effective. No American should be forced to seek safety over liberty."[111] Bulzomi concludes that although it has now become easier to protect the nation with the Patriot Act, care must be taken to ensure any actions against terrorism are employed within the constraints of the Constitution.[112]

Ruiz and Winters question the necessity of the Patriot Act:

One of the main issues underlying the Act involves balancing individual rights with governmental power. Proponents assert that the Act is necessary to combat terrorism, and that certain rights may be conceded to the government during a time of war. In 1944, the Supreme Court ruled that in times of war Congress has the authority to compromise certain rights if the circumstances warrant it (*Korematsu v. United States,* 323 U.S. 214, 1944). Conversely, opponents claim that it gives too much weight to the government's side of the balance. Furthermore, the Act is not limited solely to times of war. In fact, the "war on terrorism" is an ongoing war; whether or not it will ever end remains to be seen. A balance must be struck between the pursuit of justice and protection of the innocent.[113]

Melanie Scarborough in a briefing paper for the Cato Institute seems to agree with Ruiz and Winters: "Radical Islamic terrorists are not the first enemy that America has faced. British troops burned the White House in 1814, the Japanese navy launched a surprise attack on Pearl Harbor, and the Soviet Union deployed hundreds of nuclear missiles that targeted American cities. If policy makers are serious about defending our freedom and our way of life, they must wage this war without discarding our traditional constitutional framework of limited government."[114]

Jonathan R. White writes that supporters of the Patriot Act believe it increases federal law enforcement's ability to respond to terrorism and creates an intelligence conduit among local, state, and federal law enforcement agencies. They believe counterterrorism is strengthened by combining law enforcement and national defense intelligence. He writes that opponents of the law argue that it goes too far in threatening civil liberties while expanding police powers and are concerned about sharing noncriminal intelligence during criminal investigations and the increased power of the government to monitor the activities of its own citizens.[115]

According to the American Civil Liberties Union (ACLU), President George W. Bush and the Congress, in the aftermath of the 9/11 attacks, acted to amass an overabundance of new laws, executive orders, and regulations that expanded government powers, with little thought to their impact on traditional civil liberties or an assessment of whether the actual threat warranted such drastic measures. The ACLU believes that there is no evidence that statutory gaps in the powers of federal and state law enforcement and investigative agencies contributed to the failure to detect and prevent the attacks of 9/11.[116]

Anna R. Oller of University of Central Missouri writes that the Patriot Act and the Bioterrorism Preparedness Act have curtailed teaching and academic freedoms as teaching and research are impacted by restrictions set forth in these laws that forbid teachers from providing information that could possibly be used in any terrorist manner to students from the restricted nations list.[117]

Former FBI Special Agent James Burnett, a professor of criminal justice at Rockland County Community College, states,

> The concerns over our government's responses to the very real threat of terrorism goes far beyond the Patriot Act to NSA data mining, detentions of immigrants, material witnesses, and enemy combatants and the use of coercive interrogation techniques. In these and other policies our government's post 9/11 actions and the justifications for them have raised fundamental concerns as to whether our deliberately inefficient system of checks and balances and limitations on government power can get the job done in this new environment. Will the system itself become a casualty of this so-called war on terror and thus allow the enemy yet another powerful blow against our institutions and values?[118]

Many critics of the Patriot Act question the constitutionality of national security letters. **National security letters** can be issued if a local FBI official certifies that the information sought is relevant to an international terrorism or foreign intelligence investigation. In 2005, the FBI sent 9,254 national security letters concerning 3,501 individuals to finance, telephone, and Internet companies asking for records. National security letters can be used to retrieve the following[119]:

■ Internet and telephone data, including names, addresses, log-on times, toll records, e-mail addresses, and service providers.

■ Financial records, including bank accounts and money transfers, provided the FBI says that they are needed to "protect against international terrorism or clandestine intelligence activities."

■ Credit information from individuals' banks, loan companies, mortgage holders, or other financial institutions.

■ Consumer, financial, and foreign travel records held by "any commercial entity," if the investigation's target is an executive branch employee with a security clearance.

In February 2005, the FBI office in New Haven, Connecticut, received an e-mail that looked like a terrorist threat and hand-delivered a national security letter to the service provider, a group of Connecticut public libraries, for the real name, street address and Internet logs of the senders. The librarians refused to hand over the information and filed a federal lawsuit challenging the letters as an unconstitutional infringement on free speech.[120]

The **Foreign Intelligence Surveillance Act Court (FISA Court),** which authorizes search warrants and electronic surveillance in terrorism and spying cases, approved 2,072 warrants and wiretaps and 155 applications for business records in 2005.[121] From 1995 through 2004, FISA received 10,617 such applications and approved all but 4 of them.[122]

In 2005, it was disclosed that the National Security Agency (NSA) has been secretly keeping track of the phone calls that millions of ordinary Americans make every day. This information has been collected since 2001 from the nation's three largest phone companies and has produced what is reported to be the largest such database ever. The reasoning behind this huge database is that the NSA can sift through all that data, using a process called link analysis, searching for patterns that indicate terrorism threats. Intelligence experts say figuring out the patterns of communication helps in understanding al Qaeda. If the NSA finds a call pattern that warrants further investigation, it can take other investigatory actions. President Bush when asked about this newly revealed data-mining program stated, "We're not mining or trolling through the personal lives of millions of innocent Americans. Our efforts are focused on links to al-Qaeda terrorists and its affiliates." The day after the NSA story broke, a *Washington Post*–ABC News poll found that 63 percent of persons polled said they found the NSA program to be an acceptable way to fight terrorism, and 44 percent said they strongly approved of it.[123]

In 2006, a federal judge ruled that part of the NSA monitoring program (wiretapping the international communications of some Americans without a court warrant) violated the Constitution. The Department of Justice filed an immediate appeal and succeeded in allowing the wiretapping to continue for the time being.[124]

On March 9, 2006, President Bush signed the USA Patriot Reauthorization Act of 2005, which makes all sections of the 2001 Act permanent. Some sections were amended slightly, but none were deleted. Ruiz and Winters wrote that the bill was passed with little evidence to demonstrate the need for these measures and evidence has begun to bubble up of abuses of these wide-ranging powers. They report that on the day the bill was signed, the U.S. Department of Justice reported that the FBI had "found apparent violations of its own wiretapping and other intelligence-gathering procedures more than 100 times in the last two years, and problems appear to have grown more frequent."[125]

In a July 2006 Harris Interactive poll, a majority of Americans reported that they were in favor of increasing surveillance of suspected terrorists through cameras, banking records, and cell phones. Seventy percent of those polled reported they favored expanded camera surveillance on streets and in public places, an increase from 59 percent in June 2005 and from 63 percent shortly after September 11, 2001. Also, 62 percent of respondents said they supported police monitoring of chat rooms and other online forums, an increase from 50 percent in February 2004; 52 percent of those polled favored police monitoring of cell phones and email, but nearly 6 in 10 respondents said these techniques should only be done with authorization by Congress.[126]

The debate over security versus individual rights is sure to continue.

Summary

- 3,047 people were murdered during the terrorist attacks of September 11, 2001: 2,823 at the World Trade Center in New York City, 184 at the Pentagon in Northern Virginia, and 40 in Stony Creek Township, Pennsylvania.

- Terrorism has a long tradition in world history. Terrorist tactics have been used frequently by radical and criminal groups to influence public opinion and to attempt to force authorities to do their will. Terrorists have criminal, political, and other nefarious motives.

- Many Americans and most major U.S. firms have been targeted by terrorists in some way. Political extremists and terrorists use the violence and suspense of terrorist acts such as bombing, kidnapping, and hostage situations to put pressure on those in authority to comply with their demands and cause the authorities and public to recognize their power. They use their activities to obtain money for their causes, to alter business or government policies, or to change public opinion.

■ Two major definitions of terrorism are "the use of violence or threatened violence against innocent people to achieve a social or political goal" and "premeditated politically motivated violence perpetrated against noncombatant targets." Terrorists target civilian populations—noncombatants.

■ Some major forms of terrorism affecting the United States and its citizens are international terrorism and domestic terrorism.

■ The National Counterterrorism Center (NCTC) in 2006 reported that approximately 11,000 terrorist attacks worldwide resulted in the deaths of over 14,500 noncombatants in 2005.

■ The USA Patriot Act—Uniting and Strengthening America by Providing Appropriate Tools Required to Intercept and Obstruct Terrorism, signed into law in October 2001, gives law enforcement new ability to search, seize, detain, or eavesdrop in pursuit of possible terrorists.

■ The Transportation Security Administration (TSA) was established after the 9/11 attacks to protect the nation's transportation systems and infrastructure.

■ The cabinet-level U.S. Department of Homeland Security (DHS) was established in March 2003 and merged 22 previously disparate domestic agencies. The first DHS priority is to protect the nation against further terrorist attacks. The department's agencies analyze threats and intelligence, guard our borders and airports, protect our critical infrastructure, and coordinate the responses of our nation for future emergencies.

■ The DHS controls immigration into the United States through its US-VISIT Program. US-VISIT is part of a continuum of security measures that begins outside U.S. borders and continues through a visitor's arrival in and departure from the United States. It applies to all visitors entering the United States.

■ The FBI is the lead federal agency in the response to and investigation of terrorism.

■ Although the federal government's role in responding to and combating terrorism and promoting homeland security is extremely crucial, each act of terrorism is essentially a local problem and must be addressed by local authorities and private security professionals. State and local law enforcement agencies and private security officials have significantly increased their homeland security efforts since 9/11.

■ Private industry owns and operates about 85 percent of America's critical infrastructure and key assets.

■ In 2004, the *9/11 Commission Report: The Final Report of the National Commission on Terrorist Attacks upon the United States* made 41 major recommendations to improve homeland security and prevent future acts of terrorism against our nation. Only some of these recommendations have been implemented by the government.

■ Since 9/11, there has been a continuing debate about the tools being used by law enforcement to fight terrorism, particularly the Patriot Act.

Learning Check

1. Define and discuss terrorism.

2. Describe and discuss some of the reasons terrorists commit their acts.

3. Describe five major international terrorist incidents during the past two years.

4. Describe some of the aspects of the immediate response of the U.S. government to the September 11, 2001, terrorist attacks.

5. Describe and discuss the major subunits of the Department of Homeland Security.

6. Describe and discuss the major changes in the FBI's priorities since 9/11.

7. Describe and discuss some state and local law enforcement efforts for homeland security.

8. How does the USA Patriot Act support homeland security?

9. How does the USA Patriot Act affect citizens' civil liberties?

10. How did the former 9/11 Commission describe the nation's current state of preparedness for future terrorist acts?

Key Terms

biological weapons Weapons made from live bacterial, viral, or other microoganisms.

counterterrorism Enforcement efforts made against terrorist organizations.

Department of Homeland Security (DHS) Federal cabinet department established in the aftermath of the terrorist attacks of September 11, 2001.

domestic terrorism Terrorism committed by citizens of the United States in the United States.

Foreign Intelligence Surveillance Act **(FISA Court)** Bill passed in 1978 requiring the NSA and the FBI to seek a special court's (the FISA Court) permission to conduct searches and electronic surveillance in terrorism and spying cases.

homeland security Efforts made since the terrorist acts of September 11, 2001, to protect the U.S. against terrorist acts.

international terrorism Terrorism on an international level.

Joint Terrorism Task Forces (JTTF) concept Use of single-focused investigative units that meld personnel and talent from various law enforcement agencies.

national security letters Information requests issued by a local FBI official who certifies that the information is relevant to an international terrorism or foreign intelligence investigation.

September 11, 2001 The date of a series of terrorist attacks against the United States of America by members of al Qaeda.

terrorism Premeditated politically motivated violence perpetrated against noncombatant targets.

USA Patriot Act Public Law No. 107-56 passed in 2001 giving law enforcement new ability to search, seize, detain or eavesdrop in their pursuit of possible terrorists; full title of law is USA Patriot Act–Uniting and Strengthening America by Providing Appropriate Tools Required to Intercept and Obstruct Terrorism.

Notes

Chapter 1

1. John Ayto, *Dictionary of Word Origins* (New York: Arcade, 1990), p. 402.

2. Excesses by the military in enforcing the law in the American West led to the *Posse Comitatus Act of 1879.* See the discussion of the frontier experience later in the chapter.

3. For a brief history of investigations, see Chapter 1 of John S. Dempsey, *Introduction to Investigations,* 2nd ed. (Belmont, Calif.: Wadsworth, 2003).

4. This section on early policing is based on the following: William G. Bailey, ed., *The Encyclopedia of Police Science* (New York: Garland, 1989); John J. Fay, *The Police Dictionary and Encyclopedia* (Springfield, Ill.: Charles C. Thomas, 1988); Sanford H. Kadish, *Encyclopedia of Crime and Justice* (New York: Free Press, 1983); George Thomas Kurian, *World Encyclopedia of Police Forces and Penal Systems* (New York: Facts on File, 1989); Jay Robert Nash, *Encyclopedia of World Crime* (Wilmette, Ill.: Crime Books, 1990); Charles Reith, *The Blind Eye of History: A Study of the Origins of the Present Police Era* (London: Faber, 1912); and Philip J. Stead, *The Police of Paris* (London: Staples, 1957).

5. "The words [*vigilance* and *vigilante*] come from the Latin *vigilia,* which was derived from the adjective *vigil,* meaning 'awake, alert.' Another derivative of the Latin adjective was *vigilare,* meaning 'keep watch,' which lies behind the English *reveille, surveillance,* and *vigilant.*" Ayto, *Dictionary of Word Origins,* p. 559.

6. This section on the English roots of policing is based on the following: S. G. Chapman and T. E. St. Johnston, *The Police Heritage in England and America* (East Lansing: Michigan State University, 1962); Belton Cobb, *The First Detectives* (London: Faber & Faber, 1967), p. 51; T. A. Critchley, *A History of Police in England and Wales,* 2nd ed. rev. (Montclair, N.J.: Patterson Smith, 1972); Clive Emsley, *Policing and its Context, 1750–1870* (New York: Schocken, 1984); A. C. Germann, Frank D. Day, and Robert R. J. Gallati, *Introduction to Law Enforcement and Criminal Justice* (Springfield, Ill.: Charles C. Thomas, 1969); W. E. Hunt, *History of England* (New York: Harper & Brothers, 1938); Luke Owen Pike, *A History of Crime in England* (London: Smith, Elder, 1873–1876); Patrick Pringle, *Highwaymen* (New York: Roy, 1963); Pringle, *Hue and Cry: The Story of Henry and John Fielding and Their Bow Street Runners* (New York: Morrow, 1965); Pringle, *The Thief Takers* (London: Museum Press, 1958); Sir Leon Radiznowciz, *A History of English Criminal Law and Its Administration from 1750,* 4 vols. (London: Stevens & Sons, 1948–68); Reith, *A New Study of Police History* (London: Oliver & Boyd, 1956); Reith, *Blind Eye of History;* Thomas Reppetto, *The Blue Parade* (New York: Free Press, 1978); Albert Rieck, *Justice and Police in England* (London: Butterworth, 1936); Robert Sheehan and Gary W. Cordner, *Introduction to Police Administration,* 2nd ed. (Cincinnati, Ohio: Anderson, 1989); and John J. Tobias, *Crime and Police in England, 1700–1900* (New York: St. Martin's Press, 1979).

7. Pringle, *Hue and Cry,* p. 81.

8. New Westminster Police Service, "Sir Robert Peel's Nine Principles of Policing," retrieved October 20, 2006, from http://www.newwestpolice.org/peel.html.

9. Reppetto, *Blue Parade,* p. 19.

10. Lucia Zedner, "Policing Before and After the Police: The Historical Antecedents of Contemporary Crime Control," *British Journal of Criminology* 46 (1, January 2006), pp. 78–96.

11. The sections on American colonial and eighteenth- and nineteenth-century policing are based on the following: Bailey, *Encyclopedia of Police Science;* Carl Bridenbaugh, *Cities in Revolt: Urban Life in America, 1743–1776* (New York: Knopf, 1965); Bridenbaugh, *Cities in the Wilderness: Urban Life in America, 1625–1742* (New York: Capricorn, 1964); Emsley, *Policing and Its Context;* Robert M. Fogelson, *Big City Police* (Cambridge, Mass.: Harvard University Press, 1977); Roger Lane, *Policing the City, Boston 1822–1885* (Cambridge, Mass.: Harvard University Press, 1967); Eric Monkkonen, *Police in Urban America: 1860–1920* (Cambridge, Mass.: Harvard University Press, 1981); Reppetto, *Blue Parade;* James F. Richardson, *The New York Police: Colonial Times to 1901* (New York: Oxford University Press, 1976); Richardson, *Urban Police in the United States* (Port Washington, N.Y.: Kennikat Press, 1974); Robert C. Wadman and William Thomas Allison, *To Protect and to Serve: A History of Police in America* (Upper Saddle River, N.J.: Pearson/Prentice Hall, 2004); Samuel Walker, *A Critical History of Police Reform: The Emergence of Professionalism* (Lexington, Mass.: Lexington Books, 1977); and Walker, *Popular Justice: History of American Criminal Justice* (New York: Oxford University Press, 1980).

12. Richardson, *New York Police,* p. 31.

13. The sections on the American colonial southern experience and slave patrols are based on: Sally E. Hadden, *Slave Patrols, Law and Violence in Virginia and the Carolinas* (Cambridge, Mass.: Harvard University Press, 2001), pp. 19, 20, and 24; P. L. Reichel, "Southern Slave Patrols as a Transitional Police Type," *American Journal of Police,* 7 (1988), pp. 51–57; M. P. Roth, *Crime and Punishment: A History of the Criminal Justice System* (Belmont: Calif.: Thompson/Wadsworth, 2005), p. 64; K. B. Turner, David Giacopassi, and Margaret Vandiver, "Ignoring the Past: Coverage of Slavery and Slave Patrols in Criminal Justice Texts," *Journal of Criminal Justice Education,* 17 (1, April 2006); Wadman and Allison, "Policing Race and Violence in the South," in *To Protect and to Serve,* pp. 27–41; and Samuel Walker, *The Police in America: An Introduction,* 2nd ed (New York: McGraw-Hill, 1992), p. 6.

14. James A. Conser and Gregory D. Russell, *Law Enforcement in the United States* (Gaithersburg, Md.: Aspen, 2002), pp. 52, 258–259; Carl B. Klockars, *The Idea of Police* (Beverly Hills, Calif.: Sage, 1985), pp. 55–56.

15. Walker, *The Police in America,* p. 6.

16. Roth, *Crime and Punishment,* p. 64.

17. Wadman and Allison, *To Protect and to Serve,* pp. 32–33.

18. Wadman and Allison, *To Protect and to Serve,* pp. 32–33.

19. *Dred Scott v. Sandford,* 19 How. 393 (1857). For an excellent description of the Dred Scott case, see Fred W. Friendly and Martha J. H. Elliott, *The Constitution: That Delicate Balance* (New York: McGraw-Hill, 1984), pp. 17–22.

20. Hadden, *Slave Patrols,* pp. 185–187.

21. *Commercial Advisor,* 20 August 1840, as cited in Richardson, *New York Police,* p. 31.

22. Cited in Richardson, *New York Police,* p. 10.

23. Walker, *Popular Justice,* p. 61.

24. Luc Sante, *Low Life: Lures and Snares of Old New York* (New York: Farrar, Straus & Giroux, 1991), p. 236.

25. Walker, *Popular Justice,* p. 63.

26. Fogelson, *Big City Police,* p. 25.

27. Richard A. Staufenberger, *Progress in Policing: Essays on Change* (Cambridge, Mass.: Ballinger, 1980), pp. 8–9.

28. Walker, *Popular Justice,* p. 63.

29. Lincoln Steffens, *The Autobiography of Lincoln Steffens* (New York: Harcourt Brace Jovanovich, 1958; originally published in 1931), p. 207.

30. Wadman and Allison, "Policing Race and Violence in the South," p. 36.

31. Wadman and Allison, "Policing Race and Violence in the South," p. 36.

32. Wadman and Allison, "Policing Race and Violence in the South," pp. 36–37. Also see Paul D. Lack, "Law and Disorder in Confederate Atlanta," in *Crime and Justice in American History: The South,* Part 2, ed. Eric H. Monkkonen (Munich: K. G. Saur, 1992), pp. 249–269.

33. Wadman and Allison, "Policing Race and Violence in the South," pp. 39–40.

34. The section on the frontier experience is based on the following: James D. Horan and Howard Swiggett, *The Pinkerton Story* (New York: Putnam, 1951); Horan and Swiggett, *The Pinkertons: The Detective Dynasty That Made History* (New York: Crown, 1967); Edward Hungerford, *Wells Fargo: Advancing the American Frontier* (New York: Bonanza, 1949); David R. Johnson, *American Law Enforcement: A History* (St. Louis: Forum Press, 1981); Carolyn Lake, *Undercover for Wells Fargo* (Boston: Houghton Mifflin, 1969); Allan Pinkerton, *The Expressman and the Detective* (New York: Arno Press, 1976); Frank R. Prassel, *The Western Peace Officer: A Legacy of Law and Order* (Norman: University of Oklahoma Press, 1972); Charles A. Siringo, *A Cowboy Detective: A True Story of Twenty-Two Years with a World-Famous Detective Agency* (Lincoln: University of Nebraska Press, 1988); Bruce Smith, *Police Systems in the United States,* 2nd ed. (New York: Harper & Row, 1960); Smith, *Rural Crime Control* (New York: Columbia University Institute of Public Administration, 1933); Wadman and Allison, *To Protect and to Serve;* and Walter Prescott Webb, *The Texas Rangers: A Century of Frontier Defense* (Boston: Houghton Mifflin, 1935).

35. This section on twentieth-century policing is based on the following: Jay Stuart Berman, *Police Administration and Progressive Reform: Theodore Roosevelt as Police Commissioner of New York* (New York: Greenwood Press, 1987); William J. Bopp and Donald O. Schultz, *A Short History of American Law Enforcement* (Springfield, Ill.: Charles C. Thomas, 1972); Fogelson, *Big City Police;* Richard Kluger, *Simple Justice* (New York: Vintage, 1977); Roger Lane, *Policing the City* (New York: Atheneum, 1975); Doug McAdam, *Freedom Summer* (New York: Oxford University Press, 1988);

Wilbur R. Miller, *Cops and Bobbies: Police Authority in New York and London, 1830–1870* (Chicago: University of Chicago Press, 1977); Monkkonen, *Police in Urban America;* Edward P. Morgan, *The 60's Experience: Hard Lessons about Modern America* (Philadelphia: Temple University Press, 1991); Albert J. Reiss, *The Police and the Public* (New Haven, Conn.: Yale University Press, 1971); Richardson, *Urban Police in the United States;* Jerome H. Skolnick, *Justice without Trial: Law Enforcement in a Democratic Society,* 2nd ed. (New York: Wiley, 1975); Jerome H. Skolnick and David H. Bayley, *The New Blue Line: Police Innovation in Six American Cities* (New York: Free Press, 1986); Milton Viorst, *Fire in the Streets: America in the 1960's* (New York: Simon & Schuster, 1970); Wadman and Allison, *To Protect and to Serve;* Walker, *Popular Justice;* Walker, *Critical History of Police Reform;* Juan Williams, *Eyes on the Prize: America's Civil Rights Years, 1954–1965* (New York: Penguin, 1983); and James Q. Wilson, *Varieties of Police Behavior: The Management of Law and Order in Eight Communities* (Cambridge, Mass.: Harvard University Press, 1968).

36. Reppetto, *Blue Parade,* p. 64.

37. Reppetto, *Blue Parade,* p. 65.

38. National Commission on Law Observance and Enforcement, *Lawlessness in Law Enforcement,* vol. 2 of the *Wickersham Report* (Washington, D.C.: U.S. Government Printing Office, 1931).

39. Johnson, *American Law Enforcement,* p. 121.

40. James Q. Wilson, *Thinking About Crime* (New York: Basic Books, 1983), p. 5.

41. *Mapp v. Ohio,* 367 U.S. 643 (1961).

42. *Escobedo v. Illinois,* 378 U.S. 478 (1964).

43. *Miranda v. Arizona,* 384 U.S. 436 (1966).

44. *Brown v. Board of Education of Topeka,* 347 U.S. 483 (1954).

45. Cox Commission, *Crisis at Columbia: Report of the Fact-Finding Commission Appointed to Investigate the Disturbances at Columbia University in April and May 1968* (New York: Vintage, 1968), pp. 181–182.

46. National Advisory Commission on Civil Disorders, *Report of the National Advisory Commission on Civil Disorders* (New York: Bantam Books, 1968), p. 299.

47. Michael Cooper, "As New York Homicides Fall, Rate of Solved Cases Goes Up," *New York Times,* June 2, 1997, pp. B1, B3; Cooper, "Crime Reports Drop Sharply in New York: Murder and Car Theft Leads Declines in 1997," *New York Times,* April 1, 1997, pp. B1, B9; Federal Bureau of Investigation, *Uniform Crime Reports: Crime in the United States* (Washington, D.C.: Federal Bureau of Investigation); Fox Butterfield, "Homicides Plunge 11 Percent in U.S., FBI Report Says 'A Stunningly Low' Rate," *New York Times,* June 2, 1997, pp. A1, B10.

48. Peter C. Dodenhoff, "LEN Salutes Its 1996 People of the Year, the NYPD and Its Compstat Process: A Total Package of Re-engineering and Strategy-Making That Has Transformed the Nation's Largest Police Force—as It Will Law Enforcement in General," *Law Enforcement News,* December 31, 1996, pp. 1, 4; "There's No Going Back to Old Ways: Cities Vie to Board CompStat Bandwagon,"

Law Enforcement News, December 31, 1996, p. 5; "What's on the Grill? In New York, It's Police Commanders," *Law Enforcement News,* December 31, 1996, p. 5; Eli B. Silverman, "Mapping Change: How the New York City Police Department Re-engineered Itself to Drive Down Crime," *Law Enforcement News,* December 15, 1996, pp. 10–12.

49. Howard Safir, Police Commissioner, City of New York, *The Compstat Process* (New York: New York City Police Department, no date); William J. Bratton, Police Commissioner, City of New York, "Great Expectations: How Higher Expectation for Police Departments Can Lead to a Decrease in Crime," paper presented at the National Institute of Justice Research Institute's "Measuring What Matters" Conference, Washington, D.C., November 28, 1995; Rudolph W. Giuliani, Randy M. Mastro, and Donna Lynn, *Mayor's Management Report: The City of New York* (New York: City of New York, 1997).

50. Dodenhoff, "LEN Salutes Its 1996 People of the Year," p. 4.

51. "There's No Going Back to Old Ways," p. 5.

52. Stacey C. Koon and Robert Deitz, *Presumed Guilty: The Tragedy of the Rodney King Affair* (Washington, D.C.: Regnery Gateway, 1992).

53. James Barron, "A Father Finds Charges Hard to Believe," *New York Times,* August 15, 1997, p. A13; Dan Barry, "2d Police Officer Charged in Attack on Arrested Man: Colleague Gave Details," *New York Times,* August 15, 1997, pp. 1, 24; Barry, "A Clean Sweep for a Stained Station House: Heads of 70th Precinct Get New Assignment," *New York Times,* August 15, 1997, pp. A1, A13; and David Firestone, "A Police Case in the Context of Elector Politics: A Mayor Closely Tied to Police Successes Faces a Police Problem," *New York Times,* August 15, 1997, p. A13.

54. Donald Johnston, "Report Criticizes Scientific Testing at FBI Lab: Serious Problems Cited," *New York Times,* April 16, 1997, pp. A1, D23; Mireya Navarro, "Doubts about FBI Lab Raise Hopes for Convict: On Death Row, but Seeking a New Trial," *New York Times,* April 22, 1997, p. A8.

55. "What's Wrong at the FBI?: The Fiasco at the Crime Lab," *Time,* April 28, 1997, pp. 28–35.

56. Seth Mydans, "23 Dead after 2d Day of Los Angeles Riot: Fires & Looting Persists Despite Curfew," *New York Times,* May 1, 1992, pp. A1, A20.

57. Mydans, "Ex-Police Chief Blamed for Riot in Los Angeles: Gates Calls the Authors of the Report 'Liars,'" *New York Times,* October 22, 1992, p. A12.

58. Jennifer Nislow, "Working Together: A Case Study; PERF Report Analyzes Challenges and Successes of Beltway Sniper Investigation," *Law Enforcement News,* January 2005, pp. 1, 11; Police Executive Research Forum, *Managing a Multijurisdictional Case: Identifying Lessons Learned from the Sniper Investigation* (Washington, D.C.: Police Executive Research Forum, 2005).

59. Tom Hays, "NYC Real Time Crime Center Tracks Suspects," *Associated Press,* May 10, 2006.

60. Allison Klein, "Pr. George's Reports First-Quarter Crime Drop," *Washington Post,* April 13, 2006, p. B10.

61. Richard Winton and Hector Becerra, "Deputies Slash Compton Crime," *Los Angeles Times,* March 22, 2006.

62. Robert Moran, "Safer Streets in Phila.? Not This Year," *Philadelphia Inquirer,* April 23, 2006.

63. Sara Miller Liana, "What's at the Root of Boston's Rise in Murders?" *Christian Science Monitor,* May 10, 2006.

64. Federal Bureau of Investigation, *Uniform Crime Reports,* 2005, retrieved September 19, 2006, from http://www.fbi.com.

65. Maria Newman, "Violent Crime Rose in '05, with Murders Up by 4.8%," *New York Times,* June 13, 2006, p. A16.

66. Marie Simonetti Rosen, "Terror-Oriented Policing's Big Shadow," *Law Enforcement News,* December 2004, p. 1.

67. Richard Perez-Pena, "A Security Blanket, but with No Guarantees," *New York Times,* March 23, 2003, pp. A1, B14.

68. William K. Rashbaum, "Air Patrols and Officers at TV Stations as City Goes on Alert," *New York Times,* March 19, 2003, p. A21.

69. Jodi Wilgoren, "Higher Alert and Tighter Budgets," *New York Times,* March 19, 2003, pp. A1, A21.

70. Timothy Egan, "Pacific Northwest Keeps Watch on Many Vulnerable Points," *New York Times,* March 25, 2003, p. B13.

71. Kate Zernike and Dean E. Murphy, "Across the Nation, Protesters Carry Out a Plan to 'Stop Business as Usual,'" *New York Times,* March 21, 2003, p. B4.

72. Zernike and Murphy, "Across the Nation."

73. Leslie Eaton, "Nationwide Peace Rallies Continue, Nonviolently," *New York Times,* March 22, 2003, p. B9.

74. Leslie Eaton, "On New York's Streets and Across the Nation, Protesters Speak Out," *New York Times,* March 23, 2003, p. B14.

75. Allen G. Breed, "Looting Takes Place in View of La. Police," *Washington Post,* August 30, 2005, p. 1. See also Egan, "Uprooted and Scattered Far from the Familiar," *New York Times,* September 11, 2005, pp. 1, 33; Eric Lipton, Christopher Drew, Scott Shane, and David Rhode, "Breakdowns Marked Path from Hurricane to Anarchy: In Crisis, Federal Authorities Hesitated; Local Officials Were Overwhelmed," *New York Times,* September 11, 2005, pp. 1, 28; Jere Longman, "Scouring the Neighborhoods in a Personal Appeal to Holdouts," *New York Times,* September 6, 2006, p. A22; Joseph B. Treaster and John DeSantis, "With Some Now at Breaking Point, City's Officers Tell of Pain and Pressure," *New York Times,* September 6, 2005, pp. A21, A22; and Jodi Wilgoren, "Residents of a Parish Encountering Lost Dreams," *New York Times,* September 6, 2005, pp. A21.

76. James Varney, "Four Officers Suspended, Acting Police Chief Says," *Nola.com,* retrieved September 30, 2005, from nola.com

77. Joseph B. Treaster, "Police Quitting, Overwhelmed by Chaos," *New York Times,* September 4, 2005, p. 1.

78. Treaster and DeSantis, "With Some Now at Breaking Point," pp. A21, A22.

Chapter 2

1. Kristen A. Hughes, *Justice Expenditure and Employment in the United States, 2003* (Washington, D.C.: Bureau of Justice Statistics, 2006), p. 1.

2. Kristen A. Hughes, *Justice Expenditure and Employment,* p. 6.

3. David H. Bayley, *Forces of Order: Police Behavior in Japan and the United States* (Berkeley: University of California Press, 1976).

4. Matthew J. Hickman and Brian A. Reaves, *Local Police Departments, 2003* (Washington, D.C.: Bureau of Justice Statistics, 2006), p. 1; Reaves and Hickman, *Census of State and Local Law Enforcement Agencies, 2000* (Washington, D.C.: Bureau of Justice Statistics, 2002), p. 1; Hickman and Reaves, *Local Police Departments, 2000* (Washington, D.C.: Bureau of Justice Statistics, 2003), p. v.

5. Hughes, *Justice Expenditure and Employment,* p. 3.

6. U.S. Department of Labor, Bureau of Labor Statistics, *Occupational Outlook Handbook,* "Police and Detectives," retrieved May 15, 2003 from http://www.bls.gov/oco/ocos160.htm.

7. Sewell Chan, "Counting Heads Along the Thin Blue Line," *New York Times,* March 26, 2006.

8. Chan, "Counting Heads Along the Thin Blue Line."

9. Chan, "Counting Heads Along the Thin Blue Line."

10. Chan, "Counting Heads Along the Thin Blue Line."

11. Chan, "Counting Heads Along the Thin Blue Line."

12. Jeffrey Westcott, "Super Bowl XXXIX: The Successful Response of the FBI and its Partners," *FBI Law Enforcement Bulletin* (January 2006), pp. 1–5.

13. Alfonso Chardy, "Officers in S. Fla. Help Immigration Agents Make Arrests," *Miami Herald,* May 25, 2006.

14. William C. Cunningham, John J. Strauchs, and Clifford W. Van Meter, *The Hallcrest Report II: Private Security Trends: 1970–2000* (Boston: Butterworth-Heinemann, 1990).

15. Hughes, *Justice Expenditure and Employment,* p. 4.

16. Hickman and Reaves, *Local Police Departments, 2003,* p. 2.

17. Hickman and Reaves, *Local Police Departments, 2003,* pp. 2, 3.

18. Hickman and Reaves, *Local Police Departments, 2003,* p. iii.

19. Hickman and Reaves, *Local Police Departments, 2003,* p. iii.

20. Hickman and Reaves, *Local Police Departments, 2003,* p. iii.

21. Reaves and Hickman, *Census of State and Local Law Enforcement Agencies, 2000,* pp. 5–7; also see Reaves and Hickman, *Police Departments in Large Cities, 1990–2000* (Washington, D.C.: Bureau of Justice Statistics, 2002).

22. Hickman and Reaves, *Local Police Departments, 2003,* p. 2.

23. Hickman and Reaves, *Local Police Departments, 2003,* p. 2.

24. Hickman and Reaves, *Local Police Departments, 2003,* p. 3

25. Chan, "Counting Heads Along the Thin Blue Line"; and Steve Hymon, "Council OKs Mayor's Plan to Add to Police Force by Hiking Trash Fee," *Los Angeles Times,* May 17, 2006.

26. Chan, "Counting Heads Along the Thin Blue Line."

27. Reaves and Hickman, *Census of State and Local Law Enforcement Agencies, 2000,* pp. 12–14.

28. Lee P. Brown, "The Role of the Sheriff," in *The Future of Policing,* ed. Alvin Cohn (Beverly Hills, Calif.: Sage, 1978), pp. 237–240.

29. Matthew J. Hickman and Brian A. Reaves, *Sheriffs' Offices, 2003* (Washington, D.C.: Bureau of Justice Statistics, 2006), p. iii.

30. Hickman and Reaves, *Sheriffs' Offices, 2003,* p. iii.

31. Hickman and Reaves, *Sheriffs' Offices, 2003,* p. iii.

32. Hickman and Reaves, *Sheriffs' Offices, 2003,* p. iii.

33. Hickman and Reaves, *Sheriffs' Offices, 2003,* p. 2.

34. John Hoffman, "Rural Policing," *Law and Order* (June 1992), pp. 20–24.

35. Hoffman, "Rural Policing."

36. Christopher S. Wren, "The Illegal Home Business: 'Speed' Manufacture," *New York Times,* July 8, 1997, p. A8.

37. Wren, "The Illegal Home Business."

38. James C. Howell and Arlen Egley Jr., *Gangs in Small Towns and Rural Counties* (Tallahassee, Florida: National Youth Gang Center, 2005).

39. Dennis Lindsey and Sean Kelly, "Issues in Small Town Policing: Understanding Stress," *FBI Law Enforcement Bulletin* (July 2004), pp. 1–7.

40. John M. Violanti, "Study Concludes Police Work is a Health Hazard," *American Police Beat* (November 2002).

41. Lindsey and Kelly, "Issues in Small Town Policing," pp. 1–7.

42. Lindsey and Kelly, "Issues in Small Town Policing," p. 7.

43. "Serving the Needs of Rural Law Enforcement," Criminal Justice Institute, National Center for Rural Law Enforcement, University of Arkansas System, retrieved June 9, 2006 from http://www.ncrle.net; and Lee Colwell, "The National Center for Rural Law Enforcement: One Part of the Greater Whole," *Community Policing Exchange* (March/April 1997), p. 6.

44. Laurence French, "Law Enforcement in Indian Country," *Criminal Justice Studies,* 18 (1, March 2005), pp. 69–80. This article contains an excellent history of the history of policing Indian country.

45. National Institute of Justice, *Public Law 280 and Law Enforcement in Indian Country–Research Priorities,* retrieved June 7, 2006 from http://www.ojp.usdoj.gov/nij/pubs-sum/209839.htm.

46. M. Wesley Clark, "Enforcing Criminal Law on Native American Lands," *FBI Law Enforcement Bulletin* (April 2005), pp. 22–31.

47. Steven W. Perry, *Census of Tribal Justice Agencies in Indian Country, 2002* (Washington, D.C.: U.S. Department of Justice, 2005), pp. 1–5; Also see Clark, "Enforcing Criminal Law on Native American Lands," pp. 22–31.

48. See Federal Bureau of Investigation, *Indian Country Crime,* retrieved June 9, 2006, from http://www.fbi.gov.

49. Perry, *Census of Tribal Justice Agencies in Indian Country, 2002,* pp. 6–11.

50. Kay Falk, "Indian Country—Where Wide Open Spaces and Boundaries Blur," *Law Enforcement Technology* (February 2006), pp. 18, 20–27.

51. Hickman and Reaves, *Local Police Departments, 2003,* p. 1; and Reaves and Hickman, *Census of State and Local Law Enforcement Agencies, 2000,* p. 11.

52. Hughes, *Justice Expenditure and Employment in the United States, 2003,* p. 3.

53. Hughes, *Justice Expenditure and Employment in the United States, 2003,* p. 3.

54. Brian A. Reaves and Lynne M. Bauer, *Federal Law Enforcement Officers, 2002* (Washington, D.C.: Bureau of Justice Statistics, 2003), p. 1.

55. Hughes, *Justice Expenditure and Employment in the United States, 2003,* p. 1.

56. Federal Bureau of Investigation, *FBI Homepage,* retrieved June 9, 2006 from http://www.fbi.gov.

57. Scott L. Salley, "Preparing Law Enforcement Leaders: The FBI Academy's Leadership Fellows Program, *FBI Law Enforcement Bulletin* (July 2005), pp. 20–23.

58. See, for example, Athan Theoharis and John Stuart Cox, *The Boss* (Philadelphia: Temple University Press, 1988). There are a myriad of books in college libraries and local public libraries regarding the history and operations of the FBI and the history of Director Hoover. An interesting class project or research paper may be to compare and contrast the treatment of the FBI and Hoover in the books published before his death in 1972 and after his death. Most authors needed the prior approval of Hoover and his officials before publication. The books published after his death generally paint a much different picture of Hoover and the FBI.

59. See, for example, Tony Poveda, *Lawlessness and Reform: The FBI in Transition* (Pacific Grove, Calif.: Brooks/Cole, 1990).

60. Federal Bureau of Investigation, *National Incident-Based Reporting System,* retrieved June 9, 2006 from http://www.fbi.gov.

61. Peter Grier, "Corruption Crackdown: The FBI Has Sharpened Its Focus on Public Graft," *Christian Science Monitor,* May 30, 2006.

62. Leonard G. Johns, Gerard F. Downes, and Camille D. Bibles, "Resurrecting Cold Case Serial Homicide Investigations," *FBI Law Enforcement Bulletin* (August 2005), pp. 1–7.

63. Eugene Rugala, James McNamara, and George Wattendorf, "Expert and Risk Assessment in Stalking Cases: The FBI's NCAVC as a Resource," *FBI Law Enforcement Bulletin* (November 2004), pp. 8–17.

64. Federal Bureau of Investigation, www.fbi.gov/pressrel/speeches/speech052902.htm.

65. Lesley G. Koestner, "Law Enforcement Online," *FBI Law Enforcement Bulletin* (February 2006), pp. 1–6.

66. Suzel Spiller, "The FBI's field intelligence groups and police," *FBI Law Enforcement Bulletin* (May 2006), pp. 1–6.

67. For a complete description of the DEA and many of its major programs, as well as a complete discussion of controlled substances and drug offenses, see John S. Dempsey, *Introduction to Investigations,* 2nd ed. (Belmont, Calif.: Wadsworth, 2003), Chapter 12.

68. See Rand Corporation, *Organizing for Homeland Security* (Santa Monica, Calif.: Rand Corporation, 2002); Randall A. Yim, *National Preparedness: Integration of Federal, State, Local and Private Sector Efforts Is Critical to an Effective National Strategy for Homeland Security* (Washington, D.C.: U.S. General Accounting Office, 2002); David M. Walker, *Homeland Security: Responsibility and Accountability for Achieving National Goals* (Washington, D.C.: U.S. General Accounting Office, 2002); Michael Barletta, *After 9/11: Preventing Mass-Destruction Terrorism and Weapons Proliferation* (Monterey, Calif.: Center for Nonproliferation Studies, 2002); and JayEtta Hecker, *Homeland Security: Intergovernmental Coordination and Partnership Will Be Critical to Success* (Washington, D.C.: U.S. General Accounting Office, 2002). All of these documents are available at NCJRS at http://www.ncjrs.gov.

69. U.S. Department of Homeland Security, *DHS Organization;* retrieved October 25, 2006, from http://www.dhs.gov/xabout/structure/editorial_0644.shtm.

70. Reaves and Bauer, *Federal Law Enforcement Officers, 2002.*

71. For an interesting recent article on joint terrorist task force resources, see James Casey, "Managing Joint Terrorism Task Force Resources," *FBI Law Enforcement Bulletin* (November 2004), pp. 1–6; also see Dempsey, *An Introduction to Investigations,* pp. 365–367.

72. Sherry L. Harowitz, "The New Centurions," *Security Management* (January 2003), pp. 51–58.

73. National Advisory Commission on Criminal Justice Standards and Goals, *Report of the Task Force on Private Security* (Washington, D.C.: U.S. Government Printing Office, 1976), p. 4.

74. The coverage of the Hallcrest Reports is based on Cunningham, Strauchs and Van Meter, *The Hallcrest Report II.*

75. Cunningham, Strauchs, and Van Meter, *The Hallcrest Report II,* p. 2.

76. David H. Bayley and Clifford D. Shearing, *The New Structure of Policing: Description, Conceptualization and Research Agenda* (Washington, D.C.: National Institute of Justice, 2001).

77. Samuel Walker, *The Police in America: An Introduction,* 3rd ed. (Boston: McGraw-Hill, 1999), p. 57.

78. "Policing for Profit: Welcome to the New World of Private Security" *Economist,* April 19, 1997, pp. 20–24.

79. "ASIS display promotes security careers," *Security Management* (July 1997), pp. 137–138; Tucker Carlson, "Safety Inc.," *Policy Review* (Summer 1995), pp. 72–73; Cunningham and Taylor, *The Hallcrest Report: Private Security;* Cunningham, Strauchs, and Van Meter, *The Hallcrest Report II* (this report was also published by the National Institute of Justice, in summary form, for the government as William C. Cunningham, John J. Strauchs, and Clifford W. Van Meter, *Private Security Patterns and Trends* [Washington, D.C.: U.S.

Government Printing Office, 1991]); and "Welcome to the New World of Private Security," *The Economist,* April 19, 1997.

80. U.S. Department of Labor, Bureau of Labor Statistics, *Occupational Outlook Handbook,* retrieved on October 5, 2005, from http://www.bls.gov/oco/ocos159.htm.

81. U.S. Department of Labor, Bureau of Labor Statistics, *Occupational Outlook Handbook.*

82. U.S. Department of Labor, Bureau of Labor Statistics, *Occupational Outlook Handbook.*

83. U.S. Department of Labor, Bureau of Labor Statistics, *Occupational Outlook Handbook.*

84. See John S. Dempsey and Linda S. Forst, *An Introduction to Policing,* 3rd ed. (Belmont, Calif.: Wadsworth, 2005), Chapter 5 for a discussion of the role of the police in society and Chapter 9 for a discussion of police patrol and omnipresence.

85. ASIS Online, *Professional Development: What is Security?,* retrieved on April 20, 2000 from http://www.asionline.org/careerwhat.html.

86. Robert J. Fischer and Gion Green, *Introduction to Security,* 6th ed. (Boston: Butterworth-Heinemann, 1998), p. 96.

87. William C. Cunningham and Todd H. Taylor, *The Growing Role of Private Security* (Washington, D.C.: U.S. Government Printing Office, 1988).

88. "D.C. Passes Security Guard Training Law," retrieved June 7, 2006 from http://www.officer.com.

89. U.S. Department of Labor, Bureau of Labor Statistics, *Security Guards and Gaming Surveillance Officers,* retrieved September 15, 2004 from http://www.bls.gov/oco/ocos159.htm.

90. International Association of Security Investigative Regulators, *Licensing,* retrieved October 5, 2005, from http://www.iasir.org.

91. Jack Lichtenstein, "Bush Signs Security Officer Employment Act," *ASIS Dynamics* (March/April 2005), pp. 1, 23–24; International Association of Security and Investigative Regulators, *IASIR Regulator* (Summer 2005), p. 1.

92. ASIS International, "About ASIS," retrieved October 20, 2005, from http://www.asisonline.org/about/index.xml.

93. Mary Alice Davidson, "It IS What You Know," *Security Management* (June 2003), p. 75.

94. Cunningham, Strauchs, and Van Meter, *Private Security,* p. 4.

95. Davidson, "It IS What You Know," p. 75.

96. Davidson, "It IS What You Know," p. 70.

97. Davidson, "It IS What You Know," p. 70.

98. Davidson, "It IS What You Know," p. 69.

99. Claire Hoffman, "As Anxiety Grows, So Does Field of Terror Study," *New York Times,* September 1, 2004.

100. Claire Hoffman, "As Anxiety Grows, So Does Field of Terror Study," p. C-1; "Universities Do Their Part in Anti-Terror Effort," *Law Enforcement News,* Spring 2004, p. 4.

101. Harowitz, "The New Centurions," pp. 51–58. Also, see Teresa Anderson, "A Year of Reassessment," *Security Management* (January 2003), pp. 61–65.

102. E. Meyr, "Tactical Response to Terrorism: The Concept and Its Application," *Law and Order* (March 1999), pp. 44–47.

103. U.S. Department of Labor, Bureau of Labor Statistics, *Occupational Outlook Handbook,* "Private Detectives and Investigators," retrieved May 15, 2003, from http://www.bls.gov/oco/ocos157.htm. For a complete description of the role and jobs performed by private investigators, see Dempsey, *Introduction to Investigations,* Chapter 15.

104. Sandy Granville Sheehy, "The Adventures of Harold Smith, Art Supersleuth," *Town and Country Monthly,* October 1992, p. 118.

105. Dick Adler, "Brian Jenkin's Excellent Adventures," *Inc.,* October 1991, p. 47.

106. Thomas Bancroft, "Growth Business," *Forbes,* September 1992, p. 516.

107. Pamela Marin and Warren Kalbacker, "Love Dicks," *Playboy,* January 1991, p. 102; Steven Edwards, "The Rush to Private Eyes: Wary Lovers Check Up on Partners," *Macleans's,* March 1990, p. 49; and Bill Colligan, "Just Dial 1–900–CHEATER," *Newsweek,* July 29, 1991, p. 58.

108. Peter Wilkinson, "The Big Sleazy," *Gentlemen's Quarterly,* January 1992, p. 112.

109. L. J. Davis, "International Gumshoe," *New York Times Magazine,* August 30, 1992, p. 46.

110. "Checking Out Prospective Mates: Check-a-Mate, a Private Detective Service," *USA Today Magazine,* December 1990, p. 4.

111. Tom Dunkel, "Holy Sleuth Frees Innocent Souls," *Insight,* February 4, 1991, p. 52.

112. Scott Shuger, "Public Eye," *New York Times Magazine,* September 13, 1992, p. 56.

113. Mark Ivey, "Philip Marlowe? No. Successful? Yes," *BusinessWeek,* October 21, 1991, p. 60.

114. Amanda Gardner, "Corporate Eyes," *Inc.,* November 1991, p. 61.

115. "Doggone? Bloodhound Ron Dufault Runs Around in Circles to Help Pet Owners Find Their Missing Pooches," *People Weekly,* September 10, 1990, p. 151.

116. Ronnie Virgets, "Secret Services," *New Orleans Magazine,* March 1992, p. 36.

117. Albert Reiss, *Private Employment of Public Police* (Washington, D.C.: National Institute of Justice, 1988).

118. Cunningham, Strauchs, and Van Meter, *Private Security Patterns,* p. 3.

119. For an excellent discussion of off-duty police officers working for private security concerns and the liability and constitutional issues involved, see David H. Peck, "When Police Walk the Security Beat," *Security Management* (October 1999), pp. 39–45.

120. Walker, *The Police in America: An Introduction,* 3rd ed. Boston: McGraw-Hill, 1999, p. 58.

121. Iver Peterson, "Walking the Beat from Macy's to Sears: More police departments assign officers to a private domain, the mall," *New York Times*, December 23 1998, p. B1, B5.

122. Peterson, "Walking the Beat from Macy's to Sears," p. B1.

123. Peterson, "Walking the Beat from Macy's to Sears," p. B5.

124. Marcia Chaiken and Jan Chaiken, *Public Policing— Privately Provided* (Washington, D.C.: National Institute of Justice, 1987).

125. Walker, *The Police in America,* p. 58.

126. Julia C. Mead, "Cops as Private Guards: To Serve and Protect Whom," *New York Times*, August 8, 2004, Section 14, pp. 1, 5.

Chapter 3

1. Nicholas Henry, *Public Administration and Public Affairs,* 9th ed. (Upper Saddle River, N.J.: Pearson Education, 2004), p. 58. He cites Victor A. Thompson, *Modern Organization* (New York: Knopf, 1961), p. 5; and Chester I. Barnard, *The Functions of the Executive* (Cambridge, Mass.: Harvard University Press, 1938), p. 11.

2. Patrick O'Hara, "Why Law Enforcement Organizations Fail: Mapping the Organizational Fault Lines in Policing," *Crime and Justice International* (March/April 2006), pp. 23–26.

3. Max Weber, "Bureaucracy," in *Essays in Sociology,* eds. Hans H. Gerth and C. Wright Mills (London: Oxford University Press, 1946); renewed 1973 by Hans H. Gerth.

4. Henry, *Public Administration and Public Affairs,* pp. 59–60.

5. Henry, *Public Administration and Public Affairs,* p. 1. Henry credits the first two lines of this paragraph to Ken Auletta, "The Lost Tycoon," *New Yorker,* April 23 and 30, 2001, p. 154.

6. "Leadership," *Thinkexist.com,* retrieved June 18, 2006, from http://en.thinkexist.com.

7. "Leadership," *Thinkexist.com.*

8. "Leadership," *Thinkexist.com.*

9. "Leadership," *Thinkexist.com.*

10. "Leadership," *Thinkexist.com.*

11. See, for example, David S. Corderman, "What Is Leadership," *Police Chief* (February 2006), p. 13; Daniel W. Ford, "The Impact of Leadership Communication," *Police Chief* (May 2006), p. 7; Tracey G. Gove, "Praise and Recognition: The Importance of Social Support in Law Enforcement," *FBI Law Enforcement Bulletin* (October 2005), pp. 14–19; Jeff Green, "The Leadership Paradox," *Police Chief* (March 2006), p. 13; Wayne McFarlin, "Jump-Starting a Leadership Team," *FBI Law Enforcement Bulletin* (April 2006), pp. 1–9; Thomas Q. Weitzel, "Managing the Problem Employee: A Roadmap for Success," *Police Chief* (November 2004), pp. 25–32; Todd Wuestewald, and Brigitte Steinheider, "Shared Leadership: Can Empowerment Work in Police Organizations," *Police Chief* (January 2006), pp. 48–55; Wuestewald and Steinheider, "The Changing Face of Police Leadership," *Police Chief* (April 2006), pp. 26–32; Wuestewald and Steinheider, "How to Implement Shared Leadership," *Police Chief* (April 2006), pp. 34–37.

12. Robert C. Wadman and William Thomas Allison, *To Protect and to Serve: A History of Police in America* (Upper Saddle River: N.J.: Pearson/Prentice Hall, 2004), pp. 76–77.

13. Samuel Walker, *A Critical History of Police Reform: The Emergence of Professionalization* (Lexington, Mass.: Lexington Books, 1977), p. 67.

14. Wadman and Allison, *To Protect and to Serve,* p. 77.

15. Wuestewald and Steinheider, "Shared Leadership," pp. 48–55.

16. Weitzel, "Managing the Problem Employee," pp. 25–32.

17. Wuestewald and Steinheider, "Shared Leadership," pp. 48–55.

18. Lorie Fridell, "The results of three national surveys on community policing," in Lorie Fridell, *Community Policing: Past, Present, and Future*. (Washington, D.C.: Police Executive Research Forum, 2004).

19. K. Beck, "Optimizing the Organizational Commitment of Police Officers," *National Police Research Unit* (2005).

20. Peter Drucker, *Managing in the Next Society* (New York: St. Martin's, 2002).

21. S. Kim, "Participative Management and Job Satisfaction: Lessons for Management Learning," *Public Administration Review* 62 (2, 2002), pp. 231–241. Shared leadership concepts can be traced back to Elton Mayo's Hawthorne studies of the Western Electric Plant during the 1920s and 1930s in which worker job involvement emerged as an important aspect of job production. It can also be connected with humanist traditions of organizational psychology including the groundbreaking work of Abraham Maslow. See Henry, *Public Administration and Public Affairs,* p. 64; and Abraham H. Maslow, "A Theory of Human Motivation," *Psychological Review* 50 (July 1943), pp. 370–396.

22. Wuestewald and Steinheider, "Shared Leadership," pp. 48–55; also see Wuestewald and Steinheider, "The Changing Face of Police Leadership, *Police Chief* (April 2006), pp. 26–32; and Wuestewald and Steinheider, "How to Implement Shared Leadership," *Police Chief* (April 2006), pp. 34–37.

23. Vincent E. Henry, *The CompStat Paradigm: Management Accountability in Policing, Business and the Public Sector* (Flushing, N.Y.: Looseleaf Law, 2002).

24. Gregory P. Rothaus, "6 Strategies for Successful Team-Building Workshops," *Police Chief* (May 2006), pp. 48–52.

25. Wadman and Allison, *To Protect and to Serve,* p. 64.

26. James F. Richardson, *Urban Police in the United States* (Port Washington, N.Y.: Kennikat Press, 1974), p. 51.

27. Walker, *A Critical History of Police Reform,* p. 9.

28. Robert M. Fogelson, *Big-City Police* (Cambridge, Mass.: Harvard University Press, 1977), p. 36; Walker, *A Critical History of Police Reform,* p. 9; Wadman and Allison, *To Protect and to Serve,* p. 64.

29. Wadman and Allison, *To Protect and to Serve,* p. 76.

30. Raymond B. Fosdick, *American Police Systems* (New York: Century, 1920; reprint Montclair, N.J.: Patterson Smith, 1969), pp. 269–285.

31. George W. Griesinger, Jeffrey S. Slovak, and Joseph J. Molkup, *Civil Service Systems: Their Impact on Police Administration* (Washington, D.C.: U.S. Government Printing Office, 1979); Dorothy Guyot, "Blending Granite: Attempts to Change the Rank Structure of American Police Departments," *Journal of Police Science and Administration* 7 (1979), pp. 253–284.

32. Information received June 26, 2006 from Professor Pat Faiella of Massasoit Community College, Massachusetts. Pat is also a part-time police officer with the Hanson Police Department.

33. Scott Oldham, "Sergeant: Apathy Kills," *Law and Order* (January 2006), p. 30.

34. Scott Oldham, "Sergeant: Decision Making 101," *Law and Order* (March 2006), p. 16.

35. Robert Roy Johnson, "Captain—Workplace Dissent," *Law and Order* (April 2006), p. 16; also see Johnson, "Captain: Humor," *Law and Order* (May 2006,) p. 14.

36. John M. Collins, "Labor Relations: Promulgating a New Rule," *Police Chief*, retrieved June 12, 2006 from http://www.policechiefmagazine.org.

37. National Institute of Law Enforcement and Criminal Justice, *Employing Civilians for Police Work* (Washington, D.C.: U.S. Government Printing Office, 1975), preface.

38. President's Commission on Law Enforcement and Administration of Justice, *Task Force Report: The Police* (Washington, D.C.: U.S. Government Printing Office, 1967), p. 123.

39. International Association of Chiefs of Police, *Operational Issues in the Small Law Enforcement Agency* (Arlington, Va.: International Association of Chiefs of Police, 1990).

40. Randall Aragon, "Does Your Agency Need a Reserve Officer Program?" *Police Chief* (November 1994), pp. 27–29.

41. Geoffrey N. Calvert, *Portable Police Pensions Improving Inter-Agency Transfers* (Washington, D.C.: U.S. Government Printing Office, 1971); and President's Commission on Law Enforcement and Administration of Justice, *The Challenge of Crime in a Free Society* (Washington, D.C.: U.S. Government Printing Office, 1967), p. 112.

42. W. Hurd, "In Defense of Public Service: Union Strategy in Transition," *Working USA*, 7 (January 2005); and David KIingner and J. Nalbandian, *Public Personnel Management: Contexts and Strategies* (Upper Saddle River: N.J.: Prentice Hall, 1988).

43. Information received June 26, 2006, from Denise Owens, Project Coordinator for the Roger Williams University Justice System Training and Research Institute, and Sergeant Tom Owens, Detective Sergeant, South Kingstown, Rhode Island, Police Department.

44. M. J. Levine, "Historical Overview of Police Unionization in the United States," *Police Journal* (October/December 1988), pp. 334–343.

45. J. Zhao and N. Lovrich, "Collective Bargaining and the Police: The Consequences for Supplemental Compensation Policies in Large Agencies," *Policing: An International Journal of Police Strategies and Management*, 20 (3, 1997), pp. 508–518.

46. See Anthony V. Bouza, "Police Unions: Paper Tigers or Roaring Lions?," pp. 241–280; James B. Jacobs, "Police Unions: How They Look from the Academic Side," pp. 286–290; and Robert B. Kliesmet, "The Chief and the Union: May the Force Be with You," pp. 281–285—all from *Police Leadership in America*, ed. William A. Geller (New York: Praeger, 1985). Also see M. J. Levine, "Historical Overview of Police Unionization in the United States," pp. 334–343; Edward A. Thibault, Lawrence M. Lynch, and R. Bruce McBride, *Proactive Police Management*, 6th ed. (Upper Saddle River, N.J.: Prentice Hall, 2004), p. 425; and Wadman and Allison, *To Protect and to Serve*, pp. 85–89.

47. W. J. Bopp, "Year They Cancelled Mardi Gras—The New Orleans Police Strike of 1979," in Charles A. Salerno, *Police at the Bargaining Table* (Springfield, Ill.: Charles C. Thomas, 1981), pp. 201–221.

48. Bopp, "Year They Cancelled Mardi Gras," pp. 201–221.

49. The January 2006 edition of *Police Chief* magazine has an interesting illustrated article on new or redesigned police buildings. The IACP publishes its *Police Facility Guidelines* to help police chiefs understand the needs and requirements of police facilities, "Special Focus: Police Facilities," *Police Chief* (January 2006), pp. 41–47.

50. Robert Sheehan and Gary W. Cordner, *Introduction to Police Administration,* 2nd ed. (Cincinnati, Ohio: Anderson, 1989), pp. 113–162.

Chapter 4

1. Troy Mineard, "Recruiting and Retaining Gen-X Officers," *Law and Order,* 51 (7, July 2003), pp. 94–95.

2. Jim Weiss and Mickey Davis, "People with Abilities: The Untapped Resource," *Law and Order* (September 2003), pp. 70–73.

3. John C. Klotter, Jaqueline R. Kanovitz, and Michael I. Kanovitz, *Constitutional Law,* 9th ed. (Cincinnati, Ohio: Anderson, 2002).

4. City of Madison, Wisconsin, police recruiting website, retrieved November 1, 2006, from www.cityofmadison.com/police/recruit.html.

5. Klotter, Kanovitz, and Kanovitz, *Constitutional Law.*

6. Mike Pearl, "'Age' Ruling Backs Cops in Battle of Blue & Grey." *New York Post* (May 31, 1997), p. 12; and "Age Before Duty? Police Brass Alter Ground Rules, Leaving Some Over—35 NYPD Rookies Standing at the Altar," *Law Enforcement News* (April 1997), p. 5.

7. "The Special Appeal of Mid-Life Recruits." *Law Enforcement News,* 30 (625, Fall 2004), p. 5.

8. Matthew Hickman and Brian Reaves, *Local Police Departments, 2003* (Washington, D.C.: Bureau of Justice Statistics, 2006), NCJ#210118.

9. National Commission on Law Observance and Enforcement, *Lawlessness in Law Enforcement* (Washington, D.C.: U.S. Government Printing Office, 1931).

10. James B. Jacobs and Samuel B. Magdovitz, "At LEEPs End: A Review of the Law Enforcement Education Program,"

Journal of Police Science and Administration, 5 (1977), pp. 1–17.

11. President's Commission on Law Enforcement and Administration of Justice, *The Challenge of Crime in a Free Society* (Washington, D.C.: U.S. Government Printing Office, 1967), pp. 110.

12. R. Schanlaub, "Degree or No Degree," *Law and Order* (September 2005), pp. 76–82.

13. M. Napier, The Need for Higher Education. *Law and Order* (September 2005), pp. 86–94.

14. J. D. Dailey, "An Investigation of Police Officers Background and Performance: an Analytical Study of the Effect of Age, Time in Service, Prior Military Service, and Educational Level on Commendations" (PhD dissertation, Sam Houston State University, 2002); V. E. Kappeler, A. D. Sapp, and D. L. Carter, Police Officer Higher Education, Citizen Complaints and Department Rule Violations, *American Journal of Police,* 11 (2, 1992), pp. 37–54; B. J. Palombo, *Academic Professionalism in Law Enforcement* (New York: Garland, 1995); and S. M. Smith and M. G. Aamodt, "The Relationship Between Education, Experience, and Police Performance," *Journal of Police and Criminal Psychology,* 12 (2, 1997), pp. 7–14.

15. C. R. Baratta, "The Relationship Between Education and Police Work Performance" (masters thesis, East Tennessee State University, 1998); S. E. Buttolph, "Effect of College Education on Police Behavior: Analysis of Complaints and Commendations" (masters thesis, East Tennessee State University, 1999); and D. S. Peterson, "The Relationship Between Educational Attainment and Police Performance," (PhD diss., Illinois State University, 2001).

16. Lawrence W. Sherman and the National Advisory Commission on Higher Education for Police Officers, *The Quality of Police Education* (San Francisco: Jossey-Bass, 1978), pp. 185–188.

17. Sherman et al., *Quality of Police Education,* pp. 185–188.

18. M. D. Bostrom, "The Influence of Higher Education on Police Officer Work Habits" *Police Chief,* 72 (10, October 2005).

19. L. K. Decker and R. G. Huckabee, "Raising the Age and Educational Requirements for Police Officers: Will Too Many Women and Minority Candidates Be Excluded? *Policing: An International Journal of Police Strategies and Management,* 25 (4, 2002), pp. 789–806.

20. "Indiana State Police to drop college requirement for recruits" *Indianapolis Star,* cited in Ted Gest, *Crime and Justice News,* December 8, 2005, retrieved from http://cjj.mn-8.net/login.asp?loc=&link=.

21. "How much do college educations improve policing" *Des Moines Register,* cited in Ted Gest, *Crime and Justice News,* November 22, 2005, retrieved from http://cjj.mn-8.net/login.asp?loc=&link=.

22. Kevin Krause, "Police Agencies Mellow on Applicant's Drug Use," retrieved December 11, 2002, from www.sun-sentinel.com.

23. Arthur Sharp, "Departmental Divergences on Marijuana use and New Recruits," *Law and Order* (September 2003), pp. 80–81.

24. Hickman and Reaves, *Local Police Departments, 2003.*

25. Gary W. Cordner, Kathryn E. Scarborough, and Robert Sheehan, *Police Administration,* 5th ed. (Cincinnati, Ohio: Anderson, 2004), p. 156.

26. C. S. Koper, *Hiring and Keeping Police Officers,* Washington, D.C.: National Institute of Justice, 2004), NCJ#202289.

27. John Pomfret, "Police Finding It Hard to Fill Jobs," *Washington Post,* retrieved March 27, 2006, from Washingtonpost.com.

28. U.S. Census Bureau Public Information Office, retrieved March 18, 2004, from www.census.gov/press-release.

29. Retrieved from www.census.gov/.

30. Kathy Bushouse, "Creativity Tops off Police Recruitment," retrieved June 17, 2002, from www.sun-sentinel.com.

31. Bushouse, "Creativity Tops off Police Recruitment."

32. G. Sentementes, "Police Expand Hiring Efforts," retrieved May 23, 2006, from www.baltimoresun.com

33. B. Taylor, B. Kubu, L. Fridell, C. Rees, T. Jordan, and J. Cheney, *Cop Crunch: Identifying Strategies for Dealing with the Recruiting and Hiring Crisis in Law Enforcement* (Washington, D.C.: U.S. Department of Justice, National Institute of Justice, 2005), NCJ# 213800.

34. "Hiring Problem? What Hiring Problem? NYSP Has Answers to Recruiting Slump," *Law Enforcement News,* November 30, 2000, p. 1.

35. A. Gendar, M. Saul, "NYPD Seeking 1200 Newbies to Boost Force," retrieved March 22, 2006, from www.nydailynews.com.

36. *Guardians Association of NYC Police Department v. Civil Service Commission of New York,* 23 FEP 909 (1980).

37. D. Thompson and T. Thompson, "Court Standards for Job Analysis in Test Validation," *Personnel Psychology,* 35, pp. 865–874.

38. Hickman and Reaves, *Local Police Departments, 2003.*

39. City of Madison, Wisconsin, police recruiting website, retrieved November 1, 2006, from www.cityofmadison.com/police/recruit.html.

40. Timothy N. Oettmeier, "Perspectives on Selection Procedures," *Community Policing Exchange* (March/April 1997), p. 1.

41. Cordner, Scarborough, and Sheehan, *Police Administration,* p. 158.

42. Cordner, Scarborough, and Sheehan, *Police Administration,* p. 159.

43. E. Scrivner, *Innovations in Police Recruitment & Hiring: Hiring in the Spirit of Service* (Washington, D.C.: Department of Justice, 2006), NCJ#212981.

44. K. Johnson, "The Community Recruiter," *Police Chief,* 72 (6, June 2005).

45. L. Bowden, "Community Helps Devise Deputy Traits," *Community Links,* on The Community Policing Consortium website, retrieved from www.communitypolicing.org/publications/comlinks/.

46. K. Dayan, R. Kastan, and S. Fac, "Entry-Level Police Candidate Assessment Center: An Efficient Tool or a Hammer to Kill a Fly? *Personnel Psychology,* 55 (4, 2002), pp. 827–849.

47. M. Bromley, "Evaluating the Use of the Assessment Center Process for Entry-Level Police Officer Selection in a Medium Sized Police Agency," *Journal of Police and Criminal Psychology,* 10 (4, 1996), pp. 33–40; Dayan et al., Entry-Level Police Candidate Assessment Center; and C. Hale, "Candidate Evaluation & Scoring," *Law and Order* (December 2005), pp. 86–87.

48. Hale, "Candidate Evaluation & Scoring."

49. C. Legel, "Evaluating an Entry-Level Exam," *Law and Order* (December 2005), pp. 66–69.

50. *Dayton Daily News,* November 7, 2005, cited Ted Gest, *Crime and Justice News,* retrieved from http://cjj.mn-8.net/login.asp?loc=&link=.

51. Thomas R. Collingwood, Robert Hoffman, and Jay Smith, "Underlying Physical Fitness Factors for Performing Police Officer Physical Tasks," *Police Chief* (March 2004), pp. 32–37.

52. Dan Eggen and Shankar Vendantam, "Polygraph Results Often in Question," *Washington Post,* retrieved May 1, 2006, from www.washingtonpost.com.

53. Arnold Holzman and Mark Kirschner, "Pre-Employment Psychological Evaluations," *Law and Order* (September 2003), pp. 85–87.

54. "Guidelines for Police Psychological Service," IACP Police Psychological Services Section, *Police Chief,* 72 (9, September 2005).

55. The Americans with Disabilities Act (ADA); available at http://www.eeoc.gov/ada.

56. Hickman Reaves, *Local Police Departments 2003.*

57. Matthew Hickman, *State and Local Law Enforcement Training Academies, 2002* (Washington, D.C.: Department of Justice, January 2005), NCJ#204030.

58. Jennifer Nislow, "Who Wins with 'Pay as You Go' Pre-Academy Training Programs?," *Law Enforcement News,* Fall 2004, pp. 1, 10.

59. President's Commission on Law Enforcement and Administration of Justice, Challenge of Crime, pp. 112–113.

60. Hickman and Reaves, *Local Police Departments, 2003.*

61. Hickman and Reaves, *Local Police Departments, 2003.*

62. Jerry Hoover, "The Reno Model Police Training Officer (PTO) Program," *NAFTO News,* December 2004, pp. 10–17.

63. Hickman and Reaves, *Local Police Departments, 2003.*

64. Hickman and Reaves, *Local Police Departments, 2003.*

65. Hickman and Reaves, *Local Police Departments, 2003.*

Chapter 5

1. Herman Goldstein, *Policing a Free Society* (Cambridge, Mass: Ballinger, 1977), p. 21.

2. George L. Kirkham and Laurin A. Wollan, Jr., *Introduction to Law Enforcement* (New York: Harper & Row, 1980), p. 336.

3. Federal Bureau of Investigation, *Uniform Crime Reports,* Arrests 2005, retrieved November 3, 2006, from http://www.fbi.gov.

4. Matthew R. Durose, Erika L. Schmitt, and Patrick A. Langan, *Contacts Between Police and the Public: Findings from the 2002 National Survey* (Washington, D.C.: Bureau of Justice Statistics, U.S. Department of Justice, 2005); and Lawrence A. Greenfeld, Patrick A. Langan, and Steven K. Smith, *Police Use of Force: Collection of National Data* (Washington, D.C.: Bureau of Justice Statistics, 1997).

5. Elaine Cumming, I. Cumming, and L. Edell, "Policeman as a Philosopher, Friend and Guide," 1965, in eds. Abraham S. Blumberg and Elaine Niederhoffer, *The Ambivalent Force: Perspectives on the Police,* 3rd ed. (New York: Holt, Rinehart and Winston, 1985), pp. 212–219.

6. John Webster, "Police Task and Time Study," *Journal of Criminal Law, Criminology, and Police Science,* 61 (1970), pp. 94–100.

7. Robert Lilly, "What Are the Police Now Doing?," *Journal of Police Science and Administration,* 6 (1978), pp. 51–53.

8. Eric J. Scott, *Calls for Service: Citizen Demand and Initial Police Response* (Washington, D.C.: National Institute of Justice, 1981), pp. 28–30.

9. Michael Brown, *Working the Street* (New York: Russell Sage Foundation, 1981); Albert J. Reiss, *The Police and the Public* (New Haven, Conn.: Yale University Press, 1971); and Norman Weiner, *The Role of Police in Urban Society: Conflict and Consequences* (Indianapolis: Bobbs-Merrill, 1976).

10. Stephen Meagher, "Police Patrol Styles: How Pervasive is Community Variation?," *Journal of Police Science and Administration,* 13 (1985), pp. 36–55.

11. Egon Bittner, *The Functions of the Police in Modern Society* (Cambridge, Mass.: Oelgeschlager, Gunn, and Hain, 1979), p. 8.

12. Carl B. Klockars, *Idea of Police* (Thousand Oaks, Calif.: Sage, 1985).

13. Alan Coffey, *Law Enforcement: A Human Relations Approach* (Englewood Cliffs, N.J.: Prentice Hall, 1990), p. 247. The author cites as an excellent example Bruce J. Terris, "The Role of the Police," *Annals of the American Academy of Political and Social Science* (November 1967).

14. George Pugh, "The Police Officer: Qualities, Roles and Concepts," *Journal of Police Science and Administration,* 14 (1986), pp. 1–6.

15. Robert Sheehan and Gary W. Cordner, *Introduction to Police Administration,* 2nd ed. (Cincinnati: Anderson, 1989), p. 62. In stating this core role, the authors cite the work of Bittner, *Functions of the Police in Modern Society;* Carl B. Klockars, ed., *Thinking about Police: Contemporary Readings* (New York: McGraw-Hill, 1983), pp. 227–231; and William K. Muir, Jr., *Police: Streetcorner Politicians* (Chicago: University of Chicago Press, 1977).

16. Larry J. Siegel and Joseph J. Senna, *Introduction to Criminal Justice,* 10th ed. (Belmont, Calif.: Thomson/Wadsworth, 2005).

17. Sheehan and Cordner, *Introduction to Police Administration,* p. 16.

18. Senna and Siegel, *Introduction to Criminal Justice,* p. 217.

19. Sheehan and Cordner, *Introduction to Police Administration,* pp. 16–21.

20. Siegel and Senna, *Introduction to Criminal Justice,* p. 211. Siegel and Senna cite in this regard, Jack Kuykendall and Roy Roberg, "Police Manager's Perception of Employee Types: A Conceptual Model," *Journal of Criminal Justice,* 16 (1988), pp. 131–135.

21. Siegel and Senna, *Introduction to Criminal Justice,* p. 211. Siegel and Senna cite in this regard, William Muir, *Police: Streetcorner Politicians* (Chicago: University of Chicago Press, 1977); and James Q. Wilson, *Varieties of Police Behavior: The Munugement of Law and Order in Eight Communities* (Cambridge, Mass.: Harvard University Press, 1968).

22. John J. Broderick, *Police in a Time of Change,* 2nd ed. (Prospect Heights, Ill.: Waveland Press, 1987).

23. The discussion of Wilson's police operational styles is based on Wilson, *Varieties of Police Behavior.*

24. Muir, *Police: Streetcorner Politicians.* Note: Klockars, in his final chapter of *Idea of Police,* discusses Muir's theories of good police and good policing and his typology of four police types by using examples from the television program *Hill Street Blues.*

25. Ellen Hochstedler, "Police Types—An Empirical Test of a Typology of Individual Police Officers" (PhD diss., State University of New York at Albany, 1980); and Hochstedler, "Testing Types—A Review and Test of Police Types," *Journal of Criminal Justice,* 9 (6, 1981), pp. 451–456.

26. John Van Maanen, "Asshole," in eds. Peter K. Manning and John Van Maanen, *Policing: A View from the Street* (Santa Monica, Calif.: Goodyear, 1978), pp. 221–238.

27. John Van Maanen, "Kinsmen in Repose: Occupational Perspectives of Patrolmen," in Manning and Van Maanen, *Policing: A View from the Street,* pp. 115–128.

28. Claudia Mendias and E. James Kehoe, "Engagement of Policing Ideals and Their Relationship to the Exercise of Discretionary Powers," *Criminal Justice and Behavior* (February, 2006), pp. 70–92.

29. Wilson, *Varieties of Police Behavior,* p. 187.

30. Michael R. Gottfredson and Don M. Gottfredson, *Decision Making in Criminal Justice: Toward the Rational Exercise of Discretion* (Cambridge, Mass.: Ballinger, 1980), p. 87.

31. Kenneth Culp Davis, *Police Discretion* (St. Paul, Minn.: West 1975).

32. Gary W. Cordner, "Police Patrol Work Load Studies: A Review and Critique," *Police Studies,* 2 (4, 1979), pp. 50–60.

33. Christine N. Famega, James Frank, and Lorraine Mazerolle, "Managing Police Patrol Time: The Role of Supervisor Directives," *Justice Quarterly,* 22 (4, December 2005), pp. 540–559.

34. Christine N. Famega, "Variation in Officer Downtime: A Review of the Research," *Policing: An International Journal of Police Strategies and Management,* 28 (3, 2005), pp. 388–414.

35. John Liederbach and James Frank, "Policing the Big Beat: An Observational Study of County Level Patrol and Comparisons to Local Small Town and Rural Officers," *Journal of Crime and Justice,* 29 (1, 2006), pp. 21–44.

36. Donald Black, *The Manners and Customs of the Police* (New York: Academic Press, 1980), p. 90.

37. John A. Gardiner, *Traffic and the Police: Variations in Law Enforcement Policy* (Cambridge, Mass.: Harvard University Press, 1969).

38. Catherine H. Milton et al., *Police Use of Deadly Force* (Washington, D.C.: Police Foundation, 1977).

39. Sheehan and Cordner, *Introduction to Police Administration,* pp. 52–53.

40. Herbert Jacob, *Urban Justice* (Boston: Little, Brown, 1973), p. 27.

41. Wilson, *Varieties of Police Behavior,* pp. 83–89.

42. Larry J. Siegel, Dennis Sullivan, and Jack R. Greene, "Decision Games Applied to Police Decision Making," *Journal of Criminal Justice* (Summer, 1974), pp. 132–142.

43. Irving Pilavin and Scott Briar, "Police Encounters with Juveniles," *American Journal of Sociology,* 70 (1964), pp. 206–214.

44. John D. McCluskey, William Terrill, and Eugene A. Paoline, III, "Peer Group Aggressiveness and the Use of Coercion in Police-Suspect Encounters," *Police Practice & Research: An International Journal,* 6 (1, March 2005), pp. 19–37.

45. Wilson, *Varieties of Police Behavior.*

46. William Willbanks, *The Myth of a Racist Criminal Justice System* (Monterey, Calif.: Brooks/Cole, 1987).

47. Arrick L. Jackson and Lorenzo M. Boyd, "Minority-Threat Hypothesis and the Workload Hypothesis: A Community-Level Examination of Lenient Policing in High Crime Communities," *Criminal Justice Studies,* 18 (2005), pp. 29–50.

48. U.S. Department of Justice, *Police-Public Contact Survey, 1999* (Washington, D.C.: U.S. Department of Justice, 2001).

49. Robin Shepard Engel and Jennifer M. Calnon, "Examining the Influence of Drivers' Characteristics During Traffic Stops with Police: Results from a National Survey," *Justice Quarterly,* 21 (1, 2004), pp. 49–90.

50. Dennis Powell, "Race, Rank, and Police Discretion," *Journal of Police Science and Administration,* 9 (1981), pp. 383–389.

51. Dale Dannefer and Russel Schutt, "Race and Juvenile Justice Processing in Court and Police Agencies," *American Journal of Sociology,* 87 (1982), pp. 113–132.

52. Matthew R. Durose, Erika L. Schmitt, and Patrick A. Langan, *Contacts between Police and the Public: Findings from the 2002 National Survey* (Washington, D.C.: Bureau of Justice Statistics, U.S. Department of Justice, 2005), p. 4–15.

53. Durose, Schmitt, and Langan, *Contacts between Police and the Public.*

54. Douglas Smith, Christy Visher, and Laura Davidson, "Equity and Discretionary Justice: The Influence of Race on Police Arrest Decisions," *Journal of Criminal Law and Criminology,* 75 (1984), pp. 234–249.

55. Cecil Willis and Richard Wells, "The Police and Child Abuse, An Analysis of Police Decisions to Report Illegal Behavior," *Criminology* 26, 1988, pp. 696–716.

56. Robert A. Brown and James Frank, "Race and Officer Decision Making: Examining Differences in Arrest Outcomes Between Black and White Officers," *Justice Quarterly,* 23 (1, March 2006), pp. 96–126. For another study focused on the race of the officer, see David Eitle, Lisa Stolzenberg, and Stewart J. D'Alessio, "Police Organizational Factors, the Racial Composition of the Police, and the Probability of Arrest," *Justice Quarterly,* 22 (1, March 2005), pp. 30–57.

57. Douglas Smith and Christy Visher, "Street-Level Justice: Situational Determinants of Police Arrest Decisions," *Social Problems,* 29 (1981), pp. 167–177.

58. Christy Visher, "Gender, Police Arrest Decisions, and Notions of Chivalry," *Criminology,* 2 (1, 1983), pp. 5–28.

59. Richard J. Lundman, "Demeanor or Crime? The Midwest City Police-Citizen Encounter Study," *Criminology,* 32 (4, 1994), pp. 631–656.

60. David Klinger, "More on Demeanor and Arrest in Dade County," *Criminology,* 34 (1, 1996), pp. 61–82.

61. K. Novak, J. Frank, B. Smith, and R. Engel, "Revisiting the Decision to Arrest: Comparing Beat and Community Officers," *Crime and Delinquency,* 48 (1, 2002), pp. 70–98; and R. Worden and R. Shepard, "Demeanor, Crime, and Police Behavior: A Reexamination of the Police Services Study Data," *Criminology,* 34 (1, 1996), pp. 83–105.

62. R. J. Lundman and R. L. Kaufman, "Driving While Black: Effects of Race Ethnicity and Gender on Citizen Self-Reports of Traffic Stops and Police Actions," *Criminology,* 41 (1, 2003), pp. 195–220.

63. Engel and Calnon, "Examining the Influence of Drivers' Characteristics," pp. 49–90.

64. Durose, Schmitt, and Langan, *Contacts between Police and the Public,* pp. 4, 16.

65. Michael R. Smith, Matthew Makarios, and Geoffrey P. Alpert, "Differential Suspicion: Theory Specification and Gender Effects in the Traffic Stop Context," *Justice Quarterly,* 23 (2, June 2006), pp. 271–295.

66. See Sandra Lee Browning et al., "Race and Getting Hassled by the Police: a Research Note," *Police Studies,* 17 (1994), pp. 1–10; Darlene Conley, "Adding Color to a Black and White Picture: Using Qualitative Data to Explain Racial Disproportionality in the Juvenile Justice System," *Journal of Research in Crime and Delinquency,* 31 (1994), pp. 135–148; David Klinger, "Demeanor or Crime? Why 'Hostile' Citizens Are More Likely to Be Arrested," *Criminology,* 32 (1994), pp. 475–493; Larry Miller and Michael Braswell, "Police Perception of Ethical Decision Making: The Ideal vs. the Real," *American Journal of Police,* 11 (1992), pp. 27–45; and Eric Riksheim and Steven Cermak, "Causes of Police Behavior Revisited," *Journal of Criminal Justice,* 21 (1993), pp. 353–382.

67. Geoffrey P. Alpert, Roger G. Dunham, Meghan Stroshine, Katherine Bennett, and John MacDonald, *Police Officers' Decision Making and Discretion: Forming Suspicion and Making a Stop* (Washington, D.C.: National Institute of Justice, 2006).

68. Davis, *Police Discretion;* and Herman Goldstein, "Police Discretion: The Ideal vs. the Real," *Public Administration Review,* 23 (1963), pp. 148–156.

69. Goldstein, *Policing a Free Society,* p. 112.

70. *Tennessee v. Garner,* 471 U.S. 1 (1985).

71. Lori Rhyons and David C. Brewster, "Employee Early Warning Systems: Helping Supervisors Protect Citizens, Officers, and Agencies," *Police Chief,* 69 (11, November 2002), pp. 32–36.

72. Wilson, *Varieties of Police Behavior,* p. 33.

73. Robert Moran, "Street: Police Critics 'Unfair,'" *Philadelphia Inquirer,* May 4, 2006.

74. Durose, Schmitt, and Langan, *Contacts between Police and the Public,* pp. 16–21.

75. Joel H. Garner and Christopher D. Maxwell, *Understanding the Prevalence and Severity of Force Used by and Against the Police, Executive Summary* (Washington, D.C.: National Institute of Justice, 2002); and Garner and Maxwell, *Understanding the Prevalence and Severity of Force used by and Against the Police, Final Report* (Washington, D.C.: National Institute of Justice, 2002).

76. James Q. Wilson, "Police Use of Deadly Force," *FBI Law Enforcement Bulletin* (August 1980), p. 16.

77. James J. Fyfe, "Police Use of Deadly Force: Research and Reform," *Justice Quarterly,* 5 (1988), pp. 164–205.

78. Jodi M. Brown and Patrick A. Langan, *Policing and Homicide, 1976–1998: Justifiable Homicide by Police, Police Officers Murdered by Felons* (Washington, D.C.: National Institute of Justice, 2001).

79. Brown and Langan, *Policing and Homicide, 1976–1998.*

80. Brown and Langan, *Policing and Homicide, 1976–1998.*

81. Gerald Robin, "Justifiable Homicide by Police," *Journal of Criminal Law, Criminology, and Police Science* (May/June, 1963), pp. 225–231.

82. James J. Fyfe, "Reducing the Use of Deadly Force: The New York Experience," in National Institute of Justice, *Police Use of Deadly Force* (Washington, D.C.: National Institute of Justice, 1978), p. 29.

83. William A. Geller and Kevin J. Karales, *Split-Second Decisions* (Chicago: Chicago Law Enforcement Study Group, 1981), p. 119.

84. James Fyfe, "Shots Fired" (PhD diss., State University of New York at Albany, 1978).

85. David Lester, "Predicting the Rate of Justifiable Homicide by Police Officers," *Police Studies,* 16 (1993), p. 43.

86. Michael D. White, "Identifying Situational Predictors of Police Shootings Using Multivariate Analysis," *Policing: An International Journal of Police Strategies and Management,* 25 (4, 2004), pp. 726–752.

87. Florangela Davila, "Study: People more likely to see Blacks as a threat," *Seattle Times,* July 9, 2003, pp. B1 and B2.

88. *Tennessee v. Garner,* 471 U.S. 1 (1985).

89. Michael D. Greathouse, "Criminal Law—The Right to Run: Deadly Force and the Fleeing Felon, *Tennessee v. Garner,*"

in ed. Michael J. Palmiotto, *Police Misconduct: A Reader for the 21st Century* (Upper Saddle River, N.J.: Prentice Hall, 2001), pp. 243–255.

90. Lawrence O'Donnell, *Deadly Force* (New York: William Morrow, 1983), p. 14. See also Abraham Tennenbaum, "The Influence of the *Garner* Decision on Police Use of Deadly Force," *Journal of Law and Criminology,* 85 (1994).

91. James J. Fyfe, "Administrative Interventions on Police Shooting Discretion: an Empirical Analysis," *Journal of Criminal Justice,* 7 (1979), pp. 309–323; and Fyfe, cited in Lawrence O'Donnell, *Deadly Force.*

92. James J. Fyfe, "Police Use of Deadly Force," pp. 164–205.

93. *Law Enforcement News,* November 15, 1995, p. 1.

94. Matthew J. Hickman and Brian A. Reaves, *Local Police Departments, 2003* (Washington, D.C.: Bureau of Justice Statistics, 2006), p. iv; and Hickman and Reaves, *Sheriffs' Offices, 2003* (Washington, D.C.: Bureau of Justice Statistics, U. S. Department of Justice, 2006), p. iv.

95. Hickman and Reaves, *Local Police Departments, 2003,* p. iv; and Hickman and Reaves, *Sheriffs' Offices, 2003,* p. iv.

96. Thomas Aveni, "Special Report: Firearms Following Standard Procedure—A Long Term Analysis of Gunfights and Their Effects on Policy and Training," *Law and Order,* 51 (8, August 2003), pp. 78–87.

97. Aveni, "Special Report: Firearms Following Standard Procedure," pp. 78–87.

98. Thomas D. Petrowski, "Use of Force Policies and Training: A Reasoned Approach—Part 1," *FBI Law Enforcement Bulletin,* 71 (10, October 2002), pp. 25–32.

99. Petrowski, "Use of Force Policies and Training," pp. 24–32.

100. U.S. Government Accountability Office, *Taser Weapons: Use of Tasers by Selected Law Enforcement Agencies* (Washington, D.C.: U.S. Government Accountability Office, 2005).

101. Hickman and Reaves, *Local Police Departments, 2003,* p. iv; and Hickman and Reaves, *Sheriffs' Offices, 2003,* p. iv.

102. Karen Krause, "Boca Police Find Taser Guns Help Subdue Suspect, but Some Questions Remain," retrieved April 26, 2002, from http://www.sun-sentinel.com.

103. Christina Jewett, "CHP Weighs Adding Tasers," *Sacramento Bee,* April 7, 2006, p. A3; and Mike Saccone, "Local Taser Use Outpaces Most State Agencies," *Daily Sentinel,* June 17, 2006.

104. Hickman and Reaves, *Local Police Departments, 2003,* pp. 26–28; and Hickman and Reaves, *Sheriffs' Offices, 2003,* pp. 26–28.

105. David Standen, "Use of Force Options," *Law and Order,* 53 (8, August 2005), pp. 88–92.

106. Charles S. Petty, M.D., *Deaths in Police Confrontations When Oleoresin Capsicum Is Used* (Washington, D.C.: National Institute of Justice, 2002).

107. Jewett, "CHP Weighs Adding Tasers," p. A3; and Kevin Johnson, "Justice Department Looks into Deaths of People Subdued by Stun Guns," *USA Today,* June 13, 2006. Also see Tal Abbady and Akilah Johnson, "Report Reveals Delray Man Died of Drugs, not Taser," *Sun-Sentinel,* March 16, 2005; Alex Berenson, "The Safety of Tasers Is Questioned Again," *New York Times,* May 25, 2006; and Kevin Johnson, "Federal Bureaus Reject Stun Guns," *USA Today,* March 18, 2005, p. 3A.

108. Johnson, "Justice Department Looks into Deaths," *USA Today,* June 13, 2006.

Chapter 6

1. Richard Lezin Jones, "New York Police Officers Face Counseling on September 11 Events," *New York Times,* November 30, 2001, p. A1.

2. See, for example, Egon Bittner, *The Functions of Police in Modern Society* (Cambridge, Mass.: Oelgeschlager, 1979); Michael Brown, *Working the Street* (New York: Russell Sage Foundation, 1981); and Malcolm Sparrow, Mark Moore, and David Kennedy, *Beyond 911: A New Era for Policing* (New York: Basic Books, 1990).

3. David Jary and Julia Jary, *The HarperCollins Dictionary of Sociology* (New York: HarperPerennial, 1991), p. 101.

4. Thomas Ford Hoult, *Dictionary of Modern Sociology* (Totowa: N.J.: Littlefield, Adams, 1969), p. 93.

5. Brown, *Working the Street,* p. 82.

6. Brown, *Working the Street,* p. 82.

7. George L. Kirkham, "A Professor's Street Lessons," in *Order Under Law,* eds. R. Culbertson and M. Tezak (Prospect Heights, Ill.: Waveland Press, 1981), p. 81.

8. Bittner, *Functions of Police,* p. 63.

9. John M. Violanti, "Suicide and the Police Culture," in eds. Dell P. Hackett and John M. Violanti, *Police Suicide: Tactics for Prevention* (Springfield, Ill.: Charles C. Thomas, 2003), pp. 66–75.

10. Eugene A. Paoline III, *Rethinking Police Culture: Officers' Occupational Attitudes* (New York: LFB Scholarly, 2001).

11. Robin N. Haarr and Merry Morash, "Gender, Race, and Strategies of Coping with Occupational Stress in Policing," *Justice Quarterly,* 16 (2, June 1999), pp. 303–336.

12. Paoline III, "Taking Stock: Toward a Richer Understanding of Police Culture," *Journal of Criminal Justice,* 31 (3, May/June 2003), pp. 199–214.

13. See Richard Harris, *The Police Academy: An Inside View* (New York: Wiley, 1973); Jonathan Rubenstein, *City Police* (New York: Farrar, Straus and Giroux, 1973); and John Van Maanen, "Observations on the Making of a Policeman," in *Order Under Law,* eds. Culbertson and Tezak, p. 81.

14. Bittner, *Functions of Police,* p. 63.

15. Robert Sheehan and Gary W. Cordner, *Introduction to Police Administration,* 2nd ed. (Cincinnati, Ohio: Anderson, 1989), p. 286.

16. Sheehan and Cordner, *Introduction to Police Administration,* pp. 286–289.

17. William Westley, *Violence and the Police: A Sociological Study of Law, Custom, and Morality* (Cambridge, Mass.: MIT Press, 1970).

18. Richard J. Lundman, *Police and Policing* (New York: Holt, Rinehart and Winston, 1980); see also Jerome Skolnick, *Justice Without Trial: Law Enforcement in a Democratic Society* (New York: Wiley, 1966).

19. Skolnick, *Justice without Trial.*

20. Skolnick, *Justice without Trial.*

21. Skolnick, *Justice without Trial.*

22. Elizabeth Burbeck and Adrian Furnham, "Police Officer Selection: A Critical Review of the Literature," *Journal of Police Science and Administration,* 13 (1985), pp. 58–69.

23. Milton Rokeach, Martin Miller, and John Snyder, "The Value Gap between Police and Policed," *Journal of Social Issues,* 27 (1971), pp. 155–171.

24. Bruce Carpenter and Susan Raza, "Personality Characteristics of Police Applicants: Comparisons across Subgroups and with Other Populations," *Journal of Police Science and Administration,* 15 (1987), pp. 10–17; Richard Lawrence, "Police Stress and Personality Factors: A Conceptual Model," *Journal of Criminal Justice,* 12 (1984), pp. 247–263; and James Teevan and Bernard Dolnick, "The Values of the Police: A Reconsideration and Interpretation," *Journal of Police Science and Administration,* 1 (1973), pp. 366–369.

25. Richard Bennett and Theodore Greenstein, "The Police Personality: A Test of the Predispositional Model," *Journal of Police Science and Administration,* 3 (1975), pp. 439–445.

26. Edward A. Thibault, Lawrence W. Lynch, and R. Bruce McBride, *Proactive Police Management* (Englewood Cliffs, N.J.: Prentice Hall, 1985).

27. Van Maanen, "Observations on the Making of a Policeman."

28. Van Maanen, "Observations on the Making of a Policeman."

29. Van Maanen, "Observations on the Making of a Policeman." Also see Lundman, *Police and Policing,* pp. 73, 82, for similar observations.

30. Larry A. Gould, "Longitudinal Approach to the Study of the Police Personality: Race/Gender Differences," *Journal of Police and Criminal Psychology,* 15 (2, Fall 2000), pp. 41–51.

31. Robert Balch, "The Police Personality: Fact or Fiction?," *Journal of Criminal Law, Criminology, and Police Science* 63 (1972), p. 172; David Bayley and Harold Mendelsohn, *Minorities and the Police* (New York: Free Press, 1969); and Larry Tifft, "The 'Cop Personality' Reconsidered," *Journal of Police Science and Administration,* 2 (1974).

32. Arthur Niederhoffer, *Behind the Shield: The Police in Urban Society* (Garden City, N.Y.: Doubleday, 1967), pp. 41–42.

33. Niederhoffer, *Behind the Shield.*

34. Westley, *Violence and the Police.*

35. Niederhoffer, *Behind the Shield,* pp. 216–220.

36. Richard Anson, J. Dale Mann, and Dale Sherman, "Niederhoffer Cynicism Scale: Reliability and Beyond," *Journal of Criminal Justice,* 14 (1986), pp. 295–307.

37. Carl B. Klockars, "The Dirty Harry Problem," *Annals of the American Association of Political and Social Science* (November 1980), pp. 33–47.

38. Klockars, "The Dirty Harry Problem," pp. 33–47.

39. Klockars, "The Dirty Harry Problem," pp. 33–47.

40. Edwin S. Geffner, ed., *The Internist's Compendium of Patient Information* (New York: McGraw-Hill, 1987), sec. 30.

41. Geffner, *Internist's Compendium,* Sec. 30.

42. "Stress on the Job," *Newsweek,* 25 April 1988, p. 43.

43. Alison Mitchell, "A Night on Patrol: What's Behind Police Tensions and Discontent," *New York Times,* 19 October 1992, pp. B1, B2.

44. W. Clinton Terry, "Police Stress: The Empirical Evidence," *Journal of Police Science and Administration,* 9 (1981), pp. 67–70. This article has a substantial bibliography and discussion of the issue of police stress.

45. Clement Milanovich, "The Blue Pressure Cooker," *Police Chief,* 47 (1980), p. 20.

46. Robert J. McGuire, "The Human Dimension in Urban Policing: Dealing with Stress in the 1980's," *Police Chief* (November 1979), p. 27; and Joseph Victor, "Police Stress: Is Anybody Out There Listening?," *New York Law Enforcement Journal* (June 1986), pp. 19–20.

47. Gregory S. Anderson, Robin Litzenberger, Darryl Plecas, "Physical Evidence of Police Officer Stress," *Policing: An International Journal of Police Strategies and Management,* 25 (2, 2000), pp. 399–420.

48. See David Griffith, "Hell in High Water," *Police,* 29 (11, November 2005), pp. 32–36; and Melanie Hamilton, "Taking a Toll," *Police,* 29 (11, November 2005), pp. 38–42.

49. Merry Morash, Robin Haarr, and Dae-Hoon Kwak, "Multilevel Influences on Police Stress," *Journal of Contemporary Criminal Justice,* 22 (1, February 2006), pp. 26–43.

50. James D. Sewell, "Dealing with Employee Stress: How Managers Can Help or Hinder Their Personnel," *FBI Law Enforcement Bulletin* (July 2006), pp. 1–6.

51. Yolanda M. Scott, "Stress among Rural and Small-Town Patrol Officers: A Survey of Pennsylvania Municipalities," *Police Quarterly,* 7 (2, June 2004), pp. 237–261.

52. Scott, "Stress Among Rural and Small-Town Patrol Officers," pp. 237–261.

53. Yolanda M. Scott, "Non-Urban Police Officers' Subjective Assessments of Coping with Stress," paper presented at the 43rd Annual Meeting of the Academy of Criminal Justice Sciences, Baltimore, 2006.

54. Nancy Norvell, Dales Belles, and Holly Hills, "Perceived Stress Levels and Physical Symptoms in Supervisory Law Enforcement Personnel," *Journal of Police Science and Administration,* 6 (1978), pp. 402–416.

55. Bryan Vila, "Tired Cops: Probable Connections between Fatigue and the Performance, Health, and Safety of Patrol Officers," *American Journal of Police,* 15 (2, 1996), pp. 51–92.

56. B. Healy, "The Aerobic Cop," *Police Chief* (February 1981), pp. 67–70.

57. Ni He, Jihong Zhao, and Ling Ren, "Do Race and Gender Matter in Police Stress?: A Preliminary Assessment of the

Interactive Effects," *Journal of Criminal Justice*, 33 (6, November/December 2005), pp. 535–547.

58. Ni He, Jihong Zhao, and Carol A. Archbold, "Gender and Police Stress: The Convergent and Divergent Impact of Work Environment, Work-Family Conflict, and Stress Coping Mechanisms of Female and Male Police Officers," *Policing: An International Journal of Police Strategies and Management*, 25 (4, 2002), pp. 687–708.

59. Cheryl Wilczak, "Gender Differences in NYCPD Officer Work Stress and Trauma: September 11, 2001 and Its Aftermath," in eds. John M. Violanti and Douglas Paton, *Who Gets PTSD?: Issues of Posttraumatic Stress Vulnerability* (Springfield, Ill.: Charles C. Thomas, 2006), pp. 50–69.

60. Cheryl Wilczak, "Gender Differences in NYCPD Officer Work Stress and Trauma," pp. 50–69.

61. Susan Welch, "Suicide by Cop Takes Toll on Police," *St. Louis Post-Dispatch*, February 6, 2006.

62. Denise Buffa and Linda Massarella, "Suicide Teen Tricked Cops into Shooting Him: Dear Officer . . . Please Kill Me," *New York Post*, November 17, 1997, p. 3.

63. Welch, "Suicide by Cop Takes Toll on Police."

64. Welch, "Suicide by Cop Takes Toll on Police."

65. John O'Mahony, "'Suicide by Cop' Not So Odd: Docs," *New York Post*, November 17, 1997, p. 3; and Richard B. Parent, "Aspects of Police Use of Deadly Force in British Columbia: The Phenomenon of Victim-Precipitated Homicide" (Masters thesis, Simon Fraser University, 1996), retrieved November 6, 2006, from http://www3.telus.net/parent/pages/linksarticles.htm.

66. H. Range Huston, M.D., Diedre Anglin, M.D., et al, American College of Emergency Physicians, "Suicide by Cop," *Annals of Emergency Medicine*, 32 (6, December 1998). See also Ronnie L. Paynter, "Suicide by Cop," *Law Enforcement Technology*, 27 (6, June 2000) pp. 40–44; Anthony J. Pinizzotto, Edward F. Davis, and Charles E. Miller III, "Suicide by Cop: Defining a Devastating Dilemma," *FBI Law Enforcement Bulletin* (February 2005), pp. 8–20; and Welch, "Suicide by Cop Takes Toll on Police."

67. J. Nick Marzella, "Psychological Effects of Suicide by Cop on Involved Officers," in eds. Donald C. Sheehan and Janet I. Warren, *Suicide and Law Enforcement* (Washington, D.C.: Federal Bureau of Investigation, 2001). Also see Vivian B. Lord, *Suicide by Cop: Inducing Officers to Shoot* (Flushing, N.Y.: Looseleaf Law, 2004). In this book, experts in the fields of law, psychology and police tactics discuss how to recognize, resolve, and deal with the aftermath of suicide by cop cases.

68. Pinizzotto, Davis, and Miller, "Suicide by Cop," pp. 8–20.

69. Sue Titus Reid, *Criminal Justice*, 3rd ed. (New York: Macmillan, 1993), p. 230.

70. Dorothy Bracey, "The Decline of the Vaccination Model: Criminal Justice Education for a Changing World," *CJ, The Americas* (April 1988), p. 1.

71. "On-the-Job Stress in Policing—Reducing It, Preventing It," *National Institute of Justice Journal* (January 2000), pp. 18–24. Also see Peter E. Finn and Julie Esselman Tomz, *Developing a Law Enforcement Stress Program for Officers and Their Families* (Washington, D.C.: National Institute of Justice, 1997).

72. John Blackmore, "Are Police Allowed to Have Problems of Their Own?" *Police* 1 (1978), pp. 47–55.

73. Charles Unkovic and William Brown, "The Drunken Cop," *Police Chief* (April 1978), p. 18.

74. Chad L. Cross and Larry Ashley, "Police Trauma and Addiction: Coping with the Dangers of the Job," *FBI Law Enforcement Bulletin* (October 2004), pp. 24–32. See also John M. Violanti, *Dying from the Job: The Mortality Risk for Police Officers*, Law Enforcement Wellness Association, Inc., retrieved August 5, 2003, from http://www.cophealth.com/ articles/articles_dying_a.html.

75. Cross and Ashley, "Police Trauma and Addiction," pp. 24–32; and R. L. Richmond, A. K. Wodak, and L. Heather, "Research Report: How Healthy Are the Police? A Survey of Lifestyle Factors," *Addiction*, 93 (1998), pp. 1729–1737.

76. Cross and Ashley, "Police Trauma and Addiction," pp. 24–32; and Roger G. Dunham, L. Lewis, and G. P. Alpert, "Testing the Police for Drugs," *Criminal Law Bulletin*, 24 (1998), pp. 155–166.

77. Cross and Ashley, "Police Trauma and Addiction," pp. 24–32. In their article, they cite B. A. Arrigo and K. Garsky, "Police Suicide: A Glimpse Being the Badge," in eds. Roger G. Dunham and Gordon P. Alpert, *Critical Issues in Policing: Contemporary Readings*, 3rd ed. (Prospect Heights, Ill.: Waveland Press, 1997), pp. 609–626; Richmond, Wodak, and Heather, "How Healthy Are the Police?," pp. 1729–1737; and H. W. Stege, "Drug Abuse by Police Officers," *Police Chief*, 53, 1986, pp. 53–83.

78. James Hibberd, "Police Psychology," *On Patrol* (Fall 1996), p. 26.

79. "Dispatches," *On Patrol* (Summer 1996), p. 25.

80. See J. Michael Rivard, Park Dietz, Daniel Martell, and Mel Widawski, "Acute Dissociative Responses in Law Enforcement Officers Involved in Critical Shooting Incidents: The Clinical and Forensic Implications," *Journal of Forensic Sciences*, 47 (5, September 2002), pp. 1093–1120; and Susan Taylor, "Post Shooting Emotional Meltdown?," *Police*, 25 (9, September 2001), pp. 40–43.

81. *Justice Assistance News*, 4 (1983), p. 5.

82. David Klinger, "Police Responses to Officer-Involved Shootings," *National Institute of Justice Journal*, 253 (January 2006), pp. 21–24.

83. Jerry Dash and Martin Resier, "Suicide among Police in Urban Law Enforcement Agencies," *Journal of Police Science and Administration*, 6 (1978), p. 18.

84. David Rafky, "My Husband the Cop," *Police Chief* (August 1984), p. 65.

85. Peter Maynard and Nancy Maynard, "Stress in Police Families: Some Policy Implications," *Journal of Police Science and Administration*, 10 (1980), 309.

86. Ellen Scrivner, "Helping Families Cope with Stress," *Law Enforcement News*, June 15, 1991, p. 6.

87. Scott, "Stress among Rural and Small-Town Patrol Officers," pp. 237–261.

88. U.S. Commission on Civil Rights, *Who Is Guarding the Guardians? A Report on Police Practices* (Washington, D.C.: U.S. Government Printing Office, 1981).

89. *USA Today*, September 15, 1986, p. 3.

90. National Criminal Justice Reference Service, *Program for the Reduction of Stress for New York City Police Officers and Their Families, Final Report* (Washington, D.C.: National Criminal Justice Reference Service, 1998).

91. James J. Ness and John Light, "Mandatory Physical Fitness Standards: Issues and Concerns," *Police Chief* (August 1992), pp. 23–26.

92. Ness and Light, "Mandatory Physical Fitness Standards," p. 77.

93. Ness and Light, "Mandatory Physical Fitness Standards," p. 75.

94. Richard Lezin Jones, "New York Police Officers Face Counseling on September 11 Events," *New York Times*, November 30, 2001, p. A1.

95. "'Can We Talk?'" Officials Take Steps to Head Off 9/11 Post-Traumatic Stress," *Law Enforcement News*, November 30, 2001, p. 1.

96. John M. Madonna, Jr., and Richard E. Kelly, *Treating Police Stress: The Work and the Words of Peer Counselors* (Springfield, Ill.: Charles C. Thomas, 2002).

97. Richard Kelly, "Critical Incident Debriefing," in Madonna and Kelly, *Treating Police Stress*, pp. 139–149. Also, see "Tactical Officers Get Help from Those Who've Been There," *Law Enforcement News*, April 15, 2002.

98. "On-the-Job Stress in Policing," pp. 18–24. Also see Finn and Tomz, *Developing a Law Enforcement Stress Program*.

99. Laurence Miller, *Practical Police Psychology: Stress Management and Crisis Intervention for Law Enforcement* (Springfield, Ill.: Charles C. Thomas, 2006).

100. Samuel Walker, Stacy Osnick Milligan, and Anna Berke, *Strategies for Intervening with Officers through Early Intervention Systems: A Guide for Front-line Supervisors* (Washington, D.C.: Office of Community Oriented Policing Services, 2006). See also Violanti and Paton, *Who Gets PTSD?*; Walker, *Early Intervention Systems: A Guide for Law Enforcement Chief Executives* (Washington, D.C.: Office of Community Oriented Policing Services, 2003); and Walker, Milligan, and Berke, *Supervision and Intervention Within Early Intervention Systems: A Guide for Law Enforcement Chief Executives* (Washington, D.C.: Office of Community Oriented Policing Services, U.S. Department of Justice, 2005).

101. "On-the-Job Stress in Policing," pp. 19–24.

102. Scott, "Stress among Rural and Small-Town Patrol Officers," pp. 237–261.

103. Ronnie Garrett, "Don't Cowboy Up," *Law Enforcement Technology*, 33 (2, February 2006), pp. 40, 42–48, 50–51.

104. Hans Toch, *Stress in Policing* (Washington, D.C.: National Institute of Justice, 2002).

105. Recently, significant attention is being addressed to police suicide and the stresses that can be attributed to it. See, for example, Thomas E. Baker and Jane P. Baker, "Preventing Police Suicide," *FBI Law Enforcement Bulletin* (October 1996), pp. 24–27. See also Kevin Barrett, "More EAPs Needed in Police Departments to Quash Officers' Super-Human Self-Image," *EA Professional Report* (January 1994), p. 3; Barrett, "Police Suicide: Is Anyone Listening?," *Journal of Safe Management of Disruptive and Assaultive Behavior* (Spring 1997), pp. 6–9; Hackett and Violanti, *Police Suicide*; Steven R. Standfest, "The Police Supervisor and Stress," *FBI Law Enforcement Bulletin* (May 1996), pp. 10–16; "The Greatest Threat to Cops' Lives—Themselves," *Law Enforcement News*, 31 December 1997, p. 22; Violanti, "Police Suicide: Current Perspectives and Future Considerations"; Violanti, "The Mystery Within: Understanding Police Suicide," *FBI Law Enforcement Bulletin* (February 1995), pp. 19–23; and "What's Killing America's Cops? Mostly Themselves, According to New Study," *Law Enforcement News*, November 15, 1996, p. 1.

106. Laurence Miller, "Practical Strategies for Preventing Officer Suicide," *Law and Order*, 54 (3, March 2006), pp. 90–92.

107. Patricia Kelly and Rich Martin, "Police Suicide Is Real," *Law and Order*, 54 (3, March 2006), pp. 93–95.

108. John M. Violanti, as quoted in "What's Killing America's Cops?"

109. Violanti, "Suicide and the Police Culture," pp. 66–75.

110. Leonard Territo and Harold J. Vetter, "Stress and Police Personnel," *Journal of Police Science and Administration*, 9 (1981), p. 200.

111. Violanti, "The Mystery Within: Understanding Police Suicide," p. 22.

112. Daniel W. Clark and Elizabeth K. White, "Clinicians, Cops, and Suicide," in Hackett and Violanti, *Police Suicide: Tactics for Prevention*, pp. 16–36.

113. Miller, "Practical Strategies for Preventing Officer Suicide," pp. 90–92. See also Kelly and Martin, "Police Suicide Is Real," pp. 93–95.

114. Kelly and Martin, "Police Suicide Is Real," pp. 93–95.

115. Barbara Raffel Price, as quoted in Karen Polk, "New York Police: Caught in the Middle and Losing Faith," *Boston Globe*, December 28, 1988, p. 3.

116. Michael S. McCampbell, "Meth and Meth Labs: The Impact on Sheriffs," *Sheriff*, 58 (1, January–February 2006), pp. 16–20, 77.

117. Rich Stanek, as quoted in Mara H. Gottfried, "More Armor, Tougher Crooks," *Pioneer Press*, July 2, 2006.

118. Federal Bureau of Investigation, *Law Enforcement Officers Feloniously Killed—2005* (Washington, D.C.: Federal Bureau of Investigation, 2006), retrieved November 4, 2006, from http://www.fbi.gov.

119. Federal Bureau of Investigation, *Federal Law Enforcement Officers Killed and Assaulted—2005* (Washington, D.C.: Federal Bureau of Investigation, 2006), retrieved November 4, 2006 from http://www.fbi.gov.

120. Federal Bureau of Investigation, *Law Enforcement Officers Feloniously Killed—2005*.

121. Federal Bureau of Investigation, *Law Enforcement Officers Feloniously Killed—2005*.

122. Federal Bureau of Investigation, *Law Enforcement Officers Accidentally Killed—2005* (Washington, D.C.: Federal Bureau of Investigation, 2006), retrieved July 12, 2006 from http://www.fbi.gov.

123. Federal Bureau of Investigation, *Law Enforcement Officers Feloniously Killed—2005*; and National Law Enforcement Officers Memorial Fund, *Law Enforcement Facts*, retrieved November 5, 2006, fromhttp://www.nleomf.com/TheMemorial/Facts/polfacts.htm.

124. William Geller and Michael S. Scott, *Deadly Force: What We Know* (Washington, D.C.: Police Executive Research Forum, 1992), pp. 549–550.

125. David Lester, "The Murder of Police Officers in American Cities," *Criminal Justice and Behavior* (January 1984), pp. 101–113.

126. William Geller, "Deadly Force: What We Know," *Journal of Police Science and Administration*, 10 (1982), pp. 151–177.

127. National Law Enforcement Officers Memorial Fund, *Law Enforcement Facts*, April 3, 2006, retrieved November 5, 2006, from http://www.nleomf.com/TheFund/fund.htm.

128. Concerns of Police Survivors, Inc., retrieved July 23, 2006, from http://www.nationalcops.org.

129. Matthew R. Durose, Erica L. Schmitt, and Patrick A. Langan, *Contacts between Police and the Public: Findings from the 2002 National Survey* (Washington, D.C.: Bureaus of Justice Statistics, 2005). The statistics of these approximately 45 million contacts yearly only include persons age 16 years or older.

130. Matthew J. Hickman and Brian A. Reaves, *Local Police Departments, 2003* (Washington, D.C.: Bureau of Justice Statistics, 2006), p. iv; and Hickman, and Reaves, *Sheriffs' Offices, 2003* (Washington, D.C.: Bureau of Justice Statistics, 2006), p. iv.

131. Federal Bureau of Investigation, *Law Enforcement Officers Feloniously Killed—2005*.

132. Claire Mayhew, *Occupational Health and Safety Risks Face by Police Officers* (Canberra ACT: Australian Institute of Criminology, 2001).

133. Federal Bureau of Investigation, *Law Enforcement Officers Assaulted—2005* (Washington, D.C.: Federal Bureau of Investigation, 2006), retrieved November 4, 2006 from http://www.fbi.gov.

134. Federal Bureau of Investigation, *Law Enforcement Officers Assaulted—2005*.

135. Federal Bureau of Investigation, *Federal Law Enforcement Officers Killed and Assaulted—2005*.

136. Durose, Schmitt, and Langan, *Contacts between Police and the Public*.

137. Rich Roberts, as quoted in William Kates, "Violence Against Police Is Again on the Rise," *Associated Press*, April 15, 2006.

138. Centers for Disease Control and Prevention, U.S. Department of Health and Human Services, *HIV/AIDS Surveillance Report: HIV Infection and AIDS in the United States, 2004*, retrieved July 27, 2006, from http://www.cdc.gov/hiv/topics/surveillance/basic.htm.

139. International Association of Chiefs of Police, *HIV/AIDS Prevention: Concepts and Issues Paper* (Alexandria, Virginia, 2000).

140. Theodore M. Hammett and Walter Bond, *Risks of Infection with the AIDS Virus through Exposures to Blood* (Washington, D.C.: National Institute of Justice, 1987).

141. International Association of Chiefs of Police, *HIV/AIDS Prevention*. Also, see R. A. Thompson and J. W. Marquart, "Law Enforcement Responses to the HIV/AIDS Epidemic: Selected Findings and Suggestions for Future Research," *Policing: An International Journal of Police Strategies and Management*, 21 (4, 1998), pp. 648–665. Thompson and Marquart conducted the first study analyzing police officers' beliefs, perceptions, and attitudes about HIV/AIDS.

142. Federal Bureau of Investigation, "Collecting and Handling Evidence Infected with Human Disease-Causing Organisms," *FBI Law Enforcement Bulletin* (July 1987).

143. Theodore M. Hammett, *Precautionary Measures and Protective Equipment: Developing a Reasonable Response* (Washington, D.C.: National Institute of Justice, 1988).

144. Theodore M. Hammett, *AIDS and the Law Enforcement Officer: Concerns and Policy Responses* (Washington, D.C.: National Institute of Justice, 1987). See also, John Cooney, "HIV/AIDS in Law Enforcement: What-If Scenarios," *FBI Law Enforcement Bulletin*, 69 (2, February 2000), pp. 1–6. The author emphasizes management's role in providing their officers with proper knowledge and training regarding HIV/AIDS to reduce their fears that may result from the dissemination of false information.

Chapter 7

1. W. Marvin Dulaney, *Black Police in America* (Bloomington: Indiana University Press), p. 30.

2. Dulaney, *Black Police in America*, p. 30.

3. Dorothy Moses Schulz, *From Social Worker to Crimefighter: Women in United States Municipal Policing* (Westport, Conn.: Praeger), p. 21.

4. Schulz, *From Social Worker to Crimefighter*, p. 115.

5. U.S. Department of Justice, *Civil Service System: Affirmative Action and Equal Employment: A Guidebook for Employers* (Washington, D.C.: U.S. Government Printing Office, 1974).

6. Doug Ward, "Much to Male Cops' Surprise, the World Didn't Come to an End," *Law Enforcement News* (May 2005), pp. 12.

7. Chloe Owings, *Women Police* (Montclair, N.J.: Patterson Smith, 1969, originally published in 1925).

8. Schulz, *From Social Worker to Crimefighter*, p. 120.

9. Samuel Walker and Charles M. Katz, *Police in America: An Introduction*, 5th ed. (New York: McGraw-Hill, 2005), p. 47.

10. Dulaney, *Black Police in America*.

11. Dulaney, *Black Police in America*, p. 30.

12. Dulaney, *Black Police in America*, p. 69.

13. Nicholas Alex, *Black in Blue: A Study of the Negro Policeman* (New York: Appleton-Century-Crofts, 1969) pp. 87, 111.

14. Nicholas Alex, *New York Cops Talk Back* (New York: Wiley, 1976).

15. Steven Leinen (1984), *Black Police, White Society* (New York: University Press, 1984).

16. National Advisory Commission on Civil Disorders, *Report* (Washington, D.C.: U.S. Government Printing Office, 1968).

17. National Advisory Commission on Criminal Justice Standards and Goals, *Police* (Washington, D.C.: U.S. Government Printing Office, 1973), p. 343.

18. National Advisory Commission on Criminal Justice Standards and Goals, *Police*, p. 329.

19. R. Alan Thompson, *Career Experiences of African American Police Executives: Black in Blue Revisited* (New York: LFB Scholarly, 2003).

20. *Civil Rights Act of 1964*, Public Law 88-352, 88th Cong., *U.S. Statutes at Large* 78 (July 2, 1964), 241.

21. U.S. Department of Justice, Civil Rights Division, website, www.usdoj.gov/crt/ and www.ojp.usdoj.gov/ocr/.

22. *Equal Employment Opportunity Act of 1972*, Public Law No. 92-261.

23. *Griggs v. Duke Power Company*, 401 U.S. 424 (1971).

24. U.S. Equal Employment Opportunity Commission, *Affirmative Action and Equal Employment*, vol. 2 (Washington, D.C.: U.S. Government Printing Office, 1974), p. D-2.

25. *Mieth v. Dothard*, 418 F. Supp. 1169 (1976).

26. Larry K. Gaines, John L. Worrall, Mittie D. Southerland, and John E. Angell, *Police Administration*, 2nd ed. (New York: McGraw-Hill, 2003), p. 367.

27. Gaines et al., *Police Administration*, p. 367.

28. P. Maher, "Police Physical Ability Tests: Can They Ever Be Valid?," *Public Personnel Management Journal*, 13 (1984), pp. 173–183.

29. *Vulcan Society v. Civil Service Commission*, 490 F.2d 387, 391 (2d Cir. 1973).

30. *Guardians Association of New York City Police Department v. Civil Service Commission of New York City*, 463 U.S. 582 (1983).

31. U.S. Equal Employment Opportunity Commission, *Affirmative Action and Equal Employment*, vol. 2, pp. D15–D23.

32. B. Taylor, B. Kubu, L. Fridell, C. Rees, T. Jordan, and J. Cheney, *Cop Crunch: Identifying strategies for dealing with the recruiting and hiring crisis in law enforcement* (Washington, D.C.: U.S. Department of Justice, National Institute of Justice, 2005).

33. Zhao Jihong and Nicholas Lovrich, "Determinants of Minority Employment in American Municipal Police Agencies: The Representation of African American Officers," *Journal of Criminal Justice*, 26 (4, 1998), pp. 267–278.

34. Charles R. Swanson, Leonard Territo, and Robert W. Taylor, *Police Administration*, 5th ed. (Upper Saddle River, N.J.: Prentice-Hall, 2001).

35. *Afro-American Patrolmen's League v. Duck*, 538 F.2d 328 (1976).

36. *Detroit Police Officer Association v. Young*, 46 U.S. Law Week 2463 (E.D. Mich. 1978).

37. "The State of the Union," *Law Enforcement News*, January 15, 1996, p. 10.

38. "Affirmative Action Programs Looking a Little Black and Blue," *Law Enforcement News*, April 30, 1995, pp. 1, 7.

39. "Jury Rules Against Ex-Chief in Bias Case," *Law Enforcement News*, May 2005, p. 5.

40. Peter B. Bloch and Deborah Anderson, *Policewomen on Patrol: Final Report* (Washington, D.C.: Police Foundation, 1974); and Joyce L. Sichel, Lucy N. Friedman, Janet C. Quint, and Michael E. Smith, *Women on Patrol: A Pilot Study of Police Performance in New York City* (Washington, D.C.: Department of Justice, 1978).

41. Sichel et al., *Women on Patrol*, Foreword.

42. Sichel et al., *Women on Patrol*, Foreword.

43. James David, "Perspectives of Policewomen in Texas and Oklahoma," *Journal of Police Science and Administration*, 12 (1984), pp. 395–403.

44. Robert Homant and Daniel Kennedy, "Police Perceptions of Spouse Abuse: A comparison of Male and Female Officers," *Journal of Criminal Justice* 13 (1985), pp. 49–64.

45. Loretta J. Stalans and Mary A. Finn, "Gender Differences in Officers' Perceptions and decisions about Domestic Violence Cases." *Women and Criminal Justice*, 11 (3, 2000), pp. 1–24.

46. Merry Morash and Jack Greene, "Evaluating Women on Patrol: A Critique of Contemporary Wisdom," *Evaluation Review*, 10 (1986), pp. 230–255.

47. Sean Grennan, "Findings of the Role of Officer Gender in Violent Encounters with Citizen," *Journal of Police Science and Administration*, 15 (1988), pp. 75–78.

48. Report of the Independent Commission on the Los Angeles Police Department (Los Angeles, Calif.: Independent Commission on the Los Angeles Police Department, 1991).

49. Zev Yarolslavsky, "Gender Balance in Los Angeles Police Department," *WomenPolice* 26 (3, Winter 1992), pp. 14–15.

50. Kim Michelle Lersch, "Exploring Gender Differences in Citizen Allegations of Misconduct: An Analysis of a Municipal Police Department," *Women and Criminal Justice*, 9 (4, 1998), pp. 69–79.

51. Richard M. Seklecki, "A Quantitative Analysis of Attitude and Behavior Differences between Male and Female Police Officers toward Citizens in a Highly Conflictive and Densely Populated Urban Area," paper presented at the Academy of Criminal Justice Sciences Annual Meeting, Washington, D.C., April 2001.

52. Kristen Leger, "Public Perceptions of Female Police Officers on Patrol," *American Journal of Criminal Justice*, 21 (2, 1997), pp. 231–249.

53. Diana R. Grant, "Perceived Gender Difference in Policing: The Impact of Gendered Perceptions of Officer-Situation Fit," *Women and Criminal Justice*, 12 (1, 2000), pp. 53–74.

54. International Association of Chiefs of Police, "The Future of Women in Policing: Mandates for Action" (November 1998), retrieved April 24, 2004, from www.theiacp.org/pubinfo/researchcenterdox.htm.

55. Kimberly Lonsway, "The Role of Women in Community Policing: Dismantling the Warrior Image" (2001, September), retrieved April 12, 2004, from www.communitypolicing.org/publications/comlinks/.

56. National Center for Women and Policing, "Men, Women and Police Excessive Force: A Tale of Two Genders, A Content Analysis of Civil Liability Cases, Sustained Allegations and Citizen Complaints" (2002), retrieved April 12, 2004, from www.womenandpolicing.org.

57. Thompson, *Career Experiences of African American Police Executives*.

58. Walker, and Katz, *Police in America*, p. 161.

59. Thompson, *Career Experiences of African American Police Executives*, pp. 81–154.

60. Matthew Hickman and Brian Reaves, *Local Police Departments, 2003.* (Washington, D.C.: Bureau of Justice Statistics, 2006).

61. Schulz, Dorothy Moses, *Breaking the Brass Ceiling: Women Police Chiefs and their Paths to the Top* (Westport, Conn.: Praeger, 2004), p. 29.

62. Schulz, *Breaking the Brass Ceiling*, p. 28.

63. Schulz, *Breaking the Brass Ceiling*, p. 84.

64. Schulz, *Breaking the Brass Ceiling*, p. 72.

65. Slack, Donovan, "'I Don't Envy My Successor,' O'Toole's Departure Leaves Menino with Critical Decision on Police Leadership," *Boston Globe,* retrieved May 10, 2006, from www.boston.com/news/local/Massachusetts/articles/2006/05/.

66. Bernstein, Maxine, *Now It's Permanent: Police Chief Rosie Sizer,* retrieved June 23, 2006, from Oregonlive.com.

67. National Center for Women and Policing, "The Effect of Consent Decrees on the Representation of Women in Sworn Law Enforcement" (Spring 2003), retrieved April 12, 2004, from http://www.womenandpolicing.org/.

68. Hickman, and Reaves, *Local Police Departments, 2003.*

69. Hickman, and Reaves, *Local Police Departments, 2003.*

70. Obtained from an Interview with Sergeant Cesar Fazz of the Yuma, Arizona, Police Department, on July 26, 2006.

71. Interview with Sergeant Fazz.

72. Interview with Sergeant Fazz.

73. Remarks of the Honorable Deborah J. Daniels, Assistant Attorney General, at the Hispanic American Police Command Officers Association 29th Annual Training Conference, August 22, 2002, Albuquerque, New Mexico.

74. Interview with Sergeant Fazz.

75. Felisa Cardona, "Bias Claims Charged en Masse against Denver Department," *Denver Post,* retrieved June 9, 2006, from www.denverpost.com.

76. Hickman, Reaves, *Local Police Departments, 2003.*

77. Joseph Berger, "Influx of Asians in NJ Is Not Reflected in Police Ranks," *New York Times,* retrieved May 1, 2006, from nytimes.com.

78. John Cameron, "New Officers Reflect Diverse Face of City: More Women, Ethnic Minorities, Now Recruits." *Sacramento Bee,* retrieved May 11, 2006, from sacbee.com.

79. Schulz, *Breaking the Brass Ceiling,* pp. 177–179.

80. Pew Forum website, retrieved May 30, 2006, from http://pewforum.org/news.

81. *Law Enforcement News* (October 1990), p. 1.

82. M. L. Dantzker, *Understanding Today's Police Officer,* 3rd ed. (Upper Saddle River, N.J.: Prentice-Hall, 2003).

83. Karla D. Shores, "Manors Should Hire an Openly Gay Officer, Mayor says," retrieved January 22, 2002, from www.sunsentinel.com.

84. Wanda J. DeMarzo Steve Rothaus, "Despite Some Progress, Many Gay Officers Still in the Closet," *Miami Herald,* January 28, 2006, retrieved January 30, 2006, from www.miami.com/ mld/miamiherald/living/columnists/steve_rothaus/13733491.

85. Shores, "Manors Should Hire."

86. Donna Leinwand, "Lawsuits of 70s Shape Police Leadership Now," *USA Today,* April 26, 2004, p. 13A.

87. Sandra K. Wells, and Betty L. Alt, *Policewomen: Life with the Badge* (Westport, Conn.: Praeger, 2005), pp. 39–42.

88. Lance D. Jones, "Matrons to Chiefs in One Short Century: The Transition of Women in U.S. Law Enforcement," *WomenPolice* (2003, Summer), pp. 6–9.

89. Carole Moore, "Pregnant Officer Policies," *Law and Order,* 51 (9, September, 2003), pp. 73–78.

90. Jennifer Sinco Kelleher, "Suffolk Female Cops Win Case," *Newsday.com,* retrieved June 15, 2006, from newsday.com.

91. Moore, "Pregnant Officer Policies," p. 76.

92. Marion Gold, Top Cops: Profiles of Women in Command (Chicago: Brittany, 1999); Patricia Lunneborg, *Women Police: Portraits of Success* (New York: iUniverse, 2004); and Donna Stuccio, "Blue Moon," *Women and Criminal Justice,* 14 (1, 2002).

93. Dantzker, *Understanding Today's Police.*

94. "Always Armed, Always on Duty Questioned in Rhode Island Case," *Providence Journal,* retrieved November 28, 2005, from www.projo.com.

95. "Watch It! Shaquille O'Neal Now Carries a Badge," *USA Today,* December 9, 2005, retrieved June 12, 2006, from www.usatoday.com.

96. Thompson, *Career Experiences of African American Police Executives,* p. 32.

97. Thompson, *Career Experiences of African American Police Executives,* p. 154.

98. Interview with Officer Eric Cazares of the Yuma, Arizona Police Department on July 27, 2006.

99. Interview with Sergeant Fazz.

Chapter 8

1. Joycelyn M. Pollock (2004), *Ethics in Crime and Justice: Dilemmas & Decisions,* 4th ed. (Belmont, Calif.: Wadsworth) p. 70.

2. Douglas W. Perez and J. Alan Moore, *Police Ethics: A Matter of Character* (Belmont, Calif.: Wadsworth, 2002), pp. 49.

3. Michelle A. Mortensen and Michael Cortrite, "Ethics Training: A Passing Fad or Sustaining Component?" *Community Policing Exchange* (March/April 1998), retrieved May 2, 2003, from www.communitypolicing.org/.

4. Pollock, *Ethics in Crime and Justice,* p. 5.

5. Pollock, *Ethics in Crime and Justice,* p. 139.

6. Pollock, *Ethics in Crime and Justice,* p. 149.

7. Albert Cantara, "Ramblings about Ethics: A Shrink Speaks," *Community Policing Exchange* (March/April 1998), retrieved May 2, 2003, from www.communitypolicing.org/.

8. Sourcebook of Criminal Justice Statistics online, 2006. http://www.albany.edu/sourcebook.

9. Catherine Gallagher, Edward Maguire, Stephen D. Mastrofski, and Michael D. Reisig, "The Public Image of Police" (2001), retrieved March 27, 2003, from www. theiacp.org/.

10. Frank Schmalleger, *Criminal Justice Today,* 9th ed. (Upper Saddle River, N.J.: Prentice Hall, 2007), p. 18.

11. Perez and Moore, *Police Ethics,* p. 146.

12. National Advisory Commission on Criminal Justice Standards and Goals, *Police* (Washington, D.C.: U.S. Government Printing Office, 1973); National Commission on Law Observance and Enforcement, *Report on Police* (Washington, D.C.: U.S. Government Printing Office, 1931); President's Commission on Law Enforcement and Administration of Justice, *The Challenge of Crime in a Free Society* (Washington, D.C.: U.S. Government Printing Office, 1968); and *Standards for Law Enforcement Agencies,* 2nd. ed. (Fairfax, Va.: Commission on Accreditation for Law Enforcement Agencies, 1987).

13. Knapp Commission, *Report on Police Corruption* (New York: Braziller, 1973).

14. Vincent J. Palmiotto, "Legal Authority of Police," in Michael J. Palmiotto, *Police Misconduct* (Upper Saddle River, N.J.: Prentice Hall, 2001).

15. Herman Goldstein, *Police Corruption: A Perspective on Its Nature and Control* (Washington, D.C.: Police Foundation, 1975), p. 3.

16. Carl B. Klockars, Sanja Kutnjak Ivkovich, William E. Harver, and Maria R. Haberfeld, "The Measurement of Police Integrity," *National Institute of Justice Research in Brief* (Washington, D.C.: National Institute of Justice, 2000), p. 1.

17. Michael Palmiotto, "Police Misconduct: What Is It?" in Palmiotto, *Police Misconduct,* p. 37.

18. Richard J. Lundman, "Police Misconduct," in eds. Abraham S. Blumberg and Elaine Niederhoffer, *The Ambivalent Force: Perspectives on the Police,* 3rd. ed. (New York: Holt, Rinehart and Winston, 1985), p. 158.

19. Peter Maas, *Serpico* (New York: Bantam Books, 1974).

20. Robert Daley, *Prince of the City: The Story of a Cop Who Knew Too Much.* (Boston: Houghton Mifflin, 1978).

21. Mike McAlary, *Buddy Boys: When Good Cops Turn Bad* (New York: Putnam, 1987).

22. Michael A. Caldero, and John P. Crank, *Police Ethics: The Corruption of Noble Cause,* 2nd ed. (Cincinnati, Ohio: Anderson, 2004), p. 116.

23. Peter Pochna, "Ex-Cop Admits Stealing $180,000" retrieved April 29, 2003, from www.northjersey.com.

24. "Sentencing in City of Miami Cops Case," press release from U.S. Department of Justice, U.S. Attorney for Southern District of Florida (October 29, 2003), retrieved April 9, 2004, from www.usdoj.gov/isap/fls.

25. Christopher Drew, "Police Struggles in New Orleans Raise Old Fears," *New York Times,* retrieved June 13, 2006, from www.nytimes.com.

26. John Marzulli, "Mob Cops Guilty, Face Life in Jail," *NY Daily News,* retrieved April 7, 2006, from www. nydailynews.com.

27. Associated Press, "Former Miami City Manager Warshaw Loses Pension—Again," retrieved August 6, 2003, from www.sun-sentinel.com.

28. Paula Reed Ward, "Skosnik Gets 5-Year Prison Term" (June 2, 2006), retrieved June 5, 2006, from www. post-gazette.com.

29. William K. Rashbaum, "Kerik Described as Close to Deal on a Guilty Plea," *New York Times,* retrieved June 29, 2006, from www.nytimes.com.

30. Brad Schrade, "New Plan Rids THP of Politics in Hiring," *Tennessean,* May 19, 2006, retrieved May 23, 2006, from www.tennessean.com.

31. James Pinkerton, "Customs Agent Let Drugs Slip Through," *Houston Chronicle,* March 26, 2006, retrieved April 3, 2006, from www.HoustonChronicle.com.

32. Mimi Hall, Larry Copeland, and Wendy Koch, "Homeland Official Suspended in Sex Case," *USA Today,* April 5, 2006, retrieved April 10, 2006, from www.usatoday.com.

33. These excellent texts include the following: Tom Barker, *Police Ethics: Crisis in Law Enforcement* (Springfield, Ill.: Charles C. Thomas, 1996); Caldero and Crank *Police Ethics;* Victor Kappeler, Richard Sluder, and Geoffrey Alpert, *Forces of Deviance, Understanding the Dark Side of Policing* (Prospect Heights, Ill.: Waveland Press, 1994); Palmiotto, *Police Misconduct;* Perez and Moore, *Police Ethics;* and Jerome Skolnick and James J. Fyfe, *Above the Law: Police and the Excessive Use of Force* (New York: Free Press, 1993).

34. Frank Schmalleger, *Criminal Justice Today,* 9th ed. (Upper Saddle River, N.J.: Prentice Hall, 2007), p. 296.

35. Samuel Walker and Charles M. Katz, *Police in America: An Introduction,* 5th ed. (New York: McGraw-Hill, 2005), pp. 450–455.

36. Lawrence W. Sherman, ed., *Police Corruption: A Sociological Perspective* (Garden City, N.Y.: Doubleday, 1974), p. 1.

37. Herman Goldstein, *Policing a Free Society* (Cambridge, Mass.: Ballinger, 1977), p. 218.

38. Schmalleger, *Criminal Justice Today,* 9th ed., p. 293.

39. Knapp Commission, *Report on Police Corruption,* p. 4.

40. Walker and Katz, *Police in America,* p. 445.

41. Pollack, *Ethics in Crime and Justice,* p. 168.

42. Walker and Katz, *Police in America,* p. 447.

43. Sherman, *Police Corruption,* p. 7.

44. Sherman, *Police Corruption,* pp. 191–208.

45. Perez and Moore, *Police Ethics,* p. 134.

46. Caldero and Crank, *Police Ethics,* pp. 105–108.

47. Caldero and Crank, *Police Ethics,* p. 109.

48. Caldero and Crank, *Police Ethics,* p. 113.

49. Caldero and Crank, *Police Ethics,* p. 114.

50. Palmiotto, *Police Misconduct.*

51. U.S. General Accountability Office, *Information on Drug-Related Police Corruption* (Washington, D.C.: 1998), # GAO/GGD-98–111.

52. U.S. Department of Justice, Southern District of Florida, press release, September 12, 2002, retrieved from www.justice.gov/usao/fls.

53. Jerome H. Skolnick, "Deception by Police," in eds. Frederick A. Elliston and Michael Fieldberg, *Moral Issues in Police Work* (Totowa, N.J.: Rowman and Allanheld, 1985), pp. 76–77.

54. Tony G. Poveda, *Lawlessness and Reform: The FBI in Transition* (Pacific Grove, Calif.: Brooks/Cole, 1990), Chapters 4, 5; and Poveda, "The Effects of Scandal on Organizational Deviance: The Case of the FBI," *Justice Quarterly,* 2 (1985), pp. 237–258.

55. "Officer Sentenced for Felony," retrieved May 2, 2003, from www.wtol.com.

56. Crystal Carreon, "San Jose Officer's Deceit Raises Racial Tensions," *San Jose Mercury News,* retrieved May 25, 2003, from www.bayarea.com.

57. Petula Dvorak, "Police Reclassify 119 Injury Reports as Crimes," *Washington Post,* June 2, 2006, retrieved June 5, 2006, from www.washingtonpost.com.

58. Paula McMahon, "Broward Deputy's Trial Under Way for Allegedly Blaming Crimes on Wrong People," *South Florida Sun-Sentinel,* May 17, 2006, retrieved June 17, 2006, from www.sun-sentinel.com.

59. K. B. Kraska and V. E. Kappeler, "To Serve and Pursue: Exploring Police Sexual Violence against Women," *Justice Quarterly,* 12 (1), pp. 85–111.

60. Daniel Borunda, "Ex-Deputy Sentenced," retrieved June 18, 2003, from www.elpasotimes.com.

61. Jeremy Milarsky, "Ex-Margate Cop Gets 20 Months in Jail for Having Sex in Back seat of Cruiser," retrieved March 4, 2002, from www.sun-sentinel.com.

62. Scott Hiaassen, "Lakewood Officer Pleads to Charges, Admits to Having Sex in Back of Cruiser," retrieved May 14, 2003, from www.cleveland.com.

63. Associated Press, "Ex-LA Police Officer Sentenced to Prison for On-duty Rape," retrieved April 24, 2003, from www.bayarea.com/mid/mercurynews.

64. National Center for Women and Policing, *Police Family Violence Fact Sheet,* retrieved April 23, 2003, from www.womenandpolicing.org.

65. National Center for Women and Policing website, retrieved July 05, 2006.

66. Kimberly A. Lonsway, "Policies on Police Officer Domestic Violence: Prevalence and Specific Provisions of Large Police Agencies," retrieved November 19, 2003 from http://www.abuseofpower.info/Lonsway_Policy_Research.pdf.

67. Kenneth Peak, *Policing America: Methods, Issues, Challenges,* 5th ed. (Upper Saddle River, N.J.: Prentice Hall, 2006).

68. Michael Ko, "Brame Inquiry: Poor Judgment but No Charges," November 18, 2003, retrieved November 20, 2003, from http://seattletimes.nwsource.com.

69. U.S. Department of Justice, *A Resource Guide on Racial Profiling Data Collection Systems: Promising Practices and Lessons Learned* (Washington, D.C.: Department of Justice, 2000), NCJ#184768.

70. U.S. Department of Justice, *A Resource Guide on Racial Profiling Data Collection Systems.*

71. *Sourcebook of Criminal Justice Statistics* retrieved November 19, 2006, from www.albany.edu/sourcebook.

72. U.S. Department of Justice, *A Resource Guide on Racial Profiling Data Collection Systems.*

73. *Characteristics of Drivers Stopped by Police, 2002.* (Washington, D.C.: Department of Justice, 2006), NCJ#211471.

74. Joyce McMahon, Joel Gomer, Ronald Davis, and Amanda Kraus, *How to Correctly Collect and Analyze Racial Profiling Data: Your Reputation Depends on It* (Washington, D.C.: Department of Justice, 2003), retrieved from http://www.ncjrs.gov.

75. Matthew Hickman and Brian Reaves, *State and Local Law Enforcement Training Academies, 2002* (Washington, D.C.: Bureau of Justice Statistics, 2004), NCJ#203350.

76. Matthew Hickman and Brian Reaves, *Local Police Departments, 2003* (Washington D.C.: Bureau of Justice Statistics, 2006), NCJ#2101118.

77. U.S. Department of Justice, *A Resource Guide on Racial Profiling Data Collection Systems.*

78. U.S. Department of Justice, *A Resource Guide on Racial Profiling Data Collection Systems.*

79. Heather Ratcliffe, "Racial Gap Widens in Survey of Motorists Stopped by Police," *St. Louis Post-Dispatch,* retrieved May 26, 2006, from www.stltoday.com.

80. Jim Ruiz and Matthew Woessner, "Profiling, Cajun Style: Racial and Demographic Profiling in Louisiana's War on

Drugs," *International Journal of Police Science and Management,* 8 (3, 2006), pp. 176–197.

81. "Facing Up to an Unflattering Profile," *Law Enforcement News* (December 15/31, 2000), retrieved November 19, 2006, from www.lib.jjay.cuny.edu/len/200/12.31/coast.html.

82. "Facing Up to an Unflattering Profile."

83. "Facing Up to an Unflattering Profile."

84. "McKinney says Officer "Instigated' Incident," *Atlanta Constitution,* March 31, 2006, retrieved April 3, 2006, from www.ajc.com.

85. Caldero and Crank, *Police Ethics,* p. 194.

86. Caldero and Crank, *Police Ethics,* pp. 76–77.

87. Michael J. Sniffen, "Study Tracks Police Brutality Claims," *Associated Press,* June 25, 2006, retrieved June 29, 2006, from www.washingtonpost.com.

88. Caldero and Crank, *Police Ethics,* p. 155.

89. Goldstein, *Police Corruption,* pp. 6–8.

90. Donna Marrero, "Miami Chief Reaches Out to Rank and File after Verdicts," retrieved April 11, 2003, from www.sun-sentinel.com.

91. Lewis Kamb, "Taxpayers Foot the Bill for Keeping Bad Cops on the Job," *Seattle Post-Intelligencer,* retrieved May 15, 2006, from http://seattlepi.com/local/269669_pension11.asp.

92. "San Francisco Police Chief Retires after Brawl Cover-up Incident," *Associated Press,* retrieved on August 11, 2003, from www.newsobserver.com.

93. Carl B. Klockars, Sanja Kutnjak Ivkovich, and Maria R. Haberfeld. *Enhancing Police Integrity* (Washington, D.C.: Department of Justice, December 2005), # NCJ#209269, retrieved from www.ncjrs.gov/pdffiles1/nij/209269.pdf.

94. David Weisburd and Rosann Greenspan, with Edwin E. Hamilton, Hubert Williams, and Kellie A. Bryant, *Police Attitudes toward Abuse of Authority: Findings from a National Study* (Washington, D.C.: National Institute of Justice, 2000).

95. Samuel Walker and Geoffrey Alpert. "Early Intervention Systems: The New Paradigm," in Matthew Hickman, Alex R. Piquero, and Jack R. Greene, *Police Integrity and Ethics.* (Belmont, Calif.: Wadsworth, 2004), pp. 2.21–2.24.

96. Klockars, Ivkovich, and Haberfeld, *Enhancing Police Integrity,* NCJ#209269.

97. Walker, and Katz, *Police in America,* p. 500.

98. Larry J. Siegel and Joseph J. Senna, *Essentials of Criminal Justice,* 5th ed. (Belmont, Calif.: Wadsworth, 2006), p. 160.

99. Walker, and Katz, *Police in America,* p. 501.

100. Joe Farrow and Trac Pham, "Citizen Oversight of Law Enforcement: Challenge and Opportunity," *Police Chief,* 70 (10, October 2003), pp. 22–29.

101. Rolando V. del Carmen, *Civil Liabilities in American Policing: A Text for Law Enforcement Personnel* (Englewood Cliffs, N.J.: Prentice Hall, 1991), pp. 7–14.

102. Schmalleger, *Criminal Justice Today,* 9th ed., p. 317.

103. del Carmen, *Civil Liabilities in American Policing.*

104. Schmalleger, *Criminal Justice Today,* 9th ed., p. 315.

105. del Carmen, *Civil Liabilities in American Policing,* pp. 2–3.

106. Victor Kappeler, *Critical Issues in Police Civil Liability,* 3rd ed. (Prospect Heights, Ill.: Waveland Press, 2001), p. 26.

107. *Biscoe v. Arlington County,* 738 F.2d 1352 (D.C. Cir) (1984).

108. *Kaplan v. Lloyd's Insurance Co.,* 479 So. 2d.961 (La App.1985).

109. Sean Murphy, "City Made $500,000 Settlement in Shooting," *Boston Globe,* December 6, 1988, p. 1.

110. *Prior v. Woods* (1981), *National Law Journal,* November 2, 1981.

111. "Life, Liberty and Pursuits," *Law Enforcement News* (December 31, 1996), retrieved November 19, 2006, from www.libjjay.cuny.edu/len/96/31dec/html/26.html.

112. Richard Winton, "Accord Reached over Fatal Shooting," *Los Angeles Times,* April 13, 2006, retrieved April 17, 2006, from www.latimes.com.

113. "Oakland to Pay $ 2 Million to Protesters Injured by Cops," *New York Times,* retrieved March 20, 2006, from www.nytimes.com.

114. Caldero and Crank, *Police Ethics,* p. 87.

115. Kappeler, *Critical issues in Police Civil Liability.*

116. Kappeler, *Critical Issues in Police Civil Liability.*

117. *Canton v. Harris,* 489 U.S. 378 (1989).

118. Kappeler, *Critical Issues in Police Civil Liability.*

Chapter 9

1. Gary W. Cordner, Kathryn E. Scarborough, and Robert Sheehan, *Police Administration,* 5th ed. (Cincinnati, Ohio: Anderson, 2004), p. 365.

2. Bureau of Justice Statistics, *Law Enforcement Management and Administrative Statistics, 2000* (Washington, D.C.: Government Printing Office, 2004), NCJ#203350.

3. Samuel Walker and Charles M. Katz, *Police in America: An Introduction,* 5th ed. (New York: McGraw-Hill, 2005), p. 195.

4. O. W. Wilson and Roy Clinton McLaren, *Police Administration,* 4th ed. (New York: McGraw-Hill, 1977). A new edition was published in 1997, authored by three major researchers, in addition to Wilson and McLaren: James J. Fyfe, Jack R. Greene, William F. Walsh, O. W. Wilson, and Roy Clinton McLaren, *Police Administration,* 5th ed. (New York: McGraw-Hill, 1997).

5. Wilson and McLaren, *Police Administration,* p. 320.

6. Alejandro del Carmen and Lori Guevara, "Police Officers on Two-Officer Units: A Study of Attitudinal Responses Towards a Patrol Experiment," *Policing: An International Journal of Police Strategies and Management,* 26 (1, 2003), pp. 144–161.

7. University of Central Missouri Criminal Justice webpage, http://www.cmsu.edu/x74741.xml, retrieved November 25, 2006.

8. George L. Kelling. Tony Pate, Duane Dieckman, and Charles E. Brown, *The Kansas City Preventative Patrol Experiment: A Summary Report* (Washington, D.C.: Police Foundation, 1974).

9. Kelling et al., *Kansas City Preventive Patrol Experiment,* p. 16.

10. James Q. Wilson, *Thinking about Crime,* rev. ed. (New York: Vintage Books, 1985), p. 99.

11. Kelling et al., *Kansas City Preventive Patrol Experiment,* pp. v–vi.

12. Richard C. Larson, "What happened to Patrol Operations in Kansas City? A Review of the Kansas City Preventive Patrol Experiment," *Journal of Criminal Justice,* 3 (1975), pp. 267–297.

13. Wilson and McLaren, *Police Administration,* p. 4.

14. *Criminal Justice Newsletter,* August 27, 1979, p. 4.

15. Herbert Jacob and Michael J. Rich. "The Effects of the Police on Crime: A Second Look," *Law and Society Review,* 15 (1980–1981), pp. 109–122.

16. Cordner, Scarborough, and Sheehan, *Police Administration,* p. 368.

17. H. H. Isaacs, "A Study of Communications, Crimes, and Arrests in a Metropolitan Police Department," in President's Commission on Law Enforcement and Administration of Justice, *Task Force Report: Science and Technology* (Washington, D.C.: U.S. Government Printing Office, 1967).

18. National Advisory Commission on Criminal Justice Standards and Goals, *Police* (Washington, D.C.: U.S. Government Printing Office, 1973), p. 194.

19. Kansas City Police Department, *Response Time Analysis: Executive Summary* (Washington D.C.: U.S. Government Printing Office, 1978); and William Spelman and D. K. Brown, *Calling the Police: Citizen Reporting of Serious Crime* (Washington, D.C.: Police Executive Research Forum, 1981).

20. Gary W. Cordner, Jack R. Greene, and T. S. Bynum, "The Sooner the Better: Some Effects of Police Response Time," in *Police at Work: Policy Issues and Analysis,* ed. R. R. Bennett (Beverly Hills, Calif.: Sage, 1983).

21. Fyfe et al., *Police Administration,* p. xxiii.

22. George L. Kelling and Mary A. Wycoff, *Evolving Strategy of Policing: Case Studies of Strategic Change* (Cambridge, Mass.: Harvard University Press, 2001).

23. William G. Gay, Theodore H. Schell, and Steven Schack, *Routine Patrol: Improve Patrol Productivity,* vol. 1 (Washington, D.C.: National Institute of Justice, 1977), p. 2.

24. James Q. Wilson, *Varieties of Police Behavior: The Management of Law and Order in Eight Communities* (Cambridge, Mass.: Harvard University Press, 1968).

25. Gary W. Cordner, "The Police on Patrol," in *Police and Policing: Contemporary Issues,* ed. Dennis Jay Kenney (New York: Praeger, 1989), pp. 60–71.

26. Robert Lilly, "What Are the Police Now Doing?" *Journal of Police Science and Administration,* 6 (1978), pp. 51–53.

27. George Antunes and Eric Scott, "Calling the Cops: Police Telephone Operations and Citizen Calls for Service," *Journal of Criminal Justice,* 9 (1981), pp. 165–174.

28. Wilson, *Varieties of Police Behavior.*

29. Albert Reiss, *The Police and the Public* (New Haven, Conn.: Yale University Press, 1971).

30. Lawrence Sherman, *Repeat Calls to Police in Minneapolis* (Washington, D.C.: Crime Control Institute, 1987).

31. Cordner, "Police on Patrol," p. 62.

32. Reiss, *Police and the Public,* p. 19.

33. Egon Bittner, *The Functions of the Police in Modern Society* (Washington, D.C.: U.S. Government Printing Office, 1970), p. 127.

34. Kelling et al., *Kansas City Preventive Patrol Study.*

35. Cordner, "Police on Patrol," p. 65.

36. G. P. Whitaker, "What Is Patrol Work?" *Police Studies,* 4 (1982), pp. 13–22.

37. Jack R. Greene and Carl B. Klockars, "What Police Do," in *Thinking about Police: Contemporary Readings,* 2nd. ed., eds. Carl B. Klockars and Stephen D. Mastrofski (New York: McGraw-Hill, 1991), pp. 273–284.

38. Patrick A. Langan, Erica L. Schmitt, and Matthew R. Durose, *Contacts between Police and the Public: Findings from the 2002 National Survey* (Washington, D.C.: Bureau of Justice Statistics, 2005).

39. Sheehan and Cordner, *Introduction to Police Administration,* pp. 57–58.

40. Wilson, *Thinking about Crime,* p. x.

41. Sheehan and Cordner, *Introduction to Police Administration,* pp. 57–58.

42. Anthony V. Bouza, *Police Mystique: An Insider's Look at Cops, Crime, and the Criminal Justice System* (New York: Plenum, 1990), p. 84.

43. Bruce Smith, *Police Systems in the United States,* 2nd ed. (New York: Harper & Row, 1960), p. 14.

44. President's Commission on Crime in the District of Columbia, *A Report on the President's Commission on Crime in the District of Columbia* (Washington, D.C.: U.S. Government Printing Office, 1966), p. 53.

45. Police Department of Kansas City, *1966 Survey of Municipal Police Departments* (Kansas City, Mo.: Police Department of Kansas City, 1966), p. 53.

46. International Association of Chiefs of Police, *A Survey of the Police Department of Youngstown, Ohio* (Washington, D.C.: International Association of Chiefs of Police, 1964), p. 89.

47. Walker and Katz, *Police in America,* p. 311.

48. President's Commission on Law Enforcement and Administration of Justice, *Task Force Report: The Police,* p. 54.

49. John Heaphy, ed., *Police Practices: The General Administrative Survey* (Washington, D.C.: Police Foundation, 1978), p. 11.

50. George L. Kelling, *Foot Patrol* (Washington, D.C.: National Institute of Justice, 1988).

51. Police Foundation, *The Newark Foot Patrol Experiment* (Washington, D.C.: Police Foundation, 1981).

52. Robert C. Trojanowicz and Dennis W. Banas, *The Impact of Foot Patrol on Black and White Perceptions of Policing* (East Lansing: National Neighborhood Foot Patrol Center, School of Criminal Justice, Michigan State University, 1988).

53. Trojanowicz and Banas, *Impact of Foot Patrol.*

54. Carl J. Jensen III, "Consuming and Applying Research: Evidence-Based Policing," *Police Chief,* 73 (2, February 2006), pp. 98–101; and Lawrence Sherman, "Evidence-Based Policing," *Ideas in American Policing* (Washington, D.C.: Police Foundation, 1998).

55. Lawrence Sherman, James Shaw, and Dennis Rogan, *The Kansas City Gun Experiment* (Washington, D.C.: National Institute of Justice, 1994).

56. Larry J. Siegel and Joseph J. Senna, *Essentials of Criminal Justice,* 5th ed. (Belmont, Calif.: Wadsworth, 2007), p. 155.

57. James M. Tien, James W. Simon, and Richard C. Larson, *An Alternative Approach in Police Patrol: The Wilmington Split-Force Experiment* (Cambridge, Mass.: Public Systems Evaluation, 1977).

58. "Faced with a Crime Wave, Houston Cops 'Wave Back': Intensive Patrols Hit the Streets, but Union Blasts Directive Not to Field Calls for Service," *Law Enforcement News,* December 15, 1991, p. 3.

59. Larry K. Gaines, John L. Worrall, Mittie T. Southerland, and John E. Angell, *Police Administration,* 2nd ed. (New York: McGraw-Hill, 2003), p. 460.

60. Glen M. Mowrey and Derek Rice, "Alarm Industry steps up to Reduce False Alarm Calls through Enhanced Call Verification" *Police Chief,* 71 (9, September 2004), pp. 14, 15.

61. Walker and Katz, *Police in America,* p. 205.

62. Lorraine Mazerolle, Dennis Rogan, James Frank, Christine Famega, and John E. Eck, *Managing Calls to the Police with 911/311 Systems* (Washington, D.C.: U.S. Department of Justice, National Institute of Justice, 2005), NCJ#206256.

63. Santa Barbara Police Department web page, retrieved May 24, 2004, from http://www.santabarbaraca.gov/government/Departments/Police/Police_Tactical_Patrol_Force.htm.

64. J. E. Boydstun, *San Diego Field Interrogation: Final Report* (Washington, D.C.: Police Foundation, 1975).

65. James Q. Wilson and Barbara Boland, "The Effect of Police on Crime," *Law and Society Review,* 12 (1978), pp. 367–384.

66. Robert Sampson and Jacqueline Cohen, "Deterrent Effects of the Police on Crime: A Replication and Theoretical Extension," *Law and Society Review,* 22 (1988), pp. 163–191.

67. Lawrence Sherman, Patrick Gartin, and Michael Buerger, "Hot Spots of Predatory Crime: Routine Activities and the Criminology of Place," *Criminology,* 27 (1989), p. 27–55.

68. *Law Enforcement News,* October 31, 1995, p. 1.

69. S. J. Press. *Some Effects of an Increase in Police Manpower in the 20th Precinct of New York* (New York: Rand Institute, 1971).

70. J. M. Chaiken, M. W. Lawless, and K. A. Stenson, *The Impact of Police Activity on Crime: Robberies in the New York City Subway System* (New York: Rand Institute, 1974).

71. John F. Schnelle, Robert E. Kirchner, M. Patrick McNees, and Jerry M. Lawler, "Social Evaluation Research: The Evaluation of Two Police Patrolling Strategies," *Journal of Applied Behavior Analysis,* 8 (1975), pp. 232–240.

72. Lynn Zimmer, "Proactive Policing against Street-Level Drug Trafficking," *American Journal of Police,* 9 (1990), pp. 43-65.

73. Larry K. Gaines and Victor Kappeler, *Policing in America,* 4th ed. (Cincinnati, Ohio: Anderson, 2003), p. 531.

74. American Society for Industrial Security, "Innovations in Patrol," *Educator* (Spring/Summer 1997), p. 3.

75. Charles E. Higinbotham, "Spotlight On: Specialized Patrol Vehicles," *Police Chief,* 70 (March 2003), pp. 53–54, 56, 59–60, 62–63.

76. Higinbotham, "Spotlight On: Specialized Patrol Vehicles."

77. Seattle Police Department, *Annual Report,* Seattle: Seattle Police Department, p. 8.

78. Matthew J. Hickman and Brian A. Reaves, *Local Police Departments, 2003* (Washington, D.C.: U.S. Department of Justice, 2006).

79. Earl M. Sweeney, "Top Ten Trends: Traffic Enforcement" *Police Chief,* 72 (9, September 2005).

80. "Transportation Secretary Mineta Calls Highway Fatalities National Tragedy, Says All Americans Can Do More to Improve Road Safety," Press Release, April 20, 2006 (NHTSA # 02–06), retrieved from http://www.nhtsa.dot.gov.

81. Stacy Forster, "Crashes among Teen Drivers at 10-Year Low," *Journal Sentinel,* July 15, 2006, retrieved July 19, 2006, from http://www.jsonline.com.

82. Geoffrey Alpert and Patrick R. Anderson, "The Most Deadly Force: Police Pursuits," *Justice Quarterly,* 3 (1986), pp. 1–14.

83. Amy C. Pippel, "Orange Settles over Fatal Cop Chase," retrieved April 15, 2003, from www.sun-sentinel.com.

84. California Highway Patrol, *Pursuit Study* (Sacramento, Calif.: California Highway Patrol, 1993).

85. California Highway Patrol, *Pursuit Study,* p. 21.

86. Geoffrey P. Alpert and Roger G. Dunham, "Research on Police Pursuits: Applications for Law Enforcement," *American Journal of Police,* 7 (1988), pp. 123–131.

87. Geoffrey P. Alpert and Lorie A. Fridell, *Police Vehicles and Firearms: Instruments of Deadly Force* (Prospect Heights, Ill.: Waveland Press, 1992).

88. Ian Ith, "Seattle Police Told to Avoid High Speed Car Chases," *Seattle Times,* August 15, 2003, pp. B1, B4.

89. Michael Ko, "Harborview Researchers Tally Police Chase Toll," *Seattle Times,* retrieved April 8, 2001, from http://www.seattletimes.nwsource.com.

90. Chris Pipes and Dominick Pape, "Police Pursuits and Civil Liability," *FBI Law Enforcement Bulletin* (July 2001).

91. Hickman and Reaves, *Local Police Departments, 2003.*

92. Ith, "Seattle Police Told to Avoid High Speed Car Chases," pp. B1, B4.

93. John Specht, "Slow Pursuits Lead to Fast and Safe Apprehensions," *Police Chief*, 73 (3, March 2006).

94. "Life, Liberty and Pursuits" *Law Enforcement News*, December 31, 1996, p. 26.

95. "Los Angeles Testing GPS Dart to Avoid High-Speed Pursuits," *Los Angeles Times*, February 3, 2006.

96. "Slow Down, You're Moving Too Fast: Highway Traffic Deaths Creep Upward," *Law Enforcement News*, December 15, 1996), p. 5.

97. Heidi Coleman, "Reductions in Alcohol-Related Traffic Deaths," *Police Chief*, 72 (7, July 2005).

98. "Alcohol and Highway Safety 2001: A Review of the State of Knowledge" National Highway Traffic Safety Administration, 2001), retrieved November 28, 2006, from http://www.nhtsa.dot.gov/people/injury/research/alcoholhighway.

99. National Highway Traffic Safety Administration website, retrieved June 24, 2003, from www.nhtsa.gov.

100. "MADD Launches New Effort against Drunk Driving," Associate Press, November 25, 2006, retrieved November 25, 2006 from http://www.news8austin.com/content/top_stories/default.asp?ArID=175193.

101. "Drunk Driving: Problem-Oriented Guides for Police," Problem Specific Guides Series #36. Washington, D.C.: U.S. Department of Justice, February 2006, available at www.popcenter.org and www.cops.usdoj.gov.

102. Washington State Patrol website, retrieved June 24, 2003 from www.wsp.wa.gov.

103. Washington State Patrol website, retrieved on June 24, 2003 from www.wsp.wa.gov.

104. National Highway Traffic Safety Administration website, retrieved June 24, 2003, from www.nhtsa.gov.

105. Washington State Patrol website, retrieved on June 24, 2003, from www.wsp.wa.gov.

106. *Philadelphia Bulletin*, March 26, 1976, Section 3, p. 1.

107. Joseph Mancini, "NYPD's Hero Cops," *National Centurion* (August 1983), p. 22.

Chapter 10

1. Maria Newman, "Violent Crime Rose in '05, With Murders up by 4.8%," *New York Times*, June 13, 2006, retrieved June 13, 2006, from www.nytimes.com.

2. FBI Preliminary Annual Uniform Crime Report, 2005, retrieved November 28, 2006, from http://www.fbi.gov/ucr/oscius/data/table_12.html.

3. Amanda Paulson and Sara Miller Llana, "After Long Decline, Murders Rise in Small Cities," *Christian Science Monitor*, June 14, 2006, retrieved June 14, 2006, http://www.csmonitor.com.

4. Paulson and Llana, "After Long Decline."

5. Paulson and Llana, "After Long Decline."

6. Peter W. Greenwood and Joan Petersilia, *The Criminal Investigation Process, Volume I: Summary and Policy Implications* (Santa Monica, Calif.: Rand Corporation, 1975).

7. Greenwood and Petersilia, *Criminal Investigation Process*, p. vii.

8. William Spelman and D. K. Brown, *Calling the Police: Citizen Reporting of Serious Crime* (Washington, D.C.: Police Executive Research Forum, 1981).

9. Mark Willman and John Snortum, "Detective Work: The Criminal Investigation Process in a Medium-Size Police Department," *Criminal Justice Review*, 9 (1984), pp. 33–39.

10. Herman Goldstein, *Policing a Free Society* (Cambridge, Mass.: Ballinger, 1977), pp. 55–56.

11. Goldstein, *Policing a Free Society*, pp. 55–56.

12. Greenwood and Petersilia, *Criminal Investigation Process*, p. vii.

13. FBI *Uniform Crime Reports*, "Crime in the United States," retrieved July 29, 2006, from http://www.fbi.gov/ucr/oscium/offenses/clearances/index.html.

14. National Advisory Commission on Criminal Justice Standards and Goals, *Police* (Washington, D.C.: U.S. Government Printing Office, 1973).

15. Donald F. Cawley, H. J. Miron, W. J. Aranjo, R. Wassserman, T. A. Mannello, and Y. Huffman, *Managing Criminal Investigations: Manual* (Washington, D.C.: National Institute of Justice, 1977).

16. Cawley et al., *Managing Criminal Investigations*.

17. Cawley et al., *Managing Criminal Investigations*.

18. Ilene Greenberg and Robert Wasserman, *Managing Criminal Investigations* (Washington, D.C.: National Institute of Justice, 1975).

19. John E. Eck, *Managing Case Assignments: The Burglary Investigation Decision Model Replication* (Washington, D.C.: Police Executive Research Forum, 1979).

20. Gary W. Cordner, Kathryn E. Scarborough, and Robert Sheehan, *Police Administration*, 5th ed. (Cincinnati, Ohio: Anderson, 2004), p. 378.

21. Frank A. Colaprete, "The Case for Investigator Mentoring," *Police Chief* (October 2004), pp. 47–52.

22. Frank A. Colaprete, "Knowledge Management in the Criminal Investigation Process," *Law and Order* (October 2004), pp. 82–89.

23. G. H. Reiner, T. J. Sweeney, R. V. Waymire, F. A. Newton III, R. G. Grassie, S. M. White, and W. D. Wallace, *Integrated Criminal Apprehension Program: Crime Analysis Operations Manual* (Washington, D.C.: Law Enforcement Assistance Administration, 1977).

24. Colaprete, "Knowledge Management in the Criminal Investigation Process."

25. "Automated Information Sharing: Does It Help Law Enforcement Officers Work Better?," *National Institute of Justice Journal*, 253 (January 2006).

26. Cordner, Scarborough, and Sheehan, *Police Administration*, p. 316.

27. Paulson and Llana, "After Long Decline."

28. Testimony of Robert S. Mueller III, Director, FBI, before the Committee on Intelligence of the U.S. Senate, February 16, 2005, as cited in Frank Schmalleger, *Criminal Justice Today,* 9th ed. (Upper Saddle River, N.J.: Prentice Hall, 2007), p. 176.

29. Leon Fooksman, "Detectives from Different Agencies in Palm Beach County Team Up to Tackle Violence," *South Florida Sun-Sentinel,* June 2, 2006, retrieved June 2, 2006, from www.sun-sentinel.com.

30. Jennifer Nislow, "Working Together: A Case Study," *Law Enforcement News,* January 2005, pp. 1, 11. Report by Police Executive Research Forum is available on the Department of Justice website, http://www.ojp.usdoj.gov/BJA/pubs/SniperRpt.pdf.

31. Nislow, "Working Together."

32. Nislow, "Working Together."

33. Nislow, "Working Together."

34. Retrieved May 24, 2004, from http://unx1shsu.edu/cjcenter/trcpi7/repeat_Offender_Programs.

35. Retrieved May 24, 2004, from http://www.maricopacountyattorney.org/specialized_prosecution/gang_repeat_offenders/.

36. Susan E. Martin and Lawrence A. Sherman, "Selective Apprehension: A Police Strategy for Repeat Offenders," *Criminology* (February 1986), pp. 155–173.

37. Marcia Chaiken and Jan Chaiken, *Priority Prosecutors of High-Rate Dangerous Offenders* (Washington, D.C.: National Institute of Justice, 1991), as cited in Stephen Goldsmith, "Targeting High-Rate Offenders: Asking Some Tough Questions," *Law Enforcement News,* July/August 1991, p. 11.

38. Goldsmith, "Targeting High-Rate Offenders."

39. "Tough Chicago Neighborhood to Get Extra Attention from Police, Prosecutors," *Law Enforcement News,* March 15/31, 2003.

40. Patrick Mc Greevy, "L.A.'s Busiest Crooks to Do More Time," *Los Angeles Times,* May 8, 2006, retrieved May 11, 2006, from www.latimes.com.

41. Suzanne Smalley, "Police Planning Tight Surveillance of Worst Criminals," *Boston Globe,* May 16, 2006, retrieved May 17, 2006, from http://www.boston.com.

42. David Chipman and Cynthia E. Pappas, *Violent Crime Impact Teams (VCIT) Initiative: Focus on Partnerships* (Washington, D.C.: Department of Justice, February 2006), NCJ#214168.

43. Associated Press, "FDLE Sex Offender Site Adds Crime Detail, Vehicle Info," *South Florida Sun-Sentinel,* July 25, 2006, retrieved July 25, 2006, from www.sun-sentinel.com.

44. Elizabeth Wilkerson, "States Fight Meth Plague with Registries," retrieved June 9, 2006, from http://www.stateline.org.

45. Laura McCallum, "Pawlenty's Meth Registry: Good Policy or a Gimmick?," *Minnesota Public Radio,* July 27, 2006, retrieved August 3, 2006, from http://minnesota.publicradio.org.

46. Nikita Stewart and Allison Klein, "Council Approves Earlier Curfew," *Washington Post,* July 20, 2006, retrieved July 25, 2006, from www.washingtonpost.com.

47. Wendy Koch, "More Sex Offenders Tracked by Satellite," *USA Today,* June 6, 2006, retrieved June 7, 2006, from http://usatoday.com.

48. Robert Moran, "City Voters Approve Anticrime Cameras," *Philadelphia Inquirer,* May 17, 2006, retrieved May 17, 2006, from http://www.philly.com.

49. Information obtained from probable cause affidavit filed in Sarasota County by Detective Chris Hallisey.

50. Associated Press, "Man Guilty of Killing Girl," *Everett Herald,* November 18, 2005, retrieved July 25, 2006, from www.heraldnet.com.

51. Paula McMahon, "Prosecutors May Find It Tough to Prove First-Degree Murder in Homeless Beatings," *South Florida Sun-Sentinel,* February 3, 2006, retrieved February 3, 2006, from www.sun-sentinel.com.

52. Christina Lewis, "Solving the Cold Case: Time, Ingenuity and DNA Can Help," retrieved December 17, 2002, from www.cnn.com.

53. Sandy Haysrath, "DNA Testing Will Set You Free . . . or Not," University of Richmond School of Law, *Juris Publici,* 33 (12), retrieved August 28, 2006, from http://law.richmond.edu/.

54. Monica Davey, "Relief, and Bewilderment, Over Arrest in Kansas Killings," *New York Times* February 25, 2005, retrieved July 25, 2006, from www.nytimes.com.

55. ABT Associates, *New York City Anti-Crime Patrol: Exemplary Project Validation Report* (Washington, D.C.: U.S. Department of Justice, 1974); and Gary T. Marx, "The New Police Undercover Work," in *Thinking about Police: Contemporary Readings,* ed. Carl B. Klockars (New York: McGraw-Hill, 1983), pp. 201–202.

56. "Miami Seeks to Aid Tourist-Crime Targets," *Law Enforcement News,* October 31, 1991, p. 4.

57. Andrew Halper and Richard Ku, *New York City Police Department Street Crime* Unit (Washington, D.C.: National Institute of Justice, n.d.).

58. Patrick J. Mc Govern and Charles P. Connolly, "Decoys, Disguises, Danger—New York City's Non-Uniform Street Patrol," *FBI Law Enforcement Bulletin* (October 1976), pp. 16–26.

59. "Miami Seeks to Aid Tourist Crime Targets."

60. Bernard Edelman, "Blending," *Police* (September 1979), pp. 53–58.

61. Anthony V. Bouza, *The Police Mystique: An Insider's Look at Cops, Crime, and the Criminal Justice System* (New York: Plenum Press, 1990), p. 93.

62. Jeannie DeQuine, "High-Tech Drug Sting Zaps 93," *USA Today,* December 7, 1988, p. 3.

63. "Car Ring Sting," *USA Today,* July 13, 1988, p. 3.

64. Carl B. Klockars, "The Modern Sting," in *Thinking about Police: Contemporary Readings,* ed. Carl B. Klockars.

65. Diane Cardwell, "New York City Sues 15 Gun Dealers in 5 States, Charging Illegal Sales," *New York Times,* May 16, 2006, retrieved May 17, 2006, from www.nytimes.com.

66. Diane Cardwell, "2 Gun Dealers Settle Suit Brought by NYC," *New York Times,* August 1, 2006, retrieved August 1, 2006, from www.nytimes.com.

67. Paul McEnroe, "Illegal Guns Flooding into Minneapolis," retrieved April 29, 2006, from www.startribune.com.

68. Paul Farhi, "'Dateline' Pedophile Sting: One More Point," *Washington Post,* April 9, 2006, retrieved April 12, 2006, from www.washingtonpost.com.

69. John Sullivan, "Taking Back a Drug-Plagued Tenement, Step One: The Dealers Out," *New York Times,* August 16, 1997, pp. 25–26.

70. Evan Hess, an official with Northern Manhattan Improvement, retrieved from http://query.nytimes.com/gst/fullpage.html?res=9COE2DD133FF935A2575BC)A961958260.

71. Joseph M. Donisi, "Police Practices: Ft. Lauderdale's Code Enforcement Team," *FBI Law Enforcement Bulletin* (March 1992), pp. 24–25.

72. City of Ft. Lauderdale website, retrieved May 24, 2004, from http://info.ci.ftlaud.fl.us.

73. Retrieved August 8, 2006, from http://www.city.milwaukee.gov.

74. "Expanding Zero Tolerance (the Crackdown, not the Tolerance)," *Law Enforcement News,* April 30, 1997, pp. 1, 10.

75. Retrieved August 8, 2006, from http://www.ci.worcester.ma.us.

76. Commission on Accreditation for Law Enforcement Agencies, *Standards for Law Enforcement Agencies* (Fairfax, Va.: CALEA, 1987).

77. Robert D. McFadden, "FBI Sting: Hot Cars, Great Deals, 30 Suspects," *New York Times,* September 9, 1994, p. B1.

78. Retrieved August 7, 2006, from www.ci-wackenhut.com.

79. Retrieved August 7, 2006, from www.ci-wackenhut.com.

80. "2002 Retail Security Survey," retrieved August 7, 2006, from http://retailindustry.about.com.

81. "2002 Retail Security Survey."

82. Matthew J. Hickman and Brian A. Reaves, *Local Police Departments, 2003* (Washington, D.C.: Department of Justice, 2006), NCJ#210118.

83. George E. Rush, *The Dictionary of Criminal Justice,* 4th ed. (Guilford, Conn.: Dushkin, 1994), p. 124.

84. Craig Hemmens, John L. Worrall, and Alan Thompson, *Significant Cases in Criminal Procedure* (Los Angeles: Roxbury, 2004), p. 147.

85. Hemmens, Worrall, and Thompson, *Significant Cases in Criminal Procedure,* p. 147.

86. *United States v. Russell,* 411 U.S. 423, 1973.

87. *Hampton v. United States,* 425 U.S. 484 (1976).

88. Hemmens, Worrall, and Thompson, *Significant Cases in Criminal Procedure,* p. 148.

89. Rafael A. Olmeda, "Appeals Court Won't Toss Charges in Case of 'Cute' Detective," *South Florida Sun-Sentinel,* March 3, 2005, retrieved March 3, 2005, from www.sun-sentinel.com.

Chapter 11

1. Lee P. Brown, "Police-Community Power Sharing," in *Police Leadership in America: Crisis and Opportunity,* ed. William A. Geller (New York: Praeger, 1985), p. 71.

2. Brown, "Police-Community Power Sharing."

3. Police Foundation, *Experiments in Police Improvement: A Progress Report* (Washington, D.C.: Police Foundation, 1972), p. 28.

4. Steven M. Cox and Jack D. Fitzgerald, *Police in Community Relations,* 3rd ed. (Madison, Wisc.: Brown and Benchmark, 1996).

5. Cox and Fitzgerald, *Police in Community Relations.*

6. President's Commission on Law Enforcement and Administration of Justice, *The Challenge of Crime in a Free Society* (Washington, D.C.: U.S. Government Printing Office, 1967), p. 100.

7. Louis A. Radelet, *The Police and the Community* (Encino, Calif.: Glencoe, 1980).

8. Egon Bittner, "Community Relations," in *Police Community Relations: Images, Roles, Realities,* eds. Alvin W. Cohn and Emilio C. Viano (Philadelphia: Lippincott, 1976), pp. 77–82.

9. George Gallup, Jr., and Alec Gallup, *The Gallup Poll Monthly,* no. 420 (Princeton, N.J.: Gallup Poll, 2003).

10. *Sourcebook of Criminal Justice Statistics—1991 and 2005,* retrieved from http://www.albany.edu/sourcebook.

11. Gallup and Gallup, *Gallup Poll Monthly.*

12. James Q. Wilson, *Varieties of Police Behavior* (Cambridge, Mass.: Harvard University Press, 1968), p. 28.

13. "Avoiding Racial Conflict: A Guide for Municipalities" (Washington, D.C.: U.S. Department of Justice, 1991), retrieved December 12, 2006, from http://www.usdoj.gov/crs/publist.html.

14. U.S. Census Bureau, retrieved from http://www.census.gov/population/.

15. William Frey, as quoted in Stephen Ohlemacher, "Minority Population Increasing in States," retrieved August 15, 2006, from www.newsday.com.

16. Ohlemacher, "Minority Population Increasing."

17. Linda S. Miller, and Karen M. Hess, *The Police in the Community: Strategies for the 21st Century,* 3rd ed. (Belmont, Calif.: Wadsworth, 2002), p. 63.

18. Retrieved August 16, 2006, from http://www.census.gov.

19. *Brown v. Board of Education of Topeka,* 347 U.S. 483 (1954).

20. National Advisory Commission on Civil Disorders, *Report of the National Advisory Commission on Civil Disorders* (Washington, D.C.: U.S. Government Printing Office, 1968).

21. Steven M. Cox and Jack D. Fitzgerald, *Police in Community Relations: Critical issues,* 2nd ed. (Dubuque, Iowa: William C. Brown, 1992), p. 130.

22. "Blacks and Criminal Justice—a Grim Picture," *Law Enforcement News,* November 30, 1995, p. 11.

23. Miller and Hess, *Police in the Community*, p. 177.

24. William P. McCamey, Gene L. Scaramella, and Steven M. Cox, *Contemporary Municipal Policing* (Boston, Mass.: Allyn & Bacon, 2003), p. 209.

25. *Sourcebook of Criminal Justice Statistics Online,* retrieved August 17, 2006, from http://www.albany.edu/sourcebook/pdf/t200022005.pdf.

26. *Sourcebook of Criminal Justice Statistics Online,* retrieved August 17, 2006, from http://www.albany.edu/sourcebook/pdf/t226.pdf.

27. Ohlemacher, "Minority Population Increasing."

28. Miller and Hess, *Police in the Community*, p. 177.

29. U.S. Census Bureau, retrieved from http://www.census.gov/population/www/socdemo/foreign.html.

30. U.S. Census Bureau, retrieved from http://www.census.gov.

31. Steven W. Chalmers and Charles Tiffin, "Hispanic Outreach and Intervention Team," *Police Chief* (June 2005), pp. 58–61.

32. Thomas Kathman and Tim Chesser, "Latino Academy," *Police Chief* (June 2005), pp. 62–63.

33. U.S. Census Bureau, retrieved from http://www.census.gov.

34. "Winning Strategies Offered for Working with Different Cultures," *Cultural Diversity* (January/February 2000), retrieved on April 27, 2003, from http://www.communitypolicing.org/publications/exchange/.

35. "Winning Strategies Offered for Working with Different Cultures."

36. U.S. Census Bureau, retrieved August 18, 2006, from http://www.census.gov/population/.

37. *American Indians and Crime: A BJS Statistical Profile, 1992–2002* (Washington, D.C.: U.S. Department of Justice, 2004), NCJ#203097.

38. *American Indians and Crime.*

39. "Culture, Community and Communication: An Interview with Nancy Bill," *Building Bridges* (Summer, 1994), retrieved April 3, 2003, from http://www.edc.org/buildingsafecommunities/buildbridges/bb1.2/nancy.html.

40. International Association of Chiefs of Police (IACP), *Improving Safety in Indian Country: Recommendations from the IACP 2001 Summit* (Alexandria, Va.: IACP, 2001).

41. *American Indians and Crime.*

42. *American Indians and Crime.*

43. Community Policing Consortium, retrieved April 10, 2003, from http://www.communitypolicing.org/publications/exchange/e30_00/e30telle.htm.

44. U.S. Department of Justice, Community Relations Service, *Twenty Plus Things Law Enforcement Agencies Can Do to Prevent or Respond to Hate Incidents against Arab-Americans, Muslims, and Sikhs* (Washington, D.C.: U.S. Department of Justice), retrieved August 18, 2006, from www.usdoj.gov/crs/twentyplus.htm.

45. Andrea Elliott, "After 9/11, Arab-Americans Fear Police Acts, Study Finds," *New York Times,* June 12, 2006, retrieved June 12, 2006, from www.nytimes.com.

46. Jeff Jacoby "A Tale of 2 Stories about Anti-Semitism," *Boston Globe,* August 6, 2006, retrieved August 15, 2006, from www.boston.com.

47. "Examining Police Behavior Under Nazi Rule Offers Contemporary Lessons on Moral Responsibility and Civil Liberties," *Cultural Diversity* (January/February 2000), retrieved March 27, 2003, from http://www.communitypolicing.org/publications/exchange/e30_00/e30milog.htm.

48. Neil Santaniello, "Jewish Agency, Boca Police to Teach Terror Response," *Fort Lauderdale Sun-Sentinel,* April 2, 2003, retrieved April 2, 2003, from www.sun-sentinel.com.

49. "Data Show Surge in Female Inmates," *Los Angeles Times,* May 21, 2006, retrieved May 25, 2006, from www.latimes.com.

50. "Women and Girls in the Criminal Justice System," U.S. Department of Justice: National Criminal Justice Reference Service, retrieved June 9, 2006, from www.ncjrs.gov/spotlight/wgcjs/summary.html.

51. "Women and Girls in the Criminal Justice System."

52. "Women and Girls in the Criminal Justice System."

53. William Hermann, "Number of Arizona Women Behind Bars Escalating," *Arizona Republic,* May 31, 2006, retrieved June 5, 2006, from www.azcentral.com.

54. Sharon Coolidge, "Masked Man Really a Girl," *Cincinnati Enquirer,* August 15, 2006, retrieved from http://news.enquirer.com.

55. L. L. Brasier, "An Untold Crime: Reports of Boys Molested by Women on Rise, Experts Say," *Detroit Free Press,* August 6, 2006, retrieved August 15, 2006, from www.freep.com.

56. "D.C.'s Gay-Crime Unit Gets Recognition as It Builds Track Record of Achievement," *Law Enforcement News,* September 2005, p. 6.

57. Elizabeth Baier, "Wilton Manors Gun Group Promotes Self-Defense for Gays," *South Florida Sun-Sentinel,* May 22, 2006, retrieved May 22, 2006, from www.sun-sentinel.com.

58. Ruth Harlow, "Let's Work to Prevent, Not Just Punish, Hate Crimes," *Lambda Legal* (Spring/summer 1999), retrieved on April 19, 2003, from http://lambdalegal.org/cgi-bin/iowa/documentgs/record?record=453.

59. Bharathi Venkatraman, "Lost in Translation: Limited English Proficient Populations and Police," *Police Chief* (April 2006), retrieved May 4, 2006, from http://policechiefmagazine.org.

60. Venkatraman, "Lost in Translation."

61. Venkatraman, "Lost in Translation."

62. Jones Moy and Brent Archibald, "Reaching English-as-a–Second-Language Communities," *Police Chief* (June 2005), retrieved May 15, 2006, from http://policechiefmagazine.org.

63. Lee Bolivar, "Program Helps Brazilians Learn about the Broward Sheriff's Office," *Sun-Sentinel*, May 5, 2006, retrieved May 5, 2006, from www.sun-sentinel.com.

64. Howie Padilla, "Somali, Law Enforcement Officials Work to Curtail Gangs," *Minneapolis StarTribune*, retrieved June 8, 2006, from www.startribune.com.

65. Oren Dorell, "Towns Take Aim at Illegal Immigration" *USA Today*, August 14, 2006, retrieved August 15, 2006, from http://usatoday.com.

66. U.S. Census Bureau (2000), retrieved April 10, 2003 from www.census.gov.

67. Allan Lengel, "D.C. Police Learning to Hear the Deaf," *Washington Post*, February 11, 2002, p. B1.

68. Lori M. B. Laffel and Cynthia Pasquarello, "Diabetes and Law Enforcement," *Police Chief* (December 1996), p. 60.

69. U.S. Census, retrieved August 17, 2006, from http://www.census.gov.

70. Betsy Cantrell, "Triad: Reducing Criminal Victimization of the Elderly," *FBI Law Enforcement Bulletin* (February 1994), pp. 19–23.

71. Linda Forst, *The Aging of America: a Handbook for Police officers* (Springfield, Ill.: Charles C. Thomas, 2000), p. 7.

72. Forst, *Aging of America*, p. 31.

73. Forst, *Aging of America*. pp. 49–52.

74. William D. Miller, "The Graying of America: Implications towards Policing," *Law and Order* (October 1991), pp. 96–97.

75. Cantrell, "Triad: Reducing Criminal Victimization of the Elderly."

76. Retrieved August 17, 2006, from http://www.springspolice.com.

77. Forst, *Aging of America*, p. 136.

78. Retrieved August 17, 2006, from http://www.alz.org.

79. Office of Juvenile Justice and Delinquency Prevention (OJJDP), retrieved August 17, 2006, from http://ojjdp.ncjrs.org.

80. William DeJong, *Project DARE: Teaching kids to say "No" to Drugs and Alcohol* (Washington, D.C.: National Institute of Justice, March 1986), p. 4.

81. DARE America website, retrieved December 12, 2006, from http://www.dare.com/home/about_dare.asp.

82. University of Akron, "Initial Results Positive for New DARE Program—Media Advisory" (January 10, 2002), retrieved April 3, 2003, from http://www.dare.com/new_site/positive_results.htm.

83. U.S. Department of Justice, *The DARE Program: A Review of Prevalence, User Satisfaction, and Effectiveness* (Washington, D.C.: National Institute of Justice, 1994).

84. DARE America website, retrieved December 12, 2006, from http://www.dare.com/home/about_dare.asp.

85. DARE America website, retrieved December 12, 2006, from http://www.dare.com/home/about_dare.asp.

86. "Impact of a Drug Abuse Resistance Education (DARE) Program in Preventing the Initiation of Cigarette Smoking in Fifth and Sixth Grade Students," *Journal of National Medical Association*, 94 (2002), pp. 249–256.

87. Marnell Jameson, "Anti-Drug Overdose?," *Los Angeles Times*, May 15, 2006, retrieved May 23, 2006, from www.latimes.com.

88. Jameson, "Anti-Drug Overdose?"

89. *Evaluating GREAT: A School-Based Gang Prevention Program* (Washington, D.C.: U.S. Department of Justice, 2004), NCJ#198604.

90. Youth Crime Watch of America, retrieved March 27, 2003, from www.ycwa.org.

91. Halley Smith-La Bombard, "Bullies Find No Refuge in Oak Harbor," *Community Policing Organization* (September 2001), retrieved March 27, 2003, from www.communitypolicing.org/publications/comlinks/cl16/cl16_labom.htm.

92. Retrieved March 27, 2003, from http://www.usdoj.gov/crs/pubs/prevyouhatecrim.htm.

93. Retrieved April 2, 2003, from http://www.cert-la.com/links/CERTinSchools.htm.

94. Matthew J. Hickman and Brian A. Reaves, *Local Police Departments, 2003* (Washington, D.C.: Bureau of Justice Statistics, 2006), NCJ#210118.

95. Office of Juvenile Justice and Delinquency Prevention, http://ojjdp.ncjrs.org/ojstatbb/publications/statbb.asp?ID=T37.

96. "President Signs Protect Act," retrieved March 27, 2004, from www.Whitehouse.gov/news/releases2003/04/20030430–6.html.

97. National Association of Police Athletic Leagues (PAL), retrieved March 27, 2004, from www.nationalpal.org/Home.htm.

98. International Association of Chiefs of Police (IACP), "What Do Victims Want? Effective Strategies to Achieve Justice for Victims of Crime" (May 2000), retrieved April 28, 2004, from http://www.theiacp.org/documents/index.cfm?fuseaction=document&document_id=150.

99. IACP, "What Do Victims Want?"

100. National Center for Victims of Crime, *A Police Guide to First Response: Domestic Violence, Residential Burglary and Automobile Theft* (Washington, D.C.: U.S. Department of Justice, 2002).

101. Susan G. Parker, "Establishing Victim Services within a Law Enforcement Agency: The Austin Experience," *OVC Bulletin* (March 2001), p. 2.

102. Del Quentin Wilber, "An Open House on Open Cases," *Washington Post*, May 18, 2006, retrieved May 23, 2006, from www.washingtonpost.com.

103. Retrieved January 27, 2006, from www.philly.com.

104. Denise Kindschi-Gosselin, *Heavy Hands: An Introduction to the Crimes of Family Violence*, 2nd ed. (Upper Saddle River, N.J.: Prentice Hall, 2003).

105. Karen Collins, Cathy Schoen, Susan Joseph, Lisa Duchon, Elisabeth Simantov, and Michelle Yellowitz, "Health Concerns across a Woman's Lifespan" (1999), retrieved April 15, 2004,

from http://www.cmwf.org/programs/women/ksc_whsurvey99_3322asp.2002.

106. Callie Marie Rennison and Sarah Welchans, *Intimate Partner Violence* (Washington, D.C.: Department of Justice, 2000), NIJ#178247.

107. Patsy Klaus, *Crime and the Nation's Households, 2004* (Washington, D.C.: U.S. Department of Justice, April 2006), NCJ#211511.

108. Julie Davidow, "Doctors Urged to Look for Signs of Domestic Abuse," *Seattle Post-Intelligencer,* retrieved May 16, 2006, from http://seattlepi.nwsource.com.

109. Daniel J. Sonkin and Michael Durphy, *Learning to Live Without Violence: A Handbook for Men,* 5th ed. (Volcano, Calif.: Volcano Press, 1997).

110. Kindschi-Gosselin, *Heavy Hands.*

111. Nancy Loving, *Responding to Spouse Abuse and Wife Beating: A Guide for Police* (Washington, D.C.: Police Executive Research Forum, 1980).

112. Lawrence Sherman and Richard A. Berk, *The Minneapolis Domestic Violence Experiment* (Washington, D.C.: Police Foundation, 1984).

113. Sherman and Berk, *Minneapolis Domestic Violence Experiment.*

114. Kindschi-Gosselin, *Heavy Hands.*

115. Hickman and Reaves, *Local Police Departments, 2003,* p. 24.

116. "Victim Satisfaction with the Criminal Justice System," *National Institute of Justice Journal,* 253 (January 2006).

117. Carolyn Schleuter and Vinita Jethwani, "Integrity, Action, Justice: Leadership Committed to Ending Violence against Women," *Police Chief* (November 2004), pp. 16–18.

118. Gary W. Cordner, "People with Mental Illness," *Department of Justice: Problem-Oriented Guides for Police, Guide #40* (Washington, D.C.: U.S. Department of Justice, May 2006).

119. Richard Lamb, Linda Weinberger, and Walter DeCuir, "The Police and Mental Health," *Psychiatric Services,* 53 (10, 2002), pp. 1266–1271.

120. "Another Needless Death," *Washington Post,* May 18, 2006, retrieved May 23, 2006, from www.washingtonpost.com.

121. "Ft. Lauderdale Schedules Community Meeting Tonight on Police Shooting," *Sun-Sentinel,* July 19, 2006, retrieved July 19, 2006, from www.sun-sentinel.

122. Cordner, "People with Mental Illness."

123. *Zinermon v. Burch,* 110 S.Ct. 975 (1990).

124. Alan R. Coffey, *Law Enforcement: A Human Relations Approach* (Englewood Cliffs, N.J.: Prentice Hall, 1990), pp. 136–137.

125. Peter Finn, *Street People: Crime File Study Guide* (Washington, D.C.: National Institute of Justice, 1988), p. 1.

126. Alison Hibbert, "Police Come to the Aid of the Homeless," *Police Chief* (May 2000), retrieved April 2, 2003, from http://ci.ftlaud.fl.us.police/homeless2.html.

127. Hibbert, "Police Come to the Aid of the Homeless."

128. Michael Ko, "Police Recruits Get Look at Lives of Homeless," *Seattle Times,* July 3, 2004, retrieved July 3, 2004, from www.seattletimes.com.

129. "Attacks Prompt Homeless Advocates to Visit Schools," *USA Today,* March 8, 2006, retrieved March 8, 2006, from www.usatoday.com.

130. George L. Kelling, "On the Accomplishments of the Police," in *Control of the Police Organization,* ed. Maurice Punch (Cambridge, MA: MIT Press, 1983), p. 164.

131. The IACP Crime Prevention Committee, "Sustaining Crime Prevention and Community Outreach Programs," *Police Chief* (September 2005).

132. Lori Croy and Andrew Scott, "Crime Prevention and Community Programs: I Prevent Crime: A Crime Prevention Campaign," *Police Chief* (September 2005).

133. National Crime Watch, retrieved August 17, 2006, from http://www.ncpc.org.

134. James Garofalo and Maureen McLeod, *Improving the Use and Effective Use of Neighborhood Watch Programs* (Washington, D.C.: National Institute of Justice, 1988), p. 1.

135. Dennis Jay Kenney, "The Guardian Angels: The Related Social Issues," in *Police and Policing: Contemporary Issues,* ed. Dennis Jay Kenney (New York: Praeger, 1989), pp. 376–400.

136. Philip Messing, "Cops to Wing It with Angels in Park: Taking First Step Together—On Skates," *New York Post* (December 1996), p. 6.

137. Susan Pennell, Christine Curtis, Joel Henderson, and Jeff Tayman, "Guardian Angels: A Unique Approach to Crime Prevention," *Crime and Delinquency* (July 1989), pp. 376–400.

138. The Guardian Angels, retrieved on March 27, 2004, from www.guardianangels.org.

139. Anthony Westbury, "Guardian Angels Eager to Expand Its Ranks into Ft. Pierce/Port St. Lucie," October 20, 2005, retrieved from www.sun-sentinel.com.

140. Retrieved April 10, 2003, from http://www.police.nashville.org/get_involved/default.htm.

141. Nancy Kolb, "Law Enforcement Volunteerism," *Police Chief* (June 2005), pp. 22–30.

142. Rebecca Kanable, "Volunteers Enter the Crime Scene," *Law Enforcement Technology,* 33 (3, March 2006), pp. 14–23.

143. Retrieved March 27, 2004, from http://police.nashville.org.

144. Dennis P. Rosenbaum, Arthur J. Lurigio, and Paul J. Lavrakas, *Crime Stoppers: A National Evaluation* (Washington, D.C.: National Institute of Justice, 1986).

145. Crime Stoppers USA, retrieved March 27, 2004, from http://www.crimestopusa.com/stats.htm.

146. Virginia Beach Crime Solvers, retrieved March 27, 2004, from http://www.crimesolvers.com/stats.htm.

147. Jim Dwyer and Christopher Drew, "Fear Exceeded Crime's Reality in New Orleans," retrieved September 29, 2005, from www.nytimes.com.

148. Alston A. Morgan, "Law Enforcement Community Benefits with State-Accredited Chaplain Academy," *Sheriff Times,* 1 (10, Fall 1999), p. 1.

149. Morgan, "Law Enforcement Community Benefits."

150. Retrieved January 31, 2006, from http://www.washingtonpost.com.

151. Michele McPhee, "Cop Charity Woo$ Biz for Powwow," *Boston Herald,* April 30, 2006, retrieved May 2, 2006, from http://news.bostonherald.com.

152. McPhee, "Cop Charity."

153. McPhee, "Cop Charity."

Chapter 12

1. George L. Kelling, *Police and Communities: The Quiet Revolution, Perspectives on Policing, no. 1* (Washington, D.C.: National Institute of Justice, 1988).

2. Bureau of Justice Statistics, *Community Policing Impacts 86% of U.S. Population Served by Local Police Departments* (Washington, D.C.: Department of Justice, 2001), retrieved April 23, 2003, from www.ojp.usdoj.gov.

3. Matthew J. Hickman and Brian A. Reaves, *Local Police Departments, 2003* (Washington, D.C.: Bureau of Justice Statistics, 2006), NCJ#210118.

4. The 12 monographs in the *Perspectives on Policing* series were published in 1988 and 1989 by the National Institute of Justice, Washington, D.C.

5. Mark H. Moore and Robert C. Trojanowicz, *Corporate Strategies for Policing, Perspectives on Policing, no. 6* (Washington, D.C.: National Institute of Justice, 1988).

6. Dennis J. Stevens, *Applied Community Policing in the 21st Century* (Allyn & Bacon: Boston, 2003), p. 13.

7. James Q. Wilson and George L. Kelling, "'Broken Windows': The Police and Neighborhood Safety," *Atlantic Monthly* (March 1982), pp. 29–38.

8. Wesley G. Skogan, *Disorder and Decline: Crime and the Spiral of Decay in American Neighborhoods* (New York: Free Press, 1990), pp. 21–50.

9. Robert C. Trojanowicz, "Building Support for Community Policing: An Effective Strategy," *FBI Law Enforcement Bulletin* (May 1992), pp. 7–12.

10. Charles H. Weigand, "Combining Tactical and Community Policing Considerations," *Law and Order* (May 1997), pp. 70–71.

11. David L. Carter, *Community Policing and DARE: A Practitioner's Perspective* (Washington, D.C.: National Institute of Justice, 1995), p. 2.

12. Bonnie Bucqueroux, *What Community Policing Teaches Us about Community Criminal Justice,* retrieved August 29, 2006, from www.policing.com.

13. Retrieved August 29, 2006, from http://safestreet.org.

14. James F. Ahern, *Police in Trouble* (New York: Hawthorne Books, 1972), pp. 83–85.

15. Mary Ann Wycoff, Wesley G. Skogan, Anthony M. Pate, and Lawrence Sherman, *Citizen Contact Patrol: Executive Summary* (Washington, D.C.: Police Foundation, 1985).

16. Michael J. Farrell, "The Development of the Community Patrol Officer Program: Community Oriented Policing in the City of New York," in *Community Policing: Rhetoric or Reality?,* eds. Jack R. Greene and Stephen D. Mastrofski (New York: Praeger, 1988), pp. 73–88.

17. Joseph E. Braun, "Progress through Partnerships," *Community Links* (January 1997), retrieved April 18, 2003, from www.communitypolicing.org/publications.

18. George L. Kelling, *"Broken Windows" and Police Discretion* (Washington, D.C.: U.S. Department of Justice, 1999).

19. Herman Goldstein, "Toward Community-Oriented Policing: Potential, Basic Requirements and Threshold Questions," *Crime and Delinquency,* 33 (1997), pp. 6–36.

20. U. S. Department of Justice, *Surveys in 12 Cities Show Widespread Community Support for Police* (Washington, D.C.: National Institute of Justice, 1999).

21. Hickman and Reaves, *Local Police Departments, 2003.*

22. Samuel Walker and Charles Katz, *Police in America: An Introduction,* 5th ed. (New York: McGraw-Hill, 2005), p. 331.

23. Jack Green, "Community Policing in America: Changing the Nature, Structure, and Function of the Police," in ed. Julie Horney, *Policies, Processes, and Decisions of the Criminal Justice System* (Washington, D.C.: National Institute of Justice, 2000).

24. Police Executive Research Forum (PERF), "The Mechanics of Problem Solving Slides," retrieved September 2, 2006, from www.policeforum.org.

25. PERF, "Mechanics."

26. PERF, "Mechanics."

27. Herman Goldstein, *Problem-Oriented Policing* (New York: McGraw-Hill, 1990).

28. Rachel Boba, "What Is Problem Analysis?," *Problem Analysis in Policing: An executive Summary,* 5 (1, Winter 2003), p. 2.

29. PERF, "Mechanics."

30. Police Executive Research Forum (PERF), "2002 Herman Goldstein Award Winners," retrieved September 2, 2006, from www.policeforum.org.

31. PERF, "2002 Goldstein Winners."

32. PERF, "2002 Goldstein Winners."

33. Kenneth Weldon and Santos Hernandez, "Improving and Maintaining Public Awareness and Community Teamwork," *Police Chief* (June 2005), pp. 66–71.

34. Russell Contreras, "Homicides Reduced to Zero in Lawrence," *Boston Globe,* March 8, 2006, retrieved March 8, 2006, from www.boston.com.

35. Stevens, *Applied Community Policing in the 21st Century,* p. 237.

36. Elgin Police Department website, retrieved September 7, 2006, from www.cityofelgin.org.

37. Institute for Research Policy, Northwestern University, September 7, 2006, retrieved from www.northwestern.edu/ipr/publications.

38. Institute for Research Policy, Northwestern University.

39. IACP, 2005 Community Policing Awards, retrieved September 7, 2006, from http://www.theiacp.org.

40. IACP, 2005 Community Policing Awards.

41. IACP, 2005 Community Policing Awards.

42. Retrieved May 25, 2003, from http://www.theiacp.org/awards.

43. Retrieved May 25, 2003, from http://www.theiacp.org/awards.

44. Retrieved May 25, 2003, from http://www.theiacp.org/awards.

45. Elgin Police Department website, retrieved September 7, 2006, from www.cityofelgin.org.

46. Macon Police Department website, retrieved September 7, 2006, from http://www.maconpd.com.

47. Phoenix Police Department website, retrieved September 7, 2006, from http://www.phoenix.gov/POLICE.

48. Housing and Urban Development website, retrieved September 7, 2006, from www.hud.gov/buying/.

49. Jeffrey A. Roth and Joseph F. Ryan, "The Cops Program after 4 Years: National Evaluation," *Research in Brief* (August 2000), p. 1.

50. COPS website, retrieved September 8, 2006, from www.cops.usdoj.gov/.

51. Department of Justice, *On the Beat*, 19 (Fall, 2002), retrieved April 2, 2004, from www.cops.usdoj.gov/mime/open.pdf?item=628.

52. COPS website.

53. COPS website.

54. COPS website.

55. Department of Justice, *On the Beat*.

56. Department of Justice, *On the Beat*.

57. Department of Justice, *On the Beat*, 19 (fall, 2002).

58. Department of Justice, *On the Beat*.

59. Government Accountability Office (GAO), "Community Policing Grants COPS Grants Were a Modest Contributor to Decline in Crime in the 1990s" (October 14, 2005), GAO #06–104 retrieved from http://www.gao.gov.

60. Jihong "Solomon" Zhao and Quint Thurman, *Funding Community Policing to Reduce Crime: Have Cops Grants Made a Difference From 1994 to 2000?* (U.S. Department of Justice, Office of Community Oriented Policing Services, July 2004).

61. Community Policing Consortium Website, retrieved September 9, 2006, from www.communitypolicing.org.

62. "As Crime Rates Continue to Dip, Police Credit Community Efforts—And Their Own," *Law Enforcement News,* September 15, 1996, pp. 1, 14.

63. Lou Kilzer, "'Broken Windows' Crime-Fighting Strategy Works in N.J.," *Rocky Mountain News,* March 14, 2006, retrieved March 15, 2006, from www.insidedenver.com.

64. Christopher Osher, "Sign of the Crimes: 7.4% Fall," *Denver Post,* June 8, 2006, retrieved from www.denverpost.com.

65. Steve Berg, "How New York Got its Groove Back . . . and What It Could Mean for Minneapolis," *Minneapolis StarTribune,* June 11, 2006, retrieved from www.startribune.com.

66. Ronald Weitzer and Steven A. Tuch, "Public Opinion on Reforms in Policing," *Police Chief* (December 2004), pp. 26–30.

67. Rachel Tuffin, Julia Morris, and Alexis Poole, "Evaluation of the Impact of the National Reassurance Policing Programme" (Great Britain Home Office Research Development and Statistics Directorate, January 2006).

68. Natasha Lee, "Chief Rethinks Community Policing Policy," *Stamford Advocate,* April 10, 2006, retrieved from www. stamfordadvocate.com.

69. Wesley Skogan and Mary Ann Wycoff, "Some Unexpected Effects of a Police Service for Victims," *Crime and Delinquency,* 33 (1987), pp. 490–501.

70. William J. Bratton and George L. Kelling, "There Are No Cracks in the Broken Windows," *National Review Online,* February 28, 2006, retrieved from www.nationalreview.com.

71. "Audit Rips Houston's Policing Style as a Good Idea That Falls Short of the Mark," *Law Enforcement News,* September 30, 1991, p. 1.

72. Gary B. Schobel, Thomas A. Evans, and John L. Daly, "Community Policing: Does It Reduce Crime, or just Displace it?," *Police Chief* (August 1997), pp. 64–71.

73. Lisa M. Reichers and Roy Roberg, "Community Policing: A Critical Review of Underlying Assumptions," *Journal of Police Science and Administration* (June 1990), p. 110.

74. David Griffith, "Does Community Policing Work?," *Police,* 29 (12, December 2005), pp. 40, 42, 45.

75. Timothy Oettmeier and Mary Ann Wycoff, "Personnel Performance Evaluations in the Community Policing Context," U.S. Department of Justice & Community Policing consortium, 2006, retrieved June 9, 2006, from www. policeforum.org, p. 352.

76. Oettmeier and Wycoff, "Personnel Performance Evaluations," p. 354.

77. National Institute of Justice, "Policing Neighborhoods: A Report from St. Petersburg," *Research Preview* (July 1999).

78. Bratton and Kelling, "There Are No Cracks in the Broken Windows."

79. Rob McManamy, "Study Authors Find Cracks in 'Broken Windows,'" *University of Chicago Chronicle,* March 30, 2006, retrieved from http://chronicle.uchicago.edu/0603030/brokenwindow.shtml.

80. McManamy, "Study Authors Find Cracks in 'Broken Windows.'"

81. Bratton and Kelling, "There Are No Cracks in the Broken Windows."

82. Jacob R. Clark, "Time to Pay the Piper: COPS Funded Officers, Departments Near Day of Fical Reckoning," *Law Enforcement News,* September 30, 1997, pp. 1, 14.

83. National Institute of Justice, "Policing Neighborhoods."

84. Clark, "Time to Pay the Piper."

85. Clark, "Time to Pay the Piper."

86. "Bratton: Terror Fight Diverts Money from Crime Prevention," *Providence Journal,* March 2, 2006, retrieved March 2, 2006, from http://www.projo.com/.

87. Lee, "Chief Rethinks Community Policing Policy."

88. Retrieved May 25, 2004, from http://www.cops.usdoj.gov/mime/open.pdf?item=1046.

89. Rob Chapman and Matthew C. Scheider, "Community Policing: Now More than Ever," retrieved May 2, 2003, from http://www.cops.usdoj.gov/default.asp?item=716.

90. Quote from website by FBI Assistant Director of the Office of law enforcement coordinator Louis F. Quijas, retrieved December 13, 2006, from www.cops.usdoj.gov.

91. U.S. Department of Justice, November 2005, retrieved from www.cops.usdoj.gov/.

92. Retrieved May 3, 2006, from www.theiacp.org.

93. Stephen Doherty and Bradley G. Hibbard, "Special Focus: Community Policing and Homeland Security," *Police Chief* (February 2006), retrieved from http://policechiefmagazine.org.

94. John L. Worrall, "Does 'Broken Windows' Law Enforcement Reduce Serious Crime?," California Institute for County Government Research Brief (2002), p. 9, retrieved April 2, 2004, from http://www.cicg.org/publications.

Chapter 13

1. Federal Bureau of Investigation, *Uniform Crime Reports,* 2005, retrieved September 19, 2006, from http://www.fbi.gov.

2. *Weeks v. United States,* 232 U.S. 383 (1914).

3. *Brown v. Mississippi,* 297 U.S. 278 (1936).

4. *Mapp v. Ohio,* 367 U.S. 643 (1961); and *Miranda v. Arizona,* 384 U.S. 436 (1966).

5. *Weeks v. United States.*

6. *Silverthorne Lumber Co. v. United States,* 251 U.S. 385 (1920).

7. *Wolf v. Colorado,* 338 U.S. 25 (1949).

8. *Rochin v. California,* 342 U.S. 165 (1952).

9. *Mapp v. Ohio.*

10. U.S. Department of Justice, National Institute of Justice, *The Effects of the Exclusionary Rule: A Study of California* (Washington, D.C.: National Institute of Justice, 1982), p. 12.

11. Peter Nardulli, "The Societal Cost of the Exclusionary Rule: An Empirical Assessment," *ABF Research Journal* (1983), pp. 585–609.

12. *Atwater v. City of Lago Vista,* 532 U.S. 318 (2001).

13. *Payton v. New York,* 445 U.S. 573 (1980).

14. *Henry v. United States,* 361 U.S. 98 (1959).

15. *Brinegar v. United States,* 338 U.S. 160 (1949).

16. *Draper v. United States,* 358 U.S. 307 (1959).

17. *County of Riverside v. McLaughlin,* 500 U.S. 44 (1991).

18. *Maryland v. Pringle,* 124 S.Ct. 795 (2003).

19. For a comprehensive article of police use on force, see Thomas D. Petrowski, "When Is Force Excessive: Insightful Guidance from the U.S. Supreme Court," *FBI Law Enforcement Bulletin* (September 2005), pp. 27–32.

20. *Tennessee v. Garner,* 471 U.S. 1 (1985).

21. *Delaware v. Prouse,* 440 U.S. 618 (1979).

22. *Pennsylvania v. Mimms,* 434 U.S. 106 (1977). For a thorough discussion of *Mimms* and *Wilson,* see Lisa A. Regini, "Extending the *Mimms* Rule to Include Passengers," *FBI Law Enforcement Bulletin* (June 1997), pp. 27–32.

23. *Maryland v. Wilson,* 117 S.Ct. 882 (1997).

24. *Maryland v. Wilson,* citing Federal Bureau of Investigation, *Uniform Crime Reports: Law Enforcement Officers Killed and Assaulted* (Washington, D.C.: Federal Bureau of Investigation, 1994).

25. *Michigan Department of State Police v. Sitz,* 496 U.S. 444 (1990).

26. *City of Indianapolis v. Edmond,* 121 S.Ct. 447 (2000).

27. *Illinois v. Lidster,* 124 S.Ct. 885 (2004).

28. *Whren v. United States,* 116 S.Ct. 1769 (1996).

29. *Payton v. New York.*

30. *Minnesota v. Olson,* 495 U.S. 91 (1990).

31. *Minnesota v. Carter,* 119 S.Ct. 469 (1998).

32. *Kirk v. Louisiana,* 536 U.S. 635 (2002).

33. *Bond v. United States,* 529 U.S. 334 (2000).

34. Sophia Y. Kil, "Supreme Court Cases: 1999–2000 Term," *FBI Law Enforcement Bulletin* (November 2000), pp. 28–29.

35. *Katz v. United States,* 389 U.S. 347 (1967).

36. *Kyllo v. United States,* 533 U.S. 27 (2001); and Linda Greenhouse, "Justices Say Warrant Is Required in High-Tech Searches of Homes," *New York Times,* June 12, 2001, pp. A1, A29.

37. *United States v. Place,* 462 U.S. 696 (1983).

38. See Michael J. Bulzomi, "Drug Detection Dogs: Legal Considerations," *FBI Law Enforcement Bulletin* (January 2000), pp. 27–31.

39. Bulzomi, "Drug Detection Dogs," pp. 30–31.

40. Jayme S. Walker, "Using Drug Detection Dogs: An Update," *FBI Law Enforcement Bulletin* (April 2001), pp. 25–32.

41. *United States v. Place.*

42. *Illinois v. Caballes,* 543 U.S. 405 (2005).

43. *Illinois v. Caballes.*

44. *Wilson v. Arkansas,* 115 S.Ct. 1914 (1995). For a complete discussion of Fourth Amendment standards on search warrants, see Michael J. Bulzomi, "Knock and Announce: A Fourth Amendment Standard," *FBI Law Enforcement Bulletin* (May 1997), pp. 27–32.

45. *Aguilar v. Texas,* 378 U.S. 108 (1964); and *Spinelli v. United States,* 393 U.S. 410 (1969).

46. *Illinois v. Gates,* 462 U.S. 213 (1983).

47. For an excellent article on *Illinois v. Gates* and other cases involving probable cause and search warrants, see Edward Hendrie, "Inferring Probable Cause: Obtaining a Search Warrant for a Suspect's Home Without Direct Information That Evidence Is Inside," *FBI Law Enforcement Bulletin* (February 2002), pp. 23–32.

48. *Michigan v. Summers,* 452 U.S. 692 (1981).

49. *Maryland v. Buie,* 110 S.Ct. 1093 (1990).

50. *Illinois v. McArthur,* 121 S.Ct. 946 (2001).

51. *Muehler v. Mena,* 125 S.Ct. 1465 (2005).

52. *United States v. Banks,* 124 S.Ct. 521 (2003).

53. *Hudson v. Michigan,* 126 S.Ct. 2159 (2006); Richard G. Schott, "Knock and Announce Violations: No 'Cause' to Suppress," *FBI Law Enforcement Bulletin* (September 2006), pp. 26–32.

54. *Hudson v. Michigan.*

55. *Chimel v. California,* 395 U.S. 752 (1969).

56. *United States v. Robinson,* 414 U.S. 218 (1973).

57. *Knowles v. Iowa,* 119 S.Ct. 484 (1998). For an excellent article on the history of searches incident to arrest, see Thomas D. Colbridge, "Search Incident to Arrest: Another Look," *FBI Law Enforcement Bulletin* (May 1999), pp. 27–32.

58. *Terry v. Ohio,* 392 U.S. 1 (1968).

59. *Terry v. Ohio.*

60. *Hiibel v. Sixth Judicial District Court of Nevada, Humboldt County,* 124 S.Ct 2451 (2004).

61. *Minnesota v. Dickerson,* 113 S.Ct. 2130 (1993).

62. *Illinois v. Wardlow,* 120 S.Ct. 673 (2000).

63. *Illinois v. Wardlow,* citing *Terry,* 392 U.S. at 30.

64. Kil, "Supreme Court Cases: 1999–2000 Term," pp. 28–32. For an excellent discussion of the *Wardlow* decision and flight as justification for seizure, see Michel E. Brooks, "Flight as Justification for Seizure: Supreme Court Rulings," *FBI Law Enforcement Bulletin* (June 2000), pp. 28–32.

65. *Florida v. J. L.,* 120 S.Ct. 1375 (2000). For an interesting, informative article on *Terry* stops in response to anonymous tips, see Michael J. Bulzomi, "Anonymous Tips and Frisks: Determining Reasonable Suspicion," *FBI Law Enforcement Bulletin* (August 2000), pp. 28–30.

66. *Payton v. New York.*

67. *Arkansas v. Sanders,* 442 U.S. 753 (1979).

68. Michael L. Ciminelli, "Police Response to Anonymous Emergency Calls," *FBI Law Enforcement Bulletin* (May 2003), pp. 23–32.

69. *Warden v. Hayden,* 387 U.S. 294 (1967).

70. *Mincey v. Arizona,* 437 U.S. 385 (1978).

71. *Maryland v. Buie.*

72. *Wilson v. Arkansas.*

73. *Illinois v. McArthur.*

74. Ciminelli, "Police Response to Anonymous Emergency Calls," pp. 23–31.

75. Jayme Walker Holcomb, "Consent Searches: Factors Courts Consider in Determining Voluntariness," *FBI Law Enforcement Bulletin* (May 2002), pp. 25–31; also see Holcomb, "Obtaining Written Consent to Search," *FBI Law Enforcement Bulletin* (March 2003), pp. 26–32.

76. *Schneckloth v. Bustamonte,* 412 U.S. 218 (1973).

77. *United States v. Matlock,* 415 U.S. 164 (1974).

78. *Bumper v. North Carolina,* 391 U.S. 543 (1968).

79. *Illinois v. Rodriguez,* 110 S.Ct. 2793 (1990).

80. *Florida v. Bostick,* 111 S.Ct. 2382 (1991).

81. Edward M. Hendrie, "Consent Once Removed," *FBI Law Enforcement Bulletin* (February 2003), pp. 24–32.

82. *United States v. Pollard,* 215 F.3d 643 (6th Cir. 2000).

83. *Georgia v. Randolph,* 126 S.Ct. 1515 (2006).

84. *United States v. Matlock* and *Illinois v. Rodriguez.*

85. *Harris v. United States,* 390 U.S. 234 (1968). See also *Horton v. California,* 110 S.Ct. 2301 (1990). For a comprehensive article on plain view evidence, see Devallis Rutledge, "Seizing Evidence in Plain View," *Police* (March 2006), pp. 82–84.

86. *Arizona v. Hicks,* 107 S.Ct. 1149 (1987).

87. *Mincey v. Arizona,* 437 U.S. 385 (1978); also see *Thompson v. Louisiana,* 469 U.S. 17 (1984). Also see John S. Dempsey, *Introduction to Investigations,* 2nd ed. (Belmont, Calif.: Wadsworth, 2003), pp. 48–49; and Kimberly A. Crawford, "Crime Scene Searches: The Need for Fourth Amendment Compliance," *FBI Law Enforcement Bulletin* (January 1999), pp. 26–31.

88. Crawford, "Crime Scene Searches," pp. 26–31. For a complete discussion of crime scenes and crime scene procedures see Dempsey, *Introduction to Investigations,* chapter 3.

89. *Illinois v. Rodriquez.*

90. Crawford, "Crime Scene Searches."

91. *Abel v. United States,* 362 U.S. 217 (1960).

92. *California v. Greenwood,* 486 U.S. 35 (1988).

93. *California v. Hodari, D.,* 499 U.S. 621 (1991).

94. *Colorado v. Bertine,* 479 U.S. 367 (1987).

95. *Hester v. United States,* 265 U.S. 57 (1924).

96. *Oliver v. United States,* 466 U.S. 170 (1984).

97. *California v. Ciraola,* 476 U.S. 207 (1986).

98. *Florida v. Riley,* 488 U.S. 445 (1989).

99. *Carroll v. United States*, 267 U.S. 132 (1925).

100. *Carroll v. United States*. For a comprehensive recent article on the motor vehicle exception, see Edward Hendrie, "The Motor Vehicle Exception," *FBI Law Enforcement Bulletin* (August 2005), pp. 22–32.

101. *New York v. Belton*, 453 U.S. 454 (1981).

102. *United States v. Ross*, 456 U.S. 798 (1982).

103. *United States v. Villamonte-Marquez*, 462 U.S. 579 (1983); and *California v. Carney*, 471 U.S. 386 (1985).

104. *California v. Acevedo*, 500 U.S. 565 (1991); and *Florida v. Jimeno*, 111 S.Ct. 1801 (1991).

105. *Pennsylvania v. Labron*, 518 U.S. 938 (1996).

106. *Maryland v. Dyson*, 119 S.Ct. 2013 (1999).

107. *Florida v. White*, 526 U.S. 559 (1999).

108. *Wyoming v. Houghton*, 119 S.Ct. 1297 (1999). For an excellent article on the auto exception to the search warrant requirement, see Lisa A. Regini, "The Motor Vehicle Exception: When and Where to Search," *FBI Law Enforcement Bulletin* (July 1999).

109. *Thornton v. United States*, 124 S.Ct. 2127 (2004).

110. M. Wesley Clark, "U.S. Land Border Search Authority," *FBI Law Enforcement Bulletin* (August 2004), pp. 22–32.

111. *United States v. Martinez-Fuerte*, 428 U.S. 543 (1976). For a comprehensive article on border searches, see Clark, "U.S. Land Border Search Authority," pp. 22–32.

112. *United States v. Leon*, 468 U.S. 897 (1984).

113. *Massachusetts v. Sheppard*, 468 U.S. 981 (1984); *Illinois v. Krull*, 480 U.S. 340 (1987); and *Maryland v. Garrison*, 480 U.S. 79 (1987).

114. *Arizona v. Evans*, 514 U.S. 1 (1995).

115. *Groh v. Ramirez*, 124 S.Ct. 1284 (2004).

116. *Burdeau v. McDowell*, 256 U.S. 465 (1921).

117. *Miranda v. Arizona*.

118. Kimberly A. Crawford, "Constitutional Rights to Counsel During Interrogation: Comparing Rights Under the Fifth and Sixth Amendments," *FBI Law Enforcement Bulletin* (September 2002), pp. 28–32.

119. James W. Osterburg and Richard H. Ward, *Criminal Investigation: A Method for Reconstructing the Past* (Cincinnati, Ohio: Anderson, 1992), p. 377.

120. Louis DiPietro, "Lies, Promises, or Threats: The Voluntariness of Confessions," *FBI Law Enforcement Bulletin* (July 1993), pp. 27–32.

121. *Brown v. Mississippi*.

122. *McNabb v. United States*, 318 U.S. 332 (1943); *Mallory v. United States*, 354 U.S. 449 (1957).

123. *Escobedo v. Illinois*, 378 U.S. 478 (1964).

124. *Miranda v. Arizona*.

125. Based on *Miranda v. Arizona*.

126. Lisa A. Judge, "*Miranda* Revisited," *Police Chief* (August 2003), pp. 13–15.

127. *Oregon v. Mathiason*, 429 U.S. 492 (1977).

128. *Berkemer v. McCarty*, 468 U.S. 420 (1984); *Beckwith v. United States*, 425 U.S. 341 (1976).

129. *Moran v. Burbine*, 475 U.S. 412 (1986); *Michigan v. Mosley*, 423 U.S. 96 (1975); *Edwards v. Arizona*, 451 U.S. 477 (1981); *Arizona v. Roberson*, 486 U.S. 675 (1988); and *Minnick v. Mississippi*, 498 U.S. 146 (1991).

130. *Colorado v. Connelly*, 107 S.Ct. 515 (1986).

131. *Arizona v. Roberson*.

132. Alan M. Dershowitz, *Taking Liberties: A Decade of Hard Cases, Bad Laws and Bum Raps* (Chicago: Contemporary Books, 1988), p. 10.

133. Dershowitz, *Taking Liberties*, p. 12.

134. *Harris v. New York*, 401 U.S. 222 (1971).

135. *Michigan v. Mosley*.

136. *Brewer v. Williams*, 430 U.S. 387 (1977).

137. *Nix v. Williams*, 467 U.S. 431 (1984).

138. *Rhode Island v. Innis*, 446 U.S. 291 (1980).

139. *New York v. Quarles*, 104 S.Ct. 2626 (1984).

140. *Oregon v. Elstad*, 470 U.S. 298 (1985).

141. *Moran v. Burbine*.

142. *Illinois v. Perkins*, 110 S.Ct. 2394 (1990).

143. *Pennsylvania v. Muniz*, 496 U.S. 582 (1990).

144. *Arizona v. Fulminante*, 111 S.Ct. 1246 (1991).

145. *Minnick v. Mississippi*, 498 U.S. 146 (1991).

146. *McNeil v. Wisconsin*, 111 S.Ct. 2204 (1991).

147. *Withrow v. Williams*, 507 U.S. 680 (1993).

148. *Davis v. United States*, 114 S.Ct. 2350 (1994).

149. *Stansbury v. California*, 114 S.Ct. 1526 (1994).

150. *Oregon v. Mathiason*.

151. *Dickerson v. United States*, 530 U.S. 428 (2000). See Thomas D. Petrowski, "*Miranda* Revisited: *Dickerson v. United States*," *FBI Law Enforcement Bulletin* (August 2001), pp. 25–32.

152. *Dickerson v. United States*; Kil, "Supreme Court Cases: 1999–2000 Term," pp. 28–32.

153. Samuel C. Rickless, "*Miranda, Dickerson,* and the Problem of Actual Innocence," *Criminal Justice Ethics*, 19 (2, Summer/Fall 2000), pp. 2–55.

154. *Texas v. Cobb*, 121 S.Ct. 1335 (2001); also see Kimberly A. Crawford, "The Sixth Amendment Right to Counsel: Application and Limitations," *FBI Law Enforcement Bulletin* (July 2001), pp. 27–32.

155. *Chavez v. Martinez*, 123 S.Ct. 1994 (2003).

156. *Kaupp v. Texas*, 123 S.Ct. 1843 (2003).

157. *United States v. Patane*, 124 S.Ct. 2620 (2004).

158. *Missouri v. Seibert,* 124 S.Ct. 2601 (2004). For a comprehensive recent article on the *Seibert* case, see Lucy Ann Hoover, "The Supreme Court Brings an End to the "End Run" Around *Miranda,*" *FBI Law Enforcement Bulletin* (June 2005), pp. 26–32.

159. *Oregon v. Elstad.*

160. Kimberly A. Crawford, "Surreptitious Recording of Suspects' Conversations," *FBI Law Enforcement Bulletin* (September 1993), pp. 26–32; also see Richard G. Schott, "Warrantless Interception of Communications: When, Where, and Why It Can Be Done," *FBI Law Enforcement Bulletin* (January 2003), pp. 25–31.

161. *Stanley v. Wainwright,* 604 F.2d 379 (5th Cir. 1979).

162. *Kuhlmann v. Wilson,* 106 S.Ct. 2616 (1986).

163. *Ahmad A. v. Superior Court,* 263 Cal.Rptr. 747 (Cal.App. 2 Dist. 1989), cert. denied, 498 U.S. 834 (1990).

164. *Belmar v. Commonwealth,* 553 S.E.2d 123 (Va App. Ct. 2001).

165. Crawford, "Surreptitious Recording of Suspects' Conversations," p. 29–31.

166. *United States v. Wade,* 388 U.S. 218 (1967).

167. *Kirby v. Illinois,* 406 U.S. 682 (1972).

168. *Stoval v. Denno,* 388 U.S. 293 (1967).

169. *United States v. O'Connor,* 282 F.Supp. 963 (D.D.C. 1968).

170. *United States v. Ash,* 413 U.S. 300 (1973).

171. *Schmerber v. California,* 384 U.S. 757 (1966).

172. *Winston v. Lee,* 470 U.S. 753 (1985).

173. *Schmerber v. California.*

174. *Winston v. Lee.*

175. *United States v. Dionisio,* 410 U.S. 1 (1973).

176. *United States v. Mara,* 410 U.S. 19 (1973).

177. "Eyewitness Evidence," *FBI Law Enforcement Bulletin* (July 2001), p. 15.

Chapter 14

1. John Ashcroft, *A Resource Guide to Law Enforcement, Corrections and Forensic Technologies* (Washington, D.C.: U.S. Department of Justice, 2001), p. iii.

2. Matthew J. Hickman and Brian A. Reaves, *Local Police Departments, 2003* (Washington, D.C.: Bureau of Justice Statistics, National Institute of Justice, 2006); and Hickman, and Reaves, *Sheriffs' Offices, 2003* (Washington, D.C.: Bureau of Justice Statistics, National Institute of Justice, 2006); and U.S. Department of Justice, Bureau of Justice Statistics, *State and Local Law Enforcement Statistics* (Washington, D.C.: Bureau of Justice Statistics, 2006), p. 2.

3. Christa Miller, "Mobile Computing Options for 21st Century Law Enforcement," *Law Enforcement Technology* (July 2002), pp. 34, 36–39, 40.

4. Charles E. Higginbotham, "High-Tech Solutions to Police Problems," *Police Chief* (February 2003), pp. 32, 34–35, 36; and Donna Rogers, "CAD Selection 101: The Nuts and Bolts of Finding a CAD System That Works for You," *Law Enforcement Technology* (October 2001), pp. 120–124, 126–127.

5. Bureau of Justice Statistics, *State and Local Law Enforcement Statistics* (Washington, D.C.: Bureau of Justice Statistics, 2006), p. 2; Hickman and Reaves, *Local Police Departments, 2003;* Hickman and Reaves, *Sheriffs' Offices, 2003.*

6. Paul Egan, "Expert: 911 Rules Were Broken," *Detroit News,* April 11, 2006.

7. Roger Alford, "24 Counties Have Only Basic 911 Service," *Associated Press,* March 13, 2006.

8. Charles R. Swanson, Leonard Territo, and Robert W. Taylor, *Police Administration: Structures, Processes and Behavior,* 2nd ed. (New York: Macmillan, 1988), pp. 381–383.

9. Al Baker, "Night Out in City Ends in Slaying of Woman, 18," *New York Times,* July 28, 2006, pp. A1, B5; John Mazor and John Doyle, "Cell Phone Trace Led to 'Killer,'" *New York Post,* July 28, 2006, p. 6; Murray Weiss, Larry Celona, and Lenny Greene, "Doomed Teen's Chilling Call," *New York Post,* July 28, 2006, pp. 6, 7; and Michael Wilson, "Being Alone Raises Perils in a Night on the Town," *New York Times,* July 28, 2006, p. B5;

10. Matthew D. LaPlante, "Utah Slow on 911 Tracing," *Salt Lake Tribune,* March 14, 2006.

11. M. Wesley Clark, "Cell Phone Technology and Physical Surveillance," *FBI Law Enforcement Bulletin,* 75, 5, May 2006, pp. 25–32; *United States v. Knotts,* 460 U.S. 276 (1983); *United States v. Karo,* 468 U.S. 705 (1984).

12. M. Clark, "Cell Phone Technology and Physical Surveillance, pp. 25–32; *United States v. Knotts; United States v. Karo.*

13. Marc Robins, "Special Report: New IP Telephony Solutions for the Government Enterprise," *Homeland Defense Journal,* 4 (1, January 2006), pp. 22–27.

14. Elizabeth Daigneau, "Calling All Citizens: A Growing Number of Municipalities Are Using "Reverse 911" to Alert Residents in the Event of an Emergency," *Governance* (July 2002), pp. 44–45.

15. "Cellular Digital Packet Data (CDPD) Technology Assists Plainclothes Officers," *Police Chief* (March 1997), pp. 14–15.

16. Sam Simon, "Pocket PC Goes Tactical," *Law Enforcement Technology,* 33 (5, May 2006), pp. 112–119.

17. Federal Bureau of Investigation, *NCIC: National Crime Information Center,* retrieved August 17, 2002, from http://www.fbi.gov/hq/cjisd/ncic.htm. Also see Stephanie L. Hitt, "NCIC 2000," *FBI Law Enforcement Bulletin* (July 2000), pp. 12–15; and Christopher Swope, "Sherlock Online," *Governing* (September 2000), pp. 80–84.

18. Federal Bureau of Investigation, *NICS: National Instant Criminal Background Check System,* retrieved July 17, 2001, from http://www.fbi.gov/hq/cjisd/nics.htm.

19. For the latest on ViCAP, see Eric W. Witzig, "The New ViCAP: More User-Friendly and Used by More Agencies," *FBI Law Enforcement Bulletin* (June 2003), pp. 1–7. For a further description of ViCAP and sample ViCAP alerts, see John S. Dempsey, *Introduction to Investigations,* 2nd ed. (Belmont, Calif.: Wadsworth, 2003), chapter 10.

20. Bill Clede, "Storing Massive Records," *Law and Order* (January 1994), p. 45.

21. See William J. Bratton, "Great Expectations: How Higher Expectations for Police Departments Can Lead to a Decrease in Crime," Paper presented at the National Institute of Justice's Research Institute's "Measuring What Matters" Conference, Washington, D.C., November 28, 1995; William Bratton and Peter Knobler, *Turnaround: How America's Top Cop Reversed the Crime Epidemic* (New York: Random House, 1998); Rudolph W. Giuliani, Randy M. Mastro, and Donna Lynn, *Mayor's Management Report: The City of New York* (New York: City of New York, 1997); Vincent E. Henry, *The CompStat Paradigm: Management Accountability in Policing, Business and the Public Sector* (New York: Looseleaf Law, 2002); Howard Safir, *The CompStat Process* (New York: New York City Police Department, n.d.), Jeremy Travis, "Computerized Crime Mapping," *NIJ News* (Washington, D.C.: National Institute of Justice, 1999);

22. "Predicting a Criminal's Journey to Crime," *National Institute of Justice Journal,* 253 (January 2006), pp. 11–13.

23. Donna Rogers, "Map Quest: While Most Agree the Time Has Come for GIS Tactical Crime Analysis, the Million-Dollar Question Is Which Methodologies Are Most Accurate," *Law Enforcement Technology,* 33 (1, January 2006), pp. 60–69.

24. Spencer Chainey and Chloe Smith, *Review of GIS-Based Information Sharing Systems* (London: Great Britain Home Office Research Development and Statistics, 2006).

25. "Predicting a Criminal's Journey to Crime," pp. 11–13.

26. Preston Gralla, "Hollywood Confidential: PC Crime Fighters," *PC Computing* (January 1989), p. 188.

27. Sharon Hollis Sutter, "Holmes . . . Still Aiding Complex Investigations," *Law and Order* (November 1991), pp. 50–52.

28. Robert D. Keppel and Joseph G. Weis, "HITS: Catching Criminals in the Northwest," *FBI Law Enforcement Bulletin* (April 1993), pp. 14–19; Terry Morgan, "HITS/SMART: Washington State's Crime-Fighting Tool," *FBI Law Enforcement Bulletin* (February 2002), pp. 1–10.

29. "FBI Throws in the Towel on Overdue, Problem-Plagued Computer Upgrade," *Law Enforcement News* (January 2005), p. 1.

30. "Predicting a Criminal's Journey to Crime," pp. 11–13.

31. Robert Sheehan and Gary W. Cordner, *Introduction to Police Administration,* 2nd ed. (Cincinnati, Ohio: Anderson, 1989), p. 419.

32. Sheehan and Cordner, *Introduction to Police Administration,* p. 422.

33. "PG County Police Opt for Computer-Aided System to Red-Flag Stressed-Out Officers," *Law Enforcement News,* June 30, 1997, p. 5.

34. Swanson, Territo, and Taylor, *Police Administration,* pp. 380–381.

35. Sheehan and Cordner, *Introduction to Police Administration,* p. 428.

36. Beth Winegarner, "Police Say Online Crime Reporting Saves Officers Time," *Examiner,* April 17, 2006.

37. For a brief but interesting history of the use of fingerprints as identification, see Dempsey, *Introduction to Investigations,* pp. 123–124.

38. Federal Bureau of Investigation, *Fingerprint Identification: An Overview,* retrieved June 12, 2001 from http://www.fbi.gov/hq/cjisd/ident.htm.

39. Curtis C. Frame, "Lifting Latent Prints in Dust," *Law and Order* (June 2000), p. 75; also see Frame, "Picking Up Latent Prints in Dust," *Police Chief* (April 2000), p. 180.

40. "High-Tech Crime Hunters," *Popular Mechanics,* December 1991, p. 30.

41. T. F. Wilson and P. L. Woodard, *Automated Fingerprint Identification Systems—Technology and Policy Issues* (Washington, D.C.: U.S. Department of Justice, 1987), p. 5.

42. Harold J. Grasman, "New Fingerprint Technology Boosts Odds in Fight against Terrorism," *Police Chief* (January 1997), pp. 23–28.

43. Rongliang Ma and Qun Wei, "Chemical Fuming: A Practical Method for Fingerprint Development on Thermal Paper," *Journal of Forensic Identification,* 56 (3, May/June 2006), pp. 364–373; Stephen H. Ostrowski and Marc E. Dupre, "Fingerprint Impression Development Using a Vacuum Box," *Journal of Forensic Identification,* 56 (3, May/June 2006), pp. 356–363; Gagan deep Singh, G. S. Sodhi, and O. P. Jasuja, "Detection of Latent Fingerprints on Fruits and Vegetables," *Journal of Forensic Identification,* 56 (3, May/June 2006), pp. 374–381; and Melissa Anne Smrz, et al., "Review of FBI Latent Print Processes and Recommendations to Improve Practices and Quality," *Journal of Forensic Identification,* 56 (3, May/June 2006), pp. 402–434.

44. U.S. Congress, Office of Technology Assessment, *Criminal Justice: New Technologies and the Constitution: A Special Report* (Washington, D.C.: U.S. Government Printing Office, 1988), p. 18.

45. William Folsom, "Automated Fingerprint Identification Systems," *Law and Order* (July 1986), pp. 27–28.

46. See John Ryan, "AFIS Pays Big Dividends for a Small City," *Law and Order* (June 2000), pp. 70–72; Judith Blair Schmitt, "Computerized ID Systems," *Police Chief* (February 1992); "Something for Everyone in High-Tech," *Law Enforcement News,* December 15/31, 1998, p. 17; and William Stover, "Automated Fingerprint Identification—Regional Application of Technology," *FBI Law Enforcement Bulletin,* 53 (1984), pp. 1–4;

47. Tony Lesce, "Verafind AFIS System: Flexible and Software Based," *Law and Order* (December 1994), pp. 53–54.

48. Rebecca Kanable, "Live-Scan Is Making Its Print," *Law Enforcement Technology* (April 1999), pp. 77–81.

49. Federal Bureau of Investigation, *Integrated Automated Fingerprint Identification System (IAFIS),* retrieved June 12, 2001, from http://www.fbi.gov/hq/lab/org/systems.htm.

50. Federal Bureau of Investigation, *Latent Print Unit,* retrieved June 2, 2001, from http://www.fbi.gov/hq/lab/org/lpu.htm.

51. "INS, FBI Plan a $200M Wedding—Of Their Fingerprint Databases," *Law Enforcement News,* March 21, 2000, p. 7.

52. Rebecca Kanable, "Fingerprints Making the Case: AFIS and IAFIS Are Helping Find Matching Prints, But There Are More to Be Found," *Law Enforcement Technology* (March 2003), pp. 48, 50–53.

53. Rebecca Kanable, "Grip on Identification Information," *Law Enforcement Technology* (June 2000), pp. 122–126.

54. Dominic Andrae, "New Zealand Fingerprint Technology," *Law and Order* (November 1993), pp. 37–38; and "NAFIS Launched in South Wales," *Law and Order* (June 2000), p. 74.

55. Tony Doonan, "Palmprint Technology Comes of Age," *Law and Order* (November 2000), pp. 63–65.

56. See Ronnie Paynter, "Less-Lethal Weaponry," *Law Enforcement Technology* (October 1999), pp. 78–84; and Lois Pilant, *Less-Than-Lethal Weapons: New Solutions for Law Enforcement* (Alexandria, Va.: International Association of Chiefs of Police, 2000).

57. Bill Clede, "A Banquet of Aerosol Sprays," *Law and Order* (September 1992), pp. 57–59; and Christopher Reilly, "The Science of Pepper Spray," *Law and Order* (July 2003), pp. 124–130.

58. "Pepper Sprays Get Yet Another Shake," *Security Management* (August 2003), p. 18.

59. For a recent report on the Taser, see George T. Williams and Richard V. Simon, "Tasertron's 95HP: The Law Enforcement Taser," *Law and Order* (November 2001), pp. 80–83.

60. John Graham, "Officers Armed with Beanbags," *Law and Order* (June 1997), pp. 67–68.

61. Joan A. Hopper, "Less-Lethal Litigation: Departments and the Courts React to Less-Lethal Standards," *Law and Order* (November 2001), pp. 87–91.

62. J. P. Morgan, "Oleoresin Capsicum Policy," *Police Chief* (August 1992), p. 26.

63. Greg Meyer, "Nonlethal Weapons vs. Conventional Police Tactics: Assessing Injuries and Liabilities," *Police Chief* (August 1992), pp. 15–16.

64. Meyer, "Nonlethal Weapons vs. Conventional Police Tactics," p. 18.

65. *Michenfelder v. Sumner*, 860 F.2d 328 (9th Cir. 1988).

66. Peter D. Button, *Less-Lethal Force Technology* (Toronto: Toronto Metropolitan Police Commission, 2001).

67. T. Donnelly, *Less Lethal Technologies: Initial Prioritisation and Evaluation* (London: Great Britain Home Office, Policing and Reducing Crime Unit, 2001).

68. Dale Yeager, "Less Lethal: A New Look at the State of Tactical Training," *Law Enforcement Technology* (October 2002), pp. 52, 54–56.

69. For a comprehensive article on advanced surveillance devices, see Lois Pilant, "Spotlight on . . . Achieving State-of-the-Art Surveillance," *Police Chief* (June 1993), pp. 25–34.

70. Albert E. Brandenstein, "Advanced Technologies Bolster Law Enforcement's Counterdrug Efforts," *Police Chief* (January 1997), pp. 32–34.

71. Tom Yates, "Surveillance Vans," *Law and Order* (December 1991), pp. 52, 56.

72. Yates, "Surveillance Vans," p. 53.

73. Bill Siuru, "Seeing in the Dark and Much More: Thermal Imaging," *Law and Order* (November 1993), pp. 18–20.

74. Siuru, "Seeing in the Dark and Much More," pp. 18–20."

75. Tom Yates, "'Eyes' in the Night," *Law and Order* (November 1993), pp. 19–24.

76. Donna Rogers, "Contraband Cops: U.S. Customs and Border Patrol Agents Stem the Tide of Smuggling with High-Tech Tools," *Law Enforcement Technology* (April 2000), pp. 68–72.

77. Ronnie Paynter, "Images in the Night: Law Enforcement Sheds Light on Applications for Night Vision Technologies," *Law Enforcement Technology* (May 1999), pp. 22–26.

78. Donna Rogers, "GPS: Getting the Proper Positioning," *Law Enforcement Technology* (September 2000), pp. 44–50. See also U.S. Department of Justice, National Institute of Justice, *GPS Applications in Law Enforcement: The SkyTracker Surveillance System, Final Report* (Washington, D.C.: National Institute of Justice, 1998).

79. Keith Harries, *Mapping Crime: Principle and Practice* (Washington, D.C.: National Institute of Justice, 1999); Ron Mercer, Murray Brooks, and Paula T. Bryant, "Global Positioning Satellite System: Tracking Offenders in Real Time," *Corrections Today* (July 2000), pp. 76–80; Bill Siuru, "Tracking 'Down': Space-Age GPS Technology is Here," *Corrections Technology and Management* (September–October 1999), pp. 1–14.

80. National Sheriffs' Association, "Law Enforcement Aircraft: A Vital Force Multiplier," *Sheriff* (January–February 2000), pp. 32–60.

81. Deena Kara, Jonathan Kilworth, and Martin Gill, "What Makes CCTV Effective?" *Intersect: The Journal of International Security*, 13 (9, September 2003), pp. 293–296.

82. Chris A. Williams, "Police Surveillance and the Emergences of CCTV in the 1960s," *Crime Prevention and Community Safety: An International Journal*, 5 (3, 2003), pp. 27–37.

83. "Anti-Crime Cameras Help in 180 Arrests," *Gloucester Citizen*, February 25, 2005; Ben Brown, *CCTV in Town Centres: Three Case Studies: Crime Detection and Prevention Series Paper 68* (London: Home Office, 1995); Michael R. Chatterton and Samantha J. Frenz, "Closed-Circuit Television: Its Role in Reducing Burglaries and the Fear of Crime in Sheltered Accommodation for the Elderly," *Security Journal*, 5 (1994), pp. 133–139; Martin Gill and Karryn Loveday, "What Do Offenders Think About CCTV," *Crime Prevention and Community Safety: An International Journal*, 5 (3, 2003), pp. 17–25; *LexisNexis*, retrieved March 2, 2005, from http://www.bnp.com/security-news/new-technology.htm; Barry Poyner, "Situational Crime Prevention in Two Parking Facilities," *Security Journal*, 2 (1991), pp. 96–101; Anya Sostek, "Here's Looking at You: Electronic Surveillance Systems Make Some Law-Abiding Citizens Feel Safer, They Make Others Very Nervous," *Governing*, 15 (11, August 2002), pp. 44–45; Nicholas Tilly, *Understanding Car Parks, Crime and CCTV: Evaluation Lessons from Safer Cities: Crime Prevention Unit Paper 42* (London: Home Office, 1993); Brandon C. Welsh and David P. Farrington, "Surveillance for Crime Prevention in Public Space: Results and Policy Choices in Britain and America," *Criminology and Public Policy*, 3 (3, July 2004), pp. 497–525; and Stig Winge and Johannes Knutson,

"Evaluation of the CCTV Scheme at Oslo Central Railway Station," *Crime Prevention and Community Safety: An International Journal,* 5 (3, 2003), pp. 49–59.

84. Martin Gill and Angela Spriggs, *Assessing the Impact of CCTV* (London: Great Britain Home Office Research Development and Statistics Directorate, 2005).

85. Tom Levesley and Amanda Martin, *Police Attitudes to and Use of CCTV* (London: Great Britain Home Office Research Development and Statistics Directorate, 2005); and Angela Spriggs, Javier Argomaniz, Martin Gill, and Jane Bryan, *Public Attitudes Towards CCTV: Results from the Pre-Intervention Public Attitude Survey Carried Out in Areas Implementing CCTV* (London: Great Britain Home Office Research Development and Statistics Directorate, 2005).

86. John D. Woodward, Jr., *Privacy vs. Security: Electronic Surveillance in the Nation's Capital* (Santa Monica, Calif.: Rand Corporation, 2002).

87. Williams, "Police Surveillance and the Emergences of CCTV in the 1960s," pp. 27–37.

88. Laura J. Nichols, *Use of CCTV/Video Cameras in Law Enforcement, Executive Brief* (Alexandria, Va.: International Association of Chiefs of Police, 2001).

89. Leonor Vivanco, "More Surveillance Cameras Planned throughout Redlands," *San Bernardino County Sun,* March 24, 2005.

90. Sostek, "Here's Looking at You: Electronic Surveillance Systems," pp. 44–45.

91. Jennifer Lee, "Police Seek to Increase Surveillance; Want 400 Cameras for Public Access," *New York Times,* May 31, 2005, p. B3.

92. Grant Fredericks, as quoted in Michael E. Ruane, "Security Camera New Star Witness," *Washington Post,* October 8, 2005, p. B1.

93. Grant Fredericks, "CCTV: A Law Enforcement Tool," *Police Chief* 71 (8, August 2004), pp. 68–74.

94. Jennifer Lee, "Caught on tape, then just caught; private cameras transform police work," *New York Times,* May 22, 2005, pp. 33, 36.

95. Jennifer Lee, "Caught on tape, then just caught; private cameras transform police work," *New York Times,* May 22, 2005, pp. 33, 36.

96. Ruane, "Security Camera New Star Witness," p. B1.

97. Jolene Hernon, "CCTV: Constant Cameras Track Violators," *National Institute of Justice Journal* (249, July 2003), pp. 16–23.

98. Katherine E. Finkelstein, "Officials Admit Wrong Man Was Held in Street Attack: Morgenthau Calls Evidence Overwhelming," *New York Times,* July 27, 2000, p. B3; and Joyce Purnick, "The Truth, as Always, Is Stranger," *New York Times,* July 27, 2000, p. B1.

99. Lee, "Police Seek to Increase Surveillance," p. B3.

100. David P. Nagosky, "Admissibility of Digital Photographs in Criminal Cases," *FBI Law Enforcement Bulletin,* 74 (12, December 2005), pp. 1–8.

101. John J. Pavlis, "Mug-Shot Imaging Systems," *FBI Law Enforcement Bulletin* (August 1992), pp. 20–22.

102. "Picture This: Digital Photos Beam from Texas to Virginia via High-Tech Patrol Cars," *Law Enforcement News,* June 15, 1997, p. 1; and Darrel L. Sanders, "The Critical Role of Technology," *Police Chief* (July 1997), p. 6.

103. Stephen Coleman, "Biometrics: Solving Cases of Mistaken Identity and More," *FBI Law Enforcement Bulletin* (June 2000), p. 13.

104. "High-Tech Crime Hunters," p. 31.

105. "High-Tech Crime Hunters," p. 31. See also Gene O'Donnell, "Forensic Imaging Comes of Age," *FBI Law Enforcement Bulletin* (January 1994), pp. 5–10.

106. "High-Tech Crime Hunters," p. 31. See also O'Donnell, "Forensic Imaging Comes of Age."

107. "No More Pencils, No More Books?" *Law Enforcement News,* January 31, 1998, p. 5.

108. "The Face Is Familiar—and Computer-Generated," *Law Enforcement News,* October 31, 1999, p. 7.

109. Donna Rogers, "Drawing the Line," *Law Enforcement Technology* (May 2003), pp. 44–50.

110. Charles Jackson, "Hand-Drawn Composites," *Law and Order,* 54 (3, March 2006), pp. 36–39. Also see Charles T. Jackson, "Guide for the Artist," *Journal of Forensic Identification,* 56 (3, May/June 2006), pp. 388–401.

111. Richard Saferstein, *Criminalistics: An Introduction to Forensic Science,* 8th ed. (Upper Saddle River, N.J.: Pearson/Prentice Hall), 2004, p. 2. Saferstein recommends the following two works as excellent references for the definition and application of forensic science: Andre A. Moenssens, Fred E. Inbau, James Starrs, and Carol E. Henderson, *Scientific Evidence in Civil and Criminal Cases,* 4th ed. (Mineola, N.Y.: Foundation Press, 1995), and Werner U. Spitz, ed., *Medicolegal Investigation of Death,* 3rd ed. (Springfield, Ill.: Charles C. Thomas, 1993).

112. Dempsey, *Introduction to Investigations,* p. 133.

113. Saferstein, *Criminalistics,* p. 2.

114. Marc H. Caplan and Joe Holt Anderson, *Forensic: When Science Bears Witness* (Washington, D.C.: National Institute of Justice, 1984), p. 2. For an interesting history of criminalistics, see Dempsey, *Introduction to Investigations,* pp. 122–125. Also see Saferstein, *Criminalistics,* pp. 2–6.

115. Peter R. DeForest, N. Petraco, and L. Koblinsky, "Chemistry and the Challenge of Crime," in *Chemistry and Crime,* ed. S. Gerber (Washington, D.C.: American Chemical Society, 1983), p. 45.

116. Joseph L. Peterson, *Use of Forensic Evidence by the Police and Courts* (Washington, D.C.: National Institute of Justice, 1987).

117. David Johnston, "Report Criticizes Scientific Testing at FBI Lab: Serious Problems Cited," *New York Times,* April 16, 1997, pp. A1, D23; Mireya Navarro, "Doubts about FBI Lab Raise Hopes for Convict: On Death Row, but Seeking a New Trial," *New York Times,* April 22, 1997, p. A8.

118. "What's Wrong at the FBI?: The Fiasco at the Crime Lab," *Time*, April 28, 1997, pp. 28–35.

119. Belinda Luscombe, "When the Evidence Lies: Joyce Gilchrist Helped Send Dozens to Death Row. The Forensic Scientist's Errors Are Putting Capital Punishment under the Microscope," *Time*, May 21, 2001, pp. 37–40.

120. "Indiana: DNA Evidence Under Review," *New York Times*, July 19, 2003, p. A10.

121. Roma Khanna and Steve McVicker, "Police Lab Tailored Tests to Theories, Report Says," *Houston Chronicle*, May 12, 2006; and Steve McVicker and Roma Khanna, "More Problems Found in HPD Crime Lab Cases," *Houston Chronicle*, May 11, 2006. Also see Richard Willing, "Errors Prompt States to Watch over Crime Labs," *USA Today*, April 3, 2006.

122. "Life Imitates Art with the "CSI Effect," *Law Enforcement News* (June 2005), pp. 1, 11.

123. Jennifer Mertens, "Smoking Gun: When Real-Life CSI and Hollywood Collide," *Law Enforcement Technology*, 33 (3, March 2006), pp. 52–61.

124. Michael Biesecker, "DNA Doesn't Offer Magic Key to Case," *News & Observer*, April 12, 2006; and Patrik Jonsson, "Duke Lacrosse Case: No DNA, but Old-Fashioned Sleuthing," *Christian Science Monitor*, April 19, 2006.

125. Biesecker, "DNA Doesn't Offer Magic Key to Case"; and Jonsson, "Duke Lacrosse Case."

126. Peterson, *Use of Forensic Evidence by the Police and Courts*; and Joseph L. Peterson and Matthew J. Hickman, *Census of Publicly Funded Forensic Crime Laboratories, 2002* (Washington, D.C.: National Institute of Justice, 2005).

127. Federal Bureau of Investigation, *FBI Laboratory*, retrieved August 1, 2006 from, http://www.fbi.gov/hq/lab/labhome.htm.

128. American Society of Crime Lab Directors, *One Hundred Eighty-Day Study Report: Status and Needs of United States Crime Laboratories* (Garner, N.C.: American Society of Crime Lab Directors, 2004).

129. International Association for Identification, American Society of Crime Laboratory Directors, American Academy of Forensic Sciences, and National Association of Medical Examiners, *Status and Needs of Forensic Science Service Providers: A Report to Congress* (Washington, D.C.: National Institute of Justice, 2004. Also see American Society of Crime Lab Directors, *One Hundred Eighty-Day Study Report*; American Academy of Forensic Sciences, *AAFS Response to the 180-Day Story* (Colorado Springs, Colo.: American Academy of Forensic Sciences, 2006).

130. Alison Gendar, "Top Guns of Evil Holstered in Queens," *New York Daily News*, July 16, 2006.

131. Bureau of Alcohol, Tobacco, Firearms and Explosives, *Integrated Ballistic Identification System*, retrieved August 4, 2006, from http://www.atf.gov/firearms/nibin_ibis/index.htm; "Hey Buddy, Got a Match?: New System Does for Bullets What AFIS Did for Prints," *Law Enforcement News*, April 30, 1994, p. 1.

132. Bureau of Alcohol, Tobacco, Firearms and Explosives, *Integrated Ballistic Identification System*, retrieved August 4, 2006, from http://www.atf.gov/firearms/nibin_ibis/index.htm.

133. "ATF Tightens Screws on Illicit Gun Sales with Gun- & Bullet-Tracing Databases," *Law Enforcement News*, February 14, 2000, pp. 1, 6; and Tracy Hite, "Developments in Forensic Science: The National Integrated Ballistics Information Network," *Police Chief*, 67 (4, April 2000), pp. 173–174.

134. Julie Bykowicz, "FBI Lab Scraps Gunfire Residue," *Baltimore Sun*, May 26, 2006; and "Going Ballistic: Serious Flaws Seen in FBI Bullet-Matching Test," *Law Enforcement News* (February 2004), pp. 1, 10.

135. Bykowicz, "FBI Lab Scraps Gunfire Residue."

136. Atul K. Singla and Mukesh K. Thakar, "Establishing the Sequence of Intersecting Ballpoint Pen and Felt-Tipped Marker Strokes," *Journal of Forensic Identification*, 56 (3, May/June 2006), pp. 382–387.

137. American Society of Crime Laboratory Directors, retrieved August 4, 2006, from http://www.ascld.org.

138. Lois Pilant, "Crime Laboratory Developments," *Police Chief* (June 1997), p. 31.

139. Technical Working Group on Crime Scene Investigation, *Crime Scene Investigation: A Guide for Law Enforcement* (Washington, D.C.: National Institute of Justice, U.S. Department of Justice, 2000.)

140. National Criminal Justice Reference Center, *In the Spotlight: Forensic Science: Summary*, retrieved July 27, 2006, from http://www.ncjrs.gov/spotlight/forensic/Summary.html.

141. Saferstein, *Criminalistics: An Introduction to Forensic Science*, 8th ed., pp. 353–394.

142. Elizabeth Devine, as quoted in Judith Martin, "The Power of DNA," *Law and Order* (May 2001), pp. 31–35.

143. Peter J. Neufeld and Neville Colman, "When Science Takes the Witness Stand," *Scientific American* (May 1990), p. 46.

144. Warren E. Leary, "Genetic Record to be Kept on Members of Military," *New York Times*, January 12, 1992, p. A15.

145. C. Thomas Caskey and Holly A. Hammond, *Automated DNA Typing: Method of the Future?* (Washington, D.C.: National Institute of Justice, 1997), p. 1.

146. Federal Bureau of Investigation, *DNA Analysis*, retrieved June 2, 2001, from http://www.fbi.gov/hq/lab/org/dnau.htm.

147. National Criminal Justice Reference Center, *In the Spotlight: Forensic Science: Summary*; and National Institute of Justice, *Improved Analysis of DNA Short Tandem Repeats with Time-of-Flight Mass Spectrometry* (Washington, D.C.: National Institute of Justice, 2001).

148. CODIS was officially created by Congress through the 1994 *DNA Identification* Act. See Nicolas P. Lovrich, Michael J. Gaffney, Travis C. Pratt, and Charles L. Johnson, *National Forensic DNA Study* Report (Washington, D.C.: National Institute of Justice, 2003); and Terry L. Knowles, "Meeting the Challenges of the 21st Century," *Police Chief* (June 1997), pp. 39–43.

149. Federal Bureau of Investigation, *Combined DNA Index System (CODIS)*, retrieved June 2, 2001, from http:www.fbi.gov/hq/lab/org/systems.htm; and National Criminal Justice Reference Center, *In the Spotlight: Forensic Science:*

Facts and Figures, retrieved August 5, 2006, from http://www.ncjrs.gov/spotlight/forensic/Summary.html.

150. National Commission on the Future of DNA Testing, *The Future of Forensic DNA Testing: Predictions of the Research and Development Working Group* (Washington, D.C.: National Institute of Justice, 2000), pp. 19–20; and National Criminal Justice Reference Center, *In the Spotlight: Forensic Science: Facts and Figures.*

151. Richard Willing, "FBI Adds Uses for Its DNA Database," *USA Today*, May 30, 2006.

152. Rick Weiss, "Vast DNA Bank Pits Policing vs. Privacy," *Washington Post*, June 3, 2006, p. A1.

153. Jeff Wise and Richard Li, "The Future of DNA Evidence," *Crime and Justice International*, 19 (70, February 2003), pp. 31–32.

154. Janet C. Hoeffel, "The Dark Side of DNA Profiling: Unreliable Scientific Evidence Meets the Criminal Defendant," *Stanford Law Review*, 42 (1990), pp. 465–538.

155. *Frye v. United States*, 293 F. 1013 (1923).

156. "DNA Fingerprinting ID Method May Streamline Investigations," *Current Reports: BNA Criminal Practice Manual*, 1 (19) (1987), p. 1.

157. Ronald Sullivan, "Appeals Court Eases Rules on Genetic Evidence," *New York Times*, January 11, 1992, p. 8.

158. "Supreme Court Clarifies Ruling on Admitting Scientific Evidence," *Criminal Justice Newsletter*, December 1, 1997, p. 1; *Daubert v. Merrell Dow Pharmaceuticals*, 509 U.S. 579 (1993); and *General Electric Company v. Joiner*, 522 U.S. 136 (1997).

159. "DNA Typing Endorsed by National Academy of Sciences," *CJ Update* (Fall 1992), p. 1.

160. National Commission on the Future of DNA Evidence, *The Future of Forensic DNA Testing*, p. v.

161. National Commission on the Future of DNA Evidence, *The Future of Forensic DNA Testing*, p. 1.

162. National Commission on the Future of DNA Evidence, *The Future of Forensic DNA Testing*, pp. 3–6.

163. Diane Cardwell, "New York State Draws Nearer to Collecting DNA in All Crimes," *New York Times*, May 4, 2006; Edwin Zedlewski and Mary B. Murphy, *DNA Analysis for "Minor" Crimes: A Major Benefit for Law Enforcement* (Washington, D.C.: National Institute of Justice, 2006); Zedlewski and Murphy, "DNA Analysis for 'Minor' Crimes: A Major Benefit for Law Enforcement," *National Institute of Justice Journal* (253, January 2006), pp. 2–5; and U.S. Department of Justice, *National Forensic DNA Study Report* (Washington, D.C.: U.S. Department of Justice, 2003), p. 37.

164. "The Truth Is in Your Genes," *Law Enforcement News*, December 15/31, 2000, p. 7.

165. Rebecca S. Peterson, "DNA Databases: When Fear Goes Too Far," *American Criminal Law Review*, 37 (3, Summer 2000), pp. 1219–1237.

166. Executive Office of the President of the United States, *Advancing Justice Through DNA Technology* (Washington, D.C.: National Institute of Justice, 2003); U.S. Department of Justice, *Justice for All* Act (Washington, D.C. U.S. Department

of Justice, 2006); Zedlewski and Murphy, *DNA Analysis for "Minor" Crimes*; Zedlewski and Murphy, "DNA Analysis for 'Minor' Crimes," pp. 2–5.

167. National Commission on the Future of DNA Evidence, *What Every Law Enforcement Officer Should Know About DNA Evidence* (Washington, D.C.: National Institute of Justice, 2000); National Institute of Justice, *Understanding DNA Evidence: A Guide for Victim Service Providers* (Washington, D.C.: National Institute of Justice, 2001); and National Institute of Justice, *Mass Fatality Incidents: A Guide for Human Forensic Identification* (Washington, D.C.: National Institute of Justice, 2006).

168. Willing, "FBI Adds Uses for Its DNA Database."

169. Josee Charron, "Canada's DNA Data Bank: A Valuable Resource for Criminal Investigators," *Canadian Police Chief Magazine* (Winter 2003), pp. 19–21; W. R. Kuperus et al., "Crime Scene Links Through DNA Evidence: The Practical Experience From Saskatchewan Casework," *Journal of the Canadian Society of Forensic Science*, 36 (1, March 2003), pp. 19–28; Jenny Mouzos, *Investigating Homicide: New Responses for an Old Crime* (Canberra ACT: Australia, Australian Institute of Criminology, 2001); Zedlewski and Murphy, *DNA Analysis for "Minor" Crimes*; Zedlewski and Murphy, "DNA Analysis for 'Minor' Crimes," pp. 2–5.

170. Lovrich, Gaffney, Pratt, and Johnson, *National Forensic DNA Study Report*; and Travis C. Pratt, Michael J. Gaffney, Nicholas P. Lovrich, and Charles L. Johnson, "This Isn't CSI: Estimating the National Backlog of Forensic DNA Cases and the Barriers Associated with Case Processing," *Criminal Justice Policy Review*, 17 (1, March 2006), pp. 32–47.

171. Zedlewski and Murphy, *DNA Analysis for "Minor" Crimes*; Zedlewski and Murphy, "DNA Analysis for 'Minor' Crimes," pp. 2–5.

172. Roland A. H. van Oorschot, Sally Treadwell, et al., "Beware of the Possibility of Fingerprinting Techniques Transferring DNA," *Journal of Forensic Sciences*, 50 (6, November 2005), pp. 1417–1422.

173. Weiss, "Vast DNA Bank Pits Policing vs. Privacy," p. A1.

174. Jason Dearen, "DNA Cases Expose Problems in Oakland: Backlogs of 'Cold Hits' Drag on While Sexual Offenders Roam Streets," retrieved May 17, 2006, from http://www.insidebayarea.com.

175. Cardwell, "New York State Draws Nearer to Collecting DNA in All Crimes."

176. Sharon Coolidge, "DNA Extends Long Arm of the Law," *Cincinnati Enquirer*, January 27, 2006.

177. Katherine Aldred, "RCMP Furthers Innovation in the Forensic Sciences," *Gazette*, 65 (3, 2003), pp. 10–13.

178. J. Dearen, "DNA Cases Expose Problems in Oakland," retrieved May 17, 2006, from http://www.insidebayarea.com.

179. Stephen Kiehl, "Evidence Uncollected, Crimes Undeterred," *Baltimore Sun*, July 16, 2006.

180. Tod W. Burke and Jason M. Rexrode, "DNA Warrants," *Law and Order* (July 2000), pp. 121–124.

181. William K. Rashbaum, "New York Pursues Old Cases of Rape Based Just on DNA: Indicting with No Name: May

Allow Hundreds of Crimes to Be Prosecuted Despite Statute of Limitations," *New York Times,* August 5, 2003, pp. A1, B6.

182. Weiss, "Vast DNA Bank Pits Policing vs. Privacy," p. A1.

183. Angus J. Dodson, "DNA 'Line-Ups' Based on a Reasonable Suspicion Standard," *University of Colorado Law Review,* 71 (1, 2000), pp. 221–254.

184. Rick Weiss, "DNA of Criminals' Kin Cited in Solving Cases," *Washington Post,* May 12, 2006, p. A10.

185. Weiss, "Vast DNA Bank Pits Policing vs. Privacy," p. A1; Weiss, "DNA of Criminals' Kin Cited in Solving Cases," p. A10.

186. E. Connors, T. Lundregan, N. B. Miller, and T. McEwen, *Convicted by Juries, Exonerated by Science: Case Studies in the Use of DNA Evidence to Establish Innocence After Trial* (Washington, D.C.: National Institute of Justice, 1996).

187. Janet Reno, "Preventing the Conviction of the Innocent: A Compelling and Urgent Need," *Judicature,* 87 (4, January/February 2004), pp. 163–165.

188. Stephen Coleman, "Biometrics: Solving Cases of Mistaken Identity and More," *FBI Law Enforcement Bulletin* (June 2000), p. 13.

189. Coleman, "Biometrics: Solving Cases of Mistaken Identity and More."

190. J. A. West, *Facial Identification Technology and Law Enforcement* (Sacramento, Calif.: California Commission on Peace Officer Standards and Training, 1996).

191. Visionics Corporation, *Adaptive Surveillance: A Novel Approach to Facial Surveillance for CCTV Systems, Final Progress Report* (Jersey City, N.J.: Visionics Corporation, 2001). Also see Christopher A. Miles and Jeffrey P. Cohn, "Tracking Prisoners in Jail with Biometrics: An Experiment in a Navy Brig," *National Institute of Justice Journal* (253, January 2006), pp. 6–9.

192. Coleman, "Biometrics: Solving Cases of Mistaken Identity and More," p.13.

193. Michael A. Gips, "News and Trends," *Security Management,* March 2005, p. 14.

194. Barnaby J. Feder, "Technology Strains to Find Menace in the Crowd: Face Recognition Attempts to Heal Its Black Eye," *New York Times,* May 31, 2004, pp. C1, C2.

195. Feder, "Technology Strains to Find Menace in the Crowd," pp. C1, C2.

196. Feder, "Technology Strains to Find Menace in the Crowd," pp. C1, C2.

197. "News and Trends," *Security Management* (January 2005), p. 12.

198. Bureau of Justice Statistics, *State and Local Law Enforcement Statistics,* p. 2; Hickman and Reaves, *Local Police Departments, 2003;* and Hickman and Reaves, *Sheriffs' Offices, 2003.*

199. Michael Giacoppo, "The Expanding Role of Videotape in Court," *FBI Law Enforcement Bulletin* (November 1991), p. 3.

200. Giacoppo, "Expanding Role of Videotape"; Ronnie L. Paynter, "Patrol Car Video," *Law Enforcement Technology* (June 1999), pp. 34–37; and Dale Stockton, "Police Video: Up Close and Personal," *Law and Order* (August 1999), pp. 78–82.

201. Joseph G. Estey, "2,000 Survivors' Club Hits: In the Past 10 Years, 2,000 Officers Have 'Dressed For Survival,'" *Police Chief* (May 1997), p. 19.

202. H. G. Nguyen and J. P. Bott, *Robotics for Law Enforcement: Beyond Explosive Ordinance Disposal* (San Diego, Calif.: SPAWAR Systems Center, 2000); Douglas Page, "Get Smart: A Bomb 'Bot with Know-How," *Law Enforcement Technology* (July 2002), pp. 136–142; Douglas Page, "Small Fry Robots Becoming Big Law Enforcement Deal," *Law Enforcement Technology* (May 2002), pp. 34–37; and Lois Pilant, "Spotlight on . . . Equipping a Bomb Unit," *Police Chief* (October 1992), pp. 58–67.

203. Nguyen and Bott, *Robotics for Law Enforcement.*

204. Page, "Get Smart," pp. 136–142.

205. Page, "Get Smart," pp. 136–142.

206. U.S. Congress, Office of Technology Assessment, *Criminal Justice.*

207. "High-Tech Crime Hunters," p. 31.

208. *California v. Ciraolo,* 476 U.S. 207 (1986).

209. Alan M. Dershowitz, *Taking Liberties: A Decade of Hard Cases, Bad Laws, and Bum Raps* (Chicago: Contemporary Books, 1988), p. 209.

210. Tania Simoncelli and Carol Roses in Weiss, "Vast DNA Bank Pits Policing vs. Privacy," p. A1.

Chapter 15

1. See Jonathan R. White, *Terrorism and Homeland Security,* 5th ed. (Belmont, Calif.: Thomson/Wadsworth, 2006), p. 6.

2. White, *Terrorism and Homeland Security,* p. 7.

3. National Counterterrorism Center, *NCTC Report on Incidents of Terrorism, 2005,* retrieved August 16, 2006, from www.nctc.gov.

4. Louis J. Freeh, "Responding to Terrorism," *FBI Law Enforcement Bulletin* (March 1999), pp. 1–2.

5. Terrorism Knowledge Base of the National Memorial Institute for the Prevention of Terrorism, retrieved August 21, 2006, from http://www.tkb.org.

6. Terrorism Knowledge Base of the National Memorial Institute for the Prevention of Terrorism.

7. Karen DeYoung, "Terrorist Attacks Rose Sharply in 2005, State Dept. says," *Washington Post,* April 29, 2006, p. A1; and National Counterterrorism Center, *NCTC Report on Incidents of Terrorism, 2005.*

8. John F. Lewis, Jr. "Fighting Terrorism in the 21st Century," *FBI Law Enforcement Bulletin* (March 1999), pp. 3–10.

9. For recent coverage on Hizballah, see Christopher Allbritton and Nicolas Blanford, "Hizballah Nation," *Time,* July 31, 2006, pp. 44–45; J. F. O. McAllister, "Why Hizballah Can't Be Disarmed," *Time,* August 2, 2006, pp. 32–34; Lisa Beyer, "What Was He Thinking," *Time,* July 31, 2006, pp. 38–43; and "Hate Thy Neighbor," *Time,* July 24, 2006, pp. 24 to 30. For recent coverage on Hamas, see "Hamas in a Bind," *Economist,* June 17, 2006, pp. 51–52.

10. Lewis, "Fighting Terrorism in the 21st Century," pp. 3–10.

11. Eric Lipton, "Homeland Report Says Threat from Terrorist-List Nations Is Declining," *New York Times,* March 31, 2005, p. A5.

12. Irwan Firdaus, "Suicide Bombers Kill 25 in Bali Attacks," *Washington Post,* October 2, 2005.

13. Anna Kuchment and Frank Brown, "Stalin Lite Has Its Limits," *Newsweek,* September 20, 2004, p. 37.

14. Michael Elliott, "Rush Hour Terror," *Time,* July 18, 2005, pp. 26–49.

15. J. F. O. McAllister, "Unraveling the Plot," *Time,* July 25, 2005, pp. 42–46.

16. "London's Second Wave," *Time,* August 1, 2005, p. 5.

17. "Terrorism in Egypt," *Time,* August 1, 2005, p. 5.

18. "Punishing the West, All Things Secular and Egyptians Too," *Economist,* April 29, 2006, pp. 49–50.

19. "The Plan to Behead the Prime Minister," *Economist,* June 10, 2006, p. 33.

20. "FBI Says Suspects Sought to Form Own Army," *Associated Press,* June 24, 2006; "Homegrown Terrorists Seen as Dangerous as al Qaeda," *Christian Science Monitor,* June 26, 2006.

21. Saritha Rai and Somini Sengupta, "Series of Bombs Explode on 7 Trains in India, Killing Scores," *New York Times,* July 12, 2006. Also see "India's Horror," *Economist,* July 15, 2006, p. 10.

22. See "Courting Trouble," *Economist,* July 15, 2006, p. 11; and "The Rising Fear of a War of Proxies," *Economist,* July 15, 2006, p. 47.

23. Alan Cowell and Dexter Filkins, "Terror Plot Foiled: Airports Quickly Clamp Down," *New York Times,* August 11, 2006, pp. A1, A7.

24. Michael T. Osterholm and John Schwartz, *Living Terrors* (New York: Delta, 2000), pp. 14–23; and White, *Terrorism and Homeland Security,* p. 91.

25. "Bioterror," *Security Management* (January 2004), p. 18.

26. Department of Homeland Security, *Remarks by the President at the Signing of S.15-Project BioShield Act of 2004,* retrieved September 23, 2006, from http://www.dhs.gov.

27. White, *Terrorism and Homeland Security,* pp. 94, 350–351.

28. Lewis, "Fighting Terrorism in the 21st Century," p. 3.

29. Kevin Sack, "U.S. Says FBI Erred in Using Deception in Olympic Bomb Inquiry," *New York Times,* April 9, 1997, p. A47; and Sack, "Officials Link Atlanta Bombings and Ask for Help," *New York Times,* June 10, 1997, pp. A1, D24.

30. Mark Pitcavage, "Domestic Extremism: Still a Potent Threat" *Police Chief* (August 2003), pp. 32–35.

31. James E. Duffy and Alan C. Brantley, "Militias: Initiating Contact," *FBI Law Enforcement Bulletin* (July 1997), pp. 22–26.

32. Lois Romano, "Domestic Extremist Groups Weaker but Still Worrisome," *Washington Post,* April 19, 2005, p. A3.

33. Associated Press, "$1 Million in Luxury SUVs Destroyed in California Arson," *Everett Herald,* August 23, 2003, p. A4.

34. Bryan Denson and Mark Larabee, "U.S. Accuses 7 of Eco-Sabotage," *Oregonian,* December 9, 2005.

35. "Ruby Ridge," *Newsweek,* August 28, 1995, pp. 25–33.

36. "Ruby Ridge," pp. 25–33.

37. Mark Potok, as cited in Michael A. Gips, "Whither Domestic Terrorists?, *Security Management* (March 2004), pp. 12–14.

38. Mark Potok, as quoted in Jeffrey Ressner, "Rousing the Zealots," *Time,* June 5, 2006, p. 36.

39. John S. Dempsey, *Introduction to Investigations,* 2nd ed. (Belmont, Calif.: Thomson/Wadsworth, 2003), pp. 363–365.

40. Richard Bernstein, "Behind Arrest of Bomb Fugitive, Informer's Tip, Then Fast Action," *New York Times,* February 10, 1995, p. 1.

41. "Ashcroft Announces Plan for DOJ 'Wartime Reorganization,'" *Criminal Justice Newsletter,* November 14, 2001, pp. 1–2.

42. For example, see John Miller and Michael Stone with Chris Mitchell, *The Cell: Inside the 9/11 Plot, Why the FBI and CIA Failed to Stop It* (New York: Hyperion, 2002); and Evan Thomas et al., "The Road to September 11th," *Newsweek,* October 1, 2001, pp. 38–49.

43. "President Signs Homeland Security EO and Ridge Sworn in as Its Director," *NCIA Justice Bulletin* (October 2001), pp. 8–10.

44. Office of Homeland Security, http://www.whitehouse.gov/response/faq-homeland.html; http://www.whitehouse.gov/news/releases/2001/10/200111008.html.

45. Public Law No. 107-56, October 26, 2001, 115 Stat 272.

46. Public Law No. 107-56.

47. Transportation Security Administration, http://www.tsa.gov/Agency/mission.htm; Office of Homeland Security, http://www.whitehouse.gov/homeland/six_month_update.html.

48. "Polls: Trade Some Freedom for Security," *Law Enforcement News,* September 15, 2001, p. 1.

49. Office of Homeland Security, http://www.whitehouse.gov/deptofhomeland/.

50. Office of Homeland Security, http://www.whitehouse.gov/homeland/six_month_update.html.

51. National Commission on Terrorist Attacks upon the United States, *9/11 Commission Report: The Final Report of the National Commission Terrorist Attacks upon the United States* (New York: Norton, 2004).

52. See Michael Barletta, *After 9/11: Preventing Mass-Destruction Terrorism and Weapons Proliferation* (Monterey, Calif.: Center for Nonproliferation Studies, 2002); JayEtta Hecker, *Homeland Security: Intergovernmental Coordination and Partnership Will Be Critical to Success* (Washington, D.C.: U.S. General Accounting Office, 2002); Rand Corporation, *Organizing for Homeland Security* (Santa Monica: Calif.: Rand Corporation, 2002); David M. Walker, *Homeland Security: Responsibility and Accountability for Achieving National Goals* (Washington, D.C.: U.S. General Accounting Office, 2002); and Randall A. Yim, *National Preparedness: Integration of Federal, State, Local and Private Sector Efforts Is Critical to an Effective National Strategy for Homeland Security* (Washington, D.C.: U.S. General Accounting Office, 2002). All of these documents are available at National Criminal Justice Reference Service (NCJRS) at http://www.ncjrs.gov. See also

Joe Devanney and Diane Devanney, "Homeland Security and Patriot Acts," *Law and Order,* 51 (8, August 2003), pp. 10–12.

53. Department of Homeland Security, *Protecting Travelers and Commerce,* retrieved August 18, 2006, from http://www.dhs.gov.

54. Department of Homeland Security, *US-Visit,* retrieved December 15, 2005, from http://www.dhs.gov. Also see Department of Homeland Security, *US-Visit begins testing radio frequency identification technology to improve border security and travel; Fact sheet: Radio frequency identification technology,* retrieved December 15, 2005, from http://www.dhs.gov; and Jonathan Krim, "U.S. Passports to Receive Electronic Identification Chips," *Washington Post,* October 26, 2005.

55. Transportation Security Administration, *Federal Air Marshal Service,* retrieved August 18, 2006, from http://www.tsa.gov.

56. Thomas Frank, Mimi Hall, and Alan Levin, "Air Marshals Thrust into Spotlight," *USA Today,* retrieved December 11, 2005, from http://usatoday.com.

57. U.S. Customs and Border Protection, *A Typical Day at U.S. Customs and Border Protection (CBP),* retrieved August 18, 2006, from http://www.cbp.gov.

58. U.S. Customs and Border Protection, *The National Guard Deployment in Support of Border Security,* retrieved August 18, 2006, from http://www.cbp.gov.

59. U.S. Immigration and Customs Enforcement, *About Us,* retrieved August 18, 2006, from http://www.ice.gov.

60. Cole Maxwell and Tony Blanda, "Terror by Sea: The Unique Challenges of Port Security," *FBI Law Enforcement Bulletin* (September 2005), pp. 22–26.

61. Federal Bureau of Investigation, www.fbi.gov/pressrel/speeches/speech052902.htm; http://www.fbi.gov/page2/52902.htm.

62. Robert A. Martin, "The Joint Terrorism Task Force: A Concept That Works," *FBI Law Enforcement Bulletin* (March 1999), pp. 23–27.

63. Martin, "The Joint Terrorism Task Force," p. 27.

64. James Casey, "Managing Joint Terrorism Task Force Resources," *FBI Law Enforcement Bulletin* (November 2004), pp. 1–6.

65. Leslie Miller, "Government Misses Dozens of Security Deadlines since Sept. 11," *Associated Press,* October 30, 2005, retrieved November 2, 2005, from http://www.startribune.com.

66. D. Douglas Bodrero, "Confronting Terrorism on the State and Local Level," *FBI Law Enforcement Bulletin* (March 1999), pp. 11–18.

67. D. Douglas Bodrero, "Law Enforcement's New Challenge to Investigate, Interdict and Prevent Terrorism," *Police Chief* (February 2002), pp. 41–48.

68. Gene Voegtlin, "IACP Testifies on Local Law Enforcement Role in Homeland Defense," *Police Chief* (February 2002), p. 8.

69. Kevin Riley and Bruce Hoffman, *Domestic Terrorism: A National Assessment of State and Local Law Enforcement Preparedness* (Santa Monica, Calif.: Rand Corporation, National Institute of Justice, 1995).

70. Bodrero, "Confronting Terrorism on the State and Local Level."

71. Mike Terault, "Community Policing: Essential to Homeland Security," *Sheriff* (September/October 2002), pp. 36–37.

72. Matthew J. Hickman and Brian A. Reaves, "Local Police and Homeland Security: Some Baseline Data," *Police Chief* (October 2002), pp. 83–88.

73. Melchor C. De Guzman, "The Changing Roles and Strategies of the Police in Time of Terror," *Academy of Criminal Justice Sciences Today* (September/October 2002), pp. 8–13.

74. Erika Martinez, "NYPD's Global Eyes and Ears: Cops Abroad on Terror Beat," *New York Post,* November 28, 2005, p. 20; and Robert F. Worth, "In a Quiet Office Somewhere, Watching Terrorists," *New York Times,* February 23, 2005, pp. B1, B6.

75. Richard Perez-Pena, "A Security Blanket, but with no Guarantees," *New York Times,* March 23, 2003, pp. A1, B14, B16.

76. "Domestic Security Demands More of Local PDs," *Law Enforcement News,* December 15/31, 2002, p. 9.

77. Leon Fooksman, "Deputies to Ride Palm Beach County Trains, Buses in Search of Suspicious Activity," *South Florida Sun-Sentinel,* May 11, 2006.

78. Curt Anderson, "Police Go 'In-Your-Face' to Deter Would-Be Terrorists in Miami," *Associated Press,* November 28, 2005.

79. M. L. Brown and L. D. Maples, "No Time for Complacency: Leadership and Partnerships Are Key in Homeland Security Efforts," *Police Chief,* 73 (3, March 2006), pp. 18–20.

80. Dennis M. Rees, "Post-September 11 Policing in Suburban America," *Police Chief,* 73 (2, February 2006), pp. 72–77.

81. Michael E. Buerger and Bernard H. Levin, "Future of Officer Safety in an Age of Terrorism," *FBI Law Enforcement Bulletin* (September 2005), pp. 2–8.

82. Earl M. Sweeney, "Patrol Officer: America's Intelligence on the Ground," *FBI Law Enforcement Bulletin* (September 2005), pp. 14–21.

83. U.S. Department of Justice, National Institute of Justice, *Assessing and Managing the Terrorism Threat* (Washington, D.C.: National Institute of Justice, 2005).

84. K. Jack Riley, Gregory F. Treverton, Jeremy M. Wilson, and Lois M. Davis, *State and Local Intelligence in the War on Terrorism* (Santa Monica, Calif.: Rand Corporation, 2005).

85. Personal communication with Patrick Faiella, August 18, 2006.

86. Personal communication with Richard Martin, September 21, 2006.

87. Marie Simonetti Rosen, "Terror-Oriented Policing's Big Shadow," *Law Enforcement News* (December 2004), pp. 1, 4.

88. Karen Eschbacher, "Homicide Surge Extends Beyond Indy," *Indianapolis Star,* August 13, 2006.

89. Sherry L. Harowitz, "The New Centurions," *Security Management* (January 2003), pp. 51–58. Also see Teresa Anderson, "A Year of Reassessment," *Security Management* (January 2003), pp. 61–65.

90. "National Strategy for Prevention," *Security Management* (March 2004), p. 92.

91. U.S. Congress, Congressional Budget Office, *Homeland Security and the Private Sector* (Washington, D.C.: U.S. Congress, Congressional Budget Office, 2004).

92. Pam Belluck, "States and Cities Must Hunt Terror Plots, Governor Says," *New York Times,* December 15, 2004, p. A22.

93. "ASIS Foundation to Survey Retail Mall Security," *ASIS Dynamics* (July/August 2004), p. 6.

94. "CSO Roundtable Gathers on Capitol Hill," *ASIS Dynamics* (January/February 2005), pp. 1, 23.

95. Leonard A. Hall and Rick Adrian, "When the Front Lines Are Local," *Security Management* (February 2004), pp. 70–81.

96. Lawrence Mark Cohen, "Bombs Away: Bomb Detection Technologies Continue to Improve, and They Are Being Used in Increasingly Effective Ways," *Security Management* (August 2004), pp. 47–54.

97. David W. Dunlap, "Adding Barricades, and Trying to Avoid the Feel of a Fortress," *New York Times,* September 23, 2004, p. B3. Also see Richard Kessinger, "From Jericho to Jersey Barrier," *Security Management* (August 2004), pp. 57–66.

98. National Institute of Justice, *National Policy Summit: Building Private Security/Public Policing Partnerships to Prevent and Respond to Terrorism and Public Disorder* (Washington, D.C.: National Institute of Justice, Office of Community Oriented Policing Services, 2004); and, Joseph M. Polisar, "President's Message: Cooperation by Private Security and Public Law Enforcement," *Police Chief* (October 2004), p. 10. For a complete list of all members participating in the Summit see Appendix A of the *2004 National Policy Summit: . . .* ; Appendix B contains the pre-summit reading list; Appendix C contains the identity of all sponsors; Appendix E lists members of the Summit Advisory Committee; and Appendix F lists the members of the IACP staff participating in the report.

99. James F. Pastor, "Terrorism and Public Safety Policing," *Crime and Justice International* (March/April 2005), pp. 4–8.

100. National Commission on Terrorist Attacks upon the United States, *9/11 Commission Report,* pp. 397–398.

101. National Commission on Terrorist Attacks upon the United States, *9/11 Commission Report,* pp. 398.

102. Thomas E. Cavanagh, as cited in Benjamin Weiser and Claudia H. Deutsch, "Offices hold the line on security spending; stringent measures gather dust, experts say," *New York Times,* August 16, 2004, pp. B1, B4.

103. Andrew Scott, "Terrorism not on most companies' radar," *Fairfield County Business Journal,* August 1, 2005.

104. National Commission on Terrorist Attacks upon the United States, *9/11 Commission Report.*

105. Dan Eggen, "U.S. Is Given Failing Grades by 9/11 Panel," *Washington Post,* December 6, 2005, p. A1; and Hope Yen, "Ex-Sept. 11 Commissioners: U.S. at Risk," *Associated Press,* December 5, 2005, retrieved December 5, 2005, from http://www.washingtonpost.com.

106. Eggen, "U.S. Is Given Failing Grades by 9/11 Panel," p. A1.

107. Yen, "Ex-Sept. 11 Commissioners."

108. Thomas Rossler, "New Mission and New Challenges: Law Enforcement and Intelligence after the U.S.A. Patriot Act," *Journal of the Institute of Justice and International Studies,* 3 (2003), pp. 70–79.

109. White, *Terrorism and Homeland Security,* pp. 293–297.

110. Jim Ruiz and Kathleen H. Winters, "The USA Patriot Act: A Review of the Major Components," in ed. Craig Hemmens, *Current Legal Issues in Criminal Justice* (Los Angeles: Roxbury, 2007), 29–44. Ruiz and Winters cite National Commission on Terrorist Attacks upon the United States, *9/11 Commission Report,* pp. 79, 87, and 88.

111. Michael J. Bulzomi, "Foreign Intelligence Surveillance Act: Before and After the USA Patriot Act," *FBI Law Enforcement Bulletin,* 72 (6, June 2003), p. 25.

112. Bulzomi, "Foreign Intelligence Surveillance Act," pp. 25–32.

113. Ruiz and Winters, "The USA Patriot Act," p. 41.

114. Melanie Scarborough, *The Security Pretext: An Examination of the Growth of Federal Police Agencies* (Washington, D.C.: Cato Institute, 2005), retrieved August 17, 2006 from http://www.cato.com.

115. White, *Terrorism and Homeland Security,* pp. 295–297.

116. American Civil Liberties Union, "Insatiable Appetite: The Government's Demand for New and Unnecessary Powers after September 11," in *Homeland Security Law and Policy,* ed. William C. Nicholson (Springfield, Ill.: Charles C. Thomas, 2005), pp. 179–196.

117. Anna R. Oller, "Impact of Counter-Terrorism Legislation on Civil Liberties in the Sciences," *Journal of the Institute of Justice and International Studies,* 3 (2003), pp. 80–87.

118. Personal communication with James Burnett, August 27, 2006.

119. Richard Willing, "With Only a Letter, FBI Can Gather Private Data," *USA Today,* July 6, 2006.

120. Willing, "With Only a Letter, FBI Can Gather Private Data."

121. Willing, "With Only a Letter, FBI Can Gather Private Data." See Michael J. Bulzomi, "Foreign Intelligence Surveillance Act," pp. 25–32. The Foreign Intelligence Surveillance Act of 1978 (FISA) was passed in 1978 and established a requirement of judicial approval for the use of electronic surveillance for foreign intelligence gathering. FISA also established the FISA Court, consisting of U.S. District judges, whose purpose is to review government applications for national security electronic monitoring and searches. FISA requires a showing of probable cause to use electronic monitoring techniques.

122. Karen Tumulty, "Inside Bush's Secret Spy Net," *Time,* May 22, 2006, pp. 33–36.

123. Tumulty, "Inside Bush's Secret Spy Net," pp. 33–36.

124. Adam Liptak and Eric Lichtblau, "U.S. Judge Finds Wiretap Actions Violate the Law," *New York Times,* August 18, 2006, p. 1.

125. Ruiz and Winters, "The USA Patriot Act," p. 43. Ruiz and Winters cite E. Lichtblau, "Justice Depart. Report Cites FBI Violations," *New York Times,* March 9, 2006.

126. "Majority of Americans Support Increased Surveillance, Poll Shows," *Wall Street Journal Online,* August 17, 2006.

Glossary

A

adverse impact A form of de facto discrimination resulting from a testing element that discriminates against a particular group, essentially keeping them out of the applicant pool; when there is a significantly different rate of selection in hiring or promotion, a type of de facto discrimination.

affirmative action An active effort to improve employment or educational opportunities for minorities. This includes ensuring equal opportunity as well as redressing past discrimination.

age-progression photos Photo systems that show changes that will naturally occur to the face with age; also called age-enhanced photos.

AIDS Acquired immune deficiency syndrome.

ambiguous The concept that the police role is very diverse and dynamic.

Americans with Disabilities Act Signed into law in 1990, the world's first comprehensive civil rights law for people with disabilities. The act prohibits discrimination against people with disabilities in employment, public services, public accommodations, and telecommunications.

arrest The initial taking into custody of a person by law enforcement authorities to answer for a criminal offense or violation of a code or ordinance.

automated crime analysis The automated collection and analysis of data regarding crime (when, where, who, what, how, and why) to discern criminal patterns and assist in the effective assignment of personnel to combat crime.

automated fingerprint identification system (AFIS) Fingerprinting innovation begun in the 1980s in which a print technician can enter unidentified latent fingerprints into a computer. The computer then automatically searches its files and presents a list of likely matches.

B

background investigation The complete and thorough investigation of an applicant's past life, including education, employment, military, driving, criminal history, relationships, and character. This includes verification of all statements made by the applicant on the background form and the evaluation of detected and undetected behavior to make a determination if the candidate is the type of person suited to a career in law enforcement.

ballistics Scientific analysis of guns and bullets.

beat The smallest geographical area an individual officer can patrol.

beat system System of policing created by Sir Robert Peel for the London Metropolitan Police in 1829 in which officers were assigned to relatively small permanent posts.

biased-based policing Any police-initiated activity that relies on a person's race or ethnic background rather than on behavior as a basis for identifying that individual as being involved in criminal activity.

bike patrol Officers patrol an assigned area on bicycle rather than in a patrol car.

biological weapons Weapons made from live bacterial, viral, or other microorganisms.

biometric identification Automated identification systems that use particular physical characteristics to distinguish one person from another; can identify criminals or provide authentication.

blending Plainclothes officers' efforts to blend into an area and attempt to catch a criminal.

blue curtain A concept developed by William Westley that claims that police officers only trust other police officers and do not aid in the investigation of wrongdoing by other officers.

blue flu Informal job actions by officers in which they refuse to perform certain job functions in an attempt to win labor concessions from their employers.

blue wall of silence A figurative protective barrier erected by the police in which officers protect one another from outsiders, often even refusing to aid police superiors or other law enforcement officials in investigating wrongdoing of other officers.

bribe Payment of money or other contribution to a police officer with the intent to subvert the aim of the criminal justice system.

broken windows model Theory that unrepaired broken windows indicate to others that members of the community do not care about the quality of life in the neighborhood and are unlikely to get involved; consequently, disorder and crime will thrive.

bureaucracy An organizational model marked by hierarchy, promotion on professional merit and skill, the development of a career service, reliance on and use of rules and regulations, and impersonality of relationships among career professionals in the bureaucracy and with their clientele.

C

Carroll doctrine The legal doctrine that automobiles have less Fourth Amendment protection than other places. Arose from the landmark 1925 U.S. Supreme Court case *Carroll v. United States*.

centralized model of state law enforcement Combines the duties of major criminal investigations with the patrol of state highways.

chain of command Managerial concept stating that each individual in an organization is supervised and reports to only one immediate supervisor.

citizen oversight Also referred to as civilian review or external review. A method that allows for the independent citizen review of complaints filed against the police through a board or committee that independently reviews allegations of misconduct.

citizen patrols Program that involves citizens patrolling on foot or in private cars and alerting the police to possible crimes or criminals in the area.

citizen police academies Academies provided by the police department for the citizens of the community to enhance their understanding of the workings of their police department.

civil liability Potential liability for payment of damages as a result of a ruling in a lawsuit.

civil liability or code enforcement teams Teams used in jurisdictions to address the crime problem through the enforcement of civil laws and building and occupational codes.

Civil Rights Act of 1964 Prohibits job discrimination based on race, color, religion, sex, or national origin.

civil service system A method of hiring and managing government employees that is designed to eliminate political influence, favoritism, nepotism, and bias.

civilianization Replacing sworn positions with civilian employees; some positions that are often civilianized include call takers, dispatchers, front desk personnel, crime analysts, crime prevention specialists, accident investigators, crime scene technicians, public information officers, and training personnel.

cold hit A DNA sample collected from a crime scene that ties an unknown suspect to the DNA profile of someone in the national or a state's database.

cold-case squads Investigative units that reexamine old cases that have remained unsolved. They use the passage of time coupled with a fresh set of eyes to help solve cases that have been stagnant for years and often decades.

Combined DNA Index System (CODIS) Database that contains DNA profiles obtained from subjects convicted of homicide, sexual assault, and other serious felonies.

Community Emergency Response Team (CERT) A program in which civilians are trained in basic emergency response, first aid, and search and rescue.

community policing Philosophy of empowering citizens and developing a partnership between the police and the community to work together to solve problems.

Community Policing Consortium An organization reporting on and encouraging the latest community policing activities that comprises the International Association of Chiefs of Police (IACP), the National Organization of Black Law Enforcement Executives (NOBLE), the National Sheriffs' Association (NSA), the Police Executive Research Forum (PERF), and the Police Foundation.

community service officers (CSOs) A level of entry-level, police employee without general law enforcement powers suggested by the President's Commission on Law Enforcement and Administration of Justice.

composite sketches Sketches prepared by forensic artists or automated means of people wanted by the police for a crime.

CompStat Weekly crime strategy meetings, featuring the latest computerized crime statistics and high-stress brain storming; developed by the New York City Police Department in the mid-1990s.

computer-aided dispatch (CAD) System that allows almost immediate communication between the police dispatcher and police units in the field.

computer-aided investigations (computerized case management) The use of computers to perform case management and other functions in investigations.

consent decree An agreement binding an agency to a particular course of action for hiring and promoting minorities.

constable An official assigned to keep the peace in the mutual pledge system in England.

contract security Private security services offered by industrial security firms and guard agencies to private employers or individuals on a contract basis.

control group The group that is not acted upon, nothing is changed.

controlled experiment An experiment or study using a control group and an experimental group.

corruption Acts involving misuse of authority by a police officer in a manner designed to produce personal gain for the officer or others.

counterterrorism Enforcement efforts made against terrorist organizations.

crime Any act that the government has declared to be contrary to the public good, that is declared by statute to be a crime, and that is prosecuted in a criminal proceeding. In some jurisdictions, crimes only include felonies and/or misdemeanors.

crime analysis The use of analytical methods to obtain pertinent information on crime patterns and trends that can then be disseminated to officers on the street.

Crime Bill of 1994 The Violent Crime Control and Law Enforcement Act, signed by President Clinton in 1994.

crime scene The location where a crime occurred.

Crime Stoppers A program where a cash reward is offered for information that results in the conviction of an offender.

crime-fighting role A major view of the role of the police that emphasizes crime fighting or law enforcement.

criminal liability Subject to punishment for a crime.

criminalistics A branch of forensic science that deals with the study of physical evidence related to crime.

CSI effect The phenomenon that the popularity of the television series *CSI: Crime Scene Investigation,* and its spin-offs *CSI: Miami* and *CSI: New York* and other television shows and movies makes the public and jurors believe that the police can do what their television counterparts can.

custodial interrogation The questioning of a person in police custody regarding his or her participation in a crime.

D

de facto discrimination The indirect result of policies or practices that are not intended to discriminate, but do, in fact, discriminate.

deadly force Force that can cause death.

decentralized model of state law enforcement A clear distinction between traffic enforcement on state highways and other state-level law enforcement functions.

decoy operations Operations in which officers dress as and play the role of potential victims in the hope of attracting and catching a criminal.

defense of life standard Doctrine allowing police officers to use deadly force against individuals using deadly force against an officer or others.

deoxyribonucleic acid (DNA) The basic building code for all of the human body's chromosomes.

Department of Homeland Security (DHS) Federal cabinet department established in the aftermath of the terrorist attacks of September 11, 2001.

detective mystique The idea that detective work is glamorous, exciting, and dangerous, as it is depicted in the movies and on television.

differential response to calls for service The police response to calls for service varies according to the type and severity of the call.

directed patrol Officers patrol specific locations at specific times to address a specific crime problem.

Dirty Harry problem A moral dilemma faced by police officers in which they may feel forced to take certain illegal actions to achieve a greater good.

discretion Freedom to act or decide a matter on one's own.

discrimination Unequal treatment of persons in personnel decisions on the basis of their race, religion, national origin, gender, or sexual orientation.

DNA profiling, genetic fingerprinting, DNA typing The examination of DNA samples from a body fluid to determine whether they came from a particular subject.

domestic terrorism Terrorism committed by citizens of the United States in the United States.

double marginality The simultaneous expectation by white officers that African American officers will give members of their own race better treatment and hostility from the African American community that black officers are traitors to their race.

Dred Scott decision Infamous U.S. Supreme Court decision of 1857 ruling that slaves had no rights as citizens because they were considered to be property.

Drug Abuse Resistance Education (DARE) The most popular antidrug program in which police officers teach students in schools about the dangers of drug use.

E

enhanced CAD (enhanced 911, E911) Sophisticated CAD system using mobile digital terminals in each patrol unit that replaces voice communication.

entrapment A legal defense that holds that police originated the criminal idea or initiated the criminal action.

Equal Employment Opportunity Act of 1972 (EEOA) Extended the 1964 Civil Rights Act and made it applicable to state and local governments.

ethics The study of what constitutes good or bad conduct.

evidence-based policing Using available scientific research on policing to implement crime-fighting strategies and department policies.

exclusionary rule An interpretation of the U.S. Constitution by the U.S. Supreme Court that holds that evidence seized in violation of the U.S. Constitution cannot be used in court against a defendant.

exigent circumstances One of the major exceptions to the warrant requirement of the Fourth Amendment. Exigency may be translated as "emergency."

experimental group The group that receives the changed conditions.

F

field interrogation Unplanned questioning of an individual who has aroused the suspicions of an officer.

field training On-the-job training program that occurs after the police academy under the direction of an FTO.

field training officer (FTO) Experienced officer who mentors and trains a new police officer.

fleeing felon doctrine Doctrine widely followed before the 1960s that allowed police officers to use deadly force to apprehend a fleeing felon.

flight-or-fight response The body's reaction to highly stressful situations in which it is getting prepared for extraordinary physical exertion.

foot patrol Police officers walk a beat or assigned area rather than patrolling in a motor vehicle.

Foreign Intelligence Surveillance Act **(FISA Court)** Bill passed in 1978 requiring the NSA and the FBI to seek a special court's (the FISA Court) permission to conduct searches and electronic surveillance in terrorism and spying cases.

forensic science That part of science applied to answering legal questions.

Fourteenth Amendment Amendment to the U.S. Constitution passed in 1868 that guarantees "equal protection of the law" to all citizens of the United States; frequently used to govern employment equality in the United States.

Frye test Standard to admitting new scientific evidence into U.S. Courts; based on the U.S. Supreme Court case *Frye v. United States* (1923).

G

Gang Resistance Education and Training (GREAT) An educational program designed after DARE which addresses the issue of gangs.

Global Positioning Systems (GPS) A satellite system used to locate any position on the map.

grass-eaters Police officers who participate in the more passive type of police corruption by accepting opportunities of corruption that present themselves.

gratuities Items of value received by someone because of his or her role or job rather than because of a personal relationship.

Guardians Association of New York City Police Department v. Civil Service Commission of New York A landmark appellate court decision on the issue of job analysis.

H

Hallcrest Reports Two comprehensive reports commissioned by the National Institute of Justice on the private security industry in the United States.

Herman Goldstein First mentioned the concept of "problem-solving or problem-oriented policing" in 1979.

Hogan's Alley A shooting course in which simulated "good guys" and "bad guys" pop up, requiring police officers to make split-second decisions.

homeland security Efforts made since the terrorist acts of September 11, 2001 to protect the U.S. against terrorist acts.

hue and cry A method developed in early England for citizens to summons assistance from fellow members of the community.

human relations Everything done with each other as human beings in all kinds of relationships.

I

inked prints (ten-prints) Result of the process of rolling each finger onto a ten-print card.

in-service training Training that occurs during a police officer's career, usually on a regular basis and usually within the department; often required by department policy or state mandate.

Integrated Automated Fingerprint Identification System (IAFIS) A system for searching an individual's fingerprints against a computerized database of all fingerprints.

integrity test Proactive investigation of corruption in which investigators provide opportunities for officers to commit illegal acts.

internal affairs division The unit of a police agency that is charged with investigating police corruption or misconduct.

International Association of Chiefs of Police (IACP) An organization composed of police leaders from across the country that is very influential in setting standards for police departments throughout the country. IACP publishes *Police Chief* magazine, conducts research, and writes publications to assist law enforcement around the country.

international terrorism Terrorism on an international level.

investigative task forces A group of investigators working together to investigate one or more crimes. These investigators are often from different law enforcement agencies.

IP telephony A collection of new communication technologies, products, and services that can facilitate communication across diverse systems.

J

James Q. Wilson and George L. Kelling The authors of the seminal article in 1982 in the *Atlantic Monthly* entitled "Broken Windows: The Police and Neighborhood Safety," which came to be called the broken windows model of policing.

job analysis Identifies the important skills that must be performed by police officers, and then identifies the knowledge, skills, and abilities necessary to perform those tasks.

job relatedness Concept that job requirements must be necessary for the performance of the job a person is applying for.

joint federal and local task force Use of federal, state, and local law enforcement agents in a focused task force to address particular crime problems.

Joint Terrorism Task Forces (JTTF) concept Use of single-focused investigative units that meld personnel and talent from various law enforcement agencies.

judicial review Process by which the actions of the police in areas such as arrests, search and seizure, and custodial interrogation are reviewed by the court system to ensure their constitutionality.

K

Kansas City Patrol study The first study conducted to test the effectiveness of random routine patrol.

Knapp Commission Commission created in 1970 to investigate allegations of widespread, organized corruption in the New York City Police Department.

knowledge, skills, and abilities (KSAs) Talents or attributes necessary to do a particular job.

L

latent prints Fingerprint impressions left at a crime scene.

lateral transfers The ability and opportunity to transfer from one police department to another.

Law Enforcement Education Program (LEEP) A federal scholarship and loan program operated by the DOJ between 1968 and 1976. LEEP put money into developing criminal justice programs in colleges and provided tuition and expenses to in-service police officers to go to college.

law enforcement employee average Number of law enforcement employees for each 1,000 residents.

leadership An influence relationship among leaders and followers who intend real changes that reflect their mutual purposes.

LEMAS reports Statistical reports on law enforcement personnel data issued by the National Institute of Justice under its Law Enforcement Management and Administrative Statistics program.

less-than-lethal weapons Innovative alternatives to traditional firearms, such as batons, bodily force techniques, chemical irritant sprays, and Tasers or stun guns.

lineup Police identification procedure involving the placing of a suspect with a group of other people of similar physical characteristics so that a witness or victim of a crime can have the opportunity to identify the perpetrator of the crime.

Live Scan The electronic taking and transmission of fingerprints as opposed to traditional ink methods.

local control The formal and informal use of local or neighborhood forms of government and measures to deter abhorrent behaviors.

M

management The process of running an organization so that the organization can accomplish its goals.

Managing Criminal Investigations (MCI) Proposal recommended by the Rand Study regarding a more effective way of investigating crimes, including allowing patrol officers to follow up cases and using solvability factors in determining which cases to follow up.

meat-eaters Officers who participate in more aggressive types of corruption by seeking out and taking advantage of opportunities of corruption.

mentoring Filling a role as teacher, model, motivator, coach, or advisor in someone else's professional growth.

Minneapolis Domestic Violence Experiment An experiment conducted in Minneapolis, Minnesota, to determine the deterrent effect of various methods of handling domestic violence, including mandatory arrest.

Miranda **rules (*Miranda* warnings)** Rules established by the U.S. Supreme Court in the landmark case *Miranda v. United States* (1966) that require the police to advise suspects confronting custodial interrogation of their constitutional rights.

misdemeanor A class of criminal deviance that is usually punished by a maximum of $1,000 fine and/or up to one year in a county or city jail. A misdemeanor is less serious than a felony. Different jurisdictions classify misdemeanors and sanctions for violation thereof differently.

mitochondrial DNA (MtDNA) DNA analysis applied to evidence containing very small or degraded quantities from hair, bones, teeth, and body fluids.

mobile digital terminal (MDT) A device put into a police vehicle that allows the electronic transmission of messages between the police dispatcher and the officer in the field.

moonlight Term for police officers working in private security jobs during their off-duty hours.

mug shot imaging A system of digitizing a mug shot picture and storing its image on a computer so that it can be retrieved later.

mutual pledge A form of community self-protection developed by King Alfred the Great in the later part of the 19th century in England.

N

National Advisory Commission on Civil Disorders (Kerner Commission) Formed in 1968 to examine the civil disorders of the 1960s and recommended, among other things, that police agencies intensify their efforts to recruit more African Americans.

National Advisory Commission on Criminal Justice Standards and Goals Presidential commission formed to study the criminal justice system and recommend standards to adhere to for police agencies to reduce discrimination.

National Crime Information Center (NCIC) Computerized database of criminal information maintained by the FBI.

National Crime Victimization Survey (NCVS) National Institute of Justice survey of a random sample of U.S. households, asking them if a crime was committed against anyone in the household during the prior six months.

National Criminal Justice Reference Service (NCJRS) A national clearinghouse of criminal justice information maintained by the National Institute of Justice.

National Institute of Justice (NIJ) The research arm of the U.S. Justice Department.

National Law Enforcement Officers Memorial (NLEOM) A memorial in Washington, D.C. established to recognize the ultimate sacrifice of police officers killed in the line of duty.

national security letters Information requests issued by a local FBI official who certifies that the information is relevant to an international terrorism or foreign intelligence investigation.

Neighborhood Watch Crime prevention programs in which community members participate and engage in a wide range of specific crime prevention activities, as well as community-oriented activities.

Newark foot patrol study A study conducted to determine the effectiveness of foot patrol officers in preventing crime.

night vision devices Photographic and viewing devices that allow visibility in darkness.

noble cause corruption Stems from ends-oriented policing and involves police officers bending the rules to achieve the "right" goal of putting a criminal in jail.

nonsworn (civilian) members Police employees without traditional police powers generally assigned to noncritical or nonenforcement tasks.

O

Office of Community Oriented Policing Services (COPS) Established to administer the grant money provided by the 1994 Crime Bill and to promote community policing.

Officer Next Door (OND) program A plan initiated in 1997 allowing police officers to receive 50 percent discounts and low-cost loans to purchase homes in "distressed" areas nationwide. It is under the umbrella Good Neighbor Next Door program, which also includes teachers, firefighters, and emergency medical technicians.

Omnibus Crime Control and Safe Streets Act of 1968 Enacted to aid communities in reducing the crime problem and created the Law Enforcement Assistance Administration, which provided grants for recruitment, training, and education.

omnipresence A concept that suggests that the police are always present or always seem to be present.

Operation Identification Engraving identifying numbers onto property that is most likely to be stolen.

order maintenance Major view of the role of the police that emphasizes keeping the peace and providing social services.

organization A deliberate arrangement of people doing specific jobs, following particular procedures to accomplish a set of goals determined by some authority.

P

Peel's Nine Principles Basic guidelines created by Sir Robert Peel for the London Metropolitan Police in 1829.

Pendleton Act A federal law passed in 1883 to establish a civil service system that tested, appointed, and promoted officers on a merit system.

photo array Police identification procedure similar to a lineup, except that photos of the suspect (who is not in custody) and others are shown to a witness or victim of a crime.

physical agility test A test of physical fitness to determine if a candidate has the needed strength and endurance to perform the job of police officer.

plain view evidence Evidence seized by police without a warrant who have the right to be in a position to observe it.

platoon All of the people working on a particular tour or shift.

PODSCORB Acronym for the basic functions of management including planning, organizing, directing, staffing, coordinating, reporting, and budgeting.

police academy The initial formal training that a new police officer receives to learn police procedures, state laws, and objectives of law enforcement. The academy gives police officers the KSAs to accomplish the police job.

Police Athletic League (PAL) A large sports program involving police officers and youth.

police community relations The relationships involved in both human relations and public relations between the police and the community.

police community relations (PCR) movement The assigning of officers to a special community relations unit or public relations unit to interact with the public and attend community meetings.

police culture or police subculture A combination of shared norms, values, goals, career patterns, life styles, and occupational structures that is somewhat different from the combination held by the rest of society.

police cynicism An attitude that there is no hope for the world and a view of humanity at its worst.

police deception Form of misconduct that includes perjury and falsifying police reports.

Police Explorers A program for young adults between the ages of 14 and 20 in which they work closely with law enforcement and explore the police career.

police operational styles Styles adopted by police officers as a way of thinking about the role of the police and law in society.

police personality Traits common to most police officers. Scholars have reported that this personality is thought to include such traits as authoritarianism, suspicion, hostility, insecurity, conservatism, and cynicism.

police public relations Activities performed by police agencies designed to create a favorable image of themselves.

police pursuits The attempt by law enforcement to apprehend alleged criminals in a moving motor vehicle when the driver is trying to elude capture and increases speed or takes evasive action.

police role The concept of "what do the police do."

police storefront station or ministation A small satellite police station designed to serve a local part of the community and facilitate the community's access to the police officers.

police suicide The intentional taking of one's own life by a police officer.

polygraph Also called the lie detector test; a mechanical device designed to ascertain whether a person is telling the truth.

polymerase chain reaction-short tandem repeat (PCR-STR) One of the latest DNA technology systems; requires only pin-size samples rather than dime-size samples needed for RFLP.

posse comitatus A common law descendent of the old hue and cry. If a crime spree occurred or a dangerous criminal was in the area, the U.S. frontier sheriff would call upon the posse comitatus, a Latin term meaning "the power of the county."

Praetorian Guard Select group of highly qualified members of the military established by Roman emperor Augustus to protect him and his palace.

precinct/district/station The entire collection of beats in a given geographic area; the organizational headquarters of a police department.

President's Commission on Law Enforcement and Administration of Justice Commission that issued a report in 1967 entitled *The Challenge of Crime in a Free Society*. The commission was created following the problems of the 1960s, particularly the problems between police and citizens.

private security industry The industry that provides private and corporate security programs in the United States.

Private Security Officer Employment Authorization Act of 2004 Federal law giving employers the ability to request criminal background checks from the FBI for applicants and holders of security positions.

probable cause Evidence that may lead a reasonable person to believe that a crime has been committed and that a certain person committed it.

probationary period The period in the early part of an officer's career in which the officer can be dismissed if not performing to the departments standards.

problem-solving policing Analyzing crime issues to determine the underlying problems and addressing those underlying problems.

proprietary security Security services provided by the organization or company itself.

Q

quasi-military organization An organization similar to the military along structures of strict authority and reporting relations.

quota Numbers put into place as part of goals and objectives in affirmative action plans.

R

random routine patrol Officers driving around a designated geographic area.

rapid response to 911 calls Officers being dispatched to calls immediately, regardless of the type of call.

reasonable force The amount of force an officer can use when making an arrest.

reasonable suspicion The standard of proof that is necessary for police officers to conduct stops and frisks.

recruitment process The effort to attract the best people to apply for the police position.

Regional Community Policing Institutes (RCPIs) Part of the COPS program, the 30 RCPIs provide regional training and technical assistance to law enforcement around the country regarding community policing.

Regional Crime Analysis Geographic Information Systems (RCAGIS) Spatial Analysis Computer programs to help police locate crime "hot spots," spatially relate a list of potential suspects to actual crimes, profile crime geographically to identify where a serial criminal most likely lives, and forecast where the next crime in a series might occur.

repeat offender programs (ROPs) Enforcement efforts directed at known repeat offenders through surveillance or case enhancement.

reserve officer Either part-time compensated or noncompensated sworn police employees who serve when needed.

resident officer programs Programs through which officers live in particular communities to strengthen relations between the police and the community.

restricted fragment length polymorphism (RFLP) Traditional method of DNA technology analysis.

retroactive investigation of past crimes by detectives The follow-up investigation of crimes by detectives that occurs after a crime has been reported.

reverse discrimination The label often attached to the preferential treatment received by minority groups.

Robert C. Trojanowicz Founded the National Center for Community Policing in East Lansing, Michigan.

robotics The science of using robots to perform operations formerly done by human beings.

Rodney King incident The 1991 videotaped beating of an African American citizen by members of the Los Angeles Police Department.

"rotten apple" theory Theory of corruption in which it is believed that individual officers within the agency are bad, rather than the organization as a whole.

S

saturation patrol Assigning a larger number of uniformed officers to an area to deal with a particular crime problem.

search and seizure Legal concept relating to the searching for and confiscation of evidence by the police.

search warrant A written order, based on probable cause, signed by a judge authorizing police to search a specific person, place, or property to obtain evidence.

selection process The steps or tests an individual must progress through before being hired as a police officer.

September 11, 2001 The date of a series of terrorist attacks against the United States of America by members of al Qaeda.

serology Scientific analysis of blood, semen, and other body fluids.

shared leadership Power sharing arrangement in which workplace influence is shared among individuals who are otherwise hierarchical unequals.

shire-reeve Early English official placed in charge of shires as part of the system of mutual pledge; evolved into the modern concept of the sheriff.

showup Police identification process involving bringing a suspect back to the scene of the crime or another place (for example, a hospital where an injured victim is) where the suspect can be seen and possibly identified by a victim or witness of a crime.

silver platter doctrine Legal tactic that allowed federal prosecutors to use evidence obtained by state police officers seized through unreasonable searches and seizures.

slave patrols Police-type organizations created in the American South during colonial times to control slaves and support the southern economic system of slavery.

solvability factors Factors considered in determining whether or not a case should be assigned for follow-up investigation.

span of control The number of officers or subordinates that a superior can supervise effectively.

split-force patrol A method in which the patrol force is split and half respond to calls for service and the other half performs directed patrol activities.

squad A group of officers who generally work together all the time under the supervision of a particular sergeant.

sting operations Undercover police operations in which police pose as criminals to arrest law violators.

stop and frisk The detaining of a person by law enforcement officers for the purpose of investigation, accompanied by a superficial examination of the person's body surface or clothing to discover weapons, contraband, or other objects relating to criminal activity.

strategic policing Involves a continued reliance on traditional policing operations.

suicide by cop The phenomenon in which a person wishing to die deliberately places an officer in a life-threatening situation, causing the officer to use deadly force against that person.

sworn law enforcement employee average Number of sworn law enforcement employees for each 1,000 residents.

sworn members Police employees given traditional police powers by state and local laws, including penal or criminal laws and criminal procedure laws.

T

Tennessee v. Garner U.S. Supreme Court case that ended the use of the fleeing felon rule.

terrorism Premeditated politically motivated violence perpetrated against noncombatant targets.

terrorist attacks against the United States of America on September 11, 2001 The terrorist attacks committed by al Qaeda.

thief-takers Private English citizens with no official status who were paid by the king for every criminal they arrested. They were similar to the bounty hunter of the American West.

third degree The pattern of brutality and violence used by the police to obtain confessions by suspects.

Triad A joint partnership between the police and senior citizens to address specific problems seniors encounter with safety and quality-of-life issues.

tuition reimbursement The money a police department will pay officers to reimburse them for tuition expenses while they are employed by the police department and are pursuing a college degree.

U

undercover investigations Covert investigations involving plainclothes officers.

Uniform Crime Reports **(UCR)** Yearly collection of aggregate crime statistics prepared by the FBI based on citizens' reports of crimes to the police.

unity of command A managerial concept that specifies that each individual in an organization is directly accountable to only one supervisor.

USA Patriot Act Public Law No. 107-56 passed in 2001 giving law enforcement new ability to search, seize, detain or eavesdrop in their pursuit of possible terrorists; full title of law is USA Patriot Act–Uniting and Strengthening America by Providing Appropriate Tools Required to Intercept and Obstruct Terrorism.

V

vehicle tracking systems Transmitters that enable investigators to track a vehicle during a surveillance; also called transponders, bumper beepers, or homing devices.

Vigiles Early Roman firefighters who also patrolled Rome's streets to protect citizens.

Voice over IP (VoIP) A subset of IP telephony that is a set of software, hardware, and standards designed to enable voice transmissions over packet-switched networks, which can be either an internal local area network or the Internet. VoIP is not associated with a physical telephone line but, rather, with an IP address that is linked to a phone number.

Volstead Act (National Prohibition, Eighteenth Amendment) Became law in 1920 and forbade the sale and manufacture of alcohol.

W

watch and ward A rudimentary form of policing, designed to protect against crime, disturbances, and fire. All men were required to serve on it.

Wickersham Commission Published the first national study of the U.S. criminal justice system, in 1931.

Bibliography

Books

Ahern, James F. *Police in Trouble*. New York: Hawthorne Books, 1972.

Alex, Nicholas. *Black in Blue: A Study of the Negro Policeman*. New York: Appleton-Century-Crofts, 1969.

———. *New York Cops Talk Back*. New York: Wiley, 1976.

Alpert, Geoffrey P., and Lorie A. Fridell. *Police Vehicles and Firearms: Instruments of Deadly Force*. Prospect Heights, Ill.: Waveland Press, 1992.

American Academy of Forensic Sciences. *AAFS Response to the 180-Day Story*. Colorado Springs, CO: American Academy of Forensic Sciences, 2006.

American Society of Crime Lab Directors. *Our Hundred Eighty-Day Study Report: Status and Needs of United States Crime Laboratories*. Colorado Springs, Colo.: American Society of Crime Lab Directors, 2004.

Aristotle. *Nicomachean Ethics*.

Ayres, Richard M., and George S. Flanagan. *Preventing Law Enforcement Stress: The Organization's Role*. Washington, D.C.: National Sheriff's Association, 1990.

Ayto, John. *Dictionary of Word Origins*. New York: Arcade, 1990.

Bailey, William G., ed. *The Encyclopedia of Police Science*. New York: Garland, 1989.

Baker, Mark. *Cops: Their Lives in Their Own Words*. New York: Simon & Schuster, 1985.

Barker, Tom. *Police Ethics: Crisis in Law Enforcement*. Springfield, Ill.: Charles C. Thomas, 1996.

Barletta, Michael. *After 9/11: Preventing Mass-Destruction Terrorism and Weapons Proliferation*. Monterey, Calif.: Center for Nonproliferation Studies, 2002.

Barnard, Chester I. *The Functions of the Executive*. Cambridge, Mass.: Harvard University Press, 1938.

Bayley, David H. *Forces of Order: Police Behavior in Japan and the United States*. Berkeley: University of California Press, 1976.

Bayley, David, and Harold Mendelsohn. *Minorities and the Police*. New York: Free Press, 1969.

Bennett, R. R., ed. *Police at Work: Policy Issues and Analysis*. Beverly Hills, Calif.: Sage, 1983.

Berman, Jay Stuart. *Police Administration and Progressive Reform: Theodore Roosevelt as Police Commissioner of New York*. New York: Greenwood Press, 1987.

Bittner, Egon. *The Functions of Police in Modern Society*. Cambridge, Mass.: Oelgeschlager, Gunn, and Hain, 1979.

Black, Donald. *The Manners and Customs of the Police*. New York: Academic Press, 1980.

Bloch, Peter B., and Deborah Anderson, *Policewomen on Patrol: Final Report*. Washington, D.C.: Police Foundation, 1974.

Blumberg, Abraham S., and Elaine Niederhoffer, eds. *The Ambivalent Force: Perspectives on the Police*. New York: Holt, Rinehart & Winston, 1985.

Boba, Rachel. *What Is Problem Analysis? Problem Analysis in Policing: An Executive Summary*. Washington, D.C.: Police Foundation, 2003.

Bopp, William J., and Donald O. Schultz. *A Short History of American Law Enforcement*. Springfield, Ill.: Charles C. Thomas, 1972.

Bouza, Anthony V. *The Police Mystique: An Insider's Look at Cops, Crime, and the Criminal Justice System*. New York: Plenum Press, 1990.

Boydstun, J. E. *San Diego Field Interrogation: Final Report*. Washington, D.C.: Police Foundation, 1975.

Bratton, William, and Peter Knobler. *Turnaround: How America's Top Cop Reversed the Crime Epidemic*. New York: Random House, 1998.

Bridenbaugh, Carl. *Cities in Revolt: Urban Life in America, 1743–1776*. New York: Knopf, 1965.

———. *Cities in the Wilderness: Urban Life in America, 1625–1742*. New York: Capricorn, 1964.

Broderick, John J. *Police in a Time of Change*, 2nd ed. Prospect Heights, Ill.: Waveland Press, 1987.

Brown, Michael. *Working the Street*. New York: Russell Sage Foundation, 1981.

Caldero, Michael A., and John P. Crank. *Police Ethics: the Corruption of Noble Cause*, 2nd ed. Cincinnati, Ohio: Anderson, 2004.

Chaiken, J. M., M. W. Lawless, and K. A. Stenson. *The Impact of Police Activity on Crime: Robberies in the New York City Subway System*. New York: Rand Institute, 1974.

Chapman, S. G., and T. E. St. Johnston. *The Police Heritage in England and America*. East Lansing: Michigan State University, 1962.

Cobb, Belton. *The First Detectives*. London: Faber & Faber, 1967.

Coffey, Alan. *Law Enforcement: A Human Relations Approach*. Englewood Cliffs, N.J.: Prentice Hall, 1990.

Cohn, Alvin, ed. *The Future of Policing*. Beverly Hills, Calif.: Sage, 1978.

Cohn, Alvin W., and Emilio C. Viano. *Police Community Relations: Images, Roles, Realities*. Philadelphia: Lippincott, 1976.

Cordner, Gary, Kathryn Scarborough, and Robert Sheehan. *Police Administration*, 5th ed. Cincinnati, Ohio: Anderson, 2004.

Cox Commission. *Crisis at Columbia: Report of the Fact-Finding Commission Appointed to Investigate the Disturbances at Columbia University in April and May 1968*. New York: Vintage, 1968.

Cox, Steven M., and Jack D. Fitzgerald. *Police in Community Relations: Critical Issues*, 3rd ed. Madison, Wisc.: Brown and Benchmark, 1996.

Critchley, T. A. *A History of Police in England and Wales*, 2nd ed. rev. Montclair, N.J.: Patterson Smith, 1972.

Culbertson, R., and M. Tezak, eds. *Order under Law*. Prospect Heights, Ill.: Waveland Press, 1981.

Cunningham, William C., John J. Strauchs, and Clifford W. Van Meter. *The Hallcrest Report: Private Security and Police in America*. Portland, Oreg.: Chancellor Press, 1985.

———. *The Hallcrest Report II: Private Security Trends, 1970–2000*. Boston: Butterworth-Heinemann, 1990.

Daley, Robert. *Prince of the City: The Story of a Cop Who Knew Too Much*. Boston: Houghton Mifflin, 1978.

Dantzker, M. L. *Understanding Today's Police Officer*, 3rd ed. Upper Saddle River, N.J.: Prentice Hall, 2003.

Davis, Kenneth Culp. *Police Discretion*. St. Paul, Minn.: West, 1975.

DeForest, Peter. *Forensic Science: An Introduction to Criminalistics*. New York: McGraw-Hill, 1983.

del Carmen, Rolando V. *Civil Liabilities in American Policing: A Text for Law Enforcement Personnel*. Englewood Cliffs, N.J.: Prentice Hall, 1991.

Dempsey, John S. *An Introduction to Public and Private Investigations.* Minneapolis: West, 1996.

————. *Introduction to Investigations,* 2nd ed. Belmont, Calif.: Wadsworth, 2003.

Dempsey, John S., and Linda S. Forst, *An Introduction to Policing,* 3rd ed. Belmont, Calif.: Wadsworth, 2005.

Dershowitz, Alan M. *Taking Liberties: A Decade of Hard Cases, Bad Laws, and Bum Raps.* Chicago: Contemporary Books, 1988.

Drucker, Peter. *Managing in the Next Society.* New York: St. Martin's, 2002.

Dulaney, W. Marvin. *Black Police in America.* Bloomington: Indiana University Press, 1996.

Dunham, Roger G., and Geoffrey P. Alpert. *Critical Issues in Policing,* 3rd ed. Prospect Heights, Ill.: Waveland Press, 1997.

Eck, John E. *Managing Case Assignments: The Burglary Investigation Decision Model Replication.* Washington, D.C.: Police Executive Research Forum, 1979.

Elliston, Frederick A., and Michael Feldberg, eds. *Moral Issues in Police Work.* Totowa, N.J.: Rowman and Allanheld, 1985.

Emsley, Clive. *Policing and Its Context, 1750–1870.* New York: Schocken, 1984.

Fay, John J. *The Police Dictionary and Encyclopedia.* Springfield, Ill.: Charles C. Thomas, 1988.

Fischer, Robert J., and Gion Green, *Introduction to Security,* 6th ed. Boston: Butterworth-Heinemann, 1998.

Fogelson, Robert M. *Big City Police.* Cambridge, Mass.: Harvard University Press, 1977.

Forst, Linda. *The Aging of America: A Handbook for Police Officers.* Springfield, Ill.: Charles C. Thomas, 2000.

Fosdick, Raymond B. *American Police Systems.* New York: Century, 1920; reprint, Montclair, N.J.: Patterson Smith, 1969.

Friendly, Fred W., and Martha J. H. Elliott. *The Constitution: That Delicate Balance.* New York: McGraw-Hill, 1984.

Fridell, Lorie. *Community Policing: Past, Present, and Future.* Washington, D.C.: Police Executive Research Forum, 2004.

Fyfe, James J. "Shots Fired." Ph.D. diss., State University of New York, Albany, 1978.

Fyfe, James J., Jack R. Greene, William F. Walsh, O. W. Wilson, and Roy Clinton McLaren. *Police Administration,* 5th ed. New York: McGraw-Hill, 1997.

Gaines, Larry K., and Victor Kappeler. *Policing in America,* 4th ed. Cincinnati, Ohio: Anderson, 2003.

Gaines, Larry K., John L. Worrall, Mittie D. Southerland, and John E. Angell. *Police Administration,* 2nd ed. New York: McGraw-Hill, 2003.

Gallup, George, Jr., and Alex Gallup. *The Gallup Poll Monthly Number 420.* Princeton: N.J.: The Gallup Poll, 2003.

Gardiner, John A. *Traffic and the Police: Variations in Law Enforcement Policy.* Cambridge, Mass.: Harvard University Press, 1969.

Geffner, Edwin S. *The Internist's Compendium of Patient Information.* New York: McGraw-Hill, 1987.

Geller, William A., ed. *Police Leadership in America: Crisis and Opportunity.* New York: Praeger, 1985.

Geller, William A., and Kevin J. Karales. *Split-Second Decisions.* Chicago: Chicago Law Enforcement Study Group, 1981.

Geller, William, and Michael S. Scott. *Deadly Force: What We Know.* Washington, D.C.: Police Executive Research Forum, 1992.

Gerber, S., ed. *Chemistry and Crime.* Washington, D.C.: American Chemical Society, 1983.

Germann, A. C., Frank D. Day, and Robert R. J. Gallati. *Introduction to Law Enforcement and Criminal Justice.* Springfield, Ill.: Charles C. Thomas, 1969.

Gerth, Hans H., and C. Wright Mills eds. *Essays in Sociology* London: Oxford University Press, 1946 (renewed 1973 by Hans H. Gerth).

Gold, Marion E. *Top Cops: Profiles of Women in Command.* Chicago: Brittany, 1999.

Goldstein, Herman. *Police Corruption: A Perspective on Its Nature and Control.* Washington, D.C.: Police Foundation, 1975.

————. *Policing a Free Society.* Cambridge, Mass.: Ballinger, 1977.

————. *Problem-Oriented Policing.* New York: McGraw-Hill, 1990.

Gottfredson, Michael R., and Don M. Gottfredson. *Decision Making in Criminal Justice: Toward the Rational Exercise of Discretion.* Cambridge, Mass.: Ballinger Press, 1980.

Greene, Jack R., and Stephen D. Mastrofski. *Community Policing: Rhetoric or Reality?* New York: Praeger, 1988.

Greenwood, Peter W., and Joan Petersilia. *The Criminal Investigation Process, Volume I: Summary and Policy Implications.* Santa Monica, Calif.: Rand Corporation, 1975.

Hackett, Dell P., and John M. Violanti, eds. *Police Suicide: Tactics for Prevention.* Springfield, Ill.: Charles C. Thomas, 2003.

Hadden, Sally E. *Slave Patrols, Law and Violence in Virginia and the Carolinas.* Cambridge, Mass.: Harvard University Press, 2001.

Harris, Richard. *The Police Academy: An Inside View.* New York: Wiley, 1973.

Heaphy, John, ed. *Police Practices: The General Administrative Survey.* Washington, D.C.: Police Foundation, 1978.

Hemmens, Craig. *Current Legal Issues in Criminal Justice.* Los Angeles: Roxbury, 2007.

Hemmens, Craig, John L. Worrall, and Alan Thompson. *Significant Cases in Criminal Procedure.* Los Angeles: Roxbury, 2004.

Henry, Nicholas. *Public Administration and Public Affairs,* 9th ed. Upper Saddle River, N.J.: Pearson Education, 2004.

Henry, Vincent E. *The CompStat Paradigm: Management Accountability in Policing, Business and the Public Sector.* Flushing, N.Y.: Looseleaf Law, 2002.

Hickman, Matthew, Alex R. Piquero, and Jack R. Greene. *Police Integrity and Ethics.* Belmont, Calif.: Wadsworth, 2004.

Horan, James D., and Howard Swiggett. *The Pinkerton Story.* New York: Putnam, 1951.

————. *The Pinkertons: The Detective Dynasty That Made History.* New York: Crown, 1967.

Hoult, Thomas Ford. *Dictionary of Modern Sociology.* Totowa, N.J.: Littlefield, Adams, 1969.

Howell, James C., and Arlen Egley, Jr. *Gangs in Small Towns and Rural Counties.* Tallahassee, Fla.: National Youth Gang Center, 2005.

Hungerford, Edward. *Wells Fargo: Advancing the American Frontier.* New York: Bonanza, 1949.

Hunt, W. E. *History of England.* New York: Harper & Brothers, 1938.

Inciardi, James A. *Criminal Justice,* 3rd ed. Orlando, Fla.: Harcourt Brace Jovanovich, 1990.

International Association for Identification, American Society of Crime Lab Directors, American Academy of Forensic Sciences, and National Association of Medical Examiners.

Status and Needs of Forensic Science Service Providers: A Report to Congress. Washington, D.C.: National Institute of Justice, 2004.

International Association of Chiefs of Police. *HIV/AIDS Prevention: Concepts and Issues Paper.* Alexandria, Va.: International Association of Chiefs of Police, 2000.

———. *Improving Safety in Indian Country: Recommendations from the IACP 2001 Summit,* Alexandria, Va.: International Association of Chiefs of Police, 2001.

———. *Operational Issues in the Small Law Enforcement Agency.* Arlington, Va.: International Association of Chiefs of Police, 1990.

———. *A Survey of the Police Department of Youngstown, Ohio.* Washington, D.C.: International Association of Chiefs of Police, 1964.

Jacob, Herbert. *Urban Justice.* Boston: Little, Brown, 1973.

Jary, David, and Julia Jary. *The HarperCollins Dictionary of Sociology.* New York: HarperPerennial, 1991.

Johnson, David R. *American Law Enforcement: A History.* St. Louis: Forum Press, 1981.

Kadish, Sanford H. *Encyclopedia of Crime and Justice.* New York: Free Press, 1983.

Kappeler, Victor. *Critical Issues in Police Civil Liability,* 3rd ed. Prospect Heights, Ill.: Waveland Press, 2001.

Kappeler, Victor, Richard Sluder, and Geoffrey Alpert. *Forces of Deviance, Understanding the Dark Side of Policing.* Prospect Heights, Ill.: Waveland Press, 1994.

Kelling, George L., Tony Pate, Duane Dieckman, and Charles E. Brown. *The Kansas City Preventive Patrol Experiment: A Summary Report.* Washington, D.C.: Police Foundation, 1974.

Kenney, Dennis Jay, ed. *Police and Policing: Contemporary Issues.* New York: Praeger, 1989.

Kindschi-Gosselin, Denise. *Heavy Hands: An Introduction to the Crimes of Family Violence,* 2nd ed. Upper Saddle River, N.J.: Prentice Hall, 2003.

Kirkham, George L., and Laurin A. Wollan, Jr. *Introduction to Law Enforcement.* New York: Harper & Row, 1980.

Klingner, David, and J. Nalbandian. *Public Personnel Management: Contexts and Strategies.* Upper Saddle River, N.J.: Prentice Hall, 1988.

Klockars, Carl B., ed. *Idea of Police.* Thousand Oaks, Calif.: Sage, 1985.

———. *Thinking about Police: Contemporary Readings.* New York: McGraw-Hill, 1983.

Klockars, Carl B., and Stephen D. Mastrofski, eds. *Thinking about Police: Contemporary Readings,* 2nd ed. New York: McGraw-Hill, 1991.

Klotter, John C., Jacqueline R. Kanovitz, and Michael I. Kanovitz. *Constitutional Law,* 9th ed. Cincinnati, Ohio: Anderson, 2002.

Kluger, Richard. *Simple Justice.* New York: Vintage, 1977.

Knapp Commission. *Report on Police Corruption.* New York: Braziller, 1973.

Koon, Stacey C., and Robert Deitz. *Presumed Guilty: The Tragedy of the Rodney King Affair.* Washington, D.C.: Regnery Gateway, 1992.

Kurian, George Thomas. *World Encyclopedia of Police Forces and Penal Systems.* New York: Facts on File, 1989.

Lake, Carolyn. *Undercover for Wells Fargo.* Boston: Houghton Mifflin, 1969.

Lane, Roger. *Policing the City.* New York: Atheneum, 1975.

———. *Policing the City: Boston 1822–1885.* Cambridge, Mass.: Harvard University Press, 1967.

Leinen, Steven. *Black Police, White Society.* New York: New York University Press, 1984.

Lord, Vivian B. *Suicide by Cop: Inducing Officers to Shoot.* Flushing, N.Y.: Looseleaf Law, 2004.

Loving, Nancy. *Responding to Spouse Abuse and Wife Beating: A Guide for Police.* Washington, D.C.: Police Executive Research Forum, 1980.

Lundman, Richard J. *Police and Policing.* New York: Holt, Rinehart & Winston, 1980.

Lunneborg, Patricia. *Women Police: Portraits of Success.* New York: iUniverse, 2004.

Madonna, John M., Jr., and Richard E. Kelly. *Treating Police Stress: The Work and the Words of Peer Counselors.* Springfield, Ill.: Charles C. Thomas, 2002.

Manning, Peter K., and John Van Maanen. *Policing: A View from the Street.* Santa Monica, Calif.: Goodyear, 1978.

Maas, Peter. *Serpico.* New York: Bantam Books, 1974.

Mayhew, Claire. *Occupational Health and Safety Risks Faced by Police Officers.* Canberra ACT: Australian Institute of Criminology, 2001.

McAdam, Doug. *Freedom Summer.* New York: Oxford University Press, 1988.

McAlary, Mike. *Buddy Boys: When Good Cops Turn Bad.* New York: Putnam, 1987.

McCamey, William P., Gene L. Scaramella, and Steven M. Cox. *Contemporary Municipal Policing.* Boston: Allyn & Bacon, 2003.

McCrie, Robert D. ed. *Security Letter Source Book.* New York: Security Letter, published annually.

Miller, John, and Michael Stone with Chris Mitchell. *The Cell: Inside the 9/11 Plot, Why the FBI and CIA Failed to Stop It.* New York: Hyperion, 2002.

Miller, Laurence. *Practical Police Psychology: Stress Management and Crisis Intervention for Law Enforcement.* Springfield, Ill.: Charles C. Thomas, 2006.

Miller, Linda S., and Karen M. Hess. *The Police in the Community: Strategies for the 21st Century,* 3rd ed. Belmont, Calif.: Wadsworth, 2002.

Miller, Wilbur R. *Cops and Bobbies: Police Authority in New York and London, 1830–1870.* Chicago: University of Chicago Press, 1977.

Milton, Catherine H., Jeanne Wahl Halleck, James Lardner, and Gary L. Abrecht. *Police Use of Deadly Force.* Washington, D.C.: Police Foundation, 1977.

Moenssens, Andre A., Fred E. Inbau, James Starrs, and Carol E. Henderson. *Scientific Evidence in Civil and Criminal Cases,* 4th ed. Mineola, N.Y.: Foundation Press, 1995.

Monkkonen, Eric. *Police in Urban America: 1860–1920.* Cambridge, Mass.: Harvard University Press, 1981.

Monkkonen, Eric, ed., *Crime and Justice in American History: The South.* Munich: K. G. Saur, 1992.

Morgan, Edward P. *The 60's Experience: Hard Lessons about Modern America.* Philadelphia: Temple University Press, 1991.

Mouzos, Jenny. *Investigating Homicide: New Responses for an Old Crime.* Canberra ACT, Australia: Australian Institute of Criminology, 2001.

Muir, William K., Jr. *Police: Streetcorner Politicians.* Chicago: University of Chicago Press, 1977.

Nash, Jay Robert. *Encyclopedia of World Crime.* Wilmette, Ill.: Crime Books, 1990.

National Commission on Terrorist Attacks upon the United States. *911 Commission Report: The Final Report of the*

National Commission on Terrorist Attacks upon the United States. New York: Norton, 2004.

Niederhoffer, Arthur. *Behind the Shield: The Police in Urban Society*. Garden City, N.Y.: Doubleday, 1967.

Nichols, Laura J. *Use of CCTV/Video Cameras in Law Enforcement, Executive Brief*. Alexandria, Va.: International Association of Chiefs of Police, 2001.

Nicholson, William C., ed. *Homeland Security Law and Policy*. Springfield, Ill.: Charles C. Thomas, 2005.

Nguyen, H. G., and J. P. Bott. *Robotics for Law Enforcement: Beyond Explosive Ordinance Disposal*. San Diego, Calif.: SPAWAR Systems Center, 2000.

O'Donnell, Kenneth. *Deadly Force*. New York: William Morrow, 1983.

O'Hara, Patrick. *Why Law Enforcement Organizations Fail: Mapping the Organizational Fault Lines in Policing*. Durham, N.C.: Carolina Academic Press, 2005.

Osterburg, James W., and Richard H. Ward. *Criminal Investigation: A Method for Reconstructing the Past*. Cincinnati, Ohio: Anderson, 1992.

Osterholm, Michael T., and John Schwartz. *Living Terrors*. New York: Delta, 2000.

Owings, Chloe. *Women Police*. Montclair, N.J.: Patterson Smith, 1969. Original edition, 1925.

Palmiotto, Michael J., ed. *Critical Issues in Criminal Justice*. Cincinnati, Ohio: Anderson, 1988.

———. *Police Misconduct: A Reader for the 21st Century*. Upper Saddle River, N.J.: Prentice Hall, 2001.

Palombo, B. J. *Academic Professionalism in Law Enforcement*. New York: Garland, 1995.

Paoline, Eugene A. III. *Rethinking Police Culture: Officers' Occupational Attitudes*. New York: LFB Scholarly, 2001.

Peak, Kenneth. *Policing America: Methods, Issues, Challenges*, 5th ed. Upper Saddle River, N.J.: Prentice Hall, 2006.

Perez, Douglas W., and J. Alan Moore. *Police Ethics: A Matter of Character*. Belmont, Calif.: Wadsworth, 2002.

Pike, Owen. *A History of Crime in England*. London: Smith, Elder, 1873–1876.

Pilant, Lois. *Less-Than-Lethal-Weapons: New Solutions for Law Enforcement*. Alexandria, Va.: International Association of Chiefs of Police, 2000.

Pinkerton, Allan. *The Expressman and the Detective*. New York: Arno Press, 1976.

Police Executive Research Forum. *Managing a Multijurisdictional Case: Identifying Lessons Learned from the Sniper Investigation*. Washington, D.C.: Police Executive Research Forum, 2005.

Police Foundation. *Experiments in Police Improvement: A Progress Report*. Washington, D.C.: Police Foundation, 1972.

Pollock, Jocelyn M. *Ethics in Crime and Justice: Dilemmas and Decisions*, 4th ed. Belmont, Calif.: Wadsworth, 2004.

Poveda, Tony. *Lawlessness and Reform: The FBI in Transition*. Pacific Grove, Calif.: Brooks/Cole, 1990.

Prassel, Frank R. *The Western Peace Officer: A Legacy of Law and Order*. Norman: University of Oklahoma Press, 1972.

Press, S. J. *Some Effects of an Increase in Police Manpower in the 20th Precinct of New York*. New York: Rand Institute, 1971.

Pringle, Patrick. *Highwaymen*. New York: Roy, 1963.

———. *Hue and Cry: The Story of Henry and John Fielding and Their Bow Street Runners*. New York: Morrow, 1965.

———. *The Thief Takers*. London: Museum Press, 1958.

Punch, Maurice, ed. *Control of the Police Organization*. Cambridge, Mass.: MIT Press, 1983.

Radiznowciz, Sir Leon. *A History of English Criminal Law and Its Administration from 1750*, 4 vols. London: Stevens & Sons, 1948–1968.

Ragle, Larry. *Crime Scene*. New York: Avon, 1995.

Rand Corporation. *Organizing for Homeland Security*. Santa Monica: Calif.: Rand, 2002.

Radelet, Louis A. *The Police and the Community*. Encino, Calif.: Glencoe, 1980.

Reid, Sue Titus. *Criminal Justice*, 3rd ed. New York: Macmillan, 1993.

Reiss, Albert J. *The Police and the Public*. New Haven, Conn.: Yale University Press, 1971.

Reith, Charles. *The Blind Eye of History: A Study of the Origins of the Present Police Era*. London: Faber, 1912.

———. *A New Study of Police History*. London: Oliver & Boyd, 1956.

Reppetto, Thomas. *The Blue Parade*. New York: Free Press, 1978.

Richardson, James F. *The New York Police: Colonial Times to 1901*. New York: Oxford University Press, 1976.

———. *Urban Police in the United States*. Port Washington, N.Y.: Kennikat Press, 1974.

Rieck, Albert. *Justice and Police in England*. London: Butterworth, 1936.

Riley, K. Jack, Gregory F. Treverton, Jeremy M. Wilson, and Lois M. Davis. *State and Local Intelligence in the War on Terrorism*. Santa Monica: Calif.: Rand, 2005.

Roth, M.P. *Crime and Punishment: A History of the Criminal Justice System*. Belmont, Calif.: Thomson/Wadsworth, 2005.

Rubenstein, Jonathan. *City Police*. New York: Farrar, Straus and Giroux, 1973.

Rush, George E. *The Dictionary of Criminal Justice*, 4th ed. Guilford, Conn.: Dushkin, 1994.

Saferstein, Richard. *Criminalistics: An Introduction to Forensic Science*, 7th ed. Upper Saddle River, N.J.: Pearson Prentice Hall, 2001.

———. *Criminalistics: An Introduction to Forensic Science*, 8th ed. Upper Saddle River, N.J.: Pearson Prentice Hall, 2004.

Salerno, Charles A. *Police at the Bargaining Table*. Springfield, Ill.: Charles C. Thomas, 1981.

Sante, Luc. *Low Life: Lures and Snares of Old New York*. New York: Farrar, Straus & Giroux, 1991.

Santoro, Joseph. *DARE Works: A Police Chief's Perspective*. Los Angeles: DARE America, 2002.

Scarborough, Melanie. *The Security Pretext: An Examination of the Growth of Federal Police Agencies*. Washington, D.C.: Cato Institute, 2005.

Schmalleger, Frank. *Criminal Justice Today: An Introductory Text for the Twenty-First Century*, 9th ed. Englewood Cliffs, N.J.: Prentice Hall, 2007.

Schulz, Dorothy Moses. *From Social Worker to Crimefighter: Women in United States Municipal Policing*. Westport, Conn.: Praeger, 1995.

Schulz, Dorothy Moses. *Breaking the Brass Ceiling: Women Police Chiefs and their Paths to the Top*. Westport, Conn.: Praeger, 2004.

Shaffer, Ron, Kevin Klose, and Alfred E. Lewis. *Surprise! Surprise!* New York: Viking, 1979.

Sheehan, Robert, and Gary W. Cordner. *Introduction to Police Administration*. Cincinnati, Ohio: Anderson, 1989, 1995.

Sherman, Lawrence W. *Repeat Calls to Police in Minneapolis*. Washington, D.C.: Crime Control Institute, 1987.

———, ed. *Police Corruption: A Sociological Perspective*. Garden City, N.Y.: Doubleday, 1974.

Sherman, Lawrence W., and Richard A. Berk. *The Minneapolis Domestic Violence Experiment.* Washington, D.C.: Police Foundation, 1984.

Sherman, Lawrence W., and the National Advisory Commission on Higher Education for Police Officers. *The Quality of Police Education.* San Francisco: Jossey-Bass, 1978.

Silberman, Charles. *Criminal Violence, Criminal Justice.* New York: Vintage Books, 1978.

Siegel, Larry J., and Joseph J. Senna. *Essentials of Criminal Justice,* 5th ed. Belmont, Calif.: Wadsworth, 2007.

———. *Introduction to Criminal Justice,* 10th ed. Belmont, Calif.: Thomson/Wadsworth, 2005.

Siringo, Charles A. *A Cowboy Detective: A True Story of Twenty-Two Years with a World Famous Detective Agency.* Lincoln: University of Nebraska Press, 1988.

Skogan, Wesley G. *Disorder and Decline: Crime and the Spiral of Decay in American Neighborhoods.* New York: Free Press, 1990.

Skolnick, Jerome H. *Justice without Trial: Law Enforcement in a Democratic Society,* 2nd ed. New York: Wiley, 1966.

———. *Justice without Trial: Law Enforcement in a Democratic Society.* New York: Wiley, 1975.

Skolnick, Jerome H., and David H. Bayley. *The New Blue Line: Police Innovation in Six American Cities.* New York: Free Press, 1986.

Skolnick, Jerome H., and James J. Fyfe. *Above the Law: Police and the Excessive Use of Force.* New York: Free Press, 1993.

Smith, Bruce. *Police Systems in the United States,* 2nd ed. New York: Harper & Row, 1960.

———. *Rural Crime Control.* New York: Columbia University Institute of Public Administration, 1933.

Sonkin, Daniel J., and Michael Durphy. *Learning to Live Without Violence: A Handbook for Men,* 5th ed. Volcano, Calif.: Volcano Press, 1997.

Sparrow, Malcolm, Mark Moore, and David Kennedy. *Beyond 911: A New Era for Policing.* New York: Basic Books, 1990.

Spelman, William, and D. K. Brown. *Calling the Police: Citizen Reporting of Serious Crime.* Washington, D.C.: Police Executive Research Forum, 1981.

Spitz, Werner U., ed. *Medicolegal Investigation of Death,* 3rd ed. Springfield, Ill.: Charles C. Thomas, 1993.

Staufenberger, Richard A. *Progress in Policing: Essays on Change.* Cambridge, Mass.: Ballinger, 1980.

Stead, Philip J. *The Police of Paris.* London: Staples, 1957.

Steffens, Lincoln. *The Autobiography of Lincoln Steffens.* New York: Harcourt Brace Jovanovich, 1958. Original edition, 1931.

———. *The Shame of the Cities.* New York: Hill and Wang, 1957; original edition, 1902.

Stevens, Dennis J. *Applied Community Policing in the 21st Century.* Boston: Allyn & Bacon, 2003.

Swanson, Charles R., Leonard Territo, and Robert W. Taylor. *Police Administration: Structures, Processes, and Behavior,* 2nd ed. New York: Macmillan, 1988.

———. *Police Administration,* 5th ed. Upper Saddle River: N.J.: Prentice Hall, 2001.

Taylor, B., B. Kubu, L. Fridell, C. Rees, T. Jordan, and J. Cheney. *Cop Crunch: Identifying Strategies for Dealing with the Recruiting and Hiring Crisis in Law Enforcement.* Washington, D.C.: U.S. Department of Justice, National Institute of Justice, 2005.

Theoharis, Athan, and John Stuart Cox. *The Boss.* Philadelphia: Temple University Press, 1988.

Thibault, Edward A., Lawrence M. Lynch, and R. Bruce McBride. *Proactive Police Management.* Englewood Cliffs, N.J.: Prentice-Hall, 1985.

———. *Proactive Police Management,* 6th ed. Englewood Cliffs, N.J.: Prentice Hall, 2003.

Thompson, R. Alan. *Career Experiences of African American Police Executives: Black in Blue Revisited.* New York: LFB Scholarly, 2003.

Thompson, Victor A. *Modern Organization.* New York: Knopf, 1961.

Tien, James M., James W. Simon, and Richard C. Larson. *An Alternative Approach in Police Patrol: The Wilmington Split-Force Experiment.* Cambridge, Mass.: Public Systems Evaluation, 1977.

Tobias, John J. *Crime and Police in England, 1700–1900.* New York: St. Martin's Press, 1979.

Trojanowicz, Robert C., and Dennis W. Banas. *The Impact of Foot Patrol on Black and White Perceptions of Policing.* East Lansing: National Neighborhood Foot Patrol Center, School of Criminal Justice, Michigan State University, 1988.

Violanti, John M., and Douglas Paton, eds. *Who Gets PTSD?: Issues of Posttraumatic Stress Vulnerability.* Springfield, Ill.: Charles C. Thomas, 2006.

Viorst, Milton. *Fire in the Streets: America in the 1960's.* New York: Simon & Schuster, 1970.

Visionics Corporation. *Adaptive Surveillance: A Novel Approach to Facial Surveillance for CCTV Systems, Final Progress Report.* Jersey City, N.J.: Visionics Corporation, 2001.

Wadman, Robert C., and William Thomas Allison. *To Protect and to Serve: A History of Police in America.* Upper Saddle River, N.J.: Pearson/Prentice Hall, 2004.

Walker, Samuel. *A Critical History of Police Reform: The Emergence of Professionalism.* Lexington, Mass.: Lexington Books, 1977.

———. *The Police in America: An Introduction,* 2nd ed. New York: McGraw-Hill, 1992.

———. *The Police in America: An Introduction,* 3rd ed. New York: McGraw-Hill, 1999.

———. *Popular Justice: History of American Criminal Justice.* New York: Oxford University Press, 1980.

———. *Sense and Nonsense about Crime.* Monterey, Calif.: Brooks/Cole, 1985.

Walker, Samuel, and Vic Bumphus. *A National Survey of Civilian Oversight of the Police.* Omaha: University of Nebraska at Omaha, 1991.

Walker, Samuel, and Charles M. Katz. *Police in America: An Introduction,* 5th ed. New York: McGraw-Hill, 2005.

Wambaugh, Joseph. *The Blooding.* New York: William Morrow, 1989.

Webb, Walter Prescott. *The Texas Rangers: A Century of Frontier Defense.* Boston: Houghton Mifflin, 1935.

Weiner, Norman. *The Role of Police in Urban Society: Conflict and Consequences.* Indianapolis: Bobbs-Merrill, 1976.

Wells, Sandra K., and Betty L. Alt. *Policewomen: Life with the Badge.* Westport, Conn.: Praeger, 2005.

West, J. A. *Facial Identification Technology and Law Enforcement.* Sacramento, Calif.: California Commission on Peace Officer Standards and Training, 1996.

Westley, William. *Violence and the Police: A Sociological Study of Law, Custom, and Morality.* Cambridge, Mass.: MIT Press, 1970.

White, Jonathan R. *Terrorism and Homeland Security,* 5th ed. Belmont, Calif.: Wadsworth, 2006.

Willbanks, William. *The Myth of a Racist Criminal Justice System*. Monterey, Calif.: Brooks/Cole, 1987.

Williams, Juan. *Eyes on the Prize: America's Civil Rights Years, 1954–1965*. New York: Penguin, 1983.

Wilson, James Q. *Thinking about Crime*, rev. ed. New York: Basic Books, 1985.

———. *Varieties of Police Behavior: The Management of Law and Order in Eight Communities*. Cambridge, Mass.: Harvard University Press, 1968.

Wilson, O. W. *Police Administration*. New York: McGraw-Hill, 1950.

Wilson, O. W., and Roy Clinton McLaren. *Police Administration*, 4th ed. New York: McGraw-Hill, 1977.

Woodward, John D., Jr. *Privacy vs. Security: Electronic Surveillance in the Nation's Capital* (Santa Monica, Calif.: Rand Corporation, 2002.

Wycoff, Mary Ann, et al. *Citizen Contact Patrol: Executive Summary*. Washington, D.C.: Police Foundation, 1985.

Government Reports

ABT Associates. *New York City Anti-Crime Patrol: Exemplary Project Validation Report*. Washington, D.C.: U.S. Department of Justice, 1974.

Alpert, Geoffrey P., Dunham, Roger G., Stroshine, Meghan, Bennett, Katherine, and MacDonald, John. *Police Officers' Decision Making and Discretion: Forming Suspicion and Making a Stop* Washington, D.C.: National Institute of Justice, 2006.

Ashcroft, John. *A Resource Guide to Law Enforcement, Corrections and Forensic Technologies*. Washington, D.C.: U.S. Department of Justice, 2001.

Bayley, David H., and Clifford D. Shearing. *The New Structure of Policing: Description, Conceptualization and Research Agenda*. Washington, D.C.: National Institute of Justice, 2001.

Brown, Jodi M., and Patrick A. Langan, *Policing and Homicide, 1976–1998: Justifiable Homicide by Police, Police Officers Murdered by Felons*. Washington, D.C.: National Institute of Justice, 2001.

Bureau of Indian Affairs, Division of Law Enforcement. *Indian Law Enforcement History*. Washington, D.C.: U.S. Government Printing Office, 1975.

Bureau of Justice Statistics, *Law Enforcement Management and Administrative Statistics, 2000*. Washington, D.C.: Government Printing Office, 2004.

Button, Peter D. *Less-Lethal Force Technology*. Toronto: Toronto Metropolitan Police Commission, 2001.

California Highway Patrol. *Pursuit Study*. Sacramento, Calif.: California Highway Patrol, 1993.

Calvert, Geoffrey N. *Portable Police Pensions—Improving Inter-Agency Transfers*. Washington, D.C.: U.S. Government Printing Office, 1971.

Caplan, Marc H., and Joe Holt Anderson. *Forensic: When Science Bears Witness*. Washington, D.C.: National Institute of Justice, 1984.

Carter, David L. *Community Policing and DARE: A Practitioner's Perspective*. Washington, D.C.: National Institute of Justice, 1995.

Caskey, C. Thomas, and Holly A. Hammond. *Automated DNA Typing: Method of the Future?* Washington, D.C.: National Institute of Justice, 1997.

Cawley, Donald F., H. J. Miron, W. J. Aranjo, R. Wassserman, T. A. Mannello, and Y. Huffman. *Managing Criminal Investigations: Manual*. Washington, D.C.: U.S. Government Printing Office, 1977.

Chaiken, Marcia, and Jan Chaiken. *Priority Prosecutors of High-Rate Dangerous Offenders*. Washington, D.C.: National Institute of Justice, 1991.

———. *Public Policing—Privately Provided*. Washington, D.C.: National Institute of Justice, 1987.

Chainey, Spencer, and Chloe Smith. *Review of GIS-based Information Sharing Systems*. London: Great Britain Home Office Research Development and Statistics, 2006.

Chipman, David, and Cynthia E. Pappas. *Violent Crime Impact Teams (VCIT) Initiative: Focus on Partnerships*. Washington, D.C.: National Institute of Justice, 2006.

Commission on Accreditation for Law Enforcement Agencies. *Standards for Law Enforcement Agencies*. Fairfax, Va.: Commission on Accreditation for Law Enforcement Agencies, 1987.

Connors, Edward, T. Lundregan, N.B. Miller, and T. McEwen. *Convicted by Juries, Exonerated by Science: Case Studies in the Use of DNA Evidence to Establish Innocence after Trial*. Washington, D.C.: National Institute of Justice, 1996.

Cunningham, William C., John J. Strauchs, and Clifford W. Van Meter. *Private Security: Patterns and Trends*. Washington, D.C.: U.S. Government Printing Office, 1991.

Cunningham, William C., and Todd H. Taylor. *The Growing Role of Private Security*. Washington, D.C.: National Institute of Justice, 1984.

DeJong, William. *Project DARE: Teaching Kids to Say "No" to Drugs and Alcohol*. Washington, D.C.: National Institute of Justice, 1986.

Donnelly, T. *Less Lethal Technologies: Initial Prioritisation and Evaluation*. London: Great Britain Home Office, Policing and Reducing Crime Unit, 2001.

Durose, Matthew R., Erica L. Schmitt, and Patrick A. Langan. *Contacts between Police and the Public: Findings from the 2002 National Survey*. Washington, D.C.: Bureau of Justice Statistics, 2005.

Executive Office of the President of the United States. *Advancing Justice through DNA Technology*. Washington, D.C.: National Institute of Justice, 2003.

Federal Bureau of Investigation. *Law Enforcement Officers Feloniously Killed and Assaulted*. Washington, D.C.: Federal Bureau of Investigation, published annually.

———. *Uniform Crime Reports: Crime in the United States*. Washington, D.C.: Federal Bureau of Investigation, published annually.

Finn, Peter, *Street People: Crime File Study Guide*. Washington, D.C.: National Institute of Justice, 1988.

Finn, Peter E., and Julie Esselman Tomz. *Developing a Law Enforcement Stress Program for Officers and Their Families*. Washington, D.C.: National Institute of Justice, 1997.

Garner, Joel H., and Christopher D. Maxwell. *Understanding the Prevalence and Severity of Force Used by and against the Police, Executive Summary*. Washington, D.C.: National Institute of Justice, 2002.

———. *Understanding the Prevalence and Severity of Force Used by and against the Police, Final Report*. Washington, D.C.: National Institute of Justice, 2002.

Garofalo, James, and Maureen McLeod. *Improving the Use and Effectiveness of Neighborhood Watch Programs*. Washington, D.C.: National Institute of Justice, 1988.

Gay, William G., Theodore H. Schell, and Steven Schack. *Routine Patrol: Improve Patrol Productivity*, vol. 1. Washington, D.C.: National Institute of Justice, 1977.

Gill, Martin, and Angela Spriggs. *Assessing the Impact of CCTV.* London: Great Britain Home Office Research Development and Statistics Directorate, 2005.

Greenberg, Ilene, and Robert Wasserman. *Managing Criminal Investigations.* Washington, D.C.: U.S. Government Printing Office, 1979.

Greenfeld, Lawrence A. Patrick A. Langan, and Steven K Smith. *Police Use of Force: Collection of National Data.* Washington, D.C.: Bureau of Justice Statistics, 1997.

Griesinger, George W., Jeffrey S. Slovak, and Joseph J. Molkup. *Civil Service Systems: Their Impact on Police Administration.* Washington, D.C.: U.S. Government Printing Office, 1979.

Giuliani, Rudolph W., Randy M. Mastro, and Donna Lynn. *Mayor's Management Report: The City of New York.* New York: City of New York, 1997.

Halper, Andrew, and Richard Ku. *New York City Police Department Street Crime Unit.* Washington, D.C.: National Institute of Justice, n.d.

Hammett, Theodore M. *AIDS and the Law Enforcement Officer: Concerns and Policy Responses.* Washington, D.C.: National Institute of Justice, 1987.

———. *Precautionary Measures and Protective Equipment: Developing a Reasonable Response.* Washington, D.C.: National Institute of Justice, 1988.

Hammett, Theodore M., and Walter Bond. *Risks of Infection with the AIDS Virus through Exposures to Blood: National Institute of Justice AIDS Bulletin.* Washington, D.C.: National Institute of Justice, 1987.

Harries, Keith. *Mapping Crime: Principle and Practice.* Washington, D.C.: National Institute of Justice, 1999.

Hecker, JayEtta. *Homeland Security: Intergovernmental Coordination and Partnership Will Be Critical to Success.* Washington, D.C.: General Accounting Office, 2002.

Hickman, Matthew J. *Citizen Complaints about Police Use of Force.* Washington, D.C.: Bureau of Justice Statistics, 2006.

Hickman, Matthew J., and Brian A. Reaves. *Local Police Departments 1999.* Washington, D.C.: Bureau of Justice Statistics, 2001.

———. *Local Police Departments, 2000.* Washington D.C.: Bureau of Justice Statistics, 2003.

———. *Local Police Departments 2003.* Washington, D.C.: Bureau of Justice Statistics, 2006.

———. *Sheriffs' Offices, 2003.* Washington, D.C.: Bureau of Justice Statistics, 2006.

———. *State and Local Law Enforcement Training Academies, 2002.* Washington, D.C.: Bureau of Justice Statistics, 2004.

Horney, Julie, ed. *Policies, Processes, and Decisions of the Criminal Justice System.* Washington, D.C.: National Institute of Justice, 2000.

Howell, James C., and Arlen Egley, Jr. *Gangs in Small Towns and Rural Counties.* Washington, D.C.: Office of Juvenile Justice and Delinquency Prevention, U.S. Department of Justice, 2005.

Hughes, Kristen A. *Justice Expenditures and Employment in the United States, 2003.* Washington, D.C.: Bureau of Justice Statistics, 2006.

Kansas City Police Department. *Response Time Analysis: Executive Summary.* Washington, D.C.: U.S. Government Printing Office, 1978.

Kelling, George L. *"Broken Windows" and Police Discretion.* Washington, D.C. National Institute of Justice, 1999.

———. *Foot Patrol.* Washington, D.C.: National Institute of Justice, 1988.

———. *Police and Communities: The Quiet Revolution. Perspectives on Policing, no. 1.* Washington, D.C.: National Institute of Justice, 1988.

———. *What Works? Research and the Police.* Washington, D.C.: National Institute of Justice, n.d.

Klaus, Patsy. *Crime and the Nation's Households, 2004.* Washington, D.C.: National Institute of Justice, 2006.

Klockars, Carl B., Sanja Kutnjak Ivkovich, and Maria R. Haberfield. *Enhancing Police Integrity.* Washington, D.C.: National Institute of Justice, 2005.

Koper, C. S. *Hiring and Keeping Police Officers.* Washington, D.C.: National Institute of Justice, 2004.

Langan, Patrick A., Erica L. Schmitt, and Matthew R. Durose. *Contacts between Police and the Public: Findings from the 2002 National Survey.* Washington, D.C.: Bureau of Justice Statistics, 2005.

Levesley, Tom, and Amanda Martin. *Police Attitudes to and Use of CCTV.* London: Great Britain Home Office Research Development and Statistics Directorate, 2005.

Lovrich, Nicolas P., Michael J. Gaffney, Travis C. Pratt, Charles L. Johnson. *National Forensic DNA Study Report.* Washington, D.C.: National Institute of Justice, 2003.

Mazerolle, Lorraine, Dennis Rogan, James Frank, Christine Famega, and John E. Eck. *Managing Calls to the Police with 911/311 Systems.* Washington, D.C.: National Institute of Justice, 2005.

Moore, Mark H., and Robert C. Trojanowitz. *Corporate Strategies for Policing. Perspectives on Policing, no. 6.* Washington, D.C.: National Institute of Justice, 1988.

National Advisory Commission on Civil Disorders. *Report of the National Advisory Commission on Civil Disorders.* New York: Bantam Books, 1968.

National Advisory Commission on Criminal Justice Standards and Goals. *Police.* Washington, D.C.: U.S. Government Printing Office, 1973.

National Advisory Commission on Criminal Justice Standards and Goals. *Report of the Task Force on Private Security.* Washington, D.C.: U.S. Government Printing Office, 1976.

National Center for Victims of Crime. *A Police Guide to First Response: Domestic Violence, Residential Burglary and Automobile Theft.* Washington, D.C.: U.S. Department of Justice, 2002.

National Commission on the Future of DNA Testing. *The Future of Forensic DNA Testing: Predictions of the Research and Development Working Group.* Washington, D.C.: National Institute of Justice, 2000.

———. *What Every Law Enforcement Officer Should Know About DNA Evidence.* Washington, D.C.: National Institute of Justice, 2000.

National Commission on Law Observance and Enforcement. *Lawlessness in Law Enforcement.* Washington, D.C.: U.S. Government Printing Office, 1931.

———. *Report on Police.* Washington, D.C.: U.S. Government Printing Office, 1931.

National Criminal Justice Reference Service. *Program for the Reduction of Stress for New York City Police Officers and Their Families, Final Report.* Washington, D.C.: National Criminal Justice Reference Service, 1998.

National Institute of Law Enforcement and Criminal Justice. *Controlling Police Corruption: The Effects of Reform Policies, Summary Report.* Washington, D.C.: U.S. Department of Justice, 1978.

———. *Employing Civilians for Police Work.* Washington, D.C.: U.S. Government Printing Office, 1975.

National Institute of Justice, *Mass Fatality Incidents: A Guide for Human Forensic Identification.* Washington, D.C.: National Institute of Justice, 2006.

———. *Police Use of Deadly Force.* Washington, D.C.: National Institute of Justice, 1978.

———. *Understanding DNA Evidence: A Guide for Victim Service Providers.* Washington, D.C.: National Institute of Justice, 2001.

Oettmeier, Timothy, and Mary Ann Wycoff. *Personnel Performance Evaluations in the Community Policing Context.* Washington, D.C.: National Institute of Justice, 2006.

Petty, Charles S. *Deaths in Police Confrontations When Oleoresin Capsicum Is Used.* Washington, D.C.: National Institute of Justice, 2002.

Perry, Steven W. *Census of Tribal Justice Agencies in Indian Country, 2002.* Washington, D.C.: National Institute of Justice, 2005.

Peterson, Joseph L. *Use of Forensic Evidence by the Police and Courts.* Washington, D.C.: National Institute of Justice, 1987.

Peterson, Joseph L. and Matthew J. Hickman. *Census of Publicly Funded Forensic Crime Laboratories, 2002.* Washington, D.C.: National Institute of Justice, 2005.

Police Department of Kansas City. *1966 Survey of Municipal Police Departments.* Kansas City, Mo.: Police Department of Kansas City, 1966.

President's Commission on Crime in the District of Columbia. *A Report on the President's Commission on Crime in the District of Columbia.* Washington, D.C.: U.S. Government Printing Office, 1966.

President's Commission on Law Enforcement and Administration of Justice. *The Challenge of Crime in a Free Society.* Washington, D.C.: U.S. Government Printing Office, 1967.

———. *Task Force Report: The Police.* Washington, D.C.: U.S. Government Printing Office, 1967.

———. *Task Force Report: Science and Technology.* Washington, D.C.: U.S. Government Printing Office, 1967.

Radiznowciz, Sir Leon. *A History of English Criminal Law and Its Administration from 1750,* 4 vols. London: Stevens & Sons, 1948–68.

Reaves, Brian A., and Lynne M. Bauer. *Federal Law Enforcement Officers, 2002.* Washington, D.C.: Bureau of Justice Statistics, 2003.

Reaves, Brian A., and Mathew Hickman. *Police Departments in Large Cities, 1990–2000.* Washington, D.C.: Bureau of Justice Statistics, 2002.

———. *Census of State and Local Law Enforcement Agencies, 2000.* Washington, D.C.: Bureau of Justice Statistics, 2002.

Reiner, G. H., T. J. Sweeney, R. V. Waymire, F. A. Newton III, R. G. Grassie, S. M. White, and W. D. Wallace. *Integrated Criminal Apprehension Program: Crime Analysis Operations Manual.* Washington, D.C.: Law Enforcement Assistance Administration, 1977.

Rennison, Callie Marie, and Sarah Welchans. *Intimate Partner Violence.* Washington, D.C.: U.S. Department of Justice, 2000.

Riley, Kevin, and Bruce Hoffman. *Domestic Terrorism: A National Assessment of State and Local Law Enforcement Preparedness.* Santa Monica, Calif.: Rand Corporation, National Institute of Justice, 1995.

Reiss, Albert. *Private Employment of Public Police.* Washington, D.C.: National Institute of Justice, 1988.

Rosenbaum, Dennis P., Arthur J. Lurigio, and Paul J. Lavrakas. *Crime Stoppers: A National Evaluation.* Washington, D.C.: National Institute of Justice, 1986.

Roth, Jeffrey A., and Joseph F. Ryan. *The COPS Program after 4 Years: National Evaluation, Research in Brief.* Washington, D.C.: National Institute of Justice, 2000.

Safir, Howard. *The Compstat Process.* New York: New York City Police Department, n.d.

Scrivner, E. *Innovations in Police Recruitment & Hiring: Hiring in the Spirit of Service.* Washington, D.C.: U.S. Department of Justice, 2006, NCJ#212981.

Seattle Police Department. *Annual Report.* Seattle: Seattle Police Department, issued annually.

Sheehan, Donald C., and Janet I. Warren, eds. *Suicide and Law Enforcement.* Washington, D.C.: Federal Bureau of Investigation, 2001.

Sherman, Lawrence, James Shaw, and Dennis Rogan. *The Kansas City Gun Experiment.* Washington, D.C.: National Institute of Justice, 1994.

Sichel, Joyce, Lucy N. Friedman, Janet C. Quint, and Michael E. Smith. *Women on Patrol: A Pilot Study of Police Performance in New York City.* Washington, D.C.: Department of Justice, 1978.

Spriggs, Angela, Javier Argomaniz, Martin Gill, and Jane Bryan. *Public Attitudes towards CCTV: Results from the Pre-Intervention Public Attitude Survey Carried Out in Areas Implementing CCTV.* London: Great Britain Home Office Research Development and Statistics Directorate, 2005.

Tilly, Nicholas. *Understanding Car Parks, Crime and CCTV: Evaluation Lessons from Safer Cities: Crime Prevention Unit Paper 42.* London: Home Office, 1993.

Toch, Hans. *Stress in Policing.* Washington, D.C.: National Institute of Justice, 2002.

U.S. Bureau of Census. *Census of Population.* Washington, D.C.: U.S. Bureau of Census, published every ten years.

U.S. Commission on Civil Rights. *Who Is Guarding the Guardians? A Report on Police Practices.* Washington, D.C.: U.S. Government Printing Office, 1981.

U.S. Congress, Congressional Budget Office. *Homeland Security and the Private Sector.* Washington, D.C.: U.S. Congress, Congressional Budget Office, 2004.

U.S. Congress, Office of Technology Assessment. *Criminal Justice: New Technologies and the Constitution: A Special Report.* Washington, D.C.: U.S. Government Printing Office, 1988.

U.S. Department of Justice. *Civil Service Systems: Affirmative Action and Equal Employment: A Guidebook for Employers.* Washington, D.C.: U.S. Government Printing Office, 1974.

———. *Criminal Victimization in the United States.* Washington, D.C.: National Institute of Justice, published annually.

U.S. Department of Justice, National Institute of Justice. *American Indians and Crime: A BJS Statistical Profile, 1992–2002.* Washington, D.C.: U.S. Department of Justice, 2004.

———. *Assessing and Managing the Terrorism Threat.* Washington, D.C.: National Institute of Justice, 2005.

———. *Community Policing Impacts 86% of U.S. Population Served by Local Police Departments.* Washington, D.C.: National Institute of Justice, 2001.

———. *Crime Scene Investigation: A Guide for Law Enforcement.* Washington, D.C.: National Institute of Justice, 2000.

———. *Crime Scene Investigation: A Reference for Law Enforcement Training.* Washington, D.C.: National Institute of Justice, 2004.

———. *The DARE Program: A Review of Prevalence, User Satisfaction, and Effectiveness.* Washington, D.C.: National Institute of Justice, 1994.

———. *The Effects of the Exclusionary Rule: A Study of California.* Washington, D.C.: National Institute of Justice, 1982.

———. *Evaluating GREAT: A School-based Gang Prevention Program*. Washington, D.C.: National Institute of Justice, 2004.

———. *GPS Applications in Law Enforcement: The Sky-Tracker Surveillance System, Final Report*. Washington, D.C.: National Institute of Justice, 1998.

———. *Improved Analysis of DNA Short Tandem Repeats with Time-of-Flight Mass Spectrometry*. Washington, D.C.: National Institute of Justice, 2001.

———. *Justice for All Act*. Washington, D.C.: National Institute of Justice, 2006.

———. *National Forensic DNA Study Report*. Washington, D.C.: National Institute of Justice, 2003.

———. *National Policy Summit: Building Private Security/Public Policing Partnerships to Prevent and Respond to Terrorism and Public Disorder*. Washington, D.C.: National Institute of Justice, Office of Community Oriented Policing Services, 2004.

———. *Mass Fatality Incidents: A Guide for Human Forensic Identification*. Washington, D.C.: National Institute of Justice, 2006.

———. *Police-Public Contact Survey, 1999*. Washington, D.C.: U.S. Department of Justice, 2001.

———. *Police Use of Deadly Force*. Washington, D.C.: National Institute of Justice, 1978.

———. *A Resource Guide on Racial Profiling Data Collection Systems: Promising Practices and Lessons Learned*. Washington, D.C.: National Institute of Justice, 2000.

———. *State and Local Law Enforcement Statistics*. Washington, D.C.: National Institute of Justice, 2006.

———. *Surveys in 12 Cities Show Widespread Community Support for Police*. Washington, D.C.: National Institute of Justice, 1999.

U.S. Equal Employment Opportunity Commission, *Affirmative Action and Equal Employment*, vol. 2 (Washington, D.C.: U.S. Government Printing Office, 1974).

U.S. General Accountability Office. *Information on Drug-Related Police Corruption*. Washington, D.C.: U.S. Government Accountability Office, 1998.

———. *Taser Weapons: Use of Tasers by Selected Law Enforcement Agencies*. Washington, D.C.: U.S. Government Accountability Office, 2005.

Walker, David M. *Homeland Security: Responsibility and Accountability for Achieving National Goals*. Washington, D.C.: U.S. General Accounting Office, 2002.

Walker, Samuel. *Early Intervention Systems: A Guide for Law Enforcement Chief Executives*. Washington, D.C.: Office of Community Oriented Policing Services, 2003.

Walker, Samuel, Stacy Osnick Milligan, and Anna Berke. *Strategies for Intervening with Officers through Early Intervention Systems: A Guide for Front-line Supervisors*. Washington, D.C.: Office of Community Oriented Policing Services, 2006.

———. *Supervision and Intervention within Early Intervention Systems: A Guide for Law Enforcement Chief Executives*. Washington, D.C.: Office of Community Oriented Policing Services, 2005.

Weisburd, David, Roseann Greenspan, Edwin H. Hamilton, Hubert Williams, and Kellie Bryant. *Police Attitudes toward Abuses of Authority: Findings from a National Study*. Washington, D.C.: National Institute of Justice, 2000.

Wilson, T. F., and P. L. Woodard. *Automated Fingerprint Identification Systems—Technology and Policy Issues*. Washington, D.C.: U.S. Department of Justice, 1987.

Yim, Randall A. *National Preparedness: Integration of Federal, State, Local and Private Sector Efforts Is Critical to an Effective National Strategy for Homeland Security*. Washington, D.C.: U.S. General Accounting Office, 2002.

Zaworski, Martin J. *Final Report: Automated Information Sharing: Does It Help Law Enforcement Officers Work Better?* Washington, D.C.: National Institute of Justice, 2006.

Zedlewski, Edwin, and Mary B. Murphy. *DNA Analysis for "Minor" Crimes: A Major Benefit for Law Enforcement*. Washington, D.C.: National Institute of Justice, 2006.

Zhao, Jihong "Solomon" and Quint Thurman. *Funding Community Policing to Reduce Crime: Have Cops Grants Made a Difference From 1994 to 2000?* Washington, D.C.: National Institute of Justice, 2004.

Academic and Professional Journals and Trade Magazines

ABF Research Journal
Academy of Criminal Justice Sciences Today
Addiction
American Criminal Law Review
American Journal of Criminal Justice
American Journal of Police
American Journal of Sociology
American Police Beat
Annals of the American Academy of Political and Social Science
Annals of Emergency Medicine
ASIS Dynamics
British Journal of Criminology
Building Bridges
Canadian Police Chief Magazine
CJ, The Americas
CJ Update
Community Policing Exchange
Corrections Technology and Management
Corrections Today
Crime and Delinquency
Crime and Justice International
Crime and Social Justice
Crime Prevention and Community Safety: An International Journal
Criminal Justice and Behavior
Criminal Justice Newsletter
Criminal Justice Policy Review
Criminal Justice Review
Criminal Justice Studies
Criminal Law Bulletin
Criminology
Criminology and Public Policy
Cultural Diversity
Current Reports: BNA Criminal Practice Manual
EA Professional Report
Educator
Evaluation Review
Fairfield County Business Journal
FBI Law Enforcement Bulletin
Governance
Governing
Homeland Defense Journal
IASIR Regulator
International Journal of Police Science and Management
Intersect: The Journal of International Security
Justice Assistance News
Journal of Applied Behavior Analysis

Journal of the Canadian Society of Forensic Science
Journal of Contemporary Criminal Justice
Journal of Crime and Justice
Journal of Criminal Justice
Journal of Criminal Justice Education
Journal of Criminal Law, Criminology, and Police Science
Journal of Forensic Identification
Journal of Forensic Sciences
Journal of Law and Criminology
Journal of National Medical Association
Journal of Police and Criminal Psychology
Journal of Police Science and Administration
Journal of Research in Crime and Delinquency
Journal of Safe Management of Disruptive and Assaultive
    Behavior
Journal of Social Issues
Journal of the Institute of Justice and International Studies
Judicature
Justice Assistance News
Justice Quarterly
Lambda Legal
Law and Order
Law and Society Review
Law Enforcement Technology
National Centurion
National Institute of Justice (NIJ) Journal
National Law Journal
National Police Research Unit
NCIA Justice Bulletin
New York Law Enforcement Journal
On Patrol
PC Computing
Personnel Psychology
Police
Police Chief
Police Executive Research Forum
Police Journal
Police Practice & Research: An international Journal
Police Quarterly
Police Studies
Policing: An International Journal of Police Strategies and
    Management
Policy Review
Popular Mechanics
Psychological Review
Public Administration Review
Public Personnel Management Journal
Security Journal
Scientific American
Security
Security Management
Sheriff
Social Problems
Stanford Law Review
University of Chicago Chronicle
University of Colorado Law Review
Women and Criminal Justice
WomenPolice
Working USA

Newspapers and National Magazines

Associated Press
Atlanta Constitution

Arizona Republic
Baltimore Sun
Boston Globe
Boston Herald
Business Week
Cincinnati Enquirer
Christian Science Monitor
Commercial Advisor
Crime and Justice News
Daily News
Daily Sentinel
Denver Post
Des Moines Register
Economist
Examiner
Everett Herald
Forbes
Fort Lauderdale Sun-Sentinel
Gentlemen's Quarterly
Gloucester Citizen
Houston Chronicle
Inc.
Indianapolis Star
Insight
Journal Sentinel
Law Enforcement News
Los Angeles Times
MacLean's
Miami Herald
Minneapolis Star Tribune
NAFTO News
National Review
New Orleans Magazine
Newsday
News & Observer
Newsweek
New Yorker
New York Post
New York Times
New York Times Magazine
Oregonian
People Weekly
Philadelphia Bulletin
Philadelphia Inquirer
Pioneer Press
Playboy
Providence Journal
Rocky Mountain News
Sacramento Bee
Salt Lake Tribune
San Bernardino County Sun
San Jose Mercury News
Seattle Post-Intelligencer
Seattle Times
South Florida Sun Sentinel
St. Louis Post-Dispatch
Tampa Tribune
Tennessean
Time
Town and Country Monthly
USA Today
USA Today Magazine
Wall Street Journal
Washington Post

Index

TO THE OWNER OF THIS BOOK:

I hope that you have found *An Introduction to Policing,* Fourth Edition useful. So that this book can be improved in a future edition, would you take the time to complete this sheet and return it? Thank you.

School and address:_____

Department:_____

Instructor's name:_____

1. What I like most about this book is:_____

_____

_____

2. What I like least about this book is:

_____

_____

3. My general reaction to this book is:

_____

_____

4. The name of the course in which I used this book is:

_____

5. Were all of the chapters of the book assigned for you to read?_____

    If not, which ones weren't?_____

6. In the space below, or on a separate sheet of paper, please write specific suggestions for improving this book and anything else you'd care to share about your experience in using this book.

_____

_____

_____

_____

NO POSTAGE
NECESSARY
IF MAILED
IN THE
UNITED STATES

BUSINESS REPLY MAIL
FIRST-CLASS MAIL   PERMIT NO. 34   BELMONT CA

POSTAGE WILL BE PAID BY ADDRESSEE

Attn: Carolyn Henderson Meier, Criminal
Justice Acquisitions Editor

Wadsworth Thomson Learning
10 Davis Dr
Belmont CA 94002-9801

OPTIONAL:

Your name:_____ Date: _____

May we quote you, either in promotion for *An Introduction to Policing,* Fourth Edition,
or in future publishing ventures?

Yes: _____   No: _____

Sincerely yours,

Jack Dempsey and Linda Forst

Learn what police work is really about with this current insider's look

A "must read" for anyone considering a career in law enforcement, this book provides an up-to-date insider's look at the many rewards—as well as the stresses and challenges—that are part of police work. Written by two authors with extensive real-life experience in all ranks and assignments of policing, this text provides a solid blend of practical information and theory, creating a firm foundation for understanding the various roles of the police—who the police are, what they do, and how they do it. The book also addresses current topics that are important to today's police departments, such as homeland security, community policing, and current technological advancements.

An essential resource that you'll refer to often, both in this course and in your professional career in policing, this cutting-edge Fourth Edition includes:

- **New coverage of how the war on terror is affecting law enforcement,** including the civil liberties concerns raised by the USA Patriot Act and the diversion of funding from other police activities to homeland security initiatives.

- **Added coverage of rural, local, and small-town police forces,** with a new focus on the challenges unique to small forces.

- **Expanded coverage of ethics, as well as other key topics** such as diversity in policing and new technologies, including forensic science.

- *Guest Lectures* featuring practitioners from all areas of police work that provide a real-life glimpse into the issues officers face on the job.

ALSO AVAILABLE

Wadsworth's Guide to Careers in Criminal Justice, Third Edition
by Caridad Sanchez-Leguelinel, John Jay College of Criminal Justice. Explores opportunities in law enforcement, courts, and corrections—and how to get those jobs! **0-495-13038-9**

Writing and Communicating for Criminal Justice
Includes articles on writing skills, along with basic grammar review and a survey of verbal communication on the job, to give you an introduction to academic, professional, and research writing in criminal justice. **0-495-00041-8**

A note to instructors
Please contact your Thomson sales representative to learn about the many course preparation and lecture resources available with this book, or visit **www.thomsonedu.com/criminaljustice**.

Visit Us on the Web
www.thomsonedu.com/criminaljustice

THOMSON ™
WADSWORTH

Visit Thomson Wadsworth at **www.thomsonedu.com**

ISBN-13: 978-0-495-09545-3
ISBN-10: 0-495-09545-1

90000

9 780495 095453